INTERMEDIATE
ACCOUNTING

INTERMEDIATE
ACCOUNTING

Seventh Canadian Edition

Volume I
Chapters 1–14

Thomas R. Dyckman
Cornell University

Roland E. Dukes
University of Washington

Charles J. Davis
California State University—Sacramento

Morton Nelson
Wilfrid Laurier University

Joan E. D. Conrod
Dalhousie University

Represented in Canada by:

Times Mirror
Professional Publishing Ltd.

IRWIN

Toronto · Chicago · Bogotá · Boston · Buenos Aires
Caracas · London · Madrid · Mexico City · Sydney

Publisher: *Roderick T. Banister*
Developmental editor: *Elke Price*
Product manager: *Murray Moman*
Project editor: *Amy E. Lund*
Production supervisor: *Bob Lange*
Interior designer: *Laurie Entringer*
Cover designer: *Katherine Farmer*
Art studio: *ElectraGraphics, Inc.*
Graphics supervisor: *Heather Burbridge*
Copyeditor: *Rosalyn L. Sheff*
Compositor: *Bi-Comp, Inc.*
Typeface: *10/12 Times Roman*
Printer: *Malloy Lithographing, Inc.*

ISBN 0-256-17493-8 (Vol. I)
ISBN 0-256-17494-6 (Vol. II)
Library of Congress Catalog Card Number: 94–078192

Printed in the United States of America
1 2 3 4 5 6 7 8 9 0 ML 1 0 9 8 7 6 5 4

Purposes

Financial reporting plays a unique role in the allocation of resources in our economy by providing the information necessary for informed investment and credit decisions. Because of the importance of the financial reporting process, it is imperative that preparers and users of the information presented in financial statements understand what the data represents and how it was determined. Only then can the financial reports be used as a basis for good business decisions. Thus our main goal in writing this text is to teach students how to determine the information that should be reported and how it should be quantified and disclosed according to generally accepted accounting principles.

An essential element of this goal is to explain *why* the principles currently governing the financial reporting process have developed. This integration of theory and practice is the most effective way to impart lasting knowledge as it gives the student a reason for the existence of an accounting principle rather than just isolated facts to memorize. We emphasize that accounting principles are decided after considering the diverse views of the parties most affected by financial reporting principles: reporting firms and the investing public. This process results in a continually evolving set of accounting principles based on a conceptual framework but often reflecting significant compromises.

Another important goal of this edition is to maintain up-to-date and comprehensive coverage of GAAP relating to intermediate accounting and at the same time reduce the overall size of the text. This text is completely current as of the date of publication. It includes discussion of the relevant new *CICA Handbook* recommendations and exposure drafts that have been released since the previous edition. However, while recognizing the necessity of maintaining comprehensive coverage, we have evaluated the relative importance of topics, resulting in deletion and reduction in coverage of issues that are no longer contentious.

Each of us has taught intermediate accounting for many years. In so doing, we have developed an awareness of the issues and applications most difficult for the student to master and have exercised special care in those areas to make the presentation as clear, understandable, and stimulating as possible. We engage the student's interest in the learning process by integrating into the discussion current examples of financial reporting by actual companies. We simplify the learning process by developing the ideas within the framework of a relatively straightforward example and then proceeding step-by-step through the more difficult and controversial materials. For many topics, you will find a progression to the more complex and realistic case only after the student is first introduced to the basic idea and the reason for its importance.

Curriculum Concerns

This edition is responsive to the concerns of the Accounting Education Change Commission (AECC). These concerns suggest a new direction in accounting education that encourages students "to learn how to learn." Curricula should emphasize the importance of the underlying concepts rather than the memorization of rules and regulations. The focus is on the process of inquiry in which the student learns to identify problem situations, to search for relevant information, to analyze and interpret the information, and to reach a well-reasoned conclusion.

With these goals in mind, the seventh edition frequently asks questions and presents important contemporary issues in a manner that compels the student to think about the appropriate solution to a reporting problem. For example, the impact of lobbying and the need for compromise by standard setters is discussed in several controversial topics. One aim of this emphasis is to develop the student's ability to critically evaluate particular reporting standards. We want the students to be able to decide whether a particular accounting principle successfully fulfills the primary objective of financial statements, namely to provide information useful for decision making. A second aim is to acquaint the student with the political nature of the standard-setting process.

We view the current GAAP solutions to reporting problems as one step in the continuing evolutionary process of attempting to provide the most cost-effective and useful information possible. The text involves the student in that process. Many of the end-of-chapter cases and problems require students to identify and solve unstructured problems and consider multiple data sources. Our longer cases and problems help to stimulate a more interactive and involved process on the part of the student—learning by doing.

KEY FEATURES

Several new features have been incorporated into this edition with the intention of expanding its real-world emphasis, introducing international accounting issues, staying current with new pronouncements, and increasing the student's involvement in learning. These features are:

A Global View

A boxed element with a related end-of-chapter question appearing in some chapters.

Provides exposure to the GAAP of other countries and the International Accounting Standards Committee pronouncements; reflects an increasingly strong call for international accounting standards.

On the Horizon

A boxed element appearing in several chapters.

Introduces topics currently under consideration by standard setters and discusses their possible impact on financial reporting.

You Make the Call

New end-of-chapter item appearing in several chapters.

Presents a reporting issue that has not been considered by the accounting standard setters or an issue that continues to be controversial; requires the student to think about issues that may not have been explicitly discussed in the chapter and to render a reasoned opinion on how to resolve the issue using knowledge of accounting theory.

Analyzing Financial Statements

New end-of-chapter item appearing in most chapters.

Provides additional real-world examples by keying problems to extracts from the financial statements of actual companies; requires students to apply knowledge to a less structured situation.

Writing Assignments

End-of-chapter items appearing in all chapters.

Requires the students to write memos, reports, and other types of written communication as part of the solution to many of the problems and cases. The AECC recommends more emphasis in this area.

Ethics Assignments

End-of-chapter items appearing in some chapters.

Provides situational material involving ethical dilemmas. Students must recognize and resolve an ethical issue.

Many features of the previous edition that were well received by both students and faculty have been retained and updated. For example, real-world situations are emphasized throughout the text with numerous examples of actual companies' reporting practices, chapter introductions featuring reporting issues, frequent reference is made to the CICA's Financial Reporting in Canada, and many references taken from *The Globe & Mail, The Wall Street Jour-* *nal, Forbes, Financial Executive,* and many other sources. Magna International Inc. graciously permitted us to reproduce Magna's entire 1993 financial statements and accompanying notes. Almost all chapters have an assignment question based on this material.

Concept reviews, consisting of a brief list of questions, are placed at the end of major sections in each chapter to help students check their understanding of the basic concepts that have just been presented. These questions are answerable directly from the text and serve the same function as a short quiz. The answers are provided in the solutions manual for the convenience of the instructor. Many of the chapters contain one or more comprehensive problems that cover several of the chapter's learning objectives. Their purpose is to provide an opportunity to integrate the more important ideas into one situation.

TOPICAL CHANGES IN THE SEVENTH EDITION

Along with the new features included in the seventh edition, many changes in topical coverage have been made to reflect changes in accounting principles since the previous edition and to fine-tune the coverage by making organizational changes within each chapter.

For example, the appendixes to several chapters were shortened and incorporated into the chapter for better integration of the subject matter. Also, we have reduced the number of examples in certain chapters to focus on the more important and controversial issues and streamline the material. In this effort, our team of reviewers was especially helpful in suggesting areas that faculty across the country typically do not assign or cover.

The following list highlights the major substantive changes made to the chapters:

Chapter 1 Ethics coverage from the appendix is now integrated into the chapter.

Chapter 2 Increased emphasis has been placed on the discussion of Financial Accounting Concepts. References to U.S. material have been removed.

Chapter 4 A generalized method of determining disclosures for discontinued operations has been added.

Chapter 5 The chapter now reflects improved coverage of the statement of changes in financial position.

Chapter 7 The coverage of losses on long-term contracts has been expanded and improved, and the revenue recognition examples for when a right of return exists are more involved. A section on ethical considerations has been added.

Chapter 8 The bank reconciliation discussion now includes the treatment of a recording error. The "proof-of-cash" bank reconciliation has been deleted as it is covered more substantially in auditing classes. New to the chapter is material on Section 3025 of the *CICA Handbook*, which addresses accounting for loan impairments by creditors, as well as a discussion of income measurement after a note has become impaired.

Chapter 9 The discussion of LIFO has been somewhat reduced.

Chapter 11 The more complex cases involving interest capitalization has been removed so emphasis is on the fundamentals. A section has been added that addresses accounting for contributions made and received.

Chapter 12 The material on coinsurance (formerly an appendix) has been revised, shortened, and integrated into the chapter. The asset impairments section has been completely rewritten to reflect some new developments.

Chapter 13 The material comparing the successful efforts and full costing methods has been moved from the appendix to the chapter. An exhibit illustrating the decision process pertaining to accounting for computer software costs is presented. Expanded coverage of methods used to estimate goodwill now appears in an appendix.

Chapter 14 The appendix on consolidated financial statements has been deleted, based on reviewer comments suggesting a general lack of interest at the intermediate level. A discussion of the exposure draft, ''Financial Instruments'' has been added.

Chapter 15 The discussion of contingencies has been revised in light of the expected new *CICA Handbook* recommendations.

Chapter 16 The chapter has been shortened by reducing the coverage of certain bond accounting examples, troubled debt restructure, and debt extinguishment. The coverage on certain aspects of bond investment accounting and special mortgage notes has been reduced or eliminated. Troubled debt restructuring coverage now appears in Appendix A and serial bonds in Appendix B. A short discussion of accounting for environmental liabilities also appears in the seventh edition.

Chapter 18 Several technical revisions have been made concerning accounting for bargain purchase options, residual values, and initial direct costs. Certain material in the appendixes of the previous edition was condensed and integrated into the chapter.

Chapter 19 The appendix on settlements and curtailments has been shortened and integrated into the chapter; the appendix on financial reporting by pension plans has been deleted.

Chapter 24 The chapter has been shortened but the central emphasis on reporting accounting changes remains. The section on worksheet techniques and preparing financial statements from incomplete data has been deleted.

Chapter 25 The material includes financial statement analysis, as well as segmental disclosures and interim reporting. The discussion on segment reporting is more complete. On the advice of our reviewers and many other interested faculty, other material found in Chapter 25 of the previous edition (changing prices) has been deleted; this material was seldom assigned in intermediate accounting classes.

END-OF-CHAPTER MATERIAL

Many changes and revisions were made to the questions, cases, exercises, and problems. Cases now appear before the exercises and problems, highlighting the conceptual and more open-ended material before the more procedural and computational. Older and more repetitive items were deleted, and many new items were added.

The *questions* at the end of each chapter provide a context for in-class discussion; *cases* often require the student to integrate several issues in the chapter and provide an opinion on a reporting problem or situational aspect; *exercises* are generally structured applications of specific issues in the chapter; while *problems* generally are longer and less structured applications of one or more specific issues in the chapter. *Financial statement analysis* questions are based on actual financial statements and require understanding of underlying concepts and principles, as well as application skills.

The cases and some problems provide an opportunity for students to practice their analytical and written communication skills. Furthermore, they frequently place the student in an unstructured situation requiring a broad view to be taken of a business reporting problem. The context in which financial reporting is used must be considered in these instances.

ACCURACY

The sixth Canadian edition was extensively reviewed by seven reviewers, whose comments on content and accuracy greatly contributed to this seventh edition. Your authors have completed extensive proofreading of this text, complemented by complete proofreading at Irwin.

Every problem, exercise, and case in the U.S. text was solved independently by five accounting faculty from different universities. The U.S. authors and a team of 12 experts checked all revisions and proofread extensively. In the Canadian edition, the authors and four accounting students verified all changes. Five outside experts reviewed and checked the questions, exercises, problems, cases, analyzing financial statement questions, and the accompanying solutions.

We have made every effort to ensure that this text is as error free as it can be. If you should come upon an issue of concern, please call either of us at any time or send an E-mail message to MNELSON @MACH1.WLU.CA or JCONROD@SBACOOP. SBA.DAL.CA. We value your input and want to be of help.

SUPPLEMENTARY MATERIALS

For the Professor:

Intermediate Accounting, Seventh Edition, offers several teaching aids to assist the instructor.

Solutions Manual, Chapters 1–14 and 15–25 Done in two volumes, this comprehensive solutions manual provides complete solutions and explanations for all end-of-chapter questions, exercises, problems, and cases. The estimated completion time for each item is given in the assignment assistance schedule at the beginning of each chapter. Answers to the chapter concept review questions are included at the end of the manual.

Solutions Transparencies Acetate transparencies of solutions to even-numbered exercises and problems are free to adopters. Now increased in clarity, these transparencies are especially useful when covering problems in large classroom settings.

Spreadsheet Applications Template Software (SPATS) This is a software package developed for use with the text. SPATS includes a Lotus® 1-2-3® tutorial and innovatively designed templates that may be used with Lotus® 1-2-3® to solve many of the exercises and problems in the text. Upon adoption, this package is available to instructors for classroom or laboratory use.

Computest IV A computerized improved test generator program that allows editing of questions, provides up to 99 different versions of each test, and allows question selection based on type of question, level of difficulty, or learning objectives.

Cases Canadian Cases in Financial Accounting, by Carol E. Dilworth and Joan E. D. Conrod, contains over 100 cases that provide a variety of practical situations where professional judgment is necessary. The casebook is accompanied by an instructor's manual.

Corporate Practice Set Silicon Coast Computer Company, Ltd., by Ray Carroll, Dalhousie University, and Gerald D. Trites, Peak Marwick Thorne, is a manual practice set that can be assigned after Chapter 6 as a review of the accounting cycle.

For the Student:

Several support materials have been designed especially for the student.

Study Guide. The study guide provides the student with a summarized look at each chapter's issues. Included are outlines, chapter overviews, key concepts, review questions and exercises. The study guide was prepared by Rosita Chen and Sheng-Der Pan, both of California State University—Fresno and Frank Reichardt and Henry Funk, both of Red River Community College.

Check Figures A list of check figures for selected end-of-chapter is available.

ACKNOWLEDGMENTS

The text in its present form would not have been possible without the contributions of a great many people. We recognize and appreciate all of their efforts.

Our thanks and gratitude are extended to the outstanding faculty reviewers who provided criticism and constructive suggestions. The reviewers were:

Gerald D. Cook
University of New Brunswick

Chris J. Trunkfield
British Columbia Institute of Technology

Valorie Deluca
Laurentian University

Brian Duggan
University of Manitoba

Toni Nelson
University of Lethbridge

Michelle Foreman
St. Lawrence College

Brian J. Rothwell
Medicine Hat College

We express deep appreciation to the following individuals who reviewed the end-of-chapter material:

Don Cherry
Dalhousie University

Mauree Fizzell
Simon Fraser University

Jim Hughes
British Columbia Institute of Technology

Tilly Jensen
Northern Alberta Institute of Technology

Karen Mathews
Saskatchewan Institute of Applied Science and Technology

Christine Paradoski, Deanna Pearce, Michael Evans, and Darryl Huras at Wilfrid Laurier University and Janet Lee Brannon and Kristine Nielson at Dalhousie University, also provided valuable assistance by checking the solutions to the end-of-chapter material.

To numerous other colleagues and users whose constructive comments and suggestions have led to the improvements reflected in this latest edition, our thanks. We sincerely appreciate comments and suggestions from all sources. We also appreciate the permissions granted by several firms and organizations including the Canadian Institute of Chartered Accountants, the Certified General Accountants Association of Canada, the Society of Management Accountants of Canada, and, of course, Magna International Inc.

We are grateful to the people at Irwin for their never-ending support: Rod T. Banister, Publisher; Elke Price, developmental editor; Amy Lund, project editor; Rosalyn L. Sheff, copyeditor; Laurie Entringer, designer; Bob Lange, production supervisor; and Judy Besser, secretary—editorial.

Last, but certainly not least, we express our deepest thanks to our former co-author, Michael Zin, professor emeritus at the University of Windsor. Michael's dedication and creativity through six Canadian editions built a solid foundation for this text. We are proud to continue in his strong tradition.

We welcome your ideas and comments as you use this text and look forward to hearing from you.

Morton Nelson
Joan E. D. Conrod

"Why are textbook prices so high?"

This is, by far, the most frequently-asked question heard in the publishing industry. There are many factors that influence the price of your new textbook. Here are just a few:

• **Developmental Costs:** These are costs associated with the extensive development of your textbook. Expenses include permission fees, manuscript review costs, artwork, typesetting, printing and binding costs, and more.

• **Author Royalties:** Authors are paid based on a percentage of new book sales and **do not** receive royalties on the sale of a used book. They are also deprived of their rightful royalties when their books are illegally photocopied.

• **The Cost of Instructor Support Materials:** Your instructor may be making use of teaching supplements, many of which are provided by the publisher. Teaching supplements include transparencies, instructor's manuals, software, computerized testing materials, and more. These supplements are designed as part of a learning package to enhance your educational experience.

• **Marketing Costs:** Instructors need to be made aware of new textbooks. Marketing costs include academic conventions, remuneration of the publisher's representatives, promotional advertising pieces, and the provision of instructor's examination copies.

• **Bookstore Markups:** In order to stay in business, your local bookstore must cover its costs. A textbook is a commodity, just like any other item your bookstore may sell, and bookstores are the most effective way to get the textbook from the publisher to you.

• **Publisher Profits:** In order to continue to supply students with quality textbooks, publishers must make a profit to stay in business. Like the authors, publishers **do not** receive any compensation from the sale of a used book or the illegal photocopying of their textbooks.

We at Times Mirror Professional Publishing, representing Richard D. Irwin, Inc., hope you will find this information useful and that it addresses some of your concerns. We also thank you for your purchase of this new textbook. If you have any questions that we can answer, please write to us at:

Times Mirror Professional Publishing
College Division
130 Flaska Drive
Markham, Ontario
L6G 1B8

BRIEF CONTENTS

CONTENTS

I

FOUNDATION AND REVIEW

1 The Environment of Accounting

After you have studied this chapter, you will be able to:

1 **Explain the value of the accounting function to external users of a company's financial statements.**

2 **Explain the difference between the internal and external uses of accounting information.**

3 **Explain the impact that accounting can have on firms' decisions at all levels of the economy.**

4 **Explain the standard-setting process and the influence of various organizations' environmental factors in that process.**

5 **List the major sources of the pronouncements that constitute GAAP (generally accepted accounting principles).**

6 **Explain the political nature of the standard-setting process and its impact on accounting standards, including the relevance of economic-consequence arguments.**

7 **Discuss the ethical and international issues currently affecting accounting standard setting.**

INTRODUCTION

Financial accounting is concerned with the way businesses communicate financial information to the public—the various categories of people who either invest in, lend money to, or do business with a company. These people rely on a company's financial statements and other information reports to make investment and other financial decisions about the company. Financial accounting practices and issues apply to large, publicly owned corporations, smaller sole proprietorships, and every type and size of business enterprise in between. This text concentrates on publicly owned companies.

Other specialized branches of accounting are primarily concerned with the internal information needs of a company. Management accounting, for example, addresses the needs of internal managers, providing them with accounting information so that they can maintain control over business operations and product

3

lines, monitor budgets and profit performance, and direct the company's future success.

Financial accounting is not cut-and-dried—it can be very judgmental. Deciding how a particular transaction or event should be reflected in the financial statements can be difficult, and different methods can produce materially different results. The guiding principles of financial accounting are, by design, subject to interpretation and individual circumstances. (Tax accounting, in contrast, tends to be dominated by precise rules and regulations, leaving less room for interpretation.) Furthermore, the rule-making body that establishes financial accounting principles—the **Accounting Standards Board (AcSB)** of the Canadian Institute of Chartered Accountants (CICA)—tends to be influenced by various business and special interest groups and by circumstances that are not purely accounting in nature. Finally, financial accounting can be affected by the decisions of the various provincial securities commissions. In certain instances, these exchange commissions have established specific accounting practice rules.

To gain some appreciation for the nature and scope of accounting policy issues, consider the following account, as described in the business press.

Chambers Development Company, which became a public company in 1985, was a fast-growing waste management company. Revenues of $5 million in 1980 had grown to $322 million in 1991; annual revenue growth was as high as 51 percent over this period. Profits, too, showed respectable growth, and 1991 net income was $50 million. This picture of revenue and profit growth caused continued strong performance of the common stock price on the stock exchange.

By 1992, it had become clear that Chambers' spiraling seven-year growth pattern was mostly a mirage. The company had capitalized, as assets, costs that should have been expensed, including interest and costs associated with the initiation of new businesses and trash hauling routes. These policies, which resulted in deferrals of approximately $162 million, had been chosen to increase net income. Indeed, the majority shareholder, John G. Rangos Sr., was very concerned with reporting a positive earnings trend. When informed that 1990 profits would not meet forecasts, he was reported to have told an executive to, "Go and find the rest of it."

In March 1992, the company indicated that it was discontinuing its rather unorthodox accounting methods. Restated financial reports, issued later in 1992, showed losses of $16 million in 1989, $41 million in 1990, and $72 million in 1991.[1]

As might be expected, Chambers' share price dropped dramatically. Such a decline is not unique. Other high-growth companies, including Fidelity Medical, Valley Systems, Inc., and Phar-Mor, Inc., reported similar problems and share price effects.

These situations illustrate the need for financial reporting conventions that are accepted and followed by all companies, but especially those that are publicly traded. Investors and creditors rely on published financial reports to make investment and lending decisions. The result of better investment decisions is an improved allocation of economic resources among competing needs throughout an economy.

The institution that has the responsibility for developing financial reporting conventions in Canada is the Canadian Institute of Chartered Accountants (CICA). The CICA's Accounting Standards Board (AcSB) sets financial accounting standards. We will describe this organization later in this chapter. Understanding the nature of the process that establishes standards is a necessary precondition to understanding the standards themselves; knowing the standards is essential to understanding the messages these reports convey.

---

[1] "Audit Report Shows How Far Chambers Would Go for Profits," *The Wall Street Journal*, October 21, 1992, p. A1.

THE NATURE OF FINANCIAL ACCOUNTING

We characterize an **accounting information system** as a system whose purpose is to identify, collect, measure, and communicate information about economic entities (corporations, partnerships, and sole proprietorships) to those with an interest in the financial affairs of the enterprise.

The Chambers situation demonstrates how important an accounting information system can be. We will begin this text with a careful examination of the purpose of, or need for, an accounting information system. Because we are concerned primarily with external users of accounting information, it is necessary to first distinguish between internal and external users of information, after which the objectives of reporting accounting information to external users can be examined.

External versus Internal Accounting Information

The users of financial information can be classified as either external or internal decision makers. External decision makers are those who lack direct access to the information generated by the internal operations of a company. Included in this category are shareholders and potential investors, suppliers, creditors, rank-and-file employees, customers, competitors, financial analysts and advisers, brokers, underwriters, the stock exchanges, lawyers, economists, taxing and regulatory authorities, legislators, the financial press and reporting agencies, labour unions, trade associations, business researchers, teachers, students, and the general public.[2] These external decision makers use accounting information in deciding on matters such as whether to invest in the entity, extend it credit, or even do business with it.

External users are typically not in a position to demand specific financial information from the entity; they must rely on general-purpose financial statements. To meet the general information needs of external decision makers, the accounting profession has developed a body of financial accounting concepts, principles, and procedures intended to ensure that external financial statements are relevant and reliable. This body of concepts, principles, and procedures is known as **generally accepted accounting principles (GAAP).**

Internal decision makers are the managers of an entity. They are responsible for planning the future of the business, implementing those plans, controlling daily operations, and reporting information to other operating officers. Because of their close and direct relationship with the business, internal decision makers can usually obtain whatever financial data they need whenever they choose. Much of this information is not intended for outsiders. The reporting of financial information for internal users is called **management accounting,** and the reports generated are called **internal management reports.** Because of the confidential nature of these reports and their primary focus on internal decision-making needs, these reports need not conform to GAAP.

Objective of Financial Reporting for External Decision Makers

The objective of financial statements and their accompanying disclosure notes is to report the economic effects of completed business transactions and other events on an organization. To accomplish this purpose, two basic types of financial statements are used:

1. A statement that relates to a specific point in time: the **balance sheet,** which reports the company's assets, liabilities, and owners' equity on a specified date. This statement is also called the **statement of financial position.**
2. Statements that relate to a specified period of time are the:
   a. **Income statement,** which reports the company's revenues, gains, expenses, losses, and net income.

---

[2] Although users of accounting information for tax purposes are external users, it is worthwhile to identify this group separately. Tax law is designed to assist in the collection of moneys for public purposes and, often, to support specific economic or public policy initiatives undertaken by government. In Canada, the tax reporting requirements are often different from those followed for other accounting purposes, although this is not the case in many countries.

    b. **Statement of retained earnings** (sometimes appended to the income statement), which reports changes in the company's accumulated earnings.

    c. **Statement of changes in financial position,** which reports the company's cash flows from operating, investing, and financing activities. This statement is also called the **statement of cash flows.**

The purpose of these external financial statements is explained in Section 1000 of the *CICA Handbook:*

> It is not practicable to expect financial statements to satisfy the many and varied information needs of all external users of information about an entity. Consequently, the objective of financial statements for profit oriented enterprises focuses primarily on information needs of investors and creditors . . . Financial statements prepared to satisfy these needs are often used by others who need external reporting of information about an entity.
>
> Investors and creditors of profit oriented enterprises are interested, for the purpose of making resource allocation decisions, in predicting the ability of the entity to earn income and generate cash flows in the future to meet its obligations and to generate a return on investment . . .
>
> Investors . . . also require information about how the management of an entity has discharged its stewardship responsibility to those that have provided resources to the entity . . .
>
> **The objective of financial statements is to communicate information that is useful to investors . . . creditors and other users ("users") in making their resource allocation decisions and/or assessing management stewardship** [emphasis added]. Consequently, financial statements provide information about:
>
> (*a*) an entity's economic resources, obligations and equity/net assets;
> (*b*) changes in an entity's economic resources, obligations and equity/net assets; and
> (*c*) the economic performance of the entity.

The definitions of resources and obligations are tied to future cash flow—that is, a resource is a future cash inflow and an obligation is a future cash outflow.

Financial reporting is intended to provide information that will be useful in making decisions. This objective influences the way financial accountants prepare accounting information for financial reporting purposes. If a less decision-oriented objective were specified, the way data are measured and reported would change dramatically. For example, if the objective in financial reporting were only one of stewardship, there would be little concern with predicting future cash flows. But if the information is used to decide whether to sell shares in a company, it is important that the user be able to estimate the company's future dividend payments.

Professional Accounting

Accounting dates back at least to 3600 BC, but the first published work on the double-entry system of accounting is attributed to Luca Pacioli in AD 1494 in Venice, Italy. Pacioli's work described double-entry accounting in much the same way as it is used today. Since then, however, the need for financial accounting has grown as business has grown, starting with the industrial revolution in Europe. This growth was accelerated by the emergence of the publicly owned corporation as the major form of business entity.

Today, accountants have an important role in society. The professional accountant could be a chartered accountant (CA), a certified management accountant (CMA), or a certified general accountant (CGA). Large numbers of accountants are active in public accounting and managerial accounting.

Public Accounting Independent accountants in public practice offer services such as auditing (the attest function),[3] tax planning and determination of tax liability, and

---

[3] The auditor is required to express a written opinion on whether the firm's financial statements fairly present its financial position and operations. The auditor is said to attest to the statements.

EXHIBIT 1-1
Relationship of Preparers,
Auditors, and Users

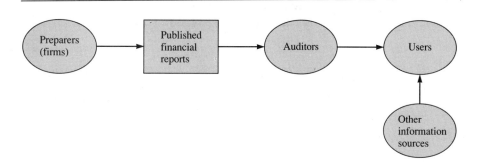

management consulting. These accountants act as independent and impartial auditors of their client's financial statements.[4] Although independent accountants are paid by their clients, they are responsible to third parties as well—the users of financial statements.

The relationship between preparers of financial statements, auditors, and users is depicted in Exhibit 1-1. Preparers (firms) are responsible for developing their financial reports. These reports are audited and attested to by the auditor to provide a reliability check to the user. Remember, though, that users also consider other sources of information when making decisions.

A professional accountant in public practice must be independent of the client whose report is to be certified. Even if the reporting of unfavorable economic results poses major problems for the reporting company, the results must be fairly and reliably presented. The public interest must be predominant.

Management Accounting   Many accountants work in business firms as managerial accountants, internal auditors, income tax specialists, systems experts, controllers, management consultants, financial vice presidents, and chief executives. Management accountants often focus on the planning and controlling functions in an enterprise and prepare internal management reports and related analyses to meet the needs of management. Accountants employed by a company are not considered independent accountants and cannot attest to the company's external financial statements.

|CONCEPT REVIEW

1. Are a firm's financial reports prepared primarily for internal or external users?
2. Who are the two basic users of financial statements? Give an example of each.
3. What is the purpose of financial statement information?

THE INTERACTION OF FINANCIAL ACCOUNTING WITH ITS ENVIRONMENT

Accounting information is essential to an economic decision. In general, accounting measurements and financial reports have an impact on society through the distribution of scarce resources, including management talent. The allocation of resources occurs as decision makers assess both opportunities for gains and the inherent risks of devoting capital to a particular venture. Accounting helps decision makers evaluate opportunities by providing measurements such as net income, total assets and equities, and cash flow. But overreliance on accounting measures is not wise. First,

---

[4] Debate continues on whether public accounting firms, which also perform consulting services for their audit clients, are fully independent.

accounting measures have limitations, as we will see. Second, other sources of information may be more relevant and more timely in any given situation.

Accounting measures play an important role in numerous situations:

- Determining tax payments.
- Evaluating an investment opportunity to buy or sell shares.
- Establishing the attractiveness of a company as a takeover target.
- Evaluating the effectiveness of individual managers in using assets committed to their charge (stewardship).
- Determining whether bond and other contract provisions are satisfied.
- Helping lenders evaluate the risk of a potential loan.

Financial reports may have indirect effects, which can be difficult to quantify. These may include:

- Influencing the attractiveness of a company to its workers.
- Suggesting bargaining strategies to unions or union organizers.
- Affecting the willingness of suppliers to enter into long-term contracts with the company.
- Alerting regulators to excessive profit performance.
- Affecting customers' willingness to purchase the company's products for economic, environmental, or ethical reasons.[5]

Choices in compiling and reporting accounting information can have a far-reaching impact on businesses and on the economy. Consider three examples:

- The alternative accounting treatments permitted for oil and gas exploration costs were alleged to have altered the willingness of some companies in this industry to develop new reserves at a time when the Organization of Petroleum Exporting Countries (OPEC) was restricting oil supplies.
- At another time, it was charged that business and industry would cut back on research activities because of accounting standards that required such expenditures to be expensed in full each year rather than capitalized as an asset and amortized. To avoid the detrimental effects of expensing research expenditures, which lowers reported net income, some companies set up separate research subsidiaries, thereby keeping research expenses off the parent company's income statement.
- Some economists contend that because Canadian businesses are required to expense goodwill (amortized over periods up to 40 years), thereby lowering net income, they are at a disadvantage relative to foreign companies that never have to amortize this intangible asset. If Canadian companies must recognize higher expenses than their foreign counterparts, these economists argue, Canadian businesses will increase their selling prices, reducing sales and contributing to the trade deficit.

Companies preparing financial statements and external decision makers using them express concerns over the adequacy of financial accounting. These concerns usually centre on the methods used to compile accounting information and report results in financial statements. Yet accounting methods and procedures are not established in a vacuum and often must accommodate a variety of interests.

Factors influencing accounting, information compilation, and reporting procedures include:

- The legal system, which stresses verifiable facts as opposed to estimates and forecasts.
- The regulatory structure. Public utility regulatory commissions, for example, decide which costs are capitalized for utility rates.
- The ethical climate, which strengthens (or weakens) the quality of the reported information.

---

[5] G. Benston and M. Kreasney, "The Economic Consequences of Financial Accounting Statements," *Economic Consequences of Financial Accounting Standards,* FASB Research Report (Norwalk, GA: FASB, 1978).

- Concerns of preparers that disclosure of certain information will reduce the company's competitive advantage.
- Demands for information by users, which might influence whether certain data, such as leases, are reported on the balance sheet as a line item with debt, in the footnotes, or not at all.
- The costs and benefits of alternative reporting methods, which play a major role in determining whether the AcSB adopts specific financial information reporting requirements.
- The timeliness versus the relevance of the information supplied. The reporting of bad debt expense and the associated allowance for uncollectibles is an example in which the need for timely information requires a forecast even though the actual loss would be more relevant.
- The development of new financial instruments.

Accounting standards and practices are constantly evolving to keep pace with and meet the changing needs and demands of society.

The Need for Financial Reporting Standards

Financial reporting standards are needed to ensure that the accounting information provided in financial statements is relevant to the types of decisions investors and other users must make. For example, creditors scrutinize financial information to evaluate a company's ability to meet its future cash obligations. Information about the past is often useful to creditors in predicting both future cash obligations and cash inflows. Reported information about current liabilities, long-term debt, and shareholders' equity can be used to compute a company's ratio of debt to equity—the portion of the company's assets that was provided by creditors.

Cash Flow Both investors and lenders find reported cash flow from operating activities useful in evaluating a company's ability to make interest payments and repay debt. At one time, companies had a choice in reporting either cash flow or the change in working capital (current assets less current liabilities) from operating activities. When studies showed that a cash flow report provides information more relevant to investor decisions and that cash flow data can be a better predictor of business failure than changes in working capital, accounting standards were changed to require a statement of changes in financial position based on cash flow.

Reported Earnings Investors are concerned with a company's reported earnings. Earnings are a major factor influencing the market price of the company's shares; share prices react to the announcement of reported earnings. Current market prices of publicly traded shares are reported daily in newspapers, accompanied by the ratio of share price to net income per share (price–earnings, or PE, ratio). Security analysts use this information to project future share prices and earnings. Companies are therefore understandably concerned about reported earnings because they want the market value of their shares to stay as high as possible. Unfortunately, as the Chambers situation discussed in the introduction to this chapter illustrates, companies that have been unable to attain their earnings goals through operations have at times resorted to deceptive accounting in an attempt to manufacture the desired result. Accounting standards have developed over time to prevent such abuses.

Earnings goals are commonly tailored to a smooth pattern of earnings growth each year or quarter. Companies thus have incentives to smooth out their earnings over time to avoid undesirable fluctuations. The smoothing may require either a reduction or an increase in earnings from the level that would otherwise be reported. Thus, if earnings appear to be above goal, equipment write-offs may be taken now, whereas such write-offs could be delayed if earnings are inadequate. Deliveries of product may be accelerated late in the fiscal year if earnings are down, and expenses may be delayed if earnings are expected to be too low. One ploy for manipulating earnings that is now prohibited in Canada but is still allowed elsewhere is to establish arbitrary reserves. If a company finds it advantageous to report lower net earnings, it might set up a reserve account for future losses due to lawsuits, asset obsolescence, fires, uncollectible trade receivables, and so on. Or, a company might want to boost its earnings artificially. In one documented case, a company sold just enough land so that the gain on the land sales, when added to income for the year, produced a constant 30 percent growth in net income each year.[6]

Practice Standards The accounting profession has, over the years, developed a structure of accounting practice standards to address comparability and reporting abuse. The chief body of practice standards is a set of generally accepted accounting principles (GAAP) intended both to guide and to govern the preparation of financial statements, with the public's needs and interest foremost in mind. The description *generally accepted* means that each principle either was established by a designated rule-making body such as the Accounting Standards Board or has achieved general acceptance through practice.

Development in the 20th century of more complex business organizations requiring large amounts of capital from diverse sources created a need to keep investors and creditors more fully informed. Enactment of the first income tax in 1917 added to the pressures for accountability. Later, the stock market crash of 1929 and the Great Depression, blamed in part on inadequate financial reporting, paved the way for adoption of many new accounting rules.

CONCEPT REVIEW
1. Describe three specific decision situations in which accounting information may play an important role.
2. Do accounting reports include data based on assumptions about the future? If so, provide an example.
3. Why is cash flow so important to financial statement users?

The Evolution of the Current Standard-Setting Process

The Canadian Institute of Chartered Accountants (CICA) was incorporated by a special act of the Canadian Parliament in 1902. The CICA has primary responsibility for developing appropriate accounting and auditing standards for business and government and for providing information to help professional accountants keep abreast of ongoing developments in theory and practice.

In 1946, a committee of the CICA issued its first accounting bulletin.[7] Twenty-six additional bulletins were issued over the next 21 years. In 1968, all bulletins that had been issued were updated and consolidated into the standards published in the *CICA Handbook*. This loose-leaf binder is regularly updated as new standards are approved.

Until 1973, the Accounting and Auditing Research Committee of the CICA was responsible for all accounting and auditing pronouncements. In 1973, separate committees for accounting and auditing were established, with the Accounting Research Committee (ARC) made responsible for accounting standards. The ARC consisted of 22 members, chosen to represent various accounting and geographical interests across Canada. In 1982 and again in 1991, this committee was renamed and reformu-

---

[6] Reported in *The Wall Street Journal,* April 27, 1971, p. 7. In another, more recent case, Mini Scribe, a manufacturer of computer disk drives, booked shipments as sales and set up inadequate reserves for bad debts, increasing profits by over 80 percent.

[7] The following discussion is based in part on *Accounting Standard-Setting in Canada* (Toronto: CICA, 1994).

lated, and is now the Accounting Standards Board (AcSB). The reformulated committee now consists of 15 members.

In 1985, the Canadian Commercial Bank (CCB) collapsed—Canada's first bank failure since 1923. This failure was estimated to have cost the federal government, and thus the Canadian taxpayer, close to $1 billion. In the subsequent enquiries and examinations, various financial reporting practices and the role of auditors were critically examined. The CICA requested a special study, which resulted in the 1988 MacDonald Commission report that made sweeping recommendations in a number of areas. Some of these were designed to improve the standard-setting process. These recommendations, designed to improve the speed and efficiency of the process and increase the level of involvement by outside parties, have strengthened the standard-setting process in Canada.

Status of *CICA Handbook* Standards   At first, the bulletins issued by the standard-setting committee did not have legal backing, and compliance was voluntary. Over time, the bulletins achieved a certain status within the accounting profession. In the early 1970s, however, the status of these standards changed. In December 1972, the Canadian Securities Administrators issued a National Policy Statement that required application of *CICA Handbook* standards for all filings required under securities legislation. This effectively meant that all Canadian public companies were required to follow the CICA's accounting standards.

Further recognition came in 1975, when the Canada Business Corporations Act (CBCA) was proclaimed in force. This legislation governs the conduct of all federally incorporated entities. The regulations of the Canada Business Corporations Act specify that financial statements required by the CBCA must be prepared in accordance with the standards of the *CICA Handbook*. This federal initiative was followed, through the 1980s, by equivalent provincial legislation. Today, all companies, whether incorporated provincially or federally, are required to follow *CICA Handbook* standards in the financial statements prepared to fulfill statutory reporting responsibilities.

Finally, the accounting profession itself enforces its standards. While the professional accounting bodies have no right to censure companies who do not follow the standards in the *CICA Handbook*, the profession can deal with its own members who are associated with noncomplying financial statements. For example, section 206.4 of the Nova Scotia Institute of Chartered Accountants' Code of Ethics states that:

> A member shall not express an opinion without reservation that financial statements are prepared in accordance with generally accepted accounting principles if such statements depart in any material respect from the recommendations of the Canadian Institute of Chartered Accountants as set out in the *CICA Handbook* as amended from time to time.

If statements are not prepared in accordance with the *CICA Handbook* standards, the accountant involved is subject to disciplinary proceedings from the provincial institute.

Acceptance of Standards   The standard-setting structure in Canada has not gone unchallenged. Since the *CICA Handbook* is adopted in the regulations of the CBCA rather than in the act itself, the requirements of the *CICA Handbook* could be overruled by a federal cabinet decision. (A change to the act itself would require formal amendment by Parliament.) In the mid-1980s, the oil and gas industry—a powerful interest group—was unhappy with the accounting treatment for a type of government assistance, Petroleum Incentive Program (PIP) grants. Accordingly, they approached the CICA for a change in the standard. This lobbying attempt was unsuccessful. They then approached the federal government, looking for a cabinet decision to allow them to use the accounting procedure they desired, one that increased income in the short run.

Such a move would have undermined the credibility of the CICA's standard-setting process and created a dangerous precedent. The accounting profession rallied behind the CICA's standard, but it was only after the Ontario Securities Commission (the largest and most influential securities commission in Canada) also indicated its support for the *CICA Handbook* standard that the initiative died. The oil and gas industry was left with the unpopular but appropriate rule. Thus, political pressure was not overtly allowed to interfere in the standard-setting process. This is in marked contrast to the U.S. experience, where powerful interest groups have sometimes had the support of the U.S. Securities and Exchange Commission and have managed to reverse accounting standards.

THE ACCOUNTING STANDARDS BOARD

The Accounting Standards Board (AcSB) consists of 13 voting and 2 nonvoting members who serve three-year terms. The two nonvoting members are the senior vice president, CICA Studies and Standards, and the CICA's Accounting Standards director. The AcSB is served by a full-time professional staff of 11 members.

The voting members of the AcSB are chosen to provide a broad range of background and experience, including public accounting, industry, commerce and finance, and academia. Care is taken to ensure that there is a balance in both occupational and regional representation. An accounting background is essential, although members do not have to be Chartered Accountants. All voting members serve as unpaid volunteers.

At least nine of the voting members are chosen by the board of directors of the CICA. The following organizations are also entitled to choose a member of the committee:

- The Canadian Council of Financial Analysts (CCFA).
- The Canadian Academic Accounting Association (CAAA).
- The Financial Executives Association of Canada (FEAC).
- The Certified General Accountants' Association of Canada (CGAAC).
- The Society of Management Accountants of Canada (SMAC).

Several features of the current AcSB make it more effective than its predecessor committees:

1. **Smaller size** The AcSB has 13 voting members, whereas its predecessor had 22.
2. **Board representation** Members are chosen to represent a broad range of occupations and interests.
3. **Increased staff and advisory support** The AcSB has its own staff and a widely based advisory body (The Standards Advisory Board) available to advise the AcSB on its agenda and proposed releases.
4. **Service** AcSB members serve for three years, and, as volunteers, do not need to sacrifice their careers to participate in the standard-setting process.
5. **Task forces** The AcSB is directed to include groups of subject area specialists in the development of a particular standard to improve the quality of input and decisions.

The current structure of the AcSB and associated organizations responsible for setting accounting standards in Canada is shown in Exhibit 1–2. The Standards Advisory Committee and the Emerging Issues Committee have specialized roles in the standard-setting process.

The **Standards Advisory Board** consists of 10 to 15 members chosen to represent a broad cross section of financial statement user groups. The Standard Advisory Board provides the opportunity for those who are affected by accounting standards, whether as preparers or users of the resulting information, to influence the standard-setting process. The board may include lawyers, economists, senior representatives from manufacturing and finance sectors of the economy, as well as the actuarial profession, labour, and the financial press. The board participates in setting priorities for the AcSB and provides input on the development of new standards and studies.

EXHIBIT 1-2
Standard-Setting Structure

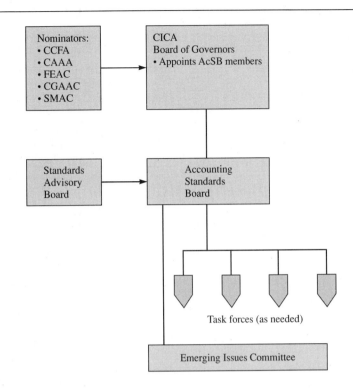

Task forces (as needed)

A committee called the **Emerging Issues Committee (EIC)** was formed by the AcSB to consider issues that are likely to receive divergent or unsatisfactory treatment in practice in the absence of some guidance. This committee provides timely guidance on specific issues without having to follow the lengthy due process required for *CICA Handbook* standards. The conclusions of this group have generally received the same status as AcSB standards.

AcSB Process

Standard setting follows a **due process,** an open format that provides an opportunity for interested parties to express their views.[8] The process involves nine steps, as illustrated in Exhibit 1–3:

1. **Write a project proposal** The proposal defines the project's term of reference and justifies the need for the standard, identifying the scope of the problem and the affected preparer and user groups.
2. **Appoint a task force** The task force, consisting of six or seven members, is established to develop material for AcSB members. These individuals will normally have specialist knowledge of the topic under consideration and attend all AcSB meetings at which the topic is debated. They serve only for the duration of their particular topic and do not vote.
3. **Develop an issues paper** (optional step) Issues papers are developed for more complex topics. The issues papers help the AcSB understand the views of interested parties on major issues before it starts to formulate its position on a particular subject.
4. **Create a statement of principles** The principles, usually developed by the task force, outline the basic response to the accounting issues raised. The principles must be approved by two-thirds of the AcSB before an exposure draft can be developed.
5. **Review with associates** Input is sought on a private and confidential basis from

[8] From *A Reference Guide for Volunteers, CICA Studies and Standards* (Toronto: CICA, 1993).

EXHIBIT 1-3
The Standard-Setting Process

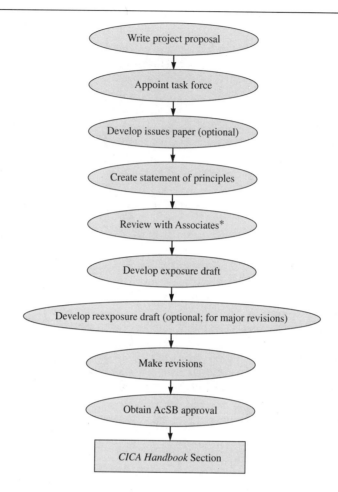

* And/or after development of exposure draft and re-exposure draft.

associates at key stages in the project's development. This may be at the statement of principles stage, it may follow the release of the exposure draft, or both. Associates provide an outside reaction to the proposed standard.

6. **Develop an exposure draft** An exposure draft is a handbook section in draft form. It is circulated, after AcSB approval, to professional accountants and other interested parties, who are asked to respond to the committee in writing.

7. **Make revisions** The responses to the exposure draft are carefully considered by the task force and the AcSB, and the exposure draft is rewritten in final form.

8. **Develop reexposure draft** (if significant change) If changes to the exposure draft are substantive, the proposed section will be reexposed and further public opinion will be solicited. For example, the exposure draft, "Financial Instruments," originally released in September 1991, was released for reexposure in March 1994 following substantive changes.

9. **Get AcSB approval** A two-thirds vote is required to approve a new section of the *CICA Handbook*.

This process is often lengthy, especially when steps are repeated.

During deliberations, all discussions are confidential. However, after the project has been completed, a public file is prepared, which includes the documents prepared and received in each of the steps along the way.

The AcSB issues two primary kinds of pronouncements:

1. *CICA Handbook* **sections** These statements establish accounting principles and procedures on specific issues and must be created by following established due process, as described.
2. **Accounting guidelines** These statements provide interpretation of existing standards or timely guidance on issues requiring immediate clarification. Guidelines are released without following the due process steps outlined above. Like the EIC pronouncements, they do not carry the full weight of a handbook section, although they are generally followed in practice.

STANDARD SETTING IN THE UNITED STATES

In Canada, many of our standards are influenced by the actions and conclusions of U.S. standard setters. This is hardly suprising. Canada's major trading partner, the United States, is significantly larger than Canada, both in population and economic activity. We share much the same financial environment, so that Canadian and U.S. accounting issues are often identical. Therefore, it is instructive to understand the history and current process of U.S. standard setting.

History

The standard-setting environment is somewhat different in the United States than in Canada. The U.S. government and the Securities and Exchange Commission (SEC) have not always been willing to support the official standards of the profession and have sometimes had an adversarial attitude toward standard-setting efforts. The SEC has published its own accounting recommendations, to be followed by public companies, when they are convinced by various interest groups that the profession's standards are flawed. This has not improved the credibility of the standard-setting process.

During the period from 1938 through 1958, the Committee on Accounting Procedure of the American Institute of Certified Public Accountants (AICPA) issued a series of pronouncements dealing with accounting principles, procedures, and terminology. Primary among these were the *Accounting Research* and *Accounting Terminology Bulletins* (with revisions). This series of statements was combined and published in 1961 by the AICPA as the *Final Edition*. Rather than attempting to develop a comprehensive statement of principles, the series dealt with specific problem areas. The *Accounting Terminology Bulletins* addressed a very serious problem of semantics: Various terms were being used by the profession rather loosely, much to the confusion of the financial community and the interested public generally.

The Accounting Principles Board (APB) was organized by the AICPA in 1959 to replace the Committee on Accounting Procedure. The APB was a volunteer committee of the AICPA, in some ways very similar to the CICA's AcSB. After a series of unsuccessful standards that did not win business or SEC support, the structure was again changed.

FASB

In 1972, the AICPA's board of directors and council replaced the Accounting Principles Board with a full-time, seven-member Financial Accounting Standards Board (FASB). The FASB is structurally different from the AcSB in several important aspects:

1. Its members are full-time, paid employees. This enables them to focus exclusively on standard setting, improving efficiency but also increasing cost.
2. The FASB is appointed by an independent board—the Financial Accounting Federation (FAF)—and is not a committee of any one professional accounting organization. The FAF is comprised of many groups that have an interest in accounting standards, including, of course, the AICPA. The FAF is funded by donations from its constituents and by revenue from publication sales. This struc-

ture ensures the independence of the standard-setting process and the inclusion of many interested parties.

3. The FASB has more research staff than its Canadian counterpart, and it regularly engages in field research to support standard-setting initiatives.
4. The FASB is smaller than the AcSB.

The due process used by the FASB involves the following steps:

1. Select and prioritize issues for the board's agenda.
2. Appoint a representative task force to identify and define the problems and alternatives related to the issue assigned to each task force.
3. Conduct research and analysis about the issue by internal staff and outside experts.
4. Prepare a decision memorandum on the issue and distribute it to interested parties, with an invitation to comment.
5. Hold a public hearing.
6. Prepare an analysis of all comments received about the issue.
7. Decide whether to issue a standard. If the decision is yes, prepare and distribute to all interested parties an exposure draft of the standard. An invitation to comment is included. Public hearings are often held.
8. Prepare an analysis of all comments received about the exposure draft. Revise the exposure draft as needed.
9. Approve (or disapprove) the exposure draft.

The FASB's due process is similar to the AcSB's in many ways. The most striking difference is that the FASB must begin its process with a discussion memorandum and hold public hearings to elicit response to the issues raised. The FASB's structure and elaborate due process are designed to create, and be seen to create, standards that are in the public interest and worthy of support.

WHAT IS GAAP?

The *CICA Handbook,* in Section 1000, paragraphs .59 and .60, describes generally accepted accounting principles (GAAP) carefully:

Generally accepted accounting principles is the term used to describe the basis on which financial statements are normally prepared. There are special circumstances where a different basis of accounting may be appropriate, for example, in financial statements prepared in accordance with regulatory legislation or contractual requirements.

The term generally accepted accounting principles encompasses not only specific rules, practices and procedures relating to particular circumstances but also broad principles and conventions of general application, including the underlying concepts described in this Section. Specifically, *generally accepted accounting principles comprise the Accounting Recommendations in the Handbook* and, when a matter is not covered by a Recommendation, other accounting principles that either:

(a) *are generally accepted by virtue of their use in similar circumstances by a significant number of entities in Canada;* or
(b) *are consistent with the Recommendations in the Handbook and are developed through the exercise of professional judgment,* including consultation with other informed accountants where appropriate, and the application of the concepts described in this Section. In exercising professional judgment, established principles for analogous situations dealt with in the Handbook would be taken into account and reference would be made to:
  (i) other relevant matters dealt with in the Handbook;
  (ii) practice in similar circumstances;
  (iii) Accounting Guidelines . . .;
  (iv) Abstracts of Issues Discussed by the CICA Emerging Issues Committee;
  (v) International Accounting Standards published by the International Accounting Standards Committee;
  (vi) standards published by bodies authorized to establish financial accounting standards in other jurisdictions;

(vii) CICA research studies; and

(viii) other sources of accounting literature such as textbooks and journals.

The relative importance of these various sources is a matter of professional judgment in the circumstances. [Emphasis added.]

CONCEPT REVIEW

1. What organization currently formulates generally accepted accounting principles?
2. What is the essence of the AcSB's due process procedure?
3. How are Canadian and U.S. due process procedures different?
4. What constitutes GAAP?

ACCOUNTING AND RELATED ORGANIZATIONS

There are a variety of bodies with an interest in accounting standards and the standard-setting process discussed in this chapter. These organizations influence the development of accounting standards.

Canadian Institute of Chartered Accountants

The CICA is the national professional organization of chartered accountants. Its efforts and publications focus on the practice of public accounting. Its primary publications include:

1. *CA Magazine:* a monthly publication containing articles, exposure drafts, and special sections of interest to independent accountants.
2. *Financial Reporting in Canada:* a biannual publication containing a survey of the characteristics of the annual financial reports of 300 public corporations.
3. *CICA Research Studies:* a series of studies that focusses on specific accounting issues, providing background information, alternative solutions, and, in many cases, recommended practices.
4. *Statements of Auditing Standards:* audit standards promulgated by the Auditing Standards Board. These standards govern auditing practice in much the same way that GAAP governs financial reporting.
5. *Statements of Accounting Standards:* accounting standards promulgated by the AcSB.

Certified General Accountants' Association of Canada

Incorporated by an act of Parliament in 1913, the Certified General Accountants' Association of Canada (CGAAC), or CGA-Canada, is currently the fastest-growing body of professional accountants in Canada. Its members are involved in managerial accounting and, in many provinces, are permitted to practice public accounting.

Of particular note is the Canadian Certified General Accountants' Research Foundation, established in 1979 to foster and promote the advancement of education and research in accounting. This foundation has been particularly active in the publication of monographs on a wide range of topical accounting issues.

CGA-Canada produces a wide range of publications to meet the needs of its members, including *CGA Magazine*, a monthly publication, and *The GAAP Guide*, which summarizes and compares Canadian, U.S., and international accounting standards.

The Society of Management Accountants

The Society of Management Accountants (SMA) is the professional organization responsible for the training, accreditation, and continuing professional development of Certified Management Accountants (CMAs). CMAs are employed in business, industry, and government and are often the preparers of financial reports issued to the public. Their interest in the standard-setting process stems from this involvement. Publications of the SMA include a variety of research studies and a monthly magazine, *Cost and Management*.

Securities Commissions

The most influential of the government regulatory agencies that influence accounting and reporting by businesses are the various provincial securities commissions. These commissions have the authority to establish and enforce accounting standards for those companies over which they have jurisdiction. Each province has such a commission, but they tend to be large and influential in provinces with public stock exchanges. Due to the prominance of the Toronto Stock Exchange, the Ontario Securities Commission (OSC) is of particular importance.

Before a company is allowed to sell an issue of securities, it must file a prospectus with the appropriate securities commission. The prospectus reports information about the company, its officers, and its financial affairs. The financial portion of the prospectus must be audited. Once its securities have been sold to the public, the company must file with the appropriate securities commission, as a matter of public record, audited financial statements each subsequent year, unaudited quarterly statements, and any other information requested by the securities commission. Disclosure requirements are extensive.

Although the securities commissions have statutory authority to prescribe financial accounting and external reporting requirements for listed companies, they rely on the accounting profession to set and enforce accounting standards and to regulate the profession. When there is disagreement within the accounting profession over significant issues, the securities commissions can exercise their influence to resolve matters.

Revenue Canada

Revenue Canada is an agency of the federal government established to interpret and enforce the nation's federal tax laws. To do so, Revenue Canada has adopted procedures and reporting requirements whose purpose is to collect money and, at times, to attain specific social objectives considered important by Parliament. These objectives include, for example, the redistribution of wealth through graduated tax rates and the encouragement of investment in plant through accelerated depreciation deductions.

The objectives of Revenue Canada's procedures and reporting requirements are not always consistent with the objective of sound financial reporting that attempts to provide useful information to investors, creditors, and others. Many small companies that keep only a single set of financial records do so on a tax basis so that the legally required reports can be made. It is natural for these firms to adopt accounting procedures designed to defer tax payments regardless of the impact on financial reporting usefulness.

Academic Associations

Canadian Academic Accounting Association (CAAA) and American Accounting Association (AAA) members are primarily accounting educators; however, members also include accountants in public practice, industry, and not-for-profit organizations. The Associations' objectives are to develop accounting theory, encourage and sponsor accounting research, and improve education in accounting. Statements of the CAAA and AAA do not constitute GAAP. The Associations operate through committees and publish monographs, committee reports, research studies, and periodicals, including *Contemporary Accounting Research, The Accounting Review, Accounting Horizons,* and *Issues in Accounting Education.* These periodicals contain articles and comments on a wide range of subjects pertaining to accounting research, concepts, and education.

The position papers relating to accounting theory and principles tend to be normative rather than descriptive. That is, they tend to express what accounting should be, rather than what accounting is, as reflected, for example, in GAAP. These organizations have a significant impact on accounting standards through responses to proposed statements and through the teaching, writing, and professional activities of their members.

Executive Associations

Executive associations are composed primarily of businesspeople with an interest in financial and accounting issues. As preparers of financial statements, they bear much of the cost of changing accounting procedures and disclosure requirements. They can represent a powerful lobby group. The two largest of these organizations are the Canadian Council of Financial Analysts (CCFA) and the Financial Executives Association of Canada (FEAC).

Other Groups

Private bodies representing special interest groups from real estate, banking, insurance, and other areas also interact with standard setters on proposed reporting practices affecting their areas of interest. These organizations, plus various business and industry representatives, make certain the AcSB is aware of their position on current issues. Sometimes, these same groups do their lobbying indirectly through government committees, bureaus, and regulatory agencies.

ATTAINING CONSENSUS IN A POLITICAL ENVIRONMENT

The primary objective in the development of accounting standards has been to develop standards that represent a consensus of the preparers, users, and independent auditors. This goal has not been wholly attained. The diverse goals, interests, and influence of each of these groups have created many difficulties and conflicts. A political process is involved that must reconcile the general interest, the conceptual and technical characteristics of accounting itself, and the specific interests of all three groups: preparers, auditors, and users. The success of this process in formulating a consensus on accounting standards depends on the conceptual soundness, absence of bias, and appropriate cost–benefit trade-offs in the decisions of the AcSB. Success also depends on the extent to which interested parties perceive their interests will be served. The participant groups and the general process of attaining a consensus are illustrated in Exhibit 1–4.

Compliance with the prescribed accounting standards is the responsibility of the preparers and the accounting profession and is primarily enforced by professional accounting bodies, the provincial securities commissions, and the courts. Many observers believe that compliance is a weak link in the chain. This view is supported by recurring oversight actions of the provincial securities commissions, increasing litigation in the courts, and the escalating cost of liability insurance premiums paid by auditing firms.

Should standard setting and compliance enforcement be the responsibility of the private sector or the public sector—that is, by legislative action of Parliament or a federal agency? Many believe that these activities should reside exclusively in the private sector. These individuals maintain that governmental regulation would not be effective. They believe that the preparers, auditors, and users can provide adequate policing action to protect the public interest. They also think that legislative action and federal oversight would result in inflexibility in meeting new challenges, slow reaction time to problems, an ineffective public forum, stereotyped reporting, and a rule-bound environment. Others believe that legislative action and a responsible government agency are necessary to serve the public interest and to oversee the rule-making and enforcement activities properly. Still others feel that a cooperative effort by the private and public sectors would be most appropriate.

Controversy is not new to the standard-setting process. Moreover, many issues, new and old, continue to challenge the AcSB. A partial list of these issues includes:
- Financial instruments.
- Use of present values for valuation of assets.
- Corporate income tax.
- Price-level adjusted financial statements.

EXHIBIT 1–4

Participants in Attaining a Consensus in Setting Accounting Standards

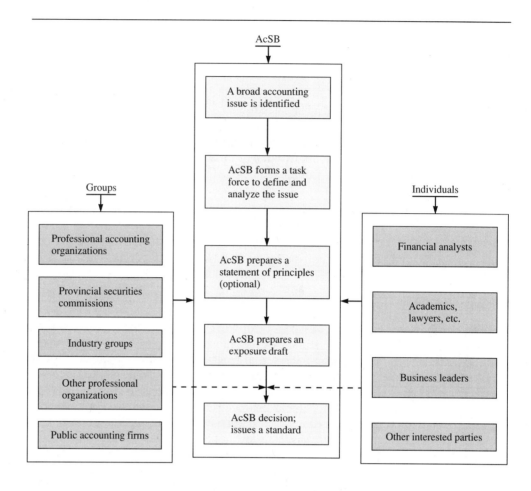

These are complex issues and have more than one reasonable solution. In each case, the choice of treatment makes a substantial difference in the dollar amounts reported in the financial statements.

Influential groups and organizations use the due process procedures of the AcSB to plead their case for alternative solutions. Their arguments include the failure of cost–benefit tests, claims that the proposed accounting treatment is not theoretically sound, statements that the reporting will not be understandable by users, implementation issues, and concerns that the economic consequences of the proposed standard will be disastrous to the firm, the industry, or the country. Government agencies, industry, and associations such as the Financial Executives Association of Canada often forcefully communicate their positions on existing and proposed standards to the AcSB. This lobbying has the positive result of informing AcSB members about issues they might otherwise overlook or underestimate.

Standard setting is carried out in a political environment that can't help but affect the process, whether we like it or not. The critical and recurring question is whether the motivation for a standard ought to be the effect of the standard on an economic outcome (e.g., the distribution of wealth, the country's trade balance, the type of compensation package offered employees, the level of research expenditures, and so on), or, alternatively, whether it should simply be a neutral reporting of financial events.

Some believe that if a standard has economic implications—and most, if not all, do—the AcSB should not ignore these implications. A few would go further and argue that standards *should* be a means of implementing economic policy. Others argue this is not the province of the AcSB. The AcSB is not elected but is rather appointed by private parties. Economic policy is appropriately left to the country's elected representatives. Further, they maintain, even were it appropriate for the

GLOBAL VIEW

In addition to Canadian organizations that influence accounting standards, international organizations concerned with accounting standards are playing an increasingly important role.

Recent times have witnessed the disappearance of both geographical and psychological barriers to globalization. The markets for products and services are increasingly international. Business thinks in market share terms with a global perspective. Financial markets, as well, have been affected as large companies raise capital worldwide where terms are most favourable.[9] Investors follow suit, making funds available globally.

The efficient operation of these financial markets is facilitated by commonly accepted accounting standards. Unfortunately, such common standards do not currently exist.

The **International Accounting Standards Committee (IASC)** was established to narrow the range of divergence in accounting standards and thereby make business easier to conduct. To date, the IASC has issued 31 standards. The Committee has 13 voting member countries, and an affirmative vote of three-quarters of its members is necessary to pass an IASC standard. However, the IASC has no means of enforcing compliance with its standards. Although its efforts are supported by the International Organization of Securities Commissioners (IOSCO), its authority is limited to the willingness of sovereign governments to adopt its views. Further, the IASC is composed primarily of representatives of national professional accounting groups such as the AICPA in the United States and the CICA in Canada, rather than being made up of members of national standard-setting bodies such as FASB or the AcSB. Yet even if this were not the case, the processes used by these national standard-setting bodies to adopt accounting standards would make substantive change difficult.

The legal and psychological hurdles to achieving common reporting standards across borders are formidable. In most continental European countries, for example, tax laws take precedence over reporting to investors and creditors. Additional issues, including language, culture, ethical standards, business practices, financial institutions, and financial instruments also differentiate the respective member countries. Differences exist as to when profit and revenues are reported, how assets are valued and amortized, capitalization requirements, the recognition of liabilities, the timing of expenses, and allowing write-offs directly to equity. Even differences in the basic financial reporting objectives in the various member companies have led to significantly different reporting guidelines. Until these differences are reconciled, cross-country company comparisons of financial statements will be difficult at best. The task of achieving harmony is going to be long and arduous.

Although it is slow, progress is being made. In 1987, the IASC began a project aimed at reducing alternative accounting treatments for like transactions and events. Ultimately, ten statements were revised, effective January 1, 1993, narrowing certain accounting alternatives. In addition, the European Union (formerly the European Community) has issued several directives that, if adopted by member states, will probably promote financial reporting harmonization.

Recently, the increasing level of international trade and cross-border financing arrangements has motivated the IASC to change its approach from one of narrowing alternatives to one of eliminating alternatives.[10] Achieving international consensus will be harder under this stricter mission.

AcSB to concern itself with economic consequences, its members are not trained to do so, given the complex and subtle nature of our economy.[11]

Regardless of the merits of the alternative positions, the important point is the AcSB's attitude toward the issue. The AcSB's objective is to ensure neutrality of information resulting from its standards. To be neutral, information must report economic activity as faithfully as possible without colouring the image it communicates for the purpose of influencing behaviour in any particular direction. After all, it is not feasible to change financial accounting standards that accountants use every time government policy changes direction, even if it were desirable to do so. Moreover, only if accounting information is neutral can it safely be used to help guide those policies as well as measure their results.

The neutrality position is not, however, easily maintained. Not only does the AcSB concern itself with implementation costs, but it also tries subjectively to balance these against the financial reporting benefits, a tough task at best.[12]

---

[9] Economists and accountants maintain that some companies could lower their cost of capital by providing reports that clearly demonstrate their financial health. "Differing Accounting Rules Snarl Europe," *The Wall Street Journal*, September 4, 1992.

[10] D. Carmichael and C. James "International Accounting Standards: Are They Coming to America?" *The CPA Journal*, October 1992, pp. 16–24.

[11] For a further discussion see S. Zeff, "The Rise and Fall of Economic Consequences," *Journal of Accountancy*, December 1978, pp. 56–63.

[12] Delays permitted in implementing new standards are perhaps the most visible sign of the AcSB's recognition of the implementation costs.

Moreover, although the fact may be difficult to document, it is likely that consideration of alleged economic consequences has influenced the AcSB's actions.

CONCEPT REVIEW

1. Name the organizations identified by the following letters: CAAA, CICA, AcSB, FASB, FEAC, SMAC, and OSC.
2. What organizations are responsible for enforcing compliance with prescribed accounting standards?
3. What is the AcSB's position on whether its standards should be set explicitly to reflect government policy?

ETHICS AND FINANCIAL REPORTING

Financial reporting is a service function. To be useful, financial information must be objective and reliable. Thus, it must be free of bias and intentional distortion. Yet because the business environment is becoming more complex, financial reporting is simultaneously becoming more complex. Complexity creates dilemmas, and these dilemmas are made more difficult to resolve by the desires of management to report improved short-term results. Pressures arise to report desired results and to ignore issues—in essence, to bend the rules. (The Chambers situation discussed in this chapter's introduction illustrates the pressures to report continuing earnings growth.) Some of the ethical dilemmas that arise are clear; others are not. The proper action is not always evident. For example, auditors may wish a company to disclose information that would be of value to a competitor. This information may raise conflicts between respecting the relationship with the client and the auditors' responsibility to disclose information to protect the public. Or, information may come to the attention of the accountant that could be used for personal gain. The accountant may be asked to use a questionable reporting method. What should be done? The answer rests on the fact that the auditors' ultimate responsibility is to the public.

The solution often is neither obvious nor easy. The question ultimately is not a legal one but an ethical one. A working rule sometimes suggested for resolving these dilemmas is to ask yourself if you would be comfortable reading about your actions on the front page of tomorrow's newspaper.

In facing a difficult ethical dilemma, the first responsibility is to recognize that an ethical issue is present. Recognition assumes a sensitivity that is developed from experience. Second, the accountant must try to understand the issues and the costs and to identify alternatives. Third, time must be spent to reflect and evaluate. Consultation is often important. Finally, an accountant will make the decision and find the best means to communicate it. The decision should meet the ''tomorrow's-newspaper'' test.

CONCEPT REVIEW

1. What is the main force behind the need to harmonize international accounting standards?
2. What is the current mission of the IASC?
3. To whom is the accountant ultimately responsible in an ethical sense?

SUMMARY OF KEY POINTS

(L.O. 1, 2, 3)   1. Accounting is an information system whose purpose is to identify, collect, measure, and communicate information about economic entities to those with interest in the entities' financial affairs. This purpose is accomplished through the periodic issuance of public financial statements.

(L.O. 2) 2. The objective of public financial statements is to disclose the economic effects of completed transactions and other events on the organization for use in decision making.

(L.O. 2) 3. Financial statements include the balance sheet, the income statement, the retained earnings statement, and the statement of changes in financial position.

(L.O. 3) 4. The reporting of such information as the composition of assets and changes in income enables decision makers to assess the opportunities for gain and the risks of loss inherent in the organization.

(L.O. 4, 5) 5. The rules and principles under which external financial statements are constructed are known as generally accepted accounting principles (GAAP) and are currently established by the Accounting Standards Board (AcSB).

(L.O. 5, 6) 6. The AcSB is a volunteer committee of the CICA operating with extensive due process procedures, broad participation, and authority delegated through the CBCA and the provincial securities commissions to formulate accounting standards.

(L.O. 4, 6) 7. Setting financial reporting standards is a complex process occurring within a political environment that influences both what reporting is required and when. Businesses, accounting organizations, trade and consumer associations, provincial securities commissions, Revenue Canada, the courts, public accounting firms, individual users, and government at both the provincial and federal levels can and do influence reporting practice.

(L.O. 3, 4, 6) 8. Standard setters attempt to adopt a neutral position toward the economic consequences of standards. However, it is not always possible for the AcSB to ignore the effect of external financial statements on the allocation of economic resources and the distribution of wealth. Estimation of the cost of a standards implementation is an example.

(L.O. 7) 9. The International Accounting Standards Committee (IASC) is the organization attempting to harmonize financial accounting standards across international borders. Differences in culture, tax laws, and reporting objectives make the task a formidable one.

(L.O. 7) 10. Accountants' ethical responsibilities arise from their obligations to serve the public.

REVIEW PROBLEM

This follow-up report was issued to the shareholders of Standard Trustco Limited:

To Our Shareholders
On July 27, 1990, Standard Trustco announced that its auditors, Peat Marwick Thorne, would conduct an audit of the June 30, 1990 financial statements to ensure that the Company's loan loss provision and policy of interest accruals accurately reflect currently depressed real estate conditions. The audit required significant adjustments to the unaudited June 30, 1990 financial statements, which have been withdrawn and replaced with the enclosed audited financial statements.

The restated results show a net loss of $50,181,000, or $7.15 per common share, for the six months ended June 30, 1990, compared with previously reported net income of $5,358,000, or $0.69 per common share. The restated results are attributable primarily to additional provisions required for losses on mortgages, notes and receivables under equipment leases of approximately $52,000,000 and to reversals of income tax recoveries, write-offs of deferred income tax debits and professional fees totalling approximately $3,000,000.

The Board of Directors and management of Standard Trustco are working closely with the Company's bankers to finalize a plan for the restructuring of its operations. The Company is segregating the portfolio of non-performing loans and intends to bring in people who specialize in this area.

If Standard Trustco is bound by the same GAAP as their auditors, why would there have been such a significant difference between the June 1990 statements prepared by Standard and those prepared by Peat Marwick Thorne?

SOLUTION

Recall that GAAP refers to broad guidelines, conventions, rules, and procedures. These human rules are subject to interpretation. Thus, there is room for differences of opinion. The difference in opinion, in this case, was in estimating the quality (collectibility) of Standard's receivables (mortgages, notes, and receivables under equipment leases) and recognition of interest revenue.

The magnitude of the differences in opinion should, of course, be of concern. While reasonable differences of opinion are acceptable, a deliberate misstatement is not only unacceptable but also illegal. The magnitude of differences is an attention getter. In the case of Standard Trustco, the *Financial Post,* January 14, 1991, Section 2, page 13, reported:

Troubled Standard Trustco Ltd. has been walking a regulatory tightrope since last spring when federal regulators began poring over the trust company's books. That rope has begun to quiver.

The Ontario Securities Commission last month began an investigation to determine whether Standard Trustco failed to prepare its June 30, 1990, financial statements and possibly prior statements in accordance with generally accepted accounting principles as required under the Ontario Securities Act.

During the first quarter of 1991, attempts to sell or merge Standard Trustco failed. In April 1991, creditors forced Standard Trustco into bankruptcy.

QUESTIONS

1. What is accounting?
2. Explain the distinction between financial and management accounting. Does this distinction mean that a company should have two accounting systems? Explain.
3. What is meant by general-purpose financial statements? What are their basic components?
4. What is the basic objective of financial reporting?
5. Why does financial accounting emphasize cash flows?
6. What are the primary areas of service provided by professional accountants?
7. The independent accountant fulfills a unique professional role that involves the concept of independence. Why is that concept important?
8. What organizations have given authority to the *CICA Handbook* standards?
9. What factors make the AcSB an effective standard-setting body?
10. Who appoints the AcSB committee members? Why are a variety of organizations included?
11. Briefly explain the due process system used by the AcSB to develop an accounting standard.
12. What is the role of the Standards Advisory Board?
13. What is the role of the Emerging Issues Committee?
14. What is the difference between an accounting guideline and a section of the *CICA Handbook?*
15. Explain how U.S. standard setting is different from Canadian standard setting, both in structure and due process.
16. Briefly explain the SEC's role in establishing U.S. accounting standards.
17. What is the CAAA? What is its role in developing accounting theory and standards?
18. Why is there widespread interest in the development of accounting standards?
19. Why is a consensus important with respect to accounting standards? How is a consensus attained at the present time?
20. What is the IASC's primary mission?

CASES

C 1-1
(L.O. 3, 4, 5)

 **Neutrality and Standard Setting**   A speaker at a recent conference stated: "Many groups, including governments, financial institutions, investors and corporations in various industries, argue that their interests are affected by present and proposed accounting pronouncements. The sometimes contradictory interests of these groups are recognized by the accounting profession. However, accounting is neutral and is not influenced by the self-interest of any one group."

Required   Write a report that discusses the issues raised.

(CICA adapted)

C 1-2
(L.O. 3, 4, 6)

Small Business and GAAP   Several authors have addressed the question of whether small business enterprises should have their own set of generally accepted accounting principles rather than be required to comply with all the recommendations presently in the *CICA Handbook*. The writers reason that many current accounting principles seem to be geared to large businesses and that small enterprises should not be asked to implement recommendations that do not justify their costs by relevance or resulting benefits.

Required   Write a report that gives the arguments for (1) having one set of generally accepted accounting principles for all sizes of businesses and (2) small businesses having their own set of generally accepted accounting principles.

(CICA adapted)

C 1-3
(L.O. 7)

Selecting a Job Offer Bill Johnson has devoted his undergraduate program to preparing for a career as a public accountant. He is currently in his senior year and has interviewed with several regional auditing firms. He has also interviewed with several manufacturing firms for a position and has received an attractive offer from one of them.

Because of his preference to work for an auditing firm, he called those that had given him a second, follow-up interview to see if they had reached a decision on his application. Two firms out of the five he visited on second interviews indicated that they continued to be interested in him but because they had not completed their second interviews with other candidates, they would not be able to give him an answer for several weeks. The other three firms said that Bill had been a strong candidate but that low hiring quotas and a stronger group of interviewees than usual meant that they could not offer him a position.

The offer from the manufacturing firm had a one-week deadline and, since he would learn nothing new in that time from the auditing firms during this period, Bill called to say he was accepting their offer. Bill felt he could not wait because he was supporting a wife and child and had no other good leads at that time. Further, he feared that the two auditing firms with a continuing interest might simply have him on a waiting list. In this case, he would receive an offer only if other priority candidates refused their offers.

Shortly after Bill called to accept the manufacturing position, one of the auditing firms called to say that the addition of two new clients enabled them to increase hiring and that they could now offer Bill a position. Bill was excited, but given his previous manufacturing job acceptance (which he did not mention to the auditing firm) he said he would talk the offer over with his wife and get back to them.

The auditing firm said they needed an answer soon but gave Bill until the end of the week to decide. Bill and his wife both preferred the auditing firm, mainly because of his long-held desire to work for an auditing firm, their belief that this would be a better starting job with a greater future, and the better location of the job with the auditing firm.

Bill comes to you as his friend for counsel on his dilemma. What do you think Bill should do, and how would you counsel him?

C 1-4
(L.O. 4)

Accounting Policy Disagreement You have been hired as the assistant in the finance department of a medium-sized publicly traded firm. Realizing the importance of accounting to your new duties, you have recently completed a two-semester introductory course in financial accounting in night school at a local community college. In this course, you learned that research costs are expensed during the period they are incurred. You also recall, however, that accountants believe in matching the costs of a given activity with the revenues resulting from that activity.

Recently, your firm has developed an important breakthrough in electronic copying equipment. The research cost has been considerable. If this cost were capitalized this year and written off against expected future revenues from the new machine, this year's earnings per share would increase by 10 percent rather than show a modest decline.

Your superior clearly favors capitalization because the firm's CEO wants to continue a 20-quarter record of increasing earnings per share figures. She has asked your opinion based on your recent exposure to accounting standards. A meeting with your superior is set for tomorrow morning.

In the meantime, you have researched your firm's past practice in this area and you have reread the accounting standard, Section 3450 of the *CICA Handbook*. Although your firm has not previously experienced the level of research expenses associated with the present project, past practice in your firm has been to expense these costs. Your reading of the accounting standard confirms what you recall from class—namely, that these expenses should be expensed.

Unfortunately, your superior is anxious to take the alternative position and has been known to be intolerant of views differing from her own. How would you handle the meeting the next day?

C 1-5
(L.O. 4)

Lobbying and Standard Setting The Accounting Standards Board is subject to lobbying from preparers and users concerning the standards it sets. Write a brief essay describing (1) the extent to which the AcSB is affected by the lobbying activities of its constituents and (2) the advantages and disadvantages created by lobbying.

C 1-6
(L.O. 3, 4, 5)

Standards and Professional Judgment Although *CICA Handbook* standards provide general guidance, application of these standards is dependent on particular circumstances. In practice, an accountant may encounter situations where *CICA Handbook* standards do not exist or may not apply. Since there is no substitute for the exercise of professional judgment in the determination of what constitutes fair presentation and good practice, it has been suggested that too much effort is being directed towards the development of standards.

Required   Write a report that discusses the issues raised in the above statements.

(CICA adapted)

C 1-7
(L.O. 3, 4, 5, 6)   **Standards and the Environment**   Several accountants have expressed the opinion that accounting principles and auditing standards cannot be regarded as static but must be viewed as evolving with the times. At any one time, those who set standards must be aware of broad social and environmental conditions. As a result, it is necessary for accountants and auditors to be aware of the assumptions and reasoning on which a pronouncement has been based and of any subsequent changes that may affect the current validity of the pronouncement. Otherwise, an outdated and less appropriate principle or standard might be applied in a current, specific situation.

Required   Write a report that discusses the issues raised above.

(CICA adapted)

EXERCISES

E 1-1
(L.O. 1, 2, 4, 5)

Chapter Overview   Indicate whether each statement is true or false.

T F   1. External decision makers lack direct access to the information generated by the internal operations of a company.
T F   2. The income statement reports the company's cash flows from operating, investing, and financing activities.
T F   3. The primary objective of financial accounting is to report on stewardship.
T F   4. All generally accepted accounting principles are the result of a designated rule-making body.
T F   5. Company earnings goals are often tailored to a smooth pattern of earnings growth through operations.
T F   6. The CBCA names *CICA Handbook* standards as the source of GAAP.
T F   7. The standard-setting process followed by the AcSB allows for due process input by the user and preparer communities before a standard is promulgated.
T F   8. The EIC provides technical guidance to the AcSB on matters of limited importance and scope.
T F   9. GAAP includes practices that have evolved and gained acceptance over time.
T F 10. The objectives of reporting to Revenue Canada are essentially in harmony with reporting under GAAP.

E 1-2
(L.O. 1, 2)

Chapter Overview   Indicate whether each statement is true or false.

T F   1. Financial accounting focuses primarily on external users of financial statements.
T F   2. GAAP must be followed for all items in management accounting and financial accounting reports.
T F   3. General-purpose financial statements are prepared primarily for internal users.
T F   4. Management accounting is directly concerned with shareholders and creditors.
T F   5. Management accounting reports are usually not subject to an independent audit.
T F   6. Management accounting reporting requires a balance sheet, an income statement, and a statement of changes in financial position.
T F   7. Accountants in public accounting practice are not permitted to become involved in management services.
T F   8. The attest and audit functions are the same.
T F   9. Disclosure notes are considered an integral part of financial statements.
T F 10. A professional accountant always serves in an independent role.
T F 11. Internal reporting (i.e., management accounting) must follow GAAP in all respects.
T F 12. External financial reports are directed primarily to shareholders, creditors, and other similarly situated groups.

E 1-3
(L.O. 2)

Distinguish between Financial and Management Accounting   The two basic types of accounting and reporting are called *financial accounting* (F) and *management accounting* (M). Fifteen characteristics of accounting and reporting are listed below. Match the types with the characteristics by entering an F or an M in each blank on the left. If not applicable, enter N.

Type	Characteristics of Accounting and Reporting
_____	1. GAAP must generally be followed.
_____	2. External users are of primary concern.
_____	3. Relates to planning and controlling the operations of an entity.
_____	4. Does not primarily use general-purpose financial statements.
_____	5. Provides information for both internal and external use.
_____	6. Is of particular interest to investors and creditors.
_____	7. Does not have to conform to GAAP.
_____	8. Provides information that is useful to external users in predicting future cash flows.
_____	9. Internal users are of primary concern.
_____10.	Is seldom, if ever, subject to independent audit.
_____11.	Does not relate primarily to internal planning and control.
_____12.	Provides information primarily for internal use.
_____13.	Is not usually available to external users.
_____14.	Uses general-purpose financial statements.
_____15.	Users have direct access to the firm's internal information.

E 1-4
(L.O. 4)

Identify Accounting Organizations Organizations involved in setting accounting standards and the designation of some required reports are listed below. To the right are commonly used abbreviations. Match the designations with the abbreviations by entering the appropriate letters to the left.

	Designation	Abbreviation
__E__	Sample: Certified General Accountants' Association of Canada.	A. EIC
_____	1. Canadian Academic Accounting Association.	B. AcSB
_____	2. Accounting Research Committee.	C. AICPA
_____	3. Emerging Issues Committee.	D. CICA
_____	4. Ontario Securities Commission.	E. CGAAC
_____	5. Accounting Standards Board.	F. SEC
_____	6. Financial Accounting Standards Board.	G. CAAA
_____	7. Canadian Institute of Chartered Accountants.	H. ARC
_____	8. Securities and Exchange Commission.	I. AAA
_____	9. Financial Executives Association of Canada.	J. IASC
_____	10. American Institute of Certified Public Accountants.	K. FASB
_____	11. Academic Accounting Association.	L. FEAC
_____	12. Standards Advisory Board.	M. SAB
_____	13. Society of Management Accountants of Canada.	N. CCFA
_____	14. Canadian Council of Financial Analysts.	O. SMAC
_____	15. International Accounting Standards Committee.	P. OSC

E 1-5
(L.O. 4)

Due Process The accounting profession has a long history of developing accounting concepts and their application that constitute generally accepted accounting principles (GAAP). Listed below are some stages in the due process that creates accounting standards. Indicate the order of the steps, and match each step with a description of the activity.

Order	Description	Step	Activity
_____	_____	1. AcSB approval.	A. A group of experts.
_____	_____	2. Statement of principles.	B. Preliminary response to issues raised.
_____	_____	3. Revisions.	C. Circulated to accountants and interested users.
_____	_____	4. Project proposal.	D. Identify accounting problems.
_____	_____	5. Exposure draft.	E. Two-thirds of committee approval necessary.
_____	_____	6. *CICA Handbook* section.	F. Comments from specific individuals.
_____	_____	7. Appoint task force.	G. Final product.
_____	_____	8. Review with associates.	H. Terms of reference.
_____	_____	9. Issues paper.	I. Changes based on written feedback.

E 1-6
(L.O. 5)

Consensus Groups in Standard Setting The process of attaining a consensus in developing accounting standards involves three major groups, each of which is directly concerned with general-purpose financial statements. Each major group is composed of various subgroups.

The three major groups and some subgroups are listed below. Identify the subgroups with respect to the major groups by entering appropriate letters to the left; provide comments when needed for clarification.

Subgroups

     1. CICA.
     2. Current shareholder.
     3. General Motors of Canada.
     4. UAW (labour union).
     5. Financial Executives Association of Canada.
     6. Ernst and Young (accounting firm).
     7. Lending institutions.
     8. Ontario Securities Commission.
     9. OK Bookkeeping Service.
     10. Financial analysts.
     11. Sole owner of a small business.
     12. Canadian Academic Accounting Association.
     13. Society of Management Accountants of Canada.
     14. Potential investors.
     15. Canadian Council of Financial Analysts.
     16. Employees of companies.
     17. Teachers and students.
     18. Taxing and regulatory authorities.
     19. Legislators.
     20. Two-member local professional accounting firm.

Major Groups

A. Preparers.
B. Users.
C. Auditors.

PROBLEMS

P 1–1
(L.O. 3, 4, 5)

Accounting Principles At the completion of the annual audit of the financial statements of Alt Corporation, the president of the company asked about the meaning of the phrase *generally accepted accounting principles,* which appears in the audit report accompanying the financial statements. She observed that the meaning of the phrase must include more than what she considers to be "principles."

You have been asked to respond in writing to the president's question. You have decided to respond by considering the following:

a. What is the meaning of the term *accounting principles* as used in audit reports (excluding what *generally accepted* means)?
b. How does one determine whether an accounting principle is generally accepted? Consider sources of evidence to determine whether there is substantial authoritative support (do not merely list titles of documents).
c. Diversity in accounting practice will, and should, always exist among companies despite efforts to improve comparability. Discuss arguments that support this statement.

(AICPA adapted)

P 1–2
(L.O. 6)

Alternative Approaches to Setting Accounting Standards Explain and assess in writing the following approaches to setting accounting standards:
a. Private sector exclusively (that is, by private professional accounting organizations).
b. Public sector exclusively (that is, by government or governmental agency).
c. Private and public sectors jointly.

Include a consideration of the politics of a standard-setting approach.

P 1–3
(L.O. 4)

Approaches to Standard Setting There are many similarities and differences between the Canadian and U.S. standard-setting process. Write a brief essay identifying these differences, and speculating on the reasons for the differences. Include an analysis of structure, due process, cost, and speed.

P 1–4
(L.O. 7)

International Harmonization of Accounting Standards What would Canada gain from achieving a greater harmonization (less diversity) in international accounting standards? Write a brief essay to support your opinion.

P 1–5
(L.O. 3, 7)

The Credibility of Financial Statements The following paragraph appeared in the November 9, 1992, edition of *Time* magazine on page 44.

"The automaking losses have put GM in the kind of financial position lately associated with dying airlines and retail chains. The company has been frantically seeking cash to meet its financial obligations. GM has sold stock and tapped credit markets to raise $5 billion in the past year alone, mostly to pay operating expenses. If the financial squeeze grows too tight, GM might even file for bankruptcy protection under Chapter 11 to force concessions in its wage, pension, and benefit packages. "This is not the company it once was," says a GM director. "There is going to have to be special oversight by the board for the next three years. Our credibility is at stake in the credit markets."

In cases similar to this, what factors do you believe will be important in establishing the credibility of the firm's financial statements?

2 Financial Statement Concepts and Principles

LEARNING OBJECTIVES

After you have studied this chapter, you will be able to:

1   **Explain the need for and importance of financial statement concepts as they relate to financial reporting.**

2   **Identify the users of financial statements, explain why they use the statements, and list the characteristics of accounting information considered of critical importance.**

3   **Define the elements of financial statements.**

4   **Describe the recognition and measurement criteria and explain how they provide the conceptual basis of accrual accounting.**

5   **Explain the essential assumptions, implementation principles, and constraints underlying generally accepted accounting principles.**

INTRODUCTION

In a public offering of new securities, Sunshine Mining Company sold an issue of corporate bonds that set stockbrokers and investors abuzz. Sunshine Mining, a major silver mining operator, proposed to redeem these bonds at maturity in a unique manner: each bondholder had the option of receiving a flat $1,000 in cash, the bond's face value, 50 ounces of silver, or the dollar equivalent of the silver.

Sunshine Mining's bonds were the first of a new breed of securities, later to be called *commodity-backed bonds*. The investing public was intrigued. If the market price for silver surpassed $1,000 per 50 ounces, the bondholders stood to make a tidy profit. If the price of silver went through the roof, the chance existed for a major killing.

The unconventional nature of this bond offering raised a few eyebrows within the business world as well. What if General Motors were to offer products as an option for redeeming bond issues, settling debt obligations in Oldsmobiles or Pontiacs instead of cash? What if Procter & Gamble used soaps and consumer products to do the same? McDonald's Corporation might join the parade, offering dividends in the form of burgers and fries.

Given a particular economic climate, almost any investment project is possible. At the time of Sunshine Mining's offering, even the so-called blue chip corporations couldn't sell new-issue securities to the public without some significant "extra" to sweeten the deal. Perceived as a risky speculative-grade company, Sunshine Mining needed a sweetener in the worst way. Thus, the option to redeem the bonds for silver—the silver market was strong at the time—was dictated by the financial situation of the company and the economic environment.

From an accounting perspective, how would these bonds be treated for accounting purposes? What impact would this offering have on the company's balance sheet and, in turn, on the company's financial integrity?

Bonds are debt obligations, carried on the issuing corporation's books as liabilities. Sunshine Mining had to determine the appropriate dollar value to record the debt. The alternatives were the face amount of the offering, $1,000 per bond, or the current equivalent dollar value of the silver for which the bonds might be redeemed.

Depending on the accounting treatment selected—and in Sunshine Mining's case, depending on what was happening in the silver market—a company could misrepresent its financial position by either overstating or understating the dollar value of its outstanding debt obligations. External users would then find it more difficult to evaluate the company. The shareholders and bondholders who rely on a corporation's financial statements for assurance that their investments are safe might be misled. Bankers and other creditors that make loans and advance credit on the basis of financial strength as reported in the financial statements might find it difficult to evaluate the financial soundness of the company. Those who supply the company's material and service needs and use the financial statements to rate the corporation's creditworthiness might find it difficult to evaluate the company's ability to pay. Or the company's customers, who rely on financial statements for assurance of contract performance, could face increased performance uncertainty.

Corporations never seem to run short of creative ideas for conducting business and finding new sources of financing. Each new business transaction typically means that new techniques are needed for accounting and disclosure. Sunshine Mining's commodity-backed bonds are a case in point.

Individual financial statement users have different information needs. Some claim they need to know everything about a company, although the evidence suggests that most actually use far less information than is made available. At the other extreme are investors who want only minimal information for their decision-making processes. *A challenge for accountants is to determine how much information to supply in general-purpose financial statements, in what format, and under what assumptions, principles, and constraints.*

Compounding the problem are managers who hold their own opinions on how much accounting information should be provided to external decision makers. Here, the spectrum of philosophies ranges from "Tell 'em only what they need to know" to "Tell 'em everything and let 'em figure it out."

This chapter discusses the accounting profession's responsibility to provide external decision makers with financial statements they can use with reasonable levels of reliability and confidence. It focusses on the Accounting Standards Board (AcSB) of the Canadian Institute of Chartered Accountants as the authoritative voice of the accounting profession. The AcSB uses its influence to keep accounting practices in step with business practices. The AcSB also determines the manner and extent to which accounting information should be communicated.

As this book goes to press, the price of silver is about $3.50 per ounce. Sunshine's bonds mature in the near future. If you were asked to offer an opinion on how these bonds should be carried on Sunshine Mining's books, what would you say?

EXHIBIT 2–1
Overview of the Financial
Statement Concepts

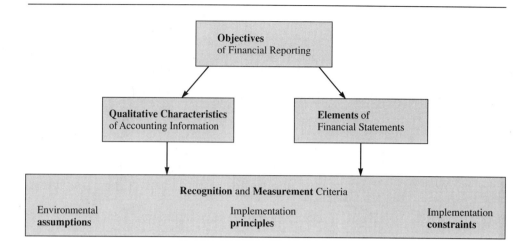

THE AcSB's
FINANCIAL
STATEMENT
CONCEPTS

In Chapter 1, we explained how the Accounting Standards Board came into existence, how it functions, and how it serves the needs of the accounting profession. The AcSB's role is to establish consensus on topical accounting issues, to interpret accounting principles, and to keep accounting practice as standardized as possible.

This chapter emphasizes the AcSB's financial statement concepts, which create a constitution used by the AcSB to guide its deliberations and thereby the development of GAAP. The concepts constitute a conceptual framework of financial accounting. The framework is the most recent attempt to develop a theoretical basis to support solutions to accounting reporting problems. The AcSB's conceptual framework is strongly reflected in the tone of its published standards. These standards are, in effect, the rules of accounting. Therefore, to understand the logic underlying the AcSB's standards, it is necessary first to understand the logic behind the conceptual framework.

Section 1000 of the *CICA Handbook,* "Financial Statement Concepts" (FSC), describes a conceptual framework to support accounting solutions. The objectives of such a framework are to:

1. Assure consistency across statements.
2. Provide a structure to address new issues.
3. Increase the understandability, relevance, reliability, and comparability of financial reporting results.
4. Improve the ability of financial statements to communicate to users.

The basic components of the FSCs are summarized in Exhibits 2–1 and 2–2.

In addition to the CICA's FSCs, the Accounting Standards Authority of Canada (ASAC), an independent body structured as a representative group of preparers and users of financial statements, published a "Conceptual Framework for Financial Reporting" (CFFR) in 1987.

The content of the CICA's 1988 FSCs and ASAC's CFFR very closely follows the FASB approach, published between 1978 and 1985. The FASB's conceptual framework project was an aggressive attack on the need for guiding theory to help set accounting standards. There are some differences between the Canadian and U.S. approaches. The overall impression, however, is that they are overwhelmingly similar. Why is this the case?

A separate Canadian framework would only be cost-efficient if benefits exceeded costs.[1] Costs include not only the cost to research and develop such a document but also the implementation cost of ensuring that all standards are consistent. Another

---

[1] J. Amernic and M. Lemon, "Do We Need a Canadian Conceptual Framework?" *CA Magazine,* July 1984, pp. 22–27.

EXHIBIT 2–2

Basic Components of the
Financial Statement Concepts

Objectives
and
Users

Qualitative Characteristics

Relevance   **Reliability**
                  Characteristics
Timeliness   Neutrality
Predictive value   Verifiability
Feedback value   Representational
                                     faithfulness

Comparability   **Consistency**

Elements of Financial Statements

(Revenues) (Expenses) (Gains) (Losses) (Assets) (Liabilities) (Equity)

Criteria for Recognition and Measurement

Recognition criteria	**Environmental assumptions**	**Implementation principles**	**Implementation constraints**
Definition	Entity	Cost	Cost-benefit
Measurability	Continuity	Revenue	Materiality
Estimation	Unit of measure	Matching	Industry peculiarities
Probability	Time period	Full disclosure	Conservatism

General-Purpose Financial Statements

cost might be created by increasing the differences between Canadian and U.S. standards and international accounting standards in general. Such differences are not necessarily bad, but they must be dictated by real differences in the environment so that benefits outweigh the costs.

Some have suggested that a separate Canadian framework would not be advisable, given our close trade links with the United States. Certainly many of Canada's largest corporations have material operating and financing transactions with U.S. entities. Many also have their shares listed for trading on the New York Stock Exchange or have raised debt in the U.S. bond markets and thus must comply with the regulations and reporting requirements of the U.S. Securities and Exchange Commission (SEC).

Environmental differences between the countries are real and include the role of government, the extent of social programs, and the nature of the litigation process. However, similarities in the business environment are obvious. The result has been a Canadian statement of concepts that leans heavily on the FASB's conceptual framework project, reflecting the commonality of our environments.

GLOBAL VIEW

 The IASC has adopted a conceptual framework similar in many ways to that developed by the AcSB and has accelerated its efforts to narrow the current variety of acceptable accounting alternatives. In the United States, the FASB has articulated its conceptual framework in the *Statements of Financial Accounting Standards* (*SFAS*) series. The *SFAS* pronouncements explain the objectives, qualitative characteristics, elements, and recognition and measurement criteria that constitute a conceptual framework. This framework is used to guide the standard-setting process and improve its credibility. The Canadian financial statement concepts are based on the FASB's work.

The European Union (formerly the European Community) has also developed financial reporting directives for member nations. Although these directives do not constitute a conceptual framework, they provide broad guidelines to which the process of promulgating future reporting principles will appeal. Two directives (the fourth and the seventh) require a higher degree of comparability in both financial reporting and corporate structure throughout the Union than existed previously.

The fourth directive, for example, requires that statements:
- Be audited.
- Give a true and fair view of the firm's financial position and profit or loss.
- Be published or made available for public inspection.
- Consist of a balance sheet and an income statement that contain explanatory notes and comparative figures.

A section dealing with valuation rules sets out certain basic concepts, including the going concern and matching concepts. Although this directive is based on historical cost, special conditions permit current values to be used.

CONCEPT REVIEW

1. Why did the AcSB develop a conceptual framework?
2. What challenge do accountants face with respect to supplying information to decision makers outside the firm?
3. Under what circumstances would a distinctly different Canadian conceptual framework (as compared to the U.S. framework) be appropriate?

Financial Statement Concepts—Background

The financial statement concepts begin by establishing a perspective on financial reporting and the limitations of information that can be reported therein. The process of financial reporting includes far more than just financial statements; it also includes other information in the annual report as well as information included in prospectuses. The FSCs relate only to the statements themselves. Remember, too, that an enterprise can communicate financial results through various media. For example, press releases and statements made in interviews result in a fast, widespread dissemination of information.

The financial statements themselves are limited to financial information about transactions and events. The information is based on past transactions, not future events, although estimates are often required concerning future transactions and events.

Finally, the basic business environment itself is acknowledged:

> In the Canadian economic environment, the production of goods and services are, to a significant extent, carried out by investor-owned business entities in the private sector and to a lesser extent by government-owned business entities. Debt and equity markets and financial institutions act as exchange mechanisms for investment resources.[2]

The nature of the environment has a profound effect on the entire conceptual framework. We have already commented on the similarities and differences between the Canadian and U.S. environments. Canadian standard setters concluded that the

---

[2] *CICA Handbook*, "Financial Statement Concepts," Section 1000, par. 1000.07 (Toronto: CICA).

similarities overwhelmed the differences to the extent that a U.S.-developed conceptual framework would be appropriate, with some modification, in Canada. This does not mean that the FASB's conceptual framework is universally applicable.

> In a country like India, for example, private investors play a much less important part in the economy than they do in the United States; government and other public agencies play a larger part. The financial reporting needs of the public sector are more important there, and the objectives of financial reporting in those countries should reflect those needs.[3]

Remember, too, that if the environment changes, we must expect the FSCs to change as well, and that what is generally applicable for the business community as a whole may not be appropriate for one firm in its own unique environment.

USERS OF FINANCIAL STATEMENTS

Different users of financial statements (also known as external decision makers) use accounting information in quite different ways. At one extreme are the individual investors who seldom look closely at the financial information contained in an annual report or the quarterly earnings statements that publicly owned companies must send to their shareholders. Being relatively unsophisticated in finance and investment matters, they may only read the introductory text, normally written by public relations people, not accountants. The accounting information contained in the audited statement typically holds little interest for them; most simply don't bother to read it, much less try to understand it. At the other extreme are securities analysts, lenders, lawyers, institutional investors, and corporate financial people who pore over a company's financial statements, sometimes more intensely than the company's own management staff.

Somewhere in the middle is the so-called prudent investor, a person who is reasonably sophisticated in business and finance matters, making informed investment decisions based on factual matters and interpretation of facts—not on intuition or hearsay. Also in the middle ground are the prudent creditors who are believed to make decisions about advancing loans or extending credit based on factual matters, not simply on gut reaction.

In the FSCs, the diversity among users is recognized. Everyone's needs cannot be accommodated at the same time. Thus, the FSCs aim at the middle-ground users, those investors and creditors most in need of accurate, reliable, and unbiased accounting information to use in making investment and credit decisions.

Within the full range of financial statement users, the target audience is investors, creditors, and others (and those who advise or represent them) who:

- Lack the authority to prescribe the information they want and must rely on information management communicates to them.
- Have a reasonable understanding of business and economic activities and are willing to study the information with reasonable diligence.

Included in the FSC's definition of users is the general class of "other users" connected with a company that is issuing financial statements. These include employees, managers and directors of the company, customers, competitors, lawyers, stock exchanges, taxing authorities, researchers, teachers, and students of business and accounting.

Because equity ownership is often separated from management, investors need an authoritative source to demand information on their behalf. In truth, the professionals and institutional investors at one end of the spectrum have the power to get virtually whatever information they want from a corporation. Unsophisticated investors at the other end would be unlikely to change their behaviour through study with reasonable diligence even if they had additional information.

There is considerable room for conflict between different user groups and even within one particular user group. For instance, consider a consumer products

---

[3] David Solomons, "The FASB's Conceptual Framework: An Evaluation," *Journal of Accountancy*, June 1986, p. 118.

company that has one major product that is selling well and two more products in the early development stage. The company wants to borrow money to finance development activities. Present shareholders would want the financial statements to support a loan application and present a rosy picture of sales growth, positive cash flows from operations, and asset growth. A potential lender might prefer a pessimistic view of assets to provide a margin of safety for collateral available for loans. The potential lender would be interested in specifics of the two products under development and market and cash flow predictions. This information, if made public, might help creditors or potential new shareholders make informed decisions. It may well also seriously damage the company's competitive position and future prospects and thus hurt current shareholders. Present and potential investors are at odds, as are investors and creditors.

There is no easy answer to the dilemma presented by such conflicts. Financial accounting principles have to be developed using professional judgment and tailored to the environment in which a firm operates.

OBJECTIVES OF FINANCIAL REPORTING

The conceptual framework seeks to identify the reasons for, or objectives of, corporate financial reporting.

Potential Objective Statements

There are a variety of objectives that could be chosen for financial reporting, including the following:

1. **Evaluation of stewardship** Statements may be used to report on the efficient and effective use of resources. This may include an evaluation of management performance and the use of assets entrusted to management. Presumably, goals have been set and the statements are one tool in the assessment of performance.
2. **Promotion of social welfare** Accounting can be viewed as a social choice mechanism if it makes some people or groups better off and others worse off—a wealth transfer. For example, if oil exploration companies could be made to appear more financially healthy or less risky by changing an accounting principle (a big if!), then their cost of capital should decline and more oil exploration programs would occur. This should lead to the discovery of more oil resources, which might benefit society as a whole.

   If social welfare is the objective of accounting, then it should be controlled by a politically appointed body, responsible to the society it affects.
3. **Facilitation of contracting** The primary purpose of financial statements may be viewed as providing data for contracts. The business entity contracts with managers, government, creditors, and owners. If this is the main objective, then agreed-on, highly reliable, nonmanipulatable rules would be the most valuable.
4. **Usefulness for decision making** Financial statements are viewed, not as an end in and of themselves, but rather as an input to a decision model. Users have to be specified and relevant information must be established. This involves understanding the decision model in force.
5. **Representational faithfulness** The portrayal of economic reality, regardless of consequences, is the goal of a financial statement that portrays "the truth." Many claim that trying to tailor a financial statement for a specific purpose (stewardship or decision making) or a particular outcome (social welfare) destroys the credibility of financial statements in the long run. In Moscow, the official government street map omits streets with "sensitive" buildings such as certain government departments or stores. Who would be willing to buy such a map? The accurate, black market map is a valuable commodity.[4]

---

[4] For a further discussion of financial statement objectives, see E. S. Hendriksen and M. F. VanBreda, *Accounting Theory*, 5th ed. (Homewood, IL: Richard D. Irwin, 1992); or R. M. Skinner, *Accounting Standards in Evolution* (Toronto: Holt, Rinehart and Winston, 1987).

FSC Objectives

The FSCs identify *decision usefulness* as the objective of financial reporting. The focus is on decision makers (financial statement users): investors, creditors, and others. The objectives state that financial reporting should provide information that assists in predicting the ability of the entity to earn income and generate cash flows in the future to meet its obligations and provide a return on investment. As a secondary objective, the statements are also used to assess how the management of an entity has performed—that is, assess stewardship.

The statements should provide information about:

a. an entity's economic resources, obligations and equity/net assets;
b. changes in an entity's economic resources, obligations and equity/net assets;
c. the economic performance of the entity.[5]

The FSCs, with their emphasis on cash flow, implicitly recognize the decision-making process that most investors and creditors use in evaluating various investment opportunities. This process helps investors predict, among other things, the future net cash receipts expected from the investment. Termed a *discounted cash flow analysis,* this process is designed to render an economic justification for making (or not making) an investment based on the investment's current price. The process requires estimates of the following:[6]

1. The timing and amounts of all expected cash flows (dividend or interest payment dates and amounts due).
2. The risk that the company may not realize cash flows needed to make future dividend and/or interest payments.
3. An appropriate interest rate for discounting all expected cash flows. (Normally, interest rates prevailing at the time the investment is being contemplated are used.)

Items 2 and 3 are interrelated because the interest rate may attempt to reflect risk. The appropriate discount rate and the future cash flows are difficult to estimate.

QUALITATIVE CHARACTERISTICS OF ACCOUNTING INFORMATION

The FSCs identify and define the attributes of accounting information that enhance its usefulness for decision making. The four principal qualitative characteristics are understandability, relevance, reliability, and comparability.

Understandability

Information must be understandable to be useful in decision making. **Understandability** does not mean that all information has to be reduced to the lowest common level or simplified so that the least sophisticated investor should understand it. The assumption is that investors and creditors have a reasonable understanding of business and economic activities, as well as some understanding of accounting. These users are expected to study the information with reasonable diligence. The user groups have been defined to include those who counsel investors and creditors; users who lack expertise are assumed to be properly advised.

Relevance

Relevance refers to the capacity of accounting information to make a difference to the external decision makers who use financial reports. They use accounting information with either or both of two viewpoints:
- Forecasting what the economic future is likely to hold.
- Confirming the accuracy of past forecasts to improve future forecasting techniques.

---

[5] *CICA Handbook,* "Financial Statement Concepts," Section 1000, par. .15 (Toronto: CICA).

[6] We discuss the analytical process by which these estimates are incorporated into the decision process in Chapter 6.

The degree to which accounting information is deemed to be relevant can be measured using three aspects of this quality:

1. **Timeliness** Accounting information should be timely if it is to influence decisions. Like the news of the world, stale financial information has less impact than fresh information. Lack of timeliness reduces relevance.
2. **Predictive value** Accounting information should be helpful to external decision makers by increasing their ability to make predictions about the outcome of future events. Decision makers working from accounting information that has little or no predictive value are merely speculating intuitively.
3. **Feedback value** Accounting information should be helpful to external decision makers who are confirming past predictions or making updates, adjustments, or corrections to predictions.

Reliability

To ensure **reliability,** accounting information must be free from error and bias and faithfully represent what it claims to represent. It must not mislead or deceive. Like relevance, reliability must meet three criteria:

1. **Representational faithfulness** This attribute is sometimes called **validity.** Information must give a faithful picture of the facts and circumstances involved. Accounting information must report the economic substance of transactions, not just their form and surface appearance. This is called *reflecting substance over form.*
2. **Verifiability** Accounting information should represent what it purports to represent and should ensure that the selected method of measurement has been used without error or bias. Verifiability pertains to maintenance of audit trails to information source documents that can be checked for accuracy. Verifiability also pertains to the existence of alternative information sources as backup. Verification implies a consensus and that independent measures using the same measurement methods would reach substantially the same conclusion.
3. **Neutrality** Accounting information must be free from bias regarding a particular viewpoint, predetermined result, or particular party. Preparers of financial reports must not attempt to induce a predetermined outcome or a particular mode of behaviour (such as to purchase a company's shares).

As an example of accountants' efforts to portray **substance over form,** or representational faithfulness, consider a company that rents, or leases, a computer system. The form of the contract is a rental agreement, which would seem to suggest that payments made by the company should simply be expensed as a rent, or lease, cost with no other financial statement impact. However, suppose that the accountant discovers that this company decided to lease the computer instead of buying one outright with money borrowed from a bank. The lease term covers the full expected useful life of the computer, cannot be cancelled by the company, and provides a full return of the cost of the computer, plus a profit margin (interest) to the lessor. Now it appears as though, *in substance,* the company has acquired property rights over the computer, far more than a rental contract would imply. In substance, they own the asset and are financing it with a lease agreement. Thus, to reflect substance over form, the asset and the obligation should be shown on the balance sheet of the lessee, and the income statement should reflect both depreciation of the computer and interest on the liability.

Comparability

The FSCs define comparability as follows:

> **Comparability** is a characteristic of the relationship between two pieces of information rather than of a particular piece of information by itself. It enables users to identify similarities in and differences between the information provided by two sets of financial statements. Comparability is important when comparing the financial state-

ments of two different entities and when comparing the financial statements of the same entity over two periods or at two different points in time . . .

Comparability in the financial statements of an entity is enhanced when the same accounting policies are used consistently from period to period.[7]

There are two aspects of comparability—**consistency,** which entails using the same accounting policies from year to year within a firm, and **uniformity,** which means that companies with similar transactions and similar circumstances use the same accounting treatment. The following example from the airline industry illustrates (a lack of) uniformity: Delta Air Lines depreciated its planes over 10 years; American Airlines used 14 to 16 years for most of its aircraft. The difference in depreciation expense represents the major explanation of Delta's reported loss of $3.06 per share in 1980 and American's income of $4.69 per share.

Consistency involves applying accounting concepts and principles from period to period in the same manner. There is a presumption that an accounting principle once used should not be changed. However, if consistency is carried too far, reliability adversely affects relevance. A change to a preferred accounting principle is permitted, even though this would impair consistency. This apparent conflict is usually resolved by retroactive restatement of financial statements to reflect the new policy and supplemental note disclosure.

On July 1, 1986, Delta increased the useful life of its aircraft to 15 years and assumed a 10% residual value, adding $69 million to net income and $1.54 to its 1987 earnings per share. Air Canada added $16 million to 1988 net income (of $96 million) by increasing the service lives and residual values of its B–767 fleet. The 1988 financial statements specify that Air Canada depreciated flight equipment over "12 to 20 years" but contain no further details. This lack of consistency in treatment (and lack of information) can make comparisons subject to error.

The income statement should be designed so that it can reasonably be used to compare revenue and expense information from other companies in the same industry and past and future revenue and expense information for the same company.

Trade-Off   There is often a trade-off between qualitative characteristics, but especially between relevance and reliability. Reliability may have to be reduced to increase the degree of relevance, or vice versa. For example, if financial statements were delayed until all the future events that affect them were to come to pass, they would be far more reliable. Uncollectable accounts, warranty reserves, and useful lives of depreciable assets would not have to be estimated. On the other hand, the timeliness of the financial statements would suffer, and thus the statements would lack relevance. Thus, a degree of reliability is sacrificed to gain relevance. The relative importance of the characteristics changes from situation to situation and calls for the exercise of professional judgment.

CONCEPT REVIEW
1. For what target user audience are financial statements primarily designed?
2. What are the primary qualitative characteristics of accounting information?
3. What three characteristics are necessary for information to be relevant? To be reliable?

---

[7] *CICA Handbook,* "Financial Statement Concepts," par. 1000.22–.23 (Toronto: CICA).

EXHIBIT 2–3   Elements of Financial Statements

Elements	Transaction Characteristics
Balance Sheet (discussed in Chapter 5)	
1. **Assets** are economic resources controlled by an entity as a result of past transactions or events from which future economic benefits may be obtained.	1. To qualify as assets, the resources involved must: *a.* Have future economic benefits (be capable of producing profits). *b.* Be under the entity's control (can be freely deployed or disposed of). *c.* Result from past transactions (meaning they are in place now, as opposed to being under contract for manufacture, creation, or delivery).
2. **Liabilities** are obligations of an entity arising from past transactions or events, the settlement of which may result in the transfer or use of assets, provision of services, or other yielding of economic benefits in the future.	2. To qualify as liabilities, obligations must: *a.* Transfer assets having future economic benefits. *b.* Be unavoidable. *c.* Result from past transactions (meaning they are binding obligations now, as opposed to obligations that will exist once pending transactions are completed).
3. **Equity/net assets** is the ownership interest in the assets of an entity after deducting its liabilities. While equity in total is a residual, it includes specific categories of items—for example, types of share capital, contributed capital, and retained earnings.	3. The dollar amounts reported represent the residual interest in the assets after deducting the liabilities. In addition, the equity element is used to report capital transactions.
Income Statement (discussed in Chapter 4)	
4. **Revenues** are increases in economic resources, either by way of inflows or enhancements of assets or reductions of liabilities, resulting from the ordinary activities of an entity, normally from the sale of goods, the rendering of services, or the use by others of entity resources yielding rent, interest, royalties, or dividends.	4. The two essential characteristics of a revenue transaction are: *a.* It arises from the company's primary earning activity (mainstream business lines) and not from incidental or investment transactions (assuming the entity is a noninvestment company). *b.* It is recurring and continuous.
5. **Expenses** are decreases in economic resources, either by way of outflows or reductions of assets or incurrences of liabilities, resulting from the ordinary revenue-earning activities of an entity.	5. The essential characteristic of an expense is that it must be incurred in conjunction with the company's revenue-generating process. Expenditures that do not qualify as expenses must be treated as either assets (future economic benefit to be derived), losses (no economic benefit), or as distributions to owners.
6. **Gains** are increases in equity from peripheral or incidental transactions and events affecting an entity and from all other transactions, events, and circumstances affecting the entity except those that result from revenues or equity contributions.	6. The transaction must not be one that meets the characteristics test of (*a*) a revenue-producing transaction or (*b*) a capital contribution transaction.
7. **Losses** are decreases in equity from peripheral or incidental transactions and events affecting an entity and from all other transactions, events, and circumstances affecting the entity except those that result from expenses or distributions of equity.	7. The transaction must not be one that meets the characteristics test of (*a*) an expense transaction or (*b*) a capital distribution (investment by owner) transaction.

Source: *CICA Handbook,* "Financial Statement Concepts," Section 1000 (Toronto: CICA).

ELEMENTS OF FINANCIAL STATEMENTS OF BUSINESS ENTERPRISES

Periodic financial statements are the primary medium used to communicate accounting information about a business enterprise. The building blocks of accrual-based financial statements are called *elements.* Elements are the classes of items that financial statements should contain. The FSCs define seven elements, as shown in Exhibit 2–3. The first three elements (assets, liabilities, and equity/net assets) relate directly to the balance sheet; the next four elements (revenues, expenses, gains, and losses) relate directly to the income statement. The definitions of these seven elements are particularly important because they provide authoritative definitions of the major classifications used in current financial statements.

Some believe that a further definition is needed to complete the conceptual framework—a definition of **comprehensive income.** This is typically defined as the measure of the effects of transactions and other events on an entity, comprising *all* recognized changes in net assets during a period except those arising from investments by owners and distributions to owners. Such things as the cumulative effect of a change in accounting policy and prior period adjustments, which are now shown on the retained earnings statement, would be part of comprehensive income. This ensures that the full impact of these items is highlighted for financial statement users. Comprehensive income has no counterpart in the current reporting model and is not calculated or disclosed at the present time.

The definitions have had a major impact because they are used directly in formulating and evaluating accounting standards. The definitions broke new ground with their emphasis on assets and liabilities as fundamental concepts. Revenues and expenses became derived concepts in that revenues represent enhancements of net assets or settlements of liabilities. Expenses represent the use of an asset or the incurrence of a liability in conducting normal operations. For many years prior to these definitions, assets and liabilities were the derived concepts. Assets, for example, were treated as costs awaiting recognition as expenses in the generation of revenues. Expenditures on research provide an example. At one time, these expenditures could be considered assets (costs to be written off over time). Now, research expenditures are written off as incurred since "the amount of future benefits and the period over which they will be received are usually uncertain."[8]

Another way to explain this is to say that the definitions emphasize the balance sheet instead of the income statement. In the past, the income statement dominated, since it was felt that matching expenses with the associated revenues to obtain income was the critical measurement issue in accounting.[9]

RECOGNITION AND MEASUREMENT CRITERIA

Recognition Criteria

Recognition is the process of including an item in the financial statements. A recognized item is given a title and numerical value. Recognition applies to all financial statement elements in all companies. The conceptual basis for the accrual basis of accounting is provided by the recognition criteria: The accrual basis of accounting recognizes the effect of transactions and events in the period in which they occur, regardless of whether there has been a cash payment or receipt.

An element should be recognized in the accounts when:

1. The item meets the **definition** of an element.
2. The item has an appropriate basis of **measurement.**
3. A reasonable **estimate** can be made of the amount involved.
4. It is **probable** that the economic benefits will be received or have to be given up.

It is entirely possible that an item that meets the first three criteria will not be recognized because of failure of the last criterion—probability. For instance, suppose a company was suing a supplier for $125,000 for damages incurred when faulty materials provided by the supplier were used in a production process. The future economic benefit, or asset, can be measured at $125,000, or a lower amount if the parties are likely to settle. The difficulty arises when assessing the probability of the receipt of the economic benefit, as the lawsuit may not be successful. It may be proven that the company ordered the wrong materials or used them incorrectly. For this reason, such items are disclosed in the notes to the financial statements as

---

[8] *CICA Handbook,* "Research and Development Costs," Section 3450.15 (Toronto: CICA).

[9] The primacy of the matching concept can be attributed to Professors William Paton and A. C. Littleton's 1940 monograph, *An Introduction to Corporate Accounting Standards.* In 1971, Professor Paton seems to have had second thoughts. "Listening to Bob Sprouse take issue with the 'matching gospel,' which the P&L [Paton and Littleton] monograph helped to foster, confirmed my dissatisfaction with the publication." William Paton, in *Foundations of Accounting Theory,* ed. Willard Stone (Gainesville: University of Florida Press, 1971), p. x.

contingencies and are not recognized until the result of the court decision is known and the probability of collection assessed.

Recognition is not the same as disclosure in the notes to the financial statements. Notes provide further details about items recognized in the financial statements, or provide information on items that do not meet the recognition criteria, such as the lawsuit just discussed.

The recognition criteria are based on the four qualitative characteristics, and there is the assumption that items, properly recognized, will have a blend of understandability, relevance, reliability, and comparability.

Measurement Criteria

Measurement is the process of determining the amount at which an item is recognized in the financial statements. If there is no appropriate basis of measurement, a transaction would fail the second recognition criterion, as previously defined. There are many alternative measurement bases, including historical cost, replacement cost, current sales value, and the sum of the cash flows an item will generate over its life, discounted at an appropriate rate. The FSCs state that, *generally,* historical cost should be used as a measurement base.

Our GAAP model is described as an historical cost model, yet there are many examples in it of other valuation bases—obsolete inventory carried at market value when this amount is less than cost, long-term liabilities with interest rates lower than market rates recorded at discounted amounts, and so on. The implication of the FSCs is that this ad hoc basis will continue and that we will continue to see a variety of measurement bases, although historical cost will dominate.

Capital Maintenance

The FSCs confirm the use of financial capital as an appropriate capital maintenance concept in financial reporting. The notion of financial capital maintenance means that income results if the closing amount of net financial assets exceeds the amount at the start, excluding transactions with owners such as additional investment or dividends. In contrast, a return on physical capital results only when the physical assets or capacity of the organization increases over the period.

For example, assume that a business is established with $1,000 of owners' equity, used to buy one unit of inventory. The unit is sold for $1,700; meanwhile, the firm's supplier increased the unit replacement cost to $1,200. How much is net income, the amount that could be distributed to owners in dividends without impairing capital? Using financial capital as a benchmark, the company has made $700, and, if this amount were paid in dividends, the company would still have the $1,000 capital that was originally invested.

The problem is that $1,000 would have bought one inventory unit at the beginning of the period; now that unit costs $1,200, and the company would be $200 short if all the income was distributed. This implies that financial capital has overstated net income. If the company reported and distributed $500 of income ($1,700 − $1,200), it would still have $1,200 to replace the inventory. Capital is viewed, not as a dollar figure ($1,000) but rather as a physical capability (one unit of inventory, now $1,200).

Physical capital may seem intuitively appealing. However, it is not always logical. For instance, not every firm replaces inventory with similar units. Also, the results are less appealing when prices are declining, not increasing. As a result, the FSCs adopt financial capital as a capital maintenance concept. It, too, has its flaws, but financial capital is more generally applicable and has stood the test of time.

|CONCEPT REVIEW

1. What are the seven elements of financial statements?
2. What has been the change in the way assets and liabilities are viewed, or defined, in the FSCs?

> 3. What criteria must be met to justify recognition of an item in the financial statements?

ENVIRONMENTAL ASSUMPTIONS

Four basic environmental assumptions significantly affect the recording, measuring, and reporting of accounting information. They are:

1. Separate entity assumption.
2. Continuity assumption.
3. Unit of measure assumption.
4. Time period assumption.

Separate Entity Assumption

Accounting deals with specific, identifiable business entities, each considered an accounting unit separate and apart from its owners and from other entities. A corporation and its shareholders are separate entities for accounting purposes, even in the case of closely held private corporations. Also, partnerships and sole proprietorships are treated as separate from their owners, although this separation does not hold true in a legal sense.

Under the **separate entity assumption,** all accounting records and reports are developed from the viewpoint of a single entity, whether it is a proprietorship, a partnership, or a corporation. The assumption is that an individual's transactions are distinguishable from those of the business he or she might own. For example, the personal residence of a business owner is not considered an asset of the business, even though the residence and the business are owned by the same person.

Continuity Assumption

Under the **continuity assumption,** also known as the **going-concern assumption,** the business entity in question is expected not to liquidate but to continue operations for the foreseeable future. That is, it will stay in business for a period of time sufficient to carry out contemplated operations, contracts, and commitments. This nonliquidation assumption provides a conceptual basis for many of the classifications used in accounting. Assets and liabilities, for example, are classified as either current or long term on the basis of this assumption. If continuity is not assumed, the distinction between current and long term loses its significance; all assets and liabilities become current. Continuity also supports the measurement and recording of assets and liabilities at historical cost.

If a business entity expects to be liquidated in the near future, conventional accounting, based on the continuity assumption, is not appropriate. Such circumstances call instead for the use of liquidation accounting, which values assets and liabilities at estimated net realizable amounts (liquidation values).

Unit-of-Measure Assumption

The **unit-of-measure assumption** means that the results of a business's economic activities are reported in terms of a standard monetary unit throughout the financial statements. Money amounts are thus the language of accounting: The common unit of measure (yardstick) enables dissimilar items such as the cost of a ton of coal and an account payable to be aggregated into a single total. The unit of measure in Canada is the dollar; in Japan, it is the yen. Different units are used in other countries.

Unfortunately, the use of a standard monetary unit for measurement purposes poses a dilemma. Unlike a yardstick, which is always the same length, a currency experiences changes in value. During periods of inflation (or deflation), dollars of different values are accounted for without regard to the fact that some have greater purchasing power than others.[10] In Canada, it is standard practice, however, to ignore changes in the purchasing power of currency. The appropriateness of this assumption depends on the level of inflation and hence on the country considered.

Time-Period Assumption

The operating results of any business enterprise cannot be known with certainty until the company has completed its life span and ceased doing business. In the meantime, external decision makers require timely accounting information to satisfy their analytical needs. To meet their needs, the **time-period assumption** (or **calendar constraint**) requires that changes in a business's financial position be reported over a series of shorter time periods.

Although the reporting period varies, one year is the standard. Some companies use a calendar year, and others use a fiscal year-end that coincides with the low point in business activity over a 12-month period. In addition, companies also report summarized financial information on an interim basis, usually quarterly.

A company may elect to use a reporting period that is either longer or shorter than the standard 12-month calendar or fiscal year, but only if doing so better fits the company's normal business cycle. Companies in the shipbuilding industry, for example, may select a longer reporting period because constructing a vessel and readying it for launch typically require more than one year's time.

The time-period assumption recognizes both that decision makers need timely financial information and that recognition of accruals and deferrals is necessary for reporting accurate information. Accrual and deferral items distinguish accrual-basis accounting. If a demand for periodic reports did not exist during the life span of a business, accruals and deferrals would not be necessary. A company's financial statements are always dated to reflect either a precise date (balance sheet) or a particular period of time covered (income statement, retained earnings statement, and statement of changes in financial position).

IMPLEMENTATION PRINCIPLES

Implementation principles govern the recognition of revenue, expense, gain, and loss items for financial statement reporting purposes. Four separate implementation principles apply to the recognition process:

1. Cost principle.
2. Revenue principle.
3. Matching principle.
4. Full disclosure principle.

Income is defined as revenues plus gains minus expenses and losses. The cost, revenue, and matching principles are the fundamental principles governing income recognition.

Cost Principle

Normally applied in conjunction with asset acquisitions, the **cost principle** specifies that the actual acquisition cost be used for initial accounting recognition purposes. The cash-equivalent cost of an asset is used if the asset is acquired via some means other than cash.

The cost principle assumes that assets are acquired in business transactions conducted at arm's length—that is, transactions between a buyer and a seller at the fair value prevailing at the time of the transaction. For non-cash transactions conducted at arm's length, the cost principle assumes that the market value of the resources given up in a transaction provides reliable evidence for the valuation of the item acquired.

When an asset is received as a gift, in exchange for common shares, or in an exchange of assets, determining a realistic cost basis can be difficult. In these situa-

---

[10] Over time, the changing value of the monetary unit, coupled with the change in the nature of goods, makes comparability difficult at best.

tions, the cost principle requires that cost be based on the market value of the assets given up or the market value of the assets received, whichever value is more reliably determined.

When an asset is acquired with debt, such as a note payable given in settlement for the purchase, the cost of the asset acquired is determined from the debt side of the transaction. The asset's cost basis is equal to the present value of the debt to be paid in the future.

The cost principle provides guidance primarily at the initial acquisition date. Once acquired, the original cost basis of some assets is then subject to depreciation, depletion, amortization, or write-down in conformity with the matching principle and the conservatism constraint, discussed later in this section. Write-ups of appreciated asset values are generally not permitted. The following information, drawn from the 1992 balance sheet of Phillips Cables Limited, illustrates this reporting:

	1992	1991
	(in thousands)	
Property, plant, and equipment at cost:		
Land	$ 335	$ 395
Buildings	23,374	24,203
Machinery and equipment	82,675	77,587
Total	$106,384	$102,185
Less: accumulated depreciation, buildings	12,418	12,691
Less: accumulated depreciation, machinery, and equipment	51,962	50,082
	$ 42,004	$ 39,412

Revenue Principle

The **revenue principle** requires the recognition and reporting of revenues in accordance with accrual-basis accounting principles. Applying this principle requires, first, that all four of the recognition criteria—definition, measurability, estimation, and probability—be met.

Revenue can be defined as inflows of cash or other enhancements of a business's assets, settlements of its liabilities, or a combination of the two. Such inflows must be derived from delivering or producing goods, rendering service, or performing other activities that constitute a company's ongoing business operations over a specific period of time. More generally, revenue is measured as the market value of the resources received or the product or service given, whichever is the more reliably determinable. This broader definition comes into play in conjunction with non-cash transactions (exchanges of goods and merchandise or services performed).

The revenue principle pertains to accrual-basis accounting and is not relevant to cash-basis accounting. Therefore, completed transactions for the sale of goods or services on credit usually are recognized as revenue for the period in which the sale or service occurs rather than in the period in which the cash is eventually collected. Furthermore, related expenses are matched to these revenues.

With regard to sales discounts, the revenue principle suggests that all discounts be viewed as adjustments of the amount of revenue earned. In determining the net cash exchange value of sales subject to discount, sales discounts should be subtracted from gross sales revenue in measuring the net amount of sales revenue.[11]

Under the revenue principle, revenue from the sale of goods is recognized at the time of sale, since the earnings process is usually completed at the time of sale. At that time, the relevant information about the asset inflows to the seller (normally either an increase in cash or accounts receivable) is known. Sales must be accompanied by transfer of ownership or the performance of services.

---

[11] Discounts not taken represent a loss to the buyer who allowed the discount to lapse and are a special revenue item to the seller. Lapsed discounts represent interest revenue, not sales revenue. Since lost discounts reflect very high interest rates, good management seldom lets them lapse. The seller, on the other hand, should expect such discounts to be taken and, hence, sales revenue should be reduced.

In general, four conditions must be met if the revenue principle is to be satisfied:

1. All significant acts required of the seller have been performed.
2. Consideration is measurable.
3. Collection is reasonably assured.
4. The risks and rewards of ownership have passed to the buyer.

Transactions that pose revenue recognition uncertainties include installment sales, long-term construction contracts, sales of land with minimal down payments, and sales of franchises that require a certain level of performance on the part of the purchaser as a condition of sale. In these transactions and in others, there are significant uncertainties concerning one or more of the listed criteria.

Matching Principle

Like the revenue principle, the **matching principle** is essential for accrual-basis accounting. Matching refers to the recognition of expenses. All expenses incurred in earning the revenue recognized for a period should be recognized during the same period. If revenue is carried over (deferred) for recognition to a future period, the related expenses should also be carried over or deferred, since they are incurred in earning that revenue.

The matching principle is one of the most pervasive principles in terms of the sheer number of accounting judgments that it affects. As a result of the matching principal, outlays that otherwise would be expensed at the time cash is disbursed, using cash-basis accounting, are carried on the books as assets. These expenditures are made for materials, purchased services, and the like, that help earn future revenue. When revenue is recognized, appropriate asset accounts are expensed. In this way, revenues and related expenses are matched across accounting periods.

A cash-basis system would report only the receipt and disbursement of cash, whereas an accrual system focuses on transactions and related events with cash consequences. A simple example illustrates the difference between the accrual- and cash-basis systems. Suppose a firm spends $100 on inventory in period 1 and sells the item in period 2. Using the accrual system, the firm would recognize the expense of $100 in period 2. Under a cash-basis system, the outflow of $100 would be recognized in period 1, when the cash is paid.

The pattern of expense recognition varies. Some expenses are linked with revenues by a direct cause-and-effect relationship, especially when the revenue and expense transactions occur simultaneously. Examples are packaging, sales commissions, and delivery expenses. Other outlays are linked to revenues by a different cause-and-effect relationship, one in which the expense is incurred at a different time from when the matching revenue occurs. Examples include purchases of inventories and supplies. In such cases, cash is disbursed in one period but the expense may often be recognized and matched with revenue in a different period. Another example is plant assets, whose cost is matched with revenues on a systematic and rational basis as depreciation expense.

Some outlays constitute expenses that have no direct relationship to either a particular type of revenue-generating transaction or a particular accounting time period. These expenses must be allocated to reporting periods subjectively. Examples are expenditures for administration and promotional activities. These items are **period costs**—they are recognized as expenses during the period in which they are incurred.

Adjusting entries may be required at the end of the accounting period to update expenses in step with recognized sales revenue. Examples include wage expense earned but not paid, estimated warranty expense, and interest expense accrued but not paid. (Adjusting entries are also used to update certain revenue accounts.)

To illustrate the matching principle, assume a home appliance is sold for cash with a 100 percent warranty on parts and labour in effect for the first 12 months from date of sale. The revenue from the sale is recognized immediately, as are the directly related costs involved in manufacturing and assembling the unit and the shipping and direct selling expenses incurred. Furthermore, the expenses involved in honoring the warranty should also be recognized in the same period as the sales revenue, even though the actual warranty cost may not be known until the next year. At the end of the year in which the sale occurs, the warranty expense should be estimated, recorded on the books, and recognized for financial statement reporting purposes. In this way, the warranty expense is matched with the revenue to which it is related even though the cash may be expended at a later time.

A simple table is helpful in summarizing the accounting disposition of costs and expenses in accordance with the matching principle:

Time Frame of Benefit	Expenditure Should Be
Future economic benefits	Recorded as an asset
Current economic benefits	Recorded as an expense
No economic benefits	Recorded as a loss

Full Disclosure Principle

The **full disclosure principle** requires that the financial statements report all *relevant* information bearing on the economic affairs of a business enterprise. The aim of full disclosure is to provide external users with the accounting information they need to make informed investment and credit decisions. Full disclosure requires that the accounting policies followed be explained in the notes to the financial statements.

Accounting information may be reported in the body of the financial statements, in disclosure notes to these statements, or in supplementary schedules and other presentation formats. For example, contracts for future delivery of goods or services are often disclosed in the footnotes. Even though the transaction has not occurred, existence of such contracts can have a material effect on a company's future financial position. For example, Rogers Communications Inc, in its 1992 annual report, disclosed in the notes to the financial statements that it had been granted one of four licences to provide cordless (cellular) telephone service in Canada. The cost of developing this service was estimated to be in the range of $25 million. This information is useful in evaluating the firm's prospects and is supplied under the full disclosure principle.

CONCEPT REVIEW

1. Why isn't the calendar year always the appropriate time period for an income statement?
2. If a company cannot be considered a going concern, how should it be valued?
3. What conditions must be met before revenue can be recognized?

IMPLEMENTATION CONSTRAINTS

Consistency in the application of accounting principles and uniformity of accounting practice within the profession may not be achievable in all cases. Exceptions to existing GAAP are allowed in special situations, categorized according to four **implementation constraints:**

1. Cost–benefit constraint.
2. Materiality constraint.
3. Industry peculiarities constraint.
4. Conservatism constraint.

These constraints exert a modifying influence on financial accounting and reporting.

Cost–Benefit Constraint

Underlying the **cost–benefit constraint** is the assumption that the benefits derived by external users of financial statements should outweigh the costs incurred by the preparers of the information. Although it is admittedly difficult to quantify these benefits and costs, standard setters often attempt to obtain information from preparers on the costs of implementing a new reporting requirement. The cost–benefit determination is essentially a judgment call.

Materiality Constraint

Materiality is defined as the magnitude of an omission or misstatement of accounting that, in the light of surrounding circumstances, makes it probable that the judgment of a reasonable person relying on the information would have been changed or influenced by the omission or misstatement. The materiality constraint is also called a **threshold for recognition.** The assumption is that the omission or inclusion of immaterial facts is not likely to change or influence the decision of a rational external user. However, the materiality threshold does not mean that small items and amounts do not have to be accounted for or reported. Furthermore, items may be material due to their nature, not their size. For example, fraud is an important event regardless of the size of the amount.

To illustrate an instance where strict conformity with GAAP is not necessary because an item is immaterial, consider a low-cost asset such as a $9.95 pencil sharpener. This item can be recorded as an expense in full when purchased rather than as an asset subject to depreciation. The dollar amount involved is simply too small for external users to worry about. Nor does it warrant distinction as a separate expense account item. The amount is lumped instead into miscellaneous expenses.

Materiality judgments are situation specific. An amount considered immaterial in one situation might be material in another. The decision depends on the nature of the item, its dollar amount, and the relationship of the amount to the total amount of income, expenses, assets, or liabilities, as the case may be. Because materiality matters tend to be case-by-case judgments, the AcSB has not specified general materiality guidelines.[12] In practice, materiality guidelines such as "5 percent or 10 percent of net income or total assets" are typically used.

The decision to expense the purchase of a pencil sharpener is an example of applying materiality. The pencil sharpener is expensed even though it lasts several years. Consider a second example involving the decisions to report separately (1) inventories and (2) interest costs in the financial statements.

	Company		
Item	A	B	C
Inventory Example			
Inventories.	$10,000	$ 10,000	$ 10,000
Current assets	20,000	20,000	200,000
Total assets	50,000	200,000	500,000
Interest Costs Example			
Sales	$10,000	$ 10,000	$ 10,000
Expenses	7,000	7,000	2,000
Interest costs.	1,000	100	600
Operating income	2,000	2,900	7,400
Net income (after tax).	$ 1,400	$ 2,030	$ 5,180

For Company A, inventories are a relatively large proportion of total assets (20 percent) and should be separately reported. This is not the case for Company B or Company C (5% and 2%, respectively), and little would be lost from merging inventories with other current assets. This is so even though inventories are 50% of Company B's current assets.

---

[12] The courts have also not been consistent in setting a single benchmark value for materiality. See K. Jeffries, "Materiality as Defined by the Courts," *The CPA Journal*, October 1981, pp. 12–17.

The question of whether to separately disclose interest costs is resolved using a similar analysis. For Company A, the interest costs are large compared with net income (71%) and should be disclosed separately. In the case of Company B, interest costs are minor (less than 5% of net income) and could be merged with other expenses. Interest costs for Company C are above 10% of net income and should be reported separately even though they are a smaller percentage of operating income.

Similarly, an expenditure for overhauling a piece of equipment might represent a major cash outlay for a small business concern and should be disclosed in its financial statements, whereas disclosure in financial statements of the same expenditure for a corporation as large as CNR or The Royal Bank would be of little consequence.

Industry Peculiarities Constraint

One of the overriding concerns of accounting is that the information in financial statements be useful. The problem is that certain types of accounting information might be critical for decision making in one industry setting, but not in another. Business practices and financial structures are very different between industries. For example, a public electricity utility has very high levels of capital assets, financed mostly by debt. A chartered bank's assets are mostly financial—loans to customers. Its capital asset section is important but is not its major asset category. The liabilities of a bank include its deposits as well as debt financing. Both these companies are very different from a mining company, with assets comprised of inventory and natural resources, financed mostly through equity investment.

Basically, each industry has its own way of doing things and its own business practices. Under the industry peculiarities constraint, selective exceptions to generally accepted accounting principles are permitted provided there is a clear precedent in the industry. Precedent is based on the uniqueness of the situation, the usefulness of the information involved, substance over form, and possible compromise of representational faithfulness. For example, Corning Glass Works follows a standard glass industry practice of accruing glass furnace repair costs before the actual repairs are made. Such repairs lead to essentially an indefinite life for a glass furnace.

Some differences in accounting also occur in response to legal requirements. This is especially so for companies that are subject to regulatory controls, such as public utilities. Another exception permits the use of a principle or accounting procedure that is at variance with an official pronouncement if it can be shown that the procedure is more useful and is necessary to avoid misleading inferences. In such cases, the choice of accounting policy must be fully disclosed in the financial statements.

Conservatism Constraint

The **conservatism** constraint holds that when two alternative accounting methods are acceptable and both equally satisfy the conceptual and implementation principles set out by the AcSB, the alternative having the less favourable effect on net income or total assets is preferable. For example:
- In recognizing assets, the lower of two alternative valuations would be recorded.
- In recognizing liabilities, the higher of two alternative amounts would be recorded.
- In recording revenues, expenses, gains, and losses where there is reasonable doubt as to the appropriateness of alternative amounts, the one having the least favourable effect on net income would be used.

Conservatism assumes that when uncertainty exists, the users of financial statements are better served by understatement than by overstatement of net income and assets. Prime examples include valuing inventories and other assets at the lower of cost or current market value (LCM, or lower of cost and market) and minimizing the estimated service life and residual value of depreciable assets. The increasingly litigious business environment contributes to conservative financial reporting. Unfortunately, the use of an overly conservative practice may also result in a negatively biased portrayal of a company's financial condition. There is no reason to believe that systematic conservative bias better serves the needs of external users.

ON THE HORIZON

The development of financial accounting concepts is an ongoing project. No doubt the AcSB will change these concepts as time passes. The development of international accounting standards will contribute to the need to reexamine the FSCs. Yet, development of the FSCs need not be complete for the framework to have a major influence over the AcSB's activities and pronouncements.

Politics also plays a role in the establishment of accounting standards. However, political factions and splinter groups within any professional association can make for healthy debate and act to safeguard the comprehensiveness and overall suitability of its pronouncements.

It is unrealistic to expect the constituency of any professional association to immediately endorse and adopt all the pronouncements handed down by its authoritative body. In the AcSB's case, differences of opinion and debate among accounting practitioners are inevitable given the scope of the matters on which the AcSB comments and rules. The issues brought to the AcSB are naturally difficult and possess no simple, ready-made solutions. Accounting contains no principles or laws to be discovered; accounting principles are based on reason, economic theory, experience, pragmatism, and general acceptability. Accounting principles are formulated by individuals, and therefore disagreements and challenges are inevitable. Thus, accounting principles change with the evolving social and economic environment within which the accounting process is applied.

CONCEPT REVIEW

1. What is the definition of materiality?
2. What is the essence of the conservatism constraint, and what is its effect on financial statements?

OVERVIEW

Refer back to Exhibit 2–1 as an overview of the financial statement concepts and the recognition criteria, environmental assumptions, implementation principles, and implementation constraints.

Many practitioners and academics have criticized the FSCs. This is to be expected: Decisions made on contentious issues will always disappoint those who championed the unchosen alternatives. Some feel that our Canadian environment demands a unique conceptual framework, that objectives were improperly formulated, and that the definitional approach is too rigid, is not rigid enough, or was simply the wrong approach.

There exists a good deal of dissatisfaction with the measurement criteria because critics argue that little guidance is supplied on measurement issues. The implication of the FSC criteria is that a case-by-case approach to the appropriate measurement basis will continue to be used, which may well include many exceptions to historical cost. The fear is that a case-by-case approach is likely to lead to inconsistency and ultimately to the unacceptability of standards in the future.

The recognition and measurement criteria have, however, resolved two other issues. First, they made clear that the information in the notes to financial statements is supplemental to, and not a substitute for, recognition in the body of the statements. Second, they support the concept of financial capital maintenance as relevant to financial reporting.

As a final cautionary note, we remind you that the value of the FSCs is seen in the results that they produce. If standards are set based on the FSCs and produce logical, intuitively appealing, consistent standards that are widely followed, then the FSCs will continue to evolve and grow in credibility. If standard setters ignore them, or if their application results in standards that do not receive support, then the worth of the initiative will be called into question.

Exhibit 2–4 provides a summary of the FSCs.

EXHIBIT 2–4   Summary of the Financial Statement Concepts

Objectives of Financial Reporting

Provide information that is:
1. Useful to investors and creditors.
2. Helpful in assessing income and cash flows.
3. Relevant to assessment of management performance.

Qualitative Characteristics	**Elements of Financial Statements**
1. Understandability.	1. Assets.
2. Relevance.	2. Liabilities.
a. Timeliness.	3. Equity.
b. Predictive value.	4. Revenues.
c. Feedback value.	5. Expenses.
3. Reliability.	6. Gains.
a. Neutrality.	7. Losses.
b. Verifiability.	
c. Representational faithfulness.	
4. Comparability.	

Recognition and Measurement Criteria

Recognition Criteria	Environmental Assumptions	Implementation Principles	Implementation Constraints
1. Definition.	1. Entity.	1. Cost.	1. Cost–benefit.
2. Measurability.	2. Continuity (going concern).	2. Revenue.	2. Materiality.
3. Estimation.	3. Unit of measure.	3. Matching.	3. Industry peculiarities.
4. Probability.	4. Time period.	4. Full disclosure.	4. Conservatism.

| SUMMARY OF KEY POINTS

(L.O. 1)   1. The financial statement concepts provide a foundation to assist standard setters in developing a consistent approach to resolving financial reporting issues.

(L.O. 2)   2. Investors and creditors are the primary users of financial statement information.

(L.O. 2)   3. The primary characteristics of accounting information are understandability, relevance, reliability, and comparability.

(L.O. 2)   4. Emphasis in reporting is placed on the usefulness of information for decision making. This means the information must have an appropriate blend of relevance and reliability, understandability, and comparability.

(L.O. 3)   5. Assets and liabilities were given greater emphasis by the financial statement element definitions, which determine the items that should appear on the balance sheet and income statement.

(L.O. 4)   6. The recognition concept provides the conceptual basis for accrual accounting. Elements are recognized when they meet the element definition, have an appropriate basis of measurement, can be estimated, and are probable.

(L.O. 4)   7. Completion of the earning process requires that all significant acts required of the seller have been performed, consideration is measurable, collection is reasonably assured, and the risks and rewards of ownership have passed to the buyer. When these conditions are satisfied, revenue can be recognized.

(L.O. 5)   8. The matching principle requires that the expenses incurred in earning revenues should be recognized during the same period in which the revenues are recognized.

(L.O. 5)   9. The environmental assumptions (separate entity, continuity, unit of measure, and time period), implementation principles (cost, revenue, matching, and full disclosure), and constraints (cost–benefit, materiality, special industry reporting needs, and conservatism) are used to implement the financial statement concepts and produce general-purpose financial statements.

(L.O. 5)   10. Conservatism in accounting suggests that the least favorable alternative be used when a choice exists and a more appropriate treatment of the item cannot be established.

REVIEW PROBLEM   When is revenue recognition appropriate in the following cases?

1. Atlantic Beverage Company (ABC) sold vending machines and soft drinks through a wholly owned subsidiary, Value Vend. Sales of vending machines by Value Vend were made under a special sales agreement called a *conditional sales contract*. Under this contract, the purchaser was required to make a $50 down payment and to pay the balance in equal monthly installments over a 48-month period. The first payment was due 120 to 210 days after purchase. ABC recognized revenue when the sales contract was signed.

2. Metro-Goldwyn-Mayer (MGM), owner of the movie *Gone with the Wind,* sold the Columbia Broadcasting Company (CBS) the rights to show the movie up to 20 times over 20 years. The sales price was $35 million. MGM reported essentially the entire amount as revenue when the contract was signed.

SOLUTION

1. In the ABC case, given the payment terms in the sales contract, there was considerable uncertainty whether collection was reasonably assured. ABC was required to delay recognizing revenue by its auditors, Alexander Grant. ABC changed auditors to a firm that permitted revenue to be recognized. Shortly thereafter, the company declared bankruptcy. Company officers and the new auditors were brought to court. The court declared that the transactions were not sales.

2. The outcome in the MGM–CBS case was quite different. In this case, the accountants argued that the sale price was known, collection was reasonably assured, no further efforts were required by the seller (MGM), and the expenses of the sale were reliably determinable. Thus, revenue was recognized immediately, even though MGM argued to delay revenue recognition until each showing.

QUESTIONS

1. What are the basic objectives of external financial reporting?
2. Identify and briefly explain the qualitative characteristics of accounting information.
3. Explain the trade-offs that can occur between relevance and reliability.
4. Explain the difference between a revenue and a gain.
5. Explain the difference between an expense and a loss.
6. What are the recognition criteria?
7. Are recognition and note disclosure synonymous? Explain.
8. Explain the four basic environmental assumptions that underlie the implementation of accounting.
9. Explain why the time-period assumption causes accruals and deferrals in accounting.
10. Relate the continuity assumption to periodicity of financial statements.
11. Which assumption or principle discussed in this chapter is most affected by the phenomenon of inflation? Give reasons for your choice.
12. Explain the cost principle. Why is it used in the basic financial statements instead of current replacement value?
13. How is cost measured in non-cash transactions?
14. Define the revenue principle.
15. How is revenue measured in transactions involving non-cash items (exclude credit situations)?
16. Explain the matching principle. What is meant by "the expense should follow the revenue"?
17. Explain why the matching principle usually necessitates the use of adjusting entries. Use depreciation expense and unpaid wages as examples.
18. Relate the matching principle to the revenue and cost principles.
19. Briefly explain the continuity assumption.
20. What accounting principle or assumption is manifested in each situation below?
    a. Prepayment for an annual license is allocated equally to expense over the next 12 months.
    b. Jerry Jenkins owns a shoe repair shop, a restaurant, and a service station. Different and independent statements are prepared for each business.
    c. Inventories at King Store are valued at lower of cost or market (LCM).
    d. Although the inflation rate for the most recent fiscal year of Clyde's Auto Dealership was 9 percent, this was not recognized in the year-end statements.
    e. While making a delivery, the driver for Cross Appliance Store collided with another vehicle, causing both property damage and personal injury. The party sued Cross for damages that could exceed Cross's insurance coverage. Existence of the suit was disclosed on Cross's most recent financial statements.
 21. In what ways does the fourth directive issued by the European Union affect financial statements?

CASES

C 2-1 (L.O. 1, 2, 4, 5)	**Discuss: Any Conceptual Violations?** The two independent cases given below may violate some financial statement concept or principle. For each case, explain the nature of any incorrect accounting and reporting and what concept or principle is violated, if any.

Case A The financial statements of Raychem Corporation included the following note: "During the current year, plant assets were written down by $8,000,000. This write-down will reduce future expenses. Depreciation and other expenses in future years will be lower, and as a result this will benefit profits of future years."

Case B During an audit of the Silvona Company, certain liabilities such as taxes appear to be overstated. Also, some semiobsolete inventory items seem to be undervalued, and the tendency is to expense rather than capitalize as many items as possible.

Management states that "the company has always taken a very conservative view of the business and its future prospects." Management suggests that it does not wish to weaken the company by reporting any more earnings or paying any more dividends than are absolutely necessary because it does not expect business to continue to be good. It points out that the lower valuations for assets and so on do not lose anything for the company but do create reserves for "hard times."

C 2-2 (L.O. 2, 5)	**Full Disclosure** Explain how each of the following items, as reported on Geoforensics Corporation's balance sheet, violated the full disclosure principle.

a. There was no comment or explanation of the fact that the company changed its inventory method from FIFO to LIFO at the beginning of the current reporting period. A large changeover difference was involved, and there was no retroactive restatement.

b. Owners' equity reported only two amounts: common shares, $150,000; and retained earnings, $130,000. The common shares have a par value of $100,000 and originally sold for $150,000 cash.

c. Sales revenue was $960,000 and cost of goods sold, $600,000; the first line reported on the income statement was "revenues, $360,000."

d. No earnings per share (EPS) amounts were reported.

e. Currents assets amounted to $314,000 and current liabilities, $205,000; the balance sheet reported as a single amount "working capital, $109,000."

f. The income statement showed only the following classifications:
   (1) Revenues.
   (2) Costs.
   (3) Net profit.

(AICPA adapted)

C 2-3 (L.O. 1, 2, 3, 4, 5)	**Concepts** The president of Richard Products Ltd. received an income statement from his controller. The statement covered the calendar year of 1993. "Fred," said the president, "this statement indicates that a net income of only $275,700 was earned last year. You know the value of the company is much more than it was this time last year. In fact, I estimate it to be over a million dollars more."

"You're probably right," replied the controller. "You see, there are factors in accounting which sometimes keep reported operating results from reflecting the change in the fair value of the company."

Present a detailed explanation of the accounting principles and practices to which the controller referred. Include justification to the extent possible for the generally accepted accounting principles and methods.

(SMA adapted)

C 2-4 (L.O. 3)	**?** *YOU MAKE THE CALL* **Elements: Application** For some time, airlines have been offering frequent-flyer mileage credits to customers. Currently there exists a huge resource of potential trips the public could sign up for at the airlines' expense. Yet the airlines do not recognize a liability for these outstanding claims on their passenger-flying capacity.

Required	1. Does an airline have a liability for unused frequent-flyer miles? 2. What argument might the airline make if it wished to avoid recognizing a liability? 3. If a liability is to be shown, how would the amount be established? What account would be debited when the liability was recognized?

C 2–5
(L.O. 5)

Constraints   The following quotation is from *Forbes* magazine, November 7, 1983, p. 106:

Last summer followers of Rockwell International probably noticed a *Wall Street Journal* article giving painful details of the company's computer-leasing fiasco with OPM Leasing Service. The story said that Rockwell has not revealed the amount of the losses, calling them "immaterial." But tucked away was the *Journal's* assertion that a member of the company's outside accounting firm, Deloitte, Haskins & Sells, told the paper that fraud-related losses that are less than 10% of the company's $2.2 billion in shareholders' equity might properly be considered not material. Both Rockwell and Deloitte insist that the comment in question was taken out of context.

Required

1. Explain the constraint on accounting information that is at issue in this quotation.
2. Assess the situation as described in the quotation.
3. Suppose the controller is informed by Rockwell's president that the amount is to be considered not material. The controller disagrees. What should the controller do?

C 2–6
(L.O. 1, 2, 4)

Valuation   The value of Coca-Cola's trademark has been estimated in excess of $1 billion. Yet even though Coca-Cola reports over $4 billion of goodwill and other intangible assets, none of this reported value is due to Coca-Cola's trademark.

Required

1. Write a paragraph indicating whether you believe that including a value for Coca-Cola's trademark would provide a better reporting of the company's assets. Explain and justify your answer.
2. What value would you expect to be reported in GAAP statements?

C 2–7
(L.O. 2, 4, 5)

Comparability, Consistency, and Matching   In 1970, the Chrysler Corporation switched its inventory method for financial reporting from LIFO to FIFO. In its letter to shareholders, Chrysler explained, "The other three [major] . . . automobile manufacturers have consistently used the FIFO method. Therefore, the reported loss for 1970 and the restated profit for 1969 are on a comparable basis as to inventory valuation with the other three companies." These companies included Ford and General Motors.

Effective January 1, 1984, Chrysler switched back to LIFO. In note 1 to Chrysler's 1985 report the company states, "The change was made to more accurately match current costs with current revenues." The results for other years reported with 1984 were restated so all years were reported on the same basis.

Required

1. Are the reasons for the changes in 1970 and 1984, taken alone, reasonable arguments for not continuing to use the same inventory cost flow assumption? Explain.
2. How does a switch to LIFO produce a more accurate matching of current costs with current revenues?
3. What inventory method do you think was being used by Ford and General Motors in 1984?
4. Should Chrysler have been permitted to make these changes in its reporting? Explain.

C 2–8
(L.O. 1)

An Ethical Issue   The December 22, 1992, edition of *The Wall Street Journal* reports that ski areas in New England were reporting more miles of trails than they actually had. The Killington ski area was no exception, overreporting its mileage by 9%. But Killington's hype was less than that of nine other competitors, and so Killington used the study (which, incidentally, Killington commissioned) "to promote its now 'honest' accounting of its terrain."

Required

1. What is the ethical issue here? Does a similar issue arise in accounting?
2. What arguments do you think other ski resort operators make when confronted by the Killington ads? Try to note comparisons with accounting.

C 2–9
(L.O. 3)

Materiality   Waste Disposal Ltd. is involved in legal proceedings related to cleaning up pollution in over 60 sites; this information is reported in the notes to the company's 1990 annual report. The extent of the future cleanup costs is reported to be "substantial."

Generally accepted accounting principles require that a company disclose a contingent liability when there is a "reasonable possibility" it has been incurred. When the liability is probable and can be reasonably estimated, the company must begin its accrual.

Required

1. Do you believe it is "reasonably possible" that the costs of cleanup will be material for Waste Disposal Ltd.? Justify.
2. If your answer to question 1 is yes, write a brief essay explaining why you believe Waste Disposal Ltd. did not at least begin to accrue the liability on its balance sheet.

C 2–10
(L.O. 1, 2)

Need for a Conceptual Framework   Various attempts have been and are being made to work toward a conceptual framework for financial accounting and reporting. These attempts have met with some success. They have helped to clarify the use and application of general accounting concepts for standard-setting bodies and for individual companies when they are making their financial reporting decisions.

Required   Write a response that discusses the usefulness, and the limitations, of a conceptual framework for financial accounting and reporting.

(CICA adapted)

C 2–11
(L.O. 1, 2, 3, 4, 5)

Concepts Application   You, a CA, a sole practitioner, are sitting in your office when your most important agricultural client, John Plowit, walks in.

"I'm sorry to barge in like this, but I've just been to see my banker. He suggested that I ask you to explain to me some matters that affect my statements.

"You will recall that I needed to renew my loans this year. The new bank manager wants some changes made to my statements before he will process my loan application.

"The banker wants me to switch from a cash basis of accounting to an accrual basis. The cash basis provides me with the information I need to evaluate my performance for a year—after all, what I make in a year is the cash in the bank once the harvest is sold.

"Also, the bank wants me to value all my cattle at their market value. Why do they want me to group all my cattle together when they aren't the same? Some are used for producing milk, some are sold as part of my beef operation, and some are used for breeding. Personally, I don't see the sense in valuing them at market when most of them won't be sold or replaced for a very long time.

"I realize that I must give the bank the information the manager wants, but I am very interested in understanding why. After all, I'm the one who has to pay for all of this!"

Required   Write a report that addresses John's concerns.

(CICA adapted)

EXERCISES

E 2–1
(L.O. 1, 2, 3, 4, 5)

Components of a Conceptual Framework   The following four interrelated components are necessary to define a complete conceptual framework:

Number	Description
1	Objectives of financial reporting.
2	Qualitative characteristics of accounting information.
3	Recognition and measurement in financial statements.
4	Elements of financial statements.

The following are primary topics of the preceding components. Match the topics to the components by entering the appropriate number in each blank to the left.

Number	Primary Topics	Number	Primary Topics
_1_	Example: Defines statement users.	___	h. Comparability.
___	a. Recognition criteria.	___	i. Balance sheet, financial statements (described).
___	b. Defines assets, liabilities, and owners' equity.	___	j. Revenues and expenses (defined).
___	c. Measurement criteria.	___	k. Predictive value.
___	d. Understandability.	___	l. Qualitative characteristics.
___	e. Reliability.	___	m. Guidance in applying recognition criteria.
___	f. Objectives of financial statements.	___	n. Capital maintenance.
___	g. Consistency.	___	o. Gains and losses (defined).

E 2–2
(L.O. 2)

Definitions—Relevance and Reliability   The FSCs established relevance and reliability as two of the primary qualitative characteristics of accounting information. Each has three characteristics. Provide a brief definition of each characteristic using the following format:

Characteristic	Brief Definition
A. Relevance.	_____
1. Timeliness.	_____
2. Predictive value.	_____
3. Feedback value.	_____
B. Reliability.	_____
1. Representational faithfulness.	_____
2. Verifiability.	_____
3. Neutrality.	_____

E 2–3
(L.O. 3)

Elements of Financial Statements   The FSCs define the elements of financial statements. To the right, some important aspects of the definitions are listed. Match the aspects with the elements by entering appropriate letters in the blanks. More than one letter can be placed in a blank.

Elements of Financial Statements	Important Aspect of the Definition of the Element
A. Revenues.	_____ 1. Residual interest in the assets after deducting liabilities.
B. Expenses.	_____ 2. Constitute the entity's ongoing major or central operation.
C. Gains.	_____ 3. Probable future economic benefits obtained by an entity.
D. Losses.	_____ 4. Using up of assets or incurrence of liabilities.
E. Assets.	_____ 5. Enhancement of assets or settlements of liabilities.
F. Liabilities.	_____ 6. From peripheral or incidental transactions of the entity.
G. Owners' equity/net assets.	_____ 7. Probable future sacrifices arising from past transactions.
H. None of the above.	_____ 8. Increases in equity from peripheral or incidental activities.

E 2–4
(L.O. 2, 3, 4, 5)

Questions on Concepts   Indicate whether each statement is true or false.

_____ 1. The users of financial statements recognized in the FSCs are limited to owners and creditors.
_____ 2. Materiality is identified as the threshold for recognition.
_____ 3. Comparability (including consistency) is a primary quality of accounting information.
_____ 4. Neutrality in accounting means that the information reported is neither biased in favor of a particular party.
_____ 5. Revenue is recognized as soon as the proceeds are measurable.
_____ 6. Relevance and reliability are necessary for recognition.
_____ 7. Both gains and losses relate to peripheral or incidental transactions of the entity.
_____ 8. All items (resulting from a transaction) must be recognized if they meet the definition of a financial statement element.
_____ 9. The matching principle is completely independent of the revenue principle.

E 2–5
(L.O. 2, 5)

Questions on Concepts   For each of the following circumstances, give the letter item(s) indicating the accounting concept or principle involved:

a. Understandability.   g. Continuity assumption.
b. Reliability.   h. Separate entity.
c. Timeliness.   i. Cost principle.
d. Comparability.   j. Revenue principle.
e. Full disclosure.   k. Unit of measure.
f. Conservatism.   l. Materiality.

1. Goodwill is only recorded in the accounts when it arises from the purchase of another entity at a price higher than the fair market value of the purchased entity's tangible assets.
2. A note describing the company's possible liability in a lawsuit is included with the financial statements even though no formal liability exists at the balance sheet date.
3. All payments out of petty cash are debited to miscellaneous expense.

4. Fixed assets are classified separately as land and buildings, with an accumulated depreciation account for buildings.
5. A retail store uses estimates rather than a complete physical count of its inventory for purposes of preparing monthly financial statements.
6. Marketable securities are valued at the lower of cost or market.
7. Long-term investments are valued at cost.
8. An advance deposit on a sale contract is reported as unearned revenue.
9. Small tools used by a large manufacturing firm are recorded as an expense when purchased.
10. Periodic payments of $1,000 per month for services of L. Ryan, who owns all of the shares of the company, are reported as salary; additional amounts paid to Ryan are reported as dividends.

E 2–6
(L.O. 2, 3, 4, 5)

Concepts Violated? The FSCs are intended to provide guidance in analyzing and recording certain transactions and events. In the following cases, indicate the assumption, principle, or constraint that applies to each case and state whether it was followed or violated.

Case A Loran Company used FIFO in 1992; LIFO in 1993; and FIFO in 1994.
Case B A tract of land was acquired on credit by signing a $55,000, one-year, noninterest-bearing note. The asset account was debited for $55,000. The going rate of interest was 10%.
Case C Loran Company always issues its annual financial report nine months after the end of the annual reporting period.
Case D Loran Company recognizes all sales revenues on the cash basis.
Case E Loran Company records interest expense only on the payment dates.
Case F Loran Company includes among its financial statement elements an apartment building owned and operated by the owner of the company.
Case G Loran Company never uses notes or supplemental schedules as a part of its financial reports.

E 2–7
(L.O. 4)

Recognition and Measurement Indicate the recognition or measurement problem associated with each of the following items:

a. Recording employee morale as an asset.
b. Recording a future liability for employees related to medical benefits to be paid after retirement.
c. Recording a liability (and expense) for cleaning up chemical dumps.
d. Recognizing the goodwill associated with increased market acceptance of a product brand name.
e. Recognizing an expense associated with the granting of a stock option to an employee at a price currently below the shares' current market price. Share prices are expected to increase.
f. Recording the value of a just-granted stock option, valid in 10 years' time.

E 2–8
(L.O. 5)

Examples of Characteristics, Assumptions, Principles, and Constraints The following characteristics, assumptions, principles, and constraints are lettered for response purposes.

Characteristics, Assumptions, Principles, and Constraints

A. Separate entity assumption.
B. Continuity assumption.
C. Unit-of-measure assumption.
D. Time period assumption.
E. Cost principle.
F. Revenue principle.

G. Matching principle.
H. Full disclosure principle.
I. Cost–benefit constraint.
J. Materiality constraint.
K. Industry peculiarities constraint.
L. Conservatism constraint.

The following list of key phrases is directly related to the preceding list. Match these phrases with the list by entering the appropriate letter to the left.

Key Phrase

_____ 1. Risks and rewards have transferred.
_____ 2. Least favourable effect on income and/or total assets.
_____ 3. Common denominator—the yardstick.
_____ 4. Expenses incurred in earning the period's revenues.
_____ 5. Preparation cost versus value of benefit to the user.
_____ 6. Separate and apart from its owners and other entities.
_____ 7. Report all relevant information
_____ 8. Reporting periods—usually one year.

_____ 9. Cash-equivalent expenditures to acquire.
_____ 10. Going concern basis.
_____ 11. Relative amount of an item that would not have changed or influenced the judgment of a reasonable person.
_____ 12. Exception to accounting principles and practices because of uniqueness of the industry.

PROBLEMS

P 2–1
(L.O. 1, 2)

Qualitative Characteristics During an audit of L. R. Grant Company, the following situations were found to exist.

Situation A The company recorded a $27.50 wrench as expense when purchased, although it had a 10-year estimated life and no residual value.
Situation B For inventory purposes, Grant switched from FIFO to LIFO to FIFO for the same items during a five-year period.
Situation C Based on estimates, the company recognizes earnings on long-term construction contracts at the end of each year of the construction period. Its major competitors recognize earnings only at the date the contract is completed, based on actual results.
Situation D Grant follows a policy of depreciating plant and equipment on the straight-line basis over a period of time that is 50% longer than the most reliable useful life estimate.
Situation E As an accounting policy, interest is reported at the end of each reporting period as the amount of interest expense less interest revenue.

Required

1. Identify and briefly explain the qualitative characteristic or constraint of accounting information that is directly involved in each situation.
2. Indicate what, if anything, the company should do in the future by way of any change in accounting policy.

P 2–2
(L.O. 3, 4)

Application of Characteristics, Assumptions, Principles, and Constraints The following list of statements pose conceptual issues.

_a._ The business entity is considered to be separate and apart from the owners for accounting purposes.
_b._ A transaction involving a very small amount does not need to be reported because of materiality.
_c._ The monetary unit is not stable over time.
_d._ GAAP always requires supplementary notes to the balance sheet.
_e._ GAAP often requires that the LCM method be used in valuing inventories.
_f._ The cost principle relates only to the income statement.
_g._ Revenue should be recognized only when the cash is received.
_h._ Accruals and deferrals are necessary because of the separate entity assumption.
_i._ Revenue should be recognized as late as possible and expenses as early as possible.

Required

1. Indicate whether each statement is correct or incorrect.
2. Identify the characteristic, assumption, principle, or constraint that is posed.
3. Provide a brief discussion of its implications.

P 2–3
(L.O. 3, 5)

Accrual and Cash Basis Compared The following summarized data were taken from the records of the Safelock Corporation at the end of the annual accounting period, December 31, 1995:

Sales for cash	$311,000
Sales on account	87,000
Cash purchases of merchandise for resale	170,000
Credit purchases of merchandise for resale	40,000
Expenses paid in cash (includes any prepayments)	72,000
Accounts receivable:	
Balance in account on January 1, 1995	27,000
Balance in account on December 31, 1995	50,000
Accounts payable:	
Balance in account on January 1, 1995	14,000
Balance in account on December 31, 1995	16,000

Merchandise inventory:
Beginning inventory, January 1, 1995 50,000
Ending inventory, December 31, 1995 62,000
Accrued (unpaid) wages at December 31, 1995 (none at January 1, 1995). 5,000
Prepaid expenses at December 31, 1995 (none at January 1, 1995). 2,000
Operational assets—equipment:
Cost when acquired 100,000
Annual depreciation 10,000

Required   1. Based on the preceding data, complete the following statements of income for 1995 to evaluate the difference between cash and accrual basis (show computations):

	Accrual Basis	Cash Basis
Sales revenue	$____	$____
Less expenses:		
Cost of goods sold	$____	$____
Depreciation expense	____	____
Remaining expenses	____	____
Total expenses	____	____
Pre-tax income	$____	$____

2. Which basis is in conformity with GAAP? Give support for your answer.

P 2–4
(L.O. 3, 5)

Application of Characteristics, Assumptions, Principles, Constraints   An inspection of the annual financial statements and the accounting records revealed that the George L. Massey Hardware Company had violated some characteristics, assumptions, principles, and constraints. The following transactions were involved:

a. Merchandise purchased for resale was recorded as a debit to inventory for the invoice price of $40,000 (accounts payable was credited for the same amount); terms were 2/10, n/30. Ten days later, the account was paid (cash was credited for $39,200).

b. Accounts receivable of $95,000 were reported on the balance sheet; this amount included a $42,000 loan to the company president. The maturity date on the loan was not specified.

c. Usual and ordinary repairs on operational assets were recorded as follows: debit operational assets, $97,500; credit cash, $97,500.

d. George L. Massey Co. sustained a $47,000 storm damage loss during the current year (no insurance). The loss was recorded and reported as follows:

Income statement: Extraordinary item—storm loss $40,000
Balance sheet (assets): Deferred charge, storm loss $ 7,000

e. Depreciation expense of $227,000 was recorded as a debit to retained earnings and was deducted directly from retained earnings on the balance sheet.

f. Income tax expense of $18,000 was recorded as a debit to retained earnings and was deducted directly from retained earnings on the balance sheet.

Required   1. For each transaction, identify the inappropriate treatment and the characteristic, assumption, principle, or constraint violated.
2. Give the entry that should have been made or the appropriate reporting.

P 2–5
(L.O. 4)

YOU MAKE THE CALL   **Recognition: Liability**   On March 24, 1989, the tanker *Exxon Valdez* spilled 11 million gallons of oil in Prince William Sound, Alaska. The tanker belonged to the Exxon Oil Company. Exxon carried insurance, but the initial estimate of the damages, which exceeded $2 billion, was beyond the firm's insurance coverage.

Required   1. Write an essay discussing whether Exxon has an ethical responsibility to pay for the cleanup (whether or not it has a legal one).
2. Is this a liability of the company? If so, how should it be recognized in the company's financial statements?

P 2–6
(L.O. 4)

Accrual- and Cash-Basis Accounting One objective of financial reporting is to provide information that is helpful to current and potential investors and creditors in assessing the ability of an entity to generate cash flows in the future to meet its obligations and provide a return on investment. Yet, revenue and matching principles are predicated on the accrual basis of accounting.

Required

Write an essay that distinguishes between the cash basis and the accrual basis and addresses any seeming conflict between the two positions. Use examples of how expenses and revenues are treated in both systems.

P 2–7
(L.O. 5)

Conservatism and Consistency Prestan Stores, a specialty retailer, has just purchased a new Canadair jet aircraft for its senior officers' travel needs. The treasurer wants to depreciate the plane for financial accounting purposes using an accelerated method because, she argues, the lower income numbers will be more conservative and this, in turn, will generate shareholder confidence in the firm. The controller, however, argues that the firm uses the straight-line method on other assets, so using an accelerated method to depreciate the plane's cost would violate the consistency of the firm's depreciation policy.

Required

Which, if either, officer's argument is correct? Write a brief memo to the president of Prestan Stores explaining your reasons for the answer given.

P 2–8
(L.O. 3, 4, 5)

Implementation of Principles The following summarized transactions were recorded as indicated for the Brown Construction Company during the current year.

a. The Brown Construction Company needed a small structure for temporary storage. A contractor quoted a price of $837,000. The company decided to build the structure itself. The cost was $643,000, and construction required three months. The following entry was made:

Buildings—warehouse.	837,000	
Cash		643,000
Revenue—self-construction		194,000

b. Brown owns a plant located on a river that floods every few years. As a result, the company suffers a flood loss regularly. During the current year, the flood was severe, causing an uninsured loss of $175,000, which was the amount spent to repair the flood damage. The following entry was made:

Retained earnings, flood loss.	175,000	
Cash		175,000

c. The company originally sold and issued 100,000 common shares. During the current year, 80,000 of these shares were outstanding and 20,000 were repurchased from the shareholders and retired. Near the end of the current year, the board of directors declared and paid a cash dividend of $4 per share. The dividend was recorded as follows:

Retained earnings.	400,000	
Cash		320,000
Dividend income ($4 × 20,000).		80,000

d. The Brown Construction Company purchased a machine that had a list price of $90,000. The company paid for the machine in full by issuing 9,000 common shares (market price $8). The purchase was recorded as follows:

Machine	90,000	
Share capital		90,000

e. On December 28, the company collected $33,000 cash in advance for merchandise to be available and shipped during February of the next accounting year (the accounting period ends December 31). This transaction was recorded on December 28 as follows:

Cash	33,000	
Sales revenue		33,000

Required

1. For each transaction, determine which implementation accounting principle was violated (if any).
2. Explain the nature of the violation.
3. In each instance, indicate how the transaction should have been recorded.

P 2-9
(L.O. 2, 3, 4, 5)

Implementation of Principles   R. H. Hall has drawn up a financial statement on December 31, 1995, employing valuation procedures as follows:

Cash	$40,000	Includes cash in the bank, $35,000, and customers' cheques that could not be cashed but that Hall feels will ultimately be recoverable, $5,000.
Marketable securities.	$90,000	Represents the value on December 31 of securities reported at the beginning of 1995 at a cost of $81,200.
Value of insurance policy	$15,000	The sum of the payments made on a life insurance policy that requires further payments through 2001. The cash surrender value of the policy at the end of 1995 is $7,000.
Intangible assets	$36,000	Recorded in 1995 when a competitor offered to pay Hall this amount for the lease entered into when the company was formed and which still has five years to run at a rental that is 7% of net sales.
Sundry payables	$ 1	Recorded as a result of a suit of $20,000 against Hall for breach of contract; Hall has offered to pay $5,000 in settlement of the suit, but this has been rejected; it is the opinion of Hall's attorney that the suit can be settled by payment of $10,000.

Required

1. Indicate what change, if any, you would make in reporting each of the preceding items.
2. In each case, discuss the concept or principle involved.

ANALYZING FINANCIAL STATEMENTS

A 2-1
(L.O. 2)

Analysis of an Annual Report: Magna International   This case relates to the 1993 financial statements of Magna International Inc., which are located at the end of the book.

Required

To become familiar with the 1993 financial statements, respond to the following:

1. The date the annual reporting period ends is _____ . Is the firm a calendar-year reporting firm?
2. Net sales for 1993 were $_____ .
3. Net increase (decrease) in cash and cash equivalents for 1993 was $_____ .
4. Total assets at the end of the 1993 reporting period were $_____ .
5. The first note to the consolidated financial statements is titled _____ . How many notes were provided? _____ .
6. What is the name of the auditing firm?
7. Do the financial statements refer to GAAP at any point?
8. How does the company apply the matching principle to the following?
   a. Goodwill.
   b. Fixed assets.
   c. Inventories.
9. When is revenue recognized?

3 Review: The Accounting Information Processing System

LEARNING OBJECTIVES

After you have studied this chapter, you will be able to:

1 **Explain the purpose of an accounting information system.**

2 **Explain the double-entry recording system and the relationships among financial statements.**

3 **Demonstrate the relationships among accounting information system components: accounts, journals, ledgers, and financial statements.**

4 **Perform the accounting cycle steps leading to the financial statements.**

5 **State the difference between two methods of recording common operating transactions and explain the effects of each on adjusting and reversing entries.**

INTRODUCTION

Early in 1992, the share price of Computer Sciences Ltd. lost significant ground as a result of uncertainties surrounding the continuation of a major government contract. One of the sticking points was "serious deficiencies" in Computer Sciences' accounting system.[1]

Eagle Hardware and Garden also found itself in a serious situation stemming from accounting system problems. These difficulties resulted in a significant overstatement of ending inventory in 1992, which in turn caused earnings to be overstated. The company withdrew its audited financial statements, saying that they could not be relied upon.[2]

In similar circumstances, Leslie Fay Company announced that the correction of numerous accounting irregularities could wipe out its 1992 earnings and force restatement of 1991 earnings. A company spokesperson indicated:

---

[1] "Investors Seem Wary over Computer Sciences as Flap over EPA Contract Clouds Prospects," *The Wall Street Journal,* March 18, 1992, p. C2.

[2] "Hot Concept, Big Following, but Stock Takes Hefty Fall," *New York Times,* December 8, 1992, p. D1.

If this [the need for restatement] proves to be true, we have a complete breakdown in terms of our financial information. There is a contradiction to what exists and what they are claiming in our books and records.[3]

These situations illustrate the problems that can result from an ineffective **accounting information system (AIS)** and lack of associated internal controls.[4] An AIS consists of physical components, including journals, ledgers, and computer hardware, used to capture transaction data and process it into usable accounting information. Supporting these physical components are company policies, procedures, and software programs that administer data collection and processing for internal management needs and external financial reporting. The corporate situations illustrated above point out the importance of an AIS to a firm's survival and success.

Internally, an AIS provides data relevant to a variety of questions. For example:

- What is the cash position?
- When must inventory be purchased?
- Is a profit being earned?
- Where can costs be cut?

With a well-designed AIS, a business can determine whether its activities are adding value for its shareholders or, rather, consuming their investment. Federal and provincial legislation requires most large for-profit companies to maintain adequate records to support the information published in financial statements. For example, Revenue Canada requires adequate evidence to substantiate tax returns.

AIS costs are substantial for most firms. These costs increase as the number and complexity of AcSB, tax, and regulatory reporting requirements grow. Many smaller businesses have difficulty coping with increased recordkeeping and reporting requirements.

Financial statements are an important output of the accounting information system. They provide investors and creditors with information useful for making decisions and for assessing a firm's profitability, its ability to generate cash flows, and the strengths and weaknesses of its financial position. This chapter reviews the fundamentals of the steps leading to those financial statements.

ACCOUNTS, TRANSACTION RECORDING, AND FINANCIAL STATEMENTS

Financial accounting information is recorded in accounts, which describe specific resources, obligations, and the changes in these items. The seven major types of accounts include permanent accounts (assets, liabilities, and owners' equity accounts) and temporary accounts (revenues, expenses, gains, and losses).[5] The permanent accounts are those appearing in the balance sheet. The descriptive term *permanent* means that balances in these accounts are carried over to future accounting periods. The **accounting identity** relates the balances of the permanent accounts:

$$\text{Assets} = \text{Liabilities} + \text{Owners' Equity}$$

The temporary accounts report events related to income-generating activities and appear in the income statement. For example, when rent is paid, the rent expense account describes the reason for the decrease in cash. Temporary accounts are closed at the end of the accounting period.

---

[3] "Leslie Fay Says Irregularities in Books Could Wipe Out '92 Profit; Stock Skids," *The Wall Street Journal*, February 2, 1993, p. A4.

[4] A firm's internal control system includes the policies and procedures designed to ensure that the firm's goals are met. These policies and procedures are designed to safeguard assets, promote reliable accounting records, encourage compliance with the firm's policies, and evaluate efficiency.

[5] Permanent accounts are also called *real* accounts, and temporary accounts are also called *nominal* accounts. Other temporary accounts are used, including cash dividends declared, income summary, and various "holding" accounts that are used for a specific purpose but are not disclosed in financial statements. The cash dividends declared account is debited when dividends are declared. Alternatively, the permanent account, retained earnings, is debited directly.

Economic events are recorded in an AIS in such a way as to change at least two accounts. This practice, called the **double-entry system,** records the change in a resource or obligation *and* the reason for, or source of, the change. In the rent example above, if only the cash decrease were to be recorded, no record of the transaction's purpose would be maintained.

The double-entry system also ensures that the accounting equation remains in balance. For example, when a company acquires $10,000 worth of equipment by tendering a note payable to the seller for that amount, both assets and liabilities increase by $10,000. The accounting identity remains in balance.

Complementing the double-entry system, the **debit–credit convention** is used as a recording and balancing procedure. This convention divides accounts into two sides. The **debit** (dr.) side is always the left side, and the **credit** (cr.) side is always the right side. These terms carry no further meaning. Depending on the account type, a debit or a credit can record an increase or decrease, as illustrated in the T accounts below. The **T account** is a form of account used for demonstrating transactions; it takes the form of the letter T.

Permanent Accounts

Assets		=	**Liabilities**		+	**Owners' Equity**	
Debit entries *increase* assets	Credit entries *decrease* assets		Debit entries *decrease* liabilities	Credit entries *increase* liabilities		Debit entries *decrease* owners' equity	Credit entries *increase* owners' equity

Temporary Accounts

Expenses		**Revenues**	
Debit entries *increase* expenses	Credit entries *decrease* expenses	Debit entries *decrease* revenues	Credit entries *increase* revenues

Losses		**Gains**	
Debit entries *increase* losses	Credit entries *decrease* losses	Debit entries *decrease* gains	Credit entries *increase* gains

An example of each type of change is illustrated below:

Permanent Accounts

Debit	**Credit**
Inventory purchased	Cash paid
Wages payable paid	Interest payable accrued
Dividends declared	Common shares issued

Temporary Accounts

Debit	**Credit**
Sales discount	Sales
Cost of goods sold	Purchases returns
Loss on sale of land	Gain on sale of equipment

The debit–credit convention helps maintain the accounting identity. For example, increases in assets (debits) are often associated with increases in liabilities (credits). Asset decreases (credits) often are associated with expenses (debits). Salary payments are an example: the dollar amount of the salary expense debit equals the dollar amount of the cash credit.

The debit–credit convention is a convenient way to check for recording errors. When the sums of debits and credits are not equal, an error is evident.[6] Without the convention, only increases and decreases in accounts would be recorded. In general, the dollar value of account increases would not equal the dollar value of account decreases for a given group of transactions. For example, paying off a long-term liability results in two decreases—to cash and to long-term liabilities. Therefore, inequality of total increases and total decreases could not be used to signal errors.

At the end of a reporting period, after all transactions and events are recorded in accounts, financial statements are prepared. The financial statements report account balances, changes in account balances, and aggregations of account balances, such as net income and total assets. The financial statements include the income statement, the balance sheet, and the statement of changes in financial position. The statement of changes in financial position is also commonly referred to as a statement of cash flows. The income statement reports the portion of the change in net assets (owners' equity) attributed to income-producing activities. The balance sheet reflects the financial position of the entity—the accounting identity. Two other statements, the retained earnings statement and the statement of shareholders' equity, are also commonly reported. The steps leading to these financial statements are discussed in the rest of this chapter.

CONCEPT REVIEW

1. How does the double-entry system increase the effectiveness of an AIS?
2. Why is the debit–credit convention used rather than mere recording of increases and decreases in account balances?
3. How does the payment of an account payable (in cash) affect the elements of the accounting identity?

THE AIS AND THE ACCOUNTING CYCLE

An AIS is designed to record accurate financial data in a timely and chronological manner, facilitate retrieval of financial data in a form useful to management, and simplify periodic preparation of financial statements for external use. Design of the AIS, to meet the company's information requirements, depends on the firm's size, the nature of its operations, the volume of data, its organizational structure, and government regulation.

The **accounting cycle,** illustrated in Exhibit 3–1, is a series of sequential steps leading to the financial statements. This cycle is repeated each reporting period, normally a year.[7] Depending on the information-processing technology used, certain accounting cycle steps can be combined or in some cases omitted. Computerized systems increase the _reliability_ of processing without compromising the _relevance_ of the information. For example, general ledger software is used to perform much of the accounting cycle work in large companies. (Worksheets also facilitate the process and are discussed in Appendix 3A.[8]) The fundamental nature of the process, however, is the same regardless of the technology used.

---

[6] The converse, however, is not true. Equality of total debits and total credits does not imply that no errors have been made.

[7] Exhibit 3–1 applies to the preparation of all financial statements except the statement of changes in financial position, which requires additional input. Firms may combine some of these steps or change their order to suit their specific needs.

[8] In manual systems, a worksheet is a sheet of accounting paper used to plot adjusting entries and develop a preliminary layout for the income statement, retained earnings statement, and the balance sheet. In automated systems, worksheets take the form of computer spreadsheets.

EXHIBIT 3–1
Steps in the Accounting
Cycle and Their Objectives

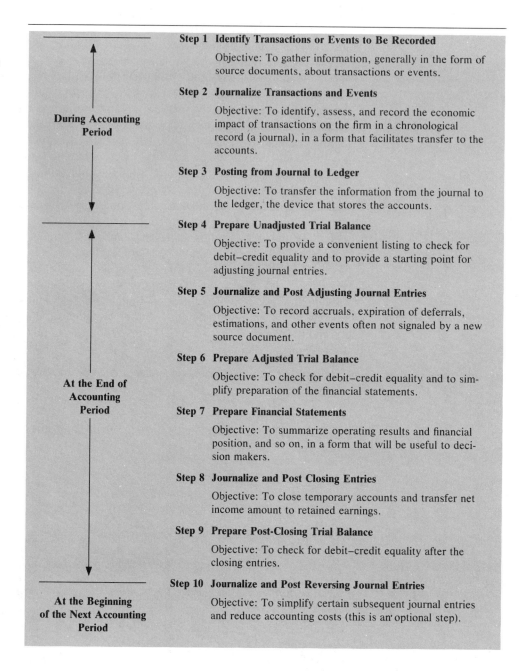

During Accounting Period

Step 1 Identify Transactions or Events to Be Recorded

Objective: To gather information, generally in the form of source documents, about transactions or events.

Step 2 Journalize Transactions and Events

Objective: To identify, assess, and record the economic impact of transactions on the firm in a chronological record (a journal), in a form that facilitates transfer to the accounts.

Step 3 Posting from Journal to Ledger

Objective: To transfer the information from the journal to the ledger, the device that stores the accounts.

At the End of Accounting Period

Step 4 Prepare Unadjusted Trial Balance

Objective: To provide a convenient listing to check for debit–credit equality and to provide a starting point for adjusting journal entries.

Step 5 Journalize and Post Adjusting Journal Entries

Objective: To record accruals, expiration of deferrals, estimations, and other events often not signaled by a new source document.

Step 6 Prepare Adjusted Trial Balance

Objective: To check for debit–credit equality and to simplify preparation of the financial statements.

Step 7 Prepare Financial Statements

Objective: To summarize operating results and financial position, and so on, in a form that will be useful to decision makers.

Step 8 Journalize and Post Closing Entries

Objective: To close temporary accounts and transfer net income amount to retained earnings.

Step 9 Prepare Post-Closing Trial Balance

Objective: To check for debit–credit equality after the closing entries.

At the Beginning of the Next Accounting Period

Step 10 Journalize and Post Reversing Journal Entries

Objective: To simplify certain subsequent journal entries and reduce accounting costs (this is an optional step).

The first three steps in the accounting cycle require the most time and effort. The frequency of Step 3, posting, depends on the volume and nature of transactions. Firms with many cash transactions post to the cash account daily. Steps 4 through 9 generally occur at the end of the fiscal year. The last step, the posting of reversing entries, is optional and occurs at the beginning of the next accounting period.

STEP 1: IDENTIFY TRANSACTIONS OR EVENTS TO BE RECORDED

The first step will identify transactions and events that cause a change in the firm's resources or obligations and will collect relevant economic data about those transactions.

Events that change a firm's resources or obligations are categorized into three types:

1. **Exchanges of resources and obligations between the reporting firm and outside parties.** These exchanges are either **reciprocal transfers** or **nonreciprocal transfers.** In

THE IMPACT OF COMPUTERIZATION

Few businesses keep manual records. Most use a customized or off-the-shelf computer program that will facilitate most of the steps in the accounting cycle (refer back to Exhibit 3–1):

- Journalizing transactions, adjustments, closing, and reversing entries.
- Posting entries.
- Preparation of trial balances.
- Preparation of financial statements.

Such programs have many advantages, including speed and accuracy.

What is left for the accountant to do? First of all, identification and control of transactions and adjustments is crucial. The accountant manages the entire process, ensuring that information entered is accurate and complete. Secondly, many elements in financial reporting require the exercise of professional judgment—choice of accounting policy, composition of the notes to the financial statements, and so on. These tasks require qualified decision makers.

Regardless of how the steps in the accounting cycle are performed, they accomplish the same task—posting is posting, manual or computerized. The accountant has to understand this process to manage it.

a reciprocal transfer, the firm both transfers and receives resources (e.g., sale of goods). In a nonreciprocal transfer, the firm either transfers or receives current or future resources (e.g., payment of cash dividends or receipt of a donation). All exchanges require a journal entry.

2. **Internal events within the firm that affect its resources or obligations but do not involve outside parties.** Examples are recognition of depreciation and amortization of capital assets and the use of inventory for production. These events also generally require a journal entry. However, other events, such as increases in the value of assets resulting from superior management and similar factors, are not recorded.

3. **External economic and environmental events beyond the control of the company.** Examples include casualty losses and changes in the market value of assets and liabilities. At the present time, accounting standards allow recording of market value changes for only a few types of assets.

Transactions[9] are often accompanied by a source document, generally a paper record that describes the exchange, the parties involved, the date, and the dollar amount. Examples are sales invoices, freight bills, and cash register receipts. Certain events, such as the accrual of interest, are not signaled by a separate source document. Recording these transactions requires reference to the underlying contract supporting the original exchange of resources. Source documents are essential for the initial recording of transactions in a journal and are also used for subsequent tracing and verification, for evidence in legal proceedings, and for audits of financial statements.

STEP 2: JOURNALIZE TRANSACTIONS AND EVENTS

This step measures and records the economic effect of transactions in a form that simplifies transfer to the accounts. Accounting principles that guide measurement, recognition, and classification of accounts are applied.

Transactions are recorded chronologically in a journal—an organized medium for recording transactions in debit–credit format. A journal entry is a debit–credit description of a transaction that includes the date, the accounts and amounts involved, and a brief description. A journal entry is a temporary recording, although journals are retained as part of the audit trail; account balances are not changed until the information is transferred to the ledger accounts in Step 3.

Much of this text is concerned with the appropriate recording of economic events. The journal entry is an important means of illustrating the application of accounting

---

[9] The term *transaction* in this text is applied to all events requiring a journal entry.

EXHIBIT 3–2
General Journal Entry

GENERAL JOURNAL

Page J-16

Date 1995	Accounts and Explanation	Post. Ref.	Amount	
			Debit	Credit
Jan. 2	Equipment	150	15,000	
	Cash	101		5,000
	Notes payable	215		10,000
	Purchased equipment for use in the business. Paid $5,000 cash and gave a $10,000, one-year note with 15% interest payable at maturity.			

principles, and it is used throughout this text. Accounting systems usually have two types of journals: the general journal and special journals. Nonrepetitive entries and entries involving infrequently used accounts are recorded in the general journal. Repetitive entries are recorded in special journals. If special journals are not used, all transactions are recorded in the general journal. Special journals are discussed in Appendix 3B. The general journal is used to illustrate most entries in this text.

The journal entry step is not absolutely essential; transaction data can be recorded directly into the accounts. However, the journal entry step has advantages. A journal is a place to record transactions when access to the ledger accounts is restricted. Transaction processing is more efficient, and less costly, if transactions are grouped in a journal and processed together. By using journals, review and analysis of transactions are much simpler and the accounts consume less storage space. Also, a chronological list of transactions is provided. Transactions can be difficult to reconstruct without a journal because the debits and credits are located in different accounts. Journals are typically part of the paper trail relied on by auditors.

Exhibit 3–2 illustrates a portion of a page from a general journal. This entry records the purchase of equipment financed with cash and debt, recorded at the value of the resources used to acquire it. The names of the accounts credited are listed below and to the right of the debited accounts.

Some companies use computerized systems to bypass the traditional journal entry step. Retailers, for example, record relevant information about a transaction by using bar codes printed on many product packages. Optical scanning equipment reads the bar code and transmits the information to a computer, which records the proper amount directly in the relevant ledger accounts. Accounting cost savings can be significant. For example, before the use of bar codes at Tate Andale, over 400 employee hours were required to record all inventory transactions each year. With bar code technology, that figure fell to 32 hours and manual data entry was eliminated. The firm also experienced substantial increases in data accuracy.[10]

CONCEPT REVIEW

1. Distinguish between reciprocal and nonreciprocal transfers.
2. Does a journal entry immediately change account balances?
3. Explain why transactions are not usually recorded directly in the accounts as they occur.

---

[10] "Wider Uses for Bar Codes," *Nation's Business*, March 1989, p. 34. The use of bar code technology does not necessarily imply a bypass of the journal entry step, however.

EXHIBIT 3-3
Portion of a General Ledger

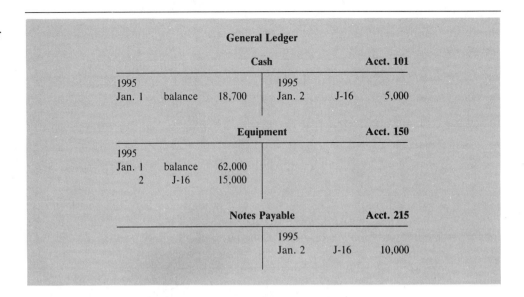

STEP 3: POSTING FROM JOURNALS TO LEDGER

Transferring transaction data from the journal to the ledger is called *posting*. Posting reclassifies the data from the journal's chronological format to an account classification format in the ledger, which stores the formal accounts. Computerized systems store ledger data on tape or disk until it is needed for processing another step in the accounting cycle.

Accounting systems usually have two types of ledgers: the general ledger and subsidiary ledgers. The general ledger holds the individual accounts, grouped according to the seven elements of financial statements. Subsidiary ledgers support general ledger accounts that are comprised of many separate individual accounts. For example, a firm with a substantial number of customer accounts receivable will maintain one ledger account per customer, stored in an accounts receivable subsidiary ledger. The individual customer account is called the **subsidiary account.** The general ledger holds only the **control account,** the balance of which reflects the sum of all the individual customer account balances. Only the control accounts are used in compiling financial statements.

For example, assume that a firm's accounts receivable consist of two individual accounts with a combined balance of $6,000. The firm's general and subsidiary ledgers might show these balances:

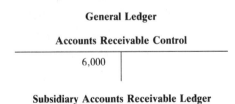

Exhibit 3-3 illustrates a section of a general ledger in T account form. This ledger depicts three general ledger accounts after posting the journal entry shown in Exhibit 3-2. Posting references and page numbers are used in both the journal and the ledger to ensure that an audit trail exists—that is, to indicate where an item in the account ledger came from and to which account the item was posted. Posting references also serve to confirm that an entry was posted. Posting references are provided automatically in a computerized system.

EXHIBIT 3–4
Unadjusted Trial
Balance Illustrated

SONORA, LTD.
Unadjusted Trial Balance
December 31, 1995

Account	Debit	Credit
Cash.	$ 67,300	
Accounts receivable .	45,000	
Allowance for doubtful accounts		$ 1,000
Notes receivable	8,000	
Inventory (January 1 balance, periodic system).	75,000	
Prepaid insurance .	600	
Land.	8,000	
Building .	160,000	
Accumulated depreciation, building		90,000
Equipment .	91,000	
Accumulated depreciation, equipment .		27,000
Accounts payable .		29,000
Bonds payable, 6% .		50,000
Common shares, nopar, 15,000 shares .		170,000
Retained earnings .		31,500*
Sales revenue.		325,200
Interest revenue.		500
Rent revenue .		1,800
Purchases .	130,000	
Freight on purchases .	4,000	
Purchase returns .		2,000
Selling expenses† .	104,000	
General and administrative expenses† .	23,600	
Interest expense.	2,500	
Extraordinary loss (pretax) .	9,000	
Totals .	$728,000	$728,000

* January 1, 1995, balance (no transactions involved retained earnings in 1995).

† These broad categories of expenses are used to conserve space.

When the $5,000 cash credit from the general journal entry of Exhibit 3–2 is posted to the cash ledger account, "101" is listed in the journal to indicate the account number to which the credit is posted. Similarly, in the cash ledger account, "J-16" indicates the journal page number from which this amount is posted. Cross-referencing is especially important for posting large numbers of transactions, detecting and correcting errors, and maintaining an audit trail.

STEP 4: PREPARE UNADJUSTED TRIAL BALANCE

An unadjusted trial balance is prepared at the end of the reporting period, after all transaction entries are recorded in the journals and posted to the ledger. The unadjusted trial balance is a list of general ledger accounts and their account balances, in the following order: assets, liabilities, owners' equity, revenues, expenses, gains, and losses. For accounts with subsidiary ledgers, only the control account balances are entered into the trial balance, after reconciliation with the subsidiary ledger.

The unadjusted trial balance is the starting point for developing adjusting entries and for the worksheet, if used. Exhibit 3–4 illustrates an unadjusted trial balance for Sonora, Ltd., a fictitious retailing company, at the end of the fiscal year. The trial balance reflects Sonora's transaction journal entries recorded during 1995 and is the basis for the remainder of our accounting cycle illustration.

The unadjusted trial balance is a convenient means for checking that the sum of debit account balances equals the sum of credit account balances. If the sums of debit and credit balances are not equal, the error must be found and corrected. A reexamination of source documents and postings is one way to discover the source of an error. Equality of debits and credits does not, however, imply that the accounts are error-free. An unposted journal entry, an incorrectly classified account, and an erroneous journal entry amount are errors that do not cause inequality of total debits and credits.

As reported in Exhibit 3–4, Sonora uses a periodic inventory system. Under this system, merchandise on hand is counted and costed at the end of each accounting period. The resulting inventory amount is used to update the inventory account balance. During the period, however, the inventory account balance remains at the January 1 amount and the cost of goods sold is not readily determinable. The unadjusted trial balance for Sonora reflects the January 1, 1995, balance.

In a perpetual inventory system, the inventory account balance is constantly updated as merchandise is purchased and sold. Thus, the inventory account balance is correctly stated at the end of the accounting period, and there will be an up-to-date cost of goods sold account before any adjustments are made.

As shown in Exhibit 3–4, Sonora's retained earnings account also reflects the January 1, 1995, balance since no transaction affected this account during 1995. Income tax expense is not listed in the unadjusted trial balance because the corporate income tax liability for the current year is not known until pretax income is computed.[11] The extraordinary loss does not yet reflect any tax effect.

CONCEPT REVIEW

1. Does the sum of the debit column in an unadjusted trial balance represent a meaningful total? If not, why is it computed?
2. Why might the retained earnings account balance in the unadjusted trial balance reflect the beginning-of-year balance?
3. Does equality of debits and credits in a trial balance assure the absence of errors in the accounts? Explain.

STEP 5: JOURNALIZE AND POST ADJUSTING JOURNAL ENTRIES

Many changes in a firm's economic resources and obligations occur continuously. For example, interest accrues daily on debts, as does rent expense on an office building. Other resources and obligations, such as employee salaries, originate as service is rendered, with payment to follow at specified dates. The end of the accounting period generally does not coincide with the receipt or payment of cash associated with these types of resource changes.

Accrual-basis accounting requires the recording of these changes at the end of the accounting period under the revenue, historical cost, and matching principles.[12] **Adjusting journal entries** (AJEs) are used to record such resource changes to ensure the accuracy of the financial statements.

AJEs generally record a resource or obligation change and usually involve both a permanent and a temporary account. AJEs are recorded and dated as of the last day of the fiscal period. They are recorded in the general journal and posted to the ledger accounts. Source documents from earlier transactions are the primary information sources for AJEs.

AJEs are classified into three categories: deferrals, accruals, and other AJEs.

Deferrals are for cash flows that occur *before* expense and revenue recognition. These AJEs are recorded when cash is paid for expenses that apply to more than one

---

[11] Companies required to pay quarterly estimated income taxes would have a balance in this account at this point.

[12] Cash-basis accounting, which generally records a journal entry only upon an exchange of cash between firms, does not typically require many adjusting entries. For example, unpaid wages at the end of a fiscal year require an adjusting entry under accrual accounting but not under cash-basis accounting. Cash-basis accounting is not acceptable under GAAP but is used by some small companies.

accounting period or when cash is received for revenue that applies to more than one accounting period. The portion of the expense or revenue that applies to future periods is deferred as a prepaid expense (asset) or unearned revenue (liability).

The AJE required for a deferral depends on the method used for recording routine operational cash payments and receipts *that precede expense and revenue recognition.* One method, here called the **standard recording method,** records an asset upon payment of cash before goods or services are received and records a liability upon receipt of cash before goods or services are provided. For example, if two months' rent is prepaid on July 1, the standard method debits prepaid rent for that amount. An adjustment later in the year recognizes rent expense and the expiration of prepaid rent.

A second method, here called the **expedient recording method,**[13] records an expense upon payment of cash before goods or services are received and records a revenue upon receipt of cash before goods or services are provided. In the case of rent paid in advance, the expedient method debits rent expense for two months' rent. This method is expedient because many cash payments and receipts relate to expenses and revenues that apply only to the year in which the cash flow occurs. No AJE is required in this example because rent expense is correctly stated at year-end. If a portion of the expense or revenue applies to a future accounting period, however, an AJE is required.

Accruals are for cash flows that occur *after* expense and revenue recognition. These AJEs are recorded when cash is to be paid or received in a future accounting period but all or a portion of the future cash flow applies to expenses or revenues of the current period. For example, unpaid wages accrued as wages payable at year-end represent wage costs matched against current-year revenues but not to be paid until next year. If the company is a landlord and rents space to tenants, uncollected rent accrued as rent receivable at year-end represents revenue earned in the current year but to be collected next year. In both cases, the expense or revenue is recognized before the cash flow occurs.

Other AJEs   The following types of journal entries are often recorded at the end of the accounting period and are listed here as adjusting journal entries for completeness. These include:
- Reclassifications of permanent accounts.
- Estimation of expenses (bad debt expenses, for example).
- Cost allocations (depreciation, for example).
- Recognition of cost of goods sold and inventory losses.
- Correction of errors discovered at year-end.

Cash generally is not involved in AJEs because transactions affecting cash are usually accompanied by source documents. However, corrections of errors involving the cash account discovered at the end of the accounting period are recorded as AJEs. Also, the entry required to adjust the cash balance upon receipt of the end-of-year bank statement, which lists service charges and other items unknown until receipt, is recorded as an AJE.

In the following discussion, Sonora's December 31, 1995, unadjusted trial balance (Exhibit 3–4) and additional information are used to illustrate AJEs.

Deferrals

Deferred Expenses   On November 1, 1995, Sonora paid a six-month insurance premium of $600 in advance. On that date, the $600 payment is recorded as a debit to prepaid insurance and a credit to cash (the standard method). On the unadjusted trial balance, the full $600 payment is reflected in prepaid insurance. One-third of this payment ($200) is applicable to 1995. The matching principle requires recognition of a $200 expense indicating the partial expiration of the asset. Sonora records insur-

---

[13] The terms *standard* and *expedient* are the authors' and are used to facilitate the discussion.

ance expense and other similar expenses in the general and administrative expense account. AJE *a* adjusts prepaid insurance and recognizes the expense:

a. December 31, 1995:

General and administrative expense 200
    Prepaid insurance   200

The credit to prepaid insurance records the reduction in the asset that took place during the last two months of 1995 as insurance benefits were received. No source document or transaction signals this entry, although the underlying insurance document was probably consulted. The remaining $400 of prepaid insurance reflects insurance coverage for the first four months of 1996.

Deferred Revenue Sonora leased a small office in its building to a tenant on January 1, 1995. The lease required an initial payment of $1,800 for 18 months rent, which is recorded as a debit to cash and a credit to rent revenue (the expedient method). On December 31, 1995, the unadjusted trial balance reports $1,800 in rent revenue, which is overstated by the $600 (one-third) relating to 1996. AJE *b* is required to reduce the revenue recognized in 1995 from $1,800 to $1,200 and to create a liability equal to the amount of rent relating to 1996 ($600).

b. December 31, 1995:

Rent revenue 600
    Rent collected in advance (liability)   600

The result of this adjustment is a liability equal to the resources received for future services. These liabilities can be substantial. For example, Maclean Hunter Limited reported $36.6 million of unearned revenue in the liabilities section of its 1992 balance sheet. A note explained the nature of the item:

Unearned Revenue

Prepaid subscriptions for business magazines that are substantially dependent on subscription revenue, for cable television and for newspapers, are deferred and taken into income as the services are provided to the subscribers . . . Net revenue pertaining to prepaid subscriptions from consumer magazines is also deferred and taken into income over the terms of the various subscriptions.

Accruals

Accrued Expense Sonora has issued, at face value, $50,000 of 6% bonds paying interest yearly each October 31. For the current accounting period, a two-month interest obligation accrues between October 31, 1995, and December 31, 1995. Under the matching principle, Sonora recognizes the appropriate amount of interest expense against the benefits obtained by using creditors' money. The amount for the two-month period is $500 ($50,000 × .06 × 2/12). Therefore, on December 31, 1995, both the interest expense and the associated payable are recognized in AJE *c:*

c. December 31, 1995:

Interest expense 500
    Interest payable   500

Accrued Revenue Sonora's unadjusted trial balance lists $8,000 in notes receivable. The interest rate on these notes is 15% payable each November 30. As of December 31, 1995, the maker of the notes is obligated to Sonora for one month's interest of $100 ($8,000 × .15 × 1/12). AJE *d* records the resulting receivable and revenue according to the revenue recognition principle.

d. December 31, 1995:

Interest receivable 100
    Interest revenue   100

Other Adjusting Entries

Depreciation Expense Property, plant, and equipment (capital assets) is the balance sheet category used to report many productive assets with a useful life exceeding one year. The capital expenditures for these assets are matched against the revenues the assets help produce. Depreciation is a systematic and rational allocation of plant asset cost over a number of accounting periods.

The amount of depreciation expense recognized depends on a number of factors:

- The original expenditure and subsequent capitalized expenditures.
- The asset's useful life.
- The method chosen for depreciation measurement.
- The asset's residual value.

Depreciation is similar to the recognition of an expense on a deferred item such as prepaid insurance in that the cash flow occurs before the expense is recognized. The main differences are the longer life and greater uncertainty of expected benefits of capital assets.

AJE *e* illustrates depreciation recorded for Sonora at the end of 1995 under the straight-line method:

Asset	Cost	Residual Value	Useful Life Years	Proportionate Use by Function	
				Selling Function	G & A* Function
Building	$160,000	$10,000	15	46%	54%
Equipment	91,000	1,000	10	40	60

* General and administrative.

Computation:

	Total	Selling	General and Administrative
Building:			
[($160,000 − $10,000) ÷ 15 yrs.] =	$10,000	× .46 = $4,600	× .54 = $ 5,400
Equipment:			
[($91,000 − $1,000) ÷ 10 yrs.] =	9,000	× .40 = 3,600	× .60 = 5,400
Totals	$19,000	$8,200	$10,800

The adjusting entry for depreciation is as follows:[14]

e. December 31, 1995:

Selling expense (depreciation)	8,200	
General and administrative expense (depreciation)	10,800	
Accumulated depreciation, building.		10,000
Accumulated depreciation, equipment		9,000

AJE *e* reduces the net book value of the building and equipment accounts. Accumulated depreciation is a **contra account.** A contra account has a balance opposite that of the account to which it relates. Thus, accumulated depreciation is subtracted from the gross building and equipment accounts, leaving the net undepreciated account balances (net book value). Sonora's balance sheet illustrates this offset. Contra accounts ensure that major assets are reported at original cost.

Many methods of depreciation are permitted under GAAP. All entail systematic and rational allocation of capital asset cost to accounting periods. Depreciation expense recognized in an accounting period does not generally equal the portion of the asset's value used up in that period. Depreciation expense recognition is not an asset valuation process. Furthermore, the undepreciated value of plant assets does not generally equal current value.

Depreciation is significant for companies with large investments in plant assets. For example, Shaw Cablesystems Ltd. reported a $23.7 million amortization ex-

---

[14] Sonora debited two expense accounts because the company uses the building and equipment assets both for selling and for general and administrative functions. Depreciation is commonly allocated to several functions, including manufacturing operations.

pense on its 1992 income statement. This was its third largest expense category: it represented 14% of revenue and 69% of pretax income.

Section 3600 of the *CICA Handbook,* Capital Assets, was revised in 1990 and established standards for the measurement, presentation, and disclosure of capital assets by profit-oriented enterprises. The section defined capital assets as property, plant, equipment, and intangibles. In practice, property, plant, and equipment are often referred to as fixed assets or plant assets, but there are many different terms used. Throughout this textbook, capital assets are usually identified by the constituent parts.

The *CICA Handbook* section refers to the allocation of cost process as follows (paragraphs .31 and .33):

> Amortization should be recognized in a rational and systematic manner appropriate to the nature of a capital asset with a limited life . . .

> Amortization may also be termed depreciation or depletion.

Throughout this textbook, allocation of cost of capital assets with limited life is generally identified as *depreciation* for physical assets, *amortization* for intangible assets, and *depletion* for natural resources. In practice, there is considerable diversity in the terminology used.

Bad Debt Expense   Often, goods and services are sold on credit. Accounts that are never collected result in bad debt expense, which is a risk of doing business on credit terms. Most large firms use a bad debt estimate to reduce income and accounts receivable in the period of sale. This practice prevents overstatement of both income and assets and is required if bad debts are probable and estimable. Recognition of bad debt expense is accomplished with an AJE that debits bad debt expense and credits the allowance for doubtful accounts, a contra–accounts receivable account.

Estimates of uncollectible accounts may be based on credit sales for the period or the year-end accounts receivable balance. Assume that Sonora extends credit on $120,000 of sales during 1995. Prior experience indicates an expected 1% average bad debt rate on credit sales. Sonora treats bad debt expense as a component of selling expenses and records AJE *f:*

f. December 31, 1995:

Selling expense ($120,000 × .01) 1,200
    Allowance for doubtful accounts   1,200

The credit is made to the allowance account, rather than to accounts receivable, because the identities of the uncollectible accounts are not yet known. In addition, the use of the contra account maintains agreement between the balance in accounts receivable control and the total of account balances in the accounts receivable subsidiary ledger.

The $1,200 allowance is the portion of 1995 credit sales not expected to be collected. Net accounts receivable, the difference between the balance in accounts receivable and the allowance account, is an estimate of the cash ultimately expected to be received from sales on account. Bad debt expense is reported in the income statement, although often not as a separate line item.

Cost of Goods Sold   The methodology used to determine cost of goods sold (a retailer's largest expense) depends on whether a perpetual or a periodic inventory system is used. In a perpetual system, no AJE is needed to establish cost of goods sold. However, an AJE might be needed to correct errors or to recognize inventory losses due to theft and economic factors. In a periodic system, cost of goods sold is determined either by an AJE or by closing entries, both of which update the inventory account and close inventory-related accounts.

A perpetual inventory system maintains an inventory record for each item stocked. This record contains data on each purchase and issue. An up-to-date balance is maintained in the inventory account. The cost of each item purchased is debited to the inventory account. Suppose an item that sells for $300 is carried in inventory at a cost of $180. A sale of this item requires two entries:

Cash or accounts receivable.	300	
Sales revenue		300
Cost of goods sold.	180	
Inventory		180

In a perpetual inventory system, the ending balance in the inventory account equals the correct ending inventory amount, assuming no errors or inventory losses. The cost of goods sold balance is also up-to-date, reflecting the recorded cost of all items sold during the period. Thus, no AJEs are needed unless the inventory account balance disagrees with the total of individual item costs determined by the annual physical count.

In contrast, a periodic system does not maintain a current balance in inventory or cost of goods sold. Instead, the physical inventory count at the end of the period is used to determine the balances of these two accounts. The purchases account, rather than the inventory account, is debited for all purchases during the period. In this case, the unadjusted trial balance at the end of an accounting period reflects the beginning inventory, and cost of goods sold does not yet exist as an account. An AJE can be used to set purchases, purchases returns, and other purchase-related accounts to zero (i.e., close these accounts), to replace the beginning inventory amount with the ending inventory amount in the inventory account; and to recognize cost of goods sold for the period.

To illustrate, Sonora determines its ending inventory to be $90,000. The company uses a periodic system, and computes cost of goods sold and records AJE g as follows:

g. December 31, 1995:

Inventory (ending).	90,000	
Purchase returns.	2,000	
Cost of goods sold (see below)	117,000	
Inventory (beginning).		75,000
Purchases.		130,000
Freight on purchases.		4,000

Cost of Goods Sold Computation
December 31, 1995

Beginning inventory (carried over from the prior period).		$ 75,000
Add (from the current-year accounts):		
Purchases.	$130,000	
Freight on purchases.	4,000	
Purchase returns.	(2,000)	
Net purchases.		132,000
Total goods available for sale.		$207,000
Less: Ending inventory (from physical count).		90,000
Cost of goods sold.		$117,000

Two sources of information contribute to entry g: the unadjusted trial balance from which several account balances are taken, and the physical inventory count indicating $90,000 of inventory on hand. Alternatively, the accounts related to cost of goods sold may be left in the adjusted trial balance, untouched, and used in detail to create the financial statements. They would then be eliminated in closing entries. Both approaches are widely used in practice and result in the same reported income and financial position. It's really a question of which method is preferred by a particular accountant or computerized reporting package.[15]

---

[15] See footnote 18 for an illustration of the closing entries.

Income Tax Expense   The recognition of income tax expense, an accrual item, is often the final AJE. Many firms pay estimated income taxes quarterly, necessitating an AJE at the end of the accounting period to record fourth-quarter taxes due. For simplicity, assume that Sonora pays its income tax once each year after the end of the full accounting period.

A worksheet or partial adjusted trial balance (prior to income tax determination) simplifies the calculation of pretax income. The amounts in parentheses indicate the account balance in the unadjusted trial balance plus or minus the effects of AJEs, denoted by letter. For Sonora:

SONORA, LTD.

Calculation of Pretax Income
December 31, 1995

Revenues:		
Sales revenue	$325,200	
Interest revenue ($500 + $100 d)	600	
Rent revenue ($1,800 − $600 b)	1,200	$327,000
Expenses:		
Cost of goods sold (g)	117,000	
Selling expenses.	113,400	
($104,000 + $8,200 e + $1,200 f)		
General and administrative expenses	34,600	
($23,600 + $200 a + $10,800 e)		
Interest expense ($2,500 + $500 c)	3,000	
Extraordinary loss (pretax)	9,000	277,000
Total pretax income		$ 50,000

Assume that Sonora faces an average income tax rate of 40%, that depreciation expense equals tax depreciation, and that the extraordinary loss and all other expenses are fully tax deductible. AJE h recognizes the resulting $20,000 ($50,000 × .40) income tax expense:

h. December 31, 1995:

Income tax expense.	20,000	
Income tax payable		20,000

For simplicity, the entire income tax expense is recorded in one account. Sonora's income statement (Exhibit 3–6), however, separates the $3,600 income tax reduction associated with the extraordinary loss ($9,000 × .40) from income tax on income before extraordinary items. This practice is called *intraperiod tax allocation.*

Additional adjusting journal entries are illustrated throughout this text. In all cases, AJEs are posted to the appropriate ledger accounts.

|CONCEPT REVIEW

1. Assuming the standard reporting method, prepare the AJE for the following situation: full payment of a $2,400, two-year insurance policy on June 30, 1995, by a firm with a December 31 year-end.
2. Prepare the AJE for the situation in (1) assuming the expedient reporting method.
3. Why is the 1995 ending balance in prepaid insurance the same under either method?

STEP 6: PREPARE ADJUSTED TRIAL BALANCE

At this point in the cycle, the transaction journal entries and the AJEs have been journalized and posted and an **adjusted trial balance** is prepared. This trial balance lists all the account balances that will appear in the financial statements (with the exception of retained earnings, which does not reflect the current year's net income

EXHIBIT 3-5
Adjusted Trial Balance
Illustrated

SONORA, LTD.
Adjusted Trial Balance
December 31, 1995

Account	Debit	Credit
Cash	$ 67,300	
Accounts receivable	45,000	
Allowance for doubtful accounts		$ 2,200
Notes receivable	8,000	
Interest receivable	100	
Inventory	90,000	
Prepaid insurance	400	
Land	8,000	
Building	160,000	
Accumulated depreciation, building		100,000
Equipment	91,000	
Accumulated depreciation, equipment		36,000
Accounts payable		29,000
Interest payable		500
Rent collected in advance		600
Income tax payable		20,000
Bonds payable, 6%		50,000
Common shares, no par, 15,000 shares		170,000
Retained earnings		31,500
Sales revenue		325,200
Interest revenue		600
Rent revenue		1,200
Cost of goods sold	117,000	
Selling expenses	113,400	
General and administrative expenses	34,600	
Interest expense	3,000	
Income tax expense	20,000	
Extraordinary loss (pretax)	9,000	
Totals	$766,800	$766,800

or dividends). The purpose of the adjusted trial balance is to confirm debit–credit equality, taking all AJEs into consideration. Exhibit 3–5 presents the adjusted trial balance for Sonora.

The account balances in the adjusted trial balance reflect the effects of AJEs. For example, the $400 balance in prepaid insurance equals the $600 balance in the unadjusted trial balance less the reduction caused by AJE *a* for this year's coverage. New accounts not appearing in the unadjusted trial balance emerge from the adjustment process. For Sonora, several accounts are created as a result of an AJE: interest receivable, interest payable, rent collected in advance, income tax payable, cost of goods sold, and income tax expense. AJE *g* has the opposite effect: It closes purchases, freight on purchases, and purchase returns. The financial statements now can be prepared from the adjusted trial balance.

STEP 7: PREPARE FINANCIAL STATEMENTS

The financial statements are the culmination of the accounting cycle. Financial statements can be produced for a period of any duration. However, monthly, quarterly, and annual statements are the most common.

The income statement, retained earnings statement,[16] and balance sheet are prepared directly from the adjusted trial balance. The income statement is prepared first

---

[16] A retained earnings statement *and* a statement of shareholders' equity generally are included in the complete set of financial statements. However, neither is considered to be a basic financial statement. Sonora chose to report only a retained earnings statement because no changes occurred in the other equity accounts during 1995.

EXHIBIT 3–6
Income and Retained
Earnings Statements
Illustrated

SONORA, LTD.
Income Statement
For the Year Ended December 31, 1995

Revenues:		
Sales	$325,200	
Interest	600	
Rent	1,200	
Total revenues		$327,000
Expenses:		
Cost of goods sold	117,000	
Selling	113,400	
General and administrative	34,600	
Interest	3,000	
Total expenses before income tax		268,000
Income before tax and extraordinary item		59,000
Income taxes on income before extraordinary item ($59,000 × .40). . . .		23,600
Income before extraordinary item		35,400
Extraordinary loss	9,000	
Less tax savings ($9,000 × .40)	3,600	5,400
Net income		$ 30,000

SONORA, LTD.
Retained Earnings Statement
For the Year Ended December 31, 1995

Retained earnings, January 1, 1995	$ 31,500
Net income	30,000
Retained earnings, December 31, 1995	$ 61,500

EXHIBIT 3–7   Balance Sheet Illustrated

SONORA, LTD.
Balance Sheet
At December 31, 1995

Assets

Current assets:		
Cash.		$67,300
Accounts receivable . .	$45,000	
Allowance for doubtful		
accounts	(2,200)	42,800
Notes receivable . . .		8,000
Interest receivable. . .		100
Inventory.		90,000
Prepaid insurance . . .		400
Total current assets .		208,600
Capital assets:		
Land.		8,000
Building	$160,000	
Accumulated deprecia-		
tion, building	(100,000)	60,000
Equipment	91,000	
Accumulated deprecia-		
tion, equipment . . .	(36,000)	55,000
Total capital assets .		123,000
Total assets		$331,600

Liabilities

Current liabilities:	
Accounts payable	$ 29,000
Interest payable	500
Rent collected in advance	600
Income tax payable.	20,000
Total current liabilities	50,100
Long-term liabilities:	
Bonds payable, 6%	50,000
Total liabilities	100,100

Shareholders' Equity

Contributed capital:		
Common shares, nopar, 15,000 shares		
issued and outstanding	$170,000	
Retained earnings.	61,500	
Total shareholders' equity		231,500
Total liabilities and shareholders'		
equity		$331,600

because net income must be known before the retained earnings statement can be completed. The temporary account balances are transferred to the income statement, and the permanent account balances (except for retained earnings) are transferred to the balance sheet. Exhibit 3–6 illustrates Sonora's 1995 income and retained earnings statements.

Total income tax expense ($20,000) in the income statement is allocated as follows: $23,600 on income before extraordinary items less $3,600 tax *savings* on the extraordinary loss.

The retained earnings statement explains the change in retained earnings for the period. If Sonora declared dividends during 1995, they would be subtracted in the retained earnings statement.

Exhibit 3–7 illustrates the 1995 balance sheet. The ending retained earnings balance is taken from the retained earnings statement rather than from the adjusted trial balance.

STEP 8: JOURNALIZE AND POST-CLOSING ENTRIES

Closing entries:
- Reduce to zero (close) the balances of temporary accounts related to earnings measurement and dividends.
- Are recorded in the general journal at the end of the accounting period.
- Are posted to the ledger accounts.

Permanent accounts are not closed because they carry over to the next accounting period. The retained earnings account is the only permanent account involved in the closing process.

Income Statement Accounts

Because net income is measured for a specific interval of time, the balances of the income statement accounts are reduced to zero at the end of each accounting period. Otherwise, these accounts would contain information from previous periods.

Some firms use the *income summary* account to accumulate the balances of income statement accounts. The income summary is a temporary clearing account—an account used on a short-term basis for a specific purpose. The balances in expenses and losses are reduced to zero and transferred to the income summary by crediting each of those accounts and debiting income summary for the total. Revenues and gains are debited to close them, and the income summary account is credited.

This process leaves a net balance in the income summary account equal to net income (credit balance) or net loss (debit balance) for the period. The income summary account is then closed by transferring the net income amount to retained earnings.[17] Sonora makes three closing entries to transfer 1995 net income to retained earnings:

December 31, 1995:

1. To close the revenue and gain accounts to the income summary:

Sales revenue	325,200	
Interest revenue	600	
Rent revenue	1,200	
Income summary		327,000

2. To close the expense and loss accounts to the income summary:

Income summary	297,000	
Cost of goods sold		117,000
Selling expenses		113,400
General and administrative expenses		34,600
Interest expense		3,000
Extraordinary loss		9,000
Income tax expense		20,000

[17] Some accountants prefer to close temporary accounts directly to retained earnings, bypassing the income summary account entirely.

3. To close the income summary (i.e., transfer net income to retained earnings):

Income summary   30,000
    Retained earnings.   30,000

After the first two closing entries are recorded and posted, the balance in the income summary equals net income ($30,000):

Income Summary

(2)	297,000	(1)	327,000
		Balance	30,000

The temporary accounts now have zero balances and are ready for the next period's accounting cycle. The third entry closes the income summary account and transfers net income to retained earnings.[18]

Dividends

When cash dividends are declared, firms debit either retained earnings or cash dividends declared, a temporary account. Dividends payable is credited. If cash dividends declared is debited, another closing entry is required:

Retained earnings . . . .   [amount of dividends]
    Cash dividends declared . . . .   [amount of dividends]

In this case, the net result of closing entries is to transfer to retained earnings an amount equal to earnings less dividends declared for a period.

STEP 9: PREPARE POST–CLOSING TRIAL BALANCE

A post–closing trial balance lists only the balances of the permanent accounts after the closing process is finished. The temporary accounts have balances of zero. This step is taken to check for debit–credit equality after the closing entries are posted. Firms with a large number of accounts find this a valuable checking procedure because the chance of error increases with the number of accounts and postings. The retained earnings account is now stated at the correct ending balance and is the only permanent account with a balance different from the one shown in the adjusted trial balance. Exhibit 3–8 illustrates the post–closing trial balance.

STEP 10: JOURNALIZE AND POST REVERSING JOURNAL ENTRIES

Depending on the firm's accounting system and its accounting policies, **reversing journal entries (RJEs)** may be used to simplify certain journal entries in the next accounting period. RJEs are *optional* entries that:
- Are dated the first day of the next accounting period.
- Use the same accounts and amounts as an AJE but with the debits and credits reversed.
- Are posted to the ledger.

---

[18] Inventory-related accounts can be adjusted and closed in the closing process as an alternative to the AJE approach illustrated previously in AJE *g*. If the closing alternative is used, the following three closing entries replace AJE *g* and the three closing entries illustrated above:

(1) Income summary	389,000		(2) Inventory (end)	90,000	
Inventory.		75,000	Sales revenue	325,200	
Purchases.		130,000	Interest revenue	600	
Freight on purchases. .		4,000	Rent revenue	1,200	
Selling expenses		113,400	Purchase returns.	2,000	
G & A expenses. . . .		34,600	Income summary . . .		419,000
Interest expense		3,000	(3) Income summary	30,000	
Extraordinary loss . . .		9,000	Retained earnings . . .		30,000
Income tax expense . .		20,000			

Using this approach, inventory-related accounts are included with expenses and revenues for closing entry purposes. The net impact on the income summary account and, in turn, income and retained earnings are identical under both approaches. However, this approach does not isolate cost of goods sold in a separate account.

EXHIBIT 3–8
Post–Closing Trial
Balance Illustrated

SONORA, LTD.
Post–Closing Trial Balance
December 31, 1995

Account	Debit	Credit
Cash.	$ 67,300	
Accounts receivable.	45,000	
Allowance for doubtful accounts		$ 2,200
Notes receivable	8,000	
Interest receivable	100	
Inventory	90,000	
Prepaid insurance.	400	
Land	8,000	
Building	160,000	
Accumulated depreciation, building		100,000
Equipment	91,000	
Accumulated depreciation, equipment.		36,000
Accounts payable.		29,000
Interest payable.		500
Rent collected in advance		600
Income tax payable.		20,000
Bonds payable, 6%		50,000
Common shares, nopar, 15,000 shares.		170,000
Retained earnings.		61,500
Totals	$469,800	$469,800

RJEs are appropriate only for AJEs that (1) defer the recognition of revenue or expense items recorded under the expedient method or (2) accrue revenue or expense items during the current period (for example, wages expense). Thus, if a deferral or accrual AJE creates or increases an asset or liability, an RJE is appropriate.

RJEs are inappropriate for AJEs that adjust assets and liabilities recorded for cash flows preceding the recognition of revenues and expenses (the standard method) and for some other AJEs, such as reclassifications, error corrections, and estimations.

In the following examples, assume a December 31 year-end.

Deferred Item—Expedient Method

Assume that on November 1, 1995, $300 is paid in advance for three months' rent: November 1, 1995—originating entry:

Rent expense	300	
Cash		300

December 31, 1995—adjusting entry:

Prepaid rent.	100	
Rent expense		100

	With Reversing Entry	Without Reversing Entry
January 1, 1996 Reversing entry:	Rent expense . . . . 100 Prepaid rent. . . 100	
1996 Subsequent entry:	(No entry needed)	Rent expense . . . . 100 Prepaid rent. . . 100

With or without an RJE, rent expense recorded in 1996 is $100. Use of the RJE, however, saves the cost and effort of reviewing the relevant accounts and source documents to determine the subsequent year's entry. The RJE makes the necessary adjustments to the accounts while the information used in making the AJE is available. The RJE is posted in 1996, the year it is recorded.

Now consider the standard method applied to the same example.

November 1, 1995—originating entry:

Prepaid rent	300	
Cash		300

December 31, 1995—adjusting entry:

Rent expense	200	
Prepaid rent		200

An RJE is not appropriate when the standard method is used for deferrals because a subsequent entry is required whether or not the AJE is reversed. No purpose is served by reinstating (debiting) prepaid rent $200 because that amount has expired.

Accrued Item

Assume that the last payroll for 1995 is December 28. Wages earned through December 28 are included in this payroll. The next payroll period ends January 4, 1996, at which time $2,800 of wages will be paid. Wages earned for the three-day period ending December 31, 1995, are $1,500, which will be paid in 1996. The following AJE is necessary to accrue these wages:

December 31, 1995—adjusting entry:

Wages expense	1,500	
Wages payable		1,500

	With Reversing Entry		Without Reversing Entry	
January 1, 1996 Reversing entry:	Wages payable 1,500			
	Wages expense	1,500		
January 4, 1996 Subsequent entry:	Wages expense 2,800		Wages expense 1,300	
	Cash	2,800	Wages payable 1,500	
			Cash	2,800

In this example, the RJE simplifies the subsequent payroll entry, which can now be recorded in a manner identical to all other payrolls. With or without reversing entries, total 1996 wage expense recognized through January 4, 1996, is $1,300. RJEs often create abnormal short-term account balances. In the above example, the January 1, 1996, RJE creates a *credit* balance in wages expense. The subsequent entry changes the net balance of wages expense to a $1,300 debit.

Some of Sonora's AJEs could be reversed:

b. Rent expense (expedient method—deferred item).

c. Interest expense (accrual).

d. Interest revenue (accrual).

h. Income tax expense (accrual).

BEYOND THE PRIMARY FINANCIAL STATEMENTS

Annual reports typically include a letter from the company president and descriptive information about the company, its products, and its key executives. Disclosure notes supplement the financial statements, providing information that is not normally recorded in accounts but can materially affect decisions. Further, a section entitled "Management Discussion and Analysis" (MD&A) is required by the Ontario, Quebec, and Saskatchewan Securities Commission.[19] This section provides managements' analysis of the firm's financial condition and results of operations.

---

[19] Firms whose shares or debt trade on public stock exchanges in these provinces must comply with the requirements of the relevant exchange commission. Annual reporting requirements are onerous.

CONCEPT REVIEW

1. Why are temporary accounts closed, but not permanent accounts?
2. Why is an AJE reversed?

SUMMARY OF KEY POINTS

(L.O. 1)	1. The AIS provides information for daily management information needs and for preparation of financial statements.
(L.O. 2)	2. There are seven basic types of accounts. The balance sheet discloses the balances of the permanent accounts, which include assets, liabilities, and owners' equity accounts. The income statement discloses the pre-closing balances of the temporary accounts, which include revenues, gains, expenses, and losses. Debits to assets, expenses, and losses increase those accounts. Credits to liabilities, owners' equity, revenues, and gains increase those accounts.
(L.O. 3, 4)	3. There are 10 steps in the accounting cycle, which culminates in the financial statements.
(L.O. 3)	4. The application of accounting principles generally occurs at the journal entry step. Journal entries are the foundation for the financial statements.
(L.O. 5)	5. Companies may use the standard or the expedient method or both to record routine operating cash receipts and payments that precede revenue and expense recognition. The choice of methods affects some AJEs and the use of RJEs.
(L.O. 4, 5)	6. AJEs are required under accrual accounting to complete the measurement and recording of changes in resources and obligations.
(L.O. 5)	7. RJEs are optional entries, dated at the beginning of the accounting period, that reverse certain AJEs from the previous period and are used to facilitate subsequent journal entries.

REVIEW PROBLEM   **Accounting Cycle Steps**   Bucknell Company developed its unadjusted trial balance dated December 31, 1995, which appears below. Bucknell uses the expedient recording method whenever possible, adjusts its accounts once per year, records all appropriate RJEs, and adjusts its periodic inventory-related accounts in an AJE. Ignore income taxes.

BUCKNELL COMPANY
Unadjusted Trial Balance
December 31, 1995

	Debit	Credit
Cash	$ 40,000	
Accounts receivable	60,000	
Allowance for doubtful accounts		$ 6,000
Inventory	90,000	
Equipment	780,000	
Accumulated depreciation		100,000
Land	150,000	
Accounts payable		22,000
Notes payable, 8%, due April 1, 2000		200,000
Common shares, nopar, 60,000 shares		400,000
Retained earnings		50,000
Sales revenue (all on account)		900,000
Subscription revenue		24,000
Purchases	250,000	
Rent expense	60,000	
Interest expense	12,000	
Selling expense	40,000	
Insurance expense	30,000	
Wage expense	110,000	
General and administrative expense	80,000	
Totals	$1,702,000	$1,702,000

Additional Information

a. Ending inventory by physical count is $70,000.

b. The equipment has a total estimated useful life of 14 years and an estimated residual value of $80,000. Bucknell uses straight-line depreciation and treats depreciation expense as a general and administrative expense.

c. Bad debt expense for 1995 is estimated to be 1 percent of sales.

d. The note payable requires interest to be paid semiannually, every October 1 and April 1.

e. $5,000 of wages were earned in December but not recorded.

f. The rent expense represents a payment made on January 2, 1995, for two years' rent (1995 and 1996).

g. The insurance expense represents payment made for a one-year policy, paid June 30, 1995. Coverage began on that date.

h. The subscription revenue represents cash received from many university libraries for a one and one-half year subscription to a journal published by Bucknell. The subscription period began July 1, 1995.

Required

1. Record the required AJEs.
2. Prepare the adjusted trial balance.
3. Prepare the income statement and balance sheet for 1995.
4. Prepare closing entries.
5. Prepare RJEs.

|SOLUTION

1. Adjusting journal entries, dated December 31, 1995:

a. Inventory (ending)	70,000	
Cost of goods sold	270,000	
Purchases		250,000
Inventory (beginning)		90,000
b. General and administrative expense ($780,000 − $80,000)/14	50,000	
Accumulated depreciation		50,000
c. Bad debt expense (.01 × $900,000)	9,000	
Allowance for doubtful accounts		9,000
d. Interest expense ($200,000 × .08 × ¼)	4,000	
Interest payable		4,000
e. Wage expense	5,000	
Wages payable		5,000
f. Prepaid rent ($60,000 × ½)	30,000	
Rent expense		30,000
g. Prepaid insurance ($30,000 × ½)	15,000	
Insurance expense		15,000
h. Subscription revenue ($24,000 × ⅔)	16,000	
Unearned subscriptions		16,000

2. Adjusted trial balance:

BUCKNELL COMPANY
Adjusted Trial Balance
December 31, 1995

	Debit	Credit
Cash	$ 40,000	
Accounts receivable	60,000	
Allowance for doubtful accounts		$ 15,000
Prepaid rent	30,000	
Prepaid insurance	15,000	
Inventory	70,000	
Equipment	780,000	
Accumulated depreciation		150,000
Land	150,000	
Accounts payable		22,000
Interest payable		4,000
Wages payable		5,000
Unearned subscriptions		16,000
Notes payable, 8%, due April 1, 2000		200,000
Common shares, nopar, 60,000 shares		400,000
Retained earnings		50,000
Sales revenue		900,000
Subscription revenue		8,000
Cost of goods sold	270,000	
Rent expense	30,000	
Interest expense	16,000	
Selling expense	40,000	
Insurance expense	15,000	
Wage expense	115,000	
Bad debt expense	9,000	
General and administrative expense	130,000	
Totals	$1,770,000	$1,770,000

3. Income statement and balance sheet for 1995:

BUCKNELL COMPANY
Income Statement
For the Year Ended December 31, 1995

Revenues:		
Sales	$900,000	
Subscription revenue	8,000	
Total revenue		$908,000
Expenses:		
Cost of goods sold	270,000	
Rent expense	30,000	
Interest expense	16,000	
Selling expense	40,000	
Insurance expense	15,000	
Wage expense	115,000	
Bad debt expense	9,000	
General and administrative expense	130,000	
Total expenses		625,000
Net income		$283,000

BUCKNELL COMPANY
Balance Sheet
December 31, 1995

Assets

Cash		$ 40,000
Accounts receivable	$ 60,000	
Allowance for doubtful accounts	(15,000)	45,000
Prepaid rent.		30,000
Prepaid insurance		15,000
Inventory		70,000
Equipment	780,000	
Accumulated depreciation	(150,000)	630,000
Land		150,000
Total assets		$980,000

Liabilities

Accounts payable		$ 22,000
Interest payable		4,000
Wages payable		5,000
Unearned subscriptions		16,000
Notes payable, 8%, due April 1, 2000 . . .		200,000
Total liabilities		$247,000

Owners' Equity

Common shares, nopar, 60,000 shares		
outstanding		400,000
Retained earnings		333,000*
Total owners' equity		733,000
Total liabilities and owners' equity		$980,000

* $50,000 + $283,000.

4. Closing entries:

Sales revenue	900,000	
Subscription revenue	8,000	
Income summary		908,000
Income summary	625,000	
Cost of goods sold.		270,000
Rent expense		30,000
Interest expense.		16,000
Selling expense		40,000
Insurance expense.		15,000
Wage expense		115,000
Bad debt expense		9,000
General and administrative expense		130,000
Income summary	283,000	
Retained earnings		283,000

5. Reversing journal entries:

Interest payable	4,000	
Interest expense		4,000
Wages payable	5,000	
Wages expense		5,000
Rent expense	30,000	
Prepaid rent		30,000
Insurance expense	15,000	
Prepaid insurance		15,000
Unearned subscriptions	16,000	
Subscription revenue		16,000

APPENDIX 3A   Worksheets

A **worksheet** is a multicolumn work space that provides an organized format for performing several end-of-period accounting cycle steps and for preparing financial statements before posting AJEs. It also provides evidence, or an audit trail, of an organized and structured accounting process that can be more easily reviewed than other methods of analysis.

In manual accounting systems, worksheet input is developed by transferring account name and balance information manually from the general ledger to the worksheet. With most computerized systems, this task is accomplished automatically. Computer **spreadsheet** and accounting software programs can be used to generate worksheets quickly and with relative ease. Computer spreadsheets also offer important labour and time savings in the planning and mechanical plotting of AJEs on the worksheet. This software is a powerful tool for accomplishing several steps in the accounting cycle.

Use of a worksheet is optional. The worksheet is not part of the basic accounting records. Worksheets assist with only a portion of the accounting cycle. Formal AJEs are recorded in addition to those entered on the worksheet. Exhibit 3A–1 compares the accounting cycle with and without a worksheet.

Illustration of the Worksheet Approach

Exhibit 3A–2 illustrates the completed worksheet for Sonora, Ltd., the company used in the chapter to present the accounting cycle. The worksheet has a debit and a credit column for each of the following: the unadjusted trial balance, the AJEs, the adjusted trial balance, the income statement, the retained earnings statement, and the balance sheet. The worksheet is prepared in four steps:

Step 1: Enter the unadjusted trial balance in the first set of columns of the worksheet by inserting the year-end balances of all ledger accounts. The inventory and retained earnings balances are the beginning-of-year balances because no transactions have affected these accounts. Confirm the debit–credit equality of the totals.

Step 2: Enter the adjusting entries, including income tax. The lowercase letters refer to the same AJEs discussed in the chapter for Sonora, Ltd.

The worksheet AJEs are facilitating entries only and are not formally recorded in the general journal at this point. If a new account is created by an AJE, it is inserted in its normal position. Interest receivable (entry *d*) is one such example. Confirm the debit–credit equality of the totals.

Determine income tax expense and payable. (Sonora's tax computation was illustrated earlier.) Enter the accounts and the amounts in the AJE columns. Income tax expense (entry *h*) is positioned below the totals of the AJE columns.

Step 3: Enter the adjusted trial balance by adding or subtracting across the unadjusted trial balance sheet columns and AJE columns, for each account. For example, the adjusted balance of the allowance for doubtful accounts is the sum of its unadjusted balance ($1,000) and the $1,200 increase from AJE (*f*).

The inventory account now displays ending inventory, purchases and related accounts no longer have balances, and cost of goods sold is present. Confirm the debit–credit equality of the totals.

Step 4: Extend the adjusted trial balance amounts to the financial statements; complete the worksheet.

Each account in the adjusted trial balance is extended to *one* of the three sets of remaining debit–credit columns. Temporary accounts are sorted to the income statement columns (revenues to the credit column, expenses to the debit column). Permanent accounts are sorted to the balance sheet columns except for the beginning balance in retained earnings, which is extended to the retained earnings columns.

Total the income statement columns before income tax expense. Pretax income is the difference between the debit and credit column totals. A net credit represents income; a net debit represents a loss. For Sonora, pretax income is $50,000 ($327,000 − $277,000). Next, determine net income after taxes by extending the income tax expense amount ($20,000) into the debit column and again totalling the columns. Net income is the difference between the columns, equaling $30,000 for Sonora ($327,000 − $297,000).

EXHIBIT 3A–1
Accounting Cycle Steps

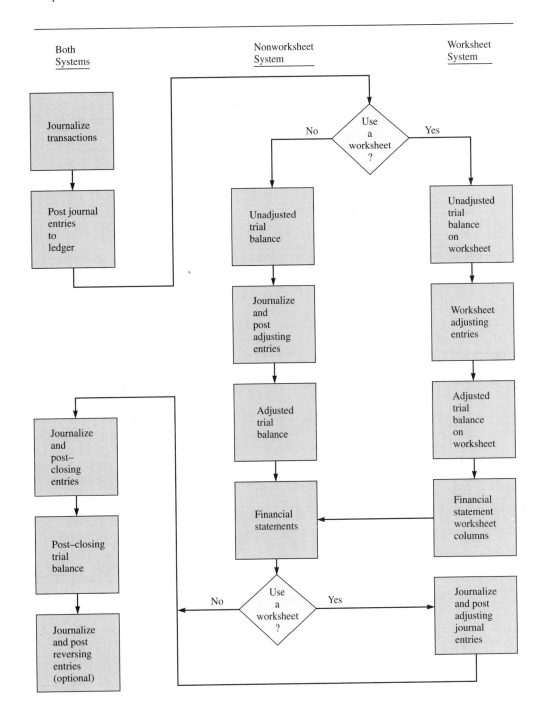

Next, add a line description (net income to retained earnings) and enter the $30,000 net income amount as a balancing value in the income statement columns: positive net income is a debit balancing value; negative income is a credit. Then complete this entry by recording $30,000 in the credit column under the retained earnings columns. (Positive net income is a credit entry, and negative income is a debit entry.)

Total the retained earnings columns and enter a balancing amount (the ending retained earnings balance) in the appropriate column to achieve debit–credit equality. For Sonora, the balancing amount is a $61,500 debit. Add a line description (retained earnings to balance sheet) and enter the balancing amount into the appropriate balance sheet column.

Total the balance sheet columns and confirm debit–credit equality.

EXHIBIT 3A–2 Completed Worksheet for Sonora, Ltd.

SONORA, LTD.
Worksheet for Year Ended December 31, 1995

	Unadjusted Trial Balance		Adjusting Entries		Adjusted Trial Balance		Income Statement		Retained Earnings Statement		Balance Sheet	
	Debit	Credit	Debit	Credit	Debit	Credit	Debit	Credit	Debit	Credit	Debit	Credit
Cash	67,300				67,300						67,300	
Notes receivable	8,000				8,000						8,000	
Accounts receivable	45,000				45,000						45,000	
Allowance for doubtful accounts		1,000		(f) 1,200		2,200						2,200
Interest receivable			(d) 100		100						100	
Inventory (periodic)	75,000		(g) 90,000	(g) 75,000	90,000						90,000	
Prepaid insurance	600			(a) 200	400						400	
Land	8,000				8,000						8,000	
Building	160,000				160,000						160,000	
Accumulated depreciation, building		90,000		(e) 10,000		100,000						100,000
Equipment	91,000				91,000						91,000	
Accumulated depreciation, equipment		27,000		(e) 9,000		36,000						36,000
Accounts payable		29,000				29,000						29,000
Interest payable				(c) 500		500						500
Rent revenue collected in advance				(b) 600		600						600
Bonds payable, 6%		50,000				50,000						50,000
Common shares, nopar, 15,000 shares		170,000				170,000						170,000
Retained earnings		31,500				31,500				31,500		
Sales revenue		325,200				325,200		325,200				
Interest revenue		500		(d) 100		600		600				
Rent revenue		1,800	(b) 600			1,200		1,200				
Purchases	130,000			(g) 130,000								
Freight on purchases	4,000			(g) 4,000								
Purchase returns		2,000	(g) 2,000									
Cost of goods sold			(g) 117,000		117,000		117,000					
Selling expenses	104,000		(e) 8,200		113,400		113,400					
			(f) 1,200									
General and administrative expenses	23,600		(a) 200		34,600		34,600					
			(e) 10,800									
Interest expense	2,500		(c) 500		3,000		3,000					
Extraordinary loss	9,000				9,000		9,000					
	728,000	728,000	230,600	230,600	746,800	746,800	277,000	327,000				
Income tax expense			(h) 20,000		20,000		20,000					
Income tax payable				(h) 20,000		20,000	297,000	327,000				20,000
					766,800	766,800						
Net income to retained earnings							30,000			30,000		
Retained earnings to balance sheet									61,500			61,500
Totals							327,000	327,000	61,500	61,500	469,800	469,800

List the general ledger accounts, leaving space for accounts that will be created by AJEs.

The account balances listed reflect all transactions during the period. Inventory (periodic system) and retained earnings show beginning balances.

Add accounts as needed to complete the AJEs.

Pretax income and income tax expense (h) are computed before the AJE for income tax is entered.

Worksheet AJEs are entered before they are formally journalized.

Each balance in the adjusted trial balance is obtained by adding across the unadjusted trial balance and AJE columns.

Cost of goods sold appears, inventory reflects the ending balance, and purchase-related accounts disappear.

Each account balance in the adjusted trial balance is extended to one financial statement column.

Net income is a balancing amount in the income statement columns and is extended to the retained earnings statement columns.

Ending retained earnings is a balancing amount in the retained earnings statement columns and is extended to the balance sheet columns.

The worksheet is now complete, and the financial statements are prepared directly from the last three sets of worksheet columns. The formal AJEs are then journalized and posted.

APPENDIX 3B   *Subsidiary Ledgers and Special Journals*

An accounting system often includes control accounts, subsidiary ledgers, and special journals. This appendix discusses these features.

Subsidiary Ledgers

The text discussed the use of control and subsidiary ledger accounts. The sum of all account balances in a subsidiary ledger must equal the related control account balance in the general ledger. To ensure that this equality exists, frequent reconciliations are made. All posting must be complete, both to the control account and to the subsidiary ledger, before a reconciliation can be accomplished. To illustrate such a reconciliation, refer ahead to the accounts receivable subsidiary ledger in Exhibit 3B–5. A reconciliation for accounts receivable control and the accounts receivable subsidiary ledger based on the information in Exhibit 3B–5 follows:

Reconciliation of
Accounts Receivable Subsidiary Ledger
at January 31, 1995

	Amount
Subsidiary ledger balances:	
112.13 Adams Co.	$ 980
112.42 Miller, J. B.	196
112.91 XY Manufacturing Co.	1,960
Total	$3,136
General ledger balance:	
Accounts receivable control	
($5,000 + $9,360 − $11,224)	$3,136

Special Journals

Both general and special journals are used in many accounting systems. Even when extensive use is made of special journals, a need exists for a general journal to record the adjusting, closing, reversing, and correcting entries and those transactions that do not apply to any of the special journals. A general journal was illustrated in Exhibit 3–2.

A special journal is designed to expedite the recording of similar transactions that occur frequently. Each special journal is constructed specifically to simplify the data processing tasks involved in journalizing and posting those types of transactions. Special journals can be custom-designed to meet the particular needs of the business. Commonly used special journals include:

1. Sales journal for recording sales of merchandise on credit only.
2. Purchases journal for recording purchases of merchandise on credit only.
3. Cash receipts journal for recording cash receipts only, including cash sales.
4. Cash payments journal for recording cash payments only, including cash purchases.
5. Voucher system, designed to replace the purchases journal and cash payments journal, composed of:
    a. A voucher register for recording vouchers payable only. A voucher payable is prepared for each cash payment regardless of purpose.
    b. A cheque register for recording all cheques written in payment of approved vouchers.

The special journals illustrated in this appendix carry page numbers preceded by letters indicating the journal name. The *S* in the page number of Exhibit 3B–1 denotes the sales journal, for example.

Sales Journal This special journal is designed to record sales on account, which otherwise would be recorded as follows in a general journal:
January 2, 1995:

Accounts receivable ($1,000 × .98) 980
   Sales revenue   980
Credit sale to Adams Company; invoice price, $1,000; terms 2/10, n/30.

Terms 2/10, n/30 mean that if the account is paid within 10 days after date of sale, a 2% cash discount is granted. The cash discount encourages early payment. If the bill is not paid within the 10-day discount period, the full amount is past due at the end of 30 days. Receipt of $1,000 after the 10-day discount period does not increase sales revenue but means that the seller has earned finance revenue of $20 ($1000 − $980). Hence, it is correct to record sales revenue of $980. Chapter 8 discusses the net (record at $980) and gross (record at $1,000) methods in detail.

Exhibit 3B–1 illustrates a typical sales journal for credit sales for a business with two sales departments. The above entry is shown as the first entry in 1995. The amount of sale is recorded only once. Each entry in the sales journal records the same information found in the traditional debit–credit format.

The posting of amounts from the sales journal to the general and subsidiary ledgers is also simplified. The two phases in posting a sales journal are the following:

1. **Daily posting:** The amount of each credit sale is posted daily to the appropriate individual account in the accounts receivable subsidiary ledger. Posting is indicated by entering the account number in the posting reference column. For example, the number 112.13 entered in the posting reference column in Exhibit 3B–1 is the account number assigned to Adams Company and shows that $980 is posted as a debit to Adams Company in the subsidiary ledger. The number 112 is the general number used for accounts receivable (see Exhibit 3B–5).
2. **Monthly posting:** At the end of each month, the receivable and sale amount column is totalled. This total is posted to two accounts in the general ledger. In Exhibit 3B–1, the $9,360 total is posted as a debit to account no. 112 (accounts receivable control) and as a credit to account no. 500 (sales revenue control). The T accounts shown in Exhibit 3B–5 illustrate how these postings are reflected in both the general ledger and the subsidiary ledger. The two ledgers show the journal page from which each amount is posted.

Purchases Journal This special journal is designed to accommodate frequent purchases of merchandise on account, which otherwise would be recorded under the net method in a general journal.[20]
January 3, 1995:

Purchases ($1,000 × .99) 990
   Accounts payable (PT Mfg. Co.).   990
(terms 1/20, n/30)

This entry is recorded as the first 1995 entry in the purchases journal illustrated in Exhibit 3B–2. The accounting simplifications found in the sales journal are present in the purchases journal as well. Each amount is posted daily as a credit to the account of an individual creditor in the accounts payable subsidiary ledger. At the end of the month, the total of the purchases and payable amount column ($6,760 in Exhibit 3B–2), is posted to the general ledger as a debit to the purchases account (no. 612) and as a credit to the accounts payable control account (no. 210).

Cash Receipts Journal A special cash receipts journal is used to accommodate a large volume of cash receipts transactions. Several different sources of cash are accommodated by including a cash debit column, several credit columns for recurring credits, and a miscellaneous accounts column for infrequent credits—all as shown in Exhibit 3B–3. Space is also provided for the names of particular accounts receivable.

---

[20] The entry assumes a periodic inventory procedure. Under a perpetual inventory system, the debit would be to the inventory account.

EXHIBIT 3B-1   Sales Journal

		SALES JOURNAL					Page S-23
Date 1995	**Sales Invoice No.**	**Accounts Receivable (name)**	**Terms**	**Post. Ref.**	**Receivable and Sale Amount**	**Dept. Sales** Dept. A	Dept. B
Jan. 2	93	Adams Co.	2/10, n/30	112.13	980		
3	94	Sayre Corp.	2/10, n/30	112.80	490		
11	95	Cope & Day Co.	net	112.27	5,734		
27	96	XY Mfg. Co.	2/10, n/30	112.91	1,960	(Not illustrated: the total of each column would also be posted to a sale subsidiary ledger.)	
30	97	Miller, J. B.	2/10, n/30	112.42	196		
31	—	Totals			9,360		
31	—	Posting			(112/500)		

EXHIBIT 3B-2
Purchases Journal

		PURCHASES JOURNAL			Page P-19
Date 1995	**Purchase Order No.**	**Accounts Payable (name)**	**Terms**	**Posting Ref.**	**Purchases and Payable Amount**
Jan. 3	41	PT Mfg. Co.	1/20, n/30	210.61	990
7	42	Able Suppliers, Ltd.	net	210.12	150
31	—	Totals	—	—	6,760
31	—	Posting	—	—	(612/210)

EXHIBIT 3B-3   Cash Receipts Journal

			CASH RECEIPTS JOURNAL				Page CR-19
				Credits			
Date 1995	**Explanation**	**Debit Cash**	**Account Title**	**Post. Ref.**	**Accounts Receivable**	**Sales Revenue**	**Misc. Accounts**
Jan. 4	Cash sales	11,200		—		11,200	
7	On acct.	4,490	Sayre Corp.	112.80	4,490		
8	Sale of land	10,000	Land	123			4,000
			Gain on sale of land	510			6,000
10	On acct.	1,000	Adams Co.	112.13	1,000		
19	Cash sales	43,600		—		43,600	
20	On acct.	5,734	Cope & Day Co.	112.27	5,734		
31	Totals	116,224		—	11,224	71,000	34,000
31	Posting	(101)		—	(112)	(500)	(NP)*

* NP—not posted as one total because the individual amounts are posted as indicated in the posting reference column.

EXHIBIT 3B–4 Cash Payments Journal

					Debits			
CASH PAYMENTS JOURNAL								**Page CP-31**
Date 1995	**Cheque No.**	**Explanation**	**Credits Cash**	**Account Name**	**Post. Ref.**	**Accounts Payable**	**Purchases**	**Misc. Accounts**
Jan. 2	141	Pur. mdse.	3,000				3,000	
10	142	On acct.	990	PT Mfg. Co.	210.61	990		
15	143	Jan. rent	660	Rent exp.	1300			660
16	144	Pur. mdse.	1,810				1,810	
31	—	Totals	98,400		—	5,820	90,980	1,600
31	—	Posting	(101)		—	(210)	(612)	(NP)

EXHIBIT 3B–5

General Ledger and
Subsidiary Ledger

```
                    General Ledger (partial)
                           Cash                        No. 101

        1995                        1995
        Jan.  1   balance   18,700   Jan. 31   CP-31   98,400
              31   CR-19    116,224

                  Accounts Receivable Control         No. 112

        1995                        1995
        Jan.  1   balance    5,000   Jan. 31   CR-19   11,224
              31   S-23       9,360

                    Sales Revenue Control             No. 500

                                    1995
                                    Jan. 31   S-23     9,360
                                          31   CR-19   71,000
```

(continued on next page)

During the month, each amount in the accounts receivable column is posted daily as a credit to an individual customer account in the accounts receivable subsidiary ledger. At the end of the month, the individual amounts in the miscellaneous account column are posted as credits to the appropriate general ledger accounts, and the totals for the cash, accounts receivable, and sales revenue columns are posted to the general ledger as indicated by the posting reference. The total of the miscellaneous accounts column is not posted because it consists of changes in different accounts. However, this column is totalled to ascertain overall debit–credit equality.

Cash Payments Journal   Many companies use some form of a cash payments journal if there are many cash disbursements. This special journal has a column for cash credits, a number of columns for recurring debits, and a miscellaneous account debit

EXHIBIT 3B-5
General Ledger and
Subsidiary Ledger
(*concluded*)

SUBSIDIARY LEDGER FOR ACCOUNTS RECEIVABLE (Accts. No. 112)					
Adams Company—Acct. No. 112.13					
Date	Post. Ref.	Explanation	Debit	Credit	Balance
1995 Jan. 1		balance			1,000
2	S-23		980		1,980
10	CR-19			1,000	980

Cope & Day Company—Acct. No. 112.27					
Jan. 11	S-23		5,734		5,734
20	CR-19			5,734	0

Miller, J. B.—Acct. No. 112.42					
Jan. 30	S-23		196		196

Sayre Corporation—Acct. No. 112.80					
Jan. 1		balance			4,000
3	S-23		490		4,490
7	CR-19			4,490	0

XY Manufacturing Company—Acct. No. 112.91					
Jan. 27	S-23		1,960		1,960

column. Exhibit 3B–4 illustrates a typical cash payments journal. Journalizing and posting follow the same procedures explained for the cash receipts journal.

Voucher Systems

Voucher systems are designed to enhance internal control over cash disbursements. A voucher is a document that describes a liability and lists information about the creditor, a description of the good or service received, authorizing signatures, and other details of the transaction, including invoice number, terms, amount due, and due date. In a voucher system, every transaction requiring payment by cheque begins with an invoice or other document that supplies information for completing a voucher.

Together, the voucher, purchase order, receiving report, and invoice form a packet of information that must be complete before a cash disbursement can be made. All authorizations must be indicated. Verification of amounts and calculations are part of the payment authorization process. Often, several departments, including the internal audit and accounting departments, are required to authorize a large cash payment.

The completed voucher is the basis for an accounting entry in a special journal called the *voucher register*. The voucher register is not restricted to purchases. Before payment is made, the authorized voucher is recorded in the voucher register. Exhibit 3B–6 illustrates an abbreviated page from a voucher register.

A new account, vouchers payable, is used to record all routine liabilities. This new account replaces accounts payable and other payables used for routine payments. When

EXHIBIT 3B–6
Voucher Register

VOUCHER REGISTER						Page VR-1
Voucher			Date	Cheque	Voucher Payable	Account
Date	Number	Payee	Paid	No.	Credit	Debited
Jan. 1, 1995	1	Crowell Co.	Jan. 2, 1995	141	$3,000	Purchases
Jan. 3, 1995	2	PT Mfg. Co.	Jan. 10, 1995	142	990	Purchases
Jan. 9, 1995	3	Williams Co.	Jan. 15, 1995	143	660	Rent Expense

EXHIBIT 3B–7
Cheque Register

CHEQUE REGISTER				Page CR-1
Date	Payee	Voucher Number	Cheque Number	Vouchers Payable Dr. and Cash Cr.
Jan. 2, 1995	Crowell Co.	1	141	$3,000
Jan. 10, 1995	PT Mfg. Co.	2	142	990
Jan. 15, 1995	Williams Co.	3	143	660

a voucher is recorded, the voucher payable credit column, it reflects the amount of the liability. The account debited reflects the good or service received. Unlike the voucher register shown in Exhibit 3B–6, most voucher registers have several debit columns for speedy recording of repetitive cash payments of the same type. The total of the vouchers payable column is posted to the vouchers payable control. The cheque number and date paid do not appear in the voucher register until a cheque is issued and payment is made to the payee. Although a voucher is prepared for each item, one cheque can be issued for the payment of several vouchers to the same creditor.

Unpaid vouchers are placed into a file pending payment and are typically filed by due date. It is important that payments be initiated within cash discount periods to obtain the lowest possible price for merchandise purchases. The unpaid voucher file is the subsidiary ledger in a voucher system.

When a voucher becomes due, it is sent by the accounting department to a person authorized to issue cheques. After a review of the authorization on the voucher is made, a cheque is prepared for the correct amount. The paid voucher is sent back to the accounting department, which enters the cheque number and payment into the voucher register. Information from the voucher is also entered in the cheque register illustrated in Exhibit 3B–7.

The total of the amount column in the cheque register is posted to the vouchers payable control account (dr.) and to the cash account (cr.). The paid voucher is retained to substantiate cash payments and for audit trail purposes. The voucher register and cheque register replace the purchases and cash payments journals.

The design and use of subsidiary ledgers, control accounts, and special journals depend on the characteristics of the business. They do not involve new accounting principles because they are only data processing tools. Their use simplifies journalizing, posting, and the subdivision of work.

QUESTIONS

1. How are the income statement and balance sheet related?
2. Explain the benefits of the double-entry system. What additional benefits does the debit–credit convention provide?
3. For each transaction entry listed below, enter the name of the relevant account affected in the appropriate column.

	Debit	**Credit**
Credit sale	_____	_____
Collection on account	_____	_____
Pay rent in advance (standard method)	_____	_____
Purchase equipment for cash	_____	_____
Declare dividends	_____	_____
Issue common shares	_____	_____
Accrue interest expense	_____	_____

4. Indicate with an X in the appropriate column whether each listed account is a temporary or permanent account.

Temporary	**Permanent**	
_____	_____	Sales revenue
_____	_____	Cash
_____	_____	Cost of goods sold
_____	_____	Prepaid rent
_____	_____	Accumulated depreciation
_____	_____	Cash dividends declared
_____	_____	Retained earnings
_____	_____	Income summary
_____	_____	Cumulative effect, accounting change
_____	_____	Unearned service fees
_____	_____	Accounts payable
_____	_____	Purchases
_____	_____	Extraordinary loss

5. Number the following steps in the accounting information processing cycle to indicate their normal sequence of completion:

_____ Journalize and post reversing entries.
_____ Posting.
_____ Identify transaction to be recorded.
_____ Journalize and post adjusting entries.
_____ Journalize and post closing entries.
_____ Prepare financial statements.
_____ Journalize current transactions.
_____ Prepare post–closing trial balance.
_____ Prepare adjusted trial balance.
_____ Prepare unadjusted trial balance.

6. Why do some companies often record an expense or revenue upon routine payment or receipt of cash, prior to the expiration of cost or the earning of revenue (the expedient method)?
7. Give two examples each for (a) a recording error that would not cause the trial balance to be out-of-balance and (b) an error that would.
8. Some adjusting entries give rise to accounts not previously represented in the ledger, while others do not. Give two examples of each type of adjusting entry.
9. A firm's unearned rent increased from $19,000 to $27,000 during the current year. The firm collected $55,000 cash in rentals. Determine the amount of rent revenue recognized in the current year.
10. Which accounts in an unadjusted trial balance might reflect their beginning balances? Which accounts in an adjusted trial balance also might reflect such balances?
11. Give some examples of internal cost allocations that require adjusting entries.
12. Briefly explain the difference between perpetual and periodic inventory systems.
13. Explain the nature and purpose of closing entries.

14. A firm first closes revenue accounts (total $25,000) and then closes expense accounts (total $15,000). What is the balance in the income summary after the second closing entry (determine the amount, and state whether it is a debit or a credit). What does the balance represent?

15. Explain the purpose and nature of reversing entries. Why are they journalized and posted?

16. Xanthon Company owes a $4,000, three-year, 9% note payable. Interest is paid each November 30. Therefore, at the end of the accounting period, December 31, the following adjusting entry was made:

Interest expense	30	
Interest payable		30

Would you recommend using a reversing entry in this situation? Explain.

17. Explain which accounting cycle steps are affected by use of a worksheet, and give their order.

18. What advantages do special journals, subsidiary ledgers, and control accounts bring to accounting systems?

19. How does a voucher system improve internal controls over cash disbursements?

CASES

C 3–1
(L.O. 2, 4)

Analysis: Correcting Financial Statements   Fannie Corporation started operations on January 1, 1995. It is now December 31, 1995, the end of the annual accounting period. A company clerk, who maintained the accounting records, has just prepared the following financial statements:

Profit and Loss Statement
December 31, 1995

Service income		$100,000
Costs:		
Salaries and wages	$30,000	
Repairs and maintenance	5,000	
Service	25,000	
Other miscellaneous	10,000	70,000
Profit		$ 30,000

Balance Sheet
December 31, 1995

Assets

Cash	$ 7,500
Note receivable, 16%	1,200
Inventory, supplies	6,000
Equipment	90,000
Other miscellaneous assets	7,300
Total assets	$112,000

Debts

Accounts payable	$ 8,000
Note payable, 15%	24,000
Total debts	32,000

Capital

Share capital, nopar, 5,000 shares	50,000
Retained earnings	30,000
Total capital	80,000
Grand total	$112,000

The above statements (unaudited) were presented to a local bank, at the bank's request, to support a major loan. The bank requested that the statements be examined by an independent accountant. You are the independent accountant, and among other accounting issues, you found that the following items were not considered by the company in preparing the income statement and balance sheet:

a. Service revenue amounting to $2,000 had been collected but not earned at December 31, 1995.

b. At December 31, 1995, wages earned by employees but not yet paid or recorded amounted to $9,000.

c. A count of the inventory of supplies at December 31, 1995, showed $4,000 supplies on hand. (Supplies are used in maintenance and repair.)

d. Depreciation on the equipment acquired on January 3, 1995, was not recorded. The estimated residual value was $10,000, and the estimated useful life, 10 years.

e. The note receivable received from a customer was dated November 1, 1995; the principal plus interest is payable April 30, 1996.

f. The note payable to the local bank was dated June 1, 1995; the principal plus interest is payable May 31, 1996.

g. Assume an average income tax rate of 20% for Fannie Corporation and that no income tax has been recorded.

h. Although you did not do a complete audit of the accounting results, your judgment is that the daily recording of transactions was appropriate.

Required

1. Recast the financial statements based on your findings. Use a format similar to the following to develop the statements:

Items	Reported Amount	Changes Due to Findings				Correct Amount
		Key	+ or −	Amount	Comments	
Income statement: (list the appropriate items here)						
Balance sheet: (list the appropriate items here)						

2. Write a brief narrative addressed to Fannie Corporation to explain the corrected statements, and give any recommendations that you would make to Fannie Corporation concerning its accounting function.

C 3-2
(L.O. 1)

 YOU MAKE THE CALL   Ethical Considerations in Transaction Recording

Required

1. Adjusting journal entries are not signaled by new source documents or exchanges of resources between parties and may therefore be more easily omitted, altered, or forgotten. Considering the adjusting entries discussed in this chapter, prepare a written description of intentional alterations of adjusting journal entries that would constitute unethical behaviour on the part of the accountant or management.

2. Briefly discuss in writing the responsibilities that the accounting staff and external auditors have toward the shareholders of a corporation, relative to transaction recording and financial reporting.

C 3-3
(L.O. 1)

Distinguishing Events and Transactions   As a staff accountant in a large suburban retailing firm, you have had significant experience developing information for financial reporting purposes. During lunch with a colleague in the marketing department, the degree to which the accounting information system is designed to record all events affecting the firm was discussed. Your colleague has always wondered why some events warrant formal recording in the accounts whereas others do not.

For example, your colleague wonders why an upturn in demand for expensive sports shoes marketed by the firm does not warrant the recording of increased income before sale. She asked,

We cannot fill all the orders we receive for these shoes. Why can't we recognize our profit as soon as we receive these items from the manufacturer? I know the firm does not wait until receipt of cash to accrue interest on its financial investments. Yet I also know that increases in the value of our company's common shares are not recognized in our accounts as increases in the value of our assets. However, outside parties have made that assessment. I guess I'm confused.

Required

Write a short memo to your colleague distinguishing three types of events that are and are not recorded in the accounts, as a way of explaining the items she has mentioned.

C 3–4
(L.O. 1)

The Need for Journals in an AIS   Systems, Inc., produces and markets a wide variety of information and communication technology products. Although current demand for its products has increased enough to justify continued growth in production systems, the VP Finance is concerned that continuing recessionary factors may reverse the good fortune of the company. Yet, if the firm is to grow, it must overhaul the AIS. The VP has discussed the AIS project with you, the controller of this company, and cannot understand your insistence that the system have a strong journalizing capability. The VP said:

> The whole purpose of the AIS is to culminate in accurate financial statements each year. Why not simply record each transaction directly into the accounts? I just do not understand the need to record transactions into a temporary record first.

The VP is removed from the day-to-day operational traffic within the firm. The volume of transactions of the medium-sized firm is substantial.

Required   Prepare a short report explaining the need for the journal entry step.

EXERCISES

E 3–1
(L.O. 1, 2)

Account Classification   The following accounts were recorded in the 1995 adjusting entries of Jackson Corporation, a nutrition research laboratory. Classify each account as asset, liability, revenue, gain, expense, or loss, and explain the classification for each:

a. Prepaid insurance.
b. Property taxes payable.
c. Rent receivable.
d. Interest payable.
e. Rent collected in advance.
f. Accumulated depreciation.
g. Allowance for doubtful accounts.

E 3–2
(L.O. 4)

Review the Accounting Information Processing Cycle   The 10 steps that constitute the accounting information processing cycle are listed in scrambled order. Also listed is a brief statement of the objective of each step, also in scrambled order.

Required   1. In the blanks to the left, number the steps in the usual sequence of completion.
2. In the blanks to the right, use the letters to match each step with its objective.

Sequence (order)	Matching (with objective)	Steps	Objectives
⸻	⸻	Journalize.	*a.* Verification after closing entries.
⸻	⸻	Journalize and post reversing entries.	*b.* Communication to decision makers.
⸻	⸻	Identify transactions.	*c.* Verification before adjusting entries.
⸻	⸻	Prepare financial statements.	*d.* Transfer from journal to ledger.
⸻	⸻	Journalize and post closing entries.	*e.* Recording of resource changes not accompanied by new source documents.
⸻	⸻	Post.	*f.* An activity based on source documents.
⸻	⸻	Journalize and post adjusting entries.	*g.* Original input into the accounting system.
⸻	⸻	Prepare adjusted trial balance.	*h.* Facilitation of subsequent entries.
⸻	⸻	Prepare unadjusted trial balance.	*i.* Obtaining a zero balance in the revenue and expense accounts.
⸻	⸻	Prepare post–closing trial balance.	*j.* Verification after adjusting entries.

E 3–3
(L.O. 2, 3)

Journalize and Post Typical Transactions   Dynamic Corporation completed the three transactions given below:

a. January 1, 1995: sold 10,000 shares of nopar common shares for $50,000 cash.
b. January 3, 1995: purchased a machine that cost $60,000. Payment was $20,000 cash plus a $30,000 one-year, 10% interest-bearing note payable and a $10,000, three-year, 12% interest-bearing note payable. Interest on each note is payable every January 2.

c. February 1, 1995: sold two unneeded lots of land for $10,000. Received $4,000 cash down payment and a $6,000, 90-day, 9% interest-bearing note (interest payable at maturity date). The two lots had a total book value of $6,500.

Required

1. Analyze each of the above transactions and enter each in the general journal.
2. Set up T accounts and post the entries in (1) above. For posting purposes, set up a numbering system for both the journal pages and the ledger accounts. Use these numbers in your posting process.

E 3-4
(L.O. 4)

Adjusting Journal Entries At December 31, 1995, the end of the fiscal year, Baker Corporation, which produces fine confectionary, has the following situations:

a. Prepaid insurance, $150; the policy was acquired on January 1, 1995, and expires on December 31, 1996.
b. Wages earned December 29–31, 1995, not yet recorded or paid, $2,400.
c. Rent collected for January 1996, $400, that was credited to rent revenue when collected.
d. Interest expense of $200 for November–December 1995 will be paid April 30, 1996.
e. An asset that cost $10,000 (residual value, $1,000) is being depreciated over five years with straight-line depreciation (i.e., an equal amount each period).

Required

1. Give the 1995 adjusting journal entry for each situation.
2. If none is needed, explain why.

E 3-5
(L.O. 3)

Resolve Errors and Correct a Trial Balance A clerk for Century Company, a consulting firm, prepared the following unadjusted trial balance, which the clerk was unable to balance:

Account	Debit	Credit
Cash	$ 71,126	
Accounts receivable	62,000	
Allowance for doubtful accounts.	(4,000)	
Inventory, supplies.		$ 36,000
Equipment	363,000	
Accumulated depreciation.		24,000
Accounts payable	36,000	
Notes payable		50,000
Common shares, nopar, 36,000 shares . .		360,000
Retained earnings (correct)		28,000
Revenues		150,000
Expenses	120,000	
Total (out of balance by $126)	$648,126	$648,000

Assume you are examining the accounts and have found the following errors:

a. Equipment purchased for $15,000 at year-end was debited to expenses.
b. Sales on credit of $1,658 were debited to accounts receivable for $1,784 and credited to revenues for $1,658.
c. A $12,000 collection on accounts receivable was debited to cash and credited to revenues.
d. The inventory amount is understated by $4,000 (supplies expense is included in expenses).

Required

Prepare a corrected trial balance. Show calculations.

E 3-6
(L.O. 4, 5)

Journalize Adjusting Entries Rivers Corporation manufactures zippers in Quebec. It adjusts and closes its accounts each December 31. The following situations require adjusting entries at the current year-end. You are requested to prepare the adjusting entries in the general journal for each situation. If no entry is required for an item, explain why.

a. Machine A is to be depreciated for the full year. It cost $90,000, and the estimated useful life is five years, with an estimated residual value of $10,000. Use straight-line depreciation.
b. Credit sales for the current year amounted to $160,000. The estimated bad debt loss rate on credit sales is 0.5%.
c. Property taxes for the current year have not been recorded or paid. A statement for the current year was received near the end of December for $4,000; if paid after February 1 in the next year, a 10% penalty is assessed.

    d. Office supplies that cost $800 were purchased during the year and debited to office supplies inventory. The inventories of these supplies on hand were $200 at the end of the prior year and $300 at the end of the current year.

    e. Rivers rented an office in its building to a tenant for one year, starting on September 1. Rent for one year amounting to $6,000 was collected at that date. The total amount collected was credited to rent revenue.

    f. Rivers received a note receivable from a customer dated November 1 of the current year. It is a $12,000, 10% note, due in one year. At the maturity date, Rivers will collect the amount of the note plus interest for one year.

E 3–7
(L.O. 2)

Compute Cost of Goods Sold The following data are available under a periodic inventory system: purchases, $70,000; sales, $150,000; returned sales, $5,000; returned purchases, $4,000; freight-in, $7,000; beginning inventory, $32,000; selling expenses, $18,000; and ending inventory, $29,000 (by count).

Required

Compute the cost of goods sold.

E 3–8
(L.O. 2, 4, 5)

Effect of Transactions The following captions are totals or subtotals on the balance sheet for Tyme Corporation:

    A. Total current assets.
    B. Total plant assets (net of accumulated depreciation).
    C. Total current liabilities.
    D. Total long-term liabilities.
    E. Total contributed capital (or share capital).
    F. Total retained earnings (including income effects).

Required

For each event listed below, indicate which subtotal(s) increased or decreased as a result of the event. Indicate with an X if there has been no subtotal increased or decreased. Consider each event to be unrelated to the others.

Events	Increase	Decrease
Example: Issued shares for cash	A, E	X
1. Wrote off an uncollectible account receivable to the allowance for doubtful accounts.	____	____
2. Sold land for cash, received more than the original cost.	____	____
3. Declared a cash dividend to be paid in 60 days' time.	____	____
4. Increased the allowance for doubtful accounts.	____	____
5. Wrote off a fully depreciated machine.	____	____
6. Converted long-term convertible bonds into common shares.	____	____
7. Paid a previously declared cash dividend.	____	____
8. Increased the supplies inventory as part of year-end adjustments; the company uses the expedient method during the year.	____	____
9. Reduced the prepaid insurance account as part of year-end adjustments; the company uses the standard method during the year.	____	____
10. Recorded depreciation on plant assets.	____	____

E 3–9
(L.O. 4, 5)

Adjusting Entries Voss Company, an accounting firm, adjusts and closes its accounts each December 31. Provide adjusting journal entries as required.

    1. On December 31, 1995, the maintenance supplies inventory account showed a balance on hand amounting to $700. During 1996, purchases of maintenance supplies amounted to $2,000. An inventory of maintenance supplies on hand at December 31, 1996, reflected unused supplies amounting to $1,000.

    Give the adjusting journal entry that should be made on December 31, 1996, under the following conditions: Case A—the purchases were debited to the maintenance supplies inventory account; Case B—the purchases were debited to maintenance supplies expense.

    2. On December 31, 1995, the prepaid insurance account showed a debit balance of $1,800, which was for coverage for the three months, January to March. On April 1, 1996, the company obtained

another policy covering a two-year period from that date. The two-year premium, amounting to $19,200, was paid and debited to prepaid insurance.

Give the adjusting journal entry that should be made on December 31, 1996.

3. On June 1, the company collected cash, $8,400, which was for rent collected in advance from a tenant for the next 12 months. Give the adjusting journal entry assuming the following at the time of the collection: Case A—$8,400 was credited to rent revenue: Case B—$8,400 was credited to rent collected in advance.

E 3-10
(L.O. 4)

Journalize Adjusting Entries Pacific Company adjusts and closes its books each December 31. It is now December 31, 1995, and the adjusting entries are to be made. You are requested to prepare, in general journal format, the adjusting entry that should be made for each of the following items:

a. Credit sales for the year amounted to $320,000. The estimated loss rate on bad debts is ⅜%.
b. Unpaid and unrecorded wages incurred at December 31 amounted to $4,800.
c. The company paid a two-year insurance premium in advance on April 1, 1995, amounting to $9,600, which was debited to prepaid insurance.
d. Machine A, which cost $80,000, is to be depreciated for the full year. The estimated useful life is 10 years, and the residual value, $4,000. Use straight-line depreciation.
e. The company rented a warehouse on June 1, 1995, for one year. It had to pay the full amount of rent one year in advance on June 1, amounting to $9,600, which was debited to rent expense.
f. The company received from a customer a 9% note with a face amount of $12,000. The note was dated September 1, 1995; the principal plus the interest is payable one year later. Notes receivable was debited, and sales revenue was credited on the date of sale, September 1, 1995.
g. On December 30, 1995, the property tax bill was received in the amount of $5,000. This amount applied only to 1995 and had not been previously recorded or paid. The taxes are due, and will be paid, on January 15, 1996.
h. On April 1, 1995, the company signed a $60,000, 10% note payable. On that date, cash was debited and notes payable credited for $60,000. The note is payable on March 31, 1996, for the face amount plus interest for one year.
i. The company purchased a patent on January 1, 1995, at a cost of $11,900. On that date, the patent account was debited and cash credited for $11,900. The patent has an estimated useful life of 17 years and no residual value.
j. Pretax income has been computed to be $80,000 after all the above adjustments. Assume an average income tax rate of 30%.

E 3-11
(L.O. 4)

Journalize Adjusting Entries Prepare journal entries for the following unrelated situations:

1. On January 1, ABC Corporation had a supplies inventory of $4,500. During the year, supplies of $21,900 were bought and recorded in temporary accounts. At the end of the year, inventory of $9,200 was on hand.
2. On December 10, ABC Corporation received a deposit of $30,000 on a consulting project it was just beginning. This was accounted for as revenue. By the end of the year, the $50,000 job was 40% complete.
3. During the year, ABC Corporation sold 10,000 units of a product that was subject to a warranty. Past history indicates that 3% of units sold require repairs at an average cost of $40 per unit. The sales have been recorded; costs incurred for the warranty to date, totalling $8,700, were debited to warranty liability when paid. No warranty expense has been recognized.
4. At year-end, the allowance for doubtful accounts had a debit balance of $26,000. The company uses the percent of sales method to calculate bad debt expense: 1% of credit sales of $6,250,000 is expected to be uncollectible.
5. In 1993, a machine was purchased for $174,000. It had a useful life of 12 years and a $24,000 residual value. A full year's depreciation was charged in 1993 and 1994. In 1995, the accountant discovered that she had forgotten to deduct the salvage value when calculating (straight-line) depreciation for these two years. Prepare a journal entry to correct the error and record 1995 depreciation. Ignore income tax.
6. ABC Corporation wrote off a $16,000 bad debt. The allowance method is used.
7. ABC Corporation buys one-year insurance policies each November 1. The year ends on December 31. On January 1, 1995, there was a balance of $9,440 in the prepaid insurance account; a cheque for $12,710 was issued on November 1, 1995, for new one-year policies and debited to the prepaid insurance account.

E 3–12
(L.O. 2, 4)

Adjusting and Closing Entries At December 31, 1995 (the end of the accounting period), Nicole Corporation reflected the following amounts on its worksheet:

Sales revenue	$380,000
Interest revenue	8,000
Beginning inventory (periodic inventory system)	60,000
Ending inventory	68,000
Freight-in (on purchases)	12,000
Purchases	216,000
Sales returns	16,000
Purchase returns	4,000
Operating expenses (including income tax)	104,000

Required

1. Compute cost of goods sold.
2. Give the adjusting entry for purchases, inventory, and cost of goods sold. If none is required, explain why.
3. Give the closing entries for (*a*) revenues, (*b*) expenses, and (*c*) net income.

E 3–13
(L.O. 4)

Adjusting and Closing Entries Seabright Company has completed its worksheet at December 31, 1995 (the end of its accounting period). The following accounts and amounts were reflected on the worksheet:

Sales revenue	$55,000
Service revenue	1,000
Operating expenses	12,000
Income tax expense	2,500
Cost of goods sold	26,500
Interest expense	2,000
Ending inventory (perpetual inventory system)	5,500

Required

1. Give the adjusting entry for inventory and cost of goods sold. If none is required, explain why.
2. Give the closing entries for (*a*) revenues, (*b*) expenses, and (*c*) net income.

E 3–14
(L.O. 5)

Reversing Entries On December 31, 1995, Nutramatics Corporation made the following adjusting entries:

a. Wages expense	32,000	
Wages payable		32,000
b. Bad debt expense	2,000	
Allowance for doubtful accounts		2,000
c. Income tax expense	48,000	
Income tax payable		48,000
d. Depreciation expense	100,000	
Accumulated depreciation		100,000

Required

1. Give the reversing entries that you think would be preferable on January 1, 1996.
2. For each adjusting entry, explain how you decided whether to reverse it.

E 3–15
(L.O. 5)

Reversing Entries At the end of the annual accounting period, Rose Garden Corporation made the following adjusting entries:
December 31, 1995:

a. Property tax expense	400	
Property taxes payable		400
These are paid once each year.		
b. Rent receivable	2,000	
Rent revenue		2,000
Rent revenue is collected at various dates each month.		
c. Patent amortization expense	1,000	
Patent		1,000
d. Warranty expense	300	
Estimated warranty liability		300
e. Wages expense	4,500	
Wages payable		4,500

Required

1. Give the reversing entries that should be made on January 1, 1996.
2. For each adjusting entry, explain how you decided whether to reverse it.

E 3-16
(L.O. 4, 5)

Adjusting Entries, Account Analysis, and Recording Methods   The following situations are unrelated.

a. Road Runner Company sells magazine subscriptions for a one-year, two-year, or three-year periods. Cash receipts from subscribers are credited to magazine subscriptions collected in advance, and this account had a balance of $1,700,000 at December 31, 1995. Information for the year ended December 31, 1996, is as follows:

Cash receipts from subscribers	$2,100,000
Magazine subscriptions revenue credited at December 31, 1996.	1,500,000

Required

In its December 31, 1996, balance sheet, what amount should Road Runner report as the balance for magazine subscriptions collected in advance?

b. Halo Company sublet a portion of its warehouse for five years at an annual rental of $18,000 beginning May 1, 1995. The tenant paid one year's rent in advance, which Halo recorded as a credit to unearned rent. Halo reports on a calendar-year basis.

Required

1. Record the adjusting entry on December 31, 1995.
2. Assume that Halo recorded the rental receipt as rent revenue. Record the adjusting entry on December 31, 1995.

c. Dane Company sells magazine subscriptions for one- and two-year periods. Cash receipts from subscribers are credited to magazine subscriptions collected in advance. This account had a balance of $2,100,000 at December 31, 1995, before the year-end adjustment. Outstanding subscriptions at December 31, 1995, expire as follows:

During 1996.	$600,000
During 1997.	900,000

Required

In its December 31, 1995, balance sheet, what amount should Dane report as the balance in magazine subscriptions collected in advance?

d. Zinnie Company assigns some of its patents to other companies under a variety of licensing agreements. In some instances, advance royalties are received when the agreements are signed; in others royalties are remitted within 60 days after each license year-end. The following data are included in Zinnie's December 31 balance sheets:

	1995	1996
Royalties receivable.	$90,000	$85,000
Unearned royalties	60,000	40,000

During 1996, Zinnie received royalty remittances of $200,000.

Required

In its income statement for the year ended December 31, 1996, how much royalty revenue should Zinnie report?

(AICPA adapted)

E 3-17

Appendix 3B, Special Journals   Next to each transaction place the letter of the journal into which that transaction would be recorded. Assume that the company uses special journals whenever appropriate.

Transactions	Journals
_____ 1. Collect cash on account.	A. General journal.
_____ 2. Purchase merchandise on account.	B. Sales journal.
_____ 3. Prepare adjusting entries.	C. Purchases journal.
_____ 4. Pay the insurance bill.	D. Cash receipts journal.
_____ 5. Receive cash for services.	E. Cash payments journal.
_____ 6. Prepare closing entries.	F. Voucher register.
_____ 7. Record a completed but unpaid voucher.	G. Cheque register.
_____ 8. Correct an erroneous journal entry.	
_____ 9. Sell merchandise on credit.	
_____ 10. Pay accounts payable.	
_____ 11. Sell merchandise for cash.	
_____ 12. Pay the voucher in (7).	

PROBLEMS

P 3–1
(L.O. 2, 4)

Journalize and Post; Unadjusted Trial Balance   The following selected transactions were completed during 1995 by Rotan Corporation, a retailer of Scandinavian furniture.

a. Sold 20,000 shares of its own nopar common shares for $12 per share and received cash in full.
b. Borrowed $100,000 cash on a 9%, one-year note, interest payable at maturity on April 30, 1996.
c. Purchased equipment for use in operating the business at a net cash cost of $164,000; paid in full.
d. Purchased merchandise for resale at a cash cost of $140,000; paid cash. Assume a periodic inventory system; therefore, debit purchases.
e. Purchased merchandise for resale on credit terms 2/10, n/60. The merchandise will cost $9,800 if paid within 10 days; after 10 days, the payment will be $10,000. The company always takes the discount; therefore, such purchases are recorded net of discount.
f. Sold merchandise for $180,000; collected $165,000 cash, and the balance is due in one month.
g. Paid $40,000 cash for operating expenses.
h. Paid three-fourths of the balance for the merchandise purchased in (e) within 5 days; the balance remains unpaid.
i. Collected 50% of the balance due on the sale in (f); the remaining balance is uncollected.
j. Paid cash for an insurance premium, $600; the premium was for two years' coverage (debit prepaid insurance).
k. Purchased a tract of land for a future building for company operations, $63,000 cash.
l. Paid damages to a customer who was injured on the company premises, $10,000 cash.

Required

1. Enter each of the above transactions in a general journal; use J1 for the first journal page number. Use the letter of the transaction in place of the date.
2. Set up appropriate T accounts and post the journal entries. Use posting reference numbers in your posting. Assign each T account an appropriate title, and number each account in balance sheet order followed by the income statement accounts; start with Cash, no. 101.
3. Prepare an unadjusted trial balance.

P 3–2
(L.O. 4)

Journalize Adjusting Entries   The following transactions and events for Stellar Manufacturing Corporation are under consideration for adjusting entries at December 31, 1995 (the end of the accounting period).

a. Machine A used in the factory cost $450,000; it was purchased on July 1, 1992. It has an estimated useful life of 12 years and a residual value of $30,000. Straight-line depreciation is used.
b. Sales for 1995 amounted to $4,000,000, including $600,000 credit sales. It is estimated, based on the experience of the company, that bad debt losses will be ¼% of credit sales.
c. At the beginning of 1995, office supplies inventory amounted to $600. During 1995, office supplies amounting to $8,800 were purchased; this amount was debited to office supplies expense. An inventory of office supplies at the end of 1995 showed $400 on the shelves. The January 1 balance of $600 is still reflected in the office supplies inventory account.
d. On July 1, 1995, the company paid a three-year insurance premium amounting to $2,160; this amount was debited to prepaid insurance.
e. On October 1, 1995, the company paid rent on some leased office space. The payment of $7,200 cash was for the following six months. At the time of payment, rent expense was debited for the $7,200.
f. On August 1, 1995, the company borrowed $120,000 from the Royal Bank. The loan was for 12 months at 9% interest payable at maturity date.
g. Finished goods inventory on January 1, 1995, was $200,000, and on December 31, 1995, it was $260,000. The perpetual inventory record provided the cost of goods sold amount of $2,400,000.
h. The company owned some property (land) that was rented to B. R. Speir on April 1, 1995, for 12 months for $8,400. On April 1, the entire annual rental of $8,400 was credited to rent collected in advance, and cash was debited.
i. On December 31, 1995, wages earned by employees but not yet paid (or recorded in the accounts) amounted to $18,000. Disregard payroll taxes.
j. On September 1, 1995, the company loaned $60,000 to an outside party. The loan was at 10% per annum and was due in six months; interest is payable at maturity. Cash was credited for $60,000 and notes receivable debited on September 1 for the same amount.
k. On January 1, 1995, factory supplies on hand amounted to $200. During 1995, factory supplies that cost $4,000 were purchased and debited to factory supplies inventory. At the end of 1995, a physical inventory count revealed that factory supplies on hand amounted to $800.

l. The company purchased a gravel pit on January 1, 1993, at a cost of $60,000; it was estimated that approximately 60,000 tons of gravel could be removed prior to exhaustion. It was also estimated that the company would take five years to exploit this natural resource. Tons of gravel removed and sold were: 1993—3,000; 1994—7,000; and 1995—5,000. Hint: Deplete on an output basis; no residual value.

m. At the end of 1995, it was found that postage stamps that cost $120 were on hand (in a "postage" box in the office). When the stamps were purchased, miscellaneous expense was debited and cash was credited.

n. At the end of 1995, property taxes for 1995 amounting to $59,000 were assessed on property owned by the company. The taxes are due no later than February 1, 1996. The taxes have not been recorded on the books because payment has not been made.

o. The company borrowed $120,000 from the bank on December 1, 1995. A 60-day note payable was signed at 9½% interest payable on maturity date. On December 1, 1995, cash was debited and notes payable credited for $120,000.

p. On July 1, 1995, the company paid the city a $1,000 license fee for the next 12 months. On that date, cash was credited and license expense debited for $1,000.

q. On March 1, 1995, the company made a loan to the company president and received a $30,000 note receivable. The loan was due in one year and called for 6% annual interest payable at maturity date.

r. The company owns three cars used by the executives. A six-month maintenance contract on them was signed on October 1, 1995, whereby a local garage agreed to do "all the required maintenance." The payment was made for the following six months in advance. On October 1, 1995, cash was credited and maintenance expense was debited for $9,600.

Required   Give the adjusting entry (or entries) that should be made on December 31, 1995, for each item. State any assumptions that you make. If an adjusting entry is not required, explain why.

P 3-3
(L.O. 4, 5)

Recording Systems, Adjusting Entries, Reversing Entries   Ronald Company, a calendar-year company that manufactures frozen hamburger for fast-food chains, employs the expedient system and reversing entries whenever appropriate. For each of the following, provide (1) the December 31, 1995, adjusting entry, (2) the January 1, 1996, reversing entry (if a reversing entry is not appropriate, explain why), and (3) the entry for the associated transaction to occur in 1996, if one is expected.

a. One of Ronald Company's liabilities is a 12%, $20,000 long-term note payable that requires interest to be paid each March 1 and September 1.

b. Ronald Company owns a $10,000, 10% bond, that it purchased at face value and that pays interest each August 1 and February 1.

c. Ronald Company performed and completed services for a customer in December for a $6,000 total fee. The customer was not billed and did not remit payment in the current year. The customer has a clean credit history.

d. Depreciation of $15,000 is to be recognized.

e. Wages totalling $7,500 were earned but not paid or recorded at year-end. Assume that the first payroll in 1996 will total $22,500.

f. Ronald Company receives the $18,000 annual rental fee on one of its real estate investments at the beginning of each contract year. The rental contract began on July 1, several years ago.

g. Estimated warranty expense on sales in the current year is $25,000. Products sold by Ronald Company carry a one-year warranty. A total of $13,000 has been spent servicing warranty claims from last year's sales, and $17,000 on this year's sales. Costs of servicing claims are debited to estimated warranty liability. Assume that Ronald Company has been able to predict total warranty costs accurately and that it will continue to do so.

P 3-4
(L.O. 2, 3)

Accounting Fundamentals and Account Analysis   Choose the correct answer among each set of four alternatives.

1. The following summary balance sheet account categories of Sure Company increased by the following amounts during 1995:

Assets.	$356,000	Liabilities.	$108,000
Share capital	264,000		

The only charge to retained earnings during 1995 was for $52,000 of dividends. What was Sure's net income for 1995?

a. $68,000.

b. $52,000.

c. $36,000.

d. $16,000.

2. How would proceeds received in advance from the sale of nonrefundable tickets for the Grey Cup be reported in the seller's financial statements published before the Grey Cup?

a. Revenue for entire proceeds.

b. Revenue less related costs.

c. Unearned revenue less related costs.

d. Unearned revenue for the entire proceeds.

3. Mello Company, a calendar-year company specializing in miniaturization of electronic products, reported the following balances:

	December 31, 1995	December 31, 1994
Inventory	$130,000	$145,000
Accounts payable	37,500	25,000

Mello paid suppliers $245,000 during 1995. What is Mello's 1995 cost of goods sold?

a. $272,500.

b. $247,500.

c. $242,500.

d. $217,500.

4. Ride! Company, a calendar-year company, sells subscriptions to a bicycling magazine for mountain bicycle enthusiasts. The magazine is published semiannually and is shipped to subscribers on April 15 and October 15. Only one-year subscriptions (for two issues) are accepted. Subscriptions received after the March 30 and September 30 cutoff dates are held for the following publication. Cash is received evenly during the year and is credited to deferred subscription revenue. During 1995, $7,200,000 of cash was received from customers. The beginning 1995 balance in deferred subscription revenue was $1,500,000. What is Ride!'s December 31, 1995, deferred subscription revenue balance?

a. $5,400,000.

b. $3,600,000.

c. $3,300,000.

d. $1,800,000.

5. A bond issued June 1, 1995, by a calendar-year company pays interest on April 1 and October 1. A bond is a financial security issued by a firm in return for cash paid in by investors. Bonds typically pay interest twice per year. The investor makes the investment on the date the bond is issued. Interest expense for 1995 is recognized on these bonds by the issuer for a period of:

a. Seven months.

b. Six months.

c. Four months.

d. Three months.

(AICPA adapted)

P 3–5
(L.O. 4)

Account Analysis and Financial Statements Multimedia, Inc., a producer of graphics and artwork for movie theatres and other media distributors, provided the following information for 1995:

Selected Accounts from the Balance Sheet January 1, 1995		Income Statement for Year Ended December 31, 1995	
Accounts receivable	$10,000	Sales	$200,000
Prepaid insurance	20,000	Insurance expense	(15,000)
Supplies	5,000	Depreciation expense	(10,000)
Equipment (net)	80,000	Supplies expense	(30,000)
Accounts payable (suppliers)	40,000*	Wages expense	(60,000)
Unearned rent	13,000	Rent revenue	12,000
Wages payable	7,000	Net income	$ 97,000
Common shares (nopar)	27,000		
Retained earnings	50,000		

* The December 31, 1995, balance is $50,000.

Statement of Changes in Financial Position
Year Ended December 31, 1995

Operating activities:

Collections from customers.	$ 90,000	
Insurance payments	(25,000)	
Payments to suppliers	(45,000)	
Payments to employees	(52,000)	
Rental receipts	19,000	
Net operating flows and cash decrease for 1995*		($13,000)
Cash balance, January 1, 1995		22,000
Cash balance, December 31, 1995		$ 9,000

* No investing or financing cash flows

Required

Prepare the 1995 balance sheet for Multimedia.

P 3–6
(L.O. 4, 5)

Account Analysis and Financial Statements   The Shirt Shack is a retail store operating in a downtown shopping mall. On January 1, 1995, it reported the following:

SHIRT SHACK
Balance Sheet
As of January 1, 1995

Cash	$ 4,000
Accounts receivable (net of allowance of $2,000)	28,000
Prepaid rent (rental deposit)	1,000
Inventory	36,000
Leasehold improvements (net)	16,000
Total assets	$85,000
Accounts payable.	$32,000
Accrued wages payable	3,500
Accrued interest payable	200
Accrued rent payable	0
Notes payable, 10%.	14,800
Common shares	10,000
Retained earnings.	24,500
Total liabilities plus equity.	$85,000

During 1995, the company reported the following:

1. Cash paid to employees (salaries and commissions), $67,000. Cash paid to suppliers, $90,000.
2. Cash collected from customers, $220,000.
3. On December 31, 1995, a physical inventory count revealed that inventory was $42,000.
4. At December 31, 1995, customers owed Shirt Shack $35,000, and the company owed its suppliers $14,000. Of the accounts receivable, aging analysis indicated that $4,000 was expected to be uncollectible. No accounts were written off in 1995.
5. Cash paid to landlord, $12,000 ($1,000 per month for 12 months). Shirt Shack is required to pay monthly rent and, at year-end, make an additional payment to bring the rent expense up to 10% of sales. This payment will be made in January of 1996.
6. Cash paid for miscellaneous operating expenses, $6,000.
7. Cash paid in dividends, $14,500; in interest, $1,680. No interest is owing at December 31, 1995.
8. Shirt Shack owed employees $500 in wages and $1,000 in commissions at year-end.
9. The leasehold improvements were acquired on January 1, 1994. They had an expected life of 10 years and were installed in leased premises that had a five-year lease on January 1, 1994.

Required

Prepare an income statement for the year ended December 31, 1995. Ignore income taxes. Show all calculations.

P 3–7
(L.O. 3, 4)

Complete All Phases of the Accounting Cycle   The post-closing trial balance of the general ledger of Wilson Corporation, a retailer of home weight-training machines, at December 31, 1994, reflects the following:

Acct. No.	Account	Debit	Credit
101	Cash	$ 27,000	
102	Accounts receivable	21,000	
103	Allowance for doubtful accounts		$ 1,000
104	Inventory (perpetual inventory system)*	35,000	
105	Prepaid insurance (20 months remaining)	900	
200	Equipment (20-year estimated life, no residual value).	50,000	
201	Accumulated depreciation, equipment		22,500
300	Accounts payable.		7,500
301	Wages payable		
302	Income taxes payable (for 1994)		4,000
400	Common shares, nopar, 80,000 shares		80,000
401	Retained earnings.		18,900
500	Sales revenue		
600	Cost of goods sold		
601	Operating expenses		
602	Income tax expense.		
700	Income summary		
		$133,900	$133,900

* Ending inventory on December 31, 1995, by physical count, $45,000.

The following transactions occurred during 1995 in the order given (use the letter at the left in place of date):

a. Sales revenue of $30,000, of which $10,000 was on credit; cost, provided by perpetual inventory record, $19,500. Hint: When the perpetual system is used, make two entries to record a sale—first, debit cash or accounts receivable and credit sales revenue; second, debit cost of goods sold and credit inventory.

b. Collected $17,000 on accounts receivable.

c. Paid income taxes payable (1994), $4,000.

d. Purchased merchandise, $40,000, of which $8,000 was on credit.

e. Paid accounts payable, $6,000.

f. Sales revenue of $72,000 (in cash); cost, $46,800.

g. Paid operating expenses, $19,000.

h. On January 1, 1995, sold and issued 1,000 common shares for $1,000 cash.

i. Purchased merchandise, $100,000, of which $27,000 was on credit.

j. Sales revenue of $98,000, of which $30,000 was on credit; cost, $63,700.

k. Collected cash on accounts receivable, $26,000.

l. Paid cash on accounts payable, $28,000.

m. Paid various operating expenses in cash, $18,000.

Required

1. Journalize each of the transactions listed above for 1995; use only a general journal.

2. Set up T accounts in the general ledger for each of the accounts listed in the above trial balance and enter the account number and December 31, 1994, balance.

3. Post the journal entries; use posting reference numbers.

4. Prepare an unadjusted trial balance.

5. Journalize the adjusting entries and post them to the ledger. Assume a bad debt rate of ½% of credit sales for the period at December 31, 1995; accrued wages were $300. The average income tax rate was 40%. Hint: Income tax expense is $11,784. Use straight-line depreciation.

6. Prepare an adjusted trial balance.

7. Prepare the income statement and balance sheet.

8. Journalize and post the closing entries.

9. Prepare a post–closing trial balance.

P 3–8   **Appendix 3A, Worksheet, Adjusting and Closing Entries, Statements**   Data Corporation is currently completing the end-of-the-period accounting process. At December 31, 1995, the following unadjusted trial balance was developed from the general ledger:

Account	Balances (unadjusted)	
	Debit	Credit
Cash	$ 60,260	
Accounts receivable	38,000	
Allowance for doubtful accounts.		$ 2,000
Interest receivable		
Inventory (perpetual inventory system)	105,000	
Sales supplies inventory	900	
Long-term note receivable, 14%	12,000	
Equipment	180,000	
Accumulated depreciation, equipment		64,000
Patent	8,400	
Accounts payable		23,000
Interest payable		
Income taxes payable.		
Property taxes payable		
Rent collected in advance		
Mortgage payable, 12%		60,000
Common shares, nopar, 10,000 shares		115,000
Retained earnings		32,440
Sales revenue		700,000
Investment revenue		1,120
Rent revenue		3,000
Cost of goods sold	380,000	
Selling expenses	164,400	
General and administrative expenses	55,000	
Interest expense	6,600	
Income tax expense		
Extraordinary gain (pretax)		10,000
	$1,010,560	$1,010,560

Additional data for adjustments and other purposes:

a. Estimated bad debt loss rate is ¼% of credit sales. Credit sales for the year amounted to $200,000; classify as a selling expense.

b. Interest on the long-term note receivable was last collected August 31, 1995.

c. Estimated useful life of the equipment is 10 years; residual value, $20,000. Allocate 10% of depreciation expense to general and administrative expense and the balance to selling expense to reflect proportionate use. Use straight-line depreciation.

d. Estimated remaining economic life of the patent is 14 years (from January 1, 1995) with no residual value. Use straight-line amortization and classify as selling expense (used in sales promotion).

e. Interest on the mortgage payable was last paid on November 30, 1995.

f. On June 1, 1995, the company rented some office space to a tenant for one year and collected $3,000 rent in advance for the year; the entire amount was credited to rent revenue on this date.

g. On December 31, 1995, the company received a statement for calendar-year 1995 property taxes amounting to $1,300. The payment is due February 15, 1996. Assume that it will be paid on that date and classify it as a selling expense.

h. Sales supplies on hand at December 31, 1995, amounted to $300; classify as a selling expense.

i. Assume an average 40% corporate income tax rate on all items including the extraordinary gain. Hint: Income tax expense is $35,132.

Required   1. Enter the above unadjusted trial balance on a worksheet.
2. Enter the adjusting entries and complete the worksheet.
3. Prepare the income statement and balance sheet.
4. Journalize the closing entries.

P 3–9   **Appendix 3B—Cash Receipts Journal** Hall Retailers uses special journals. A cash receipts journal with several selected transactions is given below.

		Debit			Credits			
Date	Explanation	Cash	Account Title	Post. Ref.	Accounts Receivable	Sales Revenue	Misc. Accounts	
1995								
Jan. 1	Cash sales	30,000				30,000		
2	On account	4,200	Riley Corp.		4,200			
5	Cash sales	10,000				10,000		
6	On account	1,240	Brown Inc.		1,240			
8	Sale of short-term		Short-term investments				4,000	
	investment	7,000	Gain on sale of					
			investments				3,000	
11	Cash sales	41,000				41,000		
12	Borrowed cash	10,000	Notes payable				10,000	
15	On account	5,500	Watson Co.		5,500			
18	Collected interest	600	Interest revenue				600	
31	Cash sales	52,000				52,000		

Required

1. Sum the cash receipts journal and post it to the appropriate accounts in the general ledger. Set up the following T accounts: cash no. 101, accounts receivable control no. 113 (beginning balance, $19,640), short-term investments no. 134, notes payable no. 326, sales revenue no. 500, interest revenue no. 509, and gain on sales of investments no. 510. Also, set up a subsidiary ledger for accounts receivable (with systematic numbers starting with 113.03). Beginning customer balances were as follows: Brown Inc., $1,240; Riley Corporation, $8,400; and Watson Company, $10,000.
2. Reconcile the subsidiary ledger with its control account.

P 3–10
(L.O. 1, 2, 3, 4)   **Perform All Accounting Cycle Steps** Spectrum Enterprises, a calendar-year firm, began operations as a retailer in January 1995. You are to perform the 10 accounting cycle steps for Spectrum for 1995. Worksheets, special journals, and subsidiary ledgers are not required. Prepare journal entries in summary (for the year) form. Post to T accounts. Spectrum uses the expedient recording system and records reversing entries whenever appropriate. Spectrum also uses a periodic inventory system and adjusts inventory in an adjusting entry.

Information about transactions in 1995:

a. Investors contributed $200,000 in exchange for 10,000 shares of nopar common shares. On the advice of its underwriter, Spectrum offered the shares at $20.
b. Spectrum obtained a 10%, $100,000 bank loan on February 1. This loan is evidenced by a signed promissory note calling for interest payments every February 1. The note is due in full on January 31, 1999.
c. A rental contract for production and office facilities was signed February 1, which required $10,000 immediate payment covering the first month's rent and a $5,000 deposit refundable in three years or upon termination of the contract, whichever occurs first. Monthly rent is $5,000. As an added incentive to pay rent in advance, Spectrum accepted an offer to maintain rent at $5,000 per month for the first three years if Spectrum paid the 2nd through the 13th (March 1995 through February 1996) month's rent immediately. In all, Spectrum paid $70,000 for rent on February 1. Spectrum intends to occupy the facilities for at least three years.
d. Equipment costing $110,000 was purchased for cash in early February. It has an estimated residual value of $10,000 and a five-year useful life. Spectrum uses the straight-line method of depreciation and treats depreciation as a separate period expense.
e. Spectrum recognized various operating expenses for the year, including the following:

Wages expense	$ 60,000
Utilities expense	40,000
Selling expenses	80,000
General and administrative expenses	100,000

f. Total merchandise purchases for the year amounted to $2,000,000. Ending inventory amounted to $200,000 at cost. Spectrum uses a periodic inventory system.

g. Total payables relating to merchandise purchases and other operating expenses are $40,000 at year-end.

h. All sales are made on credit and totalled $2,500,000 in 1995; $2,300,000 was collected on account during the year. Spectrum estimates that ½% of total sales will be uncollectible and has written off $3,000 of accounts.

i. Spectrum faces an average 40% income tax rate. Assume that all taxes for a fiscal year are payable in April of the following year.

j. Spectrum decided to declare a cash dividend of $117,000, payable in January 1996.

ANALYZING FINANCIAL STATEMENTS

A 3–1
(L.O. 2)

Collins Industries, Inc.: Account Analysis and Interpretation Collins Industries is a manufacturer of specialty vehicles (such as ambulances and school buses). A portion of its 1989 statement of cash flows follows. This report enables you to approximate certain operating information not disclosed.

COLLINS INDUSTRIES, INC.
Statement of Cash Flows
For the Period Ended October 31, 1989
(amounts in thousands)

Cash flow from operations:	
Cash received from customers	$ 131,269
Cash paid to suppliers and employees	(127,053)
Interest received	201
Interest paid	(4,173)
Cash provided by operations	244
Cash flow for investing activities:	
Capital expenditures	$ (2,358)
Proceeds from sale of fixed assets	159
Proceeds from sale of discontinued operations	246
Other	(90)
Cash used by investing activities	(2,043)
Cash flow from financing activities:	
(Not reproduced)	
Reconciliation of net income to cash provided by operations:	
Net income	$ 1,836
Non-cash charges to income	3,102
Gain on sale of fixed assets	(7)
Increase in accounts and notes receivable	(3,207)
Increase in inventories	(4,801)
Increase in prepaid expenses	(607)
Increase in accounts payable	3,492
Increase in accrued expenses	436
Cash provided by operations	$ 244

Required Estimate the following amounts for Collins for 1989 from the information given:

1. Total sales (assume that all accounts and notes receivable relate to sales).
2. Book value of fixed assets sold.
3. Cost of goods sold (assume that $60,000,000 was paid to suppliers of the total $127,053,000 paid to suppliers and employees).
4. The total of operating expenses other than cost of goods sold, non-cash expenses, and interest (assume that interest expense and revenue equal their cash counterparts).
5. Net income (this amount is given in the information, but calculate it from your previous results and other information given).

A 3–2
(L.O. 2)

Magna International Inc.: Analysis of an Annual Report   Refer to the 1993 financial statements of Magna International Inc. which appears at the end of this text, and respond to the following questions:

1. Over what period are fixed assets and goodwill amortized? Provide the journal entry that Magna would have recorded to recognize depreciation and amortization.
2. Describe and discuss Magna's policy for preproduction costs, a category of fixed asset.
3. Assuming Magna follows the expedient method and reverses all appropriate adjusting journal entries, provide the journal entries related to interest expense made in 1993. (Hint: See note 7e.)
4. Assuming Magna uses a periodic inventory method and the adjusting journal entry approach to inventory accounts, provide the adjusting journal entry that would have been made at the end of 1993.
5. What adjusting journal entry would have been made to classify the $7.6 million of long-term debt due within one year, a balance sheet current liability?
6. Does Magna use the expedient or standard method to record transactions during the year?

4 Review: The Income Statement and the Retained Earnings Statement

After you have studied this chapter, you will be able to:

1 Discuss the nature and definition of accounting income and be able to relate accounting income to other definitions of income.

2 Explain the basic purpose and elements of the income statement.

3 Describe and illustrate the single- and multiple-step forms of the income statement.

4 Illustrate the accounting treatment and disclosures of extraordinary items, unusual or infrequent items, discontinued operations, changes in accounting estimates, errors and accounting principles, and prior period adjustments.

5 Explain the basic purpose and composition of the retained earnings statement.

6 Calculate and present earnings per share on the income statement.

INTRODUCTION

In its annual report to shareholders, the Bank of Nova Scotia (Scotiabank) reported the following three-year results:

	Year Ended October 31 (amounts in millions)		
	1992	1991	1990
Net income	$676	$633	$512

Given this information and assuming no significant changes in operations at Scotiabank, what would your estimate of net income be for the year ending January 31, 1993? If your estimate is between $720 and $740 million, you are in the right range. Actual net income was $714 million for 1993, less than most of us would have predicted from the information given, but not too far off the mark.

Now consider the net income reported by Abitibi-Price Corporation over a similar three-year period:

	Year Ended December 31 (amounts in millions)		
	1992	**1991**	**1990**
Net income (loss).	$(219.3)	$(75.9)	$(50.4)

What is your estimate of net income[1] for Abitibi-Price for 1993? If you find this a more difficult number to estimate, you are not alone; it would be helpful to have more information than just net income or loss. Abitibi reported a 1993 net loss of $121.7 million, a result not readily predicted from past trends.

Is it useful to know a firm's net income? On January 19, 1993, the common share price for Wells Fargo & Co. increased from $86 per share to $99 per share when the firm reported 1992 net income of $231 million. This 15 percent increase in share price occurred on a day when the average common share on the stock exchange declined in price. Although this was an unusually large change in share price in response to an earnings announcement, it illustrates that earnings are important information to investors. Moreover, the income statement is the primary source of information for a company's current profit performance. Investors, lenders, analysts, and other financial statement readers use this and other information for predicting the amount, timing, and uncertainty of the firm's future income and cash flows. Our purpose in this chapter is to develop an understanding of what information the income statement contains, how that information is presented, and how it might be used.

The income statement links a company's beginning and ending balance sheets for a given accounting period.[2] It explains changes in owners' equity caused by operations and certain other activities during the period. When there is no new investment or disinvestment by owners (or other minor technical changes), the change in owners' equity from the beginning to the end of the period equals net income. The following diagram illustrates this point.

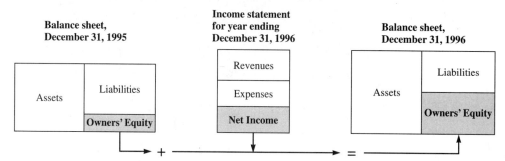

While net income is the amount that carries forward to link the two balance sheets, the components of net income found on the income statement are the things that provide important information about the sources of income. Let us return to the Abitibi-Price example. The income statements for two years[3] are presented in Exhibit 4–1. The net income (loss), or "bottom line," amounts are

---

[1] Many firms use the term *net earnings* instead of *net income*. In our usage, the two terms are synonymous.

[2] The income statement is also known as the *statement of income* (or statement of earnings), profit and loss statement, statement of operations, or by other expressions. In this text, we will most often use the term *income statement*. When two or more companies are combined for the report, the statement is identified as a *consolidated* statement.

[3] Some companies present three years of comparative data; the U.S. S.E.C. requires all listed public companies to present three-year comparative income statements, but two are all that are required by accounting standards of full disclosure.

EXHIBIT 4–1

Extracts from Consolidated
Statements of Income for
Abitibi-Price Corporation

	Year Ended December 31 (amounts in millions)	
	1993	**1992**
Net sales	$1,869.0	$1,600.8
Cost of sales.	1,727.0	1,556.6
Selling and administrative expenses	99.2	95.2
Depreciation and depletion	82.6	87.1
	1,908.8	1,738.9
Operating loss from continuing operations	(39.8)	(138.1)
Loss from newsprint joint ventures, before income taxes	(37.7)	(49.7)
Interest expense—long-term.	(38.9)	(28.6)
Interest expense—short-term	(1.3)	(3.3)
Unusual items	(21.6)	(64.8)
Other income and expense, net	(9.5)	(11.2)
Loss from continuing operations before income taxes	(148.8)	(295.7)
Recovery of income taxes.	40.5	104.2
Loss from continuing operations	(108.3)	(191.5)
Discontinued operations		
Loss from discontinued operations, net of income tax recoveries of $0.2 and $13.3, respectively	(0.3)	(21.8)
Loss on disposal of discontinued operations, net of income tax recoveries of $6.8 and $28.1, respectively	(13.1)	(6.0)
Loss from discontinued operations	(13.4)	(27.8)
Loss for the year	$ (121.7)	$ (219.3)

included, but now more detailed information is available. In particular, three additional subtotals are identified as measures of income (shown in boldface). These intermediate income measures are meant to provide the reader with information on major causes or sources of income (or loss) and assist the reader in forming estimates of the amount, timing, and uncertainty of future income and cash flows. It is now easier to understand the results of operations, continuing expenses, and non-continuing items such as unusual items and discontinued operations. However, it is still not easy to predict future income from continuing operations. Future events—paper prices—are a key forecasting variable.

Included in and following income (loss) from continuing operations in Exhibit 4–1 are several items that both require separate disclosure and are more difficult to understand and to predict:

- Unusual items.
- Loss on operation and disposal of discontinued operations.

The special reporting requirements for these items and several other categories are covered in this chapter.

WHAT THE INCOME STATEMENT REPRESENTS

Users of the financial statements must decide which earnings or income figure reported in the income statement best depicts a company's financial growth and offers the most assistance in predicting future earnings.[4] There is no simple answer to this

---

[4] Earnings trends and trend lines are important analytical tools used by investment analysts and investors in forecasting a company's future earnings. Forecasts of future earnings are one factor often used in making investment decisions. Past trends and performance do not guarantee continuation of such trends and performance in the future, but they are often useful in prediction.

question. The income statement often contains items that must be treated differently when trying to predict future income. The nature of each item must be understood in order to effectively use the information portrayed.

The Nature of Income

The term *income* means different things to different people. There are also different viewpoints on *when* to recognize income. For example, an economist defines a change in wealth, whether realized or not, as income. To illustrate, assume that a firm owns a parcel of land for which it paid $10,000 several years ago. A new highway has just been built next to the property, and several individuals have offered to pay substantially more than $10,000 for the land. The firm has not yet agreed to sell. The economist would say that an increase in wealth has occurred and would call this increase income. This is economic income, and it is based on an **events approach,** not on actual transactions.

An accountant would not recognize such an increase in wealth as income. The accountant would first require *reliable verification* of the increase in value. If the land is sold at fair value to another party in an arm's-length transaction, this transaction would provide the reliable verification the accountant seeks. Only at that point would the accountant recognize the increase in wealth as income. This is accounting income, based on the **transactions approach.**

Revenue and expense recognition are key concepts in accounting. The concepts determine when and how revenues, gains, expenses, and losses are recorded. Determining the proper treatment for a particular transaction or event is often difficult. Indeed, a large part of the study of accounting addresses measurement and recognition issues as they apply to revenues, gains, expenses, and losses, as well as to assets and liabilities.

There are two general problems with the transactions approach to reporting income. First, reliable measurement requires agreement on the rules of measurement for each type of transaction. These rules often represent a compromise between the two primary qualities of accounting information—relevance and reliability. In the $10,000 land example, knowing even the approximate increase in value may be relevant to the user's decision. However, only the actual sale of the land provides reliable information on the increase in value. If accounting measurement of income in this example were to be based on the estimated market value, more relevant but less reliable information would be found in the statements.

Second, management can often make choices about the accounting measurement method to be used. For example, assets can be depreciated on an accelerated basis or on a straight-line basis. The choice affects the amount of net income and thus the **quality of earnings** for the firm. Earnings are generally considered to be of higher quality when management chooses accounting measurement rules that recognize revenues later, rather than sooner, and that recognize expenses earlier, rather than later. From this perspective, accelerated depreciation produces a higher-quality earnings number than does straight-line depreciation because greater amounts of depreciation are expensed in the early periods of the asset's life. Accelerated depreciation reduces income in the early periods of the asset's life as it reduces the amount to be depreciated in future statements. GAAP provides considerable flexibility in the computation of net income by allowing alternative measurement methods to be used.

Overview

Although measurement and recognition issues are critical, this chapter focuses on the display of revenues, expenses, gains, and losses after they have been recorded. Our focus is on *format issues:* Where on the income statement will interest income be shown? How should the gain on the sale of a division be reported? Is the settlement of an unusual lawsuit to be reported as an expense or as an extraordinary item?

Because of their importance in assessing future earnings and cash flows, the disclosure and reporting of several items are governed by specific accounting pronouncements. These items are:

- Extraordinary items.
- Unusual or infrequently occurring items.
- Discontinued operations.

These items are discussed later in this chapter. The next section considers aspects of income statement format that can be selected by the preparing firm's management.

CONCEPT REVIEW

1. Explain the difference between economic income and accounting income.
2. Explain the difference between measurement and recognition issues and format issues.
3. Identify two limitations of the transactions approach to accounting income.

FORMAT ISSUES NOT GOVERNED BY ACCOUNTING PRONOUNCEMENTS

Many format issues are not governed by accounting pronouncements, leaving companies leeway to pick policies that suit their individual circumstances.

Fiscal Year-End   A company must choose a fiscal year-end. Normally, companies try to pick a point that represents the low point in their seasonal pattern. This is to ensure that year-end adjustments and the annual report do not have to be prepared during their busy season. However, there are other factors to consider. For example, having the same year-end as other companies in the industry facilitates comparisons. Companies who are part of a corporate group prefer to have the same year-end as their parent to allow consolidation.

Many businesses pick the calendar year as a fiscal year. According to *Financial Reporting in Canada,* a survey of 300 public Canadian companies, 61% use a December 31 year-end. The rest are fairly evenly divided among the remaining months.

Reporting Period Length and Composition   Another basic issue to decide is the length of the reporting period. Annual reports are the norm, as companies are expected to use a 12-month period. They may use the operating cycle if the operating cycle is longer than a year. The 12-month period facilitates preparation of required annual reports to shareholders and securities commissions.

Many companies are anxious to include, instead of twelve months, the same specific number of weeks in each set of financial statements. These companies typically define their reporting period as 52 weeks. This improves year-to-year trend analysis, especially of sales volume. For example, Loblaw Companies Ltd., a major grocery chain, uses a 52-week reporting period. Every so often, it must include 53 weeks in the reporting period so as to avoid moving its year-end far from a particular target date.

Reporting Currency   Companies must also determine the reporting currency used to report to shareholders. Normally, one would assume that a Canadian company, reporting with Canadian GAAP, would report in Canadian dollars. This is the norm, but it is not required. Although Canadian GAAP must always be followed, any reporting currency can be used. Why would a Canadian company choose to report in, say, U.S. dollars? One reason might be that a company's major user groups—shareholders and/or lenders—may be in the United States. Since these users perform analyses and comparisons in U.S. dollars, it is obvious that U.S. dollar reports would be more useful to them. Another reason might be that the company undertakes much of its business in U.S. dollars and keeps its records in U.S. dollars.

Display   The manner in which accounting information is displayed in an income statement may influence the reader's interpretation of the information. Positioning of items and other issues of display can confuse or clarify.

EXHIBIT 4-2
Single-Step Format—Income
Statement

> **BAILEY RETAIL COMPANY**
> **Income Statement**
> **For the Year Ended December 31, 1995**
>
> | | |
> |---|---:|
> | Revenues and gains: | |
> | Sales (less returns and allowances of $20,000) . . . . | $670,000 |
> | Rent revenue . . . . | 1,200 |
> | Interest and dividend revenue . . . . | 4,800 |
> | Gain on sale of operational assets . . . . | 6,000 |
> | Total revenues and gains . . . . | 682,000 |
> | Expenses and losses: | |
> | Cost of goods sold* . . . . | 264,000 |
> | Distribution expense* . . . . | 153,500 |
> | General and administrative expense* . . . . | 73,500 |
> | Depreciation and amortization expense . . . . | 54,000 |
> | Interest expense . . . . | 6,000 |
> | Loss on sale of investments . . . . | 5,000 |
> | Income tax expense ($126,000 × .30)† . . . . | 37,800 |
> | Total expenses and losses . . . . | 593,800 |
> | Operating income, before extraordinary items . . . . | 88,200 |
> | Extraordinary items: | |
> | Loss due to earthquake . . . . $10,000 | |
> | Less: Income tax saving ($10,000 × .30) . . . . 3,000 | 7,000 |
> | Net income . . . . | $ 81,200 |
> | EPS of common shares (20,000 shares outstanding): | |
> | Income before extraordinary item ($88,200 ÷ 20,000) . . . . . . | $4.41 |
> | Extraordinary loss ($7,000 ÷ 20,000) . . . . | (.35) |
> | Net income ($81,200 ÷ 20,000) . . . . | $4.06 |
>
> * These expenses may be detailed in the statement or condensed. Sometimes they are detailed separately in the disclosure notes to the financial statements.
>
> † Assumed average income tax rate, 30%. The income before income taxes (and before the extraordinary item) of $126,000 is determined as revenues ($682,000) less expenses to this part of the statement ($556,000).

General Formats of the Income Statement

Except for extraordinary items and discontinued operations, GAAP does not specify a standard format for organizing and presenting the elements of income on the income statement. Revenue, expense, gain, and loss items are organized in the income statement in two general ways: the single-step format and the multiple-step format.

Single-Step Format   The single-step format uses only two broad section classifications: a revenues and gains section and an expenses and losses section. It is a single-step statement because only one step is involved in computing and displaying operating income (also labelled as "income from continuing operations"). If the company has items specifically requiring separate reporting, such as discontinued operations or extraordinary items, these are reported using additional steps.

Exhibit 4-2 shows a single-step income statement for the Bailey Retail Company. It includes an extraordinary item, which adds a second subtotal to the format. In practice, numerous variations of the single-step format exist. For example, revenue items, such as interest income or investment income, are sometimes netted against related expenses. The key characteristic of a single-step statement is that only two broad classifications are used in determining the earnings from continuing operations.

Multiple-Step Format   The multiple-step format provides several classifications and intermediate subtotal measures of income. The multiple-step format typically distinguishes among various operations and activities that affect income. Use of the multiple-step format is common among public companies.

A typical multiple-step income statement would contain the following components:

I. **Operations section**   Includes the revenues and expenses of the company's primary operations.

   A. **Revenue (sales)**   A single item or a subsection that presents various revenue sources, sometimes including information on discounts, allowances, returns, and other details.

   B. **Cost of goods sold or of services provided**   Presents the direct costs of goods sold or costs of services provided in generating the revenues. Details on how these figures were determined can be provided directly on the face of the statement or in notes to the financial statements.

   Gross margin, or **gross profit,** is the difference between revenues and cost of goods sold. The gross margin percentage also provides an interesting piece of information to the company's competitors, who have access to this public financial report. For this reason, many companies conceal it by grouping cost of goods sold with other expenses.

   C. **Selling expenses**   Presents information on the expenses incurred by the company in its efforts to generate revenues. It includes salaries and marketing expenses, costs of delivering goods, and overhead items allocated to the sales-generating process.

   D. **General and administrative expenses**   Presents information on the administrative expenses of the company. It usually would include expenses related to personnel, accounting, and finance activities, operating costs of the company headquarters, and similar items.

   E. **Other operating expenses**   If a company has other operating expenses not included in the above classifications that management feels are important to identify separately, such expenses would be included here. Other expenses often include items such as research, development, and amortization expenses. Abitibi-Price, for example, reported depreciation and depletion at this point on its income statement. (See Exhibit 4–1.)

   A subtotal is often computed by deducting the above expenses from revenues or gross margin. The caption found on this subtotal is usually "income (or loss) from continuing operations," "operating income," or "operating profit."

II. **Nonoperations section**   This subsection includes income and expense items that are routine and ordinary but not components of the company's operations. Examples are interest income or expense, royalty income, dividend income, and equity in the earnings of joint ventures or unconsolidated affiliated companies. This section may also contain other revenues, gains, losses, and expenses that are unusual in nature and not expected to repeat.

III. **Other possible sections**   Occasionally, firms will display non-controlling (minority) interest in earnings or equity in the earnings of investees at this point on the statement. These items are shown separately because they arise from a different source than the operating activities of the company and receive different tax treatment. Non-controlling (minority) interest in earnings is a deduction from income that results when a company prepares financial statements combining itself with one or more additional companies that it controls, but in which it does not have a 100% ownership interest. Basically, the controlling company includes all the subsidiary's income, but then deducts the non-controlling or minority portion. Equity in earnings of investees is a revenue item. It is the pro rata share of earnings of a second company in which the reporting company has an ownership interest that gives it significant influence over, but not control of, the investee company.

Abitibi-Price computes a subtotal after this step and labels it "loss from continuing operations before income taxes." (See Exhibit 4–1.)

IV. **Income tax expenses** This subsection presents the portion of provincial and federal income tax expenses applicable to the income recognized up to this point in the statement. Even single-step format statements often display income tax expense as a separate section, with income before income taxes as an intermediary step. If the firm has experienced a loss, income taxes are a recovery of prior years' taxes paid (a refund) and represent a reduction to the reported loss.

A subtotal is usually displayed after recognition of income tax expense. If there are no subsequent subsections, this subtotal is labelled "net earnings" or "net income." If there are subsequent subsections, this intermediate amount is labelled so as to reflect these remaining subsections. Thus, Abitibi-Price, in Exhibit 4–1, calls this subtotal "Loss from continuing operations" since the results of discontinued operations follow. Extraordinary items, if any, would also follow.

Many of the above sections are found in a typical multiple-step statement, but the presentation format of this information is not specified in GAAP. Firms can alter the order of listing or grouping of the above items in a wide variety of ways.

The presentation of two special items found in some, but not all, income statements is specifically governed by accounting pronouncements. These items must be reported as separate components in the income statement, regardless of whether the company is reporting in a single-step or multiple-step format:

V. **Discontinued operations** Presents gains or losses, net of income taxes, resulting from the disposition of a segment of the business. Accounting for discontinued operations is governed by Section 3475 of the *CICA Handbook*.

VI. **Extraordinary items** Presents gains and losses, net of income taxes, resulting from extraordinary events. The criteria and reporting requirements for extraordinary items are specified in Section 3480 of the *CICA Handbook*.

Finally, firms must present earnings-per-share information on the face of the income statement. This is required by Section 3500 of the *CICA Handbook*. Computation of earnings per share is covered in detail in Chapter 22.

A multiple-step income statement, using the data from Exhibit 4–2, is presented in Exhibit 4–3. In this example, the multiple-step statement presents three intermediate subtotals not found on the single-step statement:

1. Gross margin (also called gross profit).
2. Income from operations.
3. Income before tax and extraordinary items.

Abitibi-Price follows essentially a multiple-step format in Exhibit 4–1. While it does not calculate a separate subtotal for gross profit, there are intermediate subtotals on the income statement for the loss from continuing operations, before and after various specific expense categories, and before and after tax.

Exhibits 4–1 and 4–3 contain typical classifications for a multiple-step format statement. Other formats can and should be used in operating environments where different but important relationships between revenues and expenses need to be disclosed. For example, a firm that produces and sells both goods and services might show two gross profit figures, one for activities involving the manufacturing and sale of goods and one for its service activities.

The accounting literature provides little guidance on when it is appropriate to use a single-step or a multiple-step format. The single-step format has the advantage of

EXHIBIT 4–3
Multiple-Step Format—
Income Statement

BAILEY RETAIL COMPANY
Income Statement
For the Year Ended December 31, 1995

Sales revenue			$690,000
Less: Sales returns and allowances			20,000
Net sales			670,000
Cost of goods sold:			
Beginning inventory (periodic system)		$ 52,000	
Purchases of inventory	$268,000		
Freight-in	1,200		
Cost of purchases	269,200		
Less: Purchase returns and allowances	2,700	266,500	
Total goods available for sale		318,500	
Less: Ending inventory		54,500	
Cost of goods sold			264,000
Gross margin on sales			406,000
Operating expenses:			
Distribution expense*		153,500	
General and administrative expense*		73,500	
Depreciation and amortization expense		54,000	
Total operating expenses			281,000
Income from operations†			125,000
Other revenues and gains:			
Rent revenue	1,200		
Interest and dividend revenue	4,800		
Gain on sale of operational assets	6,000	12,000	
Other expenses and losses:			
Interest expense	6,000		
Loss on sale of investments	5,000	11,000	1,000
Income before income tax and extraordinary items			126,000
Income tax expense ($126,000 × .30)‡			37,800
Income before extraordinary items			88,200
Extraordinary item:			
Loss due to earthquake		10,000	
Less: Income tax saving ($10,000 × .30)		3,000	7,000
Net income			$ 81,200
EPS of common shares (20,000 shares outstanding):			
Income before extraordinary item			
($88,200 ÷ 20,000)			$4.41
Extraordinary loss ($7,000 ÷ 20,000)			(.35)
Net income ($81,200 ÷ 20,000)			$4.06

* These expenses may be detailed in the statement or condensed. Sometimes they are detailed or reported separately in the disclosure notes to the financial statements.

† Also variously labelled earnings from operations and operating income.

‡ Assumed average income tax rate, 30%.

simplicity and avoids the need to develop names for intermediate classifications. The multiple-step format is potentially more informative to decision makers because it highlights important relationships and intermediate subtotals in the report. Advocates of the multiple-step format believe that there are important relationships in revenue and expense data and that the income statement is more useful when these relationships are explicitly shown.

EXHIBIT 4–4   Section 1520 of the *CICA Handbook*

income statement

GENERAL ACCOUNTING—SECTION **1520**

▶ The income statement should present fairly the results of operations for the period.   .01

▶ The income statement should distinguish the following: .02
(a) Income or loss before discontinued operations and extraordinary items. (See paragraph 1520.03.)
(b) Results of discontinued operations.
(c) Income or loss before extraordinary items.
(d) Extraordinary items.
(e) Net income or loss for the period.
(f) Earnings per share, when and as appropriate.

[JAN. 1990]

▶ In arriving at the income or loss before discontinued operations   .03
and extraordinary items. the income statement should distinguish at least the following items: [1]
(a) Revenue recognized.   [OCT. 1986]
(b) Income from investments, disclosing income from (i) companies subject to significant influence, (ii) joint ventures, (iii) other affiliated companies, and (iv) portfolio investments, including all other investments. Income calculated by the equity method should be separately disclosed for each of the above groups.

[JAN. 1992]

(c) Finance income from direct financing or sales-type leases.
[JAN. 1979]
(d) Income from operating leases.
[JAN. 1979]
(e) Government assistance credited direct to income.
[SEPT. 1975]
(f) The amount charged for amortization of capital assets. Disclosure should be made of the methods and rates used in such computations. The amount of any write down of a capital asset should also be disclosed. Where they are significant, disclosure of separate amounts would be desirable.

[DEC. 1990]

---

[1] Some of these items may be set out more readily in notes to the financial statements or in attached schedules. Where this is done the income statement caption which contains these items should be identified.

income statement

(g) The amount charged for amortization of property under a capital lease. The amount should be disclosed separately or as part of amortization expense for capital assets.
[DEC. 1990]
(h) The amount charged for amortization of deferred charges (except the amortization of debt discount and issue expenses included with interest expense). Disclosure should be made of the basis of amortization.
[DEC. 1974]
(i) The amount of research and development costs charged to expense for the period. The amount charged for amortization of deferred development costs should be separately disclosed.
[AUG. 1978]
(j) Interest expense, segregating interest on indebtedness initially incurred for a term of more than one year (including the amortization of debt discount or premium and issue expenses) and other interest.
(k) Interest expense related to capital lease obligations. The amount should be disclosed separately or as part of interest expense on indebtedness initially incurred for a term of more than one year.
[JAN. 1979]
(l) Revenue, expenses, gains or losses resulting from items that do not have all of the characteristics of extraordinary items but result from transactions or events that are not expected to occur frequently over several years, or do not typify normal business activities of the entity.
[JAN. 1990]
(m) Income taxes.
(n) Non-controlling interest in income or loss before discontinued operations and extraordinary items.
[JAN. 1990]

.04 Additional desirable information in the income statement includes:

(a) the amount of income from contingent rentals;

(b) the amount of income from sub-lease rentals;

(c) the amount of cost of goods sold;

(d) other major operating expenses, such as selling and administrative expenses;

(e) the amount of operating rental expense;

(f) the amount of contingent rental expense;

(g) The amount of foreign currency gain or loss included in income.

CONCEPT REVIEW

1. How might interest income be presented differently in a single-step versus a multiple-step income statement?
2. How would an extraordinary gain be shown differently in a single-step versus a multiple-step income statement?
3. What characteristics of a firm might be considered in deciding whether to report using a single- or multiple-step format?

FORMAT ISSUES GOVERNED BY ACCOUNTING PRONOUNCEMENTS

Exhibit 4–3 illustrates a multiple-step income statement that contains a fair bit of detail in the expense and revenue categories. Some expenses, such as general and administrative expenses, have been grouped. Management has considerable flexibility in presenting revenue, expense, gain, and loss items in the income statement. What dictates the decision to group an item or disclose it separately? Grouping reduces the complexity of the statement, but it may also reduce its predictive value and the information content of the statement. Grouping also hides sensitive information from competitors and other users. It's not an easy decision.

The *CICA Handbook* specifies the minimum information content of the income statement in Section 1520. This section has been reproduced in Exhibit 4–4 in its entirety. Paragraphs and items in italics are recommendations and must be followed. Paragraphs and items in regular type provide background information or desirable practices. Desirable practices are suggestions that do not have to be followed. The date after each recommendation or part of a recommendation indicates the date on which the item became effective.

Refer to paragraph .03 in Exhibit 4–4, which lists the minimum information content of the income statement. This information includes revenue (*a*), investment income of various types (*b*), lease income (*c* and *d*), and revenue from government assistance (*e*). Disclosed expenses include depreciation and amortization (*f*, *g*, and *h*), research and development expenses (*i*), interest expenses (*j* and *k*), unusual items (*l*), income taxes (*m*), and non-controlling, or minority, interest in income (*n*).

The list is probably as interesting for the things it leaves out as for the things it includes. There is no minimum disclosure *requirement* for major expense categories such as cost of goods sold, or selling, general, and administrative expenses. Many companies follow the minimum disclosure requirements and present extremely aggregated income statements.

Specific accounting pronouncements govern the presentation of several items:

1. Extraordinary gains and losses.
2. Unusual or infrequent gains and losses.
3. Discontinued operations.

Intraperiod Tax Allocation   These items are reported separately on the income statement. All except unusual or infrequent gains and losses are shown net of any related tax effect. *Net of related tax effect* means the tax consequences of the item have been determined and the reported amount is shown after these tax effects have been adjusted for. Determining this amount is the problem of **intraperiod tax allocation.** *Intra* means that the allocation is within the period and across the items shown in the income statement. **Interperiod tax allocation** is the allocation of tax expense to different reporting periods. Interperiod tax allocation is covered in Chapter 17.

To demonstrate intraperiod tax allocation, consider the following situation for the Calgary Storage Company. Sales for 1995 total $1 million and expenses before income taxes total $700,000. During 1995, the company experiences an extraordinary loss of $200,000 when an earthquake destroys several of the company's uninsured warehouses. Assume that the income tax rate is 40% and that the $200,000 earthquake loss is deductible for income tax purposes. Calgary Storage Company's income statement with and without intraperiod tax allocation is as shown on page 126.

In the column without intraperiod tax allocation, the tax expense is shown at the actual amount that will be paid, or 40% of the $100,000 taxable income (revenues of $1 million less expenses of $700,000 and less the loss of $200,000). In the column with intraperiod tax allocation, the tax effects of the two activities (operations and the earthquake loss) are shown separately. Thus, the income tax expense that would be paid if there were no loss from the earthquake would be 40% of $300,000, or $120,000. The tax effect of the earthquake loss reduces income tax for the period by 40% of the loss, or $80,000. The $80,000 tax savings resulting from the loss is subtracted from the gross loss of $200,000 to arrive at the after-tax amount of $120,000.

Canadian accounting standards require intraperiod tax allocation, as illustrated, for extraordinary items and for all other items reported separately after income from continuing operations. In Exhibit 4–1, discontinued operations are reported at their net of related tax effect amounts for Abitibi-Price.

CALGARY STORAGE COMPANY
Income Statement
For the Year Ended December 31, 1995

	Without Intraperiod Tax Allocation	With Intraperiod Tax Allocation
Sales.	$1,000,000	$1,000,000
Expenses.	700,000	700,000
Income from operations	300,000	300,000
Income tax expense:		
On operations ($300,000)(.40).		120,000
On taxable income ($100,000)(.40).	40,000	
Income before extraordinary loss	260,000	180,000
Extraordinary item:		
Loss from earthquake damage:		
Gross amount.	(200,000)	
Net of tax ($200,000)(.60)		(120,000)
Net income.	$ 60,000	$ 60,000

Reporting Extraordinary Items

It is sometimes difficult to determine whether an item is extraordinary. Before Section 3480 of the *CICA Handbook* was issued, there were inconsistencies across firms, and even over time for given firms, in the classification of items as ordinary or extraordinary. Some firms took gains that should have been classified as extraordinary and reported them in continuing operations, thereby increasing income from continuing operations. Alternatively, some firms classified all large losses as extraordinary. As a result, these firms reported a higher income from continuing operations. After the 1990 accounting standard provided specific criteria for extraordinary items, their incidence plummeted. In 1989, a survey of 300 public Canadian companies revealed 81 companies with extraordinary items; by 1992, there were only 3.

In Section 3480, the *CICA Handbook* identifies extraordinary items as those resulting from transactions or events that have *all* of the following characteristics:

1. They are not expected to occur frequently over several years.
2. They do not typify the normal business activities of the entity.
3. They do not depend primarily on decisions or determinations by management or owners.

The following examples are extraordinary items:
- The expropriation of land and buildings for a highway.
- The destruction of a large portion of a wheat crop by a tornado.
- An explosion in a nuclear reactor resulting in high-level radioactive emissions.

Gains or losses resulting from the risks inherent in an entity's normal business activities would not be considered extraordinary. The environment in which the firm operates is a consideration in determining whether an underlying event or transaction is abnormally and significantly different from the ordinary and typical activities of the business. A firm's environment includes such factors as the characteristics of the industry or industries in which it operates, the geographical location of its operations, and the nature and extent of governmental regulations. An event or transaction may be unusual for one firm, but not for another, because of differences in their respective environments. For example, the following two transactions are similar, but the first is to be treated as extraordinary while the second is not:

Extraordinary A tobacco grower's crops are destroyed by a hailstorm. Severe damage from hailstorms in the locality where the tobacco grower operates are rare.

Ordinary A citrus grower's crop is damaged by frost. Frost damage is normally experienced every three or four years.

The first situation is considered extraordinary because, given the environment in which the tobacco grower operates, hailstorms are very infrequent. In the second situation, taking into account the environment in which the company operates, the criterion of infrequency of occurrence would not be met. The history of losses by frost damage provides evidence that such damage may reasonably be expected to recur in the foreseeable future.

Section 3480 specifically identifies the following events that should not be considered as extraordinary because they are expected during the customary and continuing business activities of a firm:

- Losses and provisions for losses with respect to bad debts and inventories.
- Gains and losses from fluctuations in foreign exchange rates.
- Adjustments with respect to contract prices.
- Gains and losses from write-down or sale of property, plant, equipment, or other investments.
- Income tax reductions on utilization of prior period losses or reversal of previously recorded tax benefits. (Such reductions were once considered extraordinary and were a common example of an extraordinary item.)

Extraordinary items do not depend primarily on the decisions of managers or owners. A transaction would be considered to be outside the control of managers or owners if their decisions would not influence the transaction. For example, consider the following situations:

- A manufacturing concern sells the only land it owns. While this is an infrequent and unusual item, it results from a decision of managers or owners and thus any resulting gain or loss is considered not extraordinary.
- An airplane owned by the company is destroyed by a terrorist act. The item is infrequent, unusual, and not the result of a decision of managers or owners; any gain or loss, net of insurance proceeds, is an extraordinary item.
- A lawsuit is settled out of court. The settlement is clearly an action of management or owners, but the settlement itself is a secondary event and should not dictate classification. The nature of the event causing the lawsuit must dictate whether or not the item is extraordinary.

Sometimes, extraordinary items are described as "acts of God or government." It's a useful decision rule to remember—events such as tornados, fires, floods, expropriations, and so on, if not frequent, are normally the best examples of extraordinary items. Another decision rule is that extraordinary items are *rare*.

As is illustrated above for the Calgary Storage Company, extraordinary items are reported in the income statement under a separate classification and are net of any income tax effect. If subject to income tax, an extraordinary gain increases income tax and an extraordinary loss reduces income tax. In both cases, the extraordinary gain or loss is adjusted for its tax effects and reported net of tax. Extraordinary items are usually explained in disclosure notes.

There is still considerable room for judgment in the classification of transactions as extraordinary. One item is litigation settlements. In 1991, for example, Eastman Kodak paid Polaroid $924 million to settle a patent infringement suit. This was a large, material amount for both companies. Should it be reported as an extraordinary gain for Polaroid and an extraordinary loss for Eastman Kodak? As it turned out, neither company reported the transaction as extraordinary. They both, however, reported it as an unusual item among operating items, having decided that it represented a normal business activity.

EXHIBIT 4–5
Extracts from the Alberta
Natural Gas Company
Financial Statements

	Year Ended December 31	
	1992	1991
	(amounts in thousands)	
Income from continuing operations	$17,799	$15,659
Discontinued operations	(20,075)	(57,789)
Extraordinary items	20,181	(2,490)
Net income (loss)	$17,905	$(44,620)

Note 13 Extraordinary Items:

A fire and explosion caused substantial damage to the Sterlington facility on May 1, 1991. [The Company] maintained insurance to mitigate much of the financial impact from the resulting property damage, business interruption and liability claims. A US $150 million insurance settlement was reached in 1992.

Extraordinary items have been recorded for certain non-recurring consequences of the fire and explosion. These consequences include an "involuntary conversion" book gain due to insurance proceeds received exceeding the historical net book value of the damaged plant assets.

	1992	1991
	(amounts in thousands)	
Involuntary conversion gain	$56,733	$ 8,368
Non-reimbursed expenses and insurance deductibles	(20,429)	(7,823)
Income and other taxes	(16,123)	(3,035)
Extraordinary items	$20,181	$(2,490)

Although the amount of a gain or loss is not a factor in determining whether an item should be reported as extraordinary, only material extraordinary gains and losses must be reported separately. Extraordinary items considered immaterial in amount can be reported as a component of continuing operations. Unfortunately, there is little guidance in determining what is material. Some companies separately report only those extraordinary gains or losses that are less than 1% of income before extraordinary items.

An interesting case is presented in Exhibit 4–5. This is an example of an extraordinary item caused by fire and explosion, clearly the type of natural disaster that would be truly extraordinary. Exhibit 4–5 also represents an example of the typical note disclosure explaining an extraordinary item.

Reporting Unusual or Infrequent Gains and Losses

Some events or transactions are not extraordinary but should be disclosed separately on the income statement to emphasize their nature as unusual or infrequent. For example, assume a timber company has a material write-down of its pulp and paper inventory and timber resources (a capital asset) due to prevailing low prices in the timber industry. The write-down has been determined by management but caused by outside events. It is certainly infrequent, since it is the first time in the company's 40-year history that such a write-down has been necessary. However, risks associated with price fluctuations in a natural resource market are surely a typical business risk in the timber industry. The item is not extraordinary.

How should the company report it?

Section 1520, paragraph .03(l) of the *CICA Handbook* (see Exhibit 4–4) requires companies to report separately:

Revenues, expenses, gains or losses resulting from items that do not have all the characteristics of extraordinary items but result from transactions or events that are not expected to occur frequently over several years, or do not typify normal business activities of the entity.

Such items should *not* be shown net of tax.

For example, the unusual items shown on the Abitibi-Price income statement (Exhibit 4–1) are described in the notes as follows:

	1993	1992
		(amounts in
4. Unusual Items		millions)
Cost of employee restructuring programmes	$18.7	$ 2.8
Charges relating to the permanent closure of the Thunder Bay		
newsprint mill	3.7	60.0
Other	(0.8)	2.0
	$21.6	$64.8

Sears Canada Ltd. reported the following unusual items:

	Year Ended December 31	
	1992	1991
	(amounts in	
10. Unusual Items	millions)	
Severance costs related to the reorganization and simplification of various functions. The 1992 expense includes a reserve of $20 million for planned restructuring to occur in 1993, mainly for the conversion of Company operated catalogue selling units to independent local ownership.	$(49.4)	$(3.7)
Expenses associated with consolidating Toronto and Halifax catalogue facilities in Belleville, Ontario, excluding severance of $11.0 million included above.	(6.5)	(4.3)
Restructuring reserve related to planned 1993 conversion of catalogue selling units and closure of Together! stores..	(7.2)	—
Gain on sale of properties.	16.9	—
Total unusual items	$(46.2)	$(8.0)

Obviously, restructuring costs are common unusual items. The category is wide open to management discretion, though: Any item deemed "unusual" may be reported in this fashion. Remember, unusual items are shown as a separate line item, before tax, in a separate category after "income from operations." Refer back to the Abitibi-Price example in Exhibit 4–1.

> **|CONCEPT REVIEW**
>
> 1. What criteria are used to determine if an item is extraordinary? Unusual?
> 2. Is tornado damage an extraordinary item?
> 3. If a company has a $20,000 extraordinary loss and the tax rate is 40%, at what net amount would the extraordinary item be reported? What if the item were unusual instead of extraordinary?

Reporting Discontinued Operations

The sale or disposal of a segment of a business has important implications for predicting future income and cash flow. In a troubled economy, rationalization and restructuring of business operations and the sale or windup of business segments are common occurrences. Financial statement users need to be able to segment continuing from non-continuing results to improve predictions. Section 3475 of the *CICA Handbook* provides explicit reporting guidelines governing the disclosure of a segment of a business that is sold, abandoned, or otherwise disposed of. Specifically, two components of income resulting from **discontinued operations** must be disclosed separately on the face of the income statement:

1. Gain or loss from disposal of a segment of a business, including the income or loss from operating the business during any phaseout period.
2. Results of operations for the discontinued segment before the disposal decision.

The effects of any discontinued business are displayed on the income statement, net of tax, after income from continuing operations but before extraordinary items.

Companies have leeway in deciding what constitutes a business segment for these disclosures. Normally, a segment would be operationally distinct from other activities of the enterprise. The following are examples of segments that, if discontinued, would require disclosure as a discontinued operation:

- A manufacturer eliminates a significant and distinguishable product line.
- A tobacco and consumer products company sells its interest in an oil and gas joint venture, its only investment in the oil and gas industry.
- A food distributor who normally sells its product directly to restaurants sells its wholesale division, which sold products to retail outlets.

It is important to separately show the results of operations for discontinued operations separately on the income statement, up to the **measurement date.** This gain or loss is shown net of tax. The measurement date is the date on which the company's management adopts a formal plan to sell or wind up the segment. If there is no plan announced before disposal, then the measurement date is the disposal date. This disclosure of operating results is necessary so that users of financial statements can use the income statement for predictive purposes and project the operating results of the company without the division that is to be discontinued.

The gain or loss on disposal of a segment has two components. First, it includes the actual or estimated gain or loss on operating the segment between the date that management decides to discontinue the operation (the measurement date) and the actual date of disposal. This operating gain or loss is considered to be part of the gain or loss on the discontinuance decision, not a regular operating result. Second, the gain or loss on the sale or other disposal of the assets is included. If there is expected to be an overall loss on the decision, the loss must be accrued on the measurement date. If there is a net gain expected, it may only be recognized when realized. This is an example of conservatism in the choice of accounting practice.

Both the results of operations up to the measurement date and the gain or loss from discontinued operations are shown *net of tax* on the income statement.

A discussion of the more technical issues related to reporting discontinued operations is found in Appendix 4B.

To illustrate discontinued operations disclosure, assume that Gulf & Eastern, a large consumer products company, sold its Automatic Transmission Diagnostic Centers division for $120 million on August 1, 1995. The book value of the assets sold was $140 million, and the assets were immediately transferred to the buyer. The division had operating income before tax of $10 million in 1994 and a loss of $5 million for the first seven months of 1995. Gulf & Eastern's continuing operations earned $70 million before taxes in 1994 and $60 million in 1995. The tax rate for both the gain on sale of the division assets and for operating income or losses is 40%. Comparative income statements in the 1995 annual report shown on page 131 would show this material after the usual presentation leading up to income from continuing operations before taxes.

The pretax loss is the book value ($140 million) less the sales price of the disposed division ($120 million), or a loss of $20 million. With a tax rate of 40% there is a tax saving of $0.40 \times \$20$ million, or $8 million, and thus the net after-tax loss is $12 million. In this example, there is no income or loss during a phaseout operation since

GULF & EASTERN
Income Statements
For the Years Ending December 31 (extracts)

	1995	1994
	(amounts in millions)	
Income from continuing operations before taxes	$60	$70
Income tax expense	24	28
Income from continuing operations	36	42
Discontinued operations:		
Income (loss) from discontinued operations division, net of tax savings of $2 in 1995 and tax expense of $4 in 1994	(3)	6
Loss on disposal of Automatic Transmission Diagnostic Centers division, net of tax savings of $8	(12)	—
Net income	$21	$48

the division is transferred to the buyer on the measurement date. The amounts reported as income (loss) from operations of the discontinued division are for periods up to the disposition, net of related tax effects.

Full disclosure of a discontinued operation must include the following:

1. Identification and description of the business segment discontinued.
2. The measurement date and the actual or projected disposal date.
3. The actual or expected manner of disposition.
4. A description of the assets, by major classification, of the discontinued segment.
5. Revenue attributable to the discontinued segment for the reporting period.

Glenayre Electronics provided appropriate note disclosures in its 1992 financial statements (See Exhibit 4–6).

CONCEPT REVIEW

1. Why is separate disclosure of discontinued operations important to users?
2. What are the components of discontinued operations disclosures on the income statement?
3. What note disclosure is necessary for discontinued operations?

Earnings per Share

Earnings per share (EPS) is important to decision makers because it relates the income of the company to a single common share, helps investors make relevant profit performance comparisons among companies with different numbers of common shares outstanding, and makes relative profitability comparisons possible between companies. Section 3500 of the *CICA Handbook* requires companies to report per share data on the income statement for both income before extraordinary items and net income.[5] Although reporting per share amounts for the gain or loss on discontinued operations and for gains or losses on extraordinary items is optional, most firms also show these EPS amounts.

Earnings per share is computed by dividing reported income available to the holders of common shares by the average number of common shares outstanding

---

[5] "Earnings per Share," Section 3500 of the *CICA Handbook*, does not require reporting of EPS for extraordinary items. EPS for income before extraordinary items and net income are required. This textbook usually illustrates reporting EPS for all three amounts for completeness and because most companies follow this practice.

Discontinued operations

The Company discontinued its manufacturing operations effective November 10, 1992, its Canadian cellular operations effective May 31, 1991, its U.S. mobile data subsidiary June 28, 1991 and its Canadian paging and U.S. distribution operations effective September 30, 1991. The income from discontinued operations has been reported separately in the financial statements and consists of the following:

	1992	1991
	(amounts in thousands)	
Operations to measurement date (net of income taxes—$622,000 in 1992; $1,405,000 in 1991)	$17,696	$8,606
Gain (losses) after measurement date (net of income taxes recovered—($1,147,000) in 1992; nil in 1991)	52,001	(6,529)
	$69,697	$2,077

In 1992, net sales of the discontinued operations were $102,546,000; in 1991, $114,455,000.

The financial statements include the following net assets of the discontinued operations which are undisposed of at year end.

	1992	1991
	(amounts in thousands)	
Current assets	$ 449	$42,878
Property and equipment	1,840	15,270
Agreements and notes receivable	—	848
Goodwill and licence	965	30,156
	3,254	89,152
Current liabilities	(322)	(23,852)
Long-term debt	—	(21,203)
Net assets	$2,932	$44,097

during the year. For computation of EPS on common shares, income must be reduced by any preferred share dividend claims since such dividends are not available to common share owners and have not been subtracted in computing income. Exhibit 4–7 illustrates the calculation of EPS in three separate cases:[6]

Case A This relatively simple case involves only common and preferred shares with no changes in the number of common shares outstanding during the year and no extraordinary items on the income statement. In this case, calculation of EPS involves dividing net income applicable to common shares (which is net income less the preferred dividends) by the number of common shares outstanding.

Case B A slight complexity occurs when there is an extraordinary gain or loss on the income statement. In this case, EPS amounts are calculated and reported for (1) income before extraordinary items, (2) extraordinary items, and (3) net income.

Case C More complexity arises when there is a change during the period in the number of common shares outstanding because of the issuance of common shares or

[6] Under certain conditions (i.e., complex capital structures), Section 3500 requires two presentations of EPS on the income statement: basic EPS and fully diluted EPS. Basic EPS relates income to the company's outstanding common shares. Fully diluted EPS relates income to the maximum number of common shares that could conceivably become outstanding if all current commitments to issue shares (e.g., on conversion or exercise options) were honored. Therefore, fully diluted EPS is an estimate of the company's minimum EPS under its existing capital structure.

EXHIBIT 4–7
Calculation of Earnings per
Share: Three Cases

Assumptions	Calculating and Reporting EPS
Case A 30,000 common shares outstanding throughout the year; net income for the year, $106,000; dividends applicable to preferred shares, $10,000.	Net income applicable to common shares ($106,000 − $10,000) . . . . $96,000 Earnings per share ($96,000 ÷ 30,000 shares) . . . . . $ 3.20

Case B
30,000 common shares outstanding throughout the year; income applicable to common shares, before extraordinary item, $96,000; extraordinary loss less applicable tax saving, $21,000
	Income before extraordinary item $96,000
	Extraordinary loss (less applicable tax saving) 21,000
	Net income $75,000
	
	Earnings per share:
	    Income before extraordinary item . . . . $ 3.20
	    Extraordinary loss . . . . (.70)
	    Net income . . . . $ 2.50
	
	$96,000 ÷ 30,000 shares = $3.20
	($21,000) ÷ 30,000 shares = ($0.70)
	$75,000 ÷ 30,000 shares = $2.50

Case C
30,000 common shares outstanding from January 1 through April 1, on which date an additional 10,000 common shares were issued; other data as in Case B.
	Income before extraordinary item $96,000
	Extraordinary loss (less applicable tax saving) 21,000
	Net income $75,000
	
	Earnings per share:
	    Income before extraordinary item . . . . $ 2.56
	    Extraordinary loss . . . . (.56)
	    Net income . . . . $ 2.00
	
	Calculation of weighted-average number of shares:

Calculation of weighted-average number of shares:

Dates	Months	Shares	Weighted Shares
Jan. 1–Apr. 1	3	× 30,000 =	90,000
Apr. 1–Dec. 31	9	× 40,000 =	360,000
	12		450,000

Average: 450,000 ÷ 12 = 37,500
$96,000 ÷ 37,500 shares = $2.56
($21,000) ÷ 37,500 shares = ($0.56)
$75,000 ÷ 37,500 shares = $2.00

the purchase by the company of previously issued shares. This complexity requires calculation of the weighted-average number of shares outstanding during the year. New capital is included for the period the new shares are outstanding. The weighted average is divided into net income applicable to the common shares.

Additional complexities occur when a company has outstanding preferred shares or bonds that are convertible into common shares. These complexities involve the computation of fully diluted EPS. Chapter 22 is devoted to earnings per share calculations.

STATEMENT OF RETAINED EARNINGS

A statement of retained earnings (also called a retained earnings statement) is often presented as a supplement to the income statement and the balance sheet. Many companies instead present a *statement of owners' equity,* which shows all changes in owners' equity.

The purpose of the statement of retained earnings is to report all changes in retained earnings during the accounting period, to reconcile the beginning and ending balances of retained earnings, and to provide a connecting link between the income statement and the balance sheet. The ending balance of retained earnings is reported on the balance sheet as one element of owners' equity (see Chapter 5). The major components of a statement of retained earnings are:

1. Prior period adjustments.
2. Net income or loss for the period.
3. Dividends.
4. Other charges: capital transactions, appropriations, and restrictions.

Prior Period Adjustments

Prior period adjustments are reported on the statement of retained earnings. They do not flow through income. Current GAAP carefully defines prior period adjustments as those that have all four of the following characteristics. The items:

a. Are specifically identified with and directly related to the business activities of particular prior periods.
b. Are not attributable to economic events, occurring subsequent to the date of the financial statements for such prior periods.
c. Depend primarily on decisions or determinations by persons other than management or owners.
d. Could not be reasonably estimated prior to such decisions or determinations.[7]

Two examples of prior period adjustments are non-recurring settlements or adjustments of prior years' income tax following reassessment by Revenue Canada, and settlements of claims resulting from lawsuits. Correction of errors, while not strictly within the criteria listed above, are also accounted for in a fashion similar to prior period adjustments.

Prior period adjustments are given retroactive application, with full restatement of comparative financial statements. They are presented net of tax—that is, the opening balance of retained earnings is adjusted for the net amount of the prior period adjustment in the year that it is discovered. Opening retained earnings as restated are presented. Then, the comparative financial statements are adjusted to give effect to the prior period adjustment. In effect, the transaction is backed out of the current period and into the appropriate prior year.

A description of the prior period adjustment and its effect on the financial statements must be included in the disclosure notes.

To illustrate the recording of a retroactive adjustment for an error correction, assume that a machine that cost the Bailey Retail Company $10,000 (with a 10-year estimated useful life and no residual value) was purchased on January 1, 1992. Further, assume that the total cost was erroneously debited to an expense account in 1992. The error was discovered December 29, 1995. A correcting entry would be required in 1995. Assuming that any income tax effects are recorded separately, the entry is as follows:

December 29, 1995:

Machinery.	10,000	
Depreciation expense, straight-line (for 1995)	1,000	
Accumulated depreciation (1992 through 1995).		4,000
Error correction		7,000

The $7,000 retroactive adjustment corrects the January 1, 1995, retained earnings balance on a pretax basis. The balance is understated $7,000 before tax:

Understatement of 1992 income ($10,000 − $1,000).	$9,000
Overstatement of 1993 and 1994 income ($1,000 × 2).	(2,000)
Net pretax understatement	$7,000

---

[7] "Prior period adjustments," *CICA Handbook,* Section 3600, par. .03 (Toronto: CICA).

EXHIBIT 4–8
Retained Earnings Statement

BAILEY RETAIL COMPANY
R tained Earnings Statement
For the Year Ended December 31, 1995

Retained earnings, January 1, 1995, as previously reported (assumed)	$378,800
Correction of error (net of income tax of $2,100)	
(Note 6)	4,900
Retained earnings, January 1, 1995, as restated	383,700
Net income [See Exhibit 4–2 or Exhibit 4–3]	81,200
Cash dividends declared and paid during 1995 (assumed)	(30,000)
Retained earnings, December 31, 1995 (Note 7)	$434,900

Note 6. Error correction—During the year, the company discovered that an expenditure made in 1992 was incorrectly expensed. This error caused net income of that period to be understated and that of subsequent periods to be overstated. The adjustment of $4,900 (a $7,000 credit less income tax of $2,100) corrects the error.

Note 7. Restrictions—Of the $434,900 ending balance in retained earnings, $280,000 is restricted from dividend availability under the terms of the bond indenture. When the bonds are retired, the restriction will be removed.

Any income tax effect due to the error correction could be included in the entry or recorded separately. Assuming that the same error was made on the income tax return, the entry to record the income tax effect of the error, assuming a 30% income tax rate, would be as follows:

Error correction ($7,000 × .30)	2,100	
Income tax payable		2,100

The error correction account balance would be closed directly to retained earnings on December 31, 1995.

A prior period adjustment (net of its income tax effect) is reported on the statement of retained earnings as a *correction of the beginning balance* of retained earnings, as illustrated in Exhibit 4–8.

Reporting Accounting Changes

The retroactive effect of a change in accounting policy is also usually reflected on the retained earnings statement. The decision to change accounting policy is often forced on a company by changes in standards, but equally often, it is the result of a management decision. As such, it would not qualify as a prior period adjustment. Why, then, is it accorded treatment equivalent to a prior period adjustment? The answer is that comparability is greatly enhanced if the financial statements consistently use one set of accounting policies. Therefore, companies are encouraged to retroactively restate all prior years' results for a change in accounting policy.

Retroactive restatement is only applicable to accounting policy changes, one type of accounting change. In general, there are two types of accounting changes:

1. **Change in estimates** Estimates (such as are made in determining depreciation expense or bad debt expense) are frequently required in accounting. However, subsequent experience and additional information often make it possible to improve these estimates. For example, the estimated useful life of a machine in use (and depreciated) for six years might be changed from an original 10-year to 15-year estimated life because the machine has remained in good repair and will

be useful longer than originally expected. Changes in estimates are different from changes in accounting principle.

2. **Change in accounting policy** A change in circumstances or the development of a new accounting principle may necessitate a change in the recording and reporting approach for a particular transaction. For example, a company may change from straight-line depreciation to sum-of-the-years'-digits depreciation to conform to industry practice. This is a change from one acceptable principle to another acceptable principle.

A detailed discussion of accounting changes is delayed until Chapter 24. However, we review the reporting of changes in estimates and changes in accounting principles here as necessary background for more immediate topics.

Changes in Estimates Revisions of accounting estimates, such as useful lives or residual values of depreciable assets, the loss rates for bad debts and warranty costs, are changes in accounting estimates. As a company gains experience in such areas as depreciable assets, receivables, and warranties, it may develop a basis for revising one or more of its prior accounting estimates. Section 1506 of the *CICA Handbook* states that, in such instances, the prior accounting results are not to be disturbed. Instead, the new estimate should be used during the current and remaining periods. Thus, a change in estimate is made on a *prospective* (future-oriented) basis.

To illustrate the accounting for a change in estimate, assume that a machine that cost $24,000 is being depreciated on a straight-line basis over a 10-year estimated useful life with no residual value. Early in the seventh year, management, having had experience with the machine, determines that the total useful life will be 14 years (with zero residual value). Thus, the remaining life is eight years from the start of the year in which the revised estimate was made (year 7 in the example). The change in estimate does not require an entry to correct depreciation already recorded (years 1 to 6 in the example). Rather, new depreciation amounts will be recorded at the end of the current year (year 7) and each year during the remaining useful life of the asset. The new depreciation amounts, starting with the year of change, are based on the then *undepreciated* amounts of the asset and the new *remaining* useful life of the asset. To illustrate, the new depreciation amounts are computed and recorded as follows:

Computations (straight-line) of new annual depreciation:

Original cost.	$24,000
Accumulated depreciation to date of change ($24,000 × 6/10)	14,400
Difference—depreciated over eight years remaining life	$ 9,600
Annual depreciation over remaining life: ($9,600 ÷ 8 years)	$ 1,200

Journal entry to record year 7 depreciation expense:

Depreciation expense	1,200	
Accumulated depreciation, machinery		1,200

Section 1506 of the *CICA Handbook* suggests disclosure of changes in accounting estimates that are rare and unusual and that will affect financial statements of future periods.

Changes in Accounting Principle There are three different ways to reflect a change in accounting principle in the financial statements, according to Section 1506 of the *CICA Handbook*. This does not mean that companies can pick among the alternatives—each pertains to different circumstances. The three methods are (*a*) retroactive application, restatement of prior periods, (*b*) retroactive application, no restatement of prior periods, and (*c*) prospective application.

Retroactive Application, Restatement of Prior Periods Section 1506 of the *CICA Handbook* recommends that changes in accounting policy should be applied retroactively and comparative financial statements adjusted accordingly. The reporting guidelines are stated as follows:

a. The cumulative effect of the retroactive change in accounting policy is calculated and recorded as an adjustment to opening retained earnings. Opening retained earnings, as restated, are calculated. The disclosure of this item on the retained earnings statement is identical to the disclosure of a prior period adjustment.

b. Again as for a prior period adjustment, prior years' statements are adjusted for the new accounting policy and the effect of the accounting change is shown in all comparative financial statements. That is, if straight-line depreciation is now used, the comparative numbers for depreciation expense will be changed to straight-line amounts.

c. Disclosure of the change in policy must be made, complete with a description of the new policy, and the impact of the new policy on the financial statements (normally, the change in net assets and income). The fact that prior years' statements have been restated must also be disclosed.

Retroactive Application, No Restatement of Prior Periods   Occasionally, it is possible to determine the effect of an accounting change on the opening balances for a given year, but it is not possible (or not cost-effective) to determine the impact of the accounting change for individual prior years. For example, assume a company changes its inventory costing method from LIFO to FIFO. Data have been accumulated to determine the current year January 1 balance under FIFO. The difference between this amount and the previously reported LIFO balance represents the cumulative effect of the accounting change. But how much of that change related to last year? Two years ago? Ten years ago? The information is not available in the database to reconstruct inventory cost for the ending inventory of each prior year.

This is a practical problem, accorded a practical solution in Section 1506 of the *CICA Handbook*. In these cases, the cumulative effect of the change in accounting principle is reported on the retained earnings statement, but comparatives are not restated. The fact that prior years' financial statements have not been restated should be disclosed, in addition to a description of the accounting policy change and its impact on the financial statements (normally, the change in net assets and income).

Prospective Application   This is the method chosen to reflect the change of an accounting estimate. The company simply stops using one method, calculates the balances in the appropriate accounts, and begins to use the new method. Obviously, comparability is sacrificed. Prospective application is acceptable for changes to accounting policy only when the change in accounting policy is caused by a new accounting standard that specifically allows prospective application. Such permission is often given when standard setters decide that retroactive application would be impossible with existing data or extremely time-consuming and expensive. Companies may also use this reporting alternative if it is impossible to restate opening balances, as the effect of the accounting policy change clearly cannot be calculated in such cases. This prospective application is not deemed desirable by the AcSB, but it is all that is possible in certain cases.

If such an approach is used, the accounting policy change must be described, its impact on current statements (normally, the change in net assets and income) disclosed, and the use of prospective treatment disclosed.

Prospective treatment is also used for one more change in accounting policy. Standard setters became concerned about the large number of companies changing their depreciation policies, since this allocation often had a material impact on earnings and the appearance of income manipulation was overwhelming in certain cases. Therefore, the Handbook specifies that changes in accounting policy for depreciation caused by changed circumstances, new experience, or new information must be applied prospectively—that is, with no retroactive restatement (Section 1506, par. .23). On the other hand, if the change is made to comply with long-standing industry practice or is based on information that has always been available to the company, then the change should be made retroactively with full restatement.

To illustrate the reporting of changes in accounting principle, consider the following example. A company's management decides to change from accelerated to straight-line depreciation for its depreciable assets and has made the change to comply with industry practice. The difference between the accumulated depreciation under the accelerated method previously used and the depreciation that would have accumulated if the straight-line method had been used in all previous periods is $60,000. That is, depreciation expense has been $60,000 more using the accelerated method than would have been recorded using straight-line depreciation. Assume an income tax rate of 30%. The cumulative effect of the change in accounting principle, net of applicable income taxes, is $60,000 × .70, or $42,000. The entry to record the effect of the change in accounting principle is as follows:

Accumulated depreciation—machinery	60,000	
Cumulative effect of change in accounting principle		42,000
Deferred income tax		18,000

This is shown on the retained earnings statement as follows:

Opening retained earnings, as previously reported (assumed)	$400,000
Effect of change in accounting policy	42,000
Opening retained earnings, as restated	$442,000

Appropriate note disclosure should also be prepared.

Thus, the retained earnings statement will reflect the cumulative effect of a change in accounting policy for most policy changes. Retroactive application with full retroactive restatement is the preferable alternative. Retroactive application with no retroactive restatement will also be reflected on the retained earnings statement but reduces comparability and is less desirable. Prospective application will not trigger retained earnings statement disclosure and is the least desirable application method. Both of the less desirable methods are reactions to practical dilemmas in accounting practice.

Exhibit 4–9 provides an example of retroactive application with full restatement for a change of accounting principle. In 1992, Baton Broadcasting Ltd. began to amortize a major intangible asset, previously exempt from any amortization requirement. Appropriate disclosures accompanied the financial statements.

Capital Transactions

The retained earnings statement will also contain other increases and decreases caused by capital transactions. Most capital transactions are share transactions. Since a corporation is dealing with itself (its owners) in share transactions, gains and losses caused by these transactions are not shown on the income statement because they are not arm's-length transactions. Gains normally create contributed capital—separate shareholders' equity accounts—and losses reduce retained earnings.

For example, assume that a company has 10,000 shares outstanding, originally issued for $500,000, or $50 per share. On January 15 of the current year, 1,000 shares were bought back from the shareholders at a price of $65 per share. The shares were retired. The company has never retired shares before. The following entry would be made to record the transaction:

Common shares (1,000 × $50)	50,000	
Retained earnings	15,000	
Cash (1,000 × $65)		65,000

The debit to retained earnings has the same effect as a dividend in that earnings have been returned to a shareholder. This debit to retained earnings is reflected as a line item on the retained earnings statement.

EXHIBIT 4–9
Extracts from Baton
Broadcasting Ltd.—Change
in Accounting Policy

Consolidated Statements of Retained Earnings

	Years Ended August 31	
	1992 $	1991 $
	(amount in thousands)	
		Restated (note 2)
Retained earnings, beginning of year, as previously reported	$101,866	$134,428
Adjustment for retroactive amortization of broadcasting licences (note 2)	(8,600)	(6,100)
Retained earnings, beginning of year, as restated	93,266	128,328
Net income (loss) for the year	290	(35,062)
Retained earnings, end of year.	$ 93,556	$ 93,266

2. Change in accounting policy

In accordance with revised recommendations of The Canadian Institute of Chartered Accountants, the Company now amortizes broadcasting licences on a straight-line basis over a period of 40 years and as a result there is an additional charge against net income of $2,860,000 or 10.2¢ per share for the year ended August 31, 1992. Previously broadcasting licences were not amortized. This change in accounting policy has been applied on a retroactive basis. Accordingly, prior period earnings have been restated to account for the effect of amortization of broadcasting licences from their respective dates of acquisition and the net loss reported last year has been increased by $2,500,000 or 8.9¢ per share and retained earnings at September 1, 1990 has been reduced by $6,100,000.

Other Charges

Other charges to retained earnings result from share issue expenses incurred on the issuance of new shares, taxes resulting from a change in control or triggered by dividend payments to shareholders, and adjustments to retained earnings caused by a reorganization. These transactions are reviewed in Chapter 21.

|CONCEPT REVIEW

1. What items will appear on the retained earnings statement?
2. What criteria must be met for an item to qualify as a prior period adjustment?
3. How may a change in accounting principle be accounted for? When is each alternative appropriate?

Appropriations of and Restrictions on Retained Earnings

Appropriations of and restrictions on retained earnings limit the availability of retained earnings to support dividends.

Restrictions result from legal requirements, such as a statutory requirement that retained earnings be restricted for dividend purposes by the cost of any treasury stock held, or contractual agreements, such as a bond agreement (i.e., indenture) requiring that retained earnings of a specified amount be withheld from dividend purposes until the bonds are retired.

Appropriations of retained earnings result from formal decisions by the corporation to set aside, or appropriate, a specific amount of retained earnings (temporarily or permanently). The effect of an appropriation is to remove the specified amount of

GLOBAL VIEW

The financial reporting requirements in virtually every country include an income statement of one form or another. The measurement basis and specific measurement rules vary, but there is always some attempt to measure the results of operations.

As a general rule, income statements in non–North American reporting environments are less revealing than in Canada. Some statements are terse, with very few accounts being reported. In the extreme, an income statement consists of the single net earnings line or of the three lines: earnings before taxes, tax expense, and net earnings.

The biggest difficulty a reader has with international financial income statements is understanding what an item means and how it was measured. Although Australia, Canada, the United States and the United Kingdom identify items as "unusual or infrequent" (these items are called "exceptional" in the United Kingdom) and "extraordinary," the reporting requirements in most countries do not make these distinctions. Moreover, virtually no other country other than Canada and the United States requires separate

reporting of discontinued operations or effects of changes in accounting principle. In many countries, the accounting measurement rules are greatly influenced by tax law. For example, an item that is deducted for tax reporting may be required to be expensed in the financial statements. A firm might take a large tax deduction for an item such as bad debt expense, for example, and this same amount would have to be reported on the income statement even though it is an overestimate of the actual expense. Such reporting could mislead the reader who assumes that bad debt expense means the same thing in the foreign financial statement as in a Canadian financial statement.

When reading an income statement generated outside Canada, it is important to remember that even though it may appear very much like a statement prepared under Canadian GAAP, the terms and labels may have quite different meanings. It is important to understand how revenues, expenses, gains, and losses are defined in the environment in which the statement was prepared before trying to interpret the information in the statement.

retained earnings from dividend availability. For example, corporations often set up appropriations such as "retained earnings appropriated for future plant expansion."

The primary purpose of restrictions and appropriations is to inform statement users that a portion of retained earnings is set aside for a specific purpose (usually long term) and that these amounts are therefore not available for dividend declarations.

Exhibit 4–8 illustrates a restriction of $280,000 on the retained earnings of Bailey Retail Company. The unrestricted balance of retained earnings is $154,900 ($434,900 − $280,000 = $154,900). Bailey recorded the restriction, on the date it was imposed, as follows:

Retained earnings (unappropriated) 280,000
    Retained earnings appropriated (as required by the bond indenture) . .   280,000

When a restriction or appropriation is removed, the amount is returned to the retained earnings (unappropriated) account by reversing the above entry. Details regarding restrictions and appropriations are usually reported in a note, as illustrated in Exhibit 4–8.

SUMMARY OF KEY POINTS

(L.O. 1)   1. Accounting income is the result of applying the accrual-basis accounting system, which records transactions in accordance with established measurement rules. Because accounting income is generally based on historical cost, it is not always as relevant as desired, and because it is generally recorded only after a transaction has taken place, it is not always as timely as desired.

(L.O. 1)   2. Conceptually, economic income reflects events that change the wealth of an entity. Because economic income often requires estimations, it is not always as reliable as desired.

(L.O. 2)   3. The quality of earnings can be affected by choices management makes among acceptable alternative accounting measurement rules. The recognition of revenues later, rather than sooner, and of expenses earlier, rather than later, is generally viewed as resulting in a higher quality earnings figure.

(L.O. 2)   4. Many format issues are not governed by accounting pronouncements, and the company must make choices to create an income statement that is useful to financial statement users. Minimum disclosures are mandated by the *CICA Handbook;* additional note disclosures and format decisions are important for full disclosure.

(L.O. 3) 5. Two general formats for presenting income statement information not specifically regulated by accounting pronouncements are the single-step and the multiple-step formats.

(L.O. 3) 6. The single-step format uses only two broad classifications in its presentation: a revenues and gains section and an expenses and losses section. Total expenses and losses are deducted from total revenues and gains in a single computation to determine the net income (earnings) amount.

(L.O. 3) 7. The multiple-step format income statement presents intermediate components of income, such as gross profit, income from continuing operations, and income before tax and extraordinary items. The multiple-step format is designed to emphasize important relationships in the various revenue and expense categories.

(L.O. 4) 8. Extraordinary items result from transactions or events that are infrequent, not normal business activities, and dependent on the decision of an outsider. They are required to be reported, net of income tax effects, as a separate component of income, positioned after income from continuing operations.

(L.O. 4) 9. Unusual or infrequent items should be shown separately on the income statement, before tax.

(L.O. 4) 10. The gains or losses resulting from the sale or abandonment of a business segment, whose activities represent a separate major line of business or class of customer, must be reported, net of income tax effects, as a separate component of income, positioned after income from continuing operations and before extraordinary items. Gains or losses have two components: the operating results to the "decision day," and the gain or loss on sale, which includes the actual asset sale plus operating results after the date of the decision to sell.

(L.O. 4) 11. A change in accounting principle is to be applied retroactively, with the cumulative effect of the change shown as an adjustment to opening retained earnings. Comparative financial statements should be restated. If this treatment is not possible, only the cumulative effect is shown on the retained earnings statement. In certain circumstances, the change in principle is reflected prospectively. An accounting estimate is changed prospectively.

(L.O. 4) 12. Prior period adjustments are items that relate to a specific prior period, are not attributable to subsequent economic events, not previously estimable, and are the decisions of outsiders. The adjustment is recorded (net of tax) as a change to opening retained earnings, and comparatives are restated. Errors and corrections are accorded similar treatment.

(L.O. 5) 13. The statement of retained earnings reports all changes in retained earnings during the period, including prior period adjustments (net of tax), net income or loss, dividends declared, and capital transactions.

(L.O. 6) 14. Earnings per share amounts are required to be reported on the face of the income statement for (*a*) income from continuing operations, and (*b*) net income.

▌REVIEW PROBLEM

The following pretax amounts are taken from the adjusted trial balance of Killian Company at December 31, 1995, the end of the annual accounting period.

Sales revenue	$1,000,000
Service revenue	200,000
Interest revenue	30,000
Gain on sale of operational asset	100,000
Cost of goods sold	600,000
Selling, general, and administrative expense	150,000
Depreciation expense	50,000
Interest expense	20,000
Loss on sale of long-term investment	10,000
Extraordinary item, loss from earthquake damage	200,000
Cumulative effect of change in accounting principle (gain)	50,000
Loss on sale of business segment	60,000
Loss on operation of discontinued business segment, prior to disposal date	10,000
Income tax expense, tax rate 40% on all items	

Common shares outstanding, 100,000.

Assume simple capital structure; no preferred shares are outstanding. Assume that the disposal date and measurement date are the same for the discontinued operation.

Required

1. Prepare a single-step income statement in good form.
2. Prepare a multiple-step income statement in good form.

SOLUTION

1. Single-step income statement:

KILLIAN COMPANY
Income Statement
For the Year Ended December 31, 1995

Revenues and gains:		
Sales revenue		$1,000,000
Service revenue		200,000
Interest revenue		30,000
Gain on sale of operational asset		100,000
Total revenue and gains		1,330,000
Expenses and losses:		
Cost of goods sold		600,000
Selling, general, and administrative		150,000
Depreciation		50,000
Interest		20,000
Loss on sale of long-term investment		10,000
Income tax expense (see computations below)		200,000
Total expenses and losses		1,030,000
Income from continuing operations		300,000
Discontinued operations:		
Loss from discontinued operation, net of tax of $4,000	$ (6,000)	
Loss on disposal of business segment, net of tax of $24,000	(36,000)	(42,000)
Income before extraordinary item		258,000
Extraordinary item:		
Loss from earthquake damage, net of tax effects of $80,000		(120,000)
Net income		$ 138,000
Earnings per share:		
Income from continuing operations		$3.00
Discontinued operations		(.42)
Income before extraordinary item		2.58
Extraordinary item, loss from earthquake damage		(1.20)
Net income		$1.38

Computation of income tax expense

Revenues		$1,330,000
Expenses before income taxes:		
Cost of goods sold	$600,000	
Selling, general, and administrative	150,000	
Depreciation	50,000	
Interest expense	20,000	
Loss on sale of long-term investment	10,000	830,000
Pretax income		500,000
Tax rate		×.40
Income tax expense		$ 200,000

The discontinued operations and extraordinary item are reported net of tax, reflecting intraperiod tax allocation. The cumulative effect of a change in accounting policy is shown on the retained earnings statement.

2. Multiple-step income statement:

KILLIAN COMPANY
Income Statement
For the Year Ended December 31, 1995

Sales revenue		$1,000,000
Cost of goods sold		600,000
Gross margin		400,000
Operating expenses:		
Selling, general, and administrative expenses	$150,000	
Depreciation expense	50,000	200,000
Income from operations		200,000
Other revenues and gains:		
Service revenue	200,000	
Interest revenue	30,000	
Gain on sale of operational asset	100,000	
Total other revenues and gains		330,000
Other expenses and losses:		
Interest expense	20,000	
Loss on sale of long-term investment	10,000	
Total other expenses and losses		30,000
Net other items		300,000
Income from continuing operations before income tax		500,000
Income tax expense		200,000
Income from continuing operations		300,000
Discontinued operations:		
Loss from discontinued operation, net of tax of $4,000	(6,000)	
Loss on disposal of business segment, net of tax of $24,000	(36,000)	(42,000)
Income before extraordinary item		258,000
Extraordinary item:		
Loss from earthquake damage, net of tax effects of $80,000		(120,000)
Net income		$ 138,000
Earnings per share:		
Income from continuing operations		$3.00
Discontinued operations		(.42)
Income before extraordinary item		2.58
Extraordinary item, loss from earthquake damage		(1.20)
Net income		$1.38

Alternative arrangements of the information above the income from continuing operations line are allowed for both the single- and multiple-step formats. The presentation of the items below income from continuing operations, however, must be as shown. It is the same for both formats.

APPENDIX 4A *Conceptual Issues in the Determination of Income*

This chapter is primarily concerned with how to display the components of income in the income statement. The question, however, of what to include in net income has long been an issue in financial reporting.

What to Include in Income

The broad conceptual question is: What is income? At the practical level, the question becomes: Which items affecting shareholders' equity should be included in the computation of net income and reported in the income statement? Alternatively, what items, if any, should be recorded as direct adjustments to equity and not included in income? There are two extreme approaches to answering these questions.

Current Operating Performance At one extreme is the *current operating performance approach*. Advocates of this approach maintain that only items that are part of the ordinary recurring operations of the firm should be included in earnings. Other items related to extraordinary activities or to prior period transactions are recorded as direct adjustments to retained earnings. Advocates of this approach believe that users of financial statements attach a particular significance to the figure labelled "net income." They are concerned that some users may not be able to analyze the income statement and make adjustments for those extraordinary items and prior period adjustments that are unrelated to the company's current period operating performance.

All-Inclusive Approach At the other extreme is the *all-inclusive approach*, in which all transactions affecting the net increase or decrease in equity during the period are included in the determination of net income, except contributions by or distributions to owners. Advocates of this approach believe that the extraordinary items and prior period adjustments are all part of the earnings history of the firm and that exclusion of such items from the income statement increases the probability that they will be overlooked in a review of the operating results for a period of years. They also point out the dangers of possible manipulation of the annual earnings figure if preparers of financial statements are permitted to omit certain items in determining net income. Advocates of the all-inclusive approach believe that full disclosure in the income statement of the nature of any extraordinary items and any prior period adjustments enables income statement users to assess fully the importance of each item and its effect on operating results and cash flows.

Current GAAP Current GAAP is a compromise that tends to be closer to the all-inclusive approach. A few items are closed directly to retained earnings as advocated under the current operating performance approach, but nearly all items affecting equity (other than investment by or distributions to owners) must be included in net income. Concerns of advocates of the current operating performance approach are addressed in part by separately identifying and disclosing the various special nonoperating items on the face of the income statement. For example, income from continuing operations is measured and reported on the top portion of the statement, with the effects of nonoperating items (such as discontinued operations and extraordinary items) separately identified and reported below income from continuing operations.

Earnings and Comprehensive Income

In the United States, the FASB addressed the issue of what to include in income as part of its conceptual framework project. *Statement of Financial Accounting Concepts No. 5*, or *SFAC No. 5*, discusses two conceptual measures, one labelled *earnings*, the other, *comprehensive income*.

Earnings as Defined by *SFAC No. 5* **Earnings** is a measure of performance for a period, excluding items that are extraneous to the period—that is, items that belong to other periods.[8] The earnings measure focusses on what the firm has received or reasonably expects to receive for its output (revenues) and what it sacrifices to produce and distribute that output (expenses). Earnings also includes results of the company's incidental or

---

[8] *SFAC No. 5*, Financial Accounting Standards Board, Norwalk, CT, par. 34.

peripheral transactions and some effects of other events and circumstances stemming from the environment (gains and losses).[9]

Comprehensive Income as Defined by *SFAC No. 5*   Comprehensive income is a broad measure of the effects of transactions and other events on a company. Comprehensive income recognizes all changes in a company's equity (net assets) during a period from transactions and other events and circumstances, except those resulting from investment by owners and distributions to owners.[10]

In clarifying the difference between earnings and comprehensive income, *SFAC No. 5* lists two classes of gains and losses that would be included in comprehensive income but excluded from earnings:

1. Effects of certain accounting adjustments relating to earlier periods (such as the cumulative effects of changes in accounting principles), which, under current GAAP, are included on the retained earnings statement and excluded from income.
2. Certain other changes in net assets that are recognized in the period (principally, certain holding gains and losses), such as some changes in market values of investments in marketable securities classified as non-current assets, some changes in market values of investments in industries having specialized accounting practices for marketable securities, and foreign currency translation adjustments.[11]

The relationship between *SFAC No. 5* earnings and *SFAC No. 5* comprehensive income can best be shown by comparing a statement of earnings and a statement of comprehensive income. These two statements, in fact, complement each other (all amounts are assumed):

Statement of Earnings

Revenues.	$100,000,000
Expenses	75,000,000
	25,000,000
Add: Gains	10,000,000
Less: Losses	(15,000,000)
Earnings (per *SFAC No. 5* definition)	$ 20,000,000

Statement of Comprehensive Income

Earnings (per *SFAC No. 5* definition)	$ 20,000,000
Cumulative effect of accounting adjustments	5,000,000
Other nonowner changes in equity*	(7,000,000)
Comprehensive income (as defined by *SFAC No. 5*).	$ 18,000,000

* For example, foreign currency translation adjustments.

Future accounting pronouncements may modify reporting standards of net income so as to require the computation of earnings and comprehensive income.

APPENDIX 4B   *Discontinued Operations: Measurement Issues*

To correctly account for a discontinued operation, the components of the gain or loss on disposal must be accurately determined. This appendix explores the issues related to this measurement process.

Measurement Date and Disposal Date

To account for the discontinuance of a segment, two dates must be identified: the measurement date and the disposal date.

---

[9] Ibid., par. 38.

[10] Ibid., par. 39.

[11] Ibid., par. 42.

The **measurement date** is the date on which the company formally commits itself to a plan to dispose of a specific segment. The plan of disposal should specify at least the following:

- Identification of the major assets to be disposed.
- The method of disposal.
- The period expected to be required for disposal (normally, not longer than one year).
- An active program to find a buyer if disposal is to be a sale.
- The estimated results of operations from the measurement date to the disposal date.
- The estimated proceeds or salvage value to be realized by disposal.

The **disposal date** is either the closing date of sale of the assets (when the business segment is transferred) or the date when operations cease (if the disposal is an abandonment). The measurement date and the disposal date may be the same, but in most cases the disposal date follows the measurement date. The period between the measurement date and the disposal date is called the *phaseout period*. When the two dates differ, the seller usually continues the operations of the segment until the disposal date. Any income or loss from segment operations during this period is considered to be a component of the gain or loss on disposal.

Determination of Gain or Loss on Disposal

At the measurement date, a determination must be made of the gain or loss on disposal of the business segment. If there is a gain, recognition is delayed until the gain is realized. Losses, however, are recognized immediately at the measurement date. The gain or loss includes two components:

1. The difference between (a) the net realizable value of the segment after consideration of estimated costs and expenses directly associated with the disposal, and (b) the book value of the segment assets.
2. The estimated income or loss from operations between the measurement date and the disposal date.

In addition to the gain or loss on disposal, financial statements for accounting periods that include operating results attributable to the segment before the measurement date must separately disclose these results for those periods.

The most general situation in which the phaseout period extends over more than one accounting period is illustrated in Exhibit 4B–1. The measurement date and disposal date occur in different reporting periods. At the end of the accounting period in which the measurement date occurs, a determination must be made of the gain or loss on the disposal of the segment (the amount Z in Exhibit 4B–1). Since the income or loss from operating the segment in future periods until it is disposed (the amount X in Exhibit 4B–1) and the gain or loss on the actual sale or disposal of the segment net assets (the amount Y in Exhibit 4B–1) are included in the determination of the gain or loss on disposal, estimates must be made of these amounts. The issue is complicated further by the timing of the recognition of Z, the gain or loss on the disposal of the segment, which depends on whether there is a gain or loss.

Loss on Disposal of Business Segment

If Z is negative (that is, if there is an expected loss on the disposal of the segment), the loss is immediately recognized in the current accounting period. In addition, the operating results attributable to the segment before the measurement date (the amounts A and B in Exhibit 4B–1) must also be disclosed separately from the results of continuing operations. Assuming that there is an expected loss (Z is negative), the discontinued operations portion of the income statement in Exhibit 4B–1 would be as follows:

	1994	1995	1996
Income from continuing operations, after income taxes	xxx	xxx	xxx
Discontinued operations:			
Income (loss) from discontinued operations, net of tax	A	B	—
Loss from disposal of discontinued operations, including provision for operating loss during phaseout operations, net of tax.	—	Z	*

* If the actual value of ($X + Y$) differs from the original estimate, the difference is recognized in 1996 as a gain or loss.

EXHIBIT 4B-1   Components of Gain or Loss on Disposal of a Business Segment

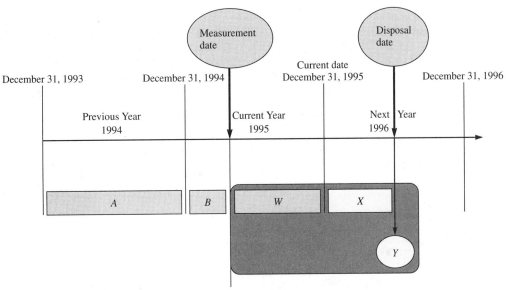

A = Income (loss) from operations of discontinued segment in 1994

B = Income (loss) from operations of discontinued segment in 1995 prior to
       measurement date

W = Realized income (loss) from operations
       of discontinued segment after measurement
       date to end of reporting period

X = Estimated income (loss) from operations
       of discontinued segment in future periods
       up to estimated disposal date

Y = Estimated gain (loss) from sale of assets
       of discontinued segment

$Z = W + X + Y$
    = Gain (loss) on disposal of segment

W, X, and Y are all components of gain
(loss) on disposal of a segment. At
December 31, 1995, W is known; X
and Y are estimates.

Note: All amounts A, B, W, X, and Y are reported net of applicable income tax effects.

**Gain on Disposal of
Business Segment**

If there is an expected net gain on the disposal (Z is positive), only the amount realized to
date, less any future estimated loss components, can be recognized in the statements of
the current year (1995). Z includes the components W, X, and Y. However, X and Y are
estimates of future amounts unknown at the reporting date, and hence at the reporting
date they can be treated as a single component, $X + Y$. There are three different cases
that give rise to an expected gain:

1. Both components, W and ($X + Y$), are positive.
2. W is positive but ($X + Y$) is negative.
3. W is negative but ($X + Y$) is positive.

Each case results in a different amount to be recognized as the gain from disposal of
business segment in the reporting period containing the measurement date. In each case
below, $Z = W + X + Y$ is positive.

Case 1 $W > 0$ and $X + Y > 0$ (both the realized and estimated components of Z are
positive). In this case, W is known and realized and no net future losses are expected, so
only W, the realized gain, is recognized in the current period.

Case 2 $W > 0$, but $X + Y < 0$ (income from discontinued operations in the current
period is positive, but the net estimated future results of discontinued operations plus

gain or loss on sale of the discontinued operation is negative). In this case, W and the estimated future loss $(X + Y)$ are both recognized, resulting in the recognition of Z.

Case 3 $W < 0$, but $X + Y > 0$ (there is a loss from operating the discontinued operations from the measurement date to the current reporting date, but sufficiently large gains are expected in the future such that an overall gain is expected). In this case, no gain or loss is recognized in the current period since the current loss is expected to be offset by gains in the future. The entire amount Z is deferred and recognized when it is realized. The income statements for these three cases are shown below.

	Case 1			Case 2			Case 3		
	1994	1995	1996	1994	1995	1996	1994	1995	1996
Income from continuing operations after income taxes	xxx	xxx	xxx	xxx	xxx	xxx	xxx	xxx	xxx
Discontinued operations:									
Income (loss) from discontinued operations, net of tax	A	B	—	A	B	—	A	B	—
Gain from disposal of discontinued operations, including provision for operating loss during phaseout operations, net of tax	—	W	$X + Y$	—	Z	*	—	0	Z

* The difference is recognized in 1996 as a gain or loss depending on whether the actual sum $X + Y$ is greater than or less than the original estimate.

Reporting Examples

Example: Identical Measurement and Disposal Dates When the measurement and disposal dates are the same, a single journal entry is made to record the full consideration received and to remove the carrying (book) values of all segment assets sold. The difference between these two amounts is the pretax gain or loss on sale of the segment. There are no phaseout operations. The gain or loss on disposal, net of tax, must be reported on the income statement after income from continuing operations and before extraordinary items.

To illustrate, assume that on September 1, 1995, TRAC Bicycle Corporation (TBC) sells its specialty products division for $200,000 cash. The carrying value of the segment's assets is $230,000. The accounting year ends December 31, and the applicable income tax rate is 30%. Assume that income from continuing operations, after income taxes, is $262,000 in 1994 and $265,000 in 1995. Also assume that the pretax income from the specialty products division is $15,000 in 1994 and totals $8,000 for the eight-month period ending September 1, 1995. The summary entry and appropriate reporting for TBC would be as follows:

September 1, 1995 (measurement and disposal date):

Cash	200,000	
Loss on disposal of segment (pretax)*	30,000	
Assets, specialty products division		230,000

* Income tax saving $30,000 × .30 = 9,000 (reflected in income tax entry).

Comparative Income Statements

	1995	1994
Income from continuing operations after taxes	$265,000	$262,000
Discontinued operations (Note 6):		
Income from discontinued operations, less income taxes of $2,400 in 1995 and $4,500 in 1994	5,600	10,500
Gain (loss) from disposal of discontinued operations, net of income tax of $9,000	(21,000)	—
	$249,600	$272,500

Note 6. Discontinued operations—On September 1, 1995, the company sold its specialty products division. This is the measurement date and the disposal date. The company received $200,000 cash for the sale of the division; a disposal loss of $30,000 (less an income tax saving of $9,000) was recognized. Pretax income from discontinued operations was $15,000 in 1994 and $8,000 in 1995.

Example: Different Measurement and Disposal Dates in Same Reporting Period   Assume the same disposal transaction as above for the TRAC Bicycle Corporation, except that the measurement date is September 1, 1995, and the disposal date is December 31, 1995.

1. September 1, 1995 (measurement date): The disposal entry may be made at this date, but the entry is usually deferred to the disposal date since it falls in the same fiscal year.
2. September 1 to December 31, 1995: Results of operations of the discontinued segments are accounted for separately and are a component of the gain or loss on disposal.
3. December 31, 1995 (end of accounting period and disposal date):
    a. Record disposal of the specialty products division:

Cash.	200,000	
Loss on disposal of segment (pretax)	30,000*	
Assets, specialty products division		230,000

* Income tax saving, $30,000 × .30 = $9,000 (reflected in income tax entry).

    b. At December 31, 1995, the accounting records provided the following pretax income data for the specialty products division: $15,000 in 1994; $8,000 from January 1 to August 31, 1995; and $4,000 from September 1 to December 31, 1995.

The $4,000 income from segment operations during the phaseout period from September 1 through December 31, 1995, and the $30,000 loss on disposal of the segment are closed to income summary at year-end. The income tax effect on each of these amounts is included in the 1995 income tax entry.

Comparative Income Statements

	1995	1994
Income from operations, net of income tax.	$265,000	$262,000
Discontinued operations (Note 6):		
Income from discontinued operations, less income taxes of $2,400 in 1995 and $4,500 in 1994 .	5,600	10,500
Gain (loss) on disposal of discontinued operations, net of tax:		
Income from operations of discontinued operations during the phaseout, net of income tax of $1,200 . . . $ 2,800		
Loss on sale of assets of discontinued segment, net of income tax of $9,000 . . . (21,000)	(18,200)	—
Net income .	$252,400	$272,500

Note 6. Discontinued operations—In 1995, the company decided to sell its specialty products division. The measurement date was September 1, 1995, and the disposal date was December 31, 1995. The company received $200,000 cash for the assets of the discontinued segment; a disposal loss of $30,000 (less an income tax saving of $9,000) is recognized. Income from the discontinued segment was $15,000 (less income tax effect, $4,500) in 1994 and $8,000 (less income tax saving, $2,400) in 1995. Income during the phaseout period was $4,000 (less income tax of $1,200). Total loss on disposal recognized in 1995 was $26,000 (i.e., $30,000 − $4,000) less the income tax effect of $7,800 (i.e., $9,000 − $1,200), yielding an after-tax loss of $18,200.

Example: Different Measurement and Disposal Dates in Different Reporting Periods
Returning to the TRAC Bicycle example, suppose that on September 1, 1995, TBC concludes an agreement to sell its specialty products division for $200,000 cash, payable on the disposal date, March 1, 1996. TBC will operate the division during the phaseout period between the measurement date, September 1, 1995, and the disposal date, March 1, 1996. The accounting period ends December 31. The carrying (or book) value of the division's net assets on the measurement date was $230,000; the income tax rate is 30%. The incomes from the discontinued operations before taxes are $15,000 in 1994 and $8,000 in 1995 (to August 31). At the end of 1995, the accounting records reflect a $6,000 pretax loss from the specialty division's operations for the period from September 1 to December 31, 1995. Further, an estimated pretax loss of $9,000 is expected for the period from January 1, 1996, to the disposal date, March 1, 1996.

The accounting and reporting for this situation are as follows:
September 1, 1995 (measurement date):

a. To record the loss on disposal:

Loss on disposal of segment.	30,000*	
Allowance to reduce segment assets to market value		30,000

* Income tax saving, $30,000 × .30 = $9,000.

The allowance account would be a contra account to the segment assets. These assets, if to be liquidated in the coming year, would be current assets, carried at market value since market value is lower than cost. With a sale agreement pending, careful disclosure of the terms and conditions of the contract would be essential to full disclosure.

This entry may be made at year-end rather than on the measurement date.
December 31, 1995 (end of the accounting period):

b. To record the loss from operations of the segment from September 1 to December 31, 1995:

Loss on disposal of segment.	6,000*	
Segment revenue and expense summary		6,000

* Income tax saving, $6,000 × .30 = $1,800.

c. To accrue the estimated loss from operations of the segment in 1996:

Loss on disposal of segment.	9,000*	
Accrued loss on segment operations (a liability)		9,000

* Income tax saving, $9,000 × .30 = $2,700.

Note: This entry may be made on the measurement date; often, however, it is not made until the end of the accounting period because a better estimate can be made at that time. The accrued loss on segment operations—the liability—will be debited as losses are incurred in 1996.

Reporting at the end of 1995:

Comparative Income Statements

	1995	1994
Income from continuing operations, after tax	$265,000	$262,000
Discontinued operations (Note 6):		
Income (loss) from discontinued operations, less income taxes of $2,400 in 1995 and $4,500 in 1994.	5,600*	10,500*

Gain (loss) on disposal of segment, including loss on sale of
    assets of discontinued segment of $30,000 and estimated operating
    loss of $15,000 from September 1, 1995, to disposal
    date of March 1, 1996, less tax savings of $13,500 . . . .
	(31,500)†	

Net income	$239,100	$272,500

Note 6. Discontinued operations—During 1995, the company arranged to sell the specialty products division for $200,000 cash. The measurement date was September 1, 1995, and the disposal date will be March 1, 1996, between which dates the company has agreed to continue the normal operations of the division. Loss from the discontinued segment operations from September 1, 1995, to the planned disposal date of March 1, 1996, is estimated at $15,000, less a $4,500 income tax saving: net loss, $10,500.

* Income of discontinued operation prior to measurement date.

† Actual loss on sale of disposed segment of $30,000 plus operating loss of $6,000 in 1995 and estimated operating loss of $9,000 in 1995, all net of income tax savings of $13,500.

Suppose that during the first two months of 1996 (from January 1 to March 1) the accounting records reflect an actual loss of $12,000 from the discontinued segment. Of this amount, $9,000 is charged (debited) against the credit balance in the account accrued loss on segment operations (see December 31, 1995, entry *c*. above), reducing the accrued loss account balance to zero. The remaining $3,000 is a component of loss on disposal of the business segment and is reported as such in the 1996 income statement:

Comparative Income Statements

	1996	1995
Income from continuing operations, after tax (assumed)	$279,000	$265,000
Discontinued operations (Note 6):		
Income from discontinued operations (less income tax of $2,400)		5,600
Gain (loss) on disposal of segment (less income tax savings of $900 in 1996 and $13,500 in 1995)	(2,100)	(31,500)
Net income.	$276,900	$239,100

Note 6. Discontinued operations—In 1995, the company arranged to sell the specialty products division for $200,000 cash, collectible on the disposal date, March 1, 1996. The company continued to operate the division until the disposal date. The loss from discontinued operations from January 1, 1996, to March 1, 1996, was $3,000 more than originally estimated. This amount, less income tax savings of $900, is reported as a loss on disposal of the specialty products division in 1996. A loss of $45,000 (less a $13,500 income tax saving) on the disposal of the division was reported in 1995.

QUESTIONS

1. Briefly explain how the income statement is a connecting link between the beginning and ending balance sheets.
2. Briefly explain the difference between economic income and accounting income.
3. What is meant by the quality of earnings?
4. What factors determine the choice of a fiscal year-end?
5. Why might a Canadian company prepare its financial statements in U.S. dollars?
6. Briefly explain the two formats used for income statements. Explain why actual income statements are often a combination of these two formats.
7. Explain how gross margin is computed for a retail business. How would gross margin be computed for a service organization?
8. Explain how cost of goods sold is reported on a single-step income statement and on a multiple-step income statement.
9. List the major income subtotals, or captions, in their order of appearance, on a typical multiple-step income statement.
10. What factors might be taken into consideration when one chooses between the two alternative formats for the income statement?

11. List the items that must be disclosed on the income statement. Why would companies choose to disclose more than minimum requirements?
12. Define an extraordinary item. How should extraordinary items be reported on (*a*) a single-step and (*b*) a multiple-step income statement?
13. How are items that are unusual or infrequent reported on the income statement?
14. Outline a situation in which a large hurricane or tornado loss could (*a*) be an extraordinary item and (*b*) not be an extraordinary item.
15. Does the amount of a gain determine whether it is classified as an extraordinary item or not?
16. Extraordinary items are sometimes described as "Acts of God or government." Why is this a useful rule of thumb?
17. Briefly define a prior period adjustment. How is a prior period adjustment reported?
18. Briefly define intraperiod tax allocation.
19. How is a change of estimate different from a change in accounting policy? How is a change in estimate accounted for?
20. Describe three different ways a change of accounting policy could be reflected in the financial statements. Under what circumstances is each appropriate?
21. How is a change in accounting principles involving a change in depreciation method treated in the financial statements?
22. How is the correction of an error treated in the financial statements?
23. Regis Publishing Corporation computed total income tax expense for 1995 of $16,640. The following pretax amounts were used: (*a*) income before extraordinary loss, $60,000; (*b*) extraordinary loss, $12,000; and (*c*) prior period adjustment, $4,000 (a credit). The average income tax rate on all items was 32%. Compute the intraperiod income tax allocation amounts.
24. Define earnings per share (EPS). Why is it required as an integral part of the income statement?
25. Wilson Sports Company reported the following amounts at the end of 1995:

Extraordinary gain.	$90,000
Net income.	50,000

Average number of common shares outstanding, 25,000.

Prepare the EPS presentation. Which EPS amount is likely to be the most relevant to a financial statement user trying to predict future income? Explain.

26. A company has a machine that cost $21,000 when acquired at the beginning of year 1. It has been depreciated using the straight-line method on the basis of a 10-year useful life and a $1,000 residual value. At the start of year 5, the residual value was changed to $3,000. Compute the amount of depreciation expense per year that should be recorded for the remaining useful life of the machine.
27. What is a discontinued operation? How is it reported in the financial statements?
28. A company has a segment that it decides to sell, effective September 1, after incurring operating losses of $45,000 to date in the fiscal year. The segment, with net assets of $310,000, was sold for $240,000 on November 1, after incurring further operating losses of $30,000. Assume a tax rate of 40%. What amounts would be disclosed in the income statement?
29. How are gains on the discontinuance of a business segment accounted for differently than losses? Why is this the case?
30. What items are reported on a statement of retained earnings? Explain how it provides a link between the current income statement and balance sheet.
31. What are capital transactions and why are they reported on the retained earnings statement?
32. What is meant by appropriations or restrictions on retained earnings? How are such items usually reported?
33. In a country where financial reporting is guided by tax reporting, how might accounting income be affected?

CASES

C 4–1
(L.O. 4)

 **Analytical: Discuss Statement Classifications** During the 1994 audit, the independent accountant encountered the following situations that caused serious concern as to proper classification on the financial statements of selected clients. Assume that all amounts are material.

a. A client was assessed additional income taxes of $100,000 plus $36,000 interest related to the past three years.
b. A client suffered a casualty loss (a fire) amounting to $500,000. The client occasionally experiences a fire, but this was significantly more than any such loss experienced before by the client company.

    c. A client company paid $175,000 damages assessed by the courts as a result of an injury to a customer on the company premises three years earlier.

    d. A client sold a large operational asset and reported a gain of $70,000.

    e. The major supplier of raw materials to a client company experienced a prolonged strike. As a result, the client company reported a loss of $150,000. This is the first such loss; however, the client has three major suppliers, and strikes are not unusual in the industry.

    f. A client owns several large blocks of common shares of other corporations. The shares have been held for a number of years and are viewed as long-term investments. During the past year, 20% of the shares were sold to meet an unusual cash demand. Additional disposals are not anticipated.

    g. A timber company wrote down inventory and natural resources (a capital asset) after five years of low pulp and paper prices on world markets. The amount was material, it was the first such write-down in the company's history, and it is not expected to recur.

Required

1. Write a brief report defining (*a*) income from ordinary business operations, (*b*) unusual gains and losses, (*c*) extraordinary gains and losses, and (*d*) prior period adjustments. Explain how the effects of each should be reported.

2. Continuing a second section of the report, explain how the financial effects of each transaction *a–g* should be classified—that is, classify as (*a*) income from ordinary business operations, (*b*) unusual items, (*c*) extraordinary gains or losses, or (*d*) prior period adjustments. Explain the basis for your decision for each situation.

C 4–2
(L.O. 4)

Analyze and Discuss Extraordinary Items   The following information was taken from an article in the *Journal of Accountancy:*[12]

Case A "XYZ Company's fruit crop was destroyed by a severe freeze. The loss was $40,000. A freeze in XYZ's location is very rare . . . ABC Company's fruit crop was also destroyed by a severe freeze. The loss was $40,000. A severe freeze in ABC's locale occurs about every two years."

Case B "Company A sold 100 shares of XYZ Company common stock for a gain of $5,000. This is the only stock that Company A owned or will ever own . . . Company B also sold 100 shares of XYZ Company common stock for a gain of $5,000. Company B has several other investments in its common stock portfolio and is frequently involved in stock transactions."

Required

1. Give the definition of an extraordinary item.
2. For Case A, explain how, and why, XYZ Company and ABC Company should report the $40,000 loss.
3. For Case B, explain how, and why, Company A and Company B should report the $5,000 gain.

C 4–3
(L.O. 4)

Unusual, Extraordinary Items; Prior Period Adjustments   Wilfrid LeClaire, the accountant of Floor Ltd., has a habit of recording items he doesn't quite know what to do with in a "suspense" account so that you, the auditor, will be sure to find and fix them.

This year, 1995, an analysis of the suspense account shows the following:

	Debit	Credit	Balance
March 31	$27,000		$ 27,000 dr.
April 22	17,000		44,000 dr.
June 16	71,000		115,000 dr.
November 2		$43,000	72,000 dr.

The entry on March 31 for $27,000 represents a write-down of inventory. The items had been purchased two years ago, and the market price steadily declined this year. This adjustment reduced inventory to the lower of cost or market. Wilfrid is inclined to believe that the $27,000 should be recorded as a prior period adjustment, since it relates to an event (purchase of inventory) that happened two years ago.

The debit on April 22 is a payment made to Revenue Canada as a result of a tax audit that covered the years 1990–1993. Wilfrid believes this amount should be part of income tax expense on the income statement, along with all the other payments to Revenue Canada.

The entry on June 16 represents the costs to rebuild and repair a plant damaged by a flash flood. Some of the older employees at the plant remember the last time it happened, 1960, but the damage

---

[12] B. Jarnigan, "Extraordinary Items: An Update," *Journal of Accountancy,* April 1984, pp. 42–44.

was not as extensive then. Wilfrid has concluded that he should set up the $71,000 as an asset, to be amortized over the expected life of the plant facilities.

Finally, the $43,000 credit of November 2 arose from the discovery of a mistake in the 1992 calculation of the pension liability. Wilfrid was checking a document and noticed a $43,000 error in addition, which resulted in a reduction of the pension liability. Since the increase in the liability was debited to pension expense, Wilfrid reasons that the credit must also be an element of current pension expense.

Required   Comment on the proper classification for each of these items. Prepare a journal entry to reallocate the suspense account; assume all items are fully taxable at 40%, except the tax reassessment, which has no further tax consequences.

EXERCISES

E 4–1
(L.O. 1, 2)

Interpreting the components of income   Excerpts from the Stanley Produce Company comparative income statements for the years 1992 through 1994 are as follows:

	1994	1993	1992
	(amounts in millions)		
Income from continuing operations, after tax.	$30	$25	$20
Discontinued operations:			
Income from operations of discontinued segment, net of tax	0	10	15
Gain on disposal of discontinued segment, net of tax	50	0	0
Extraordinary items:			
Loss from earthquake damage, net of tax	0	(40)	0
Gain on expropriation of property.	0	0	35
Net income (loss)	$80	$(5)	$70

Required   1. Stanley Produce has experienced volatile earnings over the three-year period shown. Do you expect this to continue? Why or why not?
2. Net income increased from a loss of $5 million in 1993 to a profit of $80 million in 1994. Suppose the company's common share price increased only approximately 20% during the same period. Why might this be the case? Relate the 20% increase in share price to the components of net income.
3. Would you expect net income in 1995 to be more or less than the amount reported in 1994? More specifically, assuming no new unusual, non-recurring items, what amount would you estimate net income to be in 1995?

E 4–2
(L.O. 2)

Classifications of Elements on the Income Statement   Fifteen transactions are listed to the left below that may or may not affect the income statement. Income statement element classifications are listed by letters to the right. Match each transaction with the appropriate letter to indicate the usual classification that should be used. Provide comments when appropriate.

Answer	Selected Transactions	Income Statement Element Classifications
_____	1. Sales of goods and services.	A. Revenues.
_____	2. Prepaid insurance premium.	B. Expenses.
_____	3. Loss on disposal of service trucks.	
_____	4. Cash dividends received on an investment in African diamond mine.	C. Gains (ordinary).
		D. Unusual gains.
		E. Loss (ordinary).
_____	5. Wages accrued (unpaid and unrecorded).	F. Unusual loss.
		G. Extraordinary gain.
_____	6. Cost of successful oil wells in a foreign country that are taken over (expropriated) by that country's government without compensation.	H. Extraordinary loss.
		I. None of the above.

_____ 7. Cost of goods sold.

_____ 8. Services rendered.

_____ 9. Gain (characterized as unusual but not infrequent).

_____ 10. Rent collected in advance.

_____ 11. Fire loss (characterized as not unusual but infrequent).

_____ 12. Loss due to a very rare freeze that destroys the fruit trees in the Annapolis Valley.

_____ 13. Gain on sale of long-term investments not held for resale.

_____ 14. Cash dividend declared and paid.

_____ 15. Loss due to fire that completely destroys the factory.

E 4–3
(L.O. 3, 4)

Formats of Income Statement, Extraordinary Item, and Periodic Inventory   The following selected items were taken from the adjusted trial balance of Amick Manufacturing Corporation at December 31, 1995.

Sales revenue	$950,000
Cost of goods manufactured (including depreciation, $52,000)	580,000
Dividends received on investment in shares	6,500
Finished goods inventory, January 1, 1995 (periodic inventory system)	48,000
Interest expense	4,200
Extraordinary item: fire loss (pretax)	48,000
Distribution expenses	135,300
Common shares, nopar, 20,000 shares outstanding	200,000
General and administrative expenses	113,000
Interest revenue	2,500
Finished goods inventory, December 31, 1995	53,000
Income tax, assuming an average 30% tax rate	?

Required

1. Prepare a single-step income statement (including EPS). Set up cost of goods sold as a separate schedule, including the inventory amounts and cost of goods manufactured.
2. Prepare a multiple-step income statement. Include computation of cost of goods sold within the statement.

E 4–4
(L.O. 3, 4, 6)

Formats of Income Statement, Extraordinary Item   The Sandvik Cement Company's records provided the following information at December 31, 1995 (the end of the accounting period):

Sales revenue	$95,000
Service revenue	35,000
Gain on sale of short-term investments	11,000
Distribution expense	18,000
General and administrative expense	12,000
Depreciation expense	6,000
Interest expense	4,000
Income tax expense (30% rate on all items)	?
Earthquake loss on building	15,000
Loss on sale of warehouse	3,000
Beginning inventory	20,000
Ending inventory	23,000
Purchases (including freight-in)	50,000
Purchase returns	2,000

Common shares outstanding, 10,000 shares.

Required

1. Prepare a single-step income statement (including EPS). Set up cost of goods sold as a separate schedule, including the inventory amounts and cost of goods manufactured.
2. Prepare a multiple-step income statement. Include computation of cost of goods sold within the statement.

E 4–5
(L.O. 4, 5)

Income Statement and Retained Earnings Statement: Intraperiod Tax Allocation The records of Cayuga Corporation for 1994 provided the following pretax data:

Income Statement—1994

Income before extraordinary items	$ 80,000*
Extraordinary item:	
Loss from earthquake damage	20,000*
Pretax income	$ 60,000

Statement of Retained Earnings—1994

Beginning balance	$170,000
Less: Correction of accounting error	(30,000)*
Corrected balance	140,000
Add: Net income, 1994	60,000
Less: Dividends declared and paid during 1994	(40,000)
Ending balance.	$160,000

* Subject to a 30% income tax effect.

Required Complete the above statements in good form on an after-tax basis (apply intraperiod tax allocation).

E 4–6
(L.O. 3, 4)

Formats of the Income Statement, Extraordinary Items, Discontinued Operations, and Perpetual Inventory The following items were taken from the adjusted trial balance of the Bigler Manufacturing Corporation on December 31, 1995. Assume an average 30% income tax on all items (including the divestiture loss). The accounting period ends December 31. All amounts given are pretax.

Sales revenue	$745,200
Rent revenue	2,400
Interest revenue	900
Gain on sale of operational assets	2,000
Distribution expenses.	136,000
General and administrative expenses.	110,000
Interest expense	1,500
Depreciation for the period	6,000
Extraordinary item: court-ordered divestiture loss	22,000
Common shares, 10,000 shares outstanding	100,000
Cost of goods sold (perpetual inventory system).	330,000
Operating loss of discontinued operation to measurement date	20,000
Operating loss of discontinued operation from measurement date to disposal date.	40,000
Gain on sale of assets of discontinued operation.	22,000

Required 1. Prepare a single-step income statement.
2. Prepare a multiple-step income statement.

E 4–7
(L.O. 3, 4, 5, 6)

Income and Retained Earnings Statements The following pretax amounts were taken from the adjusted trial balance of Mabel Gravel Company on December 31, 1995, the end of the annual accounting period:

Balance, retained earnings, January 1, 1995	$ 90,000
Sales revenue	600,000
Cost of goods sold	210,000
Distribution expenses.	72,000
Administrative expenses	68,000
Extraordinary gain (pretax)	20,000
Prior period adjustment, payment made to an ex-customer following a 1992 lawsuit, pretax (a debit).	40,000
Dividends declared	32,000

Assume that the income tax rate for all items is 30%. The average number of common shares outstanding during the year was 20,000.

Required 1. Prepare a multiple-step income statement.
2. Prepare a statement of retained earnings.
3. Give the entry to record income taxes payable (assumed not yet paid).

E 4–8
(L.O. 3, 4, 5, 6)

Income and Retained Earnings Statements   The following pretax amounts were taken from the adjusted trial balance of the Gilmore Equipment Corporation at December 31, 1996, the end of the annual accounting period:

Dividends declared and paid	$ 35,000
Sales revenue	300,000
Cost of goods sold	100,000
Operating expenses	60,000
Extraordinary loss (pretax)	22,000
Prior period adjustment, payment received from a 1992 lawsuit, pretax (a credit)	10,000
Common shares, nopar, 40,000 shares outstanding	200,000
Beginning retained earnings January 1, 1996	60,000

Required

1. Prepare a complete single-step income statement assuming that the income tax rate is 30% on all items.
2. Prepare a statement of retained earnings.
3. Give the entry or entries to record income taxes payable (assumed not yet paid). Assume that the extraordinary loss and prior period adjustment have been recorded on a pretax basis.

E 4–9
(L.O. 3, 4, 5, 6)

Income Statement, Retained Earnings Statement, and EPS   The following pretax amounts were taken from the adjusted trial balance of Avoca Automobile Corporation at December 31, 1995, the end of the annual accounting period:

Sales revenue	$260,000
Cost of goods sold	110,000
Operating expenses	80,000
Gain on expropriation of property (pretax)	20,000
Settlement of prior year tax audit (a debit)	22,000
Retained earnings, balance January 1, 1995	30,000
Dividends declared and paid	25,000
Common shares, nopar	
Outstanding shares, January 1, 1995	15,000
Sold and issued April 1, 1995	5,000
Sold and issued October 1, 1995	7,000
Outstanding December 31, 1995	27,000

Required

1. Prepare a single-step income statement. Assume an average 30% tax rate on all items except the settlement of the prior year tax audit. Include EPS computations and disclosures.
2. Prepare a statement of retained earnings.

E 4–10
(L.O. 3, 4, 6)

Income Statement, Unusual or Infrequent Items   The following pretax amounts were taken from the adjusted trial balance of Gonzalez Trading Corporation at December 31, 1995, the end of the annual accounting period:

Sales revenue	$220,000
Service revenue	50,000
Cost of goods sold	130,000
Operating expenses	88,000
Gain on sale of equipment (pretax)	25,000
Loss on flood damage (pretax)	20,000
Prior period adjustment, correction of error from prior period, pretax (a debit)	5,000

Common shares, nopar, 10,000 shares outstanding.

Assume an average 30% corporate tax rate on all items.

Required

1. Prepare a single-step income statement. State any assumptions necessary.
2. Give the journal entry to record income tax (assumed not yet paid).

E 4–11
(L.O. 4)

Depreciation, Change in Estimate   The Cutter Knife Company purchased a machine that cost $40,000 on January 1, 1990. The estimated useful life was 12 years, and the estimated residual value was $4,000. Straight-line depreciation is used. On December 31, 1995, before making the adjusting entry to record depreciation expense for the year, the company's chief accountant decided that the machine should be depreciated over a 15-year total useful life and that the estimated residual value at the end of the 15th year should be $1,000.

Required
1. Give the adjusting entry at the end of 1995 to record depreciation expense. Show computations.
2. Give the correcting entry required at the end of 1995. If none is required, give the reason.

E 4-12
(L.O. 4)

Change in Estimate, Error Correction   It is December 31, 1995, and Manley Delivery Company is preparing adjusting entries at the end of the accounting year. The company owns two trucks of different types. The following situations confront the company accountant:

a. Truck 1 cost $7,700 on January 1, 1993. It is being depreciated on a straight-line basis over an estimated useful life of 10 years with a $700 residual value. At December 31, 1995, it has been determined that the total useful life should have been 6 years instead of 10, with a revised residual value of $900.

b. Truck 2 cost $4,550 on January 1, 1992. It is being depreciated on a straight-line basis over an estimated useful life of seven years with a $350 residual value. At December 31, 1995, it was discovered that no depreciation had been recorded on this truck for 1992 or 1993, but it was recorded for 1994.

Required
1. For each truck, give the required adjusting entry for depreciation expense at December 31, 1995. Show computations.
2. For each truck, give the appropriate correcting entry and show computations. If no correcting entry is needed, give the reasons (ignore income tax effects).

E 4-13
(L.O. 4, 5)

Change in Policy, Retained Earnings Statement   The Hannam Company decided to change from the declining-balance method of depreciation to the straight-line method effective January 1, 1995. The following information was provided:

Year	Net Income as Reported	Excess of Declining-Balance Depreciation over Straight-Line Depreciation
1991*	$(40,000)	$10,000
1992	110,000	30,000
1993	107,000	25,000
1994	140,000	14,000

* First year of operations.

The company has a December 31 year-end. The tax rate is 40%. No dividends were declared until 1995; $35,000 of dividends were declared and paid in December of 1995. Income for 1995, calculated using the new accounting policy, was $210,000.

Required
1. Assuming that the change in policy was made to conform to long-standing industry norms, present the 1995 retained earnings statement.
2. Assuming that the change in policy was made based on the company's experience to date, explain the appropriate accounting treatment for the change in policy.

E 4-14
(L.O. 3, 4, 5, 6)

Combined Income and Retained Earnings Statement   The following pretax amounts were taken from the accounts of Ertley Products Corporation at December 31, 1995, the end of the annual accounting period:

	(amounts in thousands)
Sales revenue	$340
Cost of goods sold	170
Distribution and administrative expenses	90
Gain on expropriation of property (pretax)	30
Income tax reassessment related to 1992 (no tax; a debit)	11.2
Interest expense	2
Cash dividends declared	5
Retained earnings, January 1, 1995	103

Common shares outstanding, 10,000.

Assume an average 30% tax rate on all taxable items.

Required
Prepare a combined single-step income and retained earnings statement, including intraperiod income tax allocation and EPS.

E 4–15
(L.O. 4)

Discontinued Operations, Recording and Reporting   On August 1, 1995, Fischer Company decided to discontinue the operations of its Services Division, which qualifies as an identifiable segment. An agreement was formalized to sell this segment for $156,000 cash. The book value of the assets of the Services Division was $180,000. The disposal date was also August 1, 1995. The income tax rate is 35%, and the accounting period ends December 31. On December 31, 1995, the after-tax income from all operations, including an after-tax operating loss of $20,000 incurred by the Services Division prior to August 1, 1995, was $400,000.

Required

1. Give the entry or entries to record the sale of the Services Division.
2. Complete the 1995 income statement, starting with income from continuing operations, after tax.

E 4–16
(L.O. 4)

Gain or Loss on Disposal of Business Segment, Appendix 4B   The following table presents data for several different cases of disposal of a business segment. In each case, assume that the measurement date is September 1, 1994, and that the disposal date is April 1, 1995. The current date is December 31, 1994, which is the end of the fiscal year. Income or loss from operations of the discontinued segment for the period from September 1, 1994, to December 31, 1994, is known. Income or loss from operating the discontinued operation in the future to the disposal date and the gain or loss on sale of the assets of the discontinued segment are estimates as of December 31, 1994. Assume that these estimates are realized in 1995.

Required

Complete the table, showing the pretax amount that will be reported as the gain or loss on the disposal of the business segment in both 1994 and 1995 for all eight cases.

Case	Realized Income (Loss) from Discontinued Operations, September 1 to December 31, 1994	Estimated Income (Loss) from Discontinued Operations, January 1 to April 1, 1995	Estimated Gain (Loss) on Sale of Assets of Discontinued Segment		Gain (Loss) on Disposal of Discontinued Segment to Be Recognized in Year
1	$(600)	$(300)	$700	1994	_____
				1995	_____
2	(100)	(50)	(250)	1994	_____
				1995	_____
3	200	300	(600)	1994	_____
				1995	_____
4	(400)	(300)	800	1994	_____
				1995	_____
5	200	250	100	1994	_____
				1995	_____
6	400	(100)	(200)	1994	_____
				1995	_____
7	200	(150)	250	1994	_____
				1995	_____
8	300	(250)	200	1994	_____
				1995	_____

| PROBLEMS

P 4–1
(L.O. 3, 4, 6)

Formats of the Income Statement, Extraordinary Items   The following pretax information was taken from the adjusted trial balance of Turkey Hill Foods Corporation at December 31, 1995, the end of the accounting period:

Sales revenue	$957,000
Sales returns	7,000
Gain on sale of equipment (pretax)	8,000
Depreciation expense	25,000
Distribution expense	140,000
General and administrative expenses	92,300
Rent revenue.	18,000
Investment revenue	7,000
Gain on sale of land (pretax)	6,000
Interest expense	9,000
Gain on expropriation of property (pretax).	80,000
Loss on sale of long-term investments (pretax).	10,000
Cost of goods sold	550,000
Loss due to leak in roof (pretax)	4,000
Earthquake damage loss (pretax)	30,000

Assume an average 30% income tax rate on all items. There are 40,000 common shares outstanding.

Required

1. Prepare a single-step income statement. State any assumptions made.
2. Prepare a multiple-step income statement.

P 4–2
(L.O. 2, 3, 4)

Formats of the Income Statement, Extraordinary Item, Periodic Inventory   The following data were taken from the adjusted trial balance of Montreal Retail Corporation at December 31, 1996, the end of the accounting period:

Merchandise inventory, January 1, 1996 (periodic inventory system)	$ 71,000
Purchases	121,400
Sales revenue	405,000
Purchase returns	3,400
Sales returns	5,000
Common shares, nopar, 20,000 shares outstanding	200,000
Depreciation expense (70% administrative expense, 30% distribution expense)	50,000
Rent revenue	4,000
Interest expense	6,000
Investment revenue	2,500
Distribution expenses (exclusive of depreciation)	105,500
General and administrative expenses (exclusive of depreciation)	46,000
Gain on sale of capital asset	6,000
Loss on sale of long-term investments	3,600
Income tax expense	?
Flood loss (pretax)	10,000
Freight paid on purchases	1,000
Merchandise inventory, December 31, 1996	88,000

Assume an average 35% income tax rate on all items, including gains and losses on assets sold and extraordinary items. The company has never experienced a flood loss before.

Required

1. Prepare a single-step income statement, including EPS information, and a separate schedule of cost of goods sold to support it.
2. Prepare a multiple-step income statement (include cost of goods sold computation within the statement).

P 4–3
(L.O. 2)

Financial Statement Classifications   Listed below are the primary financial statement classifications coded with letters and, below them, selected transactions and account titles. For each transaction or account title, enter in the space provided a code letter to indicate the usual classification. Comment on doubtful items.

Financial Statement Classification
Income Statement

Code	
A.	Revenue, or ordinary gain.
B.	Expense, or ordinary loss.
C.	Unusual gain or loss.
D.	Extraordinary item.

Statement of Retained Earnings

E.	An addition to or deduction from beginning balance.
F.	Addition to retained earnings.
G.	Deduction from retained earnings.

Disclosure Notes

H.	Note to the financial statements.

Balance Sheet

I.	Appropriately classified balance sheet account.

Response   **Transaction or Account Title**

1. _____ Estimated warranties payable.
2. _____ Allowance for doubtful accounts.
3. _____ Gain on sale of operational asset.
4. _____ Hurricane damages in Quebec City.
5. _____ Payment of $30,000 additional income tax assessment on prior year's income.
6. _____ Earthquake damages in Edmonton.
7. _____ Distribution expenses.
8. _____ Total amount of cash and credit sales for the period.
9. _____ Gain on disposal of long-term investments in shares (non-recurring).
10. _____ Net income for the period.
11. _____ Insurance gain on casualty (fire)—insurance proceeds exceed the book value of the assets destroyed.
12. _____ Cash dividends declared and paid.
13. _____ Rent collected on office space temporarily leased.
14. _____ Interest paid during the year plus interest accrued on liabilities.
15. _____ Dividends received on shares held as an investment.
16. _____ Damages paid as a result of a lawsuit by an individual injured while shopping in the store; the litigation lasted three years.
17. _____ Loss due to expropriation of a plant in a foreign country.
18. _____ A $100,000 bad debt is to be written off—the receivable had been outstanding for five years. The company estimates bad debts each year and has an allowance for bad debts.
19. _____ Adjustment due to correction of an error during current year; the error was made two years earlier.
20. _____ On December 31 of the current year, paid rent expense in advance for the next year.
21. _____ Cost of goods sold.
22. _____ Interest collected on November 30 of the current year from a customer on a 90-day note receivable, dated September 1 of the current year.
23. _____ Year-end bonus of $50,000 paid to employees for performance during the year.
24. _____ Cumulative effect of a change in accounting policy.
25. _____ A meteor destroys manufacturing facilities ($5 million book value, no insurance).

P 4–4
(L.O. 3)

Identify Reporting Deficiencies, Redraft Income Statement   Quad Graphics Company prepared the following income statement at the end of its annual accounting period, December 31, 1995.

Profit and Loss Report
December 31, 1995
QUAD GRAPHICS COMPANY
(amounts in thousands)

Sales income		$196.0
Inventory	$24.0	
Merchandise	68.0	
Freight.	2.0	
Inventory	(30.0)	
Cost of sales		64.0
Gross profit		132.0
Costs:		
Labour.	30.0	
Depreciation	12.0	
Sales	42.0	
Overhead	16.0	
Interest	6.0	
Extraordinary.	10.0	
Sale of used equipment	8.6	122.8
Other incomes:		
Service	7.4	
Interest	2.8	10.2
Taxable profit.		19.4
Tax (25%)		4.9
Net profit		$14.5

EPS: $14.5 ÷ 5,000 shares = $2.90.

Required

1. List all of the defects that you can identify on the above statement. (*Hint:* There may be errors in computing various subtotals in the report).
2. Recast the above statement in good multiple-step format using good terminology.

P 4–5
(L.O. 1, 2)

Relationships between Income Statement and Balance Sheet   Analyze the relationships and amounts for each case and complete the following schedule by entering the appropriate amount in the blank spaces:

a.

Case	Owners' Equity at Start of Period	Additional Investment by Owners	Dividends	Prior Period Adjustment	Owners' Equity at End of Period	Net Income (loss)
A	$10,000	$2,000	$1,000	0	$17,400	$ ____
B	28,000	3,000	____	0	22,000	4,700
C	____	0	800	$1,200 cr.	30,000	(2,200)
D	15,500	600	____	0	12,950	(2,000)
E	18,000	____	700	2,000 dr.	22,000	4,700

b.

Case	Sales Revenue	Beginning Inventory	Purchases	Ending Inventory	Cost of Goods Sold	Gross Margin	Total Remaining Expenses	Net Income
F	$ ____	$25,000	$60,000	$ ____	$67,000	$23,000	$ ____	$1,000
G	80,000	____	48,000	2,000	____	23,000	18,000	____
H	____	20,000	____	36,000	59,000	18,000	____	8,000

P 4–6
(L.O. 3, 4, 5, 6)

Combined Income and Retained Earnings Statement   The following amounts were taken from the accounting records of Curtis Recyclers Corporation at December 31, 1995, the end of the annual accounting period:

Sales revenue	$340,000
Service revenue	64,000
Cost of goods sold	170,000
Distribution and administrative expenses	86,000
Investment revenue	6,000
Interest expense	4,000
Loss on sale of long-term investment (pretax)	10,000
Earthquake damage loss (pretax)	14,000
Cash dividends declared	8,000
Correction of error from prior period, pretax (a debit)	12,000
Balance, retained earnings, January 1, 1995	80,300

Common shares, 30,000 shares outstanding.
Restriction on retained earnings, $50,000 per bond payable indenture.

Assume an average 35% income tax rate on all items.

Required

Prepare a combined single-step income and retained earnings statement, including tax allocation and EPS. Show computations. State any necessary assumptions.

P 4–7
(L.O. 4)

Prior Period Adjustments, Correcting Entries   Cheyenne Express Corporation underwent its annual audit by the independent auditor at December 31, 1995, the end of the annual accounting period. During the audit, the following situations were found to need attention:

a. On December 29, 1993, an asset that cost $12,000 was debited in full to 1993 operating expenses. The asset has a six-year estimated life and no residual value. The company uses straight-line depreciation.

b. Late in 1995, the company constructed a small warehouse using its own employees at a total cost of $90,000. However, before the decision was made to self-construct the asset, Cheyenne obtained a $100,000 bid from a contractor. Upon completion of the warehouse, Cheyenne made the following entry in the accounts:

Warehouse (an operational asset)	100,000	
Cash		90,000
Other income (nonoperating)		10,000

c. Prior to recording 1995 depreciation expense, the management decided that a large machine that originally cost $128,000 should have been depreciated over a useful life of 14 years instead of 20 years. The machine was acquired January 2, 1990. Assume that the residual value of $8,000 was not changed and 1995 depreciation has not been recorded.

d. During December 1995, the company disposed of an old machine for $6,000 cash. Annual depreciation for 1995, which was not recorded, was $2,000. At the beginning of 1995, the accounts reflected the following:

Machine (cost)	$18,000
Accumulated depreciation	13,000

At date of disposal, the following entry was made:

Cash	6,000	
Machine		6,000

e. A patent that originally cost $3,400 is being amortized over its legal life of 17 years at $200 per year. After the 1994 adjusting entry, it was amortized down to a book value of $800. At the end of 1995, it was determined in view of a competitor's patent that the patent has no remaining economic value.

f. As the result of a tax audit, the company had to pay $27,000 of additional tax relating to the 1990 and 1991 fiscal years. The following journal entry was made on the payment:

Tax expense	$27,000	
Cash		$27,000

Required

For each of the above situations, write a one-paragraph summary explaining the nature of each item and what should have been recorded in the accounts. If a journal entry is needed to correct the accounts, provide it, along with supporting computations. Ignore income tax considerations.

P 4–8
(L.O. 4, 5)

Change in Accounting Principle, Retained Earnings Statement Moncton Developments Ltd. was formed in 1992. During the year ended December 31, 1994, the company changed its method of accounting for product development expenses from expensing such items to capitalizing them and amortizing them over the period of expected benefit. The 1994 statements have been prepared using this new policy. Preliminary statements appear as follows:

MONCTON DEVELOPMENTS LTD.

Comparative Statements of Income and Retained Earnings
For the Years Ended December 31, 1994 and 1993

	1994	1993
Sales	$2,400,000	$2,160,000
Costs and expenses	1,282,000	1,040,000
Product development	—	150,000
Depreciation and amortization	118,000	70,000
	1,400,000	1,260,000
Income before tax	1,000,000	900,000
Tax expense (40%)	400,000	360,000
Net income	600,000	540,000
Retained earnings, opening	690,000	200,000
	1,290,000	740,000
Dividends, ($1 per share)	50,000	50,000
Retained earnings, closing	$1,240,000	$ 690,000
EPS	$12	$10.80

The following pretax information was gathered:

	1994	1993	1992
Net income	$600,000*	$540,000	$210,000
Product development costs	200,000	150,000	250,000
Depreciation and amortization, prior to change	70,000	70,000	60,000
Depreciation and amortization, after change	118,000	110,000	90,000

* Using new policy.

Required

1. Prepare a revised comparative 1994 income and retained earnings statement, giving appropriate treatment to the change in accounting policy. All amounts are taxable at 40%. Include note disclosure.
2. If insufficient information is available to treat the accounting policy change as in (1), what other options does the company have? Describe the impact of the alternatives on the financial statements in a brief report.

P 4–9
(L.O. 3, 4, 5, 6)

Combined Income and Retained Earnings Statement, Intraperiod Income Tax Allocation The following pretax amounts were taken from the accounts of Stone Container Corporation at December 31, 1995, the end of the annual accounting period:

Sales revenue	$550,000
Cost of goods sold	280,000
Distribution expenses	100,000
Administrative expenses	70,000
Interest revenue	1,000
Interest expense	3,000
Gain on sale of long-term investment not held for resale (pretax)	20,000
Loss from earthquake damage (pretax)	40,000
Balance, retained earnings, January 1, 1995	95,000
Cash dividends declared	15,000
Payment made after lawsuit filed by a customer; litigation lasted three years (pretax; a debit)	8,000

Common shares outstanding, 40,000.
At December 31, 1995, there is a restriction on retained earnings amounting to $25,000 as required by the indenture agreement on bonds payable.

Assume an average 35% income tax rate on all items.

Required   Prepare a combined multiple-step income and retained earnings statement, including intraperiod income tax allocation and EPS. Show computations.

P 4–10
(L.O. 2, 3, 4)   **Identify Statement Deficiencies and Redraft Statements**   The following income statement and retained earnings statement were prepared by the bookkeeper for Airco Supply Corporation:

AIRCO SUPPLY CORPORATION
Profit Statement
December 31, 1995

Sales income		$123,000
Service income		20,000
Total		143,000
Cost of sales:		
Inventory	$34,000	
Purchases (net)	71,000	
Inventory	(40,000)	65,000
Gross profit		78,000
Costs:		
Salaries, wages, etc.	35,000	
Depreciation and write-offs	7,000	
Rent	3,000	
Taxes, property	500	
Utilities	2,100	
Promotion	900	
Sales returns	2,000	
Sundry	6,700	(57,200)
Special items:		
Profit on asset sold		6,000
Inventory shortage		(2,800)
Pretax profit		24,000
Income tax		3,200
Net profit		$ 20,800

AIRCO SUPPLY CORPORATION
Earned Surplus
December 31, 1995

Balance, earned surplus		$ 27,000
Add:		
Profit		20,800
Correction of inventory error of 1994 (pretax)		5,000
Total		52,800
Deduct:		
Earthquake loss (pretax)	$13,000	
Dividends	15,000	27,000
Balance		$ 25,800

Required   1. Write a brief report evaluating Airco Supply's financial statement presentation and format. There may be arithmetic errors in the report. List items that you believe should be changed, and give your recommendations with respect to appropriate reporting, terminology, and format. The average income tax rate is 20%, and 10,000 common shares are outstanding. Assume that the earthquake loss is the first in the company's 20-year history.

2. Prepare a complete multiple-step income statement and a complete statement of retained earnings.

P 4–11
(L.O. 2, 3, 4)   **Discontinued Operations**   At its September 1, 1995, meeting, the board of directors of Hazelton Candy Company approved a plan for disposing of its candy vending division. The vending machine

operation has separately identifiable assets and operations and had incurred a loss before tax of $150,000 for the eight-month period ending September 1, 1995. A tentative agreement has been reached with McAdoo Corporation to buy the vending division for $2,000,000 with delivery of all the assets and operations to McAdoo as of April 1, 1996. Hazelton will continue operating the division until it is delivered to McAdoo. It is expected that the sale will result in a loss of $250,000 on the net assets of the division.

An operating loss of $30,000 before tax effects was experienced during the last four months of 1995; an additional loss of $50,000 is expected during the time Hazelton will be operating the division in 1996. Assume an income tax rate of 30%.

Required

1. Show the discontinued operations section of the 1995 income statement for Hazelton Candy Company. Assume that the after-tax income from continuing operations in 1995 is $500,000.
2. Actual operations of the vending machine division for the first three months of 1996 result in an operating loss before taxes of $40,000, and the sale of the net assets of the division results in an actual pretax loss of $230,000. Show the discontinued operations section of comparative income statements for 1995 and 1996 for Hazelton Candy Company. Assume that after-tax income from continuing operations is $600,000 in 1996.

P 4–12
(L.O. 2, 3, 4)

Discontinued Operations, Unusual Item   Hess Products Company, a diversified manufacturing company, had four separate operating divisions, each engaged in the manufacture of products in one of the following areas: paper products, health aids, textiles, and office equipment.

Pretax data for the two years ended December 31, 1995 and 1994, are presented below:

	Net Sales		Cost of Goods Sold		Operating Expenses	
	1995	1994	1995	1994	1995	1994
Paper products.	$3,500,000	$3,000,000	$2,400,000	$1,800,000	$ 550,000	$ 275,000
Health aids	2,000,000	1,270,000	1,100,000	700,000	300,000	125,000
Textiles	1,580,000	1,400,000	500,000	900,000	200,000	150,000
Office equipment.	920,000	1,330,000	800,000	1,000,000	650,000	750,000
	$8,000,000	$7,000,000	$4,800,000	$4,400,000	$1,700,000	$1,300,000

Additional pretax data:

a. On January 1, 1995, Hess agreed to sell the assets and product line of the office equipment division and expected to realize a gain on this disposal. An offer was accepted on this date and a contract signed. On September 1, 1995, the division's assets and product line were sold for $2,100,000 (two-thirds cash collected on this date), resulting in a gain of $640,000 (exclusive of operations during the phaseout period). The office equipment division had operating losses of $420,000 in 1994 and $530,000 through September 1, 1995.
b. The company's textiles division had six manufacturing plants that produced a variety of textile products. In April 1995, the company sold one of these plants and realized a gain of $130,000 (carrying value, $200,000). After the sale, the operations at the plant that was sold were transferred to the remaining five textile plants that the company continued to operate.
c. In August 1995, the main warehouse of the paper products division, located on the banks of the Bayer River, was flooded when the river overflowed. The resulting damage of $420,000 is not included in the financial data given above. Historical records indicate that the Bayer River normally overflows every four to five years, causing flood damage to adjacent property; this loss was not covered by insurance.
d. For the two years ended December 31, 1995 and 1994, the company had interest revenue earned on investments of $70,000 and $40,000, respectively. This is not included in the above information.
e. For the two years ended December 31, 1995 and 1994, the company's net income (after income tax) was $1,152,000 and $804,000, respectively.
f. Income tax expense for each of the two years should be computed at a rate of 40%.

Required

1. Prepare in proper form a comparative income statement of Hess Products Company for the two years ended December 31, 1995, and December 31, 1994.
2. Give or explain the entries related to the discontinued segment on (a) the measurement date and (b) the disposal date.

(AICPA adapted)

P 4–13
(L.O. 4)

Discontinued Operations   On April 1, 1995, Carter Electronics Company signed a contract to sell its Teck Products Division to Baker Company for $300,000 cash: one-third on April 1, 1995; the remainder on July 1, 1995. Carter transferred control of the Teck Products Division to Baker on April 1, 1995. The book (i.e., carrying) value of the net assets of the Teck Division on March 31, 1995, was $280,000. The income tax rate is 40% and the annual reporting period ends December 31. The income (pretax) of the Teck Division for the period from January 1 to March 31, 1995, was $15,000.

At December 31, 1995, the accounting records provide the following pretax income from the operations of the Teck Products Division: 1994, $16,500; 1995, $15,000. Teck Products had sales of $640,000 in 1994 and $210,000 in 1995. Carter's after-tax income from operations (excluding income from Teck Products Division) was $600,000 for 1994 and $630,000 for 1995.

Required

1. Give the entries by Carter Company for 1995 related to the sale of the Teck Products Division, including explanations.
2. Prepare the comparative income statements dated December 31, 1994, and December 31, 1995, including an appropriate disclosure note.

P 4–14
(L.O. 2, 3, 4, 5, 6)

 Format of Income Statement, Discontinued Operations, Prior Period Adjustment, Retained Earnings Statement   The following trial balance of the Puget Petroleum Corporation at December 31, 1995, has been adjusted, except that income tax expense has not been allocated.

PUGET PETROLEUM CORPORATION
Trial Balance*
December 31, 1995

	Debit	Credit
Cash.	$ 675,000	
Accounts receivable (net)	1,695,000	
Inventory	2,185,000	
Property, plant, and equipment (net)	8,660,000	
Accounts payable and accrued liabilities		$ 1,895,000
Income tax payable		360,000
Deferred income tax.		285,000
Common shares.		5,975,000
Retained earnings, January 1, 1995		3,350,000
Net sales, regular		10,750,000
Net sales, plastics division		2,200,000
Cost of sales, regular	5,920,000	
Cost of sales, plastics division	1,650,000	
Selling and administrative expenses, regular	2,600,000	
Selling and administrative expense, plastics division	660,000	
Interest income, regular		65,000
Gain on litigation settlement		200,000
Depreciation adjustment from accounting change, regular	350,000	
Gain on disposal of plastics division.		150,000
Income tax expense	835,000	
Totals	$25,230,000	$25,230,000

* Accounts identified as regular include all but plastics division for that account.

Other financial data for the year ended December 31, 1995:

a. **Income tax expense:**

Tax payments	$475,000
Accrued	360,000
Total charged to income tax expense*	$835,000
Tax rate on all types of income	40%

The gain from litigation settlement is a taxable gain, and relates to 1993.

* The $835,000 does not reflect intraperiod income tax allocation as is required for financial statement purposes.

b. **Discontinued operations** On October 31, 1995, Puget sold its Plastics Division for $2,950,000, when the carrying amount was $2,800,000. For financial statement reporting, this sale was considered a disposal of a segment of a business. The measurement date and the disposal date were both October 31, 1995.

c. **Change in depreciation method** On January 1, 1995, Puget changed to the declining-balance method from the straight-line method of depreciation to conform to industry practice. The pretax cumulative effect of this accounting change was determined to be a charge of $350,000. There was no change in depreciation method for income tax purposes.

d. **Capital structure** Common shares, nopar, traded on a national exchange:

	Shares
Outstanding at January 1, 1995.	200,000
Issued on July 1, 1995 at $11.50 per share	30,000
	230,000

Required   Using the multiple-step format, prepare an income statement for Puget for the year ended December 31, 1995. Also, prepare a retained earnings statement. All components of income tax expense should be appropriately shown.

(AICPA adapted)

P 4–15
(L.O. 4)

Discontinued Operations, Appendix 4B Below are data for four different cases of disposal of a business segment. In all cases, assume that the disposal measurement date is August 1, 1995, and that the actual disposal does not occur until March 1, 1996. Ignore income taxes.

	Case 1	**Case 2**	**Case 3**	**Case 4**
Income (loss) from operations of discontinued segment from January 1 to August 1, 1995	$(150)	$ 40	$(150)	$(150)
Actual income (loss) from operations of discontinued segment from August 1 to December 31, 1995. . . .	(30)	30	30	(30)
Estimated income (loss) from operations of discontinued segment in future periods until actual disposal date	(50)	20	20	(20)
Estimated gain (loss) on disposal of assets of discontinued segment.	250	100	(100)	(100)

Required
1. For each case, show the computation of the amount to be recorded as the pretax gain or loss on disposal of the business segment in 1995 and 1996, assuming that the estimates for 1996 are the actual results.

2. On the disposal date, the following amounts are known:

	Case 1	**Case 2**	**Case 3**	**Case 4**
Actual income (loss) from operations of discontinued segment from January 1, 1996, to the actual disposal date	$(40)	$20	$30	$(20)
Actual gain (loss) on disposal of assets of discontinued segment	180	90	(120)	(80)

Show the computation of the actual amounts to be recorded as the pretax gain or loss on disposal of the business segment in both years, assuming that the computations in requirement 1 were appropriately recorded and that the actual amounts given at the disposal date are known at the disposal date in 1996.

ANALYZING FINANCIAL STATEMENTS

A 4–1
(L.O. 2, 3,
4, 5, 6)

Mark's Work Wearhouse: Format of Income Statement, Retained Earnings Statement, Disclosure of Special Items   In its 1992 annual report, Mark's Work Wearhouse identified the following accounts and amounts* (amounts in thousands):

	52 weeks ended	
	Jan. 25, 1992	**Jan. 26, 1991**
Sales	$132,742	$178,318
Front line (retail and franchise operation) expenses	39,089	51,653
Opening retained earnings.	?	11,560
Discontinued operations—loss on disposal	2,250	—
Franchise revenue	3,000	3,817
Settlement with ex-senior executive	1,959	—
Loss on closure of retail operations	—	1,384
Income taxes (recovery)	(443)	(4,400)
Purchase of common shares—excess of redemption price over original proceeds	—	15
Back line (support) expenses	15,491	17,246
Discontinued operations—loss from operations	196	13
Cost of goods sold	85,959	122,593

Common shares outstanding: 9,875

* The income statement provides more detail than reproduced; amounts have been aggregated for illustration purposes.

Required   Assume that Mark's Work Wearhouse wished to present the above accounts in a multiple-step format income statement. Prepare an income statement and a retained earnings statement in good form.

A 4–2
(L.O. 4)

National Semiconductor: Disposal of Business Segment   National Semiconductor Corporation (NSC) has a May 30 fiscal year-end. NSC disposed of its Information Systems Group (ISG) on January 31, 1989, during NSC's third quarter. The measurement date was the disposal date. The division was sold for $475,600,000 in cash plus future royalties through May 30, 1990, which were guaranteed to be $30,000,000. The guaranteed royalties were included in the computation of the gain on the sale of the division. Excerpts from comparative income statements found in the May 30, 1990, financial statements are as follows:

	Year Ended May 30		
	1990	**1989**	**1988**
	(amounts in millions)		
Earnings (loss) from continuing operations	$(29.3)	$(205.5)	$30.1
Discontinued operations:			
Earnings (loss) from operations (net of income taxes of $6.5 in 1989 [recoveries] and $10.5 in 1988)	—	(37.7)	32.6
Gain on sale of discontinued operation (net of incomes taxes of $1.2 in 1990 and $40.5 in 1989)	4.3	220.0	—
Net income (loss).	$(25.0)	$ (23.2)	$62.7

Required   1. Determine the net book value of ISG as of the measurement date.
2. Why does NSC report a gain on the sale of the discontinued operation of $4,300,000 in the year ending May 30, 1990?
3. NSC reports an after-tax loss from discontinued operations of $37,700,000 for the year ending May 30, 1989, and earnings from discontinued operations of $32,600,000 for the year ending May 30, 1988. Over what period was the loss accrued? Over what period were the earnings accrued?
4. How would the reporting differ if NSC had adopted a formal disposal plan at the beginning of the 1988 fiscal year?

A 4–3
(L.O. 4)

Mead Corporation: Discontinued Operations, Unusual Item, Change in Accounting Principle   In December 1990, the board of directors of Mead Corporation approved a plan to curtail the development of the company's imaging products division. As a result, the company established a provision before tax totalling $77,000,000 for (a) the loss expected on the disposal of the division's assets and (b) future losses of $29,300,000 expected to be incurred in fulfilling contract obligations over the next four years. The imaging products division had incurred before-tax losses of $50,000,000 in 1989 and $41,700,000 in 1990.

In addition, during 1990, the company retired an issue of bonds early. Assume that the bonds retired early had a carrying value of $170,000,000 and were retired at a cost of $159,000,000, resulting in a pretax gain of $11,000,000. The company had never had such a transaction before.

The tax rate on all the above items is Mead Corporation's average income tax rate of 37%.

Assume that earnings from continuing operations before income taxes were $392,500,000 in 1989 and $168,900,000 in 1990. This does not include the bond retirement transaction. The average number of common shares outstanding were 65,100,000 shares in 1989 and 62,200,000 shares in 1990. Mead Corporation has no preferred shares outstanding.

Required

1. Prepare the income statements for Mead Corporation for 1989 and 1990, beginning with income from continuing operations. Include appropriate earnings per share computations.
2. In 1991, the imaging products division was operated by Mead as a discontinued business, and it incurred a pretax operating loss of $6,500,000. The original provision for the disposal of the division is still considered to be a reasonable estimate. In addition, Mead adopted a new accounting principle to record the expected future costs of postretirement benefits other than pensions. The cumulative effect of the change in accounting principle was a debit of $93,500,000 ($53,700,000 net of income tax benefit). Except for this item, the average tax rate is 37%. Income from continuing operations after tax was $75,600,000 in 1991, and they had an average of 58,600,000 common shares outstanding during the year. Show the income statements for 1991 and 1990, beginning with income from continuing operations. Include appropriate earnings per share computations.

A 4–4
(L.O. 2, 3, 4, 5)

Magna International Inc.: Statement Analysis   A set of financial statements for Magna International Inc. appears at the end of the book. Examine them carefully and respond to the following questions (for 1993 only, unless otherwise specified):

1. Are the statements comparative? Why are comparative statements usually presented?
2. Are the statements consolidated? What do you understand this to mean?
3. Is this a retail, financial, or a manufacturing company? Explain.
4. Compare the income statement disclosures of Magna with the list of required disclosures in the chapter. What does Magna disclose that is not required?
5. Were any unusual or extraordinary items reported on the income statement?
6. How many EPS amounts were reported? How were they calculated?
7. Does Magna use a single-step or a multiple-step income statement? Comment.
8. What was the profit margin (net income dividend by revenue)?
9. What was the total amount of dividends declared? Dividends paid?
10. Are there any charges to retained earnings other than dividends in 1993 or 1992? Describe these items, if any.

5

Review: The Balance Sheet and the Statement of Changes in Financial Position

LEARNING OBJECTIVES

After you have studied this chapter, you will be able to:

1   Describe balance sheet formats and the classification of asset, liability, and equity accounts.

2   Explain the different methods used to value assets, liabilities, and equities and why the use of market values is uncommon in balance sheets.

3   Understand the importance of precise terminology, comparative statements, and disclosure notes in communicating accurate information about the financial status of a company. Describe appropriate disclosure for various items, including contingencies and subsequent events.

4   Describe the uses and limitations of the balance sheet.

5   Explain alternative formats for structuring a statement of changes in financial position.

6   Define the major elements of the statement of changes in financial position.

7   Describe the uses and limitations of the statement of changes in financial position.

INTRODUCTION

Balance sheet information can be less than fully informative. For example, Brascan Limited reported a $505.1 million asset as of December 31, 1992—its investment in the common shares and convertible debentures of John Labatt Limited. On February 13, 1993, Brascan sold its investment for $993 million. Cost was materially lower than market value!

In 1986, IBM and MCI Communications entered into an agreement in which Satellite Business Systems, one of IBM's subsidiaries, was sold to MCI. In lieu of cash, IBM accepted 47 million shares of MCI's stock, which was worth $528 million at the time of the sale, based on the shares' then-current market value. The agreement specified that IBM hold the MCI shares for a period of three years. In 1989, MCI repurchased the shares for $677 million, an amount $149 million above the figure of $528 million shown at the time on IBM's balance sheet.

Critics might charge that Brascan and IBM were deliberately undervaluing their assets. Defenders could answer that both companies were simply following generally accepted accounting principles.

In 1992, Fisheries Products International (FPI) was forced to recognize substantial write-downs on certain of its assets. FPI recognized a $65 million unusual item on the income statement, which included a $57.2 write-down of its Newfoundland-based harvesting and processing assets. This write-down was caused by a significant decline in the company's Newfoundland ground fish resource base—basically, a lack of fish. The write-down was a major reduction in reported asset amounts. In this case, cost-base assets were overstated in 1991.

In 1985, Clayton & Dubilier, an investment firm specializing in corporate takeovers, gained a controlling interest in Uniroyal and took the big tire company private. Having bought out the public shareholders, Clayton planned to strip the company and sell off Uniroyal's operating divisions at juicy profits. But Uniroyal's employees got in the way. They sued Clayton & Dubilier, charging that they were owed retirement benefits not shown as liabilities on Uniroyal's balance sheet. The employees won, costing Clayton & Dubilier $75 million and putting an end to the planned breakup. Uniroyal was later sold intact to a Japanese tire maker.

How could Clayton & Dubilier have ignored Uniroyal's pension and retirement benefit obligations? Companies used to insist that future pension funding obligations were not liabilities and, therefore, did not need to be recognized as such on the balance sheet. The courts, however, have consistently ruled that future pension and retirement benefits are legal contract obligations. Accounting standards now require disclosure of these liabilities.

This chapter examines the balance sheet and the statement of changes in financial position. The emphasis is on the value of these statements to a company's investors and creditors, the way the statements are structured, and the relevance of individual line items. How an item appears on a company's balance sheet can affect understanding the item, and what does not appear on the balance sheet can be as important as what does appear.

THE BALANCE SHEET

The balance sheet provides economic information about an entity's resources (**assets**), claims against those resources (**liabilities**), and the remaining claim accruing to the owners (**owners' equity**). **Statement of financial position** is the formal term, but the more common term among statement preparers and users is *balance sheet*. The term *balance sheet* reflects an important aspect of this report; namely, the statement balances in conformity with the **basic accounting identity:**

$$\text{Assets} = \text{Liabilities} + \text{Owners' Equity}$$
$$A \quad = \quad L \quad + \quad OE$$

Format of the Balance Sheet

Net Assets Form   The basic accounting identity or model can be rearranged to reflect the owners' viewpoint. Thus, $A - L = OE$. The recorded value of the firm to the owners, called *owners' equity*, is what remains after the liabilities are subtracted from the assets. This amount is reported periodically to the owners.

Financing Form   The financing form follows the classic accounting identity, $A = L + OE$.

EXHIBIT 5-1
Alternative Presentations of
the Balance Sheet

	Emphasis	
	Net Assets Form A − L = OE	Financing Form A = L + OE
	(thousands of dollars)	
Current assets:		
Cash	$ 575.1	$ 575.1
Short-term investments	518.4	518.4
Accounts receivable	1,736.9	1,736.9
Inventories and prepayments	1,569.3	1,569.3
Total current assets	4,399.7	4,399.7
Capital assets:		
Land, building, and equipment	5,767.4	5,767.4
Construction in progress	763.5	763.5
Accumulated amortization	(2,259.8)	(2,259.8)
Total capital assets	4,271.1	4,271.1
Investments and other assets	2,415.2	2,415.2
Total assets	$11,086.0	$11,086.0
Current liabilities	$ 3,617.3	$ 3,617.3
Long-term debt	495.7	495.7
Other liabilities	1,970.1	1,970.1
Total liabilities	$ 6,083.1	$ 6,083.1
Assets minus liabilities	$ 5,002.9	
Shareholders' equity:		
Common shares	204.7	204.7
Retained earnings	4,798.2	4,798.2
Total shareholders' equity	$ 5,002.9	$ 5,002.9
Total liabilities and shareholders' equity		$11,086.0

Expressing the balance sheet using the accounting identity A = L + OE can be viewed as emphasizing the means of financing the organization's assets. Funds must be raised from creditors (liabilities) or from owners (owners' equity), often by retaining the organization's earnings. Exhibit 5–1 shows alternative balance sheet presentations of the accounting identity.

Most companies in Canada use the financing form. Two versions exist—one lists assets at the top of the statement, followed vertically by liabilities and then equities. This is called the **report form.** Alternatively, assets can be listed on the left of the statement and liabilities and equities on the right. This is called the **account form.** According to *Financial Reporting in Canada,* a survey of 300 Canadian public companies, 82% used the report form in 1992, while 14% used the account form. The remainder used the net assets form or a version thereof.

Exhibit 5–2 provides the balance sheet for Dominion Textiles Inc. This statement has a total for assets and another for liabilities and equities, so it is in the financing form. It lists assets, then liabilities, then equities down the statement, so it is in report form. The balance sheet provides two years of comparative information instead of the more common one comparative year. Some stock exchanges require disclosure of the extra year of comparative data for the income statement; companies are encouraged to make disclosures useful to financial statement users and can exceed minimum requirements if they wish.

Basic Definitions

Assets, liabilities, and owners' equity are key concepts and therefore require precise definitions. Section 1000 of the *CICA Handbook* provides the definitions shown on the following page:

EXHIBIT 5–2
Balance Sheet, Financing
Form: Dominion Textile Inc.

Consolidated Balance Sheets
As at 30 June

	1993	1992	1991
	(in thousands of dollars)		
Assets			
Current assets:			
Cash and cash equivalents	$ 156,674	$ 46,956	$ 39,119
Receivables			
Trade, less allowances of $13,416			
(1992—$17,573, 1991—$14,218)	246,650	262,964	226,796
Other	17,512	21,225	19,215
Inventories.	160,782	181,118	200,750
Prepaid expenses and other current assets	16,529	15,177	11,049
	598,147	527,440	496,929
Investments and advances	19,979	28,748	64,282
Property, plant, and equipment, net.	556,358	627,021	649,214
Intangible assets, net	119,486	116,088	120,665
Other assets	35,142	23,858	26,716
Total assets	$1,329,112	$1,323,155	$1,357,806
Liabilities and Shareholders' Equity			
Current liabilities:			
Short-term borrowings.	$ 40,041	$ 39,790	$ 55,649
Accounts payable and accrued liabilities.	197,234	218,578	184,099
Dividends payable	1,260	1,283	1,320
Income taxes payable	15,154	9,242	7,071
Long-term debt due within one year	122,519	26,471	29,682
	376,208	295,364	277,821
Long-term debt.	361,616	517,380	527,853
Other non-current liabilities	41,637	45,611	38,238
Deferred income taxes.	41,009	22,623	17,712
Minority interest	61,684	64,089	59,825
Shareholders' equity:			
Capital stock			
Preferred.	71,441	73,041	73,052
Common	463,897	408,115	408,001
	535,338	481,156	481,053
Deficit	(77,848)	(100,715)	(20,728)
Cumulative translation adjustment	(10,532)	(2,353)	(23,968)
Total shareholders' equity	446,958	378,088	436,357
Total liabilities and shareholders' equity	$1,329,112	$1,323,155	$1,357,806

Assets: Economic resources controlled by an entity as a result of past transactions or events and from which future economic benefit may be obtained.

Liabilities: Obligations of an entity arising from past transactions or events, the settlement of which may result in the transfer or use of assets, provision of services, or other yielding of economic benefits in the future.

Owners' equity: The residual ownership interest in the assets of an entity that remains after its liabilities are deducted.

To make accounting information as understandable and usable by decision makers as possible, items are grouped and arranged in the balance sheet according to certain guidelines:

- Assets are classified and presented in decreasing order of liquidity (convertibility into cash). Those items nearest to cash (that is, readily convertible at any time without restriction) are ranked first. Assets with least liquidity (or least likely to be converted to cash) are listed last.
- Liabilities are classified and presented based on time to maturity. Thus, obligations currently due are listed first, and those carrying the most distant maturity dates are listed last. (Several exceptions are discussed later.)
- Owners' equity items are classified and presented in order of permanence. Thus, paid-in capital contribution accounts, which typically change the least, should be listed first. Equity accounts used to report accumulated earnings and profit distributions are listed last.

Classification of information reported in the balance sheet and the items under each classification are determined by accounting standards, although such classifications are also strongly influenced by the unique characteristics of each industry and each business enterprise. The balance sheet of a financial institution such as a bank reflects classifications different from those of a manufacturing company. For example, financial institutions do not use current asset and liability designations.[1] Format and classifications should be designed for a particular enterprise to comply with the full disclosure principle, which specifies that reporting be informative and sufficiently inclusive to avoid misleading inferences.

Classification

The classification and presentation order below are representative of current reporting practice and terminology.

A. Assets.
    1. Current assets.
        a. Cash.
        b. Short-term investments.
        c. Receivables.
        d. Inventories.
        e. Prepayments.
    2. Non-current assets.
        a. Investments and funds.
        b. Tangible capital assets (also called property, plant, and equipment).
        c. Intangible capital assets.
        d. Other assets.
        e. Long-term deferred charges.
B. Liabilities.
    1. Current liabilities (including the current portion of long-term liabilities).
    2. Long-term (non-current) liabilities.
    3. Long-term deferred credits.
C. Owners' equity.
    1. Contributed (or paid-in) capital.
        a. Share capital.
        b. Other contributed (or paid-in) capital.
    2. Retained earnings.

The balance sheet must be dated at a specific date, such as "December 31, 1995." In contrast, the income statement and the statement of changes in financial position are dated to cover a specific period of time, such as "For the Year Ended December 31, 1995."

---

[1] Banking institutions are government-regulated. As such, they are required to furnish financial statement information in formats prescribed by the federal Bank Act. Regulators have decided that there is no need to distinguish between a bank's current and non-current assets because the nature of a bank's primary assets (marketable debt securities and loan portfolios) is such that they are all fairly liquid, at least in theory.

CONCEPT REVIEW

1. Describe the difference between structuring the balance sheet to reflect the owners' view as compared to reflecting the financing of the business.
2. In what order are assets presented on the balance sheet? Liabilities? Equities?
3. Where would a long-term deferred charge be presented on a balance sheet?

Assets

Current Assets Current assets include cash and other assets that are *reasonably expected to be realized in cash or to be sold or consumed during the normal operating cycle* of the business or within one year from the balance sheet date, whichever is longer.

The normal operating cycle of a business is the average length of time from the expenditure of cash for inventory, to sale, to accounts receivable, and finally back to cash. This is sometimes called the cash-to-cash cycle. Most companies use one year as the time period for classifying items as current or long-term because either the operating cycle is less than one year or the length of the operating cycle may be difficult to measure reliably.

Current assets are relatively easy to define. However, judgment is required in operationalizing the phrases *normal operating cycle* and *reasonably expected to be realized in cash*. When there is uncertainty, management may be inclined to classify certain items as current assets in order to produce a positive effect on working capital (current assets minus current liabilities), a key financial measure. For example, an investment in marketable securities could be classified as a current or noncurrent asset, depending on the intended holding period. The placement of this asset on a company's balance sheet could be based on the actual intention of management or, alternatively and inappropriately, on management's desire to show its accounts in a better light; this is a problem both for the auditors and for external decision makers.

The following items are *not* current assets:

1. Cash and claims to cash that are restricted for uses other than current operations.
2. Receivables with an extended maturity date.
3. Long-term prepayments of expenses.
4. Investments made in securities that are not readily marketable, or where the intention is to hold them as a long-term investment.

Cash Cash available for operating activities is a current asset. Accounts held for designated purposes (e.g., bond sinking funds) are long term.

Short-Term Investments Investments in debt securities, such as Canadian government treasury bills (T-bills), money market funds, and commercial paper, are short-term investments. Short-term investments also include corporate equity securities. Any significant amounts of short-term investments in debt or in equity securities should be listed separately among the current assets. Short-term investments are reported at the lower of their cost or current market value. Current market value for any marketable securities should be disclosed.

Receivables Receivables should be reported net of any anticipated reduction because of uncollectible amounts. Receivables pledged as security for an obligation of the firm should be disclosed.

Inventories Inventories are reported at the lower of cost or market (LCM). In addition, the valuation basis and the completion stage should be indicated (e.g., raw materials, work in process, or finished goods). Dominion Textile reports this information in a disclosure note, shown in Exhibit 5–3.

EXHIBIT 5–3

Inventory: Note Disclosure
from Dominion Textile's
Financial Statements

Note 7. Inventories

	1993	1992	1991
	(in thousands of dollars)		
Raw materials	$25,814	$31,227	$35,666
Work in process, including greige fabric for further processing	51,330	50,391	59,485
Finished goods	72,670	87,046	89,991
Supplies	10,968	12,454	15,608
	$160,782	$181,118	$200,750

Inventory Valuation [from the Accounting Policies note]

Materials and supplies in inventories are valued at the lower of average cost and replacement cost. Work in process and finished goods inventories are valued at the lower of cost and net realizable value. Cost includes raw materials, direct labour and certain manufacturing overhead expenses. Adequate provision is made for slow moving and obsolete inventories.

Prepaid Expenses   Prepaid expenses are cash outlays made in advance of receipt of service. Rent paid May 31 for the month of June is an example. A short-term prepayment should be classified as a current asset, whereas a long-term prepayment should be classified as a non-current asset. Prepaid expenses are current assets because an investment is made by paying cash in advance, thereby reducing cash outlays for the coming reporting period.

Non-Current Assets   The important distinctions between current, or short-term, assets and non-current, or long-term, assets are one or both of the following:

1. Long-term assets may not be used up in a single operating cycle.
2. Management plans to retain long-term assets beyond one year from the balance sheet date or beyond the operating cycle if it is longer.

Investments and Funds   The investments and funds classification includes the following non-current investments:

1. Long-term investments in the share capital of another company not intended for sale in the year. Such shares should be recorded at original cost or adjusted cost arising from the application of the equity method, where appropriate.
2. Long-term investments in the bonds of another company (any unamortized premium is added to the investment, and any unamortized discount is subtracted).
3. Investments in subsidiaries, including long-term receivables from subsidiaries. If the statements are consolidated, these accounts are eliminated.
4. Funds set aside for long-term future use, such as bond sinking funds (to retire bonds payable), expansion funds, share retirement funds, and long-term savings deposits. Funds are shown at the accumulated amount in the fund—contributions plus interest earned to date.
5. Cash surrender value of life insurance policies carried by the company.
6. Long-term investments in tangible assets, such as land and buildings, that are not used in current operations (including operational assets that are only temporarily idle).

Although long-term investments are usually shown at their original cost, some are not. Marketable equity securities, for example, may be reported at market.[2] The

---

[2] See Chapter 14 on investments for a full discussion. In brief, market value is appropriate when market value is lower than cost and the decline in value is permanent.

basis of valuation must be disclosed. If securities are carried at cost, market value must be disclosed. Major classifications of long-term investments should be disclosed separately.

Tangible Capital Assets   Capital assets are defined in the *CICA Handbook*, Section 3060, paragraph .04, as assets that:

(a) are held for use in the production or supply of goods and services, for rental to others, for administrative purposes or for the development, construction, maintenance or repair of other capital assets;
(b) have been acquired, constructed or developed with the intention of being used on a continuing basis; and
(c) are not intended for sale in the ordinary course of business.

Historically, capital assets were called *fixed assets* because of their relative permanence, or by the more descriptive term *property, plant, and equipment* (P,P&E). A wide variety of terminology is found in practice. Tangible capital assets include items that are depreciable, such as buildings, machinery, and fixtures; items that are subject to depletion, including mineral deposits, timber stands, and agricultural land; and items that are not subject to depreciation, such as land. Land should be reported separately. Capital assets also include certain leased assets if the lease arrangement is deemed to be a method of financing a permanent acquisition of the facilities.

The balance sheet or the related notes must report additional information on capital assets, including the following:

1. Balances of major classes of capital assets.
2. Accumulated depreciation, by major class of capital assets.
3. A description of the methods used in computing depreciation for the major classes of capital assets.

Tangible capital assets are usually shown on the balance sheet at their original cash equivalent cost less any accumulated depreciation or depletion to date.

Intangible Capital Assets   Intangible capital assets are those that lack physical substance. Examples of intangible properties include brand names, copyrights, franchises, licenses, patents, software, subscription lists, and trademarks. These assets are reported as a separate element in the balance sheet. Major items should be listed separately and recorded at cost. The accumulated amount of amortization should be disclosed in the notes or elsewhere in the financial statements. By convention, the contra account accumulated amortization is seldom listed separately and the asset is shown net of the contra account. Refer to the disclosure given to intangible assets in Dominion Textile's financial statements. Intangibles are listed as one net item on the balance sheet, augmented by note disclosure (Exhibit 5–4).

Some important intangible assets are not valued at all on company balance sheets. This is because intangibles are usually capitalized only when they are purchased as part of the acquisition of another firm or when expenditures such as legal fees are made in regard to them. Legal fees protecting future use of intangible assets are capitalized and written off over the future period benefitted, in accordance with the matching principle.

Most promotional expenditures and research expenditures are expensed in the period made. These expenditures are usually made with a clear expectation of future economic benefits. However, the connection between these expenditures and a resulting valuable asset is too indirect to permit capitalization and subsequent amortization of the outlays. Yet the write-off, while being conservative and practical, can substantially understate the intangible assets of the firm. Moreover, financial analysts might ignore reported intangible values when calculating return on assets, thereby producing misleading higher rates of return.

EXHIBIT 5–4

Intangible Assets: Note
Disclosure from
Dominion Textile's
Financial Statements

Note 10. Intangible Assets, Net

Goodwill, which represents the excess of cost over the fair value of companies acquired, is amortized on a straight-line basis over 40 years. Other intangible assets are amortized on a straight-line basis over periods ranging between 4 and 25 years. The net value of intangible assets is computed as follows:

	1993	1992	1991
	(in thousands of dollars)		
Goodwill	$140,147	$131,644	$130,072
Other intangibles.	3,389	3,170	7,962
	143,536	134,814	138,034
Less: Accumulated amortization.	24,050	18,726	17,369
	$119,486	$116,088	$120,665

The omission of these intangibles from the balance sheet stems from the lack of an arm's-length transaction for establishing a verifiable value or from the difficulty associated with establishing the probability of future economic benefits. Firms whose major assets are intangible present problems for financial statement users and preparers.

Other Assets   The other assets classification is used for assets that are not easily included under alternative asset classifications. Examples include long-term receivables from company officers and employees and idle operational assets (such as a mothballed plant). An asset should be analyzed carefully before it is classified among other assets in case there is a logical basis for classifying it elsewhere. Classification as an other asset is a last resort, and amounts should not be material. The nature of, and valuation basis for, these assets should be clearly disclosed. If a reported asset has no future economic benefit, it should be written off and reported in the income statement as a loss.

Long-Term Deferred Charges   Deferred charges may be the result of the prepayment of long-term expenses. These expenses have reliably determinable future economic benefits useful in earning future revenues. On this basis, they are viewed as assets until they are used. The only conceptual difference between a prepaid expense (classified as a current asset) and a deferred charge is the length of time over which the amount is amortized.

Also included under the deferred charges caption are such things as organization costs, machinery rearrangement costs, bond issue costs, and pension costs paid in advance. Deferred charges are sometimes inappropriately reported as other assets, but they should be reported separately. They are items that have economic benefit and qualify for deferral because they will benefit future periods. To promote good matching, they are deferred and amortized in future periods. The nature of these items, their valuation base, and the method and period of amortization must be clearly disclosed.

|CONCEPT REVIEW

1. How are the items in the current assets section ordered?
2. When is an investment in marketable securities long term?
3. Why are major intangible assets often not on the balance sheet?

Liabilities

Current Liabilities   Current liabilities include those obligations expected to be liquidated using current assets or refinanced by other short-term liabilities. Liabilities are usually classified in the order in which they will be paid. Current liabilities include the following:

1. Accounts payable for goods and services that enter into the operating cycle of the business (sometimes called *trade payables*).
2. Special short-term payables for nonoperating items and services.
3. Short-term notes payable.
4. Short-term bank debt.
5. Current maturities of long-term liabilities (including capital lease obligations).
6. Collections in advance of unearned revenue (such as rent collected in advance).
7. Accrued expenses for payrolls, interest, and taxes (including unpaid income taxes and property taxes).
8. The current portion of deferred income taxes.

The difference between total current assets (CA) and total current liabilities (CL) is an important measure of solvency called **working capital** (WC):

$$\text{Working capital} = \text{Current assets} - \text{Current liabilities}$$
$$WC = CA - CL$$

The **working capital ratio,** commonly called the *current ratio,* is defined as current assets (CA) divided by current liabilities (CL):

$$\text{Current or working capital ratio} = \frac{CA}{CL}$$

A ratio of 1 or more implies that the company can discharge its current obligations with current assets over the operating cycle, usually one year.

Dominion Textile has $221,939 ($598,147 less $376,208) in working capital, and a working capital ratio of 1.59 ($598,147 ÷ $376,208) (figures from Exhibit 5–2). Working capital is a rough indicator of current liquidity. Norms vary between industries and among companies.

Long-Term Liabilities   A long-term (non-current) liability is an obligation that does not require the use of current assets or the incurrence of another current liability for payment during the next operating cycle or during the next reporting year, whichever is longer.

All liabilities not appropriately classified as current liabilities are reported as long term. Typical long-term liabilities are bonds payable, long-term notes payable, pension liabilities, deferred long-term revenues (advances from customers), and long-term capital lease obligations. Most long-term liabilities are recorded at the exchange value of the assets or services received.

Disclosure provisions for long-term debt can be extensive, especially if the debt issue contains unusual features. Disclosure includes the interest rate, maturity date, sinking fund requirements (if any), and redemption and conversion provisions (if any). Further, the aggregate payments (cash flow) required over each of the next five years must be disclosed. Security given for particular debt issues, and details of loan covenants are also to be disclosed.

Long-Term Deferred Credits   When the amount of taxes legally payable is less than the tax expense recorded on the income statement, a **deferred tax credit** results. This is a common state of affairs, as capital assets qualify for fast write-off for tax purposes but are amortized more slowly for accounting purposes. Taxable income is lower than accounting income in the early years of capital asset ownership; in later years, the situation will be reversed and the deferred credit will be reduced.

This deferred tax credit is generally not classified as a liability since it is not owing to anyone nor does it have a repayment schedule or an interest rate. It is the result of matching. Therefore, long-term deferred taxes are shown as a separate component on the balance sheet.

Another common deferred credit is called a **non-controlling (or minority) interest in the assets of consolidated subsidiaries.** If the company controls a subsidiary, all its assets and liabilities are added into a consolidated balance sheet for corporate reporting purposes. The percentage of those assets owned by the non-controlling (minority) interest is established as a deferred credit. For example, if a company has an 80% controlling ownership of the voting shares of another company, all the investee's assets would be consolidated with the parent company and a 20% minority interest will be reported. Dominion Textile reports minority interests of $61,684 on its 1993 balance sheet (as shown in Exhibit 5–2).

Owners' Equity

Owners' equity for a corporation is called **shareholders' equity,** for a partnership, **partners' equity,** and for a sole proprietorship, **proprietor's equity.** Owners' equity is the owners' residual interest in the firm since it is the amount left after the liabilities are subtracted from the firm's assets. Owners' equity includes contributed (or paid-in) capital and retained earnings.

Contributed Capital   Because of legal requirements, contributed capital is subclassified to reflect detailed sources. For corporations, the most commonly reported subclassifications are:

a. Share capital.
b. Other contributed capital.

Share Capital   Share capital is the firm's stated or legal capital. It is the paid-in value or par value of the issued or outstanding preferred and common shares of the corporation. This amount is not available for dividend declarations.

Each share class, common and preferred, should be reported at its paid-in amount, or, in the case of par value shares, at par value. Par value shares are only found in a few provincial jurisdictions in Canada. Details of each class of share capital should be reported separately, including the number of shares authorized, issued, outstanding, and subscribed; also disclosed are conversion features, callability, preferences, dividend rates, and any other special features. Changes in share capital accounts during the period must be disclosed.

Other Contributed Capital   Other contributed capital arises from such transactions as the retirement of shares for less than the original investment made and capital arising from recapitalizations. Details and changes during the period should be disclosed.

Other contributed capital also includes, for corporations able to issue par value shares, an account called contributed capital in excess of par. If shares are sold for an amount in excess of par value, contributed capital is created. Details and changes during the period should be disclosed.

Retained Earnings   Retained earnings is essentially a corporation's accumulated net earnings, less dividends paid out, since the company's inception. In many corporations, retained earnings is the largest amount in the owners' equity section. Over a corporation's life, dividends are distributed to the shareholders in amounts that are usually less than the corporation's earnings. This policy establishes a continuing source of internally generated funds. Companies that are in their growth phase normally pay few, if any, dividends to their shareholders; instead, they retain all or most of their earnings for reinvestment and business expansion. Companies that are beyond their growth phase commonly pay out a higher percentage of their earnings in the form of shareholder dividends. A negative balance in retained earnings is called a **deficit** and usually arises when a company experiences operating losses.

Retained earnings may be divided between the amount available for dividends (unappropriated or unrestricted retained earnings) and any amounts restricted for other purposes (appropriated or restricted retained earnings). This practice ensures retention of a certain level of internally generated funds. Retained earnings may be restricted (i.e., dividend payments restricted) due to the provisions of bond agreements, because of an impending adverse lawsuit, or because of future expansion plans. During the period of restriction or appropriation, the specified amount is unavailable for dividends. After the restriction is removed, the restricted amount is again included in the total available for dividends. Restrictions and appropriations must be disclosed.

CONCEPT REVIEW

1. How are the items in the current liabilities section ordered?
2. What is working capital and why is it important to financial statement users?
3. What are the major elements of owners' equity?

ADDITIONAL REPORTING ISSUES

Offsetting Assets and Liabilities

Offsetting assets and liabilities in financial reporting is usually improper. Offsetting is a procedure by which a liability is subtracted from an asset or vice versa and the resulting net amount is disclosed. Such practice circumvents full disclosure and could permit a business to show a more favourable current ratio than actually exists. For example, if Dominion Textile were to offset its accounts payable of $197,234 against its accounts receivable, the current ratio would be computed as ($598,147 − $197,234) ÷ ($376,208 − $197,234) = 2.24 instead of the correct ratio of 1.59.

Offsetting is permissible only when a legal right to offset exists. For instance, it would be permissible to offset a $5,000 overdraft in one bank account against another account reflecting $8,000 on deposit in that same bank because the bank can legally offset the two deposit accounts.

Valuations Reported in the Balance Sheet

Although current market values may be more relevant for decision making, the balance sheet reports historical cost valuations because they are considered to be more objective. The market values of most assets are known reliably only when they are bought or sold in completed transactions. Hence, the determination of market value is generally subjective and thus susceptible to manipulation, bias, and misrepresentation. In contrast, historical cost information is measurable and verifiable and is therefore reliable. Furthermore, many assets are not held for sale (e.g., capital assets) and thus market values would be irrelevant.

When an asset is first acquired or created, it is entered on the books at its acquisition cost. Normally, if an asset is acquired through a non-cash transaction, the asset is valued at the fair market value of the consideration paid or the fair market value of the asset itself, if more readily determinable. Once acquired, most assets continue to be reported at their acquisition cost.

Amortizing capital assets are not reported at cost subsequent to acquisition. For these assets, that portion of the cost allocated to the production of goods and services is subtracted from cost, and the asset is reported at its amortized (net book) value. Examples include property, plant, and equipment less accumulated depreciation, mineral deposits less depletion, and goodwill less amortization. This net book value is not equal to market value.

Valuations other than cost, or amortized cost, are also reported, including net realizable values, present values, and market values. For example, receivables are usually valued at estimated net realizable amounts, marketable equity securities at market if market value is less than cost, and bonds held to maturity at discounted present values. Users of financial statements need to know which valuation method is being used in order to evaluate the company's financial position; disclosure of valuation method is required.

Terminology

Consistency and precision are essential in preparing financial statements to ensure the effective communication of accounting information. Accountants should refrain from using jargon or vague terminology. Captions and titles should be selected carefully because the statements are read and used by a wide range of decision makers.

Confusing terminology is illustrated by the use of the term *reserve* in the following examples:

- A contra asset account, such as "reserve for doubtful accounts." Instead, use the more descriptive "allowance for doubtful accounts."
- An estimated liability, such as "reserve for warranties." Instead, use "estimated warranty liability."
- An appropriation of retained earnings, such as "reserve for future expansion." Instead, use "retained earnings appropriated for future expansion."

The term *reserve* should be restricted to retained earnings appropriations. Even with this restriction, some accountants do not believe that the term *reserve* is a suitable description because it suggests that a fund of money is set aside somewhere, earmarked for a specific purpose. Similarly, the term *surplus* should be avoided.

Comparative Statements

Trends in financial information are much more revealing than information for only one period. In recognition of this fact, Section 1500, paragraph .09 of the *CICA Handbook* requires that comparative figures be presented when they are meaningful. Presentation of one year's comparative information is the norm, although some companies present two years' comparative results on the income statement to comply with the U.S. SEC regulation requiring this expanded disclosure.[3] As previously mentioned, Dominion Textile presents two years' comparative information for all its financial statements.

Many companies also include in their annual reports special tabulations of selected financial items going back 5 to 10 years or more. Typical items often included are total revenues, income before extraordinary items, net income, depreciation expense, earnings per share, dividends, total assets, total owners' equity, and average number of common shares outstanding. Such long-term summaries are particularly useful.

Disclosure Notes

Disclosure notes are an integral part of the financial statements. They are audited by an external auditor and must be presented if the statements are to be complete. Notes provide descriptive explanations regarding various items included (and not included) in the body of the statements that are deemed to be potentially meaningful to users. Unlike the purely quantitative financial statements, information in disclosure notes can be provided in qualitative terms. Readers can then make their own assessment of the potential quantitative ramifications of the information presented. Notes sometimes take on a complex and highly technical nature. In many instances, they provide invaluable information.

In general, notes can fulfill several functions:

1. **Disclosure of significant accounting policies** Knowledge of the various accounting policies used in generating a set of financial statements is essential when developing an understanding of the specific figures presented in the statements. Knowing, for example, that a firm is using the LIFO method of inventory valuation rather than the FIFO method provides the reader with a basis for interpreting both the inventory value and the cost of goods sold amount found in the financial statements.

---

[3] Canadian firms whose securities are traded on U.S. stock exchanges must comply with SEC rules.

Section 1505 of the *CICA Handbook*, "Disclosure of Accounting Policies," requires disclosure of accounting policies used by the firm. The policies used are those that are judged by management to be the most appropriate in order to fairly present the financial position, cash flows, and results of operations in accordance with GAAP. Accounting policies include specific accounting principles and the methods of applying these principles. In general, disclosure should encompass important judgments as to principles relating to revenue recognition and allocation of asset costs to current and future periods. More specifically, the disclosures must include those accounting principles and methods that involve:

- A selection from existing acceptable alternatives, and
- Principles and methods particular to the industry.

The information may be presented as the first note to the financial statements, or in a separate summary of significant accounting policies. The specific items found in this disclosure note will vary from firm to firm.

For example, Magna International Inc.'s summary of significant accounting policies, contained in the financial statements at the end of this book, disclose policies related to:

• Consolidation.	• Revenue recognition.
• Cash.	• Government financing.
• Inventories.	• Foreign exchange.
• Fixed assets.	• Income taxes.
• Goodwill.	• Earnings per share.

2. **Provide detail** If detail is included on the face of a financial statement itself, the resulting clutter may reduce the understandability of the statement. Thus, details concerning accounts receivable, inventory, fixed assets, debt, and share capital are usually found in the notes.

3. **Explain transactions** The nature of major acquisitions or disposals during the year must be disclosed in the notes to the financial statements to comply with various accounting standards. Transactions involving share capital or other ownership interests, including stock options, are also described in the notes.

4. **Explain unrecorded items** Some contracts or business arrangements are not recorded in the financial statements even though they are important to an understanding of the entity's financial position or results of operations. These items are disclosed in the notes. Examples such as contingencies and subsequent events are described in following sections of this chapter.

5. **Provide new information** Many important pieces of information cannot be incorporated into a financial statement due to the nature of the item or the nature of the financial statement itself. The information is still crucial for decision making. Examples include:

- Assets pledged as collateral for long-term debt.
- Pension fund assets and pension fund liabilities. While these do not have to be recorded on the balance sheet, they are required in the notes.
- Information about lines of business and geographical spread of operations. Such segmented information provides valuable data to assess operations and risk.
- Non-arm's-length transactions. Data on **related party transactions** may be significant in evaluating risk and profitability.

Contingencies

Section 3290 of the *CICA Handbook* requires that a contingent loss should be accrued in the financial statements when both of the following conditions are met:

a. It is likely that a future event will confirm that an asset has been impaired or a liability incurred at the date of the financial statements.

b. The amount of the loss can be reasonably estimated.

Few situations meet both conditions and, therefore, few contingent losses are recorded by journal entry. If a loss is probable or estimable but not both, or if there is at least a reasonable possibility that a liability may have been incurred, the nature of the contingency must be disclosed in a note along with an estimate of the possible loss or the range of the possible loss if an estimate can be made. Most companies refrain from estimating any expected loss, arguing that no recognition is necessary because:

1. The situation does not meet the required reasonable probability level.
2. It is not possible to estimate the loss.

Companies are particularly reluctant to disclose potential losses arising from litigation because such disclosure might provide the appearance of guilt. The desire not to release information that might be unfavourable to the company coupled with the vagueness of such words as "it is likely that a future event will confirm" allows many contingencies to go unreported.

Although contingent gains are also possible, the accounting profession has adopted a conservative position of nonrecognition, as it has in countless other areas. Contingent gains may at most be disclosed in notes, and then only if there is a high probability of realization. Many instances of this take-the-loss-but-defer-the-gain approach are found throughout accounting. The conservative position is often advocated by those charged with setting accounting standards. These individuals believe that they should protect external decision makers such as creditors and investors who rely on the financial statements. When there is no logically preferable alternative, conservatism is appealed to in resolving the reporting issue. Critics, however, believe the lack of symmetry in this approach is logically unjustifiable.

DMR Group Inc. disclosed the following contingency in its 1992 disclosure notes:

> During 1988, the Company filed a court action against a customer for cancellation of a contractual obligation and claimed a sum of $1,553,367 for amounts due and damages. The same customer instituted a counteraction against the Company, claiming damages and breach of contract for an amount of $4,100,000. As at the date of the Auditors' Report, management and counsel are unable to provide estimates on the outcome. Settlements, if any, concerning this contingency, will be recorded as a prior year adjustment.

Subsequent Events

Subsequent events are important events with a material effect on the financial statements that occur after the balance sheet date but prior to the actual issuance of the financial statements (ordinarily one to four months later). Such events *must* be reported because they involve information that could influence a user's evaluation of the future prospects of the business.

The effects of some subsequent events must be reported in the financial statements themselves. They provide additional evidence about conditions that existed at the balance sheet date or affect assumptions made in preparing the financial statements. For example, assume that as of the balance sheet date, a company is unaware that collection of one of its major accounts receivable is doubtful. During the period between the balance sheet's preparation and its publication, the customer in question declares bankruptcy and therefore collection in full is extremely doubtful. The expected loss should be recognized as of the balance sheet date, assuming an insufficient allowance for doubtful accounts.

Some subsequent events, although unrelated to the period covered by the financial statements, would have a profound effect on elements reported in the financial statements and are important to financial statement users. These subsequent events are disclosed in the notes, rather than in the body of the statement, if they result from conditions that did not exist at the balance sheet date, arose after that date, and do not merit adjustment to the current financial statements. Examples are:

1. The issuance of a long-term debt or share capital.
2. Litigation related to an event occurring subsequent to the date of the balance sheet.

3. Losses caused by a condition that arose after the balance sheet date, such as a fire or flood.
4. Purchase of a business after the balance sheet date.

Subsequent events that do not require disclosure include changes in the market price of the company's shares, a strike, new product developments, management changes, and the recognition or decertification of a union.

The Auditors' Report

The auditors' report is typically the first item presented in the financial statements, although it sometimes follows the financial reports. The report expresses the auditors' professional opinion on the financial statements.

The auditors have sole responsibility for all opinions expressed in the auditors' report, while company management has the primary responsibility for the financial statements, including the supporting notes. Compilation and presentation of the accounting information and all supporting text contained in a company's financial statements is company management's concern and responsibility; the auditors, in rendering their opinion, affirm or disaffirm what management has compiled and presented.

Seven required elements in the auditors' report have special significance. They are identified by number in Exhibit 5–5, Dominion Textile's audit report.

1. Salutation.
2. Identification of the statements examined.
3. Statement of scope of the examination.
4. Opinion.
5. Reference to fair presentation in conformity with generally accepted accounting principles.
6. Signature of the independent accountant.
7. Date.

When an audit is finished, the auditors are required to draft an opinion paragraph that communicates their professional opinion about the company's financial statements. The auditors can render one of four opinions, although an unqualified opinion is most common.

1. **Unqualified opinion** An unqualified opinion is given when the auditor concludes that the statements fairly present the results of operations, financial position, and changes in financial position in conformance with GAAP and provide reasonable assurance that the financial statements are free of material misstatement. Dominion Textile's audit report is unqualified.
2. **Qualified opinion** A qualified opinion is given when the auditor takes limited exception to the client's financial statements in a way that does not invalidate the statements as a whole. A qualified opinion must explain the reasons for the exception and its effect on the financial statements.
3. **Adverse opinion** An adverse opinion is given when the financial statements do not fairly present the results of operations, financial position, and changes in financial position. An adverse opinion means that the statements, taken as a whole, are not presented in accordance with GAAP. Adverse opinions are rare.
4. **Disclaimer of opinion** When the auditors have not been able to obtain sufficient evidence, they must state that they are unable to express an opinion (i.e., they issue a disclaimer). The disclaimer must provide the reasons the auditor did not give an opinion.

A major purpose of the auditors' report is to assure the reader that the financial statements conform to GAAP. Without such assurance, an investor or creditor would be ill-advised to rely on a company's statements when making investment or lending decisions.

EXHIBIT 5-5   Audit Report: Dominion Textile's Independent Audit Report

To the Shareholders of Dominion Textile Inc.   } 1

We have audited the consolidated balance sheets of Dominion Textile Inc. as at 30 June 1993, 1992 and 1991 and the consolidated statements of income, retained earnings (deficit) and changes in financial position for the years then ended. These consolidated financial statements are the responsibility of the corporation's management. Our responsibility is to express an opinion on these consolidated financial statements based on our audits.   } 2

We conducted our audits in accordance with generally accepted auditing standards. Those standards require that we plan and perform an audit to obtain reasonable assurance whether the financial statements are free of material misstatement. An audit includes examining, on a test basis, evidence supporting the amounts and disclosures in the financial statements. An audit also includes assessing the accounting principles used and significant estimates made by management, as well as evaluating the overall financial statement presentation.   } 3

In our opinion, these consolidated financial statements present fairly, in all material respects, the financial position of the corporation as at 30 June 1993, 1992 and 1991 and the results of its operations and the changes in its financial position for the years then ended in accordance with generally accepted accounting principles.   } 4 and 5

Deloitte + Touche   } 6

Chartered Accountants

9 August 1993   } 7

Usefulness of the Balance Sheet

The balance sheet provides information concerning liquidity, the financial flexibility of an organization, and is the basis used to determine rates of return on assets and equity.

Liquidity in the form of working capital is evidence of a company's ability to pay short-term debts from its current assets as well as to meet short- and long-term obligations. Creditors are obviously interested in assessing liquidity. Beyond this, equity investors are interested in liquidity because it affects dividend payments. Unions examine liquidity to establish bargaining positions. Employees are concerned with the company's continuing ability to pay wages. Liquidity is a major concern to many financial statement users.

The balance sheet can also provide insight into the risk profile of a business and its financial flexibility. Has the company acquired new businesses? Has it disposed of any? If so, how do these activities relate to the company's mainstream business? Are managers doing what they know best or merely diversifying to reduce risk? Are the company's assets old and fully depreciated or relatively new? Is the organization in a position to finance new activities with relative ease without incurring excessive debt?

The balance sheet also provides data needed to determine rates of return, including return on equity (ROE), return on assets (ROA), the ratio of total debt to owners' equity, and a variety of other ratios. These ratios are very important to financial statement users, both lenders and equity investors. They help determine the company's credit rating and share price.

Limitations of the Balance Sheet

A balance sheet based on GAAP has limitations. Balance sheet values are not current values or meant to be current values. The amounts reported for major asset categories such as plant and equipment may be significantly out-of-date. Given even a modest level of inflation, combining various assets into totals, such as total assets, is of questionable value. In particular, ratios such as return on assets have a numerator (income) measured in current dollars and denominator (assets) measured in older, historical, dollars. Individual companies are affected by this problem differently, depending on the date and rate of capital acquisitions. Comparisons between companies can therefore be misleading.

The typical balance sheet also includes many estimated amounts, such as the estimated loss from uncollectible receivables and the estimated liability arising from warranties. Other estimates are accumulated depreciation, depletion, amortization, income taxes, contingencies, and pension liabilities. The usefulness of these estimates and of the values of certain other items commonly found on balance sheets may be limited. Examples include intangible asset values and amounts recorded as deferred tax liabilities.

Finally, certain assets and liabilities simply do not appear on the balance sheet. Such assets include the loyalty and morale of the workforce, licenses to do business (such as a liquor license), and the value of research activity. On the liability side, omitted items include operating leases, hazardous waste cleanups required by law, and unrecorded commitments (such as frequent-flier miles). Difficulties in quantifying most of these items and a lack of authoritative accounting principles help explain their exclusion from the balance sheet.

CONCEPT REVIEW

1. What requirements must be met before a contingency is recorded on the balance sheet?
2. Identify an asset or liability that is valued on the balance sheet:
   a. At historical cost.
   b. At market value.
   c. At an estimated amount.
3. What is the purpose of an audit report?

THE STATEMENT OF CHANGES IN FINANCIAL POSITION

On October 2, 1975, W. T. Grant, the largest specialty store chain in the United States at the time, filed for protection of the court under Chapter 11 of the U.S. National Bankruptcy Act. Only two years earlier, Grant's stock had sold at nearly 20 times earnings. "But Grant's demise should not have come as a surprise . . . A careful analysis of the company's cash flows would have revealed the impending problems as much as a decade before the collapse."[4] Exhibit 5–6 dramatically illustrates the point. Although net income and working capital remained satisfactory through 1973, as did ratios such as return on equity, turnover, the current ratio, and debt to equity, cash flow from operations had been unhealthy since at least 1966—plunging to a disastrous $100 million deficit figure in 1973.

In addition to the income statement and the balance sheet, companies now present a **statement of changes in financial position (SCFP)**. According to Section 1540, paragraph .01 of the *CICA Handbook:*

The objective of the statement of changes in financial position is to provide information about the operating, financing and investing activities of an enterprise and the effects of those activities on cash resources. The statement of changes in financial position assists users of financial statements in evaluating the liquidity and solvency of an enterprise, and in assessing its ability to generate cash from internal sources, to

---

[4] J. Largay and C. Stickney, "Cash Flow, Ratio Analysis and the W. T. Grant Company Bankruptcy," *Financial Analysts Journal,* July–August, 1980, p. 51.

EXHIBIT 5–6

W. T. Grant Company
Net Income, Working
Capital, and Cash Flow
from Operations for
Fiscal Years Ending
January 31, 1966 to 1975

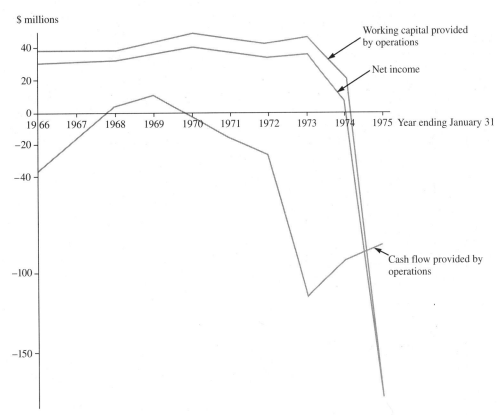

Source: J. Largay and C. Stickney, "Cash Flow, Ratio Analysis and the W. T. Grant Company Bankruptcy," *Financial Analysts Journal*, July–August, 1980, p. 54.

repay debt obligations, to reinvest and to make distributions to owners. This information is not provided or is only indirectly provided in the balance sheet, income statement and statement of retained earnings. Thus, the statement of changes in financial position complements, and presents information different from that provided in, the other financial statements.

Exhibit 5–7 shows Dominion Textile's comparative SCFP.

Basic Definitions

A statement of changes in financial position reports three types of cash flows into and out of the firm. It does not report accrual amounts. The report is designed to show the change in "cash plus cash equivalents." Cash plus cash equivalents would normally include *cash and temporary investments, net of short-term borrowings.* It may, in some cases, include certain other elements of working capital when they are equivalent to cash. Cash equivalents must be defined consistently over time.

The classifications used in the SCFP are defined as follows:

1. **Cash flows from operating activities** Reported under this classification are both the cash inflows and the cash outflows that are related to net income. They may be listed directly, or arrived at indirectly through a reconciliation of the net income number to cash flow. The usual cash flows identified are the following:

Inflows—cash received from:
- Customers.
- Interest on receivables.
- Dividends from investments.
- Refunds from suppliers.

Outflows—cash paid for:
- Purchase of goods for resale.
- Interest on liabilities.
- Operating expenses and income taxes.
- Salaries and wages.

EXHIBIT 5-7 Statement of Changes in Financial Position: Dominion Textile

Consolidated Statements of Changes in Financial Position
For the Years Ended 30 June

	1993	1992	1991
	(in thousands of dollars)		
Operating activities:			
Net income (loss)	$ 30,334	$ (74,823)	$(128,827)
Depreciation and amortization.	65,733	73,348	76,091
Financial expense, net of income taxes.	43,055	50,777	55,735
Deferred income taxes	16,477	4,206	(22,650)
Share in net income of associated companies	(6,900)	(5,462)	(4,327)
Dividends received from associated companies	12,133	5,770	4,151
Restructuring and other non-recurring charges	—	74,904	62,557
Other non-cash items.	5,084	5,742	(3,130)
Financial resources generated from earnings	165,916	134,462	39,600
Changes in non-cash working capital.	6,158	(6,632)	29,338
Foreign currency translation adjustment	(2,188)	23,316	(9,548)
Net cash inflow from operating activities*	169,886	151,146	59,390
Financing activities:			
Issue of common shares	55,782	114	23,264
Share issue expenses.	(2,456)	—	—
Issue of long-term debt.	23,425	100,946	112,768
Repayment of long-term debt	(100,982)	(154,291)	(32,799)
Redemption of preferred shares by a subsidiary	(6,590)	—	—
Payment related to termination of accounts receivable sale programs	—	—	(79,724)
Other items.	(1,600)	(11)	(1,000)
Net cash outflow for financing activities*	(32,421)	(53,242)	22,509
Investing activities:			
Additions to property, plant, and equipment	(46,491)	(37,996)	(59,629)
Proceeds from disposal of property, plant, and equipment	3,515	6,151	13,798
Proceeds from sale of businesses	68,583	11,808	—
Note receivable from sale of business	(12,032)	—	—
Decrease (increase) in investments and advances	2,568	(1,651)	3,152
Other items.	3,925	3,421	(2,020)
Net cash inflow from investing activities*.	20,068	(18,267)	(44,699)
Payments to investors:			
Dividends.	(5,011)	(5,164)	(12,370)
Financial expense, net of income taxes.	(43,055)	(50,777)	(55,735)
Net cash outflow for payments to investors*	(48,066)	(55,941)	(68,105)
Increase (decrease) in net cash position:	$ 109,467	$ 23,696	$ (30,905)
Cash and cash equivalents	$ 109,718	$ 7,837	$ (22,999)
Short-term borrowings	(251)	15,859	(7,906)
Increase (decrease) in net cash positions	$ 109,467	$ 23,696	$ (30,905)

* Captions added for clarity.

The difference between these inflows and outflows is called the *net cash inflow (outflow) from operating activities*. Typically, the net amount will be an inflow because, over the long term, cash collections from operations should exceed cash outflows for a going concern. Dominion Textile reports $169,886 as the cash flow from operations. (See Exhibit 5-7.)

2. **Cash flows from investing activities** This classification includes cash inflows and outflows related to the acquisition or disposal of capital assets (plant, property, and

equipment), the sale or purchase of investments, and other investments. Outflows are investments of cash by the entity to acquire non-cash assets. Inflows under this classification occur only when cash is received from the sale or disposal of prior investments. The following are typical cash flows under investing activities:

Inflows—cash received from:
- Disposal/sale of property, plant, and equipment.
- Disposal/sale of investments.
- Collection of a loan receivable (excluding interest, which is an operating activity).

Outflows—cash paid for:
- Acquisition/purchase of property, plant, and equipment.
- Long-term investments in debt and equity securities.
- Loans to other parties.
- Acquisition of other assets used in production, such as patents or other intangible assets (excluding inventories, which are included in operating activities).

The difference between these cash inflows and outflows is called *net cash inflow (outflow) from investing activities*. Dominion Textile reports a $20,068 cash inflow from investing activities.

3. **Cash flows from financing activities** This classification includes both cash inflows and outflows related to the financing activities used to obtain cash for the business. Outflows occur only when cash is paid to the owners and creditors for their earlier investments. The usual cash flows under this classification are:

Inflows—cash received from:
- Owners—issuing equity securities.
- Lenders—issuing long-term debt.

Outflows—cash paid to:
- Owners—dividends and other distributions.
- Owners—retiring shares.
- Creditors—for repayment of amounts borrowed (excluding interest, which is included in operating activities).

The difference between these cash inflows and outflows is called *net cash inflow (outflow) from financing activities*. Dominion Textile reports a $32,421 cash outflow for financing activities.

4. **Other categories** There is some disagreement among reporting companies concerning the proper classification for dividends paid to investors and interest paid to lenders. According to the *CICA Handbook,* interest paid to lenders is an operating outflow, while dividends paid to investors represent a financing outflow. However, many companies feel that because these two outflows are returns to investors, they are similar and are not appropriately disclosed in any of the operating, investing, or financing sections. These companies disclose these amounts in a separate, fourth section of the SCFP. Dominion Textile is such a company; refer to Exhibit 5–7, where payments to investors are listed as a separate category, total outflows for interest and dividends, $48,066.

Fully 26% of surveyed Canadian public companies adopted this separate classification disclosure, at least for dividends, in 1992. While this separate classification is not contemplated by the accounting standard, it is GAAP by virtue of general acceptance. This variation of classification practice makes comparisons tricky, especially cash flows from operating activities, which could be before or after interest payments. Analysts must proceed carefully. In this text, dividend payments will always be classified as a financing outflow and interest as an operating outflow, to be consistent with current standards.

The cash flow from the activities (operating, investing, financing, etc.) is totalled at the bottom of the statement to arrive at the net increase or decrease in cash during the period. For Dominion Textile, this amount is $109,467. This amount is then compared to the change in cash and cash equivalents.

The definitions of cash and cash equivalents must be clearly disclosed.

Non-cash Investing and Financing Activities   Some transactions are significant financial events that do not involve any cash inflows or outflows. For example, a piece of land may be acquired in exchange for a long-term note payable. Or, capital assets may be acquired in exchange for common shares. These transactions are financing and/or investing transactions, but do they belong on the statement of changes in financial position? They do not involve cash flow.

The *CICA Handbook* takes the position that these transactions do affect capital and asset structure and thus have to be disclosed. However, companies may either disclose significant non-cash transactions in a note to the financial statements, or they can include them on the SCFP itself, as both a source and a use of cash. The transactions would be cross-referenced to each other. For example, the issuance of common shares for land could be disclosed in a note, bypassing the SCFP, or could be on the SCFP, listed as a financing activity (an inflow, issuance of common shares for land) and an investing activity (an outflow, acquisition of land in exchange for common shares). This text will generally record the item on the SCFP.

Statement Formats

Two formats are available for displaying cash flow information. They differ only in the approach used to calculate net cash flows from operating activities. Computation and presentation of information pertaining to investing and financing activities remain the same.

Using the **indirect method,** the cash flow from operating activities section starts with net income before extraordinary items and makes adjustments to arrive at cash flow. There are two basic types of adjustments:

1. Adjustments for non-cash expenses (e.g., amortization) or revenues that do not increase cash (e.g., investment income under the equity method). These items are on the income statement and included, properly, in net income, but they do not increase or decrease cash flow. In order to alter income to cash flow, they must be included in the reconciliation: Amortization is added, and non-cash revenues subtracted, to arrive at cash flow from operating activities.
2. Changes to working capital (e.g., accounts payable) or other balance sheet accounts (e.g., long-term accounts receivables) caused by income elements. If accounts payable for operating expenses have increased over the year, then the amount of expense listed, properly, on the income statement was not all paid out in cash. Some of it will be paid out next year. If long-term receivables from the sale of goods increased, then some of the revenue on the income statement did not produce cash flow. To reconcile income to cash flow, these changes in balance sheet accounts must be adjusted. Increases in payables are added back to income and increases to receivables are subtracted to arrive at cash flow from operating activities.

Dominion Textile, in Exhibit 5–7, uses the indirect approach. Net income is adjusted for non-cash revenues and expenses and then for changes in working capital. Net income of $30,334 generated cash of $169,886.

Alternatively, a company may use the **direct method** to present the cash flow from operating activities. The end result will be the same. The direct method lists the individual cash inflows (from customers, investments, etc.) and the individual cash outflows (to suppliers, employees, interest to lenders, taxes to governments, etc.). The net amount of the inflows from revenues and outflows for expenses is the cash from operating activities.

Exhibit 5–8 provides an example of the operating activities section using the direct method.

Regardless of whether the indirect or direct method is used in the operating activities section, the investing and financing sections are identical. They list suitably classified significant financial events with appropriate descriptions.

EXHIBIT 5-8   Consolidated Statement of Changes in Financial Position, Collins Industries, Inc, Direct Method, Operating Section

For Each of the Three Years in the Period Ended October 31, 1991			
	1991	1990	1989
Cash flow from operations:			
Cash received from customers.	$ 138,870,245	$ 144,770,135	$ 131,269,180
Cash paid to suppliers and employees	(133,747,096)	(130,525,771)	(127,053,481)
Interest received.	188,842	203,836	201,356
Interest paid.	(4,121,217)	(4,372,288)	(4,173,072)
Income taxes paid	(392,031)	(220,000)	—
Cash provided by operations	$ 798,743	$ 9,855,912	$ 243,983

Regardless of whether the indirect or direct method is used in the operating activities section, the investing and financing sections are identical. They list suitably classified significant financial events with appropriate descriptions.

Although the indirect format is preferred by preparers, many financial statement users' preference is for the more straightforward direct method format. If a company elects to use the direct method, the operating activity information that would have been reported under the indirect method must appear in a supplementary schedule. Only 1.3% of the 300 firms covered by *Financial Reporting in Canada* used the direct method in 1992; the indirect method is widely used.

Usefulness of the Statement of Changes in Financial Position

Information about the cash available from various sources for debt payments, dividends, investments by the entity, and the support of future growth is important to decision makers, be they investors or creditors. Of particular interest is the amount of cash a company generates from its operating activities, which must eventually pay for the company's debts and dividends and provide for growth. The SCFP also provides useful information about a company's borrowing patterns, subsequent repayments, new investments by owners, and dividends.

On a broader scale, the SCFP helps decision makers assess the financial strength of a business, which is indicated by the relationship between the company's assets and liabilities and is reflected in the company's credit standing with financial institutions and other lenders. Analysts see the SCFP as providing information on whether a company is generating sufficient cash to pay its bills, replace assets, take advantage of new opportunities, and pay the dividends it has declared.[5] In this sense, the SCFP is an indispensable complement to the balance sheet and income statement.

The statement of changes in financial position is not useful in isolation. In any one year, unusual events can occur, which might be interpreted incorrectly or prompt inaccurate evaluations of the company's longer-term financial position. A series of SCFPs covering several years is essential. There is no substitute for a careful analysis based on a complete set of financial statements. Further, whatever else is known about a particular company should also be considered. Annual reports are but one source of financial information available to decision makers.

---

[5] Cash available from operations may be insufficient to replace equipment because of inflation and changing technology.

GLOBAL VIEW

The fourth directive from the European Union requires that financial statements include a balance sheet and an income statement.

The specific items included in the balance sheet, however, continue to vary from country to country, even within the European Union. The predominant practice in the United Kingdom, for example, is not to record goodwill as an asset. Accounting for leased assets and lease obligations also varies greatly across countries. For example, leased assets are not recorded as assets in France. Finally, the valuation basis used in preparing the balance sheet in many international environments differs from Canadian GAAP. For example, fixed assets such as property, plant, and equipment can be revalued using current prices in Belgium,

Finland, and the Netherlands. Comparisons between Canadian balance sheets and those prepared in international settings are at best difficult because the principles underlying the preparations of the two differ greatly. Specific differences are discussed in later chapters.

The International Accounting Standards Committee (IASC) issued *IAS No. 7*, "Cash Flows Statements," in 1992. This revised standard has provisions very similar to those of the *CICA Handbook*. The statement requires that cash flows be classified by operating, investing, and financing activities. The statement applies to the financial statements of all enterprises and is effective for periods beginning after January 1, 1994.

MANAGEMENT DISCUSSION AND ANALYSIS

As part of the annual report, companies often include a section entitled "Management Discussion and Analysis" (MD&A). This section is required for firms that must comply with the rules of the Ontario, Quebec, and Saskatchewan Securities Commissions. The MD&A section provides information about the firm's earnings and financial position for the reporting period, the effects of laws and other environmental aspects, and the effects of economic and business trends on the firm. It is expected to place particular emphasis on the future.

For example, the MD&A section of the 1992 annual report of PanCanadian Energy Ltd. includes a discussion of future capital spending:

> The Company's 1993 capital spending is projected to be approximately $425 million, up 25 percent from 1992 levels. It is anticipated that this program will result in the drilling of over 700 wells. The 1993 capital programs will be largely financed from cash flow. PanCanadian continually monitors its planned expenditures in light of changing industry conditions and its own record of operational success. The 1993 program contains no material long-term commitments. The Company will continue to seek out attractive investment opportunities and is financially well-positioned to utilize additional debt leverage to generate enhanced returns for its shareholders.

Most companies are reluctant to discuss future events because positive expectations may not be fulfilled and negative projections are viewed with concern by the investing community; most respondents to a 1987 request for public comment on the issue indicated that disclosures about future events were inadequate.[6]

CONCEPT REVIEW

1. What are the major headings in a statement of changes in financial position?
2. What are the major differences between the direct and indirect methods for the SCFP?
3. How can the net change in cash from the SCFP be confirmed using the balance sheet?

---

[6] "'What If' Accounting," *Forbes*, May 30, 1988, p. 112.

SUMMARY OF KEY POINTS

(L.O. 1)   1. The balance sheet reflects the basic accounting identity and the means of financing the organization's assets:

$$\text{Assets} = \text{Liabilities} + \text{Owners' Equity}$$

In an alternate format, the identity reflects the residual interests of the owners:

$$\text{Assets} - \text{Liabilities} = \text{Owners' Equity}$$

(L.O. 2)   2. The elements of the balance sheet are recorded primarily using historic costs, although different
valuation approaches will be encountered, including market values, net realizable values, and
present values.

(L.O. 2)   3. The working capital of a firm is its current assets less its current liabilities. Together with the
working capital ratio (current assets divided by current liabilities), working capital provides information on the financial strength and flexibility of the firm.

(L.O. 3)   4. The ability of a decision maker to use the balance sheet effectively is enhanced by the use of
consistent and precise terminology, comparative statements, the reporting of subsequent events,
contingencies, and informative note disclosure.

(L.O. 3   5. Note disclosure should include disclosure of significant accounting policies, detail on statement
elements, explain transactions and unrecorded information, and explain important new information.

(L.O. 4)   6. Although the balance sheet provides information on the financial strength and flexibility of a firm,
many amounts are estimated, omitted, or of limited usefulness. Aggregate figures are particularly
problematic.

(L.O. 5)   7. The statement of changes in financial position is designed to provide information on the cash
generated (or used) by the operating, investing, and financing activities of a company.

(L.O. 6)   8. The statement of changes in financial position may use one of two formats for the cash flows from
operating activities section. The common indirect method reconciles income to cash flows, while
the direct method lists cash flows from revenues and expenses separately.

(L.O. 7)   9. The statement of changes in financial position is particularly valuable in assessing a company's
short-term financial strength, but the trends suggested by several statements of changes in financial
position combined with the other statements and with future-oriented information are more useful.

REVIEW PROBLEM

Answer the following questions based on Dominion Textile's balance sheet (Exhibit 5–2),
statement of changes in financial position (Exhibit 5–7), and audit report (Exhibit 5–5).

1. What is the date of the end of the fiscal or reporting year?
2. Do the statements include Dominion Textile's subsidiaries? Explain the meaning of
the minority interest on the balance sheet.
3. What percentage of total assets are property, plant, and equipment (PP&E) in 1993?
4. What was the amount of cash and cash equivalents reported at the end of 1993?
5. What was the amount of working capital reported at the end of 1993? How has it
changed since 1991?
6. What was the income tax obligation at the end of the current year? The dividend
obligation?
7. What percentage of total assets was provided by (a) creditors and (b) owners in
1993?
8. What is the definition of cash on the SCFP?
9. What items represented the three largest uses of cash in 1993?
10. What items represented the three largest sources of cash in 1993?
11. What do the auditors claim is involved in an audit?
12. Who is responsible for the preparation and integrity of the company's financial
statements?

SOLUTION

Dollar amounts are in thousands.

1. The fiscal or reporting year ends on each June 30.
2. Yes, the financial statements are labelled to include subsidiaries and are called *consolidated*. The minority interest is the share of the consolidated subsidiary's assets
owned by other shareholders.
3. PP&E is 41.8% ($556,358 ÷ $1,329,112) of total assets.
4. Cash and cash equivalents equalled $156,674 at the end of 1993.

5. Current assets, $598,147, minus current liabilities, $376,208, equals working capital, $221,939, at the end of 1993. In 1991, working capital was $219,108, almost equivalent.

6. Income taxes payable was $15,154. Dividends payable were $1,260.

7. (a) Total assets provided by creditors: total liabilities ($376,208 + $361,616 + $41,637 + $41,009 + $61,684) ÷ total assets ($1,329,112) = 66.4%. Some items may not be considered liabilities (deferred taxes, minority interests), but have been included for completeness.

   (b) Total assets provided by owners: total owners' equity ($446,958) ÷ total assets ($1,329,112) = 33.6%.

8. Cash is defined as cash and cash equivalents less short-term debt.

9. The three largest uses of cash were debt repayment, interest payment, and buying capital assets.

10. The three largest sources of cash were operations, sale of a business, and issuance of common shares.

11. The audit report states that an audit includes examining, on a test basis, evidence to support the financial statements, assessment of accounting principles, estimates, and overall presentation.

12. Management is responsible for the preparation and integrity of the financial statements.

QUESTIONS

1. What is the basic purpose of a balance sheet?
2. What is a balance sheet? Why is it dated differently from the income statement and the statement of changes in financial position?
3. Basically, what valuations are reported on the balance sheet?
4. Define assets, liabilities, and equities.
5. What is the difference between the net assets and financing form of the balance sheet? The report and account form?
6. Explain the relation between the balance sheet and full disclosure.
7. Define current assets and current liabilities and emphasize their interrelationship.
8. Define working capital. What is the working capital ratio?
9. Why aren't market values used exclusively in balance sheets?
10. Is it proper to offset current liabilities against current assets? Explain.
11. What would the "investments and funds" caption cover in a balance sheet?
12. What are capital assets? Distinguish between tangible and intangible capital assets.
13. Comment on the difficulties associated with evaluating the balance sheet of an entity whose primary assets are intangible.
14. Why is the caption "other assets" sometimes necessary? Name two items that might be reported under this classification.
15. Explain the term *deferred charge*.
16. Distinguish between current and non-current liabilities. Under what conditions would a non-current liability amount be reclassified as a current liability?
17. What disclosure should accompany a long-term liability? Why is this disclosure important?
18. What is the nature of deferred tax such that this item is classified as a deferred credit?
19. Explain the term *non-controlling (minority) interest*.
20. What is owners' equity? What are the main components of owners' equity?
21. What is a restriction, or appropriation, of retained earnings? How are restrictions and appropriations reported?
22. What kinds of information are normally found in the disclosure notes?
23. When is a contingency recorded versus disclosed?
24. When is a subsequent event recorded versus disclosed?
25. What is the purpose of the statement of changes in financial position?
26. Explain the major sections in the statement of changes in financial position.
27. What items are included in cash in the statement of changes in financial position?
28. What is meant by "non-cash investing and financing activities" in the statement of changes in financial position?
29. Explain the relation between the balance in the cash account and the statement of changes in financial position.
30. Explain the position of the accounting profession with respect to use of the term *reserves*. Why is careful attention to terminology important in financial statements?

31. What are comparative financial statements? Why are they important?
32. What is the auditors' report? What are its basic components? Why is it especially important to the statement user?
33. Are the financial statements the representations of the management of the enterprise, the independent auditor, or both? Explain.
 34. Does the IASC require a cash flow statement? If so, is it similar to the SCFP and when was the requirement effective?

CASES

C 5–1
(L.O. 1, 2, 4)

Criticize a Deficient Balance Sheet   The president of Artar Manufacturing Company is a personal friend. She reports that the company has never had an audit and is contemplating having one, principally because she suspects that the financial statements are not well prepared. As an example, the president hands you the following statement for review:

ARTAR MANUFACTURING COMPANY
Balance Sheet
Year Ended December 31, 1995

Resources

Liquid assets:

Cash in banks	$ 8,700
Receivables from various sources net of reserve for bad debts ($200)	4,500
Inventories	10,000
Cash for daily use	800
Total	24,000

Permanent assets:

Artar common shares, cost, 400 shares	4,000*
Fixed assets (net of depreciation)	26,000
Grand total	$54,000

Obligations and Net Worth

Short-term:

Trade payables	$ 4,500
Salaries accrued	600
Total	5,100

Fixed:

Mortgage	8,000

Net worth:

Capital stock, 2,500 shares	25,000
Earned surplus	15,900
Total	$40,900
Grand total	$54,000

* Shares bought back from shareholder; to be retired.

Required

1. List and explain in writing your criticisms of the above statement.
2. Using the above data, prepare a balance sheet that meets your specifications in terms of format, terminology, and classification of data. Assume capital assets at cost of $30,000 and that the Artar common share assets should be retired.

C 5–2
(L.O. 1, 2, 3, 4)

 Criticize and Redraft a Deficient Balance Sheet   The most recent balance sheet of Blackstone Tire Corporation appears below:

BLACKSTONE TIRE CORPORATION
Balance Sheet
For the Year Ended December 31, 1995

Assets

Current:			
Cash		$ 23,000	
Marketable securities		10,000	
Accounts receivable		15,000	
Merchandise		31,000	
Supplies		5,000	
Shares of Wilmont Co. (not a controlling interest)		17,000	$101,000
Investments:			
Cash surrender value of life insurance			82,500
Tangible:			
Building and land ($10,000)	$86,000		
Less: reserve for depreciation	40,000	46,000	
Equipment	$20,000		
Less: reserve for depreciation	15,000	5,000	51,000
Deferred:			
Prepaid expenses		2,000	
Discount on bonds payable		3,000	5,000
Total			$239,500

Debt and Capital

Current:			
Accounts payable		$ 16,000	
Reserve for income tax		17,000	
Customers' accounts with credit balance		100	$ 33,100
Fixed (interest paid at year-end):			
Bonds payable		45,000	
Mortgage, 11%		12,000	57,000
Reserve for bad debts			900
Capital:			
Capital stock, authorized 10,000 shares, nopar		117,000	
Earned surplus		22,500	
Capital surplus		9,000	148,500
Total			$239,500

Required   1. List and explain in writing your criticisms of the above statement.
2. Prepare a complete balance sheet; use appropriate format, captions, and terminology.

C 5–3
(L.O. 2, 3, 4)

Valuing an Asset   The federal Bank Act establishes accounting policies to be followed by banking institutions. For many years, these rules were very different from GAAP. One rule, called *loan loss deferral,* allowed banking institutions to sell loans at a loss to investment firms and write off the loss over the life of the loan.

Required

Write a brief letter to the Inspector General for banks, commenting on this accounting rule as it would affect the balance sheet. Suggest how you believe the sale should be handled.

C 5–4
(L.O. 2, 4)

A New Asset?   On August 19, 1992, press reports indicated that, under an expropriation settlement of oil interests, the government of Iran agreed to pay Sun Company and Atlantic Richfield Company $130 million each for oil wells and refineries located in Iran that had been expropriated in prior years.

Required

Write a brief report commenting on the appropriate accounting treatment that should have been followed by the companies at the date of expropriation and at the (later) date of the settlement announcement.

C 5–5
(L.O. 3)

Contingencies, Subsequent Events   Zero Growth Ltd. has just completed financial statements for the year ended December 31, 1996. Discuss the appropriate accounting treatment for the following items:

1. The office building housing administrative staff burned to the ground on January 15, 1997.
2. On November 15, 1996, a customer sued the company for $1,000,000 based on a claim of negligence leading to personal injury; Zero Growth is actively defending the suit and claims it is unfounded. Nothing was recorded in the 1996 financial statements in relation to this event.
3. On February 1, 1997, Zero Growth received an income tax reassessment for 1995.
4. On December 20, 1996, Zero Growth applied for a bank loan to replace an existing line of credit. The loan was granted on January 2, 1997. Nothing was recorded in the 1996 financial statements in relation to this event.
5. Zero Growth has reinterpreted a legal agreement entitling it to commission revenue for the sale of a client's products. Zero Growth's interpretation would entitle it to an extra $60,000 over and above amounts recognized in 1996. The client was billed for this amount in 1996 but has disagreed with Zero Growth on the contract interpretation. Both parties have consulted their lawyers; resolution of the issue is not expected soon.
6. On March 1, 1997, Zero Growth issued common shares for cash.

C 5–6
(L.O. 5, 6, 7)

SCFP Interpretation   A friend, knowing of your expertise in accounting, has given you the SCFP of The Davison Corporation and has asked you to explain it. He has asked some specific questions:

- How can a company that lost $10,750 have such a large ($101,250) cash flow from operations?
- Why are depreciation and goodwill write-offs listed as a source of cash?
- Why does the change in receivables affect cash flow?
- Why is the increase in short-term bank debt not on the statement?
- How much cash did it take to buy the land? Why is this transaction on the statement?
- Overall, what did the company do with, or do to get, cash?

THE DAVISON CORPORATION

Statement of Changes in Financial Position
For the Year Ended December 31, 1995

Operating activities:

Net income (loss) . . . . $(10,750)

Plus (Less): Changes in working capital accounts:

Decrease in accounts receivable	$27,000	
Increase in accounts payable	39,000	
Increase in inventory	(46,500)	19,500

Less (Plus): Non-cash charges or revenues

Depreciation	27,000	
Goodwill write-off	70,000	
Loss on sale of equipment	4,200	
Gain on sale of investments	(6,500)	
Gain on bond retirement	(2,000)	
Premium amortization	(200)	92,500

Net cash flow from operations $101,250

Investing activities:

Sale of investments	36,500	
Sale of equipment	1,800	
Acquisition of land for common shares	(40,000)	
Acquisition of equipment	(60,000)	

Net cash flow for investing . . . .   (61,700)

Financing activities:

Share issuance, for cash	210,950	
Share issuance, for land	40,000	
Bond retirement	(42,000)	
Preferred share retirement	(110,000)	
Cash dividends	(50,000)	

Net cash flow from financing   48,950

Net increase in cash and cash equivalents*	88,500
Opening cash (overdraft)	(11,250)
Closing cash and cash equivalents*	$ 77,250

* Cash plus short-term investments less short-term bank debt.

Required   Write a brief response to your friend's questions.

C 5-7
(L.O. 1, 2, 3)

 Balance Sheet Interpretation   The balance sheet of Karmax Ltd. discloses the following assets:

KARMAX LTD.
Extracts from the Balance Sheet
As at Year Ended December 31, 1996
(amounts in thousands)

Assets

Current assets:
Cash		$ 710
Short-term investments		416
Accounts receivable		1,011
Inventory		2,600
Prepaid expenses		410
Total current assets		$ 5,147
Tangible capital assets, net		14,755
Long-term investments		1,077
Intangible capital assets, net		984
Total assets		$21,963

The following information has been established in relation to market values:

	Amount	Source
Short-term investments	$501	Quoted stock market price
Inventory	$4,190	Karmax price list
Tangible capital assets	$20,000–$25,000	Real estate appraisal
Long-term investment	$3,000	(note 1)
Intangible capital assets	$10,000	(note 2)

Note 1

The long-term investment is an investment in the shares of a company owned and operated by Karmax's major shareholder's two sons. The Karmax investment is 25% of the outstanding shares. The sons' company has never sold shares to a nonfamily investor. The Karmax shareholder provided this estimate of value.

Note 2

Karmax holds patents on a successful consumer product, licensed to various manufacturers. Significant annual royalties are earned; the recorded balance sheet value consists of legal fees paid during patent infringement cases. The $10 million estimate of market value is based on discounted future cash flow.

Required   Prepare a brief report that contains:

1. An analysis of the reliability of the various market value estimates.
2. An assessment of the usefulness of the historical cost balance sheet to:
   a. A banker making a lending decision.
   b. An investor evaluating return on investment.

EXERCISES

E 5-1
(L.O. 2, 3)

Valuations on the Balance Sheet   Below to the left are some items from a typical balance sheet for a corporation. Below to the right are some brief statements of the valuations usually reported on the balance sheet for specific items.

Required

Use the code letters given below to the right to indicate the usual valuation reported in the balance sheet. Comment on any doubtful items. Some code letters may be used more than once or not at all. The first item is completed for you as an example.

Balance Sheet Items

___C___ 1. Land (held as investment).
_____ 2. Merchandise inventory, FIFO.
_____ 3. Short-term investments.
_____ 4. Accounts receivable (trade).
_____ 5. Long-term investment in bonds of another company held to maturity (purchased at a discount; the discount is a credit balance).
_____ 6. Land used as a plant site (in use).
_____ 7. Plant and equipment (in use).
_____ 8. Patent (in use).
_____ 9. Accounts payable (trade).
_____10. Bonds payable (sold at a premium; the premium is a credit balance).
_____11. Common shares, nopar.
_____12. Other contributed capital.
_____13. Retained earnings.
_____14. Land (future plant site).
_____15. Idle plant (awaiting disposal).
_____16. Natural resource (in use).

Valuations Usually Reported

A. Amount payable when due (usually no interest is involved because of the short term).
B. Lower of cost or market.
C. Original cost when acquired.
D. Market value at date of the balance sheet.
E. Original cost less accumulated amortization over estimated economic life.
F. Amount received on sale.
G. Face amount of the obligation plus unamortized premium.
H. Realizable value expected.
 I. Cost of the asset less unamortized discount.
J. Current market value less accumulated depreciation.
K. Accumulated income less accumulated losses and dividends.
L. Excess of average issue price over amount to retire common shares.
M. No valuation reported (explain).
N. Expected net disposal proceeds, if below book value; otherwise, net book value.
O. Cost less accumulated depletion.
P. None of the above (when this response is used, explain the valuation approach usually used).

E 5-2
(L.O. 2, 3)

Classifications on the Balance Sheet   A typical balance sheet has the following subcaptions:

A. Current assets.
B. Investments and funds.
C. Capital assets (property, plant, and equipment).
D. Intangible assets.
E. Other assets.
F. Deferred charges.
G. Current liabilities.
H. Long-term liabilities.
 I. Share capital (common or preferred).
J. Additional contributed capital.
K. Retained earnings.

Required

Use the code letters above to indicate the usual classification for each balance sheet item listed below. If an item is a contra amount (i.e., a deduction) under a caption, place a minus sign before the lettered response. The first item is completed for you as an example.

___-C___ 1. Accumulated depreciation.
_____ 2. Bonds payable (due in 10 years).
_____ 3. Accounts payable (trade).
_____ 4. Investment in shares of X Company (long term).
_____ 5. Plant site (in use).
_____ 6. Restriction or appropriation of retained earnings.
_____ 7. Office supplies inventory.
_____ 8. Loan to company president (collection not expected for two years).
_____ 9. Accumulated income less accumulated dividends.
_____ 10. Unamortized bond discount (on bonds payable; a debit balance).
_____ 11. Bond sinking fund (to retire long-term bonds).
_____ 12. Prepaid insurance.
_____ 13. Accounts receivable (trade).
_____ 14. Short-term investment.
_____ 15. Allowance for doubtful accounts.

_____ 16. Building (in use).

_____ 17. Common shares, nopar.

_____ 18. Interest revenue earned but not collected.

_____ 19. Patent.

_____ 20. Land, held for investment.

_____ 21. Land, idle plant.

E 5–3
(L.O. 1, 2, 3)

Determining Values in the Balance Sheet The consolidated balance sheet of Mutron Lock, Inc., is given below.

MUTRON LOCK, INC.
Consolidated Balance Sheet
As of December 31, 1995

Assets

Current assets:		
Cash and cash equivalents		$10,195
Marketable securities		*a*
Accounts receivable	$153,682	
Allowance for doubtful accounts	*b*	147,421
Inventories		201,753
Prepaid expenses		8,902
Total current assets		*c*
Capital assets:		
Land	12,482	
Building	*d*	
Equipment and machinery	195,467	
Accumulated depreciation	(103,675)	
Total capital assets		261,056
Investments		14,873
Other assets		7,926
Total assets		$661,774

Liabilities and Shareholders' Equity

Current liabilities:		
Accounts payable	$ 85,476	
Notes payable	*e*	
Income taxes payable	6,421	
Current portion of long-term debt	4,893	
Accrued expenses	5,654	
Total current liabilities		$110,763
Long-term debt		122,004
Deferred income taxes		*f*
Minority interests		35,136
Total liabilities		*g*
Shareholders' equity:		
Preferred shares, nopar value (authorized 10,000 shares, issued 2,400 shares for $14,281)		*h*
Common shares, nopar value (authorized 400,000 shares, issued 20,000 shares)		*i*
Additional paid-in capital		51,916
Total contributed capital		*j*
Retained earnings:		
Appropriated	25,000	
Unappropriated	*k*	181,471
Total shareholders' equity		$347,668
Total liabilities and shareholders' equity		$ *l*

1. For each of the items (*a*) through (*l*) identify the amounts that should appear on the balance sheet.
2. Indicate appropriate note disclosure for any balance sheet account that would normally require a disclosure note.

E 5–4
(L.O. 1, 2, 3)

Prepare a Classified Balance Sheet and Compute Ratios   The ledger of the Alberta Manufacturing Company reflects obsolete terminology, but you find its accounts have been, on the whole, accurately kept. After the books were closed at December 31, 1995, the following accounts were submitted to you for preparation of a balance sheet:

Accounts payable	$33,200
Accounts receivable	9,500
Accrued expenses (credit)	800
Bonds payable, 14%	25,000
Share capital, 700 shares	70,000
Cash	10,000
Earned surplus (to be determined)	xx,xxx
Factory equipment	31,200
Finished goods	13,100
Investments	13,000
Office equipment	9,500
Raw materials	9,600
Reserve for bad debts	500
Reserve for depreciation	9,000
Rent expense paid in advance	3,000
Sinking fund	7,000
Land held for future plant site	14,000
Note receivable	6,600
Work in process	23,300

Two-thirds of the depreciation relates to factory equipment and one-third to office equipment. Of the balance in the investments account, $4,000 will be converted to cash during the coming year; the remainder represents a long-term investment. Rent paid in advance is for the next year. The note receivable is a loan to the company president on October 1, 1995, and is due in 1997, when the principal amount ($6,600) plus 9% interest per annum will be paid to the company. The sinking fund is being accumulated to retire the bonds at maturity.

Required

1. Prepare a balance sheet using preferred format, classifications, and terminology.
2. Compute (*a*) the amount of working capital and (*b*) the current (working capital) ratio.

E 5–5
(L.O. 1, 3)

Prepare a Classified Balance Sheet Using Preferred Terminology   The following trial balance was prepared by Vantage Electronics Corporation as of December 31, 1995. The adjusting entries for 1995 have been made, except for any specifically noted below.

Cash	$15,000	
Accounts receivable	15,000	
Inventories	17,000	
Equipment	22,400	
Land	6,400	
Building	7,600	
Deferred charges	1,100	
Accounts payable		$ 5,500
Note payable, 10%		8,000
Share capital, nopar, 2,500 shares outstanding		38,500
Earned surplus		32,500
Totals	$84,500	$84,500

You find that certain errors and omissions are reflected in the above trial balance, including the following:

a. The $15,000 balance in accounts receivable represents the entire amount owed to the company; of this amount, $12,400 is from trade customers and 5% of that amount is estimated to be uncollectible. The remaining amount owed to the company represents a long-term advance to its president.
b. Inventories include $1,000 of goods incorrectly valued at double their cost (i.e., reported at $2,000). No correction has been recorded. Office supplies on hand of $500 are also included in the balance of inventories.
c. When the equipment and building were purchased new on January 1, 1990 (i.e., six years earlier), they had estimated lives of 10 and 25 years, respectively. They have been depreciated using the

straight-line method on the assumption of zero residual value, and depreciation has been credited directly to the asset accounts. Depreciation has been recorded for 1995.

   d. The balance in the land account includes a $1,000 payment made as a deposit on the purchase of an adjoining tract. The option to buy it has not yet been exercised and probably will not be exercised during the coming year.

   e. The interest-bearing note dated April 1, 1995, matures March 31, 1996. Interest on it has not been recorded.

Required

1. Prepare a correct balance sheet with appropriate captions and subcaptions. Use preferred terminology and the financing report form format. Show the computation of the ending balance in retained earnings.
2. How would your balance sheet be different if the net assets form were used? The account form?

E 5–6
(L.O. 1, 3, 4)

Analyzing Data and Reporting on the Balance Sheet   Akeman Seed Corporation is preparing its balance sheet at December 31, 1995. The following items are at issue:

   a. Note payable, long term, $80,000. This note will be paid in instalments. The first instalment, $10,000, will be paid August 1, 1996.

   b. Bonds payable, 12%, $200,000; at December 31, 1995, unamortized premium amounted to $6,000.

   c. Bond sinking fund, $40,000; this fund is being accumulated to retire the bonds at maturity. There is a restriction on retained earnings required by the bond indenture equal to the balance in the bond sinking fund.

   d. Rent revenue collected in advance for the first quarter of 1996, $6,000.

   e. After the balance sheet date, but prior to issuance of the 1995 balance sheet, one-third of the merchandise inventory was destroyed by flood (January 13, 1996); estimated loss, $150,000.

   f. Ending balance of unappropriated retained earnings (December 31, 1995), $35,000.

Required

Show by illustration, with appropriate captions, how each of these items should be reported on the December 31, 1995, balance sheet.

E 5–7
(L.O. 3)

Note Disclosures   Note disclosures provide the following information:

1. Disclosure of significant accounting policies.
2. Detail of items summarized on the financial statements.
3. Explanation of specific transactions recorded in the financial statements.
4. Explanation of unrecorded items.
5. New information not in the financial statements (not contained in the financial statements in their present form).

Typical notes include:

   a. Description of income statement item, discontinued operations.
   b. Revenue recognition policy.
   c. Breakdown of balance sheet total, other assets.
   d. Description of contingent loss that is not measurable.
   e. Depreciation policy and amounts of accumulated depreciation by asset class.
   f. Inventory note—breakdown of inventory into component parts and description of valuation method.
   g. Consolidation policy.
   h. Description of subsequent event not relating to conditions before balance sheet date.
   i. Information on key operating segments of the business.
   j. Description of related party transactions.
   k. Long-term debt note—interest rates, terms to maturity, five-year cash flow.
   l. Details of outstanding stock options.
   m. Description of subsequent events relating to conditions existing before balance sheet date.
   n. Details of pension plan assets and obligations.

Required

For each note *a* to *n* above, indicate the type(s) of disclosure (numbers 1 to 5) provided. A note may provide more than one type of disclosure. Explain your choice.

E 5–8
(L.O. 5, 6)

Statement of Changes in Financial Position Classification　The main parts of a statement of changes in financial position are shown below with letter identification. Next, several transactions are given. Match the transactions with the statement parts by entering a letter in each blank space. Assume loans and notes receivable are long-term investments not related to operating activities.

Statement of Changes in Financial Position

A. Cash inflows (outflows) from operating activities.
B. Cash inflows (outflows) from investing activities.
C. Cash inflows (outflows) from financing activities.
D. Not a cash flow.

Transactions

———— 1. Acquisition of operational assets; paid cash.
———— 2. Cash dividends declared but not paid.
———— 3. Proceeds from note payable.
———— 4. Sale of operational assets.
———— 5. Issue a loan.
———— 6. Purchase of a long-term security as an investment.
———— 7. Collections on notes receivable (principal only).
———— 8. Change in inventory.
———— 9. Depreciation expense.
———— 10. Payment of debt, 60% cash and 40% common shares issued.
———— 11. Issuance of the company's common shares, for cash.
———— 12. Sales revenue, cash.
———— 13. Repurchase and retirement of common shares.
———— 14. Payment on notes payable.
———— 15. Paid cash dividend.

E 5–9
(L.O. 5, 6)

Prepare a Statement of Changes in Financial Position　The records of Rangler Paper Company provided the selected data given below for the reporting period ended December 31, 1995.

Balance sheet data

Paid cash dividend	$ 10,000
Established restricted construction fund to build a new building at 8% interest	60,000
Increased inventory of merchandise	14,000
Borrowed on a long-term note	25,000
Acquired five acres of land for a future site for the company; paid in full by issuing 3,000 shares of Rangler common shares, nopar, when the quoted market price per share was $15	45,000
Increase in prepaid expenses	3,000
Decrease in accounts receivable	7,000
Payment of bonds payable in full	97,000
Increase in accounts payable	5,000
Cash from disposal of old operational assets (sold at book value)	12,000
Decrease in rent receivable	2,000

Income statement

Sales revenue	$400,000
Rent revenue	10,000
Cost of goods sold	(190,000)
Depreciation expense	(20,000)
Remaining expenses	(97,000)
Net income	$103,000

Required　Prepare a statement of changes in financial position (in thousands). Use the indirect method. Assume a beginning cash balance of $62,000.

E 5–10
(L.O. 5, 6, 7)

Recast a Deficient Statement of Changes in Financial Position: Direct Method　The following statement was incorrectly prepared by Yankee Auto Supply Corporation.

YANKEE AUTO SUPPLY CORPORATION
Cash Statement
December 31, 1995

Cash received:
  From operations:

Net income	$102,000
Depreciation expense	40,000
Amortization of patent	9,000
Decrease in accounts receivable balance	5,000
Increase in inventory balance	(10,000)
Increase in wages payable balance	4,000
Machinery, old (sold at book value on credit)	7,000
Long-term note payable given for land purchased	29,000
Total funds received	$186,000

Cash spent:

Retirement of mortgage	$ 60,000
Cash dividends	20,000
Machinery (new)	50,000
Acquired land; issued common shares in full payment (6,000 shares)*	36,000
Invested in common shares of Bittle Corporation	10,000
Increase in cash balance	10,000
Total funds spent	$186,000

Income statement:

Sales revenue	$320,000
Cost of goods sold	(120,000)
Depreciation expense	(40,000)
Amortization of patent	(9,000)
Salaries and wages	(11,000)
Remaining expenses (all cash)	(38,000)
Net income	$102,000

* Market price per share, $6. Total land acquisition was $65,000 ($29,000 + $36,000).

Required Using the direct method, recast the above statement (in thousands). Assume a beginning cash balance of $28,000.

E 5–11
(L.O. 5, 6)

Recast a Deficient Statement of Changes in Financial Position: Indirect Method Recast the information given in Exercise 5–10 using the indirect method.

E 5–12
(L.O. 6)

Statement of Changes in Financial Position: Classification The main categories of the statement of changes in financial position are shown below with letter identifications. Next, several transactions are given, preceded by a blank space.

A. Operating activity—addition to net income (indirect method).
B. Operating activity—subtraction from net income (indirect method).
C. Cash flows from operating activities (direct method).
D. Cash flows from investing activities.
E. Cash flows from financing activities.
F. Reported as a non-cash transaction, either on the statement or in the notes.

     1. Purchase of equity securities as an investment.
     2. Increase in prepaid expenses during the year.
     3. Increase in unearned rent revenue.
     4. Payment of cash dividends by the firm.
     5. Purchase of raw materials for cash.
     6. Depreciation expense.
     7. Declared a cash dividend for payment in the next fiscal year.
     8. Proceeds from sale of land.
     9. Retirement of bonds through the issuance of common shares.
   10. Proceeds from issuance of preferred shares.

———— 11. Interest payments on long-term debt.
———— 12. Amortization of goodwill.
———— 13. Issuance of bonds.
———— 14. Purchased short-term marketable securities.
———— 15. Payment on mortgage.
———— 16. Collection of accounts receivable for the year.
———— 17. Proceeds from settlement of patent infringement lawsuit.
———— 18. Loss on write-off of obsolete plant.
———— 19. Proceeds from sale of used equipment.
———— 20. Repaid short-term bank loans.

Required   Match the transactions with the statement parts by entering a letter in each blank space. Add a plus sign next to the letter if the transaction represents a cash inflow and a minus sign next to the letter if the transaction represents a cash outflow. If the transaction does not appear on the SCFP or the notes related to the SCFP, leave the blank space blank. Cash is defined as cash plus short-term investments less short-term bank debt.

PROBLEMS

P 5–1
(L.O. 1)

Classification on the Balance Sheet Typical balance sheet classifications along with a code letter for each classification are as follows:

A. Current assets.
B. Investments and funds.
C. Capital assets, tangible (property, plant and equipment).
D. Intangible assets.
E. Other assets.

F. Deferred charges.
G. Current liabilities.
H. Long-term liabilities.
I. Share capital.
J. Additional contributed capital.
K. Retained earnings.

Typical balance sheet items are as follows:

———— 1. Cash.
———— 2. Cash set aside to meet long-term purchase commitment.
———— 3. Land (used as plant site).
———— 4. Accrued salaries.
———— 5. Investment in the common shares of another company (long term; not a controlling interest).
———— 6. Inventory of damaged goods.
———— 7. Idle plant.
———— 8. Investment in bonds of another company.
———— 9. Cash surrender value of life insurance policy.
———— 10. Goodwill.
———— 11. Natural resource (timber tract).
———— 12. Allowance for doubtful accounts.
———— 13. Share subscriptions receivable (no plans to collect in near future).
———— 14. Organization costs.
———— 15. Discount on bonds payable.
———— 16. Service revenue collected in advance.
———— 17. Accrued interest payable.
———— 18. Accumulated amortization on patent.
———— 19. Prepaid rent.

———— 20. Short-term investment (common shares).
———— 21. Rent revenue collected but not earned.
———— 22. Net amount of accumulated revenues, gains, expenses, losses, and dividends.
———— 23. Trade accounts payable.
———— 24. Current maturity of long-term debt.
———— 25. Land (held for speculation).
———— 26. Notes payable (short-term).
———— 27. Special cash fund accumulated to build plant five years hence.
———— 28. Bonds issued—to be repaid within six months out of bond sinking fund.
———— 29. Long-term investment in rental building.
———— 30. Copyright.
———— 31. Accumulated depreciation.
———— 32. Deferred plant rearrangement costs.
———— 33. Franchise.
———— 34. Revenue earned but not collected.
———— 35. Premium on bonds payable (unamortized).
———— 36. Common shares (nopar).
———— 37. Petty cash fund.
———— 38. Deficit.
———— 39. Contributed capital on share retirement.
———— 40. Earnings retained in the business.

Required   Enter the appropriate code letter for each item to indicate its usual classification on the balance sheet. When it is a contra item (i.e., a deduction), place a minus sign before the lettered response.

(AICPA adapted)

P 5–2
(L.O. 1, 3)

Setting Up the Balance Sheet   Below is a typical chart of accounts for Altar Paving Corporation for 1995.

Accounts payable.
Accounts receivable.
Accrued expenses.
Accumulated amortization, all intangible assets.
Accumulated depreciation, all tangible assets.
Allowance for decline in value of marketable securities.
Allowance for doubtful accounts.
Amortization expense.
Bad debt expense.
Bonds payable.
Bond sinking fund.
Buildings.
Cash.
Cash surrender value of life insurance policies.
Common shares.
Cost of goods sold.
Deferred tax credits.
Depreciation expense.
Discount on bonds payable.
Dividends payable.
Equipment.
Finished goods.
Gain on sale of marketable securities.
General and administrative expense.

Goodwill.
Income tax expense.
Income tax payable.
Interest payable.
Investment in common shares, not intended for resale.
Investment in subsidiaries.
Land.
Licences.
Loss on sale of land.
Marketable securities.
Miscellaneous expense.
Overhead.
Contributed capital from share retirement.
Patents.
Prepaid expense.
Purchases.
Raw materials.
Restricted cash for long-term debt retirement.
Retained earnings.
Sales revenue.
Travel and entertainment expense.
Wages expense.
Wages payable.
Work in process.

Required   Prepare a blank, classified balance sheet in proper form using the financing format.

P 5–3
(L.O. 1, 2, 3, 4)

Prepare Balance Sheet, Analytical Questions The following data were taken from the accounts of Fuere Spice Corporation on December 31, 1995, the end of the current reporting year.

Cash	$ 16,000
Accounts receivable, trade	37,000
Short-term investment in marketable securities (cost $42,000)	40,000
Inventory of merchandise, FIFO	95,000
Prepaid expense (short term)	1,000
Bond sinking fund (to pay bonds at maturity)	35,000
Advances to suppliers (short term)	4,000
Dividends (cash) declared during 1995	10,000
Rent receivable	2,000
Investment in shares of Life Systems Corporation (long term, at cost, which approximates market)	22,000
Unamortized discount on bonds payable	2,000
Loans to employees (company president; payment date uncertain)	25,000
Land (building site in use)	30,000
Building	450,000
Equipment	60,000
Franchise (used in operations)	12,000
Deferred equipment rearrangement cost (long term)	4,000
Total debits	$845,000
Mortgage payable (14%)	$ 50,000
Accounts payable, trade	6,000
Dividends (cash) payable (payable March 1, 1996)	10,000
Deferred rent revenue	3,000
Interest payable	4,000
Accumulated depreciation, building	210,000
Accumulated depreciation, equipment	20,000
Allowance for doubtful accounts	2,000
Bonds payable (12.5%, maturity 2003)	100,000
Common shares, nopar (50,000 shares outstanding)	200,000
Preferred shares, nopar (8,000 shares outstanding)	96,000
Unappropriated retained earnings, January 1, 1995	17,000
Net income for 1995	88,000
Appropriation of retained earnings for plant expansion (set up prior to 1995)	39,000
Total credits	$845,000

Required

1. Prepare a complete balance sheet. Assume that all amounts are correct, and round to the nearest thousand dollars. Use the account titles as given. Show computation of the ending balance in retained earnings and include any restrictions on retained earnings on the statement.
2. In interpreting the foregoing data, refer to your response to (1) and respond to the following:
   a. Give the amount of working capital and the working capital ratio.
   b. Give the amount of total retained earnings.
   c. By what percent was the building depreciated?
   d. What were the per share issue prices of the preferred and common shares?
   e. Give the entry that was made to record the 1995 dividend declaration.
   f. Give the entry that was made for the appropriation of retained earnings.
   g. Give the entry that probably was made to record the issuance of (1) the preferred shares and (2) the common shares. Assume cash transactions.
   h. Give the entry that was made for the advances to suppliers. Assume cash transactions.
   i. Give the adjusting entry that probably was made for rent receivable.
   j. Give the adjusting entry that probably was made for deferred rent revenue.
   k. Give the probable closing entry for net income.

P 5–4
(L.O. 1, 2, 3, 4)

Income Statement and the Balance Sheet; Format, Disclosures The adjusted trial balance and other related data for Amana Cement Corporation, at December 31, 1995, are given below. Although the company uses obsolete terminology, the amounts are correct. Certain amounts may have to be reported separately. Assume that a perpetual inventory system is used.

AMANA CEMENT CORPORATION
Adjusted Trial Balance
December 31, 1995

Debit Balance Accounts

Cash	$ 38,600
Land (used for building site)	29,000
Cost of goods sold	125,500
Short-term securities (shares of Sanders Co.)	42,000
Goodwill (net)	12,000
Merchandise inventory	29,000
Office supplies inventory	2,000
Patent	7,000
Operating expenses	55,000
Income tax expense	17,500
Bond discount (unamortized)	7,500
Prepaid insurance	900
Building (at cost)	150,000
Land (held for speculation)	31,000
Accrued interest receivable	300
Accounts receivable (trade)	22,700
Note receivable, 10% (long-term investment)	20,000
Cash surrender value of life insurance policy	9,000
Deferred plant rearrangement costs	6,000
Dividends, paid during 1995	15,000
Correction of error from prior year—no income tax effect	15,000
	$635,000

Credit Balance Accounts

Reserve for bad debts	$ 1,100
Accounts payable (trade)	15,000
Revenues	245,000
Reserve for income taxes	7,500
Note payable (short term)	12,000
Common shares, nopar, authorized 50,000 shares, 10,000 shares outstanding	115,000
Reserve for depreciation, building	90,000
Retained earnings, January 1, 1995	37,000
Accrued wages	2,100
Reserve for estimated damages (set up in 1994)	10,000
Reserve for patent amortization	4,000
Cash advance from customer	3,000
Accrued property taxes	800
Note payable (long-term)	16,000
Rent revenue collected in advance	1,500
Bonds payable, 11% ($25,000 due June 1, 1996)	75,000
	$635,000

Additional information (no accounting errors are involved):

a. Market value of the short-term marketable securities is $44,000.

b. Merchandise inventory is based on FIFO, lower of cost or market (LCM).

c. Goodwill is being amortized (written off) over a 20-year period. The amortization for 1995 has already been recorded (as a direct credit to the goodwill account and a debit to expense). Amortization of other intangibles is recorded in this manner except for the patent, for which a contra account is used.

d. Reserve for income taxes represents the estimated income taxes payable at the end of 1995. Reserve for estimated damages was recorded as a credit to this reserve account and a debit to retained earnings during 1994. The $10,000 was the estimated amount of damages that would have to be paid as a result of a damage suit against the company. At December 31, 1995, the appeal was still pending. The $10,000 represents an appropriation, or restriction, placed on retained earnings by management.

e. Operating expenses as given include interest expense, and revenues include interest and investment revenues.

f. The cash advance from customer was for a special order that will not be completed and shipped until March 1996; the sales price has not been definitely established because it is to be based on cost (no revenue should be recognized for 1995).

Required

1. Prepare a single-step income statement and a separate retained earnings statement.
2. Prepare a balance sheet. Use preferred terminology, captions and subcaptions.
3. Indicate the likely note disclosure for balance sheet items.

P 5-5
(L.O. 1, 2, 3, 4)

Income Statement and Balance Sheet: Disclosure The adjusted trial balance for Deck Manufacturing Corporation at December 31, 1995, is given below in no particular order. Debits and credits are not indicated; however, debits equal credits. All amounts are correct. Assume the usual type of balance in each account and a perpetual inventory system, FIFO, and LCM.

Work in process inventory.	$ 29,000
Accrued interest on notes payable	1,000
Accrued interest receivable	1,200
Accrued income on short-term investments	1,000
Common shares, nopar, authorized 100,000 shares, issued 40,000	150,000
Cash in bank.	30,000
Trademarks (amortized cost)	1,400
Land held for speculation	27,000
Supplies inventory	600
Goodwill (amortized cost)	18,000
Raw materials inventory.	13,000
Bond sinking fund	10,000
Accrued property taxes	1,400
Accounts receivable (trade)	29,000
Accrued wages.	2,100
Mortgage payable (due in three years)	10,000
Building.	130,000
Prepaid rent	1,900
Organization expenses (amortized cost)	7,800
Deposits (cash collected from customers on sales orders to be delivered next quarter: no revenue yet recognized)	1,000
Long-term investment in bonds of Kaline Corp. (at cost)	50,000
Patents (amortized cost).	14,000
Reserve for bond sinking fund*	10,000
Reserve for depreciation, office equipment	1,600
Reserve for depreciation, building	5,000
Cash on hand for change	400
Preferred shares, $1, nopar, authorized 5,000 shares, issued 600 shares, noncumulative, nonconvertible.	68,000
Precollected rent income	900
Finished goods inventory	43,000
Notes receivable (short term)	4,000
Bonds payable, 12% (due in 6 years)	50,000
Accounts payable (trade)	17,000
Reserve for bad debts.	1,400
Notes payable (short term)	7,200
Office equipment	25,000
Land (used as building site)	8,000
Short-term investments (at cost)	15,500
Retained earnings, unappropriated (January 1, 1995)	13,200
Cash dividends on preferred and common shares declared and paid during 1995	20,000
Revenues during 1995.	500,000
Cost of goods sold for 1995	300,000
Expenses for 1995 (including income taxes)	100,000
Income taxes payable.	40,000

* This is a restriction on retained earnings required by the bond indenture equal to the bond sinking fund that is being accumulated to retire the bonds.

Required

1. Prepare a single-step income statement; use preferred terminology. To compute EPS, deduct $6,000 from net income as an allocation to nonconvertible preferred shares.
2. Prepare a complete balance sheet; use preferred terminology, format, captions, and subcaptions. Indicate likely note disclosure.
3. Assume that between December 31, 1995, and issuance of the financial statements, a flood damaged the finished goods inventory in an amount estimated to be $20,000. This event has not been and should not have been recorded in 1995. However, disclosure in the 1995 statements is required. Prepare the necessary disclosure.

P 5–6
(L.O. 5, 6)

Statement of Changes in Financial Position: Indirect Method   The items from the December 31, 1996, SCFP for Star Limited are given below, in no particular order.

Closing cash	?
Repayment of long-term debt	$297,139
Depreciation	186,176
Issuance of common shares to finance land acquisition	40,500
Decrease in inventories	97,760
Capital expenditures	286,292
Proceeds from issuance of common shares	21,056
Decrease in accounts and taxes payable.	90,000
Income before extraordinary items	37,668
Dividends paid	48,020
Net proceeds from expropriation of land	90,600
Opening cash.	116,714
Decrease in prepaid expenses	660
Increase in deferred tax	32,400
Net proceeds from the sale of a long-term investment	280,020
Increase in long-term borrowings.	30,245
Depletion	59,540
Increase in accounts receivable	67,090
Acquisition of land in exchange for common shares	40,500

Required

1. Using the above information, prepare a SCFP in good format, using the indirect method.
2. Based on this statement, what would you conclude about the company's cash flows for 1996?

P 5–7
(L.O. 5, 6)

Prepare Statement of Changes in Financial Position Showing a Net Loss   At the end of the current reporting year, December 31, 1995, Felch Construction Company's executives were very concerned about the ending cash balance of $4,000; the beginning cash balance of $34,000 had been considered serious the year before.

During 1995, management undertook numerous actions to attain a better cash position. In view of the decreasing cash balance, they asked the chief accountant to prepare a statement of changes in financial position. The following information was developed from the accounting records:

 a. Debt:
   1. Borrowing on long-term note, $10,000.
   2. Payments on maturing long-term debt, $110,000.
   3. Settled short-term debt of $50,000 by issuing Felch common shares.
 b. Cash payments:
   1. Regular cash dividends, $18,000.
   2. Purchase of new operational assets, $22,000.
 c. Cash received:
   1. Sold and issued Felch common shares, $11,000.
   2. Sold old operational assets at their book value, $1,000.
   3. Sold investment (long-term) in shares of Tech Corporation purchased this year and made the following entry:

Cash	90,000	
Loss on sale of investment	30,000	
Investment in Tech Corporation shares		120,000

d. Relevant balance sheet accounts:
   1. Increase in income tax payable, $10,000.
   2. Decrease in inventory, $38,000.
   3. Increase in accounts receivable, $5,000.

e. Income statement data:

Sales	$ 160,000
Cost of goods sold	(150,000)
Depreciation expense	(58,000)
Amortization of patent	(2,000)
Income tax expense	(4,000)
Remaining expenses	(41,000)
Loss on sale of long-term investment	(30,000)
Net income (loss)	$(125,000)

Required

Based on the above data, prepare a statement of changes in financial position (in thousands). Use the indirect method; non-cash significant transactions should be shown in a note to the SCFP.

P 5–8
(L.O. 5, 6)

Prepare Statement of Changes in Financial Position: Indirect Method Linda Ray, the president of Zabron Electric Corporation, has asked the company controller for a statement of changes in financial position for the reporting year ended December 31, 1995. The following balance sheet data have been obtained from the accounting records.

a. Cash account balances: January 1, 1995, $43,000; December 31, 1995, $18,000.
b. The balance in accounts receivable decreased by $10,000 during the year. Wages payable decreased by $5,000.
c. Inventory increased $9,000, and accounts payable increased $3,000 during the year.
d. Income tax payable increased $4,000 during the year.
e. During December 1995, the company settled a $10,000 note payable by issuing its own common shares with equivalent value.
f. Cash expenditures during 1995 were (1) payment of long-term debts, $64,000; (2) purchase of new operational assets, $74,000; (3) payment of a cash dividend, $16,000; and (4) purchase of land as an investment, $25,000.
g. Sale and issuance of shares of Zabron share capital for $20,000 cash.
h. Issuance of a long-term mortgage note, $30,000.
i. Some capital assets were sold; the following entry was made:

Cash	5,000	
Accumulated depreciation	12,000	
Capital assets		15,000
Gain on sale of capital assets		2,000

j. Income statement data:

Sales revenue	$ 295,000
Cost of goods sold	(140,000)
Depreciation expense	(14,000)
Patent amortization	(1,000)
Income tax expense	(17,000)
Remaining expenses	(42,000)
Gain on sale of capital assets	2,000
Net income	$ 83,000

Required

Prepare a statement of changes in financial position in thousands of dollars using the indirect method. Non-cash significant transactions should be disclosed in the body of the SCFP.

P 5–9
(L.O. 5, 6)

Prepare Statement of Changes in Financial Position: Direct Method Prepare a statement of changes in financial position using the direct method with the data in Problem 5–8.

ANALYZING FINANCIAL STATEMENTS

A 5–1
(L.O. 1, 2, 3, 4)

Inco Limited: Current Assets The 1993 balance sheet of Inco Limited lists seven items under current assets:

a.	Accounts receivable	$224,716
b.	Cash	9,993
c.	Deferred income and mining taxes	26,900
d.	Income and mining tax refunds receivable.	60,026
e.	Inventories	813,492
f.	Marketable securities	36,683
g.	Prepaid expenses	12,368

Required

1. Show how these items would be reported in Inco's financial statements.
2. Indicate the note disclosure that could be expected.
3. What kinds of items would be contained in "prepaid expenses"?
4. Why might deferred taxes be a current asset?

A 5–2
(L.O. 1)

Balance Sheet Items: Classification The items in the left-hand column are taken from the actual balance sheets of the identified companies. The right-hand column gives alternative balance sheet classifications. Use the letters in the right-hand column to indicate where the items in the left-hand column would appear on the balance sheet.

_____ 1. Prepaid income taxes (Sun Microsystems).

_____ 2. Intangibles (D. A. Stuart Ltd.).

_____ 3. Unearned revenue (Dow Jones & Company, Inc.).

_____ 4. Cash and cash equivalents (Noranda, Inc.).

_____ 5. Minority interest in consolidated subsidiary (Alberto-Culver Company).

_____ 6. Equipment under capital leases (Gesco Industries Ltd.).

_____ 7. Deferred subscription costs (*New York Times*).

_____ 8. Investments in joint ventures (Internetco Ltd.).

_____ 9. Investments in and advances to affiliated companies (W. R. Grace & Co.).

_____ 10. Contributed surplus (Loblaw Ltd.).

_____ 11. Cash surrender value of life insurance policies (Affiliated Publications, Inc.).

_____ 12. Excess of cost over fair value of assets acquired from investees (Seagram Ltd.).

_____ 13. Arena development costs (Northwest Sports Enterprises Ltd., owner of the Vancouver Canucks).

_____ 14. Development costs (M-Corp. Ltd.).

_____ 15. Perpetual 4% consolidated debentures (Canadian Pacific Ltd.).

A. Current asset.
B. Noncurrent asset (various categories).
C. Current liability.
D. Long-term liability.
E. Owners' equity.

A 5–3
(L.O. 5, 6)

Locating Items within the Statement of Changes in Financial Position   The following items were taken from the actual SCFPs of the indicated companies. Match each item to its location under the direct and indirect method. Use the following symbols:

O. Cash flows from operations.
 I. Cash flows from investing activities.
F. Cash flows from financing activities.
N. Item does not appear directly in the SCFP.

| | Form of Statement | |
Item (company)	Direct	Indirect
a. Capital expenditures (Imperial Oil).		
b. Paid to suppliers and employees (Lubrizol Corporation).	___	___
c. Net earnings (General Electric Company).	___	___
d. Proceeds from sale of common stock (Safeway, Inc.).	___	___
e. Depreciation, depletion, and amortization (Sun Company).	___	___
f. Cash dividends (Power Corp. of Canada).	___	___
g. Interest received (Compaq Computer Corporation).	___	___
h. Decrease in taxes payable (Astrosystems, Inc.).	___	___
i. Cash received from customers (Collins Industries, Inc.).	___	___
j. Net gain on divestiture of business (Domtar Inc.).	___	___
k. Proceeds from sale of fixed assets (George Weston Ltd.).	___	___
l. Change in operating working capital (MT&T Ltd.).	___	___
m. Cash flow used in discontinued operations (Spar Aerospace Ltd.)	___	___
n. Dividends from life insurance policies (Crown X Ltd.).	___	___
o. Debentures repaid (Domtar Inc.).	___	___
p. Loss on sale of capital assets (Panorama Industries Inc.).	___	___
q. Redemption of preferred shares (Dofasco Inc.).	___	___
r. Funding of pension obligation (Rothmans Inc.).	___	___
s. Increase in other assets (UAP Inc.).	___	___

A 5–4
(L.O. 1, 2, 4,
6, 7)

 Magna International Inc.: Analysis of Actual Financial Statements   The following questions deal with Magna's financial statements, located at the end of the text.

a. Does the Magna balance sheet reflect the net asset or financing form? Account or report form?
b. What are the major limitations of the balance sheet Magna presents to its financial statement users? In what way is it incomplete?
c. Why do you think the convertible subordinated bonds and debentures are disclosed separately and not as part of long-term debt?
d. What are the major reconciling items between 1993 income, $140,400,000, and cash from operations, $302,700,000?
e. Are there any significant non-cash events on the SCFP? Explain.
f. What does the comparative SCFP tell you about Magna's cash flows and strategy?

6 Interest: Concepts of Future and Present Value

LEARNING OBJECTIVES

After you have studied this chapter, you will be able to:

1 **Explain the concept of the time value of money, which underlies all interest calculations and a wide range of accounting issues.**

2 **Describe the difference between simple and compound interest.**

3 **Explain the difference between future value and present value as these terms apply to both single-payment amounts and annuities.**

4 **Describe the distinction between an ordinary annuity and an annuity due.**

5 **Compute future and present values of both single payments and annuities.**

6 **Solve valuation problems by combining present and future value computations for single payments and annuities.**

INTRODUCTION

During the fourth quarter of 1988, Imasco Limited wrote down (reduced capital assets) by $110 million. These assets were being sold by Imasco, and the company did not expect to recover the costs invested to date. To establish the amount of the write-down, Imasco compared the balance sheet cost to the total cash expected to be received from the sale of these assets in the years ahead. After the write-down, the assets were valued at the amount of future cash receipts expected.

In 1985, Diamond Shamrock Oil Company wrote down its oil and gas reserves in Sumatra, Indonesia, by $600 million. Rather than basing the write-down on the total expected future cash flows, Diamond Shamrock discounted its future cash flows. That is, if Diamond Shamrock expected the asset to be sold for $1 million in cash a year from now, that asset would be valued at less than $1 million today. Hence, the write-down would exceed the write-down Imasco would recognize under the same circumstances.[1]

---

[1] Interest, especially when compounded (interest on interest as well as on principal), has large and often underestimated effects. For example, consider the $24 paid to the Indians for the Island of Manhattan in 1626 by Peter Minuit of the Dutch West India Company. Historians tell us this was a real bargain, even though that $24 invested at 10% compounded yearly yields a value today of $2.5 quadrillion.

These different approaches to essentially a similar situation result in radically different values for assets and income. How should market value be estimated? This chapter suggests that a measure using discounted future cash flows, the Diamond Shamrock approach, is the most logical.

TIME VALUE OF MONEY

In general business terms, **interest** is defined as the cost of using money over time. This definition is in close agreement with the definition used by economists, who prefer to say that interest represents the **time value of money.**

One hundred dollars in hand today will be worth more in one year's time than a second $100 received one year from today. The assumption is that today's dollars can be put to work earning interest. Thus, today's money has a future value equal to its principal (face amount) plus whatever interest can be earned over the period of time, one year in this case. If the interest rate on money invested for one year is 10%, the **future value** of today's $100 principal at the end of 12 months is $110 ($100 principal + $10 interest). Numerically, $110 = $100 + $100(.10).

The second $100, the amount coming in at the end of 12 months, is tomorrow's money, scheduled to be received (or paid) at some future date—in this example, one year. Just as today's money has a future value, calculated by adding interest to principal, tomorrow's money has a **present value,** calculated by subtracting interest. For example, if the interest rate on money invested for one year is 10%, the present value of $110 a year from now is the principal necessary to invest today to obtain $110 in a year. We already know that this required principal is $100, because $100 + $100(.10) yields $110 in one year. Suppose, instead, that $100 is to be received in one year. What is its present value? If the interest rate is again 10%, the present value is the principal needed today to yield $100 in one year at 10%. This principal amount is $91, because $91 plus 10% of $91 gives (approximately) $100 in one year ($91 principal + $9 interest). Numerically, $100 = $91 + $91(.10), approximately.

Accounting involves many applications of the concepts of present and future value. Some of the more prominent applications covered in this book relate to:

- Receivables and payables.
- Bonds.
- Leases.
- Pensions.
- Asset valuation.

The purpose of this chapter is to provide the concepts necessary to facilitate measurement of the time value of money and its impact on transactions.

BASIC INTEREST CONCEPTS

Concept of Interest

Interest is the excess of resources (usually cash) received or paid over and above the amount of resources loaned or borrowed at an earlier date. The amount loaned or borrowed is called the **principal.** The cost of the excess resources to the borrower is called **interest expense.** The benefit of the excess resources to the lender is called **interest revenue.**

To illustrate measurement of interest in a simple situation, assume that the Debont Company borrows $10,000 cash and promises to repay $11,200 one period later. The interest on this contract is as follows:

Resources repaid at maturity	$11,200
Resources borrowed	10,000
Interest	$ 1,200
Analysis:	
Interest in dollars	$ 1,200
Interest rate for one period ($1,200 ÷ $10,000)	12%

Interest calculations and the time value of money are also key considerations in negotiating transactions that call for payment over one or more future time periods.

Interest and time value are considerations in decisions involving expenditures for business investments and the acquisition of operating assets; both types of expenditures are expected to produce future cash inflow over one or more future periods.

Consistent Interest Periods and Rates

Interest usually is expressed as a **rate per year,** such as 12%, although interest is often required to be paid for periods of less than one year, such as monthly, quarterly, or semiannually.[2] This is called compound interest. Thus, a 12% annual interest rate would be 1% monthly, 3% quarterly, or 6% semiannually, depending on when interest is paid. If an interest rate is specified with no indication of an interest period less than one year, an annual rate should be assumed.[3] In the case of compound interest, the interest rate and compounding period must be clearly stated. The amount of interest is a function of the principal amount, the interest rate, and the number of interest periods.

Simple versus Compound Interest

Business transactions subject to interest state whether simple or compound interest is to be calculated. **Simple interest** is the product of the principal amount multiplied by the period's interest rate (a one-year rate is standard). The equation for computing simple interest is:

$$\text{Interest amount} = (P)(i)(n)$$

where

P = Principal
i = Interest rate per period
n = Number of interest periods

When applied to long-term transactions extending over multiple years, simple interest is based on the principal amount outstanding during the year. If there are no changes caused by repayments or additional borrowing, this will equal the principal outstanding at the beginning of each year. Interest is paid periodically (typically yearly or at the end of the contract) and not added to the principal. Thus, interest is paid only on the initial principal and not on interest accumulated but not yet paid. The yearly interest remains the same. Thus, a three-year $10,000 loan at a rate of 10% simple interest produces the following numbers, assuming that no installment payments are made on the principal:

Simple Interest Calculation,
Three Years @ 10%, No Principal Payments

Year	Principal Beginning Balance	Annual Interest @ 10%	Total Interest	Simple Interest	
1995	$10,000	$1,000	$1,000	$10,000(.10)	$1,000
1996	10,000	1,000	2,000	$10,000(.10)	1,000
1997	10,000	1,000	3,000	$10,000(.10)	1,000
				Total	$3,000

Compound interest is based on the principal amount outstanding at the beginning of each interest period, to which accumulated interest from previous periods has been added. In compound interest problems, it is assumed that interest is allowed to accumulate rather than being paid (by the borrower) or withdrawn (by the lender). This means that compound interest includes interest on previously computed and

---

[2] Throughout this textbook and in the problem materials, short-term periods are used to facilitate comprehension. Also, for instructional convenience, amounts are usually rounded to the nearest dollar.

[3] In recent years, the term *annual percentage rate (APR)* has become common, especially in conjunction with consumer lending and consumer product financing. *Rate per year, annual rate,* and *annual percentage rate* are synonymous.

recorded interest. The following table illustrates compound interest calculations on a bank deposit:

Compound Interest Calculation,
Three Years @ 10%, No Principal Payments, Yearly Compounding

Year	Principal Beginning Balance	Annual Interest @ 10%	Total Interest	Compound Interest	
1995	$10,000	$1,000	$1,000	$10,000(.10)	$1,000
1996	11,000	1,100	2,100	($10,000 + $1,000)(.10)	1,100
1997	12,100	1,210	3,310	($10,000 + $1,000 + $1,100)(.10).	1,210
				Total	$3,310

The compound interest calculation produces $310 more interest than the simple interest calculation over three years. Interest periods of less than one year would yield even more. Semiannual, quarterly, monthly, weekly, and daily compounding are all in common use. Even continuous compounding is possible.

When interest periods of less than one year are used, the annual interest rate given must be converted to an equivalent rate for the time period specified for compounding purposes. To demonstrate, we add quarterly compounding to the interest calculation example. The interest rate is now 10% compounded quarterly, or 2.5% (10% ÷ 4) per quarter. The first year's interest calculations are as follows:

Compound Interest Calculation,
One Year at 10%, No Principal Payments, Quarterly Compounding

Quarter 1995	Principal Beginning Balance	Quarterly Interest @ 2.5%	Total Interest	Compound Interest 10% Annual Rate Equivalent to 2.5% Quarterly Rate	
1st	$10,000.00	$250.00	$ 250.00	$10,000.00(.025).	$ 250.00
2nd	10,250.00	256.25	506.25	($10,000.00 + $250.00)(.025).	256.25
3rd	10,506.25	262.66	768.91	($10,000.00 + $250.00 + $256.25)(.025).	262.66
4th	10,768.91	269.22	1,038.13	($10,000.00 + $250.00 + $256.25 + $262.66)(.025)	269.22
				Total	$1,038.13

In the above example, quarterly compounding for the first year produces $38.13 more interest than annual compounding. Quarterly compounding of a 10% interest rate is equivalent to an annual interest rate of 10.38% ($1,038.13 ÷ $10,000).[4] This rate, 10.38%, is said to be the effective, or true, interest rate.

CONCEPT REVIEW

1. Is it more of a burden on a borrower to owe $50,000 to be paid back in one payment without interest (a) 1 year from now, or (b) 10 years from now?
2. Which stipulation of an obligation places a larger financial burden on a borrower?
   a. The borrower of $10,000 agrees to repay the loan in equal instalments. No interest rate is specified in the loan agreement.
   b. The borrower of $10,000 agrees to repay the loan in equal instalments plus interest calculated at 10% per year.
3. Which of the following produces the larger value?
   a. $100,000 invested for 10 years at 10% simple interest.
   b. $100,000 invested for 10 years at 10% compound interest.

---

[4] In an attempt to prevent fraud and consumer deception, certain legislation has been enacted that requires disclosure of the true annual rate of interest on loans quoted at rates other than an annual percentage rate. For example, an advertised 1% loan rate may seem enticing. But if the 1% rate is a monthly compounding rate, the true annual rate is 12.68%.

OVERVIEW OF FUTURE VALUE AND PRESENT VALUE

Future value (*FV*) and present value (*PV*) pertain to compound interest calculations.[5] Future value involves a current amount that is increased in the future as the result of compound interest accumulation. Present value, in contrast, involves a future amount that is decreased to the present as a result of compound interest discounting.

The fact that investments have starting points and ending points makes it easier to understand present and future values. Present value in general refers to dollar values at the starting point of an investment, and future value refers to end-point dollar values. If the dollar amount to be invested at the start is known, the future value of that amount at the end can be projected, provided the interest rate and number of interest compounding periods are also specified. Similarly, if the dollar amount available at the end of an investment period (future value) is known, the amount of money needed at the start of the investment period (present value) can be determined, again if the interest rate and number of interest compounding periods are known.

Present value and future value apply to interest calculations on both single principal amounts and periodic equal payment (annuity) amounts.

Single Principal Amount

Also known as a lump-sum amount, the single principal amount is based on a one-time-only investment amount that earns compound interest from the start to the end of the investment time frame.

Application	**Example**
Find the future value of a single current payment.	If $100,000 is available for investment today (present value date) and the current annual interest rate is 11% compounded semiannually, what total investment amount will result at the end of two years (future value date)?
Find the present value of a single future payment.	It is known that $100,000 will be needed in two years (future value date), and the current annual interest rate is 11% compounded semiannually. What total amount must be invested today (present value date) to produce $100,000 in two years?

Annuity Amount

An **annuity** is a series of uniform payments (also called *rents*) occurring at uniform intervals over a specified investment time frame, with all amounts earning compound interest at the same rate. Annuity amounts may take the form of either cash payments into an annuity type of investment or cash withdrawals from an annuity type of investment.

Application	**Example**
Find the future value of a series of uniform periodic payments.	If $10,000 is invested on January 1 of *each* of the next five years at an annual interest rate of 11% compounded semiannually, what total amount will result at the end of the investment period (future value date)?
Find the present value of a series of uniform periodic payments.	If it is known that $10,000 is needed from an investment at the end of *each* of the next five years and the current annual interest rate is 11% compounded semiannually, what total amount today (present value date) must be invested to yield these receipts?

The Ordinary Annuity and the Annuity Due

There are two distinct types of annuities: ordinary annuities and annuities due. The distinction is in the timing of the payments. With an **ordinary annuity,** the more

---

[5] Notation and abbreviations vary considerably; alternative designations are *f* for future value and *p* for present value.

EXHIBIT 6–1

Comparison of an Ordinary
Annuity with an Annuity Due

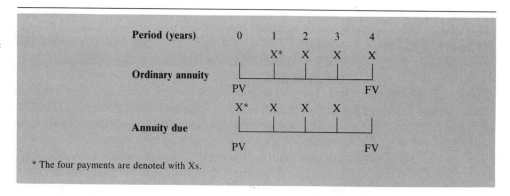

* The four payments are denoted with Xs.

common type, the payments (or receipts) occur at the end of each interest compounding period. With an **annuity due,** payments (or receipts) occur at the beginning of each interest compounding period.

The difference between an ordinary annuity and an annuity due is illustrated in Exhibit 6–1. With an ordinary annuity, the first payment occurs one period after the present value is established and the last payment coincides with the determination of future value. For an annuity due, the first payment coincides with the date the present value is established and the last payment occurs one period before the future value is determined.

A series of equal payments beginning today, an annuity due, has a greater present value than the same set of payments beginning one year from now, an ordinary annuity. Similarly, a set of payments starting today, an annuity due, discharges a debt with lower payments than the payments required under an ordinary annuity.

Future Value and Present Value Tables and Formulas

There are four methods used to compute future and present values:

1. Make successive interest calculations.
2. Use a formula.
3. Use tables.
4. Use a financial calculator or personal computer, likely a spreadsheet package.

All methods will produce the same results. Most accountants prefer to use a calculator or computer spreadsheet, since the result is accurate and the application of the technique is not restricted to the values displayed in the tables.

Any calculation method should use all the decimal places throughout, rounding only after all calculations have been completed.

Appendix 6 includes the following tables:

Table No.	Table Title (and use)	Formula*
6–1	Future value of 1 (FV1): Used to compute the future value of single payments made now.	$FV1 = (1 + i)^n$ Also expressed (FV1, i, n)
6–2	Present value of 1 (PV1): Used to compute the present value of single payments made in the future.	$PV1 = \dfrac{1}{(1 + i)^n}$ Also expressed (PV1, i, n)
6–3	Future value of ordinary annuity of 1 (FVA): Used to compute the future value of a series of payments made at the *end* of each interest compounding period.	$FVA = \dfrac{(1 + i)^n - 1}{i}$ Also expressed (FVA, i, n)

Table No.	Table Title (and use)	Formula*
6–4	Present value of ordinary annuity of 1 (PVA): Used to compute the present value of a series of payments made at the *end* of each interest compounding period.	$PVA = \dfrac{1 - \dfrac{1}{(1+i)^n}}{i}$ Also expressed (PVA, i, n)
6–5	Future value of annuity due of 1 (FVAD): Used to compute the future value of a series of payments made at the *beginning* of each interest compounding period.	$FVAD = \left[\dfrac{(1+i)^n - 1}{i}\right] \times (1+i)$ Also expressed (FVAD, i, n) = $(1+i)(FVA, i, n)$
6–6	Present value of annuity due of 1 (PVAD): Used to compute the present value of a series of payments made at the *beginning* of each interest compounding period.	$PVAD = \left[\dfrac{1 - \dfrac{1}{(1+i)^n}}{i}\right] \times (1+i)$ Also expressed (PVAD, i, n) = $(1+i)(PVA, i, n)$

* In these equations and throughout this text, i is the compound interest rate and n is the number of interest periods.

VALUES OF A SINGLE PAYMENT

Future Value of 1

The future value of 1 (FV1) is the future value of a single payment of 1 ($1) after a specified number of interest periods (n) when increased at a specified compound interest rate (i). For example, to find the future value of $1 left on deposit for six interest periods at an interest rate of 8% per period (FV1, 8%, 6), use either the formula for calculating the future value of 1 or Table 6A–1. According to the formula, the calculation is as follows:

$$FV1 = (1+i)^n \qquad \text{expressed as (FV1, } i, n)$$
$$FV1 = (1 + .08)^6$$
$$FV1 = 1.58687, \text{ or } 1.59$$

The same result can be obtained by using Table 6A–1 in Appendix 6. Exhibit 6–2, an excerpt from Table 6A–1, illustrates how the appropriate number, 1.58687, is obtained. First locate the appropriate interest rate column, and then read down the column to the intersecting line representing the number of interest periods involved. The number of interest periods is listed on the left-hand side of the table. Once the correct future value factor is located, multiply it by the principal amount involved. For example, the future value of $5,000 at 8% for six interest periods is $7,934.35, or $5,000(1.58687).

Present Value of 1

The present value of 1 (PV1) is the present value of a single payment of 1 ($1) for a specified number of interest periods (n) at a specific interest rate (i). For example, to find the present value of $1 to be received six interest periods from today at 8% (PV1, 8%, 6), use either the formula to calculate the present value of 1 or Table 6A–2. According to the formula, the calculation is as follows:

$$PV1 = \frac{1}{(1+i)^n} \qquad \text{expressed as (PV1, } i, n)$$
$$PV1 = \frac{1}{(1 + .08)^6}$$
$$PV1 = \frac{1}{1.58687}$$
$$PV1 = .63017, \text{ or } .63$$

EXHIBIT 6–2
Excerpt from Table 6–1, in Appendix

Number of Periods (n)*	Selected Interest Rates (i)†					
	6%	7%	8%	9%	10%	
1	1.06000	1.07000	1.08000	1.09000	1.10000	. . . . .
2	1.12360	1.14490	1.16640	1.18810	1.21000	. . . . .
3	1.19102	1.22504	1.25971	1.29503	1.33100	. . . . .
4	1.26248	1.31080	1.36049	1.41158	1.46410	. . . . .
5	1.33823	1.40255	1.46933	1.53862	1.61051	. . . . .
6	1.41852	1.50073	1.58687	1.67710	1.77156	. . . . .
7	1.50363	1.60578	1.71382	1.82804	1.94872	. . . . .
8	1.59385	1.71819	1.85093	1.99256	2.14359	. . . . .
9	1.68948	1.83846	1.99900	2.17189	2.35795	. . . . .
10	1.79085	1.96715	2.15892	2.36736	2.59374	. . . . .

* Compounding periods may be annual, semiannual, quarterly, monthly, or daily.

† Interest rates are compounded regardless of the length of the period.

These notes hold for all the tables in the appendix to this chapter.

Table 6A–2 produces the same answer. First locate the 8% interest rate column, and then read down the column to the intersecting line representing the number of interest periods involved, 6, found at the left-hand side of the table. Once the correct present value of 1 factor is located, multiply it by the principal amount involved. For example, the present value of $5,000 at 8% for six interest periods is $3,150.85, or $5,000(.63017).

Future Value and Present Value of 1 Compared

Future values and present values of 1 are the same in one respect: they both relate to a single payment. The future value looks forward from present dollars to future dollars. The present value looks back from future dollars to present dollars. This distinction is shown by the time lines in Exhibit 6–3, which compares the present and future values of $1 for six periods at 8% ($.63 versus $1.59). The directions of the arrows help illustrate the difference between present and future value computations.

Present value and future value, for a given i and n, are reciprocals.

$$PV1 = \frac{1}{FV1} \quad \text{and} \quad FV1 = \frac{1}{PV1}$$

This reciprocal relationship is illustrated in Exhibit 6–3 and is summarized below.

a. The future value of $1 invested at 8% for six periods is $1.59 (rounded).
b. The present value of $1 discounted at 8% for six periods is $.63.

The reciprocal relationship is as follows:

For (a): $1 \div 1.59 = 0.63$
For (b): $1 \div 0.63 = 1.59$

Remember, future value is the single payment plus all subsequent accumulated compound interest. It is always larger than the single payment. Present value is always less than the single payment, as it takes a future payment and factors out compound interest.

EXHIBIT 6–3
Future Value and Present
Value of a Single Payment of
$1 Compared

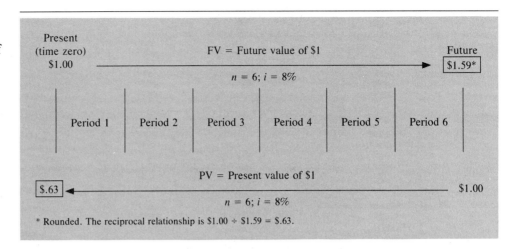

CONCEPT REVIEW

1. Which is larger at any positive interest rate?
   a. The present value of an annuity of $1,000 for 10 periods.
   b. The future value of an annuity of $1,000 for 10 periods.
2. Calculate the present value of $10,000 to be received five years from now if interest is 12% compounded semiannually.
3. Explain how an annuity due differs from an ordinary annuity.

ACCOUNTING APPLICATIONS OF A SINGLE PAYMENT

We now turn to several examples of interest calculations involving single payments. These examples illustrate the variety of questions raised in typical business contexts that can be answered with single-payment interest mathematics. The various examples are all solved using the tables, but any computation method could be employed.

Future Value of a Single Payment

Case A   On January 1, 1995, Able Company deposited $100,000 in a special construction fund. The fund earns 10% interest compounded annually for three years. Interest earned each period is added to the fund.

1. The amount that will be in the fund at the end of 1997 is found using Table 6A–1:

   $$\$100{,}000(FV1, 10\%, 3) = \$100{,}000(1.33100) = \$133{,}100$$

2. The total amount of accumulated interest is:

   $$\$133{,}100 - \$100{,}000 = \$33{,}100$$

3. The fund accumulation schedule is:

   Fund Accumulation Schedule

Date	Interest Earned	Fund Balance
January 1, 1995		$100,000
December 31, 1995	$100,000 × .10 = $10,000	110,000
December 31, 1996	110,000 × .10 = 11,000	121,000
December 31, 1997	121,000 × .10 = 12,100	133,100

4. The journal entries related to the fund are:
   January 1, 1995:

Special construction fund	100,000	
Cash		100,000

Each December 31:

	1995	1996	1997
Special construction fund	10,000	11,000	12,100
Investment revenue		10,000	11,000	12,100

Case B On January 1, 1995, Baker Company deposited $100,000 in a special savings account. The fund earns 10% interest compounded quarterly for three years. Interest earned is added to the fund. The three years encompass 12 interest periods, and the interest rate for each quarterly interest period is 10% ÷ 4 = 2½%.

1. The amount that will be in the fund at the end of 1997 is found using Table 6A–1:

$$\$100,000(FV1, 2.5\%, 12) = \$100,000(1.34489) = \$134,489$$

2. The total amount of accumulated interest is:

$$\$134,489 - \$100,000 = \$34,489$$

Case B results in more accumulated interest than Case A ($34,489 versus $33,100) because of more frequent compounding.

Determination of an Unknown Interest Rate or Unknown Number of Periods

In some situations, either the interest rate (i) or the number of periods (n) is not known, but sufficient data are available for their determination. For example, in Case A above, three values were provided: principal, $100,000; interest rate, 10%; and number of periods, 3. These three values were used to compute the future value, $133,100. Now consider two situations in which the unknown variable is not the future value but, rather, the interest rate or required number of payments.

Interest Rate Is Unknown A $100,000 investment will yield $146,933 in five periods. What is the implicit interest rate earned on the investment?

1. $146,933 ÷ $100,000 = 1.46933, which is the future value of 1 for five periods.
2. Use Table 6A–1 and read across the row corresponding to five interest periods to find 1.46933 in the table.
3. The table value 1.46933 is found under the 8% column.
4. The interest rate, therefore, is 8%.

If the exact value computed in step 1 above is not found in the table, the interest rate can be approximated using interpolation, described below, or determined precisely using a computer or calculator.

Number of Interest Periods Is Unknown A family can invest $150,000 today to provide for the college education of their child. The family believes that $285,000 will be necessary for four years of college by the time the student graduates from high school. If the family can invest at 6%, how many years will it take to accumulate $285,000?

1. $285,000 ÷ $150,000 = 1.90000, which is the future value of 1 at 6% interest.
2. In Table 6A–1, read down the 6% column to find 1.90000.
3. The table value 1.89830 is found on the line for 11 years, and the value 2.01220 is found on the line for 12 years.
4. The number of interest periods required is just over 11 years.

Interpolation of Table Values

Determination of an unknown interest rate or number of periods with greater accuracy requires interpolation, because the table values are given only in whole interest percentages. Assume that $5,000 is deposited in a savings account with compound interest and that a $15,000 balance is expected at the end of year 10. What is the implicit interest rate, assuming annual compounding?

1. $15,000 = $5,000(FV1, i, 10) where i is the unknown implicit interest rate. So (FV1, i, 10) = $15,000 ÷ $5,000 = 3.00000.
2. In the excerpt from Table 6A–1 in Appendix 6 displayed below, the 3.00000 value

found in step 1 for 10 periods falls somewhere between 2.83942 (which is compounded at 11%) and 3.10585 (which is compounded at 12%):[6]

	i	
n	11%	12%
.	.	.
.	.	.
.	.	.
9	2.55804	2.77308
10	2.83942	3.10585
11	3.15176	3.47855
.	.	.
.	.	.
.	.	.

3. The difference between these two factors is .26643 (3.10585 − 2.83942). An additional .16058 (3.00000 − 2.83942) is needed above the 11% PV factor.

   Therefore, the interest rate is 11% plus (approximately) .6 (.16058 / .26643), or approximately 11.6%.[7]

Present Value of a Single Payment

Assume that on January 1, 1995, Cary Company purchased a machine. Cary immediately paid $25,000 cash and gave a $50,000 noninterest-bearing note, due on December 31, 1996. Assume that similar transactions carry interest at 10% compounded annually. The present value of the noninterest-bearing note is equal to the face amount ($50,000) discounted at 10% for two years, which is $41,323.[8] Therefore:

1. The cost of the machine is as follows:

Cash paid.	$25,000
Note at present value $50,000(PV1, 10%, 2) = $50,000 (.82645).	41,323
Cost of the machine	$66,323

2. The entry to record the acquisition of the machine using the net method is as follows:

Machine	66,323	
Cash.		25,000
Note payable		41,323*

   * Alternatively, this note could be recorded at $50,000 (the gross method) with an accompanying debit for $8,677 made to a discounts on notes payable account. Discounts on notes payable is a contra liability, with the balance (which represents interest yet to be recognized) deducted from the face value to arrive at the net note payable ($50,000 − $8,677 = $41,323).

3. The debt payment schedule is:

Date	Interest Expense Incurred (payable at maturity)	Liability (note payable)	
		Increase	Balance
January 1, 1995			$41,323
December 31, 1995.	$41,323 × .10 = $4,132	$4,132	45,455
December 31, 1996.	45,455 × .10 = 4,545	4,545	50,000

4. The remaining entries related to this example, assuming the note was originally recorded at $41,323:

---

[6] It is often sufficient simply to use the closest rate given in the table.

[7] An even more precise answer can be obtained by using a calculator to solve $5,000(1 + i)^{10} = $15,000 to obtain $i =$ 11.612%. This answer is more precise because the linear interpolation used to obtain 11.6% is itself an approximation.

[8] If the note had specified interest at 10%, the cost of the machine would have been $75,000 ($25,000 cash plus the $50,000 note) and, in addition, interest would have been paid on $50,000.

	December 31	
	1995	**1996**
Interest expense	4,132	4,545
Note payable	4,132	4,545
Note payable	50,000	
Cash		50,000

Unknown interest rates or time periods are found for problems involving present values in the way illustrated in the previous section for future values.

Selecting an Interest Rate

Future and present values are affected by the interest rate used. The effect can be substantial, especially when the time period is long. For example, the future value of $100,000 for 20 periods at 10% per period is $672,750. If the interest rate is 8%, the future value is $466,096.

Occasionally, an accountant will be faced with a transaction in which the time value of money is obviously important but there are too many unknown factors to establish the interest rate used in the payment scheme. In these circumstances, the going or market interest rate for transactions of similar risk should be used, as long as the resulting present or future value calculation is logical.

|CONCEPT REVIEW

1. Calculate the following:
   a. The present value of $1,500 at 8% interest for five years compounded annually (PV1, 8%, 5).
   b. The future value of $1,800 at 4% interest for seven years compounded annually (FV1, 4%, 7).
2. What annual compound interest rate is implicit in a loan that provides a borrower with $8,264 today based on the promise to repay $10,000 two years from today?
3. Suppose $10,000 is invested today at 12% interest compounded quarterly. About how long would it take for this amount to grow to $20,000?

|VALUES OF AN ANNUITY

Future Value of an Ordinary Annuity

The future value of an ordinary annuity (FVA) is the future value of a series of payments (or receipts) in equal dollar amounts being made over a specified number of equally spaced interest periods (n) at a specified interest rate (i). Unless otherwise stated, all annuities are assumed to be ordinary annuities, meaning that every payment occurs at the end of the interest period. The future value of an ordinary annuity can be determined by any of the four methods discussed earlier to find the future value of 1. To find the future value of an annuity of $5,000 invested at 8% for six interest periods (FVA, 8%, 6) by formula, compute:

$$FVA = \frac{(1 + i)^n - 1}{i} \qquad \text{expressed as (FVA, } i, n)$$

$$FVA = \frac{(1 + .08)^6 - 1}{.08}$$

$$FVA = \frac{1.58687 - 1}{.08}$$

$$FVA = 7.33588, \text{ or } 7.34$$

To find the future value of an ordinary annuity of 1 using Table 6A–3 in Appendix 6, proceed in the same way as illustrated in Exhibit 6–2. First locate the proper interest rate column, and then read down the column to the intersecting line representing the number of interest periods involved, at the left of the table.

Once the correct future value factor is located, simply multiply the factor by the payment involved. According to Table 6A–3, the future value of an ordinary annuity consisting of $5,000 payments at 8% for six interest periods is $36,679.65, or $5,000(7.33593).

Present Value of an Ordinary Annuity

The present value of an ordinary annuity (PVA) is today's equivalent dollar amount of a series of payments (or receipts) made over a predetermined time frame. The assumption is that the payments are made at equal intervals (at the end of each interest period in the case of an ordinary annuity) and at a constant rate of interest. The present value of an ordinary annuity can be determined using a formula or an appropriate table (Table 6A–4). To find the present value of an ordinary annuity of $5,000 invested at 8% for six interest periods (PVA, 8%, 6) by formula, compute:

$$PVA = \frac{1 - \dfrac{1}{(1 + i)^n}}{i} \qquad \text{expressed as (PVA, } i, n)$$

$$PVA = \frac{1 - \dfrac{1}{(1 + .08)^6}}{.08}$$

$$PVA = \frac{1 - .63017}{.08}$$

$$PVA = 4.62287 \text{ or } 4.62$$

To find the present value of an ordinary annuity of 1 using a table, proceed in the same way as in determining the future value of an annuity, except now use Table 6A–4. First locate the proper interest rate column, then read down the column to the intersecting line representing the number of interest periods involved, at the left of the table.

Once the correct present value factor is located, multiply this factor by the payment involved. According to Table 6A–4 in Appendix 6, the present value of a series of $5,000 payments invested at 8% for six interest periods is $23,114.40, or $5,000(4.62288).

The present value of an annuity is also the sum of the present values of the individual payments. For example, the present value (PVA, 8%, 6), which was just calculated to be 4.62288, is the sum of the first six entries in the 8% column of Table 6A–2.

Future Value of an Annuity Due

The best way to understand an annuity due is to compare its cash flows with those of an ordinary annuity. Exhibit 6–4 shows two time lines that compare the future value of an ordinary annuity (FVA) of 1 with the future value of an annuity due (FVAD) of 1 for the same interest rate and annuity period.

The future value of the ordinary annuity illustrated in Exhibit 6–4 involves three payments but only two interest periods. The annuity due involves three payments and three interest periods. For each of the three values illustrated in the last column of Exhibit 6–4, FVA × (1 + i) = FVAD. This relationship means that if the FVA is

EXHIBIT 6–4

Future Value of an Ordinary Annuity of 1 Compared with the Future Value of an Annuity Due: (FVA, 10%, 3) versus (FVAD, 10%, 3)

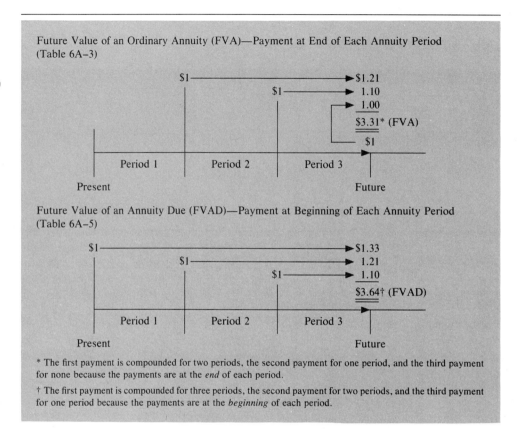

Future Value of an Ordinary Annuity (FVA)—Payment at End of Each Annuity Period (Table 6A–3)

Future Value of an Annuity Due (FVAD)—Payment at Beginning of Each Annuity Period (Table 6A–5)

* The first payment is compounded for two periods, the second payment for one period, and the third payment for none because the payments are at the *end* of each period.

† The first payment is compounded for three periods, the second payment for two periods, and the third payment for one period because the payments are at the *beginning* of each period.

known, it can be multiplied by $(1 + i)$ to determine the FVAD value for the same i and n.[9] For the example in Exhibit 6–4:

$$(FVAD, 10\%, 3) = 3.64 \quad \text{or} \quad (FVA, 10\%, 3)(1 + .10) = 3.31000(1.10) = 3.64$$

Present Value of an Annuity Due

Exhibit 6–5 shows two time lines that compare the present value of an ordinary annuity (PVA) with the present value of an annuity due (PVAD) of 1 for the same interest rate and number of payments.

The present value of the ordinary annuity illustrated in Exhibit 6–5 involves three payments and three discounting periods. The annuity due involves three payments but only two discounting periods. The annuity due is discounted for one fewer period than the ordinary annuity, so the ordinary annuity amount is less than the corresponding annuity due amount by a factor of $1/(1 + i)$; therefore, PVA $\times (1 + i) =$ PVAD. This relationship means that a known PVA value can be multiplied by $(1 + i)$ to yield its corresponding PVAD value.

ACCOUNTING APPLICATIONS OF AN ANNUITY

In most situations, the amount of the equal periodic payments ($X), the number of payments (n), and the constant interest rate per period (i) are known. To determine the future amount, the appropriate future value from Table 6A–3 or 6A–5 (both in Appendix 6) is multiplied by the amount of the periodic payment.

---

[9] Another procedure frequently used when the future value of an annuity due is needed but an annuity due table is not available is to find the future table value of an ordinary annuity for one more payment (i.e., $n + 1$) than the number of payments specified in the annuity problem, and then subtract 1.0 from that table value. The effect of this is to add one more period of compound interest while keeping the payments the same. This procedure frequently is expressed as ($n + 1$ payments) − 1.0. If the present value of an annuity due is needed, the relationships are essentially the opposite; thus, the procedure is ($n − 1$ payments) + 1.0. Calculators often are programmed to compute both ordinary annuity and annuity due values.

EXHIBIT 6-5

Present Value of an Ordinary Annuity of 1 Compared with the Present Value of an Annuity Due: (PVA, 10%, 3) versus (PVAD, 10%, 3)

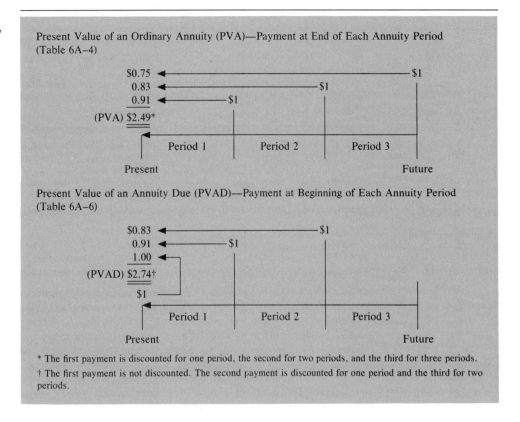

Future Value of an Annuity

A typical accounting application of the future value of an annuity is the establishment of a fund by equal annual contributions, perhaps for the future expansion of a facility or payment of a debt.

Case A On April 1, 1995, Delta Company decided to accumulate a fund (an asset) to pay a debt that matures on March 31, 1998. The company deposited $10,000 cash in a debt retirement fund on March 31, 1996, 1997, and 1998. The fund will earn 10% compound interest, which is added to the fund balance. The debt matures on the date of the last deposit, which is when the annuity terminates. Delta's fiscal year ends March 31.

1. This is an ordinary annuity because the payments are deposited at the end of each of the three annuity periods. The last payment is deposited on the last day that the annuity is in existence, March 31, 1998.

   The time line for this ordinary annuity is shown below:

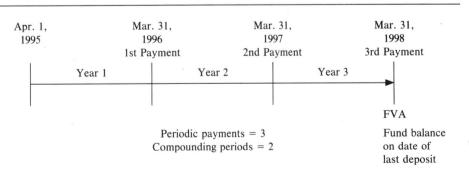

2. The amount in the fund at the end of the annuity's existence is found using Table 6A–3:

$$\$10,000(FVA, 10\%, 3) = \$10,000(3.31000) = \$33,100$$

3. The fund accumulation schedule is:

Case A: Fund Accumulation Schedule—Ordinary Annuity

Date	Cash Deposit	Interest Revenue	Fund Change	Fund Balance
March 31, 1996.	$10,000		+$10,000	$10,000
March 31, 1997.	10,000	$10,000(.10) = $1,000	+ 11,000	21,000
March 31, 1998.	10,000	21,000(.10) = 2,100	+ 12,100	33,100*
Totals	$30,000	$3,100	$33,100	

* Ordinary annuity balance, as of the date of the last deposit.

4. The journal entries required at each year-end, March 31, are:

	1996	1997	1998
Investment in debt retirement fund	10,000	11,000	12,100
Cash		10,000	10,000	10,000
Interest revenue.			1,000	2,100

5. The journal entry to record withdrawal of the fund balance on March 31, 1998, is:

Cash (or debt retired). 33,100
    Investment in debt retirement fund. 33,100

Determination of Other Values Related to the Future Value of an Annuity

In Case A, *three* values were given: the periodic payment (P), $10,000; the number of periodic payments (n), 3; and periodic interest rate (i), 10%. A fourth value, the future value of an ordinary annuity, was unknown; however, it was obtained from Table 6A–3 in Appendix 6 as follows:

$$\$10,000(FVA, 10\%, 3) = \$10,000(3.31000) = \$33,100$$

In some situations, either P, n, or i is unknown. If any three of the four variables are given, however, the fourth can be computed.

1. For example, to compute the periodic payment, P, given that the future value of an ordinary annuity = $33,100, $n = 3$, and $i = 10\%$ and using Table 6A–3:

$$P = \$33,100 \div (FVA, 10\%, 3) = \$33,100 \div 3.31000 = \$10,000$$

2. To compute the periodic interest rate (i) given a future value of an ordinary annuity of $33,100, a periodic payment of $10,000, and three periodic payments ($n = 3$):

$$\$33,100 \div \$10,000 = 3.31000$$

which is the value shown in Table 6A–3 for $n = 3$ periods. The row for $n = 3$ in Table 6A–3 indicates a periodic interest rate of 10%.

3. To compute the number of payments (n) given the future value of an ordinary annuity of $33,100, payment of $10,000, and $i = 10\%$:

$$\$33,100 \div \$10,000 = 3.31000$$

which is the Table 6A–3 value for $i = 10\%$. The column for $i = 10\%$ in Table 6A–3 indicates that the number of payments is 3.

Present Value of an Annuity

Tables of the present value of an annuity of 1 are used to calculate the present value of a series of future payments (n) at a specific compound discount rate (i). In most cases, the following variables are known: the amount of each equal payment, the number of payments, and the constant rate of interest per discounting period. To determine the present value in a specific situation, the appropriate present value factor from Table 6A–4 or Table 6A–6 is multiplied by the amount of the periodic payment.

A typical accounting application of the present value of an annuity is the determination of the equal annual payment required in a debt contract. Two cases will demonstrate the accounting for a debt contract. Case B is an ordinary annuity, and Case C is an annuity due.

Case B On April 1, 1995, Echo Company owed a $15,000 liability (a present value amount). The creditor agreed to allow Echo Company to pay the debt in three equal annual instalments at 10% compound interest. Thus, payments of $6,032 are payable March 31, 1996, 1997, and 1998. Each payment includes principal and interest. Echo's fiscal year ends March 31.

1. This is an ordinary annuity because the three payments are due at the end of each year during the three-year extended credit period. The first payment is to be made 12 months from the current date. The time line for this ordinary annuity is:

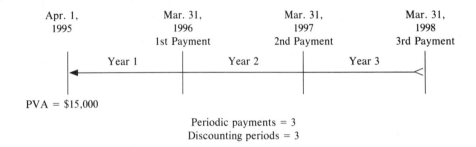

2. The present value of the three payments, obtained from Table 6A–4, is:

$$\$6,032(\text{PVA}, 10\%, 3) = \$6,032(2.48685) = \$15,000$$

3. The amount of each equal annual payment is computed to be:

$$\$15,000 \div (\text{PVA}, 10\%, 3) = \$15,000 \div 2.48685 = \$6,032$$

4. The debt payment schedule is:

Case B: Debt Payment Schedule—Ordinary Annuity

Date	Cash Payment	Interest Expense	Liability Change	Liability Balance
April 1, 1995				$15,000
March 31, 1996.	$ 6,032	$15,000(.10) = $1,500	−$ 4,532	10,468
March 31, 1997.	6,032	10,468(.10) = 1,047	− 4,985	5,483
March 31, 1998.	6,032	5,483(.10) = 549*	− 5,483	0
Totals	$18,096	$3,096	$15,000	

* Rounded to balance.

5. The entries required each March 31 are:

	1996	1997	1998
Interest expense.	1,500	1,047	549
Liability	4,532	4,985	5,483
Cash	6,032	6,032	6,032

Case C Assume the same facts as in Case B, except that three equal annual payments of $5,483 are to be made on each April 1 in 1995, 1996, and 1997.

1. This is an annuity due because the payments are due at the beginning of each year; the first payment is paid immediately and there is no interest included in it.

The time line for this annuity due is:

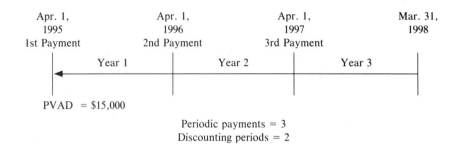

2. The present value of the three payments obtained from Table 6A–6 is:

$$\$5,483 \times (PVAD, 10\%, 3) = \$5,483(2.73554) = \$15,000$$

3. The amount of each equal annual payment is computed to be:

$$\$15,000 \div (PVAD, 10\%, 3) = \$15,000 \div 2.73554 = 5,483$$

4. The debt payment schedule is:

Case C: Debt Payment Schedule—Annuity Due

Date	Cash Payment	Interest Expense	Liability Change	Balance
April 1, 1995				$15,000
April 1, 1995	$ 5,483		−$ 5,483	9,517
March 31, 1996		$9,517(.10) = $ 952	+ 952	10,469
April 1, 1996	5,483		− 5,483	4,986
March 31, 1997		4,986(.10) = 497*	+ 497	5,483
April 1, 1997	5,483		− 5,483	0
Totals	$16,449	$1,449	$15,000	

* Rounded to balance.

5. The entries required on March 31 are:

	1995	1996	1997
Interest expense*		952	497
Liability	5,483	4,531	4,986
Cash		5,483	5,483	5,483

* The interest expense and cash payment are recognized and recorded on March 31 rather than April 1 here for convenience. Accruals would be made on March 31.

Determination of Other Values Related to the Present Value of an Annuity

Determining an implicit interest rate for the present value of an annuity due or an ordinary annuity involves the same procedure as illustrated previously for future values. For example, assume that an overdue debt of $83,398 is paid in five equal instalments of $20,000 each. The first payment is to be paid immediately; therefore, this calculation involves the present value of an annuity due. The implicit compound interest rate is determined as follows:

$$\$83,398 \div \$20,000 = 4.1699 = (PVAD, i, 5).$$

The row corresponding to $n = 5$ in Table 6A–6 indicates a periodic interest rate of 10%. To prove this:

$$\$20,000(PVAD, 10\%, 5) = \$20,000(4.16987) = \$83,398 \text{ (rounded)}$$

Using Multiple Present and Future Values

Some transactions require application of two or more future or present value amounts. These more complex problems require careful analysis. Two cases are given below to illustrate the application of multiple future and present values.

Case D: Deferred Annuity   A deferred annuity occurs in two phases: (1) capital is invested over a period to accumulate maximum interest compounding and principal growth, and (2) the principal is paid out in uniform amounts until the total accumulated principal is exhausted. Investment during the accumulation phase may be in the form of either periodic payments or a lump-sum payment at the beginning. During the second phase, while withdrawals are being distributed to the annuitant, the remaining principal continues to earn interest.

To illustrate, assume that on January 1, 1995, Fox Company invests in a $100,000 deferred annuity for the benefit of an employee, George Golf, who was injured while at work. The terms call for Fox Company to make an immediate $100,000 lump-sum payment, which will earn interest at 11% for four years (the capital accumulation phase of the annuity). Then, beginning on January 1, 1999, when George Golf retires, the total amount of the annuity will be paid to him in five equal annual instalment payments.

First, the fund grows at 11% for four years. At that time, the fund will equal:

$$\$100,000(FV1, 11\%, 4) = \$100,000(1.51807) = \$151,807$$

Second, the fund is used in total to pay Golf a five-year annuity beginning January 1, 1999. The fund is assumed to continue to earn 11% until the last payment is made. The fund will be used up by the payments, so:

$$\text{Payment} \times (PVAD, 11\%, 5) = \$151,807$$

$$\text{Payment} \times 4.10245 = \$151,807$$

$$\text{Payment} = \$151,807 \div 4.10245$$

The yearly payment to Golf is $37,004. The procedure can be diagrammed as follows and a fund schedule follows the diagram:

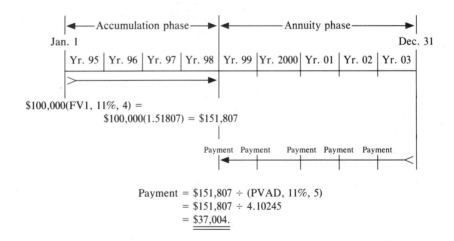

$$\text{Payment} = \$151,807 \div (PVAD, 11\%, 5)$$
$$= \$151,807 \div 4.10245$$
$$= \underline{\underline{\$37,004.}}$$

Fund Schedule

Date	Interest Revenue	Fund Change	Fund Balance
Accumulation			
January 1, 1995	Single deposit	+ $100,000	$100,000
December 31, 1995	$100,000(.11) = $11,000	+ 11,000	111,000
December 31, 1996	$111,000(.11) = 12,210	+ 12,210	123,210
December 31, 1997	$123,210(.11) = 13,553	+ 13,553	136,763
December 31, 1998	$136,763(.11) = 15,044	+ 15,044	151,807

Fund Schedule

Date	Interest Revenue	Fund Change	Fund Balance
Annuity			
December 31, 1998			$151,807
January 1, 1999	Payment	− $37,004	114,803
December 31, 1999	$114,803(.11) = 12,628	+ 12,628	127,431
January 1, 2000	Payment	− 37,004	90,427
December 31, 2000	$ 90,427(.11) = 9,947¹	+ 9,947	100,374
January 1, 2001	Payment	− 37,004	63,370
December 31, 2001	$ 63,370(.11) = 6,971	+ 6,971	70,341
January 1, 2002	Payment	− 37,004	33,337
December 31, 2002	$ 33,337(.11) = 3,667	+ 3,667	37,004
January 1, 2003	Payment	− 37,004	0

Case E: Annuity and Salvage   Explo Company is negotiating to purchase four acres of land containing a gravel deposit that is suitable for development. Explo Company has completed a survey that provides the following reliable estimates:

Expected net cash revenues over life of resource:

End of 1995	$ 5,000
End of 1996 to 1999 (per year)	30,000
End of 2000 to 2003 (per year)	40,000
End of 2004 (last year—resource exhausted)	10,000
Estimated sales value of four acres after exhaustion of gravel and net of land restoration costs (end of 2004)	2,000

What is the maximum amount Explo Company could offer on January 1, 1995, for the land, assuming that Explo requires a 12% after-tax return on the investment? We will assume that all amounts are measured at year-end and that the above amounts are net of income taxes. This case requires computation of the present value of the future expected cash inflows. The amount that the company would be willing to pay is the sum of the present values of the net future cash inflows for the various years. The calculation is complex because both single payments and annuities are involved. Because equal but different future cash inflows are expected for years 2 to 5 and years 6 to 9, two annuities must be calculated. Because the cash inflows are assumed to be received at year-end, the annuities are ordinary.

This case is best solved in several steps in which the cash flows are separated into single payments and annuities and each expressed in present value terms. Thus:

(1) $5,000(PV1, 12%, 1) = $5,000(.89286)   = $ 4,464

(2) $30,000(PVA, 12%, 4)(PV1, 12%, 1)
        = $30,000(3.03735)(.89286)   =   81,358

(3) $40,000(PVA, 12%, 4)(PV1, 12%, 5)
        = $40,000(3.03735)(.56743)   =   68,939

(4)   ($10,000 + $2,000)(PV1, 12%, 10) = $12,000(.32197) =   3,864
                                                          $158,625

Explo should offer no more than $158,625 for the properties. The cash flows are depicted graphically as follows:

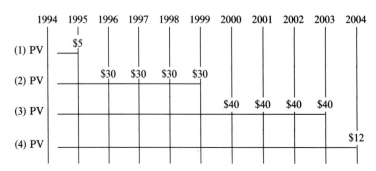

The present value of the annuity shown in equation (2) is first calculated as of December 31, 1995, as $30,000(PVA, 12%, 4). It is then discounted for one period using (PV1, 12%, 1). The present value of the annuity shown in equation (3) is first calculated as of December 31, 1999, as $40,000(PVA, 12%, 4) and is then discounted to December 31, 1994, using the value for (PV1, 12%, 5).

SUMMARY TABLE   Exhibit 6–6 provides a summary of interest concepts discussed in this chapter.

EXHIBIT 6–6   Summary of Interest Concepts

Title (Symbol)	Basic Concept Summarized	Formula	Table	Illustrative Table Values	
				$n = 5; i = 10\%$	$n = 6; i = 10\%$
Simple interest i	Interest on principal only, regardless of any prior accrued interest	$P \times i \times n$	—	—	—
FV of 1 (FV1, i, n)	FV of a single payment increased by compound interest i for n periods	$(1 + i)^n$	6A–1	1.61051 (always more than 1)	1.77156 (more by compound interest for one period)
PV of 1 (PV1, i, n)	PV of a single payment decreased by compound discount i for n periods	$\dfrac{1}{(1 + i)^n}$	6A–2	.62092 (always less than 1)	.56447 (less by the discount for one period)
FV of Annuity of 1: (a) Ordinary annuity (FVA, i, n)	FV of a series of n equal end-of-period payments at compound interest i	$\dfrac{(1 + i)^n - 1}{i}$	6A–3	6.10510 (always more than sum of payments)	7.71561 (more by one payment, plus compound interest for one period)
(b) Annuity due (FVAD, i, n)	FV of a series of n equal beginning-of-period payments at compound interest i	$\left[\dfrac{(1 + i)^n - 1}{i}\right] \times (1 + i)$	6A–5	6.71561, or (6.10510 × 1.10)	8.48717, or (7.71561 × 1.10)
PV of Annuity of 1: (a) Ordinary annuity (PVA, i, n)	PV of a series of n equal end-of-period payments in the future decreased at compound discount i.	$\dfrac{1 - \dfrac{1}{(1 + i)^n}}{i}$	6A–4	3.79079 (always less than sum of payments)	4.35526 (more by one payment, less discount for one period)
(b) Annuity due (PVAD, i, n)	PV of a series of n equal beginning-of-period payments in the future decreased at compound discount i.	$\left[\dfrac{1 - \dfrac{1}{(1 + i)^n}}{i}\right] \times (1 + i)$	6A–6	4.16987, or (3.79079 × 1.10)	4.79079, or (4.35526 × 1.10)

ON THE HORIZON

The AcSB is currently involved in a major project relating to the recognition, measurement, and disclosure of financial instruments, a broad range of financial statement elements that result in the transfer of cash between entities. This project is being carried out in conjunction with the IASC and seeks to establish general principles for financial instruments, some of which are quite exotic. The 1991 exposure draft and the 1994 reexposure draft call for the use of present value methods to establish the value attached to certain financial assets and liabilities,

primarily those that are to be settled with scheduled payments of fixed or determinable amounts (loans, and so on—par. 66). Such a valuation would take place yearly, and gains or losses caused by this regular remeasurement would be deferred until recognition.

When these provisions are in force, the use of present values in the financial statements will be expanded. The rules would likely have a significant effect on the financial statements of financial institutions and other entities with sizeable investments in loans and mortgages.

CONCEPT REVIEW

1. Calculate the following:
   a. The future value of an ordinary annuity of $1,000 for 10 years accumulated at an annual compound interest rate of 12% (FVA, 12%, 10).
   b. The present value of an ordinary annuity of $15,000 for five years assuming an annual compound interest rate of 9%.
   c. Repeat (a) and (b) for an annuity due.
2. A company deposits $1,000 semiannually in the retirement annuity for an employee. How much will the retirement annuity amount to in 10 years at an annual compound interest rate of 4%? Payments are made at the start of the period.
3. A bond agreement promises to pay interest of $10,000 per year for 10 years and to return the principal amount of $100,000 at the end of the 10-year period. Payments are made at the end of the year.
   a. What is the implicit market interest rate in this contract?
   b. What is the present value of this contract?
   c. If the bond did not offer annual interest payments but the market interest rate did not change from part (a), what is the present value of the obligation?

SUMMARY OF KEY POINTS

(L.O. 1)	1. Interest is the cost of using money over time. Interest is an acknowledgment that there is a time value to money, meaning that a dollar in hand today is worth more than a dollar to be collected one year from now.
(L.O. 2)	2. Simple interest is computed on the principal each period. Compound interest is computed on the principal amount and on all prior interest accrued and not paid.
(L.O. 3)	3. The future value (FV) of a current amount is the amount that will have accumulated by a specified date, given a specific interest rate. The present value (PV) of a future amount is the amount today that, with interest at a specific rate, will accumulate to a given sum at a specified future date.
(L.O. 3)	4. An annuity is a stream of constant and regular periodic cash payments over a specified period of time.
(L.O. 4)	5. Ordinary annuities are annuities in which regular payments occur at the end of the period. An annuity due is an annuity for which payments occur at the beginning of the period.
(L.O. 5)	6. The selection of the appropriate interest rate for present or future value calculations is not an easy task. The rate selected can have a significant effect on present and future value calculations if the time period is long. In general, the prevailing market rate for transactions of similar risk should be used.

(L.O. 5) 7. The tables in Appendix 6 (Tables 6A–1 to 6A–6) can be used to solve PV and FV calculations. When tables are not available, or if more precise results are required, a calculator or spreadsheet programmed to solve present and future values may be used.

(L.O. 6) 8. Complex interest problems can be solved by breaking them into components and calculating the answer to each component separately.

REVIEW PROBLEM

Air Canada is negotiating to acquire four new Airbus planes. Three alternatives are available:

1. Purchase the aircraft for $35 million each, payment due immediately.
2. Purchase the aircraft by paying $20 million immediately and $20 million at the beginning of each year for 11 more years.
3. Lease the aircraft for $21.5 million payable at the end of each year for 12 years.

The relevant market rate of interest (the discount rate) for ventures of this type is 10%. Assuming that Air Canada has sufficient resources, which alternative is least expensive? Ignore tax considerations.

SOLUTION

The value of each alternative is:

1. $35 million × 4 planes = $140 million.
2. $20(PVAD, 10%, 12) = $20(7.49506) = $149.9 million.
3. $21.5(PVA, 10%, 12) = $21.5(6.81369) = $146.5 million.

The least expensive option is to buy the aircraft for cash, alternative 1. If the discount rate is made sufficiently large, alternative 1 would no longer be the least expensive choice. A higher discount rate would reflect a lower burden to Air Canada for the future yearly $20 million payments. With a 20% discount rate, the burden of the 12 payments of $20 million is $20(PVAD, 20%, 12); $20(5.32706) = $106.5 million.

TABLE 6A–1   Future Value of 1: $FV1 = (1 + i)^n$, also expressed as (FV1, i, n)

This table shows the compound amount (future value) of 1 at various interest rates and for various time periods. It is used to compute the future value of single payments.

Number of Periods n	2%	2½%	3%	4%	5%	6%	7%	8%	9%	10%
1	1.02000	1.02500	1.03000	1.04000	1.05000	1.06000	1.07000	1.08000	1.09000	1.10000
2	1.04040	1.05063	1.06090	1.08160	1.10250	1.12360	1.14490	1.16640	1.18810	1.21000
3	1.06121	1.07689	1.09273	1.12486	1.15763	1.19102	1.22504	1.25971	1.29503	1.33100
4	1.08243	1.10381	1.12551	1.16986	1.21551	1.26248	1.31080	1.36049	1.41158	1.46410
5	1.10408	1.13141	1.15927	1.21665	1.27628	1.33823	1.40255	1.46933	1.53862	1.61051
6	1.12616	1.15969	1.19405	1.26532	1.34010	1.41852	1.50073	1.58687	1.67710	1.77156
7	1.14869	1.18869	1.22987	1.31593	1.40710	1.50363	1.60578	1.71382	1.82804	1.94872
8	1.17166	1.21840	1.26677	1.36857	1.47746	1.59385	1.71819	1.85093	1.99256	2.14359
9	1.19509	1.24886	1.30477	1.42331	1.55133	1.68948	1.83846	1.99900	2.17189	2.35795
10	1.21899	1.28008	1.34392	1.48024	1.62889	1.79085	1.96715	2.15892	2.36736	2.59374
11	1.24337	1.31209	1.38423	1.53945	1.71034	1.89830	2.10485	2.33164	2.58043	2.85312
12	1.26824	1.34489	1.42576	1.60103	1.79586	2.01220	2.25219	2.51817	2.81266	3.13843
13	1.29361	1.37851	1.46853	1.66507	1.88565	2.13293	2.40985	2.71962	3.06580	3.45227
14	1.31948	1.41297	1.51259	1.73168	1.97993	2.26090	2.57853	2.93719	3.34173	3.79750
15	1.34587	1.44830	1.55797	1.80094	2.07893	2.39656	2.75903	3.17217	3.64248	4.17725
16	1.37279	1.48451	1.60471	1.87298	2.18287	2.54035	2.95216	3.42594	3.97031	4.59497
17	1.40024	1.52162	1.65285	1.94790	2.29202	2.69277	3.15882	3.70002	4.32763	5.05447
18	1.42825	1.55966	1.70243	2.02582	2.40662	2.85434	3.37993	3.99602	4.71712	5.55992
19	1.45681	1.59865	1.75351	2.10685	2.52695	3.02560	3.61653	4.31570	5.14166	6.11591
20	1.48595	1.63862	1.80611	2.19112	2.65330	3.20714	3.86968	4.66096	5.60441	6.72750
21	1.51567	1.67958	1.86029	2.27877	2.78596	3.39956	4.14056	5.03383	6.10881	7.40025
22	1.54598	1.72157	1.91610	2.36992	2.92526	3.60354	4.43040	5.43654	6.65860	8.14027
23	1.57690	1.76461	1.97359	2.48472	3.07152	3.81975	4.74053	5.87146	7.25787	8.95430
24	1.60844	1.80873	2.03279	2.56330	3.22510	4.04893	5.07237	6.34118	7.91108	9.84973
25	1.64061	1.85394	2.09378	2.66584	3.38635	4.29187	5.42743	6.84848	8.62308	10.83471

	11%	12%	14%	15%	16%	18%	20%	22%	24%	25%
1	1.11000	1.12000	1.14000	1.15000	1.16000	1.18000	1.20000	1.22000	1.24000	1.25000
2	1.23210	1.25440	1.29960	1.32250	1.34560	1.39240	1.44000	1.48840	1.53760	1.56250
3	1.36763	1.40493	1.48154	1.52088	1.56090	1.64303	1.72800	1.81585	1.90662	1.95313
4	1.51807	1.57352	1.68896	1.74901	1.81064	1.93878	2.07360	2.21533	2.36421	2.44141
5	1.68506	1.76234	1.92541	2.01136	2.10034	2.28776	2.48832	2.70271	2.93163	3.05176
6	1.87041	1.97382	2.19497	2.31306	2.43640	2.69955	2.98598	3.29730	3.63522	3.81470
7	2.07616	2.21068	2.50227	2.66002	2.82622	3.18547	3.58318	4.02271	4.50767	4.76837
8	2.30454	2.47596	2.85259	3.05902	3.27841	3.75886	4.29982	4.90771	5.58951	5.96046
9	2.55804	2.77308	3.25195	3.51788	3.80296	4.43545	5.15978	5.98740	6.93099	7.45058
10	2.83942	3.10585	3.70722	4.04556	4.41144	5.23384	6.19174	7.30463	8.59443	9.31323
11	3.15176	3.47855	4.22623	4.65239	5.11726	6.17593	7.43008	8.91165	10.65709	11.64153
12	3.49845	3.89598	4.81790	5.35025	5.93603	7.28759	8.91610	10.87221	13.21479	14.55192
13	3.88328	4.36349	5.49241	6.15279	6.88579	8.59936	10.69932	13.26410	16.38634	18.18989
14	4.31044	4.88711	6.26135	7.07571	7.98752	10.14724	12.83918	16.18220	20.31906	22.73737
15	4.78459	5.47357	7.13794	8.13706	9.26552	11.97375	15.40702	19.74229	25.19563	28.42171
16	5.31089	6.13039	8.13725	9.35762	10.74800	14.12902	18.48843	24.08559	31.24259	35.52714
17	5.89509	6.86604	9.27646	10.76126	12.46768	16.67225	22.18611	29.38442	38.74081	44.40892
18	6.54355	7.68997	10.57517	12.37545	14.46251	19.67325	26.62333	35.84899	48.03860	55.51115
19	7.26334	8.61276	12.05569	14.23177	16.77652	23.21444	31.94800	43.73577	59.56786	69.38894
20	8.06231	9.64629	13.74349	16.36654	19.46076	27.39303	38.33760	53.35764	73.86415	86.73617
21	8.94917	10.80385	15.66758	18.82152	22.57448	32.32378	46.00512	65.09632	91.59155	108.42022
22	9.93357	12.10031	17.86104	21.64475	26.18640	38.14206	55.20614	79.41751	113.57352	135.52527
23	11.02627	13.55235	20.36158	24.89146	30.37622	45.00763	66.24737	96.88936	140.83116	169.40659
24	12.23916	15.17863	23.21221	28.62518	35.23642	53.10901	79.49685	118.20502	174.63064	211.75824
25	13.58546	17.00006	26.46192	32.91895	40.87424	62.66863	95.39622	144.21013	216.54199	264.69780

TABLE 6A–2 Present Value of 1: $PV1 = 1 \div (1 + i)^n$, also expressed as $(PV1, i, n)$

This table shows the present value of 1 discounted at various rates of interest and for various time periods. It is used to compute the present value of single payments.

Number of Periods n	2%	2½%	3%	4%	5%	6%	7%	8%	9%	10%
1	.98039	.97561	.97087	.96154	.95238	.94340	.93458	.92593	.91743	.90909
2	.96117	.95181	.94260	.92456	.90703	.89000	.87344	.85734	.84168	.82645
3	.94232	.92860	.91514	.88900	.86384	.83962	.81630	.79383	.77218	.75131
4	.92385	.90595	.88849	.85480	.82270	.79209	.76290	.73503	.70843	.68301
5	.90573	.88385	.86261	.82193	.78353	.74726	.71299	.68058	.64993	.62092
6	.88797	.86230	.83748	.79031	.74622	.70496	.66634	.63017	.59627	.56447
7	.87056	.84127	.81309	.75992	.71068	.66506	.62275	.58349	.54703	.51316
8	.85349	.82075	.78941	.73069	.67684	.62741	.58201	.54027	.50187	.46651
9	.83676	.80073	.76642	.70259	.64461	.59190	.54393	.50025	.46043	.42410
10	.82035	.78120	.74409	.67556	.61391	.55839	.50835	.46319	.42241	.38554
11	.80426	.76214	.72242	.64958	.58468	.52679	.47509	.42888	.38753	.35049
12	.78849	.74356	.70138	.62460	.55684	.49697	.44401	.39711	.35553	.31863
13	.77303	.72542	.68095	.60057	.53032	.46884	.41496	.36770	.32618	.28966
14	.75788	.70773	.66112	.57748	.50507	.44230	.38782	.34046	.29925	.26333
15	.74301	.69047	.64186	.55526	.48102	.41727	.36245	.31524	.27454	.23939
16	.72845	.67362	.62317	.53391	.45811	.39365	.33873	.29189	.25187	.21763
17	.71416	.65720	.60502	.51337	.43630	.37136	.31657	.27027	.23107	.19784
18	.70016	.64117	.58739	.49363	.41552	.35034	.29586	.25025	.21199	.17986
19	.68643	.62553	.57029	.47464	.39573	.33051	.27651	.23171	.19449	.16351
20	.67297	.61027	.55368	.45639	.37689	.31180	.25842	.21455	.17843	.14684
21	.65978	.59539	.53755	.43883	.35894	.29416	.24151	.19866	.16370	.13513
22	.64684	.58086	.52189	.42196	.34185	.27751	.22571	.18394	.15018	.12285
23	.63416	.56670	.50669	.40573	.32557	.26180	.21095	.17032	.13778	.11168
24	.62172	.55288	.49193	.39012	.31007	.24698	.19715	.15770	.12640	.10153
25	.60953	.53939	.47761	.37512	.29530	.23300	.18425	.14602	.11597	.09230

	11%	12%	14%	15%	16%	18%	20%	22%	24%	25%
1	.90090	.89286	.87719	.86957	.86207	.84746	.83333	.81967	.80645	.80000
2	.81162	.79719	.76947	.75614	.74316	.71818	.69444	.67186	.65036	.64000
3	.73119	.71178	.67497	.65752	.64066	.60863	.57870	.55071	.52449	.51200
4	.65873	.63552	.59208	.57175	.55229	.51579	.48225	.45140	.42297	.40960
5	.59345	.56743	.51937	.49718	.47611	.43711	.40188	.37000	.34111	.32768
6	.53464	.50663	.45559	.43233	.41044	.37043	.33490	.30328	.27509	.26214
7	.48166	.45235	.39964	.37594	.35383	.31393	.27908	.24859	.22184	.20972
8	.43393	.40388	.35056	.32690	.30503	.26604	.23257	.20376	.17891	.16777
9	.39092	.36061	.30751	.28426	.26295	.22546	.19381	.16702	.14428	.13422
10	.35218	.32197	.26974	.24718	.22668	.19106	.16151	.13690	.11635	.10737
11	.31728	.28748	.23662	.21494	.19542	.16192	.13459	.11221	.09383	.08590
12	.28584	.25668	.20756	.18691	.16846	.13722	.11216	.09198	.07567	.06872
13	.25751	.22917	.18207	.16253	.14523	.11629	.09346	.07539	.06103	.05498
14	.23199	.20462	.15971	.14133	.12520	.09855	.07789	.06180	.04921	.04398
15	.20900	.18270	.14010	.12289	.10793	.08352	.06491	.05065	.03969	.03518
16	.18829	.16312	.12289	.10686	.09304	.07078	.05409	.04152	.03201	.02815
17	.16963	.14564	.10780	.09293	.08021	.05998	.04507	.03403	.02581	.02252
18	.15282	.13004	.09456	.08081	.06914	.05083	.03756	.02789	.02082	.01801
19	.13768	.11611	.08295	.07027	.05961	.04308	.03130	.02286	.01679	.01441
20	.12403	.10367	.07276	.06110	.05139	.03651	.02608	.01874	.01354	.01153
21	.11174	.09256	.06383	.05313	.04430	.03094	.02174	.01536	.01092	.00922
22	.10067	.08264	.05599	.04620	.03819	.02622	.01811	.01259	.00880	.00738
23	.09069	.07379	.04911	.04017	.03292	.02222	.01509	.01032	.00710	.00590
24	.08170	.06588	.04308	.03493	.02838	.01883	.01258	.00846	.00573	.00472
25	.07361	.05882	.03779	.03038	.02447	.01596	.01048	.00693	.00462	.00378

TABLE 6A–3　Future Value of an Ordinary Annuity of n Payments of 1 Each: $FVA = [1 + i)^n - 1] \div i$, also expressed as (FVA, i, n)

This table shows the future value of an ordinary annuity of 1 at various rates of interest and for various time periods. It is used to compute the future value of a series of payments made at the end of each interest compounding period.

Number of Periods n	2%	2½%	3%	4%	5%	6%	7%	8%	9%	10%
1	1.00000	1.00000	1.00000	1.00000	1.00000	1.00000	1.00000	1.00000	1.00000	1.00000
2	2.02000	2.02500	2.03000	2.04000	2.05000	2.06000	2.07000	2.08000	2.09000	2.10000
3	3.06040	3.07563	3.09090	3.12160	3.15250	3.18360	3.21490	3.24640	3.27810	3.31000
4	4.12161	4.15252	4.18363	4.24646	4.31013	4.37462	4.43994	4.50611	4.57313	4.64100
5	5.20404	5.25633	5.30914	5.41632	5.52563	5.63709	5.75074	5.86660	5.98471	6.10510
6	6.30812	6.38774	6.46841	6.63298	6.80191	6.97532	7.15329	7.33593	7.52333	7.71561
7	7.43428	7.54753	7.66246	7.89829	8.14201	8.39384	8.65402	8.92280	9.20043	9.48717
8	8.58297	8.73612	8.89234	9.21423	9.54911	9.89747	10.25980	10.63663	11.02847	11.43589
9	9.75463	9.95452	10.15911	10.58280	11.02656	11.49132	11.97799	12.48756	13.02104	13.57948
10	10.94972	11.20338	11.46388	12.00611	12.57789	13.18079	13.81645	14.48656	15.19293	15.93742
11	12.16872	12.48347	12.80780	13.48635	14.20679	14.97164	15.78360	16.64549	17.56029	18.53117
12	13.41209	13.79555	14.19203	15.02581	15.91713	16.86994	17.88845	18.97713	20.14072	21.38428
13	14.68033	15.14044	15.61779	16.62684	17.71298	18.88214	20.14064	21.49530	22.95338	24.52271
14	15.97394	16.51895	17.08632	18.29191	19.59863	21.01507	22.55049	24.21492	26.01919	27.97498
15	17.29342	17.93193	18.59891	20.02359	21.57856	23.27597	25.12902	27.15211	29.36092	31.77248
16	18.63929	19.38022	20.15688	21.82453	23.65749	25.67253	27.88805	30.32428	33.00340	35.94973
17	20.01207	20.86473	21.76159	23.69751	25.84037	28.21288	30.84022	33.75023	36.97370	40.54470
18	21.41231	22.38635	23.41444	25.64541	28.13238	30.90565	33.99903	37.45024	41.30134	45.59917
19	22.84056	23.94601	25.11687	27.67123	30.53900	33.75999	37.37896	41.44626	46.01846	51.15909
20	24.29737	25.54466	26.87037	29.77808	33.06595	36.78559	40.99549	45.76196	51.16012	57.27500
21	25.78332	27.18327	28.67649	31.96920	35.71925	39.99273	44.86518	50.42292	56.76453	64.00250
22	27.29898	28.86286	30.53678	34.24797	38.50521	43.39229	49.00574	55.45676	62.87334	71.40275
23	28.84496	30.58443	32.45288	36.61789	41.43048	46.99583	53.43614	60.89330	69.53194	79.54302
24	30.42186	32.34904	34.42647	39.08260	44.50200	50.81558	58.17667	66.76476	76.78981	88.49733
25	32.03030	34.15776	36.45926	41.64591	47.72710	54.86451	63.24904	73.10594	84.70090	98.34706

n	11%	12%	14%	15%	16%	18%	20%	22%	24%	25%
1	1.00000	1.00000	1.00000	1.00000	1.00000	1.00000	1.00000	1.00000	1.00000	1.00000
2	2.11000	2.12000	2.14000	2.15000	2.16000	2.18000	2.20000	2.22000	2.24000	2.25000
3	3.34210	3.37440	3.43960	3.47250	3.50560	3.57240	3.64000	3.70840	3.77760	3.81250
4	4.70973	4.77933	4.92114	4.99338	5.06650	5.21543	5.36800	5.52425	5.68422	5.76563
5	6.22780	6.35285	6.61010	6.74238	6.87714	7.15421	7.44160	7.73958	8.04844	8.20703
6	7.91286	8.11519	8.53552	8.75374	8.97748	9.44197	9.92992	10.44229	10.98006	11.25879
7	9.78327	10.08901	10.73049	11.06680	11.41387	12.14152	12.91590	13.73959	14.61528	15.07349
8	11.85943	12.29969	13.23276	13.72682	14.24009	15.32700	16.49908	17.76231	19.12294	19.84186
9	14.16397	14.77566	16.08535	16.78584	17.51851	19.08585	20.79890	22.67001	24.71245	25.80232
10	16.72201	17.54874	19.33730	20.30372	21.32147	23.52131	25.95868	28.65742	31.64344	33.25290
11	19.56143	20.65458	23.04452	24.34928	25.73290	28.75514	32.15042	35.96205	40.23787	42.56613
12	22.71319	24.13313	27.27075	29.00167	30.85017	34.93107	39.58050	44.87370	50.89495	54.20760
13	26.21164	28.02911	32.08865	34.35192	36.78620	42.21866	48.49660	55.74591	64.10974	68.75958
14	30.09492	32.39360	37.58107	40.50471	43.67199	50.81802	59.19592	69.01001	80.49608	86.94947
15	34.40536	37.27971	43.84241	47.58041	51.65951	60.96527	72.03511	85.19221	100.81514	109.68684
16	39.18995	42.75328	50.98035	55.71747	60.92503	72.93901	87.44213	104.93450	126.01077	138.10855
17	44.50084	48.88367	59.11760	65.07509	71.67303	87.06804	105.93056	129.02009	157.25336	173.63568
18	50.39594	55.74971	68.39407	75.83636	84.14072	103.74028	128.11667	158.40451	195.99416	218.04460
19	56.93949	63.43968	78.96923	88.21181	98.60323	123.41353	154.74000	194.25350	244.03276	273.55576
20	64.20283	72.05244	91.02493	102.44358	115.37975	146.62797	186.68800	237.98927	303.60062	342.94470
21	72.26514	81.69874	104.76842	118.81012	134.84051	174.02100	225.02560	291.34691	377.46477	429.68087
22	81.21431	92.50258	120.43600	137.63164	157.41499	206.34479	271.03072	356.44323	469.05632	538.10109
23	91.14788	104.60289	138.29704	159.27638	183.60138	244.48685	326.23686	435.86075	582.62984	673.62636
24	102.17415	118.15524	158.65862	184.16784	213.97761	289.49448	392.48424	532.75011	723.46100	843.03295
25	114.41331	133.33387	181.87083	212.79302	249.21402	342.60349	471.98108	650.95513	898.09164	1054.79118

TABLE 6A–4   Present Value of an Ordinary Annuity of n Payments of 1 Each: $PVA = [1 - (1 \div (1 + i)^n)] \div i$, also expressed as (PVA, i, n)

This table shows the present value of an ordinary annuity of 1 at various interest rates and for various time periods. It is used to compute the present value of a series of payments made at the end of each interest compounding period.

Number of Periods n	2%	2½%	3%	4%	5%	6%	7%	8%	9%	10%
1	.98039	.97561	.97087	.96154	.95238	.94340	.93458	.92593	.91743	.90909
2	1.94156	1.92742	1.91347	1.88609	1.85941	1.83339	1.80802	1.78326	1.75911	1.73554
3	2.88388	2.85602	2.82861	2.77509	2.72325	2.67301	2.62432	2.57710	2.53129	2.48685
4	3.80773	3.76197	3.71710	3.62990	3.54595	3.46511	3.38721	3.31213	3.23972	3.16987
5	4.71346	4.64583	4.57971	4.45182	4.32948	4.21236	4.10020	3.99271	3.88965	3.79079
6	5.60143	5.50813	5.41719	5.24214	5.07569	4.91732	4.76654	4.62288	4.48592	4.35526
7	6.47199	6.34939	6.23028	6.00205	5.78637	5.58238	5.38929	5.20637	5.03295	4.86842
8	7.32548	7.17014	7.01969	6.73274	6.46321	6.20979	5.97130	5.74664	5.53482	5.33493
9	8.16224	7.97087	7.78611	7.43533	7.10782	6.80169	6.51523	6.24689	5.99525	5.75902
10	8.98259	8.75206	8.53020	8.11090	7.72173	7.36009	7.02358	6.71008	6.41766	6.14457
11	9.78685	9.51421	9.25262	8.76048	8.30641	7.88687	7.49867	7.13896	6.80519	6.49506
12	10.57534	10.25776	9.95400	9.38507	8.86325	8.38384	7.94269	7.53608	7.16073	6.81369
13	11.34837	10.98318	10.63496	9.98565	9.39357	8.85268	8.35765	7.90378	7.48690	7.10336
14	12.10625	11.69091	11.29607	10.56312	9.89864	9.29498	8.74547	8.24424	7.78615	7.36669
15	12.84926	12.38138	11.93794	11.11839	10.37966	9.71225	9.10791	8.55948	8.06069	7.60608
16	13.57771	13.05500	12.56110	11.65230	10.83777	10.10590	9.44665	8.85137	8.31256	7.82371
17	14.29187	13.71220	13.16612	12.16567	11.27407	10.47726	9.76322	9.12164	8.54363	8.02155
18	14.99203	14.35336	13.75351	12.65930	11.68959	10.82760	10.05909	9.37189	8.75563	8.20141
19	15.67846	14.97889	14.32380	13.13394	12.08532	11.15812	10.33560	9.60360	8.95011	8.36492
20	16.35143	15.58916	14.87747	13.59033	12.46221	11.46992	10.59401	9.81815	9.12855	8.51356
21	17.01121	16.18455	15.41502	14.02916	12.82115	11.76408	10.83553	10.01680	9.29224	8.64869
22	17.65805	16.76541	15.93692	14.45112	13.16300	12.04158	11.06124	10.20074	9.44243	8.77154
23	18.29220	17.33211	16.44361	14.85684	13.48857	12.30338	11.27219	10.37106	9.58021	8.88322
24	18.91393	17.88499	16.93554	15.24696	13.79864	12.55036	11.46933	10.52876	9.70661	8.98474
25	19.52346	18.42438	17.41315	15.62208	14.09394	12.78336	11.65358	10.67478	9.82258	9.07704

	11%	12%	14%	15%	16%	18%	20%	22%	24%	25%
1	.90090	.89286	.87719	.86957	.86207	.84746	.83333	.81967	.80645	.80000
2	1.71252	1.69005	1.64666	1.62571	1.60523	1.56564	1.52778	1.49153	1.45682	1.44000
3	2.44371	2.40183	2.32163	2.28323	2.24589	2.17427	2.10648	2.04224	1.98130	1.95200
4	3.10245	3.03735	2.91371	2.85498	2.79818	2.69006	2.58873	2.49364	2.40428	2.36160
5	3.69590	3.60478	3.43308	3.35216	3.27429	3.12717	2.99061	2.86364	2.74538	2.68928
6	4.23054	4.11141	3.88867	3.78448	3.68474	3.49760	3.32551	3.16692	3.02047	2.95142
7	4.71220	4.56376	4.28830	4.16042	4.03857	3.81153	3.60459	3.41551	3.24232	3.16114
8	5.14612	4.96764	4.63886	4.48732	4.34359	4.07757	3.83716	3.61927	3.42122	3.32891
9	5.53705	5.32825	4.94637	4.77158	4.60654	4.30302	4.03097	3.78628	3.56550	3.46313
10	5.88923	5.65022	5.21612	5.01877	4.83323	4.49409	4.19247	3.92318	3.66186	3.57050
11	6.20652	5.93770	5.45273	5.23371	5.02864	4.65601	4.32706	4.03540	3.77569	3.65640
12	6.49236	6.19437	5.66029	5.42062	5.19711	4.79322	4.43922	4.12737	3.85136	3.72512
13	6.74987	6.42355	5.84236	5.58315	5.34233	4.90951	4.53268	4.20277	3.91239	3.78010
14	6.98187	6.62817	6.00207	5.72448	5.46753	5.00806	4.61057	4.26456	3.96160	3.82408
15	7.19087	6.81086	6.14217	5.84737	5.57546	5.09158	4.67547	4.31522	4.00129	3.85926
16	7.37916	6.97399	6.26506	5.95423	5.66850	5.16235	4.72956	4.35673	4.03330	3.88741
17	7.54879	7.11963	6.37286	6.04716	5.74870	5.22233	4.77463	4.39077	4.05911	3.90993
18	7.70162	7.24967	6.46742	6.12797	5.81785	5.27316	4.81219	4.41866	4.07993	3.92794
19	7.83929	7.36578	6.55037	6.19823	5.87746	5.31624	4.84350	4.44152	4.09672	3.94235
20	7.96333	7.46944	6.62313	6.25933	5.92884	5.35275	4.86958	4.46027	4.11026	3.95388
21	8.07507	7.56200	6.68696	6.31246	5.97314	5.38368	4.89132	4.47563	4.12117	3.96311
22	8.17574	7.64465	6.74295	6.35866	6.01133	5.40990	4.90943	4.48822	4.12998	3.97049
23	8.26643	7.71843	6.79206	6.39884	6.04425	5.43212	4.92453	4.49854	4.13708	3.97639
24	8.34814	7.78432	6.83514	6.43377	6.07263	5.45095	4.93710	4.50700	4.14281	3.98111
25	8.42174	7.84314	6.87293	6.46415	6.09709	5.46691	4.94759	4.51393	4.14742	3.98489

TABLE 6A–5 Future Value of an Annuity Due of n Payments of 1 Each: FVAD $= [((1 + i)^n - 1) \div i] \times (1 + i)$, also expressed as (FVAD, i, n) = $(1 + i)$ (FVA, i, n)

This table shows the future value of an annuity due of 1 at various rates of interest and for various time periods. It is used to compute the future value of a series of payments made at the beginning of each interest compounding period.

Number of Periods n	2%	2½%	3%	4%	5%	6%	7%	8%	9%	10%
1	1.02000	1.02500	1.03000	1.04000	1.05000	1.06000	1.07000	1.08000	1.09000	1.10000
2	2.06040	2.07563	2.09090	2.12160	2.15250	2.18360	2.21490	2.24640	2.27810	2.31000
3	3.12161	3.15252	3.18363	3.24646	3.31013	3.37462	3.43994	3.50611	3.57313	3.64100
4	4.20404	4.25633	4.30914	4.41632	4.52563	4.63709	4.75074	4.86660	4.98471	5.10510
5	5.30812	5.38774	5.46841	5.63298	5.80191	5.97532	6.15329	6.33593	6.52333	6.71561
6	6.43428	6.54743	6.66246	6.89827	7.14201	7.39384	7.65402	7.92280	8.20043	8.48717
7	7.58297	7.73612	7.89234	8.21423	8.54911	8.89747	9.25980	9.63663	10.02847	10.43589
8	8.75463	8.95452	9.15911	9.58280	10.02656	10.49132	10.97799	11.48756	12.02104	12.57948
9	9.94972	10.20338	10.46388	11.00611	11.57789	12.18079	12.81645	13.48656	14.19293	14.93742
10	11.16872	11.48347	11.80780	12.48635	13.20679	13.97164	14.78360	15.64549	16.56029	17.53117
11	12.41209	12.79555	13.19203	14.02581	14.91713	15.86994	16.88845	17.97713	19.14072	20.38428
12	13.68033	14.14044	14.61779	15.62684	16.71298	17.88214	19.14064	20.49530	21.95338	23.52271
13	14.97394	15.51895	16.08632	17.29191	18.59863	20.01507	21.55049	23.21492	25.01919	26.97498
14	16.29342	16.93193	17.59891	19.02359	20.57856	22.27597	24.12902	26.15211	28.36092	30.77248
15	17.63929	18.38022	19.15688	20.82453	22.65749	24.67253	26.88805	29.32428	32.00340	34.94973
16	19.01207	19.86473	20.76159	22.69751	24.84037	27.21288	29.84022	32.75023	35.97370	39.54470
17	20.41231	21.38635	22.41444	24.64541	27.13238	29.90565	32.99903	36.45024	40.30134	44.59917
18	21.84056	22.94601	24.11687	26.67123	29.53900	32.75999	36.37896	40.44626	45.01846	50.15909
19	23.29737	24.54466	25.87037	28.77808	32.06595	35.78559	39.99549	44.76196	50.16012	56.27500
20	24.78332	26.18327	27.67649	30.96920	34.71925	38.99273	43.86518	49.42292	55.76453	63.00250
21	26.29898	27.86286	29.53678	33.24797	37.50521	42.39229	48.00574	54.45676	61.87334	70.40275
22	27.84496	29.58443	31.45288	35.61789	40.43048	45.99583	52.43614	59.89330	68.53194	78.54302
23	29.42186	31.34904	33.42647	38.08260	43.50200	49.81558	57.17667	65.76476	75.78981	87.49733
24	31.03030	33.15776	35.45926	40.64591	46.72710	53.86451	62.24904	72.10594	83.70090	97.34706
25	32.67091	35.01171	37.55304	43.31175	50.11345	58.15638	67.67647	78.95442	92.32398	108.18177

	11%	12%	14%	15%	16%	18%	20%	22%	24%	25%
1	1.11000	1.12000	1.14000	1.15000	1.16000	1.18000	1.20000	1.22000	1.24000	1.25000
2	2.34210	2.37440	2.43960	2.47250	2.50560	2.57240	2.64000	2.70840	2.77760	2.81250
3	3.70973	3.77933	3.92114	3.99338	4.06650	4.21543	4.36800	4.52425	4.68422	4.76563
4	5.22780	5.35285	5.61010	5.74238	5.87714	6.15241	6.44160	6.73958	7.04844	7.20703
5	6.91286	7.11519	7.53552	7.75374	7.97748	8.44197	8.92992	9.44229	9.98006	10.25879
6	8.78327	9.08901	9.73049	10.06680	10.41387	11.14152	11.91590	12.73959	13.61528	14.07349
7	10.85943	11.29969	12.23276	12.72682	13.24009	14.32700	15.49908	12.76231	18.12294	18.84186
8	13.16397	13.77566	15.08535	15.78584	16.51851	18.08585	19.79890	21.67001	23.71245	24.80232
9	15.72201	16.54874	18.33730	19.30372	20.32147	22.52131	24.95868	27.65742	30.64344	32.25290
10	18.56143	19.65458	22.04452	23.34928	24.73290	27.75514	31.15042	34.96205	39.23787	41.56613
11	21.71319	23.13313	26.27075	28.00167	29.85017	33.93107	38.58050	43.87370	49.89495	53.20766
12	25.21164	27.02911	31.08865	33.35192	35.78620	41.21688	47.49660	54.74591	63.10974	67.75958
13	29.09492	31.39260	36.58107	39.50471	42.67199	49.81802	58.19592	68.01001	79.49608	85.94947
14	33.40536	37.27971	42.84241	46.58041	50.65951	59.96527	71.03511	84.19221	99.81514	108.68684
15	38.18995	41.75328	49.98035	54.71747	59.92503	71.93901	86.44213	103.93450	125.01077	137.10855
16	43.50084	47.88367	58.11760	64.07509	70.67303	86.06804	104.93056	128.02009	156.25336	172.63568
17	49.39594	54.74971	67.39407	74.83636	83.14072	102.74028	127.11667	157.40451	194.99416	217.04460
18	55.93949	62.43968	77.96923	87.21181	97.60323	122.41353	153.74000	193.25350	243.03276	272.55576
19	63.20283	71.05244	90.02493	101.44358	114.37975	145.62797	185.68800	236.98927	302.60062	341.94470
20	71.26514	80.69874	103.76842	117.81012	133.84051	173.02100	224.02560	290.34691	376.46447	428.68087
21	80.21431	91.50258	119.43600	136.63164	156.41499	205.34479	270.03072	355.44323	468.05632	537.10109
22	90.14788	103.60289	137.29704	158.27638	182.60138	243.48685	325.23686	434.86075	581.62984	672.62636
23	101.17415	117.15524	157.65862	183.16784	212.97761	288.49448	391.48424	531.75011	722.46100	842.03295
24	113.41331	132.33387	180.87083	211.79302	248.21402	341.60349	470.98108	649.95513	897.09164	1053.79118
25	126.99877	149.33393	207.33274	244.71197	289.08827	404.27211	566.37730	794.16526	1113.63363	1318.48898

TABLE 6A–6   Present Value of an Annuity Due of n Payments of 1 Each: $PVAD = [1 - (1 \div (1 + i)^n)] \div i \times (1 + i)$, also expressed as $(PVAD, i, n) = (1 + i)(PVA, i, n)$

This table shows the present value of an annuity due of 1 at various rates of interest and for various time periods. It is used to compute the present value of a series of payments made at the beginning of each interest compounding period.

Number of Periods n	2%	2½%	3%	4%	5%	6%	7%	8%	9%	10%
1	1.00000	1.00000	1.00000	1.00000	1.00000	1.00000	1.00000	1.00000	1.00000	1.00000
2	1.98039	1.97561	1.97087	1.96154	1.95238	1.94340	1.93458	1.92593	1.91743	1.90909
3	2.94156	2.92742	2.91347	2.88609	2.85941	2.83339	2.80802	2.78326	2.75911	2.73554
4	3.88388	3.85602	3.82861	3.77509	3.72325	3.67301	3.62432	3.57710	3.53130	3.48685
5	4.80773	4.76197	4.71710	4.62990	4.54595	4.46511	4.38721	4.31213	4.23972	4.16987
6	5.71346	5.64583	5.57971	5.45182	5.32948	5.21236	5.10020	4.99271	4.88965	4.79079
7	6.60143	6.50813	6.41719	6.24214	6.07569	5.91732	5.76654	5.62788	5.48592	5.35526
8	7.47199	7.34939	7.23028	7.00205	6.78637	6.58238	6.38929	6.20637	6.03295	5.86842
9	8.32548	8.17014	8.01969	7.73274	7.46321	7.20979	6.97130	6.74664	6.53482	6.33493
10	9.16224	8.97087	8.78611	8.43533	8.10782	7.80169	7.51523	7.24689	6.99525	6.75902
11	9.98259	9.75206	9.53020	9.11090	8.72173	8.36009	8.02358	7.71008	7.41766	7.14457
12	10.78685	10.51421	10.25262	9.76048	9.30641	8.88687	8.49867	8.13896	7.80519	7.49506
13	11.57534	11.25776	10.95400	10.38507	9.86325	9.38384	8.94269	8.53608	8.16073	7.81369
14	12.34837	11.98319	11.63496	10.98565	10.39357	9.85268	9.35765	8.90378	8.48690	8.10336
15	13.10625	12.69091	12.29607	11.56312	10.89864	10.29498	9.74547	9.24424	8.78615	8.36669
16	13.84926	13.38139	12.93794	12.11839	11.37966	10.71225	10.10791	9.55948	9.06069	8.60608
17	14.57771	14.05500	13.56110	12.65230	11.83777	11.10590	10.44665	9.85137	9.31256	8.82371
18	15.29187	14.71220	14.16612	13.16567	12.27407	11.47726	10.76322	10.12164	9.54363	9.02155
19	15.99203	15.35336	14.75351	13.65930	12.68959	11.82760	11.05909	10.37189	9.75563	9.20141
20	16.67846	15.97889	15.32380	14.13394	13.08532	12.15812	11.33560	10.60360	9.95012	9.36492
21	17.35143	16.58916	15.87747	14.59033	13.46221	12.46992	11.59401	10.81815	10.12855	9.51356
22	18.01121	17.18455	16.41502	15.02916	13.82115	12.76408	11.83553	11.01680	10.29224	9.64869
23	18.65805	17.76541	16.93692	15.45112	14.16300	13.04158	12.06124	11.20074	10.44243	9.77154
24	19.29220	18.33211	17.44361	15.85684	14.48857	13.30338	12.27219	11.37106	10.58021	9.88322
25	19.91393	18.88499	17.93554	16.24696	14.79864	13.55036	12.46933	11.52876	10.70661	9.98474

	11%	12%	14%	15%	16%	18%	20%	22%	24%	25%
1	1.00000	1.00000	1.00000	1.00000	1.00000	1.00000	1.00000	1.00000	1.00000	1.00000
2	1.90090	1.89286	1.87719	1.86957	1.86207	1.84746	1.83333	1.81967	1.80645	1.80000
3	2.71252	2.69005	2.64666	2.62571	2.60523	2.56564	2.52778	2.49153	2.45682	2.44000
4	3.44371	3.40183	3.32163	3.28323	3.24589	3.17427	3.10648	3.04224	2.98130	2.95200
5	4.10245	4.03735	3.91371	3.85498	3.79818	3.69006	3.58873	3.49364	3.40428	3.36160
6	4.69590	4.60478	4.43308	4.35216	4.27429	4.12717	3.99061	3.86364	3.74538	3.68928
7	5.23054	5.11141	4.88867	4.78448	4.68474	4.49760	4.32551	4.16692	4.02047	3.95142
8	5.71220	5.56376	5.28830	5.16042	5.03857	4.81153	4.60459	4.41551	4.24232	4.16114
9	6.14612	5.96764	5.63886	5.48732	5.34359	5.07757	4.83716	4.61927	4.42122	4.32891
10	6.53705	6.32825	5.94637	5.77158	5.60654	5.30302	5.03097	4.78628	4.56550	4.46313
11	6.88923	6.65022	6.21612	6.01877	5.83323	5.49409	5.19247	4.92318	4.68186	4.57050
12	7.20652	6.93770	6.45273	6.23371	6.02864	5.65601	5.32706	5.03540	4.77569	4.65640
13	7.49236	7.19437	6.66029	6.42062	6.19711	5.79322	5.43922	5.12737	4.85136	4.72512
14	7.74987	7.42355	6.84236	6.58315	6.34322	5.90951	5.53268	5.20277	4.91239	4.78010
15	7.98187	7.62817	7.00207	6.72448	6.46753	6.00806	5.61057	5.26456	4.96160	4.82408
16	8.19087	7.81086	7.14217	6.84737	6.57546	6.09158	5.67547	5.31522	5.00129	4.85926
17	8.37916	7.97399	7.26506	6.95424	6.66850	6.16235	5.72956	5.35673	5.03330	4.88741
18	8.54879	8.11963	7.37286	7.04716	6.74870	6.22233	5.77463	5.39077	5.05911	4.90993
19	8.70162	8.24967	7.46742	7.12797	6.81785	6.27316	5.81219	5.41866	5.07993	4.92794
20	8.83929	8.36578	7.55037	7.19823	6.87746	6.31624	5.84350	5.44152	5.09672	4.94235
21	8.96333	8.46944	7.62313	7.25933	6.92884	6.35275	5.86958	5.46027	5.11026	4.95388
22	9.07507	8.56200	7.68696	7.31246	6.97314	6.38368	5.89132	5.47563	5.12117	4.96311
23	9.17574	8.64465	7.74294	7.35866	7.01133	6.40990	5.90943	5.48822	5.12998	4.97049
24	9.26643	8.71843	7.79206	7.39884	7.04425	6.43212	5.92453	5.49854	5.13708	4.97639
25	9.34814	8.78432	7.83514	7.43377	7.07263	6.45095	5.93710	5.50700	5.14281	4.98111

QUESTIONS

1. Explain what is meant by the time value of money.
2. Assuming that the annual rate of interest is specified as 12%, what would simple interest rates be for the following periods: (a) semiannual, (b) quarterly, (c) monthly?
3. What is the fundamental difference between simple interest and compound interest?
4. Briefly explain each of the following:
   a. Future value of 1.
   b. Present value of 1.
   c. Future value of annuity of n payments of 1 each.
   d. Present value of annuity of n payments of 1 each.
5. Assume that $10,000 is borrowed on a two-year, 10% note payable. Compute the total amount of interest that would be paid on this note assuming (a) simple interest and (b) compound interest.
6. Match columns 2 and 3 with column 1 by entering the appropriate letter from column 1:

Column 1	Column 2	Column 3
A. Future value of 1.	FV1 _____	$\dfrac{1}{(1 + i)^n}$ _____
B. Present value of 1.	PV1 _____	$(1 + i)^n$ _____
C. Future value of an ordinary annuity of 1.	PVA _____	$\dfrac{1 - [1 \div (1 + i)^n]}{i}$ _____
D. Present value of an ordinary annuity of 1.	FVA _____	$\dfrac{(1 + i)^n - 1}{i}$ _____

7. Match the following by entering the appropriate letter from column 1 in column 2 (n and i are the same for each value). (Hint: Which number in column 2 is most easily identified with the definition in column 1? Use it to find n and i .)

Column 1	Column 2
A. Future value of 1.	17 51851
B. Present value of 1.	4.60654 _____
C. Future value of annuity of 1 (ordinary).	.26295 _____
	3.80296 _____
D. Present value of annuity of 1 (ordinary).	20.32147 _____
	5.34359 _____
E. Future value of annuity of 1 (due).	
F. Present value of annuity of 1 (due).	

8. Contrast a future value of 1 with the present value of 1.
9. The future value of 1 at 15% interest for 12 years is 5.35025: (a) What is the present value of 1 in this situation? (b) If the present value of 1 at 12% interest for 17 years is .14564, what is the future value of 1 at 12% for 17 years? Do not use tables.
10. (a) If the table value for a future value of 1 is known, how can it be converted to the table value for present value of 1? (b) Show the computations to convert the following future values of 1 to the equivalent present values of 1: 1.46933, 3.18547, and 216.54199.
11. If $15,000 is deposited in a savings account at 8% compound interest, what would be the balance in the savings account at the end of (a) 10 years? (b) 15 years? (c) 25 years?
12. Assume that you have a legal contract that specifies that you will receive $200,000 cash in the future. Assuming a 9% interest rate, what would be the present value of that contract if the amount will be received (a) 10 years, (b) 15 years, or (c) 25 years from now?
13. Assume that you deposited $20,000 in a savings account for a three-year period. How much cash would you receive at the end if 12% simple interest per annum is accumulated in the fund at the end of each quarter? There is no compounding.
14. Assume that you will receive $100,000 cash from a trust fund six years from now. What is the present value of the $100,000 assuming 12% interest compounded on a quarterly basis?
15. What are the three characteristics of an annuity? Explain what would happen if any of these characteristics were changed.
16. Table 6–3 gives a future value of an ordinary annuity of 1 of 3.09 (rounded) for n = 3 and i = 3%. Explain the meaning of this table value.

17. If $20,000 is deposited in a savings account at the end of each of *n* annual periods and will earn 9%, what will be the balance in the savings account at the date of the last deposit (i.e., an ordinary annuity), assuming that *n* = 10 years, 15 years, and 25 years?

18. Explain the difference between (*a*) future value of an ordinary annuity and (*b*) future value of an annuity due.

19. Explain the difference between (*a*) present value of an ordinary annuity and (*b*) present value of an annuity due.

20. Compute the present value of an annuity of five payments of $9,000 each using a 12% interest rate, assuming (*a*) an ordinary annuity and (*b*) an annuity due. Explain why the two amounts are different.

21. Compute the future value of an annuity of six payments of $5,000 each using a 10% interest rate, assuming (*a*) an ordinary annuity and (*b*) an annuity due. Explain why the two amounts are different.

22. Room Company will create a building fund by contributing $100,000 per year to it for 10 years; the fund will be increased each year at a 7% compound interest rate. Assume that this is the current year: (*a*) Explain how you would determine whether this situation is an ordinary annuity or an annuity due. (*b*) In each instance, how many payments and compounding periods would be involved?

23. J. Reed purchased a Mercedes for a cash "bargain" price of $40,000. Cash of $10,000 was paid at purchase date and the remainder was paid in eight quarterly payments (ordinary annuity) of $4,274 each. The going rate of annual interest used for typical car deals was 16%. How much did Reed pay for the auto? How much interest was paid? Was the interest implicit in the $4,274 payment greater or less than 16%?

CASES

C 6–1
(L.O. 1)

Select Your Bonus   Linda Reed is an executive of VIP Company and has earned a performance bonus. She has the option of taking the $30,000 bonus now or $57,000 five years from now. Write a brief report explaining which option she should elect. Explain why, identifying the interest rate at which Linda would be indifferent.

C 6–2
(L.O. 1, 5, 6)

Compare the Cost of Two Alternatives   Viable Corporation purchases large machines for use in its plant. Machine Type A is typical of these machines. Currently, Viable is considering the purchase of a new Type A machine. Two different brand names are being considered, as follows:

	Brand A	Brand B
Cost (cash basis)	$100,000	$90,000
Operating expense to operate the machine (per year)	$ 7,000	$ 8,000
Estimated useful life (years)	8	8
Estimated residual value (% of cost)	20%	10%

Viable expects a 20% return on its investments.

Required

1. Write a one-page report analyzing and comparing the relative cost of the two brands. Assume that all variables, other than the four listed above, are the same for both brands.
2. Which machine should Viable purchase? Why? Are any other factors relevant in addition to your computations?

C 6–3
(L.O. 1, 5)

Compute an Implicit Interest Rate   Slick Real Estate Tax Shelters, Ltd. advertised that its special tax-shelter partnerships "earn 21% interest for the investor each year." An independent analysis of the actual figures (obtained from a prior partner after considerable effort) showed that an individual who invested $100,000 would receive a projected return of $310,000 at the end of year 10 from the investment date. (Adapted from "How to Fool with Averages," *Forbes Magazine,* December 7, 1984, pp. 33–34.)

Required

1. Compute the actual interest rate implicit in the tax shelter (round to the nearest percent).
2. Was the advertised rate of return of 21% correct or was it misleading? Explain.

C 6–4
(L.O. 1, 5)

Mortgages   Laura Ray buys a house for $150,000. She makes a down payment amounting to $30,000 and takes out a 12% mortgage for the balance. The bank requires that she pay off the mortgage in 25 equal annual instalments, beginning one year from now.

Required

1. Determine the amount of these instalments.
2. What is the total amount paid by Ray (over the 25 years) for the $150,000 house?
3. How much of this total represents interest charges?

C 6–5
(L.O. 1, 5, 6)

Investment Alternatives   Nancy Sly wishes to sell her business and receives the following three offers:

a. $284,000 cash (receivable immediately).
b. $100,000 cash now plus an annual instalment of $30,000 at the end of each year for 10 years, a total of $400,000.
c. An offer to manage the property for 10 years that would yield her $48,000 cash at the end of each of the 10 years. She would, however, have to make an initial investment of $10,000 cash now. Total net cash to be received is $470,000.

Which offer should be accepted if Sly has equally risky alternative opportunities that will yield a return of 10% per year?

C 6–6
(L.O. 1, 3, 4, 5, 6)

Decision to Overhaul or Replace   A component is presently being manufactured on equipment that is fully depreciated. Although this old machine has a $20,000 cash value on the open market now, with suitable annual overhauls it can be used by the firm for the next three years. The cost of these overhauls is expected to be $40,000 per year (payable at the beginning of each year), and at the end of the third year the "overhauled" machine is expected to have a salvage value of $10,000.

On the other hand, a new machine with an expected life of three years and no expected salvage value at that time can be acquired at a cost of $134,350. The projected sales and cost of operations for each of the next three years are as follows:

Data on Component	Old Machine	New Machine
Unit sales (transfer to other production departments) per year	20,000	20,000
Out-of-pocket operating costs per unit*	$8.00	$7.50

* These cash flows are assumed to occur at the end of each year.

Assume that the time value of money for the firm is 10% per annum, and ignore income taxes.

Required

1. Should the old machine be overhauled or the new equipment acquired? Why?
2. If the component can be purchased at a cost of $10.30 per unit from outside suppliers, should it then be purchased or manufactured internally? Explain. Assume that payments to external suppliers are made at the end of each year.
3. At what level of output (unit sales per year) would management be indifferent (*a*) to buying the component from outside suppliers at $10.30 per unit and (*b*) to manufacturing it internally on the new equipment?

C 6–7
(L.O. 1, 3, 4, 5, 6)

Debt Funds   Included in Cherry Corp.'s long-term debt as of December 31, 1991, were $154.2 million of long-term bonds due December 31, 2017. The interest rate is 8.75%. Interest is paid semiannually.

1. Suppose Cherry Corp. were to establish a fund by making a single lump-sum payment on January 1, 1993. If the fund would earn 10% interest compounded annually, what single amount is necessary on January 1, 1993, to retire the long-term bonds on December 31, 2017? (The sinking fund would not be used to pay interest.)
2. Suppose, instead, that equal payments into the fund are to begin January 1, 2001, and end January 1, 2017. What is the amount of each annual payment required to retire the long-term bonds on December 31, 2017? Interest on the fund will be 10% compounded annually.
3. How many consecutive payments of $4.1 million each January 1 would have to be made into the fund beginning on January 1, 1993, to retire the debt December 31, 2017, if interest at 10% compounded annually is earned on the fund?

EXERCISES

E 6–1
(L.O. 5)

Compounding for Periods Less than One Year The Wittink Company plans to deposit $80,000 today into a special building fund that will be needed at the end of six years. A financial institution will serve as the fund trustee and will pay 12% interest on the fund balance.

Required

Compute the fund balance at the end of year 6 assuming:

a. Annual compounding.
b. Semiannual compounding.
c. Quarterly compounding.

E 6–2
(L.O. 3, 4, 5)

Lump Sums and Annuities: Multiple Choice Each situation is independent. Select the best solution.

1. On May 1, 1995, a company purchased a new machine for which it does not have to pay until May 1, 1997. The total payment on May 1, 1997, will include both principal and interest. Assuming 10% interest, the cost of the machine will be the total payment multiplied by what time value of money?
   a. Future amount of an annuity of 1.
   b. Future amount of 1.
   c. Present value of an annuity of 1.
   d. Present value of 1.

2. For which one of the following transactions would the use of the present value of an annuity due be appropriate in calculating the present value of the asset obtained or liability owed at the date of incurrence?
   a. A capital lease is entered into with the initial lease payment due one month after the signing of the lease agreement.
   b. A capital lease is entered into with the initial lease payment due immediately.
   c. A 10-year 8% bond is issued on January 2 with interest payable semiannually on July 1 and January 1 yielding 7%.
   d. A 10-year 8% bond is issued on January 2 with interest payable semiannually on July 1 and January 1 yielding 9%.

   (AICPA adapted)

E 6–3
(L.O. 1, 5)

Compounding Complete the following questions:

1. Suppose you invested $10,000 in a savings account at 8% compound interest. What balance would be in your savings account at the end of five years assuming:
   a. Annual compounding?
   b. Semiannual compounding?
   c. Quarterly compounding?
   Explain why these amounts are different.
2. Suppose you wish to accumulate a fund of $40,000 at the end of six years by making a single deposit now. The fund will earn 8% compound interest. What amount must you deposit now to accumulate the $40,000 fund assuming:
   a. Annual compounding?
   b. Semiannual compounding?
   c. Quarterly compounding?
   Explain why these amounts are different.

E 6–4
(L.O. 1, 3, 4, 5)

Annuities, Time Value, Lump Sums, and Future Value Each case is independent. Select the best solution.

On January 15, 1995, Cart Corporation adopted a plan to accumulate funds for environmental improvements beginning July 2, 1999, at an estimated cost of $2,000,000. Cart plans to make four equal annual deposits in a fund that will earn interest at 10% compounded annually. The first deposit was made on July 1, 1995.

1. Cart should make four annual deposits (rounded) of which of the following amounts?
   a. $573,584.
   b. $391,765.
   c. $430,942.
   d. $630,941.

2. On January 1, 1995, Ott Company sold goods to Fox Company. Fox signed a noninterest-bearing note requiring payment of $60,000 annually for seven years. The first payment was made on January 1, 1995. The prevailing rate of interest for this type of note at date of issuance was 10%. Ott should record sales revenues in January 1995 of which of the following amounts?
   a. $321,316.
   b. $287,447.
   c. $261,316.
   d. $292,105.

3. Rex Company accepted a $10,000, 10% interest-bearing note from Brooks Company on December 31, 1995, in exchange for a machine with a list price of $8,000 and a cash price of $7,500. The note is payable on December 31, 1998. In its 1995 income statement, Rex should report the sale at which amount?
   a. $7,500.
   b. $8,000.
   c. $10,000.
   d. $10,400.

(AICPA adapted)

E 6-5
(L.O. 1, 4, 5)

Annuities, Interest Rates, Payment Periods Compute each of the following amounts. Each case is independent. Round to the nearest dollar or percentage.

a. On January 1, 1994, Marcon Corporation borrowed $120,000 from the Canadian Bank. Repayment is to be in six equal annual instalments, including both principal and interest. Compounding is annual. Calculate the annual payment for:

   1. December 31 payment, 10% annual interest $ _____.
   2. December 31 payment, 6% annual interest $ _____.
   3. January 1 payment, 10% annual interest $ _____.
   4. January 1 payment, 6% annual interest $ _____.

b. On January 1, 1993, Marcon Corporation borrowed $40,000 from the Canadian Bank. Repayment is to be made in equal annual instalments, including both principal and interest. Compounding is annual.

   Calculate the implicit interest rate associated with:
   1. December 31 payment of $10,856, 6 payments   _____.
   2. January 1 payment of $5,323, 10 payments   _____.
   Calculate the number of payments needed for:
   3. December 31 payment of $4,074, 8% rate   _____.
   4. January 1 payment of $4,936, 10% rate   _____.

(CGAAC adapted)

E 6-6
(L.O. 1, 5)

Fund Accumulation, Schedule, and Entries R. Ball has decided to set up a fund to provide for his young child's college education. A local financial institution will handle the fund and increase it each year on a 10% annual compound interest basis. Ball desires to make a single deposit on January 1, 1997, and specifies that the fund must have a $90,000 balance at the end of 2012.

Required

1. Compute the amount of cash that must be deposited on January 1, 1997.
2. Prepare a fund accumulation schedule through 1999.
3. Give the journal entries for the first year of the fund. Assume that Ball's reporting year ends December 31.

E 6-7
(L.O. 1, 5)

PV, Acquisition of Equipment, Cost, Debt Schedule, and Entries Act Company purchased some additional equipment that was needed because of a new contract. The equipment was purchased on January 1, 1996. Because the contract would require two years to complete and Act was short of cash, the vendor agreed to accept a down payment of $10,000 and a two-year, noninterest-bearing note for $45,000 (this amount includes the principal and all interest) due in two years. Assume that the going rate of interest for this debt was 20% because of the extremely high risk.

Required

1. Compute the cost of the equipment. Show computations.
2. Give Act's entry at date of acquisition of the equipment. Record the note at its net value.
3. Prepare a debt payment schedule.
4. Give all additional entries related to the debt. Assume that Act's reporting year ends December 31.

E 6–8
(L.O. 2)

Savings Account; Simple and Compound Interest Compared   Assume that a deposit of $500,000 is made in a special savings account on January 1; the interest rate is 8%.

Required

1. Compute the balance in the savings account at the end of five years assuming (*a*) simple interest and (*b*) compound interest.
2. Calculate and explain the cause of the difference.

E 6–9
(L.O. 1, 5)

Fund Accumulation, Interest Rate or Time Unknown   The two following cases are independent.

a. At the present date, Lot Company has $40,000 that will be deposited in a savings account until needed. It is anticipated that $111,000 will be needed at the end of 10 years to expand some manufacturing facilities.. What approximate rate of interest would be required to accumulate the $111,000, assuming compounding on an annual basis? Show computations. Do not interpolate.
b. Lot Company is planning an addition to its office building as soon as adequate funds can be accumulated. The company has estimated that the addition will cost approximately $250,000. At the present time, $90,600 cash is on hand that will not be needed soon. A local savings institution will pay 8% interest (compounded annually). How many periods would be required to accumulate the $250,000? Show computations. Do not interpolate.

E 6–10
(L.O. 1, 5)

Debt Retirement, Interest Rate Not Known   The two following cases are independent:

a. On September 1, Luft Company decided to deposit $400,000 in a debt retirement fund. The company needs $947,000 cash to pay a debt 10 years later. What rate of compound interest must the fund earn to meet the cash requirement to pay the debt? Do not interpolate.
b. Flame Company owes a $200,000 debt that is payable eight years from now. Flame wants to pay the debt in full immediately. The creditor has agreed to settle the debt in full for $108,100 cash. What rate of compound discount is the creditor applying to the note? Do not interpolate.

E 6–11
(L.O. 1, 5)

Compounding with Increasing Interest Rate; Compute Expected Selling Price   The following two cases are independent.

a. Jason Fine decides to invest $10,000 today in a mutual fund. He anticipates leaving this investment in the fund for 12 years. The fund will be increased each year-end by specified compound interest rates as follows: years 1 to 4 inclusive, 8%; 5 to 8 inclusive, 9%; and 9 to 12 inclusive, 10%. Compute the balance that will be in the fund at the end of year 12.
b. Bob Nixon owns a special kind of property that he wants to sell for cash. Bob estimates that this property will produce two net cash inflows as follows: end of year 5 (from now), $120,000, and end of year 8, $80,000. He also deems it reasonable to use compound discount interest rates of 6% for the $120,000 cash inflow and 10% for the $80,000 cash inflow. (The $80,000 is riskier to the buyer.) Given these estimates, compute the approximate selling price that Bob should expect.

E 6–12
(L.O. 1, 3)

Applications of Future and Present Value of 1   Each of the following cases is independent.

a. A compound interest table (or formula) value is .72198. Is this a future value of 1 or a present value of 1? Explain without consulting the tables.
b. What table value should be used to compute the balance in a fund at the end of year 11 if $100,000 is deposited at the date the fund is established, assuming 6% annual compound interest and semi-annual compounding?
c. What table value should be used to compute the present value of $50,000, assuming 8% compound interest, quarterly compounding, and six years of discounting?
d. A fund is established by depositing $6,000 at compound interest; the fund will have a balance of $48,822 at the end of 15 years. What is the approximate annual rate of interest?
e. A discounted note payable of $40,000 (including both principal and interest) is due three years hence. Assuming 7% annual compound interest, at what amount should this debt be settled today (i.e., three years before maturity) on a cash basis?

E 6–13
(L.O. 1, 5)

Fund Balance with Changing Interest Rate   On January 1, Stan Zeff invested $30,000 cash in a savings account. It will be increased by the compound interest each year-end. The fund will earn 8% for the first three years, 9% for the next three years, and 10% for the last four years.

Required

Compute the balance in the fund at the end of year 10.

E 6-14
(L.O. 4)

Ordinary and Annuity Due Compared   United Company has decided to accumulate a fund by making equal periodic contributions. The fund will be increased each interest period by 8% interest compounded annually. The current date is January 1.

Required

1. Complete the following tabulation to compare an ordinary annuity with an annuity due:
   a. Ordinary annuity (end-of-period):

Compounding	Contribution	n	i	Table Value	Fund Balance
Annual	$5,000	5			$____
Semiannual	2,500	___	___	___	___
Quarterly	1,250	___	___	___	___

   b. Annuity due (beginning of period):

Compounding	Contribution	n	i	Table Value	Fund Balance
Annual	$5,000	5			$____
Semiannual	2,500	___	___	___	___
Quarterly	1,250	___	___	___	___

2. Explain why the ordinary annuity and annuity due fund balances are different.
3. Give the journal entry at the end of the first compounding period for each of the six situations above (indicate dates and use simple interest because the differences are insignificant). Assume that United's reporting year ends December 31.

E 6-15
(L.O. 3)

Understanding Future and Present Value Concepts   Complete the following table, assuming that $n = 9$ and $i = 18\%$.

Concept	Symbol	Formula	Table Value	Table (source)
1. Future value of 1.	___	___	___	___
2. Present value of 1.	___	___	___	___
3. Future value of ordinary annuity of n payments of 1 each.	___	___	___	___
4. Present value of ordinary annuity of n payments of 1 each.	___	___	___	___
5. Future value of annuity due of n payments of 1 each.	___	___	___	___
6. Present value of annuity due of n payments of 1 each.	___	___	___	___

E 6-16
(L.O. 1, 4, 5)

Fund, Ordinary Annuity, Schedule, Entries   Zoltar Moving Company has decided to accumulate a debt retirement fund by making three equal annual deposits of $15,000 beginning December 31, 1997. Assume that the fund will accumulate annual compound interest at 7% per year, which will be added to the fund balance. The fund will be used for debt retirement on December 31, 1999.

Required

1. What kind of annuity is this? Explain.
2. What will be the balance in the fund in three years (immediately after the last deposit)?
3. Prepare an accumulation schedule for this fund.
4. Prepare the journal entries for the three-year period. Assume that Zoltar's reporting year ends December 31.
5. What would be the balance in the fund at the end of three years if it were set up on an annuity due basis?

E 6-17
(L.O. 1, 4, 5)

Debt Payment, Annuity Due, Schedule, Entries   On September 1, 1996, Sault Company incurred a $60,000 debt. Arrangements have been made to pay this debt in three equal annual instalments starting immediately at compound interest of 10%.

Required

1. Is this an ordinary annuity or an annuity due? Explain.
2. Compute the amount of the equal annual payments.
3. Prepare a debt payment schedule.
4. Give the journal entries related to the debt. Assume that Sault's reporting year ends August 31.
5. Compute the annual payment assuming that the debt payments are made annually beginning at the end of each year.

E 6–18
(L.O. 1, 3, 4, 5)

Understanding Present and Future Value Cases   Each of the following cases is independent.

a. Julie Able has $25,000 in a fund that earns 10% annual compound interest. If she desires to withdraw it in five equal annual amounts, starting today (i.e., beginning of period), how much would she receive each year?

b. Julie will deposit $250 each semiannual period starting today (i.e., beginning of period); this savings account will earn 6% compounded each semiannual period. What will be the balance in Julie's savings account at the end of year 10?

c. Julie purchased a new automobile that cost $14,000. She received a $4,000 trade-in allowance for her old auto and signed a 16% note for $10,000. The note requires eight equal quarterly payments starting at the end of the first quarter from date of purchase. What is the amount of each payment?

d. Julie deposited $2,000 at the end of each year in a savings account for five years at compound interest. The fund had a balance of $12,456 at the date of the last deposit. What rate of interest did she earn?

e. On January 1, Julie owed a debt of $15,131.14. An agreement was reached that she would pay the debt plus compound interest in 24 monthly instalments of $800, the first payment to be made at the end of January. What rate of annual interest is she paying?

E 6–19
(L.O. 3, 5)

Funds, Single Plus Periodic Deposits   Wolf Company established a construction fund on July 1, 1996, by making a single deposit of $180,000. Also at the end of each year, on June 30, the company will make a $30,000 deposit in the fund. The fund will earn 14% compound interest each year, which will be added to the fund balance.

Required

1. Compute the balance that will be in the fund June 30, 2000.
2. Give the journal entries that would be made for the first year. Assume that Wolf's reporting year ends December 31.

E 6–20
(L.O. 1, 3, 5)

Compute the Price of a Used Machine   Rye Company is considering purchasing a used machine that is in excellent mechanical condition. The company plans to keep the machine for 10 years, at which time the residual value will be zero. An analysis of the capacity of the machine and the costs of operating it (including materials used in production) provided an estimate that the machine would increase after-tax net cash inflow by approximately $200,000 per year.

Required

1. Compute the approximate amount that Rye should be willing to pay now for the machine assuming a target earnings rate of 20% per year. Assume also that the revenue is realized at each year-end. Show your computations.
2. What price should be paid assuming a $50,000 residual value at the end of the 10 years?

| PROBLEMS

P 6–1
(L.O. 5)

Future Values, Different Compounding Periods   Herts Company deposited $100,000 in a special expansion fund on May 1, 1996, for future use as needed. The fund will accumulate 12% compounded interest per year.

Required

1. Complete the following table:

Compounding Assumption	Periodic Interest Rate	Fund Balance at End of	
		Two Years	Four Years
Annual			
Semiannual			
Quarterly			

2. Prepare a fund accumulation schedule based on the first cell (annual, for two years).
3. Give journal entries for the fund based on the first cell (annual, for two years). Assume that Herts' reporting year ends December 31.

P 6–2
(L.O. 1, 5)

How Much to Deposit to Build a Fund, Different Compounding Periods   Story Company anticipates that it will need $200,000 cash for an expansion in the next few years. Assume an annual compound interest rate of 8%. The company desires to make a single contribution on January 1, 1997, so that the $200,000 will be available when needed.

Required

1. Complete the following schedule:

		Amount to Be Deposited Now			
		Two Years		Three Years	
Compounding Assumption	Interest Rate	n	$	n	$
Annual	————	————	————	————	————
Semiannual	————	————	————	————	————

2. Prepare a fund accumulation schedule based on $n = 2$ and $i = 8\%$.
3. Give journal entries for years 1 and 2 based on $n = 2$ and $i = 8\%$. Assume that Story's reporting year ends December 31.

P 6–3
(L.O. 1, 5)

Building a Fund, Three Cases, Unknown Time or Rate, Schedule

Case 1.   On January 1, 1995, Joy Brown deposited $10,000 in a savings account that would accumulate at 11% annual compound interest for four years.

Required

1. Compute the balance that would be in the savings account at the end of the fourth year.
2. Prepare a fund accumulation schedule for this case.

Case 2.   On March 1, 1995, Phil Gray deposited $15,000 in a savings account that would accumulate to $16,873 at the end of three years, assuming annual compound interest. Do not interpolate.

Required

1. Compute the interest rate that would be necessary. Show computations.
2. Prepare a fund accumulation schedule for this case.

Case 3.   On September 1, 1995, Dan Jones deposited $7,000 in a savings account that would accumulate to $11,108, assuming 8% annual compound interest.

Required

1. Compute the number of periods that would be necessary. Show computations.
2. Prepare a fund accumulation schedule for this case.

P 6–4
(L.O. 1, 5)

Funds, Time or Rate Unknown, Fund Balance

Case 1.   On September 1, 1995, Betty Mason deposited $30,000 in a savings account that was expected to accumulate to $32,700 by August 31, 1996.

Required

1. Compute the implicit compound annual interest rate.
2. What would be the balance in the fund on August 31, 2000, 2005, and 2015 assuming no withdrawals?

Case 2.   On May 1, 1996, Jim Bolton deposited $100,000 in a savings account that would accumulate to $125,971 on April 30, 1999. Interest is compounded annually.

Required

1. Compute the implicit compound annual interest rate. Interpolate if necessary.
2. Prepare the three-year fund accumulation schedule.

Case 3.   On October 1, 1996, Phil Hardy deposited $10,000 in a savings account, and he expects the fund to have a balance of $25,000 at the end of 10 years. Interest is compounded annually.

Required

1. Compute the implicit interest rate. Show the interpolation that would be required to approximate the interest rate to two decimal places.
2. What would be in the fund at the end of 20 years? (Use a programmed calculator, if available; otherwise round the answer in [1] to the nearest percent.)

P 6–5
(L.O. 1, 2, 5)

Settle Old Debts with New Debt, Present and Future Value   The Bush Tree Company is planning to pay some of its debts. On January 1, 1995, the company has savings accounts as follows:

Date Established	Amount Deposited (single deposit for each)	Annual Compound Interest Rate
January 1, 1984	$20,000	8%
January 1, 1990	30,000	10%

The outstanding debts on January 1, 1995, to be paid off are as follows:

Due Date	Type of Note	Face of Note*
December 31, 1998	Noninterest bearing	$ 60,000
December 31, 2005	Noninterest bearing	200,000

* These amounts include both principal and all interest thereon. The amount given for each note is the single sum to be paid at maturity date.

Required

1. Compute the amount of cash that Bush will receive from the two savings accounts on January 1, 1995.
2. Compute the amount for which the two debts can be settled on January 1, 1995, assuming a going rate of interest of 18%.
3. Assuming that all cash is withdrawn from the savings accounts and all payments are made on the debts on January 1, 1995, would Bush have a cash shortage or an excess? How much?

P 6–6
(L.O. 1, 4, 5)

Annuity: Ordinary and Due Compared, Schedules, Entries   Strong Tools Company will establish a special debt retirement fund amounting to $100,000. A trustee has agreed to handle the fund and to increase it each year on a 20% annual compound interest basis. Strong Tools will make equal annual contributions to the fund during the next four years, starting in 1997.

Required

1. Compute the amount of the required annual deposit assuming that they are made on (a) December 31 and (b) January 1. If your answers are different, explain why.
2. Prepare a fund accumulation schedule for each starting date (a) and (b) above.
3. Give the journal entries related to each starting date for all four years. Date each entry. Assume that Strong's reporting year ends December 31.

P 6–7
(L.O. 1, 5)

Annuity versus Annuity Due; Compute Payments, Schedule   It is January 1, 1994, and Terry Corporation is about to borrow $100,000 from the Canadian Bank. The loan will be repaid in five equal instalments, including both principal and compound interest at 10%; interest is compounded annually.

Required

1. Compute the annual loan payment that would be made if (a) the first payment is made on January 1, 1994, or (b) the first payment is made on December 31, 1994.
2. Prepare a debt amortization schedule for each alternative, as follows:

Date	Beginning Principal	Instalment Payment		Ending Principal
		Interest	Principal	

(CGAAC adapted)

P 6–8
(L.O. 1, 5)

Annuity, Debt Schedule, Entries   It is January 1, 1996, and Delux Specialties Company owes a $100,000 past-due debt to City Bank. The bank has agreed to permit Delux to pay the debt in three equal instalments, each payment to include principal and compound interest at 10%. One issue has not yet been settled. The bank desires that the first instalment be paid immediately; however, because of a cash liquidity problem, Delux is asking to make the first payment at year-end, December 31.

Required

1. Compute the amount of the three equal annual payments if (a) the first payment is on January 1 and (b) the first payment is on December 31. If the amounts are different, explain why.
2. Prepare a debt payment schedule for each payment.
3. Give the journal entries related to each payment date through the last payment. Assume that Delux's reporting year ends December 31.

P 6–9
(L.O. 5)

Present Values, Compounding Periods   Compute each of the following amounts. Each case is independent. Round to the nearest dollar.

a. On January 1, 1993, Dardon Corporation signed a contract agreeing to pay $40,000 on December 31, 1995. What is the present value of the payment, assuming the following:

1. Annual compounding, 8% annual interest $_____.
2. Semiannual compounding, 8% annual interest $_____.
3. Quarterly compounding, 8% annual interest $_____.

b. On January 1, 1993, Dardon Corporation agreed to pay Servicon Corporation $4,000 per year for five years in exchange for the right to use a patented process. What is the present value of the payment stream, assuming the following:

1. Payments each January 1, 12% annual interest, annual compounding $_____
2. Payments each January 1, 12% annual interest, semiannual compounding $_____
3. Payments each December 31, 12% annual interest, annual compounding $_____
4. Payments each December 31, 12% annual interest, semiannual compounding $_____

c. On January 1, 1994, Dardon Corporation agreed to pay Canadian Finance Co., as follows:

December 31, 1994, $6,000
December 31, 1995, $6,000
December 31, 1996, $6,000
December 31, 1997, $6,000
December 31, 1998, $106,000

Canadian Finance Co. advanced the present value of this payment stream to Dardon Corporation on January 1, 1994; the present value of the payment stream is the principal amount of the loan, while the rest is interest. Complete the following table:

	Present Value	
	Principal	Interest
1. 6% annual interest, annual compounding	$_____	$_____
2. 8% annual interest, annual compounding	$_____	$_____
3. 4% annual interest, annual compounding	$_____	$_____
4. 6% annual interest, semiannual compounding	$_____	$_____
5. 8% annual interest, semiannual compounding	$_____	$_____

d. On January 1, 1994, Dardon Corporation agreed to lease a machine, with the following terms required by the lease contract:

December 31, 1994–1998, per year, $40,000
December 31, 1999–2003, per year, $20,000
December 31, 2004, $10,000
December 31, 2005, $ 5,000

What is the present value of the payment stream, assuming:

1. 6% annual interest, annual compounding $_____
2. 16% annual interest, annual compounding $_____

(CGAAC adapted)

P 6–10
(L.O. 1, 5)

Annuity, Fund Schedule On January 1, the Wiek Company agreed with its president, J. May, to make a single deposit immediately to establish a fund with a trustee that will pay May $80,000 per year for each of the three years following retirement. May will retire in 10 years on December 31, and the three equal annual payments are to be made by the trustee each December 31 starting in the 11th year. The trustee will add to the fund 8% annual compound interest each year-end. The fund is to have a zero balance on December 31 of year 13, immediately after the last payment to May.

Required

1. Compute the single amount that the Wiek Company must deposit in the fund on January 1 to meet the specified payments to May.
2. Prepare a fund payout schedule to show the use of the fund during the payment period. Use captions similar to the following: date, cash payments to May, interest revenue earned on the fund, net fund decreases, and fund balance.
3. How much of the amount paid to May during the payout period was provided by interest earned during the payout period?

P 6–11
(L.O. 4, 5)

Annuities Compared, Ordinary and Due For each of the independent cases given below, assume that the interest rate is 12% and that compounding is semiannual.

1. How much will accumulate by the end of eight years if $3,000 is deposited each semiannual interest period in a savings account (a) at the end of each period and (b) at the start of each period? Verify your answers, by calculating the answer to (a) with your answer to (b).
2. What will be the periodic payments each period on a $67,000 debt that is to be paid in semiannual instalments over a six-year period, assuming compound interest, if payments are made (a) at the beginning of each period and (b) at the end of each period?

3. A special machine is purchased that had a list price of $45,000. Payment in full is $9,000 cash and five equal semiannual payments of $6,000 each. The first payment will be made at the end of the first semiannual period from purchase date. How much should be recorded in the accounts as the cost of the machine?

4. A special investment is being contemplated. This investment will produce an estimated end-of-period cash income of $26,000 semiannually for five years. At the end of its productive life, the investment will have an estimated recovery value of $4,500. Determine a reasonable estimate of the present value of the investment.

P 6–12
(L.O. 1, 5)

Annuity, Debt, Computation, Entry   The following situations are independent:

1. On June 1, Hill Rover Company owed a $90,000 overdue debt. The bank agreed to allow payment over the next three years at 12% compound interest, with payments to be made each quarter. Compute the periodic payments assuming that (a) the first payment is made May 31 and (b) the first payment is made June 1. If you get different answers, explain why they are different.

2. Swerin Tool Company rents a warehouse from William Smith, Inc., for $20,000 annual rent, payable in advance on each January 1. Swerin Tool Company proposed to sign a three-year lease and to pay the three years' rent in advance. The owner agreed to the proposal with the stipulation that the $60,000 be paid immediately (i.e., on January 1). The company has this proposal under consideration because it expected some discount in view of the fact that funds currently are earning above 8% per annum. Develop a counterproposal as to the amount the company should pay. Give the entry the company should make on January 1 to record your proposal, assuming that it is accepted by Jones.

P 6–13
(L.O. 1, 3, 4, 5)

Overview of Future and Present Value Application   Compute each of the following amounts. Each situation is independent of the others. Round to the nearest dollar or percent.

a. On January 1, year 1, $30,000 is deposited in a fund at 16% compound interest. At the end of year 5, what will the fund balance be, assuming:
   1. Annual compounding?
   2. Semiannual compounding?
   3. Quarterly compounding?

b. On January 1, year 1, a machine is purchased at an invoice price of $20,000. The full purchase price is to be paid at the end of year 5. Assuming 12% compound interest, what did the machine cost if compounding is:
   1. Annual?
   2. Semiannual?
   3. Quarterly?

c. If $6,000 is deposited in a fund now and will increase to $12,798 in 13 years, what is the implicit compound interest rate? Do not interpolate.

d. If the present value of $15,000 is $5,864 at 11% compound annual discount, what is the number of periods?

e. On January 1, year 1, a company decided to establish a fund by making 10 equal annual deposits of $6,000, starting on December 31. The fund will be increased by 9% compounded interest. What will be the fund balance at the end of year 10 (i.e., immediately after the last deposit)?

f. On January 1, year 1, a company decided to establish a fund by making 10 equal annual deposits of $9,000, starting on January 1. The fund will be increased by 7% compound interest. What will be the balance in the fund at the end of year 10?

g. John Day is at retirement and has a large amount of ready cash. He wants to deposit enough cash in a fund to receive back $40,000 each December 31 for the next five years, starting on December 31 of this year. Assuming 10% compound interest, how much cash must Day deposit on January 1?

h. Ace Company is considering the purchase of a unique asset on January 1, year 1. The asset will earn $8,000 net cash inflow each January 1 for five years, starting January 1, year 1. At the end of year 5, the asset will have no value. Assuming a 14% compound interest rate, what should Ace be willing to pay for this unique asset on January 1, year 1?

i. In January of year 1, Bigbay Company decided to build a fund to equal $552,026 in seven years by making seven equal annual deposits of $60,000, starting on December 31 of year 1. What is the implicit compound interest rate for this fund? Interpolate if necessary.

j. The present value of several future equal annual cash payments at year-end of $30,000 each is $141,366, assuming 11% compound discount. What is the implicit number of cash payments?

k. Mike Moe will retire 10 years from now and wants to establish a fund now that will pay him $30,000 cash at the end of each of the first five years after retirement. Specific dates are: date of a single deposit by Mike, January 1, year 1; date of first cash payment from the fund to Moe, December 31, year 11. The fund will pay 10% compound interest. How much cash must Mike deposit on January 1, year 1, to provide the five equal annual year-end cash payments from the fund?

P 6–14
(L.O. 1, 2, 3, 5)

Valuing Liabilities   Linden, Inc., had the following long-term receivable account balances at December 31, 1995:

> Note receivable from sale of division $1,500,000
> Note receivable from officer   400,000

Transactions during 1996 and other information relating to Linden's long-term receivables were as follows:

a. The $1,500,000 note receivable is dated May 1, 1994, bears interest at 9%, and represents the balance of the consideration received from the sale of Linden's electronics division to Pitt Company. Principal payments of $500,000 plus appropriate interest are due on May 1, 1996, 1997, and 1998. The first principal and interest payment was made on May 1, 1996. Collection of the note instalments is reasonably assured.
b. The $400,000 note receivable is dated December 31, 1993, bears interest at 8%, and is due on December 31, 1998. The note is due from Robert Finley, president of Linden, Inc., and is collateralized by 10,000 of Linden's common shares. Interest is payable annually on December 31, and all interest payments were paid on their due dates through December 31, 1996. The quoted market price of Linden's common shares was $45 per share on December 31, 1996.
c. On April 1, 1996, Linden sold a patent to Bell Company in exchange for a $100,000 noninterest-bearing note due on April 1, 1997. There was no established exchange price for the patent, and the note had no ready market. The prevailing rate of interest for a note of this type at April 1, 1996, was 15%. The collection of the note receivable from Bell is reasonably assured.
d. On January 1, 1996, Linden sold a parcel of land to Carr Company for $200,000 under an instalment sale contract. Carr made a $60,000 cash down payment on January 1, 1996, and signed a four-year 16% note for the $140,000 balance. The equal annual payments of principal and interest on the note will be $50,000 payable on January 1, 1997, through January 1, 2000. Circumstances are such that the collection of the instalments on the note is reasonably assured.

Required   What value should be attached to each item as of December 31, 1996?

(AICPA adapted)

ANALYZING FINANCIAL STATEMENTS

A 6–1
(L.O. 1)

Denison Mines Ltd: Liabilities and Present Values   The 1992 balance sheet for Denison Mines Limited shows the following liabilities:

Liabilities	1992 (in thousands)
Bank indebtedness	$ —
Accounts payable and accrued liabilities	34,084
Income and mining taxes	6,057
Long-term debt	80,449
Provision for Elliot Lake decommissioning and reclamation costs	91,801
Advances on concentrate sales contracts	170,500
Deferred income and mining taxes	74,829

Additional information:

1. Income and mining taxes are current liabilities.
2. Long-term debt includes corporate loans and mortgage loans payable, all interest bearing.
3. The Elliot Lake mine, a uranium site, is to be decommissioned. Site reclamation costs are estimated and subject to government agency approval. They will be incurred over the next three years; total costs of $105,353,000, less spending to date of $13,552,000, have been accrued.
4. Advances on concrete sales contracts represent customer prepayments.

5. Deferred taxes represent the difference between tax expense and taxes payable, where tax expense exceeds the payable because of tax provisions that allow speedy expensing of capital assets. The taxes will become payable when and if accounting expenses are greater than tax expenses at some time in the future. Date of reversal cannot be predicted with certainty.

Required   Which of the amounts on the 1992 balance sheet would have been originally recorded at a present value or discounted amount? Are there any amounts recorded on the 1992 balance sheet for which discounting could be considered?

A 6–2
(L.O. 1)

Anheuser-Busch: Credit Agreement   Anheuser-Busch reported the following credit agreement in Note 5 of its 1991 consolidated financial statements:

The company has in place revolving credit agreements totaling $500 million. The agreements, which expire in 1993, provide that the company may select among various loan arrangements with differing maturities and among a variety of interest rates, including a negotiated rate. At December 31, 1991 and 1990, the company had no outstanding borrowings under these agreements. Fees under these agreements amounted to $.7 million in 1991, $.6 million in 1990 and $.6 million in 1989.

Required   What amount (denoted by an interest rate) did the company pay to maintain its line of credit in 1991? Is this an unusual rate? Write a brief paragraph explaining the situation.

A 6–3
(L.O. 1)

Magna International Inc.: Deferred Taxes and Discounting   Because the tax law specifies different timing for certain expense deductions than is required under GAAP, deferred tax liabilities are commonly found in company balance sheets. For example, if a $1,000,000 machine is depreciated over 10 years for book purposes using the straight-line method but more rapidly for establishing the liability for taxes payable to the government, the book tax expense exceeds the tax expense payable to the government. The difference is a deferred tax liability, which is payable in future periods when depreciation for book purposes exceeds that allowed for tax. Magna International Inc., for example, shows a deferred tax liability of $90,800,000 as of July 31, 1993.

Required   Would it be logical to show the deferred tax liability at its discounted value on the balance sheet? Explain in writing.

A 6–4
(L.O. 1, 5)

ConPak Seafoods, Inc.: Present Value and Long-Term Debt   ConPak Seafoods, Inc., in its 1993 annual financial statements, discloses the following information with respect to long-term debt:

Long-term debt consists of the following:

	1993	1992
	(in thousands)	
Term bank loans bearing interest at prime plus 1%	$ 781	$1,013
Term bank loan bearing interest at 8.845%	938	1,061
Government of Newfoundland and Labrador loan bearing interest at 9.25%	56	64
Term loan bearing interest at prime plus 1%	75	107
	1,850	2,245
Current portion of long-term debt	404	391
Total long-term debt	$1,446	$1,854

Assume that principal is due as follows:

1. Term bank loans ($781 and $938) due 20% per year starting in 1994, at year-end.
2. Government of Newfoundland and Labrador loan, due in 1997, at year-end.
3. Term loan ($75) due in 1994, at year-end.

Required   Assume that interest is paid annually and that all payments are made at the end of the year.

1. Assume that prime rates are expected to remain at 7% over the medium term. Calculate the present value of the debt—and related interest—obligations as of December 31, 1993.
2. Assume that prime rates are expected to increase to 10%. Repeat (1).
3. Comment on the different values calculated. Where was there the most change?
4. Is the change in present value caused by fluctuating interest rates reflected on the balance sheet? Why or why not?

A 6–5
(L.O. 1, 2, 3, 4,
5, 6)

International Paper Co: Long-Term Debt: Single Payments and Annuities   The 1991 balance sheet of International Paper Company (IPC), dated December 31, shows $132,000,000 of 8.85% sinking fund debentures due from December 31, 1992, through December 31, 2000. IPC is a large paper products manufacturer. Assume that the principal amount of these debentures must be retired in equal amounts on December 31 of each year. It is now December 31, 1991. Assume that the sinking fund earns interest at 10% compounded annually.

Required

1. If IPC sets up a fund by investing a single amount on January 1, 1992, to fund only the principal amount of the debentures due on December 31, 1997, what amount is required?
2. Repeat (1), assuming that the single amount is deposited December 31, 1992.
3. Repeat (1), assuming that a sinking fund is used with equal payments each December 31, beginning in 1992 and ending December 31, 1997.
4. Repeat (3), assuming that the payments begin December 31, 1991, and end December 31, 1997.
5. Repeat (3), assuming that the payments begin December 31, 1991, and end December 31, 1996. The fund continues to earn interest during 1997.

A 6–6
(L.O. 1, 5)

Gesco Industries Inc: Present Value; Leases and the Balance Sheet   Gesco Industries Inc. is one of Canada's largest independent floor-covering distributors. Gesco is active in manufacturing, distributing, and marketing a wide range of floor-covering products. Gesco was formed 55 years ago and currently employs 325 employees. Due to the lingering recession, the company has not been profitable recently, but it has restructured and has a solid equity base.

One operating policy the company follows is to lease capital assets where possible. If the company were to buy these assets outright, it would report higher capital assets and higher levels of debt. Operating leases are often called *off balance sheet financing,* since the obligations to make payments in the future are not recorded as liabilities.

Gesco, as is required, discloses the extent of its commitments under operating leases in the notes to the financial statements.

Excerpts from the 1993 financial statements follow:

	1993	1992
Current assets	$33,075,363	$40,701,659
Fixed assets	3,787,461	4,126,103
Equipment under capital leases	—	142,583
Deferred portion of leasehold interest	111,480	148,640
Deferred income taxes	1,058,437	95,758
	$38,032,741	$45,214,743
Liabilities		
Current:		
Bank indebtedness, secured	$10,039,262	$6,679,144
Accounts payable and accrued liabilities	14,495,733	14,271,803
Obligation under capital leases, current	—	115,882
Current portion of long-term debt	—	4,023,713
	24,534,995	25,090,542
Obligation under capital leases	—	50,937
Long-term debt	—	5,000,000
	24,534,995	30,141,479
Shareholders' Equity		
Share capital	2,571,327	2,571,327
Retained earnings	10,926,419	12,501,937
	13,497,746	15,073,264
	$38,032,741	$45,214,743

Annual rentals payable under long-term operating leases for premises and computer equipment are as follows for the year ending in:

1994	$ 2,448,123
1995	1,933,862
1996	1,718,676
1997	1,705,780
1998	1,079,409
After 1998	2,530,729
	$11,416,579

Required   How would Gesco's balance sheet change if it were required to capitalize its operating leases? To answer this question, calculate the present value of the minimum lease payments at the market interest rate, assumed to be 10%. Assume that payments due after 1998 are due 50% in 1999 and 50% in the year 2000. Assume all payments occur at the beginning of the year. Then, increase assets and long-term debt by this amount. Consider the effect on the balance sheet by calculating a debt-to-equity ratio and a debt-to-capital-assets ratio. Use year-end figures, not averages, in your ratio calculations.

II ASSET RECOGNITION AND MEASUREMENT

7 Revenue and Expense Recognition

LEARNING OBJECTIVES

After you have studied this chapter, you will be able to:

1   Explain the theory and conceptual framework underlying revenue recognition practices.

2   Explain the revenue and matching principles as they apply to revenue and expense recognition.

3   Apply acceptable methods of accounting for revenue from long-term contracts and identify the circumstances where each is appropriate.

4   Use the instalment method and the cost recovery method of revenue recognition, and identify the circumstances where each is appropriate.

5   Properly account for revenue when the right of return exists.

6   Apply the four different methods of revenue recognition for service sales: (*a*) specific performance, (*b*) proportional performance, (*c*) completed performance, and (*d*) collection.

7   Apply the theory and conceptual framework linking expense recognition to revenue recognition.

INTRODUCTION

In December 1992, Bombardier Inc. announced that it had received an order for 216 advanced-technology subway cars, together with four options totalling 286 additional cars, for the Toronto Transit Commission system (TTC).[1] The company would not begin to deliver the cars until well into 1993 and 1994.

Consider the accounting ramifications attached to this contractual commitment between Bombardier and the TTC. Will Bombardier recognize any revenue from this order before the first car is delivered? Your prior accounting knowledge should lead you to answer no, which is indeed the case. Did Bombardier incur significant costs essential to obtaining this order? The answer is a most assured yes. The advanced-technology subway car design and development effort took several years and incurred costs of millions of dollars before a single car was ordered.

---

[1] Bombardier Inc., *Annual Report*, year ended January 31, 1993.

In the Bombardier example, enormous effort was made to develop a competitive vehicle, a firm order for the cars was placed, and the securities market made known its opinion that Bombardier was better off. However, Bombardier's accounting system will not record one cent of revenue from this transaction until the first car is delivered. Bombardier has *economic income* when the order is received, but not *accounting income*.[2] To comprehend this treatment of accounting income, it is first necessary to understand the principles of revenue and expense recognition.

The measurement and reporting of income is one of the most important and difficult issues in financial accounting. The timing of revenue recognition is complex, given today's innovative marketing and selling methods. Some other examples demonstrate the issues.

In a recent year, a mining company produced 12,000 ounces of gold at a production cost of $1.2 million. Administrative costs for the year were $0.5 million. Even though the gold could have been sold immediately at a market price of $400 per ounce, management elected not to sell, expecting the price of gold to increase in the future. What will the company show as revenue for the period? What will it report as income? Is the company better or worse off at the end of the year, compared with the beginning of the year?[3]

Book sales provide another example of revenue recognition problems. College textbooks, for example, are typically ordered and shipped about eight weeks before the beginning of a new term, with orders based on anticipated enrolment. Upon receipt of an order, the publisher ships books in time for stocking before the term begins. The accompanying invoice calls for payment in 30 days, and the bookstore pays the invoice amount in full. Several weeks into the term, a number of copies of the text remain unsold. Most publishers provide retailers with the right to return unsold, damage-free books 60 days or more from the original shipping date.[4] At what point during this sequence of events should the publisher record revenue and related expenses on its sales?

Thousand Trails, Inc., develops campgrounds and sells usage rights to campers for a membership fee of several thousand dollars. Membership allows the use of existing campgrounds and campgrounds planned for future development. One of the attractions of membership is the promise of the interesting campgrounds that the company claims will be developed in the future, although it has limited, if any, legal obligation to develop any. Membership fees can be paid in full when the contractual arrangement is signed, but the most typical arrangement is for the member to pay a small percentage down and the balance in periodic instalments over a period of up to seven years. Again, the question is when revenue and related expenses should be recognized.[5]

These examples demonstrate how even minor departures from ordinary sales transactions can complicate revenue and expense recognition. This chapter first covers the conceptual guidelines for determining when revenue and expense should be recognized and then covers several specific accounting applications that have been developed for use in resolving various types of revenue recognition problems.

---

[2] The conclusion that Bombardier Inc. has economic income is arrived at indirectly by observing the increase in shareholder wealth. The owners of the company, the shareholders, see increases in the value of the shares they own; thus, it is reasonable to conclude that the value of the net assets of the company has increased.

[3] This example is, in fact, a simplification of the situation faced by the Alaska Gold Company, a placer gold–dredging company. Alaska Gold mined gold for three straight years without selling any of its production. In its annual report to shareholders, Alaska Gold reported zero revenues from gold operations for these periods and thus reported sizable losses each year because of period expenses. This is one of many interesting cases in G. Pfeiffer and R. Bowen, *Financial Accounting: A Casebook* (Englewood Cliffs, NJ: Prentice Hall, 1985), pp. 24–29.

[4] The CICA has attempted to resolve this particular problem in handbook Section 3400, paragraph .18.

[5] Thousand Trails, Inc., is another case found in Pfeiffer and Bowen, *Financial Accounting*.

THE CONCEPTS OF REVENUE AND EXPENSE

To understand the conceptual issues involved in income measurement, it is necessary first to consider the nature of revenues and expenses as defined in Section 1000 of the *CICA Handbook:*

> **Revenues** are increases in economic resources, either by way of inflows or enhancements of assets or reductions of liabilities, resulting from the ordinary activities of an entity, normally from the sale of goods, the rendering of services or the use by others of entity resources yielding rent, interest, royalties, or dividends.

> **Expenses** are decreases in economic resources, either by way of outflows or reductions of assets or incurrences of liabilities, resulting from the ordinary revenue-earning activities of an entity.

> **Gains** are increases in equity from peripheral or incidental transactions and events affecting an entity and from all other transactions, events and circumstances affecting the entity except those that result from revenues or equity contributions.

> **Losses** are decreases in equity from peripheral or incidental transactions and events affecting an entity and from all other transactions, events and circumstances affecting the entity except those that result from expenses or distributions of equity.

The definitions contain the terms *assets* and *liabilities*. That is, revenues and expenses are concepts derived from assets and liabilities. Therefore, clear knowledge of assets and liabilities is needed in order to understand revenues and expenses.

> **Assets** are economic resources controlled by an entity as a result of past transactions or events from which future economic benefits may be obtained.

> **Liabilities** are obligations of an entity arising from past transactions or events, the settlement of which may result in the transfer or use of assets, provision of services or other yielding of economic benefits in the future.

Although our attention in this chapter is focussed on recognition and measurement of revenues and expenses, these issues are not separable from the questions of asset and liability recognition and measurement.

THE EARNINGS PROCESS

At a conceptual level, a firm earns revenue as it engages in activities that increase the utility or value of an item or service. For example, an automobile parts manufacturer increases the utility (value) of sheet metal when it undertakes activities to cut, shape, and weld the sheet metal into automobile fenders. Transporting completed fenders to a regional wholesale warehouse increases utility because it makes the fenders readily available for purchase and use by automobile repair shops. The earnings process is fully completed when the fenders are sold and delivered to a customer for an agreed sales price. All of these activities, and many more, are part of the earnings process.

Exhibit 7–1 graphically illustrates the concept of the earnings process in a highly simplified setting. It focusses on the process of earning revenue; costs are not included on the graph. A firm undertakes many different activities, over the five periods shown, for the purpose of earning a profit. The top graph depicts the cumulative amount of revenue the firm has earned over time. For ease of illustration, the graph assumes a constant rate of increase in utility over time and thus a constant rate of revenue earned as the different activities are performed. The graph also assumes that we know what the total amount of revenue will be when the earnings process is complete. Usually, there is considerable uncertainty at the earlier stages of the earnings process (for example, during the design of a new product) as to whether a revenue is really being earned (that is, whether the new product will sell) and in what amount. It is only when there is a sale at an agreed price and delivery of the product to a customer that this uncertainty is removed.

The bottom graph in Exhibit 7–1 shows the amount of revenue that could *conceptually* be recognized in each accounting period as activities in the earnings process are completed. Because we assume that a constant rate of revenue is earned at each stage in the earnings process, the amount of revenue is the same for each period. The

EXHIBIT 7–1
Conceptual Representation of
the Earnings Process

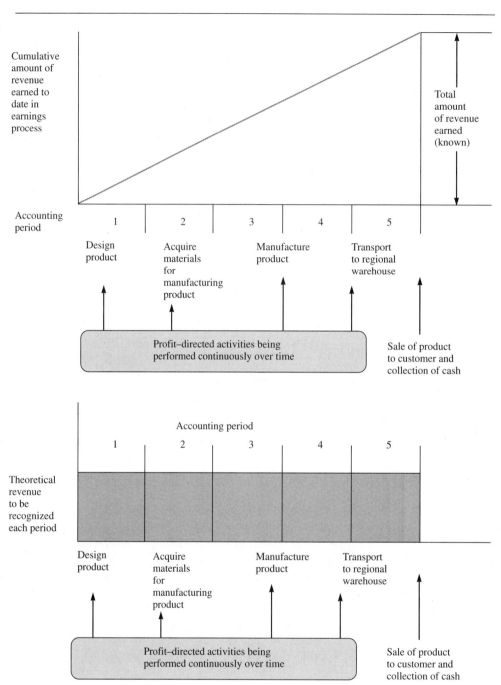

shaded area in the bottom graph equals the total amount of revenue earned over the completed earnings process, which is represented in the top graph by the height of the cumulative revenue earned at the end of the fifth period.

The earnings process for most companies involves incurring costs to increase the utility of an in-process product. Sometimes the process is very long. The design and development process for a new subway car can take 5 to 10 years from initial design efforts to the delivery of the first car to a customer. Conceptually, revenue is being earned as each of the many activities is completed, assuming that the activity brings the company closer to having a salable product.

Companies are required to provide periodic reports on earnings even when the earnings process extends over several accounting periods. In these situations, the question of how much revenue (and expense) to recognize and report in each period must be resolved. Because earnings processes are not often as simple as that depicted in the top graph in Exhibit 7–1 and because of uncertainty about the total amount of revenue that will be earned, determining the amount of revenue to recognize each period is a difficult and important accounting problem. Guidelines have been established to assist in this determination.

THE RECOGNITION PROCESS

Section 1000 of the *CICA Handbook* defines *recognition* as the process of including an item in the financial statements of an entity. Recognition consists of the addition of the amount involved into the statement totals together with a narrative description of the item in a statement.

The recognition criteria an item must satisfy are as follows:

a. The item has an appropriate basis of measurement and a reasonable estimate can be made of the amount involved.

b. For items involving obtaining or giving up future economic benefits, it is probable that such benefits will be obtained or given up. (paragraph 1000.44)

Thus, revenues are normally recognized when performance is achieved and reasonable assurance exists with respect to measurement and collectibility of the consideration. Gains are recognized when realized. Expenses and losses are normally recognized when an expenditure or a previously recognized asset does not retain any future economic benefit. When revenues and expenses are linked together in a cause-and-effect relationship, the expense is matched with the revenue and included in income in the same accounting period. In other situations, expenses may not be linked with revenues but be related to a period on the basis of transactions or events taking place in that period or by allocation. The cost of assets that benefit more than one period is allocated over the periods benefited.

Relevance and reliability are two primary qualitative characteristics of accounting information. Further guidance on the importance of these two criteria follows:

To be relevant information must have feedback value or predictive value (or both) for users, and must be *timely*. It must have the capability for making a difference in the decision-making process of investors, creditors, and others who use and rely on a company's financial statements for relevant, reliable information. The relevance of a particular piece of information cannot be determined in isolation. Rather, relevance should be evaluated in the context of the principal objective of financial reporting, which is to provide information that is useful in making informed investment, credit, and other related decisions.

To be reliable, information about an item or event must be representationally faithful, verifiable, and neutral. Reliability may affect the *timing of recognition*. For example, the first available information about a business transaction or event that could result in recording an asset or a liability (or change to an existing asset or liability) is sometimes too uncertain (too speculative) to be recognized. Based on the financial effects of a given business transaction or event, it may be too early to properly classify the matter and report it as one of the financial statement elements. The financial outcome of the matter in question may not be easily measured for accounting purposes, at least not yet. Or it may be cost-prohibitive to investigate such matters to the extent needed to resolve the uncertainties that surround them. Indeed, situations may develop where a piece of accounting information is never recognized, simply because it cannot be categorized, or cannot be made measurable without incurring inordinate costs.

On the other hand, while the unavailability or unreliability of information may delay recognition of an item or event, waiting too long for more complete information to develop—or for the cost involved in gathering more complete information to justify itself—may result in the information losing its relevance. At some intermediate point, uncertainty may be reduced at a justifiable cost to a level tolerable in view of the perceived relevance of the information. If other criteria are met, this is the appropriate time for recognition. In short, *recognition may sometimes involve a trade-off between relevance and reliability.*[6] [Emphasis added.]

The preceding interpretation points out the difficulty of establishing a point in time for recognition of revenue, especially in more complex situations. For example, Bombardier investors and others at the time of the TTC order immediately wanted to know what the income effects would be for Bombardier. But the vehicle in question was new, and production costs were uncertain at that point. Any information immediately released on estimated expenses associated with the order would have had relevance but would have been of questionable reliability. In general, relevance indicates early recognition, while reliability suggests later recognition.

The four recognition criteria—definition, measurability, relevance, and reliability—apply to all items to be recognized in the financial statements. Since information about earnings and its components are primary measures of a company's financial performance, the *CICA Handbook* goes on to provide further guidance for recognizing the components of earnings. This additional guidance is intended in part to provide more stringent requirements for recognizing components of earnings than is required for recognizing other changes in assets or liabilities.

THE REVENUE PRINCIPLE

In addition to the general recognition criteria discussed above, the revenue principle provides that revenue should be recognized in the financial statements when two additional specific criteria are met. That is:

1. It is earned, and
2. It is realized or realizable.

Revenues are *earned* when the company has substantially accomplished all that it must do to be entitled to receive the associated benefits of the revenue. In general, revenue is recognizable when the earnings process is completed or virtually completed. However, revenue can be recognized even though the earnings process is not completed as long as the costs required to complete the earnings process can be reliably estimated.

Revenue is *realized* when cash is received for the goods or services sold. Revenue is considered *realizable* when claims to cash (for example, non-cash assets such as accounts or notes receivable) are received that are determined to be readily convertible into known amounts of cash. This criterion is also met if the product is a commodity such as gold or wheat for which there is a public market in which essentially unlimited amounts of the product can be bought or sold at the known market price.

Revenues are recognized as soon as these two criteria are met. The accounting issue is to determine when these criteria are met for different types of revenue-generating transactions.

As a general rule, revenue recognized early in the earnings process is viewed as highly relevant information. On the other hand, when the recording of revenue is delayed, it is often because there are concerns about the reliability of the revenue information at the earlier stages of the earnings process. In this situation, reliability is increased by delaying the recognition, but the revenue information may have less relevance. Thus, whether to recognize revenue early or late is often linked to whether its relevance or reliability is more important.

The delivery of goods or services to a customer is a significant event that occurs in

---

[6] FASB, *SFAC No. 5,* "Recognition and Measurement in Financial Statements of Business Enterprises" (Norwalk, Conn., 1984), par. 73–77.

EXHIBIT 7–2   Alternative Methods of Revenue Recognition Relative to Delivery of Product or Service to Customer

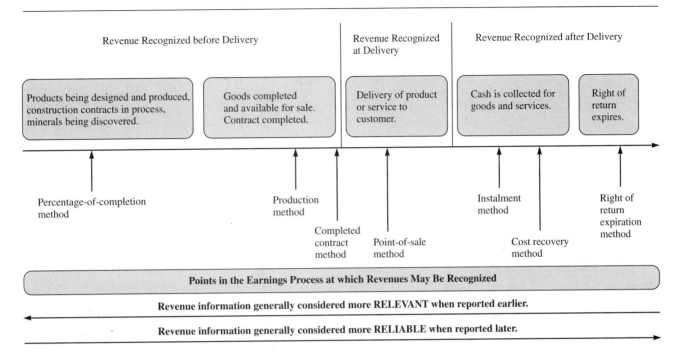

virtually all revenue-generating transactions. Given this, three broad timing categories of revenue recognition can be identified:

1. Revenue recognized at the delivery of the product or service (the point of sale).
2. Revenue recognized *after* delivery of the product or service.
3. Revenue recognized *before* delivery of the product or service.

Exhibit 7–2 illustrates several alternative methods of revenue recognition from early to late in the earnings process. Not all possible methods are shown. There are several alternatives for recognizing revenue before the product or service is delivered to the customer and several for recognizing revenue after delivery. Although in some circumstances both are applicable, some general characteristics of the methods for recognizing revenue before delivery distinguish them from those that recognize revenue after delivery.

In general, revenue is recognized before delivery when the earnings process extends over several accounting periods and it is important (i.e., relevant) to provide revenue information before the earnings process is complete. When there is a contract to produce the product for a known amount that will be received when the product is delivered (i.e., it is realizable), revenue can be recognized as it is earned, which may be before the product is delivered to the customer.

Revenue is recognized after delivery generally because there are concerns about the amount of revenue that will be realized. In this case, revenue is often deemed to have been earned, but recognition is delayed until the amount realizable is determined. In these situations, providing reliable revenue information is considered more important than early, potentially more relevant but less reliable, revenue information.

For most companies and for most goods and services, however, revenue is recognized at the time of delivery of the goods or services to the customer. Revenue is then considered both earned and realized or realizable when the product or service is delivered.

CONCEPT REVIEW

1. What fundamental criteria must be met before a transaction or event can be formally recognized in the financial statements?
2. What are the additional requirements of the revenue principle?
3. Discuss the application of the revenue principle to the gold-mining example presented in this chapter. Determine the application of the revenue principle in terms of the two specific criteria.

REVENUE RECOGNIZED AT DELIVERY (POINT OF SALE)

The two conditions for revenue recognition—when the revenue is realized or realizable and when it is earned—are usually met at the time goods or services are delivered. Thus, revenue from the sale of products is usually recognized at the date of sale, meaning the date the product is delivered to the customer. Revenue from services rendered is likewise recognized when the services have been performed. This is the **point-of-sale method,** sometimes called the *sales method* or the *delivery method* of revenue recognition.

Some transactions do not result in a one-time delivery of a product or service but rather in continual delivery. For example, revenue from contractual arrangements allowing others to use company assets (such as revenues from rent, interest, lease payments, and royalties) is *recognized as time passes* or as the asset is used. Revenue is earned with the passage of time and is recognized accordingly.[7]

The costs associated with servicing a product or service sold with a guaranty or warranty may be incurred after delivery. When these costs can be reasonably estimated, revenue is still recognized at the date of sale, with a provision made for future warranty costs. In this case, revenue is considered earned and realizable.

When a company sells a magazine subscription or an airline sells a ticket for future air travel, cash is received before delivery of the product or service. The realizability criterion is met, but the earnings process is not completed until the product is delivered. In this case, cash inflow does not result in a revenue but in an obligation to produce and deliver the product—a liability. This liability is called **deferred revenue** or unearned revenue. The revenue is not recognized until the product or service is delivered.

REVENUE RECOGNIZED AFTER DELIVERY

Under some circumstances, the revenue recognition criteria are not met until some time after delivery of the good or service to the customer. Such is the case when:

1. The substance of the transaction is different from the form, such as in product-financing arrangements.
2. There is a right to return the product.
3. The ultimate collectibility of the sales price is highly uncertain, such as with some long-term instalment sales.

The list is not exhaustive but rather gives examples of failure to meet the revenue recognition criteria until after the point of sale.

Product-Financing Arrangements

Product-financing arrangements include agreements in which a sponsoring company sells a product to another company and in a related transaction agrees to repurchase the product.[8] Motivations for such transactions include the following: (1) the spon-

---

[7] If, however, the contract is a lease and is essentially a noncancellable transfer of all the risks and rights of ownership of the asset, the transaction qualifies as a sale. Such transactions, called *capital leases,* are considered later in Chapter 18.

[8] In another form of this transaction, one firm (the sponsoring firm) arranges for a second firm to purchase the product on its behalf and in a related transaction agrees to repurchase the product from the second firm at a later time. There may well be a legal transfer of title to the second firm, but the economic substance of the transaction is such that all the business risk is borne by the sponsoring firm.

soring firm can share the business risks of the second firm in order to market its own product, and (2) the sponsoring company can finance its inventory without debt or inventory being shown in its financial statements (assuming that the transaction is treated as a sale). In the latter case, the second firm borrows in order to purchase the inventory, using the inventory as collateral, and the proceeds from the borrowing are used to pay for the purchase. This latter case gives rise to a description of the transaction as a **product-financing arrangement.**

In any case, the sponsoring company bears all the business risk even though it does not have legal title to the inventory. In regard to this transaction, the second company is an extension of the sponsoring company. If revenue were to be recognized upon delivery of the goods to the second company, it would be recognized sooner than is appropriate because the realizability criterion is not met.

In these kinds of product-financing agreements, the sponsoring company must record a liability at the time the proceeds are received. It can neither record a sale nor remove the product from its inventory account. Only when the product is sold to an outside party without a related repurchase agreement can the sponsoring company record a sale.[9]

Revenue Recognition When Right of Return Exists

In several industries—for example, book publishing and equipment manufacturing—the sales terms allow customers the right to return goods under certain circumstances and over long periods of time. Thus, when the product is delivered, it is not known what amount will ultimately become realizable.

Concerning the right of return, *CICA Handbook* Section 3400, paragraph .18 states:

> Revenue would not be recognized when an enterprise is subject to significant and unpredictable amounts of goods being returned, for example, when the market for a returnable good is untested. If an enterprise is exposed to significant and predictable amounts of goods being returned, it may be sufficient to provide therefor.

When the uncertainty of realization is deemed high enough, a provision should not be used. Instead, a variation of the point-of-sale method is used. With this variation, sales revenue, costs of goods sold, and, therefore, gross margin are deferred to the period in which the return privilege expires.

Example: Recognition When Right of Return Exists   On September 30, 1995, Brantford Publishing sells 10,000 copies of a new hardcover book to bookstores. Brantford Publishing sells the book for $50 per book, and it requires payment by the bookstores in 30 days, but gives the bookstores the right to return unsold books for a full cash refund until March 31, 1996. Brantford uses a perpetual inventory system and has a fiscal year-end of December 31. Brantford's unit cost of the book is $30. The bookstores pay the $500,000 due, as required, on October 30.

Case 1   Assume that the book's market appeal is unknown and that the number of books that will be returned therefore cannot be estimated. In this case, there is sufficient uncertainty of realization, so no revenue is recorded until the right of return expires. Brantford will record the transfer of the books, recognize accounts receivable, and record **deferred gross margin** associated with the sale. Gross margin, also called gross profit, is defined as sales less the cost of goods sold. The entries Brantford would make in 1995 are as follows:

a. To record the transfer of the books and record deferred gross margin:

Accounts receivable (10,000 books × $50)	500,000	
Inventory (10,000 books × $30)		300,000
Deferred gross margin*		200,000

* The deferred gross margin account may be reported as a contra account to accounts receivable.

---
[9] *CICA Handbook*, Section 3400, paragraph .18.

b. To record the receipt of payment from the bookstores:

Cash	500,000	
Accounts receivable		500,000

No revenue, expense, or profit is reported for 1995 because the criteria for revenue recognition are not met.

Assume that 4,000 books are returned in March 1996, just before the right of return privilege expires, and that Brantford Publishing refunds the appropriate amount for these returns. The entries to record these returned books are as follows:

c. To record return of books to inventory, cash refund to bookstores, and reduction of deferred gross margin:

Inventory (4,000 books × $30)	120,000	
Deferred gross margin.	80,000	
Cash (4,000 books × $50)		200,000

When the right of return expires on March 31, 1996, Brantford records revenue related to the sales transaction:

Cost of goods sold (6,000 books × $30)	180,000	
Deferred gross margin.	120,000	
Sales revenue (6,000 books × $50)		300,000

The effect of these entries is to defer until 1996 the recognition of revenue, expense, and gross margin related to the sale of these books.

Case 2 Suppose all facts are as presented above except that Brantford has experience selling this type of book and estimates that returns will be 20%. In this case, the conditions of Section 3400, paragraph .18 are met and revenue can be recognized at delivery:

To record sales and cost of goods sold in 1995:

Accounts receivable	500,000	
Sales revenue		500,000
Cost of goods sold	300,000	
Inventory		300,000

At December 31, 1995, Brantford must make an adjusting entry to reflect the estimated sale returns, to reduce cost of goods sold, and to defer the gross margin that is related to the estimated sales returns:

Estimated sale returns (0.20 × $500,000)*	100,000	
Cost of goods sold (0.20 × $300,000)		60,000
Deferred gross margin.		40,000
* Estimated sales returns is a contra revenue account.		

If the estimate for returns is exactly correct, 2,000 books will be returned to Brantford in 1996. The entry to record the returns is as follows:

Inventory (2,000 books × $30)	60,000	
Deferred gross margin.	40,000	
Accounts receivable (or cash)		100,000

Case 3 Make the same assumptions as in Case 2, except assume that only 1,500 books are returned before the right of return expires. The entry to record the returns and recognize the additional sales in 1996 is as follows:

Inventory (1,500 books × $30)	45,000	
Cost of goods sold (500 × $30)	15,000	
Deferred gross margin.	40,000	
Accounts receivable (or cash)		75,000
Sales (500 × $50)		25,000

In Case 3, because the rate of returns is lower than expected, sales are recognized in 1996 for the books not returned. This is an example of a change in estimate. A change in estimate is recorded in the period in which it occurs.

There are other situations in which recognition conditions are not met. In order to recognize revenue, the buyer's obligation to pay the seller must not be contingent on the resale of the product. If payment is contingent, this is a **consignment**—a marketing arrangement in which the owner of the product (the consignor) ships the product to another party (the consignee) who acts as a sales agent. The consignee does not purchase the goods but assumes responsibility only for their care and resale. Upon sale, the consignee remits the proceeds (less specified expenses and commission) to the consignor. **Goods on consignment** are part of the inventory of the consignor until sold by the consignee. They are not a sale of the consignor when shipped to the consignee but only when they are sold by the consignee.

Instalment Sales Method of Revenue Recognition

When collection of the sales price is not reasonably assured, revenue recognition is deferred until the uncertainty is resolved. The **instalment sales method** and the cost recovery method are alternatives for deferring the recognition of revenue and income until cash is received.[10]

Many consumer products are sold on an instalment or deferred payment plan, but they are not necessarily accounted for using the instalment sales method. Immediate revenue recognition is possible at the point of sale when the company has a reasonable basis for estimating an allowance for uncollectible accounts. A retail customer instalment sale, which calls for a purchaser to make payments in accordance with a periodic payment plan, does not imply the use of the instalment sales method, which is a method of revenue recognition employed only under special circumstances and for certain limited types of instalment sales.

Revenue under the instalment sales method is recognized when cash is collected rather than at the time of sale. It is used only when the point-of-sale method or other GAAP revenue recognition method is not appropriate. It is a conservative method of revenue recognition that is used only when there is such a high degree of uncertainty about whether the sales price will be collected that an allowance for bad debts cannot be reasonably estimated. For instance, it is used to account for sales of real estate when the down payment is relatively small and ultimate collection of the sales price is not reasonably assured.[11] The instalment sales method has very limited application under GAAP.[12]

Procedure for Deferring Gross Margin Under the instalment sales method, both sales and cost of sales are actually recorded in the period of sale, but recognition of the related gross margin is deferred to the period when cash is collected. Deferring gross margin has the same effect on income as deferring both sales and cost of sales, but only one deferred account is needed. The procedure for calculating the deferred gross margin is as follows:

1. Record sales and cost of sales for instalment sales in the usual way during the year, but keep records of these items separately in order to compute a gross margin rate and to recognize gross margin in the future.
2. Compute the gross margin rate for the instalment sales as gross margin (sales less cost of sales) divided by sales.

---

[10] Use of the instalment sales method for revenue recognition is controversial, in part because it lacks a firm conceptual basis. A full presentation of the controversial issues surrounding instalment sales method is found in R. A. Scott and R. K. Scott, "Installment Accounting: Is It Consistent?" *Journal of Accountancy,* November 1979, pp. 52–58.

[11] "Accounting for Sales of Real Estate," *SFAS No. 66,* par. 35, describes the accounting requirements for real estate sales. Paragraph 47 of *SFAS No. 66* explicitly requires use of the instalment sales method when the sale of real estate does not meet the criteria for application of the point-of-sale method or the percentage-of-completion method (to be described in a later section).

[12] The Accounting Principles Board greatly limited the situations in which the instalment sales method may be used. "Omnibus Opinion," *APB Opinion No. 10,* par. 12, requires use of the point-of-sale method for instalment sales except when "there are exceptional cases where receivables are collectible over an extended period of time and when, because of the terms of the transactions or other conditions, there is no reasonable basis for estimating the degree of collectibility." In the absence of these circumstances, the instalment method is not appropriate.

3. At year-end, apply the gross margin rate to cash collections on the current year's instalment sales to determine realized gross margin on the current year's instalment sales. Gross margin not realized in the current year is deferred to future years when additional cash is collected.

4. For cash collected in the current year on instalment sales made in prior years, apply the gross margin rate for the prior year to the amount of the cash collections to determine the amount of realized gross margin to be recognized on that year's instalment sales.

The instalment sales method requires special recordkeeping. Separate accounts for instalment sales must be maintained, as well as separate accounts for gross margin on instalment sales for each year. The amounts collected on each year's instalment sales must be known so that the appropriate amount of deferred gross margin related to each year's instalment sales can be realized.

Example   Assume that Truro Company has the following transactions for 1994 and 1995 regarding sales and cost of goods sold to be accounted for using the instalment sales method:

	1994		1995	
Instalment sales	$80,000	100%	$120,000	100%
Cost of goods sold	60,000	75%	80,000	67%
Gross margin on instalment sales	$20,000	25%	$ 40,000	33%

	Applicable to 1994 Instalment Sales	Applicable to 1995 Instalment Sales
Cash collections:		
Customer payments in 1994	$10,000	
Customer payments in 1995	40,000	$ 45,000
Customer payments in 1996	30,000	55,000
Customer payments in 1997		20,000
Totals	$80,000	$120,000

The accounting entries to record the above instalment sales and customer collections for 1994 and 1995 are:

1994 Entries   To record $80,000 of instalment sales with a cost of goods sold of $60,000:

Instalment accounts receivable, 1994	80,000	
Instalment sales revenue		80,000
Cost of instalment sales	60,000	
Inventory		60,000

To record the collection of $10,000 on the instalment sale receivable:

Cash	10,000	
Instalment accounts receivable, 1994		10,000

As of December 31, 1994, Truro Company must establish an account for the deferred gross margin on instalment sales for 1994. The amount to be credited to this account initially is $20,000, which is 25% of the instalment sales in 1994 of $80,000. The entry to record the deferred gross margin and to close the instalment sales revenue and the cost of instalment sales accounts for 1994 is as follows:

Instalment sales revenue	80,000	
Cost of instalment sales		60,000
Deferred gross margin on instalment sales, 1994		20,000

Also as of December 31, 1994, Truro Company will record the recognition of gross margin based on the amount of cash collected and the gross margin percentage. With $10,000 collected and a gross margin of 25%, $2,500 of gross margin is recognized:

Deferred gross margin on instalment sales, 1994	2,500	
Realized gross margin on instalment sales		2,500

The realized gross margin on instalment sales account is an income statement account and will be closed to the income summary. The instalment accounts receivable and deferred gross margin accounts are reported on the December 31, 1994, balance sheet as follows:

Instalment accounts receivable.	$70,000
Less: Deferred gross margin	(17,500)
Net instalment accounts receivable	$52,500

1995 Entries Accounting entries for 1995 instalment sales activities and cost of instalment sales are handled similarly:

Instalment accounts receivable, 1995	120,000	
Instalment sales revenue		120,000
Cost of instalment sales	80,000	
Inventory		80,000

The gross margin percentage on 1995 instalment sales is 33% (gross margin of $40,000 divided by instalment sales of $120,000). The entry to record the deferral of gross margin on the instalment sales and close the revenue and cost of sales accounts as of December 31, 1995, is as follows:

Instalment sales revenue	120,000	
Cost of instalment sales		80,000
Deferred gross margin on instalment sales, 1995		40,000

During 1995, there are collections of $40,000 on the 1994 instalment sales and $45,000 on the 1995 instalment sales, which are recorded as follows:

Cash	85,000	
Instalment accounts receivable, 1994		40,000
Instalment accounts receivable, 1995		45,000

At December 31, 1995, Truro Company recognizes gross margin from instalment sales made in 1994 and 1995 for which cash is collected in 1995. The computation of total realized gross margin in 1995 on instalment sales is as follows:

Collections from instalment receivables of 1994.	$40,000	
Gross margin rate for 1994	× .25	
Realized gross margin from 1994 instalment sales		$10,000
Collection from instalment receivables of 1995	$45,000	
Gross margin rate for 1995	× .33	
Realized gross margin from 1995 instalment sales		15,000
Total realized gross margin in 1995		$25,000

The entry to record realized gross margin in 1995 is the following:

Deferred gross margin on instalment sales, 1994	10,000	
Deferred gross margin on instalment sales, 1995	15,000	
Realized gross margin on instalment sales		25,000

Financial statements prepared under the instalment sales method can be presented in several ways. If instalment sales are a small part of a company's total revenue, it may be appropriate to include only the realized gross margin in the income statement as an item following gross margin on sales. Suppose the Truro Company has other sales in 1995 of $500,000 at a cost of $450,000 for which the point-of-sale method is used for revenue recognition. Truro's income statement would include the following:

TRURO COMPANY
Income Statement
For the Year Ended December 31, 1995

Sales.	$500,000
Cost of sales	450,000
Gross margin on sales	50,000
Realized gross margin on instalment sales	25,000
Gross margin on sales and instalment sales	$ 75,000

Truro Company could provide more complete information with a disclosure format such as the following:

TRURO COMPANY
Income Statement
For the Year Ended December 31, 1995

	Instalment Sales	Other Sales	Total Sales
Sales	$120,000	$500,000	$620,000
Cost of sales	80,000	450,000	530,000
Gross margin on sales	40,000	50,000	90,000
Less: Deferred gross margin on instalment sales	(25,000)		(25,000)
Realized gross margin on current year sales	15,000	50,000	65,000
Add: Realized gross margin on instalment sales of prior years	10,000		10,000
Total gross margin realized.	$ 25,000	$ 50,000	$ 75,000

On the Truro Company balance sheet at December 31, 1995, the remaining account balances relating to instalment sales to be disclosed are instalment accounts receivable, $105,000 ($30,000 for 1994 plus $75,000 for 1995), and deferred gross margin on instalment sales, $32,500 ($7,500 arising from 1994 instalment sales and $25,000 from 1995 instalment sales). This information is disclosed as follows:

Instalment receivable	$105,000
Less: Deferred gross margin on instalment sales	32,500
Net instalment receivable	$ 72,500

The deferred gross margin is presented as a contra account to instalment accounts receivable because it is conceptually an asset valuation—that is, a reduction of an asset. Deferred gross margin has frequently been reported as a current liability, which would be appropriate if the deferred gross margin were viewed as unearned revenue. But the earnings process is complete, and the revenue being deferred has been earned; the only issue is whether it will be collected. When collectibility is not assured, recording instalment accounts receivable at the gross amount results in an overstatement of assets. Classifying the deferred gross margin as a contra to this receivable corrects this overstatement. Despite the logic of this approach, many companies continue reporting deferred gross margin on instalment sales as a current liability.

Interest Computations and the Instalment Sales Method   When interest is charged under the instalment method, on the unpaid balance of accounts receivable, the accounting procedure is conceptually the same as that outlined above but a bit more complex.

Example   Alberta Land Company is in the business of selling undeveloped land for future homesites. It sells a parcel of land for $60,000 on December 31, 1994. The buyer makes a $10,000 down payment and signs a note payable for the remaining $50,000, payable in equal annual instalments over 10 years, due December 31 of each year, with interest at 15%. The cost of the property to Alberta Land was $45,000. The collectibility of the payments is uncertain enough that the instalment sales method is deemed appropriate. The entries to record the initial transaction are as follows:

December 31, 1994—to record the instalment sale, including the cash down payment:

Cash	10,000	
Instalment receivable	50,000	
Instalment sales		60,000

To record the cost of the land sold:

Cost of land sold	45,000	
Land inventory		45,000

At December 31, 1994, the gross margin on the sale is deferred, with an appropriate amount realized because of the $10,000 down payment. The gross margin rate is 25%—($60,000 − $45,000) ÷ $60,000—so the amount of gross margin realized on the $10,000 down payment is $2,500:

Instalment sales	60,000	
Cost of land sold		45,000
Deferred gross margin		15,000
Deferred gross margin	2,500	
Realized gross margin		2,500

At December 31, 1994, the net instalment receivable is $50,000 less the deferred gross margin ($12,500), or $37,500. This is the unrecovered cost of the land sold in this transaction.

1995   The amount of the equal annual payments is determined as follows. The present value of the remaining balance ($50,000) is set equal to the 10-period annuity payments at a 15% rate of interest:

$$\$50,000 = \text{Annual payment (PVA, 15\%, 10)}$$
$$= \text{Annual payment (5.01877)}$$

Solving for the annual payment (and rounding to whole dollars) yields $9,963. Each payment consists of two components: interest revenue (earned on the unpaid receivable balance) and principal (payment on the receivable balance). The payment received on the principal balance also has two components: return of cost and realized gross margin. The initial principal amount is the $50,000, the amount that would have been received had this been a cash sale. This is the amount on which interest revenue is computed for the first period. Interest revenue in 1995 is thus $50,000 times 0.15, or $7,500. Interest is deducted from the payment ($9,963) to determine the amount applied to principal, which must be divided into profit and cost in the same way as in the Truro Company example. The specific computations and entries for Alberta Land, assuming that payments are received as expected, are as follows.[13]

1995 Payment Receipt   At December 31, 1995, the first annual payment of $9,963 on the instalment sale receivable is received. Interest on the unpaid instalment receivable balance is $7,500 ($50,000 × .15); thus, payment on the receivable is the difference, $9,963 − $7,500, or $2,463. Of the $2,463 payment on the receivable, 25%, or $616, is the *realized* gross margin from this payment. The entries to record the payment and recognition of gross margin are as follows:

Cash	9,963	
Interest revenue (.15 × $50,000)		7,500
Instalment receivable		2,463
Deferred gross margin (.25 × $2,463)	616	
Realized gross margin		616

The components of the first $9,963 payment can be diagrammed as follows:

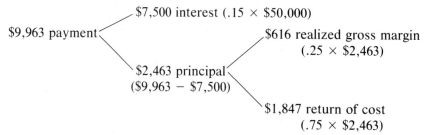

At December 31, 1995, the Alberta Land balance sheet would disclose the following:

Instalment receivable ($50,000 − $2,463)	$47,537
Less: Deferred gross margin ($12,500 − $616)	(11,884)
Net instalment sales accounts receivable	$35,653

The net instalment receivable is the unrecovered cost of the parcel of land sold. This is verified:

Original cost of land sold		$45,000
Cost recovered to date from:		
Initial down payment ($10,000 × .75)	7,500	
First annual payment ($2,463 × .75)	1,847	9,347
Unrecovered cost of land sold, Dec. 31/95		$35,653

1996 Payment Receipt   The entries to be made at December 31, 1996, to record the receipt of the second annual payment are the following:

Cash	9,963	
Interest revenue (.15 × $47,537)		7,131
Instalment receivable		2,832
Deferred gross margin (.25 × $2,832)	708	
Realized gross margin		708

Similar entries are made each year through the year 2004. Exhibit 7–3 is a schedule of the allocation of each payment to interest, principal, and realized gross margin

---

[13] Some advocate recording the gross instalment receivable as the sum of the payments—in this example, 10 times $9,963, or $99,630. A contra account called unearned interest is then established for the amount of interest to be collected in future periods ($49,630 in this example) and is deducted from the gross receivable, leaving an instalment receivable that includes deferred gross margin ($50,000 in this example). When payments are received, they are credited in full to the gross instalment receivable. Separately, interest revenue is credited, and unearned interest is debited, with the appropriate amounts. The effects of this approach are the same as those of the net approach illustrated.

EXHIBIT 7–3

Schedule of Allocation of Annual Payments to Interest Revenue, Instalment Receivable, and Realized Gross Margin for Alberta Land Company

Date	(1) Annual Payment	(2) Interest Revenue (15% of beginning instalment receivable)*	(3) Payment on Instalment Receivable (col. 2 less col. 3)	(4) Realized Gross Margin (25% of col. 4)	(5) Gross Instalment Receivable (beginning balance less col. 4)	(6) Deferred Gross Margin (beginning balance less col. 5)
Dec. 31/94	—	—	—	—	$50,000	$12,500
Dec. 31/95	$ 9,963	$ 7,500	$ 2,463	$ 616	47,537	11,884
Dec. 31/96	9,963	7,131	2,832	708	44,705	11,176
Dec. 31/97	9,963	6,706	3,257	814	41,448	10,362
Dec. 31/98	9,963	6,218	3,745	936	37,703	9,426
Dec. 31/99	9,963	5,656	4,307	1,077	33,396	8,349
Dec. 31/00	9,963	5,010	4,953	1,238	28,443	7,111
Dec. 31/01	9,963	4,267	5,696	1,424	22,747	5,687
Dec. 31/02	9,963	3,412	6,551	1,638	16,196	4,049
Dec. 31/03	9,963	2,430	7,533	1,883	8,663	2,166
Dec. 31/04	9,963	1,300	8,663	2,166	0	0
Totals	$99,630	$49,630	$50,000	$12,500		

* Rounded

Note: Column headers numbered (1) Annual Payment, (2) Interest Revenue, (3) Payment on Instalment Receivable, (4) Realized Gross Margin, (5) Gross Instalment Receivable, (6)... (7) Deferred Gross Margin.

for the 10-year period. The inclusion of interest in the computations delays the recognition of gross profit, with increasing amounts recognized each period. This occurs because earlier payments include a larger component of interest revenue, since more principal is outstanding in the earlier periods.

Repossessions under the Instalment Method   Repossessions are common under the instalment sales method because this method is used only when there is substantial uncertainty of collection. When a repossession is made, it is necessary to ensure that all accounts related to the instalment sale are current as of the date of repossession. A repossession entry records the asset recovered in an inventory account, reduces the related instalment accounts receivable and deferred gross margin to zero balances, and records any gain or loss on repossession. The inventory amount is the estimated net realizable value of the item, which is never more than the current market value of the item in its present condition.

Suppose in the Alberta Land example that the company repossesses the land in January 1997 because no payment was made in December 1996. The repossessed land is assumed to have a net realizable value of $30,000. The net instalment receivable at December 31, 1995, was $35,653 ($47,537 gross instalments receivable less $11,884 deferred gross margin). This represents the unrecovered cost at that date, and therefore the loss on repossession is $35,653 less $30,000, or $5,653. The entry to record the repossession is the following:

```
Land inventory. . . . . . . . . . . . . . . . . . . . . . . . . . . . . . .   30,000
Deferred gross margin (balance as of December 31, 1995) . . . . . . . . . .   11,884
Loss on repossession . . . . . . . . . . . . . . . . . . . . . . . . . . .    5,653
      Instalment receivable (balance as of December 31, 1995) . . . . . . .           47,537
```

The instalment sales method has a significant conceptual flaw. The key reason for using it is that the amount expected to be uncollectible cannot be estimated. Yet the implicit assumption underlying partial recognition of income with each dollar collected is that the *full* amount of the sale will be collected! If anything less than the full amount is collected, the amount recognized as income is overstated. Thus, only if the total sales price is certain to be collected (contradicting the premise for using the instalment sales method) is it appropriate to calculate a profit component equal to the gross margin rate for every dollar collected.[14]

The Cost Recovery Method

The **cost recovery method** is sometimes called the **sunk cost method.** A company must recover all the related costs incurred (the sunk costs) before it recognizes any profit. The cost recovery method is used only for highly speculative transactions when the ultimate realization of revenue or profit is unpredictable. An example is Lockheed Corporation's use of the cost recovery method in the early 1970s when it faced great uncertainty regarding the ultimate profitability of its TriStar Jet Transport program. Lockheed had invested more than $500 million in the initial planning, tooling, and production start-up costs of its wide-body aircraft, the L-1011 TriStar. These costs were to be amortized over the production and sale of the first 300 planes, but considerable uncertainty developed concerning how many airplanes might ultimately be sold—the TriStar program might not generate enough sales to recover the development costs. Note 2 to Lockheed's 1973 annual report reported the company's decision to use the cost recovery method for revenue recognition for its TriStar program:

> All of the development costs and the normal production costs on the TriStar Jet Transport have been included in the inventory except for General and Administrative expenses which are charged to income in the year incurred. G & A expenses amounted to $70 million in 1973 and $81 million in 1972. Since the cumulative development costs to date have been substantial, it is estimated that 300 aircraft will have to be delivered to make the total program profitable. Since 56 aircraft have been delivered to date (all during 1972 and 1973), the Company does not expect a final determination of recoverability of Inventoried Cost can be made until a later date. *Zero gross profit was recorded on the $730 million of sales in 1973 and $302 million in sales in 1972 (for deliveries in those years) and no gross profit will be recorded on deliveries until uncertainties are reduced.* [Emphasis added.]

Lockheed's income statements reported the effects of the cost recovery method for the TriStar program as follows:[15]

(in millions)	1973			1972		
	TriStar	**Other**	**Total**	**TriStar**	**Other**	**Total**
Sales	$730	$2,027	$2,757	$302	$2,171	$2,473
Costs and expenses.	800	1,875	2,675	383	2,021	2,404
Profit (loss)*	$(70)	$ 152	$ 82	$(81)	$ 150	$ 69

* The losses for the TriStar program reflect the general and administrative expenses of $70 million in 1973 and $81 million in 1972 included in cost and expenses.

The cost recovery method is also justified when there is uncertainty regarding the ultimate collectibility of an instalment sale. The *CICA Handbook* Section 3400, paragraph .16 explicitly states that "When there is uncertainty as to ultimate collection, it may be appropriate to recognize revenue only as cash is received."

Example   Suppose Peninsula Land Sales Company sells undeveloped land during 1994, with an original cost of $80,000 for a contract sales price of $140,000. During

---

[14] Many accountants believe the instalment sales method should be discontinued. If collection uncertainty is so great that computation of an allowance for uncollectibles is not appropriate, the best procedure would be to view every dollar collected as recovery of product cost until that total is recovered in full. This procedure is the cost recovery method, which is discussed in the next section.

[15] In 1975, Lockheed reclassified TriStar's initial planning, tooling, and unrecovered production start-up costs as deferred charges and began amortizing them in the amount of approximately $50 million per year. This was done because of "increased uncertainties" regarding the number and timing of future TriStar deliveries. This write-off procedure was a means of spreading the loss over future years. A preferred alternative would have been to write off the entire amount immediately.

1994, collections on these sales total $35,000. In 1995, an additional $55,000 is collected, and it is determined at year-end that an amount totalling $15,000 will be uncollectible. Property with an estimated net realizable value of $4,000 is recovered from the defaulted accounts.

To record land sales in 1994 and defer the gross margin, the following entries would be made:

Land sales instalment receivable	140,000	
Land sales.		140,000
Cost of land sold	80,000	
Inventory of land held for sale		80,000
Land sales.	140,000	
Deferred margin on land sales		60,000
Cost of land sold		80,000

The entry to record $35,000 in collections in 1994 is as follows:

Cash	35,000	
Land sales instalment receivable		35,000

There is no recognition of realized gross margin in 1994, even though $35,000 in cash is collected. Under the cost recovery method, all cash collected from customers is first applied to the recovery of product costs. In Peninsula's case, the cost of the product (land) sold is $80,000. Applying this $35,000 against the $80,000 cost of sales figure leaves $45,000 still to be recovered. The deferred gross margin on land sales (like the deferred gross margin on instalment sales) is treated as a contra account to the land sales instalment receivable account. After the $35,000 collection in 1994, the balance in the land sales instalment receivable account is reduced from $140,000 to $105,000, and thus the net receivable is reduced by $35,000 as well:

Land sales instalment receivable	$105,000
Less: Deferred gross margin on land sales.	60,000
Net land sales instalment receivable	$ 45,000

In 1995, the cash collection of $55,000 is recorded first as a recovery of the remaining $45,000 cost of land sold, with the $10,000 treated as realized gross margin. The entries to record the $55,000 in collections in 1995 and to record the $10,000 as realized gross margin are the following:

Cash	55,000	
Land sales instalment receivable		55,000
Deferred gross margin on land sales	10,000	
Realized gross margin on land sales		10,000

At this point, the cost of the land sold has been fully recovered and all additional cash collections are recorded entirely as realized gross margin.

Next, consider $15,000 of the receivable that has been identified as uncollectible. The recognition of an amount as uncollectible does not by itself affect income. This amount must be removed from both the receivable and the deferred gross margin accounts:

Deferred gross margin on land sales	15,000	
Land sales instalment receivable		15,000

Now assume that land having a net realizable value of $4,000 is recovered. Since the original cost of all land sold has already been recovered in our example, the value of the land recovered is recorded in the land inventory account and (along with any future collection) is treated as an increase in realized gross margin. The entry to record the recovery of the land is as follows:

Land inventory.	4,000	
Realized gross margin on land sales		4,000

Finally, the net balance of the instalment receivable is equal to zero after the entries above:

Land sales instalment account receivable, original balance		$140,000
Less: Cash collections, 1994 . . . . $35,000		
Cash collections, 1995 55,000		
Uncollectible accounts recognized 15,000		105,000
Balance, December 31, 1995		35,000
Deferred gross margin, original amount.	$60,000	
Less: Realized gross margin in 1995 . . . . $10,000		
Uncollectible accounts written off in 1995 15,000	25,000	
Balance, December 31, 1995		35,000
Net land sales instalment account receivable balance, Dec. 31, 1995		$ 0

On the income statement, revenues and cost of sales are reported as in the instalment sales method except that no gross margin is realized until cash collections exceed the cost of sales. Income statement presentation for Peninsula Land Sales would be as follows:

PENINSULA LAND SALES COMPANY
Partial Income Statement

	1994	1995
Land sales.	$140,000	$ 0
Cost of land sold	80,000	0
Gross margin	60,000	0
Less: Deferred gross margin	(60,000)	0
Add: Realized gross margin	0	14,000
Total gross margin	$ 0	$14,000

The cost recovery method is a conservative method of revenue and expense recognition that makes no attempt to match revenue and expense. It is justified only under extreme uncertainty about collection of the receivables or ultimate recovery of capitalized production start-up costs.

| CONCEPT REVIEW

1. What is the key difference between revenue recognition under the instalment sales method and under the cost recovery method?
2. Why is revenue recognition a problem when there are product-financing arrangements?
3. If products are sold with right-of-return privileges, when is revenue to be recognized?

REVENUE RECOGNITION BEFORE DELIVERY

In some instances, the earnings process extends over several accounting periods. Delivery of the final product may occur years after the initiation of the project. Examples are construction of large ships, bridges, office buildings, and development of oil-exploration equipment. Contracts for these projects often provide for progress billings at various points in the construction process.

If the builder (seller) waits until the construction is completed to recognize revenue, the information on revenue and expense included in the financial statements will be reliable, but it may not be relevant for decision making because the information is not timely. It is often worthwhile to trade off reliability in order to provide more timely, relevant earnings information. This is the case for a company engaging in long-term construction contracts.

GAAP allows two methods of accounting for revenue on long-term contracts:

1. **Completed-contract method** Revenues, expenses, and gross profit are recognized only when the contract is completed. As construction costs are incurred, they are accumulated in an inventory account (construction in process). Progress billings are not recorded as revenues but are accumulated in a contra inventory account (billings on construction in process). At the completion of the contract, all the accounts are closed and the gross profit from the construction project is recognized.

2. **Percentage-of-completion method** Revenues, expenses, and gross profit are recognized each accounting period based on an estimate of the percentage of completion of the construction project. Construction costs and gross profit to date are accumulated in the inventory account (construction in process). Progress billings are accumulated in a contra inventory account (billings on construction in process).

The percentage-of-completion method recognizes revenue on a long-term project before the contract is completed so that timely information is provided.

Guidance on the Choice between the Two Methods

Management has little freedom of choice in deciding between these alternative methods of accounting for long-term construction contracts. The *CICA Handbook* states:

> In the case of . . . long-term contracts, performance should be determined using either the percentage of completion method or the completed contract method, whichever relates the revenue to the work accomplished. Such performance should be regarded as having been achieved when reasonable assurance exists regarding the measurement of the consideration that will be derived from . . . performing the long-term contract.[16]

One of the arguments in favour of the percentage-of-completion method is a view that revenue is deemed to be earned over the production period and should be recognized gradually on a basis related to accomplishment. The criteria for determining whether to use the percentage-of-completion method focus on the measurability of revenues and expenses. The critical criteria are whether the seller can estimate (1) the progress toward completion of the contractual obligation and (2) the costs to complete the project. If not, the completed-contract method should be used. The completed-contract method is often used when the contractor is engaged primarily in short-term contracts in situations for which the risks involved in completing the contract are beyond the normal, recurring risks of business. In such cases, the ability of the contractor to complete the contractual obligations may be uncertain. However, the vast majority of construction companies use the percentage-of-completion method.

MEASURING PROGRESS TOWARD COMPLETION

Measuring progress toward completion of a long-term construction project is accomplished with input measures or output measures:

1. **Input measures** The effort devoted to a project to date is compared with the total effort expected to be required in order to complete the project. Examples are costs incurred to date compared with total estimated costs for the project and

---

[16] *CICA Handbook* Section 3400, paragraph .08.

labour hours worked compared with total estimated labour required to complete the project.

2. **Output measures** Results to date are compared with total results when the project is completed. Examples are number of storeys of a building completed compared with total number of storeys to be built and kilometers of highway completed compared with total kilometers to be completed.

The goal is to have a realistic measure of progress made toward completion of the project. Neither input nor output measures are always ideal. Output measures are useful when it is easy to measure the percentage that a project is completed and when the estimated cost to complete each portion of the project is constant. Building a 20-kilometer highway across a flat area where the estimated construction cost is $50,000 for each kilometer would lend itself to use of output measures. The measure of completion would be kilometers completed divided by total kilometers of highway to be constructed.

Output measures can be misleading, however, when the output units require different amounts of effort to complete. For example, suppose the terrain varies greatly where the 20 kilometers of highway are to be constructed, and the estimated construction costs of the first 10 kilometers are $50,000 per kilometer, but the second 10 kilometers involve mountainous terrain and have an estimated cost of $80,000 per kilometer. Using kilometers completed, an output measure to measure progress would lead to the conclusion that the project is 50% completed when the initial 10 kilometers of highway are completed. However, the most difficult and costly construction is yet to be done. In this case, the output measure overstates the percentage of the project that is completed. An input measure comparing cost incurred with total estimated costs to complete the project gives the following percentage complete:

$$\text{Percent complete} = (\$50,000 \times 10 \text{ kilometers}) \div [(\$50,000 \times 10) + (\$80,000 \times 10)]$$
$$= 38.5\%$$

In this case, the input measure (costs incurred) appears to be more accurate than the output measure (kilometers completed).

Input measures are often used when it is difficult to measure progress using output measures but when it is possible to estimate total costs to complete the project. The construction of a large ship, for example, does not easily lend itself to output measures of progress. However, a reasonably accurate estimate of total construction costs for the ship usually can be obtained. Many long-term construction projects tend to have nonhomogeneous parts and therefore lend themselves to use of input measures for progress.

However, input measures can also be misleading when no relatively constant relationship between the input measure and productivity exists. Consider measuring progress on a project using input measures when output measures are available. Suppose a contract calls for a road construction company to build 20 kilometers of highway across a fairly flat area, and the contractor estimates that the construction costs will be $50,000 per kilometer of road built for every part of the project. At the end of the first year of the project, 4 kilometers of highway have been completed at a cost of $250,000. The costs are $50,000 greater than originally estimated because bad weather interrupted the construction schedule and thus more overtime than originally planned was used. This bad weather is not expected to continue for the remainder of the project. What percentage of this project is completed? If we use an output measure, the project is 4 kilometers divided by 20 kilometers, or 20% completed. Using an input measure (cost), the project is 23.8% completed: $250,000 divided by a total estimated cost for the project of $1,050,000 ($50,000 per kilometer times 20 kilometers, plus the extra $50,000 incurred for unexpected overtime). In this case, the project is only 20% completed. The input measure is biased upward because unexpected costs were incurred.

Costs incurred may also be misleading as a measure of progress if costs include one-time, up-front expenditures for quantities of materials and supplies to be used during the construction period. Even though costs have been incurred, progress toward project completion is not made until the materials are actually used. Thus, suppose that paving materials for all 20 kilometers of highway were purchased for $400,000 at the outset of the construction project. Treating all $400,000 as costs incurred on construction leads to the misleading conclusion that the highway project is 40% completed before the first kilometer is constructed. The input measure should include only costs incorporated in the project and not purchases that are expected to be used in the project.

For any given contract, the circumstances must be analyzed carefully to determine which type of measure—input or output—is most useful. Input measures are most frequently used. Among input measures, the **cost-to-cost method** is the most common. The cost-to-cost method measures the percentage completed by the ratio of the costs incurred to date to the current estimate of the total costs required to complete the project:

$$\text{Percent complete} = \frac{\text{Total costs incurred to date}}{\substack{\text{Most recent estimate of} \\ \text{total costs of project}}}$$

The most recent estimate of total project costs is the sum of the total costs incurred to date plus the estimated costs yet to be incurred to complete the project. Once the percentage completed has been computed, the amount of revenue to recognize in the current period is determined as:

$$\substack{\text{Current} \\ \text{period} \\ \text{revenue}} = \left[\substack{\text{Percent} \\ \text{complete}} \times \substack{\text{Total revenue} \\ \text{from contract}} \right] - \substack{\text{Total revenue} \\ \text{recognized in} \\ \text{prior periods}}$$

Illustration of Alternative Methods of Accounting for Long-Term Contracts

There can be dramatic differences between the revenue and income effects of the completed-contract and percentage-of-completion methods. The completed-contract method is the simplest and most straightforward and is discussed first.

Completed-Contract Method   Assume that the Ace Construction Company has contracted to erect a building for $1.5 million, starting construction on February 1, 1994, with a planned completion date of August 1, 1996. Total costs to complete the contract are estimated at $1.35 million, so the estimated gross profit is projected to be $150,000. Progress billings payable within 10 days after billing will be made on a predetermined schedule.

Assume that the following data pertain to the three-year construction period:

ACE CONSTRUCTION COMPANY
Construction Project Fact Sheet
Three-Year Summary Schedule
Contract price: $1,500,000

	1994	1995	1996
1. Estimated total costs for project	$1,350,000	$1,360,000	$1,365,000
2. Costs incurred during current year	350,000	550,000	465,000
3. Cumulative costs incurred to date.	350,000	900,000	1,365,000
4. Estimated costs to complete at year-end.	1,000,000	460,000	0
5. Progress billings during year	300,000	575,000	625,000
6. Cumulative billings to date	300,000	875,000	1,500,000
7. Collections on billings during year	270,000	555,000	675,000
8. Cumulative collections to date	270,000	825,000	1,500,000

Estimated completion costs increased by $10,000 in 1995 and then by another $5,000 in 1996. The total cost to complete the project turns out to be $1,365,000. Contract profit therefore drops from $150,000 to $135,000.

Progress billings are debited to accounts receivable and credited to billings on contracts, which is a contra account to the construction-in-process inventory. If the net of the construction-in-process inventory (inventory less billings on contracts) results in a debit balance, it is reported as a current asset, inventory. This account balance represents the contractor's net ownership interest in the construction project; it is sometimes referred to as the *contractor's draw*. If the net amount in the construction-in-process inventory is a credit balance, it represents the developer's (buyer's) interest in the project and is referred to as the *developer's draw*. A credit balance is reported as a liability in the contractor's financial statements.

The journal entries to record the construction-in-process inventory, progress billings, and collections of progress billings each year for Ace Construction are as follows:

	1994		1995		1996	
Construction-in-process inventory	350,000		550,000		465,000	
Cash, payables, etc.		350,000		550,000		465,000
Accounts receivable	300,000		575,000		625,000	
Billings on contracts		300,000		575,000		625,000
Cash	270,000		555,000		675,000	
Accounts receivable		270,000		555,000		675,000

At the completion of the contract, income is recognized as the difference between the accumulated credit balance in the billings on contracts account and the debit balance in the construction-in-process inventory account, assuming that the total price of the contract has been billed. The accumulated amount of billings on contracts is recognized as sales revenue, and the accumulated amount of construction-in-process inventory on completion of the contract is recognized as cost of goods sold. The journal entries to recognize revenue and expense upon completion of Ace's contract in August 1996 are as follows:

Billings on contracts	1,500,000	
Revenue from long-term contracts		1,500,000
Costs of construction	1,365,000	
Construction-in-process inventory		1,365,000

On balance sheets during the construction period, the construction-in-process inventory is reported as total accumulated costs to date less the total progress billings to date.

Percentage-of-Completion Method   Under the percentage-of-completion method, a portion of revenue and expense (and thus income) is recognized as it is earned in each accounting period. The amount of income that is recognized is added to the construction-in-process inventory. *Total actual* income on the contract will not be known until the project is completed; what is recognized each period is an estimate of income.

The cost-to-cost method is used to determine percentage completed as follows:

	1994	1995	1996
Costs incurred to date	$ 350,000	$ 900,000	$1,365,000
Estimated total costs	1,350,000	1,360,000	1,365,000
Percent completed	25.926%	66.176%	100%

The percent completed is computed as costs incurred to date divided by the estimate of total costs. For example, estimated total costs at the end of 1994 ($1,350,000) equals costs incurred to date ($350,000) plus estimated costs to complete at the end of 1994 ($1,000,000). The next step is to compute the total cumulative amount of revenue recognizable through each year-end by multiplying the total contract revenue by the percentage completed for each year:

	1994	1995	1996
1994 $1.5 million × .25926	$388,890	—	—
1995 $1.5 million × .66176	—	$992,640	—
1996 $1.5 million × 1.0000	—	—	$1,500,000

To determine revenue for each year, revenue recorded in prior years is subtracted from the total revenue recognizable. In 1995, for instance, the revenue to be recognized is the total revenue recognizable of $992,640 less the revenue recognized in 1994 of $388,890, or $603,750.

The gross profit to be recognized is the difference between revenue and costs incurred in the period:

	1994	1995	1996	Total
Revenue for the current period	$388,890	$603,750	$507,360	$1,500,000
Costs incurred in current period	350,000	550,000	465,000	1,365,000
Gross profit for the period	$ 38,890	$ 53,750	$ 42,360	$ 135,000

The journal entries to record the costs incurred on the construction, the progress billings, and the collections of progress billings are the same as those of the completed-contract method. An additional entry is needed to record the recognition of revenue and expense in each period. The gross profit is debited to the construction-in-process inventory:

	1994	1995	1996
Construction-in-process inventory (gross profit for the period)	38,890	53,750	42,360
Costs of construction	350,000	550,000	465,000
Revenue from long-term contracts	388,890	603,750	507,360

The construction-in-process inventory account is greater under the percentage-of-completion method than under the completed-contract method by the amount of gross margin recognized to date. The costs of construction account measures the expense of construction and is an income statement account.

A journal entry is also needed to remove the costs of the contract and the progress billings from the accounts of Ace Construction at the completion of the project:

| Billings on contracts | 1,500,000 | |
| Construction-in-process inventory | | 1,500,000 |

Exhibit 7–4 compares the financial statement presentations for the completed-contract method and the percentage-of-completion method. Under the completed-contract method, inventory is carried at cost. Under the percentage-of-completion method, inventory is carried at cost plus recognized gross profit. The difference between year-end inventory amounts under the two methods is the accumulated gross margin recognized under the percentage-of-completion method. Exhibit 7–4 also shows the dramatic difference in gross profit between the two methods on a year-to-year basis. Total gross profit over the three years is the same for both methods:

ACCOUNTING FOR LOSSES ON LONG-TERM CONTRACTS

When the costs necessary to complete a contract result in losses, two situations are possible:

1. The loss results in an unprofitable contract.
2. The contract remains profitable but there is a current-year loss.

EXHIBIT 7–4   Financial Statement Presentation of Accounting for Long-Term Construction Contracts

Completed-Contract Method

	1994	1995	1996
Balance Sheet			
Current assets:			
Accounts receivable	$ 30,000	$ 50,000	
Inventory:			
Construction in process.	$350,000	$900,000	
Less: Billings on contracts	300,000	875,000	
Construction in process in excess of billings. . . .	$ 50,000	$ 25,000	
Income Statement			
Revenue from long-term contracts	$ 0	$ 0	$1,500,000
Costs of construction.	0	0	1,365,000
Gross profit	$ 0	$ 0	$ 135,000

Note 1. Summary of Significant Accounting Policies

Long-term construction contracts. Revenues and income from long-term construction contracts are recognized under the completed-contract method. Such contracts are generally for a duration in excess of one year. Construction costs and progress billings are accumulated during the periods of construction. Only when the project is completed are revenue, expense, and income recognized on the project.

Percentage-of-Completion Method

	1994	1995	1996
Balance Sheet			
Current assets:			
Accounts receivable	$ 30,000	$ 50,000	
Inventory:			
Construction in process.	$388,890	$992,640	
Less: Billings on contracts	300,000	875,000	
Construction in process in excess of billings. . . .	$ 88,890	$117,640	
Income Statement			
Revenue from long-term contracts	$388,890	$603,750	$ 507,360
Costs of construction.	350,000	550,000	465,000
Gross profit	$ 38,890	$ 53,750	$ 42,360

Note 1. Summary of Significant Accounting Policies

Long-term construction contracts. Revenues and income from long-term construction contracts are recognized under the percentage-of-completion method. Such contracts are generally for a duration in excess of one year. Construction costs and progress billings are accumulated during the periods of construction. The amount of revenue recognized each year is based on the ratio of the costs incurred to the estimated total costs of completion of the construction contract.

Gross Profit Recognized Each Year

Year	Completed-Contract Method	Percentage-of-Completion Method
1994	$ 0	$ 38,890
1995	0	53,750
1996	135,000	42,360
Total	$135,000	$135,000

Loss on an Unprofitable Contract   Suppose that at the end of 1995, Ace's costs incurred are as shown ($350,000 in 1994 and $550,000 in 1995), but the estimate of the costs to complete the contract in 1996 increases to $625,000. Since costs incurred through 1995 total $900,000, the total estimated cost of the contract becomes $1,525,000, and there is now an expected loss on the contract of $25,000.

For both methods, the projected loss is recognized in full in the period in which it is established. For the completed-contract method, the journal entry to record the loss in 1995 is as follows:

```
Loss on construction contracts (an income statement account)  . . . . . . .   25,000
     Construction-in-process inventory . . . . . . . . . . . . . . . . . .              25,000
```

For the percentage-of-completion method, the gross margin of $38,890 recognized in 1994 must be reversed, and the overall loss of $25,000 must be recognized. The sum of these two amounts is a net loss on construction contracts to be recognized in 1995 of $63,890. The amount of revenue recognized in 1995 is computed in the usual way:

```
Percent complete ($900,000 ÷ $1,525,000) . . . . . . . . . . . .   59.016%
Revenue recognizable to Dec. 31/95 ($1,500,000 × .59016). . . . .   $885,240
Less: Revenue recognized in prior periods . . . . . . . . . . . .    388,890
Revenue to be recognized in 1995 . . . . . . . . . . . . . . . .    $496,350
```

The cost of construction in 1995 is computed as follows:

```
Estimated net loss (to be fully recognized in current period) . . . . . . . . . .         $ 25,000
Remaining total project cost ($1,525,000 − $25,000). . . . . . . . . . . .   $1,500,000
Times percent complete at Dec. 31/95. . . . . . . . . . . . . . . . . .        × .59016
Portion of costs to be recognized by Dec. 31/95 . . . . . . . . . . . . .                 885,240
  Total . . . . . . . . . . . . . . . . . . . . . . . . . . . . . . .                      910,240
Less: Cost recognized in prior periods . . . . . . . . . . . . . . . . . .                 350,000
Cost of construction to be recognized in 1995* . . . . . . . . . . . . . . .              $560,240
```

* An easier way to compute the amount of costs of construction for 1995 is to add the amount of the loss to be recognized to the amount of revenue to be recognized:

```
Loss to be recognized in 1995 . . . . . . . . . . . . .   $ 63,890
Revenue to be recognized in 1995 . . . . . . . . . . .     496,350
Costs of construction to be recognized in 1995  . . . . .  $560,240
```

A journal entry is recorded to recognize revenue, costs of construction, and the loss in 1995:

```
Costs of construction . . . . . . . . . . . . . . . . . . . . . . . .   560,240
     Revenue from construction contracts . . . . . . . . . . . . . . . .            496,350
     Construction-in-process inventory . . . . . . . . . . . . . . . . .             63,890
```

Actual costs of construction for 1995 were $550,000, but $560,240 is expensed. The difference of $10,240 is offset in 1996 when actual costs of construction are $625,000 but revenue and costs of construction expensed are $614,760:

Computation of 1996 revenue:

```
Total revenue to be recognized on contract . . . . .         $1,500,000

Amount recognized in prior years:
  1994 revenue . . . . . . . . . . . . . . . . . .   $388,890
  1995 revenue . . . . . . . . . . . . . . . . . .    496,350       885,240
Revenue to be recognized in 1996 . . . . . . . . .               $ 614,760
```

Computation of 1996 costs of construction:

Total costs to be recognized on contract		$1,525,000
Amount recognized in prior years:		
1994 costs of construction	$350,000	
1995 costs of construction	560,240	910,240
Costs of construction to be recognized in 1996		$ 614,760

Because the entire loss was recognized in 1995, the gross margin in 1996 is zero. The construction-in-process inventory account has an ending balance of $1,500,000 before it is closed:

Construction-in-Process Inventory

1994 construction costs	350,000		
1994 gross profit	38,890		
1995 construction costs	550,000	1995 loss recognition	63,890
1996 construction costs	625,000		
Dec. 13/96 balance	1,500,000		

The balance in the construction-in-process account equals the amount of the progress billings. When the contract is completed, a journal entry is made to close the construction-in-process inventory and the progress billings accounts:

Progress billings.	1,500,000	
Construction-in-process inventory.		1,500,000

Current Period Loss on Overall Profitable Contract   Suppose Ace's costs incurred to the end of 1995 are as shown, but the estimate of costs to complete the contract has increased to $550,000. Costs totalling $900,000 have already been incurred; thus, the total estimated cost of completing the construction contract is $1,450,000. The overall contract still generates a gross profit of $50,000.

Under the completed-contract method, no entry is needed in 1995. At completion of the contract, the usual revenue, costs of construction, and gross margin entries are made, but now the gross margin is reduced to $50,000.

The percentage-of-completion method requires an entry to recognize revenue and expense in 1995. The computation of revenue for 1995 is as follows:

Construction costs to Dec. 31/95	$ 900,000
Estimated costs to complete	550,000
Estimated total costs of contract	$1,450,000
Percent complete ($900,000 ÷ $1,450,000)	62.069%
Revenue recognizable as of Dec. 31/95 ($1,500,000 × .62069)	$ 931,035
Revenue recognized in prior periods	388,890
Revenue to be recognized in 1995	542,145
Costs of construction in 1995	550,000
Loss on construction contract in 1995	$ 7,855

The journal entry to record revenue, costs of construction, and loss for 1995 is the following:

Costs of construction	550,000	
Construction-in-process inventory.		7,855
Revenue from construction contracts		542,145

In 1996, Ace Construction recognizes the remaining revenue of $568,965 ($1,500,000 less the $931,035 recognized in prior years) and costs of $550,000, yielding a gross profit of $18,965. The total gross profit over the three years of the contract totals $50,000 ($38,890 in 1994, a loss of $7,855 in 1995, and $18,965 in 1996). This is equal to the total revenue of $1,500,000 less the total costs of construction of $1,450,000 ($350,000 in 1994, $550,000 in 1995, and $550,000 in 1996).

In summary, when a loss on the contract is probable, the construction-in-process inventory is reported at estimated net realizable value under both the completed-contract method and percentage-of-completion method. When the contract is profitable, construction-in-process inventory is reported at cost plus recognized gross profit. Changes in projected profitability of the construction contracts are accounted for prospectively as a change in accounting estimate.

The completed-contract method is both more objective and more conservative than the percentage-of-completion method. Income is recognized only when all costs and revenues are known, and all revenue and income recognition is delayed until all income is earned. Yet many accountants view this method as deficient because income recognition does not reflect income earned during each period of construction. The percentage-of-completion method is supported by these accountants because it recognizes income as it is earned over the life of the contract. Others consider the percentage-of-completion method deficient because income is measured subjectively according to estimates of work done (percentage of completion) and estimated total contract costs. Either estimate can be wrong and result in potentially misleading information. Section 3400 of the *CICA Handbook* allows either method depending on the relationship of revenue to the work accomplished. Thus, it is necessary to apply professional judgment.

| CONCEPT REVIEW

1. Under what conditions may a company use the percentage-of-completion method of accounting for long-term contracts?
2. If a loss is expected on a long-term contract after one or more periods of recording a gross profit, what are the requirements for recording the loss if (*a*) the contract is still profitable overall and (*b*) the loss causes the overall contract to have a net loss?
3. How does the construction-in-process inventory balance differ between the percentage-of-completion method and the completed-contract method?

ALTERNATIVE METHODS OF REVENUE RECOGNITION BEFORE DELIVERY

Three additional methods for recognizing revenue before the delivery of the product are discussed in the accounting literature. They are (1) completion of production, (2) accretion basis, and (3) discovery basis. Each has theoretical merit, but each also poses significant problems in implementation. The completion-of-production method is GAAP in certain circumstances. Neither the accretion basis nor the discovery basis method is currently acceptable under GAAP.

Completion of Production

In certain situations, revenue can reasonably be recognized at the completion of production. The key criterion for using this method is that realizability be assured. That is, the product must be marketable immediately at quoted prices that cannot be influenced by the producer. Units of the production must be interchangeable, and there must be no significant costs involved in product distribution. Examples are some precious metals, agricultural products, and other commodities for which there is a ready market. The completion-of-production method can provide the producer with valuable information on the profit from production activities, with separate recognition of any gains or losses that arise if the product is not sold upon completion of production. Such gains or losses arise because the producer becomes a speculator in the commodity. Separation of the sources of profit (production or speculation) is potentially important for decision making.

Accretion Basis

Accretion is an increase in value resulting from natural causes such as the growth of timberland or the ageing of wines and liquors. As the product's value increases, revenue is being earned, and some accountants believe that it should be recognized. Recognition may be important when the natural process is very long and knowing the change in value is relevant information for decision making. There remain difficulties in determining future prices or value even if current prices are known, and in estimating future costs of activities such as harvesting or otherwise bringing the product to market. Accretion-basis accounting is not currently acceptable, even though from an economic perspective it is logical.

Discovery Basis

The discovery method was suggested in the early 1980s as a means of providing timely, relevant information to users of financial statements of oil- and gas-producing companies. The SEC labelled the proposed method the "reserve recognition method." The logic is that upon discovery of a valuable mineral deposit such as oil and gas, the company has earned revenue. Many would agree that the firm is better off as a result of the discovery and that it would be useful to reflect this information in the financial statements. The argument against such recognition is that there is too much uncertainty regarding costs and future prices to develop accurate measures of revenue and expense at the time of discovery. That is, the revenue and expense amounts are not sufficiently reliable. The discovery basis is not currently an acceptable method for revenue recognition under GAAP.

REVENUE RECOGNITION FOR SERVICE SALES

For companies that provide services rather than products, revenue recognition follows procedures similar to those for tangible goods transactions. The four methods of revenue recognition for service sales are (1) specific performance, (2) proportional performance, (3) completed performance, and (4) collection.

Specific Performance Method

The **specific performance method** is used to account for service revenue that is earned by performing a single act. For example, a real estate broker earns sales commission revenue on completion of a real estate transaction; a dentist earns revenue on completion of a tooth filling; a laundry earns revenue on completion of the cleaning.

Franchise Revenue   *CICA Accounting Guideline,* "Franchise Fee Revenue," July 1984, deals with a particular case of service sales—franchises. The *Guideline* prescribes the specific performance method to account for franchise fee revenue, which the franchisor earns by selling a franchise to the franchisee. For revenue recognition purposes, it is often difficult to determine the point at which the franchisor has "substantially performed" the service required to earn franchise fee revenue. In this regard, the *Guideline* (par. 5) states:

> Revenue from initial franchise fees relating to the sale of an individual franchise or an area franchise would ordinarily be recognized, with an appropriate provision for estimated uncollectable amounts, when all material conditions relating to the sale have been substantially performed by the franchisor. Substantial performance is considered to have occurred when:
>
> a. The franchisor has performed substantially all of the initial services required by the franchise agreement or volunteered by the franchisor as a result of normal business practice.
> b. The franchisor has no remaining obligation or intent—by agreement, industry practice or legislation—to refund amounts received or forgive unpaid amounts owing.
> c. There are no other material unfulfilled conditions affecting completion of the sale.
>
> In practice, these conditions will not normally be met before the franchisee commences operations.

Example Assume that on April 1, 1994, Regina Pizza Corporation (franchisor) sold a franchise to Arthur Wilson (franchisee) for $20,000 cash, and a note that required five annual payments of $8,739 beginning on March 31, 1995. The interest rate is 14%, and the note therefore has a present value of $30,000 [(PVA, 14%, 5) × $8,739 = 3.43308 × $8,739].

Case A If no additional services are to be performed by the franchisor and collectibility is reasonably assured, Regina Pizza should recognize the entire amount (the $20,000 cash payment and $30,000 note receivable) as revenue on April 1, as follows:

Cash	20,000	
Note receivable	30,000	
Franchise fee revenue		50,000

Case B If Regina Pizza has additional services to perform for the franchisee, such as outfitting the new pizza restaurant, no franchise fee revenue would be recognized on April 1, 1994. Rather, the entry would be as follows:

Cash	20,000	
Note receivable	30,000	
Deferred franchise fee revenue		50,000

The deferred franchise fee revenue account will appear as a liability on Regina Pizza's 1994 balance sheet. Although the franchisee has made cash payment and has executed a note that obligates payments in the future, this is not earned revenue because Regina Pizza still has significant obligations it must complete.

On December 31, 1994, Regina Pizza would make the following entry to accrue interest on the note receivable:

Interest receivable	3,150	
Interest revenue ($30,000 × .14 × 9/12)		3,150

Assume that Regina Pizza completes its obligations to the franchisee in January 1995, after having spent $2,000 in the process. The entry to record this expenditure and recognize revenue would be as follows:

Deferred franchise fee revenue	50,000	
Franchise service expense	2,000	
Franchise fee revenue		50,000
Prepaid expense, franchise services		2,000

Expenditures in 1994 by the franchisor related to the franchise would be deferred as prepaid expenses until the associated franchise fee revenue is recognized, in conformity with the matching principle.

Proportional Performance Method

The **proportional performance method** is used to recognize service revenue that is earned by more than a single act and only when the service extends beyond one accounting period. Under this method, revenue is recognized based on the proportional performance of each act. The proportional performance method of accounting for service revenue is similar to the percentage-of-completion method. Proportional measurement takes different forms depending on the type of service transaction.

1. **Similar performance acts** An equal amount of service revenue is recognized for each such act (for example, processing of monthly mortgage payments by a mortgage banker).
2. **Dissimilar performance acts** Service revenue is recognized in proportion to the seller's direct costs to perform each act (for example, providing lessons, examinations, and grading by a correspondence school).[17]

---

[17] If the direct cost of each act cannot be measured reliably, the total service sales revenue should be prorated to the various acts by the relative sales value method. If sales values cannot be identified with each act, the straight-line method to measure proportional performance should be used.

3. **Similar acts with a fixed period for performance** Service revenue is recognized by the straight-line method over the fixed period unless another method is more appropriate (for example, providing maintenance services on equipment for a fixed periodic fee).

Completed-Performance Method

The **completed-performance method** is used to recognize service revenue earned by performing a series of acts of which the last is so important in relation to the total service transaction that service revenue is considered earned only after the final act occurs. For example, a trucking company earns service revenue only after delivery of freight, even though packing, loading, and transporting preceded delivery. The method is similar to the completed-contract method, used for long-term contracts.

Collection Method

The **collection method** is used to account for service revenue when the uncertainty of collection is so high or the estimates of expenses related to the revenues are so unreliable that the requirement of reliability is not satisfied. Revenue is recognized only when cash is collected. This method is similar to the cost recovery method, used for product sales.

EXPENSE RECOGNITION

CICA Handbook Section 1000, paragraph .33, "Financial Statement Concepts," defines expenses as follows:

> Expenses are decreases in economic resources, either by way of outflows or reductions of assets or incurrences of liabilities, resulting from the ordinary revenue-earning activities of an enterprise.

After the revenue of the accounting period is measured and recognized in conformity with the revenue principle, the matching principle is applied to measure and recognize the expenses of that period.

Both the revenue principle and the matching principle are often categorized as "implementation principles." Some people believe that these two principles do not appear to be as fundamental to income measurement as the definitions of financial statement elements. This was not always the case. For years, accounting theory has treated matching as a fundamental cornerstone of income measurement. As such, it sometimes led to the recording of an expense even though no asset was used up nor liability created. The amount debited to expense was credited to an account called deferred credits. Deferred credits were often not liabilities, at least not in conformity with the definition of liabilities as found in Section 1000. However, Section 1000, paragraph .26 does not preclude the existence of other items, so that "a balance sheet may include, as a category of assets or liabilities, items that result from a delay in the recognition of revenue, expense, gains and losses." These items are typically called deferred credits or deferred debits.

Matching: An Implementation Principle

The matching principle requires that once revenues are determined in conformity with the revenue principle for any reporting period, the expenses incurred in generating the revenue should be recognized in that period. The essence of the matching principle is that as revenues are earned, certain assets are consumed (such as supplies) or sold (such as inventory), and services are used (such as employee effort). The costs of those assets and services used up should be recognized and reported as expenses of the period during which the related revenue is recognized.

Expenses can be classified in three categories:

1. **Direct expenses** are expenses such as cost of goods sold that are associated directly with revenues. These expenses are recognized based on recognition of revenues that result directly and jointly from the same transactions or other events as the expenses.

2. **Period expenses** are expenses such as selling and administrative salaries which are not associated directly with revenues. These expenses are recognized during

the period in which cash is spent or liabilities are incurred for goods and services that are used up either simultaneously at acquisition or soon after.

3. **Allocated expenses** are expenses such as depreciation and insurance. These expenses are allocated by systematic and rational procedures to the periods during which the related assets are expected to provide benefits.

Direct Expenses

Expenses Directly Related to Sales of Products   Expenses directly related to the sales of products during the period usually include:

- Costs of materials and labour for manufacture, or the cost to purchase inventory that is sold during the period (i.e., cost of goods sold).
- Selling expenses such as sales commissions, salaries, rent, and shipping costs.
- Warranty expense on products sold.

Under the matching principle, these costs should be recognized as expenses during the reporting period in which the related sales revenue is recognized. Some expenses have less clear relationships to sales revenue. For example, advertising and research and development (R&D) expenditures are made to enhance the marketability of a company's products, but it is difficult to establish a direct causal link between them and specific revenues. Allocation of such costs is subjective, so GAAP requires that such costs be expensed as incurred.

Expenses Directly Related to Sales of Services   Expenses directly related to the sales of services can be classified as follows:

- **Initial direct costs**   These are directly associated with negotiating and consummating service transactions. They include commissions, legal fees, salespersons' compensation other than commissions, and nonsales employees' compensation that is applicable to negotiating and consummating service transactions.
- **Other direct costs**   These have an identifiable causal effect on service sales. Examples include the cost of repair parts and service labour included as part of a service contract.

All initial direct costs and other direct costs should be recognized as expenses during the period in which the related service revenue is recognized under the *specific performance* and *completed-performance methods* for an appropriate matching of revenues and expenses. Similarly, initial direct costs and other direct costs that are incurred prior to the recognition of revenue from performance of the service should be *deferred* as prepayments and expensed when the related service revenue is recognized.

Under the *proportional performance method*, initial direct costs should be expensed as the related service revenue is recognized. However, other direct costs should be expensed as incurred because of the high correlation between the amount of other direct costs incurred and the service revenue recognized in this method.

Under the *collection method*, all initial direct costs and other direct costs should be expensed as incurred.

Indirect Expenses

Expenses not directly related to the sales of products or services are *period* expenses and *allocated* expenses. Examples include certain types of advertising expense, compensation for time spent in negotiating transactions that are not consummated, and general administrative expenses, depreciation expense, and amortization expense. With no objective basis for relating period expenses to product or service sales revenue of the period, these costs should be expensed as they are incurred. The same is true for allocated expenses, which are assigned to periods on a systematic and rational basis.

RECOGNITION OF GAINS AND LOSSES

Gains and losses are distinguished from revenues and expenses in that they result from peripheral or incidental transactions, events, or circumstances. Whether an item is a gain or loss or an ordinary revenue or expense depends in part on the reporting company's primary activities or businesses. When a company primarily involved in manufacturing and marketing products, for example, sells some of its land, the transaction is accounted for as a net gain or loss because this is not the primary business of the company. When a real estate sales company sells land, however, the transaction gives rise to revenues and expenses. A gain or loss may also result from purely internal transactions, such as a write-down related to a plant closing. Such gains and losses are also recognized in the period when the transaction occurs.

Most gains and losses are recognized when the transaction is completed. Thus, gains and losses from disposal of operational assets, sale of investments, and early extinguishment of debt are recognized in the entry made to record the transaction. For example, an entry to record the disposal of a tract of land for cash would reflect a debit to cash, a credit to land (for its recorded cost), and a debit to loss (or credit to gain) on disposal.

Estimated losses are recognized before their ultimate realization if they are both likely and can be reasonably estimated (*CICA Handbook* Section 3290, paragraph .12, "Contingencies."). Examples are unrealized losses on write-downs of temporary investments to market value below cost, disposal of a segment of the business, pending litigation, and expropriation of assets. If both conditions are not met, the nature and estimated amount of the contingent loss must be disclosed in a note to the financial statements.

In contrast, gains are not recognized before the completion of a transaction that establishes the existence and amount of the gain.[18] For example, in the case of a likely but as yet unrealized gain on disposal of a segment of the business, *CICA Handbook* Section 3475, paragraph .08 states that if a gain is expected, it "should be recognized only when realized." In some cases, potential gains may be disclosed in notes to the financial statements, provided the notes are written carefully to "avoid misleading implications as to the likelihood of realization" (*CICA Handbook,* Section 3290, paragraph .18).

Accounting for gains and losses reflects a conservative approach. Losses may be recognized before they actually occur, but gains are not recognized before a completed transaction or event. *SFAC No. 5* (par. 81) states:

> In assessing the prospect that as yet uncompleted transactions will be concluded successfully, a degree of skepticism is often warranted. Moreover, as a reaction to uncertainty, more stringent requirements historically have been imposed for recognizing revenues and gains than for recognizing expenses and losses, and those conservative reactions influence the guidance for applying the recognition criteria to components of earnings.

---

[18] Contingencies that might result in gains are not usually reflected in the accounts since to do so might be to recognize revenue prior to its realization.

Companies can generally control the timing of transactions or events that give rise to gains or losses (e.g., disposal of investment securities or of an unprofitable division of the business, early extinguishment of debt, or a change in accounting principle), providing considerable discretion as to the net income they report in a given period. This explains in part why GAAP contains relatively strict disclosure requirements for such gains and losses.

ETHICAL CONSIDERATIONS

Revenue recognition is an area where firms anxious to show growing sales and profits have followed a number of questionable and even improper accounting procedures. A relatively innocent-looking example occurs when a firm ships and records as a sale goods that have been ordered for a later delivery. Suppose a firm receives an order in December for goods that the customer desires to receive in mid-January. By accelerating the shipment of the goods to December, the selling firm records a revenue in the current fiscal year (assume a December 31 fiscal year-end), thereby increasing sales and profits in that period. The ethical nature of this transaction is at best questionable; many would view such reporting as improper.

Even more questionable would be a transaction in which goods are shipped (and recorded as a revenue) to a customer who regularly purchases such goods in approximately the amounts shipped, but who has not yet ordered the goods! There have also been cases where the invoices for goods shipped after the fiscal year-end are backdated to the current fiscal year in order to record them as sales in that period. The February 23, 1993, issue of *The Wall Street Journal* suggests this might have been the case at Leslie Fay Company. The article also raises the issue of whether Leslie Fay engaged in another questionable practice in its attempt to achieve its sales and profit goals:

> But by early spring, several large retailers sensed growing anxiety at Leslie Fay. They said [the Chief Executive Officer of Leslie Fay] had, at that point, been calling them to take more of his company's merchandise and offering to pay "markdown money"—compensation that manufacturers give stores, in cash or discounts on future orders, to guarantee profit margins if they have to mark down goods that aren't moving.

There is nothing improper with offering customers markdown money, but the amount should be estimated and recorded as a contra revenue in the period in which the goods with the markdown provision are shipped to the customers. If the seller does not record such an "allowance for markdowns," revenues and profits for the current period are overstated.

Finally, the choice of method used to record revenues is an area where ethical questions are sometimes raised. Thousand Trails, the company mentioned in the introduction to this chapter, used the point-of-sale method to recognize revenue on its membership rights transactions. Because most of these transactions were instalment sales and the default rate was high and, some would argue, very difficult to estimate with reasonable accuracy, it has been suggested that the instalment sales method would have been a more appropriate choice for revenue recognition. The company and its auditor maintained, however, that the point-of-sale method was appropriate because they felt they could estimate the future default amounts on the instalment receivables with reasonable accuracy. By using the point-of-sale method, Thousand Trails reported rapid growth in sales and profits even though the company had received only a very small portion of the reported revenue in cash. Again, this is appropriate so long as the receivables do eventually convert into estimated amounts of cash. The fact that the company eventually got into severe financial difficulty in part because of an unexpectedly large number of defaults on the receivables reinforced concerns about whether the point-of-sale method was appropriate in the first place.

Choice of method and implementation of accounting procedures for revenue recognition must be done with a careful consideration of what is ethical and appropriate for the circumstances.

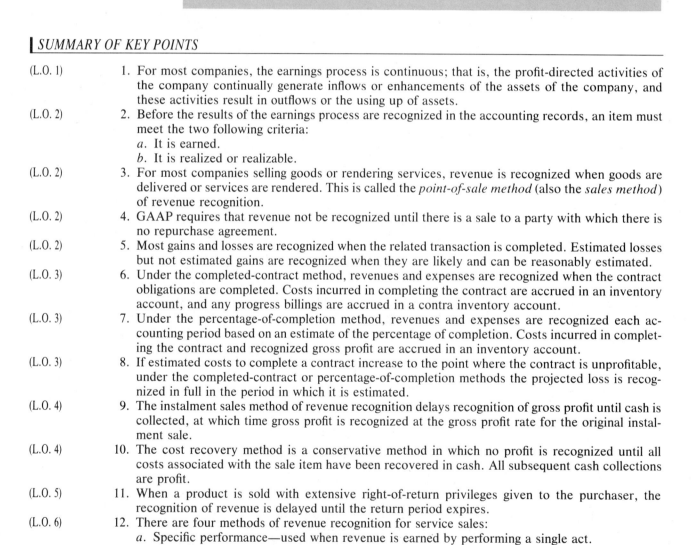

CONCEPT REVIEW

1. What distinguishing characteristics influence the choice of specific performance, proportional performance, or the completed-performance method of revenue recognition for service sales?
2. What are direct expenses? Period expenses? Allocated expenses? How are these different expenses accounted for under the different methods of revenue recognition for service sales?
3. Chartered Bank decides to close several branches, and it estimates that it will lose $1 million on the closings. The branches will be physically shut down next year. When will the bank recognize the loss on the closings?

SUMMARY OF KEY POINTS

(L.O. 1) 1. For most companies, the earnings process is continuous; that is, the profit-directed activities of the company continually generate inflows or enhancements of the assets of the company, and these activities result in outflows or the using up of assets.

(L.O. 2) 2. Before the results of the earnings process are recognized in the accounting records, an item must meet the two following criteria:
   a. It is earned.
   b. It is realized or realizable.

(L.O. 2) 3. For most companies selling goods or rendering services, revenue is recognized when goods are delivered or services are rendered. This is called the *point-of-sale method* (also the *sales method*) of revenue recognition.

(L.O. 2) 4. GAAP requires that revenue not be recognized until there is a sale to a party with which there is no repurchase agreement.

(L.O. 2) 5. Most gains and losses are recognized when the related transaction is completed. Estimated losses but not estimated gains are recognized when they are likely and can be reasonably estimated.

(L.O. 3) 6. Under the completed-contract method, revenues and expenses are recognized when the contract obligations are completed. Costs incurred in completing the contract are accrued in an inventory account, and any progress billings are accrued in a contra inventory account.

(L.O. 3) 7. Under the percentage-of-completion method, revenues and expenses are recognized each accounting period based on an estimate of the percentage of completion. Costs incurred in completing the contract and recognized gross profit are accrued in an inventory account.

(L.O. 3) 8. If estimated costs to complete a contract increase to the point where the contract is unprofitable, under the completed-contract or percentage-of-completion methods the projected loss is recognized in full in the period in which it is estimated.

(L.O. 4) 9. The instalment sales method of revenue recognition delays recognition of gross profit until cash is collected, at which time gross profit is recognized at the gross profit rate for the original instalment sale.

(L.O. 4) 10. The cost recovery method is a conservative method in which no profit is recognized until all costs associated with the sale item have been recovered in cash. All subsequent cash collections are profit.

(L.O. 5) 11. When a product is sold with extensive right-of-return privileges given to the purchaser, the recognition of revenue is delayed until the return period expires.

(L.O. 6) 12. There are four methods of revenue recognition for service sales:
   a. Specific performance—used when revenue is earned by performing a single act.
   b. Proportional performance—used when revenue is earned by the performance of several acts.
   c. Completed performance—used when the revenue can be considered earned only after the performance of the last act.
   d. The collection method—used when uncertainty is high or estimates of expenses are unreliable.

(L.O. 7) 13. The matching principle provides guidance for expense recognition. The matching principle states that for any reporting period, the expenses recognized in that period are to be those incurred in generating the revenues recognized in that period.

(L.O. 7)

14. Expenses directly related to the sale of products or to the rendering of services are matched with the related sales. Expenses not directly related to the sale of products or to the rendering of services are one of the following:

a. Period expenses, which are expensed in the period in which they are incurred.

b. Allocated expenses, which are expensed by a systematic and rational allocation of costs to the periods during which they are expected to provide benefits.

REVIEW PROBLEM

Precision Punctual Construction Company has agreed to build a 10-storey office building for Mountain Bank Limited. The contract calls for a contract price of $15,000,000 for the building, with progress payments being made by Mountain as the construction proceeds. The period of construction is estimated to be 30 months. The contract is signed on February 1, 1995, and construction begins immediately. The building is completed and turned over to Mountain Bank on December 1, 1997.

Data on costs incurred, estimated costs to complete, progress billings, and progress payments over the period of construction are as follows:

	1995	1996	1997
		(in thousands)	
Costs incurred this period	$ 1,500	$ 7,875	$ 3,825
Costs incurred to date	1,500	9,375	13,200
Estimated costs to complete at year-end	10,500	3,125	0
Estimated total costs of project	12,000	12,500	13,200
Progress billings this period	1,200	6,000	7,800
Progress payments received this period	825	6,300	7,875

1. Show the entries to account for this project over the period of construction, assuming that PPC uses the completed-contract method of recognizing revenue.
2. Show the entries to account for this project over the period of construction, assuming that PPC uses the percentage-of-completion method of recognizing revenue.
3. Show the relevant balance sheet and income statement items for 1995, 1996, and 1997 for PPC, assuming that the company uses:
   a. The completed-contract method of recognizing revenue.
   b. The percentage-of-completion method of recognizing revenue.

SOLUTION

1. and 2. The entries to record the construction of the building for both the completed-contract method and the percentage-of-completion method are as follows (all amounts in thousands):

Entries for 1995:

	Completed-Contract	Percentage-of-Completion
a. To record incurrence of construction costs:		
Construction-in-progress inventory	1,500	1,500
Cash, payables, etc..	1,500	1,500
b. To record progress billings:		
Accounts receivable	1,200	1,200
Billings on contract	1,200	1,200
c. To record billing collections:		
Cash	825	825
Accounts receivable	825	825
d. To record revenue recognition for the percentage-of-completion method:*		
Construction-in-progress inventory	—	375
Cost of earned construction revenue	—	1,500
Revenue from long-term contracts	—	1,875

* The percentage of completion is cost incurred to date divided by total estimated project costs or $1,500 divided by $12,000, or 12.50%. The total amount of revenue recognizable to this point is .1250 × $15,000, or $1,875.

Entries for 1996:

	Completed-Contract		Percentage-of-Completion	
a. To record incurrence of construction costs:				
Construction-in-progress inventory	7,875		7,875	
Cash, payables, etc..		7,875		7,875
b. To record progress billings:				
Accounts receivable.	6,000		6,000	
Billings on contract		6,000		6,000
c. To record billing collections:				
Cash	6,300		6,300	
Accounts receivable.		6,300		6,300
d. To record revenue recognition for the percentage-of-completion method:*				
Construction-in-progress inventory	—		1,500	
Cost of earned construction revenue	—		7,875	
Revenue from long-term contracts		—		9,375

* The percentage of completion is cost incurred to date divided by total estimated project costs, or \$9,375 divided by \$12,500, which equals 75%. The total amount of revenue recognizable to this point is .75 × \$15,000, or \$11,250. Since \$1,875 was recognized in 1995, the amount recognizable in 1996 is \$11,250 − \$1,875, or \$9,375.

Entries for 1997:

	Completed-Contract		Percentage-of-Completion	
a. To record incurrence of construction costs:				
Construction-in-progress inventory	3,825		3,825	
Cash, payables, etc..		3,825		3,825
b. To record progress billings:				
Accounts receivable.	7,800		7,800	
Billings on contract		7,800		7,800
c. To record billing collections:				
Cash	7,875		7,875	
Accounts receivable.		7,875		7,875
d. To record revenue recognition for the percentage-of-completion method:				
Cost of earned construction revenue	—		3,825	
Revenue from long-term contracts*		—		3,750
Construction-in-progress inventory		—		75

* The project is completed; thus, any remaining portion of the contract price not previously recognized as revenue should be recognized this period. In prior years, \$1,875 plus \$9,375 (totalling \$11,250) has been recognized; thus, \$3,750 is to be recognized in this year.

	Completed-Contract		Percentage-of-Completion	
e. To record elimination of contract costs from inventory:				
Billings on contract	—		15,000	
Construction-in-progress inventory		—		15,000
f. To record revenue recognition for the completed-contract method:				
Billings on contract	15,000			
Cost of earned construction revenue	13,200			
Revenue from long-term contracts		15,000		
Construction-in-progress inventory		13,200		

Computations for percentage-of-completion method:

	1995	1996	1997
		($ thousands)	
Contract price	$15,000	$15,000	$15,000
Actual costs to date	1,500	9,375	13,200
Estimated costs to complete	10,500	3,125	nil
Total estimated costs	12,000	12,500	13,200
Total estimated margin	$ 3,000	$ 2,500	$ 1,800
Apportionment			
Actual costs to date	$ 1,500	$ 9,375	$13,200
Total estimated costs	12,000	12,500	13,200
Percent complete	12.5%	75%	100%
Revenue to be recognized			
1995: ($15,000 × .125)	$ 1,875	—	—
1996: ($15,000 × .75) − $1,875	—	$ 9,375	—
1997: ($15,000 − $1,875 − $9,375)	—	—	$ 3,750

3. The relevant financial statement presentations for both the completed-contract and the percentage-of-completed methods of revenue recognition are found in Exhibit 7–5.

EXHIBIT 7–5 Comparison of Completed-Contract and Percentage-of-Completion Financial Statement Presentations for Precision Punctual Construction

	December 31, 1995		December 31, 1996		December 31, 1997	
	Completed-Contract	Percentage-of-Completion	Completed-Contract	Percentage-of-Completion	Completed-Contract	Percentage-of-Completion
Balance Sheet						
Accounts receivable	$ 375	$ 375	$ 75	$ 75	0	0
Inventory:						
Construction in progress	$1,500	$1,875	$9,375	$11,250	0	0
Less: Billings on contract	(1,200)	(1,200)	(7,200)	(7,200)	0	0
Construction in progress in excess of billings	$ 300	$ 675	$2,175	$ 4,050	0	0
Income Statement						
Revenue from long-term contracts	—	$1,875	—	$ 9,375	$15,000	$3,750
Cost of construction	—	1,500	—	7,875	13,200	3,825
Gross profit	—	$ 375	—	$ 1,500	$ 1,800	$ (75)*

* This is an example of a current year loss on a contract that is profitable overall.

| QUESTIONS

1. Explain the relation between revenue recognition, the definition of income, and the definitions of assets and liabilities.
2. State the conditions that must be met for revenue to be recognized when a customer has the right to return purchased products. What accounting procedures are used until all conditions are met?
3. Explain the difference between the cash basis and the accrual basis of accounting. Explain why accounting uses the accrual basis.

4. What are the fundamental criteria for revenue recognition identified in Section 3400 of the *CICA Handbook?*

5. How may the criterion of reliability affect the timing of recognition?

6. What do the terms *realization* and *earned* mean in the context of revenue recognition?

7. Give two typical examples of revenues for which recognition occurs on the basis of the passage of time.

8. When is sales revenue recognized under the point-of-sale method?

9. A three-year, $360 subscription to a business periodical is paid, and delivery of it starts immediately. When should the publishing company recognize revenue?

10. Explain why accretion is not accepted as a basis for recognizing revenue.

11. When is income recognized, assuming the following:
    a. Completed-contract method?
    b. Cost recovery method?
    c. Percentage-of-completion method?

12. Explain the difference between the two acceptable methods of accounting for long-term construction contracts.

13. What are two different approaches for determining the extent of progress toward completion of a construction project? Identify some specific types of measurement for each.

14. Why is the ending inventory of construction in process different in amount when the percentage-of-completion method is used compared with the completed-contract method? Explain how much the amounts will differ.

15. When a loss is projected on a long-term construction contract, in what period(s) is the loss recognized under (*a*) percentage-of-completion and (*b*) completed-contract methods of accounting for long-term construction projects?

16. Describe the instalment sales method of recognizing revenue and when it is appropriately used.

17. Describe the cost recovery method of recognizing revenue. When is it appropriate?

18. What is a consignment? How is revenue recognized on a consignment transaction?

19. Distinguish among the specific performance method, the proportional performance method, the completed-performance method, and the collection method of recognizing revenue associated with service sales.

20. Identify the different types of costs for service types of transactions. What are the guidelines for expensing these costs?

21. Give a definition of expense. Provide three broad categories of expense.

22. What special characteristic distinguishes gains and losses from revenues and expenses?

23. In general, how does revenue and expense recognition differ in international accounting settings from Canadian GAAP?

CASES

C 7–1 (L.O. 1, 7)	**Deferral of Revenue: Analysis** Assume that in 1989, the Federal Power Commission (FPC) issued a ruling raising the ceiling price on regulated (interstate) gas, but with a "vintaging" system: gas suppliers could charge $1.42 per thousand cubic feet on "new gas" drilled after January 1, 1988, and $1.01 on gas drilled between January 1, 1986, and December 31, 1987. The old price had been 52 cents per thousand cubic feet and remained at this for all "old" gas (i.e., pre-1986 gas). The FPC soon reduced the $1.01 rate to 93 cents and retained the $1.42 rate. As a result of a lawsuit against the FPC seeking a rollback to the old 52-cent rate, a circuit court of appeals decided that gas suppliers should go ahead and collect the higher prices provided they would agree to refund the money if the final decision went against the FPC.
Required	1. If you were part of the management of a gas supplier at the time of the circuit court decision, what position would you take with respect to recognition of the extra amounts of revenue from the sale of new gas? Give reasons for whatever position you take. 2. Disregard the answer you gave to (1) above. If the revenue is deferred, how would it be accounted for until a final court decision is rendered? How would the deferred revenue be recognized if the final court decision is delayed until a new accounting year and then is favourable?
C 7–2 (L.O. 1)	**Magazine Subscriptions Collected in Advance: Analysis** At a meeting of the board of directors of Vanguard Publishing Company, where you are the controller, a new director expressed surprise that the company's income statement indicates that an equal proportion of revenue is earned with the publication of each issue of the magazines the company publishes. This director believes that the most important event in the sale of magazines is the collection of cash on the subscriptions and expresses

the view that the company's practice smooths its income and that its subscription revenue is actually earned as subscriptions are collected.

Required Discuss the propriety of timing the recognition of revenue on the basis of:

1. Cash collections on subscriptions.
2. Number of magazines delivered each month.
3. Both events, by recognizing part of the revenue with cash collections of subscriptions and part with delivery of the magazines to subscribers.

(AICPA adapted)

C 7–3
(L.O. 1, 2)
Liberalism versus Conservatism in Using Accounting Practices Two associates—Tom, an accountant, and Jerry, an engineer—are discussing the role of accounting in managing an enterprise and reporting on its operating results. Jerry argues, "When things are so-so or are going badly, the management uses current accounting practices to portray the picture reasonably accurately, but when things are going well, these practices are applied either liberally or conservatively to the extent that a company sometimes fails to tell the true story." You join their discussion.

Required
1. Cite some specifics that support Jerry's general line of argument.
2. How can Tom respond to justify current accounting practices in good times as well as bad?

C 7–4
(L.O. 2, 4)
Revenue Recognition Scientific Development Company (SDC) conducts research and development on specific projects under contract for clients; SDC also conducts basic research and attempts to market any new products or technologies it develops.

In January 1994, scientists at SDC began research to develop a new industrial cleaner. During 1994, $1,560,000 of costs were incurred in this effort. Late in July 1995, potentially promising results emerged in the form of a substance the company called Blast. Costs incurred through the end of July 1995 were $840,000. At this point, SDC attempted to sell the formula of and rights to Blast to Pride and Glory Industries Ltd. (P&G), for $10,000,000. P&G, however, was reluctant to sign before further testing was done. It did wish, though, to have the first option to acquire the rights and formulas to Blast if future testing showed the product to be profitable. Therefore, P&G paid SDC $40,000 for an option to acquire the formulas and rights to Blast anytime before December 31, 1995. Testing costs on the product incurred by SDC for the remainder of 1995 amounted to $1,080,000.

In late December 1995, P&G exercised its option and agreed to purchase the formulas and rights to Blast for $10,000,000. P&G paid $500,000 immediately with the balance payable in five equal annual instalments on December 31, 1996, to 2000.

In April 1996, SDC delivered the formulas and samples of Blast to P&G Industries. Additional costs incurred by SDC during 1996 amounted to $480,000.

Required
1. When should revenue be recognized by SDC from its work on Blast? Why?
2. Assume that the total costs of $3,960,000 actually incurred by SDC over the years 1994 to 1996 were accurately estimated in 1994. Determine the amount of revenue and expense that should be recognized each year from 1994 to 2000, assuming revenue is to be recognized:
   a. At the time the option is sold.
   b. At the time the option is exercised.
   c. At the time the formulas are delivered.
   d. As cash is collected (use the instalment method).

EXERCISES

E 7–1
(L.O. 1)
Revenue Principle: Special Applications This exercise focusses on the revenue principle. Respond to each of the following:

1. Define revenue.
2. What should be the dollar amount of revenue recognition under the revenue principle in the case of (a) product sales and services for cash and (b) product sales and services rendered in exchange for non-cash considerations?
3. How might revenue be recognized when there is a highly speculative transaction involving potential revenue that cannot be reliably estimated?
4. When should revenue be recognized in the case of long-term, low-down-payment sales, for which collectibility is very uncertain?
5. When should revenue be recognized for long-term construction contracts?

E 7–2
(L.O. 1)

Review of Definitions of Elements of Financial Statements Listed below are the seven elements of financial statements. To the right are key phrases from each definition. Match the key phrases with the elements by entering one letter in each blank.

Key Phrase	**Element**
_____ 1. Residual interest.	A. Revenues.
_____ 2. Decreases in net assets from peripheral or incidental transactions.	B. Expenses.
_____ 3. Enhancement of assets from ongoing major or central operations.	C. Gains.
_____ 4. Future sacrifices of economic benefits, results from past transactions or events.	D. Losses.
_____ 5. Increases in net assets from peripheral or incidental transactions.	E. Assets.
_____ 6. Using assets or incurring debts for ongoing major or central operations.	F. Liabilities.
_____ 7. Future economic benefits resulting from past transactions or events.	G. Equity.

E 7–3
(L.O. 2)

Alternative Revenue Recognition Methods For each of the following independent items, indicate when revenue should be recognized, and why.

a. Interest on loans made by a financial institution, receivable in annual payments.

b. Interest on loans made by a financial institution, receivable in three years when the customer, who has an excellent credit rating, will make payment.

c. Interest on loans made by a financial institution, where the loans are in default and payment is highly uncertain.

d. Collection of airline ticket fares, where the travel purchased will occur in the next fiscal period.

e. Transportation of freight by a trucking company for a customer; the customer is expected to make payment in accordance with the terms of the invoice in 60 days.

f. Growing, harvesting, and marketing of Christmas trees; the production cycle is 10 years.

g. Building houses in a subdivision, where the project will take two years to complete and each house must be individually sold by the contractor.

h. Building houses in a subdivision, where the project will take two years to complete and the contractor is building the houses under a contract from the local government.

i. Selling undeveloped lots for future retirement homes in a western province, with very low down payment and long-term contracts.

j. Sale of a two-year parking permit by a Montreal parking garage, with one-half the sale price received on the sale, and the remainder to be received in equal monthly payments over the period of the permit.

k. A fixed-price contract with the government to design and build a prototype of a space arm; the costs to complete the project cannot be reliably estimated.

l. A silver-mining company produces one million ounces of silver but stores the silver in a vault and waits for silver prices to increase.

E 7–4
(L.O. 2, 4)

Revenue Recognition: Four Special Cases—Amounts and Explanations The York Lumber Company has been involved in several transactions that require interpretation of the revenue principle. For each of the following 1995 transactions, write a brief one- or two-paragraph report, stating (1) the amount of revenue that you believe should be recognized during 1995 and (2) the basis for your answer.

a. Regular credit sales amounted to $500,000, of which two-thirds was collected by the end of 1995; the balance will be collected in 1996.

b. Regular services were rendered on credit amounting to $290,000, of which three-fourths will be collected in 1996.

c. An item that had been repossessed from the first purchaser and carried in inventory at $4,000 was sold again for $5,000. A $3,000 cash down payment was received in 1995. The balance is to be paid on a quarterly basis during 1996 and 1997. Repossession again would not be a surprise.

d. On January 1, 1994, the company purchased a $10,000 note as a speculative investment. Because the collectibility of the note was highly speculative, the company was able to acquire it for $1,000 cash. The note specifies 8% simple interest payable each year (disregard interest prior to 1994). The first collection on the note was $1,500 cash on December 31, 1995. Further collections are highly speculative.

E 7-5
(L.O. 2)

 Revenue Recognition: Three Cases—Entries and Reporting Three independent cases are given below for 1995. The accounting period ends December 31.

Case A On December 31, 1995, Zulu Sales Company sold a special machine (serial no. 1713) for $100,000 and collected $40,000 cash. The remainder plus 10% interest is payable December 31, 1996. Zulu will deliver the machine on January 5, 1996. The buyer has an excellent credit rating.

Case B On November 15, 1995, Victor Cement Company sold a ton of its product for $500. The buyer will pay for the product with two units of its own merchandise. The buyer promised to deliver the merchandise around January 31, 1996.

Case C On January 2, 1995, Remer Publishing Company collected $900 cash for a three-year subscription to a monthly, *Investors Stock and Bond Advisory*. The March 1995 issue will be the first one mailed.

Required Write a brief report covering the following:

1. The revenue recognition method that should be used.
2. Any entry that should be made on the transaction date.
3. An explanation of the reasoning for your responses to (1) and (2).

E 7-6
(L.O. 3)

Percentage-of-Completion Method: Analysis of Criteria It has been argued that before the percentage-of-completion method can be used properly, the following criteria must be met:

a. There is a written contract executed by buyer and seller that clearly specifies what is to be provided and received, the consideration to be exchanged, and the manner and terms of settlement.
b. The buyer can satisfy obligations under the contract.
c. The seller has the ability to perform the contractual obligations.
d. The seller can reliably estimate both the cost to complete and the percentage of completion of the contract.
e. The seller has a cost accounting system that adequately accumulates and allocates cost to final cost objectives in a manner consistent with the estimating process.

Required 1. Are the foregoing criteria adequate? What, if anything, would you add or delete?
2. Is (*d*), concerning the ability to estimate cost to complete, consistent with the quality of reliability?

E 7-7
(L.O. 3)

Completed-Contract and Percentage-of-Completion Methods Compared—Entries Watson Construction Company contracted to build a plant for $500,000. Construction started in January 1994 and was completed in November 1995. Data relating to the contract are summarized below:

	1994	1995
Costs incurred during year	$290,000	$120,000
Estimated additional costs to complete	125,000	
Billings during year	270,000	230,000
Cash collections during year	250,000	250,000

Required Give the journal entries for Watson in parallel columns, assuming (*a*) the completed-contract method and (*b*) the percentage-of-completion method. Use costs incurred to date divided by total estimated construction costs to measure percent completed.

E 7–8
(L.O. 3)

(Continuation of E 7–7) Financial Statements: Can Be Assigned Separately or Jointly   Use the data given in E 7–7 to complete the following schedule:

	Completed-Contract Method	Percentage-of-Completion Method*
Income Statement		
Income:		
1994	$_____	$_____
1995	_____	_____
Balance Sheet		
Receivables:		
1994	_____	_____
1995	_____	_____
Inventory—construction in process, net of billings:		
1994	_____	_____
1995	_____	_____

* Use costs incurred to date divided by total estimated construction costs to measure percentage of completion.

E 7–9
(L.O. 3)

Percentage-of-Completion and Completed-Contract Methods Compared: Analysis of Account Balances   Mullen Construction Company contracted to build a municipal warehouse for the city of Moncton for $750,000. The contract specified that the city would pay Mullen each month the progress billings, less 10%, which was to be held as a retention reserve. At the end of the construction, the final payment would include the reserve. Each billing, less the 10% reserve, must be paid within 10 days after submission of a billing to the city.

Transactions relating to the contract are summarized below:

1994   Construction costs incurred during the year, $200,000; estimated costs to complete, $400,000; progress billing, $190,000; and collections per the contract.

1995   Construction costs incurred during the year, $350,000; estimated costs to complete, $115,000; progress billings, $280,000; and collections per the contract.

1996   Construction costs incurred during the year, $100,000. The remaining billings were submitted by October 1 and final collections completed on November 30.

Required

1. Complete the following schedule:

Year	Method	Income Recognized	Receivables Ending Balance	Construction-in-Process Inventory Ending Balance	Costs in Excess of Billings Ending Balance
1994	Completed contract				
	Percentage of completion*				
1995	Completed contract				
	Percentage of completion*				
1996	Completed contract				
	Percentage of completion*				

* Use costs incurred to date divided by total estimated construction costs to measure percentage of completion.

2. Explain what causes the ending balance in construction in process to be different for the two methods.
3. Which method would you recommend for this contractor? Why?

E 7–10
(L.O. 3)

Percentage-of-Completion and Completed-Contract Methods Compared—Entries   Pedlar Construction Company contracted to build an apartment block for $2,800,000. Construction began in October 1994 and was scheduled to be completed in April 1996. Pedlar has a December 31 year-end. Data related to the contract are summarized below:

	1994	1995	1996
	(amount in thousands)		
Costs incurred during year	$ 400	$1,500	$ 700
Estimated additional costs to complete	2,200	900	
Billings during year	350	1,450	1,000
Cash collections during year	325	1,300	1,175

Required

1. Prepare the journal entries for Pedlar, assuming the completed-contract method.
2. Prepare the journal entries for Pedlar, assuming the percentage-of-completion method. Use costs incurred to date divided by total estimated construction costs to measure percent complete.

E 7–11
(L.O. 4)

Instalment Sales Method: Entries Barr Machinery Corporation had credit sales of $55,000 in 1995 that required use of the instalment method. Barr's cost of the merchandise sold was $44,000. Barr collected cash related to the instalment sales of $25,000 in 1995 and $30,000 in 1996. A perpetual inventory system is used.

Required

1. Give journal entries related to the instalment sales for 1995 and 1996.
2. Give the ending 1995 balances (before the closing entries) in the following accounts: instalment accounts receivable, instalment sales revenue, cost of instalment sales, deferred gross margin on instalment sales, and realized gross margin.

E 7–12
(L.O. 5)

Unconditional Right of Return: Entries McLaughlin Novelty Corporation developed a new product, an electric shoe tree, in 1995. To increase acceptance by retailers, McLaughlin sold the product to retailers with an unconditional right of return, which expires on February 1, 1996. McLaughlin has no basis for estimating returns on the new product. The following information is available regarding the product:

Sales—1995	$180,000
Cost of goods sold—1995	120,000
Returns—1995	12,000 (cost, $8,000)
Returns—January, 1996	15,000 (cost, $10,000)

All sales are on credit. Cash collections related to the sales were $40,000 in 1995 and $113,000 in 1996. McLaughlin uses the perpetual inventory system.

Required

Give journal entries for sales, returns, and collections related to the new product. The closing or reversing entries are not required. How much sales revenue should McLaughlin recognize in 1995?

E 7–13
(L.O. 4)

Cost Recovery Method The Trusett Merchandising Company has an inventory of obsolete products that it formerly stocked for sale. Efforts to dispose of this inventory by selling the products at low prices have not been successful. At the end of the prior year (1994), the company reduced the value to a conservative estimate of net realizable value of $22,000. On March 1, 1996, Watson Trading Company purchased this entire inventory for $10,000 cash as a speculative investment. Watson hopes to be able to dispose of it in some foreign markets for approximately $30,000. However, prior to purchase, Watson concluded that there was no reliable way to estimate the probable profitability of the venture. Therefore, Watson decided to use the cost recovery method. Subsequent cash sales have been as follows: 1996, $4,000; 1997, $5,000; and 1998, $8,000. Approximately 12% of the inventory remains on hand at the start of 1999.

Required

Give the 1996, 1997, and 1998 entries for Watson Trading Company to record revenues and cost of sales.

PROBLEMS

P 7–1
(L.O. 3)

Long-Term Construction: Percentage-of-Completion Method—Entries and Reporting Thrasher Construction Company contracted to construct a building for $975,000. The contract provided for progress payments. Thrasher's accounting year ends December 31. Work began under the contract on July 1, 1995, and was completed on September 30, 1997. Construction activities are summarized below by year:

1995 Construction costs incurred during the year, $180,000; estimated costs to complete, $630,000; progress billings during the year, $153,000; and collections, $140,000.

1996 Construction costs incurred during the year, $450,000; estimated costs to complete, $190,000; progress billing during the year, $382,500; and collections, $380,000.

1997 Construction costs incurred during the year, $195,000. Because the contract was completed, the remaining balance was billed and later collected in full per the contract.

Required

1. Give Thrasher's entries assuming that the percentage-of-completion method is used. Show computation of income apportionment on a cost basis. Assume that percentage of completion is measured by the ratio of costs incurred to date divided by total estimated construction costs.

2. Prepare income statement and balance sheet presentations for this contract by year; assume that the percentage-of-completion method is used.
3. Prepare income statement and balance sheet presentations by year; assume that the completed contract method is used. For each amount that is different from the corresponding amount in (2), explain why it is different.
4. Which method would you recommend to this contractor? Why?

P 7–2
(L.O. 3)

Long-Term Construction: Methods Compared—Entries and Reporting Wallen Corporation contracted to construct an office building for Ragee Company for $1,000,000. Construction began on January 15, 1994, and was completed on December 1, 1995. Wallen's accounting year ends December 31. Transactions by Wallen relating to the contract are summarized below:

	1994	1995
Costs incurred to date	$400,000	$ 850,000
Estimated costs to complete	420,000	
Progress billings to date	410,000	1,000,000
Progress collections to date	375,000	1,000,000

Required

1. In parallel columns, give the entries on the contractor's books; assume (*a*) the completed-contract method and (*b*) the percentage-of-completion method. Assume that percentage of completion is measured by the ratio of costs incurred to date divided by total estimated construction costs.
2. For each method, prepare the income statement and balance sheet presentations for this contract by year.
3. What is the nature of the item "costs in excess of billings" that would appear on the balance sheet?
4. Which method would you recommend that the contractor use? Why?

P 7–3
(L.O. 3)

Percentage-of-Completion and Completed-Contract Methods Compared—Entries and Reporting Banks Construction Company contracted to build an office block for $3,200,000. Construction began in September 1994 and was scheduled to be completed in May 1996. Banks has a December 31 year-end. Data related to the contract are summarized below:

	1994	1995	1996
	(amount in thousands)		
Costs incurred during year	$ 500	$1,800	$1,000
Estimated additional costs to complete	2,500	1,100	
Billings during year	450	1,300	1,450
Cash collections during year	400	1,100	1,700

Required

1. Prepare the journal entries for Banks, assuming the completed-contract method.
2. Prepare the balance sheet and income presentations for this contract by year, assuming the completed-contract method is used.
3. Prepare the journal entries for Banks, assuming the percentage-of-completion method. Use costs incurred to date divided by total estimated construction costs to measure percent complete.
4. Prepare the balance sheet and income presentations for this contract by year, assuming the percentage-of-completion method is used.

P 7–4
(L.O. 2, 4)

Accounting for Instalment Sales: Entries Baxter Land Corporation made a number of sales in 1994 and 1995 that required use of the instalment method. The following information regarding the sales is available:

	1994	1995	1996
Instalment sales	$200,000	$150,000	$ 0
Cost of instalment sales	160,000	112,500	0
Collections on 1994 sales	40,000	50,000	60,000
Collections on 1995 sales		30,000	75,000

Baxter uses a perpetual inventory system.

Required

1. Give journal entries relating to instalment sales for the years 1994 to 1996.
2. What is the year-end balance in instalment accounts receivable (net of any deferred gross margin) for 1994, 1995, and 1996?
3. If the sales qualified for application of the sales method, what amounts of gross margin would Baxter report in 1994, 1995, and 1996?

P 7-5
(L.O. 4)

Instalment Sales Method: Entries and Reporting Ontario Retail Company sells goods for cash, on normal credit (2/10; n/30). However, on July 1, 1994, the company sold a used computer for $2,200; the inventory carrying value was $440. The company collected $200 cash and agreed to let the customer make payments on the $2,000 whenever possible during the next 12 months. The company management stated that it had no reliable basis for estimating the probability of default. The following additional data are available: (*a*) collections on the instalment receivable during 1994 were $300 and during 1995 were $200, and (*b*) on December 1, 1995, Ohio Retail repossessed the computer (estimated net realizable value, $700).

Required

1. Give the required entries for 1994 and 1995; assume that the instalment method is used.
2. Give the balances in the following accounts that would be reported on the 1994 and 1995 income statements and balance sheets: realized gross margin on instalment sales, gain (loss) on repossession, instalment accounts receivable, and inventory of used computers.

P 7-6
(L.O. 2, 4)

Instalment Sales Method with Interest Computations On January 1, 1994, Wonderland Vacation Homes, Inc. (WVH), a developer of potential vacation home sites located in Chester, N.S., sold vacation home sites to 100 purchasers. All were sold under an instalment sales contract, with no down payment and with 10 annual payments of $1,000, beginning December 31, 1994. Purchasers could purchase the home sites outright with a cash payment of $6,150, but few buyers ever exercised this option. The home sites had cost an average of $3,690 to acquire and develop.

The home sites, located on a ridge overlooking Mahone Bay, were quite rustic and not usable year-round. Very aggressive marketing efforts were used to find buyers for the properties, and the company had a serious default problem on the instalment payments. In fact, the company could not reliably estimate the rate of default and thus decided to use the instalment sales method for recognizing revenue.

Required

1. Show the entry to record the instalment sale of the 100 home sites on January 1, 1994. WVH desires to record the gross amount of instalment receivables, with deferred gross margin and unearned interest deducted to determine the net instalment receivable. (Hint: First determine the rate of interest implicit in the contract sale terms.)
2. Assume that all 100 buyers make the required payment on December 31, 1994. Show the entry to record receipt of the payments and to recognize instalment sales revenue, interest revenue, costs of instalment sales, and realized gross margin for 1994.
3. Assume that at the end of 1995, 10 buyers return the titles to their properties and refuse to make further payment. WVH determines it can sell the returned properties back to a local farmer for $20,000. All other buyers make the required payment. Show the journal entries to record all these transactions.
4. Show the income statement and ending balance sheet accounts and amounts that would be reported for these transactions for 1994 and 1995.

P 7-7
(L.O. 6)

Accounting for a Franchise: Entries On October 1, 1995, Baker Latte Shops, Inc., (a franchisor) sold a franchise to J. Johns. Under the terms of the sale, Johns paid $20,000 in cash and issued a note payable in four equal annual instalments of $10,000 beginning on October 1, 1996. The note payments were based on a 12% interest rate. In return, Baker agreed to locate a suitable site for the franchise and assist in training personnel for the Latte shop.

A site was located on December 15, 1995, at a cost to Baker of $3,000. Training of Johns's personnel cost Baker $5,000 and was completed on February 1, 1996. The franchise began operation on February 15, 1996.

Required

Give journal entries for Baker associated with the franchise sale for 1995 and 1996.

P 7-8
(L.O. 4)

Cost Recovery Method Slatt Department Store has accumulated a stock of obsolete merchandise of the type it used to sell. Routine efforts have been made to dispose of it at a low price. This merchandise originally cost $60,000 and was marked to sell for $132,000. The management decided to set up a special location in the basement to display and (it was hoped) sell this stock starting in January 1995. All items will be marked to sell at a cash price that is 30% of the original marked selling price. On December 31, 1994, the company accountant transferred the purchase cost to a perpetual inventory account called "inventory, obsolete merchandise," at 30% of its purchase cost, which approximates estimated net realizable value. The management knows that a reliable estimate of the probable sales cannot be made. Therefore, the cost recovery method will be used. Subsequent sales were $9,000 in 1995 and $7,000 in 1996, and in 1997 the remaining merchandise was sold for $8,000.

Required

Give the entries that Slatt should make for 1994 through 1997.

P 7–9
(L.O. 6, 7)

Revenue Recognition: Proportional Performance Fly and Mattox, a professional corporation, contracted to provide legal services for Brown Company. The contract specified a lump-sum payment of $60,000 on November 15, 1994. Assume that Fly and Mattox can reliably estimate future direct costs associated with the contract. The following services were performed based on the estimate by Fly and Mattox:

	Direct Costs	Date Completed
Research potential lawsuit	$ 5,000	December 15, 1994
Prepare and file documents	15,000	March 1, 1995
Serve as Brown's counsel during legal proceedings	15,000	October 15, 1995

Required

1. What method of revenue recognition is appropriate for Fly and Mattox? Explain.
2. Give entries to recognize revenues related to this contract for Fly and Mattox.

P 7–10
(L.O. 1, 7)

Recognizing and Matching Expenses with Revenue The general ledger of Airtime, Inc., a corporation engaged in the development and production of television programs for commercial sponsorship, contains the following asset accounts before amortization at the end of 1995:

Account	Balance
"Sealing Wax and Kings"	$75,000
"The Messenger"	36,000
"The Desperado"	19,000
"Shin Bone"	8,000
Studio rearrangement	7,000

An examination of contracts and records revealed the following information:

a. The first two accounts listed above represent the total cost of completed programs that were televised during 1995. Under the terms of an existing contract, "Sealing Wax and Kings" will be rerun during 1996 at a fee equal to 60% of the fee for the first televising of the program. The contract for the first run produced $300,000 of revenue. The contract with the sponsor of "The Messenger" provides that at the sponsor's option, the program can be rerun during the 1996 season at a fee of 75% of the fee for the first televising of the program. There are no present indications that it will be rerun.

b. The balance in "The Desperado" account is the cost of a new program that has just been completed and is being considered by several companies for commercial sponsorship.

c. The balance in the "Shin Bone" account represents the cost of a partially completed program for a projected series that has been abandoned.

d. The balance of the studio rearrangement account consists of payments made to a firm of engineers that prepared a report about a more efficient utilization of existing studio space and equipment.

Required

Write a brief report addressed to the chief executive officer of Airtime, Inc., responding to the following:

1. State the general principle (or principles) of accounting that are applicable to recognizing revenue and expense for the first four accounts.
2. How would you report each of the first four accounts in the financial statements of Airtime? Explain.
3. In what way, if at all, does the studio rearrangement account differ from the first four? Explain.

(AICPA adapted)

P 7–11
(L.O. 1, 6, 7)

Matching Expense with Revenue Pepper Publishing Company prepares and publishes a monthly newsletter for an industry in which potential circulation is limited. Because information provided by the newsletter is available only piecemeal from other sources and because no advertising is carried, the subscription price for the newsletter is relatively high. Ogden recently engaged in a campaign to increase circulation that involved extensive use of person-to-person long-distance telephone calls to research directors of nonsubscriber companies in the industry. The telephone cost of the campaign was $38,000, and salary payments to persons who made the calls amounted to $51,000.

As a direct result of the campaign, new one-year subscriptions at $175 each generated revenue of $164,500. New three-year subscriptions at $450 each generated revenue of $324,000, and new five-year subscriptions at $625 generated $157,500. Cancellations are rare, but when they occur, refunds are made on a half-rate basis (e.g., if a subscriber has yet to receive $100 worth of newsletters, $50 is refunded).

Aside from the two direct costs of the campaign cited above, indirect costs, consisting of such items as allocated office space, fringe benefit costs for employees making telephone calls, and supervision, amounted to $21,000.

Required

1. Identify the specific accounting issues involved in recognizing revenue and expense for Ogden and give the accounting principles that are important in resolving each issue.
2. Assume that the campaign was begun and concluded in November, new subscriptions begin with the January issue of the monthly newsletter, and the company's accounting year ends December 31. How should costs of the campaign be allocated among current and future accounting years? Show calculations.

P 7–12
(L.O. 5)

Unconditional Right of Return   Following the success of its electric shoe tree product, McLaughlin Novelty Corporation developed a second unusual product, electric clip-on eyeglass wipers. McLaughlin felt the product would appeal to hikers, joggers, and cyclists who engaged in their sports in rainy climates. Because retail establishments were skeptical about the market appeal of the product, McLaughlin sold the product with a declining unconditional right of return for up to 10 months, with 10% of the right-of-return amount of the purchase expiring each month for 10 months. Thus, after the retailer had the product for one month, only 90% could be returned. After two months, only 80% could be returned, and after 10 months, the right of return was fully expired.

McLaughlin had no basis for estimating the amount of returns. Consistent with the terms McLaughlin offered its customers, all retailers paid cash when purchasing the clip-on eyeglass wipers. McLaughlin had its first sales of the product in September 1995. Sales for the remainder of the year, and returns prior to December 31, 1995, were as follows:

Month of Sale	Units Sold	Sales Price	Monthly Sales	Units Returned
Sept.	10,000	$10	$100,000	2,500
Oct.	12,000	10	120,000	1,000
Nov.	15,000	12	180,000	1,000
Dec.	11,000	12	132,000	0
Totals	48,000		$532,000	4,500

Each unit of product costs McLaughlin $6 to produce.

Required

1. Show the journal entries to record the four months of sales transactions, including the deferral of gross margin. You may use summary entries.
2. Show the entries to record the returns in 1995.
3. Compute and give the journal entry to record the amount that McLaughlin can record as realized gross margin for 1995.
4. For the above transactions, returns in 1996 were as follows:

Month of Sale	Units Returned
September	1,000
October	2,000
November	2,500
December	4,000

Show the entries to record the returns in 1996 and to record sales revenue and cost of sales from the 1995 shipments of this product.

8 Cash and Receivables

After you have studied this chapter, you will be able to:

1 **Explain the composition of cash and receivables accounts.**

2 **Prepare a bank reconciliation and explain other internal control procedures for cash.**

3 **Determine the conditions under which receivables may be recorded.**

4 **Perform the adjustments to accounts receivable, including uncollectible accounts, discounts, and returns and allowances.**

5 **Determine when the transfer of a receivable is reported as a sale or a liability.**

6 **Explain and apply appropriate valuation concepts to the reporting of notes receivable; in particular, how to establish their present value.**

INTRODUCTION

A full-page advertisement by Continental Bank featured a picture of Rumpelstiltskin feverishly spinning straw. It began:

> Sure, he could change straw into gold. But could he convert accounts receivable into cash?[1]

The ability of firms to convert accounts receivable into cash on a timely basis is an important element of their cash management strategy. Banks and other financial institutions aggressively compete for the opportunity to provide loans secured by accounts receivable. Firms also issue securities based on their receivables. Intrawest Corporation noted in its 1993 annual report that it had assigned its mortgages and notes receivable, amounting to $15 million, as part security for its general corporate debt.

An objective of financial reporting is to help users assess the amounts, timing, and uncertainty of future cash flows. Those assessments are affected by how a firm reports its liquidity position. Concern about ability to pay debts was evident when Sequoia Systems Inc. was forced to reduce its reported 1992 sales and accounts receivables. In a competitive market, Sequoia aggressively sought to increase sales of computers by liberalizing credit terms to buyers who ultimately were unable to pay. At one point, receivables were almost 50% of annual sales, a level double that of its competitors. Restatement of Sequoia's financial results was

---

[1] *The Wall Street Journal,* November 19, 1992, p. B3.

necessary to correct both the earnings figures and the receivables, the main source of its future operating cash inflows.[2]

Gitano Group Inc., a New York manufacturer of popular apparel marketed to youthful customers, found itself in a similar situation. As part of a general restructuring effort, the company recognized an immediate $28 million charge (of a total $78 million restructuring charge) for uncollectible receivables.[3] Even accountants are having trouble collecting their receivables; as the managing partner of a large Los Angeles CPA firm lamented "You can't eat receivables."[4]

Some companies have gone to great lengths to improve their reported receivables and income. Peabody International Corporation was particularly creative in this regard. In 1979, Peabody was a $600 million company. That year, 42% of its fourth-quarter profit resulted from anticipated victories in lawsuits against subcontractors: lawsuits receivable![5]

These examples illustrate the need for accounting principles related to receivables. This chapter develops the accounting principles for the recognition, measurement, and reporting of a primary category of liquid resources: cash, accounts receivable, and notes. We also discuss accounting for financing of receivables through third parties.

ACCOUNTING FOR CASH

Characteristics of Cash and Cash Equivalents

The cash account includes only those items immediately available to pay obligations. Cash includes balances on deposit with financial institutions,[6] coins and currency, petty cash, and certain negotiable instruments accepted by financial institutions for immediate deposit and withdrawal. These negotiable documents include ordinary cheques, cashier's cheques, certified cheques, and money orders. The balance of the cash control account reflects all items included in cash.

Cash equivalents are items similar to cash but not classified as such. They include Treasury bills,[7] commercial paper,[8] and money market funds.[9] Cash equivalents are very near cash but are not in negotiable form, and hence they are not included in the cash account.

Cash also excludes postage stamps, travel advances to employees (prepaid expenses), receivables from company employees, and cash advances to either employees or outside parties (receivables).

At the end of the accounting period, undelivered cheques are not deducted from the balance in the cash account. Entries already made to record such cheques are reversed before the financial statements are prepared because no resources were exchanged. Some companies do not reduce the cash account balance until cheques are presented for payment.

An **overdraft** is a negative bank account balance and is reported as a current liability. Overdrafts occur when the dollar amount of cheques honoured by the bank exceeds the account balance. However, if a depositor overdraws an account but has

---

[2] "Sequoia Systems Remains Haunted by Phantom Sales," *The Wall Street Journal*, October 30, 1992, p. B4.

[3] "Gitano Group to Take a $78 Million Charge for the Second Quarter," *The Wall Street Journal*, August 3, 1992, p. C16.

[4] "CPA Firms Weed Out Late Payers," *Accounting Today*, January 20, 1992, p. 1.

[5] "Slick Accounting Ploys Help Many Companies Improve Their Income," *The Wall Street Journal*, June 20, 1980, p. 1. Recording anticipated gains is not an accepted accounting procedure.

[6] Chequing accounts are considered cash. With normal savings accounts, the bank typically has the right to demand advance notification of a withdrawal but rarely invokes this authority. Therefore, savings accounts are generally also included in cash.

[7] Treasury bills are noninterest-bearing obligations of the government of Canada with a maturity of less than one year from issue date. They are sold at a discount and are redeemed at maturity. The difference between the maturity and issue amounts is interest revenue to the purchaser.

[8] Commercial paper is short-term notes issued by corporations as a means of financing short-term cash needs.

[9] Money market funds consist of government securities, commercial paper, certificates of deposit, and other short-term debt securities.

positive balances in other accounts with that bank, it is appropriate to offset the negative and positive balances. In this case, the bank is both a creditor and debtor. Accounts with different financial institutions are not offset against each other.

A **compensating balance** is a minimum balance that must be maintained in a depositor's account as support for funds borrowed by the depositor. Compensating balances are not included in the cash account because they are not currently available for use, although many companies include these balances in cash and disclose the restrictions in notes to the financial statements. Either disclosure option avoids overstating the firm's liquidity position.[10]

Compensating balances increase the effective rate of interest on loans because the borrower can use only the net amount. For example, assume that a firm borrows $15,000 for one year at 10% but must maintain a $1,000 compensating balance in an account with the bank. The compensating balance increases the effective interest rate to 10.71% ($1,500 interest ÷ $14,000 loan). A compensating balance is an example of a *restricted* cash balance, cash held for a specific purpose and not intended for general payment use. Another common restricted cash balance is a *sinking fund*, an amount of cash set aside for debt retirement. Restricted cash balances are classified as short- or long-term investments, depending on the duration of the restriction.

As an example, the March 31, 1993, balance sheet of United Rayore Gas Ltd. included "Cash" amounting to $2.23 million as a long-term asset. The notes to the financial statements explain that this cash is held under the "Canadian Immigrant Investor Program" and would be paid back if permanent resident visas were not issued.

Items properly included in cash generally do not present valuation problems because they are recorded at nominal value. That is, they are worth their face value in terms of Canadian dollars. The Canadian dollar value of holdings in foreign currency, however, fluctuates with changes in the relevant exchange rate. Only foreign currencies convertible to Canadian dollars without restriction are included in cash. The valuation of foreign currency and other foreign currency accounting issues are considered in advanced accounting courses.

Although maintaining separate ledger accounts for cash and cash equivalents is normal practice, 61% of surveyed companies combine cash and cash equivalents for external reporting purposes.[11]

Internal Controls for Cash

The need to safeguard cash is crucial in most businesses. Cash is easy to conceal and transport, carries no mark of ownership, and is universally valued. The risk of theft is directly related to the ability of individuals to access the accounting system and obtain custody of cash. Firms address this problem through the internal control system. An internal control system is a set of policies and procedures designed to:
- Protect assets.
- Ensure compliance with laws and company policy.
- Provide accurate accounting records.
- Evaluate performance.

A sound internal control system for cash increases the likelihood that the reported values for cash and cash equivalents are accurate and may be relied on by financial statement users.

Internal controls for cash should:
- Separate custody of and accounting for cash.

---

[10] *Legally restricted deposits* held as compensating balances against short-term borrowing arrangements should be reported as non-cash current assets, and if they are held against long-term borrowing, they should be reported as non-current assets.

[11] *Financial Reporting in Canada 1993* (Toronto: CICA, 1993), p. 86. The trend toward combining cash with cash equivalents for reporting purposes is likely to accelerate further because *CICA Handbook* Section 1540, "Statement of Changes in Financial Position," requires cash and cash equivalents as the basis for SCFPs.

- Account for all cash transactions.
- Maintain only the minimum cash balance needed.
- Provide for periodic test counts of cash balances.
- Reconcile ledger and bank cash account balances.
- Achieve an adequate return on idle cash balances.
- Physically control cash.

Control of Cash Receipts   Cash inflows have many sources, and cash control procedures vary across companies. These minimum procedures apply in most situations:

1. Separate the responsibilities for handling cash, recording cash transactions, and reconciling cash balances. This separation reduces the possibility of theft and of concealment through false recording.
2. Assign cash-handling and cash-recording responsibilities to different people to ensure an uninterrupted flow of cash from receipt to deposit. This control requires immediate counting, immediate recording, and timely deposit of all cash received.
3. Maintain close supervision of all cash-handling and cash-recording functions. This control includes both routine and surprise cash counts, internal audits, and daily reports of cash receipts, payments, and balances.

Control of Cash Disbursements   Most firms disburse cash to a large number of different payees. Although cash disbursement control systems are tailored to each firm's specific needs, certain fundamentals apply:

1. Separate the responsibilities for cash disbursement documentation, cheque writing, cheque signing, cheque mailing, and recordkeeping.
2. Except for internal cash funds (petty cash), make all cash disbursements by cheque.
3. If petty cash funds are employed, develop tight controls and authorization procedures for their use.
4. Prepare and sign cheques only when supported by adequate documentation and verification.
5. Supervise all cash disbursements and recordkeeping functions.

The following discussion highlights two of the most common elements of cash control and management: petty cash funds and bank accounts.

Petty Cash Funds

A **petty cash** fund is a type of *imprest* fund, providing ready currency for routine disbursements.[12] Amounts can vary from $50 or less to more than $10,000. A large organization may have several petty cash funds in a variety of offices and production facilities. Although the amount in any one location may be relatively minor, the total of all petty cash can be significant. The balance of the petty cash account, which is part of the total cash balance, changes only when the fund is established, changed in amount, or discontinued.

Petty cash funds are intended to handle many types of small payments, including employee transportation costs, postage, office supplies, and delivery charges. Generally, control of cash in a petty cash system is informal. Increased economy and convenience often justify the use of petty cash funds.

The following chronological steps illustrate a typical petty cash fund operation:

1. Assume that a $3,000 petty cash fund is established at a specific location. The cash is placed in a secured location (usually a strongbox or safe under custodial control). The journal entry is as follows:

Petty cash	3,000	
Cash		3,000

---

[12] Imprest funds are funds created for specific purposes and periodically replenished by reimbursement for amounts disbursed, which requires authorization.

2. The custodian reviews authorization on vouchers for cash requests and dispenses the required cash. The vouchers are kept with the fund. The sum of cash and vouchers should equal $3,000. Journal entries are not made for disbursements.

3. At the end of the first month, $560 remains in the fund, indicating that $2,440 was disbursed during the month ($3,000 − $560) and that the custodian should have $2,440 in supporting payout vouchers. The following individual vouchers accompany the fund: postage, $900; office supplies, $700; and taxi fares, $800 ($2,400 in total). There is a $40 cash shortage ($2,440 − $2,400). Presumably, a voucher was lost, or a voucher understates the amount disbursed. The shortage is reflected in a replenishment entry:

Postage expense	900	
Office supplies expense	700	
Transportation expense	800	
Cash short and over	40	
Cash		2,440

This entry is recorded by the accounting department, not the custodian. Replenishment of the petty cash fund occurs whenever the fund runs low and at the end of each fiscal period for proper reporting of expenses and cash balance.

Cash short and over is an expense (debit balance) or revenue account (credit balance). A shortage or overage is caused by recording or disbursing errors. If a shortage is larger than normal or if shortages occur regularly with the same fund, theft should be suspected. When fraud or theft is suspected, a loss is recorded rather than cash short and over.

4. When a petty cash fund is increased, decreased, or closed, an entry is made affecting both the petty cash and cash accounts. For example, if the fund is increased to $5,000 because of increased office cash needs, the entry is as follows:

Petty cash	2,000	
Cash		2,000

Petty cash systems foster internal control through the requirement that someone other than the recipient of cash must authorize the disbursement. A record of each disbursement is made, the fund is created and replenished by cheque and is reconciled, and the replenishment cheque is written by someone other than the custodian of the fund.

Control of Cash through Bank Accounts

Bank accounts are an important means of cash control and provide several advantages:
- Cash is physically protected by the bank.
- A separate record of cash is maintained by the bank.
- Cash handling and theft risk are minimized.
- Customers may remit payments directly to the bank.
- Financial institutions provide cash management services such as chequing privileges, investment advice, and interest revenue on accounts.

Large companies with widely dispersed activities often use banks to facilitate cash collection and to take advantage of float. Float consists of uncollected or undeposited cheques in transit between companies. Firms attempt to maximize *payment* float to increase interest earned on the funds supporting cheques written to other firms, and minimize *collection* float to reduce interest lost on cheques received from other firms.

Lockbox systems can reduce collection float. In lockbox systems, customers mail their payments to a local bank or post office box. A local bank is authorized (for a fee) to empty the box daily and deposit the funds to the company's account with the local bank.

Electronic funds transfer (EFT), the transferring of funds between banks and firms by telephone, wire, or computer, is also a means of reducing float. EFT facilitates immediate posting of transactions to accounts. Its advantages include reduced paperwork, fewer errors, and lower transaction costs. Chief disadvantages are the cost of new equipment and the required internal control systems.[13]

Debit cards, another form of EFT, have recently been introduced in Canada. Payment for a purchase is electronically transferred from the purchaser's account to the vendor's account when authorized by the purchaser at the point of sale.

Reconciliation of Bank and Book Cash Balances   Banks send monthly statements showing beginning and ending balances and transactions occurring during the month: cheques clearing the account, deposits received, and service charges. Monthly reconciling of the bank balance with the depositor's cash account balance is an essential cash control procedure.

Generally, several items listed in the bank statement have not been recorded by the firm. These include interest credited, notes collected by the bank, and service charges. **Debit** and **credit** memos inform the firm about changes in the cash account. For a bank, a depositor's cash balance is a liability, the amount the bank owes to the firm. Therefore, a debit memo describes the amount and nature of a decrease in the firm's cash account. A credit memo indicates an increase in the cash account. The balance per the bank does not reflect outstanding cheques (those that have not cleared the bank) and deposits reaching the bank after preparation of the bank statement.

Bank reconciliations are used to:

1. Determine whether the bank account and the company's cash balance are in agreement after taking into account unrecorded items.
2. Isolate recording errors and other problems in the bank records or company's recording system.
3. Establish the correct ending cash balance.
4. Supply information for adjusting entries.

Reconciliation Procedures   The bank and book balance to correct cash balance method[14] begins with the two cash balances and lists the differences between those balances and the true ending cash balance. Assume the information in Exhibit 8–1 for West Company. The bank statement reported an ending $38,660 balance, and the cash account reflects an ending $34,880 cash balance. These figures are reconciled to $35,650, as shown in Exhibit 8–2.

I. Items are entered to reconcile the bank statement balance to the correct cash balance. This is information the bank did not have at August 31.
  A. **Cash on hand** This is the cash held by the company but not deposited at August 31. This amount, usually representing undeposited cheques, is added to the bank balance.
  B. **Deposits in transit** These are deposits made too late to be reflected in the bank statement. This amount is determined by comparing the firm's record of deposits with the deposits listed in the bank statement or by using a schedule:

Deposits in transit at end of prior period	$ 5,000
Deposits for the current period (per books)	75,300
Total amount that could have been deposited	80,300
Deposits shown in bank statement	(77,300)
Deposits in transit at end of current period	$ 3,000

---

[13] Westinghouse Corporation estimated that EFT would reduce routine transaction costs from $1.05 to $0.15 per item; $1.4 million would be saved on cheque collections alone. See R. Caruso, "Paying Bills the Electronic Way," *Management Accounting*, April 1984, pp. 25–27. Also, EFT reduced cheque-processing costs from $0.59 to $0.07 per cheque at the U.S. Treasury Department. See T. Hanley, C. D'Arista, and N. Mitchell, "Electronic Banking: Key to the Future— If Properly Planned and Integrated," *American Banker*, May 21, 1984, pp. 4–26.

[14] Other methods are also used. A proof of cash method is used by auditors as one test of the internal controls for cash; this method is covered in auditing texts.

EXHIBIT 8–1
Information for Bank
Reconciliation

WEST COMPANY
Information for Bank Reconciliation
August 31, 1995

Bank Statement		Company's Cash Account	
August 1 balance	$32,000	August 1 balance	$30,000
Deposits recorded in		August deposits	75,300
August	77,300	August disbursements*	(70,420)
Cheques cleared in		August 31 balance	$34,880
August	(71,240)		
Note collected			
(including $100			
interest)	1,100		
NSF cheque, J. Fox	(300)		
August service charges	(200)		
August 31 balance	$38,660		

* Per cash payments journal. Additional data, end of July: Deposits in transit, $5,000, and cheques outstanding, $8,000 (these two amounts were taken from the July bank reconciliation). End of August: Cash on hand (undeposited), $990. This amount will be deposited September 1. A cheque written by West in the amount of $240 for a repair bill in August is included in the cleared cheques. West recorded the cheque for $420, the correct amount, debiting repair expense. The payee will bill West for the remaining $180 due.

C. **Outstanding cheques** This amount is determined by comparing cheques written with cheques cleared or by using a schedule:

Outstanding cheques at end of prior period	$ 8,000
Cheques written during the current period (per cash payments journal, as corrected: $70,420 − $180 payment overstatement)	70,240
Total cheques that could have cleared	78,240
Cheques cleared shown in bank statement	(71,240)
Outstanding cheques at end of current period	$ 7,000

The reconciling items result in a correct cash balance of $35,650.

II. Items are entered to reconcile the firm's cash ledger account to the correct cash balance. These are amounts the firm did not know about at August 31. Each of these items requires an adjusting journal entry to correct the cash balance.

A. **Note collected by bank** A note receivable with a face value of $1,000 plus $100 accrued interest was collected by the bank but was not recorded by West.[15] The entry is as follows:

Cash	1,100	
Notes receivable		1,000
Interest revenue		100

B. **Nonsufficient funds (NSF) cheque** A $300 cheque from customer J. Fox, which was not supported by sufficient funds in Fox's chequing account, was returned to West by the bank.[16] West had deposited the cheque, increased cash, and decreased accounts receivable, but the bank was unable to credit West's account. The $300 amount is included in the $75,300 deposits recorded in August.

Accounts receivable, J. Fox	300	
Cash		300

---

[15] Banks normally transmit credit advices, confirming collection and detailing the amounts involved immediately to the company, so the accounting entry to record the collected note could be prepared during the month.

[16] In practice, banks notify companies immediately that a cheque has been returned rather than wait to inform the company through the bank statement. In this case, the entry to record the NSF cheque could have been recorded earlier.

EXHIBIT 8–2   Bank Reconciliation

WEST COMPANY
Bank Reconciliation
August 31, 1995

Bank Statement		**Book Balance**	
Ending bank balance, August 31	$38,660	Ending book balance, August 1	$34,880
Additions:		Additions:	
Cash on hand (undeposited)	990	Note collected by bank:	
Deposits in transit, August 31 ($5,000		Principal	1,000
+ $75,300 − $77,300)	3,000	Interest	100
		Error in recording repair payment	180
Deductions:		Deductions:	
Cheques outstanding ($8,000 +		NSF cheque, J. Fox	(300)
$70,240 − $71,240) August 31	(7,000)	Bank service charges	(200)
		Total	$35,660
		Cash shortage*	(10)
Correct cash balance	$35,650	Correct cash balance	$35,650

* Discovered in making the reconciliation.

C. **Bank service charges** The bank debited West's account for $200 of bank charges in August for cheque printing, chequing account privileges, and collection of customer cheques and notes. West deducts this amount from the cash account.

Miscellaneous expenses	200	
Cash		200

D. **Error in recording** West recorded a $240 cheque in the cash payments journal as $420, causing the book balance to be understated by $180 ($420 − $240). West corrects the recording error with the following entry:

Cash	180	
Miscellaneous payables		180

(Repair expense is correctly stated at $420.) This entry corrects the cash disbursement amount and establishes a payable for the amount due.

E. **Cash shortage** This is the amount by which the cash balance to this point in the reconciliation ($35,660) exceeds the correct cash balance, previously determined to be $35,650. Such a small amount ($10) is written off. If a shortage occurs regularly, if the difference is larger, or if West suspects theft, further investigation is warranted. The write-off is accomplished with the following entry:

Miscellaneous expenses	10	
Cash		10

Book and bank balances are now reconciled to the same value. The cash ledger balance is increased $770 ($1,000 + $100 + $180 − $300 − $200 − $10) as a result.

When more than one bank account exists, each is reconciled separately with an individual subsidiary cash ledger account. The sum of the correct ending subsidiary cash ledger balances then equals the cash balance for reporting purposes.

Separation of duties is an important internal control attribute and applies to personnel involved in reconciling bank accounts. For example, a person having responsibility for the bank reconciliation, cash disbursements, and accounting for cash could write and deliberately fail to record an unauthorized cheque. When the canceled cheque is returned, outstanding cheques could be understated by the amount of the cheque, in turn overstating the correct cash balance by the amount of the cheque. The cash account would appear reconciled. Someone other than the cashier should prepare the bank reconciliation.

|CONCEPT REVIEW

1. Why is a distinction made between those items qualifying as cash and other items that are similar to cash but are not cash?
2. How does a bank reconciliation provide internal control for cash?
3. Why are adjusting entries made only for items reconciling the book balance to the correct cash balance?

ACCOUNTING FOR RECEIVABLES

Receivables represent claims for money, goods, services, and other non-cash assets from other firms. Receivables may be current or non-current, depending on the expected collection date. Accounts receivable are often supported only by a sales invoice. Notes receivable are usually supported by formal promissory notes. Trade receivables describe amounts owed the company for goods and services sold in the normal course of business. Non-trade receivables arise from many other sources, such as tax refunds, contracts, investees, finance receivables, instalment notes, sale of assets, and advances to employees. The main accounting issues pertaining to receivables are recognition and valuation. Both are affected by collectibility.

Recognition and Measurement of Accounts Receivable

Accounts receivable are amounts owed by customers for goods and services sold in the firm's normal course of business. These receivables are supported by sales invoices or other documents rather than by formal written promises, and they include amounts expected to be collected either during the year following the balance sheet date or within the firm's operating cycle, whichever is longer. Generally, a 30- to 60-day period is allowed for payment, beyond which the account is considered past due. Individual accounts receivable for customers with credit balances (from prepayments or overpayments) are reclassified and reported as liabilities. The credit balances are not netted against other accounts receivable.

The average age of receivables (average number of days required for collection) is an important statistic to analysts. Ultimate Corporation experienced financial problems as reflected in the age of its receivables, which increased from 120 days (twice the industry average) to 158 days. Contributing to the increasing incidence of uncollectibility was the firm's practice of shipping computers to dealers before receiving orders. Payment terms and return privileges were liberal, so dealers did not protest. Ultimate recorded these shipments as sales. After a year or two, the company was forced to recognize large write-offs of receivables, resulting in a $1.2 million second-quarter loss in 1988 as compared with $6.2 million of income for the same quarter of 1987.[17]

Accounts receivable are recognized only when the criteria for recognition are fulfilled. They are valued at the original exchange price between the firm and the outside party, less adjustments for cash discounts, sales returns, and allowances and

---

[17] "No Question, It Looks Bad," *Forbes*, November 28, 1988.

uncollectible accounts, yielding an approximation to net realizable value, the amount of cash expected to be collected.

Cash Discounts   Companies frequently offer a **cash discount** for payment received within a designated period. Cash discounts are used to increase sales, to encourage early payment by the customer, and to increase the likelihood of collection. Typical sales terms are 2/10, n/30. This means that the customer is given a 2% cash discount if payment is made within 10 days from sale; otherwise, the full amount net of any returns or allowances is due in 30 days.

The incentive to pay within the discount period is generally significant, although in percentage terms this does not always appear to be the case. Assume that West Company purchased merchandise with a $1,000 gross sales price on 2/10, n/30 terms. West decides to settle on the 30th day following the sale, paying $1,000 without taking advantage of the $20 cash discount available.

Although this decision to delay payment cost West $20, the annualized interest rate it pays is 37.2%! It is computed as follows:

$$\frac{.02(\$1,000)}{\$980} \times \frac{365}{20} = 37.2\%$$

The $20 "interest," or amount of discount lost paid by West, is slightly over 2% of $980, an amount which would have satisfied the seller if paid within the discount period. This rate was paid for a "borrowing" period of only 20 days, however. The factor $365 \div 20$ represents the number of 20-day periods in a year, which yields the substantial annualized rate. Few investments can offer such a rate of return, so most buyers benefit by paying within the discount period. A well-designed accounting information system signals the accounts payable staff to pay bills within the discount period.

Gross and Net Methods   When cash discounts are offered, the receivable and sale is recorded either at the gross or net amount (gross invoice price less available cash discount). The key distinction between the two is the treatment of sales discounts. The **gross method** records sales discounts only if the customer pays within the discount period. The **net method** records sales discounts only if the customer fails to pay within the discount period. Both approaches are found in practice.[18]

To illustrate the two methods, assume that North Company sells merchandise to South Company at a gross sales price of $1,000. Credit terms are 2/10, n/30. Entries for selected events follow.

Entry to record credit sale:

Gross Method			**Net Method**		
Accounts receivable	1,000		Accounts receivable	980*	
Sales revenue		1,000	Sales revenue		980
			* $1,000(.98)		

North's offer of a cash discount supports the net valuation of sales and accounts receivable. North is satisfied with $980 if payment is made within 10 days of sale. Therefore, the additional $20 is a finance charge for delaying payment.

Entry to record collection within the 10-day discount period:

Gross Method			**Net Method**		
Cash	980		Cash	980	
Sales discounts	20		Accounts receivable		980
Accounts receivable . . .		1,000			

---

[18] Although billing and valuation of accounts are different functions, the gross method predominates in practice because companies find it convenient to use the gross price for both billing and accounting purposes.

Sales discounts is a contra account to sales, reducing net sales by the amount of cash discounts taken. The gross method specifically identifies discounts taken by customers.

Entry to record collection after the 10-day discount period:

Gross Method		**Net Method**	
Cash 1,000		Cash 1,000	
Accounts receivable . .	1,000	Accounts receivable . . .	980
		Sales discounts forfeited .	20

Sales are measured at the gross price under the gross method when collection is received after the end of the discount period. The date of payment affects the amount of recorded sales under this method because the finance charge is included in sales if the gross price is paid.

Sales discounts forfeited, a revenue account, is similar to interest revenue. The net method specifically identifies discounts forfeited by customers. Regardless of the payment date, the net method reports sales and receivables at the net amount, the amount acceptable to the seller for complete payment.

Year-End Adjusting Entries   Under the gross method, if a material amount of cash discounts is expected to be taken on outstanding accounts receivable at year-end, and if this amount can be estimated reliably, an adjusting entry is required under the matching principle to decrease net sales and accounts receivable to the estimated amount collectible. To illustrate, assume that North has $2 million of accounts receivable, all on 2/10, n/30 terms, recorded at gross at year-end and expects 60% of these accounts to be collected within the discount period. North records an adjusting entry on December 31, 1995:

Gross Method

Sales discounts $2,000,000(.02)(.60).	24,000	
Allowance for sales discounts		24,000

The allowance account is a contra account to accounts receivable. During 1996, assuming that the estimates were correct, a summary entry records the receipts during 1996:

Gross Method

Allowance for sales discounts	24,000	
Cash.	1,176,000	
Accounts receivable $2,000,000(.60)		1,200,000

A material discrepancy between estimated and actual discounts taken is treated as a change in accounting estimate and may affect future estimates of sales discounts.[19]

Under the net method, if the discount period on a material amount of accounts receivable has lapsed, an adjusting entry is required to recognize forfeited discounts and increase accounts receivable. For example, assume that at the end of 1995, North has $980,000 of accounts receivable recorded at net on which the discount period has lapsed. Assuming 2/10, n/30 terms, an adjusting entry is made on December 31, 1995:

Net Method

Accounts receivable (.02)($980,000 ÷ .98)	20,000	
Sales discounts forfeited		20,000[20]

---

[19] Under *CICA Handbook* Section 1506, "Accounting Changes," changes in estimates are handled prospectively; prior periods are not affected.

[20] *Estimated* lapsed discounts on outstanding accounts receivable at year-end are not recorded under the net method because a gain contingency would result. *CICA Handbook* Section 3290, "Contingencies," does not endorse the recording of gain contingencies in the accounts.

If proper adjusting entries are made, both methods yield similar results. In practice, adjusting entries for sales discounts are not common when the relevant amounts from year to year are similar.

Trade Discounts Typically, a single invoice price for a product is published. Then, several different discounts may apply, depending on customer type and quantity ordered. These **trade discounts** reduce the final sales price and are not affected by date of payment.

For example, suppose an item priced at $50 is offered at a trade discount of 40% for quantities over 1,000 units. The unit price for an order of 1,100 units is therefore $30 ($50 × .60). The percentage discount can be changed for different order quantities without changing the basic $50 price.[21]

For accounting purposes, the listed invoice price less the trade discount is treated as the gross price to which cash discounts apply. Trade discounts are not accounted for separately but rather help define the invoice price.

Sales Returns and Allowances Return privileges are frequently part of a comprehensive marketing program required to maintain competitiveness. Sales returns are unacceptable merchandise taken back; sales allowances are price reductions made to encourage customers to keep merchandise not meeting their preferences or having minor damage.

Sales returns and allowances are material in some industries, including retailing and book publishing. For example, in 1988, Regina Corporation experienced a return rate between 20% and 25% on sales of vacuum cleaners.[22]

Sales returns and allowances reduce both net accounts receivable and net sales. Assume that Maas Company grants $16,000 of returns and allowances in 1995, the first year of operations. The summary entry to record actual returns and allowances during the year is the following:

Sales returns and allowances (contra sales)	16,000	
Accounts receivable		16,000

Under certain conditions, discussed in Chapter 7, Maas must also estimate and recognize the remaining returns and allowances expected for 1995. Assume that total estimated sales returns and allowances are 2% of the $1 million sales for 1995. Maas records an adjusting entry on December 31, 1995:

Sales returns and allowances $1,000,000(.02) − $16,000	4,000	
Allowance for sales returns and allowances		4,000

The allowance account is contra to accounts receivable. The effect of the two entries in this example is to reduce 1995 net sales and net accounts receivable by $20,000, the total estimated returns and allowances on sales during 1995. In 1996, assuming that the estimates were correct, an entry records returns and allowances on 1995 sales:

Entry to record actual sales returns and allowances:

Allowance for sales returns and allowances	4,000	
Accounts receivable		4,000

A material discrepancy between estimated and actual returns and allowances is treated as a change in accounting estimate and may affect future estimates. If returns and allowances are either immaterial or relatively stable across periods, companies often do not estimate returns and allowances at year-end.

---

[21] Several discounts (*chain* discounts) may apply to the same item. The actual price paid for a $500 item subject to both a 15% and a 20% trade discount is $340 [$500(1 − .15)(1 − .20)]. An employee discount applied to already discounted merchandise is an example.

[22] "Cute Tricks on the Bottom Line," *Fortune*, April 24, 1989.

MEASUREMENT OF UNCOLLECTIBLE ACCOUNTS RECEIVABLE

When credit is extended, some amount of uncollectible receivables is generally inevitable. Firms attempt to develop a credit policy neither too conservative (leading to excessive lost sales) nor too liberal (leading to excessive uncollectible accounts). Past records of payment and the financial condition and income of customers are key inputs to the credit-granting decision.

If uncollectible receivables are both likely and estimable, an estimate of uncollectible accounts must be recognized in the period of sale, under the matching principle.[23] This approach is called the *allowance method*. Accounts receivable and income are reduced to reflect future uncollectibles from current-year sales. Estimated uncollectibles are recorded in *bad debt expense,* an operating expense usually classified as a selling expense.

If uncollectible accounts are not likely or estimable, no adjustment to income or accounts receivable is required; rather, accounts are written off when considered uncollectible. This approach is called the *direct write-off method*.

Events and Journal Entries for Uncollectible Accounts—The Allowance Method

If uncollectible accounts are likely and estimable, an adjusting entry is needed at the end of an accounting period. For example, if a company estimates $9,000 of bad debts at year-end, the adjusting entry is as follows:

Bad debt expense. 9,000
    Allowance for doubtful accounts   9,000

Allowance for doubtful accounts is a contra account to accounts receivable and is used because the identity of specific uncollectible accounts is unknown at the time of the above entry. *Net* accounts receivable (gross accounts receivable less the allowance account) is an estimate of the net realizable value of the receivables.

CICA Handbook Section 3020, paragraph .01 "Accounts and Notes Receivable," states, "Since it is to be assumed that adequate allowance for doubtful accounts has been made if no statement is made to the contrary, it is not considered necessary to refer to such an allowance." In 1992, reference to an allowance was made by 9% of the companies surveyed.[24]

Two subsequent events must be considered: (1) the write-off of a specific receivable and (2) collection of an account previously written off. The adjusting entry for bad debt expense creates the allowance for doubtful accounts for future uncollectible accounts. When specific accounts are determined to be uncollectible, they are removed from the accounts receivable and that part of the allowance is no longer needed. The bad debt estimation entry previously recognized the estimated economic effect of future uncollectible accounts. Thus, write-offs of specific accounts do not further reduce total assets unless they exceed the estimate.

For example, the following entry is recorded by a company deciding not to pursue collection of R. Knox's $1,000 account:

Allowance for doubtful accounts 1,000
    Accounts receivable, R. Knox   1,000

This write-off entry affects neither income nor the net amount of accounts receivable outstanding. Instead, it is the culmination of the process that began with the adjusting entry to estimate bad debt expense. The write-off entry changes only the components of net accounts receivable, not the net amount itself:

	Before Knox Write-Off (assumed)	After Knox Write-Off
Accounts receivable	$160,000	$159,000
Allowance for doubtful accounts.	(14,000)	(13,000)
Net accounts receivable.	$146,000	$146,000

---

[23] *CICA Handbook* Section 3400, paragraph .17, "Revenue."

[24] *Financial Reporting in Canada 1993* (Toronto: CICA, 1993), p. 90.

The write-off entry is recorded only when the likelihood of collection does not support further collection efforts. When should an account be written off? In one collection expert's opinion, it should be written off:

> not more than three or four months after delivery of the product or service. The typical business won't resolve bad debts for nine or ten months. They're just unwilling to confront the fact they've lost. The time factor of money has to be factored in.[25]

When amounts are received on account after a write-off, the write-off entry is reversed to reinstate the receivable and cash collection is recorded. Assume that R. Knox is able to pay $600 on account some time after the above write-off entry was recorded. These entries are required:

Accounts receivable, R. Knox.	600	
Allowance for doubtful accounts.		600
Cash .	600	
Accounts receivable, R. Knox.		600

The debit and credit to accounts receivable record the partial reinstatement and collection of the account for future reference.[26]

Estimating Bad Debt Expense

Two acceptable methods of estimating bad debt expense are the *credit sales* (income statement) method and the *accounts receivable* (balance sheet) method. The objective of the credit sales method is accurate measurement of the expense caused by uncollectible accounts. The objective of the accounts receivable method is accurate measurement of the net realizable value of accounts receivable. Some companies use both methods. A third method, called the *specific identification* method, is often used by auditors in conjunction with either of the other two methods. Troublesome receivables, which may be identified in the ageing schedule, are examined and a reasonable allowance for that account is estimated.

Exhibit 8–3 presents background information for several examples. The current $500 debit balance in Rally's allowance account does not necessarily indicate that past estimates of bad debt losses were too low. It is possible that some receivables originating in 1995 were written off and the debit balance does not yet reflect the estimate for bad debts based on 1995 sales.

Credit Sales Method This method emphasizes the matching principle and income statement. The average percentage relationship between actual bad debt losses and net credit sales is estimated on the basis of experience. This percentage is then applied to a period's net credit sales to determine bad debt expense.

Assume that in the past, 1.2% of Rally's credit sales have not been collected. Barring changes in Rally's credit policies or major changes in the economy, Rally expects this rate to continue. Under this method, the following is the required 1995 adjusting entry:

Bad debt expense $500,000(.012) .	6,000	
Allowance for doubtful accounts .		6,000

After this entry is posted, the balance in the allowance account is $5,500 ($6,000 from the adjusting entry less the prior $500 debit balance). This method *directly* computes bad debt expense *without regard* to the prior balance in the allowance

---

[25] "Collecting Overdue Bills Involves Walking Delicate Line," *The Wall Street Journal*, October 10, 1990, p. B2.

[26] In some cases, the accounts receivable department records the second entry without immediate knowledge that it relates to a written-off account. R. Knox's account would show a credit balance until the reinstatement entry is recorded. That Knox was able to pay $600 may also support reinstatement of the entire $1,000 amount, depending on Knox's situation.

EXHIBIT 8–3

Information for Bad Debt
Estimation Examples

RALLY COMPANY

January 1, 1995, balances:

Accounts receivable (debit)	$101,300
Allowance for doubtful accounts (credit).	3,300

Transactions during 1995:

Credit sales	500,000
Cash sales	700,000
Collections on accounts receivable	420,000
Accounts written off as uncollectible during 1995.	3,800

After posting of sales, collections, and write-offs, accounts receivable
and allowance for doubtful accounts appear as follows:

Accounts Receivable

Jan. 1/95 balance	101,300	Collections	420,000
Credit sales	500,000	Write-offs	3,800
Dec. 31/95 balance	177,500		

Allowance for Doubtful Accounts

Write-offs	3,800	Jan. 1/95 balance	3,300
Dec. 31/95 balance			
before adjustment	500		

---

account.[27] Rally would disclose $172,000 ($177,500 − $5,500) of net accounts receivable in the 1995 balance sheet as follows:

Accounts receivable	$177,500
Less: Allowance for doubtful accounts	5,500
Net accounts receivable	$172,000

The credit sales method emphasizes the income statement because its primary focus is on bad debt expense. The matching principle is the conceptual basis for this method because bad debt expense is based on sales. The method is simple and economical to implement. The percentage applied to credit sales should be updated periodically to approximate the rate of actual write-offs.

Accounts Receivable Method This method emphasizes the net realizable value of net accounts receivable and uses historical data to estimate the percentage of accounts receivable expected to become uncollectible. The accounts receivable method results in a net accounts receivable balance that more closely fulfills the *CICA Handbook* Section 1000 definition of an asset because it directly considers the collectibility of the accounts receivable.

In contrast to the credit sales method, the accounts receivable method estimates the ending allowance account balance required to state net accounts receivable at estimated net realizable value. The current balance in the allowance account then is updated through the adjusting entry so that it equals this required balance. Bad debt expense is debited for the amount of this adjustment. Bad debt expense therefore is computed *indirectly*.

---

[27] One variation of this method applies a percentage to total net sales rather than to credit sales. This percentage would be less than the percentage based on credit sales alone because cash sales are included in the base used for estimation. If the ratio of cash sales to credit sales is reasonably constant, this variation produces acceptable results.

To estimate the required ending allowance balance, either a single composite rate based on total accounts receivable or a series of rates based on the age of individual accounts receivable (ageing of accounts receivable) can be used.

Single Composite Rate   Assume that experience leads Rally Company (Exhibit 8–3) to use a single 3% composite rate. Therefore, the *required* ending allowance credit balance is $5,325 (.03 × $177,500). The allowance account currently reflects a $500 debit balance, so the adjusting entry increases the allowance account $5,825 ($5,325 + $500), yielding the $5,325 ending credit balance:

Bad debt expense.	5,825	
Allowance for doubtful accounts		5,825

Rally's 1995 current assets include the following:

Accounts receivable	$177,500
Less: Allowance for doubtful accounts	5,325
Net accounts receivable	$172,175

The estimated net realizable value of accounts receivable is $172,175 in this case. Previously discussed adjustments, including allowance for sales discounts and allowance for sales returns and allowances, could reduce this amount further.

Ageing of Accounts Receivable   The ageing approach categorizes the individual receivables according to age (the ageing schedule) and applies a historical collection loss percentage to each age category to determine the required ending allowance balance.

The age categories are based on the extent to which accounts are past due. An account is past due if it is not collected by the end of the period specified in the credit terms. For example, an account arising from a November 1 sale with terms 2/10, n/30, is due December 1. If the account remains unpaid at December 31, the ageing analysis classifies the account as 30 days past due.

Exhibit 8–4 illustrates Rally's ageing schedule and the application of the collection loss percentages. The $177,500 receivable balance is divided into four age classifications with a collection loss percentage applied to each age category. Rally's collection loss percentages increase with the age of the accounts. As accounts are collected and removed from each category, the proportion represented by uncollectible accounts increases.

The computation in Exhibit 8–4 yields a required ending balance in the allowance account at December 31, 1995, of $5,690 (credit). Because the allowance balance is $500 (debit) before adjustment, the allowance account is increased $6,190, yielding an ending $5,690 balance.

Bad debt expense ($5,690 + $500)	6,190	
Allowance for doubtful accounts		6,190

In the single composite rate and ageing examples, had the allowance balance been a $500 credit before adjustment, bad debt expense would have been $4,825 ($5,325 − $500) and $5,190 ($5,690 − $500), respectively.

Which Method to Use?   The credit sales and accounts receivable estimation methods may be used together. Each is used to validate the other although only one may be used in the accounts. For interim financial statements, many companies base monthly or quarterly adjusting entries on the credit sales method because of its low cost. At the end of the year, they may age their accounts receivable to check the reasonableness of the allowance balance.

Computerization has reduced costs of implementing the ageing method, and increasing cash flow problems prompt companies to monitor the age of their receivables more closely to reduce losses. In addition, the ageing method corrects for prior

EXHIBIT 8–4
Ageing of Accounts
Receivable

RALLY COMPANY
Accounts Receivable Ageing Schedule
December 31, 1995

Ageing Schedule

Customer	Receivable Balance Dec. 31, 1995	Current	Past due		
			1–30 days	31–60 days	Over 60 Days
Denk	$ 500	$ 400	$ 100		
Evans	900	900			
Field	1,650		1,350	$ 300	
Harris	90			30	$ 60
King	800	700	60	40	
Zabot	250	250			
Total	$177,500	$110,000	$31,000	$29,500	$7,000

Application of Collection Loss Percentages to Age Categories

Age Category	Total Balances	Collection Loss Percentage	Amount Estimated to Be Uncollectible
Not past due (current).	$110,000	.2%	$ 220
1–30 days past due	31,000	1.0	310
31–60 days past due.	29,500	8.0	2,360
Over 60 days past due.	7,000	40.0	2,800
	$177,500		$5,690

errors in estimating uncollectible accounts because it regularly reevaluates the loss percentages in each age category.

The general condition of the economy, the economic health of specific customers, and the seller's credit policy and collection effort affect the rate of account write-offs. Over time, this rate changes, necessitating adjustment to the percentages applied to credit sales or receivables. If the balance in allowance for doubtful accounts is found to increase each year, the estimate of uncollectibles is decreased to reflect actual experience.

Depending on the firm's fortunes, estimated uncollectible accounts can be a very significant expense item. For the fiscal year ended January 29, 1993, Hughes Supply, Inc., recognized $1.73 million of bad debt expense, which was 77% of earnings that year. Other firms have recognized bad debt expense in amounts sufficient to cause an overall loss for the accounting period.

Direct Write-Off of Uncollectible Accounts

Companies in the first year of operation or in new lines of business may have no basis for estimating uncollectibles. In such cases, and when uncollectible accounts are immaterial, GAAP allows receivables to be written off directly as they become uncollectible. The entry for the direct write-off of a $2,000 account receivable from M. Lynx is as follows:

Bad debt expense. 2,000
    Accounts receivable, M. Lynx 2,000

No adjusting entry is made at the end of an accounting period under the direct write-off method.

GLOBAL VIEW

The IASC's *Framework for the Preparation and Presentation of Financial Statements,* the international counterpart to *CICA Handbook* Section 1000, fundamentally embraces the same general accounting principles supporting the reporting of receivables and recognition of uncollectibles. The accrual basis of accounting is the foundation for recognition:

> Under this basis, the effects of transactions and other events are recognized when they occur (and not as cash or its equivalent is received or paid) [par. 22].

In addition, the *Framework* requires that the following two criteria be fulfilled before a financial statement element is recognized (par. 83):

a. It is probable that any future economic benefit associated with the item will flow to or from the enterprise.
b. The item has a cost or value that can be measured with reliability.

Although no specific IASC standard governs measurement of uncollectible receivables, the accrual concept and requirements for recognition of financial statement elements support the use of the allowance method of recognizing uncollectibles.

Uncollectible receivables are an expected aspect of business. Uncollectible loans were a major contributing factor to the savings and loan crisis in the United States during the 80s. But firms all over the world are affected by this problem, as exemplified by Credit Lyonnais, in France, which suffered a 15% decline in 1991 earnings as a result of sharply higher provisions for bad debts.

At the present time, few IASC standards directly address reporting for cash and receivables. Although firms in most industrialized nations follow principles similar to those followed in Canada, there are minor differences. Under *International Accounting Standard No. 13,* cash may include restricted balances if the term of the restriction is one year or less. Similarly, all trade receivables may be classified as current if the amount not expected to be realized within one year is disclosed.

The inability to estimate uncollectible accounts creates several unavoidable problems. First, receivables are reported at more than their net realizable value, even though it is virtually certain that not all receivables are collectible. Second, the period of write-off is often after the period of sale, violating the matching principle. And third, direct write-off opens the potential for income manipulation by arbitrary selection of the write-off period.

CONCEPT REVIEW

1. What are the advantages of the net method of recording cash discounts?
2. Explain the computation of the annual rate of interest for cash discounts lost.
3. What are the advantages and disadvantages of the two approaches to the allowance method of accounting for bad debt expense?

USE OF ACCOUNTS RECEIVABLE TO OBTAIN IMMEDIATE CASH

Companies frequently sell or use their accounts receivable as collateral to secure loans. The objective is to obtain more immediate access to cash. Sales of accounts receivable (also called **factoring**), **assignment,** and **pledging** are common forms of financing. The original holder of the accounts receivables is called the **transferor** (in factoring), **assignor** (in assignment), or the **pledger** (in pledging). Similarly, the company providing the cash is called the **transferee, assignee,** or **pledgee,** respectively and is usually a finance company or bank.

Using receivables to obtain financing effectively shortens the operating cycle, hastens the return of cash to productive purposes, and alleviates short-run cash flow problems. The costs of these arrangements include initial fees and interest on loans collateralized by the receivables. Also, certain risks may be retained by the transferor, including bearing the cost of bad debts, cash discounts, and sales returns and allowances.

Agreements to transfer accounts receivable are made on a **recourse** or **nonrecourse** basis. In recourse financing arrangements, the transferee can collect from the transferor if the original debtor (customer) fails to pay. If the arrangement is without recourse, the transferee assumes the risk of collection losses. The fee is therefore higher under nonrecourse arrangements because more risk is transferred.

Agreements are made on either a **notification** basis (customers are directed to remit to the new party holding the receivables) or a nonnotification basis (customers continue to remit to the original seller). Factoring arrangements are usually made on a notification basis.

The CICA's Accounting Standards Board (AcSB), in conjunction with the International Accounting Standards Committee (IASC), issued the Re-Exposure Draft "Financial Instruments" in April 1994. Paragraph .028 of the proposed standard states:

> A recognized financial asset or financial liability should be removed from an entity's balance sheet when:
> (a) substantially all of the risks and rewards associated with the asset or liability have been transferred to others and the fair value of any risks and rewards retained can be measured reliably; or
> (b) the underlying right or obligation has been exercised, discharged or cancelled, or has expired.

Therefore, the key financial reporting issue in a receivable-financing arrangement is whether the transaction is a sale or loan. In a sale, the transferor removes the receivables from the books and records a gain or loss. In a loan, the receivables remain on the transferor's books and a liability is recorded. Generally, recording a sale is preferred, especially if a transferor's total debt is already substantial.

Factoring Accounts Receivable

Factoring transfers ownership of the receivables to the transferee (the **factor**). In some instances, the factor performs credit verification, receivables servicing, and collection agency services—in effect, taking over a company's accounts receivable and credit operations. Other factoring arrangements are less inclusive.

Factoring is common in the textile industry. Many apparel makers will not risk shipping merchandise to retailers without assurance that a factor will purchase the resulting receivables. The factor charges a fee in return for accepting the risk of default by retailers. If that risk is too great, the factor will suspend credit to the apparel maker. For example, Home Shopping Network, Inc., began experiencing financial difficulties. Several factors then suspended credit to a number of apparel makers supplying Home Shopping, in fear that the retailer would be unable to meet its payments. Home Shopping's ability to purchase merchandise was sharply reduced as a result.[28]

Factoring without Recourse   A nonrecourse factoring arrangement generally constitutes an ordinary sale of receivables because the factor has no recourse against the transferor for uncollectible accounts. Control over the receivables passes to the factor. The factor typically assumes legal title to the receivables, the cost of uncollectible accounts, and collection responsibilities. However, any adjustments or defects in the receivables (sales discounts, returns, and allowances) are borne by the transferor because these represent preexisting conditions.

The receivables are removed from the transferor's books, cash is debited, and a financing fee is recognized immediately as a financing expense or loss on sale. Normally, the factor withholds an amount to cover probable sales adjustments (sales discounts, returns, and allowances). This amount is recorded as a receivable on the seller's books.

Example   To illustrate factoring without recourse, consider the following case. Largo, Inc., factors without recourse $200,000 of accounts receivable on August 15, 1995, with a finance company on a notification basis. The factor charges a 12%

---

[28] "Home Shopping Is Dealt Blow from Factors," *The Wall Street Journal*, April 16, 1993, p. A3.

financing fee and retains an amount equal to 10% of the accounts receivable for sales adjustments. Largo does not record bad debt expense on these receivables because, in nonrecourse transfers, the finance company bears the cost of uncollectible accounts. The entry to record the transfer is:

Largo, Inc.

Cash $200,000 − (.12 + .10)$200,000	156,000	
Receivable from factor (.10)$200,000	20,000	
Loss on sale of receivables (.12)$200,000	24,000	
Accounts receivable . .		200,000

Finance Company

Accounts receivable	200,000	
Payable to Largo . . .		20,000
Financing revenue . .		24,000
Cash		156,000

Largo's loss equals the finance fee. This amount is also the book value of the receivables factored less the assets received from the finance company ($200,000 − $156,000 − $20,000). As customer sales adjustments occur, Largo records these deductions in the proper contra sales accounts and credits the receivable from factor. After all adjustments are recorded, any excess in the receivable is remitted to Largo. If adjustments exceed the amount withheld by the factor ($20,000 in this case), either the finance company or the seller absorbs this amount as a loss or the two parties agree to allocate it in some other manner.

Assuming that 1% of the receivables ($2,000) is estimated to be uncollectible, the finance company makes the following entry:

Finance Company

Bad debt expense	2,000	
Allowance for doubtful accounts		2,000

Assume that there were altogether $4,000 of cash discounts, $12,000 of sales returns and allowances, and $2,000 of uncollectible accounts. Therefore, customers remitted $182,000 ($200,000 − $4,000 − $12,000 − $2,000) to the finance company.

The next two entries for Largo record the sales adjustments, and the return of the excess amount held back by the finance company.

Largo, Inc.

Sales returns and allowances	12,000	
Sales discounts	4,000	
Receivable from factor		16,000
Cash	4,000	
Receivable from factor ($20,000 − $4,000 − $12,000)		4,000

The finance company records customer collections, reduces the payable to Largo by the amount of actual sales adjustments ($16,000), records actual write-offs, and settles the remaining payable to Largo.

Finance Company

Cash	182,000	
Payable to Largo	16,000	
Accounts receivable		198,000
Allowance for doubtful accounts	2,000	
Accounts receivable		2,000
Payable to Largo	4,000	
Cash		4,000

The final entry for each firm is not recorded until all the receivables are either collected, written off, or otherwise reduced by sales adjustments. The sales adjustments are recorded on Largo's books because Largo recorded the original sale.

EXHIBIT 8–5
Income and Cash Flow
Summary of Nonrecourse
Factoring Example

Largo

Assumed gross margin percentage: 24%

Net cash received on $200,000 of financed receivables:

Original proceeds	$156,000
Settlement payment	4,000
Net cash received	$160,000

Increase in net income from sales and financing of receivables:

Gross sales	$200,000
Sales returns and allowances	(12,000)
Sales discounts	(4,000)
Net sales to Largo	184,000
Gross margin percentage	.24
Gross margin on net sales	44,160
Loss on sale of receivables	(24,000)
Increase in net income	$ 20,160

Finance Company

Net cash received from financed receivables:

Collections on account	$182,000
Proceeds to Largo	(156,000)
Settlement payment	(4,000)
Net cash received	$ 22,000

Increase in net income from financing of receivables:

Financing revenue	$ 24,000
Bad debt expense	(2,000)
Increase in net income	$ 22,000

Reconciliation of Cash and Factored Receivables Schedule

Cash received by both parties:		Receivables sold to finance company:	
Largo	$160,000	Gross receivables	$200,000
Finance company	22,000	Sales discounts	(4,000)
		Sales returns and allowances	(12,000)
		Bad debt expense	(2,000)
Total cash received	$182,000	Net receivables collected	$182,000

Exhibit 8–5 summarizes the income and cash flow effects of the financing arrangement for both parties.

Credit Card Operations   Although bank credit card companies such as Visa and MasterCard are not factors, they are sometimes considered in the same category for accounts receivable financing purposes. Two benefits accrue to the merchant who accepts credit cards. First, the merchant receives immediate cash on sales that otherwise would be made on credit (or not made at all). Second, unless the merchant prefers to maintain its own credit card operation in addition to accepting national cards (which many department stores do), the merchant saves the cost of customer screening and servicing functions.

Normally, a merchant accumulates credit card sales in batches, depending on volume. Credit card vouchers are deposited with a bank acting as agent for the credit card company, and the amount remitted is discounted by the credit card company. Assume that a merchant accumulates $2,000 in credit card sales. The discount fee is 6%. The appropriate entry at the time of deposit is as follows:

To deposit credit card vouchers:

Cash	1,880	
Credit card fees expense (.06) ($2,000)	120	
Sales		2,000

If sales are posted daily with deposits made less frequently, a receivable is debited rather than cash.[29]

Factoring with Recourse   When receivables are factored with recourse, the transferor bears the risk and cost of sales adjustments and bad debts because the finance company has recourse against the transferor. Whether all the benefits of receivables are transferred in recourse arrangements is not as clear as in nonrecourse arrangements. The transferor records a sale or a loan depending on the transfer of risks and rewards of the receivables and on whether the transferor can estimate future obligations to the transferee under the contract.

The CICA's Emerging Issues Committee provides guidance in EIC-9, "Transfer of Receivables," which states that:

> for a transaction involving a transfer of receivables to be recognized as a sale, both of the following conditions should exist:
> i. the transferor has transferred the significant risks and rewards of ownership of the receivables; and
> ii. reasonable assurance exists regarding the measurement of the consideration derived from the transfer of the receivables.

If the transferor retains the option to repurchase the receivables, risks and rewards may not pass to the transferee and the first criterion fails.

If the transferor cannot estimate the ultimate collectibility of the receivables, criterion 2 fails. This situation is similar to sales made with right of return, discussed in Chapter 7. If estimates of sales returns are not possible, a sale is not recognized until the right of return expires.

If the obligations of the transferor are limited to estimable payments under the recourse provisions (payments to the transferee for bad debt losses, cash discounts, returns, and allowances), there is no obligation to repay the proceeds from the transfer. In this case, a sale is properly reported, assuming that the other criteria are met.

A recourse provision requiring the transferor to repurchase receivables in the event of default by the original customer does not imply the existence of a liability at date of transfer. However, the recourse provisions must be reasonable in relation to the losses expected to be incurred on the receivables transferred. What is reasonable is a matter of professional judgment. It is unlikely that a sale of receivables has occurred if the total recourse exceeds 10% of the proceeds received.

Exhibit 8–6 continues the Largo, Inc., example with additional data to illustrate accounting for factoring with recourse. Below, we describe the transferor's entries accounting for the transfer as a sale or a loan. All entries shown are recorded by Largo because the entries for the transferee are similar to the nonrecourse example described earlier.

Case 1: Factoring with Recourse Recorded as a Sale   In a recourse factoring recorded as a sale, the transferor recognizes the *probable* sales adjustments. The difference between the book value of receivables transferred and assets received from the factor is recognized immediately as a gain or loss on the sale:

Largo, Inc.

Cash $200,000 − (.06 + .10)$200,000		168,000
Receivable from factor ($20,000 − $9,000 − $5,000 − $3,000)		3,000
Bad debt expense		3,000
Sales returns and allowances		9,000
Sales discounts		5,000
Loss on sale of receivables		12,000*
Accounts receivable		200,000

* Book value of receivables less assets received = ($200,000 − $3,000 − $9,000 − $5,000) − ($168,000 + $3,000).

---

[29] Some banks and credit card companies sell their receivables to other parties. Banc One Corporation of Columbus, Ohio, is credited with starting the securitization of credit card accounts. In 1986, it sold $50 million of its credit card receivables as securities. See *The Wall Street Journal*, Centennial Issue, June 23, 1989, p. A2.

EXHIBIT 8–6
Largo, Inc., Information for
Factoring with Recourse

Largo, Inc., factors with recourse $200,000 of accounts receivable on August 15, 1995, with a finance company on a notification basis. The factor retains 10% of the accounts receivable to protect against sales adjustments.

Additional Information for Sale Example (Case 1):

1. Both criteria are met, and the transfer is recorded as a sale.
2. The financing fee is 6% (less than in the nonrecourse example).
3. Largo estimates the following sales adjustments:
   a. Sales returns and allowances of $9,000 ($12,000 of returns and allowances are experienced, as in the previous illustration).
   b. Sales discounts of $5,000 ($4,000 actually occurred).
   c. Uncollectible accounts of $3,000 ($2,000 of accounts are actually written off).

Additional Information for the Loan Example (Case 2):

1. Largo is unable to estimate sales discounts and sales returns and allowances and retains the option to repurchase the receivables. Therefore, the transfer is recorded as a loan.
2. The financing fee is 6%.
3. Largo estimates $3,000 of uncollectible accounts ($2,000 of accounts are actually written off).

In general, the cash debit equals the gross accounts receivable factored less the finance fee and any amount held back by the factor. The receivable from the factor represents the total amount held back less the estimated sales adjustments and uncollectibles. These adjustments are immediately recognized and matched against the previously recorded sales. The extra $3,000 held back by the transferee is a buffer for estimation errors.

The recognized loss also equals the product of the finance fee and gross accounts receivable (.06 × $200,000). The cost of uncollectibles is assumed by Largo in recourse factoring.

After all collections are received by the finance company, the final settlement is recorded:

Largo, Inc.

Cash	2,000	
Sales expenses	1,000*	
Receivable from factor		3,000

* ($12,000 + $4,000 + $2,000) − ($9,000 + $5,000 + $3,000)

The $1,000 difference between actual and estimated adjustments is expensed. The difference is the result of an estimation error and is therefore treated as a change in estimate.

Case 2: Factoring with Recourse Recorded as a Loan In a recourse factoring recorded as a loan, the transferor recognizes the difference between the assets received from the factor and the book value of the receivables as interest over the term of the loan. This is in contrast to the sale example, in which the difference was immediately recognized as a loss. In this example, the transaction is treated as a loan because Largo retains the option to repurchase the receivables. Entries to record the loan and estimated uncollectible accounts are:

Largo, Inc.

Cash $200,000 − (.06 + .10)$200,000	168,000	
Receivable from factor (.10)$200,000	20,000	
Discount on payable to factor (.06)$200,000	12,000	
Payable to factor		200,000
Bad debt expense	3,000	
Allowance for doubtful accounts		3,000

Receivables are not removed from the transferor's books in a loan transaction. Rather, a liability is recorded. The discount account is a contra account to the payable to factor account and represents the total interest to be paid by Largo. This contra account is amortized as interest expense over the loan term. While an interest approach would be appropriate, the discount can also be amortized based on collections.

Largo records sales adjustments as they occur and reduces the payable as customers remit cash to the factor.

Largo, Inc.

Sales discounts.	4,000	
Sales returns and allowances.	12,000	
Accounts receivable		16,000
Payable to factor	182,000	
Accounts receivable ($200,000 − $12,000 − $4,000 − $2,000)		182,000
Notification basis: customers remit to the finance company.		

The entries to record write-offs, and final settlement are:

Largo, Inc.

Allowance for doubtful accounts	2,000	
Accounts receivable		2,000
Payable to factor	18,000	
Cash ($20,000 − $12,000 − $4,000 − $2,000)	2,000	
Receivable from factor		20,000

Assume that Largo recognizes interest expense in proportion to collections on accounts receivable. That proportion is a measure of the expired portion of the loan term. The following entry records interest expense, assuming that all collections were received by the end of the fiscal year.

Largo, Inc.

Interest expense	12,000	
Discount on payable to factor		12,000

If accounts receivable are outstanding at the end of the year, a pro rata portion of the discount is amortized in a later period of collection. For example, if $20,000 of the accounts receivable (10% of the total factored) were outstanding at the end of 1995, only $10,800 of interest expense (.90 × $12,000) would be recognized in the above entry.

Assignment and Pledging of Accounts Receivable

Assignment and pledging entail the use of receivables as collateral for a loan. An assignment of accounts receivable requires the assignor to assign the rights to specific receivables. Frequently, the assignor and the finance company enter into a long-term agreement whereby the assignor receives cash from the finance company as sales are made. The accounts are assigned with recourse, and the assignee has the right to seek payment from the specific receivables.

The assignor usually retains title to the receivables, continues to receive payments from customers (nonnotification basis), bears collection costs and the risk of bad debts, and agrees to use any cash collected from customers to pay the loan. A formal promissory note often allows the assignee (lender) to seek payment directly from the receivables if the loan is not paid when due.

The loan proceeds are typically less than the face value of the receivables assigned in order to compensate for sales adjustments and to give the assignee a margin of protection. The assignee charges a service fee and interest on the unpaid balance each month.

The receivables are reclassified as accounts receivable assigned, a separate category within accounts receivable used to disclose their status as collateral. The subsidiary accounts are also reclassified for internal accounting purposes to indicate their use as collateral. The loan balance is reported among the assignor's other liabilities.

Example　Assume that on November 30, 1995, Franklin Corporation assigns $80,000 of its accounts receivable to a finance company on a nonnotification basis. Franklin agrees to remit customer collections as payment on the loan. Loan proceeds are 85% of the receivables less a $1,500 flat-fee finance charge. In addition, the finance company charges 12% interest on the unpaid loan balance, payable at the end of each month.

In the entries below, accounts receivable assigned is a current asset listed under accounts receivable in the balance sheet. All entries are for Franklin.

To record receipt of loan proceeds:

Cash .85($80,000) − $1,500	66,500	
Finance expense	1,500	
Notes payable .85(80,000)		68,000

To classify accounts receivable as assigned:

Accounts receivable assigned	80,000	
Accounts receivable		80,000

By the end of December, assume that Franklin has collected $46,000 cash on $50,000 of the assigned accounts less $3,000 sales returns and $1,000 sales discounts, and remits the proceeds to the finance company.

To record sales adjustments:

Cash ($50,000 − $3,000 − $1,000)	46,000	
Sales discounts	1,000	
Sales returns and allowances	3,000	
Accounts receivable assigned		50,000

To remit collections to finance company:

Notes payable	45,320	
Interest expense $68,000(.12) ($\frac{1}{12}$)	680	
Cash		46,000

Assigned accounts receivable are part of the total balance in accounts receivable. If the assigned amounts are material, they should be reported as a separate subtotal within accounts receivable. GAAP significantly restricts the offsetting of accounts and specifies, among other requirements, that in order for accounts to be offset, the entity:

(a) has a legally enforceable right to set off the recognized amounts; and
(b) intends either to settle on a net basis, or to realize the asset and settle the liability simultaneously.[30]

When accounts receivable are assigned, only the assignor is a debtor and there is no legal right of setoff. Therefore, the note payable is reported in the assignor's liability section.

Assume, now, that in January 1996, $2,000 of the accounts are written off as uncollectible (the original $80,000 of receivables is included in the normal bad debt estimation process). Also, $25,000 is collected on account. The remaining entries complete the process, assuming that the loan is paid in full at the end of January.

To record collection and write-off in January:

Cash	25,000	
Allowance for doubtful accounts	2,000	
Accounts receivable assigned		27,000

---

[30] *CICA Re-Exposure Draft*, "Financial Instruments," par. .062.

January 31, 1996—Payment of remaining loan balance:

Notes payable	22,680	
Interest expense $22,680(.12) (1/12)	227	
Cash		22,907

To record reclassification of remaining accounts:

Accounts receivable ($80,000 − $50,000 − $27,000)	3,000	
Accounts receivable assigned		3,000

Pledging of accounts receivable is a less formal way of using receivables as collateral for loans. Proceeds from receivables must be used to pay the loan, but accounts receivable are not reclassified. If the pledger (borrower) defaults on the loan, the pledgee (creditor) has the right to use the receivables for payment. The accounting for the receivables or the loan is not affected by pledging. When the loan is extinguished, the pledge is voided.

Disclosure of Accounts Receivable Financing Arrangements

Income statement and balance sheet disclosure of receivable financing arrangements is not specifically required in the *CICA Handbook*. However, Section 1500, paragraph .12 requires disclosure of "the nature, and where practicable, the carrying value" of any assets pledged as security against liabilities. This general provision would seem to require appropriate disclosure so that the users of the financial statements are able to determine the risk associated with the pledged assets.

> *CONCEPT REVIEW*
>
> 1. Why is a sale implied when the criteria of EIC-9 are fulfilled?
> 2. What effect does a recourse provision have on reporting of transfers of receivables?
> 3. If a factored account (with recourse) becomes uncollectible, must the factoring be recorded as a loan? Explain.

RECOGNITION AND MEASUREMENT OF NOTES RECEIVABLE

A note receivable is a written promise to pay specified amounts over a series of payment dates. Notes receivable provide:
- Extended payment terms.
- More security than sales invoices and other commercial trade documents.
- A formal basis for charging interest.
- Negotiability.

Most notes receivable represent loans. Notes receivable also arise from normal sales, extension of the payment period of accounts receivable, exchanges of long-term assets, and advances to employees. The borrower is the *maker* of the note and the lender is the payee (note holder). When goods are transferred between a buyer and seller and a trade note receivable is involved, the buyer is the maker and the seller is the payee.

The interest rate stated in a note may not equal the market rate prevailing on obligations involving similar credit rating or risk, although the stated rate is always used to determine the cash interest payments. If the stated and market rates are different, the market rate is used to value the note and to measure interest revenue. The market rate is the rate accepted by two parties with opposing interests engaged in an arm's-length transaction. If the value of the consideration given is known, the rate can be determined by equating the present value of the cash flows called for in the note to the market value of the consideration. The rate can be determined with a computer program or calculator that iteratively locates the correct rate.

For example, assume that on June 30, 1995, a firm sells equipment with a cash price of $10,000 and receives in exchange a note with the following payment schedule: $6,000 due on June 30, 1996, and on June 30, 1997. The note does not explicitly require interest, but $2,000 of interest is implicit in the note. The interest rate is computed using the present value of an annuity as follows:

$$\$10,000 = \$6,000(\text{PVA}, i, 2)$$
$$\$10,000/\$6,000 = 1.66667 = (\text{PVA}, i, 2)$$

The value 1.66667 does not appear in the table for the present value of an ordinary annuity, but through a calculator equipped for present value, $i = 13.066\%$. Interpolation (see Chapter 6) could also be used.

In some cases, the value of the consideration given may also be difficult to determine and an **imputed interest rate** must be estimated from other similar transactions in the market. This rate must at least equal the rate incurred by the debtor on similar financing.[31]

For accounting purposes, the **principal amount** of a note is measured by the fair market value or cash equivalent value of goods or services provided in exchange for the note, if this value is known, or the present (discounted) value of all cash payments required under the note using the market rate. The principal is also the amount initially subject to interest. The principal represents the sacrifice by the payee, and therefore the present value of the future payments, at the date of the transaction. Any amount paid in excess of the principal is interest. Short-term notes need not be reported at present value, because the difference between present and maturity value is generally not significant.

The **face value,** or **maturity value,** is the dollar amount stated in the note. The face value is the amount, excluding interest, payable at the end of the note term, unless the note requires that principal repayments be made according to an instalment schedule. The principal value equals the maturity value if the stated interest rate equals the market interest rate. The total interest over the life of the note equals the total cash receipts less the principal amount.

Notes may be categorized as interest-bearing or noninterest-bearing notes. Interest-bearing notes specify the interest rate to be applied to the face amount in computing interest payments. Noninterest-bearing notes do not state an interest rate but command interest through face values that exceed the principal amount.

Interest-bearing notes in turn can be divided into two categories according to the type of cash payment required: (1) notes whose cash payments are interest only except for final maturity payment and (2) notes whose cash payments include both interest and principal.[32]

A 10%, $4,000, two-year note received by Vancouver Sealines, which requires interest to be paid on its face value, is an example of the first type. The annual interest of $400 ($4,000 × .10) is payable at the end of each year of the note term. The $4,000 face amount is paid at the end of the second year. In total, $800 of interest is required over the term of the note. In notes of this type, the original principal is not decreased by the yearly payment.

Now assume that Vancouver's note is instead a note of the second type, requiring two equal annual amounts payable at the end of each year. These payments each contain interest and principal in the amount necessary to discharge the debt at 10% in two payments. The payment is computed as follows:

$$\$4,000 = \text{Present value of an annuity} = \text{Payment (PVA, 10\%, 2)}$$
$$\$4,000 \div (\text{PVA}, 10\%, 2) = \text{Payment}$$
$$\$4,000 \div 1.73554 = \$2,304.76 = \text{Payment}$$

---

[31] "Interest on Receivables and Payables," *APB Opinion No. 21* (New York: AICPA, 1971), par. 13.

[32] These categorizations are made for expository purposes only. There are an unlimited number of principal and repayment options. Payment schedules are not limited to those used in the examples.

Payment	Interest Component	Principal Component
1	$400 ($4,000 × .10)	$1,904.76 ($2,304.76 − $400)
2	$209.52*	$2,095.24 ($2,304.76 − $209.52)
		$4,000.00

* ($4,000 − $1,904.76)(.10)

Total interest for the second type of note ($609.52) is less than for the first note because part of the first payment is a principal payment, which reduces the principal on which interest is paid in the second period.[33]

Notes Receivable and Accounts Receivable Compared

Recognition and valuation of notes receivable and accounts receivable are both affected by collectibility. If estimates of uncollectible notes can be made, procedures similar to those discussed for accounts receivable apply. If estimates cannot be made, the direct write-off method is used.

Long-term notes involve two additional reporting issues not considered in accounts receivable: the time value of money and the recognition of interest revenue. *CICA Re-Exposure Draft, "Financial Instruments,"* par. .074 suggests that long-term notes should be recorded at "the present value of the expected future payments discounted at the interest rate currently applied in financial markets to instruments having similar terms, conditions, risk and collateral." This rate is not changed, for accounting purposes, over the life of the note.

Notes Receivable Accounting Illustrations

In the following examples, assume that adjusting entries are not reversed.

Example 1: Simple Interest Note On April 1, 1995, Lionel Company loaned $12,000 cash to Baylor Company and received a three-year, 10% note. Interest is payable each March 31, and the principal is payable at the end of the third year. The stated and market interest rates are equal. The entry to record the note is as follows:

April 1, 1995:

Notes receivable	12,000	
Cash		12,000

The present value of the principal and interest payments on April 1, 1995, is $12,000 because the stated and market rates are equal. Cash interest received also equals interest revenue recognized over the terms of the note, as indicated in the remaining entries. The computation for interest assumes months of equal length.[34]

December 31, 1995, 1996, 1997—Adjusting entries:

Interest receivable $12,000 (.10) (9/12)	900	
Interest revenue		900

March 31, 1996, 1997:

Cash	1,200	
Interest receivable		900
Interest revenue $12,000 (.10) (3/12)		300

---

[33] Other types of notes also exist. For example, negative amortization is found in some mortgage notes. These notes allow the mortgagor to make payments early in the mortgage term that are less than the amount required to extinguish the debt over the mortgage. The difference between these payments and those required to pay off the mortgage is added to the principal and increases future amounts of interest.

[34] For very short-term notes such as a 30-day note, a convention is often followed for calculating interest: The day the note is issued is not counted in the 30 days. Rather, the first day of the note term is the day after the note is issued. A 10%, $1,000, 30-day note issued April 16 requires an April 30 adjusting entry to recognize $3.84 interest revenue (14 ÷ 365 × $1,000 × .10).

March 31, 1998:

Cash 13,200
    Notes receivable 12,000
    Interest receivable 900
    Interest revenue 300

Example 2: Different Market and Stated Rates   Fox Company, which sells specialized machinery and equipment, sold equipment on January 1, 1995, and received a two-year, $10,000 note with a 3% stated interest rate. Interest is payable each December 31, and the entire principal is payable December 31, 1996.

The equipment does not have a ready market value. The market rate of interest appropriate for this note is 10%. The present value (and principal) of the note is computed as follows (amounts are rounded to the nearest dollar):

Present value of maturity amount:
$10,000(PV1, 10%, 2) = $10,000(.82645)   = $8,265

Present value of the nominal interest payments:
$10,000(.03)(PVA, 10%, 2) = $300(1.73554)   =   521

Present value of the note at 10%: $8,786

Before *APB Opinion No. 21,* there were no definitive guidelines to use when the stated and market rates were unequal. Some companies recorded notes at face value even though the market rate exceeded the stated rate, thereby inflating notes receivable and sales. *APB Opinion No. 21,* however, requires the recording of the substance of the transaction over its form. The effect of the *CICA Re-Exposure Draft* would essentially be the same.

Notes with stated interest rates below market may be used by companies to increase sales. The Fox Company note, for example, uses a low nominal (stated) interest rate offset by an increased face value. Many buyers of big-ticket items, including automobiles, home appliances, and even houses, are more concerned about the monthly payment than the final maturity payment—the balloon payment, as it is called. A note with an $8,786 face value and a 10% stated rate achieves the same present value to Fox. A 3% interest payment on $10,000 ($300) may be more attractive than a 10% payment on $8,786 ($879). Fox earns 10% over the two-year term either way.[35]

As the Fox Company example illustrates, when the stated and market interest rates are different, the face value and principal differ. Notes are recorded at gross (face) value plus a premium or minus a discount amount (the gross method), or at the net principal value (the net method). The two methods are illustrated for the Fox example:

January 1, 1995:

	Gross		Net
Notes receivable	10,000		8,786
Discount on notes receivable		1,214	
Sales		8,786	8,786

Under either method, the net book value of the note is $8,786, the principal value. Discount on notes receivable is a contra account to notes receivable. The gross method discloses both the note's face value and the interest to be received over the remaining term. The entries at the end of the fiscal year are as follows:

---

[35] Under the alternative structuring, Fox would receive two $879 payments plus $8,786, totalling $10,544, which is less than the total cash receipts under the original structuring ($10,600). Fox receives cash more quickly under the alternative arrangement.

December 31, 1995:

	Gross		Net	
Cash $10,000(.03)	300		300	
Discount on note receivable.	579			
Notes receivable.			579	
Interest revenue $8,786(.10).		879		879

The balance sheet dated December 31, 1995, discloses the following:

	Gross	Net
Notes receivable	$10,000	
Discount on notes receivable.	635*	
Net notes receivable	$9,365	$9,365†

* $1,214 − $579.

† $8,786 + $579.

Under both methods, the previous entry increases net notes receivable by $579. Under the gross method, the discount amount is amortized, increasing net notes receivable. A substantial portion of the interest revenue is reflected in the increase in net notes receivable. The present value of the note on January 1, 1996, is the net note receivable—namely, $9,365. This value can also be computed as:

$$\$10,300(PV1, 10\%, 1) = \$10,300(.90909) = \$9,365 \text{ (rounded)}$$

The market rate of interest is applied to the beginning balance in the net note receivable to compute interest revenue. This approach, called the *interest method,* results in a constant rate of interest throughout the life of the note. Another method, the *straight-line method,* which amortizes a constant amount of discount each period but which produces a varying rate of interest, is allowed only if the results are not materially different from the interest method. In this example, the straight-line method results in discount amortization of $607 ($1,214 ÷ 2 years) and interest revenue of $907 ($607 + $300) in both years.

Continuing with the interest method, the entry at the end of 1996 is the following: December 31, 1996:

	Gross		Net	
Cash $10,000(.03)	300		300	
Discount on note receivable.	636			
Notes receivable.			636	
Interest revenue $9,365(.10).		936		936

After the December 31, 1996, entry, the net notes receivable balance is $10,000, the present value at that date. The discount account balance is now zero (rounded), and the note is collected at this time:
December 31, 1996:

	Gross		Net	
Cash	10,000		10,000	
Notes receivable.		10,000		10,000

Example 3: Note Issued for Non-Cash Consideration   Siever Company sold specialized equipment originally costing $20,000 with a net book value of $16,000 on January 1, 1995, to Bellow. The market value of the equipment was not readily determinable.

Siever received a $5,000 down payment and a $10,000, 4% note payable in four equal annual instalments starting December 31, 1995. The current market rate on notes of a similar nature and risk is 10%. With the stated rate of 4%, the payment (P) is determined as follows:

$$\$10,000 = P(PVA, 4\%, 4) = P(3.62990)$$
$$\$10,000/3.62990 = \$2,755 = P$$

Therefore, the note's principal equals the present value of four $2,755 payments at 10%:

$$\$2,755(PVA, 10\%, 4) = \$2,755(3.16987) = \$8,733$$

The present value of the consideration received is $13,733 ($5,000 + $8,733), which is therefore the agreed-on value of the equipment. The entry to record the sale (net method) is the following:

January 1, 1995:

Cash	5,000	
Notes receivable	8,733	
Accumulated depreciation ($20,000 − $16,000)	4,000	
Loss on sale of equipment	2,267	
Equipment		20,000

The loss on sale equals the net book value of the equipment ($16,000) less the present value of consideration received ($13,733). The following entry is made at the end of the fiscal year:

December 31, 1995:

Cash	2,755	
Interest revenue (.10)$8,733		873
Notes receivable		1,882

The note's book value on January 1, 1996, is $6,851 ($8,733 − $1,882). Therefore, 1996 interest revenue is $685 (.10 × $6,851).

Example 4: Notes Exchanged for Cash and Other Privileges   Long-term notes must be recorded at their present value using the appropriate interest rate. Companies may accept a note with a stated interest rate lower than the market rate in exchange for cash or other consideration worth the face value of the note. To make this a reasonable transaction, other rights or privileges must be received by the party accepting the note, beyond the cash payments required in the note.

On January 1, 1995, Quail Corporation loaned River Corporation $10,000 and accepted a $10,000 note due December 31, 1996, with 5% interest payable annually each December 31, beginning 1995. The market interest rate is 12%. River agreed to provide Quail with agricultural materials at a discount price over the note term. Two-thirds of the supplies are to be furnished during the first year. The present value of the note itself is significantly less than $10,000:

$$\text{Principal value of note} = \$10,000(PV1, 12\%, 2) + \$10,000(.05)(PVA, 12\%, 2)$$
$$= \$10,000(.79719) + \$10,000(.05)(1.69005)$$
$$= \$8,817$$

In this example, Quail would lend only $8,817 if only the note were received in exchange. The additional $1,183 ($10,000 − $8,817) is a prepayment for discount pricing. Quail thus receives two payments of $500, one payment of $10,000, and discount pricing on purchases over the note term. The value of the other privileges should be recorded as an asset equal to the difference between the note's present and face values. The entries on Quail's books are as follows (gross method):

January 1, 1995:

Notes receivable	10,000	
Prepaid purchases	1,183	
Discount on notes receivable		1,183
Cash		10,000

Two-thirds of the prepaid purchases account is a current asset on January 1, 1995, and one-third is a long-term asset. The entries to record receipt of cash and to recognize two-thirds of the discount are as follows:

December 31, 1995:

Cash	500	
Discount on notes receivable	558	
Interest revenue (.12)$8,817		1,058
Purchases (⅔ × $1,183)	789	
Prepaid purchases		789

The remaining prepaid purchases account is now a current asset for 1996. The entries on December 31, 1996, when the contract concludes are as follows:

December 31, 1996:

Cash	500	
Discount on notes receivable	625	
Interest revenue (.12)($8,817 + $558)		1,125
Purchases (⅓)$1,183	394	
Prepaid purchases		394
Cash	10,000	
Notes receivable		10,000

Accounting for Loan Impairments

According to *CICA Handbook* Section 3025, paragraph .03, "Impaired Loans," a note receivable or other loan is considered impaired when the creditor (investor or holder) "no longer has reasonable assurance of timely collection of the full amount of principal and interest." This situation arises if principal or interest payments are likely not to be collected or if payments will not be received as scheduled. Virtual certainty that a loss has occurred is not necessary for a loan to be impaired.

CICA Handbook Section 3025, paragraph .02, "Impaired Loans," defines a loan as:

> a financial asset resulting from the delivery of cash or other assets by a lender to a borrower in return for a promise to repay on a specified date or dates, or on demand, usually with interest.

The extent of impairment of a loan would depend on numerous factors, including economic conditions, delays in payment, independent credit reports, failure to meet debt covenants, downgrading of the borrower's credit status, or the decline in market value of a traded debt instrument. A serious decline in the value of a loan's collateral could also indicate that the loan is impaired. An insignificant delay or shortfall in payments would not constitute a loan impairment, nor is a loan impaired if the creditor expects to collect interest for the period of delay.

Recording a Loan Impairment   The **net carrying value** of an impaired loan is either:

1. The present value of expected future cash flows discounted at the loan's effective interest rate (the rate implicit in the original agreement).
2. The loan's market value (or market value of collateral if the collateral is expected to provide the sole payment).

Creditors can measure impaired loans on a loan-by-loan basis. Otherwise, they can aggregate loans with similar risk characteristics and apply a composite effective rate, an average recovery period, and an average recoverable amount.

A creditor's investment in a loan is the amount initially recorded plus accrued interest. If the loan is impaired, the net carrying value is less than the recorded investment, necessitating a write-down to carrying value. The write-down is accomplished with a debit to charge for loan impairment (an expense) and a credit to a valuation allowance account (contra to notes receivable).

Example   Swiss Army, Inc., a calendar-year firm, sold merchandise (selling price, $5,000) to Finnair, Inc., on January 1, 1994, and received a two-year, 6%, $5,000 note. The note calls for annual interest to be paid each December 31. Swiss Army collected the 1994 interest on schedule. At December 31, 1995, however, based on Finnair's recent financial problems, Swiss Army expects that the 1995 interest payment will not be collectible and that only $3,000 of the principal will be collected. The principal payment is expected to be delayed until December 31, 1997 (two years late).

Swiss Army records the following entries for 1995 accrued interest, and the impairment:

December 31, 1995:

Notes receivable (.06)$5,000	300	
Interest revenue		300
Charge for loan impairment	2,630	
Allowance for loan impairment.		2,630

Investment in note	$5,300
Carrying value of note: $3,000(PV1, 6%, 2) = $3,000(.89)	2,670
Amount of write-down	$2,630

The write-down entry recognizes the impairment loss in 1995, the year it is determined, and reduces the net carrying value of the note to $2,670 (estimated realizable value). Swiss Army's December 31, 1995, balance sheet reflects the following:

Noncurrent assets:	
Notes receivable	$5,300
Allowance for loan impairment.	(2,630)
Net carrying value	$2,670

Assuming no change in future estimated cash flows, Swiss Army would accrue interest on the net carrying value at 6% until the final payment is received. The allowance account is reduced (carrying value increased) when $160 ($2,670 × .06) of interest revenue is recognized on December 31, 1996, and $170 on December 31, 1997 [($2,670 + $160) × .06]. Alternatively, loan impairment expense may be credited rather than interest revenue. The net carrying value equals $3,000, the amount collected, on December 31, 1997.

The AcSB concluded that loan impairments should reflect the loss from deterioration of the debtor's ability to pay but that the original loan agreement remains unchanged. Therefore, rather than change the interest rate to reflect general changes in interest rates, the creditor applies the original effective rate.

Subsequent Changes in Loan Value   Changes in the amount or timing of an impaired loan's expected future cash flows or in the market value of the loan may occur after the initial write-down. During the remaining term of the loan, these changes require adjustments to the allowance account and to the impairment expense account. The carrying value can be increased or decreased but may not exceed the investment in the loan. For example, if new information about Finnair at December 31, 1996, implies that $4,000 will be collected on December 31, 1997, rather than the previous estimate of $3,000, Swiss Army makes the following adjustment, which increases net income:

December 31, 1996:

Allowance for loan impairment.	1,104	
Charge for loan impairment		1,104

New carrying value balance: $4,000(PV1, 6%, 1) = $4,000(.9434)	$3,774
Carrying value, December 31, 1995	2,670
Reduction in allowance account balance	$1,104

If the creditor can distinguish the interest portion of the increase in present value (due to the passage of time) from the portion due to changes in amounts or timing of future cash flows, the interest portion may be recorded as interest revenue. Swiss Army chose to recognize the entire change as a credit to the loan impairment expense. The method of recording the change in present value should be used consistently. If market value is the basis for measuring the loan, the adjustment is charged or credited entirely to loan impairment expense.

When the last payment on the Swiss Army's impaired loan is collected, a final adjustment to the loan impairment expense may be needed. Assume that Finnair pays $3,600 on December 31, 1997, and that payment is the last to be received. Swiss Army makes the final entry:

Cash	3,600	
Allowance for loan impairment ($2,630 − $1,104)	1,526	
Charge for loan impairment	174	
Notes receivable		5,300

Discounting Notes Receivable

Rather than hold a note to maturity, payees often discount the note with a bank or financial institution. Notes can be discounted, or sold, by any holder, as well as the original payee, at any time before the note's maturity date. The process has three steps, as indicated in Exhibit 8–7. In the first step, the maker receives goods, services, or cash from the payee in exchange for the note. In the second step, the payee discounts the note with a bank and receives the maturity value of the note less a discount (a fee) charged by the bank. In the third step, the maker pays the bank at the maturity of the note.

Notes are discounted with or without recourse and are recorded as a borrowing or a sale. Most note discountings are with recourse, fulfill the criteria of *CICA Handbook* Section 3290, and are recorded as sales of receivables. The payee records a gain or loss equal to the difference between the proceeds and book value of the note, including accrued interest, and has a contingent liability until the note is paid by the maker.[36] If the note is discounted without recourse, the payee has no contingent liability.

If a discounted note is recorded as a borrowing, a liability is recorded and interest expense is recognized over the term of borrowing. The proceeds to the payee are not affected by the reporting alternatives and are based on the total of principal value plus interest to maturity, whether or not the note is interest bearing. The bank charges its discount rate on this total amount for the period between the date of discounting and the date of maturity of the note. The sum of principal and interest is the amount at risk, from the bank's point of view.

Notes Receivable Discounting Recorded as a Sale   On April 1, 1995, Winnipeg Company received a $3,000, 10%, one-year note from a sale of equipment to Nell

EXHIBIT 8–7
Three Steps in
Discounting a Note

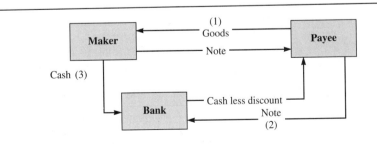

---

[36] This contingent liability is for the face value plus interest to maturity.

Company. Interest on the note is due at maturity. Winnipeg discounted the note on August 1, 1995, with recourse. Assume that the discounting qualifies as a sale and that the bank charges 15%. The proceeds to Winnipeg are as follows:

Principal value	$3,000
Interest to maturity $3,000(.10)	300
Total maturity value subject to discount	3,300
Interest charged by bank $3,300(.15)(8/12)	330
Proceeds to Winnipeg[37]	$2,970

The bank charges interest on the maturity value a full eight months before that value is reached, effectively raising the interest cost to Winnipeg Company. Winnipeg records the following entries to discount the note:

August 1, 1995:

Interest receivable $3,000(.10)(4/12)	100	
Interest revenue		100
Cash	2,970	
Loss on discounting of note	130	
Notes receivable		3,000
Interest receivable		100

The note is no longer an asset of Winnipeg and is removed from the books. The loss equals the book value of the note plus accrued interest ($3,100) less the proceeds. Two factors contribute to the loss: The note was transferred relatively early in its term, and the bank charged a higher interest rate. If the note had been held longer before it was discounted, the total interest charged by the bank would have been reduced, thus increasing the proceeds.

A second acceptable method for recording the Nell note discounting is as follows:

August 1, 1995:

Cash	2,970	
Interest expense	30	
Notes receivable		3,000

Interest expense represents the face value less the proceeds and is the net cost to Winnipeg of this financing arrangement. The interest expense in this case is determined by offsetting the loss with the interest revenue. The first alternative recognizes the increase in the note's value through the date of discounting. The *CICA Handbook* supports the recording of a gain or loss on discounting the note; it defines gains and losses as changes in owners' equity other than from revenues, expenses, and transactions with owners. In addition, Winnipeg recognizes interest revenue for the period the note was held.

Either way, a contingent liability exists. Two ways of reporting that contingent liability are available.[38]

1. Winnipeg reports in the disclosure notes to its financial statements that it is contingently liable for $3,300 of notes receivable.
2. Winnipeg credits notes receivable discounted rather than notes receivable in the August 1, 1995, entry above, subtracting this $3,000 contra account from total notes receivable in the balance sheet. Total notes receivable thus includes the note discounted. This alternative reduces net notes receivable by $3,000 and also discloses that $3,000 of total notes receivable is discounted. For example, assume $10,000 of notes receivable before discounting. After discounting, the notes are disclosed as follows:

---

[37] In practice, banks charge interest on a daily basis.

[38] In most cases, defaults on notes are less than likely, and therefore no actual liability need be recorded. However, the reporting of a contingent liability is required by the *CICA Handbook* Section 3290 for discounted notes.

```
Current assets:
  Notes receivable . . . . . . . . .    $10,000
  Notes receivable discounted. . . . .      3,000
Net notes receivable . . . . . . . .    $ 7,000
```

When the contingency is removed (upon payment of the note by the maker), the following entry is made:

```
Notes receivable discounted . . . . . . . . . . . . . . . . . . . . . . . . . .   3,000
  Notes receivable . . . . . . . . . . . . . . . . . . . . . . . . . . . . .           3,000
```

The advantages of note disclosure are that the maturity value including interest ($3,300) is disclosed, and a smaller number of accounts are affected. However, the notes receivable discounted account is more noticeable because it appears in the balance sheet. Either way, the contingency is removed when the maker pays the note. When the bank does not notify the payee of default by the maker, the contingency is removed a few days after the maturity date. For a note discounted without recourse, the entries are the same (although the notes receivable discounted account is not used), but no contingent liability exists.

Notes Receivable Discounting Recorded as a Borrowing

If the discounting does not qualify as a sale (perhaps the payee has the option to repurchase the note), Winnipeg makes these entries on August 1, 1995:

August 1, 1995:

```
Interest receivable 3,000(.10)(4/12) . . . . . . . . . . . . . . . . . . . .      100
  Interest revenue . . . . . . . . . . . . . . . . . . . . . . . . . . . . .           100
Cash . . . . . . . . . . . . . . . . . . . . . . . . . . . . . . . . . . . .    2,970
Interest expense . . . . . . . . . . . . . . . . . . . . . . . . . . . . . .      130
  Liability on discounted notes receivable . . . . . . . . . . . . . . . . .         3,000
  Interest receivable . . . . . . . . . . . . . . . . . . . . . . . . . . . .           100
```

There is no loss because an asset was not sold. The note remains on Winnipeg's books. The net of interest revenue and interest expense is $30 interest expense. When the maker pays the note at maturity, the following entry is made:

After April 1, 1996:

```
Liability on discounted notes receivable . . . . . . . . . . . . . . . . . .    3,000
  Notes receivable . . . . . . . . . . . . . . . . . . . . . . . . . . . . .         3,000
```

Dishonoured Notes

A note receivable not renewed or collected at maturity is considered a **dishonoured note.** Interest continues to accrue on the face value plus any previously accrued interest at the interest rate on the note. The payee generally transfers the note to a special receivable account and initiates collection efforts. If the Nell Company note were held to maturity (i.e., not discounted), the default would be recorded as follows:

April 1, 1996:

```
Notes receivable past due . . . . . . . . . . . . . . . . . . . . . . . . .    3,300
  Notes receivable . . . . . . . . . . . . . . . . . . . . . . . . . . . . .         3,000
  Interest receivable $3,000(.10)(9/12) . . . . . . . . . . . . . . . . . . .          225*
  Interest revenue $3,000(.10)(3/12) . . . . . . . . . . . . . . . . . . . .           75
```

* Interest receivable recorded December 31, 1995.

The accounting for discounted notes dishonoured by the maker depends on the discounting transaction. If the note was discounted without recourse and recorded as a sale, no entry is required and no contingent liability exists to be removed.

If the note was discounted with recourse (the more likely case) and recorded as a sale, the payee pays the maturity value, including interest and any fee charged by the bank, and debits a special receivable account for the amount paid.

Assume that the note discounted by Winnipeg and recorded as a sale is dishonoured. The bank charges a $15 fee (called a *protest* fee) for the additional task of notifying Winnipeg of the default. Assuming note disclosure of the contingent liability, the entry upon notification by the bank is as follows:

After April 1, 1996:

Notes receivable past due	3,315	
Cash		3,315

This amount is the maturity value plus bank fee. If the account method of disclosing the contingent liability were used, the entry would be the following:

After April 1, 1996:

Notes receivable past due	3,315	
Notes receivable discounted	3,000	
Cash		3,315
Notes receivable		3,000

This entry removes the contingent liability and establishes the special receivable.

Finally, assume that the note Winnipeg discounted is recorded as a liability and is then dishonoured. The entry to record the default, with the $15 protest fee, is as follows:

Notes receivable past due	3,315	
Liability on discounted notes receivable	3,000	
Cash		3,315
Notes receivable		3,000

If efforts to collect the past-due note fail, the accounting for the loss depends on whether notes are included in the bad debt estimation process. If notes are included, the account is closed against the allowance for doubtful accounts at its carrying value. If notes are not included, the direct write-off method is used. The note is credited for the carrying value and a loss is debited.

CONCEPT REVIEW

1. Why are long-term notes receivable recorded at the present value of future cash receipts using the market rate of interest?
2. When is the principal amount of a long-term note not equal to its face value?
3. Under what conditions must an interest rate be imputed? How does imputation affect the valuation of a note?

SUMMARY OF KEY POINTS

(L.O. 1)   1. Cash includes only those items immediately available to pay obligations.

(L.O. 2)   2. Bank reconciliations and petty cash funds are cash control and management tools. The reconciliation of book balance to correct cash balance provides the data for end-of-month adjusting entries for cash.

(L.O. 3)   3. Revenue recognition, valuation at estimated net realizable value, the use of present value for long-term notes, and the full-disclosure principle are the main principles affecting accounting for receivables.

(L.O. 4)   4. Bad debt expense, cash discounts, and sales returns and allowances represent adjustments to the initial recorded value of sales and receivables. Subtracting these adjustments yields an estimate of net realizable value and the net recognizable sales for the period under the matching concept.

(L.O. 5)   5. Factoring, assignment, and pledging are methods of obtaining immediate cash from accounts receivable. The key accounting issue is whether the transfer is treated as a sale or loan. When the risks and rewards are transferred and the transferor's obligation can be estimated, the transfer is handled as a sale. Otherwise, it is treated as a loan.

(L.O. 6)   6. Long-term notes are recorded at the present value of the consideration given or at the present value of all cash payments to be received using the appropriate market rate of interest, whichever is more clearly determinable. Interest revenue is based on that rate and the outstanding principal balance at the beginning of the period. Impaired notes are reduced to present value.

(L.O. 3, 5, 6)   7. Disclosure of contingent liabilities for transfers of receivables, including discounted notes receivable, is required under *CICA Handbook* Section 3290.

REVIEW PROBLEM

At the end of 1995, three companies have asked you to record journal entries in three different areas associated with receivables. All reporting years end December 31.

A. **Mandalay Company—Uncollectible accounts receivable** Mandalay Company requests that you record journal entries for its bad debt expense and uncollectible accounts receivable in 1995. Mandalay's January 1, 1995, balances relevant to accounts receivable are as follows:

Accounts receivable . . . . $400,000 (dr.)
Allowance for doubtful accounts. . . . .   20,000 (cr.)

During 1995, $45,000 of accounts receivable is considered uncollectible, and no more effort to collect these accounts will be made. Total sales for 1995 are $1,200,000, of which $200,000 are cash sales; $900,000 was collected on account during 1995.

1. Assuming that Mandalay uses the credit sales method to estimate bad debt expense and uses 4% of credit sales as its estimate of bad debts, provide the journal entries to record write-offs and bad debt expense for 1995. Also, provide the December 31, 1995, balance sheet disclosure for net accounts receivable.
2. Assuming that Mandalay uses the accounts receivable method to estimate net accounts receivable and uses 9% of accounts receivable as its estimate of uncollectibles, provide the journal entries to record write-offs and bad debt expense for 1995. Also, provide the December 31, 1995, balance sheet disclosure for net accounts receivable.

B. **Berkshire Company—Assigning accounts receivable** Berkshire company requests that you record journal entries for the listed events related to accounts receivable it assigned in 1995.

1. On January 1, 1995, Berkshire borrows cash from a finance company and assigns $40,000 of accounts receivable (nonnotification) as collateral. A note is signed, and the finance company advances an amount equal to 75% of the receivables. The note requires that interest at the rate of 24% be paid on the outstanding note balance at the end of each month. No finance fee is charged because of the high rate of interest.
2. During January, $19,700 is collected on account and $800 of returns and allowances are granted to customers.
3. On January 31, 1995, Berkshire remits the cash collected on the receivables plus interest due.
4. During February, the remainder of the accounts receivable assigned is collected except for $200, which is written off as uncollectible. Berkshire uses the credit sales method to estimate bad debt expense.
5. On February 28, 1995, Berkshire remits the balance of the note and interest due the finance company.

C. **White Mountain Company—Accounting for long-term notes** White Mountain Company requests that you record journal entries for a note it received in 1995. On April 1, 1995, White Mountain Company sold merchandise for $12,000 and received a $12,000, three-year, 10% note (10% is also the market rate). The note calls for three equal annual payments to be made beginning March 31, 1996. Provide the first three journal entries for this note.

SOLUTION

A. **Mandalay Company**
1. During 1995 (write-offs):

Allowance for doubtful accounts 45,000
   Accounts receivable (various).   45,000

December 31, 1995:

Bad debt expense (.04)$1,000,000 40,000
   Allowance for doubtful accounts   40,000

December 31, 1995, accounts receivable disclosure:

Accounts receivable	$455,000*
Allowance for doubtful accounts	(15,000)†
Net accounts receivable	$440,000

* $400,000 + $1,000,000 − $900,000 − $45,000.

† $20,000 − $45,000 + $40,000.

2. During 1995 (write-offs):

Allowance for doubtful accounts	45,000	
Accounts receivable (various)		45,000

December 31, 1995:

Bad debt expense	65,950	
Allowance for doubtful accounts		65,950

Ending gross accounts receivable from (1)		$455,000
Required allowance balance:		$40,950*
Allowance balance before adjusting entry:		
January 1, 1995, balance	$20,000	
1995 write-offs	(45,000)	(25,000)
Required increase to allowance account		$65,950

* .09($455,000)

December 31, 1995, accounts receivable disclosure:

Accounts receivable	$455,000
Allowance for doubtful accounts	(40,950)
Net accounts receivable	$414,050

B. Berkshire Company

1.
Accounts receivable assigned	40,000	
Accounts receivable		40,000
Cash $40,000(.75)	30,000	
Note payable		30,000

2.
Cash	19,700	
Sales returns and allowances	800	
Accounts receivable assigned		20,500

3.
Interest expense $30,000(1/12)(.24)	600	
Note payable	19,700	
Cash		20,300

4.
Cash ($40,000 − $20,500 − $200)	19,300	
Allowance for doubtful accounts	200	
Accounts receivable assigned		19,500

5.
Interest expense ($30,000 − $19,700)(1/12)(.24)	206	
Note payable	10,300	
Cash		10,506

C. White Mountain Company

The equal annual payment (P) is computed as follows:

$$\$12,000 = P(PVA, 10\%, 3) = P(2.48685)$$
$$\$12,000/2.48685 = P = \$4,825$$

1. April 1, 1995:

Note receivable	12,000	
Sales revenue		12,000

2. December 31, 1995:

Interest receivable $12,000(.10)(9/12)	900	
Interest revenue		900

3. March 31, 1996:

```
Cash . . . . . . . . . . . . . . . . . . . . . . . . . . . .   4,825
     Note receivable  . . . . . . . . . . . . . . . . . . . . .        3,625
     Interest receivable . . . . . . . . . . . . . . . . . . .          900
     Interest revenue $12,000(.10)(3/12). . . . . . . . . . . . .        300
```

QUESTIONS

1. Define *cash* as it is used for accounting purposes.
2. In what circumstances, if any, is it permissible to offset a bank overdraft against a positive balance in another bank account?
3. Define a compensating balance and explain the related reporting requirements.
4. Why is a petty cash fund replenished at the end of a reporting period?
5. Which of the following items should not be recorded in the cash account?
   - *a.* Money orders.
   - *b.* Postdated cheques.
   - *c.* Ordinary cheques.
   - *d.* Postage stamps.
   - *e.* Currency.
   - *f.* Cash deposited in savings accounts.
   - *g.* Certificates of deposit.
   - *h.* Deposits in chequing accounts.
6. Where (if at all) do items in (*a*) through (*g*) belong in the following bank reconciliation?

```
Balance from bank statement, June 30 . . . . . . . .   $x,xxx.xx
     Additions . . . . . . . . . . . . . . . . . .          _____
     Deductions . . . . . . . . . . . . . . . . . .          _____
June 30 correct cash balance . . . . . . . . . . .   $ 9,600.00

Balance from company cash account, June 30. . . . .   $x,xxx.xx
     Additions . . . . . . . . . . . . . . . . . .          _____
     Deductions . . . . . . . . . . . . . . . . . .          _____
June 30 correct cash balance . . . . . . . . . . .   $ 9,600.00
```

   - *a.* Note collected by bank for the depositor on June 29; notification was received July 2 when the June 30 bank statement was received.
   - *b.* Cheques drawn in June that had not cleared the bank by June 30.
   - *c.* Cheque of a depositor with a similar name that was returned with cheques accompanying June 30 bank statement and was subtracted from the company's bank account.
   - *d.* Bank service charge for which notification was received on receipt of bank statement.
   - *e.* Deposit mailed June 30 that reached bank July 1 (not yet included in the bank statement).
   - *f.* Notification of charge for imprinting the company's name on blank cheques was received with the June 30 bank statement.
   - *g.* Upon refooting the cash receipts journal, the company discovered that one receipt was omitted in arriving at the total that was posted to the cash account in the ledger.
7. Briefly explain the basic purposes of a bank reconciliation.
8. Define the following terms related to accounting for cash:
   - *a.* Deposits in transit.
   - *b.* Cheques outstanding.
   - *c.* NSF cheque.
   - *d.* Correct cash balance.
   - *e.* Cash short and cash over.
9. A company sold merchandise for $500, terms 2/10, n/30. Explain these terms and give the journal entry for the sale under the net approach and gross approach. Which approach is preferable? Why?
10. Briefly describe the different methods of estimating bad debt expense and the allowance for doubtful accounts for trade receivables. State which financial statement each method emphasizes. What is the conceptual basis for each emphasis?
11. It sometimes happens that a receivable that has been written off as uncollectible is subsequently collected. Describe the accounting procedures in such an event.
12. What is the difference between a cash discount and a trade discount?
13. How should customer accounts receivable with credit balances be reported in the financial statements?
14. A company has a credit balance of $600 in its allowance for doubtful accounts. The amount of credit sales for the period is $80,000, and the balance in accounts receivable is $15,000. Assume

that the bad debt estimates are as follows: (*a*) related to accounts receivable, 9%, and (*b*) related to credit sales, 0.5%. Complete the following tabulation after the adjusting entry is made for bad debts.

Account	(a) Based on Accounts Receivable	(b) Based on Credit Sales
Bad debt expense	$_____	$_____
Allowance for doubtful accounts	$_____	$_____

15. Illustrate the differences between a one-year note received for a $5,000 credit sale and a going rate of interest of 12%, assuming (*a*) an interest-bearing note and (*b*) a noninterest-bearing note (interest included in face value). Ignore adjusting entries but provide the entry for the date the note is received and the date it is collected.

16. A company received from a customer a $1,000, 9% interest-bearing note that will mature in three months. Two months later, the note was sold to the bank to yield 12%. Compute the proceeds. Give the required journal entry made by the company at the time the note was sold.

17. A company sold accounts receivable of $10,000 (allowance for doubtful accounts, $300) for $9,000, with recourse. Estimated obligations due to the with-recourse provision amounted to $700 (uncollectible accounts, discounts, and sales returns). Give the required entry.

18. Under what circumstances should the direct write-off method for bad debts be used?

19. How does fulfilling the criteria of *EIC–9,* "Transfers of Receivables," imply a *sale* of receivables?

20. Why are long-term notes recorded at the present value of all future cash flows specified in the note, using the market interest rate?

21. Why are certain short-term notes not valued at present value?

22. On December 31, 1995, Johnson holds a 6%, $1,000 note due in one year. Johnson expects to receive only $600 on the due date. The note was issued at face value, but the market interest rate on similar notes is 7% on December 31, 1995. At what amount should the note be carried on Johnson's balance sheet dated December 31, 1995?

23. When is a current receivable recognized under international accounting standards?

CASES

C 8–1
(L.O. 4)

Gross and Net Methods of Recording Sales   Both the gross and net methods of recording sales with terms that include cash discounts are allowed by GAAP and are used in practice. In certain situations when material amounts are involved, an adjusting entry is required at the end of the year for correct financial reporting.

Required

1. Assuming material amounts of cash discounts, when is an adjusting entry required under each method? Cite any applicable accounting standards in your answer.
2. Give the adjusting entry without using amounts.

C 8–2
(L.O. 5)

Receivable Financing: Sale or Loan?   The following situations involve transactions that should be classified as either a sale or a loan.

a. Sherman Company assigns $400,000 of accounts receivable as collateral for a loan (notification basis). Interest is charged on the monthly outstanding loan balance, and a 2% finance fee is charged immediately on the accounts assigned.

b. Hopper Company factors $50,000 of accounts receivable on a nonrecourse basis. The finance company charges an 8% fee and withholds 10% to cover sales adjustments. The finance company obtains title to the receivables and assumes collection responsibilities.

c. Pineapple Company factors $40,000 of accounts receivable on a recourse basis. Pineapple assumes the cost of all sales adjustments. The receivables are part of a much larger group of receivables. Pineapple's business is stable, and sales adjustments are readily estimable. Pineapple is compelled under the financing agreement to reimburse the finance company for any losses due to default by original customers.

d. Helms Company factors $80,000 of accounts receivable on a recourse basis. Helms assumes the cost of all sales adjustments. At the finance company's option, if it appears that the receivables are not collected as quickly as expected, Helms must repurchase the receivables.

e. Gilbert Company discounts on a nonrecourse basis a $20,000 note received in a sale.

f. Franklin Company discounts on a recourse basis a $10,000 note received in a sale. The only provision of the financing agreement is that Franklin must reimburse the bank in the event of default by the original maker of the note.

g. Puget Company discounts on a recourse basis a $30,000 note received in a sale. The bank allows repurchase of discounted notes at face value for a small fee.

h. Bellingham Company discounts on a recourse basis a $35,000 note received in a sale. The bank can compel Bellingham to repurchase the note if the maker's current ratio falls below 2.3 within five months of the note's due date.

i. Pobedy Company pledges all of its accounts receivable as collateral for a loan. Pobedy must use the proceeds from the accounts receivable to service the loan. Pobedy retains title to the receivables. In the event of default by Pobedy on the loan, the finance company has a claim against any of these receivables for payment of the loan.

Required

For each of the preceding situations, explain whether the financing of the receivables should be recorded as a sale or a loan.

C 8–3
(L.O. 2)

Ethical Considerations: Bank Reconciliation   Blueridge Company recently hired you as a junior accountant. Blueridge is a closely held, medium-sized retailing firm. One of your first assignments is to prepare the June bank reconciliation. You find the following information from the June bank statement and company records:

Deposits in transit	$ 7,200
Balance per bank statement	16,500
Bank service charges	30
Outstanding cheques	9,750
NSF cheque returned	3,000
$3,300 deposit incorrectly recorded by the company as	3,030

Your immediate supervisor, the chief accountant for the company, who also has limited cash disbursement responsibilities, tells you that the unadjusted balance of cash per the ledger at the end of June is unavailable. However, he must have the reconciliation immediately for a report to the vice president of finance. Furthermore, he asks you to reduce the above outstanding cheque total by $2,600 "to adjust for certain errors before you were hired."

Accompanying the bank statement are the cancelled cheques. Among them is a $2,600 cheque written to an individual not employed with the company signed by your superior.

Required

1. Assuming that the information in the above list is correct and complete, prepare the June bank reconciliation.

2. Comment on why the superior might have withheld information and made his unusual request for adjusting the bank reconciliation.

3. Discuss your options and responsibilities in this situation, including ethical considerations and possible effects on yourself.

C 8–4
(L.O. 4)

Interest Rate on Cash Discounts   Maxfield Company sells $2,000 worth of merchandise on credit, terms 4/10, n/30. The buyer paid on the 15th day following the sale.

Required

Assuming a 365-day year, prepare a report addressing the following questions:

1. What is the effective annual interest rate paid by the buyer in this case?

2. How sensitive is the annual interest rate to (*a*) the number of days between the last day of the discount period and payment date, (*b*) the gross purchase price, and (*c*) the cash discount percentage? What implications does this sensitivity have for buyers?

C 8–5
(L.O. 4)

Trade Accounts Receivable: Magna International Inc.   The 1993 Magna International Inc. annual report, reproduced at the end of this text, presents few details about the firm's trade receivables. Therefore, let's assume the following in addition to the information contained in the report:

a. All sales are made on credit.

b. The ageing method of estimating uncollectible accounts receivable is used. The ageing schedule for Magna's receivables at July 31, 1993, follows:

Age Category	Aggregate Amount	Probability of Noncollection
Not overdue	$198,950,000	.005
1–30 days overdue.	57,850,000	.03
31–60 days overdue	43,400,000	.06
More than 60 days overdue	14,400,000	?

c. Write-offs of accounts receivable during 1993 were $12,000,000.

d. The allowance at July 31, 1993 is $7,494,250; 1992, $7,850,450.

Required

1. What is the probability of noncollection for accounts more than 60 days overdue?
2. With the assumptions given, what amount of bad debt expense did Magna recognize for 1993?

EXERCISES

E 8–1
(L.O. 1)

Cash Terminology   Match the descriptions given below with the terms listed to the left by entering one capital letter in each blank space:

Term	Brief Description
_____ 1. Petty cash.	A. Cash inflows.
_____ 2. Cheques outstanding.	B. Negotiable instruments that are accepted by a bank for immediate deposit and withdrawal.
_____ 3. Bank reconciliation.	
_____ 4. Compensating balance.	C. Certificates of deposit.
_____ 5. Cash debits.	D. A special cash fund used to make small payments.
_____ 6. Cash equivalents.	E. A negative balance in a bank account.
_____ 7. Deposits in transit.	F. Caused by theft, unintentional counting errors, and inappropriate accounting.
_____ 8. Lockbox system.	
_____ 9. NSF.	G. Cheques that have been drawn and mailed but have not yet cleared the bank.
_____ 10. Overdraft in bank.	
_____ 11. Cash that is not reported as a current asset.	H. A loan constraint that requires a minimum balance at all times in a bank account.
	I. Cash outflows.
_____ 12. CDs.	J. A deposit made but not included on the periodic bank statement.
_____ 13. Cash credits.	K. A system to reduce the mail time for delivery of collections from customers; uses a post office box number.
_____ 14. Cash short and over.	
	L. Insufficient funds to support an account on which a cheque is written.
	M. A schedule that shows the correct cash balance for both the bank and the company.
	N. A cash fund set aside to pay a long-term debt.

E 8–2
(L.O. 2)

Petty Cash Entries   Main Company decided to use a petty cash system for making small payments. The following transactions were completed during December 1995:

a. On December 1, 1995, the company treasurer prepared an $800 cheque payable to petty cash; the cash was given to the custodian.

b. Expenditures by the custodian (and signed receipts received) through December 20 were postage, $160; office supplies, $140; newspapers, $72; office equipment repairs, $240; coffee room supplies, $60; and miscellaneous items, $48.

c. On December 20, the treasurer fully replenished the fund.

d. Expenditures by the custodian through December 31 were postage, $52; office supplies, $72; newspapers, $28; office equipment repairs, $84; coffee room supplies, $40; and miscellaneous items, $24. The fund was replenished on December 31.

Required

1. Give all the journal entries that should be made relating to the petty cash fund through December 31, 1995 (end of the annual accounting period), assuming that petty cash expenditures were for administrative expenses.

2. Show how the petty cash fund should be reported on the balance sheet. The regular cash account showed an ending cash balance of $186,000.
3. How should the petty cash transactions affect the 1995 income statement?

E 8–3
(L.O. 1)

Define Cash   Carbine Company is preparing its December 31 Bank A reconciliation (end of the annual accounting period), and it must determine the proper balance sheet classification of the items listed below. You have been asked to complete the tabulation provided.

	Balance Sheet	
Item	Include in Cash Amount	Classification if Not Cash
1. Coins and currency, $1,000.		
2. Cheques on hand received from customers, $12,000.		
3. Certificates of deposit (CDs), $16,000.		
4. Petty cash fund, $800.		
5. Postage stamps, $120.		
6. Bank A, chequing account balance, $42,000.		
7. Postdated cheque, customer, $200.		
8. Money order from customer, $300.		
9. Cash in savings account, $20,000.		
10. Bank draft from customer, $800.		
11. Cash advance received from customer, $160.		
12. Utility deposit to the gas company, refundable, $100.		
13. Certified cheque from customer, $2,000.		
14. NSF cheque, R. Roe, $400.		
15. Cash advance to company executive, collectible upon demand, $40,000.		
16. Bank B, chequing account, overdraft, $4,000.		
17. IOUs from employees, $240.		

E 8–4
(L.O. 1)

Define Cash   Maze Company is preparing its 1995 financial statements; the accounting period ends December 31. The following items, related to cash, are under consideration. You have been asked to indicate how each item should be reported on the balance sheet and to explain the basis for your responses.

a. A $900 cheque received from a customer, dated February 1, 1996, is on hand.
b. A customer's cheque was included in the December 20 deposit. It was returned by the bank stamped NSF. No entry has yet been made by Maze to reflect the return.
c. A $20,000 CD on which $1,000 of interest accrued to December 31 has just been recorded by debiting interest receivable and crediting interest revenue. The chief accountant proposes to report the $20,000 as cash in bank.
d. Maze has a $200 petty cash fund. As of December 31, the fund cashier reported expense vouchers covering various expenses in the amount of $167 and cash of $32.
e. Postage stamps that cost $30 are in the cash drawer.
f. A cashier's cheque of $200 payable to Maze Company is in the cash drawer; it is dated December 29.
g. Three cheques, dated December 31, 1995, totalling $465, payable to vendors who have sold merchandise to Maze Company on account, were not mailed by December 31, 1995. They have not been entered as payments in the cheque register and ledger.
h. Prior to December 30, Maze company left a note that matures December 31, 1995, with its bank for collection. The note is $20,000 and bears interest at 9%, having been outstanding for three months. As yet, Maze has not heard from the bank about collection but is confident of a favourable outcome because of the high credit rating of the maker of the note. The company plans to include the $20,000 plus interest in its cash balance.

E 8-5
(L.O. 2)

Petty Cash Entries   As a part of its newly designed internal control system, Dorothy Corporation established a petty cash fund. Transactions for the first month were as follows:

a. Wrote a cheque for $500 on August 1 and gave the cash to the fund custodian.
b. Summary of the petty cash expenditures made by the custodian:

	August 1–15	August 16–31
Postage used	$ 40	$ 58
Supplies purchased and used	265	190
Delivery expense	98	178
Miscellaneous expenses	35	40
Totals	$438	$466

c. Fund replenished on August 16.
d. Fund replenished on August 31 and increased by $300.

Required

Give all of the entries indicated through August 31.

E 8-6
(L.O. 2)

Bank Reconciliation and Journal Entries   Foster Company, as a matter of policy, deposits all cash receipts and makes all payments by cheque. The following were taken from the cash records of the company:

	May 31	June 30
Deposits in transit	$ 2,200	$ 3,900
Cheques outstanding	1,400	800

June transactions:

	Bank	Books
Balance, June 1	$ 5,000	$ 5,800
June deposits	10,600	12,300
June cheques	14,500	13,900
June note collected (including 10% interest)	2,200	—
June bank charges	10	—
Balance, June 30	3,290	4,200

Required

1. Based on the above data only, show how to prove the deposits in transit and cheques outstanding as of June 30.
2. Reconcile the bank account as of June 30 using the bank and book balance to correct cash format.
3. Give any journal entries that should be made based on the June bank reconciliation.

E 8-7
(L.O. 2)

Bank Reconciliation, NSF Cheques, Journal Entries   Reconciliation of Crabtree Company's bank account at May 31 was as follows:

Balance from bank statement	$5,250
Deposits in transit	750
Cheques outstanding	(75)
Correct cash balance	$5,925
Balance from books	$5,932
Bank service charge	(7)
Correct cash balance, May 31	$5,925

June transactions:

	Bank	Books
Cheques recorded	$5,750	$5,900
Deposits recorded	4,050	4,500
Service charges recorded	6	—
Collection by bank ($1,000 note plus interest)	1,050	—
NSF cheque returned with June 30 statement (will be redeposited; assumed to be good)	25	—
Balances, June 30	4,569	4,525

Required

1. Compute deposits in transit and cheques outstanding at June 30 by comparing bank and books for deposits and cheques.

2. Prepare a bank reconciliation for June using the bank and book balance to correct cash balance format.

3. Give all journal entries that should be made based on the June bank reconciliation.

E 8–8
(L.O. 2)

Bank Balance to Book Balance Reconciliation   The bank to book balance method is a popular alternative to the bank and book balance to correct cash balance method of reconciling bank accounts. To use this alternative, start with the bank balance and use the table below to place items into the reconciliation:

	Cash Increases Reflected Only in the:	Cash Decreases Reflected Only in the:
Bank balance	Subtract: (Example: note collected by bank)	Add: (Example: bank service charges)
Book balance	Add: (Example: deposits in transit)	Subtract: (Example: outstanding cheques)

The result is the book balance.

Required

1. Using the information in E 8–7, provide the bank balance to book balance reconciliation.
2. Explain why the bank service charges are added to the bank balance in your reconciliation.

E 8–9
(L.O. 2)

Bank Reconciliation Based on Bank Statement and Cash Account

Required

a. Jones Company shows the following June 30 bank statement:

Statement Summary

Balance June 1.	$23,000
Deposits and other credits.	11,600
Cheques and other debits	(12,120)
Interest earned on this statement.	100
Ending balance, June 30.	$22,580

Account transactions:

Deposits

6–1	$ 2,000
6–8	3,000
6–17	4,500
6–22	2,100
Total. . . .	$11,600

Cheques

6–2 #61	$1,000	6–17 #65	$ 400
6–7 #63	2,000	6–23 #60	1,100
6–9 #66	3,000	6–27 #67	2,100
6–14 #64	1,420	6–28 #59	1,100
			$12,120

b. **Cash Account**

Balance June 1	$23,900	Cheques			$13,220
Deposits	12,300	60	$1,100	65	$ 400
6–8	$3,000	61	1,000	66	3,000
6–17	4,500	62	900	67	2,100
6–22	2,100	63	2,000	68	1,300
6–30	2,700	64	1,420		

c. Bank reconciliation at May 31:

Bank balance, $23,000, add deposit outstanding, $2,000,
Deduct cheque #59 outstanding, $1,100,
Book balance, $23,900.

Required

Prepare the June bank reconciliation and give any entries required. Use the bank and book balance to correct cash balance format.

E 8–10
(L.O. 3)

Correcting Ledger Accounts for Receivables During the annual audit of Coil Corporation, you encountered the following account, entitled "receivables and payables":

Items	Debit	Credit
Due from customers	$156,000	
Payables to creditors for merchandise		$62,000
Note receivable, long term	80,000	
Expected cumulative losses on bad debts.		4,000
Due from employees, current	2,200	
Cash dividends payable.		24,000
Special receivable, dishonoured note*	22,000	
Accrued wages		2,400
Deferred rent revenue		1,600
Insurance premiums paid in advance	1,200	
Mortgage payable, long term		40,000

* Collection probable in two years.

Required

1. Give the journal entry to eliminate the above account and set up the appropriate accounts to replace it.
2. Show how the various items should be reported on a current balance sheet.

E 8–11
(L.O. 4)

Accounting for Sale on Credit: Net versus Gross Methods On December 29, 1995, Sabre Company sold merchandise for $4,000 on credit terms, 3/10, n/60. The accounting period ends December 31.

Required

1. Give the following entries under the net method and the gross method:
   a. To record the 1995 sale.
   b. To record collection of the account: assumption A, on January 5, 1996; assumption B, on April 1, 1996.
2. Show what should be reported on the 1995 and 1996 balance sheets and income statements under each approach and for each assumption for the above transactions.

E 8–12
(L.O. 4)

Recording Bad Debt Expense Based on Credit Sales At January 1, 1995, the credit balance in the allowance for doubtful accounts of the Master Company was $400,000. The provision (expense) for doubtful accounts is based on a percentage of net credit sales. Total sales revenue for 1995 amounted to $150 million, of which one-third was on credit. Based on the latest available facts, the 1995 provision needed for doubtful accounts is estimated to be three-fourths of 1% of net credit sales. During 1995, uncollectible receivables amounting to $440,000 were written off.

Required

1. Prepare a schedule to compute the balance in Master's allowance for doubtful accounts at December 31, 1995. Show supporting computations.
2. Give all 1995 entries related to doubtful accounts.

(AICPA adapted)

E 8–13
(L.O. 4)

Bad Debt Estimates Based on Credit Sales, Accounts Receivable, and Ageing At December 31, 1995, end of the annual reporting period, the accounts of Bader Company showed the following:

a. Sales revenue for 1995, $360,000, of which one-sixth was on credit.
b. Allowance for doubtful accounts, balance January 1, 1995, $1,800 credit.
c. Accounts receivable, balance December 31, 1995 (prior to any write-offs of uncollectible accounts during 1995), $36,100.
d. Uncollectible accounts to be written off, December 31, 1995, $2,100.
e. Ageing schedule at December 31, 1995, showing the following breakdown of accounts receivable:

Status	Amount
Not past due	$20,000
Past due 1–60 days	8,000
Past due over 60 days	6,000

Required	1. Give the 1995 entry to write off the uncollectible accounts.
	2. Give the 1995 adjusting entry to record bad expense for each of the following independent assumptions concerning bad debt loss rates:
	a. On credit sales, 1.5%.
	b. On total receivables at year-end, 2.5%.
	c. On ageing schedule: not past due, 0.5%; past due 1–60 days, 1%; and past due over 60 days, 8%.
	3. Show what would be reported on the 1995 balance sheet relating to accounts receivable for each assumption.

E 8–14
(L.O. 6)

Short-Term, Interest-Bearing Note Receivable: Entries and Reporting On April 15, 1995, Welsch Company sold merchandise to Customer Rodriguez for $18,000, terms 2/10, n/EOM (i.e., end of month). Because of nonpayment by Rodriguez, Welsch received an $18,000, 15%, 12-month note dated May 1, 1995. The annual reporting period ends December 31. Customer Rodriguez paid the note in full on its maturity date.

Required

1. Give all entries related to the above transactions. Assume the net method.
2. Show what should be reported on the 1995 income statement and balance sheet.

E 8–15
(L.O. 6)

Short-Term, Noninterest-Bearing Note Receivable: Entries and Reporting On May 1, 1995, Darby Company sold merchandise to Customer Domo and received a $26,400 (face amount), one-year, noninterest-bearing note. The going (i.e., market) rate of interest is 10%. The annual reporting period for Darby Company ends on December 31. Customer Domo paid the note in full on its maturity date.

Required

1. Give all entries related to the above transactions.
2. Show what should be reported on the 1995 income statement and balance sheet.

E 8–16
(L.O. 6)

Interest-Bearing and Noninterest-Bearing Notes Receivable: Entries at Net and Gross and Reporting On November 1, 1995, Rouse Company sold merchandise on credit to Customer A for $14,000 and received a six-month, 12%, interest-bearing note. On this same date, Customer B purchased identical merchandise for the same price and credit terms except that the note received by Rouse was noninterest-bearing (the interest was included in the face value of the note). The annual accounting period for Rouse ends December 31.

Required

1. Give all required entries for each note from the date of sale of the merchandise through the maturity dates of the notes. For the noninterest-bearing note, give the entries for both the net and gross alternatives.
2. Show how the effects of these two notes should be reported on the 1995 income statement and balance sheet.

E 8–17
(L.O. 6)

Discounting an Interest-Bearing Note: Entries On May 1, 1995, Mark Company sold merchandise to Customer Kim for $20,000, credit terms 2/10, n/EOM. At the end of May, Customer Kim could not make payment. Instead, a six-month, 12% note receivable of $20,000 was received by Mark (dated June 1, 1995). Mark Company's accounting period ends December 31. On August 1, 1995, Mark discounted (i.e., sold) this note, with recourse, to City Bank at 14% interest. On maturity date, Customer Kim paid the bank in full for the note.

Required

Give all required entries for Mark Company on May 1, 1995, through the maturity date, November 30, 1995. Record sales at net.

E 8–18
(L.O. 6)

Noninterest-Bearing Note: Other Privileges On January 1, 1995, Jacobs Company provides a $40,000 loan to Andress Company by issuing a $40,000 noninterest-bearing note. Andress agrees (1) to repay the $40,000 proceeds on December 31, 1996, and (2) to sell a specified amount of construction materials to Jacobs at a 20% discount off the regular invoice price. The prevailing interest rate on similar notes, without the special purchase privilege, is 14%. Assume that Jacobs purchases materials at an even rate throughout the note term.

Required

Provide all entries for Jacobs over the note term.

E 8–19
(L.O. 6)

Discounting an Interest-Bearing Note: Entries Aerobic Sports Company completed the following 1995 transactions related to a special note receivable:

    a. February 1, 1995—Received a $200,000, 9%, interest-bearing, six-month note from Temple Company for a tract of land that had a carrying value of $60,000.
    b. March 1, 1995—Discounted (sold with recourse) the note to Local Bank at a 12% interest rate.
    c. July 31, 1995—Maturity date of the note:
        1. *Case A*—Temple Company paid the bank for the note and all interest.
        2. *Case B*—Temple Company defaulted on the note. The bank charged a $1,000 protest fee.

Required

Give all journal entries that Aerobic Sports Company should make for the term of the note, February 1, 1995, through July 31, 1995.

E 8–20
(L.O. 5)

Sale of Accounts Receivable with and without Recourse: Entries On April 1, 1995, DOS Company transferred $20,000 accounts receivable to PS2 Finance Company to obtain immediate cash. The related allowance for doubtful accounts was $800.

Required

1. The financial agreement specified a price of $16,000 on a without-recourse, notification basis. Give the entry(s) that DOS Company should make. Explain the basis for your response.
2. The financial agreement specified a price of $17,000 on a with-recourse, notification basis. DOS estimated $400 of transfer obligations related to the with-recourse provision. Give the entry(s) that DOS should make. Explain the basis for your response.

E 8–21
(L.O. 5)

Assignment of Accounts Receivable with Recourse: Entries Fence, Inc., assigned $120,000 of its receivables to Gate Finance Company. A note payable was executed. The contract provided that Gate would advance 85% of the gross amount of the receivables. The contract specified recourse and nonnotification; therefore, Fence's debtors continue to remit directly to it; the cash from customers is then remitted to the finance company. The cash remitted is first applied to the finance charges, with the remainder applied to principal.

During the first month, customers owing $82,000 paid cash, less sales returns and allowances of $3,200. The finance charge at the end of the first month was $700.

During the second month, the remaining receivables were collected in full except for $800 written off as uncollectible. Final settlement was effected with the finance company, including payment of an additional finance charge of $300.

Required

1. Give the entries for Fence to record (*a*) the assignment of the receivables and (*b*) the note payable.
2. Give the entries for Fence to record (*a*) the collections and (*b*) the payment to Gate for the first month.
3. Give the entries for Fence to record (*a*) the collections for the second month and (*b*) the final payment to Gate.

E 8–22
(L.O. 5)

Factoring Accounts Receivable: Sale or Loan? Appa Apparel manufactures fine sportswear for many national retailers and frequently sells its receivables to factors as a means of accelerating cash collections. Appa transferred $100,000 of receivables from retailers to a factor. The receivables were transferred without recourse on a notification basis. The factor charged 8% and held back 5% for sales adjustments.

Required

1. Should Appa record the transfer of receivables as a sale or as a loan, and why?
2. Record all entries related to the transfer for both parties, assuming that $92,000 in total was collected by the factor, $5,000 of accounts were found to be uncollectible, and $3,000 of merchandise was returned by retailers for full credit. The factor wrote off the uncollectible accounts.

E 8–23
(L.O. 5)

Factoring Accounts Receivable: Sale or Loan? Bappa Apparel manufactures fine sportswear for many national retailers and frequently sells its receivables to factors as a means of accelerating cash collections. Bappa transferred $100,000 of receivables from retailers to a factor. The receivables were transferred with recourse on a notification basis. The factor charged 6% and held back 5% for sales adjustments. Bappa has no obligation to the factor other than to pay the account of a retailer in the event of a default. However, Bappa is unable to estimate the amount of factored accounts that will be uncollectible. In addition, Bappa bears the cost of sales returns, allowances, and discounts.

Required

1. Should Bappa record the transfer of receivables as a sale or as a loan, and why?
2. Record all of Bappa's entries related to the transfer, assuming that $92,000 in total was collected by

the factor, $5,000 of accounts were found to be uncollectible (Bappa uses the direct write-off method for these receivables), and $3,000 of merchandise was returned by retailers for full credit. All transactions are related to the factoring of receivables that occurred within one fiscal year.

E 8-24
(L.O. 5)

Factoring Accounts Receivable: Sale or Loan?   Cappa Apparel manufactures fine sportswear for many national retailers and frequently sells its receivables to factors as a means of accelerating cash collections. Cappa transferred $100,000 of receivables from retailers to a factor. The receivables were transferred with recourse on a notification basis. Cappa's remaining responsibility for the factored accounts is limited to the recourse provisions and sales adjustments. The factor charged 6% and held back 10% for sales adjustments. For the factored accounts, Cappa estimates $4,000 uncollectible accounts and $4,000 sales returns and allowances.

Required

1. Should Cappa record the transfer of receivables as a sale or as a loan, and why?
2. Record all of Cappa's entries related to the transfer, assuming that $96,000 in total was collected by the factor, $3,000 of accounts were found to be uncollectible, and $3,000 of merchandise was returned by retailers for full credit.

E 8-25
(L.O. 4)

Accounting for an Account Receivable over a Six-Year Period   Given below is the history of a sale on credit by Airport Company to J. Doe:

a. December 24, 1991—Sold merchandise to J. Doe, $2,000, terms 2/10, n/30.
b. January 2, 1992—Doe paid half of the receivable and was allowed the discount.
c. December 31, 1994—Because of the disappearance of Doe, Airport Company wrote Doe's account off as uncollectible.
d. December 31, 1996—Doe reappeared and paid the debt in full, including 6% annual interest (not compounded, compute to the nearest month).

Required

1. Give the entry(s) that Airport Company should make at each of the above dates. Record at net.
2. Show how Doe's account should be reported each December 31 (end of Airport Company's annual reporting period).

E 8-26
(L.O. 6)

Long-Term Notes: Interest-Bearing versus Noninterest-Bearing   Wilma Company sells large construction equipment. On January 1, 1995, the company sold Cather Company a machine at a quoted price of $30,000. Wilma collected $10,000 cash and received a $20,000, two-year, 10% note (simple interest payable each December 31).

Required

1. Give Wilma's required entries for the two years, assuming an interest-bearing note, face value $20,000.
2. Give Wilma's required entries for the two years, assuming a noninterest-bearing note, face value $20,000.
3. Compare the interest revenue, sales revenue, and asset cost under (1) and (2).

E 8-27
(L.O. 6)

Interest-Bearing Long-Term Note: Entries   Felix Company sold a pickup truck to RV Company on January 1, 1995, at a quoted price of $24,000. Felix collected $6,000 cash and received an $18,000 note. The note is payable in three equal (December 31) instalments that include both principal and compound interest at 10%.

Required

1. Compute the equal periodic collections.
2. Prepare a collection schedule and give the entries for Felix Company.

E 8-28
(L.O. 6)

Noninterest-Bearing Note Receivable: Entries   On January 1, 1995, Electro Company sold a special machine that had a list price of $39,995. The purchaser paid $9,995 cash and signed a $30,000 note. The note specified that it would be paid off in three equal annual payments of $13,798 each (starting on December 31, 1995).

Required

1. Determine the implied rate of interest on the note.
2. Prepare a collection schedule for Electro.
3. Give all entries for Electro through 1997.

E 8-29
(L.O. 6)

Note Receivable with Unrealistic Interest Rate   On July 1, 1995, Stealth Company sold a large machine that had a list price of $36,000. The customer paid $6,000 cash and signed a three-year, $30,000 note that specified a stated interest rate of 3%. Annual interest on the full amount of the principal is payable each June 30. The principal is payable on June 30, 1998. The market (going) rate of interest for this transaction is 10%.

Required
1. Compute the present value of this note.
2. Prepare a collection schedule for this note.
3. Give all entries required through maturity date.

E 8–30
(L.O. 6)
Impairment of a Loan   Gumco Inc., a calendar-year firm, carries an 8%, $12,000 note received from the sale of merchandise worth $12,000 at sales value. The note is due December 31, 1998. Annual interest is due each December 31.

On December 31, 1995, Gumco reviews the collectibility of its loans and determines that only $9,000 is likely to be received on the due date.

Although Gumco received the 1995 interest payment, the firm does not expect to receive further interest payments. On December 31, 1998, Gumco received $8,800, and it expects no further payments.

Required
1. Prepare the entry to record the loan impairment, and the portion of the balance sheet showing the note.
2. Prepare the December 31, 1996 and 1997, entries to accrue interest. Gumco chooses to recognize the normal growth in present value as interest revenue and assumes no change in the amount collectible.
3. Prepare the entry to record the final receipt.

PROBLEMS

P 8–1
(L.O. 2)
 Bank Reconciliation Errors: Journal Entries   It is March 31 and Fry Company is ready to prepare its March bank reconciliation. The following information is available:

a.

Company Cash Account			
March 1 balance	28,350	Cheques	53,000
Deposits	51,468		

b. Bank statement, March 31:

Balance, March 1	$30,800
Deposits	51,198
Cheques cleared	(54,118)
NSF cheque (Customer Zinny)	(100)
Note collected for depositor (including interest, $80)	1,680
Interest on bank balance	36
Bank service charge	(14)
Balance, March 31	$29,482

c. Additional information:
(1) The company overstated one of its deposits by $20; the bank recorded it correctly.
(2) The bank cleared a $178 cheque as $187; the error has not been corrected by the bank.
(3) End of February: deposits in transit, $1,550; cheques outstanding, $4,000.

Required
1. Based on the data given above, compute the March 31 deposits in transit and cheques outstanding.
2. Prepare a bank reconciliation for March. (Hint: A check figure, $28,400). Use bank and book balance to correct cash balance format.
3. Give all journal entries that should be made based on your bank reconciliation.

P 8–2
(L.O. 2)
 Reconciliation—Collection, Deduction, Transfer: Entries   Ample Company carries its chequing account with Commerce Bank. The company is ready to prepare its December 31 bank reconciliation. The following data are available:
a. The November 30 bank reconciliation showed the following: (1) cash on hand (held back each day by Ample Company for change), $400 (included in Ample's Cash account); (2) deposit in transit, #51, $2,000; and (3) cheques outstanding, #121, $1,000; #130, $2,000; and #142, $3,000.

b. Ample Company Cash account for December:

Balance, December 1	$ 64,000
Deposits: #52–#55, $186,500; #56, $3,500	190,000
Cheques: #143–#176, $191,000; #177, $2,500; #178, $3,000; and #179, $1,500	(198,000)
Balance, December 31 (includes $400 cash held each day for change)	$ 56,000

c. Bank statement, December 31:

Balance, December 1	$ 67,600
Deposits: #51–#55	188,500
Cheques: #130, $2,000; #142, $3,000; #143–#176, $191,000	(196,000)
Note collected for Ample Co. (including $720 interest)	6,720
Fund transfer received for foreign revenue (not yet recorded by Ample Co.)	10,000
NSF cheque, Customer Belinda	(200)
United Fund (per transfer authorization signed by Ample Co.)	(50)
Bank service charges	(20)
Balance, December 31	$ 76,550

Required

1. Identify by number and dollars the December 31 deposits in transit and cheques outstanding.
2. Prepare the December 31 bank reconciliation. Use bank and book balance to correct cash balance format.
3. Give all journal entries that should be made at December 31, based on your bank reconciliation.

P 8–3
(L.O. 2)

Bank Reconciliation Error   Your first assignment as a summer intern with a local public accounting firm is to prepare the bank reconciliation for a client firm, which provides you with the following information for June:

Client cheques written but that have not yet cleared the bank	$3,000
Client deposits placed into night depository June 30, not appearing on bank statement	8,000
Cheque written on the account of a customer of the client, returned by the client's bank marked NSF	2,000
Balance per June bank statement for the client account	9,000
Bank service charges for June	60
Proceeds from a note owed by a customer to the client remitted directly to the client bank (includes $30 interest not yet recorded by the client)	930
Cheque written by client for a $472 advertising bill returned with the other canceled cheques. The client recorded the cheque and expense for $472, the correct amount, in the journal, but the cheque was written for $427. The client has already been notified by the advertiser, who decided to cash the cheque and bill the client for the remainder due	?
Balance per ledger account	?

Required

1. Prepare the bank reconciliation for June.
2. Prepare the required adjusting entry(ies) implied by the reconciliation.

P 8–4
(L.O. 1)

Classification of Cash   For each of the items listed in the table below, place an X in the column indicating the correct classification for balance sheet purposes. The first one is completed for you.

	Balance Sheet Classification			
	Cash	**Cash Equivalent**	**Short-Term Investments**	**Other**
Chequing account	X			
Savings account				
Rare coins kept for long-term speculation				
Post-dated cheques received				
Money orders received				
Petty cash fund				
Treasury bills purchased when two months remain in term				
Compensating balance for a short-term loan				
Sinking fund to retire a bond in five years				
Certificate of deposit (six-month term)				
Short-term investment in marketable equity securities				

P 8-5
(L.O. 3)

Classification of Receivables   When examining the accounts of St. Tropez Company, you ascertain that balances relating to both receivables and payables are included in a single controlling account called "receivables" that has a $23,050 debit balance. An analysis of the details of this account revealed the following:

Items	Debit	Credit
Accounts receivable—customers.	$40,000	
Accounts receivable—officers (current collection expected).	2,500	
Debit balances—creditors.	450	
Expense advances to salespersons	1,000	
Common share subscriptions receivable	4,600	
Accounts payable for merchandise.		$19,250
Unpaid salaries		3,300
Credit balances in customer accounts.		2,000
Cash received in advance from customers for goods not yet shipped		450
Expected bad debts, cumulative		500

Required

1. Give the journal entry to eliminate the above account and to set up the appropriate accounts to replace it.
2. How should the items be reported on St. Tropez Company's balance sheet?

P 8-6
(L.O. 1, 2, 4)

Cash, Receivables, and Cash-Basis Accounting   Choose the correct statement among the alternatives for each question.

1. The following information pertains to Deekers, a men's clothier, at December 31, 1995:

Bank statement balance.	$20,000
Chequebook balance	28,000
Deposits in transit	10,000
Outstanding cheques	2,000

In Deekers's December 31, 1995, balance sheet, at what amount should cash be reported?
   a. $18,000.
   b. $20,000.
   c. $28,000.
   d. $30,000.

2. When the allowance method of recognizing doubtful accounts is used, the entries to record collection of a small account previously written off would:
   a. Increase the allowance for doubtful accounts.
   b. Increase net income.
   c. Decrease the allowance for doubtful accounts.
   d. Have no effect on the allowance for doubtful accounts.

3. Roundtree Company, a manufacturer of natural foods, reported sales of $2,300,000 in 1995. Roundtree also reported the following balances:

	Dec. 31, 1994	Dec. 31, 1995
Accounts receivable	$500,000	$650,000
Allowance for doubtful accounts	(30,000)	(55,000)

Roundtree wrote off $10,000 of accounts during 1995. Under the cash basis of accounting, Roundtree would have reported 1995 sales of:
   a. $2,450,000.
   b. $2,175,000.
   c. $2,150,000.
   d. $2,140,000.

4. Brynn Company, a hard disk servicing company, reported $80,000 of gross cash sales (on which there were $4,000 of actual returns and allowances) and $120,000 of gross credit sales (on which $6,000 of cash discounts were taken) in 1995. The beginning and ending balances of accounts receivable in 1995 were $40,000 and $30,000, respectively. Brynn uses the direct write-off method

for bad debts and recorded no bad debts in 1995. Under the cash basis of accounting, what amount of revenue would Brynn record in 1995?

a. $200,000.

b. $190,000.

c. $170,000.

d. $76,000.

(AICPA adapted)

P 8–7
(L.O. 3)

Returns and Allowances: Gross and Net Methods   On August 12, Camel Company sells merchandise worth $20,000 (gross sales price) to Pyramid Company, terms 4/10, n/30. Camel grants cash discounts on amounts remitted within the discount period.

Required

1. Record journal entries in general journal form for the following transactions under both the net and the gross methods.
   a. The sale.
   b. Returns and allowances of $3,000 (gross) are granted Pyramid on August 17.
   c. Camel collects on $12,000 (gross) of the account on August 19.
   d. Returns and allowances of $2,400 (gross) are granted Pyramid on August 24 on items not yet paid for.
   e. The remaining account is collected on August 27.
   f. Returns and allowances of $1,000 cash (gross) are granted Pyramid on September 12 on merchandise paid for on August 19.
   g. Returns and allowances of $1,000 cash (gross) are granted Pyramid on September 14 on merchandise paid for on August 27.
2. Prepare a schedule showing the effect on Camel's net income of the above events under both methods (ignoring cost of goods sold), and compare that effect with the net cash inflow from these events.

P 8–8
(L.O. 4)

Comparison of Four Ways to Estimate Bad Debt Expense   The accounting records of Helsinki Company provided the following data for 1995:

Cash sales	$600,000
Credit sales	450,000
Balance in accounts receivable, January 1, 1995	90,000
Balance in accounts receivable, December 31, 1995	100,000
Balance in allowance for doubtful accounts, January 1, 1995	1,500 (cr.)
Accounts written off as uncollectible during 1995	2,500

Recently, Helsinki's management has become concerned about various estimates used in its accounting system, including those relating to receivables and bad debts. The company is considering various alternatives with a view to selecting the most appropriate approach and related estimates.

For analytical purposes, the following 1995 alternative estimates have been developed for consideration:

a. Bad debt expense approximates 0.6% of credit sales.

b. Bad debt expense approximates 0.25% of total sales (cash plus credit sales).

c. Two percent of the uncollected receivables at year-end will be uncollectible.

d. Ageing of the accounts at the end of the period indicated that three-fourths of them would incur a 1% loss, while the other one-fourth would incur a 6% loss.

The reporting period ends December 31.

Required

For each of the four alternatives listed above, give the following: 1995 adjusting entry, ending 1995 balance in the allowance account, and an evaluation of the alternative.

P 8–9
(L.O. 4)

Comparison and Evaluation of Three Ways to Estimate Bad Debt Expense   The accounts of Long Company provided the following 1995 information at December 31, 1995 (end of the annual period):

Accounts receivable balance, January 1, 1995	$ 51,000
Allowance for doubtful accounts balance, January 1, 1995	3,000
Total sales revenue during 1995 (⅙ on credit)	960,000
Uncollectible account to be written off during 1995 (ex-customer Slo)	1,000
Cash collected on accounts receivable during 1995	170,000

Estimates of bad debt losses:

a. Based on credit sales, 1%.
b. Based on ending balance of accounts receivable, 8%.
c. Based on ageing schedule:

Age	Accounts Receivable	Probability of Noncollection
Less than 30 days	$28,000	2%
31–90 days	7,000	10
91–120 days	3,000	30
More than 120 days	2,000	60

Required

1. Give the entry to write off customer Slo's long-overdue account.
2. Give all entries related to accounts receivable and the allowance account for the following three cases:

   Case A—Bad debt expense is based on credit sales.
   Case B—Bad debt expense is based on the ending balance of accounts receivable.
   Case C—Bad debt expense is based on ageing.

3. Show how the results of applying each case above should be reported on the 1995 income statement and balance sheet.
4. Briefly explain and evaluate each of the three methods used in Cases A, B, and C.
5. On August 1, 1996, customer Slo paid his long-overdue account in full. Give the required entries.

P 8–10
(L.O. 4)

Establish an Allowance for Doubtful Accounts   Pawn Company has been in business for five years but has never had an audit of its financial statements. Engaged to make an audit for 1995, you find that the company's balance sheet carries no allowance for doubtful accounts; instead, uncollectible accounts have been expensed as written off, and recoveries have been credited to income as collected. The company's policy is to write off, at December 31 of each year, those accounts on which no collections have been received for three months. The credit terms usually provide for equal monthly collections over two years from date of sale.

Upon your recommendation, the company agreed to revise its accounts for 1995 in order to account for bad debts on the allowance basis. The allowance is to be based on a percentage of credit sales that is derived from the experience of prior years.

Data for the past five years are as follows:

Year	Credit Sales	Accounts Written Off and Year of Sale			Recoveries and Year of Sale
		(1991)			
1991	$100,000	$ 550			
		(1991)	(1992)		(1991)
1992	250,000	1,500	$1,000		$300
		(1991)	(1992)	(1993)	(1992)
1993	300,000	500	4,000	$1,300	850
		(1992)	(1993)	(1994)	(1993)
1994	325,000	1,200	4,500	1,500	500
		(1993)	(1994)	(1995)	(1994)
1995	275,000	2,700	5,000	1,400	600

Accounts receivable at December 31, 1995, were as follows:

1994 sales	$ 15,000
1995 sales	135,000
	$150,000

Required Prepare the journal entry or entries, with appropriate explanations, to establish the allowance for doubtful accounts. Debit prior period adjustment because this is the correction of an accounting error. Support each item with computations; ignore income tax implications. The books have been adjusted but not closed at December 31, 1995.

(AICPA adapted)

P 8–11
(L.O. 5)

Assignment of Accounts Receivable: Entries   Verona Company finances some of its current operations by assigning accounts receivable to Adams Finance Company. On July 1, Verona Company assigned, with recourse, notification basis, accounts amounting to $100,000. The finance company advanced 80% of the accounts assigned (20% of the total to be withheld until the finance company has made full recovery), less a commission charge of 0.5% of the total accounts assigned.

On July 31, Verona Company received a statement from the finance company that it had collected $52,000 of these accounts, and in conformity with the contract, an additional charge of 0.5% of the total accounts outstanding as of July 31 was deducted.

On August 31, Verona Company received a second statement from the finance company, together with a check for the amount due. The statement indicated that the finance company had collected an additional $32,000 and had made a charge of 0.5% of the balance outstanding as of August 31.

Required
1. Give Verona's entry to record (*a*) the assignment of the accounts and (*b*) the liability on July 1.
2. Give Verona's entry to record the data from the July 31 report from the finance company.
3. Reconstruct the report submitted to Verona by Adams Finance Company on August 31; show details to explain cash remitted and the uncollected accounts still held by the finance company.
4. Give Verona's entry to record the data in the report of August 31.
5. Give Verona's entry to record the collection of the remaining assigned accounts receivable on September 15.

P 8–12
(L.O. 6)

PV of a Note: Collection Schedule, Entries   Savoy Company sold a building and the land on which it is located on January 1, 1995, and received a $150,000 noninterest-bearing note receivable that matures December 31, 1997. The $150,000 is to be paid in full on the note's maturity date. The sale was recorded as follows by Savoy Company:

Note receivable.	150,000	
Accumulated depreciation, building.	100,000	
Building		150,000
Land		60,000
Gain on sale of assets		40,000

It has been determined that 12% is a realistic interest rate for this particular note. The annual reporting period ends December 31. The accounts have not been adjusted or closed for 1995.

Required
1. Compute the present value of the note. Use compound interest.
2. Prepare a correction and collection schedule as follows:

		Note Receivable	
Date	Explanation and Interest Revenue	Change	Balance
Jan. 1, 1995	Originally recorded		$150,000
Dec. 31, 1995	Corrections to present value	?	?

3. Give all entries through 1997.

P 8–13
(L.O. 6)

Notes Receivable   Choose the correct statement among the alternatives for each question.

1. On December 31, 1995, Hangtown Company, a Manitoba real estate firm, received two $20,000 notes from customers in exchange for services rendered. On both notes, simple interest is computed on the outstanding principal balance at 3% and payable at maturity. The note from El Dorado Company is due in nine months, and the note from Newcastle Company is due in five years. The market interest rate for similar notes on December 31, 1995, was 8%. At what amounts should the two notes be reported in Hangtown's December 31, 1995, balance sheet?

	El Dorado	Newcastle
a.	$18,868	$13,624
b.	$18,519	$15,653
c.	$20,000	$13,624
d.	$20,000	$15,653

2. EPPA, an environmental management firm, sold to DUMPCO a $10,000, 8%, five-year note that required five equal annual year-end payments. This note was discounted to yield a 9% rate to DUMPCO. What is the total amount of interest revenue to be recognized by DUMPCO on this note?

   a. $4,500.
   b. $4,000.
   c. $2,781.
   d. $2,523.

3. On August 15, 1995, Edu-Trust Inc., a firm specializing in educational software, sold software for which it received a four-month note dated July 15, 1995, bearing the market rate of interest on that date. The principal and interest on the note are due November 15, 1995. When the note is recorded on August 15, which of the following accounts is increased?

   a. Unearned discount.
   b. Interest receivable.
   c. Prepaid interest.
   d. Interest revenue.

4. On July 1, 1995, Lezix Company, maker of denim clothing, sold goods in exchange for a $100,000, eight-month, noninterest-bearing note. At the time of the sale, the market rate of interest was 12% on similar notes. What amount did Lezix receive when it discounted the note at 10% on September 1, 1995?

   a. $97,000.
   b. $96,900.
   c. $95,000.
   d. $94,000.

(AICPA adapted)

P 8-14
(L.O. 6)
Note Receivable with Equal Collections and Long-Term Note Receivable, with Unrealistic Interest Rate During the annual reporting period (ends on December 31), Koke Company received two notes related to the sale of products (commercial autos). These notes are identified as Note A and Note B.

Note A: On August 1, 1995, Koke Company sold a special van with a price of $31,000. Koke received cash, $11,000, and a $20,000 six-month note that matures January, 31, 1996. This note specifies equal monthly payments of $3,451, starting on August 31, 1995, which included principal and interest. The going, or market, rate of interest for this loan is 12%.

Note B: On March 1, 1995, Koke Company sold a large vehicle equipped with a special crane mounted to it. The quoted price was $80,000. Koke Company received $20,000 cash and a $60,000, five-year note receivable. The note had a stated rate of 3%, although the imputed (going, or market) rate for this transaction was 9%. The interest concession was made to "beat a strong competitor." The note is payable in five equal annual payments starting on February 28, 1996.

Required

For Note A:

1. Prepare a schedule of collections that shows, by date, cash collections, interest revenue, and note receivable (reduction and balance).
2. Give all entries from August 1, 1995, through January 31, 1996.

For Note B:

1. Compute the annual cash collections and the present value of the note.
2. Prepare a schedule of collections to show, by date, cash collections, interest revenue, and note receivable (reduction and balance).
3. Give all entries from March 1, 1995, through February 28, 1996.

P 8-15
(L.O. 6)
Discounting Notes: Interest-Bearing and Noninterest-Bearing On October 15, 1995, Farb Company sold identical merchandise for $12,000 on credit terms 2/10, n/30, to two different customers, Customer X and Customer Y. Farb's annual reporting period ends December 31. These sales were recorded as follows:

	Customer X	Customer Y
Accounts receivable.	11,760	11,760
Sales revenue.	11,760	11,760

For each customer, the following events occurred:

Customer X

Nov. 1, 1995	Could not pay the account; signed a note payable for $12,000, 10% interest-bearing, due in six months, on April 30, 1996.
Dec. 1, 1995	Sold (discounted) the X note to Provincial Bank, with recourse, at 12% interest per annum.
April 30, 1996	Customer X defaulted, and the bank charged a $20 protest fee.
July 31, 1996	Collected in full on the defaulted note plus an additional interest charge of 10% per annum.

Customer Y

Nov. 1, 1995	Could not pay the account; signed a $12,600 noninterest-bearing note; maturity date, on April 30, 1996.
Dec. 1, 1995	Sold (discounted) the Y note to Provincial Bank, with recourse, at 12% interest per annum.
April 30, 1996	Customer Y paid the note in full on maturity date.

Required

1. Give all of the entries related to the Customer X note from date initiated through July 31, 1996.
2. Give all of the entries related to the Customer Y note from date initiated through its final settlement, assuming that (*a*) the net approach is used and (*b*) the gross approach is used. No need to recompute when the same as (1).
3. Show the effect of each note on the 1995 income statement and balance sheet of Farb Company. Set up the following column headings and side captions:

	Customer	Customer Y Note	
Items	X Note	Net Basis	Gross Basis
Income Statement			
[List items]			
Balance Sheet			
[List items]			

P 8–16
(L.O. 6)

Overview of Notes: Four Different Notes   Resolve Company had a critical cash problem related to collections from four customers: Smith, Johnson, Karnes, and Cates. The transactions, in order of date, are given below. You will notice discounting, defaults, and extensions, but everyone finally paid in full. Resolve's annual accounting period ends December 31.

May	1	Received a $16,000, 90-day, 9% interest-bearing note from E. M. Smith, a customer, in settlement of an account receivable for that amount.
June	1	Received a $24,000, six-month, 9% interest-bearing note from M. Johnson, a customer, in settlement of an account receivable for that amount.
Aug.	1	Discounted (i.e., sold), with recourse, the Johnson note at the bank at 10%.
Aug.	1	Smith defaulted on the $16,000 note.
Sept.	1	Received a one-year, noninterest-bearing note from D. Karnes, a customer, in settlement of a $10,000 account receivable. The face of the note was $10,800, and the imputed going rate of interest was 8% (use the net method).
Oct.	1	Received a $40,000, 90-day note from R. M. Cates, a customer. The note was in payment for goods Cates purchased and was interest bearing at 15%.
Oct.	1	Collected the defaulted Smith note plus accrued interest to September 30 (10% per annum on the total amount due for two months).
Dec.	1	Johnson defaulted on the $24,000 note. Resolve Company paid the bank the total amount due plus a $50 protest fee.
Dec.	30	Collected Cates note in full.
Dec.	30	Collected Johnson note in full, including additional interest on the full amount due at the legal rate of 10% since default date.
Dec.	31	Accrued interest on outstanding notes.

Required

1. Give Resolve's entry to record each of the above transactions. Show computations.
2. Show how the outstanding notes at December 31 would be reported on the balance sheet.

P 8–17
(L.O. 6)

Notes Receivable with Unrealistic Interest Rate   Watt Service Company completed a major renovation contract and billed the customer $56,000 on January 1, 1995. Cash of $16,000 was collected, and a 5% note was received for the remaining $40,000, payable in three equal annual instalments (including principal plus interest) each December 31. The going rate of interest for notes with comparable risk is 12%.

Required

1. Compute the amount of the annual payments.
2. Compute the present value of the note.
3. Prepare a schedule of collections.
4. Give the entries on January 1, 1995, December 31, 1995, December 31, 1996, and December 31, 1997 (use the net method).

P 8–18
(L.O. 6)

Note Interest Rate Using Calculator or Computer   Falconcrest Company sold 10,000 cases of wine (cost: $80,000) to a large restaurant for an agreed-on cash price of $300,000 and accepted $50,000 as a down payment. A note was signed for the remainder, which calls for two years of $13,500 monthly payments beginning one month after the sale.

Required

Compute the implied monthly interest rate using a calculator equipped for interest calculations or a computer program you may have available. Compare that result with the result of interpolation, using Table 6A–4.

P 8–19
(L.O. 6)

Impairment of a Loan; Change in Present Value   On January 1, 1995, Robertson Inc. sold merchandise (cost, $8,000; sales value, $14,000) to Russell, Inc., and received a noninterest-bearing note in return. The note requires $17,636 to be paid in a lump sum on December 31, 1997.

On January 1, 1996, Russell requested that the terms of the loan be modified as follows: $7,000 to be paid in five years, balance due in six years. Robertson refused Russell's request.

During 1996, however, news of Russell's deteriorating financial condition prompted Robertson to reevaluate the collectibility of the note. Consequently, the modified terms requested by Russell were used as the estimate of future cash flows to be received, as of December 31, 1996. Russell was not informed of the reestimation, however.

To make matters worse, at the end of 1997, Robertson's accountants estimated that the most likely amount to be received from Russell would be $12,000, on December 31, 1999. This estimation was based on payments made by Russell to other creditors.

Required

1. Prepare the entry to record the sale by Robertson, assuming a perpetual inventory system, and the December 31, 1995, adjusting entry. Use the net method.
2. Prepare the entry to record the impairment.
3. Prepare the entry to record the adjustment in the note's value on December 31, 1997. Robertson makes no attempt to record interest revenue separately.

P 8–20
(L.O. 3, 4, 5)

Accounts Receivable Factoring   Michael Company sells merchandise for $100,000 on credit and factors the receivables with a finance company. All events occur within the reporting year.

Required

Make summary journal entries to account for all events of the following three independent situations:

1. The receivables are factored on a nonrecourse basis. The factor charges 8% as a financing fee and withholds 10% of the receivables for sales returns, allowances, and discounts. The factor absorbs sales adjustments beyond 10%. The factor estimates that 0.5% of the receivables are uncollectible. Actual adjustments are as follows: uncollectible accounts, $500; sales returns and allowances, $6,000; and sales discounts, $6,000. Record all entries for both Michael and the factor.
2. The receivables are factored on a recourse basis. The fee is 4%, and 15% is withheld. Michael estimates $5,000 each of sales returns and allowances, and sales discounts. Michael also expects $500 of uncollectibles. Michael bears the cost of all sales adjustments, including uncollectible accounts. The factor can neither compel nor allow Michael to repurchase the receivables. Assume the actual sales adjustments in (1). Record entries only for Michael.
3. Assume the facts in (2) except that the factor can compel Michael to repurchase uncollected receivables at any time. Record entries only for Michael.

ANALYZING FINANCIAL STATEMENTS

All questions in this section are based on information adapted from the financial statements of actual companies.

A 8–1
(L.O. 4, 6)

 Bad Debt Expense and Long-Term Notes

1. McGraw-Hill's 1989 statement of cash flows disclosed the following:

Statement of Cash Flows
For the Year Ended December 31, 1989
($000s)

Cash flows from operating activities:
Net income $47,791
Provision for losses on accounts receivable   44,880

The firm's bad debt expense (provision) of $44,880,000 is substantial in relation to earnings. Assume that McGraw-Hill uses the allowance method of accounting for bad debts.

2. O'Sullivan Corporation's 1989 statement of cash flows disclosed the following information:

Statement of Cash Flows
For the Year Ended December 31, 1989
($000s)

Cash flows from operating activities:
Net income $16,098
Gain on disposal of assets . . . .   (1,253)

Cash flows from investing activities:
Proceeds from disposal of assets. . . . . . $ 1,087

Supplemental Schedule of Non-Cash Investment Activities: A note receivable of $1,500,000 was received by the Corporation in 1989 for a portion of the proceeds due from the sale of certain real estate investments.

Assume that O'Sullivan's gain on disposal of assets, proceeds from disposal of assets, and receipt of the note all resulted from the sale of real estate investments at the end of 1989. Also assume that the note is noninterest-bearing and due in six years. The market interest rate on similar notes is 12%.

Required

1. For McGraw-Hill, what effect would each of the following have on 1989 earnings and ending balance sheet accounts: (*a*) failure to estimate bad debts and (*b*) failure to write off a worthless account of $600,000? Ignore differences between tax and financial reporting principles.
2. Reconstruct the summary entry for disposal of real estate assets by O'Sullivan Corporation. (Ignore tax effects.)

A 8–2
(L.O. 4)

Doubtful Accounts   Excerpts from Ameritech's 1991 income statement and statement of cash flows and from its 1990 and 1991 comparative balance sheets follow:

	1991	1990
	(amount in millions)	
Income Statement		
Revenues	$10,818.4	$10,662.5
Balance Sheet		
Current assets:		
Receivables, less allowance for uncollectibles		
of $124.6 and $134.7, respectively	$ 1,981.7	$ 1,824.2
Statement of Cash Flows		
Cash flows from operating activities:		
Net income	$ 1,165.5	$ 1,253.8
Provision for uncollectibles	165.0	121.0

Required

Answer the following questions assuming that (*a*) Ameritech uses the allowance method to estimate bad debts (provision for uncollectibles) and (*b*) all revenues are credit sales.

1. Are estimated uncollectible accounts increasing or decreasing as a percentage of revenues?
2. How much were net write-offs of accounts receivable during 1991?
3. What was cash collected on receivables during 1991?
4. Why is the provision for uncollectibles added to net income in the operating section of the statement of cash flows, and why was the amount of cash collections from receivables not available in the annual report?

A 8–3
(L.O. 4, 5, 6)

 Methods of Recognizing Bad Debts: The 1989 annual report of Brunswick Corporation included the following disclosure note:

Accounts and notes receivable. During the second quarter of 1989, the Company discontinued its Corporate collection department, which was responsible for the collection of receivables deemed to be uncollectible by the Company's operating units. As a result of this discontinuance, the collection effort for these receivables was shifted outside the Company. Consequently, receivables approximating $7.7 million, which were administered by the collection department and carried on the Company's books, were written off along with an equal amount of allowances for doubtful accounts.

In the same year, Eagle-Picher Industries, Inc., listed the following item in a disclosure note explaining the components of "other income":

Notes receivable write-off . . . . ($2,918,000)

The notes receivable write-off recognizes the uncollectibility of several notes received from the previous sale of certain assets.

Required

Briefly comment on which method you believe was used to account for uncollectible receivables by these two companies.

A 8–4
(L.O. 4)

Methods of Recognizing Cash Discounts: The annual reports of the following two companies provided information about cash discounts:
1. Knape & Vogt Manufacturing (from 1989 balance sheet):

Current assets:
   Accounts receivable, less allowance of $297,000
     for doubtful accounts and cash discounts $16,938,624

2. Genesco, Inc. (from 1990 disclosure notes):

Total receivables	$61,781,000
Allowance for bad debts and cash discounts	(3,173,000)
Net receivables	$58,608,000

Required

Briefly comment on which method you believe was used to account for cash discounts by these two companies.

A 8–5
(L.O. 5, 6)

Notes Receivable:

1. The 1989 annual report of Frozen Food Express Industries reported the following:

Current assets:
    Notes receivable (note 8) $413,000

Note 8

In connection with these sales [of tractors], total assets at December 31, 1989 include notes receivable of $973,000 of which $413,000 was classified as a current asset.

2. The 1989 annual report of McKesson Corporation listed total notes receivable but did not provide other detail regarding notes. Included in the disclosure notes was the following:

At March 31, 1989, the Company was contingently liable for $35.5 million of customer financing notes receivable. These notes were sold to a bank by the Company's finance subsidiary with recourse to the Company for certain uncollectible amounts.

Required

1. Assume that the non-current portion of the notes due Frozen Food Express specifies 3% interest on the $700,000 *maturity* value (the amount in excess of the current portion) due each December 31 through 1994. The $700,000 maturity value is due in one lump sum on December 31, 1994. Set up an equation to determine the market interest rate at the date of the tractor sales. Approximate the market interest rate through trial and error. A calculator or computer program capable of solving the equation also may be used.
2. Can you determine from the above information whether McKesson recorded the financing of the notes as a sale or as a borrowing?

COMPARATIVE ANALYSIS

Information pertaining to uncollectible accounts receivable for three firms appears below.

 Apogee Enterprises   This high-technology firm and manufacturer of robotic systems disclosed the following in its 1993 and 1992 annual reports:

($ in thousands)	1993	1992	1991
Bad debt expense	$ 2,061	$ 6,261	$ 2,064
Net accounts receivable*	106,421	93,093	96,006
Allowance for doubtful accounts*	6,339	9,049	5,070
Sales	572,450	596,281	599,525

  * Ending balances

Avnet, Inc.   This multinational firm with interests in electronics and computer technology disclosed the following in its 1991 and 1990 annual reports:

($ in thousands)	1991	1990	1989
Bad debt expense	$ 6,816	$ 7,728	$ 7,597
Net accounts receivable*	250,610	257,467	262,019
Allowance for doubtful accounts*	11,212	10,804	10,150
Sales	1,740,770	1,751,345	1,918,678

  * Ending balances

Double Eagle Petroleum and Mining Company   This natural resource exploration and development company disclosed the following note in its 1992 annual report:

Note 1. C. Bad Debts—The direct write-off method of accounting for uncollectible accounts is utilized whereby an account is written off only when determined to be uncollectible. The results of this method do not vary materially from the preferred method.

In addition, a supplemental schedule to Double Eagle's statement of cash flows disclosed the following:

Net income	$ XXXXXX
Subtract accounts receivable increase	(11,862)

Required

1. For each firm, determine (a) the method chosen to account for uncollectible accounts receivable and (b) the actual write-offs of accounts receivable (net of recoveries) for the most recent two years indicated in the data (for Double Eagle, explain why you cannot determine the amount of accounts receivable written off in 1992).

2. For the firms using the allowance method of accounting for uncollectible accounts receivable, provide an opinion on whether the credit sales or accounts receivable method of estimating bad debt expense was used.

3. For Double Eagle Petroleum and Mining, why is the increase in accounts receivable subtracted from net income in the supplemental schedule to the statement of cash flows? Assuming only a minor amount of write-offs in 1992 (use $500), what does the $11,862 amount in the schedule to the statement of cash flows consist of?

9 Inventory: Basic Valuation Methods

LEARNING OBJECTIVES

After you have studied this chapter, you will be able to:

1 **Explain the characteristics of inventories.**

2 **Describe the components of inventory cost.**

3 **Apply the periodic and perpetual inventory methods.**

4 **Explain the various alternative cost flow assumptions used to value inventory, their effect on reported income, and the reasons for management's choice among the alternatives.**

INTRODUCTION

Inventory turnover, defined as the cost of product sold divided by the average inventory level, is often used as one measure of firm efficiency. Maple Leaf Foods Inc., and the Oshawa Group Limited, both firms in the food products business, show inventory turnover ratios for 1993 of 13.16 and 17.70, respectively. Dominion Textile Inc. (Domtex), a textile manufacturer, had an inventory turnover ratio of 6.21 for 1993. Does this mean that Oshawa is more efficient than Maple Leaf and over twice as efficient as Domtex? Initially, comparing firms across industries may not be reasonable. Even firms apparently in the same business may serve different markets. For example, Maple Leaf manufactures food, Oshawa does not. On the other hand, Maple Leaf has a greater presence in the United States. But is this all there is to the difference? Could different inventory valuation methods have an impact on these values?

An article in *The Wall Street Journal* reports "The recent rise in inventory fraud is one of the biggest single reasons for the proliferation of accounting scandals."[1] The article notes several examples.

One case involves Comptronix. On December 1, 1992, the company admitted "fraudulent" accounting practices involving false entries to increase inventory

---

[1] L. Beiten, "Inventory Chicanery Tempts More Firms, Fools More Auditors," *The Wall Street Journal,* December 12, 1992, pp. A1 and A4. The quote is attributed to Professor Paul R. Brown of the City University of New York's Baruch College.

and decrease the company's cost of sales. Senior management capitalized to inventory the salaries and start-up costs related to expansion activities.

Another involved the Laribee Wire Manufacturing Company that recorded shipments of inventory between its own plants as stock located in both plants. Some "shipments" never left the originating plant, and supporting documentation "appeared to be largely fictitious." In one case, copper rod worth more than $5 million would have required a storage capacity three times that of the warehouses in which the inventory was supposedly located.

Creating nonexistent inventory magnified Laribee's profits because the cost-of-goods-sold expense is determined by subtracting ending inventory amounts from goods available for sale. Laribee filed for bankruptcy court protection in early 1991. Felix Pomerantz, a noted accountant and director of Florida International University's Center for Accounting, Auditing, and Tax Studies, observed in the *Wall Street Journal* article that "when companies are desperate to stay afloat, inventory fraud is the easiest way to produce instant profits and dress up the balance sheet."

An alternative means of producing instant profits is illustrated by Terex Corporation. Terex followed a practice of buying (often bankrupt) companies with substantial inventories at a fraction of their book value.[2] The inventories were then written down to artificially low values relative to their selling prices, ostensibly because they were obsolete. Later, when the inventory was sold, at premiums ranging up to 40%, the result was a substantial boost to net income in the short run.

Because this approach to generating profits rests on acquisitions rather than production and sales activities, it is hard to sustain over time. Indeed, *Business Week* observes that Terex "has been willing to speculate in deals that most prudent businesses would not consider. That may be the reason Terex . . . is crumbling."

Inventory levels are important to companies to ensure production schedules and meet customer requirements. At the same time, holding inventories is costly. Japanese firms achieve higher profits by shortening production set-up times, improving the quality of both incoming materials and finished goods, and attaining better working relationships with suppliers so that inventory is received just in time (JIT) for production.

Results of just-in-time systems have been impressive. Until recently, North American manufacturers carried on average over four times the monthly inventories carried by Japanese firms. Although this ratio has recently declined, Japanese firms are still more effective. Some of the difference, however, is due to the Japanese environment, including the geographical proximity of firms to each other, an effective railway system, and a relative lack of work disruptions.

THE IMPORTANCE OF INVENTORIES

Inventories are an important asset to most businesses and typically represent the largest current asset of manufacturing and retail firms. In today's competitive economic climate, inventory accounting methods and management practices have become profit-enhancing tools. Better inventory systems can increase profitability; poorly conceived systems can drain profits and put a business at a competitive disadvantage.

Inventory effects on profits are more noticeable when business activity fluctuates. During prosperous times, sales are high and inventory moves quickly from purchase to sale. But when economic conditions decline, sales levels retreat, inventories

[2] "The Accounting Questions at Terex," *Business Week,* October 12, 1992, pp. 148–150. Companies acquired by Terex include Koehring, Fruehauf Trailer, and Clark Equipment's Forklift Division.

accumulate and may need to be sold at a loss. Management must monitor inventory types and levels continuously if profits are to be maintained.

In many companies, inventories are a significant portion not only of current assets but also of total assets. Although many inventory items may appear to be relatively insignificant (for example, hardware such as nuts and bolts), in the aggregate they can have considerable value, so safeguarding inventories is as important as protecting cash. The need to stock adequate items for sale coupled with the need to avoid the cost of overstocking represent critical management planning and control problems. Failure either to control physical inventories or to account for inventory costs properly can even lead to business failure.

This chapter and the one to follow cover the various accounting methods used to value and report inventories on the balance sheet and simultaneously measure the cost of goods sold required to determine income. This chapter emphasizes inventory accounting in the manufacturing sector, and Chapter 10 focusses on retail establishments. However, several topics are relevant in both settings.

INVENTORY CATEGORIES

Inventories consist of goods owned by a business and held either for use in the manufacture of products or as products awaiting sale. We typically think of inventories as raw materials, work in process, finished goods, or merchandise held by retailers. But depending on the nature of the company's business, inventory may consist of virtually any tangible good or material. An inventory might consist of component pieces of equipment, bulk commodities such as wheat or milling flour, fuel oil awaiting sale during the winter heating season, unused storage space, or the airline seats available each day on Air Canada between Toronto and Vancouver. Machinery and equipment, for example, are considered operational assets by the company that buys them, but before sale they are part of the inventory of the manufacturer who made them. Even a building, during its construction period, is an inventory item for the builder.

Inventories are classified as follows:

1. **Merchandise inventory** Goods on hand purchased by a retailer or a trading company such as an importer or exporter for resale. Generally, goods acquired for resale are not physically altered by the purchaser company; the goods are in finished form when they leave the manufacturer's plant. In some instances, however, parts are acquired and then further assembled into finished products. Bicycles that are assembled from frames, wheels, gears, and so on and sold by a bicycle retailer are an example.

2. **Manufacturing inventory** The combined inventories of a manufacturing entity, consisting of:

   a. **Raw materials inventory** Tangible goods purchased or obtained in other ways (e.g., by mining) and on hand for direct use in the manufacture of goods for resale. Parts or subassemblies manufactured before use are sometimes classified as component parts inventory.

   b. **Work-in-process inventory** Goods requiring further processing before completion and sale. Work-in-process, also called goods-in-process inventory, includes the cost of direct material, direct labour, and allocated manufacturing overhead costs incurred to date.[3]

   c. **Finished goods inventory** Manufactured items completed and held for sale. Finished goods inventory cost includes the cost of direct material, direct labour, and allocated manufacturing overhead related to its manufacture.

   d. **Manufacturing supplies inventory** Items on hand, such as lubrication oils for the machinery, cleaning materials, and other items that make up an insignificant part of the finished product.

---

[3] The term *allocated overhead* refers to nontraceable indirect expenses such as heat, light, and administrative salaries added to the cost of goods manufactured.

EXHIBIT 9-1

Typical Cost Flow and
Physical Flow for a
Manufacturing Company:
Men's Suit Maker

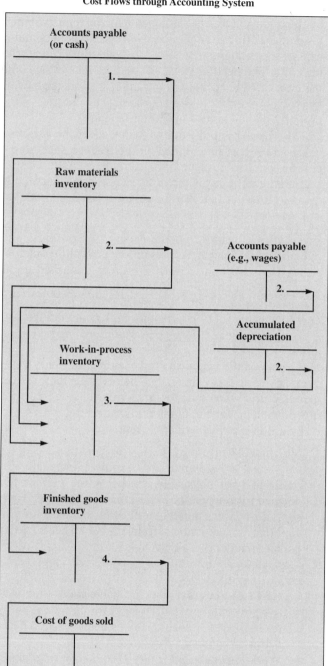

Cost Flows through Accounting System

Physical Flow of Goods Through Manufacturing System

1. Purchases of raw materials are made, with bolts of cloth, sewing thread, buttons, zippers, and other items of production received. Debit raw materials inventory and credit cash or accounts payable.

2. Items are requisitioned from raw materials to be used in the production of a run of men's suits. Employees are hired to cut cloth, operate sewing machines, sweep, and clean up the shop area. Power and heat are acquired, and depreciation is incurred on building and machines. Debit work-in-process inventory and credit raw materials or appropriate payable or accumulated depreciation.

3. Men's suits are completed, inspected, and transferred to a warehouse for shipping to customers. Costs of each unit are determined and transferred. Debit finished goods inventory and credit work-in-process inventory.

4. Orders are received and filled for men's suits. Suits are packaged and shipped to customers. Debit cost of goods sold (assuming perpetual inventory system) upon shipment and credit finished goods inventory.

3. **Miscellaneous inventories** Items such as office, janitorial, and shipping supplies. Inventories of this type are typically used in the near future and are usually recorded as selling or general expense when purchased.

The major classifications of inventories depend on the operations of the business. A wholesale or retail trading entity acquires merchandise for resale. A manufacturing entity acquires raw materials and component parts, manufactures finished products, and then sells them. The flow of inventory costs in a manufacturing setting is shown in Exhibit 9–1.

The majority of inventory accounting issues stem from the need to determine the cost of goods sold as reported on the income statement and, simultaneously, the inventory values to be reported on the balance sheet. This means that the dollar amount of inventories must be allocated between expense (cost of goods sold) and assets (closing inventory). This allocation involves two distinct phases:

1. **Phase 1** Identification and measurement of the quantity of physical goods (items and quantities) that should be included in inventory at the end of the accounting period.
2. **Phase 2** Assignment of an accounting value to the physical amount of inventory at the end of the accounting period.

ITEMS INCLUDED IN INVENTORY

All goods owned by the company on the inventory date should be included in inventory, regardless of their location. At any time, a business may hold goods that it does not own or own goods that it does not hold. Therefore, care must be taken to identify the goods properly includable in inventory.

Goods purchased and in transit should be included in the purchaser's inventory provided ownership has passed to the purchaser. If the goods are shipped **FOB (free on board) destination,** ownership passes when the buyer receives the goods from the common carrier, a railroad or independent trucker.

Goods on consignment, those held by agents and goods located at branches, should be included in inventory. Goods *held* (but owned by someone else) for sale on commission or on consignment and goods received from a vendor but rejected and awaiting return to the vendor for credit should be excluded from inventory.[4]

Some companies enter into *repurchase agreements* to sell and buy back inventory items at prearranged prices. This practice has several advantages. Inventory sold is, in effect, "parked" outside the company, so the selling company may be able to avoid finance expenses that would be incurred if the inventory stayed in house. This saving is possible because the buyer pays all or most of the retail value of the inventory covered in the repurchase agreement until the goods are reacquired by the seller, again at a prearranged price.

Another motivation for repurchase agreements is to avoid the reporting of direct borrowing on the balance sheet when debt-to-equity ratios are high and the reporting of more debt would make matters worse. However, when a repurchase agreement covers all costs, including holding (financing) costs, the inventory must remain on the seller's books. In effect, repurchase agreements are normally loans rather than sales. Hence, these agreements should not be used to reduce reported debt. A repurchase agreement offers the buyer an opportunity to earn the equivalent of financing fees from the predetermined price spread between the buy and sell-back sides of the transaction.

Special sales agreements exist for many firms, including those selling items to retailers (sporting goods manufacturers and book publishers provide examples). These agreements permit goods to be returned if not sold. Should such goods be considered sold when delivered to the retailer? *CICA Handbook* Section 3400 allows these goods to be considered as sales only if returns can be reasonably estimated or, if the return privilege has expired. If not, the items remain in the seller's inventory account.

A similar result applies when sales are made on an instalment basis. Sellers may require a conditional sales contract, withholding legal title until all payments have

---

[4] Consignment is a marketing arrangement whereby the consignor (the owner of the goods) ships merchandise to another party, known as a consignee, who acts as a sales agent only. The consignee does not purchase the goods but assumes responsibility for their care and sale. Upon sale, the consignee remits the proceeds, less specified expenses and a commission, to the consignor. Goods on consignment, because they are owned by the consignor until sold, should be excluded from the inventory of the consignee and included in the inventory of the consignor.

been made. Nevertheless, the sale may be included in revenues if a reasonable estimate can be made of the percentage of uncollectible accounts.

Although legal ownership is a useful starting point to identify items that should be included in inventory, a strict legal determination is often impractical. In such cases, the sales agreement, industry practices, and other evidence of intent should be considered.

COMPONENTS OF INVENTORY COST

Inventory cost is measured by the total cash equivalent outlay made to acquire the goods and to prepare them for sale. These costs include the purchase cost and incidental costs incurred until the goods are ready for use or for sale to the customer.

Certain incidental costs, although theoretically a cost of goods purchased, are often not included in inventory valuation but are reported as separate expenses. Examples include insurance costs on goods in transit, sales taxes paid, and material-handling expenses. These expenditures are usually not included in determining inventory costs because they are not directly related to the purchase or manufacture of goods for sale.

General and administrative (G&A) expenses are appropriately treated as *period* expenses because they relate more directly to accounting periods than to inventory. Selling and distribution costs are also considered period operating expenses and are not allocated to inventories. The difficulty in allocating these items and the cost of doing so exceed the benefits.

Freight-In (Freight on Purchases)

Freight charges and other incidental costs incurred in connection with the purchase of inventory are additions to inventory cost. When these costs can be attributed to specific goods, they should be added to the cost of such goods. However, in some cases, specific identification is impractical. Therefore, freight costs are often recorded in a special account, such as freight-in, which is reported as an addition to cost of goods sold in the case of a retail company, and to cost of materials used in the case of a manufacturing firm. This practical procedure may overstate cost of goods sold and understate inventory by the amount of costs that should be allocated to inventory. When the amounts are material and it is practical, freight-in should be apportioned between cost of goods sold and the ending inventory.

Purchase Discounts (Cash Discounts on Credit Purchases)

Many companies offer cash discounts on purchases to encourage timely payment from buyers (which speeds up cash flow and may save on borrowing costs). Most buyers make timely payments and take advantage of cash discounts because the savings are normally quite substantial. In fact, some companies borrow money in order to take advantage of cash discounts. This tactic makes sense because the typical purchase discount terms of 2/10, n/30 are equivalent to an annualized interest rate of about 37%, if payment is delayed to the 30th day after purchase. Lost discounts are a cost of financing and should not be included in inventory amounts.

INVENTORY RECORDING METHODS

The physical quantities in inventory may be measured by use of either a **periodic inventory system** or a **perpetual inventory system.** Exhibit 9–2 compares these two systems in a manufacturing environment. The essential difference between these two systems from an accounting point of view is the frequency with which the physical flows are assigned a value. In the periodic system, the inventory value is determined only at particular times, such as at the end of a reporting period. This approach to valuation is used even when an ongoing record of physical flows is maintained. A good example is provided by supermarkets that use automated scanners at checkout stations to keep track of physical inventory levels but place accounting values on the physical flows only periodically.

In a perpetual system of inventory valuation, the ongoing physical flow is monitored and the cost of the items is maintained on a continual basis.

EXHIBIT 9–2   Comparison of the Periodic and the Perpetual Inventory Systems

Transaction or Event	Periodic Inventory System	Perpetual Inventory System
Routine purchases of various inventory items.	All inventory item values are debited to the purchases account regardless of the particular items acquired.	As in an accounts receivable subsidiary ledger, individual accounts are maintained for each type of inventory item, along with an inventory control account. This control account is debited for all purchases, with supporting entries made to individual inventory accounts.
Items removed from inventory for use in production.	No accounting entries are made.	Individual credit entries are made to each inventory account (plus a combined credit to the inventory control account) with an offsetting debit entry to the work-in-process (WIP) account.
End-of-period accounting entries and related activities.	Physical count of the ending inventory is taken and dollar values are assigned. This activity is a prerequisite to computing the cost of goods sold (CGS) for the period. Adjusting entries are made to compute the cost of goods sold (CGS) using the following formula: CGS = Beginning inventory + Purchases − Ending inventory	Physical count of inventory is not needed for calculation of cost of goods sold for the period, but such inventory counts are usually made in order to verify the accuracy of the perpetual system and to identify inventory overages and shortages. Cost of goods sold is automatically determined from the sum of the daily postings to this account.

Periodic Inventory System   In a periodic inventory system, an actual *physical count* of the goods on hand is taken at the end of each accounting period for which financial statements are prepared. The goods are counted, weighed, or otherwise measured, and the quantities are then multiplied by unit costs to value the inventory. An ongoing inventory record may, but need not, be kept of the units and amounts purchased or sold (or issued) and of the balance on hand.[5] Purchases are debited to a purchases account, and end-of-period entries are made to close the purchases account, to close out beginning inventory, and to record the ending inventory as an asset (i.e., the ending inventory replaces the beginning inventory in the accounts).[6]

Cost of goods sold (also commonly called *cost of sales*) is computed as a residual amount (beginning inventory plus net purchases less ending inventory) and for all practical purposes cannot be verified independently of an inventory count. To illustrate, consider the following data for the Lea Company:

	Units	Unit Cost	Total
Beginning inventory	500	$4.00	$2,000
Purchases	1,000	4.00	4,000
Goods available for sale	1,500		$6,000
Sales	900		
Ending inventory	600		

[5] If the physical flow is monitored continuously, the physical count serves only as an accuracy check. Statistical methods are commonly used to ease the task of verifying inventory levels.

[6] The purchase returns and allowances and the purchases discount accounts are also closed at this time. These accounts are contra to purchases.

Based on this data, the computation of the cost of goods sold yields:

Beginning inventory (carried forward from the prior period): 500 × $4.00 . . . . $2,000
Merchandise purchases (accumulated in the purchases account): 1,000 × $4.00.   4,000
    Total goods available for sale during the period   6,000
Less: Ending inventory (quantity determined by a physical count): 600 × $4.00   2,400
    Cost of goods sold (a residual amount). $3,600

Perpetual Inventory System

When a perpetual inventory system is used, detailed perpetual inventory records, in addition to the usual ledger accounts, are maintained for each inventory item, and an inventory control account is maintained in the general ledger on a current basis. The perpetual inventory record for each item must provide information for recording receipts, issues, and balances on hand, usually both in units and in dollar amounts. With this information, the physical quantity and the valuation of goods on hand at any time are available from the accounting records. Therefore, a physical inventory count is unnecessary except to verify the perpetual inventory records. A physical count is made annually for auditing purposes to compare the inventory on hand with the perpetual record and to provide data for any adjusting entries needed (errors and losses, for example).

When a difference is found between the perpetual inventory records and the physical count, the perpetual inventory records are adjusted to the physical count. In such cases, the inventory account is debited or credited as necessary for the correction, and an inventory correction account, such as inventory shortages (loss) or overages (gain), is debited or credited. The inventory correction account is closed to income summary at the end of the period. The balance in the inventory shortage account is usually reported separately on internal financial statements for control purposes, but any balance is combined with the cost of goods sold amount on external statements.

For improved inventory management, a perpetual inventory system is especially useful when inventory consists of items with high unit values or when it is important to have adequate but not excessive inventory levels. Although perpetual inventory systems are better for inventory management, problems remain. For example:

▪ **Accounting information control versus physical property control** Thanks to robotics and computer technology, today there are automated inventory systems that not only account for the inventory but also manage the stocking and handling of inventory goods and materials. However, even with automated systems, certain aspects of physical inventory management and control are problematic. Theft and pilferage, breakage and other physical damage, misorders and misfills, and inadequate inventory supervision practices must be dealt with regardless of the type of inventory accounting system used.

▪ **Higher costs associated with perpetual inventory systems** Perpetual inventory systems, which involve detailed accounting records, tend to be more costly to implement and maintain (at least initially) than periodic systems, which tend to be less complex. Here again, computers have made perpetual inventory systems more popular today than ever before.

Accounting for Periodic and Perpetual Systems

Journal entries for the periodic and perpetual inventory systems differ.

1. **Entries at date of purchase** In the periodic inventory system, acquisitions of goods during the accounting period are entered in the purchase account. In this example, the unit cost of three kinds of inventory has remained constant:

Item	Unit Cost
A	$50
B	75
C	80

Four units of each item are purchased on three different dates during January (amounts in dollars), and recorded as follows.

Purchases*		Accounts Payable (or Cash)	
Jan. 15 Item A 200		Jan. 15 Item A 200	
Jan. 18 Item B 300		Jan. 18 Item B 300	
Jan. 20 Item C 320		Jan. 20 Item C 320	

* $50(4); $75(4); $80(4).

In the perpetual inventory system, purchases are debited instead to an inventory control account and concurrently recorded in a subsidiary inventory ledger. Assume that the opening balance reflects one unit each of A, B and C.

Inventory Control		Accounts Payable (or Cash)	
Jan. 1 Balance 205*		Jan. 15 Item A 200	
Jan. 15 Item A 200		Jan. 18 Item B 300	
Jan. 18 Item B 300		Jan. 20 Item C 320	
Jan. 20 Item C 320			

* $50 + $75 + $80.

The subsidiary inventory ledger accounts are as follows:

Inventory Item A		Inventory Item B	
Jan. 1 Balance 50		Jan. 1 Balance 75	
Jan. 15 Purchase 200		Jan. 18 Purchase 300	

Inventory Item C	
Jan. 1 Balance 80	
Jan. 20 Purchase 320	

2. **Entries at date of sale** In the periodic inventory system, only one entry is made to record each sale. Assume that during the period three units of each item are sold. Unit selling prices are A, $75; B, $225; C, $300.

Accounts Receivable		Sales Revenue*	
Jan. 25 Item A 225		Jan. 25 Item A 225	
Jan. 27 Item B 675		Jan. 27 Item B 675	
Jan. 29 Item C 900		Jan. 29 Item C 900	

* $75(3); $225(3); $300(3)

In the perpetual inventory system, two entries are required to record each sale: one to account for the sales revenue and another to account for the cost of goods sold. Only the perpetual inventory system provides a current accounting of goods sold as sales are made.

Accounts Receivable		Sales Revenue	
Jan. 25 Item A 225		Jan. 25 Item A 225	
Jan. 27 Item B 675		Jan. 27 Item B 675	
Jan. 29 Item C 900		Jan. 29 Item C 900	

Cost of Goods Sold*		Inventory Control	
Jan. 25 Item A 150		Jan. 1 Balance 205	
Jan. 27 Item B 225		Jan. 15 Item A 200	Jan. 25 Item A 150
Jan. 29 Item C 240		Jan. 18 Item B 300	Jan. 27 Item B 225
		Jan. 20 Item C 320	Jan. 29 Item C 240

* $50(3); $75(3); $80(3)

Inventory Item A				Inventory Item B			
Jan. 1 Balance	50	Jan. 25 Sale	150	Jan. 1 Balance	75		
Jan. 15 Purchase	200			Jan. 18 Purchase	300	Jan. 27 Sale	225

Inventory Item C			
Jan. 1 Balance	80		
Jan. 20 Purchase	320	Jan. 29 Sale	240

3. **Inventory balances** In the periodic inventory system, the beginning balance in the merchandise inventory account remains unchanged throughout the accounting period. The beginning inventory balance in this case is $205.

Inventory	
Jan. 1 Balance 205	

In the perpetual inventory system, all inventory purchase costs and individual cost of goods sold (CGS) per sale are accounted for in the inventory control account.

4. **Entries at end of accounting period** In the periodic inventory system, the cost of goods sold during the period and the ending inventory must be computed. For these computations, the beginning balance in the inventory account ($205) and the total in the purchases account ($820) are first closed to the cost of goods sold account. At the same time, a physical count of the remaining inventory is taken, with the value of the remaining inventory recorded as the ending inventory. This value is debited to the merchandise inventory account and credited to the cost of goods sold account. The cost of goods sold is then closed to the income summary account.

Inventory				Purchases			
Jan. 1 Balance	205	Jan. 31 Close to CGS	205	Jan. 15 Item A	200	Jan. 31 Close to CGS	820
Jan. 31 Ending Inv.	410			Jan. 18 Item B	300		
				Jan. 20 Item C	320		

Cost of Goods Sold			
Jan. 31 Beginning Inv.	205	Jan. 31 Ending Inv.	410
Jan. 31 Purchases	820		
Jan. 31 Balance	615		

In the perpetual inventory system, no end-of-period entries are needed to compute the cost of goods sold and ending inventory values (although adjustments due to shortages and possible breakage may be necessary). Both the merchandise inventory control and the cost of goods sold accounts will show their current balances.

Inventory Control				Cost of Goods Sold			
Jan. 1 Balance	205	Jan. 25 Sale A	150	Jan. 25 Item A	150		
Jan. 15 Purchase A	200	Jan. 27 Sale B	225	Jan. 27 Item B	225		
Jan. 18 Purchase B	300	Jan. 29 Sale C	240	Jan. 29 Item C	240		
Jan. 20 Purchase C	320			Jan. 31 Balance	615		
Jan. 31 Balance	410						

Inventory Item A			Inventory Item B		
Jan. 1 Balance 50 Jan. 15 Purchase 200	Jan. 25 Sale	150	Jan. 1 Balance 75 Jan. 18 Purchase 300	Jan. 27 Sale	225
Jan. 31 Balance 100			Jan. 31 Balance 150		

Inventory Item C		
Jan. 1 Balance 80 Jan. 20 Purchase 320	Jan. 29 Sale	240
Jan. 31 Balance 160		

5. **Closing entries to income summary account** Whichever inventory system is used, the sales revenue account ($1,800) and the cost of goods sold account ($615) are closed to the income summary account, which will report a gross margin figure of $1,185 ($1,800 − $615). The next step is to deduct expenses for the period (not covered in this illustration) to arrive at net income before taxes.

6. **Income statement reporting** In both inventory systems, for this example the income statement would appear as follows:

Income Statement

Sales revenue.	$1,800
Less: Cost of goods sold.	615
Gross margin on sales	$1,185

The following additional information may be shown in a note or supporting schedule under the periodic inventory system:

Sales revenue		$1,800
Less: Cost of goods sold:		
Beginning inventory	$ 205	
Purchases	820	
Goods available for sale.	$1,025	
Less: Ending inventory	410	
Cost of goods sold		615
Gross margin on sales.		$1,185

7. **Balance sheet reporting** Whichever inventory system is used, the balance sheet reports only the ending balance in the merchandise inventory account.

Partial Balance Sheet
Periodic or Perpetual Inventory System

Current assets:	
Inventory	$410

8. **Treatment of purchase returns** When a purchaser returns goods, the goods are removed from inventory. The entry using the perpetual method to record $200 of returns is:

Accounts payable*	200	
Inventory.		200

* Or a receivable, if payment has already been made to the seller.

The appropriate inventory subsidiary account is also credited for the return. Cost of goods sold will be correctly determined with this approach.

If the periodic inventory method is used, the entry is:

```
Accounts payable. . . . . . . . . . . . . . . . . . . . . . . . . . . . .  200
     Purchase returns . . . . . . . . . . . . . . . . . . . . . . . . . .         200
```

At the end of the accounting period, the purchase returns account is contra to the purchases and is closed to cost of goods sold. Since the goods have been removed from inventory, the cost of goods calculation will be correct.

9. **Treatment of purchase discounts** Chapter 8 discussed accounting for cash discounts from the seller's point of view. The same concepts hold for the purchaser, and either the gross or net method may be used. The following chart illustrates the entries to record purchase discounts, depending on whether the periodic or perpetual system is used. Assume the purchase of goods with a gross invoice cost of $100 on terms 2/10, n30.

	Gross Method		Net Method	
	Periodic System	Perpetual System	Periodic System	Perpetual System

Record purchase	Purchases 100
	   Accounts payable 100
		Inventory 100
		   Accounts payable 100
			Purchases 98
			   Accounts payable 98
				Inventory 98
				   Accounts payable 98

Remit payment within 10 day discount period	Accounts payable 100
	   Purchase discounts 2
	   Cash 98
		Accounts payable 100
		   Inventory 2
		   Cash 98
			Accounts payable 98
			   Cash 98
				Accounts payable 98
				   Cash 98

Remit payment after discount period lapses	Accounts payable 100
	   Cash 100
		Accounts payable 100
		   Cash 100
			Accounts payable 98
			Purchase discounts
			   forfeited 2
			   Cash 100
				Accounts payable 98
				Purchase discounts
				   forfeited 2
				   Cash 100

Purchase discounts are contra to purchases and closed to cost of goods sold. Purchase discounts forfeited represent a finance charge and are merged with miscellaneous expenses. Inventory (or net purchases), in theory, should not be increased if an available cash discount is lost. However, the gross method includes this finance charge in net purchases if the discount period is allowed to lapse.

MEASUREMENT OF INVENTORY VALUES FOR ACCOUNTING PURPOSES

At date of acquisition, inventory items are recorded at their cash equivalent cost in accordance with the cost principle. Subsequently, when an item is sold, its cost is matched with the revenue from the sale in accordance with the matching principle. Inventory items remaining on hand at the end of an accounting period are assigned an accounting value based on the cost principle except when their value has declined below cost because of damage, obsolescence, or a decrease in replacement cost. In such a case, the items in inventory are typically assigned a lower value for accounting purposes, in accordance with the conservatism constraint. For example, the item's net realizable value may be assigned.

The cost value assigned to the end-of-period inventory of merchandise and finished goods is an allocation of the total cost of goods available for sale between that portion sold (cost of goods sold) and that portion held as an asset for subsequent sale (ending inventory). The nature of this allocation is shown in Exhibit 9–3, based on the data given in the previous example (page 383).

Measurement of acceptable accounting values for inventory involves two distinct tasks:

1. **Inventory unit cost** Selection of an appropriate unit cost for valuation of the items in inventory. The principal inventory valuation methods are:

EXHIBIT 9–3
Allocation of Costs to
Inventory and Cost of
Goods Sold

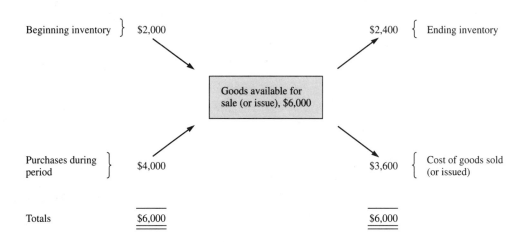

a. The cost basis.
b. Departures from the cost basis:
   (1) Lower of cost or market (LCM).   (4) Current cost.
   (2) Net realizable value.   (5) Selling price.
   (3) Replacement cost.
   This chapter uses the cost basis. Under certain circumstances, inventory is written down to market value if cost exceeds market. This adjustment (LCM), and
   other departures from cost are discussed in Chapter 10.
2. **Inventory cost flow** Selection of an inventory cost flow method; that is, selection
   of an *assumed flow* of inventory unit costs during the accounting period. The
   principal inventory cost flow methods discussed in this chapter are:
   a. Specific cost identification.
   b. Average cost.
   c. First-in, first-out (FIFO).
   d. Last-in, first-out (LIFO).

CONCEPT REVIEW

1. Explain the essential differences in accounting for inventories under the periodic
   and perpetual inventory systems.
2. Which of the following items should be included in inventory or the cost of
   inventory?
   a. Goods out on consignment.
   b. Sales with right of return agreements when sales returns cannot be reasonably
      estimated.
   c. Freight-in expenditures on purchases.
3. What two tasks are involved in the measurement of acceptable accounting values
   for inventory?

**INVENTORY COST
FLOW METHODS**

**Underlying Concepts of
Cost Flow**

An appropriate cost allocation procedure must be selected to allocate the total cost
of goods available for sale during each period between the cost of goods sold and the
cost of the ending inventory. If inventory unit acquisition costs are constant over
time, the choice of an allocation process will not affect the result. However, inventory item costs—both acquisition and manufacturing costs—typically vary, trending
up or down in response to prevailing conditions in the economy. For inventory
accounting purposes, this price variability creates a need for management to select
an explicit cost flow method (assumption) for use in allocating the total cost of

goods available for sale between expense (cost of goods sold) and assets (ending inventory).

The physical movement of goods is nearly always on a first-in, first-out basis, especially if the product is perishable or subject to obsolescence. But the cost flow method used to account for the value of both the inventory used up during the period and the inventory on hand at the end of the period can be quite different from the actual flow of goods. Inventory accounting concerns the flow of costs through the accounting system, not the flow of goods physically in and out of a stockroom. On this issue, the *CICA Handbook* states:

> The method selected for determining cost should be one which results in the fairest matching of costs against revenues regardless of whether or not the method corresponds to the physical flow of goods.[7]

The inventory cost flow methods discussed in this chapter conform to the cost principle. The central issue is the order in which the actual unit costs incurred are assigned to the ending inventory and to cost of goods sold. Selection of an inventory cost flow method determines the cost of goods sold, which is deducted from sales revenue for the period.

In a periodic inventory system, the quantity of the ending inventory is established at the end of the period. The unit costs are then applied to derive the ending inventory valuation by using a particular cost flow method. Cost of goods sold (or used) is determined by subtracting the ending inventory valuation from the cost of goods available for sale.

In a perpetual inventory system, each receipt and each issue of an inventory item is recorded in the inventory records to maintain an up-to-date perpetual inventory balance at all times. Thus, the perpetual inventory records provide the units and costs of ending inventory and cost of goods sold at any given time. The unit costs applied to each issue or sale are determined by the cost flow method used.

Four inventory cost flow methods—specific cost identification, average cost, FIFO, and LIFO—are discussed in this chapter.

Specific Cost Identification Method

The **specific cost identification method** requires that each item stocked be specifically marked so that its unit cost can be identified at any time. When the items involved are large or expensive, or only small quantities are handled, it may be feasible to tag or number each item when purchased or manufactured. This method makes it possible to identify at date of sale the specific unit cost of each item sold and each item remaining in inventory. Thus, the specific cost identification method relates the cost flow directly with the specific flow of physical goods. It is the only method to do so.

Evaluation of the Specific Cost Identification Method   The specific cost identification method requires careful identification of each item, which is a practical limitation because of the detailed records that are required. However, computerized inventory systems can mitigate this problem.

An undesirable feature of the method is the opportunity to manipulate income by arbitrary selection of items at time of sale. Assume that three identical stereo sets are for sale that cost $800, $850, and $900. When one is sold for $1,500, the reported cost of goods sold (and reported income) would depend on the unit (arbitrarily) selected to be sold.

Automobile dealers use the specific cost method for two reasons. First, the dealer's specific cost is an important determinant of the sales price. Second, this method is easily applied because there is an identification number for each vehicle and a known invoice cost. In this case, the specific cost identification method has the advantage that it establishes a specific gross margin on each item sold.

---

[7] *CICA Handbook*, Section 3030, paragraph .09, "Inventories."

EXHIBIT 9–4
Data on Inventories: Chase
Container Corporation

	Units		
Transaction Date	**Purchased**	**Sold**	**On Hand**
Jan. 1 Inventory @ $1.00.			200
Jan. 9 Purchases @ $1.10.	300		500
Jan. 10 Sales.		400	100
Jan. 15 Purchases @ $1.16.	400		500
Jan. 18 Sales.		300	200
Jan. 24 Purchases @ $1.26.	100		300

The costs to be allocated are the total costs of the goods
available for sale:

Beginning inventory.	200 × $1.00 =	$ 200
Purchases	300 × $1.10 = $330	
	400 × $1.16 = 464	
	100 × $1.26 = 126	920
Cost of goods available for sale*		$1,120

* The $1,120 is allocated between ending inventory and cost of goods sold, using one of the cost flow assumptions described in the next subsections.

Average Cost Method

The **average cost method** assumes that the cost of inventory on hand at the end of a period and the cost of goods sold during a period is representative of all costs incurred during the period. Application depends on the inventory system:

- **Periodic inventory system** The *weighted-average unit cost* is used for the entire accounting period.
- **Perpetual inventory system** The *moving-average unit cost* is used.

Data for the Chase Container Corporation are given in Exhibit 9–4 and are used to illustrate the calculations.

Weighted-Average Cost (Periodic Inventory System) A weighted-average unit cost is computed by dividing the sum of the beginning inventory cost plus current period purchase costs by the number of units in the beginning inventory plus units purchased during the period. The formula is:

$$\frac{\text{Beginning inventory cost} + \text{Current purchase cost}}{\text{Beginning inventory units} + \text{Current purchase units}} = \text{Weighted-average unit cost}$$

The weighted-average unit cost is then applied to the units in the ending inventory to compute the ending inventory balance and to the units sold to compute cost of goods sold. Exhibit 9–5 illustrates application of the weighted-average method under a periodic system using the data given in Exhibit 9–4 for the Chase Container Corporation.

Evaluation of the Weighted-Average Cost Method The weighted-average cost method is generally viewed as objective, consistent, not readily subject to manipulation, and easy to apply. The method is used with a periodic inventory system because the physical inventory is not counted until the end of the period and the period's weighted-average unit cost can be determined only at the end of the period. Thus, the measurements needed to compute ending inventory and cost of goods sold are determined concurrently at the end of the accounting period. Also, the amounts reported in the balance sheet (ending inventory) and the income statement (cost of goods sold) are valued consistently because the same unit costs are used on both statements.

EXHIBIT 9–5

Weighted-Average Inventory Cost Method (Periodic Inventory System): Chase Container Corporation

	Units	Unit Price	Total Cost
Goods available:			
Jan. 1 Beginning inventory.	200	$1.00	$ 200
9 Purchase.	300	1.10	330
15 Purchase.	400	1.16	464
24 Purchase.	100	1.26	126
Total available	1,000	1.12*	1,120
Ending inventory at weighted-average cost:			
Jan. 31	300	1.12	336
Cost of goods sold at weighted-average cost:			
Sales during January	700†	1.12	$ 784

* Weighted-average unit cost ($1,120 ÷ 1,000 = $1.12).

† 400 units on January 10 plus 300 units on January 18.

EXHIBIT 9–6

Moving-Average Inventory Cost (Perpetual Inventory System): Chase Container Corporation

Date	Purchases			Sales (issues)			Inventory Balance		
	Units	Unit Cost	Total Cost	Units	Unit Cost	Total Cost	Units	Unit Cost	Total Cost
Jan. 1							200*	$1.00	$200
9	300	$1.10	$330				500	1.06†	530
10				400	$1.06	$424	100	1.06	106
15	400	1.16	464				500	1.14‡	570
18				300	1.14	342	200	1.14	228
24	100	1.26	126				300	1.18§	354
Ending inventory									$354
Cost of goods sold						$766			

* Beginning inventory.

† $530 ÷ 500 = $1.06.

‡ $570 ÷ 500 = $1.14.

§ $354 ÷ 300 = $1.18.

Moving-Average Cost (Perpetual Inventory System) When a perpetual inventory system is used, the weighted-average approach just described cannot be applied. Instead, a moving-average unit cost is used. The moving average provides a new unit cost after each purchase. When goods are sold or issued, the moving-average unit cost at the time is used. Application of the moving-average concept in a perpetual inventory system is shown in Exhibit 9–6, based on Exhibit 9–4. For example, on January 9, the $1.06 moving-average cost is derived by dividing the total cost ($530) by the total units (500). The January ending inventory of 300 units is costed at the latest moving-average unit cost of $1.18 ($354 ÷ 300). The cost of goods sold for the period is the sum of the sales in the total cost column, $766.

Evaluation of Moving-Average Cost Method The moving-average method is generally viewed as objective, consistent, and not subject to easy manipulation. It is used

EXHIBIT 9–7
FIFO Inventory Costing
(Periodic Inventory System):
Chase Container Corporation

Beginning inventory (200 units at $1)		$ 200
Add purchases during period (computed as in Exhibit 9–4)		920
Cost of goods available for sale		1,120
Deduct ending inventory (300 units per physical inventory count):		
100 units at $1.26 (most recent purchase—Jan. 24)	$126	
200 units at $1.16 (next most recent purchase—Jan. 15)	232	
Total ending inventory cost		358
Cost of goods sold (or issued)		$ 762*

* Also 200 units on hand Jan. 1 at $1 plus 300 units purchased Jan. 9 at $1.10, plus 200 units purchased Jan. 15 at $1.16.

with the perpetual inventory system because it provides a current average cost on an ongoing basis.

Overall Evaluation of the Average Cost Methods   The average cost methods do not match the *latest* unit costs with current sales revenues. Rather, they match the average costs of the period against revenues and value the ending inventory at average cost. Therefore, when unit costs are steadily increasing or decreasing, average cost methods provide inventory and cost of goods sold amounts between the LIFO and FIFO extremes.

First-In, First-Out Cost Method

The **first-in, first-out (FIFO) method** treats the first goods purchased or manufactured as the first units costed out on sale or issuance. Goods sold (or issued) are valued at the oldest unit costs, and goods remaining in inventory are valued at the most recent unit cost amounts. FIFO can be used with either a periodic or a perpetual inventory system, and no attempt is made to match the specific cost incurred in purchasing or manufacturing specific inventory unit items with the revenue from the sale of the item. Particularly when goods are fungible (identical in appearance and interchangeable in use), individual piece identification for inventory cost flow tracking and accounting purposes is not practical.

Periodic Inventory System   Exhibit 9–7 demonstrates FIFO results for the data given in Exhibit 9–4.

Perpetual Inventory System   Application of FIFO with a perpetual inventory system requires the maintenance of *inventory layers* by unit costs throughout the period in order to assign the appropriate cost to each issue or sale.

A sale or issue is costed out either currently throughout the period each time there is a withdrawal, or entirely at the end of the period, with the same results. In Exhibit 9–8, issues from inventory on January 10 and 18 (FIFO basis) are costed out as they occur. FIFO produces the same results whether a periodic or perpetual system is used.

Evaluation of FIFO Cost Method   FIFO is the most common method used for inventory costing purposes:
- It is easy to apply with either periodic or perpetual inventory systems.
- It produces an inventory value for the balance sheet that approximates current cost.
- The flow of costs tends to be consistent with the usual physical flow of goods.
- It is systematic and objective.
- It is not subject to manipulation.

Some accountants believe that FIFO results in a proper profit measure under the historical cost approach, particularly when the cost flow assumption parallels the

EXHIBIT 9–8
FIFO Inventory Costing (Perpetual Inventory System): Chase Container Corporation

Date	Purchases			Sales (issues)			Inventory Balance		
	Units	Unit Cost	Total Cost	Units	Unit Cost	Total Cost	Units	Unit Cost	Total Cost
Jan. 1							200*	$1.00	$200
9	300	$1.10	$330				200	1.00	200
							300	1.10	330
10				200	$1.00	$200			
				200	1.10	220	100	1.10	110
15	400	1.16	464				100	1.10	110
							400	1.16	464
18				100	1.10	110			
				200	1.16	232	200	1.16	232
24	100	1.26	126				200	1.16	232
							100	1.26	126
Ending inventory									$358
Cost of goods sold						$762			

* Beginning inventory.

physical inventory flow. A criticism of FIFO is that it does not match the current cost of goods sold with current revenues; rather, the oldest unit costs are matched with current sales revenue. When costs are rising, reported income under FIFO is higher than under LIFO or average cost. This effect on income is often called an *inventory* (or *phantom*) *profit,* because this portion of gross profit is needed to replace inventory in the next period. This inventory profit is the difference between the cost of goods sold at FIFO cost and the cost of goods sold measured at their current cost. When inventory replacement costs are rising, companies that use FIFO report more income than those using LIFO or average cost, all other factors constant.[8]

Last-In, First-Out Cost Method

The **last-in, first-out (LIFO) method** of inventory costing matches inventory valued at the most recent unit acquisition cost with current sales revenue. The units remaining in ending inventory are costed at the oldest unit costs incurred, and the units included in cost of goods sold are costed at the newest unit costs incurred, the exact opposite of the FIFO cost assumption. Like FIFO, application of LIFO requires the use of inventory cost layers for different unit costs.

Unit Cost Approach for LIFO Periodic Inventory System   Under a periodic inventory system, LIFO results are determined as shown in Exhibit 9–9. The ending inventory is costed at the oldest unit costs. Cost of goods sold is determined by deducting ending inventory from the cost of goods available for sale. The periodic LIFO system permits the costs of purchases occurring after the last sale to be included in cost of sales, which cannot occur in the perpetual system. For the current example, the LIFO cost of the January 18th sale includes the cost of the January 24th purchase. The ending inventory therefore consists of two layers, one at $1.00 and one at $1.10.

---

[8] The opposite is true during periods of declining prices.

EXHIBIT 9–9
LIFO Inventory Costing (Periodic Inventory System): Chase Container Corporation

Cost of goods available (see Exhibit 9–4).	$1,120
Deduct ending inventory (300 units per physical inventory count):	
200 units at $1 (oldest costs available, from Jan. 1 inventory). $200	
100 units at $1.10 (next oldest costs available; from Jan. 9 purchase) . . . 110	
Ending inventory	310
Cost of goods sold	$ 810*

* Also 100 units at $1.26 plus 400 units at $1.16 plus 200 units at $1.10.

EXHIBIT 9–10
LIFO Inventory Costing (Perpetual Inventory System): Chase Container Corporation

	Purchases			Sales (issues)			Inventory Balance		
Date	Units	Unit Cost	Total Cost	Units	Unit Cost	Total Cost	Units	Unit Cost	Total Cost
Jan. 1							200*	$1.00	$200
9	300	$1.10	$330				200	1.00	200
							300	1.10	330
10				300	$1.10	$330			
				100	1.00	100	100	1.00	100
15	400	1.16	464				100	1.00	100
							400	1.16	464
18				300	1.16	348	100	1.00	100
							100	1.16	116
24	100	1.26	126				100	1.00	100
							100	1.16	116
							100	1.26	126
Ending inventory									$342
Cost of goods sold						$778			

* Beginning inventory.

Unit Cost Approach for LIFO, Perpetual Inventory System   When LIFO is applied with a perpetual inventory system, as shown in Exhibit 9–10, sales are costed currently throughout the accounting period as each sale occurs. In Exhibit 9–10, in both sales transactions (January 10 and January 18), sales were costed using the newest inventory items then available.

Compare this with Exhibit 9–8, in which FIFO is illustrated and the same sales were costed using the oldest inventory items available. Under FIFO (Exhibit 9–8), the cost of goods sold for the January 10 sale is $420, but the same sale under LIFO (Exhibit 9–10) produces a cost of goods sold amount of $430, a $10 increase. Similar cost of goods sold amount differences are produced in connection with the January 18 sale. Also, the difference in the cost of the ending inventory with LIFO under a periodic inventory system (Exhibit 9–9) and LIFO under a perpetual inventory system (Exhibit 9–10) is $32, ($342 − $310). The ending inventory consists of three distinct layers (at $1.00, $1.16, and $1.26 unit costs respectively).

Exhibits 9–8 and 9–10 illustrate the rather tedious nature of the perpetual inventory system under both FIFO and LIFO. Thanks to computers, some degree of relief from the burdensome nature of this work has been made possible, but extensive recordkeeping is still required.

Comparison of LIFO with FIFO

Using LIFO rather than FIFO can cause significant differences in the income statement and the balance sheet, depending on whether unit costs are increasing or decreasing. If unit costs remain constant, the two methods give the same results. With rising prices, FIFO matches low (older) costs with current (higher) sales revenue. However, FIFO provides an inventory valuation approximating higher current costs. In contrast, LIFO matches high (newer) costs with current (higher) sales revenue but provides an inventory valuation on a low (older) cost basis.

Conversely, with declining costs, FIFO matches high (older) costs with current sales revenue and provides an inventory valuation approximating lower current cost. LIFO matches low (newer) costs with current sales revenue and provides an inventory on a high (older) cost basis.

Why So Many Methods?

Since nearly all organizations process physical inventories on a FIFO (first-in, first-out) physical flow, why are so many alternative cost flow assumptions used in practice to establish the values given to inventory and to cost of sales in the financial statements? The simplest method would seem to be one that used the cost of the specific item involved. Indeed, specific identification is used for high-cost, distinguishable items, especially when the item's cost is an important determinant of the final price charged. Specific identification is also appropriate when units are not physically interchangeable—for example, in car dealerships.

As a business becomes more complex, specific identification of the cost of an item can become increasingly burdensome. Using either an average cost method or a flow assumption reduces the difficulty of recordkeeping. Average values are appealing where a mixing of inventories of different purchase values occurs (e.g., liquids such as crude oil) or is expedient (small, interchangeable items such as bolts). The FIFO assumption represents a convenient and logical cost flow assumption for other items; thus, a tradition has been created for the use of these two approaches (average and FIFO).

Use of a FIFO cost flow assumption is not only consistent with the physical flow of goods and therefore with the matching concept, but it also provides a system that is easy to use. Essentially, it's just easier to keep inventory records on a FIFO basis. Even companies that report on some other basis, such as last-in, first-out, typically keep their internal records on a FIFO basis and convert the cost flow to a LIFO value only at the time financial reports are needed.

The use of the LIFO cost flow assumption is relatively recent. During the latter half of the 1930s, the economy experienced increased inflation. At the same time in the United States, the Internal Revenue Service (IRS) required the same system for establishing a company's tax liability as the company used for financial reporting. Hence, most firms using FIFO found that the cost of the goods they sold—and hence their taxes—were based on older and lower prices, whereas replacement inventory required more current and higher prices. Firms believed that the funds necessary to replace higher cost inventory were being unfairly taxed away. They requested that the IRS let them charge their more recent costs, thereby reducing their tax liability and leaving more funds to replace inventories at their current prices. Ultimately, the IRS agreed, but only on the condition that firms using LIFO for establishing their tax liability also report on a LIFO basis in their published financial reports. Thus, firms wishing to save on taxes and faced with rising prices for the goods they bought were required to prepare their external financial reports on a LIFO basis as well.

The LIFO and FIFO assumptions have different effects on reported earnings. When prices are rising, using FIFO charges older and therefore lower costs to cost of goods sold. The result is higher earnings. Where management compensation is based in part on the particular level of reported earnings, salary incentives may be considered in the choice of reporting method. The effects can be large. In its 1988 financial reports, Consolidated Paper indicated that its inventories would have been 25% greater had it reported using FIFO. Consolidated's 1988 income is substantially smaller under LIFO reporting, as is its tax liability.

The same pressures existed in Canada as in the United States with respect to the use of LIFO for tax purposes. However, in 1955, the Privy Council decided in the *Anaconda American Brass Ltd.* case that while there was no quarrel that LIFO was a sound basis for the valuation of inventories for accounting purposes, it was not acceptable for tax purposes. Although many consider it unfortunate that taxation policies should result in the determination of accounting practices, the existence of this phenomenon is, indeed, a reality. Consequently, inventory valuation on the LIFO basis is seldom used in Canadian practice today.

The concept of *opportunity cost* has also been used to support alternative inventory cost flow approaches. The argument stresses the importance of matching the opportunity cost of the item sold with the revenue from the sale. The opportunity cost is created by the need to replace the item sold if business is to continue. A logical approach to establish the opportunity cost would be to use the cost of the item to be bought, a next-in, first-out (NIFO) concept. Because an unambiguous NIFO value is unavailable, accountants relying on the opportunity cost idea use instead the most recent costs actually incurred as the next best measure. Thus, the economists' opportunity cost concept becomes, in practice, an argument for using LIFO.

REPORTING INVENTORIES

The discussion so far suggests that reporting inventories is relatively simple. In fact, companies often use several methods concurrently to report their inventories. *Financial Reporting in Canada* discussed the methods of cost determination disclosed by various companies in a recent survey. In some cases, different methods were used for various components of the inventory, so that the total number of bases in the following summary does not tie in with the total number of companies responding. Note that many of the methods disclosed apply only to part of the inventory.

	Number of Companies*			
	1992	**1991**	**1990**	**1989**
First-in, first out	125	132	128	127
Average cost	92	97	93	92
Retail method	12	12	12	12
Last-in, first-out	10	9	7	7
Specific item	7	6	7	8
Actual cost	3	4	5	5
Base stock	3	3	3	3
Standard cost	3	3	3	3
Various other bases	7	7	7	9

Of the 10 companies in 1992 that used last-in, first-out (LIFO) as a method of determining the cost of inventories, 5 companies used LIFO for certain inventories, 2 companies disclosed that LIFO was used for substantially all inventories, 2 companies indicated that LIFO was used only by U.S. subsidiaries, and 1 company disclosed that LIFO was used by U.S. and other subsidiaries.

* *Financial Reporting in Canada—1993* (Toronto: CICA, 1993), p. 92.

Information on which method a firm is using to value its inventories usually appears in the notes to the financial statements. This information is often in the initial note describing accounting policies adopted by the firm. More detailed disclosure is commonly provided in additional notes. Moore Corporation Limited provides an example of inventory disclosure:

Consolidated Balance Sheet
As at December 31

	1993	1992
	(in thousands of U.S. dollars)	

Assets

Current assets:

	1993	1992
Cash.	$ 7,807	$ 12,846
Short-term securities, at cost that approximates market value	253,930	299,147
Accounts receivable, less allowance for doubtful accounts of $15,305 ($17,032 in 1992)	419,805	426,215
Inventories (note 2)	255,347	272,974
Prepaid expenses	19,429	17,654
Deferred taxes	54,123	34,308
Total current assets	$1,010,441	$1,063,144

1. Summary of Accounting Policies

Inventories

Inventories of raw materials and work in process are valued at the lower of cost and replacement cost and inventories of finished goods at the lower of cost and net realizable value. The cost of the principal raw material inventories and the raw material content of finished goods inventories in the United States is determined on the last-in, first-out basis. The cost of all other inventories is determined on the first-in, first-out basis.

2. Inventories

	1993	1992
	(in thousands)	
Raw materials	$ 77,141	$ 78,966
Work in process	26,321	26,970
Finished goods	141,827	153,725
Other.	10,058	13,313
	$255,347	$272,974

The excess of the current cost over the last-in, first-out cost of those inventories determined on the latter basis is approximately $43,370,000 at December 31, 1993 (1992—$44,100,000).

CONCEPT REVIEW

1. Compute the inventory value as of June 5, assuming the data below, according to specific cost identification, average cost, FIFO, and LIFO under both the perpetual and the periodic inventory approaches. Assume a zero beginning balance.

> June 1 . . . . .   Bought one case of Red Hook Ale @ $10
> June 2 . . . . .   Bought one case of Red Hook Ale @ $16
> June 3 . . . . .   Sold one case of Red Hook Ale @ $20*
> June 4 . . . . .   Bought one case of Red Hook Ale @ $18

* The case of Red Hook Ale sold was purchased on June 2.

	Ending Inventory	
	Periodic	Perpetual
a. Specific identification	_____	_____
b. Average cost	_____	_____
c. FIFO	_____	_____
d. LIFO	_____	_____

2. Explain why a company might elect to use a FIFO cost flow approach.
3. Which inventory cost flow assumption permitted under GAAP is most compatible with the matching principle?

GLOBAL VIEW

Accounting for inventories, called *stocks* in some English-speaking countries, is similar throughout the world, with one exception—the use of LIFO. LIFO, which is widely used in the United States, is not generally acceptable in the rest of the world, including Canada, Australia, France, the Netherlands, and the United Kingdom.

Germany does permit LIFO, but average cost is the most frequently used method because it is allowed for tax purposes. Belgium permits LIFO, but only if it is used on an item-by-item basis. Italy does not formally permit LIFO, but a pricing method acceptable for tax purposes is basically a LIFO approach. In Japan, LIFO can be used for financial reporting but not for tax reporting.

The International Accounting Standards Committee recently revised its *Standard No. 2*, "Inventories," to allow LIFO for certain inventories. However, FIFO remains the benchmark method, the method identified as the point of reference for firms making a choice from among allowable alternatives.

SPECIAL TOPICS

Adoption of LIFO

Switching from another inventory method to LIFO for *external reporting* purposes involves a change in accounting principle. *CICA Handbook* Section 1506, "Accounting Changes," requires that the cumulative effect of a change in accounting principle be reported as an adjustment to the opening balance of retained earnings of the current period. However, Section 1506 does not require reporting of the cumulative effect when it is impossible to measure. Usually it is impossible to reconstruct the composition of old inventory cost layers that a company would have reported in prior periods under LIFO. The difficulty of computing the cumulative effect of a change to LIFO is due in part to the arbitrariness of deciding how far back in time to go to identify the base layer of LIFO inventory and, in part, due to the unavailability of past cost and price data. Therefore, when a company changes to LIFO, the year in which the change is made is used as the base year. The base year LIFO cost for the beginning inventory of that year is the ending inventory for the prior year valued by the method then used. The base layer of LIFO inventory must be changed to cost regardless of the prior method used. This means that any write-downs of the prior year's ending inventory below cost (such as might occur under LCM) must be eliminated.

Suppose, for example, that the Erie Valve Company uses FIFO and follows the lower-of-cost-or-market rule of writing its inventory down to current market values when the market value at the end of the accounting period is below its original FIFO cost. At the end of 1995, Erie shows an inventory value of $90,000, marked down from its FIFO cost of $100,000. For 1996, when Erie plans to switch to LIFO for financial reporting, the Company would make an entry to write the inventory back up to $100,000:

January 1, 1996:

Inventory*. 10,000
    Retained earnings; change in accounting principle FIFO to LIFO   10,000

* This entry assumes that the direct inventory method of recording LCM is used. If the allowance method is used, the debit would be made to the allowance to reduce inventory to LCM account (discussed in Chapter 10).

LIFO Liquidation

A problem occurs under LIFO when a company ends the year with a lower inventory quantity than when it began the year. This is called LIFO liquidation. To illustrate LIFO inventory liquidation, assume the following:

	Units	Unit Cost	Total Cost
Beginning inventory (assumed to be a single layer of LIFO inventory)	10,000	$1.00	$10,000
Purchases	40,000	1.50	60,000
Total available for sale	50,000		$70,000

	Units	Unit Cost	Total Cost
Sales (44,000 units, costed on LIFO basis) from:			
Purchases	40,000	1.50	$60,000
Beginning inventory layer*	4,000	1.00	4,000
Cost of goods sold	44,000		64,000
Ending inventory	6,000	1.00	$ 6,000

* Beginning layer partially used.

In this example, the company did not maintain the base year inventory of 10,000 units. This liquidation could have been voluntary or involuntary:

1. **Voluntary** Management decides to reduce normal inventory quantity for some reason, such as a decline in demand, anticipation of reduced inventory replenishment costs, or anticipated changes in the product.[9]
2. **Involuntary** An inventory reduction may be forced by uncontrollable causes such as shortages, strikes, delayed delivery dates, or unexpected demand.

As a result of the liquidation of part of the base inventory, cost of goods sold includes 4,000 units with an old cost ($1 per unit) matched against current revenue. This liquidation of part of the LIFO base layer distorts reported income relative to income under the normal LIFO relationship of cost and revenue.

Inventory liquidation may well occur sporadically during the year. A company will typically replenish inventory liquidations, especially involuntary ones, before the end of the year to avoid a lower cost of goods sold and thereby avoid higher taxable income. When replacement is anticipated, entries can be made quarterly to avoid misleading readers of interim financial statements.

SUMMARY OF KEY POINTS

(L.O. 1) 1. Inventories are assets consisting of goods owned by the business and held for future sale or for use in the manufacture of goods for sale.

(L.O. 2) 2. Cost at acquisition, including the costs to obtain the inventory, such as freight, is used to value inventory.

(L.O. 2) 3. All goods owned at the inventory date, including those on consignment, should be counted and valued.

(L.O. 3) 4. Either a periodic or a perpetual inventory system may be used, but computer technology now makes it easier and less costly to use a perpetual system, which also provides up-to-date inventory records.

(L.O. 4) 5. Several cost flow assumptions are in current use, including specific identification, average cost, LIFO, and FIFO.

(L.O. 4) 6. LIFO has several disadvantages, including increased recordkeeping requirements, that cause many firms to use other cost flow assumptions.

REVIEW PROBLEM

Bay City Explosives bought and sold the following items in January for cash:

Cash: January 1 balance	$21
Bought: 1 barrel of powder, January 2	$15
Sold: 1 barrel of powder, January 30	$20
Bought: 1 barrel of powder, January 31	$18

1. Using FIFO, LIFO, and the average cost method, determine Bay City's ending inventory value and income for January. Assume a periodic inventory system.
2. What profit did Bay City make in January?
3. What dividend could Bay City pay for January without contracting the size of the business? (Ignore all considerations except the effect suggested by net income and the possible implications of the cost numbers given.)

---

[9] One criticism of LIFO is that it is subject to income manipulation. For example, a year-end purchasing policy can be used to reduce reported income by heavy buying if prices have increased, or increase reported income by permitting inventories to decline and old, low prices to be included in cost of goods sold.

SOLUTION

1.

	FIFO	LIFO	Average Cost
Inventory value	$18	$15	$16.50*
Income:			
Sales	$20	$20	$20.00
Cost of sales	15	18	16.50
Income	$ 5	$ 2	$ 3.50

* ($15 + $18) ÷ 2

2. Bay City's profits could be measured by any one of the three income measures calculated in (1) above. This result illustrates the difficulty of comparing the incomes of companies using different inventory costing methods.

3. Deciding what dividend would not cause Bay City to contract in size is more complex. One answer would be to pay out the income earned, which depends on the cost flow assumption used.

   After purchasing the barrel of powder on January 31, the firm has $8 in cash remaining:

$$\$21 - \$15 + \$20 - \$18 = \$8$$

After paying out cash equal to its January earnings, Bay City would have cash under each alternative, as follows:

FIFO	LIFO	Average Cost
$3	$6	$4.50

Bay City would also have one barrel of powder. If Bay City pays its $2 of LIFO earnings as a dividend, the firm would have cash of $6 left and one barrel of powder. This result is equivalent to having $21 in cash January 1, which was used at that time to buy one barrel of powder at the price of $15, leaving $6 in cash.

But if the firm is initially viewed as having $21 in value on January 1, and if the current barrel is valued at $18, its most recent cost, rather than the historical cost of $15, then $5 could be paid out, leaving $3 in cash and $18 in powder, a total of $21 in value ($3 + $18). This approach pays a dividend equal to the FIFO earnings.

Still another answer, based on an opportunity cost approach, would support Bay City paying a dividend of only $.80. The cost of a barrel of powder has risen from $15 to $18, an increase of 20% over the month. If the initial assets of the firm (cash of $21) must therefore also increase by 20% for the firm to be undiminished economically, Bay City's asset values must increase to 1.20 ($21) = $25.20 by the end of January. For this to happen, cash of $7.20 must be added to the barrel's value of $18. The firm has only $8 in cash on January 31. Therefore, the firm could pay a dividend of only $.80. If the barrel of powder is valued at its current selling price of $20, Bay City's assets are worth $8 + $20 = $28, permitting a dividend of $2.80 ($28 − $25.20) to be paid without contracting the company.

APPENDIX 9   *Additional Cost Flow Methods*

This appendix discusses three inventory cost methods used less often than average cost, FIFO, LIFO, and specific identification. Three methods are discussed: **JIT (just-in-time) costing, standard costing,** and **variable (or direct) costing.** These methods are not generally allowed under GAAP, but they are used for internal accounting purposes.

Just-in-Time Inventory Systems

Just-in-time (JIT) inventory systems are a response to the high costs associated with stockpiling inventories of raw materials, parts, supplies, and finished goods. Rather than keeping ample quantities on hand awaiting use, the idea is to reduce inventories to the lowest levels possible and thus save costs. As the name suggests, the ultimate goal is to see goods and materials arrive at the company's receiving dock *just in time* to be moved directly to the plant's production floor for immediate use in the manufacturing or assembly process. Then, taking the concept one step further, finished goods roll off the production floor and move directly to the shipping dock *just in time* for shipment to the customers. The ideal net impact is zero inventory levels and zero inventory costs.

Physical Inventory Management In practice, inventories are still not zero under JIT systems, but they are at substantially diminished levels. Minimum inventories are needed. If inventory levels are kept too lean, an unexpected surge in business can cause the company to run out of stock, thus halting production. Or a batch of defective parts might be encountered, again causing a work suspension.

Like other inventory systems, the success of a JIT system depends on how well it is conceived and implemented for a particular production setting (or selling situation—JIT techniques apply to merchandise inventories carried by retail outlets as well). Purely from a management standpoint, inventory problems shift from the cost of stockpiling production parts and materials needs—one week's expected needs or one month's or whatever—to coordinating inventory to meet production needs. At the extreme, under a JIT system, some of the inventory may be in-house (today's needs), some of it may be in transit to the plant (tomorrow's needs), some of it may be in the process of being fabricated or otherwise finished by the supplier (the day after tomorrow's needs), and some of it may not have been ordered yet (next week's needs). Extremes aside, minimal inventory levels normally result in reduced need for storage space, materials moving and handling equipment, property and casualty insurance coverage, and materials obsolescence or deterioration.

JIT Inventory Accounting Practices JIT systems tend to result in simplified inventory accounting procedures, primarily because inventory levels are kept low, but also because raw materials and work-in-process inventories are in many cases combined. At Hewlett-Packard, for example, raw materials are charged to a combined account and then transferred to finished goods upon completion of production.[10]

JIT systems also affect the way companies account for production costs. Conversion costs (labour and direct overhead costs) are charged directly to the cost of goods sold account as a matter of expediency. The working premise is that almost everything being produced is in response to orders from customers. Therefore, all conversion costs are charged to the cost of goods sold account and charge backs are made (finished items not sold or unfinished items still in production as of the end of the accounting period) to finished goods or work-in-process inventories, respectively. In effect, JIT systems work backward in comparison with traditional inventory accounting systems. Under traditional systems, the cost of goods sold is derived from inventory balances. Under the JIT system, the cost of goods sold is the starting point for determining the inventory balances as of the end of the accounting period.

To illustrate the workings of a typical JIT inventory accounting system, the assumed facts about a particular manufacturing process and the resulting accounting entries are provided:

Manufacturing Facts and Transactions

1. The company purchases 420 kg. of raw materials @ $8/kg. ($3,360) at the start of a production cycle. All or nearly all of these materials are expected to be used during the current production cycle (based on sales estimates) at the rate of 2 kg. per finished unit.

2. Working from sales estimates of slightly more than 200 units, the plant manager authorizes a production run of 210 units. As of the end of the account-

Corresponding Accounting Entries

Work-in-process inventory 3,360
    Accounts payable   3,360
To record purchase of 420 kg. of raw materials @ $8/kg. for current production run needs.

Cost of goods sold 1,030
    Conversion costs   1,030
To close conversion costs (labour charges of 103 hours @ $10/hour) to cost of goods sold as of the end of cur-

[10] B. Newmann and P. Jaouen, "Kanban, Zips and Cost Accounting: A Case Study," *Journal of Accountancy*, August 1986, pp. 132–41.

Manufacturing Facts and Transactions	**Corresponding Accounting Entries**

ing period, labour charges (conversion costs) at the rate of $10/hour amounting to 103 hours ($1,030) are attributable to this production run.

rent accounting period. (Conversion costs is a temporary holding account for labour and overhead.)

3. As of the end of the accounting period, 200 units of the 210-unit production run are fully assembled and ready for shipment to customers.

Finished goods inventory 3,200
　　Work-in-process inventory. . . . .　　3,200

To transfer material costs on 200 units to finished goods at rate of 2 lb. × $8/kg. × 200 units.

4. As of the end of the accounting period, 190 units of the 200 units in finished goods inventory have been sold.

Cost of goods sold 3,040
　　Finished goods inventory . . . . .　　3,040

To transfer material costs on 190 units to cost of goods sold at the rate of 2 lb × $8/kg. × 190 units.

5. As of the end of the accounting period, conversion costs (labour charges) applicable to production run units not sold and other runs still not complete are determined to be:
- Finished goods inventory—5 hours @ $10/hour ($50).
- Work-in-process inventory—3 hours @ $10/hour ($30).

Finished goods inventory . . . .　50
Work-in-process inventory. . . . . . .　30
　　Cost of goods sold . . . .　　　80

To transfer conversion (labour) costs from costs of goods sold to finished goods (5 hours @ $10/hour) and work in process (3 hours @ $10/hour).

The events just described can be shown using T-accounts:

Work-In-Process Inventory

1.	3,360	3.	3,200
5.	30		
Balance	190		

Accounts Payable

		1.	3,360

Finished Goods Inventory

3.	3,200	4.	3,040
5.	50		
Balance	210		

Conversion Costs

		2.	1,030

Cost of Goods Sold

2.	1,030		
4.	3,040	5.	80
Balance	3,990		

The appeal of JIT and other systems aimed at minimizing physical inventory levels appears to be growing as companies seek better ways to reduce investments in inventory assets, to encourage production efficiencies, and on-time product delivery to customers. 3M Corporation, for example, observed in a recent annual report that a JIT system increased total production capacity in one of its plants by 15%.

Standard Cost Method

In manufacturing entities using a standard cost system, the inventories are valued, recorded, and reported for internal purposes on the basis of a standard unit cost. The standard cost, which approximates an ideal or expected cost, prevents the overstatement of inventory values because it excludes from inventory losses and expenses due to inefficiency, waste, and abnormal conditions. Under this method, the differences between actual cost (which includes losses due to inefficiencies, etc.) and standard cost (which excludes losses due to inefficiencies, etc.) are recorded in separate variance accounts. These accounts are written off as a current period loss rather than capitalized in inventory. Standard costing may be applied to raw materials, work in process, and finished goods inventories. Standard costing is particularly useful for cost control in manufacturing situations. To illustrate, assume that a manufacturing company has just

EXHIBIT 9A–1
Standard Cost Method

Results for the Period		
Purchases at actual cost:		
10,000 units at $1.10 .... $11,000		
2,000 units at $.95 1,900		
Total		$12,900
Issues at standard cost:		
8,000 units at $1 8,000		
Ending inventory at standard cost:		
4,000 units at $1 4,000	12,000	
Raw materials purchase price variance (debit—charged against current income as a loss) ($1,000 − $100)		$ 900

adopted standard cost procedures and that the beginning inventory is zero. During the current period, the company makes two purchases and one issuance and records them as follows:

1. To record the purchase of 10,000 units of raw material at $1.10 actual cost; standard cost has been established at $1:

Raw materials (10,000 units × $1)	10,000	
Raw materials purchase price variance (10,000 units × $.10)	1,000	
Accounts payable (10,000 units × $1.10)		11,000

2. To record issuance of 8,000 units of raw material to the factory for processing:

Material in process	8,000	
Raw materials (8,000 units × $1)		8,000

3. To record the purchase of 2,000 units of raw materials at 95 cents:

Raw materials (2,000 units × $1)	2,000	
Raw materials purchase price variance (2,000 units × $.05)		100
Accounts payable (2,000 units × $.95)		1,900

Under the standard cost method procedures, shown in Exhibit 9A–1 for raw material, there would be no need to consider inventory cost flow methods (such as LIFO, FIFO, and average) because only one cost—standard cost—appears in the records. In addition, perpetual inventory records can be maintained in units because all issues and inventory valuations are at the same standard cost. Because standard cost represents a departure from the cost principle, it may not be acceptable under GAAP.[11] For external reporting, the standard cost inventory is usually restated by applying one of the generally accepted methods discussed in the chapter.

Variable, or Direct, Cost Method

Manufacturing firms often use variable costing (also called direct costing) for internal management planning and control purposes. Under this approach, fixed costs (those that relate to time, such as depreciation) and variable costs (those that vary with productive activities, such as direct material and direct labour) are segregated. An important aspect of this concept is that the cost of goods manufactured is the sum of the variable costs only, which include direct materials, direct labour, and variable manufacturing overhead. All fixed costs, including fixed manufacturing overhead, are treated as period costs and are expensed when incurred rather than being capitalized and carried forward in inventory. Hence, fixed costs are not reported as part of cost of inventory or cost of goods sold.

---

[11] Standard cost figures may be used if the effect on inventory values is not material. Standard costs are widely used for internal management planning and control. A detailed discussion of standard cost procedures can be found in any cost accounting textbook.

Valuation of inventories only at variable production costs, although useful for internal management purposes, is *not* GAAP for external financial reporting purposes. Also, it cannot be used for tax purposes except in special circumstances. Companies using variable costing internally convert the inventory and cost of goods sold to actual cost by using the other costing methods discussed in this chapter.

QUESTIONS

1. In general, why should accountants and management be concerned with inventories?
2. List and briefly explain the usual inventory classifications for a trading entity and a manufacturing entity.
3. What general rule is applied by accountants in determining what goods should be included in inventory? How does the location of inventory affect this rule?
4. Complete the following:

	Include in Inventory	
	Yes	**No**
a. Goods held by our agents for us.	——	——
b. Goods held by us for sale on commission.	——	——
c. Goods held by us but awaiting return to vendor because of damaged condition.	——	——
d. Goods returned to us from buyer, reason unknown to date.	——	——
e. Goods out on consignment.	——	——
f. Goods held on consignment.	——	——
g. Merchandise at our branch for sale.	——	——
h. Merchandise at conventions for display purposes.	——	——

5. Assume that you are in the process of adjusting and closing the books at the end of the accounting period (for the purchaser of inventory). For inventory purposes, how would you treat the following goods in transit?
   a. Invoice received for $10,000, shipped FOB shipping point.
   b. Invoice received for $18,000, shipped FOB destination.
   c. Invoice received for $6,000, shipped FOB shipping point and delivery refused on the last day of the period because of damaged condition.
6. Explain the principal features of a periodic inventory system.
7. Why is cost of goods sold sometimes characterized as a residual amount? In which inventory system is this characterization appropriate?
8. Which of the following items should be included in determining the unit cost for inventory purposes?
   a. Purchase returns.
   b. Cash discounts on credit purchases.
   c. Freight on goods purchased.
9. Should cash discounts on credit purchases be (*a*) deducted in part on the income statement and in part from inventory on the balance sheet or (*b*) deducted in total on the income statement for the period in which the discounts arose? Assume that three-fourths of the goods purchased were sold by year-end. Explain.
10. What is meant by the accounting value of inventory? What accounting principles predominate in measuring this value?
11. Assuming the LIFO method, what is meant by inventory liquidation? Why is it a serious problem for LIFO but not FIFO?
12. What are the primary purposes to be considered in selecting a particular inventory cost flow method? Why is the selection important?
13. Briefly explain the differences between periodic and perpetual inventory systems. Under what circumstances is each generally used?
14. Does the adoption of a perpetual inventory system eliminate the need for a physical count or measurement of inventories? Explain.
15. Explain the specific identification cost inventory method and explain when the method is not appropriate.
16. Distinguish between a weighted average and a moving average in determining inventory unit cost. When is each generally used? Explain.
17. Explain the essential features of first-in, first-out (FIFO). What are the primary advantages and

disadvantages of FIFO? Explain the difference in the application of FIFO under a periodic and perpetual inventory system.

18. Explain the essential features of last-in, first-out (LIFO). What are the primary advantages and disadvantages of LIFO? Explain the differences in application of LIFO under the periodic and perpetual inventory systems.

19. What is meant by inventory layers? Why are they significant with respect to the FIFO and LIFO methods?

20. Compare the balance sheet and income statement effects of FIFO with those of LIFO when prices are rising and when prices are falling.

21. Which accounting method leads to "inventory profits" in a rising-cost market? In a declining-cost market?

22. What is the major difficulty in harmonizing accounting for inventories on a worldwide basis?

CASES

C 9–1
(L.O. 4)

 Ethics, LIFO, Profit Manipulation Butte Company uses a periodic inventory system and LIFO, unit basis, to cost the ending inventory for external reporting purposes. Near the end of 1995, the records and related estimates provided the following annual data for one item sold regularly:

	Units	Unit Cost
Beginning inventory (LIFO basis):		
Base inventory (normal minimum level)	8,000	$20
Increment No. 1	5,000	25
Purchases (actual)	60,000	35
Sales* (at $50 per unit)	65,000	
Expenses* (excluding income taxes), $700,000.		

* Including estimates for remainder of 1995.

On December 26, 1995, the company has an opportunity to purchase no fewer than 30,000 units of the above item at $30 (a special price) with 10-day credit terms. Delivery is immediate, and the offer will expire January 3, 1996. The question has been posed whether the purchase (and delivery) should be consummated in 1995 or 1996; the management has tentatively decided to make the purchase in 1995.

Required

1. What purchase date do you recommend? Support your recommendation with reasons and pro forma (as if) income statement and balance sheet data. Include computations.
2. Explain and illustrate why EPS would be changed if the purchase is made in 1995.
3. Would you suspect profit manipulation in this situation if Butte elected to make the purchase in 1995? Does this create an ethical problem? Explain.

C 9–2
(L.O. 4)

Ethics, LIFO, Profit Manipulation R. Babinski, S. Chasnoff, and T. Doland formed a partnership to import furniture. Their initial partnership agreement provided for equal investments, equal sharing of responsibilities, equal work, equal salaries, and equal shares of the partnership income. After a few years of operation, sales took off and the business prospered. On January 1, 1994, they incorporated as BCD, Inc., with each of the former partners owning 33⅓% of the shares of the corporation. The board of directors of BCD was comprised of Babinski, Chasnoff, and Doland. The board elected Chasnoff as chair of the board of directors, Babinski as president of the corporation in charge of operations, and Doland as vice president and controller (Doland was a public accountant). Annual compensation of the three officers was set as follows:

Chasnoff	$130,000	plus bonus equal to 2% of annual net income
Babinski	135,000	plus bonus equal to 1% of annual net income
Doland	140,000	plus 5% of annual decrease in income tax payments

The compensation plan was intended as an incentive device as well as to reflect the relative contributions of the three officers to corporate success. In particular, the bonus plan was intended to motivate Chasnoff and Babinski (who represented the corporation in the business community) to increase sales and to encourage Doland (the accountant) to decrease income tax payments. During 1995, 1996, and 1997, sales and income increased steadily. In the year ended December 31, 1997, net income of the corporation was $500,000, which put the annual earnings of all three officers at $140,000 (this amount cannot be verified). Income tax payments for 1997 were $150,000. During 1998, net income, computed on the basis of the FIFO inventory method, which BCD used, increased to $750,000. This increase in corporate income was destined to put Chasnoff's annual earnings at $145,000 and Babinski's at $142,500, but to leave Doland's at $140,000 (neither Babinski nor Chasnoff were aware of this). A major reason for the increase in corporation income was Doland's skill at controlling costs; however, the compensation plan did not adequately reflect this factor. Doland tried to persuade Chasnoff and Babinski to renegotiate his salary, but they refused because they knew very little about finance and accounting and were therefore unable to appreciate Doland's effectiveness at controlling expenses. They were convinced that the reason for the success of BCD was their superlative sales and management skills.

The cost to BCD of its imported furniture was rising rapidly near the end of 1998, and, due to increased competition, the outlook for the company's sales was not bright for 1999. Without notifying Chasnoff or Babinski, Doland changed inventory methods from FIFO to LIFO, effective January 1, 1998. Also, near year-end 1998, Doland, who controlled all purchases of inventory, stocked up on inventory in response to a pending 20% cost increase announced by BCD's suppliers; the price increase was to become effective in January 1999. Because of the change to LIFO, income tax payments for 1998 decreased to $70,000.

Required

1. What was the likely effect of the change in inventory method on reported income of BCD for 1998, and on the annual bonuses of Babinski and Chasnoff?
2. What was the likely effect of stocking up of inventory on reported income of 1998 and on the annual earnings of Babinski and Chasnoff?
3. What was the likely effect of Doland's actions on his annual bonus? Does this raise any ethical issues? Explain.
4. What conclusions about accounting income can you draw from this situation?

C 9–3
(L.O. 1, 4)

 Magna   Study Magna's financial statements, provided at the back of this text.

Required

1. How does Magna value its inventory?
2. What comprises Magna's inventories?
3. Is it likely that a different cost flow assumption would materially affect Magna's results?

EXERCISES

E 9–1
(L.O. 2)

Items to Include in Inventory: Classification, Correction   On December 31, 1995, Patco computed an ending inventory valuation of $250,000 based on a periodic inventory system. The accounts for 1995 have been adjusted and closed. Subsequently, the independent auditor located several discrepancies in the 1995 ending inventory. These were discussed with the company accountant, who then prepared the following schedule:

a. Merchandise in store (at 50% above cost)	$250,000
b. Merchandise out on consignment at sales price (including markup of 60% on selling price)	10,000
c. Goods held on consignment from Davis Electronics at sales price (sales commission, 20% of sales price, included)	4,000
d. Goods purchased, in transit (shipped FOB shipping point, estimated freight, not included, $800), invoice price	5,000
e. Goods out on approval, sales price, $2,500, cost, $1,000	2,500
Total inventory as corrected	$271,500

Average income tax rate, 40%.

Required

1. The auditor did not agree with the "corrected" inventory amount of $271,500. Compute the correct ending inventory amount (show computations) by modifying the corrected balance of $271,500.
2. List the items on the income statement and balance sheet for 1995 that should be corrected for the above errors; give the amount of the error in the balance of each item affected.
3. The accounts have been closed for 1995. Therefore, a correcting entry in January 1996 is needed. Give the required correcting entry.

E 9–2
(L.O. 1)

Perpetual and Periodic Inventory: Income Statement, Closing Entries   The records of Ferris Fashions reflected the following data for 1995: sales revenue, $200,000; purchases, $140,000; net income as a percentage of sales revenue, 15%; beginning inventory, $25,000; and expenses, including income tax, $45,000. The tax rate for 1995 is 25%.

Required

1. Reconstruct the income statement. Assume a periodic inventory system.
2. Give the required journal entries at the end of the period for the inventories and the closing entries for revenues and expenses; assume in Case A a periodic inventory system, and in Case B a perpetual inventory system.

E 9–3
(L.O. 3)

Periodic and Perpetual Inventory: Journal Entries The records for Cummings Company at December 31, 1995, reflected the following:

	Units	Unit Price
Sales during period (for cash)	10,000	$10 (sales price)
Inventory at beginning of period	2,000	6 (cost)
Merchandise purchased during period (for cash)	16,000	6 (cost)
Purchase returns during period (cash refund)	100	6 (cost)
Inventory at end of period	?	6 (cost)
Total expenses (excluding cost of goods sold), $30,000		

Required

In parallel columns, give entries for the above transactions, including all entries at the end of the period. Assume in Case A a periodic inventory system and in Case B a perpetual inventory system. Use the following format:

	Case A		Case B	
Accounts	**Dr.**	**Cr.**	**Dr.**	**Cr.**

E 9–4
(L.O. 2)

Multiple Choice: Content of Inventory Cost The following information was available for Mason Corporation for 1995:

Sales	$100,000
Beginning inventory	36,000
Freight out	9,000
Purchases	43,000
Sales commissions	5,000
Cost of goods sold	60,000

Required

1. Mason's ending inventory is:
   a. $28,000.
   b. $19,000.
   c. $47,000.
   d. $14,000.
2. Mason's gross margin is:
   a. $31,000.
   b. $35,000.
   c. $40,000.
   d. $26,000.
3. Which of the following *theoretically* correctly indicates the treatment of the indicated items in inventory cost?

	Warehouse Costs	Insurance on Raw Materials in Transit
a.	Included	Excluded
b.	Included	Included
c.	Excluded	Included
d.	Excluded	Excluded

4. Kemp Company had the following consignment transactions during December 1995:

Inventory on consignment to Ace Company	$9,000
Freight paid by Kemp	450
Inventory received on consignment from Fenn Company	6,000
Freight paid by Fenn	250

No sales of consigned goods were made through December 31, 1995. Kemp's December 31, 1995, balance sheet should include consigned inventory at:

a. $9,450.

b. $9,000.

c. $6,250.

d. $6,000.

(AICPA adapted)

E 9–5
(L.O. 3)

Multiple Choice: Inventory Systems Ward Hardware had an inventory of 1,600 saws valued at $4 each to begin the month. Ward purchased 2,400 saws on the last day of the month at $4.80 each and sold 800 saws on the 15th of the month.

Required

1. The moving-average cost at the beginning of the next month is:
   a. $4.80.
   b. $4.60.
   c. $4.48.
   d. $4.40.
2. Ward's inventory on a FIFO basis as of the beginning of the next month is:
   a. $14,080 under the periodic system only.
   b. $14,720 under either inventory system.
   c. $14,720 under the perpetual system only.
   d. $14,720 under the periodic system only.
3. Ward's inventory on a LIFO basis as of the beginning of the next month is:
   a. $14,080 under the perpetual system only.
   b. $14,720 under the periodic system.
   c. $14,720 under the perpetual system.
   d. $14,080 under both inventory systems.

(AICPA adapted)

E 9–6
(L.O. 3)

Perpetual Inventory: Shortage, Entries Perforated Pipe Company uses a perpetual inventory system. The items on hand are inventoried on a rotation basis throughout the year so that all items are checked twice each year. At the end of the year, the following data relating to goods on hand are available:

Product	From Perpetual Inventory Units	Unit Cost	From Physical Count (units)
A.	450	$12	390
B.	1,500	5	1,520
C.	2,000	4	1,950
D.	8,000	2	7,980
E.	13,000	6	13,100

Required

Determine the amount of the net inventory overage or shortage and give the adjustment to the perpetual inventory records. Give any entry needed to record the final disposition of any discrepancy. (Note: An inventory shortage is a loss.)

E 9–7
(L.O. 1)

Inventory Cost with a Rebate Majestic Stores, Inc., a dealer in radio and television sets, buys large quantities of a television model that costs $500. The contract reads that if 100 or more are purchased during the year, a rebate of $20 per set will be made. On December 15, the records showed that 150 sets had been purchased and that 50 more were ordered FOB destination. The sets were received on December 22, and a request for the rebate was made. The rebate cheque was received on January 20, after Majestic's books were closed.

Required

1. At what valuation should the inventory be shown on December 31? Why?
2. What entry should be made relative to the rebate on December 31? Why?
3. What entry would be made on January 20? Why?

E 9–8
(L.O. 4)

Manufacturing Inventory Accounts   Assume the following information for Murphy Manufacturing during 1995:

	Jan. 1, 1995	Dec. 31, 1995
Raw materials inventory	$10,400	$14,600
Work-in-process inventory	28,100	31,300
Finished goods inventory	15,700	12,500

In addition, direct labour and manufacturing overhead totalled $364,600, and cost of goods manufactured equalled $461,200 in 1995.

Required   Calculate the correct amounts for raw materials purchased, raw materials used, and cost of goods sold for 1995.

E 9–9
(L.O. 2)

Inventory and CGS; Five Cost Inventory Methods   The inventory records of Acme Appliances showed the following data relative to a food processor item in inventory (assume that the transactions occurred in the order given):

Transaction	Units	Unit Cost
1. Inventory	30	$19.00
2. Purchase	45	20.00
3. Sale	50	
4. Purchase	50	20.80
5. Sale	50	
6. Purchase	50	21.60

Required   Compute the cost of goods sold for the period and the ending inventory, assuming the following (round unit costs to nearest cent):

a. Weighted averaged (periodic inventory system).
b. Moving average (perpetual inventory system).
c. FIFO.
d. LIFO (periodic inventory system).
e. LIFO (perpetual inventory system).

E 9–10
(L.O. 4)

Inventory and CGS: Four Inventory Cost Methods   The inventory records of Gilman Company provided the following data for one item of merchandise for sale (assume that the six transactions occurred in the order given):

Goods Available for Sale	Units	Unit Cost	Total Amount
Beginning inventory	500	$6.00	$ 3,000
1. Purchases	600	6.10	3,660
2. Sales	900		
3. Purchases	600	6.20	3,720
4. Sales	500		
5. Purchases	400	6.30	2,520
6. Sales	300		
Total available for sale	2,100		$12,900

Required   1. Complete the following schedule (round unit costs to nearest cent and total amounts to nearest dollar):

	Valuation	
Costing Method	Ending Inventory	Cost of Goods Sold
a. FIFO	$_____	$_____
b. LIFO (periodic inventory system)	$_____	$_____
c. Weighted average	$_____	$_____
d. LIFO (perpetual inventory system)	$_____	$_____

2. Compute the amount of pretax income and rank the methods in order of the amount of pretax income (highest first), assuming that FIFO pretax income is $50,000.

3. Which method is preferable in this instance? Explain your choice.

E 9–11
(L.O. 4)

Inventory and CGS: Five Inventory Cost Methods   The College Store inventory records showed the following data relative to a particular item sold regularly (assume transactions in the order given):

Transaction	Units	Unit Cost
1. Inventory	2,000	$5.00
2. Purchases	18,000	5.20
3. Sales (at $13 per unit)	7,000	
4. Purchases	6,000	5.50
5. Sales (at $13.50 per unit)	16,000	
6. Purchases	3,000	6.00

Required

Complete the following schedule (round unit costs to nearest cent and total costs of inventory to the nearest $10):

	Ending Inventory	Cost of Goods Sold	Gross Margin
a. FIFO	——	——	——
b. Weighted average	——	——	——
c. LIFO (periodic inventory system)	——	——	——
d. LIFO (perpetual inventory system)	——	——	——
e. Moving average (show computations)	——	——	——

E 9–12
(L.O. 4)

Ending Inventory: Three Inventory Cost Methods   Leven Company was formed on December 1, 1995. The following information is available from the company's inventory records for hair blow dryers:

	Units	Unit Cost
January 1, 1996 (beginning inventory)	800	$ 9.00
Purchases:		
January 5, 1996	1,500	10.00
January 25, 1996	1,200	10.50
February 16, 1996	600	12.00
March 26, 1996	900	13.00

A physical inventory taken on March 31, 1996, showed 1,500 units on hand. Leven uses a periodic inventory system.

Required

Prepare schedules to compute the ending inventory at March 31, 1996, under each of the following inventory flow methods: FIFO, LIFO, and weighted average. Show supporting computations.

E 9–13
(L.O. 4)

LIFO Liquidation   Chloride Chemical's lube oil storage facility was shut down due to a strike in December 1995, resulting in a drastic reduction in inventory. The firm had switched to LIFO effective January 1, 1995. Assume the following data:

	Units	Unit Cost
Beginning inventory (Base layer of LIFO—Jan. 1/95)	20,000	$1.00
Lube oil purchases during 1995	450,000	1.25
Total available for sale	470,000	
Sales (costed on LIFO basis) from:		
Purchases	450,000	1.25
Base inventory layer	10,000	1.00
Total	460,000	
Ending inventory (Dec. 31/95)	10,000	

Management believes that the base layer will be replaced at a cost of $1.40 per unit in January 1996. Chloride Chemical is on a calendar-year reporting basis.

Required

1. Assume that management decides to increase cost of goods sold by the estimated replacement cost of the base layer of LIFO. What journal entries should be made in December 1995 and January 1996? The actual unit replacement cost is $1.35 per unit, and management uses a perpetual inventory system.
2. Do you agree with management's decision? Justify your response.

PROBLEMS

P 9–1
(L.O. 3)

Perpetual and Periodic Inventory Systems Compared: Entries   Carlisle Company completed the following selected transactions during 1995 for men's slacks:

	Units	Unit Price
Beginning inventory	6,000	$18 (cost)
Purchases	20,000	18 (cost)
Purchase returns	1,000	18 (cost)
Sales (gross)	18,000	25 (selling price)
Sales returns	100	25 (selling price)
Damaged merchandise (unsalable)	100	18 (cost)
Ending inventory or physical count (salable)	6,900	
Inventory shortage	?	

Expenses (excluding damaged goods, cost of goods sold, and income taxes) were $47,800.

Required

1. In parallel columns, give entries for the above transactions, including entries at the end of the accounting period, December 31, 1995, for the following cases (assume a 40% income tax rate and cash transactions):
   Case A—periodic inventory system.
   Case B—perpetual inventory system.
2. Prepare a multiple-step income statement, assuming a periodic inventory system and 10,000 common shares outstanding.
3. What amounts, if any, would be different on the income statement if a perpetual inventory system is used? Explain.

P 9–2
(L.O. 4)

Inventory, CGS, Gross Margin—Five Inventory Cost Methods   The records of Clayton Company showed the following transactions, in the order given, relating to the major inventory item:

	Units	Unit Cost
1. Inventory	3,000	$6.90
2. Purchase	6,000	7.20
3. Sales (at $15)	4,000	
4. Purchase	5,000	7.50
5. Sales (at $15)	9,000	
6. Purchase	11,000	7.66
7. Sales (at $18)	9,000	
8. Purchase	6,000	7.80

Required

Complete the following schedule for each independent assumption (round unit costs to the nearest cent for inventory; show computations):

Independent Assumptions	Units and Amounts		
	Ending Inventory	Goods Sold	Gross Margin
a. FIFO.	_____	_____	_____
b. LIFO, periodic inventory system.	_____	_____	_____
c. LIFO, perpetual inventory system.	_____	_____	_____
d. Weighted average, periodic inventory system.	_____	_____	_____
e. Moving average, perpetual inventory system.	_____	_____	_____

P 9–3
(L.O. 4)

Inventory Cost Flow Issues: Four Methods, Two Inventory Systems   The records of Johnson Brothers showed the following data about one raw material used in the manufacturing process. Assume that the transactions occurred in the order given.

	Units	Unit Cost
1. Inventory	4,000	$7.00
2. Purchase 1	3,000	7.70
3. Issue 1	5,000	
4. Purchase 2	8,000	8.00
5. Issue	7,000	
6. Purchase 3	3,000	8.40

Required

1. Compute cost of materials issued (to work in process) and the valuation of raw materials ending inventory for each of the following independent assumptions (round unit costs to the nearest cent for inventory; show computations).
    a. FIFO.
    b. LIFO, periodic inventory system.
    c. Weighted average, periodic inventory system.
    d. Moving average, perpetual inventory system.
2. In parallel columns, give all entries indicated for FIFO, assuming a count of the raw material on hand at the end of the period showed 6,000 units.
    Case A—periodic inventory system.
    Case B—perpetual inventory system.

P 9–4
(L.O. 4)

Inventory, CGS, Gross Margin—Three Inventory Cost Methods   The records of Betsworth Company showed the following data relative to one of the major items being sold. Assume that the transactions occurred in the order given.

	Units	Unit Cost
Beginning inventory	8,000	$4.00
Purchase No. 1	6,000	4.20
Sale No. 1 (at $12)	9,000	
Purchase No. 2	8,000	4.50
Sale No. 2 (at $13)	4,000	

Required

1. Complete the following schedule under each independent assumption given (round unit costs to nearest cent):

	Units and Amount		
Independent Assumptions	**Ending Inventory**	**Cost of Goods Sold**	**Gross Margin**
a. Weighted-average cost, periodic inventory system.	———	———	———
b. FIFO, perpetual inventory system.	———	———	———
c. LIFO, periodic inventory system.	———	———	———

2. Give all transaction entries indicated by the above data, assuming FIFO and a perpetual inventory system, (b) above.

P 9–5
(L.O. 4)

Ending Inventory, CGS, Five Inventory Cost Methods—Two Inventory Systems   Kim Corporation's records showed the following transactions, in order of occurrence, relative to inventory item A:

	Units	Unit Cost
1. Inventory	400	$5.00
2. Purchase	600	5.50
3. Sale	700	
4. Purchase	900	5.70
5. Sale	800	
6. Purchase	200	5.80

Required Compute the cost of goods sold and ending inventory in each of the following independent situations (round unit costs to the nearest cent for inventory; show computations):

	Units and Amount	
Assumption	**Ending Inventory**	**Cost of Goods Sold**
a. Weighted average.	————	————
b. Moving average.	————	————
c. FIFO.	————	————
d. LIFO, perpetual inventory system.	————	————
e. LIFO, periodic inventory system.	————	————

P 9–6
(L.O. 4)

Ending Inventory, CGS, Income—Three Inventory Cost Methods Patterson Corporation maintains a periodic inventory system. The following transactions occurred during 1995 for its major inventory item (in order of occurrence):

	Units	Unit Cost
1. Beginning inventory.	1,000	$50
2. Purchase.	900	40
3. Sale (at $100).	800	
4. Purchase.	800	51
5. Sale (at $100).	200	

Other expenses (excluding income taxes) during 1995 were $20,000. Patterson's tax rate is 40%.

Required 1. Complete the following schedule for each of the independent assumptions given (show supporting computations):

Independent Assumptions	**Ending Inventory**	**Cost of Goods Sold**	**Net Income**
a. Weighted average	————	————	————
b. FIFO	————	————	————
c. LIFO	————	————	————

2. Which method results in the highest net income? Explain why this occurred.

P 9–7
(L.O. 4)

A Hypothetical Inventory Riddle to Solve! Stigler and Sons sells two main products. The records of the company showed the following information relating to one of the products:

	Units	Unit Cost
Beginning inventory	500	$3.00
Purchases and sales (in order given):		
Purchase 1	400	3.10
Purchase 2	600	3.15
Sale 1.	1,000	
Purchase 3	800	3.25
Sale 2.	700	
Sale 3.	500	
Purchase 4	700	3.30

In considering a change in inventory policy, the following summary was prepared:

	Illustration			
	(1)	**(2)**	**(3)**	**(4)**
Sales	$16,000	$16,000	$16,000	$16,000
Cost of goods sold	7,110	6,996	6,905	6,930
Gross margin	$ 8,890	$ 9,004	$ 9,095	$ 9,070

Required   Identify the inventory flow method used for each illustration, assuming that only the ending inventory was affected. Show computations.

(AICPA adapted)

P 9–8
(L.O. 3)

An Overview of Perpetual Inventory: Entries, Partial Income Statement   Walsh Company maintains perpetual inventory records on a FIFO basis for the three main products distributed by the company. A physical inventory is taken at the end of each year in order to check the perpetual inventory records.

The following information relating to one of the products, blenders, for the year 1995, was taken from the records of the company:

	Units	Unit Cost
Beginning inventory	9,000	$8.10
Purchases and sales (in order given):		
Purchase 1	5,000	8.15
Sale 1	10,000	
Purchase 2	16,000	8.20
Sale 2	11,000	
Purchase 3	4,000	8.40
Purchase 4	7,000	8.25
Sale 3	14,000	
Purchase 5	5,000	8.10
Ending inventory (per count)	10,500	
Replacement cost (per unit), $8.10.		

Required
1. Reconstruct the perpetual inventory record for blenders.
2. Give all entries indicated by the above data, assuming that the selling price is $22 per unit.
3. Prepare the income statement through gross margin for this product.

P 9–9
(L.O. 4)

Appendix 9A: Standard Costs—Perpetual versus Periodic   Walton Woodstompers specializes in snowshoe manufacturing. Three raw materials (fine ash, leather hides, and laminated wax) are used in the production process. The company carries all manufacturing inventory accounts at standard cost. The following data apply to the first quarter of 1995, just ended:

	Ash		Leather		Wax	
	Units	Cost	Units	Cost	Units	Cost
Beginning inventory	75	$7.60	170	$5.60	20	$4.80
Purchases:						
Jan. 7/95	50	$7.70	110	$5.60	10	$4.60
Feb. 10/95	100	$7.50	145	$6.20	40	$4.50
Mar. 24/95	55	$7.80	120	$5.40	10	$4.80
Issues:						
Jan. 5/95	60		120		15	
Feb. 17/95	100		200		25	
Mar. 28/95	50		100		10	
Ending inventory:						
Physical count (Mar. 31/95)	70		120		30	
Standard cost		$7.60		$5.60		$4.80

Required
1. Determine ending inventories and provide journal entries for the three raw material accounts during the period (assume periodic inventory system).
2. Redo your answer to (1) using a perpetual inventory system.

P 9–10
(L.O. 4)

Manufacturing Firm: Perpetual Inventory Method   Cofer Manufacturing produces sporting goods. The following data pertain to its wooden baseball bat inventory accounts for January:

			Units
Jan. 1	Beginning balance:		
	Raw materials (@ $3.50)	100	
	Work in process (@ $8.40)	300	
	Finished goods (@ $12.80)	220	
Jan. 4	Purchased wood (@ $3.75)	100	
Jan. 11	Sold bats at retail (@ $16.50)	120	
Jan. 15	Issued to work in process.	100	
Jan. 17	Completed production	300	
Jan. 25	Sold bats at retail (@ $16.75)	240	
Jan. 28	Purchased wood (@ $3.60)	200	
Jan. 30	Issued work in process	180	

Required

1. Prepare journal entries for each of the above transactions using a FIFO perpetual flow. Assume that it takes $10 in labour and overhead to complete one finished item (this figure is constant throughout the month), that beginning work in process is 50% completed, and that ending work in process is 40% completed.
2. What is the dollar value of the three ending inventory accounts at January 31? Assume that work in process is 40% completed at this time.

P 9–11
(L.O. 4)

Appendix 9: Standard Costs   Wood Manufacturing Company manufactures one main product. Two raw materials are used in the manufacture of this product. The company uses standard costs in the accounts and carries the raw material, work-in-process, and finished goods inventories at standard. The records of the company showed the following:

	Material A	**Material B**
Beginning inventory (units)	8,000	5,000
Standard cost per unit	$2.00	$7.00
Purchases during period:		
Purchase 1	10,000 at $2.00	7,000 at $7.00
Purchase 2	20,000 at $1.90	8,000 at $7.20
Issues during period (units)	28,000	16,000
Ending inventory per physical count (units).	10,000	3,900

Required

1. Give all entries indicated relative to raw materials, assuming standard costs (assume a perpetual system).
2. Determine the value of the ending inventory and cost of issues for each raw material.
3. Accumulate the amount of the variations from standard for each raw material. Explain or illustrate the reporting and accounting disposition of these amounts.

ANALYZING FINANCIAL STATEMENTS

All questions in this section are based on information taken from the financial statements of actual companies.

A 9–1

LIFO versus FIFO Inventory Value Effects   Eli Witt, a distribution subsidiary of Culbro Corporation, holds inventories consisting of tobacco, confectionery, grocery, and paper products. Culbro uses FIFO to value its inventories except for those held by Eli Witt, which are valued on the LIFO basis. Eli Witt's inventories are described in the following portion of note 5 to Culbro's 1991 financial statements, dated November 30, 1991:

Note 5 [in part]: Supplementary Financial Statement Information

Inventories ($000)
Inventories consist of:

	Nov. 30, 1991	**Dec. 1, 1990**
Raw materials and supplies	$62,872	$ 63,524
Work-in-process	4,180	3,938
Finished goods	31,080	56,288
	$98,132	$123,750

The cost of Eli Witt's inventories at LIFO was $20,752 and $37,435 at November 30, 1991 and December 1, 1990, respectively. On a FIFO basis, the cost of the inventories would have been $34,418 and $60,996, respectively. Cost of sales on a FIFO basis would have been higher by $9,895 in 1991, and lower by $3,035 in 1990.

At November 30, 1991 and December 1, 1990, Eli Witt's cigarette inventory quantities were less than at the end of the respective previous years, which resulted in liquidations of LIFO inventory quantities carried at lower costs. The effect in 1991 and 1990 was to increase pretax income by $17,045 and $5,225, respectively. The aforementioned supplemental information is presented for comparative purposes.

Required

Assume that Eli Witt's inventories have been valued on a LIFO basis for the last several years.

1. What would have been the effect on Culbro's pretax income for 1991 if Eli Witt's inventories had always been valued on a FIFO basis?
2. What would have been the effect on Culbro's retained earnings as of November 30, 1991, if Eli Witt's inventories had always been valued on a FIFO basis? (Use a 34% tax rate.)
3. Suppose Eli Witt had not experienced a liquidation of LIFO layers in either 1990 or 1991. What would the effect have been on Culbro's pretax income in 1991? Was the increase in Culbro's pretax income a welcome event?

A 9-2

Adopting LIFO and a Change Back to FIFO   Chrysler Corporation is the third largest producer of cars and trucks in North America.[12] It also manufactures vehicles for the armed services. Despite its size, the firm has been dominated by its major competitors, Ford and General Motors. This has caused Chrysler's competitive position to deteriorate sharply in bad times.

The industry generally, and Chrysler in particular, was experiencing substantial problems in 1970. Inflationary pressures were strong and labour unrest was on the rise in the automobile industry. General Motors had, for example, recently emerged from a strike that had idled production for over 10 weeks.

Chrysler's sales and net earnings had dropped precipitously during the fourth quarter of 1970, a period when new models are released and sales are normally strong. These pressures were reflected in the company's shares, which fell as low as $16 from a high of $72 in 1968, as well as in drops in overseas sales and in Chrysler's poor competitive situation with respect to smaller cars then gaining in popularity with consumers.

Under these pressures, Chrysler found it necessary to take a number of actions to improve its financial situation. These included tightening cost control, organizational changes designed to increase efficiency, a review and cutback of large capital expenditures, and a vigorous marketing effort related to its existing products.

It was at this time that the firm also reviewed its accounting policies. Chrysler, as well as Ford and General Motors, used essentially conservative accounting procedures. All three companies expensed research and development costs in the year in which they arose. All three used accelerated depreciation methods for most if not all of their fixed assets. They deferred any investment tax credits. Finally, current pension costs were funded, although all three companies had a substantive potential liability for past service costs.

One of two main differences in the accounting practices followed by the three firms related to inventories. Ford and General Motors were essentially on a FIFO system. Chrysler, on the other hand, used what was basically a LIFO system. In 1970, however, Chrysler elected to convert to a FIFO system and retroactively restate its 1969 operational data to be comparable. In making this change, Chrysler, in a letter to its shareholders, noted, "The other three U.S. automobile manufacturers have consistently used the FIFO method. Therefore, the reported loss for 1970 and the restated profit for 1969 are on a comparable basis as to inventory valuation with the other three companies."

The impact of the accounting change could only be discerned by a careful examination of the company's financial reports and the accompanying footnotes. The major footnote is as follows:

> Inventories are stated at the lower of cost or market. For the period January 1, 1957 through December 31, 1969 the last-in first-out (LIFO) method of inventory valuation had been used for approximately 60% of the consolidated inventory. The cost of the remaining 40% of inventories was determined using the first-in, first-out (FIFO) or average cost methods. Effective January 1, 1970 the FIFO

---

[12] This case was prepared from publicly available sources. The situation was suggested by a case written by Professor John K. Shank.

method of inventory valuation has been adopted for inventories previously valued using the LIFO method. This results in a more uniform valuation method throughout the Corporation and its consolidated subsidiaries and makes the financial statements with respect to inventory valuation comparable with those of the other automobile manufacturers. As a result of adopting FIFO in 1970, the net loss reported is less than it would have been on a LIFO basis by approximately $20.0 million, or $0.40 a share. Inventory amounts at December 31, 1969 and 1970 are stated higher by approximately $110.0 million and $150.0 million, respectively, than they would have been had the LIFO method been continued.

The Corporation has retroactively adjusted financial statements of prior years for this change. Accordingly, the 1969 financial statements have been restated resulting in an increase in Net Earnings of $10.2 million, and Net Earnings Retained for Use in the Business at December 31, 1969 and 1968 have been increased by $53.5 million and $43.3 million, respectively.

For income tax purposes, the adjustment to inventory amounts will be taken into taxable income ratably over 20 years commencing January 1, 1971.

The Wall Street Journal commented on Chrysler's decisions:

The change improved Chrysler's 1970 financial results several ways. Besides narrowing the 1970 loss by $20 million it improved Chrysler's working capital. The change also made the comparison with 1969 earnings look somewhat more favourable because, upon restatement, Chrysler's 1969 profit was raised by only $10.2 million from the original figures.

Finally, the change helped Chrysler's balance sheet by boosting inventories, and thus current assets, by $150 million at the end of 1970 over what they would have been under LIFO. As Chrysler's profit has collapsed over the last two years and its financial position tightened, auto analysts have eyed warily Chrysler's shrinking ratio of current assets to current liabilities.

To get the improvements in its balance sheet and results, however, Chrysler paid a price. Roger Helder, vice president and comptroller, said Chrysler owed the government $53 million in tax savings it accumulated by using the LIFO method since it switched from FIFO in 1957. The major advantage of LIFO is that it holds down profit and thus tax liabilities. The other three major auto makers stayed on the FIFO method. Mr. Helder said Chrysler now has to pay back that $53 million to the government over 20 years, which will boost Chrysler's tax bills about $3 million a year.

In note 1 to its financial statements for 1985, Chrysler states:

Effective January 1, 1984, Chrysler changed its method of accounting (for inventories) from First-In, First-Out (FIFO) to Last-In, First-Out (LIFO) for substantially all of its domestic automotive inventories. The change to LIFO was made to more accurately match current costs with current revenues.

Required

1. How much did the change cost Chrysler:
   a. In 1970?
   b. In future years?
2. Do you believe the change in 1970 was in the best interest of Chrysler's shareholders?
3. What entry is necessary on January 1, 1970?
4. Compare the reasons for the shift to FIFO in 1970 and back to LIFO in 1984. What observations would you make?
5. Why did the U.S. Internal Revenue Service allow Chrysler to pay the $53 million over 20 years?

COMPARATIVE ANALYSIS

Chrysler and Ford are two of the three major automobile producers in North America. The two firms use different inventory assumptions. This problem asks you to determine some of the differences due to the reporting. The two firms report the following selected information for 1991 for their automotive activities:

	Chrysler	Ford
	(in millions)	
Earnings from continuing operations	($538)	($3,432)*
Cost of sales	24,803	71,826
Net earnings per share (continuing operations)	(2.22)	(7.21)*
Assets (total)	43,076	174,429
Inventories	3,571	6,215
Total shareholders' equity	6,109	22,690
Cars and trucks sold: US and Canada	1.661	3.114
Worldwide	1.866	5.346

* Estimated.

Chrysler Corporation

Note 1: Summary of Significant Accounting Policies

Inventories are valued at the lower of cost or market. The cost of approximately 41 percent and 49 percent of inventories at December 31, 1991, and 1990, respectively, is determined on a Last-In, First-Out (LIFO) basis. The balance of inventory cost is determined on a First-In, First-Out (FIFO) basis.

Note 2: Inventories and Cost of Sales

Inventories are summarized by major classification as follows (in millions of dollars):

	December 31	
	1991	1990
Finished products, including service parts	$1,192	$1,114
Raw materials, finished, production parts, and supplies	873	1,100
Vehicles held for short-term lease	1,476	911
Other	30	25
Total	$3,571	$3,150

Inventories valued on the LIFO basis would have been $239 million and $208 million higher than reported had they been valued on the FIFO basis at December 31, 1991, and 1990, respectively (see Note 1).

Total manufacturing cost of sales aggregated $24.81 billion, $24.13 billion and $27.42 billion for 1991, 1990, and 1989 respectively.

Ford Motor Company

Note 1: Accounting Policies (Inventory Valuation—Automotive)

Inventories are stated at the lower of cost or market. The cost of substantially all US inventories is determined by the last-in, first-out ("LIFO") method. The cost of the remaining inventories is determined substantially by the first-in, first-out ("FIFO") method.

If FIFO were the only method of inventory accounting used by the company, inventories would have been $1,323 million and $1,331 million higher than reported at December 31, 1991, and 1990, respectively.

The major classes of inventory for the company's automotive business segment at December 31 were as follows:

(in millions)	1991	1990
Finished products	$2,979.2	$3,628.2
Raw materials and work-in-process	2,800.9	3,025.7
Supplies	435.2	461.5
Total	$6,215.3	$7,115.4

Required:
1. Are prices rising or falling in the 1991 factor markets in which Ford (and by implication, Chrysler) buys? How do you know?
2. If Ford's United States inventories are proportional to its North American car and truck sales, what percentage of its December 31, 1991, inventory would be valued on LIFO? How does this compare to Chrysler's percentage?
3. If Ford were to compute its earnings from continuing operations on the same basis (same percentage of inventory valued on FIFO, estimate what Ford would report for earnings from continuing operations? (Use a 36% tax rate.) Indicate any assumptions in your analysis.
4. Compare Ford's and Chrysler's inventory levels and comment on the comparison.
5. Does Chrysler appear to be using FIFO to value some of its US inventories? Why do you think they are doing so?

10 Inventory: Alternative Valuation Methods

LEARNING OBJECTIVES

After you have studied this chapter, you will be able to:

1 **Determine inventory values based on the lower-of-cost-or-market (LCM) approach.**

2 **Explain and apply the gross margin method of estimating inventories.**

3 **Use the retail inventory method to value inventory and explain what types of businesses use it.**

4 **Explain and apply several special inventory problems, including the valuation of inventories using other methods, losses on purchase commitments, and the effects of errors in valuing inventories.**

INTRODUCTION

Imagine you have been assigned to a team of accountants and given responsibility for constructing the balance sheet and income statement for Hudson's Bay Company. Imagine computing the carrying value of the thousands of items The Bay stocks in its stores, catalogue operations, and distribution centers across the country as of the end of the company's fiscal year—with sales taking place up to the last minute, the firm's buyers making purchases throughout the period, and sales returns occurring each day.

Fortunately, hand-held price scanners and other forms of automation now remove much of the drudgery. With a quick pass over the bar code affixed to each item of merchandise, the scanner automatically records the current retail sales price, which may have changed several times during the product's inventory shelf life. Even more important, the bar code, which the scanner electronically registers in a network of mainframe computers, includes the product's inventory identification number. This number controls a host of critical inventory accounting details, most of which are discussed in this chapter.

Despite the use of scanners and other types of automated equipment, inventory accounting remains one of the most significant areas of accounting, in terms of both its importance to the integrity of a company's financial statements and the effort involved in gathering, processing, and reporting the required accounting information.

In any large business—for example, Kmart or Loblaw, on the retailing side, or Procter & Gamble or Dominion Textile, on the product supply side—inventory valuation methods provide only a basic estimate of inventory values. Taking inventory is somewhat like taking a population census—actually counting each member of the group (let alone assigning a value to each piece of merchandise) is simply not feasible. Although counting the physical inventory is a necessary part of the inventory control process (even when perpetual inventory record systems are in use), valuing the inventory is equally important and substantially more difficult.

Over the years, accountants have developed a number of estimation methods for valuing inventories that are within acceptable error-tolerance levels. Chapter 10 presents three methods for estimating inventory values: the lower-of-cost-or-market (LCM) method, the gross margin method, and the retail inventory method. The LCM method is an inventory valuation approach that is used with other valuation methods to obtain an alternative value often required for reporting purposes.

LCM INVENTORY VALUATION METHOD

GAAP requires that inventories be valued either at cost or at current market value, whichever is less. This is something of a departure from the historical cost principle that applies in most other asset valuation practices. Using the approach known as **lower of cost or market (LCM)** means that during inflationary economic periods (when prices are rising), inventories should be carried on the books and reported in financial statements at their original acquisition cost, even though the inventory's replacement value may be substantially higher according to current market prices. In deflationary conditions (when prices are trending down), however, inventories must be carried and reported at their market value.

When prices are rising, conservative accounting practices ignore holding gains resulting from higher current market values; instead, such gains are recognized only when the inventory is sold or otherwise disposed of at this higher market value.[1] When prices are declining, holding losses may result if current market prices decline below the inventory's original cost. When this occurs, the holding losses are recognized and inventories are reported at the lower market value. This conservative approach is applied to inventory accounting, because the inventory has less utility value to the company.

That the inventory has less utility value means that it has less revenue-generating power—that is, a lower selling price, which may or may not cover the cost to produce the inventory (or acquire the merchandise, in the case of a retailer). With raw materials and work-in-process inventories, less utility value refers to the diminished sales revenue expected to be generated after such inventories are converted to finished goods in the normal flow of production.

An inventory valuation loss occurring because of a decline in current market prices below original cost must be recognized in the period during which the price decline (and loss) occurs. When the cost of a component of a larger unit declines without affecting the unit's sales value, however, the component's cost is not written down to LCM. In general, for a loss to be recognized under the LCM method, a decline in both replacement cost and the expected final sales value should have occurred.

To illustrate the basic operation of the LCM inventory valuation method, assume that a retailer has an inventory consisting of a single line of office electronics prod-

---

[1] Gains in market value are recognized in volatile market situations where market prices have declined below cost (and were previously reported as losses) and have now recovered. Gain recognition in such instances is limited to the amount of the previously established loss, which means market value recoveries up to the amount of the original inventory cost. Any gains above original cost are disregarded, in keeping with the LCM rule.

ucts, all purchased during 1995 at a cost of $165 per unit, the going wholesale price at the time the merchandise was acquired. Late in the year, stiff competition in the electronics and office products market causes wholesale prices for the retailer's products in inventory to drop substantially, with retail prices following suit. As of the end of the year, manufacturers are quoting wholesale prices of $125 per unit. Assume that none of the retailer's inventory has been sold. The retailer's ending inventory for 1995 should be valued and reported at $125 per unit, which represents a $40 loss per unit based on the $165 original purchase cost. This $40-per-unit loss must be reported in the retailer's 1995 financial statements, the period during which the market price decline took place.

Assume that the retailer's inventory is sold in 1996. For each unit sold, the cost of goods sold is now $125, not $165. Assuming that retail selling prices dropped commensurate with last year's decline in wholesale prices, the lower cost of goods sold provides the retailer with approximately the same gross margin on sales as would have been available in 1995, when both wholesale and retail prices were higher. The net effect of the LCM application in this instance is to shift the $40-per-unit loss from the period when the inventory was sold to the period in which the replacement cost decreased.

Net Realizable Value, Replacement Cost, and Net Realizable Value Less a Normal Profit Margin

The Meaning of *Market* Canada has no recommendations as to the meaning of *market* in the term *lower of cost or market*. The *CICA Handbook* provides the following comment:

> In view of the lack of precision in meaning, it is desirable that the term *market* not be used in describing the basis of valuation. A term more descriptive of the method of determining market, such as *replacement cost, net realizable value* or *net realizable value less normal profit margin,* would be preferable.[2]

The first of these bases, replacement cost, is the primary market referent used in accounting practice in the United States. The AICPA has, however, constrained "market" value to a maximum value equivalent to the net realizable value and a minimum value equivalent to the net realizable value less normal profit.

1. **Net realizable value** is defined as the estimated selling price of the goods in the ordinary course of business less reasonably predictable costs of completion and disposal. This is considered to be a maximum, or **ceiling,** value.
2. **Replacement cost** is the current cost of replacing the goods as they would be obtained by purchase or reproduction.
3. Market should not be less than the **net realizable value less a normal profit margin.** A normal profit margin is that profit margin, expressed as a percentage achieved on the item or on similar items in normal circumstances. This is considered to be a minimum, or **floor,** value.

The ceiling and floor values for one unit of inventory, item A, for a manufacturing company are illustrated in Exhibit 10–1.

Line *a:* Inventory item A is currently valued at $70, which includes raw materials, direct labour, and allocated overhead expenses incurred to date in bringing item A to its present condition. (If this were a retail merchandise item, the $70 would represent the item's original purchase price.)

Line *b:* For a variety of reasons, inventory item A, which originally sold for $122, has declined in sales value, perhaps because another manufacturer lowered its selling price, forcing all other manufacturers to lower their prices in order to compete. Thus, the current selling price of item A is down to $100. (If this were a retailing example, the same price-cutting practice by a competitor could force the other retailers to cut their prices as well.)

---

[2] *CICA Handbook,* Section 3030, paragraph .11, "Inventories."

EXHIBIT 10–1

Net Realizable Value and Net Realizable Value Less a Normal Profit Margin

a. Inventory item A, at original cost	$ 70
b. Inventory item A, at estimated current selling price in completed condition.	$100
c. Less: Estimated costs to complete and sell*.	40
d. **Net realizable value**	$ 60
e. Less: Allowance for normal profit (10% of sales price)	10
f. **Net realizable value less normal profit**.	$ 50

* For goods already completed, as in a retail company, this amount would be the cost to sell.

Line *c:* Assume that currently item A is not quite ready to be transferred to finished goods inventory. The company estimates that $5 of additional direct labour and overhead is needed to complete the conversion, with $35 in selling expenses expected to be incurred to transfer the fully assembled item A to the retailer's selling floor. Thus, $40 is estimated as the completion and selling costs for item A. (If this were a retailing inventory situation, the additional conversion costs would have been included in the retailer's purchase price.)

Line *d:* The net realizable value of inventory item A is $60 ($100 selling price less $40 in completion and selling costs), which represents item A's maximum utility value to the manufacturer. (In a retailing situation, the same maximum utility value to the seller applies.)

Line *e:* The normal profit margin for items similar to item A is on average 10% of selling price, or in this case $10.

Line *f:* The net realizable value less normal profit is the lowest cost recovery amount expected by the manufacturer based on a selling price of $100. Thus, the minimum utility value of inventory item A is $50 ($100 selling price less $40 in completion and selling costs and $10 in profit).

Establishing Inventory Valuations under LCM

When the current replacement cost exceeds original cost, the original cost is used to value the inventory. When the current replacement cost is below the original cost, the net realizable value, (*d*) in Exhibit 10–1, represents the ceiling price for inventory valuation purposes, and the net realizable value less normal profit margin, (*f*) in Exhibit 10–1, represents the floor price. If the current replacement cost of the inventory is higher than the ceiling price (net realizable value), the ceiling price is used for valuing the inventory; if the current replacement cost is below the floor price (net realizable value less normal profit margin), the floor price is used for valuing the inventory. If the current replacement cost falls between the floor and the ceiling prices, the current replacement cost figure is used.[3] In short, market according to LCM is the middle value of the ceiling value, the floor value, and the replacement cost.

The ceiling and floor constraints prevent inventory from being stated at an amount in excess of net selling price or below net selling price less a normal margin of profit. The ceiling (maximum value) applies to obsolete, damaged, or out-of-style items, so these losses are recognized in the period of occurrence instead of being carried forward in inventory.

The floor (minimum value) deters the establishment of unreasonably low inventory values, causing losses on these items to be recognized before sale while increas-

---

[3] LCM represents a conservative approach to inventory accounting. When LIFO is used to obtain the cost value used in LCM, the accounting approach is even more conservative because LIFO usually produces lower inventory values. Precisely because of its conservative nature, the floor constraint to LCM (net realizable value less a normal profit margin) is often not needed when LIFO is used to establish cost because the LIFO cost is already very low.

ing profits in future periods when the items are sold. For example, consider this situation for a specific item:

Cost	$1,200
Current replacement cost	700
Cost to complete and sell	150
Normal profit margin	100
Current sales price	1,150

In this situation, net realizable value is $1,000 = $1,150 − $150 and the floor inventory value under LCM is $900 = $1,000 − $100. Market cannot be the replacement cost of $700 since that is below $900. The $900 value is used to value the inventory. If management were instead permitted to value the inventory at the $700 current replacement cost, an additional loss of $200 = $900 − $700 would be recognized this period, only to be recognized as a gain in the next period when the item is sold: $1,150 − ($150 + $700) = $300, which is the sum of the $100 normal profit plus the $200 loss recognized in the prior period. Such a practice would enable management to increase income by $200 in the second period regardless of the final sales price.

These ceiling and floor constraints were adopted by the AICPA and incorporated into the LCM rule to prevent abuses and unethical manipulation of reported inventory values. For similar reasons, the ceiling price exists to prevent a company from overstating its inventory and not recognizing the full extent of an inventory loss for the current year. Failure to recognize a current loss causes overstatement of the cost of goods sold in future years, which in turn understates gross margins on sales in future years.

Accounting studies in both Canada and England argue for the use of net realizable value alone for the market valuation of inventories. In 1963, the CICA conducted a research study into "The Use and Meaning of 'Market' in Inventory Valuation." The conclusion to this study noted that:

> [selling] prices do not necessarily fluctuate with [replacement] costs and that, as a result, a decline in the cost of replacement or reproduction, in itself, is not conclusive evidence that a loss will be incurred . . .
>
> Because of its obvious limitations and because consistent use may produce unreasonable results, the lower of cost and replacement cost can hardly be classified as a practical interpretation of the lower of cost and market basis of valuing inventories.
>
> The only reasonable choice of interpretation seems to be between net realizable value and net realizable value less normal profit. Both of these interpretations have the desired quality of being capable of consistent application. The choice between the two reduces itself to the question of which interpretation provides the more accurate measurement of the loss which will actually be experienced. Under the net realization theory, the loss charged against the income of the current period is limited to irrecoverable cost which is, in effect, the true loss (cost incurred without return or benefit) that is expected to be suffered. Under the net realizable value less normal profit theory, all or part of the charge against current income does not represent a true loss.
>
> Since any departure from cost disrupts the normal process of matching costs with related revenues and is an arbitrary shifting of income from one period to another, it would seem most logical to insist on that interpretation of market which causes the lesser disruption of or shift away from the normal matching process. Net realizable value wins over net realizable value less normal profit because the latter interpretation results in a larger inventory adjustment and, therefore, unnecessarily accentuates the shift in income.[4]

Applications of the LCM Rule

Exhibit 10–2 illustrates how the LCM rule is applied in five different cases; it assumes, for convenience, a single unit of inventory. The same procedures apply to an entire inventory, provided it consists of homogeneous goods or materials.

---

[4] Gertrude Mulcahy, "The Use and Meaning of 'Market' in Inventory Valuation" (Toronto: The Canadian Institute of Chartered Accountants, 1963), p. 19.

EXHIBIT 10–2

Determination of Lower of
Cost or Market (LCM)
Illustrated

Information for Five Cases	Case I	II	III	IV	V
Estimated selling price (later period)	$ .85	$ .90	$ .80	$ .75	$ .70
Less: Estimated cost to complete and sell	.25	.30	.20	.15	.12
Net realizable value (ceiling)	$ .60	$ .60	$ .60	$ .60	$ .58
Less: Estimated normal profit*	.09	.09	.08	.08	.07
Net realizable value less profit (floor)	$ .51	$ .51	$ .52	$ .52	$ .51
Original cost	$1.00	$1.00	$1.00	$ .45	$ .40
Current replacement cost.	.55	.65	.45	.40	.45

Computations	Case I	II	III	IV	V
a. Cost (per unit).	$1.00	$1.00	$1.00	$.45	$.40
b. Current replacement cost (per unit)	.55	.65	.45	.40	.45
c. Ceiling (net realizable value—i.e., estimated sales price less predictable costs of completion and sale)	.60	.60	.60	.60	.58
d. Floor (net realizable value less a normal profit margin).	.51	.51	.52	.52	.51
e. Market, selected from (*b*), (*c*), and (*d*) values . . .	.55	.60	.52	.52	.51
f. Inventory valuation selected from lower of (*a*) and (*e*).	.55	.60	.52	.45	.40

* 10% of selling price rounded for instructional convenience.

For Case V, the current $.45 replacement cost is higher than the original cost. Case V, therefore, is disposed of under the LCM rule simply by maintaining the original cost of the inventory ($.40) for end-of-period valuation purposes. In the other four cases, it is necessary to determine which amount to use as market under the LCM rule because the current replacement cost is below original cost.

In Case I, the $.55 current replacement cost is used as market because it falls between the floor and ceiling prices; thus, $.55 is used to value the inventory. In Case II, the ceiling price ($.60) applies because the current replacement cost ($.65) exceeds this ceiling. In Case III, the floor price ($.52) applies because the current replacement cost ($.45) is below this floor price. In Case IV, the original cost ($.45) takes precedence because it is lower than market ($.52). Case V, once again, was disposed of immediately because the original cost is lower than the current replacement cost.

Exhibit 10–3 draws on the data used in the preceding illustration and compares the valuation of inventories under the CICA guidelines to the valuation achieved under the AICPA rule. Note that in Cases II, IV, and V, the valuation of inventory under the two methods is the same; in the other two instances, the CICA guidelines result in a higher inventory valuation than is indicated under the AICPA rule. Further, this higher valuation of ending inventory results in the "lesser disruption or shift away from the normal matching process" that was noted in the CICA Research Study.

EXHIBIT 10–3

Lower of Cost or
Market—Comparison of
CICA and AICPA Methods

	Case I	II	III	IV	V
a. Cost (line *a*, Exhibit 10–2)	$1.00	$1.00	$1.00	$.45	$.40
b. Net realizable value (line *c*, Exhibit 10–2)	.60	.60	.60	.60	.58
c. Lower of cost or market—CICA guidelines (from *a* and *b* above).	.60	.60	.60	.45	.40
d. Lower of cost or market—AICPA rule (line *f*, Exhibit 10–2)	.55	.60	.52	.45	.40

The determination of a market price for use in LCM calculations is well established in practice. Because inventory is acquired for resale, the relevant market price is the price attained when the sale is ultimately achieved, as opposed to the assumed selling price at the balance sheet date.

The net realizable value for raw materials and work in process is more difficult to determine because the costs to complete and ultimate selling prices are more uncertain. Therefore, replacement costs for raw materials, plus manufacturing costs to date for work in process, is often used on the expectation that selling prices tend to move in step with replacement costs. Nevertheless, a write-down may still be required if realizable values have declined despite no decline in replacement costs.

As seen in the following CICA survey, the majority of Canadian companies use net realizable value as the determination of market value. However, companies use various methods as shown by the examples below.

Methods of Market Determination

	Number of Companies			
	1992	**1991**	**1990**	**1989**
Net realizable value	226	229	233	228
Replacement cost	68	72	69	74
Net realizable value less normal profit margin	13	12	11	11
Estimated net realizable value	9	10	9	10
Lower of replacement cost and net realizable value	5	4	4	4
Estimated realizable value	4	4	5	5
Various other bases	11	14	13	13

The category "Various other bases" includes methods such as current replacement cost, replacement cost that is not in excess of net realizable value, lower of estimated replacement cost and estimated net realizable value, and current selling prices.

Source: CICA, *Financial Reporting in Canada 1993* (Toronto: CICA, 1993), p. 92.

Examples of Inventory Accounting Policies

Notes to the Consolidated Financial Statements (partial): Accounting Policies—Inventories

Moore Corporation Limited—December 31, 1993

Inventories of raw materials and work in process are valued at the lower of cost and replacement cost and inventories of finished goods at the lower of cost and net realizable value. The cost of the principal raw material inventories and the raw material content of finished goods inventories in the United States is determined on the last-in, first-out basis. The cost of all other inventories is determined on the first-in, first-out basis.

The Oshawa Group Limited—January 22, 1994

Warehouse inventories are valued at the lower of cost and net realizable value with cost being determined on a first-in, first-out basis. Retail inventories are valued at the lower of cost and net realizable value less normal profit margins as determined by the retail method of inventory valuation.

Mark's Work Warehouse—January 29, 1994

Inventories are accounted for by the retail method and are carried at the lower of estimated cost and anticipated selling price, less an expected average gross margin.

The Molson Companies—March 31, 1994

Inventories, other than returnable containers and retail lumber inventories, are valued at the lower of cost and net realizable value. Returnable containers are valued at amortized cost while retail lumber inventories are valued at the lower of cost and replacement cost.

EXHIBIT 10–4
Application of LCM to
Inventory Categories

Inventory	Cost	Market	LCM Applied to		
			Individual Items	Classifications	Total
Classification A:					
Item 1.	$10,000	$ 9,500	$ 9,500		
Item 2.	8,000	9,000	8,000		
	18,000	18,500		$18,000	
Classification B:					
Item 3.	21,000	22,000	21,000		
Item 4.	32,000	29,000	29,000		
	53,000	51,000		51,000	
Total	$71,000	$69,500			$69,500
Inventory valuation.			$67,500	$69,000	$69,500

Accounting Problems in Applying LCM

Two accounting problems arise in applying LCM:

1. How should LCM be applied to determine the overall inventory valuation?
2. How should the resulting inventory valuation be recorded in the accounts and reported on the financial statements?

Determination of Overall Inventory Valuation   Three approaches are available to determine the overall inventory valuation:

- Comparison of cost and market separately for each item of inventory.
- Comparison of cost and market separately for each classification of inventory.
- Comparison of total cost with total market for the inventory.

Exhibit 10–4 shows the application of each approach. Consistency in application over time is essential. The individual unit basis produces the most conservative inventory value because units whose market value exceeds cost are not allowed to offset items whose market value is less than cost. This offsetting occurs to some extent in the other approaches.

A problem arises when different unit costs of a particular commodity must be compared with a single-unit market price. This occurs frequently under first-in, first-out cost flow. In such cases, the aggregate cost for the commodity is compared with the aggregate market as defined under LCM, as shown in the Total column ($69,500) in Exhibit 10–4.

Recording and Reporting Lower of Cost or Market   When inventory items on hand can be replaced for less than their original cost, there is an **inventory holding loss.** The basic issue, then, is whether the inventory holding loss should be separately recorded in the accounts and separately reported on the financial statements or merged into cost of goods sold. Two methods of recording and reporting the effects of the application of LCM are used in practice:

1. **Direct inventory reduction method** The inventory holding loss is not separately recorded and reported. Instead, the LCM amount, if it is less than the original cost of the inventory, is recorded and reported each period. Thus, the inventory holding loss is automatically included in cost of goods sold, and ending inventory is reported at LCM.
2. **Inventory allowance method** The inventory holding loss is separately recorded using a contra inventory account, allowance to reduce inventory to LCM. Thus, the inventory and cost of goods sold amounts are recorded and reported at original cost, while any inventory holding loss is recognized separately. The entry for a loss of $1,000 would be as follows:

EXHIBIT 10–5 Recording and Reporting LCM (Periodic Inventory System)

Case Data
In Thousands of Dollars

	1995		1996		1997	
	Beginning	Ending	Beginning	Ending	Beginning	Ending
a. Cost.	0	$10	$10	$20	$20	$30
b. Market.	0	11	11	17	17	26
c. LCM, lower of (a), (b).	0	10	10	17	17	26
d. Inventory holding loss.	0	0	0	3	3	4

End-of-Period Inventory Entries	Direct Inventory Reduction Method		Inventory Allowance Method	
1995 (no holding loss):*				
a. Beginning inventory—none				
b. Ending inventory:				
Inventory (ending).	(cost) 10		(cost) 10	
Income summary (cost of goods sold)		10		10
1996 (holding loss, $3):				
a. To close beginning inventory:				
Income summary (cost of goods sold)	(cost) 10		(cost) 10	
Inventory (beginning)		10		10
b. To record ending inventory:				
Inventory (ending).	(LCM) 17		(cost) 20	
Income summary (cost of goods sold)		17		20
c. To record holding loss in ending inventory:				
Holding loss on inventory ($20 − $17)			3	
Allowance to reduce inventory to LCM				3
1997 (holding loss, $1):				
a. To close beginning inventory:				
Income summary (cost of goods sold)	(LCM) 17		(cost) 20	
Inventory (beginning)		17		20
b. To record ending inventory:				
Inventory (ending).	(LCM) 26		(cost) 30	
Income summary (cost of goods sold)		26		30
c. To record holding loss in ending inventory:				
Holding loss on inventory			1	
Allowance to reduce inventory to LCM†				1

* There is no entry for holding loss in 1995 because market is above cost.

† 1997 balance required in allowance account, $30 − $26, less 1996 balance in allowance account, $3, equals $1.

Holding loss on inventory 1,000

Allowance to reduce inventory to LCM. 1,000

Each method yields exactly the same income and total asset amounts. The only difference is the detail in the entries and disclosures on the income statement and balance sheet. Exhibit 10–5 illustrates the accounting entries under both methods (assuming a periodic inventory system). Exhibit 10–6 presents the related balance sheet and income statement amounts.

Under the direct inventory reduction method, the LCM amount of the ending inventory, rather than the inventory's original cost, is recorded directly in the accounts and reported on the financial statements. The amount of ending inventory at LCM is carried forward to the next period as the beginning inventory. Thus, both the beginning and ending inventory amounts are reflected at LCM.

In contrast, under the inventory allowance method, the entries and financial statements retain the actual costs for inventory and cost of goods sold. The entries also

EXHIBIT 10–6

Financial Statement Reporting—LCM for Inventory: Direct Inventory Reduction and Inventory Allowance Methods Compared

Reporting LCM—Direct Inventory Reduction Method
Inventory Holding Loss Merged with Inventory and Cost of Goods Sold

	1995	1996	1997
Balance Sheet			
Current assets:			
Merchandise inventory.	$10	$17	$26
Income Statement			
Sales revenue (assumed)	$50	$65	$81
Cost of goods sold:			
Beginning inventory (at LCM)	$ 0	$10	$17
Purchases (assumed).	40	47	61
Total goods available for sale.	40	57	78
Ending inventory (at LCM)	(10)	(17)	(26)
Cost of goods sold	30	40*	52*
Gross margin	20	25	29
Expenses (assumed).	(10)	(13)	(16)
Income (pretax).	$10	$12	$13

Reporting LCM—Inventory Allowance Method
Holding Losses Reported Separately from Inventory and Cost of Goods Sold

	1995		1996		1997	
Balance Sheet						
Current assets:						
Merchandise inventory (at cost). . . .	$10		$20		$30	
Less: Allowance to reduce inventory to LCM	(0)	$10	(3)	$17	(4)	$26
Income Statement						
Sales revenue (assumed)		$50		$65		$81
Cost of goods sold:						
Beginning inventory (at cost)	$ 0		$10		$20	
Purchases (assumed).	40		47		61	
Total goods available for sale.	40		57		81	
Ending inventory (at cost)	(10)		(20)		(30)	
Cost of goods sold (at cost)		30		37		51
Gross margin		20		28		30
Expenses (assumed).		(10)		(13)		(16)
Deduct net holding loss:						
1995		0				
1996				(3)		
1997						(1)
Income (pretax).		$10		$12		$13

* The holding loss merged with these amounts is 1996, $3; and 1997, $1. For 1996, $40 = $37 + $3, and for 1997, $52 = $51 + $1. The $37 and $52 amounts are the CGS values reported under the allowance method.

record and report the holding loss each period in a contra inventory account, allowance to reduce inventory to LCM. The net holding loss (which is the net effect of the holding losses in the beginning and ending inventories) is reported separately on the income statement.

The LCM method shifts a portion of the inventory cost as an expense or loss to the year of the write-down. In the year of the sale, the remaining portion of the original purchase cost is expensed. Ultimately, the entire historical cost of the inventory is expensed. However, this shifting affects earnings in both years. So to determine the effect of applying LCM to earnings of a particular year, both the beginning and ending effects on inventory must be considered.

For example, in Exhibit 10–5, the $3 write-down of the 1996 ending inventory also reduces the 1997 beginning inventory by $3, thereby increasing 1997 earnings by $3. The $4 write-down of 1997 ending inventory reduces 1997 earnings by $4. The net effect of LCM on 1997 earnings is therefore only a $1 decrease. The inventory allowance method captures the net earnings effect in any year in the holding loss or gain.

A net gain from holding inventory is also possible if market declines below cost in one period and partly or completely recovers in a subsequent period. For example, if the market value of the 1997 ending inventory were $32 rather than $26, a holding gain of $3 would be recognized under the allowance method. The market value of the inventory would have shown a positive gain of $5 from the beginning of the year, when the market value of the inventory was $17 ($3 below the inventory's $20 cost and thus a loss), to the end of the year, when the market value of the inventory was $32 ($2 above the inventory's $30 cost and thus a gain). With the direct method, the $3 write-down for the 1997 beginning inventory increases 1997 income by $3, as it does with the allowance method. Only the amount of the previously recognized loss ($3) can be recovered in the form of holding gains, however. Gains beyond the amount of the holding loss are ignored, in keeping with the LCM rule. Inventory is never written up to an amount higher than original cost.

The direct inventory reduction method is widely used because it is less complex than the allowance method when the periodic inventory system is used and the inventory holding loss amount for the period is not material or unusual. Disclosure notes can be used to report the holding loss information. Some companies prefer the inventory allowance method because it provides full disclosure of the effects of LCM on inventories.[5] It is less complex than the direct inventory reduction method when the perpetual inventory system is used (perpetual records usually are maintained at cost, not LCM).

CONCEPT REVIEW

1. What does *market* mean in LCM terms?
2. What are the arguments for and against deducting a normal profit margin when using net realizable value as the definition of *market?*
3. What is the difference in reporting holding losses under the direct inventory reduction method and the inventory allowance method?

GROSS MARGIN METHOD AND INVENTORY ESTIMATION

Imagine how many people it would take to maintain a physical count of all the different items in The Bay's inventory. Fortunately, there are simpler approaches to estimate inventory values. One is called the **gross margin method.** Although generally unacceptable for use in external financial statements, it is still used by many companies to estimate the cost of an inventory for other purposes. The gross margin method (also known as the *gross profit method*) assumes that a constant gross margin estimated on recent sales can be used to estimate inventory values from

---

[5] *ARB No. 43*, Chapter 7, statement 7, par. 14, recommends that "when substantial and unusual losses result from the application of this rule (LCM), it will frequently be desirable to disclose the amount of the loss in the income statement as a charge separately identified from . . . *cost of goods sold*" [emphasis added]. The inventory allowance method provides for separate reporting of the holding loss. The direct inventory reduction method merges the holding loss with cost of goods sold automatically; therefore, to some accountants it does not appear compatible with this recommendation when the difference is unusual and substantial in amount.

EXHIBIT 10–7   Gross Margin Method Applied

	Known Data	Computations*	Computation (step)†
Net sales revenue (base amount).	$10,000	100%	
Cost of goods sold:			
Beginning inventory	$ 5,000		
Add: Purchases	8,000		
Goods available for sale.	13,000		2
Less Ending inventory	?	$13,000 − $6,000 = $7,000	5
Cost of goods sold	?	$10,000 − $4,000 = $6,000	4
Gross margin rate (estimated as percent of sales) Step 1.	40%† ?	40% × $10,000 = $4,000	3

* These computations can be arranged in numerous ways. The most abbreviated one is $13,000 − [$10,000 × (1.00 − .40)] = $7,000, ending inventory.

† Step 1 has already been done, and the result was 40%.

current sales. The gross margin method provides a test check on the accuracy of the results of other inventory methods. The method assumes that the gross margin rate (gross margin divided by sales), based on recent past performance, is reasonably constant in the short run. The gross margin method has two basic characteristics—it requires the development of an estimated gross margin rate, and it applies the rate to groups of items (such as all items sold in a Bay's sporting goods department).

Estimating the ending inventory by the gross margin method requires five steps:

1. Estimate the gross margin rate on the basis of prior years' sales: (sales − cost of goods sold) ÷ sales.
2. Compute total cost of goods available for sale in the usual manner (beginning inventory plus purchases), based on actual data provided by the accounts.
3. Compute the estimated gross margin by multiplying sales by the estimated gross margin rate.
4. Compute cost of goods sold by subtracting the computed gross margin from sales.
5. Compute ending inventory by subtracting the computed cost of goods sold from the cost of goods available for sale.

Application of the gross margin method is illustrated in Exhibit 10–7.

The gross margin method has two significant limitations. First, the past gross margin rate may not appropriately reflect markup changes relating to the current or future periods. Second, gross markup rates may vary widely on different types of inventory. Most companies, including The Bay, carry a number of different lines of merchandise, each having a different markup rate. A change during the period in the markup rate on one or more lines or a shift in the relative quantities of each line sold (shifts in sales mix) changes the average gross margin rate. This change affects the reliability of the results.

When the gross margin method is applied in a situation that involves broad aggregations of inventory items with significantly different markup rates, the computations should be developed for each separate class. The estimate of the total inventory is then determined by summing the estimates for the separate classes.

The gross margin method can be used with different inventory cost flow assumptions (FIFO, LIFO, average cost) because the cost of goods sold used to determine the gross margin rate reflects the cost flow assumption used.

Sometimes the gross margin method uses a cost percentage (cost of goods sold divided by sales) rather than the gross margin percentage (gross margin divided by sales). If either percentage is known, the other can be determined because the two percentages must sum to 100%. In Exhibit 10–7, the gross margin rate is 40% of sales; therefore, the cost percentage is 60% (100% − 40%) of sales.

Also, the gross margin rate, or markup, may be available as a percentage of selling price, total sales, cost, or cost of goods sold. In Exhibit 10–7, for example, the markup is given as a percentage of selling price. If necessary, the markup on sales can be converted to a markup on cost based on the following relationship:

$$\text{Sales} = \text{Cost of goods sold} + \text{Gross margin}$$

or:

$$1 = \frac{\text{Cost of goods sold}}{\text{Sales}} + \frac{\text{Gross margin}}{\text{Sales}}$$

For the situation described in Exhibit 10–7, a 40% gross margin on sales implies that the cost of goods sold is 60% of the selling price:

$$1.0 = 0.6 + 0.4$$

Thus, the markup on cost is (1.0 − 0.6) ÷ 0.6 = 0.4 ÷ 0.6 = 0.6667, or 66.67%.

The gross margin method is used to:

1. Test the reasonableness of an inventory valuation determined by some other means such as a physical inventory count or from perpetual inventory records. For example, assume the company in Exhibit 10–7 submitted to an auditor an ending inventory valuation of $10,000. The gross margin method provides an approximation of $7,000, which suggests that the inventory may be overvalued and should be examined.
2. Estimate the ending inventory for interim financial reports prepared during the year when it is impractical to count the inventory physically and a perpetual inventory system is not used.
3. Estimate the cost of inventory destroyed by an accident such as fire or storm. Valuation of inventory lost is necessary to account for the accident and to establish a basis for insurance claims and income taxes. This is an example of a case where it would be helpful to know the markup on cost since cost is used for the insurance claim and to establish the tax deductible loss.
4. Develop budget estimates of cost of goods sold, gross margin, and inventory consistent with a sales revenue budget.

THE RETAIL INVENTORY METHOD AND INVENTORY ESTIMATION

The **retail inventory method** is often used by retail stores, especially department stores that sell a wide variety of items. In such situations, perpetual inventory procedures may be impractical, and a complete physical inventory count is usually taken only annually. The retail inventory method is appropriate when items sold within a department have essentially the same markup rate and articles purchased for resale are priced immediately. Two major advantages of the retail inventory method are its ease of use and reduced recordkeeping requirements.

The retail inventory method uses both retail value and actual cost data to compute a *ratio of cost to retail* (referred to as the *cost ratio*), calculates the ending inventory at retail value, and converts that retail value to a cost value by applying the computed cost ratio to the ending retail value.

Application of the retail inventory method requires that internal records be kept to provide data on:

- Sales revenue.
- Beginning inventory valued at both cost and retail.
- Purchases during the period valued at both cost and retail.
- Adjustments to the original retail price, such as additional markups, markup cancellations, markdowns, markdown cancellations, and employee discounts.
- Other adjustments, such as interdepartmental transfers, returns, breakage, and damaged goods.

EXHIBIT 10–8
Retail Inventory Method
Illustrated, Average Cost

	At Cost	At Retail
Goods available for sale:		
Beginning inventory (January 1, 1996)	$ 15,000	$ 25,000
Purchases during January 1996	195,000	275,000
Total goods available for sale	$210,000	300,000
Cost ratio:		
$210,000 ÷ $300,000 = .70 (average, January 1996)		
Deduct January sales at retail		260,000
Ending inventory (January 31, 1996):		
At retail		$ 40,000
At cost ($40,000 × .70)	$ 28,000	

The retail inventory method differs from the gross margin method in that it uses a computed cost ratio based on the actual relationship between cost and retail for the current period, rather than an historical ratio. The computed cost ratio is an average across several different kinds of goods sold. Although the computed inventory amount is an estimate, it is acceptable for external financial reporting.

The retail inventory method is illustrated in Exhibit 10–8. The objective of the retail inventory method is to find the ending inventory value at cost. To do this, the following information is needed:

- The total cost of goods available for sale at both cost and retail.
- Sales for the current period at retail.

The steps are as follows:

1. The total cost of goods available for sale during January 1996 is determined to be $210,000 at cost and $300,000 at retail, as shown in Exhibit 10–8.
2. Next, the cost ratio (ratio of cost to sales) is computed. This is done by dividing the total cost of goods available for sale at cost ($210,000) by the same items at retail ($300,000). In this instance, the cost ratio is ($210,000 ÷ $300,000) = .70, or 70%, as shown in Exhibit 10–8. This is an average cost application of the retail method, because both beginning inventory and purchases are included in determining the cost ratio.
3. The next step is to subtract January sales ($260,000) from the total cost of goods available for sale at retail ($300,000), resulting in the value of the ending inventory at retail ($40,000), as shown in Exhibit 10–8.
4. The last step is to compute the ending inventory at cost. This is done by applying the cost ratio (.70), derived in (2), to the ending inventory at retail ($40,000), derived in (3). The result is an ending inventory of $28,000 at cost ($40,000 × .70).

Markups and Markdowns

The data used for Exhibit 10–8 assumed no changes in the sales price of the merchandise as originally set. Frequently, however, the original sales price on merchandise is changed, particularly at the end of the selling season or when replacement costs are changing. The retail inventory method requires that a careful record be kept of all changes to the original sales price because these changes affect the inventory cost computation. To apply the retail inventory method, it is important to distinguish among the following terms:

- **Original sales price** Sale price first marked on the merchandise.
- **Markup** The original or initial amount that the merchandise is marked up above cost. It is the difference between the purchase cost and the original sales price, and it may be expressed either as a dollar amount or a percentage of either cost or sale prices. Sometimes this markup is called *initial markup* or *markon*.

EXHIBIT 10–9
Computation of Final
Sales Price

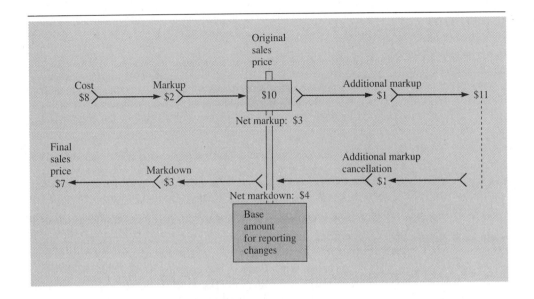

- **Additional markup** Any increase in the sales price above the original sales price. The original sales price is the base from which additional markup is measured.
- **Additional markup cancellation** Cancellation of all, or some, of an additional markup. Additional markup less additional markup cancellations is usually called net additional markup.
- **Markdown** A reduction in the original sales price.
- **Markdown cancellation** An increase in the sales price (that does not exceed the original sales price) after a reduction in the original sales price markdown.

The definitions are illustrated in Exhibit 10–9. An item that cost $8 is originally marked to sell at $10. This item is subsequently marked up $1 to sell at $11, then marked down to $10, and finally reduced to a sales price of $7.

Application of the Retail Inventory Method

The retail inventory method can be applied in different ways to estimate the cost of ending inventory under alternative inventory cost flow assumptions such as FIFO with LCM, average cost with LCM, and LIFO. In each case, the cost of the ending inventory is given by:

$$\frac{\text{Ending inventory}}{\text{cost}} = \frac{\text{Ending inventory}}{\text{at retail}} \times \frac{\text{The appropriate}}{\text{cost ratio}}$$

Since LCM is a required valuation process under GAAP, we use it with FIFO and average cost for illustration.

To illustrate the FIFO and average cost bases, assume the information in Exhibit 10–10 is provided by the accounting records of the Sandia Company at the end of the accounting period. Data on units are not used, only dollars.

FIFO Basis The cost and retail amounts of the beginning inventory are excluded from the computation of the cost ratio because FIFO takes the cost of ending inventory from purchases made during the current period, not from beginning inventory. Thus, the FIFO basis cost ratio is derived from the relationship of cost to retail values for current period purchases only.

$$\text{FIFO cost ratio} = \frac{\text{Cost of net purchases}}{\text{Retail value of (net purchases} + \text{net markups} - \text{net markdowns)}}$$

In instances where the ending inventory exceeds the amount of purchases for the accounting period, the cost ratio no longer represents the current period relationship

EXHIBIT 10–10
Data Used to Illustrate the
Retail Inventory Method,
Sandia Company

	At Cost	At Retail
Inventory at beginning of period	$ 550	$ 900
Purchases during period	6,290	8,900
Additional markups during period		225
Additional markup cancellations during period		25
Markdowns during period		600
Markdown cancellations during period		100
Sales revenue for the period		8,500

only. The ending inventory, in this case, includes a portion of the previous period's ending inventory.

Average Cost Basis   The average cost basis cost ratio is computed on total goods available for sale (i.e., the sum of beginning inventory plus purchases) because the cost of the ending inventory is assumed to represent the total goods available for sale during the period. Thus, this cost ratio reflects the relationship of cost to retail values for all inventory items available for sale, including the beginning inventory:

$$\text{Average cost ratio} = \frac{\text{Cost of (beginning inventory + net purchases)}}{\text{Retail value of (beginning inventory + net purchases + net markups − net markdowns)}}$$

LCM Basis (the conventional method)   To estimate the LCM value of ending inventory, the denominator of the cost ratio *excludes net markdowns,* causing the retail value of goods available (the denominator of the cost ratio) to be higher. This reduces the cost ratio and thus produces a conservative estimate of the value of ending inventory. Although the resulting cost value would only coincidentally be equal to the actual LCM value based on replacement cost, the result is an acceptable approximation. The previous two cost ratio formulas are adjusted to exclude net markdowns.

In Exhibit 10–11, LCM is applied only to FIFO and average cost. The LCM method is not applied to LIFO under the retail method. This is in part because the conventional retail method is designed to approximate the lower of average cost or market.

Retail Method, FIFO with LCM, Illustrated

When FIFO is used, ending inventory is costed at the current period's unit costs. Therefore, the costs in the beginning inventory are included in cost of goods sold rather than in the ending inventory. To accomplish this result with the retail method, the beginning inventory is excluded from computation of the cost ratio. The result will approximate the FIFO cost of the ending inventory. Then, to approximate LCM, net markdowns are excluded from the cost ratio. (It is assumed that all markups and markdowns relate to purchases and not to beginning inventory.) The LCM computations on the FIFO basis are shown for the Sandia Company in Exhibit 10–11. When any version of the retail inventory method is used, cost of goods sold is computed in the usual manner—cost of goods available for sale minus ending inventory at cost.

Retail Method, Average Cost with LCM, Illustrated

When the average cost basis is used, the cost ratio is derived by dividing total goods available for sale at cost by total goods available for sale at retail. Both totals include the beginning inventory. Because the cost ratio includes the beginning inventory, the retail method approximates average cost. To approximate LCM, net markdowns are excluded from the cost ratio. The LCM computation using the average cost basis is also shown for the Sandia Company in Exhibit 10–11.

EXHIBIT 10–11
Retail Inventory Method
Illustrated: Sandia Company
(FIFO with LCM and
Average Cost with LCM)

	At Cost	At Retail
Goods available for sale:		
Beginning inventory	$ 550	$ 900
Purchases during period	6,290	8,900
Additional markups during period	$225	
Less: Additional markup cancellations	(25)	
Net additional markups		200
Markdowns	(600)	
Less: Markdown cancellations	100	
Net markdowns		(500)
Total goods available for sale	$6,840	9,500
Deduct:		
Sales		(8,500)
Ending inventory:		
At retail		$1,000
At approximate FIFO cost with LCM ($1,000 × .691*)	$ 691	
At approximate average cost with LCM ($1,000 × .684†)	$ 684	

* FIFO basis with LCM cost ratio:

$$\frac{\$6,290}{\$8,900 + \$225 - \$25} = .691$$

Based on current period costs and retail values; beginning inventory excluded from numerator and denominator; net markdowns excluded from denominator in computation of cost ratio.

† Average cost basis with LCM cost ratio:

$$\frac{\$550 + \$6,290}{\$900 + \$8,900 + \$225 - \$25} = .684$$

Based on average costs and retail values; beginning inventory included in numerator and denominator; net markdowns excluded from denominator in computation of cost ratio.

Markdowns occur because the utility of the merchandise has declined. That is, the current purchase price of identical new goods decreased, or, stated differently, the goods had a replacement cost lower than historical cost, perhaps because of obsolescence, spoilage, or excess supply. Therefore, to value the inventory at LCM, the net markdowns are omitted from computation of the cost ratio for both FIFO and average cost.

For example, assume that two items are purchased for $4 and first marked up to sell at $12 each. Later markdowns amount to $8 in total. Using the LCM (conventional) retail method, which does not recognize markdowns, the cost ratio is 2($4) ÷ 2($12) = .3333. If markdowns are considered, the ratio is 2($4) ÷ [2($12) − $8] = .500. When applied to the ending retail value of $16 ($24 − $8), the LCM value is obtained by applying the .3333 ratio to obtain $5.33 for ending inventory at cost. If the .50 cost ratio were applied, the resulting inventory at cost would be $8 per unit, which is historical cost. By definition, however, markdowns represent a decline in the inventory's utility, so the conventional retail method produces results that better reflect that decline.

Special Items Related to the Retail Inventory Method

Several items may complicate computation of the ending inventory value using the retail inventory method. In overcoming such complications, it is essential to protect the integrity of the computed cost ratio and the estimated ending inventory at retail. The treatment of the six complicating items that follow is illustrated in Exhibit 10–12.

1. **Freight-in** An expenditure for freight adds to the cost of merchandise; therefore, it is added to goods available for sale (or directly to purchases) at cost (but not at retail).

EXHIBIT 10–12

Retail Inventory Method (Average Cost, LCM), with Special Items, Illustrated: Data Assumed*

	At Cost	At Retail
Goods available for sale:		
Beginning inventory	$ 6,050	$ 11,000
Purchases	57,120	102,000
Freight-in (1)	1,020	
Purchase returns (2)	(560)	(1,000)
Net additional markups		600
Casualty loss:† (3)		
At cost	(3,630)	
At retail		(6,600)
Total	$60,000	106,000

Cost ratio: $60,000 ÷ $106,000 = .566

Deduct:		
Gross sales	$71,200	
Sales returns (merchandise returned to stock) (4)	(1,200)	
Net sales		(70,000)
Discounts to employees (5)		(200)
Normal spoilage (6)		(1,300)
Net markdowns		(4,500)
Ending inventory:		
At retail		$ 30,000
At average cost, LCM ($30,000 × .566)	$16,980	

* The numbers in parentheses refer to the factors discussed in the text.
† The casualty loss could be recorded as follows:

Cash (from insurance company: assumed)	2,000	
Casualty loss (fire damage)	1,630	
Purchases (or cost of goods sold)		3,630

2. **Purchase returns** Because purchase returns, as distinguished from allowances, reduce the amount of goods available for sale, they are deducted from goods available for sale at both cost and retail.

3. **Abnormal casualty losses** A purchase allowance is deducted only in the "At Cost" column. Any associated sales price reduction would be reflected in the markdowns. Merchandise missing because of unusual or infrequent events (such as fire or theft) are deducted from goods available for sale at both cost and retail because they will not be sold; removal from both cost and retail eliminates their effect on the cost ratio as if they had not been purchased in the first place. Damaged merchandise is set up in a special inventory account at its net realizable value.

4. **Sales returns and allowances** Because this is a contra account to the sales revenue account, sales return and allowances are deducted from gross sales. If the returned merchandise is placed back into inventory for resale, no change in the At Cost column in Exhibit 10–11 is needed because the cost has already been included in the purchases amount. Merchandise not returned to inventory (because of damage, for example), is deducted, at retail, from gross sales. The original cost of the merchandise is deducted from ending inventory at cost after applying the cost ratio to ending inventory at retail. The merchandise is set up in a special inventory account at its net realizable value.

5. **Discounts to employees and favoured customers** Discounts that result from selling merchandise below the normal sales price and that are not caused by market value decreases are different from markdowns. Such discounts are deducted after cal-

culation of the cost ratio, which means they reduce ending inventory at retail but not the total cost of goods available for sale. In Exhibit 10–12, $200 of discounts were allowed on goods sold to employees. Assume that employees paid $500 in total for these goods (other customers would be charged $700). If the discounts were not subtracted, ending inventory at retail would be overstated relative to the physical quantity of goods.

6. **Normal spoilage** This amount is the retail value of the units lost under normal conditions including expected shrinkage and breakage. This amount is also deducted below the cost ratio at retail because the expected cost of normal spoilage is included implicitly in determining the selling price and does not reflect market value changes. Normal spoilage, then, is not included in the cost-to-retail ratio calculation but is deducted in determining ending inventory at retail, because it represents goods not available for sale at the end of the period. Abnormal spoilage and theft are another matter. They are not deducted from the total cost of goods available for sale but are deducted, instead, in establishing the cost ratio.

Application of the retail inventory method assumes that the goods included in a single set of computations are similar in markup percentage and relative proportion of the total inventory. In individual departments, this is usually the case, although on a storewide basis, often it is not. For example, three-fourths of the total inventory may have a markup of 80%, and one-fourth of the inventory, a markup of 50%. The essential data should be accumulated for each sales department and the retail inventory computations made on a departmental basis. Departmental inventories are summed to derive the total ending inventory.

| CONCEPT REVIEW

1. When is the gross margin method used? Explain, using a major grocery chain as an example.
2. How is the retail method related to the gross margin method of estimating inventories? Why are markdowns excluded from the cost ratio in applications of the retail method?
3. Explain how to compute the cost ratios for the inventory methods discussed in this section.

Evaluation of the Retail Inventory Method

The retail inventory, which is supported by the Retail Merchants Association, can be used for both financial accounting and income tax purposes. Like the gross margin method, it is used only to estimate the amount of the ending inventory and cost of goods sold. A physical inventory count should be taken at least annually as a check on the accuracy of the estimated inventory amounts. Differences between the physical inventory count and the retail inventory valuation may indicate:

- Inventory losses due to breakage, loss, or theft.
- Incorrect application of the retail method.
- Incorrect reporting of markdowns, additional markups, or cancellations.
- Errors in the inventory records.
- Errors in the physical inventory.
- Inventory manipulation.

The inventory accounts must be changed to the actual count by using a correcting entry.

Uses of the Retail Inventory Method

The primary uses of the retail inventory method are to provide:

- Estimates of inventory cost for interim periods (e.g., monthly or quarterly) when it is not practical to count the inventory and a perpetual inventory system is not used. The method provides estimated inventory valuations needed for interim statements, analyses, and purchasing policy considerations.

- A means for converting inventory amounts determined by a physical count of inventory, priced at retail, to a cost basis. Some retail establishments, after physically counting the inventory, extend the inventory sheets at retail. The retail value then is converted to cost by applying the retail inventory method without reference to the costs of individual items.
- A basis for control of inventory, purchases, theft, markdowns, and additional markups when neither a traditional periodic nor a perpetual inventory system is used for these interim purposes.
- Inventory cost data for external financial reports.
- Inventory cost data for income tax purposes.
- A test of the overall reasonableness of a physical inventory costed using a traditional cost flow assumption (e.g., FIFO).

ADDITIONAL INVENTORY ISSUES

Four additional issues affect inventory valuation:

1. Inventory valuation at current replacement cost and net realizable value.
2. Relative sales value method.
3. Losses on purchase commitments.
4. Effects of inventory errors.

Methods of Inventory Valuation

Inventories Valued at Current Replacement Cost and Net Realizable Value   Special inventory categories often include items for resale that are damaged, shopworn, obsolete, defective, trade-ins, or repossessions. These inventory items are assigned a cost related to their condition—namely, their *current replacement cost*—if it can be determined reliably in an established market for the items in their current condition.

Current replacement cost is defined as the price for which the items can be purchased in their present condition. To illustrate a situation in which the current replacement cost can be determined reliably, assume that Allied Appliance Company has on hand a repossessed TV set that had an original cost of $650 when new. The set, which originally sold for $995, was repossessed when $500 was owed by the customer. Similar used TV sets can be purchased in the wholesale market for $240. The repossessed item should be recorded as follows:

Inventory, repossessed merchandise	240	
Loss on repossession*	260	
Accounts receivable		500

* In some situations, there may be a gain. If losses such as this one are included in bad debt estimates, the allowance for doubtful accounts is debited.

Assume, further, that during the following year, the repossessed TV set is sold for $270 cash. The entry to record the sale would be recorded as follows (assuming a perpetual inventory system):

Cash	270	
Sales revenue, repossessed merchandise		270
Cost of goods sold	240	
Inventory, repossessed merchandise		240

When the replacement cost cannot be determined reliably, such items should be valued at their estimated *net realizable value* (NRV). NRV is defined as the estimated sale price less all costs expected to be incurred in preparing the item for sale. Replacement cost is preferred over NRV because it is typically a more objective value, established by existing market forces rather than by managerial estimates. To illustrate accounting for inventory at NRV when replacement cost cannot be determined reliably, assume that Allied suffers fire damage to 100 units of its regular inventory. The item, which originally cost $10 per unit (as reflected in the perpetual inventory records), was marked to sell before the fire for $18 per unit. No established used market exists. The company should value the item for inventory purposes at its

EXHIBIT 10-13
Relative Sales Value
Method Applied

Grade	Quantity (bushels)	Unit Sales Price	Total Sales Value	Fraction of Total Sales Value	Apportioned Cost
A	200	$5.00	$1,000	$1,000/$3,450	$ 600*
B	300	4.00	1,200	1,200/ 3,450	720
C	500	2.50	1,250	1,250/ 3,450	750
	1,000		$3,450		$2,070

Entry indicated (assuming a perpetual inventory system):
Inventory—Grade A apples, 200 units 600
Inventory—Grade B apples, 300 units 720
Inventory—Grade C apples, 500 units 750
    Cash 2,070

* ($1,000 ÷ $3,450) × $2,070 = $600. Or, alternatively, $2,070 ÷ $3,450 = 60%; $1,000 × 60% = $600; $1,200 × 60% = $720; and $1,250 × 60% = $750.

NRV. Allied estimates that after cleaning and making repairs, the items would sell for $7 per unit; the estimated cost of the repairs for all the units is $150, and the estimated selling cost is 20% of the new selling price. Given these data, the total inventory valuation for the items is as follows:

Estimated sale price (100 × $7)		$700
Less:		
Estimated cost to repair.	$150	
Estimated selling costs ($700 × 20%).	$140	(290)
NRV for inventory		$410

Assuming no insurance reimbursement, the casualty loss and the inventory would be recorded as follows (assuming a perpetual inventory system):

Inventory, damaged merchandise (NRV) 410
Casualty loss, fire damage. 590
    Inventory (regular merchandise) (100 × $10) 1,000

Relative Sales Value Method

Two or more different types of inventory items may be purchased for a lump sum. A separate cost for each type is required for accounting purposes. The apportionment of the total cost should be related to the economic utility of each kind or group of items. If the sales value of a particular item is a reasonable indication of its relative utility, the cost apportionment can be made on the basis of the relative sales value of the several items. Also, additional joint costs incurred subsequent to purchase may be allocated on the basis of relative sales value.

Assume, for illustration, that a packing plant purchases 1,000 bushels of apples (ungraded) for $2,000. After purchase, the apples are sorted into three grades at a cost of $70 (giving a total cost of $2,070), with the following results: grade A, 200 bushels; grade B, 300 bushels; and grade C, 500 bushels. The sorted apples sell at different retail prices per bushel: grade A, $5; grade B, $4; and grade C, $2.50. The cost apportionment is made as shown in Exhibit 10–13.

In joint cost allocations, quantities lost due to shrinkage or spoilage are assigned no cost, thus increasing the unit cost for the remaining units.

Losses on Purchase Commitments

To lock in prices and ensure sufficient quantities, companies often contract with suppliers to purchase a specified quantity of materials during a future period at an agreed unit cost. Some purchase commitments (contracts) are subject to revision or cancellation before the end of the contract period; others are not. Each case requires different accounting and reporting procedures.

In the case of purchase contracts subject to revision or cancellation where a future loss is possible and the amount of the commitment can be reasonably estimated and is material in amount, the full-disclosure principle requires note disclosure of the contingency. To illustrate, assume that the Bayshore Company enters into a purchase contract during October 1995 that states, "During 1996, 50,000 tanks of compressed chlorine will be purchased at $5 each. On 60 days' notice, this contract is subject to revision or cancellation by either party." If the current cost of the inventory under contract for purchase at the end of 1995 is $240,000, this fact is revealed in a disclosure note such as the following:

Note

At the end of 1995, a contract was in effect that will require the Company to pay $250,000 for materials during 1996. The purchase contract can be revised or cancelled upon 60 days' notice by either party. At the end of 1995, the materials under contract had a current replacement cost of $240,000.

This note gives the relevant aspects of the contingency. No entry is required for the $10,000 ($250,000 − $240,000) contingent loss, which is not likely because the contract can be revised or cancelled.

When purchase contracts are not subject to revision or cancellation, and when a loss is likely and material and can be reasonably estimated, the loss and related liability should be recorded in the accounts and reported. Suppose the contract above is not cancelable, the $240,000 current replacement cost is measured reliably, and the $10,000 loss is likely. In this case, the loss on the purchase commitment should be recorded at the end of 1995 as follows:

Estimated loss on purchase commitment ($250,000 − $240,000)	10,000	
Estimated liability on noncancellable purchase commitment		10,000

The estimated loss is reported on the 1995 income statement, and the liability is reported on the balance sheet.[6] When the goods are acquired in 1996, merchandise inventory (or purchases) is debited at the current replacement cost, and the estimated liability account is debited. Assume that the above materials have a replacement cost at date of delivery of $235,000. The purchase entry would be as follows:

Materials inventory (or purchases)	235,000	
Estimated liability on noncancellable purchase commitment	10,000	
Loss on purchase contract	5,000	
Cash		250,000

This treatment records the loss in the period when it became likely in accordance with the provisions of *CICA Handbook* Section 3290, "Contingencies."

If there were a full or partial recovery of the purchase price, the recovery would be recognized (as a gain) in the period during which the recovery took place. Thus, if in 1996 the materials had a replacement cost at date of delivery of $255,000, the purchase entry would be as follows:

Materials inventory (or purchases)	250,000	
Estimated liability on noncancellable purchase commitments	10,000	
Recovery of loss on purchase commitment (gain)		10,000
Cash		250,000

An increase above the contract price of $250,000 is not recognized because Bayshore has a noncancellable contract to buy at that price. Gains are not recognized until the earnings process is complete. The $5,000 gain ($255,000 − $250,000) will be realized through higher gross margins for Bayshore's products.

Accounting for commitments, including purchase commitments, is controversial among accountants. Some believe these contracts should be given formal recognition

---

[6] Even if no loss is likely, *CICA Handbook,* Sections 3280, "Contractual Obligations," and 3290, "Contingencies," require disclosure, either in a note or by way of entries in the accounts, as appropriate, of the nature and term of the obligation, the fixed amount of the obligation, and any amounts purchased to date under the obligation.

EXHIBIT 10–14
Effects of Inventory Errors
Illustrated—Periodic
Inventory System
(in $ thousands)

		Income Statement							Balance Sheet
			Cost of Goods Sold						
		Sales −	(BI +	PUR −	EI =	CGS) =	GM −	EXP = NI	Asset EI
Case	Correct ⟶	10	3	12	8	7	3	1 2	8
	Error								
A	EI, 1*	10	3	12	9*	6†	4*	1 3*	9*
B	EI and PUR, 1*	10	3	13*	9*	7	3	1 2	9*
C	EI, 1†	10	3	12	7†	8*	2†	1 1†	7†
D	EI and PUR, 1†	10	3	11†	7†	7	3	1 2	7†
E	BI, 1*	10	4*	12	8	8*	2†	1 1†	8
F	BI, 1†	10	2†	12	8	6†	4*	1 3*	8

Abbreviations: BI = Beginning inventory, PUR = Purchases, EI = Ending inventory, CGS = Cost of goods sold, GM = Gross margin, EXP = Expenses, and NI = Pretax net income.

* Overstatement $1 relative to correct amount.

† Understatement $1 relative to correct amount.

Hence, for case A, EI, 1 means the ending inventory is overstated by $1.

at the time binding agreements are signed. Others prefer recognition at the date of delivery. We prefer recognition at the date of the contract and support disclosure regardless of the decision concerning formal recognition.

Effects of Inventory Errors

Errors in measuring inventory quantities or values may occur because of the size of the inventory, the number of different kinds of items, their physical characteristics, and their means of storage. Inventory errors affect the financial statements. Overstatement of the *ending* inventory understates cost of goods sold and therefore overstates pretax income by the same amount. Understatement of the *ending* inventory understates pretax income by the same amount. Conversely, an overstatement of the *beginning* inventory understates pretax income, and an understatement of the beginning inventory overstates pretax income. Overstatement of purchases (assuming correct measurement of beginning and ending inventories) overstates cost of goods sold and understates pretax income by the same amount.

Inventory and purchases errors are common.[7] Exhibit 10–14, using the periodic inventory system, shows the *pretax effects* of several $1 errors, using the following relationships:

1. Cost of goods sold = Beginning inventory + Purchases − Ending inventory
2. Gross margin = Sales − Cost of goods sold
3. Income = Gross margin − Operating expenses

In cases A through F, assume that the *correct* figures are:

Sales $10
Beginning inventory 3
Purchases 12
Ending inventory 8
Expenses 1

Then the correct cost of goods sold is:

$$\$3 + \$12 - \$8 = \$7$$

---

[7] The dollar effects of these errors will differ depending on the cost flow method used (FIFO, LIFO, etc.).

The gross margin is:

$$\$10 - \$7 = \$3$$

And net income is:

$$\$3 - \$1 = \$2$$

Situation 1 Ending inventory *overstated*, beginning inventory *correct:*

Case A Ending inventory is overstated by $1, but the purchases amount is correct. This error causes cost of goods sold to be understated and both gross margin and income to be overstated by the same amount.

$$\text{Cost of goods sold} = \$3 + \$12 - \$9 = \$6 \text{ (understated by \$1)}$$
$$\text{Gross margin} = \$10 - \$6 = \$4 \text{ (overstated by \$1)}$$
$$\text{Net income} = \$4 - \$1 = \$3 \text{ (overstated by \$1)}$$

Case B Ending inventory and purchases are both overstated by the same amount, $1. These two errors have opposite effects; therefore, gross margin and income are correct. However, on the balance sheet, both inventory and accounts payable are overstated by the same amount.

$$\text{Cost of goods sold} = \$3 + \$13 - \$9 = \$7 \text{ (correct)}$$
$$\text{Gross margin} = \$10 - \$7 = \$3 \text{ (correct)}$$
$$\text{Net income} = \$3 - \$1 = \$2 \text{ (correct)}$$

Situation 2 Ending inventory *understated*, beginning inventory *correct:*

Case C Ending inventory is understated by $1, but the purchases amount is correct. This error causes cost of goods sold to be overstated and both gross margin and income to be understated by the same amount.

$$\text{Cost of goods sold} = \$3 + \$12 - \$7 = \$8 \text{ (overstated by \$1)}$$
$$\text{Gross margin} = \$10 - \$8 = \$2 \text{ (understated by \$1)}$$
$$\text{Net income} = \$2 - \$1 = \$1 \text{ (understated by \$1)}$$

Case D Ending inventory and purchases are both understated by the same amount, $1. These two errors have opposite effects; therefore, gross margin and income are correct. On the balance sheet, both inventory and accounts payable are understated by the same amount, $1.

$$\text{Cost of goods sold} = \$3 + \$11 - \$7 = \$7 \text{ (correct)}$$
$$\text{Gross margin} = \$10 - \$7 = \$3 \text{ (correct)}$$
$$\text{Net income} = \$3 - \$1 = \$2 \text{ (correct)}$$

Situation 3 Beginning inventory *overstated*, ending inventory *correct:*

Case E Beginning inventory is overstated by $1, but the purchases amount is correct. This error causes cost of goods sold to be overstated, while gross margin and net income are understated by the same amount, $1.

$$\text{Cost of goods sold} = \$4 + \$12 - \$8 = \$8 \text{ (overstated by \$1)}$$
$$\text{Gross margin} = \$10 - \$8 = \$2 \text{ (understated by \$1)}$$
$$\text{Net income} = \$2 - \$1 = \$1 \text{ (understated by \$1)}$$

Situation 4 Beginning inventory *understated*, ending inventory *correct:*

Case F   Beginning inventory is understated by $1, but the purchases amount is correct. This error causes cost of goods sold to be understated, while gross margin and net income are overstated by the same amount, $1.

$$\text{Cost of goods sold} = \$2 + \$12 - \$8 = \$6 \text{ (understated by \$1)}$$

$$\text{Gross margin} = \$10 - \$6 = \$4 \text{ (overstated by \$1)}$$

$$\text{Net income} = \$4 - \$1 = \$3 \text{ (overstated by \$1)}$$

Errors like these not only cause errors in current financial statements but also frequently in future amounts. That is, an error in the ending inventory, if not corrected, will cause a counterbalancing error in the next period because the ending and beginning inventories have opposite effects on the income amounts of the two consecutive periods.

For example, assume that case A in Exhibit 10–14 refers to 1995. Then net income is overstated by $1 in 1995. Thus, beginning inventory is overstated by $1 in 1996, causing income to be understated by $1 in 1996 (case E). Assuming no new errors in 1996, inventories would be reported at the correct amount. The 1995 and 1996 errors counterbalance each other because the effect of the errors in 1995 and 1996 net income cancel each other. Ending 1996 retained earnings is correctly stated. However, cost of goods sold and net income for each year are incorrect by the same amount. Chapter 24, "Accounting Changes and Error Corrections," considers the reporting guidelines for errors and error corrections.

CONCEPT REVIEW

1. What are the major uses of the retail inventory method?
2. Under what circumstances might inventories be valued at selling price?
3. Suppose there is an error in the ending inventory that results in an overstatement of $1. If no further errors are made, what accounts are affected for the current and next periods?

SUMMARY OF KEY POINTS

(L.O. 1)	1. The lower-of-cost-or-market (LCM) method of estimating inventory recognizes declines in market value (but not gains) in the period of decline. The inventory value obtained is conservative.
(L.O. 1)	2. The lower-of-cost-or-market method values inventories at market if market is below cost. Market may be interpreted to be net realizable value or replacement cost.
(L.O. 2)	3. The gross margin method is used to estimate inventory values when it is difficult or impractical to take a physical count of the goods. Items are grouped in broad categories, and different cost flow assumptions can be accommodated.
(L.O. 2)	4. The gross margin method is generally unacceptable for external financial reporting.
(L.O. 3)	5. The retail method of estimating inventory, used extensively by department stores, applies the ratio of actual cost to sales value to the ending inventory at sales value to estimate the inventory's cost.
(L.O. 4)	6. Returned, repossessed, and damaged items not in new condition are valued at replacement cost or net realizable value.
(L.O. 4)	7. The relative sales value method can be used to allocate the cost of different items purchased together when sales is the best indicator of their relative values.
(L.O. 4)	8. Losses on firm purchase commitments, when they can be reasonably estimated and are material, are recognized in the accounts if the loss is likely and can be estimated. But they need only be disclosed in the notes if the loss is just possible.
(L.O. 4)	9. Errors in establishing inventory values should be corrected because they produce both current and future mistakes in the accounts and financial statements.

REVIEW PROBLEM

Jensen Hardware experienced substantial damage to its inventory of 100 snow shovels carried over from the prior winter season. These shovels had originally cost Jensen $10 each when new, and Jensen sells them for $15 each. Jensen estimates it will take $400 to put the shovels in salable condition and another $200 to advertise them for special sale. Jensen believes the repaired shovels will sell for $12 each. Similarly damaged shovels from Jensen's current supplier of new shovels could be obtained for $5 each.

1. Assuming that the lower-of-cost-or-market rule can be used:
   a. Establish a net realizable value for the shovels.
   b. Determine a value for net realizable value less a normal profit margin.
   c. What value should be assigned to the repaired shovels using the lower-of-cost-or-market rule?
2. If these items were valued as damaged or distressed merchandise, what value should be used?
3. Should Jensen repair and sell the items?

SOLUTION

1. a. The net realizable value is:

$$\$12 - (\$4 + \$2) = \$6$$

   b. The only information available on normal profit margins is based on the new shovels, where the margin is $5 on a selling price of $15, or 33⅓%. Assuming that it is reasonable to apply the same margin to the repaired shovels, the net realizable value less a normal profit margin is:

$$\$6 - .333(\$12) = \$2$$

   c. Since replacement cost, $5, is between net realizable value, $6, and net realizable value less a normal profit margin, $2, the inventory would be valued at $5 a shovel, or a total of $500.
2. If the shovels were valued as damaged or distressed merchandise, Jensen would probably use the net realizable value of $6 a shovel, or $600 in total, because the shovels cannot be purchased in their present condition.
3. Jensen should repair and market the shovels since it can obtain $6 each for them. If Jensen does so, the firm will obtain a net of $600. This is likely to exceed their junk value. The $600 also exceeds the wholesale value of damaged shovels, estimated here at $5 each. Jensen should attempt to repair and market the shovels even though the company would need to write the current inventory down and recognize a loss of either $500 ($1,000 − $500, using LCM) or $400 ($1,000 − $600, using NRV).

QUESTIONS

1. Why is the LCM rule applied to inventory valuation?
2. Why are the ceiling and floor values used in determining market in the application of the LCM concept?
3. What is the holding loss (gain) recognized using the LCM, inventory allowance method, for each of the following years?

	Cost	Market
1994 Beginning inventory	$ 0	$ 0
Ending inventory	12,000	14,000
1995 Ending inventory	15,000	13,000
1996 Ending inventory	18,000	17,000
1997 Ending inventory	20,000	16,000
1998 Ending inventory	22,000	23,000

4. What basic assumption is implicit in the gross margin method?
5. Approximate the value of ending inventory, assuming the following data:

Cost of goods available for sale	$170,000
Sales	150,000
Gross margin rate (on sales)	25%

6. Assume that the 25% given in question 5 is the markup on cost of goods sold. Approximate the value of ending inventory.
7. Distinguish between (a) gross margin rate on sales, (b) gross margin percentage on cost of goods sold, (c) cost percentage, (d) markup on cost, and (e) markup on sales.
8. List four uses of the gross margin method.
9. Why is it frequently desirable to apply the gross margin method by classes of merchandise?
10. Explain the basic approach of the retail method of estimating inventories (FIFO and average). What data must be accumulated in order to apply the retail method?
11. The ending inventory estimated by the retail inventory method is $90,000. A physical inventory of the merchandise on hand extended at retail shows $75,000. Suggest possible reasons for the discrepancy.
12. What are the primary uses of the retail method of estimating inventories?
13. When are markdowns and markdown cancellations excluded in computing the cost ratio in the retail inventory method?
14. Explain the difference between the FIFO method with LCM and the average cost method with LCM, both under the retail method of estimating inventories.
15. How should damaged or obsolete merchandise on hand at the end of the period be valued for inventory purposes?
16. What types of inventory does GAAP allow to be measured at selling price in excess of cost?
17. What are the basic assumptions underlying the relative sales value method when used in allocating costs for inventory purposes?
18. Briefly outline the accounting and reporting of losses on purchase commitments when (a) the purchase contract is subject to revision or cancellation and (b) it is noncancellable and a loss is probable.
19. Explain the effect of each of the following errors in the ending inventory of a retail business (ignore income taxes):
    a. Incorrectly excluded 300 units of commodity C, valued at $3 per unit, from the ending inventory; the purchase was recorded.
    b. Incorrectly excluded 400 units of commodity D, valued at $4 per unit, from the ending inventory; the purchase was not recorded.
    c. Incorrectly included 100 units of commodity A, valued at $5 per unit, in the ending inventory; the purchase was recorded.
    d. Incorrectly included 200 units of commodity B, valued at $3 per unit, in the ending inventory; the purchase was not recorded.
20. Assume that inventory, cost $1,000, was sold on credit for $1,200 and held pending pickup by the customer. The goods were incorrectly included in the ending inventory. What is the pretax effect of this error if (a) the sale was not recorded or (b) the sale was correctly recorded? Assume that a periodic inventory system is used.

CASES

C 10–1
(L.O. 2)

Estimate the Inventory of Books   The manager of Seton Book Company, a book retailer, requires an estimate of the inventory cost for a quarterly financial report to the owner on March 31, 1995. In the past, the gross margin method was used because of the difficulty and expense of taking a physical inventory at interim dates. The company sells both fiction and nonfiction books. Due to their lower turnover rate, nonfiction books are typically marked up at a 60% rate on cost. Fiction, on the other hand, has a 40% markup rate on cost. The manager has used an average markup of 50% to estimate interim inventories.

You have been asked by the manager to estimate the book inventory cost as of March 31, 1995. The following data are available from Seton's accounting records:

	Fiction	Nonfiction	Total
Inventory, Jan. 1/95.	$100,000	$ 40,000	$140,000
Purchases	600,000	200,000	800,000
Freight.	5,000	2,000	7,000
Sales	590,000	160,000	750,000

Required

Round gross margin ratios to three decimal places.

1. Using an estimated markup on cost of 50%, compute the estimate of inventory as of March 31, 1995, based on the gross margin method applied to combined fiction and nonfiction books.

2. Compute the estimate of ending inventory as of March 31, 1995, based on the gross margin method applied separately to fiction and nonfiction books.

3. Which method is preferable in this situation? Explain.

C 10–2
(L.O. 4)

 Repurchase Commitment: Probable Loss   Stauffer Chemical Company is a major agricultural chemical supplier. The following excerpts are from an article in *The Wall Street Journal* (August 14, 1984, p. 2):

> Stauffer, which relies on agricultural chemicals for more than half its profits, has been hammered in the past three years by bad weather, depressed farm prices, and lowered farm output caused by a federal price-support program. In the summer of 1982, "aware that agricultural chemical sales for its 1982–83 season would probably fall off sharply," Stauffer undertook a plan to accelerate sales of certain products to dealers during fiscal 1982, according to the SEC.
>
> The commission charged that the plan was "tantamount to consignment sales which shouldn't have been recognized in 1982," and that Stauffer's annual report to shareholders for that year failed to reflect this fact.
>
> Stauffer, the SEC charged, offered its dealers incentives to take products during the fourth quarter of 1982. As a result, the company reported $72 million of revenue that ordinarily wouldn't have been booked until early 1983. By March 1983, according to the commission, Stauffer realized that it would have to "offer its distributors relief" from the oversupply of unsalable products. Stauffer offered dealers refunds for as much as 100% of unsold products taken in 1982, compared with 32% the previous year.
>
> Stauffer ended up refunding nearly 40% of its 1982 agricultural chemical sales, but failed to disclose the "substantial uncertainties" surrounding the sales in the annual report filed with the SEC in April 1983. The omission was "materially false and misleading," according to the SEC.
>
> "Their business was down and they wanted to accelerate sales," said a government official familiar with the year-long SEC investigation.
>
> H. Barclay Morley, Stauffer's chief executive officer, conceded that fears about the fading popularity of the company's best-selling farm products had prompted some of the accounting policies questioned by the SEC. "Our theory was that if the distributor had title on the product he would have more incentive to move it," Mr. Morley said. But he declined to comment on the SEC charge that the company was aware of severe problems with a substantial portion of its agricultural chemical sales when it filed its annual report.

Required   Discuss the appropriate accounting treatment and disclosures by Stauffer for its agricultural chemical inventories and sales in 1982.

C 10–3
(L.O. 1)

Magna   The 1992 annual report of Magna Corporation is reproduced at the end of this text.

Required
1. What method does Magna use to report its inventories? What cost flow approach is used?
2. Is this method permitted under GAAP?

EXERCISES

E 10–1
(L.O. 1)

Lower of Cost or Market

1. Ward Distribution Company has determined its December 31, 1995, inventory on a FIFO basis at $200,000. Information pertaining to that inventory follows:

Estimated selling price	$204,000
Estimated cost of disposal	10,000
Normal profit margin	30,000
Current replacement cost	180,000

Ward records losses that result from applying the lower-of-cost-or-market rule. At December 31, 1995, the loss that Ward should recognize is:

a. $0.
b. $6,000.
c. $14,000.
d. $20,000.

2. Under the lower-of-cost-or-market method, the replacement cost of an inventory item would be used as the designated market value:

    a. When it is below the net realizable value less the normal profit margin.

    b. When it is below the net realizable value and above the net realizable value less the normal profit margin.

    c. When it is above the net realizable value.

    d. Regardless of net realizable value.

3. The original cost of an inventory item is above the replacement cost. The replacement cost is above the net realizable value. Under the lower-of-cost-or-market method, the inventory item should be reported at its:

    a. Original cost.

    b. Replacement cost.

    c. Net realizable value.

    d. Net realizable value less the normal profit margin.

4. The original cost of an inventory item is above the replacement cost and above the net realizable value. The replacement cost is below the net realizable value less the normal profit margin. Under the lower-of-cost-or-market method the inventory item should be priced at its:

    a. Original cost.

    b. Replacement cost.

    c. Net realizable value.

    d. Net realizable value less the normal profit margin.

(AICPA adapted)

E 10–2
(L.O. 2, 3)

Gross Margin and Retail Inventory

1. Dart Company's accounting records included the following information:

Inventory, Jan. 1/96	$ 500,000
Purchases during 1996	2,500,000
Sales during 1996	3,200,000

A physical inventory taken on December 31, 1996, resulted in an ending inventory of $575,000. Dart's gross margin on sales has remained constant at 25% in recent years. Dart suspects that some inventory may have been taken by a new employee. At December 31, 1996, what is the estimated cost of missing inventory?

    a. $25,000.

    b. $100,000.

    c. $175,000.

    d. $225,000.

2. Lin Co. sells its merchandise at a gross margin of 30%. The following figures are among those pertaining to Lin's operations for the six months ended June 30, 1996:

Sales	$200,000
Beginning inventory	50,000
Purchases	130,000

On June 30, 1996, all of Lin's inventory was destroyed by fire. The estimated cost of this destroyed inventory was:

    a. $120,000.

    b. $70,000.

    c. $40,000.

    d. $20,000.

3. Dean Company uses the retail inventory method to estimate its inventory for interim statement purposes. Data relating to the computation of the inventory at July 31, 1997, are as follows:

	Cost	Retail
Beginning inventory, Feb. 1/97	$ 180,000	$ 250,000
Purchases	1,020,000	1,575,000
Markups, net		175,000
Sales		1,705,000
Estimated normal shoplifting losses		20,000
Markdowns, net		125,000

Under the approximate lower-of-average-cost-or-market retail method, Dean's estimated inventory at July 31, 1997, is:

 a. $90,000.
 b. $96,000.
 c. $102,000.
 d. $150,000.

4. At December 31, 1995, the following information was available from Palo Company's accounting records:

	Cost	Retail
Inventory, Jan. 1/95	$ 73,500	$101,500
Purchases	416,500	577,500
Additional markups	—	21,000
Available for sale	$490,000	$700,000

If sales were $553,000 and markdowns totalled $7,000, under the retail method (LCM), Palo Company's inventory at December 31, 1995 is:
 a. $98,000.
 b. $140,000.
 c. $102,900.
 d. $105,840.

E 10-3
(L.O. 1)

LCM: Maximum and Minimum The Updyck Company had 1,000 units of analog microchips in inventory at the end of the accounting period. The unit cost was $60; estimated distribution cost was $3 per unit; and the normal profit is $5 per unit. Compute the unit valuation of the inventory based on LCM under each separate case listed below.

Case	Anticipated Sales Price	Current Replacement Cost
a	$61	$50
b	66	57
c	68	61
d	50	44
e	59	57
f	53	48
g	73	59
h	65	61
i	70	62
j	60	59

E 10-4
(L.O. 1)

LCM: Maximum and Minimum The management of Tarry Hardware Company has taken the position that under the LCM procedure the two items listed below should be reported in the ending inventory at $16,600 (total). Do you agree? If not, indicate the correct inventory valuation by item. Show computations.

Handyman edgers: 300 on hand; cost, $22 each; replacement cost, $16; estimated sale price, $30; estimated distribution cost, $3 each; and normal profit, 10% of the sales price.

Handyman hedge clippers: 200 on hand; cost $50 each; replacement cost, $36 each; estimated sales price, $90; estimated distribution cost, $28; and normal profit, 20% of the sales price.

E 10-5
(L.O. 1)

LCM: Compute the Holding Gain or Loss The records of Loren Moving Company showed the following inventory data:

		Cost	Market
1994	Beginning inventory	$ 4,000	$ 4,000
1994	Ending inventory	5,000	6,000
1995	Ending inventory	8,000	7,500
1996	Ending inventory	4,000	3,000
1997	Ending inventory	12,000	10,000
1998	Ending inventory	8,000	7,000
1999	Ending inventory	10,000	11,000

Required

Compute the holding gain or loss recognized by Loren in each year due to the use of LCM.

E 10–6
(L.O. 1)

 LCM: Direct and Allowance Compared The inventories for years 1995 and 1996 are shown below for Colbert Corporation.

Inventory Date	Original Cost	LCM	Difference	Purchases
Jan. 1/95	$6,000	$6,000	0	—
Dec. 31/95	7,000	6,800	$400	$50,000
Dec. 31/96	9,000	9,000	0	56,000

Required

1. Give the journal entries to apply the LCM procedure to the inventories for 1995 and 1996, assuming that the company uses the inventory allowance method and periodic inventory procedures.
2. Give the journal entries to apply the LCM procedure to the inventories for 1995 and 1996, assuming that the company uses the direct inventory reduction method and periodic inventory procedures.
3. What are the primary advantages and disadvantages of each method?

E 10–7
(L.O. 2)

Gross Margin Method: Estimate the Ending Inventory You are auditing the records of Coldridge Corporation. A physical inventory has been taken by the company under your observation. However, the valuation extensions have not been completed. The records of the company provide the following data: sales, $315,000 (gross); return sales, $5,000 (returned to stock); purchases (gross), $155,000; beginning inventory, $100,000; freight-in, $7,000; and purchase returns and allowances, $2,000. The gross margin last period was 35% of net sales; you anticipate that it will be 25% for the year under audit.

Required

Estimate the cost of the ending inventory using the gross margin method. Show computations.

E 10–8
(L.O. 2)

 Gross Margin Method: Results Evaluated The records of Carson Company provided the following data for January for two products sold:

	Product A	Product B
Beginning inventory, January 1	$ 50,000	$ 60,000
Purchases during January	147,000	180,000
Freight-in on purchases	3,000	4,000
Sales revenue during January.	300,000	400,000

Gross margin rates on sales for the prior year were as follows: company overall, 45%; product A, 42%; and product B, 47%.

Required

1. Estimate the cost of the ending inventory separately, by products, and in the aggregate.
2. Under what conditions would one of your responses to (1) above be suspect?

E 10–9
(L.O. 2)

Gross Margin Method: Estimate a Fire Loss On November 15, 1995, a fire destroyed Youngstown Corporation's warehouse where croquet mallets were stored. It is estimated that $10,000 can be realized from sale of usable damaged inventory. The accounting records concerning croquet mallets reveal the following:

Inventory at Nov. 1/95.	$120,000
Purchases from Nov. 1/95 to Nov. 15/95.	140,000
Net sales from Nov. 1/95 to Nov. 15/95	200,000

Based on recent history, the gross margin has averaged 35% of net sales.

Required

Prepare a schedule to calculate the estimated loss of inventory based on the gross margin method. Show supporting computations.

(AICPA adapted)

E 10–10
(L.O. 2)

Gross Margin Method: Markup on Sales and Cost Compared Assume the following data for Cressy Company for the year 1996:

Sales revenue.	$120,000
Beginning inventory.	16,000
Purchases	80,000

Required

For each of the separate situations below, estimate the ending inventory (round all ratios to three decimal places):

a. Markup is 50% on cost.
b. Markup is 60% on sales.
c. Markup is 25% on cost.
d. Markup is 40% on sales.
e. Markup is 60% on cost.

E 10–11
(L.O. 2)

Gross Margin Method: Estimate Inventory Loss, Markup on Sales versus Costs   The books of Butler Company provided the following information:

Inventory, January 1	$ 10,000
Purchases to July 19	100,000
Net sales to July 19	85,000

Before the company opened for business on July 20, its assets were totally destroyed by flood. The insurance company adjuster found that the average rate of gross margin for the past few years had been 40%.

Required

What was the approximate value of the inventory destroyed, assuming the gross margin percentage given was based on (*a*) sale and (*b*) cost of goods sold? Round all ratios to two decimal places.

E 10–12
(L.O. 3)

Retail Inventory Method: Average LCM   Dan's Clothing Store values its inventory using the retail inventory method at the lower of average cost or market. The following data are available for the month of June 1995:

	Cost	Selling Price
Inventory, June 1	$ 53,800	$ 80,000
Markdowns		21,000
Markups		29,000
Markdown cancellations		10,000
Markup cancellations		9,000
Purchases	173,200	223,600
Sales		250,000
Purchase returns and allowances	3,000	3,600
Sales returns and allowances		10,000

Required

Prepare a schedule to compute the estimated inventory at June 30, 1995, at the lower of average cost or market using the retail inventory method. Round the cost ratio to three decimals.

(AICPA adapted)

E 10–13
(L.O. 3)

Retail Inventory Method: FIFO and Average   Chic Department Store uses the retail method of inventory. At the end of June, the records of the company provided the following information:

Purchases during June: at cost, $240,000; at retail, $400,000.

Sales during June: $350,000.

Inventory, June 1: at cost, $40,000; at retail, $75,000.

Required

Estimate the ending inventory and cost of goods sold for June, assuming (*a*) FIFO cost basis and (*b*) average cost basis. Show all computations (round cost ratios to two decimals).

E 10–14
(L.O. 3)

Retail Inventory Method: FIFO and Average   The records of Rainey Retailers showed the following data for January: beginning inventory at cost, $20,000, and $26,000 at selling price; purchase at cost, $150,000, and $300,000 at selling price; gross sales, $310,000; return sales, $5,000 (returned to stock); purchase returns at cost, $3,000, and $6,000 at selling price; and freight-in, $9,000.

Required

Determine the approximate valuation of the ending inventory using the retail inventory method (*a*) at average cost and (*b*) at FIFO. Show all computations. Round all cost ratios to two decimal places. Which is lower? What may have accounted for the result? Was LCM applied implicitly by Rainey? If so, explain.

E 10–15
(L.O. 1, 3)

Retail Inventory Method: FIFO and Average, LCM   Use the retail inventory method to estimate the ending inventory (*a*) at average cost with LCM and (*b*) FIFO with LCM for Post Corporation based on the following data (round all cost ratios to three decimal places):

	At Cost	At Retail
Beginning inventory.	$101,000	$150,000
Purchases	323,000	563,000
Purchases returned	6,000	10,000
Freight-in	8,000	
Additional markups.		12,000
Additional markup cancellations		5,000
Markdowns		9,000
Markdown cancellations.		2,000
Sales		540,000
Sales returned (and restored to inventory).		6,000

Required   How is LCM introduced into the computations? Explain the logic of this procedure. Will LCM always produce a lower inventory cost estimate under the retail method than FIFO or average without LCM?

E 10–16
(L.O. 1, 3)   **Retail Inventory Method: Average LCM, Discrepancy**   Jefferson Retail Company has just completed the annual physical inventory, which involved counting the goods on hand and then pricing them at selling prices. The inventory valuation derived in this manner amounted to $106,000. The records of the company provided the following data: beginning inventory, $80,000 at retail and $60,000 at cost; purchases (including freight-in and returns), $750,000 at retail and $500,000 at cost; additional markups, $20,000; additional markup cancellations, $8,000; gross sales, $733,000; return sales (restored to inventory), $13,000; and markdowns, $10,000.

Required   Round cost ratios to three decimal places.

1. Estimate the cost of the ending inventory, assuming average cost with LCM based on sales.
2. Estimate any inventory shortage.
3. Note any discrepancies and give possible reasons for them.

E 10–17
(L.O. 1, 3)   **Retail Inventory Method: LCM with Shrinkage**   Dundas Department Store uses the retail inventory method. Information relating to the computation of inventory for 1996 is as follows:

	At Cost	At Retail
Beginning inventory	$ 40,000	$ 80,000
Sales		600,000
Purchases.	300,000	590,000
Freight-in	8,000	
Markups		60,000
Markup cancellations		20,000
Markdowns		25,000
Markdown cancellations		5,000
Estimated normal shrinkage is 2% of sales.		

Required   Calculate the estimated ending inventory for 1996 at the lower of average cost or market. Show supporting calculations. Round all cost ratios to three decimal places.

(AICPA adapted)

E 10–18
(L.O. 4)   **Net Realizable Value of Damaged Goods: Entries**   A fire damaged some of the merchandise held for sale by AAA Appliance Company. Seven television sets and six stereo sets were damaged. They were not covered by insurance. The sets will be repaired and sold as used sets. Data are as follows:

	Per Set	
	Television	Stereo
Inventory (at cost)	$400	$250
Estimated cost to repair	50	30
Estimated cost to sell	20	20
Estimated sales price	200	110

Required
1. Compute the appropriate inventory net realizable value for each set.
2. Give the separate entries to record the damaged merchandise inventory for the television and stereo sets. Assume a perpetual inventory system.
3. Give the entries to record the subsequent repair of the television sets and the stereo sets (credit cash).

4. Give the entry to record sale for cash of two television sets and one stereo set; credit distribution costs in the entry to record the sale (it will be necessary to record payment of the distribution costs in a separate entry). Assume that the actual sales prices equalled the estimated sales prices.

E 10–19
(L.O. 4)

Relative Sales Value Method Chewy Nut, Inc., purchased 1,200 bags of pecans that cost $4,200. In addition, the company incurred $300 for transportation and grading. The pecans graded out as follows:

Grade	Quantity (bags)	Current Market Price per Bag
A	400	$6.75
B	600	6.00
C	100	4.50
Waste	100	

Required

The relative sales value method is used to apportion the joint costs. Give:

1. The entry for purchase, assuming a perpetual inventory system (show computations).
2. Valuation of ending inventory, assuming that the following quantities are on hand: grade A, 100 bags; grade B, 80 bags; and grade C, 40 bags.
3. The entry for sale of 20 bags of the grade A pecans at the above market price for cash.

E 10–20
(L.O. 4)

Relative Sales Value Method: Entries Acton Land Developers purchased and subdivided a tract of land that cost $900,000. The subdivision was divided on the following basis:

10% used for streets, alleys, and parks.
50% divided into 100 lots to sell for $4,000 each.
30% divided into 200 lots to sell for $3,000 each.
10% divided into 100 lots to sell for $2,000 each.

Required

1. Give the entry for the purchase of the lots. Use the relative sales value method to apportion the total cost of $900,000 to the three categories of lots. Assume a perpetual inventory system.
2. During the final month of the year, the paving was completed (included in the $900,000 cost), and sales were made. At the end of the first year, 20 of the $4,000 lots, 50 of the $3,000 lots, and 10 of the $2,000 lots are on hand. Compute the valuation of the inventory at year-end, and record the sales and cost of goods sold amounts for each category of lots. Assume cash sales only.

E 10–21
(L.O. 4)

Relative Sales Value Method: Land, Entries Alberta Development Company purchased a tract of land for development purposes. The tract was subdivided as follows: 30 lots to sell at $4,000 per lot and 80 lots to sell at $6,000 per lot. The tract cost $225,000, and an additional $15,000 was spent in general development costs, including streets and alleys.

Required

Assuming cost apportionment is based on the relative sales value method, give entries for (a) purchase of the tract and payment of the development costs, (b) sale of one $4,000 lot, and (c) sale of one $6,000 lot. Alberta uses a perpetual inventory system. Assume cash transactions.

E 10–22
(L.O. 4)

Relative Sales Value Method: Entry Quick Company purchased 2,630 bushels of ungraded apricots at $2 per bushel. The apricots were sorted as follows: grade 1, 1,000 bushels; grade 2, 700 bushels; grade 3, 900 bushels; and spoilage, 30 bushels. Handling and sorting costs amounted to $140. The current market prices for graded apricots were as follows: grade 1, $5 per bushel; grade 2, $3 per bushel; and grade 3, $1 per bushel. The company uses a perpetual inventory system.

Required

What entry should be made to record the purchase? Show computations of total costs for each grade, assuming the relative sales value method of cost apportionment is used.

E 10–23
(L.O. 4)

Loss on Purchase Commitment During 1995, Mossback Company signed a contract with Alpha Corporation to "purchase 15,000 subassemblies at $30 each during 1996."

Required

1. On December 31, 1995, end of the annual accounting period, the financial statements are to be prepared. Under what additional contractual and economic conditions should disclosure of the contract terms be made only by means of a note in the financial statements? Prepare an appropriate note. Assume that the cost of the subassemblies is dropping and the estimated current replacement cost is $425,000.
2. What contractual and economic conditions would require accrual of a loss? Give the accrual entry.

3. Assume that the subassemblies are received in 1995 when their cost was at the estimate given in (1) above. The contract was paid in full. Give the required entry.

E 10–24
(L.O. 4)

Loss on Purchase Commitments On November 1, 1995, Xit Corporation entered into a purchase contract (not subject to revision or cancellation) to purchase 10,000 units of Material X at $7 per unit (to be used in manufacturing). The contract period extends through February 1996. Xit's accounting period ends December 31. On December 31, 1995, Material X was being sold at a firm price of $5 per unit. On January 25, 1996, Xit purchased the 10,000 units; however, the market price per unit of Material X on this date was $4.75. The company uses a perpetual inventory system.

Required

Give all relevant entries or disclosure notes on November 1, 1995, December 31, 1995, and January 25, 1996. Explain the basis for each entry.

E 10–25
(L.O. 4)

Correct Four Inventory Errors on the Income Statement The records of Largo Company reflected the following:

Sales revenue		$205,000
Cost of goods sold:		
Beginning inventory	$ 10,000	
Purchases	105,000	
Goods available for sale.	115,000	
Ending inventory	25,000	90,000
Gross margin		115,000
Expenses		60,000
Income (pretax)		$ 55,000

The following errors were found that had not been corrected:

a. Revenues collected in advance amounting to $5,000 are included in the sales revenue amount.
b. Accrued expenses not recognized, $7,000.
c. Goods costing $10,000 were incorrectly included in the ending inventory (they were being held on consignment from Carter Company). No purchase was recorded.
d. Goods costing $5,000 were correctly included in the ending inventory; however, no purchase was recorded (assume a credit purchase).

Required

1. Prepare the income statement on a correct basis.
2. What amounts would be incorrect on the balance sheet if the errors are not corrected?

PROBLEMS

P 10–1
(L.O. 1)

Lower of Cost or Market Hanlon Company purchased a significant amount of raw materials inventory for a new product it is manufacturing. Hanlon purchased insurance on these raw materials while they were in transit from the supplier.

Hanlon uses the lower-of-cost-or-market rule for these raw materials. The replacement cost of the raw materials is above the net realizable value, and both are below the original cost.

Hanlon uses the average cost inventory method for these raw materials. In the last two years, each purchase has been at a lower price than the previous purchase, and the ending inventory quantity for each period has been higher than the beginning inventory quantity for that period.

Required

1. What is the theoretically appropriate method that Hanlon should use to account for the insurance costs on the raw materials incurred while they were in transit from the supplier? Why?
2. a. At what amount should Hanlon's raw materials inventory be reported on the balance sheet? Why?
   b. In general, why is the lower-of-cost-or-market rule used to report inventory?
3. What would have been the effect on ending inventory and cost of goods sold had Hanlon used the LIFO inventory method instead of the average cost inventory method for the raw materials? Why?

(AICPA adapted)

P 10–2
(L.O. 1)

 LCM: Three Ways to Apply   The information shown below relating to the ending inventory was taken from the records of Fast Print Company.

Inventory Classification	Quantity	Per Unit Cost	Per Unit Market
Paper:			
Stock X	200	$300	$330
Stock Y	60	250	230
Ink:			
Stock D	20	70	65
Stock E	10	55	62
Toner fluid:			
Stock A	8	75	70
Stock B	4	95	80
Stock C	7	100	110

Required

1. Determine the valuation of the above inventory at cost and at LCM, assuming application by (*a*) individual items, (*b*) classifications, and (*c*) total inventory. The unit costs of the three categories are significantly different; however, within each category the unit costs are similar.
2. Give the entry to record the ending inventory for each approach, assuming periodic inventory and the allowance method.
3. Of the three applications described in (1) above, which one appears preferable in this situation? Explain.

P 10–3
(L.O. 1)

LCM, Allowance Method: Recording and Reporting   The records of Cool Aire Company provide the following data relating to inventories for the years 1996 and 1997:

Inventory Date	Original Cost	At LCM
Jan. 1/96	$40,000	$40,000
Dec. 31/96	50,000	46,000
Dec. 31/97	46,000	45,000

Other data available are as follows:

	1996	1997
Sales	$240,000	$260,000
Purchases	135,000	150,000
Administrative and selling expenses	49,000	61,000

The company values inventories on the basis of LCM and uses the periodic inventory system. For problem purposes, ignore income taxes.

Required

1. In parallel columns, give the entries to apply the LCM procedure under the allowance method for 1996 and 1997.
2. Prepare an income statement for 1996 and 1997, and show the inventory amounts for the balance sheet.

P 10–4
(L.O. 1)

LCM: Allowance and Direct Methods Compared   Neutra Fresh Corporation uses a perpetual inventory system. The following data are available from company records:

	1995	1996
Sales revenue	$80,000	$120,000
Cost of goods sold	40,000	60,000
Remaining expenses	20,000	35,000

The cost of goods sold is based on inventories valued at cost. Additional information regarding inventories are as follows:

	Cost	Market
January 1, 1995	$ 6,000	$ 8,000
December 31, 1995	10,000	9,000
December 31, 1996	13,000	10,000

Required

1. In parallel columns, give the entries to apply the LCM procedure under the allowance method for 1995 and 1996. Prepare an income statement for 1995 and 1996. Ignore income taxes.
2. In parallel columns, give the entries to apply the LCM procedure under the direct inventory reduction method for 1995 and 1996. Prepare an income statement for 1995 and 1996. Ignore income taxes.

P 10–5
(L.O. 1)

LCM: Allowance and Direct Methods Compared   York Corporation's summarized income statements for 1995 and 1996 are shown below. The inventories given below were valued at cost.

	1995	1996
Sales	$107,000	$97,000
Cost of goods sold:		
Beginning inventory	25,000	20,000
Purchases	75,000	73,000
Total	100,000	93,000
Ending inventory	20,000	15,000
Cost of goods sold	80,000	78,000
Gross margin	27,000	19,000
Less: Operating expenses	14,000	12,000
Pretax income	$ 13,000	$ 7,000

The inventories valued at LCM would have been as follows: at the beginning of 1995, $25,000 (the same as cost); end of 1995, $18,000; and end of 1996, $12,000.

Required

1. Restate the 1995 and 1996 income statements applying the LCM rule for each of the following procedures. Disregard income taxes.
   a. Direct inventory reduction method, where the inventory holding loss is not reported separately.
   b. Allowance method.
2. Which procedure is preferable? Why?

P 10–6
(L.O. 2)

Gross Margin Method: Inventory Fire Loss, Evaluation   The records of Georgetown Company provided the following information on September 1, 1995:

Inventory, Jan. 1/95	$ 50,000
Purchases, January 1 to September 1	300,000
Sales, January 1 to September 1	400,000
Purchase returns and allowances	3,000
Sales returns (goods returned to stock)	5,000
Freight-in	4,000

A fire completely destroyed the inventory on September 1, 1995, except for goods marked to sell at $6,000, which had an estimated residual value of $4,000, and for goods in transit to which Georgetown had ownership; the purchase had been recorded. Invoices recorded on the latter show merchandise cost of $2,000 and freight-in of $100. The average rate of gross margin on sales in recent years has been 30%.

Required

1. Compute the inventory fire loss.
2. Under what conditions would your response to (1) above be questionable?

P 10–7
(L.O. 2)

Gross Margin Method: Use in Profit Planning   The Bach Company is developing a profit plan. The following data were estimated for 1996 and 1997.

a. January 1, 1996, estimated inventory, $85,000.
b. Estimated average rate of gross margin on sales, 40%.

Required   Complete the following profit plan:

	Profit Plan Estimates	
	1996	1997
Sales planned	$160,000	$190,000
Cost of goods sold:		
Beginning inventory	?	?
Purchases budget	120,000	130,000
Total goods available	?	?
Less: Ending inventory	?	?
Cost of goods sold	?	?
Gross margin planned	?	?

P 10–8
(L.O. 2)   **Gross Margin Method: Inventory Burned, Indemnity**   Wood Wholesale Company's warehouse burned on April 1, 1996. The following information (up to the date of the fire) was taken from the records of the company: inventory, January 1, $30,000; gross sales, $160,000; purchases, $90,000; sales returns (restored to stock), $5,000; purchase returns and allowances, $2,000; and freight-in, $8,000. The cost of goods sold and gross margin for the past three years were as follows:

Year	Cost of Goods Sold	Gross Margin
1993	$500,000	$125,000
1994	460,000	120,000
1995	500,000	120,000

Required   1. Estimate the cost of the inventory destroyed in the fire.
2. Under what conditions would your response to (1) above be questionable?
3. The insurance company pays indemnity on market value at date of the fire. What amount would you recommend that Wood submit as an insurance claim? Explain.

P 10–9
(L.O. 2)   **Gross Margin Method: Inventory Records Destroyed, Income Statement**   In the past, Swat Corporation valued inventories at cost. At the end of the current period, the inventory was valued at 25% of selling price as a matter of convenience. However, the cost ratio is not 25%. The current financial statements have been prepared and the inventory sheets inadvertently destroyed; consequently, you find it impossible to reconstruct the ending inventory at actual cost per the physical count. Fortunately, the following data are available:

Sales	$400,000
Ending inventory (at 25% of selling price)	25,000
Purchases (at cost)	150,000
Pretax income	40,000
Beginning inventory (at cost)	30,000

Required   Prepare a corrected (and detailed) income statement. Show computations and round the cost ratio to two decimal places.

P 10–10
(L.O. 3)   **Retail Inventory Method**   Hudson Company, which is both a wholesaler and a retailer, purchases its inventories from various suppliers. Additional facts for Hudson's wholesale operations are as follows:
- Hudson incurs substantial warehousing costs.
- Hudson uses the lower-of-cost-or-market method.
- The replacement cost of the inventories is below the net realizable value and above the net realizable value less the normal profit margin. The original cost of the inventories is above the replacement cost and below the net realizable value.

Additional facts for Hudson's retail operations are as follows:
- Hudson determines the estimated cost of its ending inventories held for sale at retail using the retail inventory method, which approximates lower of average cost or market.
- Hudson incurs markups and net markdowns.

Required

1. Theoretically, how should Hudson account for the warehousing costs related to its wholesale inventories? Why?
2. *a.* In general, why is the lower-of-cost-or-market method used to report inventory?
   b. At which amount should Hudson's wholesale inventories be reported on the balance sheet? Explain the application of the lower-of-cost-or-market method in this situation.
3. In the calculation of the cost (to retail) ratio used to determine the estimated cost of its ending retail inventories, how should Hudson treat:
   a. Freight-in costs?
   b. Net markups?
   c. Net markdowns?
4. Why does Hudson's retail inventory method approximate lower of average cost or market?

(AICPA adapted)

P 10–11
(L.O. 3)

Retail Inventory Method: Average, FIFO, and LCM The records of Diskount Department Store provided the following data for 1995:

Sales (gross)	$800,000
Return sales (restored to inventory)	2,000
Additional markups	9,000
Additional markup cancellations	5,000
Markdowns	7,000
Purchases:	
At retail	850,000
At cost	459,500
Purchase returns:	
At retail	4,000
At cost	2,200
Freight on purchases	7,000
Beginning inventory:	
At cost	45,000
At retail	80,000
Markdown cancellations	3,000

Required

Estimate the valuation of the ending inventory and cost of goods sold, assuming the following cases. Show computations, carry cost ratios to four decimal places, and round inventory to the nearest dollar.

Case A—average cost (for illustrative purposes only).

Case B—average cost with LCM.

Case C—FIFO cost (for illustrative purposes only).

Case D—FIFO cost with LCM.

P 10–12
(L.O. 3)

Retail Inventory Method: An Audit Test Auditors are examining the accounts of Acton Retail Corporation. They were present when Acton's personnel physically counted the Acton inventory; however, the auditors made their own tests. Acton's records provided the following data for the current year:

	At Retail	At Cost
Inventory, January 1	$ 300,000	$180,500
Net purchases	1,453,000	955,000
Freight-in		15,000
Additional markups	31,000	
Additional markup cancellations	14,000	
Markdowns	8,000	
Employee discounts	2,000	
Sales	1,300,000	
Inventory, December 31 (per physical count valued at retail)	475,000	

Required

1. Compute the ending inventory at average cost and LCM as an audit test of the overall reasonableness of the physical inventory count. Round the cost ratio to three decimals.

2. Note any discrepancies indicated. What factors should the auditors consider in reconciling any difference in results from the analysis?
3. What accounting treatment (if any) should be accorded the discrepancy?

P 10–13
(L.O. 1, 4)

 Inventory Concepts, Recording, Adjusting, Closing, Reporting Gamit Company completed the following selected (and summarized) transactions during 1995:

a. Merchandise inventory on hand January 1, 1995, $105,000 (at cost, which was the same as LCM).
b. During the year, purchased merchandise for resale at quoted price of $200,000 on credit, terms 2/10, n/30. Immediately paid 85% of the cash cost.
c. Paid freight on merchandise purchased, $10,000 cash.
d. Paid 40% of the accounts payable within the discount period. The remaining payables were unpaid at the end of 1995 and were still within the discount period.
e. Merchandise that had a quoted price of $3,000 (terms 2/10, n/30) was returned to a supplier. A cash refund of $2,940 was received because the items were unsatisfactory.
f. During the year, sold merchandise for $370,000, of which 10% was on credit, terms 2/10, n/30.
g. A television set caught fire and was damaged internally; it was returned by the customer because it was guaranteed. The set was originally sold for $600, of which $400 cash was refunded. The set cost the company $420. Estimates are that the set, when repaired, can be sold for $240. Estimated repair costs are $50, and selling costs are estimated to be $10.
h. Operating expenses (administrative and distribution) paid in cash, $120,000; includes the $10 in (g).
i. Excluded from the purchase given in (b) and from the ending inventory was a shipment for $7,000 (net of discount). This shipment was in transit, FOB shipping point at December 31, 1995. The invoice was on hand.
j. Paid $50 cash to repair the damaged television set; see (g) above.
k. Sold the damaged television set for $245; selling costs allocated, $10.
l. The ending inventory (as counted) was $110,000 at cost, and $107,000 at market. Assume an average income tax rate of 40%.

Accounting policies followed by the company are (1) the annual accounting period ends December 31, (2) a periodic inventory system is used, (3) purchases and accounts payable are recorded net of cash discounts, (4) freight charges are allocated to merchandise when purchased, (5) all cash discounts are taken, (6) used and damaged merchandise is carried in a separate inventory account, (7) inventories are reported at LCM and the allowance method is used, and (8) sales are recorded at gross.

Required
1. Give the entries for transactions (b) through (k).
2. Give the end-of-period entries (adjusting and closing).
3. Prepare a multiple-step income statement (1995). Assume that 20,000 common shares are outstanding.
4. Show how the ending inventory should be reported on the balance sheet at December 31, 1995.

P 10–14
(L.O. 4)

Relative Sales Value Method Hill Top Grocers Co-op purchased a large quantity of mixed grapefruit for $41,000, which was graded at a cost of $1,000, as indicated below. Sales (at the sales prices indicated) and losses (frozen, rotten, etc.) are also listed.

Grade	Baskets Bought	Sales Price per Basket	Baskets Sold	Baskets Spoiled
A	5,000	$4.00	2,000	50
B	4,000	3.00	3,000	70
C	10,000	2.00	8,000	30
Culls.	1,000	.50	900	

Required
1. Give the entry for the purchase, assuming a perpetual inventory system. Show computations.
2. Give entries to record the sales and cost of goods sold.
3. Give the entry for the losses, assuming that the losses are recorded separately from cost of goods sold.
4. Determine the valuation of the ending inventory.
5. Compute the direct contribution to pretax income for each grade of grapefruit. (Disregard operating, administrative, and selling expenses.)

P 10–15
(L.O. 4)

Relative Sales Value Method: Land   On January 1, 1994, Bob and Sam each invested $100,000 cash in a partnership for the purpose of purchasing and subdividing a tract of land for residential building purposes.

On June 1, they purchased a 30-acre subdivision at $5,000 per acre, paying $50,000 in cash and giving a one-year, 15% interest-bearing note (with mortgage) for the balance. Development costs amounted to an additional $110,000 (paid in cash).

The property was subdivided into 300 lots, 200 of which were to sell at $4,000 each and the balance at $5,000 each.

During July through December 1994, the following sales were made for half cash and half interest-bearing notes receivable due in six months from date of sale.

	Lots
Group A (sold at $4,000 each)	50
Group B (sold at $5,000 each)	60

Cash collections on the notes receivable up to December 31, 1994, amounted to $49,000 principal plus $1,000 interest. Accrued interest recorded at December 31, 1994, amounted to $1,000.

Operating and selling expenses amounted to $125,000 by the end of December 1994. No payment was made on the note payable.

Required
1. Give the entries for all of the above transactions. Disregard income taxes.
2. Prepare an income statement for 1994.
3. Compute the valuation of the inventory of unsold lots on December 31, 1994.

P 10–16
(L.O. 4)

Correcting Errors on an Income Statement   Dexter Company has completed the income statement and balance sheet (summarized and uncorrected, shown below) at December 31, 1995. Subsequently, during an audit, the following items were discovered:

a. Expenses amounting to $7,000 were not accrued.
b. A conditional sale on credit for $12,000 was recorded on December 31, 1995. The goods, which cost $8,000, were included in the ending inventory; they had not been shipped because the customer's address was not known and the credit had not been approved. Ownership had not passed.
c. Merchandise purchased on December 31, 1995, on credit for $6,000 was included in the ending inventory because the goods were on hand. A purchase was not recorded because the accounting department had not received the invoice from the vendor.
d. The ending inventory was overstated by $15,000 because of an addition error on the inventory sheet.
e. A sale return (on account) on December 31, 1995, was not recorded: sales amount was $15,000 and cost, $8,000. The ending inventory did not include the goods returned.

Required
Set up a schedule similar to the one below; make the corrections and derive the corrected amounts. Indicate increases and decreases for each transaction. Explain any assumptions made with respect to doubtful items. Disregard income taxes.

	Uncorrected Amounts	Items for Correction (a)	(b)	(c)	(d)	(e)	Corrected Amounts
Income Statement							
Sales revenue.	$90,000						
Cost of goods sold	50,000						
Gross margin	40,000						
Expenses	30,000						
Income	$10,000						
Balance Sheet							
Accounts receivable	$42,000						
Inventory	20,000						
Remaining assets	30,000						
Accounts payable	11,000						
Remaining liabilities	6,000						
Common stock	60,000						
Retained earnings	15,000						

P 10–17
(L.O. 4)

Correcting Inventory Errors   On January 3, 1996, Jonah Corporation engaged an independent accountant to perform an audit for the year ended December 31, 1995. The company used a periodic inventory system. The accountant did not observe the inventory count on December 31, 1995; as a result, a special examination was made of the inventory records.

The financial statements prepared by the company (uncorrected) showed the following: ending inventory, $72,000; accounts receivable, $60,000; accounts payable, $30,000; sales, $400,000; net purchases, $160,000; and pretax income, $51,000.

The following data were found during the audit:

a. Merchandise received on January 2, 1996, costing $800, was recorded on December 31, 1995. An invoice on hand showed the shipment was made FOB supplier's warehouse on December 31, 1995. Because the merchandise was not on hand at December 31, 1995, it was not included in the inventory.

b. Merchandise that cost $18,000 was excluded from the inventory, and the related sale for $23,000 was recorded. The goods had been segregated in the warehouse for shipment; there was no contract for sale but a "tentative order by phone."

c. Merchandise that cost $10,000 was out on consignment to Bar Distributing Company and was excluded from the ending inventory. The merchandise was recorded as a sale of $25,000 when shipped to Bar on December 2, 1995.

d. A sealed packing case containing a product costing $900 was in Jonah's shipping room when the physical inventory was taken. It was included in the inventory because it was marked "Hold for customer's shipping instructions." Investigation revealed that the customer signed a purchase contract dated December 18, 1995, but that the case was shipped and the customer billed on January 10, 1996. A sale was recorded on December 18, 1995.

e. A special item, fabricated to order for a customer, was finished and in the shipping room on December 31, 1995. The customer had inspected it and was satisfied. The customer was billed in full on that date. The item was included in inventory at cost, $1,000, because it was shipped on January 4, 1996.

f. Merchandise costing $1,500 was received on December 28, 1995. The goods were excluded from inventory, and a purchase was not recorded. The auditor located the related papers in the hands of the purchasing agent; they indicated, "On consignment from Baker Company."

g. Merchandise costing $2,000 was received on January 8, 1996, and the related purchase invoice recorded January 9. The invoice showed the shipment was made on December 29, 1995, FOB destination. The merchandise was excluded from the inventory.

h. Merchandise that cost $11,000 and was sold on December 31, 1995, for $16,000 was included in the ending inventory. The sale was recorded. The goods were in transit; however, a clerk failed to note that the goods were shipped FOB shipping point.

i. Merchandise that cost $6,000 was excluded from the ending inventory and not recorded as a sale for $7,500 on December 31, 1995. The goods had been specifically segregated. According to the terms of the contract of sale, ownership will not pass until actual delivery.

j. Merchandise that cost $15,000 was included in the ending inventory. The related purchase has not been recorded. The goods had been shipped by the vendor FOB destination; and the invoice, but not the goods, was received on December 30, 1995.

k. Merchandise in transit that cost $7,000 was excluded from inventory because it was not on hand. The shipment from the vendor was FOB shipping point. The purchase was recorded on December 29, 1995, when the invoice was received.

l. Merchandise in transit that cost $13,000 was excluded from inventory because it had not arrived. Although the invoice had arrived, the related purchase was not recorded by December 31, 1995. The merchandise was shipped by the vendor FOB shipping point.

m. Merchandise that cost $8,000 was included in the ending inventory because it was on hand. The merchandise had been rejected because of incorrect specifications and was being held for return to the vendor. The merchandise was recorded as a purchase on December 26, 1995.

Required

1. Prepare a schedule with one column for each of the six financial statement items given in the problem introduction (starting with the uncorrected balances) plus a column for explanations. Show the specific corrections to each balance and the corrected balances. Explain the basis for your decision on all items.

2. Give the entry to correct the accounts, assuming that the accounts for 1995 have been closed.

(AICPA adapted)

ANALYZING FINANCIAL STATEMENTS

All questions in this section are based on information taken from the financial statements of actual companies.

A 10–1
(L.O. 1)

 Lower of Cost or Market   The partial note reproduced here describes the inventory accounting of American Home Products for 1992. American Home Products makes prescription drugs, nutritionals, food products, over-the-counter medications, and medical devices, supplies, and instruments. The company's products include Premarin, Advil, Anacin, Dristan, Robitussin, and the Chef Boyardee prepared pasta line.

Inventories are valued at the lower of cost or market. Inventories valued under the last-in, first-out (LIFO) method amounted to $265,816,000 at December 31, 1992 and $234,929,000 at December 31, 1991. Current value exceeded LIFO value by $52,894,000 and $56,428,000 at December 31, 1992 and 1991, respectively. The remaining inventories are valued under the first-in, first-out (FIFO) or the average cost method.

Inventories at December 31 consisted of:

	1992	1991
	(in thousands)	
Finished goods	$477,226	$404,477
Work in progress	197,368	166,193
Materials and supplies.	269,974	271,374
	$944,568	$842,044

Required

1. What is your estimate of the replacement cost of the company's inventories on December 31, 1992?
2. Do you see any limitations to your answer?
3. Assuming that your answer to (1) is correct, what would be the impact on the company's accounts if the replacement cost were used to value inventories? Describe in general terms rather than with specific numerical values.

A 10–2
(L.O. 1, 4)

Inventory Valuation: Distress Situation   The following quotes are taken from "Costly Postponement," written by Graham Button and appearing in the September 3, 1990, issue of *Forbes*.

In March 1988 investors in General Homes Corp. learned that the Houston-based home builder was marking down the value of its assets, primarily land inventories, by $91 million. Last year came another shocker—a $113 million writedown.

All told, General Homes' losses have exceeded $285 million over the last two years—no small feat for a company that earned $19 million in 1983. Its stock, which traded as high as 21¼, was selling at ⅜ before trading was suspended in April.

What's going on here? Did the assets really decline by almost 40% in just two years? Or should some of those writedowns have come earlier? After all, the Texas real estate market hit bottom in 1987, and yet the company's total chargeoffs between 1984 and 1987 were a mere $8 million.

Finally, in March 1988, the company changed its accounting method on many of its troubled properties from the "lower of cost or net realizable value" to the "lower of cost or fair market"—resulting in the $91 million hit. It made the same switch last year on just about all of its remaining properties—writing off another $113 million and finally acknowledging that development was impossible.

Given the market context and the fact that General Homes had had negative cash flow since autumn 1986, bondholders argue that General Homes should have made that admission years earlier and that assets and earnings were way overstated in 1986 and 1987. Which in turn kept the company from running afoul of its revolving credit agreement.

Required

1. Was an earlier write-down of General Homes land inventories appropriate? Explain why or why not. Give a supporting example.
2. If you argued for a write-down, when should it have been made, given the facts as reported? Why do you believe the firm did not write down its land inventories?
3. Where would you look for support for your position?

A 10–3
(L.O. 4)

Inventory Values: Replacement Cost, International Firm   The British Petroleum Company (BP) is the parent company of one of the world's largest international petroleum and petrochemical groups. It engages in exploration and production, refining and marketing, and chemicals. BP also has interests in nutrition.

BP provides the following in the notes to its 1991 annual report:

The accounts are prepared under the historic cost convention . . . The historic cost results include stock holding gains or losses.* Stock holding gains or losses represent the difference between the replacement cost of sales and the historical cost of sales calculated using the first-in, first-out method.

BP's income statement contains the following before-tax figures (in millions of British pounds):

	1991	1990
Replacement cost operating profit	£2,555	£2,962
Stock holding gains (losses)	(629)	477
Total	£1,926	£3,439

* Under British accounting, inventories are often called *stocks*.

Required

1. What other title would you give to the amount indicated as Total?
2. What would you estimate BP's income to be in 1991 if BP used a LIFO cost flow assumption to value its inventories?

A 10–4
(L.O. 2, 3)

Gross Margin and Retail Inventory Method   On pages D1 and D8 of the December 8, 1992, *New York Times,* Floyd Norris reported that Eagle Hardware and Garden's shares had dropped over 20% the previous day. Eagle operates home improvement stores.

At one point in the prior month, Eagle's shares sold for over $40. On closing December 7, they were at $26.75.

The problem was in Eagle's reported inventories. Audited statements presented in February 1992 were later withdrawn because the figures were not reliable. The following paragraph appears in the article on page D8:

The inventory problems reflect the way companies calculate profits. Sales for a retailer like Eagle are relatively easy to measure, but to get a gross profit number the retailer must estimate the original cost of the items that were sold. To do that, Eagle has relied on estimates of gross profit margins. It now appears those estimates were higher than reality called for. With its new systems, many of those mistakes should be eliminated. In the meantime, Mr. Takata (Eagle's president) said, "We will be as conservative as we can be" in making the estimates.

Required

1. What method do you believe Eagle is using to determine its inventory values?
2. What do you believe the problem is?

11 Capital Assets: Acquisition, Disposal, and Exchange

LEARNING OBJECTIVES

After you have studied this chapter, you will be able to:

1 **Apply the general accounting principle for valuation of capital assets at acquisition.**

2 **Distinguish between expenditures that are capitalized to plant assets and those that are expensed.**

3 **Apply specific valuation principles for capital assets acquired by means other than cash purchase.**

4 **Determine the interest to be capitalized during the construction of capital assets, and present the arguments for and against interest capitalization.**

5 **Account for the disposal of capital assets and the ensuing gains and losses.**

6 **Account for exchanges of nonmonetary assets.**

7 **Apply the general principle underlying accounting for post-acquisition costs and the alternate accounting approaches.**

INTRODUCTION

How a company measures and classifies its expenditures for capital assets, the long-term assets a company employs in its main revenue-generating activities, can have a considerable effect on earnings and balance sheet reporting. When Tridel Enterprises Inc. took a $135 million write-down, shareholders' equity was more than wiped out and the price of Tridel shares dropped by almost 40%.[1]

Chambers Development Company reported a similar earnings restatement for 1991 when it announced a write-off of nearly $50 million. The write-off corrected earlier capitalization into fixed assets (landfills) of costs such as executive salaries for time spent in developing landfills, public relations and legal costs, and

---

[1] "Tridel Holders Hit with Bad News," *Report on Business,* April 28, 1994, p. B9.

executive travel expenses. As a result of the accounting change, the price of Chambers shares fell 63% in one day.[2]

These examples point to the importance of correct recognition of expenditures as capital assets or expenses and the degree to which investors rely on the resulting earnings figures. Closely related to this issue is whether interest should be capitalized during construction. Chambers's restated earnings of $1.5 million reflect only 20% of its total interest cost. The remaining 80%, or $29 million, was capitalized to projects under construction. Did Chambers's economic position improve because it incurred a liability for interest cost? Does the firm have $29 million more disposable income as a result?

The common shares of firms that have large holdings in land and natural resources can become attractive investments simply by virtue of these holdings. Consider that St. Joe Paper, which produces 2% of the supply of corrugated paper boxes in the United States, owns 3% of all the land in Florida! Several stock analysts have recommended St. Joe Paper common shares on that basis alone, especially because some of the property is believed to hold reserves of oil.[3] The market price of St. Joe Paper common shares fluctuates in part as the prospects for exploiting its real estate holdings change, even though the recorded value of land on St. Joe Paper's balance sheet remains unchanged.

Capital assets often constitute the largest single asset category for corporations, and the recorded value of plant assets is the basis for subsequent depreciation. This chapter discusses the valuation of plant assets acquired using debt, equity securities, or other assets; the valuation of self-constructed assets; accounting for the disposal and exchange of nonmonetary assets; and accounting for post-acquisition costs.

VALUATION OF CAPITAL ASSETS AT ACQUISITION

The focus of this chapter and the next two is on assets often described as *capital* or *operational assets* because they are used in the operations of a business and are not held for resale.

Classifying Capital Assets

For accounting purposes, capital assets are usually classified into tangible and intangible assets.

Tangible capital assets:
- Are actively used in operations rather than held as an investment or for resale.
- Are expected to provide benefits beyond the current accounting period.
- Have physical substance.

Tangible capital assets are typically reported in the balance sheet under headings such as *property, plant, and equipment,* or *plant assets,* or *tangible fixed assets.* Tangible capital assets are grouped into three subclassifications:
- Assets subject to depreciation, such as buildings, equipment, furniture, and fixtures.
- Assets subject to depletion, such as mineral deposits and timber tracts.
- Land, which is not subject to depreciation or depletion.

Intangible capital assets:
- Are actively used in operations rather than held as an investment or for resale.
- Are expected to provide future benefits beyond the current accounting period.
- Do not have their value tied to physical substance.

The value of intangible assets is represented by rights that produce an operating, financial, or income-producing benefit. Examples are goodwill, patents, copyrights,

---

[2] "Chambers Development Co. May Face Further Write-Offs over Accounting," *The Wall Street Journal,* April 10, 1992, p. A5.

[3] "St. Joe Paper Stock Wins Analysts' Plaudits, but Real Estate Slump May Defer Rewards," *The Wall Street Journal,* March 17, 1992, p. C2.

and trademarks. The cost of an intangible asset is periodically amortized over the asset's useful life. Intangible assets are discussed in Chapter 13.

Expenditures related to the acquisition and use of capital assets are either capital expenditures or revenue expenditures. **Capital expenditures** are expenditures expected to yield benefits beyond the current accounting period. Therefore, such expenditures are **capitalized,** meaning they are treated as asset acquisitions and debited to an appropriate asset account. The cost of a capital asset is recognized as an expense in current and future periods through depreciation, amortization, or depletion. **Revenue expenditures,** such as ordinary repairs, are expected to yield benefits only in the current accounting period. Therefore, they are recorded in expense accounts and matched against the revenue of the period.

It is important to classify expenditures correctly. An incorrect classification affects reported income for the entire life of the asset. If costs are misclassified as capital expenditures and carried as asset accounts, for example, then current income is overstated and future income is understated by depreciation of those costs.

General Principles for the Valuation of Capital Assets

Section 3060, paragraph .07 of the *CICA Handbook* defines cost as:

> the amount of consideration given up to acquire, construct, develop, or better a capital asset and includes all costs directly attributable to the acquisition, construction, development or betterment of the capital asset including installing it in the location and in the condition necessary for its intended use.

Historical cost, representing arm's-length transactions between unrelated parties, is considered objective and reliable.

Historical acquisition cost is the cash outlay, or equivalent, made to acquire an asset and prepare it for use. It represents the fair market value of the asset at time of acquisition. When plant assets are acquired for non-cash consideration, the assets are recorded at either the market value of the consideration or the market value of the acquired asset, whichever amount is more objective. Accounting for asset exchanges includes an exception to this principle and is discussed later.

The list (sticker) price of a plant asset is not necessarily the asset's market value. List prices are often merely a starting point for negotiations between buyer and seller, with each party using experience and knowledge to bargain for a favourable price.

Historical cost is often criticized as irrelevant when prices of specific assets change. Price changes can render the recorded book value of assets meaningless. An extreme example arose when Power Corporation purchased the Polo Ralph Lauren building in New York City in 1989 for $43 million, paying a record $1,600 per square foot. The building was built in 1894 at a cost of $500,000, less than $19 per square foot.[4] Valuation bases other than historical cost exist, although they are not in common use. These alternative valuation bases include replacement cost (a measure of entry value), net realizable value (a measure of exit value), and price-level-adjusted values (a measure of current value).

In addition to the net invoice price, many other kinds of costs are incurred to acquire plant assets, including sales tax, freight, back property taxes assumed by the buyer, import duties, ownership registration, installation, commissions, interest during construction, and break-in costs. Break-in costs include practice runs with machinery and initial setup before the first production run. Expenditures to make the asset ready for use are also capitalized because they are required to obtain the benefits expected of the asset.

The matching principle requires that costs be deferred or held in asset accounts until revenues are generated. As plant assets are placed into service, the historical acquisition cost is matched against revenues through depreciation. Depreciation is not recognized until the asset begins to produce benefits.

---

4 "Power Corp. Buys New York Building for $1,600 a Foot," *The Wall Street Journal,* July 31, 1989, p. A5.

Costs Not Capitalized   Not all expenditures associated with acquiring plant assets are capitalized. For example, a discount is deducted from the invoice price whether taken or not, for purposes of valuing the asset. Discounts not taken are recorded as a financing expense; they do not increase the value of the asset, but rather represent a financing cost, as in the case of inventories, discussed in Chapter 9.

Interest on debt incurred to purchase plant assets is not capitalized because the asset is already in its intended condition for use. Prepaid interest, called *points,* and loan origination fees charged by lending institutions are also period expenses.

The costs of training employees to use plant assets are not capitalized. Training costs enhance the value of employees, not assets.[5] Annual property taxes and insurance costs are not capitalized either. These costs only maintain or protect the asset over the period. In addition, the costs of dismantling and disposing of an old asset are not added to the cost of its replacement. Rather, such costs are treated as adjustments to any gain or loss on disposal of the old asset.

Make-Ready Costs   Subsequent to acquisition, but prior to use of a plant asset, all expenditures incurred to ready the asset for use are included in its cost. This includes any outlays for repair, reconditioning, remodeling, and installation of a second-hand asset. Machinery reinstallation and rearrangement costs, renovations, and structural changes are capitalized as part of the original asset's cost.

During renovation, overhead expenditures directly related to refurbishing a used asset, including insurance, taxes, and supervisory salaries, are capitalized. These expenditures increase the value of the asset and generate long-term benefits to the firm. In general, costs that do not enhance the expected utility of the asset are not capitalized. For example, an expenditure to repair damage resulting from improper installation is not capitalized.

Classification with Property, Plant, and Equipment   Plant assets are subdivided into the following:
- Buildings.
- Machinery and equipment.
- Land.
- Land improvements.
- Natural resources.

Subsidiary ledgers are maintained for individual assets in each of these categories as a basis for internal control of fixed assets. Natural resources, which raise accounting issues not pertinent to other plant assets, are discussed in Chapter 13.

Section 3060, paragraph .58 of the *CICA Handbook* requires disclosure of the balances of all major classes of depreciable assets. Correct classification is important because different depreciation methods and useful lives are applied to the various account classifications. For internal accounting purposes, accurate records in the individual accounts are important for complying with income tax laws, determining the gain or loss on disposal or exchange, assisting external audits, and evaluating capital budgeting decisions.

Buildings   The cost of buildings includes architectural fees, cost of permits, and excavation costs. Excavations vary according to the building specifications and are a necessary cost of construction.

Machinery and Equipment   Machinery and equipment (M&E) includes special platforms, foundations, and other required installation costs. The costs of building modifications necessary for specific equipment are also debited to equipment, whereas the costs of general rearrangement of plant facilities to accommodate major changes in the production process are capitalized to the building account. **Furniture and**

---

[5] The matching principle could be invoked to justify capitalizing training costs, but the absence of an assured connection to specific revenues causes recountants to be conservative and expense these costs.

fixtures may often be included under machinery and equipment or, if significant, under its own heading, particularly in nonmanufacturing companies.

Land   Land is not depreciated because its value is expected neither to diminish over time nor to be exhausted by production activities. Expenditures are capitalized to the land account only for properties currently in service as a building site or in other productive use. General land preparation costs, including grading, filling, draining, and surveying, are capitalized to land. In contrast to excavation costs, which are capitalized to buildings, these activities are required for general land use and add permanent value to the land.

If land is acquired for redevelopment or use as a building site, the cost of removing structures and other obstructions is capitalized to land. Such razing costs are necessary for many land uses. Proceeds from salvaged materials reduce the costs capitalized. If a building constructed *after* the land acquisition is later removed to make way for new construction, razing costs are not associated with the land but rather increase the loss or reduce the gain on disposal of the structure.

Special assessments for local government-maintained improvements, including streets, sidewalks, sewers, and streetlights, are also capitalized to land. The rationale is that the assessed company has no responsibility to maintain or replace these structures, and the benefits derived are perpetual.

Property taxes, insurance, and other holding costs are incurred on land not in current productive use. Treatment of these costs varies. Some accountants contend that capitalization is proper because the land is not currently producing benefits, although the costs do not increase the value of land. In most cases, though, these costs are expensed on grounds of expedience and conservatism.

Land held by real estate development companies and land sales organizations is classified as inventory rather than as land. For most other firms, idle land constitutes an investment and is not included in the land account. If idle land is held for investment or lease, property taxes and insurance should be capitalized only during periods in which the property is prepared for sale or lease.

Certain types of landscaping and other property enhancements are included in land if they are permanent. Examples are terracing and artificial lakes. Treatment of these enhancements contrasts with land improvements.

Land Improvements   Land improvements are depreciable site enhancements that are not permanent, including driveways, parking lots, fencing, and landscaping. Although a parking lot appears to be permanent, it is subject to weather damage, requires maintenance, and must eventually be replaced. The cost of land improvements is not added to the land account but is capitalized to the land improvements account and depreciated.

Example of Plant Asset Classification   A disclosure note to the 1993 financial statements of Dynacare Inc. demonstrates the variety of account classifications in fixed assets.

5. Fixed Assets

	1993	1992
	(in thousands of dollars)	
Land.	$ 3,874	$ 3,874
Buildings.	6,903	6,886
Medical equipment	8,014	7,020
Leasehold improvements.	7,450	6,087
Furniture and fixtures	2,882	2,398
Computer equipment	5,948	4,817
Motor vehicles.	185	297
	35,256	31,379
Accumulated depreciation and amortization	(11,539)	(8,534)
	$ 23,717	$22,845

EXHIBIT 11–1 Example of Cost Classification: Vita-Life Company

Vita-Life Company recently acquired several plant assets and began construction on a building. The costs incurred by Vita-Life are classified into the indicated accounts.

Cost Incurred	Equipment	Land	Building under Construction*	Land Improvements	Current Period Expense
Invoice price of equipment	$50,000				
3% cash discount not taken on equipment purchase	(1,500)				$1,500†
4% sales tax on equipment	2,000				
Insurance and freight costs on equipment purchase	600				
Cost of land parcel		$100,000			
Commission and title insurance on land purchase		7,000			
Setup, testing, and practice runs on equipment	2,000				
Cost to train employees on equipment					500
Interest on debt incurred to purchase equipment					1,200
Cost to remove structures from land		30,000			
Proceeds on materials salvaged from structures removed		(2,000)			
Excavation of foundation			$ 3,500		
Surveying and grading		12,000			
Concrete and labour for foundation			26,000		
Property tax paid four months after acquisition of land					550
Asphalt for parking lot				$11,000	
Fencing for property				6,000	
Ending account balance	$53,100	$147,000	$29,500	$17,000	—

* Reclassified to building account on completion.

† Finance expense.

Exhibit 11–1 provides an example of cost classification related to the acquisition of several plant assets.

Lump-Sum Purchase of Several Assets Occasionally, several assets are acquired for a single lump-sum price that may be lower than the sum of the individual asset prices to induce a larger purchase. In other cases, the assets are attached, as in the case of a land and building. This type of acquisition, called a **basket, group,** or **lump-sum purchase,** requires allocation of a portion of the single lump-sum price to each asset acquired.

The portions of the lump-sum price directly attributable to particular assets in the group are assigned in full to those assets. Land appraisal costs are assigned only to the land account, for example. Allocation of the remaining lump-sum price to each asset is necessary. Under the cost principle, the sum of the individual asset account balances at acquisition is limited to the lump-sum price.

The allocation is based on the best available indicator of the relative values of the several assets involved. Possible indicators include market prices for similar assets, current appraised value, assessed value for property tax purposes, expected manufacturing cost savings, and the present value of estimated future net cash flows. The seller's book values generally do not reflect the current value of the assets in the group.

Each asset is valued according to the ratio of its value to the total value of the group; this valuation is called the *proportional* method. If the value of only the first of two assets in a group is determinable, the second asset is valued at the cost remaining to be allocated. This procedure is called the *incremental* method.

To illustrate the proportional method, assume that $90,000 is the negotiated acquisition price paid for land, a building, and machinery. These assets are appraised (as the best available indication of value in this case) individually as follows: land, $30,000; building, $50,000; and machinery, $20,000. The cost apportionment of the single lump-sum price and the entry to record the transaction are as follows:

Asset	Appraised Value	Apportionment of Cost	Apportioned Cost
Land	$ 30,000	.3*($90,000)	$27,000
Building	50,000	.5(90,000)	45,000
Machinery	20,000	.2(90,000)	18,000
Total	$100,000		$90,000

* .3 = $30,000 ÷ $100,000.

To record the lump-sum purchase:

Land	27,000	
Building	45,000	
Machinery	18,000	
Cash		90,000

CONCEPT REVIEW

1. Why are costs such as freight and insurance in transit capitalized to fixed assets?
2. Why are annual property taxes on land not capitalized to land?
3. Why is the cost of excavating a building foundation debited to the building when the excavation is performed on the land site?

ACCOUNTING FOR NON-CASH ACQUISITIONS OF CAPITAL ASSETS

Capital assets may be acquired in several ways:
- With cash.
- On credit.
- In exchange for equity securities of the acquiring company.
- Through donation from another entity.
- Through construction.
- In exchange for non-monetary assets.[6]

The general principles for valuation of capital assets apply regardless of the type of consideration or method used to acquire capital assets, although non-cash acquisition of capital assets involves additional considerations.

Capital Assets Purchased on Credit

In accordance with the cost principle, the recorded cost of an asset purchased on credit is based on one of the following, whichever is more objective and reliable:
- The cash equivalent price (market value).
- The present value of the future cash payments required by the debt agreement discounted at the prevailing (market) interest rate for that type of debt.

If the debt instrument does not bear interest and the current cash price of the asset is determinable, the excess to be paid over the cash price is treated as interest

---

[6] Non-monetary assets are not readily convertible into fixed amounts of cash. Their value fluctuates with demand and supply. All capital assets are non-monetary. Cash is an example of a monetary asset.

expense and is apportioned over the term of the debt. If the cash price is not determinable, the prevailing interest rate is used to determine total interest cost and to compute the asset's present value for recording purposes. The valuation of assets acquired in exchange for debt securities is similar to the valuation of long-term notes receivable, discussed in Chapter 8.

To illustrate the purchase of a capital asset on credit, assume that Cobb Corporation purchases equipment on January 1, 1995, with a $600 cash down payment and a 12%, $1,000, one-year note with interest payable on December 31, 1995. The stated interest rate is equal to the current market rate. Its present value equals its face value. The asset is recorded at the sum of the cash down payment plus the present value of the note because the cash equivalent price of the asset is not available. The recorded amount is:

$$\text{Equipment valuation} = \text{Cash down payment} + \text{Present value of note}$$
$$= \$600 + \$1,000 = \$1,600$$

Cobb records the entry:
January 1, 1995:

Equipment.	1,600	
Cash		600
Note payable.		1,000

Cobb will pay and recognize as expense $120 in interest ($1,000 × .12) for the year ended December 31, 1995.

Assume now that Feller Company acquires a machine on January 1, 1995, with a note that requires $8,615 to be paid on December 31, 1995, 1996, and 1997. The note has no stated rate, but the prevailing interest rate is 14% on liabilities of similar risk and duration. The face amount of the note is $25,845 ($8,615 × 3). The cash equivalent cost of the machine is unknown, so the asset is recorded at the present value of the three payments discounted at 14%:

$$\text{Recorded cost} = \$8,615(\text{PVA}, 14\%, 3)$$
$$= \$8,615(2.32163)$$
$$= \$20,000 \text{ (rounded)}$$

Feller's entries to record the asset and recognize interest expense on the note are as follows:
January 1, 1995:

	Gross Method	Net Method
Equipment	20,000	20,000
Discount on note payable.	5,845	
Note payable	25,845*	20,000

* $8,615 × 3.

Discount on note payable is a contra note payable account. It reduces the net note payable balance to the present value of the future cash flows ($20,000). Subsequent entries record the debt payments, each composed of principal and interest.

December 31 (gross method):

	1995		1996		1997	
Interest expense	2,800*		1,986†		1,059‡	
Note payable	8,615		8,615		8,615	
Discount on note payable		2,800		1,986		1,059
Cash		8,615		8,615		8,615

* $2,800 = $20,000(.14).

† $1,986 = ($20,000 − Principal reduction in 1995)(.14) = [$20,000 − ($8,615 − $2,800)](.14) = $14,185(.14).

‡ $1,059 = [$14,185 − ($8,615 − $1,986)](.14) (rounded).

Under the net method, the 1995 entry would be the following:

Interest expense		2,800
Note payable		5,815
Cash		8,615

Capital Assets Acquired in Exchange for Equity Securities

When equity securities are issued to acquire capital assets, the assets are recorded either at the fair market value of the asset or at the fair market value of the securities issued, whichever is more objective and reliable.

The market value of the securities issued is reliable for publicly traded securities if the number of shares in the exchange is below the typical daily market volume. Assume that Medford Corporation purchases used equipment in 1995. The equipment is in reasonable condition but is not normally sold before the end of its useful life. Thus, it has no reliable market value. In payment for this equipment, Medford issues 2,000 common shares. Medford's common shares are listed on the Toronto Stock Exchange and currently trade at $10 per share. Medford has 10 million common shares outstanding. Therefore, the proper valuation for the equipment is 2,000 × $10, or $20,000.

Several factors can complicate the situation, however. The effect of a substantial share offering on the market price of the shares is often not known until after issuance. Also, the shares of many companies are not traded with sufficient frequency to establish a daily market price. In other cases, organizers of a newly formed corporation may be willing to exchange a substantial number of shares for capital assets, when there is no clear value for the shares or the assets. Unexplored or unproven mineral deposits, manufacturing rights, patents, chemical formulas, and mining claims increase uncertainty about a share's value.

If the market value of the securities (in the volume exchanged) cannot be determined reliably, the market value of the assets acquired is used if it can be determined reliably. In the absence of recent cash sale evidence, an independent appraisal can be used to value the assets.

If no reliable market value can be determined for either the securities issued or the assets acquired, the board of directors of the corporation establishes a reasonable valuation. The directors have considerable discretion in establishing values, and firms experiencing financial difficulty may be tempted to overstate asset values, overstating owners' equity as well. A disincentive to overvaluation, however, is the increased depreciation expense in future years.

Donated Assets

Shareholders and other parties occasionally donate assets and services to corporations. For example, shareholders may contribute shares of the donee company to assist it during difficult financial times. Other shareholder donations include rare paintings and similar assets to enhance the corporate boardroom. Municipalities donate land and buildings to induce a company to locate in the area, improving the local tax base and increasing employment.

Contribution Defined FASB issued *SFAS No. 116,* "Accounting for Contributions Received and Contributions Made," in November 1993, which defines a **contribution** to be:

> an unconditional transfer of cash or other assets to an entity or a settlement or cancellation of its liabilities in a voluntary nonreciprocal transfer by another entity acting other than as an owner. [par. 5]

In the definition, "other assets" includes securities, property, use of facilities, and **unconditional promises** to transfer assets in the future. An unconditional promise must depend only on the passage of time or demand by the donee. If an entity transfers an asset to another entity in exchange for another asset valued substantially lower and no other rights or privileges are involved, the transaction is in part an exchange of assets and in part a contribution.[7]

Sometimes the donor imposes restrictions on the use of contributed resources. Although restrictions may affect the donee's use of the property, a restriction does not alter the transfer's status as a contribution for purposes of recognition in the accounts.

Recognition of Contributions   Before *SFAS No. 116,* donees credited owners' equity for the market value of donated assets. Now, consistent with the *SFAC No. 6* definition of comprehensive income, which includes all changes in equity except those resulting from investments by owners, contributions are to be included in income. Both unrestricted and restricted contributions are recognized, at fair market value, as *revenues or gains in the period received* and as assets, decreases of liabilities, or expenses, depending on the form of benefits received. Contributed depreciable assets are depreciated on the basis of fair market value.

The CICA's Accounting Standards Board has addressed this issue in the Re-Exposure Draft, "Not-For-Profit Organizations." In the Re-Exposure Draft, the treatment of donated assets is similar to the FASB recommendations. However, *SFAS No. 116* applies to both profit and nonprofit oriented entities, but the CICA proposed standard will apply only to nonprofit entities. In Canada, therefore, it would appear that profit-oriented entities would continue to credit donated assets to contributed capital and not to income.

The donation of a capital asset is a non-reciprocal transfer, the transfer of resources in one direction, in this case from an outside party to the firm. The absence of a fixed value for the donated non-monetary asset, and the one-way nature of the transfer, necessitated the development of an accounting principle to measure the transfer. Since no asset or service is given up, a non-monetary asset received in a non-reciprocal transfer would be valued at "the fair value of the asset or service received" (*CICA Handbook* Section 3830, paragraph .05).

The asset and a contributed capital account (owners' equity) should be increased by a realistic appraisal of the current market value of the donated asset, provided the donation is unconditional. The increase to the contributed capital account represents the source of the donated asset and the increase in the value of the firm. Net income is not affected by donations received because the firm has not earned these resources. Future revenue may increase, however, on their use. Depreciation based on the market value of the donated asset is matched against that revenue.

If the donor imposes restrictions on the use of the asset donated, the expected cost of complying with those restrictions should be estimated and deducted from the market value of the asset in determining the valuation to be recorded.[8] Depreciable assets received by donation should be depreciated in the normal manner on the basis of the valuation recorded in the accounts.

Example   To illustrate accounting by a donee, assume a building (fair market value $400,000), and the land on which it is located (fair market value $100,000) are given by a city to Stanford Limited. A $5,000 legal and deed transfer cost is borne by Stanford, which records the donation as follows:

Plant building	400,000	
Plant land	105,000	
Cash		5,000
Contributed capital—Donated plant building and land		500,000

---

[7] *SFAS No. 116* does not apply to contributions made by governments to businesses or to tax exemptions, incentives, or abatements. *SFAS No. 116* is effective for financial statements issued for fiscal years beginning after December 15, 1994.

[8] When the restrictions are removed on fulfillment of the conditions by the firm, the resulting expenditure is treated as an expense or increase to the donated asset, depending on the expected benefit period.

Government Assistance

Instead of being donated directly, assets are often acquired with the assistance of various levels of governments. Often these programs require the firm to maintain certain employment levels or pollution control levels, for example, for the assistance (or loan) to be forgivable. If the conditions of the assistance are not met, the firm may be required to refund the amounts received to the granting agency.

There are two schools of thought in relation to the receipt of assistance particularly from governments (*CICA Handbook* Section 3800). The capital approach argues that (1) the assistance reduces the amount of capital required by the firm, (2) it is inappropriate to reflect the assistance as income because the donor's policies may change, and (3) the assistance is gratuitous and not earned. Therefore, the value of assistance received should be credited to a capital surplus account.

The income approach argues that (1) the receipt of assistance confers a benefit to the firm and should be reflected in income, (2) the assistance received generally offsets costs and thus should be reflected, (3) assistance is a factor in the overall results of the operation and the income statement should report this factor, and (4) most assistance is not entirely gratuitous and thus, in some sense, is earned. Therefore, the assistance received should be credited to income either by an increase in revenues or a reduction in expenses during the period(s) to which it relates.

The CICA Accounting Standards Board concluded that the income approach arguments are more persuasive. Section 3800, paragraph .10 of the *CICA Handbook* provides that (government) assistance received affects income in current or future accounting periods.

An analysis of the terms of the assistance will indicate the accounting procedure to be used on its receipt.

1. Assistance toward current expenses or revenues should be included in the determination of net income for the period.
2. Assistance relating to future periods should be deferred and amortized to income as related expenses are incurred.
3. Assistance toward the acquisition of fixed assets should be either deducted from the related fixed asset with any depreciation calculated on the net amount or deferred and amortized to income on the same basis as the related depreciable fixed assets are depreciated.[9]

Example To illustrate accounting for a government grant, assume that machinery costing $100,000 was eligible for assistance of 30%. The machinery has a 10-year life with no salvage value. Because both the net and deferral methods of accounting are acceptable, both sets of journal entries are provided.

Net Method	Deferral Method

To record purchase:

Net Method			Deferral Method		
Machinery	100,000		Machinery	100,000	
Cash		100,000	Cash		100,000

To record the receipt of the grant:

Net Method			Deferral Method		
Cash	30,000		Cash	30,000	
Machinery		30,000	Deferred government grant		30,000

To record depreciation expense at the end of years 1 to 10:

Net Method			Deferral Method		
Depreciation expense ($1/10 \times \$70,000$)	7,000		Depreciation expense ($1/10 \times \$100,000$)	10,000	
Accumulated depreciation		7,000	Accumulated depreciation		10,000
			Deferred government grant ($1/10 \times \$30,000$)	3,000	
			Depreciation expense		3,000

---

[9] *CICA Handbook* (Toronto: The Canadian Institute of Chartered Accountants), Section 3800, paragraphs .20, .24, and .26.

The effect on income is the same under either method. The difference would appear on the balance sheet where with the deferral method the gross amount of the fixed asset would appear with an offsetting credit consisting of the unamortized grant—as opposed to the net method, which would present the net cost of the long-term asset. Either method is acceptable.

Forgivable loans should be accounted for in the same manner as outlined earlier—when the firm becomes entitled to receive the loan, not when it is forgiven. Any amount not yet forgiven should be disclosed by means of a note to the financial statements. Should the loan become repayable, this event should be accounted for prospectively and not as a prior period adjustment.

Self-Constructed Assets

Companies sometimes construct plant assets for their own use. Suppose a utility employs its personnel to extend transmission lines and construct pipelines. All costs directly associated with the construction are capitalized to the constructed asset. These costs include incremental material, labour, and overhead costs. Overhead includes general costs not directly related to production, such as utility costs, maintenance on equipment, and supervision.

Under certain conditions, some of the general overhead and interest expense incurred during construction is included in the cost of these assets. Determining the amount of general overhead cost to allocate to a construction project is not well established in practice. One view is that self-constructed assets should bear the incremental overhead cost and the portion of general overhead cost that would be assigned to any regular production displaced by the special project. According to this view, if general overhead is allocated on the basis of labour-hours, and 8% of labour-hours are associated with self-construction, then 8% of total general overhead during construction should be included as a cost of the self-constructed asset. Many accountants contend that failure to allocate some portion of the general overhead to self-construction projects causes an undervaluation of self-constructed assets and overstatement of inventory and cost of goods sold on regular production.

The actual cost of a self-constructed asset does not necessarily equal fair market value. Consistent with the valuation of other assets, the maximum valuation allowed by GAAP for self-constructed assets is fair market value. If total construction cost (including overhead and interest during construction) exceeds the market value of a similar asset of equal capacity and quality, the excess is recognized as a loss. Failure to do so carries forward cost elements that have no future benefit, causes overstated depreciation in future years, and violates the conservatism constraint.

In the opposite case, a self-constructed asset costing less than its external acquisition or replacement cost is recorded at total construction cost. Using the higher market value would imply a gain on construction. Conservatism in this situation requires waiting for more objective evidence, perhaps lower operating costs or increased revenues, to support increased income. The lower construction cost is ultimately reflected in higher net income through lower depreciation expense.

Accumulated construction costs are generally recorded in an account such as plant asset under construction and classified as an investment or "other asset" until completion of the project. Upon completion and placement into service, the account is reclassified as a plant asset and is subject to depreciation.

To illustrate the accounting for a self-constructed asset, assume that Kelvin Corporation completes a project with total construction costs as follows:

Material	$200,000
Labour	500,000
Incremental overhead	60,000
Applied general overhead	40,000
Capitalized interest	100,000
Total	$900,000

Kelvin has recorded costs in the equipment under construction account. If the asset's market value at completion equals or exceeds $900,000, the summary entry is:

Equipment.   900,000
    Equipment under construction   900,000

If the asset's market value is only $880,000, the entry is:

Equipment.   880,000
Loss on construction of equipment   20,000
    Equipment under construction   900,000

│CONCEPT REVIEW

1. At what amount would you record a capital asset purchased on credit, if the asset does not have a ready market value?
2. If a large, publicly held corporation whose shares are actively traded issues a small number of shares in exchange for a capital asset, what value would most likely be used to record the asset?
3. What is the justification for including at least some overhead as part of the cost of self-constructed assets?

CAPITALIZATION OF INTEREST DURING CONSTRUCTION

The period required for construction of capital assets can be lengthy. There is general agreement that time-related costs, including taxes and insurance during construction, should be capitalized to the asset under construction. Consistent logic supports **capitalization of interest** during the construction period. Moreover, if the company chose to apply the funds used in construction to retire debt, a certain amount of interest cost would be avoided. In addition, if the asset were purchased rather than self-constructed, the purchase price would normally include a cost component to cover the seller's financing expenses. Finally, many firms would be unable to construct assets without debt financing.

Under GAAP, interest cost incurred *during construction* of assets is considered to be a cost necessary for placing the asset into its intended condition. That is, the asset cannot generate revenue until it is completed, so the interest incurred until completion should be capitalized. The capitalized interest is subsequently expensed as part of the periodic depreciation.

When interest is capitalized, interest expense is reduced and plant assets are increased. For example, the following entry capitalizes $2,000,000 of previously recorded interest expense to equipment under construction:

Equipment under construction   2,000,000
    Interest expense   2,000,000

Both total assets and current pretax income are increased by the amount of capitalized interest.[10]

A contrasting view is that interest incurred during construction does not increase the value of constructed assets but is rather a finance cost, as in the case of purchased assets. Proponents of this view maintain that the asset's value is independent of the method of financing. A debt-free company using its own funds to construct an asset does so without interest cost. Another company with debt would construct the identical asset at a cost including capitalized interest. This anomaly occurs because the two firms have different capital structures.

---

[10] This example assumes that interest is capitalized as an adjustment to interest expense already recorded. In practice, some companies capitalize interest charges directly to the equipment under construction account as they are incurred.

Independent of this debate, an opportunity cost arises when a company uses its own funds for construction. If those funds come from owners' equity, some accountants argue that an **imputed interest** rate should be estimated to assign the cost of funds to a project. All financing, they argue, has an implicit cost. Furthermore, many firms have continuing credit agreements with financial institutions that make it impossible to relate a specific self-construction project to a specific source of debt financing. Capitalizing only imputed interest would solve the problem of associating a project with a specific source of financing.

Public utilities have traditionally capitalized interest during construction. If construction-related interest were recognized as a current expense, current customers would pay increased utility rates to cover the added expense, thereby financing facilities for future customers. Including the interest (both actual and imputed) in the cost of the constructed assets (thereby raising the future depreciation amount) means that future customers who benefit from those assets pay for the interest incurred in creating the assets and the related utility service.

During the 1970s, a growing number of nonutility companies began capitalizing interest, thereby increasing both current income and total assets. The lack of uniformity in accounting for interest during construction and an SEC moratorium[11] on interest capitalization by nonutility registrants led to *SFAS No. 34* on the capitalization of interest.

Section 3060, paragraph .26 of the *CICA Handbook,* "Capital Assets," states the following:

> The cost of property, plant and equipment that is acquired, constructed, or developed over time includes carrying costs directly attributable to the acquisition, construction, or development activity such as interest costs when the enterprise's accounting policy is to capitalize interest costs. For a rate-regulated capital asset, the cost includes the directly attributable allowance for funds used during construction allowed by the regulator.

Twenty-six percent of the companies surveyed in *Financial Reporting in Canada—1993,* indicated that they followed a policy of capitalizing interest charges during construction.

Not everyone agrees with the capitalization of interest. Many accountants and financial statement users contend that the earnings of many companies are artificially increased by interest capitalization while the quality of earnings is diminished. Capitalized interest increases net income without increasing liquidity. However, Section 3850 of the *CICA Handbook* requires disclosure of interest capitalized, allowing financial statement users to determine the effect of capitalized interest on earnings and assets.

Avoidable Interest

The rationale behind interest capitalization is that interest could be avoided if expenditures on constructed assets are applied instead to retire debt. The interest on this debt, **avoidable interest,** is the amount capitalized in the construction period. The **average accumulated expenditures (AAE)** on a constructed asset, which is a measure of the debt that could have been retired, is the average cash investment *during* the construction period.

Suppose the cost to date of a partially finished building represents average cash expenditures of $1.4 million during the construction period. Assuming that at least that much debt was outstanding during that period, the company could have retired $1.4 million of debt instead of embarking on the construction project. Consequently, the interest on $1.4 million of debt could have been avoided in that period.

The *CICA Handbook* provides for interest capitalization but does not provide guidelines for the methodology. Therefore, we look to *SFAS No. 34,* which provides

---

[11] "Capitalization of Interest by Companies Other than Public Utilities," *Accounting Series Release No. 163* (Washington, DC: SEC, 1974).

guidelines on qualifying assets, qualifying expenditures to be capitalized, the conditions under which interest is capitalized, and the calculation of capitalized interest. Immaterial amounts of interest need not be capitalized.[12]

Qualifying Assets

Interest is capitalized on assets constructed for a company's own use and on assets constructed as *discrete* projects for sale or lease, such as ships or real estate developments. Qualifying assets are not routinely produced and require significant construction time. Firms incur a significant opportunity cost (the interest expense that otherwise could be avoided) during the construction of qualifying assets. Expenditures made to construct qualifying assets are included in AAE. Inventories routinely manufactured or otherwise produced in large quantities, even those such as whiskey and tobacco that require an extended maturation period, do not qualify for interest capitalization.

Assets in use or ready for use do not qualify for capitalization because construction is completed and the asset is presumably contributing to revenue. For example, only certain assets of an oil and gas company qualify for interest capitalization. These assets may include unproved projects under development and not currently being depleted, and properties in cost centers with no production.

Land deserves special mention. When land is developed for sale, interest is capitalized and added to the land cost based on expenditures made for its development. If land is to be used as a building site, the amount of interest capitalized on the land expenditures becomes part of the building cost. Idle land is not a qualifying asset; however, once construction commences, the historical cost of the land and expenditures to make the land ready for use are included in AAE.

Qualifying Expenditures

Qualifying expenditures are included in AAE because they represent an opportunity cost for the firm. They include cash payments for construction, transfer of other assets, and incurrence of interest-bearing liabilities. Interest-bearing liabilities are similar to cash expenditures in that they create an opportunity cost. Short-term noninterest-bearing liabilities do not qualify because they cause no interest expense.

Conditions for Capitalizing Interest

Three conditions must be met for interest to be capitalized for a period:

1. Qualifying expenditures were made.
2. Construction and related activities occurred for substantially the entire period.
3. Interest cost was incurred.

Interest capitalization *ceases* when any one of the three conditions is not met or when the asset is substantially completed. If the first condition is not met, the conceptual basis for interest capitalization is absent. If the second condition is not met, construction activities are not the cause of the opportunity cost. If the third condition is not met, there is no interest to capitalize.

Brief construction interruptions that are part of the normal construction process do not stop the capitalization process. Intentional delays do. Stopping construction of a building for a substantial period to allow the customer to choose fixtures is an example. Interest during these periods is a financing, rather than an acquisition, cost.

Calculating Capitalized Interest

The amount of **interest potentially capitalizable (IPC)** for a given period is determined by applying the appropriate interest rate to the AAE amount. This result is capitalized if it is less than or equal to actual interest expense for the period. Interest capitalized is limited to the actual interest *expense* recognized in the period. Interest

---

[12] Paragraphs 7 and 10 of *SFAS No. 42*, "Determining Materiality for Capitalization of Interest Cost," require that the usual tests for materiality be applied to interest capitalization.

expense does not necessarily equal interest paid.[13] A set of four general steps with an example illustrates the calculation.

Assume that York Company hires Superior Builders on January 2, 1995, to construct a warehouse.

Debt	10%, $2 million warehouse construction loan obtained January 3, 1995.
	12%, $5 million mortgage loan obtained January 3, 1990 (unrelated to the construction project).
Construction payments	$1 million paid January 3, 1995.
	$4 million paid evenly throughout 1995.
Warehouse completion	December 29, 1995.

Step 1: Compute Actual Interest Expense for the Period   This is the maximum capitalizable amount; for York in 1995 it is:

$$\text{Interest expense for 1995} = \$2,000,000(.10) + \$5,000,000(.12)$$
$$= \$800,000$$

Step 2: Compute AAE for the Period   York need not analyze each payment to the contractor if payments are made on a reasonably even basis throughout the year. AAE for York is:

$$\text{AAE} = \$1,000,000 + \$4,000,000(.5) = \$3,000,000$$

The $1 million payment is invested in the project for the entire year and therefore receives a weight of 1 (or $12/12$). The $4 million is spread evenly throughout 1995 and has the same effect as $2 million invested at the beginning of the year. Therefore, a weight of 0.5 (or $6/12$) is applied to it. This result can also be achieved by computing one-half of the beginning ($1 million) and ending ($5 million) cash investment balances because of the even payment assumption:

$$\text{AAE} = (\$1,000,000 + \$5,000,000) \div 2 = \$3,000,000$$

York's cash investment has reached a total of $5 million by the end of 1995. However, many other construction payment schedules would have yielded the same $3 million AAE figure. For example, had York's construction expenditures consisted solely of one $3 million construction payment on January 1, 1995, AAE again would be $3 million [($3 million + $3 million) ÷ 2]. AAE represents the debt *outstanding the entire period* that could have been retired.

When construction payments are not made evenly throughout the year, each payment is weighted for the portion of the period it was incorporated in the project. For example, if York had instead made a $1 million payment on January 3 and a $4 million payment on October 1, AAE would be computed as follows:

$$\text{AAE} = \$1,000,000 + \$4,000,000(3/12) = \$2,000,000$$

AAE is considerably less under this alternative assumption because cash was invested in the project much later in the year. Assuming equal payments during 1995 under this assumption would be inappropriate.

Step 3: Compute the Interest Potentially Capitalizable (IPC)   Using the original data, York's 1995 AAE ($3 million) exceeds the principal balance of the specific

---

[13] For example, unpaid accrued interest and amortization of discount on bonds payable are included in interest expense but are not included in interest paid for the current period.

construction loan ($2 million). Therefore, the 12% interest rate on the mortgage is applied to the excess of AAE over the specific debt ($3 million − $2 million), and IPC is computed as follows:

IPC = Interest on construction loan + Interest on excess of AAE over construction loan

$$= \$2,000,000(.10) + (\$3,000,000 - \$2,000,000).12$$
$$= \$320,000.$$

The IPC represents the interest that could have been avoided if the funds used in the construction project were applied to retire debt. Avoidable interest is not limited to interest on construction debt.

Step 4: Capitalize the Smaller of Actual Interest and IPC   In York's case:

Capitalized interest in 1995 = Smaller of IPC and actual interest
= Smaller of $320,000 and $800,000
= $320,000

Assuming that York has already recorded interest expense for 1995 and has recorded the construction payments in building under construction, an adjusting entry is made:

December 31, 1995

Building under construction	320,000	
Interest expense		320,000

Interest expense recognized for 1995 is therefore $480,000 ($800,000 − $320,000). The building under construction account has a $5,320,000 ending balance ($1,000,000 + $4,000,000 + $320,000). The capitalized interest will be matched against revenues during the asset's service period, in the form of increased depreciation.

Had the building not been completed as of the end of 1995, the calculation for AAE in 1996 would begin by applying a weight of 100% to the opening cash investment amount of $5,320,000, which includes capitalized interest from 1995. Thus, previously capitalized interest is compounded when construction activities span more than one period.

Some flexibility is allowed in calculating capitalized interest. If a project is financed with specific construction debt, the rate on that debt can be applied first to AAE. If AAE exceeds the principal amount of that specific debt, the weighted-average interest rate on all other interest-bearing debt is applied to the excess. This procedure is called the **specific method** and is the one used in the York example.

In other cases, it is difficult to associate borrowings and projects. Companies often have continuing lines of credit with financial institutions, that enable them to borrow up to the credit limit in amounts unrelated to specific projects. In these cases, it is easier to apply the weighted-average interest rate on all interest-bearing debt to AAE in order to determine IPC. This is called the **weighted-average method.**

Only steps 3 and 4 are affected by the choice of method, and the two methods can yield the same amount of capitalized interest. The weighted-average method applied to step 3 of the York example yields:

$$\frac{\text{Weighted-average interest}}{\text{rate on all interest-bearing debt}} = \frac{\text{Total actual interest}}{\text{Total interest-bearing debt}}$$
$$= \$800,000 \div \$7,000,000 = .1143$$

IPC = $3,000,000(.1143) = $342,900

In this instance, IPC is different because a higher overall interest rate is applied to AAE under the weighted-average method. IPC is again less than actual interest; thus, $342,900 is capitalized (step 4).

GLOBAL VIEW

Capitalization of interest is a controversial issue in international accounting. Revised *International Accounting Standard (IAS) No. 23*, "Borrowing Costs" (effective January 1, 1995), was one of the original standards the IASC considered in its comparability and improvement project started in the 1980s. Although one of the goals of this project was to reduce the number of acceptable accounting alternatives, the International Accounting Standards Committee decided to allow two alternative treatments with respect to interest capitalization.

The revised standard states that all borrowing costs should be expensed in the period incurred, regardless of how the borrowings are applied. This is the benchmark treatment, the treatment the IASC identifies as the point of reference when making a choice among accounting alternatives.

However, as is the case with a few IASs, an alternative treatment is allowed under certain circumstances. Borrowing costs directly attributable to the acquisition, construction, or production of a qualifying asset may be capitalized as part of the cost of the asset. If the borrowing costs were avoidable had the asset not been acquired, such costs are considered to be directly attributable to the asset under this alternative accounting treatment. Thus, a choice exists for those firms complying with IASC standards and meeting the requirements for capitalizing interest—expense or capitalize the qualifying interest.

Although Revised *IAS No. 23* is less detailed than *SFAS No. 34*, most of the fundamental requirements are similar. For example, interest may not be capitalized on inventories, and only actual interest expense may be capitalized under international rules.

Canada provides for interest capitalization when an enterprise has a policy to do so. Other countries allowing, but not requiring, interest capitalization include Austria, Belgium, France (but the practice is not widespread), Germany, Greece (interest charges relating to fixed asset construction debt can be expensed or capitalized and amortized over a five-year period), Sweden (which also allows interest capitalization on inventory), and the United Kingdom.

Firms are free to adopt either method. Firms wishing to maximize income would choose the specific method when interest rates on specific construction loans exceed rates on other debt. The specific method would first exhaust the interest on the higher interest rate construction loans before applying the lower interest rate. The result is higher capitalized interest, greater income, and greater net assets. The difference between the two methods is not material unless interest rates are significantly different and AAE exceeds specific construction debt by a considerable amount.

For simplicity, we ignored the cost of the land site on which the warehouse was constructed. Assuming the land was owned by York, the historical cost of the land would be included in AAE with a weight of 100% because the expenditures for land were invested in the project during the entire construction period.

The capitalization of interest calculation is affected by two additional factors. First, it can be performed monthly, quarterly, or over interim periods of any length. Monthly calculations are preferable when significant changes in debt structure occur during the year. Public companies publish quarterly earnings reports and therefore capitalize interest on a quarterly basis. The annual capitalized interest, however, is limited to annual recognized interest expense.

Second, not all interest-bearing debt need be considered. The objective is to achieve a reasonable measure of the financing cost involved in construction. If interest rates on older debt are significantly different from current interest rates, the older debt can be ignored for interest capitalization purposes.

CONCEPT REVIEW

1. What are the major arguments for and against interest capitalization?
2. What is the justification for capitalizing interest on debt not related to construction of plant assets?
3. What does the average accumulated expenditures amount for a period represent?

ACCOUNTING FOR DISPOSALS OF CAPITAL ASSETS

The disposal of capital assets may be voluntary (as a result of a sale, exchange, or abandonment) or involuntary (as a result of a casualty such as a fire, storm, or of a government's exercise of its right of eminent domain).

If the asset to be disposed of is subject to depreciation, it is depreciated up to the date of disposal in order to update the recorded book value. Applicable property taxes, insurance premium costs, and similar costs are also accrued up to the date of disposal. At the date of disposal, the original cost of the asset and its related accumulated depreciation are removed from the accounts.

The difference between the book value of a plant asset and the amount received on disposal is recorded as a gain or loss. Ideally, the gain or loss is segregated from ordinary income and reported in the income statement as part of income from continuing operations unless extraordinary. If the gain or loss meets the criteria in Section 3480, paragraph .02 of the *CICA Handbook,* it is classified with extraordinary items. This treatment is often applied to involuntary conversions.

To illustrate the disposal of a capital asset, assume that on February 1, 1991, Brown Company paid $32,000 for office equipment with an estimated service life of five years and an estimated residual value of $2,000. Brown uses straight-line depreciation and decides to sell the asset on July 1, 1995, for $8,000. The entries for Brown, a calendar-year company, at date of disposal are as follows:

```
Depreciation expense  . . . . . . . . . . . . . . . . . . . . . . . .   3,000*
     Accumulated depreciation—equipment. . . . . . . . . . . . . .             3,000

* ($32,000 − $2,000)(⅕)(⁶⁄₁₂).

Cash . . . . . . . . . . . . . . . . . . . . . . . . . . . . . . . .   8,000
Accumulated depreciation—equipment. . . . . . . . . . . . . . . . .  26,500*
     Equipment . . . . . . . . . . . . . . . . . . . . . . . . . . .           32,000
     Gain from disposal of equipment . . . . . . . . . . . . . . . .            2,500

* ($32,000 − $2,000)(53 months used) ÷ 60 months total useful life.
```

The $26,500 accumulated depreciation balance includes the $3,000 depreciation recognized on July 1. The gain from disposal is the difference between the $8,000 cash received and the $5,500 book value of the asset at disposal ($32,000 − $26,500).

However, the economic value of Brown Company is unaffected by the disposal. Brown received an asset worth $8,000 (cash) for an asset worth $8,000. Why is a gain recognized? Brown depreciated the equipment faster than it declined in value. The book value ($5,500) is less than market value ($8,000) at date of disposal. If depreciation reflected market value changes, there would be no gain or loss from disposal. The accounting gain in this example is a correction for excessive depreciation charges recognized before disposal. In effect, the gain is a "change in estimate."

The disposal of an asset with no market value is handled similarly. The loss recognized equals the book value of the asset at disposal. If the Brown Company asset has no market value, the loss recognized is $5,500. Involuntary conversions (e.g., uninsured casualty losses) are handled in a similar fashion. No cash is received, and the loss recognized equals book value.

The costs of dismantling, removing, and disposing of plant assets are treated as reductions of any proceeds obtained from disposal. Therefore, the resulting gain is reduced, or the resulting loss is increased by these costs. If Brown Company incurs $500 in disposal costs, the net cash debit is $8,000 − $500, or $7,500, reducing the gain to $2,000.

When the decision to abandon plant assets is made near the end of a fiscal year, an estimated loss from disposal is recognized in that year if the loss is estimable according to Section 3290, "Contingencies." Gains are not recognized before disposal, however.

Because of the rapid rise in real estate values that occurred in many parts of North America in the 1980s, many companies own land and buildings with market values greatly exceeding book value. These companies would have realized large gains if the properties were sold. The difference between market and book value is so great in certain cases that some analysts have recommended investing in these companies on the basis of their undervalued real estate holdings alone.

For example, in 1989, Bassett Furniture Industries owned a square mile of land in Virginia, which it carried on its books at $4.5 million, but whose market value was estimated at $130 million.[14]

Companies have long included gains from disposal of assets in operating income, although accountants recommend that disposal gains be segregated from operating income to prevent misleading reporting. A firm wishing to increase earnings, for example, might sell an asset at a large gain at the end of the reporting period. The argument is that gains from asset disposals cannot be expected to continue. Both gains and losses on plant asset disposals are substantial in many cases. For example, International Semi-Tech Microelectronics Inc. reported a gain of $22.2 million from the sale of one of its operations. The gain amounted to 37% of its 1992 net income of $60 million.

Disposal by Donation

Corporations occasionally donate assets to other organizations. Computer manufacturers donate computing equipment to universities, for example. The donor recognizes contribution expense equal to the market value of the donated asset.[15] Market value rather than book value represents the economic sacrifice of the donor. A gain or loss equal to the difference between book value and market value is recorded on donation. An expense and a payable are recognized when an unconditional promise is made.

In the Brown Company example, if the asset had been donated rather than sold, the entries would have been the same, except that contribution expense would have been debited instead of cash, and the gain would have referred to the donation.

Reclassification of Plant Assets Removed from Service

A plant asset removed from service before its usefulness expires is removed from the plant asset accounts. Depreciation is recorded up to the date of reclassification, and the accumulated depreciation and asset accounts are closed to other assets. If the market value of the asset is less than book value, a loss is recorded and the other assets account is debited for the market value. If the market value exceeds book value, the other assets account is debited for the book value, but no gain is recorded.

In the Brown Company example, if the equipment had been removed from service, other assets would have been debited for $5,500, because the book value is less than the market value ($8,000). A gain is not recognized, because the reclassification is internal. An arm's-length transaction is generally required to support increased asset values. The conservatism constraint justifies the recognition of a loss.

| CONCEPT REVIEW

1. Why would a company dispose of a capital asset at a loss? Is the company in a worse position economically after doing so?
2. How would you interpret the gain on the disposal of a capital asset?
3. How might income be manipulated by capital asset disposals?

---

[14] "Hidden Value of Real Estate Assets May Be One Clue to Stocks with a Strong Potential," *The Wall Street Journal,* June 23, 1989, p. C2.

[15] "Accounting for Contributions Received and Contributions Made," *SFAS No. 116,* 1993.

ACCOUNTING FOR EXCHANGES OF NON-MONETARY ASSETS

Capital assets are often exchanged for other non-monetary assets. The book value and market value of non-monetary assets are normally not equal because market value fluctuates with supply and demand. The valuation of the acquired asset is the substantive issue in non-monetary asset exchanges. This valuation determines whether a gain or loss is recognized.

Non-monetary transactions are:

> exchanges of non-monetary assets, liabilities or services for other non-monetary assets, liabilities or services with little or no monetary consideration involved. In general, if the fair value of the monetary consideration is less than 10% of the estimated fair value of the total consideration given up or received, the transaction would be considered non-monetary.[16]

A General Valuation Principle

In general, the valuation of a non-monetary asset acquired in exchange for another non-monetary asset depends on whether cash is paid or received and on which non-monetary asset has a more readily determinable market value. The **general valuation principle (GVP)** for valuing non-monetary assets acquired through exchange is given by the following equation:

General valuation of non-monetary asset acquired through exchange =

$$\text{Market value of asset transferred} \quad \begin{array}{l} + \text{ cash paid} \\ or \\ - \text{ cash received} \end{array}$$

or

Market value of asset acquired (if more readily determinable)

For example, if Bull Company exchanges a plant asset worth $4,000 for another plant asset and receives $300 on the exchange, the recorded value of the acquired asset is $3,700 according to the GVP. This principle makes sense because Bull's net sacrifice to acquire the asset is $3,700.

If the exchanged assets are dissimilar, the earnings process is considered complete and the exchange is treated like a monetary transaction. Both gains and losses are recognized in full regardless of cash received or paid. Determination and disclosure of gains and losses on exchange are similar to plant asset disposals. The gain or loss is the difference between the book value and the market value of the asset transferred and is disclosed in the income statement. When book value exceeds market value, a loss results; when market value exceeds book value, a gain results. Gains and losses do not represent increases (gains) or decreases (losses) in the value of the firm but rather are corrections to previously recognized depreciation.

Exception: Exchange of Similar Non-Monetary Assets

CICA Handbook Section 3830, which governs the accounting for non-monetary exchanges, includes a major exception to the general valuation principle for non-monetary asset exchanges and corresponding recognition of gains and losses. The accounting for exchanges of non-monetary assets depends on whether there is a culmination (completion) of an earnings process.[17] An earnings process is not complete when the non-monetary assets exchanged are similar. Non-monetary assets are similar if they are held for resale in the same line of business or if they are productive assets used for comparable purposes. An exchange of land parcels is an exchange of similar non-monetary assets, while an exchange of equipment for a building is an exchange of dissimilar non-monetary assets.

Exchanges of similar assets do not complete an earnings process because the operations of the business are not altered substantively by the exchange. Replacement of an assembly line with another assembly line does not change how the firm

---

[16] *CICA Handbook* Section 3830, "Non-monetary Transactions."

[17] In the earlier discussion of disposals of plant assets for cash (a monetary asset), the earnings process is completed. Therefore, a gain or loss is recognized. The value of the disposed asset is substantiated by the arm's-length transaction.

uses assembly lines. In contrast, the exchange of a fleet of rental cars for an office building concludes the rental car business and its earnings.

Gains and losses are not normally recognized on exchanges of similar assets. The earnings process has not been completed and the acquired asset merely replaces the asset exchanged. The future earnings of the firm will reflect any increase or decrease in productivity inherent in the acquired asset. The acquired asset is thus recorded at the book value of the asset transferred plus any cash paid or minus any cash received.

One further point must be considered: The highest value at which any asset received may be recorded is its fair market value at the time of the transfer. Therefore, when cash is paid, the paying enterprise must be careful to check that the sum of the book value of the asset transferred, plus the cash paid, is not greater than the market value of the asset being received. If this is so, the asset must be written down to its market value and a loss recorded on the transaction.

In general, the accounting for exchanges of non-monetary assets does not imply symmetry in the values recorded by the two enterprises. The amounts recorded by each enterprise depend on the book values of the assets on their respective balance sheets.

Examples of Non-Monetary Asset Exchanges

The following information for Regina Corporation is used in the examples that follow:[18]

Asset transferred: crane
Original cost.	$50,000
Accumulated depreciation at date of exchange.	$40,000

1. **Dissimilar assets**

   a. **Exchange does not involve cash** Assume that the crane has a fair value of $12,000 and is exchanged for a used truck whose value is not more clearly determinable; no cash is paid or received. The book value of the crane is $10,000; therefore, a $2,000 gain is recognized and the entry is:

Machinery (truck)	12,000	
Accumulated depreciation—crane	40,000	
Machinery (crane)		50,000
Gain on exchange		2,000

   The gain represents the difference between the market value and book value of the crane. If we assume the fair value of the crane was $9,000, the truck would be valued at that amount and a $1,000 loss would be recognized.

   b. **Exchange includes cash paid or received** Assume that the crane still has a fair value of $12,000 but that Regina also pays $900 to obtain the used truck. In this case, the truck would be valued at $12,900 (the fair value of the crane plus the cash paid)—that is, the fair value of the assets given up. If Regina received $900, the gain would be recorded as $2,900; the fair value of the asset given up is still $12,000 and the cash received increases the gain or decreases the loss on the exchange. The two situations are illustrated:

   $900 is paid by Regina:

Machinery (truck)	12,900	
Accumulated depreciation—crane	40,000	
Machinery (crane)		50,000
Cash		900
Gain on exchange		2,000

---

[18] Although depreciation is recognized (updated) on the asset transferred up to the date of exchange, for simplicity this entry is omitted. The balance of the accumulated depreciation account at the date of exchange reflects this depreciation update.

$900 is received by Regina:

Machinery (truck)	12,000	
Accumulated depreciation—crane	40,000	
Cash	900	
Machinery (crane)		50,000
Gain on exchange		2,900

2. **Similar assets**

   a. **Exchange does not involve cash** When similar assets are exchanged and no cash is involved, the asset being received is recorded at the book value of the asset given up. Normally no gain or loss is recorded. Assume that Regina exchanges the crane in the preceding example for another crane. Because both machines perform essentially the same function, there is no culmination of an earnings process. Therefore, the entry for the transaction would be:

Machinery (new crane)	10,000	
Accumulated depreciation (old crane)	40,000	
Machinery (old crane)		50,000

   b. **Exchange involves cash paid or received** The cash paid or received when similar assets are exchanged alters the value at which the asset received is recorded. Two situations are illustrated:

   $900 is received by Regina:

Cash	900	
Machinery (new crane)	9,100	
Accumulated depreciation (old crane)	40,000	
Machinery (old crane)		50,000

   $700 is paid by Regina:

Machinery (new crane)	10,700	
Accumulated depreciation (old crane)	40,000	
Cash		700
Machinery (old crane)		50,000

Normally, no gain or loss is recorded when similar assets are exchanged. However, the maximum amount at which the asset received may be recorded is its fair value. Therefore, when the asset received has a fair value lower than the book value of the asset given up, it must be recorded at that fair value.

Assume, in the previous example, that the crane being received by Regina has an estimated fair value of $8,500 and that this value is more clearly determinable. The recorded value for the new crane, in all three entries, would then be $8,500 and a loss of $1,500 ($10,000 − $8,500), $600 ($9,100 − $8,500), and $2,200 ($10,700 − $8,500), respectively, would be recorded.

Section 3830, paragraph .13 of the *CICA Handbook* requires the following:

> The nature, basis of measurement, amount and related gains and losses of non-monetary transactions, other than exchanges that do not represent the culmination of the earnings process, should be disclosed in the financial statements for the period.

Fair Market Value Determination

When a quoted cash price is unavailable, a company can invite bids for the asset to be exchanged. The highest bid for the asset, subsequently exchanged, is used as the market value. A less defensible but commonly used alternative is published information on the average price of specific used assets, such as the *Kelley Blue Book Auto Market Report* for automobiles.

In the absence of a reasonably determinable market value for either asset, the valuation of the acquired asset is based on the book value of the asset transferred, adjusted for any cash paid or received. For example, if a plant asset ($10,000 book value) and $4,000 cash are exchanged for another plant asset, the asset acquired is recorded at $14,000, assuming that the market value of neither plant asset is determinable.

CONCEPT REVIEW

1. What is the general valuation principle for capital assets received through exchange of non-monetary assets when cash is also paid on the exchange?
2. Why is an exception made to the general valuation principle for gains on exchanges of similar non-monetary assets?
3. Under what circumstances would a loss be recognized on exchange of similar non-monetary assets?

POST-ACQUISITION EXPENDITURES

After acquisition, many costs related to plant assets are incurred. Examples include repairs, maintenance, betterments, and replacements. Correct balance sheet classification is necessary for accurate depreciation calculations.

General Accounting Principles

Expenditures that increase the original useful life or productivity of an asset (the quantity or quality of service) above the *original* level estimated at acquisition are capitalized. A capitalized post-acquisition expenditure is depreciated over the number of periods benefited, which can be less than the remaining useful life of the original asset.

The service potential of assets and their estimated useful life at acquisition assume a certain minimum level of maintenance and repair. Costs for maintenance are revenue expenditures expensed in the period incurred. Some companies expense all post-acquisition expenditures less than a certain dollar amount (for example, $500). This policy is acceptable under the materiality constraint. The policy is also applied to material expenditures if the expenditures are relatively stable over time.

Expenditures that result from accident, neglect, intentional abuse, or theft are recognized as losses. For example, if a computer workstation is damaged during installation, the repair cost is recognized as a loss. After repair, the asset is no more valuable than it was before the mishap. Outlays made to restore uninsured assets damaged through casualty are also recorded as losses. They do not enhance the utility of the asset beyond the value before the casualty. If such a loss meets the criteria in Section 3480, paragraph .02 of the *CICA Handbook,* it is treated as an extraordinary loss.

If the asset's useful life or utility is increased upon restoration, the costs are capitalized to the extent of the improvement.

Significant post-acquisition expenditures fall into four major categories:

1. Maintenance and ordinary repairs.
2. Betterments.
3. Additions.
4. Rearrangements and other adjustments.

Maintenance and Ordinary Repairs

Maintenance expenditures include lubrication, cleaning, adjustment, and painting, incurred on a continuous basis to keep plant assets in usable condition. Ordinary repair costs include outlays for parts, labour, and related supplies that are necessary to keep assets in operating condition but neither add materially to the use value of assets nor prolong their useful life significantly. Ordinary repairs usually involve relatively small expenditures.

Two approaches are used to account for these revenue expenditures.

1. **Incurred approach** This approach records actual maintenance and repair expenditures as expenses as they occur and presumes an even distribution of expenditures over time. When annual expenditures for repairs and maintenance are not evenly distributed, the periods in which they occur bear a disproportionate

amount of maintenance cost. In these circumstances, the next approach is appropriate.

2. **Allocation approach** This approach is based on estimated repair and maintenance amounts. It is especially useful when repairs are seasonal in nature and material in amount. The total cost of repairs and maintenance expected is estimated and allocated on the basis of time or production, depending on the situation. If based on time, an equal amount of repair and maintenance expense is recognized each interim period, and a contra plant asset account is credited for the estimated amount. Actual expenditures for ordinary repairs and maintenance are charged against this contra account.

To illustrate the allocation approach, assume that $18,000 of ordinary repairs and maintenance are estimated for a year. This amount is allocated equally to each month. Suppose the total repair and maintenance cost incurred for the first month is $1,100. The entry to record the estimated expense and the related contra plant asset account for the month are as follows:

Repair and maintenance expense ($18,000 ÷ 12 months)	1,500	
Allowance for repairs and maintenance		1,500

The entry to record actual outlays in the first month for ordinary repairs and maintenance is:

To record actual repair costs:

Allowance for repairs and maintenance	1,100	
Cash or payables		1,100

The income statement reports $1,500 of repair and maintenance expense each month. The $400 credit balance in the allowance account is reported in the interim balance sheet as a reduction from the appropriate assets. The allowance account carries a credit balance whenever the expense recognized to date exceeds actual expenditures. At the end of the year, any remaining credit balance in the allowance account is closed to repair and maintenance expense, reducing the expense to the actual level. The allocation approach provides a better matching of interim expense and revenue.

Betterments

A betterment is the replacement of a major component of a capital asset with a significantly improved component. Examples include the replacement of an old shingle roof with a modern fireproof tile roof, installation of a more powerful engine in a ship, and significant improvement of the electrical system in a building.

A replacement is the substitution of a major component of a plant asset with one of comparable quality. Replacement of a truck engine with a similar engine is an example.

Renewals involve large expenditures, are not recurring in nature, and usually increase the utility or the service life of the asset beyond the original estimate. Major overhauls of equipment and strengthening of a building foundation are examples.

All these categories of expenditure increase the useful life or productivity of the original asset. Three different approaches have evolved to account for these expenditures, all causing the book value of the original asset to increase.

1. **Substitution** This approach removes the cost of the old component and related accumulated depreciation, recognizes a loss equal to the remaining book value, and increases the original asset account in the amount of the expenditure. To illustrate, assume that a shingle roof with an original cost of $20,000 and 80% depreciated is replaced by a fireproof tile roof costing $60,000. The two entries to record the betterment are as follows:

   To remove old component accounts:

Accumulated depreciation (old roof, $20,000 × .80)	16,000	
Loss on asset improvement	4,000	
Building (old roof)		20,000

To record cost of new component:

Building (new roof). 60,000
    Cash   60,000

The loss represents the undepreciated portion of the original roof cost. This approach is applied only when the original cost and accumulated depreciation are known. It is not used for extraordinary repairs that do not involve replacement of components.

2. **Increase asset account** This approach is used when the costs and depreciation amounts of the old component are not known and when the primary effect is to increase efficiency rather than the economic life of the basic asset. The cost of the betterment is debited to the original asset account under the historical cost principle. One result of this treatment is an overstatement of the basic asset's book value and subsequent depreciation, although this value is usually relatively minor at time of replacement.

3. **Reduce accumulated depreciation** This is the traditional approach used when the primary effect is to lengthen the remaining life of the related asset. The expenditure is debited to the relevant accumulated depreciation account on the grounds that some of the useful life is restored. The cost of the unit replaced is not removed from the accounts. Often, the depreciation rate must be revised. In light of the provisions in Section 3060 of the *CICA Handbook,* this method would appear to have questionable legitimacy.

Sometimes, replacements are required by law to ensure public safety or to meet environmental standards. For example, many localities require removal of asbestos insulation for health reasons. Is asbestos removal and replacement capitalizable, or should it be expensed? A case can be made either way. The useful life of the building is likely to remain unchanged as will the overall productivity of the building. On the other hand, employee safety is increased, and the firm has less exposure to health-related lawsuits.

Additions

Additions are extensions, enlargements, or expansions of an existing asset. An extra wing or room added to a building is an example. Additions represent capital expenditures and are recorded in the capital asset accounts at cost. Related work on the existing structure, such as shoring up the foundation for the addition or cutting an entranceway through an existing wall, is a part of the cost of the addition and is capitalized. If the addition is an integral part of the older asset, its cost, less any estimated residual value, is normally depreciated over the shorter of its own service life or the remaining life of the original asset. If the addition is not an integral part, it is depreciated over its own useful life.

Many firms retrofit production facilities with pollution control equipment to comply with laws and court orders. When the cost of antipollution devices exceeds the cost of the polluting assets, the devices are capitalized separately and depreciated as plant additions.

Rearrangements and Other Adjustments

The costs of reinstallation, rerouting, or rearrangements of factory machinery to increase efficiency are capital expenditures if the benefits of the rearrangement extend beyond the current accounting period. Such costs are capitalized as an other asset, a deferred charge, or a specific plant asset and amortized over the periods benefiting from the rearrangement.

> ## CONCEPT REVIEW
>
> 1. Why are ordinary maintenance and repair costs expensed if they prolong the useful life of a plant asset?
> 2. What is a limitation of the accepted accounting for the replacement of a major asset component when the cost of the original component is unknown?
> 3. What is the general principle for capitalizing post-acquisition expenditures?

SUMMARY OF KEY POINTS

(L.O. 1)   1. The historical cost of a capital asset equals the cash paid plus the market value of all other consideration transferred, or the market value of the asset received, whichever is more reliably determinable.

(L.O. 1, 2)   2. To be capitalized as a plant asset, an expenditure must contribute to placing the asset into its intended condition and location. Other costs are expensed.

(L.O. 3)   3. If debt is incurred for the acquisition of plant assets, the present value of the debt is used to value the asset. If equity securities are issued, the market value of the securities or the market value of the asset acquired, whichever is more objective, is used to value the asset.

(L.O. 4)   4. The general rule for capitalizing expenditures as plant assets and the matching principle support interest capitalization during construction.

(L.O. 4)   5. The interest that could have been avoided had the construction expenditures been applied to debt retirement constitutes the interest to be capitalized. The debt need not have been incurred specifically for construction.

(L.O. 5)   6. The gain or loss recognized on disposal of plant assets equals the difference between the market value of the consideration received and the book value of the asset at date of disposal.

(L.O. 6)   7. A plant asset acquired by exchanging a non-monetary asset is valued at its market value or the market value of assets exchanged, whichever is more objective. The non-monetary exchange of similar assets is recorded at the book value of the asset given up.

(L.O. 7)   8. Expenditures made on plant assets after their acquisition are classified as capital expenditures and debited to an asset account if either the useful life or productivity of the asset is enhanced. Otherwise, the expenditures are classified as expenses.

REVIEW PROBLEM

The following five short cases are independent.

1. **Plant asset cost classification** Maldive Company completes the construction of a building. The following independent items are the costs and other aspects relevant to the purchase of the lot and construction:

Cash payments to contractor.	$100,000
Total sales tax on materials used in construction in addition to payments made to contractor	3,000
Cost of land (building site).	50,000
Gross cost to raze old building on land	20,000
Proceeds from old building salvage	5,000
Power bill for electricity used in construction	2,000
Interest on purchase of materials.	1,000
Capitalized interest on construction.	3,000

What is the final recorded value of the land and building, respectively?

2. **Accounting for debt incurred on acquisition** The Round Wheel Barn Company purchases a tractor by making a down payment of $10,000. In addition, Round Wheel Barn signs a note requiring monthly payments of $2,000, starting one month after purchase and continuing for a total of 20 months. The contract calls for no interest, yet the prevailing interest rate is 24% on similar debts. What is the correct recorded value

of the asset at purchase? What is the interest expense recognized one month after purchase?

3. **Interest capitalization** Whitehouse Company spent a total of $300,000 cash on a construction project during 1993 and 1994. During 1995, Whitehouse spends an additional $200,000 evenly during the year on the project and completes it at the end of 1995. Debt outstanding during 1995 is:

Accounts payable average balance	$ 50,000
10% bonds payable.	700,000
12% construction loan	200,000

a. What is average accumulated expenditures for 1995?

b. Assume that average accumulated expenditures for 1995 is $600,000, without prejudice to your answer in (a). Using the specific method of capitalization of interest, compute the amount of interest capitalized in 1995.

c. Again assume that average accumulated expenditures for 1995 is $600,000. Using the weighted-average method of capitalization of interest, compute the interest capitalized in 1995.

4. **Accounting for exchange of plant asset** Ocular Company trades an electron microscope with an original cost of $200,000 and accumulated depreciation of $80,000 for new optical equipment (a similar asset). The old equipment has a fair market value of $160,000 at trade-in time, and Ocular receives $30,000 on the trade-in. Give the entry to record the exchange.

5. **Post-acquisition costs** After one-fourth of the useful life had expired on equipment with an original cost of $100,000 and no salvage value, a major component of the equipment is unexpectedly replaced. The old component was expected to last as long as the equipment itself, and the company records on the component indicates it originally cost $20,000 and had no expected salvage value. The replacement component cost $30,000 and has no usefulness beyond that of the equipment. Give the entry(ies) to record the company replacement. Assume straight-line depreciation.

SOLUTION

1.

Land		**Building**	
Land cost	$50,000	Cash payments—contractor	$100,000
Razing cost	20,000	Sales tax on materials	3,000
Salvage proceeds	(5,000)	Power bill	2,000
		Capitalized interest	3,000
Total land cost	$65,000	Total building cost	$108,000

2. Recorded value of tractor
$$= \$10,000 + \$2,000(PVA,2\%,20)$$
$$= \$10,000 + \$2,000(16.35143)$$
$$= \$42,703$$

Interest expense after one month $= (\$42,703 - \$10,000)(1/12)(.24)$
$$= \$654$$

3. a. AAE $= \$300,000 + \$200,000 \div 2 = \$400,000$

   b. Actual interest $= .10(\$700,000) + .12(\$200,000) = \$94,000$
   IPC $= .12(\$200,000) + .10(\$400,000 - \$200,000) = \$44,000$
   Therefore:

   Capitalized interest $= \$44,000$

   c. Weighted-average interest rate on all interest-bearing debt $= \dfrac{\$94,000}{\$900,000} = .10444$

   IPC $= .10444(\$400,000) = \$41,776$

   Therefore:

   Capitalized interest $= \$41,776$

4.

Equipment	90,000	
Accumulated depreciation	80,000	
Cash	30,000	
Equipment		200,000

5.	Loss	15,000	
	Accumulated depreciation $20,000 ÷ 4	5,000	
	Equipment.		20,000
	Equipment.	30,000	
	Cash		30,000

QUESTIONS

1. Capital assets are classified as tangible or intangible; distinguish between the two, and give examples. Under what balance sheet caption are tangible capital assets reported? Give at least one synonym for whatever caption you specify.
2. How does the historical cost principle apply to the acquisition of capital assets? What implications does the matching principle have for capital asset accounting?
3. Distinguish between capital and revenue expenditures. What accounting implications are involved?
4. To determine the cost of a capital asset, how should the following items be treated: (*a*) invoice price, (*b*) freight-in, (*c*) discounts, (*d*) title verification costs, (*e*) installation costs, (*f*) break-in costs, and (*g*) cost of a major overhaul before operational use?
5. A machine was purchased on the following terms: cash, $100,000, plus five annual payments of $5,000 each. How should the acquisition cost of the machine be determined? Explain.
6. How is an asset's acquisition cost determined when the consideration given consists of equity securities?
7. Basically, how are assets recorded when they are acquired by exchanging another asset?
8. When does the "culmination (completion) of an earnings process" occur upon exchange of assets?
9. When dissimilar assets are exchanged, what value is used as the cost of the asset acquired?
10. When several operational assets are purchased for a single lump-sum consideration, cost apportionment is usually employed. Explain the procedure. Why is apportionment necessary?
11. Should donated assets be recorded in the accounts? If so, how should they be recorded and at what value?
12. Under what conditions should general overhead be allocated to a self-constructed asset?
13. Some businesses construct plant assets for their own use. What costs should be capitalized for these assets? Explain what to do about (*a*) general company overhead and any incremental costs incurred and (*b*) costs of construction in excess of the purchase price from an outsider.
14. Basically, what amount of interest should be capitalized as a part of the cost of an asset?
15. For what types of assets requiring a substantial completion or processing time is interest capitalization inappropriate?
16. If interest can be capitalized on an asset requiring a substantial completion period, when must interest capitalization begin and cease?
17. Wembley Company borrowed $2 million at 10% to finance construction of a new loading pier, which turned out to cost $3 million aside from capitalized interest. Wembley has other debt. To what extent, if any, can interest in excess of $200,000 be capitalized in any full year the pier is under construction? As to the other debt, how is the interest rate determined for capitalization purposes?
18. Miller Corporation added a new wing to a plant building at a cost of $300,000 plus $10,000 spent in making passageways through the walls of the old structure. The plant was 10 years old and was being depreciated by an equal amount each year over a 30-year life. Over what period should the new wing be depreciated?
19. When are post-acquisition costs capitalized rather than expensed?
20. What is the nature of a gain or loss on disposal of an operational asset when cash is received?
21. Outline the accounting steps related to the disposition of an operational asset, assuming it is not traded in on another asset.
22. If interest is capitalized, what is the effect on income in the current year? What is the effect on income in future years?
23. Briefly explain how to compute the amount of gain or loss to be recognized in an exchange of similar operational assets when cash is received.
24. What value is assigned to an operational asset received in exchange for a dissimilar asset when cash is also received and the market value of the asset transferred is known?
25. What are the two treatments with respect to interest capitalization allowed by the IASC?

CASES

C 11–1
(L.O. 1, 2, 7)

Acquisition Cost: Expenditures Subsequent to Acquisition Assume that the market value of equipment acquired in a non-cash transaction is not determinable by reference to a cash purchase.

Required

1. Explain how the acquiring company should determine the capitalizable cost of equipment obtained through each of the following exchanges:
   a. Bonds that have an established market price.
   b. Common shares that do not have an established market price.
   c. Similar equipment that has a determinable market price.
2. Assume that the equipment was acquired and has been used by the acquiring company for three years. Expenditures related to the equipment must be made. Identify the various types of expenditures that might be involved and explain the appropriate accounting for each.

(AICPA adapted)

C 11–2
(L.O. 1)

Court Settlement: Capitalize versus Expense Consolidated Smelting Company, which operates in the east, agreed in a court settlement to:

a. Install pollution control equipment on its smelters at an estimated cost of $18 million.
b. Pay specified medical expenses for children living near its facilities who were suffering from lead poisoning; tentatively estimated cost of $2,000,000 is to be paid as families incur expenses.
c. Pay a civil penalty of $200,000 over a four-year term in equal $50,000 instalments.

Required

1. For each item above, discuss the propriety of capitalizing versus expensing the cost.
2. What amount should be attributed to each item immediately after the settlement (before any payments are made) and how should each be accounted for or disclosed?

C 11–3
(L.O. 1)

Asset Cost: Related Incidental Costs The invoice price of a machine is $20,000. Various other costs relating to the acquisition and installation of the machine amount to $5,000 and include such things as transportation, electrical wiring, special base, and so forth. The machine has an estimated life of 10 years and no residual value.

The owner of the business suggests that the incidental costs of $5,000 be debited to expense immediately for three reasons: (1) if the machine should be sold, these costs could not be recovered in the sales price; (2) the inclusion of the $5,000 in the machinery account will not necessarily result in a closer approximation of the market price of this asset over the years because of the possibility of changing price levels; and (3) debiting the $5,000 to expense immediately will reduce federal income taxes.

Required

Discuss each of the points raised by the owner of the business.

(AICPA adapted)

C 11–4
(L.O. 1)

Asset Cost: After Acquisition but before Use One of your clients, a savings bank with several local branches, recently acquired ownership of a lot and building located in a historical part of the city. The building was dilapidated, unsuitable for human habitation. The bank thought at the time that it was acquiring a site for a new branch. Although a firm of architects recommended demolition, the city council, in whose discretion such activity rests, refused consent to demolish the building in view of its historical and architectural value.

In order to comply with safety requirements and to make the building suitable for use as a branch location, the bank spent $250,000 restoring and altering the old building. It had paid $90,000 for the building and lot and had contemplated spending $200,000 on a new building after demolishing the old structure. Somewhat similar old buildings in less run-down condition could have been bought in the same area for about the same $90,000 price. It is possible, even likely, that some of these that were not so old could have been demolished without governmental intervention, and the bank could have carried out its original plan.

Now that the restoration is finished and the bank is making final plans to open its newest branch in the restored building, the bank has been informed by the Municipal Historical Commission that the building qualifies for and will receive a plaque designating it as a historical site. The designation will be of some value in attracting traffic to the site, the building will probably be pointed out during tours of the city, and so on. Under present laws, receipt of the designation may well mean that the bank can never demolish the structure and is obligated to preserve it, even if the property is later vacated.

Required

1. Discuss the pros and cons of capitalizing the entire $250,000 spent on restoration of the building.
2. How should the $90,000 original expenditure be treated? What would have been the cost of the land if the bank had been able to carry out its original plans?
3. Sooner or later, your client is likely to seek advice as to proper accounting for subsequent costs—repairs, depreciation, possible improvements, and so on. What advice would you give?

C 11–5
(L.O. 4)

Interest Capitalization: Rationale and Discussion   Two competing publicly held firms in the same city, Infosystems Company and Data Capability Company, built very similar buildings in the same year. Both buildings were built at a hard-dollar cost of approximately $30,000,000. This amount included material, labour, and other incremental costs. The common shares (voting ownership shares) of both companies are traded on the same stock exchange.

Infosystems, which has been in business several decades, has very little debt. Consequently, it capitalized only $2,000,000 of interest, bringing the total cost of its building to $32,000,000. Data Capability, a relatively new company, is highly leveraged and capitalized $12,000,000 of interest, bringing its building cost up to $42,000,000.

Required

Discuss the rationale for interest capitalization by these two companies. Include in your discussion reasons for and against interest capitalization, the matching principle, and the CICA definition of an asset.

C 11–6
(L.O. 1, 4, 5, 7)

Ethical Considerations   Robert Baker, accountant for Miller Motor Company, is aware that the rules for interest capitalization are relatively flexible. He understands that either the specific or the weighted-average method may be used to compute interest potentially capitalizable (IPC). He also understands that either a continuous expenditure assumption (construction payments are assumed to be evenly distributed throughout the construction period) or a discrete assumption (each payment receives a weight based on the time it is invested in the project) may be used.

Bob was recently congratulated on his choice of accounting methods at the annual holiday dinner held for management and top-level staff. Among his choices were FIFO for inventories, straight-line depreciation, and long useful lives for operational assets. Bob, without informing management, also consistently employs the IPC calculation method that capitalizes the greatest amount of interest. When current interest rates are high and specific construction debt balances are high, he chooses the specific method. When interest rates moderate, especially after a period of relatively high general interest rates, he goes back to the weighted-average method.

He also times payments to contractors, through his influence over the accounts payable department, so that significant payments are made near the end of the year. He also uses the continuous expenditure assumption to measure average accumulated expenditures when the result will increase IPC.

Required

Discuss the propriety of Bob's accounting methods. Why might they have been chosen? Do you think that any ethical considerations are relevant to the case?

C 11–7
(L.O. 1)

Accounting for Land Costs   Write a brief report comparing and contrasting the accounting for the following expenditures related to land for your client, Caspar Golfing, a golfing supply retailer. In your discussion, refer to the general principle for inclusion of expenditures in property, plant, and equipment, and why you believe the expenditure should or should not be included in the land account.

1. The cost of constructing a paved parking lot on land already owned by Caspar. Presently, customers must park on a gravel lot next to Caspar's retail outlet.
2. The net cost, after salvage proceeds, to raze an old building on a tract of land just purchased by Caspar. A practice putting green will be constructed in its place.
3. The net cost, after salvage proceeds, to raze the original building constructed several years ago by Caspar to house the retail operations. Caspar intends to build a larger building to be used for the same purpose.
4. The allocated cost of a building on a second tract of land just purchased by Caspar. The land and building were valued separately by a reliable appraiser, but Caspar was able to purchase the package at a lump-sum price considerably less than the sum of the land and building market values. Caspar plans to demolish the building and construct a second retail outlet on the property.

EXERCISES

E 11-1
(L.O. 1)

Acquisition of Land: Non-Cash Considerations   Under the cost principle, what cost should be used for recording the land acquired in each of the following independent cases? Give reasons in support of your answer.

a. At the middle of the current year, a cheque was given for $40,000 for the land, and the buyer assumed the liability for unpaid taxes in arrears at the end of last year, $1,000, and those assessed for the current year, $900.

b. A company issued 14,000 shares of capital stock with a market value of $6 per share (based on a recent sale of 10 shares) for the land. The land was recently appraised at $80,000 by independent and competent appraisers.

c. A company rejected an offer to purchase the land for $8,000 cash two years ago. Instead, the company issued 1,000 shares of capital stock for the land (market value of the shares, $7.80 per share based on several recent large transactions and normal weekly share trading volume).

d. A company issued 1,000 shares of capital stock for the land. The market value (shares sell daily with an average daily volume of 5,000 shares) was $60 per share at time of purchase of the land. The vendor earlier offered to sell the land for $59,000 cash. Competent appraisers valued the land at $61,000.

E 11-2
(L.O. 3)

Asset Acquisition: Note Payable   Vee Corporation acquired equipment on credit. Terms were $7,000 cash down payment plus payments of $5,000 at the end of each of the next two years. The seller's implicit interest rate was 14%. The list price of the equipment was $17,000.

Required

Round to the nearest dollar.

a. Give the entry to record the purchase.
b. Give the entry to record the last $5,000 payment.

E 11-3
(L.O. 2)

Assets Acquired: Note Payable, Discount   The following situations are independent:

a. Delivery equipment with a list price of $30,000 was purchased; terms were 2/10, n/30. Payment was made within the discount period.

b. Delivery equipment with a list price of $20,000 was purchased; terms were 2/10, n/30. Payment was made after the discount period.

c. Delivery equipment listed at $9,000 was purchased and invoiced at 2/10, n/30. In order to take advantage of the discount, the company borrowed $8,000 of the purchase price by issuing a 60-day, 15% note, which was paid with interest at the maturity date.

Required

Give entries in each separate situation for costs, borrowing, and any expenses involved.

E 11-4
(L.O. 1)

Acquisition of Multiple Assets for a Single Price   Freeman Company purchased a tract of land on which were located a warehouse and an office building. The cash purchase price was $140,000 plus $10,000 in fees connected with the purchase. The following data were collected concerning the property:

	Tax Assessment	Vendor's Book Value	Original Cost
Land	$20,000	$10,000	$10,000
Warehouse	40,000	20,000	60,000
Office building.	60,000	50,000	80,000

Required

Give the entry to record the purchase; show computations.

E 11-5
(L.O. 3)

Asset Acquisition: Time Payment Plan   Wolf Company bought a machine on a time payment plan. The cash purchase price was $25,615. Terms were $7,000 cash down payment plus four equal annual payments at year-end of $6,000, which include interest on the unpaid balance at 11% per annum.

Required

1. Give the entry to record the purchase. Show computations (round to nearest dollar).

2. Prepare a schedule to reflect the accounting entries for each of the four instalment payments. Round amounts in the schedule to the nearest dollar.

E 11-6
(L.O. 5)

Similar and Dissimilar Assets Exchanged   Bloem Corporation has some old equipment that cost $70,000; accumulated depreciation is $40,000. This equipment was traded in on a new machine that had a list price of $80,000; however, the new machine could be purchased without a trade-in for $75,000 cash. The difference between the market value of the new asset and the market value of the old asset will be paid in cash.

Required

Give the entry to record the acquisition of the new machine under each of the following independent cases:

a. The new machine was purchased for cash with no trade-in.
b. The equipment and the machine are dissimilar. The old equipment is traded in, and $50,000 cash is paid.
c. Same as (b) except that the equipment and the machine are similar.

E 11-7
(L.O. 5)

Assets Exchanged: Five Different Cases   Seismographics Corporation exchanged old equipment that cost $10,000 (accumulated depreciation, $4,500) for new equipment. The market value of the new equipment was $8,000. The market value of the old equipment could not be reliably estimated.

Required

Give the entry to record the acquisition of the new equipment under each of the following independent cases:

a. The assets are dissimilar. No cash was involved.
b. The assets are dissimilar. Cash of $3,000 was paid by Seismographics.
c. The assets are similar. No cash was involved.
d. The assets are similar. Cash of $500 was paid by Seismographics.
e. The assets are similar. Cash of $700 was received by Seismographics.

E 11-8
(L.O. 1)

Acquisition of Multiple Assets for a Single Price   Brushy Machine Shop purchased the following used equipment at a special auction sale for $40,000 cash: a drill press, a lathe, and a heavy-duty air compressor. The equipment was in excellent condition except for the electric motor on the lathe, which will cost $900 to replace with a new motor. Brushy has determined that the selling prices for the used items in local outlets are approximately as follows: drill press, $8,400; lathe, with a good motor, $24,000; and air compressor, $10,500.

Required

Give the entry to record (a) acquisition of the operational assets and (b) replacement of the motor.

E 11-9
(L.O. 3)

Donated Assets   A wealthy shareholder donated a building and the land on which it is located to a company. The property was reliably appraised at a value of $160,000 (one-fourth related to the land). The company paid transfer costs of $4,000. The building has an estimated remaining life of 25 years (no residual value).

Required

Give the entries to record the (a) transfer and (b) depreciation expense at the end of the first year. Assume a full year of depreciation and the straight-line method.

E 11-10
(L.O. 3)

Government Assistance   The Weipert Widget Company installed at a cost of $2,200,000 a new portable factory in an isolated area of Quebec. In consideration for locating in this area, Weipert Widget received a grant from the federal government in the amount of $800,000 for the factory purchase, as well as a grant of $150,000 from the province of Quebec to defray the cost of the necessary land purchase. The building was put into use in early March 1995, shortly after the beginning of the fiscal year, and has the capability of producing a new improved line of widgets for 15 years, with no residual value expected.

Required

Prepare the journal entries necessary to account for the government assistance and for depreciation expense for the fiscal year ending February 28, 1996, under each of the two alternative treatments suggested by the *CICA Handbook*. Label your solution by method.

(SMA adapted)

E 11–11
(L.O. 3)

Self-Constructed Asset: Rationale for Accounting Treatment   Amethyst Company constructed a building and incurred the following costs directly associated with construction:

Materials.	$25,000
Labour.	40,000
Incremental overhead	15,000
Interest on the construction loan incurred before completion.	2,500
Interest on the construction loan incurred after completion	1,000
Total.	$83,500

The building was worth $77,500 (market value) upon completion.

Required

1. Provide summary journal entries to record construction and completion of the building. Assume that all qualifying interest during the current year is to be capitalized to the building.
2. Discuss the rationale for the limitation on the valuation of Amethyst's building in terms of the historical cost principle.

E 11–12
(L.O. 4)

Capitalization of Interest: Specific Method   Weld Corporation is constructing a plant for its own use. Weld capitalizes interest on an annual basis. The following expenditures were made during the current year: January 1, $15,000; July 1, $145,000; September 1, $400,000; and December 31, $1,055,000. The following debts were outstanding throughout the year:

Construction note, 12%.	$ 50,000
Short-term note payable, 15%	200,000
Accounts payable (noninterest-bearing).	200,000

Weld capitalizes interest first using the interest rate on debt directly associated with the construction and then using the weighted-average rate of all other debt (i.e., the specific method).

Required

1. Compute the amount of interest to be capitalized and the amount of interest to be expensed.
2. Give the entry to record the construction expenditures and interest.

E 11–13
(L.O. 4)

Capitalization of Interest: Weighted-Average Method

Required

Using the information in E 11–12, compute the amount of interest to be capitalized under the weighted-average method.

E 11–14
(L.O. 1, 5)

Multiple Choice: Acquisition and Exchange   Choose the correct statement among the alternatives.

1. Deal Company traded a delivery van and $10,000 cash for a newer delivery van owned by East Corporation. The following information relates to the values of the vans on the exchange date:

	Carrying Value	Fair Value
Old van	$60,000	$ 90,000
New van.	80,000	100,000

What amount should Deal report as a gain on exchange of the vans?
   a. $30,000.
   b. $20,000.
   c. $10,000.
   d. $0.

2. Valley Company traded equipment with an original cost of $50,000 and accumulated depreciation of $20,000 for similar productive equipment with a fair value of $30,000. In addition, Valley received $5,000 cash in connection with this exchange. What should be Valley's carrying amount for the equipment received?
   a. $15,000.
   b. $20,000.
   c. $25,000.
   d. $30,000.

3. Bengal Company purchased a $200,000 tract of land for a factory site. Bengal razed an old building on the property and sold the materials it salvaged from the demolition. Bengal incurred additional costs and realized salvage proceeds as follows:

Demolition of old building	$25,000
Legal fees for purchase contract and recording ownership.	5,000
Title guaranty insurance	6,000
Proceeds from sale of salvaged materials	4,000

As a result, what balance should Bengal report in the land account?

a. $232,000.

b. $230,000.

c. $221,000.

d. $211,000.

4. On July 1, one of Renee Company's delivery vans was destroyed in an accident. On that date, the van's carrying value was $5,000. On July 15, Renee received and recorded a $1,400 invoice for a new engine installed in the van earlier in May and another $1,000 invoice for various repairs. In August, Renee received $7,000 under its insurance policy on the van, which it plans to use to replace the van. What amount should Renee report as a gain (loss) on disposal of the van in its income statement?

a. $2,000.

b. $600.

c. $0.

d. $(400).

5. Lamont Company's forest land was condemned for annexation to a national park. Compensation for the condemnation exceeded the land's carrying value. Lamont purchased similar, but larger, replacement forest land for an amount greater than the condemnation award. As a result of the condemnation and replacement, what is the net effect of the carrying value of forest land reported in Lamont's balance sheet?

a. The amount is increased by the excess of the replacement forest land's cost over the condemned forest land's carrying amount.

b. The amount is increased by the excess of the replacement forest land's cost over the condemnation award.

c. The amount is increased by the excess of the condemnation award over the condemned forest land's carrying amount.

d. There is no effect, because the condemned forest land's carrying amount is used as the replacement forest land's carrying amount.

(AICPA adapted)

E 11–15
(L.O. 1, 2)

Asset Acquisition   During the current year, Candle Soap Company began a project to construct its new corporate headquarters. Candle purchased land with an old building for $375,000. The land was valued at $350,000 and the building at $25,000. Candle plans to demolish the building. Additional expenditures on the project include:

a. Interest of $73,500 on construction financing incurred after completion of construction of the headquarters building.

b. Interest of $93,000 on construction financing paid during construction of the headquarters building.

c. Payment of $9,250 for delinquent real estate taxes assumed by Candle on purchase of the land and building.

d. Liability insurance premium of $6,000 covering the construction period.

e. Cost of $32,500 for razing the existing building.

f. Costs of $68,000 to move into new headquarters.

Required

Assuming no previous acquisitions of plant assets, determine Candle's ending balance in all relevant plant asset accounts given the above information. Also note the total amount of expense, if any, to be recognized.

(AICPA adapted)

E 11–16
(L.O. 7)

Ordinary Repairs: Incurred Approach versus Allocation Approach   Jenkins Company operates two separate plants. In Plant A, the accounting policy is to expense all ordinary (minor) repairs as incurred. In contrast, in Plant B, the accounting policy is to use the allocation approach that debits repair and maintenance expense equally each period. Jenkins Company has little seasonality in its production. Selected data for 1995 are as follows:

	Plant A	Plant B
Estimated repair costs budgeted for year	$5,000	$5,000
Actual repair costs incurred and paid:		
First quarter	1,200	400
Second quarter	800	1,500
Third quarter	1,000	1,100
Fourth quarter	2,100	2,200

Required

1. Give the entries in parallel columns for each plant for each of the four quarters.
2. Would you recommend any changes in the accounting policies? Explain and justify your response.

E 11–17
(L.O. 7)

Repairs, Replacements, Betterments, and Renovations   The plant building of Xon Corporation is old (estimated remaining useful life, 12 years) and needs continuous maintenance and repairs. The company's accounts show that the building originally cost $600,000; accumulated depreciation was $400,000 at the beginning of the current year. During the current year, the following expenditures relating to the plant building were made:

a. Continuing, frequent, and low-cost repairs . . . . $ 34,000
b. Added a new storage shed attached to the building; estimated useful life, eight years   72,000
c. Removed original roof; original cost, $80,000; replaced it with guaranteed, modern roof   100,000
d. Unusual and infrequent repairs due to damage from flood in desert; repairs did not
   increase the use value or the economic life of the asset   12,000
e. Complete overhaul of the plumbing system (old costs not known).   25,000

Required

Give the journal entry to record each of the above items. Explain the basis for your treatment of each item.

E 11–18
(L.O. 5)

Disposal of Operational Assets: Interpretation of Resulting Gain or Loss   Renny Company sells a machine on June 1, 1995, for $139,000. Renny incurred $800 of removal and selling costs on disposal. The machine cost $250,000 when it was purchased on January 2, 1992. Its estimated residual value and useful life were $40,000 and 10 years, respectively. Renny uses straight-line depreciation and records annual depreciation on December 31.

Required

1. Provide the journal entries needed to record the disposal.
2. How would the gain or loss in (1) be affected if the machine were abandoned (zero market value)?
3. Provide an interpretation of the gain or loss in (1) for someone with little or no background in accounting.

E 11–19
(L.O. 5)

Disposal of Asset   On April 1, 1995, one of the two large production machines used by Unlucky Company stripped a gear, causing major internal damages. On April 10, 1995, the company decided to purchase a new machine (cost, $182,500) so that production could continue. On January 1, 1995, the accounts showed the following for the old machine: original cost, $90,000; accumulated depreciation, $63,000 (20-year life; no residual value). The company would not accept a trade-in offer of $13,500. Instead, the old machine was sold on May 1, 1995, to another company for $24,000. Unlucky spent $3,000 cleaning and moving the old machine prior to shipping, which cost another $1,000. Insurance premium (prepaid) for 1995 on the old machine was $45; the unused portion of the premium will be applied to the new machine. The insurance was paid on January 1, 1995, and covered the period January 1, 1995, through December 31, 1995.

Required

Give all entries, by date, that Unlucky Company should make from April 1 through May 1, 1995.

E 11–20
(L.O. 1, 2)

Asset Cost—Seven Cases   Select the best answer for each of the following. Briefly justify your choice for each item.

1. May Company purchased certain plant assets on credit. May agreed to pay $10,000 per year for five years. The plant assets should be valued at:
   a. $50,000.
   b. $50,000 plus a charge for the market rate of interest.
   c. Present value of a $10,000 annuity for five years at the market interest rate.
   d. Present value of a $10,000 annuity for five years discounted at the bank prime interest rate.

2. The debit for a sales tax properly levied and paid on the purchase of machinery preferably would be to:
   a. A separate deferred charge account.
   b. Miscellaneous tax expense (which includes all taxes other than those on income).
   c. Accumulated depreciation, machinery.
   d. The machinery account.
3. When a closely held corporation issues preferred shares for land, the land should be recorded at the:
   a. Total par value of the shares issued.
   b. Total book value of the shares issued.
   c. Appraised value of the land.
   d. Total liquidating value of the shares issued.
4. An improvement made to a machine increased its market value and its production capacity by 25% without extending the machine's useful life. The cost of the improvement should be:
   a. Expensed.
   b. Debited to accumulated depreciation.
   c. Capitalized in the machine account.
   d. Allocated between accumulated depreciation and the machine account.

Items (5), (6), and (7) are based on the following information. Two independent companies, Ball and Brown, are in the home-building business. Each owns a tract of land for development, but each company would prefer to build on the other's land. Accordingly, they agree to exchange their land. An appraiser was hired, and from the report and the companies' records, the following information was obtained:

	Ball Co.'s Land	Brown Co.'s Land
Cost (same as book value)	$ 80,000	$50,000
Market value based on appraisal.	100,000	90,000

The exchange of land was made, and based on the difference in appraised values, Brown paid $5,000 cash to Ball.

5. For financial reporting purposes, Ball would recognize a pretax gain on this exchange in the amount of:
   a. $0.
   b. $10,000.
   c. $20,000.
   d. $30,000.
6. For financial reporting purposes, Brown would recognize a pretax gain on this exchange in the amount of:
   a. $0.
   b. $10,000.
   c. $30,000.
   d. $40,000.
7. After the exchange, Ball would record its newly acquired land at:
   a. $50,000.
   b. $75,000.
   c. $80,000.
   d. $85,000.

(AICPA adapted)

PROBLEMS

P 11–1
(L.O. 3)

Asset Acquired: Instalment Payments   Acme Cement Company contracted to buy equipment, agreeing to make an equal annual payment of $10,832 at the end of each of the next four years. The equipment has a list price of $32,900 (which is also the cash price), an estimated service life of five years, and an estimated residual value of $2,000.

Required   Round to the nearest dollar.

1. Determine the approximate interest rate implicit in the contract and prepare a debt amortization schedule for the four-year period. Record the purchase of the equipment in conformity with GAAP.
2. Assuming that Acme's fiscal year coincides with the payment dates, record (a) the first payment and (b) the depreciation at the end of the first year (use straight-line depreciation).
3. Give similar entries at the end of the fourth year.

P 11–2
(L.O. 3)

Asset Acquisition: Non-Cash Consideration   Machinery with a market value of $30,000 is acquired in a non-cash exchange. Below are five independent assumptions (a to e) as to the consideration given in the non-cash exchange:

a. Bonds held as a long-term investment to be held to maturity, which originally cost $56,000 and had been written down 50% because of a perceived permanent loss of their value.
b. Inventory carried at $19,000 on the most recent balance sheet as part of a perpetual inventory carried at LCM. When originally acquired, the goods had cost $19,800.
c. Similar used machinery with a book value of $12,000 and a market value of $13,400 plus cash of $16,600. When new, the used machinery cost $17,600.
d. Land with a book value of $15,000 and a market value of $30,000.
e. A noninterest-bearing note for $34,500 maturing in one year. Notes of similar risk required 15% interest at the date of the exchange.

Required   Give the journal entry required for each of the above independent assumptions.

P 11–3
(L.O. 1, 2, 7)

Acquisition Cost: Six Cost Changes   An examination of the property, plant, and equipment accounts of James Company on December 31, 1995, disclosed the following transactions:

a. On January 1, 1994, a new machine was purchased having a list price of $30,000. The company did not take advantage of a 1% cash discount available upon full payment of the invoice within 10 days. Shipping cost paid by the vendor was $100. Installation cost was $400, including $100 that represented 10% of the monthly salary of the factory superintendent (installation period, two days). A wall was moved two feet at a cost of $800 to make room for the machine.
b. During January 1994, the first month of operations, the newly purchased machine became inoperative due to a defect in manufacture. The vendor repaired the machine at no cost; however, the specially trained operator was idle during the two weeks the machine was inoperative. The operator was paid regular wages ($650) during the period, although the only work performed was to observe the repair by the factory representative.
c. On January 1, 1994, bought fixtures with a list price of $4,500; paid cash $1,500 and gave a one-year, noninterest-bearing note payable for the balance. The current interest rate for this type of note was 15%.
d. On July 1, 1994, a contractor completed construction of a building for the company. The company paid the contractor by transferring $400,000 face value, 20-year, 8% James Company bonds payable, at which time financial consultants advised that the bonds would sell at 96 (i.e., $384,000).
e. During January 1995, exchanged the electric motor on a machine for a heavier motor and paid $400 cash. The market value of the new motor was $1,250. The parts list showed a $900 cost for the original motor (estimated life, 10 years).
f. On January 1, 1994, purchased an automatic counter to be attached to a machine in use, cost $700. The estimated useful life of the counter was 7 years, and the estimated life of the machine was 10 years.

Required

1. Prepare the journal entries to record each of the above transactions as of the date of occurrence. Explain and justify your decisions on questionable items. James Company uses straight-line depreciation.
2. Record depreciation at the end of 1994. None of the assets is expected to have a residual value except the fixtures (residual value is $500). Estimated useful lives: fixtures, 5 years; machinery, 10 years; and building, 40 years. Give a separate entry for each asset.

P 11–4
(L.O. 1, 7)

Multiple Choice: Asset Acquisition and Post-Acquisition Costs   Choose the correct answer for each of the following questions.

1. Discounts available for early payment of liabilities incurred for the purchase of operational assets should be:
   a. Recorded and reported as a contra account to the related liability account.

     b. Given no recognition until taken or until the discount period has expired; if not taken, the discounts should be added to the cost of the asset.

     c. Deducted from the invoice price, whether taken or not.

     d. Capitalized as a part of the cost of the asset, whether taken or not, and subsequently included in depreciation expense.

2. Able Corporation purchased an old building and the land on which it is located. The old building will be demolished at a net cost of $10,000. A new building will be built on the site. The net demolition cost (after salvage proceeds) should be:

     a. Depreciated over the remaining life of the new building.

     b. Written off as an extraordinary loss in year of demolition.

     c. Capitalized as part of the cost of the land.

     d. Written off as an expense.

3. Shwee Corporation purchased land by signing a note with the seller calling for $10,000 down, $12,000 one year from purchase, and $8,000 three years from purchase. The note is not interest-bearing, but the going rate for similar land purchase notes is 10%. What value should be recorded in the land account?

     a. $25,019.

     b. $26,920.

     c. $27,000.

     d. $30,000.

4. The cost to train employees to run new robotic technology used in manufacturing should be debited to:

     a. Machinery.

     b. Deferred charge.

     c. Manufacturing expense.

     d. Office salaries.

5. At great cost, a special plastic film was applied to all the south- and west-facing windows of a 12-storey office building. This film reduces the radiant energy entering the building and is expected to pay for itself in reduced air-conditioning costs in five years. The useful life of the windows is not affected. The cost of this film should be debited to:

     a. Maintenance and repair expense.

     b. Building.

     c. Leasehold improvement.

     d. Other expense.

6. A music system was added to the office building and elevators to create a more pleasant environment. The system consists of new wiring, speakers, and state-of-the-art amplification equipment. The cost of the system should be debited to:

     a. Entertainment expense.

     b. Furniture.

     c. Building.

     d. Employee expenses.

7. The cost of repaving a parking lot with a new, longer-life asphalt should be debited to which of the following accounts? The company owns the land and the lot. The new asphalt will increase the life of the present lot significantly over the original expected useful life.

     a. Land improvements.

     b. Land.

     c. An expense account.

     d. Deferred charge.

P 11–5
(L.O. 1, 2, 3)

Asset Acquisition   At December 31, 1994, certain accounts included in the property, plant, and equipment section of Hine Corporation's balance sheet had the following balances:

Land	$ 600,000
Buildings	1,300,000
Leasehold improvements	800,000
Machinery and equipment.	1,600,000

During 1995, the following transactions occurred:

     a. Land site number 101 was acquired for $3,000,000. Additionally, to acquire the land, Hine paid a $180,000 commission to a real estate agent. Costs of $30,000 were incurred to clear the land. During the course of clearing the land, timber and gravel were recovered and sold for $16,000.

b. A second tract of land (site number 102) with a building was acquired for $600,000. The closing statement indicated that the land value was $400,000 and the building value was $200,000. Shortly after acquisition, the building was demolished at a cost of $40,000. A new building was constructed for $300,000 plus the following costs:

Excavation fees	$12,000
Architectural design fees	16,000
Building permit fee	4,000

The building was completed and occupied on September 30, 1995.

c. A third tract of land (site number 103) was acquired for $1,500,000 and was put on the market for resale.

d. Extensive work was done to a building occupied by Hine under a lease agreement that expires on December 31, 2004. The total cost of the work was $250,000, as follows:

Item	Cost	Estimated Useful Life (years)
Painting of ceilings	$ 10,000	1
Electrical work	90,000	10
Construction of extension to current working area	150,000	25
	$250,000	

The lessor paid half the costs incurred for the extension to the current working area.

e. During December 1995, $120,000 was spent to improve leased office space. The related lease will terminate on December 31, 1998, and is not expected to be renewed.

f. A group of new machines was purchased under a royalty agreement, which provides for payment of royalties based on units of production for the machines. The invoice price of the machines was $270,000, freight costs were $2,000, unloading costs were $3,000, and royalty payments for 1995 were $44,000.

Required

Disregard the related accumulated depreciation accounts.

1. Prepare a detailed analysis of the changes in each of the following balance sheet accounts for 1995. (Hint: Set up a separate analysis for land, buildings, leasehold improvements, and machinery and equipment.)
   a. Land.
   b. Buildings.
   c. Leasehold improvements.
   d. Machinery and equipment.
2. List the amounts in the items (a to d) that were not used to determine the answer to (1) above, and indicate where, or whether, these items should be included in Hine's financial statements.

(AICPA adapted)

P 11–6
(L.O. 3)

Operational Asset Acquisition through Debt: Gross and Net Methods of Recording   Lien Company purchased machinery on January 1, 1995, and gave a two-year, 6%, $2,000 note that pays interest each December 31. The market interest rate is 12% on such notes.

Required

Record the purchase of the asset, the two interest payments, and note extinguishment under the following two methods:

1. Gross method.
2. Net method.

P 11–7
(L.O. 6)

Assets Exchanged: Similar and Dissimilar Compared   Trader Joe, Inc., has a policy of trading in equipment after one year's use. The following information is available from Trader Joe's records:

January 1, 1992—Acquired asset A for $12,000 cash.
January 1, 1993—Exchanged asset A for asset B. Asset B had a market value of $14,000.
   Paid $1,000 in cash in the exchange.
January 1, 1994—Exchanged asset B for asset C. Asset C had a market value of $16,000.
   Paid $1,500 in cash in the exchange.
January 1, 1995—Exchanged asset C for asset D. Asset D had a market value of $11,000.
   Received $2,000 in cash in the exchange.

Assume a five-year estimated useful life and no residual value for all assets. Trader Joe uses straight-line depreciation.

Required

1. Assume that the assets are all similar. Give the journal entries required for each exchange.
2. Assume that the assets are all dissimilar. Give the journal entries required for each exchange.

P 11-8
(L.O. 6)

Assets Exchanged: Similar and Dissimilar, No Cash versus Cash Paid   This problem presents two independent cases—case A, similar assets, and case B, dissimilar assets.

a. **Case A**   Two similar operational assets were exchanged when the accounts of the two companies involved reflected the following:

Account	Company M (designate as asset M)	Company N (designate as asset N)
Operational asset.	$4,000	$4,100
Accumulated depreciation.	2,750	2,400

The market value of asset M was reliably determined to be $1,400; no reliable estimate could be made of asset N.

Required   Round amounts to the nearest dollar.

1. Give the exchange entry for each company, assuming that no cash difference is involved.
2. Give the exchange entry for each company, assuming that a cash difference of $400 was paid by Company M to Company N.

b. **Case B**   Two dissimilar operational assets were exchanged when the accounts of the two companies involved reflected the following:

Account	Company A (designate as asset A)	Company B (designate as asset B)
Operational asset.	$5,000	$7,000
Accumulated depreciation.	3,500	5,250

The market value of asset A was reliably determined to be $2,250; no reliable estimate could be made for asset B.

Required

1. Give the exchange entry for each company, assuming that no cash difference was involved.
2. Give the exchange entry for each company, assuming that a cash difference of $600 was paid by Company A to Company B.

P 11-9
(L.O. 6)

Assets Exchanged, Entries for Both Parties: Five Transactions   In this problem, all items of property refer to operational assets, not inventory, unless specified to the contrary. List prices are not necessarily market values.

Required   Give journal entries where specified to record the following transactions:

1. Land carried on the books of Company A at $18,000 is exchanged for a computer carried on the books of Corporation B at $25,000 (cost, $35,000; accumulated depreciation, $10,000). Market value of both assets is $30,000. Give the journal entry for both A and B.
2. A truck, which cost Company A $6,000 ($3,000 accumulated depreciation), has a market value of $3,400. It is traded to a dealer, plus a $5,600 cash payment, for a new truck that has a $12,400 list price. Give the journal entry for Company A.
3. A truck that cost Company A $6,000, on which $5,000 depreciation has been accumulated, is traded to a dealer along with $6,300 cash. The new truck would have cost $7,000 if only cash had been paid; its list price is $7,500. Give the journal entry for Company A.
4. Land carried on the books of Company A at $90,000 is exchanged for land carried on the books of Corporation B at $78,000. Market value of each tract is $100,000. Give the journal entry for Corporation B.
5. Fixtures that cost Company A $15,000 ($9,000 accumulated depreciation) and are worth $8,000 are traded to Corporation B along with $500 cash. In exchange, A receives fixtures from B carried by B at a cost of $13,000 less $6,000 accumulated depreciation. Give the journal entries for both A and B; if necessary, round amounts to the nearest dollar.

P 11–10
(L.O. 3)

Donated Assets   Hermanson Company received a vacant building as a donation. The building has a 20-year estimated useful life (no residual value), which was recognized in the donation agreement at the time that the company was guaranteed occupancy. Transfer costs of $12,000 were paid by the company. The building originally cost $300,000, 10 years earlier. The building was recently appraised at $160,000 market value by the city's tax assessor. Anticipating occupancy within the next 10 days, the company spent $36,000 for repairs and internal rearrangements (good for 10 years). There are no unresolved contingencies about the building and Hermanson's permanent occupancy.

Required

Give all entries for Hermanson Company related to (a) the donation, (b) the renovation, and (c) any depreciation or amortization at the end of the first year of occupancy, assuming that Hermanson uses straight-line depreciation and that the assets have no residual value.

P 11–11
(L.O. 3)

Government Assistance   The Gysbers Company Limited has embarked on a three-year pollution control program that will require the purchase of smoke stack scrubbers costing a total of $600,000. The federal government will lend Gysbers 50% of the cost, provided that emissions are reduced 95% during the fourth year, at which time the loans will be forgiven. The federal funds are received as the expenditures are made. If the standards are not met, the loan will have to be repaid.

Gysbers will depreciate the devices over 20 years, straight-line (no residual value), and will take a full year's depreciation in the year installed. The purchase and installation schedule is as follows:

			Cost
January 1995.	Device 1	$200,000
January 1996.	Device 2	200,000
January 1997.	Device 3	200,000
Total		$600,000

Required

    a. Journal entries to record the purchase of device 1 and the receipt of the federal loan.
    b. Journal entries to record depreciation and amortization for the year ending December 31, 1996.
    c. Partial balance sheet showing the relevant information regarding the pollution control devices as at December 31, 1997.
    d. Assume that after testing, it is found that the emissions have been reduced only 85%. After negotiations, it was agreed that 60% of the loans will be refunded to the government in November 1998. The balance of the loan will be forgiven. Prepare the journal entries to record the refund and depreciation for the year ended December 31, 1998.

P 11–12
(L.O. 1, 2)

Asset Cost: Numerous Related Expenditures   The following transactions relate to operational assets:

    a. Purchased land and buildings for $157,800 cash. The purchaser agreed to pay $1,800 for taxes already assessed. The purchaser borrowed $100,000 at 15% interest (principal and interest due in one year) from the bank to help make the cash payment. The property was appraised for taxes as follows: land, $50,000; and building, $100,000.
    b. Prior to use of the property purchased in (a) above, the following expenditures were made:

Repair and renovation of building.	$16,000
Installation of 220-volt electrical wiring	4,000
Removal of separate shed of no use (sold scrap lumber for $100).	600
Construction of new driveway	3,000
Repair of existing driveways	1,200
Deposits with utilities for connections.	100
Painting company name on two sides of building	1,800
Installation of wire fence around property	5,000

    c. Purchased a tract of land for $64,000; assumed taxes already assessed amounting to $360. Paid title fees, $100, and attorney fees of $600 in connection with the purchase. Payments were in cash.
    d. The land purchased in (c) above was leveled, and two retaining walls were built to stop erosion that had created two rather large gulleys across the property. Total cash cost of the work was $6,000. The property is being held as a future plant site.

e. Purchased a used machine at a cash cost of $17,000. Subsequent to purchase, the following expenditures were made:

General overhaul prior to use.	$2,400
Installation of machine.	600
Cost of moving machine	300
Cost of removing two small machines to make way for larger machine purchased.	200
Cost of reinforcing floor prior to installation	800
Testing costs prior to operation.	120
Cost of tool kit (new) essential to adjustment of machine for various types of work.	440

Required   Prepare journal entries to record the above transactions. Give special attention to the cost of each asset. Justify your position on doubtful items.

P 11–13
(L.O. 3)

Self-Constructed Assets: Factory Case   Shear Corporation used its own facilities to construct a small addition to its office building. Construction began on February 1 and was completed on June 30 of the same year. Before the decision to construct the asset with its own facilities, Shear accepted bids from outside contractors; the lowest bid was $240,000. Costs accumulated during the construction period are summarized as follows:

Materials used (including $120,000 for normal production)	$180,000
Direct labour (including $300,000 for normal production)	450,000
General supplies used on construction	6,000
Rent paid on construction machinery.	5,000
Insurance premiums on construction.	2,000
Supervisory salary on construction	7,000
Total general overhead for year	115,000
Total factory overhead for year:	
Fixed ($10,000 due to construction)	100,000
Variable	60,000
Direct labour-hours (including 100,000 hours for normal production).	120,000

Shear allocates factory overhead to normal production on the basis of direct labour-hours.

Required   Compute the amounts that might be capitalized, under the following independent assumptions:

1. The plant capacity was 120,000 direct labour-hours, and the construction displaced production for sale to the extent indicated.
2. The plant capacity was 200,000 direct labour-hours, and idle capacity (80,000 hrs.) was used for the construction. This company allocates general overhead to self-constructed assets.

Hint: Use separate fixed and variable overhead rates for factory overhead (i.e., overhead cost ÷ direct labour-hours.)

P 11–14
(L.O. 7)

Replacements and Ordinary Repairs: Entries   The plant asset records of Reston Company reflected the following at the beginning of the current year:

Plant building (residual value, $30,000; estimated useful life, 20 years).	$150,000
Accumulated depreciation, plant building.	90,000
Machinery (residual value, $35,000; estimated useful life, 10 years)	180,000
Accumulated depreciation, machinery	90,000

During the current year ending December 31, the following transactions (summarized) relating to the above accounts were completed:

a. Expenditures for non-recurring, relatively large repairs that tend to increase economic utility but not the economic lives of assets:

Plant building	$45,000
Machinery.	15,000

b. Replacement of original electrical wiring system of plant building (original cost, $18,000). ... 29,000

c. Additions:

Plant building—added small wing to plant building to accommodate new equipment acquired; wing has useful life of 18 years and no residual value ... 54,000

Machinery—added special protection devices to 10 machines; devices are attached to the machines and will have to be replaced every five years (no residual value) ... 10,000

d. Outlays for maintenance parts, labour, and so on to keep assets in normal working condition:

Quarter	Plant Building	Machinery
1	$1,600	$ 1,900
2	1,800	6,100
3	1,600	1,000
4	2,000	10,000

Required

1. Give appropriate entries to record transactions (*a*) through (*c*). Explain the basis underlying your decisions.
2. In parallel columns, give the appropriate entries by quarter for the transactions in (*d*) under each of the following assumptions: (*a*) the accounting policy is to record all ordinary repairs as expense when incurred, and (*b*) the accounting policy requires use of the allocation approach. The annual budgeted amounts for repair and maintenance expense were plant building, $7,200, and machinery, $17,000.
3. Which approach used in (*b*) above do you prefer? Explain.

P 11–15
(L.O. 5)

Disposal of Asset: Addition, Depreciation, Reporting   Equipment that cost $18,000 on January 1, 1991, was sold for $10,000 on June 30, 1996. It had been depreciated over a 10-year life by the straight-line method, assuming its residual value would be $1,500.

A warehouse that cost $150,000, residual value $15,000, was being depreciated over 20 years by the straight-line method. When the structure was 15 years old, an additional wing was constructed at a cost of $90,000. The estimated life of the wing considered separately was 15 years, and its residual value is $10,000. The accounting period ends December 31.

Required

1. Give all required entries to record:
   a. Sale of the equipment.
   b. The addition; cash was paid.
   c. Depreciation on the warehouse and its addition after the latter has been in use for one year.
2. Show how the building and attached wing would be reported on a balance sheet prepared immediately after entry (1*c*) was recorded.

P 11–16
(L.O. 6)

Multiple Choice: Exchanges of Operational Assets   Choose the correct answer for each of the following questions.

1. Silo Corporation owns an asset originally costing $75,000, with accumulated depreciation of $38,000. Its current market value is $38,000. Silo traded in this old asset and paid $4,500 for a similar asset. The new asset should be recorded at:
   a. $54,000.
   b. $41,500.
   c. $42,500.
   d. $40,500.
2. DDD traded in its old textbook building (cost $350,000, accumulated depreciation $100,000) for a new building whose market value is $180,000, and received $80,000 on the trade. The new building should be recorded on DDD's books at which of the following values?
   a. $170,000.
   b. $180,000.
   c. $100,000.
   d. $270,000.
3. Choose the correct statement concerning operational asset exchanges.
   a. Gains are not allowed on exchanges of similar assets for the corporation receiving cash since the value of the new asset is not objectively determinable.
   b. When cash is received on the exchange of a dissimilar asset, the full gain derived from debiting the new asset with its fair market value is recognized.
   c. Gains are allowed on all operational asset exchanges.
   d. Losses are not allowed on non-cash exchanges of similar assets.

The following information relates to questions (4), (5), and (6), which are independent.

Original cost of an operational asset, $10,000.

Accumulated depreciation on the asset, 6,000.

XOR Corporation is the owner of the asset.

4. The old asset is traded for a dissimilar new asset with a $12,000 fair market value. XOR paid $7,000 on the exchange. The new asset's recorded value is:
   a. $12,000.
   b. $11,000.
   c. $10,000.
   d. $13,000.

5. The old asset is traded for a similar new asset with a $12,000 fair market value. XOR paid $700 on the exchange. The new asset's recorded value is:
   a. $12,000.
   b. $10,000.
   c. $6,000.
   d. $4,700.

6. The old asset is traded for a similar new asset. XOR received $1,000 on the exchange. The fair market values of the assets are indeterminate, but the new asset has a list price of $14,000. The new asset's recorded value is:
   a. $14,000.
   b. $0.
   c. $10,000.
   d. $3,000.

P 11–17
(L.O. 4)

Capitalization of Interest, Weighted-Average Method Rose Company began construction of a small building on January 1, 1995. The company's only debt during the first quarter was an unrelated long-term $300,000 note bearing interest at 11% per annum, maturity date, December 31, 1997. On May 1, 1995, the company borrowed $100,000 on a 9% construction note (interest-bearing); the note matures on April 30, 1996. The company capitalizes interest on the building on the basis of average quarterly cumulative expenditures. As of the end of each quarter of the six-month construction period, construction expenditures (not including interest) are as shown below. Rose's reporting year ends on December 31. Interest is paid quarterly.

The construction expenditures were as follows:

Date, 1995	Expenditure		Date, 1995	Expenditure	
Jan. 1	Land	$ 20,000	April 30	Construction	$200,000
Jan. 31	Construction	70,000	May 31	Construction	170,000
Feb. 28	Construction	100,000	June 30	Construction	80,000
March 31	Construction	180,000			

Required

1. Compute the amount of interest cost to be capitalized and expensed each quarter. Use the weighted-average method.
2. Give all journal entries related to construction and interest cost.

P 11–18
(L.O. 4)

Capitalization of Interest, Weighted-Average Method Dobie Industries began construction of a new plant for its own use on January 1, 1995. During 1995, Dobie had the following debt outstanding:

Accounts payable (noninterest-bearing)	$ 80,000
Short-term note payable (14%)	500,000
Bonds payable (12%, issued at par)	1,300,000

On April 1, 1995, Dobie borrowed an additional $500,000 on a 14%, one-year construction note to finance the plant construction. Interest on all debt is paid at the end of each quarter. The average accumulated expenditures on construction for each quarter of 1995 have already been computed. Assume that these amounts include the correct amounts of previously capitalized interest. The payments and average accumulated expenditures are as follows:

Quarter	Payments to Contractors	Average Accumulated Expenditures
1	$150,000	$150,000
2	450,000	300,000
3	750,000	675,000
4	950,000	850,000

Required   Dobie capitalizes interest using the weighted-average method (based on a weighted-average interest rate on all debt). Compute the amounts of interest to be capitalized and expensed for each quarter in 1995. Also, give the required entry in each quarter.

P 11–19   **Capitalization of Interest, Specific Method**   Use the information given in P 11–18.
(L.O. 4)

Required   Assume that Dobie capitalizes interest using the specific method (first applying the interest rate on loans identified with self-construction, and then applying a weighted-average interest rate based on all other debt). Compute the amounts of interest to be capitalized and expensed for each quarter in 1995, and give the entry in each quarter.

P 11–20   **Self-Constructed Asset and Interest Capitalization**   Mannheim Company begins construction of a
(L.O. 1, 2, 3, 4)   factory facility on January 4 of the current year. Mannheim uses its own employees and subcontractors to complete the facility. The following list provides information relevant to the construction. The facility is completed December 27 of that year.

a. At the beginning of January, Mannheim obtains construction financing: A 10%, $12,000,000 loan with principal payable at the end of construction provides significant financing for the project. Interest on the loan is payable semiannually. Mannheim pays the interest and principal when due.

b. Mannheim also has (1) $40,000,000 of 12% bonds payable issued at face value seven years before, which pay interest every June 30 and December 31, and (2) an 11%, $20,000,000 note paying interest every December 31, outstanding the entire year.

c. Mannheim owns the land site (cost, $4,000,000). In January, a subcontractor is employed to raze the old building (cost, $800,000; accumulated depreciation, $600,000) on the site for $80,000. Mannheim received $10,000 from salvaged materials.

d. Also in January, subcontractors survey, grade, and prepare the land for construction at a cost of $200,000 and excavate the foundation of the new facility for $1,000,000.

e. In January, a subcontractor poured and finished the foundation for $1,500,000. This work is financed separately through a one-year, 9% loan. Mannheim secured the financing at the beginning of January. The principal and interest were paid on December 30.

f. The total material cost for construction, excluding other items in this list, is $8,000,000.

g. Payments to subcontractors, excluding others in this list, amount to $2,000,000.

h. Payments to Mannheim employees for work on construction are $16,000,000.

i. In October, a subcontractor constructed a parking lot and fences for $300,000.

j. Incidental fees and other costs associated with facility construction were $150,000.

k. The market value of the building upon completion is $25,000,000.

l. For purposes of interest capitalization, Mannheim assumes an even distribution of cash payments for all construction costs throughout the year and capitalizes interest once per year as an adjusting entry. The specific method is used. Construction costs are accumulated in Mannheim's facility under a construction account.

Required   Provide general journal entries to account for all aspects of construction and related events. Your entries should lead to the correct total cost to record for the building. You may record the events in any order you feel is easiest for you. For simplicity and materiality, include the cost of any land improvements in the average accumulated expenditures for the building.

ANALYZING FINANCIAL STATEMENTS

All questions in this section are based on information adapted from the financial statements of actual companies.

A 11–1   **Asset Disposals**   Northern Bell Company is the parent corporation of five Bell companies
(L.O. 5)   serving the Great Lakes region. The firm's 1991 annual report included the following information (in millions of dollars):

From Disclosure Notes

Depreciation is based on the straight-line method and group methods of depreciation.

Gross capital expenditures $2,200

From Statement of Cash Flows   Investing activities section: net capital expenditures   2,152

From Balance Sheet	Increase in accumulated depreciation	454
From Income Statement	Depreciation expense	1,915

The group method of depreciation treats all assets within a group as having a uniform useful life and applies a depreciation rate based on the total cost of the group. No gain or loss is recognized on disposal under this method. Accumulated depreciation is reduced by the difference between the cost of the assets disposed of and cash proceeds.

Required

1. Assuming that all plant assets are depreciated on the group basis, estimate the original cost of plant assets retired in 1991.
2. Assuming that the straight-line method is applied individually to all plant assets and that gains and losses on plant asset disposals were approximately equal in amount during 1991, estimate the average proportion of useful life remaining at disposal on the plant assets retired in 1991. What additional information would be helpful in answering this question?

A 11–2
(L.O. 4)

Interest Capitalization General Steel Corporation's 1991 annual report disclosed the following information related to its construction project, debt, and interest cost (in thousands of dollars):

Construction in progress, a component of total property, plant, and equipment, increased from $51,043 to $126,804 in 1991.

Interest capitalized in 1991 was $8,342. This amount was in the disclosure notes and on the income statement as a deduction from total interest cost to derive interest expense.

Interest-bearing debt outstanding at the end of 1990: $95,000 of 11.4% notes, and $15,000 of 13.0% notes.

Required

Based on the information provided in the annual report, estimate the amount of interest to be capitalized in 1991. Give reasons why the amount you compute differs from the amount reported by General Steel. Assume that construction payments were made uniformly during the year.

A 11–3
(L.O. 3)

Plant Assets Acquired on Credit Super Valu Stores, Inc., a large food marketing company, disclosed the following information in a note to its 1991 annual report. Independent retailers use funds provided by Super Valu to finance acquisitions of property used in retail food operations. Super Valu records these loans in its long-term notes receivable account.

	Ending Balances	
	1991	**1990**
	($ thousands)	
Long-term notes receivable (net)	$53,088	$59,762

Additional information from the disclosure note:

Unearned finance charges are amortized to interest income using a method which approximates the interest method. The notes range in length from 1 to 20 years, with a majority being 7 years, and may be non-interest bearing or bear interest at rates ranging from 7 to 15 percent.

Now, for purposes of this problem, assume the following:

a. The notes receivable account is comprised of one 11-year, 11% note with four years remaining at the end of 1991.
b. Super Valu financed 100% of the asset acquisitions for the retailer.
c. Annual payments on the note are received at the end of each year, include principal and interest, and are a constant amount each year.

Required

Determine the market value of the assets financed by Super Valu at the date of acquisition by the retailer (debtor).

A 11–4
(L.O. 1)

Property, Plant, and Equipment Refer to the 1993 financial statements of the Magna International Inc. that appear at the end of this text. Determine the change in net fixed assets during 1993, and try to explain that change in terms of its component parts. Indicate any additional information you would like to have available in order to completely answer this question.

COMPARATIVE ANALYSIS

(L.O. 4)   **Capitalized Interest**   Following are notes to the 1992 financial statements relating to capitalized interest for each of three companies.

ABC Corporation   is a large international firm that develops, constructs, and operates electrical generating facilities (December 31, 1992, total assets: $1.55 billion).

Note: Construction in progress — Construction progress payments, engineering costs, insurance costs, wages, interest and other costs relating to construction in progress are capitalized. Construction in progress is transferred to electric and steam generating facilities when the related assets or group of assets are ready for their intended use. Capitalized interest totalled $21 million, $20 million, and $37 million in 1992, 1991, and 1990, respectively.

Air Freight Corporation   is an air freight carrier (December 31, 1992, total assets: $.96 billion).

Interest incurred during the construction period of certain facilities and on aircraft purchase and modification costs are capitalized as an additional cost of the asset until the date the asset is placed in service. Capitalized interest was $2,466,000; $4,476,000; and $4,107,000 for 1992, 1991, and 1990, respectively.

Toys 4 U Inc.   is a large retailer of toys and other items for children (January 30, 1993, total assets: $5.3 billion).

Interest on borrowed funds is capitalized during construction of property and is amortized by charges to earnings over the depreciable lives of the related assets. Interest of $8,403,000, $12,237,000 and $9,437,000 was capitalized during 1992, 1991 and 1990, respectively.

Additional information from the 1992 annual report for each firm appears below (amounts in millions of dollars):

	ABC	Air	Toys 4 U
Interest expense	$ 97	$ 19	$ 69
Earnings from continuing operations before tax	66	9	689
Net property, plant, and equipment, ending	1,250	730	2,803
Capital expenditures	123	253	422
Average long-term debt*	1,170	228	520

* (Beginning total long-term debt + Ending total long-term debt)/2

Required   1. Assuming the three firms use the weighted average method to capitalize interest, estimate average accumulated expenditures for each firm for 1992. Use an estimated average interest rate applicable to all long-term debt.
2. What percentage of total property, plant, and equipment was AAE for each firm in 1992 (use ending property, plant, and equipment)?
3. By what percentage did each firm's 1992 earnings from continuing operations before tax increase as a result of capitalizing interest?
4. For each firm, what percentage of total interest cost was capitalized in 1992?
5. Comment on the effect of interest capitalization on the quality of earnings, given your findings.

12 Capital Assets: Depreciation and Impairment

After you have studied this chapter, you will be able to:

1 **Explain the concept of depreciation.**

2 **Apply several depreciation methods and explain the incentives for choosing them.**

3 **Explain the relationships among depreciation, taxes, cash flows, and dividends.**

4 **Calculate and account for fractional-year depreciation and depreciation of post-acquisition costs.**

5 **Explain the circumstances under which special depreciation systems are used and then apply them.**

6 **Account for impairments and casualty insurance.**

7 **Explain the capital cost allowance system and calculate depreciation for tax purposes (chapter appendix).**

INTRODUCTION

Trizec Corporation Limited lost $312 million in 1993 while reporting $67.5 million in net cash flow from operations. Depreciation of $89.4 million was a major reason for the disparity between the two measures. Depreciation, one of the largest expenses for companies, reduces earnings but causes no cash outflow. Few areas in accounting offer greater choice of accounting treatment. The magnitude of the expense for most companies amplifies the implications of this flexibility.

In 1993, National Sea Products Limited announced a $49 million restructuring charge to cover plant closings and other losses. Such losses are sometimes taken in a "big bath," in which a firm recognizes a number of discretionary losses in a period of below-normal performance. Such losses generally include large write-downs of assets due to permanent impairment of value. These immediate reductions in the book value of plant assets contrast with the gradual effects of depreciation.

Depreciation and asset impairments are major issues in international accounting as well. With demand sagging during the economic recession of the early 1990s, several Japanese manufacturing firms, including Nissan and Mazda, reported significantly lower earnings due to massive depreciation charges on idle facilities.[1] Bramalea Ltd. was forced to recognize a write-down of $939 in real estate assets, reflecting a general drop in property values in 1992.[2]

These examples reflect the major topics covered in this chapter. Chapter 11 focussed on accounting events that *increase* plant asset carrying values. This chapter focusses on depreciation and asset impairments that *decrease* plant asset carrying values.

DEPRECIATION CONCEPTS

Terminology

Capital assets produce revenue through use rather than through resale. They can be viewed as quantities of economic service potential to be consumed over time in the earning of revenues. Accounting principles call for matching the costs of all types of operational assets against revenue over their useful lives. The accounting terminology for this process differs depending on the asset category:

1. **Depreciation** The periodic allocation of the cost of *plant assets* against the periodic revenue earned.
2. **Depletion** The periodic allocation of the cost of *natural resources,* such as mineral deposits and timber, against the periodic revenue earned.
3. **Amortization** The periodic allocation of *intangible assets* against the periodic revenue earned. The term amortization also applies to financial assets and liabilities.

These three terms are generically known as *amortization* and refer to the same process of cost allocation. Traditionally, they apply to the different capital asset categories.

Depreciation recognition transfers a portion of both acquisition cost and capitalized post-acquisition cost of plant assets to an expense account called *depreciation expense*. This expense is recorded in an adjusting entry at the end of each reporting period. Depreciation expense for a nonmanufacturing company is classified as a selling or administrative expense, depending on the asset's function. Manufacturing companies include depreciation on plant assets used in manufacturing in the cost of goods produced. When goods are sold, depreciation becomes part of cost of goods sold expense.

The corresponding credit is to accumulated depreciation, a contra plant asset account that reduces gross plant assets to net undepreciated plant assets (book value). This account appears in the balance sheet parenthetically or as a line item deduction from gross property, plant, and equipment, as illustrated by the following excerpt from Alcan Aluminium Limited's 1993 balance sheet:

	1993	1992	1991
Property, plant and equipment			
Cost	$11,092	$11,015	$11,144
Accumulated depreciation.	5,087	4,759	4,619
	$ 6,005	$ 6,256	$ 6,525

Separate asset and related accumulated depreciation accounts are maintained to preserve records on the historical cost of the asset. These individual records are necessary to account for estimate changes and changes in depreciation method and to support internal control procedures for plant assets.

---

[1] "Gearing Down: As Japan's Rapid-Growth Economy Slumps, Past Recession Cures May No Longer Work," *The Wall Street Journal,* December 7, 1992, p. A1.

[2] "Bronfman-Controlled Firms Write Down Total of $1.03 Billion in Property Assets," *The Wall Street Journal,* December 18, 1992, p. A4.

Accumulated depreciation does not represent cash set aside for replacement of plant assets; nor does depreciation recognition imply the creation of reserves for asset replacement. Most firms do not specifically reserve cash for replacement of plant assets.

The book value (carrying value) of an asset is its original cost plus any capitalized post-acquisition cost less accumulated depreciation to date. **Depreciable cost** is the total amount of depreciation to be recognized over the useful life of the asset, and it equals total capitalized asset cost less estimated residual value (salvage value). Book value includes residual value at any balance sheet date. The minimum book value is residual value, the amount not subject to depreciation.

Nature of Depreciation

A new automobile is said to depreciate by several thousand dollars once it leaves the dealer's premises. However, the meaning of the terms *depreciation* or *amortization* as used in accounting is different from this common usage of the term. Section 3060, paragraph .31 of the *CICA Handbook* states that:

> Amortization should be recognized in a rational and systematic manner appropriate to the nature of the capital asset.

The phrase *rational and systematic* implies that depreciation methods should be both precisely specified, rather than haphazard or arbitrary, and defensible on the grounds that the result follows logically from the asset's use.

For financial reporting purposes, the cost of property, plant, and equipment can be thought of as a long-term prepayment of an expense. A portion of the cost is assumed to benefit each period of use, and depreciation expense is the systematically determined amount recognized for this purpose. Depreciation expense is not recognized for sudden and unexpected factors, such as damage from natural phenomena, sudden changes in demand, or radical misuse of assets that impair their revenue-generating ability.

Depreciation is not a valuation process. Gradual market value changes are not recorded in the capital asset accounts, and the book value of a capital asset typically does not equal its market value. To understand this concept better, consider the following partial balance sheet:

GRANGE COMPANY
Partial Balance Sheet Information
December 31, 1995

			Underlying Measurement Concept
Assets			
Accounts receivable	$200,000		
Less allowance for doubtful accounts . . .	(20,000)		
Net accounts receivable		$180,000	Net realizable value
Buildings.	$200,000		
Less accumulated depreciation	(20,000)		
Net buildings, at book value		$180,000	Undepreciated acquisition cost

Although the two net amounts in Grange's partial balance sheet have identical book values, they have quite different interpretations. The net accounts receivable is an estimate of net realizable value, the cash reasonably expected to be collected from Grange's receivables. The net book value of the buildings, however, represents only the undepreciated acquisition cost at the end of 1995. The realizable value or replacement cost of the buildings is most likely some other amount.

Periodic market value changes are not a sufficiently reliable or objective basis for depreciation accounting, and they are not the result of arm's-length transactions. The cost principle supports the objective original cost as the depreciation base. Furthermore, the conservatism constraint prohibits the recording of a market value increase in the absence of a transaction supporting the increased value.

Two Causes for Decline in Capital Asset Value   The amount of depreciation recognized is not necessarily linked to the decline in an asset's utility or market value over time. However, the eventual decline in value justifies periodic recognition of depreciation. The decline in utility of capital assets is caused by *physical factors* (wear and tear from operations, action of time and the elements, and deterioration and decay) and *obsolescence*. Obsolescence is usually the result of new technology; older assets become less efficient and therefore more expensive to operate. Obsolescence also occurs when facility expansion renders certain assets unusable under new operating conditions or when demand for the product or service supplied by the asset declines. Assets rendered obsolete are often in good condition and still capable of supplying the service originally expected of them.

Technological change does not automatically render older equipment obsolete, however. If the older equipment meets the present needs of the company, obsolescence is not a factor. For example, in the computer industry, new computer chips may substantially increase computer speeds and capabilities. The 486 chip eclipsed the 386 chip, for example, although PCs built around the 386 chip continued to be in widespread use, fully supported by software and maintenance agreements. For many companies, changing to the more expensive computers based on the 486 chip was not immediately cost-effective.

Factors in Determining Depreciation Expense

Four factors are relevant in determining periodic depreciation expense:

1. Acquisition cost and capitalized post-acquisition costs.
2. Estimated residual value.
3. Estimated useful life.
4. Method of depreciation.

Generally, *acquisition cost* is the most definite of the four factors, although even here, variation in accounting practice exists. For example, landscaping is included in land or in land improvements, depending on the permanence of the landscaping and the firm's capitalization policy. Also, different approaches to the treatment of interest capitalization and post-acquisition costs affect the depreciation base.

The *residual value* is the estimated net recoverable amount from disposal or trade-in of the asset. It is the portion of an asset's acquisition cost not consumed through use, and it is not matched against revenues through depreciation.

To estimate residual value, allowance is made for the costs of dismantling, restoring, and disposing of the retired asset. For example, if the estimated realizable value upon retirement of an asset is $2,500 and estimated dismantling and selling costs are $500, the residual value is $2,000. Net residual value is negative if disposal costs exceed the expected proceeds from sale of the asset. Using the same example, if estimated dismantling and selling costs are $3,000, residual value is −$500. When negative, residual value increases the asset's depreciable cost but not the recorded value of the asset, because the disposal costs will be incurred in the future and do not enhance the asset's value.

In practice, residual values are often ignored. This is acceptable when recovery proceeds and disposal costs are expected to offset or when the amounts involved are immaterial. However, if a firm expects to retire an asset relatively early in its useful life, a substantial residual value can be involved.

The *useful life* (economic life) generally has a greater impact on depreciation than estimated residual value. The useful life of an asset must be finite to justify depreciation recognition. Land is not depreciated, for example. Estimates of useful life require assumptions about potential obsolescence, severity of use, and maintenance. Inadequate maintenance is a short-run cost-saving strategy that can both result in higher future cost and contribute to a shortening of useful life.

Where possible, the measurement standard should describe the primary causes of the decline in value. For example, assume that a delivery truck has an estimated useful life of five years or 300,000 kilometres. Depreciation based on distance driven might yield a more accurate matching of expense and revenue than depreciation based on useful life in years.

Depreciation is not recognized (that is, useful life does not begin) until the asset is in its intended condition and location and is contributing to revenue. When facilities are temporarily idle, recognition of depreciation continues when the method used is based on the passage of time, reflecting increased obsolescence and the reduced economic usefulness of the asset.

In certain regulated industries, companies must maintain equipment in superior condition for public safety reasons. There are no definite guidelines for useful life in the airline industry, for example, because airlines must maintain their planes as long as they are used. Economic considerations govern the choice of useful life and lead to different decisions by the firms in this industry.[3]

Useful life can affect earnings significantly. Longer useful lives mean lower annual depreciation charges and higher net income. General Motors was once more conservative in depreciating manufacturing equipment than its major competitors. Its useful lives were half those of Ford and one-third of Chrysler's.[4] In 1987, GM increased the useful lives of plant assets to be more consistent with its competitors, thus increasing earnings.[5] GM has since returned to more conservative accounting practices.

Among the four factors affecting depreciation computations, the *method of depreciation* chosen usually has the greatest effect on periodic depreciation expense. The rational and systematic requirement of the *CICA Handbook* places few constraints on depreciation policy. The selection from among the various depreciation methods is management's choice. Depreciation, as measured and reported in practice, is related only incidentally to ageing or deterioration.

Depreciation expense is typically not equal to the decline in market value of the asset for the period, nor is it equal to the portion of original cost (or asset utility) consumed in the period. Depreciation is usually some other value because:

- Market value changes are ignored in the depreciation process.
- The portion of original cost consumed in a period is not observable and cannot be directly measured.
- GAAP does not mandate a depreciation method based on the pattern of benefits derived from the asset, the pattern of its use, or its decline in usefulness or value.
- The amount of revenue or cash produced by a plant asset's use is usually impossible to determine unequivocally.[6]

---

[3] "The Wild Blue Yonder," *Forbes*, November 9, 1981, p. 94.

[4] Therefore, GM would depreciate plant assets more rapidly. This was a more conservative practice because it produced lower earnings than would otherwise be the case.

[5] "Fiddling with Figures While Sales Drop," *Forbes*, August 24, 1987, p. 32.

[6] Arthur Thomas, in "The FASB and the Allocation Fallacy," *Journal of Accountancy*, November 1975, p. 66, argues that all allocations of the costs of assets that interact are inherently arbitrary. Revenues are not generated by assets used in isolation. Rather, they are produced by a number of assets and people working together. Therefore, it is impossible to associate specific revenues (benefits) to specific assets, and thus impossible to allocate the cost of most operational assets on the basis of benefits or revenues produced.

CONCEPT REVIEW

1. What are the main causes of the decline in value or usefulness of plant assets over time?
2. Why is depreciation expense not necessarily an accurate measure of the decline in value of capital assets?
3. What is the conceptual difference between the amounts reported as accumulated depreciation for capital assets and the allowance for doubtful accounts?

DEPRECIATION METHODS

In this text, depreciation measurement procedures are classified into depreciation methods and depreciation systems. Depreciation methods are typically applied individually to assets, and depreciation systems are applied to groups of assets. The following methods and systems are discussed here:

I. Depreciation Methods.
  A. Based on equal allocation to each time period—the straight-line (SL) method.
  B. Based on inputs and outputs.
    1. Service-hours (SH) method.
    2. Productive output (PO), or units-of-production, method.
  C. Accelerated methods.
    1. Sum-of-the-years'-digits (SYD) method.
    2. Double-declining-balance (DDB) methods.
  D. Present value–based methods.
II. Depreciation systems.
  A. Inventory appraisal system.
  B. Group and composite systems.
  C. Retirement and replacement systems.

Fixed-asset software packages streamline the process of calculating, recording, and posting depreciation in the accounts for both methods and systems. The aggregate nature of depreciation systems serves to lower accounting information system costs in certain instances.

Assets are not depreciated below residual value under any method or system. Although declining balance methods do not use residual value in calculating periodic depreciation expense, a determination is made at the end of each accounting period to ensure that book value is at least equal to residual value.

Exhibit 12–1 presents information for a hypothetical plant asset used to illustrate five of the depreciation methods.

EXHIBIT 12–1
Data Used to Illustrate
Depreciation Methods

Item	Illustrative Amount
Acquisition cost, January 1, 1995	$ 6,600
Residual value	600
Estimated useful life:	
Years	5
Service-hours	20,000
Productive output in units	10,000

EXHIBIT 12–2
Depreciation
Schedule—Straight-Line
Method

Year	Depreciation Expense (debit)	Accumulated Depreciation (credit)	Balance, Accumulated Depreciation	Undepreciated Asset Balance (book value)
January 1, 1995				$6,600
December 31, 1995	$1,200	$1,200	$1,200	5,400
December 31, 1996	1,200	1,200	2,400	4,200
December 31, 1997	1,200	1,200	3,600	3,000
December 31, 1998	1,200	1,200	4,800	1,800
December 31, 1999	1,200	1,200	6,000	600 (residual value)
Total	$6,000	$6,000		

Straight-Line Method

The **straight-line (SL) method** is based on the assumption that a plant asset declines in usefulness at a constant rate. The SL method relates depreciation directly to the passage of time rather than to the asset's use, resulting in a constant amount of depreciation recognized per time period. The formula for computing periodic SL depreciation, with its application to the asset in Exhibit 12–1, is:

$$\text{Annual SL depreciation} = \frac{\text{Acquisition cost} - \text{Residual value}}{\text{Estimated useful life in years}}$$

$$= (\$6,600 - \$600) \div 5 = \$1,200 \text{ per year}$$

SL depreciation frequently is expressed in terms of a percentage rate: the ratio of annual depreciation expense to depreciable cost. The asset in Exhibit 12–1 has a 20% SL rate ($1,200 ÷ $6,000). Each year, 20% of depreciable cost is recognized as depreciation. This rate also equals the reciprocal of useful life, or 1/5 (20%). Exhibit 12–2 illustrates the SL method over the useful life of the asset described in Exhibit 12–1.

Evaluation   The SL method is logically appealing as well as rational and systematic. It is especially appropriate when the decline in service potential is approximately the same each period, the use of the asset is essentially the same each period, and repairs and maintenance expenditures are constant over the useful life. The method is not appropriate for assets whose decline in service potential or benefits produced relates not to the passage of time but rather to other variables, such as units produced or hours in service. The SL method is also inappropriate when obsolescence is the primary factor in depreciation.

The SL method is the most popular method in use. Of 300 firms surveyed by the CICA in 1993, 262 used this method. Ease of use partially explains the method's popularity. SL also results in the highest long-run earnings levels for growth firms, an effect that is attractive to managers whose compensation is tied to earnings performance.

Methods Based on Inputs and Outputs

Depreciation methods that associate periodic depreciation with a measurable attribute of capital assets include the service-hours method and productive output method (also called the units-of-production method). These methods do not relate depreciation to the passage of time, as the other individually applied methods do. Hence, depreciation expense under these methods is not recorded when assets are idle.

EXHIBIT 12–3   Depreciation Schedule—Service-Hours Method

Year	Service-Hours Worked	Depreciation Expense (debit)	Accumulated Depreciation (credit)	Balance, Accumulated Depreciation	Undepreciated Asset Balance (book value)
January 1, 1995					$6,600
December 31, 1995.	3,800	(3,800 × $.30) = $1,140	$1,140	$1,140	5,460
December 31, 1996.	4,000	(4,000 × $.30) = 1,200	1,200	2,340	4,260
December 31, 1997.	4,500	(4,500 × $.30) = 1,350	1,350	3,690	2,910
December 31, 1998.	4,200	(4,200 × $.30) = 1,260	1,260	4,950	1,650
December 31, 1999.	3,500	(3,500 × $.30) = 1,050	1,050	6,000	600 (residual value)
Total	20,000	$6,000	$6,000		

Service-Hours Method   The **service-hours (SH) method** is based on the assumption that the decrease in useful life of a plant asset is directly related to the amount of time the asset is in use. The depreciation rate per service-hour is:

$$\text{Depreciation rate per service-hour} = \frac{\text{Acquisition cost} - \text{Residual value}}{\text{Estimated service life in hours}}$$

Periodic depreciation expense is then found by multiplying the hours used during the period by the depreciation rate. This method generally results in varying amounts of depreciation expense per period, depending on the extent of asset use. For the asset in Exhibit 12–1, the depreciation rate is:

$$\frac{\$6,600 - \$600}{20,000} = \$.30 \text{ per service-hour}$$

Assuming 3,800 hours of running time, 1995 depreciation is $1,140 (3,800 × $.30). Exhibit 12–3 illustrates the service-hours method for the life of the asset, assuming an estimated and actual life of 20,000 hours.

Productive Output Method   The **productive output (PO) method** is similar except that the number of units of output is used to measure asset use. A constant amount of depreciable cost is allocated to each unit of output as a cost of production, so annual depreciation amounts fluctuate with changes in the volume of output.

The depreciation rate per unit is:

$$\text{Depreciation rate per unit of output} = \frac{\text{Acquisition cost} - \text{Residual value}}{\text{Estimated productive output in units}}$$

For the asset in Exhibit 12–1, the rate is:

$$\frac{\$6,600 - \$600}{10,000} = \$.60 \text{ per unit of output}$$

Assuming that 1,800 units are produced, 1995 depreciation is $1,080 ($1,800 × $.60). Exhibit 12–4 illustrates the PO method over the life of this asset, assuming an estimated and actual productive output of 10,000 units.

The service-hours and productive output methods can produce different results, depending on the ratio of machine-hours to units produced. For the asset under study, 2.11 machine-hours were required to produce one unit in 1995 (3,800 ÷ 1,800), while in 1996 that figure was reduced to 2.00 (4,000 ÷ 2,000), indicating a greater efficiency (see Exhibits 12–3 and 12–4). The SH method, therefore, yielded slightly higher depreciation per unit of output in 1995 than in 1996.

EXHIBIT 12–4   Depreciation Schedule—Productive Output Method

Year	Units of Output	Depreciation Expense (debit)	Accumulated Depreciation (credit)	Balance, Accumulated Depreciation	Undepreciated Asset Balance (book value)
January 1, 1995					$6,600
December 31, 1995	1,800	(1,800 × $.60) = $1,080	$1,080	$1,080	5,520
December 31, 1996	2,000	(2,000 × $.60) = 1,200	1,200	2,280	4,320
December 31, 1997	2,400	(2,400 × $.60) = 1,440	1,440	3,720	2,880
December 31, 1998	1,800	(1,800 × $.60) = 1,080	1,080	4,800	1,800
December 31, 1999	2,000	(2,000 × $.60) = 1,200	1,200	6,000	600 (residual value)
Total	10,000	$6,000	$6,000		

Evaluation   The input–output methods are rational and systematic and logically match expense and revenue if the asset's utility is measurable in terms of service time or units of output. However, a problem arises when the running time of an asset varies without a corresponding effect in the output of service. For example, the increasingly heavy traffic in urban areas causes vehicles to run many more hours per week with no increase in their productive service. Also, for many assets such as buildings, furniture, and office equipment, application of these methods is impracticable because no measure of service or output is available.

Of 300 firms surveyed by the CICA in 1993, 68 used a depreciation method based on inputs or outputs. Mining, oil-drilling, and steel-making equipment is often depreciated using these methods.

Accelerated Depreciation Methods

Accelerated depreciation methods recognize greater amounts of depreciation early in the useful life of plant assets and lesser amounts later. Thus, they *accelerate* the recognition of depreciation.

Accelerated methods are based on the assumption that newer assets produce more benefits per period because they are more productive and require less maintenance and repair. Accelerated methods match more of the acquisition cost against the revenue of these earlier periods when greater benefits are obtained. A smoother pattern of total annual operating expense is often the result, with the sum of annual depreciation and maintenance expense more constant than is likely with SL depreciation. The principal accelerated method in use today is the declining-balance method. The sum-of-the-years'-digits method is not nearly as popular but is useful as a surrogate for other declining-balance methods.

Declining-Balance Methods

Declining-balance (DB) methods are significantly different from other methods in two ways:
- Residual value is not subtracted from cost when computing depreciation.
- The depreciation rate is applied to a declining balance rather than to a constant depreciable cost.

Care must be taken to ensure that assets are not depreciated below their residual value, which is the minimum book value for a plant asset.

Double-Declining-Balance (DDB) Method   Accelerated depreciation methods have been imposed for tax purposes in Canada since January 1, 1949. The rates of depreciation allowed (described in the act as capital cost allowance) were usually set at

EXHIBIT 12–5 Depreciation Schedule—Double-Declining-Balance Method

Year	Annual Rate	Depreciation Expense (debit)	Accumulated Depreciation (credit)	Balance, Accumulated Depreciation	Undepreciated Asset Balance (book value)
January 1, 1995					$6,600
December 31, 1995.	40%*	(40% × $6,600) = $2,640	$2,640	$2,640	3,960
December 31, 1996.	40%	(40% × $3,960) = 1,584	1,584	4,224	2,376
December 31, 1997.	40%	(40% × $2,376) = 950	950	5,174	1,426
December 31, 1998.	40%	(40% × $1,426) = 570	570	5,744	856
December 31, 1999.	40%	256†	256	6,000	600
Total		$6,000	$6,000		

* 40% = 2/5.

† Depreciation expense stops when accumulated depreciation equals the $6,000 depreciable cost, leaving the $600 residual value intact. Thus, the maximum depreciation for 1999 is $256 ($6,000 − $5,744) rather than $342 (40% of $856).

twice the old straight-line rates.[7] Thus, the method has been referred to as double-declining balance. Under this method, the fixed percentage used is simply double the straight-line rate ignoring salvage value. This rate is multiplied each year by the declining book value. The double-declining-balance (DDB) rate is $2/n$ or twice the straight-line rate of $1/n$.[8] Based on the illustrative data given in Exhibit 12–1, the DDB rate would be 40% (i.e., 20% × 2). The depreciation would be computed as shown in Exhibit 12–5.

For example, using double-declining balance, depreciation expense for 1995 and 1996 on the asset in Exhibit 12–1 (useful life of five years) is:

$$1995 \text{ depreciation} = \$6,600 \times 40\% = \$2,640$$

$$1996 \text{ depreciation} = (\$6,600 - \$2,640) \times 40\% = \$1,584$$

Annual depreciation expense declines along with the declining book value under these methods. The book value at the beginning of any year is reduced by the depreciation in all previous years.

In recent years, the double-declining-balance method has lost some significance because from time to time the taxing authorities have allowed more rapid write-offs of fixed asset cost. The primary aim of the tax method is not the apportionment of fixed asset costs over their useful life; often, it is used as a tool to stimulate economic activity.

---

[7] R. M. Skinner, *Accounting Standards in Evolution* (Toronto: Holt, Rinehart and Winston of Canada, Limited, 1987), p. 172.

[8] A way to directly compute double-declining-balance depreciation for any year is:

$$\text{Depreciation in year } t \text{ of the asset's life} = (\text{Acquisition cost}) \left(\frac{2}{\text{Useful life}} \right) \left(1 - \frac{2}{\text{Useful life}} \right)^{Years\ depreciated}$$

For example, 1997 (year 3) depreciation is:

$$\$6,600 \left(\frac{2}{5} \right) \left(1 - \frac{2}{5} \right)^2 = \$950$$

The book value at the beginning of any year may be determined as follows:

$$(\text{Acquisition cost}) \left(1 - \frac{2}{\text{Useful life}} \right)^{Years\ depreciated}$$

For example, book value at the beginning of 1997 (year 3) = $\$6,600(1 - 2/5)^2 = \$2,376$.

EXHIBIT 12–6   Depreciation Schedule—SYD Method

Year	Depreciation Expense (debit)	Accumulated Depreciation (credit)	Balance, Accumulated Depreciation	Undepreciated Asset Balance (book value)
January 1, 1995				$6,600
December 31, 1995	($\frac{5}{15} \times$ $6,000) = $2,000	$2,000	$2,000	4,600
December 31, 1996	($\frac{4}{15} \times$ $6,000) = 1,600	1,600	3,600	3,000
December 31, 1997	($\frac{3}{15} \times$ $6,000) = 1,200	1,200	4,800	1,800
December 31, 1998	($\frac{2}{15} \times$ $6,000) = 800	800	5,600	1,000
December 31, 1999	($\frac{1}{15} \times$ $6,000) = 400	400	6,000	600 (residual value)
Total	$6,000	$6,000		

Strict application of the double-declining-balance methods eventually yields a book value less than residual value. In this situation, firms can change to the SL method when depreciation under the double-declining-balance method is equal to or less than SL depreciation. Alternatively, a firm can change to the SL method the year the declining-balance method would reduce the book value below residual value (the approach taken in Exhibit 12–5 for 1999—the last year of useful life).

Evaluation   The declining-balance method is rational and systematic and is especially appropriate for assets supplying proportionately greater benefits early in their useful life. For example, computers and other high-technology equipment often provide more benefits early in their life and then become obsolete as technology changes. Of 300 firms surveyed by the CICA in 1993, 87 used a declining-balance method.

Sum-of-the-Years'-Digits Method   The **sum-of-the-years'-digits (SYD) method** computes annual depreciation by multiplying an asset's depreciable cost by a fraction made up as follows:

Numerator   The number of years remaining in the useful life at the *beginning* of the period. The numerator declines with each year of asset use. For the asset in Exhibit 12–1, the numerator for 1997 is 3 because at the beginning of 1997, three years of useful life remain.

Denominator   The sum of the integers from 1 up to the number of years of useful life (the sum of the years' digits). For an asset with a useful life of five years, the denominator is $1 + 2 + 3 + 4 + 5$, or 15. This sum also equals $n(n + 1) \div 2$: $5(5 + 1) \div 2 = 15$, where n is the useful life in years.

Depreciation expense in 1995 for the Exhibit 12–1 asset is:

$$1995 \text{ SYD depreciation} = (\$6,600 - \$600)(\tfrac{5}{15}) = \$2,000$$

Exhibit 12–6 illustrates the SYD method over the life of the Exhibit 12–1 asset.

Evaluation   The declining-balance and SYD methods are appropriate under similar conditions. Both methods are acceptable under GAAP, yield similar results, and recognize depreciation on an accelerated basis.

Accelerated methods are applicable when obsolescence is an important factor in the estimate of useful life. An asset with a three-year useful life is 50% depreciated at the end of its first year under the SYD method: $3 \div (3 + 2 + 1) = 3 \div 6$, or 50%. If the asset becomes obsolete in its second year, most of the asset is already depreciated. However, of 300 firms surveyed by the CICA in 1993, only 1 used this method.

The Raytheon Company disclosed its use of SYD in a note to its 1992 annual report:

> Provisions for depreciation are computed generally on the sum-of-the-years'-digits method, except for certain operations which use the straight-line or declining-balance method.

Present Value–Based Depreciation Methods

Under the present value, or interest, method of depreciation, the cost of a plant asset represents the present value of the stream of cash receipts generated by the asset. Each receipt consists of interest (return on investment) and principal (depreciation expense or return of investment).

For example, assume that a firm purchases an asset with a two-year useful life on January 1, 1995, for $10,000. The firm anticipates a 6% return on its investment in the asset, equivalent to a net cash flow of $5,454 per year, computed as follows:

$$\$10,000 = (PVA, 6\%, 2)(\text{Annual net cash inflow})$$
$$\$10,000/1.83339 = \text{Annual net cash inflow} = \$5,454$$

The following schedule illustrates the interest method of depreciation:

Date	Estimated Net Cash Inflow	Return on Investment	Depreciation Expense	Asset Book Value
January 1, 1995				$10,000
December 31, 1995	$ 5,454	$600 ($10,000 × .06)	$ 4,854 ($5,454 − $600)	5,146 ($10,000 − $4,854)
December 31, 1996	5,454	308 ($5,146 × .06)	5,146 ($5,454 − $308)	0
	$10,908	$908	$10,000	

The interest method treats a plant asset as a monetary asset. Before income is recognized, the firm must be reimbursed for its investment. In 1995, the $5,454 net cash inflow from the asset consists of $4,854 return of investment (depreciation expense) and $600 of return on investment (or interest income). Depreciation expense increases as time passes because less investment remains on which to earn an income return.

EXHIBIT 12–7
Depreciation Methods Used
by 300 Firms in 1993
(surveyed by the CICA)

	Number of Companies			
	1992	**1991**	**1990**	**1989**
Straight line	262	260	263	263
Diminishing balance	86	90	94	97
Unit of production	68	69	68	68
Sinking fund	4	4	3	3
Modified sum-of-the-years'-digits	1	1	—	—

Note: Total responses exceed 300 because some firms use more than one method.

Source: *Financial Reporting in Canada—1993* (Toronto: CICA, 1993), p. 154.

DEPRECIATION POLICY

Exhibit 12–7 illustrates the variety of methods used in practice. The choice of depreciation method hinges on a variety of factors. Accounting information system costs are an important factor, the computer revolution notwithstanding. Detailed information about acquisition costs, post-acquisition costs, useful life, residual value, and accumulated depreciation must be maintained. The system must facilitate retrieval of this information for depreciation calculations. In addition, complexity influences the choice of method.

Expected obsolescence can also affect the choice of method. Accelerated methods are appropriate in this instance. Most Canadian firms employ SL depreciation for financial accounting but must use accelerated depreciation for tax reporting, typically resulting in higher earnings reported to shareholders and lower tax liabilities. Resistance to change is another factor. Firms may use a method not only because it satisfies their reporting needs but also to avoid the cost of changing methods.

Other factors affecting depreciation policy are a belief that depreciation methods that maximize net income have a positive effect on share price, and management's desire to maximize its own financial well-being through compensation contracts based on earnings. Although both factors may contribute to the dominance of the straight-line method, research suggests that share prices are not directly affected by the choice of depreciation method.

The latitude in adoption of depreciation methods and the variety of estimates of useful life and residual value are at odds with the uniformity and consistency objectives of financial reporting. The large dollar amount of depreciation expense reported combined with the inherently approximate nature of depreciation result in a potentially difficult comparison problem for financial statement users. Many firms also use more than one depreciation method, further complicating the problem of comparing income across firms.

Compounding the comparability problem is the ability of firms to change depreciation estimates and methods when significant changes in economic conditions and new information dictate. For example, unanticipated obsolescence could necessitate a reduction in useful life. Alternatively, a prolonged recession can reduce demand for the firm's products, which could prompt a switch from an accelerated depreciation method. To inform financial statement users, GAAP imposes significant disclosure requirements on firms that change estimates and methods. The accounting and rationale for these depreciation policy decisions are discussed in Chapter 24.

Depreciation, Cash Flow, and Dividend Policy

Although it is not a cash outflow, depreciation reduces reported income and retained earnings. Depreciation over the life of a depreciable asset reduces retained earnings by the depreciable cost less the associated tax savings. Because dividends are generally limited by law to the amount of earnings retained in the business, depreciation,

EXHIBIT 12–8
Effect of Depreciation on
Amount of Retained Earnings
Available for Dividends

STABLE COMPANY
Two-Year Period Ending December 31, 1996

Start of Stable Company's operations: January 1995
Assets under consideration for purchase: land (option 1) or equipment (option 2)
Cost: $6,000 each (only one asset is purchased)
Useful life of equipment: 2 years
Residual value of equipment: $0
Annual sales revenues: $20,000 regardless of the asset acquired
Tax rate: 30%
Annual cash expenses: $7,000 regardless of the asset acquired
Method of depreciation: SL for accounting and tax purposes

Combined Results for 1995 and 1996	Option 1 Purchase Land	Option 2 Purchase Equipment
Sales revenue	$40,000	$40,000
Cash expenses	(14,000)	(14,000)
Depreciation expense		(6,000)
Pretax income	26,000	20,000
Income tax expense (30%)	(7,800)	(6,000)
Net income for two-year period, and December 31, 1996 retained earnings balance	$18,200	$14,000

like any other expense, may reduce the amount of dividends paid. To illustrate this effect, Exhibit 12–8 compares the earnings generated by a depreciable asset (option 2) with those of a nondepreciable asset (option 1).

Depreciation on the equipment in option 2 reduces income and retained earnings by $4,200 ($18,200 − $14,000) relative to option 1. This difference equals the after-tax income effect of depreciation:

Depreciation for two years	$6,000
Less tax savings (.30)$6,000	1,800
Net effect of depreciation on income and retained earnings for two years	$4,200

If Stable's policy is to pay out 100% of retained earnings in dividends, the company pays $18,200 under option 1 and $14,000 under option 2. Option 2 (depreciable asset) thus conserves a total of $6,000 cash compared with option 1 (nondepreciable asset), computed as follows:

Dividends saved ($18,200 − $14,000)	$4,200
Tax savings (.30)$6,000	1,800
Total assumed cash savings	$6,000

The Stable Company example illustrates that depreciation can indirectly conserve resources in an amount equal to the acquisition cost of depreciable assets, depending on the dividend payout and tax depreciation.

Depreciation, however, does not guarantee that sufficient capital will be available for asset replacement. The replacement cost of most plant assets normally exceeds the original cost, especially during periods of inflation. As for dividends, few firms pay out the maximum allowed by law. In general, depreciation does not conserve resources in the amount recognized as expense.

A related misconception is that depreciation generates cash inflows equal to the amount of depreciation expense. The frequent references by the financial press to "cash provided by depreciation" are misinterpretations of published cash flow statements. An excerpt from Dofasco's 1993 financial statements, shown below, provides an example.

DOFASCO INC.
Notes to Consolidated Financial Statements
For Years Ended December 31

13. Cash Derived from Operations

	1993	1992
	(in millions)	
Net income (loss) for year	$138.6	$(207.1)
Items not involving cash:		
Unusual items	(74.8)	323.9
Depreciation and amortization	179.8	166.8
Deferred income taxes	(11.9)	(163.8)
Loss from equity investments	4.8	10.5
Pension and other post-employment benefits	6.5	(2.7)
Other	12.3	4.6
Operating working capital components providing (utilizing) cash	(74.7)	46.8
	$180.6	$ 179.0

The $179.8 million adjustment (almost 100% of total cash provided by operating activities) should not be interpreted as the contribution that depreciation and amortization made to net operating cash inflow. Actually, depreciation and amortization are added to net income because they did not cause a cash outflow but were deducted from revenues in determining income. Tax savings are the only definite contribution made by depreciation to cash inflows.

Depreciation and Price Level Changes

Total depreciation on capital assets is limited to historical depreciable cost. No allowance is made for the increase in the replacement cost of plant assets.[9] Moreover, advances in technology and changing market demands often require replacement of plant assets with more expensive ones.

Many accountants and others interested in improving financial reporting contend that depreciation based on the historical cost of capital assets significantly understates the cost on a going-concern basis, thereby overstating reported income. The understatement of depreciation and overstatement of income result in overstatement of various rates of return that relate earnings to investment, to total assets, and to owners' equity, ratios commonly used for evaluating performance.[10]

Another problem occurs when companies disinvest permanent capital by maintaining dividends based on historical cost earnings. In 1979, for example, the Ford Motor Company reported historical cost earnings per share of $9.75 but earned only $1.78 per share based on the current cost of plant facilities. Ford paid dividends of $3.90 per share that year. Assuming eventual replacement of facilities, many contend that Ford paid out $2.12 per share ($3.90 − $1.78, an amount representing $225 million) that should have been retained for replacement of facilities. This phenomenon is not an isolated problem. Most capital-intensive firms fell victim to overstated earnings due to inflation in the 1970s and early 1980s.

---

[9] For example, the consumer price index for Canada, published by Statistics Canada and used as a primary measure of inflation, increased 365% between 1973 and 1993. A new plant asset costing $100,000 in 1973 would have cost $365,000 in 1993 if replacement cost had kept pace with inflation.

[10] Both the numerator and the denominator of these ratios are changed in a way that increases the ratio. The numerator is overstated because it is an income measure. The denominators are understated because book values of operational assets often understate their true market value during times of inflation. The numerator and denominator effects combine to cause historical rates of return for some firms to exceed rates based on current-cost values by hundreds of percentage points.

Other accountants point out that selling prices of products can be expected to keep pace with inflation, with net income growing to replace outdated assets at higher prices when the need arises. Whichever point of view is correct, financial statement users should be aware of the potential distortion of historical cost depreciation and its effect on performance measures.

To reduce the overstatement of reported earnings relative to price-level-adjusted earnings, firms can choose accelerated depreciation methods.[11] The higher depreciation amounts recognized early in the useful life of plant assets more closely approximates depreciation based on price-level-adjusted cost.

ADDITIONAL DEPRECIATION ISSUES

Additional depreciation issues include fractional-year depreciation, depreciation of post-acquisition costs, and depreciation systems.

Fractional-Year Depreciation

Most capital assets are not placed in service at the beginning of a reporting period, nor are disposals typically made on an asset's service-entry anniversary date. Firms adjust for fractional periods in two different ways. Some compute the exact amount of depreciation for each fractional period, and others apply an accounting policy convention.

For the following examples, assume that an asset costing $20,000 with a residual value of $2,000 and useful life of four years is placed into service on April 1, 1995. The firm has a calendar-year reporting cycle.

Exact Calculation Approach   This approach computes the precise amount of depreciation for each fractional period. The asset in question is used only $9/12$ of a year in 1995. Under SL depreciation, the asset's fractional service period is applied to the annual depreciation amount, as illustrated:

$$\text{Depreciation expense, 1995} = (\$20{,}000 - \$2{,}000)(1/4)(9/12) = \$3{,}375$$

$$\text{Depreciation expense, 1996–1998} = (\$20{,}000 - \$2{,}000)(1/4) \qquad = \$4{,}500$$

$$\text{Depreciation expense, 1999} = (\$20{,}000 - \$2{,}000)(1/4)(3/12) = \$1{,}125$$

The service-hours and productive output methods automatically adjust for fractions of a year. The number of hours used or units produced in the partial-year period is applied to the depreciation rate in the normal manner.

Under accelerated depreciation methods, first compute depreciation for each *whole year* of the asset's useful life (without regard to the fiscal year). Then apply the relevant fraction of the fiscal year to the appropriate whole-year depreciation amount. This process applied to the asset for the double-declining-balance method (the double-declining-balance rate is $2/4$ years = 50%) yields:

Whole Year	Double-Declining-Balance Depreciation for Whole Year	
1. April 1, 1995 to March 31, 1996	.50($20,000)	= $10,000
2. April 1, 1996 to March 31, 1997	.50($20,000 − $10,000)	= $ 5,000
3. April 1, 1997 to March 31, 1998	.50($20,000 − $15,000)	= $ 2,500
4. April 1, 1998 to March 31, 1999	.50($20,000 − $17,500)	= $ 1,250*

Recognized Depreciation

1995 depreciation = $10,000($9/12$)		= $ 7,500
1996 depreciation = $10,000($3/12$) + $5,000($9/12$)		= $ 6,250
1997 depreciation = $5,000($3/12$) + $2,500($9/12$)		= $ 3,125
Depreciation through December 31, 1997		$16,875

* Using this amount causes total depreciation to exceed depreciable cost. The switch to straight-line depreciation is explained in the text.

---

[11] See R. Mohr and S. Dilley, ''Current Cost and ACRS Depreciation Expense: A Comparison,'' *Accounting Review* 59, no. 4 (October 1984).

Depreciation for 1995 includes only the *first* $9/12$ of the first whole-year depreciation amount because the asset is in service only $9/12$ of 1995. Fiscal year 1996 contains the last $3/12$ of whole-year 1 and the first $9/12$ of whole-year 2.[12]

Continuing to apply the fractional calculation to 1998 yields $1,562.5 of depreciation ($2,500 $\times$ $3/12$ + $1,250 $\times$ $9/12$). Total depreciation through December 31, 1998, would then amount to $18,437.50 ($16,875 + $1,562.50), which *exceeds* depreciable cost ($18,000). Therefore, assume that the firm switches to straight-line depreciation beginning January 1, 1998. The remaining depreciation is computed as follows:

Remaining depreciable cost, January 1, 1998

$$= \$20,000 - \$2,000 - \$16,875 = \$1,125$$

Remaining months in useful life at January 1, 1998 = 15 months
1998 depreciation = $1,125($12/15$) = $900
1999 depreciation = $1,125($3/15$) = $225

Total depreciation from 1995 through 1999 equals $18,000 (depreciable cost).[13] The whole-year approach just illustrated also is applicable to the sum-of-the-years'-digits method.

Accounting Policy Convention   To avoid the complexities of fractional-year depreciation, many firms adopt a policy convention. Examples in conventions in current use are:

1. Compute annual depreciation solely on the basis of the balance in the capital asset accounts at the beginning of the period. Assets disposed of during a period are depreciated a full period, and assets purchased during a period are not depreciated that period. (No depreciation is recognized in 1995 on the asset in the example.)
2. Compute annual depreciation solely on the basis of the balance in the asset account at the end of the period. Assets purchased during a period are depreciated a full period, and assets disposed of during a period are not depreciated that period. ($4,500, or $18,000 $\div$ 4, of SL depreciation is recognized in 1995 on the asset.)
3. Compute a full year's depreciation on assets placed into service before midyear, and none on assets placed into service after midyear. Assets retired before midyear are not depreciated that year; those retired after midyear are depreciated a full year. ($4,500 of SL depreciation is recognized in 1995 on the asset.)
4. Compute a full month's depreciation on assets placed into service on or before the 15th of the month, and none on assets placed into service after the 15th. Assets retired on or before the 15th of the month are not depreciated that month; those retired after the 15th are depreciated a full month. ($3,375 of SL depreciation is recognized in 1995 on the asset, the same amount as under the exact computation.)[14]

---

[12] Accelerated depreciation methods are accelerated only in terms of whole years. Within each whole year, a constant rate of depreciation applies.

[13] A faster approach to computing exact depreciation under the declining-balance methods is to multiply the asset's book value at the beginning of each period by the appropriate declining-balance rate. This approach, applied to the asset for the first three years, yields:

1995 depreciation = .50($20,000)($9/12$)   = $7,500
1996 depreciation = .50($20,000 − $7,500)   = $6,250
1997 depreciation = .50($20,000 − $7,500 − $6,250) = $3,125

The depreciation recognized in the disposal year, however, generally does not equal that under the whole year approach. The gain or loss on disposal also differs. The differences are generally not material.

[14] However, if the asset were purchased on April 9, the exact calculation would depreciate the asset for the period April 9 through December 31, resulting in a different amount of expense. The amount under the fourth convention would remain $3,375.

5. Compute half a year's depreciation in both the year of purchase and the year of retirement, regardless of the date of purchase or retirement. This is similar to the half-year convention used for income tax purposes. ($2,250, or ½ × $18,000 ÷ 4, of SL depreciation is recognized in 1995 on the asset.)

These conventions satisfy GAAP if the results are not materially different from the exact calculation. The same policy must be used consistently to achieve similar results from period to period. The exact approach to fractional-year depreciation should be used only if the information advantages justify the added cost.

Depreciation of Post-Acquisition Costs

Capitalized post-acquisition costs as well as the original acquisition cost of plant assets must be depreciated. The example below applies the straight-line method, but the general approach is the same regardless of method: Depreciate the new expenditure over its economic useful life.

How this is accomplished depends on which account is capitalized with the amount of the post-acquisition cost: the original asset, accumulated depreciation, or a separate new asset. The useful life of the post-acquisition item relative to that of the original asset must also be considered. Depreciation on the original asset is recognized to the date of the post-acquisition expenditure. Depreciation on the new balance begins on the date the new item is placed into service.

Subsequent Cost Combined with Original Asset   If the new item is an integral part of the original asset, is expected to be retired with the original asset, or only extends the life of the original asset, the expenditure need not be classified and depreciated as a separate capital asset. Although accumulated depreciation might sometimes be debited for the cost of an extraordinary repair, other types of post-acquisition expenditures are debited to the original asset account. Either way, depreciation from the date of the post-acquisition expenditure is based on the increased book value of the original asset.

For example, assume the following information for Macro Corporation:

Original asset: office building purchased January 1, 1990.
Useful life: 20 years.
Original cost: $800,000.
Straight-line depreciation is used.
Post-acquisition cost: wall partitions added to the third-floor executive office suite to increase the number of private offices (an addition). The partitions do not extend the life of the building and have no separate utility apart from the building. The partitions were installed July 1, 1996, at a cost of $150,000.

Macro debits the building account for the cost of the partitions.

Book value of building on July 1, 1996:
Original cost	$800,000	
Depreciation through Jan. 1, 1996 ($800,000 ÷ 20)(6 years).	(240,000)	
1996 depreciation through June 30, 1996 ($800,000 ÷ 20)½	(20,000)	$20,000
Post-acquisition cost—partitions	150,000	
Building book value July 1, 1996	$690,000	

Remaining useful life of building at July 1, 1996:
20 years original life—6.5 years in use = 13.5 years

1996 depreciation on building, July 1 through December 31 ($690,000 ÷ 13.5)(½) .		25,556
Total 1996 depreciation		$45,556

Subsequent Cost Not Combined with Original Asset   If the new item is not an integral part of the original asset and has separate utility or is not expected to be retired with the original asset, it should be depreciated separately.

Suppose that removable refrigeration units with a useful life of 10 years are added to railroad boxcars with a remaining useful life of 5 years (an addition). Because the refrigeration units can be used in other rolling stock, the units should be depreciated independently over their respective useful lives. In this case, the subsequent expenditure has no effect on the depreciation of the original asset.

Depreciation Systems

Unique features of certain depreciable assets, as well as practical considerations, may cause firms to modify the application of standard depreciation methods. We call these adaptations **depreciation systems** because they apply depreciation computations to groups of assets:

1. Inventory appraisal systems.
2. Group and composite systems.
3. Retirement and replacement systems.

Depreciation systems reduce accounting costs because fewer depreciation calculations are required and accumulated depreciation records are not maintained on individual assets.

Inventory Appraisal System Under the **inventory appraisal system,** capital assets are appraised at the end of each accounting period in their present condition through application of a deterioration percentage to the cost of the assets in place or through an outside assessment of replacement cost. This system is especially suitable for firms with numerous low-cost capital assets.

The decline in the total appraisal value during the period is recorded directly in the asset account as depreciation expense. Cash received on disposal is recorded as a credit to depreciation expense. The book value (appraisal value) of the assets at the end of the period is an estimate of current acquisition cost that takes into account current condition and usefulness.

To illustrate how this system works, assume this information on the hand tools capital asset account of Miller Company, which began operations in 1995:

Purchases of hand tools in 1995: $1,900.

Appraisal value of tools at the end of 1995: $1,080.

Proceeds from disposal of tools in 1995: $70.

The entries for 1995 are as follows:
During 1995:

Hand tools.	1,900	
Cash		1,900
Cash	70	
Depreciation expense		70

December 31, 1995:

Depreciation expense	820	
Hand tools ($1,900 − $1,080)		820

The value of tools on hand decreased $820, but the $70 received on disposal offsets that decline, resulting in $750 of net depreciation expense.

Accounting cost savings are evident from the elimination of individual subsidiary accounts, with depreciation recorded only for the group. Disposals do not require retrieval of accumulated depreciation information, and no gain or loss is recorded. Furthermore, the appraisal is made for the entire group rather than for each individual asset.

Evaluation Although inventory appraisal systems appear to be a departure from the historical cost principle, assets are not written up in value, and the resulting depreciation expense must be consistent with results obtained with historical cost-based depreciation methods. The method is open to criticism, however, because appraisals can be quite subjective.

EXHIBIT 12–9
Case Data for Composite
Depreciation Example:
Components of Operating
Assembly Acquired
Early 1995

Component	Quantity	Unit Original Cost	Unit Residual Value	Unit Useful Life	Unit Annual SL Depreciation
A	10	$50,000	$5,000	15 years	$3,000
B	4	20,000	4,000	10 years	1,600
C	6	7,000	600	8 years	800
D	20	3,000	0	3 years	1,000

Total annual depreciation:
10($3,000) + 4($1,600) + 6($800) + 20($1,000) = $61,200

Total asset acquisition cost:
10($50,000) + 4($20,000) + 6($7,000) + 20($3,000) = $682,000

Total depreciable cost:
$682,000 − 10($5,000) − 4($4,000) − 6($600) = $612,400

Composite annual depreciation rate = $61,200 ÷ $682,000 = 0.0897

Composite group useful life = $612,400 ÷ $61,200 = 10 years

Group and Composite Systems Plant assets are sometimes grouped together for application of an average depreciation rate that reflects the characteristics of the group. There are two approaches:

1. **Group depreciation** is used for homogeneous assets. Example: delivery trucks having similar costs, useful lives, and residual values.
2. **Composite depreciation** is used for heterogeneous assets. Example: industrial equipment with different costs, useful lives, and residual values.

However, these systems are identical with respect to calculation and journal entries.

Although the original cost for each asset acquired is maintained, only a control account for accumulated depreciation is used. As with the inventory appraisal method, gains and losses are not recognized on disposal. Instead, the asset control account is credited for the original cost of the item, and the accumulated depreciation account is debited for the difference between cash received and the original cost of the item.

Exhibit 12–9 presents information and calculations for an example that uses heterogeneous assets. Annual depreciation expense is the product of an average depreciation rate and the balance in the asset control account. The composite depreciation rate equals the percentage of total cost depreciated each year:

$$\frac{\text{Annual group SL depreciation}}{\text{Total group acquisition cost}} = \text{Composite rate}$$

Residual value is taken into account because the numerator used in determining the composite rate reflects the SL method.[15] The advantage of using total acquisition cost as the denominator is that future depreciation can then be computed by applying the composite rate to the remaining balance in the asset control account, and depreciable cost need not be computed each year.

Annual depreciation expense for the group of assets in Exhibit 12–9 is:

$$\begin{array}{ccc}
\text{Annual group} \\
\text{depreciation expense} \end{array} = \text{Composite rate} \times \begin{array}{c} \text{Total group} \\ \text{acquisition cost} \end{array}$$

$$\$61,200 \quad = (.0897)(\text{rounded}) \quad \$682,000$$

---

[15] The double-declining-balance method can also be used in composite and group systems. In the example, twice the straight-line rate (.1794) would be used for depreciation purposes. Other declining-balance methods are also appropriate. The sum-of-the-years'-digits method, however, cannot be applied when the assets have different useful lives; the numerator and denominator of the fractional rates used each year cannot be computed.

The composite useful life of the group is also the ratio of two values: total depreciable cost and annual depreciation. The ratio yields the number of years over which depreciation is taken (in this case, 10 years, from Exhibit 12–9). In 10 years, the group is fully depreciated and has a net book value equal to total group residual value. The composite life is not the simple average useful life of the group but rather depends on the relative contribution each type of asset makes to the total depreciable cost of the group. For example, component A contributes $450,000 of depreciable cost to the group, and each unit of component A has a useful life of 15 years, whereas component D contributes only $60,000 to depreciable cost, and each unit has a useful life of 3 years. The composite life is therefore closer to the useful life of component A.

If no changes occur in the makeup of the group during the entire composite life, annual depreciation does not change. When assets are added or disposed of before the end of their useful life, the original depreciation rate is maintained if the changes are not significant to the overall depreciable cost and useful life composition of the group. Depreciation is computed with the old rate and the new balance in the group asset control account, which reflects the addition or deletion of assets. Material changes in the makeup of composite groups may require changes in depreciation rates because these assets are heterogeneous.

The following entry is made to dispose of one unit of component B sold for $18,000 in 1996:

Cash	18,000	
Accumulated depreciation—operating assembly (to balance)	2,000	
Operating assembly.		20,000

The disposal affects 1996 depreciation, computed as:

$$(\$682,000 - \$20,000).0897 = \$59,381$$

The original rate continues to be applied because no significant change in the group has occurred.

Evaluation The variance in the useful life and depreciable cost among group assets is the basis for criticisms about group and composite systems. The group of assets in the example is depreciated for 10 years. Before the end of the first 10 years, components C and D have probably been retired. After the group is fully depreciated, component A remains in service. Critics charge that composite and group systems compromise the matching of acquisition costs against periods of use.

However, group and composite systems are widely used in companies reporting the use of the straight-line method. For example, Ameritech Corporation disclosed its use of composite methods in its 1992 financial statements:

> The provision for depreciation is based principally on straight-line remaining life and straight-line equal life group methods of depreciation applied to individual categories of plant with similar characteristics . . . When depreciable plant is retired, the amount at which such plant has been carried in property, plant and equipment is charged to accumulated depreciation.

Retirement and Replacement Systems These depreciation systems are used by public utilities and railroads to reduce recordkeeping costs. Such companies typically own large numbers of items dispersed over extensive geographic areas, including rolling stock, track, wire, utility poles, and microwave telephone equipment. The cost to depreciate these items individually is prohibitive.

Under both the **retirement system** and the **replacement system,** depreciation is not recorded for individual assets, no gain or loss is recognized on disposal, and an accumulated depreciation account is not used. The total original cost of acquisitions is maintained although often not on an individual asset basis. Residual value is treated as a reduction from depreciation expense in the disposal period. Depreciation expense under both systems is based on assets *retired* during the period.

The key difference between the two systems is the assumed cost of the retired assets, which can be substantial. Depreciation under the *retirement* system equals the original cost of the item retired less residual value. If the cost of acquisition cannot be associated with specific physical units, the oldest remaining cost of the type of asset retired less residual value is used for depreciation purposes. This is essentially a FIFO system.

Depreciation under the *replacement* system equals the cost of the most recent acquisition of the type of item retired less residual value. This is essentially a LIFO system. The most recent acquisition is considered the replacement for the item retired.

To illustrate these systems, assume this information for Western Power Utility:

1. In 1984, its first 100 kilometers of power lines are installed for a total of $300,000 at an average cost of $3,000 per kilometer.
2. In 1992, 12.5 kilometers of additional lines are installed for $50,000 at an average cost of $4,000 per kilometer.
3. In 1995, 16 kilometers of new lines are installed for $80,000 at an average cost of $5,000 per kilometer. Also in 1995, 20 kilometers of lines installed in 1984 at an original cost of $60,000 are retired. $5,000 is received on the disposal.

The following entries are made under each system to record the acquisitions, which total $430,000:

	1984		1992		1995	
Transmission lines.	300,000		50,000		80,000	
Cash		300,000		50,000		80,000

The retirement system recognizes the cost of the asset retired ($60,000) less the $5,000 residual as depreciation in 1995. The replacement system uses the *latest* acquisition cost for calculating depreciation:

All 1995 lines installed: 16 kilometers @ $5,000/kilometer.	$80,000
Part of 1992 installation: 4 kilometers @ $4,000/kilometer.	16,000
1995 replacement system depreciation before residual	96,000
Proceeds on disposal.	5,000
1995 replacement system depreciation	$91,000

The following entries record 1995 depreciation under the two systems:

	Retirement System		Replacement System	
Depreciation expense	55,000		91,000	
Cash	5,000		5,000	
Transmission lines		60,000		96,000

The ending balances in the transmission line account are $370,000 ($430,000 − $60,000) for the retirement system and $334,000 ($430,000 − $96,000) for the replacement system.

Evaluation   Retirement and replacement systems can result in depreciation amounts that bear no relationship to those of individually applied methods. For example, some deterioration of Western Power Utility's assets very likely occurred between 1984 and 1994, but no depreciation is recognized during that period. Furthermore, the replacement system asset balances can be distorted to the point of meaninglessness. The results of the retirement system are opposite those of the replacement system: relatively greater reported values for assets, and smaller reported values for depreciation expense.

Neither system meets the requirement of being rational and systematic. Because a preset, orderly procedure is not followed, the results are heavily influenced by retirement of assets. Nor do these systems match depreciable cost to periods of use. Severe distortion of profitability and economic position occurs in early years when few assets are retired. Only if a firm replaces assets on a regular basis do depreciation results approximate those of one of the more traditional methods.

|CONCEPT REVIEW

1. What is the main difference between the retirement and replacement depreciation systems?
2. How is annual depreciation expense computed under the inventory appraisal system?
3. What are the main criticisms of the group and composite systems?

IMPAIRMENT OF PLANT ASSETS

Plant assets that lose a significant portion of utility or value suffer an **impairment of value.** Asset impairments are caused by casualty, obsolescence, lack of demand for a company's products, negligence, or mismanagement. Other reasons for recognizing an impairment include decisions to close a plant or sell a product line, orders to take a product off the market, and expropriation of assets by a foreign government.[16] Asset impairments lead to a write-down of assets to fair value.

Asset write-downs accelerated in the 1980s.[17] Between 1986 and the middle of 1988, the firms constituting the Dow Jones industrials recognized $10 billion in write-downs.[18] Losses from discontinued operations had been relatively common, but now firms were writing down assets that they were keeping. Changes in technology and a high level of merger activity contributed to this phenomenon.

Asset write-downs often result from a corporate restructuring, a partial or complete overhauling of the organization that changes employee composition, corporate policy, product, operating location, and company strategy. For example, in the fourth quarter of 1993, Tridel Enterprises Inc. recognized a $135 million write-down of plant assets.[19] The management of a reorganized firm often prefers to publish financial statements reflecting new starting values for major classes of plant assets. When companies face difficult times, entire groupings of plant assets may be determined to be overvalued and written down.

Land, although not depreciated, is also subject to impairment loss. Land can be written down to market value as a result of:

- Permanent erosion.
- Natural and man-made pollutants making land unusable.
- Excessive depletion of underground aquifers causing sinkholes.
- Encroachment from competing businesses.
- Impairment caused by changing demographics and competition.

---

[16] Squibb, for example, took a $68 million write-down of its pharmaceuticals operations in South America and Asia fearing unfavourable political and economic conditions, although it continued to operate there. See "You Know It When You See It," *Forbes,* July 25, 1988, p. 84.

[17] The dollar amount and frequency of write-offs increased during 1980–1985. In "Impairments and Writeoffs of Long-Lived Assets," *Management Accounting,* August 1989, D. Fried, M. Schiff, and A. Sondhi found, for 702 companies during that period, that the average pretax write-off increased from $28.3 million (38 write-offs) to $117.5 million (207 write-offs).

[18] "You Know It When You See It," *Forbes,* July 25, 1988, p. 84.

[19] "Tridel Holders Hit with Bad News," *Globe and Mail,* April 28, 1994, p. B9.

Accounting Guidelines

In practice, accounting for impairment losses has not been uniform. The amount and timing of recognized impairment losses have varied depending on the particular situation. In the *CICA Handbook,* Section 3060, "Capital Assets," several paragraphs deal with the write-down of capital assets. In particular, paragraphs .42 and .43 state:

> When the net recoverable amount of a capital asset falls below the net carrying amount, the net carrying amount should be written down, by a charge to income, to the net recoverable amount.
>
> A write-down to net recoverable amount should not be reversed if the net recoverable amount subsequently increases.

The net recoverable amount may be estimated either on the basis of net cash flows from use or on net realizable value, given the intention and ability to sell the assets. The write-down of capital assets usually arises out of the risks inherent in an entity's normal business activities. As such, the write-downs would not be considered extraordinary, although they could be sufficiently significant to warrant separate disclosure on the income statement as part of income before extraordinary items.

Conditions Suggesting an Asset Impairment An asset's carrying value (cost less depreciation to date) is recoverable if it is exceeded by the asset's expected future net cash inflows from use or disposal. One of the assumptions inherent in reporting assets at cost less depreciation is that the carrying value (book value) will be recovered. Otherwise, an impairment is implied and a new cost basis should be established. The following factors may suggest that an asset currently in use is impaired:

- A decline in market value of the asset.
- A change in the manner in which the asset is used.
- A change in legal or business considerations affecting the value of the asset.
- A cost overrun on assets being constructed.
- A forecast demonstrating continuing future losses associated with the asset.

Only when there is reason to believe an asset in use is impaired must it be tested for recoverability of carrying value. Routine investigations for impairments are not required.

Specific Test for Asset Impairment When circumstances suggest that an asset's carrying value is not recoverable, the future net cash inflows expected from the asset's use and disposal are estimated. An impairment loss is recognized if the undiscounted sum of the future net cash inflows is less than the carrying value of the asset. The asset then is written down to fair value.

Measurement of the Impairment Loss The impairment loss for assets in use is the difference between the carrying value of the asset and the fair value of the asset. If no active market exists for the asset, then the selling prices of similar assets may be used to approximate fair value. Otherwise, the present value of the asset's expected future net cash inflows, discounted at a rate commensurate with the risk involved, may be used. The impairment loss for assets designated for disposal is the difference between carrying value and fair value less estimated disposal costs.

Illustration

Assume that Galt Limited owns $2,000,000 (cost) of specialized equipment used in the production of video display terminals (VDTs). The equipment was purchased and installed in January 1985 and has an expected useful life of 20 years and a residual value of $200,000. Galt uses straight-line depreciation. In January 1995, one of Galt's competitors completed the development of a reduced-radiation VDT. The demand for Galt's VDTs immediately declined by 90%.[20]

---

[20] This example was suggested by an actual development in the computer industry. IBM planned to lower the electromagnetic fields generated by its VDTs in 1989. See "IBM's Plan to Reduce VDT Radiation Fails to Impress Most Computer Makers," *The Wall Street Journal,* November 24, 1989, p. B3.

As a result, Galt estimates the total future net cash inflows from operating the equipment to be $550,000, and the fair value to be $400,000 in use. The equipment is expected to have no residual value and will be used only during the five remaining years that the older model VDTs are manufactured. The following entries recognize the impairment loss, reduce the carrying value of the equipment to fair value, and recognize 1995 depreciation.

January 1995:

Impairment loss	700,000*	
Accumulated depreciation		700,000

* Original cost of equipment	$2,000,000
Depreciation 1985–1994:	
($^{10}\!/_{20}$)($2,000,000 − $200,000)	900,000
Carrying value, January 1995	1,100,000
Fair value, and new carrying value, January 1995	400,000
Impairment loss	$ 700,000

December 31, 1995:

Depreciation expense ($400,000 ÷ 5)	80,000	
Accumulated depreciation		80,000

In this example, the equipment is examined for impairment because of the change in market conditions. The undiscounted sum of future net cash inflows ($550,000) is less than the equipment's carrying value ($1,100,000). Therefore, the equipment is written down to fair value and an impairment loss is recognized.

The use of the undiscounted sum of cash flows for *determining when* an impairment has occurred may appear to be inconsistent with the use of fair (or present) value to *measure* the impairment loss. An asset is impaired when its carrying value is not recoverable using the most liberal definition of recovery—the nominal sum of future cash flows. This definition produces fewer asset impairment losses than would a discounted cash flow definition and is consistent with the need to investigate for impairment losses on an exception basis only. The test, based on the nominal sum of future cash flows, will require only those assets that are clearly impaired to be written down.

Future Changes in Fair Value   After the impairment loss is recognized on assets in use, the reduced carrying value becomes the new basis for future depreciation. Recoveries of previous impairment losses on assets in use are not permitted.

Disclosures   Impairment losses are reported as a component of income from continuing operations before income tax. If not separately itemized in the income statement, the loss should be shown in the disclosure notes.

| CONCEPT REVIEW

1. Although land is not subject to depreciation, under what conditions is it written down?
2. When is an impairment loss recognized on an asset presently used in operations?
3. How is an impairment loss on an asset presently used in operations computed?

Casualty Insurance

An asset impairment caused by casualty will not result in a complete loss if the asset is covered by casualty insurance. Casualty insurers normally impose a **coinsurance requirement** compelling firms wishing to guarantee a full recovery in the event of a casualty to carry a substantial amount of insurance. Otherwise, the insured becomes a coinsurer of the property and must absorb some of the loss.

GLOBAL VIEW

International accounting practice is characterized by a variety of approaches to recognizing asset impairments. For example, French firms recognize temporary impairments, those that may be recovered, as a charge to an allowance account instead of reducing current earnings. For other countries, the cause of the impairment affects the recognition and classification of the impairment loss. In Japan, write-downs related to casualties are treated as extraordinary losses, whereas impairments from obsolescence are absorbed through changes in depreciation rates.

The Fourth Directive of the European Union requires write-downs of permanently impaired assets to be recognized in earnings immediately. The directive also requires reversal of write-downs upon recovery. Although such practice is not allowed in Canada, it is consistent with the standards of the International Accounting Standards Committee.

Revised *International Accounting Standard No. 16* (effective January 1, 1995), "Property, Plant, and Equipment," establishes two different approaches to accounting for asset impairments. The two acceptable approaches depend on the treatment chosen for measuring asset carrying value.

The first, or benchmark, treatment is to carry plant assets at cost less accumulated depreciation. Under this treatment, the first part of which is similar to Canadian GAAP, if the recoverable amount of a plant asset declines below carrying value, an expense is recognized in the amount necessary to reduce the carrying value to the asset's recoverable amount. Recoverable amount is the expected future value to be obtained through use and disposal of the asset. However, if circumstances after the write-down imply that the asset's value has been recovered, the write-down is reversed and the carrying value increased to the prewrite-down amount less depreciation to the current date. This reversal of the write-down is not allowed under Canadian GAAP.

The second "allowed alternative" treatment, which is markedly different from the more conservative Canadian GAAP, permits revaluation of plant assets above or below carrying value. Thus, when a plant asset becomes impaired, the asset is written down and an expense recognized unless the asset had been revalued above carrying value previously. In this case, the reduction is charged first to an owners' equity account credited when the asset was written up.

Casualty Insurance Policy Settlement   The amount of insurance proceeds from a casualty insurance policy with an 80% coinsurance requirement is the lowest of the following three potential settlement amounts:[21]

1. Face value of the policy, which depends on the premium cost and is the maximum recoverable amount.

2. Loss at replacement cost:

$$\text{Replacement cost of property before casualty} - \text{Replacement cost of property after casualty}$$

3. Indemnity amount:

$$\frac{\text{Face value of policy}}{80\% \times \text{Replacement cost of property before casualty}} \times \text{Loss at replacement cost}$$

The second of the three values above is the economic loss from the casualty before insurance proceeds are collected. This value is generally not equal to the loss for financial accounting purposes, which is the difference between insurance proceeds and the portion of the book value lost. The denominator of the first term of the indemnity amount (the third item above) is the coinsurance requirement.

Full Recovery   A firm receives full recovery on an insured casualty loss when the insurance proceeds are at least equal to the loss at replacement cost. For purposes of the discussion, assume that there is an 80% coinsurance requirement and that losses are classified as small or large depending on whether the loss exceeds the coinsurance requirement:

1. Small losses: ≤80% of replacement cost before casualty.
2. Large losses: >80% of replacement cost before casualty.

---

[21] For an insurance policy with no coinsurance clause, the recoverable amount is the lower of the first two potential reimbursement amounts.

Also assume the following information for Chance Company (amounts in thousands):

Replacement cost of property before casualty, $100.

Coinsurance requirement, 80%.

Small Losses The minimum face value of the policy required to achieve full recovery for a small loss is the coinsurance requirement. For Chance, this amount is $80 (.80 × $100). Assume that the property is worth $70 after the casualty and that face value is $80. The three potential proceeds amounts are:

1. Face value: $80.
2. Loss at replacement cost:

$$\$100 - \$70 = \$30$$

(The loss is less than the $80 coinsurance requirement.)
3. Indemnity amount:

$$\frac{\$80}{.80(\$100)} \times \$30 = \$30$$

Chance's insurance proceeds equal $30, the lowest of the three values, and provide full recovery of the loss. If the face value had been less than $80, the indemnity amount would have been less than $30, resulting in proceeds less than the loss. Therefore, the lowest face value for Chance to achieve a full recovery is $80, the coinsurance requirement.

A policy face value exceeding the loss does not necessarily guarantee full recovery. For example, had Chance's policy face value been $70, an amount more than double the loss, the proceeds would have equalled the $26.25 indemnity value [($70 ÷ $80) × $30]. This example illustrates the role of the coinsurance requirement in transferring part of the risk from the insurance company to the insured. The requirement effectively obliges the policyholder to carry insurance well beyond the expected loss to guarantee full recovery. Most casualty losses are not total losses. Without the coinsurance requirement, companies would insure property for considerably less than 80% of value, thus lowering their insurance costs. Insurance firms would be responsible for 100% of small-percentage losses even though the property was insured for much less than full value.

Large Losses The minimum face value of the policy required to achieve full recovery for a large loss is the loss itself. Assume now that the replacement cost of the property after the casualty is only $10 and that the face value is $90 for Chance. The three potential proceeds amounts are:

1. Face value: $90.
2. Loss at replacement cost:

$$\$100 - \$10 = \$90$$

(The loss is greater than the $80 coinsurance requirement.)
3. Indemnity amount:

$$\frac{\$90}{.80(\$100)} \times \$90 = \$101.25$$

Chance's insurance proceeds equal $90, the lowest of the three values, and provide full recovery of the loss. If the face value had been less than $90 (the loss), the loss would no longer have been the lowest of the competing values, and the recovery would not have been complete. Therefore, the lowest face value for Chance to achieve a full recovery is $90, the amount of the loss.

Accounting for Casualty Losses   To illustrate the accounting for a casualty, assume that Hazard Company experienced a fire that destroyed equipment insured under a casualty insurance policy:

1. Equipment originally costing $140,000 has a $20,000 accumulated depreciation balance on January 1, 1995. It is depreciated $20,000 per year.
2. The equipment has a replacement cost of $90,000 on June 30, 1995, just prior to a fire on that date that caused major damage to the equipment. The equipment is worth $40,000 after the fire. The loss at replacement cost is therefore $50,000 ($90,000 − $40,000). Thus, 55.56% of the equipment's replacement value is lost ($50,000 ÷ $90,000).
3. The equipment is insured under a $70,000 casualty insurance policy with an 80% coinsurance requirement. The annual $1,600 premium is paid on January 1, 1995, and prepaid insurance is debited. The policy apportions the premium on face value; face value is reduced by insurance proceeds in the event of a casualty.

The three potential settlement amounts for Hazard are:

1. Face value: $70,000.
2. Loss at replacement cost:

$$\$90,000 - \$40,000 = \$50,000$$

3. Indemnity formula value:

$$\frac{\$70,000}{.80(\$90,000)} \times \$50,000 = \$48,611$$

Hazard receives $48,611 from the insurance company (the lowest of the three values), which is less than full recovery of the economic loss.

The following entries, dated June 30, 1995, are recorded by Hazard:
Depreciation for ½ year:

Depreciation expense	10,000	
Accumulated depreciation		10,000

Insurance expense for ½ year:

Insurance expense	800	
Prepaid insurance		800

Recognition of casualty loss:

Cash	48,611	
Accumulated depreciation	16,668*	
Casualty loss	13,061	
Prepaid insurance		556†
Equipment		77,784‡

* ($20,000 + $10,000)(.5556).

† ($48,611 ÷ $70,000)($800).

‡ $140,000(.5556).

The casualty loss represents the net asset reduction resulting from the fire, considering insurance proceeds, and is measured in terms of the book value of assets involved. The percentage of replacement cost lost (55.56%) is applied to the book value of the equipment. The face value of the insurance policy is reduced by the proceeds. Therefore, $556 of the premium is absorbed in the fire loss. The remaining $244 ($800 − $556) of prepaid insurance relates to the $21,389 face value remaining in the policy ($70,000 − $48,611) for the remainder of 1995.

Multiple Insurance Policies   Companies can purchase more than one policy to insure an asset against casualty. If there is more than one policy, the recoverable cash amount from policy A (with an 80% coinsurance clause) is determined from the following formula:

$$\left[\frac{\text{Face value of policy A}}{\substack{\text{Greater of: 80\% of replacement cost} \\ \text{of property at date of casualty} \\ \text{or} \\ \text{Sum of face values of all} \\ \text{policies on asset}}}\right]\left(\substack{\text{Loss at} \\ \text{replacement} \\ \text{cost}}\right)$$

This formula is similar to the indemnity value for single policies. Firms cannot expect to insure property with a number of policies of small face value and reap full recovery if a casualty occurs. The coinsurance clause produces a large denominator (due to the coinsurance requirement), resulting in a smaller fraction and lower ultimate cash recovery. The policyholder again is a coinsurer.

Using the Hazard example again ($50,000 loss at replacement cost), assume that two policies each with 80% coinsurance clauses are maintained on the equipment. The face value of policy A is $10,000, and that of policy B is $45,000. The sum of the face values is $55,000, and 80% of the replacement cost of the property at date of casualty is $72,000. The denominator of the formula is the greater of $72,000 or $55,000. Thus the amounts recoverable from each policy are:

$$
\begin{array}{lr}
\text{Policy A: } (\$10,000 \div \$72,000)\$50,000 = & \$\ 6,944 \\
\text{Policy B: } (\$45,000 \div \$72,000)\$50,000 = & \underline{31,250} \\
\text{Total amount recovered} & \underline{\underline{\$38,194}}
\end{array}
$$

Hazard did not insure the property for at least 80% of its $90,000 replacement value and thus bears 24% of the loss ($1 - \$38,194 \div \$50,000$). If the sum of the face values of the policies were $72,000 (the total 80% coinsurance requirement), full recovery would be achieved.

Companies generally insure assets at market value. Therefore, casualty insurance proceeds can exceed the book value of the damaged asset, causing large gains. For example, Delta Air Lines recognized a $5.5 million gain on the crash of one of its 727 aircraft in Dallas in 1988. The plane was insured for $6.5 million, but had a book value of only $1 million.[22]

PLANT ASSET AND DEPRECIATION DISCLOSURES

The *CICA Handbook,* Section 3060, requires the following disclosures related to depreciation and depreciable assets to be made for each major category of capital asset:

1. Cost.
2. Accumulated amortization, including the amount of any write-downs.
3. Amortization method used, including the amortization period or rate.

The amount of amortization of a capital asset charged to income for the period should be disclosed.

Information about the depreciation methods employed helps financial statement users interpret the meaning and impact of depreciation on income and financial position.

An excerpt from the disclosure notes to the 1993 financial statements of Canadian Pacific Limited (shown in Exhibit 12–10) illustrates disclosure of depreciation method and information on capital assets.

[22] "Crash Accounting," *Forbes,* October 17, 1988, p. 13.

EXHIBIT 12–10
Canadian Pacific
Limited—Notes to
Consolidated Financial
Statements

1. Significant Accounting Policies

Properties

Transportation: Accounting for railway properties is carried out in accordance with the Uniform Classification of Accounts issued by the National Transportation Agency in Canada and in accordance with Interstate Commerce Commission rules in the United States. Fixed asset additions and major renewals are recorded at cost. Maintenance and repairs are charged to expense as incurred with the exception of material costs of programmed track replacement in Canada which are capitalized. When depreciable property is retired or otherwise disposed of in the normal course of business, the book value, less salvage, is charged to accumulated depreciation.

Depreciation is calculated on the straight-line basis at rates based upon the estimated service lives of depreciable property, except for rail and other track material in the United States which is based on usage. For railway properties, the rates used by CP Rail System are as authorized by the National Transportation Agency of Canada for CP Rail, and by the Interstate Commerce Commission for the Soo Line Railroad Company (a wholly-owned subsidiary of Soo Line Corporation) and the Delaware and Hudson Railway Company, Inc. As a result of depreciation studies required by the National Transportation Agency, the estimated service lives of certain categories of assets have been extended.

Estimated service lives used for principal categories of transportation properties are as follows:

	Years
Railway	
Diesel locomotives	27 to 40
Freight cars	17 to 51
Ties	28 to 60
Rails—in first position	21 to 62
in other than first position	45 to 62
Ships	20
Trucks and trailers	7 to 12

Energy: CP Limited follows the full cost method of accounting for oil and gas properties, whereby all costs relating to the exploration for, and the development of, conventional crude oil and natural gas reserves are capitalized on a country-by-country cost centre basis. Costs accumulated within each cost centre are depleted and depreciated using the unit of production method, based on estimated proved reserves, with net production and reserve volumes of natural gas converted to equivalent energy units of crude oil. Proceeds from disposal of properties are normally deducted from the full cost pool without recognition of gain or loss.

Acquisitions and exploration costs in new cost centres are excluded from costs subject to depletion until it is determined whether or not proved reserves are attributable to the properties, or if impairment has occurred.

In determining depletion and depreciation provisions for conventional crude oil and natural gas assets, CP Limited includes any excess of the net book value of those oil and natural gas assets over the unescalated, undiscounted future net operating revenues from its proved oil and natural gas reserves for each cost centre (ceiling test). A second ceiling test calculation is conducted on an enterprise basis, by including in the depletion and depreciation provisions any excess of the net book value of conventional oil and natural gas assets for all cost centres over the total unescalated, undiscounted future net operating revenues from proved oil and natural gas reserves, less future general and administrative expenses, financing costs and income taxes. The ceiling test calculations utilize CP Limited's weighted average product prices prevailing at year end.

Depreciation of conventional crude oil and natural gas plant, production and other equipment is provided for using the unit of production method. Natural gas liquids extraction and Syncrude oil sands facilities are depreciated on a straight-line basis over the estimated service lives of the assets.

Estimated future dismantlement and site restoration costs for conventional crude oil, natural gas and Syncrude oil sands assets are provided for using the unit of production method. Such costs for extraction facilities of natural gas liquids are provided for over the estimated service lives of the assets. Expenditures incurred to dismantle facilities and restore well sites are charged against the related restoration liability.

Expenditures by CP Limited to acquire, explore for and develop identified mineral properties are capitalized, net of costs relating to production during the development phase, pending evaluation and completion. Expenditures on general exploration for producing properties and abandoned properties are charged against income.

EXHIBIT 12–10
(*concluded*)

Depletion on producing properties is provided using a unit of production method based upon the proven mineral reserve position.

CP Limited provides for the eventual reclamation of mineral properties based upon current production.

Interest on funds borrowed to finance major energy projects is capitalized during the development and construction periods.

Real Estate and Hotels: Real estate held for investment is stated at the lower of cost less accumulated depreciation, and net recoverable amount which is the estimated undiscounted future cash flow from the ongoing use and residual value of a capital asset. Real estate held for sale is stated at the lower of cost and estimated net realizable value. Cost includes carrying costs, principally real estate taxes, interest, the imputed value of free rent, directly attributable salaries and expenses of development personnel and, for income properties, initial leasing costs.

Hotel properties are recorded at cost including interest capitalized during major renewals.

The sinking fund method of providing depreciation is used for buildings. This method will amortize the cost of the buildings over a maximum period of 40 years in a series of annual instalments increasing at the rate of 5% compounded annually.

Telecommunications and Manufacturing: Property, plant and equipment are recorded at cost which, in the case of new manufacturing facilities, includes interest during construction. Maintenance and repairs are expensed as incurred.

Depreciation of plant and equipment is provided principally on a straight-line basis at rates intended to amortize the cost of these assets over their estimated economic lives. Rates for telecommunications equipment are approved by the Canadian Radio-television and Telecommunications Commission.

SUMMARY OF KEY POINTS

(L.O. 1)   1. Depreciation is a rational and systematic process of allocating depreciable cost (acquisition cost less residual value) to the periods in which capital assets are used. Depreciation expense for a period does not represent the change in market value of assets, nor does it necessarily equal the portion of the asset's utility consumed in the period. Depreciation is justified on the basis of physical deterioration, reduction in utility, and obsolescence.

(L.O. 1)   2. Four factors contribute to the determination of periodic depreciation expense: original acquisition cost and any capitalized post-acquisition costs, estimated residual value, estimated useful life or productivity measured either in service-hours or units of output, and the depreciation method chosen.

(L.O. 2)   3. Several methods of depreciation are acceptable under GAAP: the straight-line, service-hours, productive output, and accelerated methods. For all methods, the estimated residual value is the minimum book value. Except for the declining-balance methods, depreciable cost is multiplied by a rate to determine periodic depreciation.

(L.O. 3)   4. In some cases, depreciation may reduce the amount of dividends that would otherwise be paid. Tax depreciation reduces the tax liability and thereby reduces the outflow of cash.

(L.O. 4)   5. Fractional-year depreciation is necessary when capital asset acquisitions and disposals do not coincide with the fiscal year. Depreciation is computed on a whole-year basis, with the appropriate fraction of a period applied to the depreciation for the relevant whole year of the asset's life.

(L.O. 4)   6. Depreciation of any capitalized post-acquisition cost is affected by the remaining useful life of the original asset relative to that of the subsequent cost and whether or not the subsequent cost is combined with the original asset for accounting purposes.

(L.O. 5)   7. Three depreciation systems (appraisal, composite and group, and replacement/retirement) are alternatives to depreciation methods applied individually to assets. These systems save accounting costs and are justified under cost-benefit and materiality constraints.

(L.O. 6)   8. An impairment loss is recognized when the sum of undiscounted expected future net cash inflows from use and disposal of an asset is less than the asset's carrying value. The loss equals the difference between the asset's carrying value and fair value.

(L.O. 6)   9. The recognized gain or loss from an insured casualty is the difference between the insurance proceeds and book value of the asset involved. Coinsurance clauses effectively require insured companies to carry substantial insurance, based on the market value of assets, to guarantee a full recovery of any loss.

REVIEW PROBLEM

The following short cases are independent.

1. **Partial-year depreciation** Whitney Company purchases equipment on July 1, 1994, for $34,000. This equipment has a useful life of five years and a residual value of $4,000. What is depreciation for 1995 under the double-declining-balance method?

2. **Asset impairment** Rancho Company purchases equipment on January 1, 1993, for $34,000. This equipment has a useful life of five years, a residual value of $4,000, and is depreciated using the SYD method. At the beginning of 1995, Rancho suspects that the original investment in the asset will not be realized: The total remaining future cash inflows expected to be produced by the equipment, including the original residual value, is $10,000. The equipment's fair value at January 1, 1995, is $7,000. Determine whether the asset is impaired and if so, the impairment loss at January 1, 1995. Also compute depreciation for 1995.

3. **Composite depreciation** Baja Company uses the composite method of depreciation and has a composite rate of 25%. During 1995, it sells assets with an original cost of $100,000 (residual value of $20,000) for $80,000 and acquires $60,000 worth of new assets (residual value $10,000). The original group of assets has the following characteristics:

Total cost $250,000
Total residual value.   30,000

Assuming that the new assets conform to the group and that the company does not revise the depreciation rate, what is depreciation in 1995?

4. **Retirement and replacement depreciation systems** Rolling Company at the end of 1994 has $250,000 in its plant asset account. During 1995, it acquires $100,000 of new property and sells property with an original cost of $50,000, receiving only 10% of the original cost on disposal. Assume the units acquired replace the units retired.

   a. Under the retirement system of depreciation, what is depreciation expense for 1995, and what is the December 31, 1995, balance in the property account?

   b. Under the replacement system of depreciation, what is depreciation expense for 1995, and what is the December 31, 1995, balance in the property account?

SOLUTION

1.

Depreciation (1994) = .50(2/5)($34,000) = $6,800
Depreciation (1995) = (2/5)($34,000 − $6,800) = $10,880

2.

Original cost of equipment $34,000
Accumulated depreciation, Jan. 1/95 =
    ($34,000 − $4,000)(5 + 4) ÷ 15 = ...   18,000
Book value, Jan. 1/95, before impairment loss $16,000

The asset is impaired because the sum of future cash flows ($10,000) is less than book value ($16,000).

Impairment loss   = $16,000 − $7,000 (fair value) = $9,000.
New book value, Jan. 1/95 = $7,000 (fair value); 3 years remain in useful life.
1995 depreciation   = ($7,000 − $4,000)[3 ÷ (1 + 2 + 3)] = $1,500.

3.

Depreciation (1995) = ($250,000 − $100,000 + $60,000).25
                = $52,500

4*a.*

Depreciation (1995) = $50,000 − (.10 × $50,000) = $45,000
Balance in property account (Dec. 31/95)
                = $250,000 − $50,000 + $100,000 = $300,000

4*b*.

$$\text{Depreciation (1995)} = \$100,000 - (.10 \times \$50,000) = \$95,000$$

Balance in property account (Dec. 31/95)
$$= \$250,000 + \$100,000 - \$100,000 = \$250,000$$

APPENDIX 12: *Depreciation and Income Taxes*

Depreciation under GAAP and depreciation under the Income Tax Act are different matters. Under both authorities, depreciation acts to reduce income before tax, and total depreciation over the life of an asset is limited to original cost. But there the similarity ends. Under GAAP, depreciation guidelines are intended to allocate an asset's historical cost to the accounting periods in which the asset is used, in accordance with the matching principle.

In contrast, tax depreciation is geared to the revenue needs of the federal government, which change in response to economic conditions and the fiscal policies of Parliament. For example, tax depreciation currently provides an incentive for replacement, modernization, and expansion of industrial facilities through accelerated depreciation schedules.

The Capital Cost Allowance System

The Income Tax Act does not allow the deduction of depreciation expense in the determination of taxable income. Instead, it provides that a taxpayer may deduct a **capital cost allowance (CCA)** as specified by the act. Therefore, depreciation expense is added to, and capital cost allowance is deducted from, income before income taxes to determine taxable income.

The capital cost allowance system relies on the grouping of assets into various classes established by the act. Most classes provide a rate to use in calculating the equivalent of declining-balance depreciation, although some classes use the equivalent of straight-line depreciation. Classes and rates for some of the more common assets follow:

Declining-Balance

Class 1 (4%)	Buildings or other structures, including component parts acquired after 1987.
Class 3 (5%)	Buildings or other structures, including component parts acquired before 1988.
Class 8 (20%)	Tangible capital property and machinery or equipment not included in another class.
Class 10 (30%)	Automotive equipment and electronic data processing or decoding equipment.
Class 12 (100%)	Jigs, patterns, tools, utensils costing less than $200, linens, videotape, certified feature films, computer software.

Straight-Line

Class 13	Leasehold interest (life of lease plus one renewal period; minimum 5 years, maximum 40 years).
Class 14	Patent, franchise, concession, or licence (life of asset).

The basic rules for the capital cost allowance system can be explained for most classes as follows:

1. When assets are purchased, their purchase price **(capital cost)** is added to the balance **(undepreciated capital cost)** of the appropriate asset class.
2. When assets are sold, the lesser of the proceeds or the capital cost is deducted from the balance in that asset's class.
3. Assets are considered to be purchased in the middle of the taxation year (half-year rule).
4. The maximum capital cost allowance deductible for a particular class is the balance of undepreciated capital cost, after adjusting for the half-year rule, multiplied by the CCA rate for that class.

Exhibit 12A–1 provides an example of a calculation for capital cost allowance. Iles Machine Shop begins business in January 1995 and purchases four lathes (class 8) for $5,000 each. A fifth lathe is purchased in 1996 for $5,700. In 1997, one of the original lathes is sold for $1,200 and is replaced with another lathe costing $6,500. In 1998 one of the lathes was sold for $1,100.

EXHIBIT 12A–1
Calculation of Capital Cost
Allowance

1995	UCC opening balance		0
	Additions; 4 × $5,000		$20,000
	CCA for 1995; $20,000 × 20% × ½		(2,000)
1996	UCC opening balance		$18,000
	Additions		5,700
	CCA for 1996; ($18,000 × 20%) + ($5,700 × 20% × ½)		(4,170)
1997	UCC opening balance		$19,530
	Additions	$ 6,500	
	Proceeds on disposal	(1,200)	
	Net additions		5,300
	CCA for 1997; ($19,530 × 20%) + ($5,300 × 20% × ½)		(4,436)
1998	UCC opening balance		$20,394
	Proceeds on disposal		(1,100)
	CCA for 1998; ($20,394 − $1,100) × 20%		(3,859)
1999	UCC opening balance		$15,435

When net asset additions take place, the net addition is subject to the half-year rule (see 1996 and 1997 in Exhibit 12A–1). However, when there is a net asset disposal, the entire amount is deducted prior to determining the CCA for the year (see 1998 in Exhibit 12A–1).

The amount deducted on an asset disposal is the lesser of the proceeds and the asset's capital cost. Any proceeds on disposal in excess of the capital cost are treated, for tax purposes, as a capital gain. Any amount in excess of the asset's undepreciated capital cost (UCC) is considered to be a recapture of CCA (depreciation) claimed and reduces the future CCA claimable in that class.

When all of the assets in a class are disposed of, any remaining balances are treated as follows: A positive UCC balance is deducted as a terminal loss in determining taxable income. A negative UCC balance is added to taxable income as recaptured depreciation. In effect, this treatment is similar to the gain or loss on disposal of plant assets on the assumption that either too little or too much depreciation (i.e., CCA) was taken over the lives of the assets. Any proceeds received in excess of the assets' capital (original) cost are treated as a capital gain for tax purposes.

QUESTIONS

1. Explain and compare amortization, depletion, and depreciation.
2. A company reported $2 million of depreciation expense in its income statement. Explain what this means to a friend who has little or no background in accounting. Also explain what it does not imply.
3. List several factors a firm would consider in choosing a depreciation method.
4. Explain the difference in meaning between the balances in the following two accounts: (a) accumulated depreciation and (b) allowance to reduce inventory to LCM.
5. What are the primary causes of depreciation? What effect do changes in the market value of the asset being depreciated have on the depreciation estimates?
6. Explain the three factors (other than depreciation method) that must be considered in allocating the cost of a capital asset.
7. Explain the effects of depreciation on (a) the income statement and (b) the balance sheet.
8. In estimating the service life of an operational asset, obsolescence should be considered. Explain this factor.
9. Explain the relationship of depreciation to (a) cash flow and (b) tangible capital assets.
10. Explain the relationship between depreciation and replacement of the assets being depreciated.
11. Compare the effect of the straight-line and productive output methods of depreciation on the per unit cost of output for a manufacturing company.
12. What is meant by accelerated methods of depreciation? Under what circumstances would these methods generally be appropriate?

13. Which method, SYD or DDB, will always produce the larger amount of depreciation in the first year of an asset's useful life? Show why by example and in general.

14. Explain the basic accounting policy problems that arise with respect to depreciation when a firm's reporting year and the asset year do not coincide. Consider the case of a company that closes its books on June 30 and has purchased a depreciable asset on January 1.

15. Explain the inventory appraisal system of depreciation. Under what circumstances is such a system appropriate?

16. Compare retirement and replacement depreciation systems. Explain when each of these systems would be appropriate.

17. When would the replacement method of depreciation result in lower depreciation expense than the retirement system?

18. How are the composite and group depreciation systems similar?

19. Explain the difficulties that may arise when group or composite depreciation is used.

20. What are some of the advantages of using depreciation systems?

21. What are the three values to be considered when determining the settlement from an insurance company for a casualty loss covered by a casualty insurance policy with an 80% coinsurance clause?

22. What does an 80% coinsurance clause mean to the insured company?

23. Explain what is meant by capital cost allowance (CCA). Explain why CCA may not conform to GAAP.

24. In computing a corporation's tax liability, is tax or GAAP depreciation used?

 25. What is a major difference between *International Accounting Standards* and Canadian GAAP with regard to accounting for asset impairments?

CASES

C 12–1
(L.O. 1, 3)

 Depreciable Tangible Assets Fully Depreciated but Still in Use

1. Baker Corporation has certain fully depreciated tangible operational assets that are still used in the business.
   a. Discuss the possible reasons why this could happen.
   b. Comment on the significance of the continued use of these fully depreciated assets.

2. In the past, these fully depreciated assets and their accumulated depreciation have been merged with other operational assets and related depreciation on the balance sheet. Discuss the propriety of this accounting treatment, including a consideration of other possible treatments and the circumstances in which they would be appropriate.

(AICPA adapted)

C 12–2
(L.O. 1)

Depreciation and Gain or Loss on Disposal   Some of the major car rental companies account for the gain or loss on disposal of their used cars as an adjustment to depreciation expense in the period of disposal rather than reporting gains or losses on disposal.

Required

On what grounds, if any, can such a procedure be justified? Would your answer be different if the procedure were used by relatively few (instead of most) companies in the industry?

C 12–3
(L.O. 5)

Depreciation: Single Asset Unit or Separate Subunits   In situations where depreciable properties are treated as units rather than as part of a group of assets depreciated on a composite or group basis, the question sometimes arises as to what constitutes an appropriate property unit for accounting purposes. For example, a building as a single entity may be designated as the basic property unit. Alternatively, the elevators, escalators, heating and air-conditioning system, other mechanical equipment, plumbing, electrical system, and basic building structure could be accounted for as separate property units.

Required

1. What accounting problems arise if an item that could be accounted for as a single property unit is instead accounted for as a number of separate asset units?

2. Identify and explain some advantages of accounting separately for smaller property units as opposed to aggregation as a single property unit.

C 12-4
(L.O. 1, 4)

Ethical Considerations Discuss ethical factors relevant to each of the following examples of financial reporting and disclosure. Comment on the propriety of the accounting chosen, GAAP flexibility, and the degree to which underlying economic effects are disclosed.

a. The manager of a large division of a major corporation has significant input to accounting policy for the division and has authority over all line decisions, including purchasing, maintenance, and capital expenditures. The manager has occupied the position for three years; the average time for promotion to the corporate staff level is five years.

 The manager has successfully endorsed capitalizing all post-acquisition costs, including improvements and general maintenance and repair. His justification is that all maintenance increases the useful life or productivity of assets relative to lower levels of such costs. In addition, he has recommended postponing many routine repairs on equipment used in manufacturing the division's product. Furthermore, he has resisted requests from lower managers to upgrade and expand facilities in several important areas. Divisions are evaluated on rate of return on investment (ROI), the ratio of divisional income to divisional investment.

b. "Earnings Helper," *Forbes,* June 12, 1989, p. 150, discussed the cases of two firms that chose somewhat unusual accounting practices for depreciating and amortizing assets. Cineplex Odeon amortizes its movie theatre seats, carpets, and related equipment over 27 years. Blockbuster Entertainment changed the period of amortization of the videotapes it rents from 9 months to 36 months. In Blockbuster's case, an article in *The Wall Street Journal* critical of its accounting practices was followed by significant declines in the price of its common shares. In both cases, these firms have adopted accounting practices that are unrepresentative of those chosen by most firms in their respective industries. One effect of these policies is increased income.

C 12-5
(L.O. 5)

Composite Depreciation MotoCross Bicycles, Inc., uses straight-line depreciation for all its depreciable plant assets. All assets are depreciated individually except manufacturing machinery, which is depreciated using the composite method. During the year, MotoCross exchanged a delivery truck with Trike Company for a larger delivery truck. MotoCross paid cash equal to 5% of the larger truck's value.

Required

1. What factors should have influenced MotoCross's selection of the straight-line method?
2. How should MotoCross account for and report the truck exchange transaction?
3. a. What benefits should MotoCross derive from using the composite method rather than the individual basis for manufacturing machinery?
   b. How should MotoCross have calculated the manufacturing machinery's annual depreciation expense in its first year of operations?

(AICPA adapted)

EXERCISES

E 12-1
(L.O. 2)

Depreciation Schedules Stoner Company acquired an operational asset at a cost of $10,000 that is estimated to have a useful life of five years and a residual value of $2,500.

Required

1. Prepare a depreciation schedule for the entire life of the asset using the following methods (show computations and round to the nearest dollar):
   a. Straight-line method.
   b. SYD method.
   c. DDB method.
2. What criteria should be considered in selecting a method?

E 12-2
(L.O. 2)

Several Methods of Depreciation Computation To demonstrate the computations involved in several methods of depreciating an operational asset, the following data are used:

Acquisition cost	$12,500
Residual value	500
Estimated service life:	
Years	5
Service-hours	10,000
Productive output (units)	24,000

Required Give the formula and compute the annual depreciation amount using each of the following methods (show computations and round to the nearest dollar):

1. Straight-line depreciation; compute the depreciation rate and amount for each year.
2. Service-hours method; compute the depreciation rate and amount for the first year, assuming 2,200 service-hours of actual operation.
3. Productive output method of depreciation; compute the depreciation rate and amount for the first year, assuming 4,000 units of output. Is all of the depreciation amount (computed in your answer) expensed during the current period?
4. DDB method; compute the depreciation amount for each year.

E 12–3
(L.O. 1, 2)

Depreciation Computation Mace Company acquired equipment that cost $18,000, which will be depreciated on the assumption that it will last six years and have a $1,200 residual value. Several possible methods of depreciation are under consideration.

Required

1. Prepare a schedule that shows annual depreciation expense, accumulated depreciation, and book value for the first two years, assuming the following (show computations and round to the nearest dollar):
   a. DDB method.
   b. Productive output method. Estimated output is a total of 105,000 units, of which 12,000 will be produced the first year; 18,000 in each of the next two years; 15,000 the fourth year; and 21,000 the fifth and sixth years.
2. What criteria would you consider important in selecting a method?

E 12–4
(L.O. 2)

Identify Depreciation Methods: Depreciation Schedules Veto Company bought equipment on January 1, 1995, for $45,000. The expected life is 10 years, and the residual value is $5,000. Based on three acceptable depreciation methods, the annual depreciation expense and cumulative balance of accumulated depreciation at the end of 1995 and 1996 are shown below.

| | Case A | | Case B | | Case C | |
| | Annual Expense | Accumulated Amount | Annual Expense | Accumulated Amount | Annual Expense | Accumulated Amount |
Year						
1995	$9,000	$ 9,000	$4,000	$4,000	$7,273	$ 7,273
1996	7,200	16,200	4,000	8,000	6,545	13,818

Required

1. Identify the depreciation method used in each case.
2. Based on your answer to (1), prepare a depreciation schedule for each case for 1995 through 1998.

E 12–5
(L.O. 2)

Identify Three Depreciation Methods On January 1, 1995, Gopher Company acquired a machine for $15,000. The estimated residual value of the machine is $1,000 and the estimated useful life is five years. Gopher's year-end is December 31.

Required Identify the method of depreciation used by Gopher if 1996 depreciation expense is (a) $3,600, (b) $2,800, (c) $3,733.

E 12–6
(L.O. 5)

Application of the Inventory Appraisal System Mite Engineering Company acquired a large number of small tools at the beginning of operations on January 1, 1995, for $4,000. During 1995 and 1996, Mite disposed of several used tools, receiving cash salvage value of $400 in 1995 and $500 in 1996. During 1996, Mite acquired additional tools at a cost of $1,600. Inventories of tools on hand, valued at current acquisition cost adjusted for the present condition of the tools, indicated a value of $2,800 on December 31, 1995, and $3,600 on December 31, 1996. Mite uses the inventory appraisal system of depreciation for small tools.

Required Give the entries for the inventory appraisal system to record the above transactions. Include adjusting entries for depreciation and the related closing entries.

E 12–7
(L.O. 1, 2, 3)

Multiple Choice: Depreciation Select the best answer for each of the following.

1. As generally used in accounting, which of the following is correct about depreciation?
   a. It is a process of asset valuation for balance sheet purposes.
   b. It applies only to long-lived intangible assets.

    c. It is used to indicate a decline in market value of a long-lived asset.

    d. It is an accounting process that allocates long-lived asset cost to accounting periods.

2. Property, plant, and equipment should be reported at cost less accumulated depreciation on a balance sheet dated December 31, 1995, unless:

    a. Some obsolescence is known to have occurred.

    b. An appraisal made during 1995 disclosed a higher value.

    c. The amount of insurance carried on the property is well in excess of its book value.

    d. Some of the property still on hand was written down in 1993 because of permanent impairment of its use value.

3. Upon purchase of certain depreciable assets used in its production process, a company expects to be able to replace these assets by adopting a policy of never declaring dividends in amounts larger than net income (after depreciation is deducted). If a net income is earned each year, recording depreciation will coincidentally result in retention of sufficient assets within the enterprise. If in liquid form, these assets could be used to replace those fully depreciated assets if:

    a. Prices remain reasonably constant during the life of the property.

    b. Prices rise throughout the life of the property.

    c. The retirement depreciation system is used.

    d. Obsolescence was an unexpected factor in bringing about retirement of the assets replaced.

4. On which of the following assumptions is straight-line depreciation based?

    a. The operating efficiency of the asset decreases in later years.

    b. Service value declines as a function of time rather than of use.

    c. Service value declines as a function of obsolescence rather than of time.

    d. Physical wear and tear are more important than economic obsolescence.

(AICPA adapted)

E 12–8
(L.O. 1, 2, 4)

Multiple Choice: Depreciation   Choose the correct answer for each of the following questions, assuming a calendar-year reporting period. Accounting conventions are not used for fractional-period depreciation.

1. Accumulated depreciation, as used in accounting, represents:

    a. Funds set aside to replace assets.

    b. The portion of asset cost written off as an expense since the acquisition date.

    c. Earnings retained in the business that will be used to purchase another operational asset when the related asset becomes fully depreciated.

    d. An expense on the income statement.

2. Corporations A and B purchased identical equipment having an estimated service life of 10 years. Corporation A uses straight-line depreciation and B uses DDB. Assuming that the companies are identical in all other respects, choose the correct statement below.

    a. Corporation B will record more depreciation on this asset over the entire 10 years than A.

    b. At the end of the third year, the book value of the asset will be lower for A than for B.

    c. Net income will be lower for A in the ninth year than for B.

    d. Depreciation expense will be higher the first year for A than for B.

3. Depreciation:

    a. Is an allocation of property, plant, and equipment cost in a rational and systematic manner to periods in which such items are used.

    b. Is a process of recognizing the decreasing value of an asset over time.

    c. Is a cash expense.

    d. Expense of $2,000 reflects a $2,000 increase in liquid funds.

4. Group or composite depreciation:

    a. Is not based on historical cost.

    b. Requires changing the composite rate each year.

    c. Does not provide effective results if the group members' useful lives are widely different.

    d. Usually records a gain or loss on retirement of assets.

5. What is 1995 depreciation using the DDB method on an asset purchased October 1, 1994, costing $10,000, with a residual value of $2,000 and a three-year useful life?

    a. $4,000.   *c.* $6,667.

    b. $5,000.   *d.* $5,556.

6. Pepple Company purchased a computer on June 30, 1995, for $21,000. The computer had a salvage value of $6,000 and useful life of six years. Using double-declining-balance depreciation, determine depreciation expense for 1996.

    a. $4,167.   *c.* $5,833.

    b. $4,667.   *d.* $4,863.

E 12-9
(L.O. 4)

Depreciation of Post-Acquisition Costs   Fender Company purchased a mainframe computer on January 2, 1995, for $1,200,000. The system has a useful life of six years, considering obsolescence. Its residual value is $20,000. Fender uses the straight-line method. The following events took place in 1996:

a.   March 1: Peripheral equipment costing $30,000 was added to the mainframe. This equipment has a useful life of seven years and residual value of $2,000. This equipment can be used with several different mainframes. Fender may replace the mainframe before the disposal of this equipment.

b.   September 1: An additional memory device was added to the mainframe, costing $250,000. This device has no utility apart from the mainframe but will increase the total residual of the mainframe to $40,000.

Required   Provide the general journal entry to record depreciation expense for 1996 on the mainframe and related equipment.

E 12-10
(L.O. 5)

Group Depreciation: Asset Torn Down, Entries   Manitoba Company owned 10 warehouses of similar type except for varying size. The group system of depreciation is applied to the 10 warehouses, and the rate is 6% each year on cost. At the end of 1995, the asset account warehouses showed a balance of $2,650,000 (residual value $150,000), and the accumulated depreciation account showed a balance of $1,200,000. Shortly after the end of 1995, warehouse 8, costing $200,000, was torn down. Materials salvaged from the demolition were sold for $26,500, and $7,500 was spent on demolition.

Required   Give entries to record (*a*) depreciation for 1995, (*b*) disposal of the warehouse, and (*c*) depreciation for 1996.

E 12-11
(L.O. 5)

Composite Depreciation System Applied   Wilson Company owned the following machines, all acquired on January 1, 1995:

Machine	Original Cost	Estimated Residual Value	Estimated Life (years)
A	$ 7,000	None	4
B	10,000	$1,200	8
C	18,000	2,000	10
D	19,000	1,000	12

Required   1.   Prepare a schedule based on straight-line depreciation for each machine that shows the following: cost, residual value, depreciable cost, life in years, and annual depreciation.
2.   Compute the composite depreciation rate (based on cost) and the composite life if the machines are depreciated using the composite system.
3.   Give the entry to record 1995 composite depreciation.

E 12-12
(L.O. 5)

Composite Depreciation System Applied   Alberta Utilities owned a power plant that consisted of the following, all acquired on January 1, 1995:

	Cost	Estimated Residual Value	Estimated Life (years)
Building.	$250,000	$25,000	30
Machinery, etc.	125,000	5,000	10
Other equipment.	50,000	5,000	5

Required   Carry decimals to the nearest two places.

1.   Compute the total straight-line depreciation for 1995 on all items combined.
2.   Compute the composite depreciation rate (based on cost) and the composite life on the plant.
3.   Give the entry to record 1995 composite depreciation.

E 12-13
(L.O. 5)

Replacement and Retirement Systems Compared   Brunswick Power Company purchased 600 poles at $220 per pole, debiting the poles inventory account (a special plant asset account). These poles were immediately placed into service; 100 of the new poles were used to replace an equal number of old poles (debit transmission line). The old poles originally cost $140 each and had an estimated residual value of $20 per pole (debit salvage inventory).

Required

1. Give all indicated entries (*a*) assuming that the replacement system is employed and (*b*) assuming that the retirement system is used.
2. Compare the effect of these two systems on depreciation expense and the related asset accounts.

E 12–14
(L.O. 4)

Fractional-Year Depreciation: SL and DDB Compared   Jackson Company's records show the following property acquisitions and disposals during the first two years of operations:

| | | | Disposals | |
| | Acquisition Cost of | Estimated Useful Life | Year of | |
Year	Property	(years)	Acquisition	Amount
1995	$50,000	10	—	—
1996	20,000	10	1995	$7,000

Property is depreciated for one-half year in the year of acquisition. Property disposed of is depreciated for one-half year in its year of disposal. Assume no residual values. There are no sale proceeds upon retirement.

Required

1. Compute depreciation expense for 1995 and for 1996 and the balances of the property and related accumulated depreciation accounts at the end of each year under the following depreciation methods. Show computations and round to the nearest dollar. (Hint: Set up separate schedules for property and for accumulated depreciation.)
   a. Straight-line method.
   b. DDB method.
2. Give entries for the acquisition, periodic depreciation, and retirement of the property, assuming:
   a. Straight-line method.
   b. DDB method.
   (Hint: Set up parallel columns for 1995 and 1996.)

(AICPA adapted)

E 12–15
(L.O. 6)

Impairment of Value: Operational Assets   Down Manufacturing Company has a small facility, Plant XT, that has not been used for several years because of low product demand. The company does not expect to use the facility in the foreseeable future. Efforts are being made to sell the plant for $35,000, but a realistic recovery amount is $20,000 (net of disposal costs). The accounting records show cost, $145,000; accumulated depreciation, $80,000.

Required

Give the entry that Down should make to record the impairment of value.

E 12–16
(L.O. 6)

Multiple Choice: Casualty Losses   Choose the correct answer for each of the following questions.

1. A company carries casualty insurance on one of its buildings. The policy features an 80% coinsurance requirement.
   a. If the company carries insurance equal to or exceeding 80% of the fair value of the building prior to a casualty, it is guaranteed a full recovery.
   b. The company must bear 20% of any casualty loss.
   c. The company will receive full recovery on any loss that is less than or equal to 80% of the fair value of the building prior to a casualty.
   d. The company has less of a chance of a full recovery than if it had a 65% coinsurance requirement.
   e. If the policy's face value exceeds a loss at replacement cost, a full recovery is guaranteed.
2. Mabel Corporation suffered fire damage to one of its buildings. The building was insured by a casualty insurance policy that had a face value of $50,000 and a 65% coinsurance requirement. The fair market values of the building before and after the fire were $77,500 and $32,500, respectively. Mabel will receive which of the following amounts from the insurance company?
   a. $50,000.   *c*. $45,000.
   b. $32,500.   *d*. $44,665.
3. A casualty insurance policy was written on a building with a fair market value of $175,000. If a fire caused $75,000 damage and there was an 80% coinsurance requirement, what is the minimum face value of the policy required to guarantee a full settlement of this loss?
   a. $140,000.   *c*. $175,000.
   b. $75,000.   *d*. $100,000.
4. The market and book value of a building partially destroyed by fire are $50,000 prior to the fire and $35,000 after the fire. The casualty insurance policy covering the property carried an 80% coinsur-

ance requirement. What is the net loss for accounting purposes if face value of the policy is $30,000?

a. $15,000.   c. $6,000.

b. $3,750.   d. There was no loss.

E 12–17
(L.O. 6)

Fire Loss, Coinsurance   Grife Company operates retail branches in various cities. Branches in four cities are served out of warehouse 16, which sustained fire damage to part of the inventory on April 10.

Between January 1 and April 10, shipments from warehouse 16 to its four stores were recorded as follows: branch W, $80,500; X, $92,000; Y, $69,000; and Z, $23,000.

Shipments to branches are marked up 15% above cost, and sales prices are reflected in the foregoing amounts. The January 1 inventory at warehouse 16 was $48,100; purchases between January 1 and April 10 totalled $224,600; freight-in was $2,300; and purchase returns totalled $9,200.

To arrive at the total replacement cost of the April 10 inventory for insurance settlement purposes, it was agreed to deduct 10% for goods that were shopworn and damaged prior to the fire.

A compromise agreement between the insurance adjuster and Grife Company management set the current replacement cost of inventory lost in the fire at $21,480.

Required

1. Estimate the total replacement cost of inventory in the warehouse at April 10.
2. Determine the indemnity claim if the warehouse contents were insured by a single $20,000 policy having a 65% coinsurance requirement. Calculate to the nearest dollar.

E 12–18
(L.O. 6)

Fire Loss, Coinsurance   On January 1, Carson's Store had a fire insurance policy with a face amount of $15,000 and an 80% coinsurance requirement. At that date, the company had $360 recorded in its records for unexpired insurance for one year. On January 1, the inventory was $20,000; Carson uses a perpetual inventory system. January purchases were $44,000, and January sales were $60,000. A fire on February 1 destroyed the entire stock on hand. At that time, the historical cost of the inventory represented replacement cost as well. The policy apportions the premium on face value; face value is reduced by insurance proceeds.

Required

Give journal entries to record the estimated inventory and the fire loss, assuming a 30% gross margin rate on sales.

E 12–19
(L.O. 2)

CCA Depreciation Calculations   Delton Company purchased equipment in 1995 for $200,000, which qualifies as a class 8 asset for tax depreciation purposes. The equipment has a useful life of six years, after which it will be scrapped.

Required

1. Compute Delton's CCA deduction for each year.
2. Compute the present value of tax benefits from depreciating this asset for tax purposes, assuming that (a) Delton has an applicable 14% after-tax minimum rate of return, (b) it has sufficient income to obtain the tax benefits of depreciation in each year, (c) tax payments for a tax year are made at year-end, and (d) the applicable tax rate is 30%. What is the effect of this amount on the total economic cost of the asset?

| PROBLEMS

P 12–1
(L.O. 1, 2)

Multiple Choice: Depreciation   Choose the correct statement among the alternatives.

1. Silhouette Company purchased a machine that was installed and placed in service on January 1, 1995, at a cost of $120,000 including acquisition cost. Salvage value was estimated at $20,000. The machine is being depreciated over 10 years by the double-declining-balance method. For the year ended December 31, 1996, what amount should Silhouette report as depreciation expense?

a. $24,000.
b. $19,200.
c. $16,000.
d. $10,800.

2. Which of the following must be true in order to use the units-of-production method of depreciation?

a. Total units to be produced can be estimated.
b. Production is constant over the life of the asset.
c. Repair costs increase with use.
d. Obsolescence is expected.

3. A machine with a five-year estimated useful life and an estimated 10% salvage value was acquired on January 1, 1995. On December 31, 1998, the balance of accumulated depreciation on this asset, using the sum-of-the-years'-digits method, would be:
   a. (Original cost − Salvage) × $\frac{1}{15}$.
   b. (Original cost − Salvage) × $\frac{14}{15}$.
   c. Original cost × $\frac{1}{15}$.
   d. Original cost × $\frac{14}{15}$.
4. On January 1, 1995, Aptos Company installed cabinets to display its merchandise in its retail stores. Aptos expects to use these cabinets for five years. The 1995 multistep income statement of Aptos should include:
   a. One-fifth of the cabinet costs in cost of goods sold.
   b. One-fifth of the cabinet costs in selling, general, and administrative expenses.
   c. All of the cabinet costs in cost of goods sold.
   d. All of the cabinet costs in selling, general, and administrative expenses.

(AICPA adapted)

P 12–2
(L.O. 2)

 Depreciation Schedule Quick Producers acquired factory equipment on January 1, 1995, costing $39,000. In view of pending technological developments, it is estimated that the machine will have a resale value upon disposal in four years of $8,000 and that disposal costs will be $500.
Data relating to the equipment follow:

Estimated service life:
Years 4
Service-hours. 20,000

Actual operations:

Calendar Year	Service Hours
1995	5,700
1996	5,000
1997	4,800
1998	4,400

Required

Round to the nearest dollar and show computations.

1. Prepare a depreciation schedule for the service-hours method assuming the accounts are closed each December 31.
2. Compute depreciation expense for the first and second years assuming (a) straight-line and (b) DDB depreciation.

P 12–3
(L.O. 1, 3)

Discussion: Overview of Depreciation Depreciation continues to be one of the more important problem areas in accounting.

Required

1. Explain the factors that should be considered when applying the conventional concept of depreciation to determine how the value of a newly acquired computer system should be assigned to expense for financial reporting purposes. (Ignore income tax considerations.)
2. What depreciation methods might be used for the computer system in (1)?
3. Explain the conventional accounting concept of depreciation accounting.
4. Discuss the merits of depreciation accounting under current GAAP with respect to (a) the value of the asset, (b) periodic amounts of expense, and (c) the discretion of management in selecting the method.

(AICPA adapted)

P 12–4
(L.O. 2)

Depreciation Schedules Constar Company purchased a machine that cost $145,000. The firm estimated that the machine would have a net resale value of $8,000 at the end of its useful life. Data relating to the machine over its service life were as follows: estimated service life in years, 5; output (units), 8,000. Actual operations in units of output were as follows: 1995, 1,600; 1996, 1,900; 1997, 1,000; 1998, 1,800; and 1999, 1,700.

Required

Prepare a depreciation schedule for the asset over the useful life for each of the following methods: (a) straight-line, (b) output, (c) DDB. Show computations and round to the nearest dollar.

P 12-5
(L.O. 2)

Analysis of Four Depreciation Methods: Maximize Income   On January 1, 1995, Vello Company, a tool manufacturer, acquired new industrial equipment for $2 million. The new equipment had a useful life of four years, and the residual value was estimated to be $200,000. Vello estimates that the new equipment can produce 14,000 tools in its first year. Production is then estimated to decline by 1,000 units per year over the remaining useful life of the equipment.

The following depreciation methods are under consideration: (a) DDB, (b) straight-line, (c) SYD, and (d) units of output.

Required

Which depreciation method would result in maximum income for financial statement reporting for the three-year period ending December 31, 1997? Prepare a schedule showing the amount of accumulated depreciation at December 31, 1997, under the method selected. Show supporting computations in good form. Ignore present value, income tax, and deferred income tax considerations in your answer.

(AICPA adapted)

P 12-6
(L.O. 2, 3)

Analyze Cash Flows: Depreciation   Bryan Company acquired equipment on January 1, 1995, for $80,000. It is estimated that the equipment has a four-year life and a residual value of $5,000. Assume Bryan may use the same method of depreciation for financial reporting and tax purposes and is taxed at a 30% rate.

Required

1. Calculate the cash flow effect of depreciation on income taxes for each year of the equipment's useful life, assuming:
   a. Straight-line depreciation.
   b. DDB depreciation.
2. Assume that Bryan can invest any idle cash to yield an annual return of 12%. Which depreciation method is preferable from a tax perspective? Show computations to support your answer.

P 12-7
(L.O. 2)

Match Four Depreciation Methods with Depreciation Expense   Equipment was acquired for $40,000 that has a six-year estimated life and a residual value of $4,000. The equipment will be depreciated by various amounts in this third full year, depending on the depreciation method used.

Third-year depreciation expense under the four methods listed below (but not in the same order) amounted to (1) $6,000, (2) $5,926, (3) $6,857, and (4) $9,900. The depreciation methods used were (a) DDB, (b) productive output, (c) straight-line, and (d) SYD.

The productive output method assumed that 800,000 units could be produced; the actual output in the first three years was 200,000 units, 180,000 units, and 220,000 units.

Required

Analyze the above data. Based on this analysis, alongside each letter (a) through (d), which identify the four methods, write the number (1) through (4) associated with the amount of third-year depreciation for that method. Support each answer with calculations.

P 12-8
(L.O. 1, 2)

Analyze Asset and Accumulated Accounts   Selected accounts included under property, plant, and equipment on Abel Company's balance sheet at December 31, 1995, had the following balances (at original cost):

Land	$220,000
Land improvements.	75,000
Buildings	600,000
Machinery and equipment (acquired Jan. 1/88).	650,000

During 1996, the following transactions occurred:

a. A plant facility consisting of land and building was acquired from Club Company in exchange for 10,000 of Abel's common shares. On the acquisition date, Abel's shares had a closing market price of $39 per share on a national stock exchange. The plant facility was carried on Club's accounts at $95,000 for land and $130,000 for the building at the exchange date. Current appraised values for the land and building, respectively, are $120,000 and $240,000.
b. A tract of land was acquired for $85,000 as a potential future building site.
c. Machinery was purchased at a total cost of $250,000. Additional costs were incurred as follows:

Freight and unloading.	$ 5,000
Sales taxes.	10,000
Installation.	25,000

d. Expenditures totalling $90,000 were made for new parking lots, streets, and sidewalks at the corporation's various plant locations. These improvements had an estimated useful life of 15 years.

e. A machine that cost $50,000 on January 1, 1988, was scrapped on June 30, 1996. DDB depreciation has been recorded on the basis of a 10-year life.

f. A machine was sold for $25,000 on July 1, 1996. Original cost of the machine was $37,000 at January 1, 1993, and it was depreciated on the straight-line basis over an estimated useful life of eight years and a residual value of $1,000.

Required

1. Prepare a detailed analysis of the changes in each of the following balance sheet accounts for 1996 (disregard accumulated depreciation): (*a*) land, (*b*) land improvements, (*c*) buildings, and (*d*) machinery and equipment. Hint: Analyze each asset separately.

2. List the information items in the problem that were not used to determine the answer to (1) above, showing the relevant amounts and supporting computations for each item. In addition, indicate where, or if, these items should be included in Abel's financial statements. (Hint: Set up three schedules: (*a*) loss or gain on scrapping the machine, (*b*) accumulated depreciation, DDB method, and (*c*) loss or gain on sale of machine.)

P 12–9
(L.O. 5)

Multiple Choice: Depreciation Systems Choose the correct answer for each of the following questions.

1. Information relevant to the assets designated as small equipment for a corporation follows:

Beginning balance. $32,000
Acquisitions this year 6,000
Cash from disposals 200
Ending inventory at appraisal value. 29,000

Assuming that the inventory appraisal system is used, depreciation expense for this year for small equipment equals:
a. $9,000.   c. $6,000.
b. $8,800.   d. $3,000.

The following information is used for questions 2 and 3:

Mills Corporation began 1995 with 100 railroad cars each with a $8,000 unit book value. During 1995, Mills purchased 50 cars for $12,000 each and retired 60 cars. Mills received $120,000 in total from the disposal of the railroad cars. What is the balance in the ledger account for railroad cars on January 1, 1996, using the:

2. Retirement system?
a. $720,000.   c. $360,000.
b. $920,000.   d. $560,000.

3. Replacement system?
a. $720,000.   c. $360,000.
b. $920,000.   d. $560,000.

4. Endo Corporation uses the retirement system of depreciation. At the beginning of 1995, Endo had 200 trucks (cost $16,000 each) in use. During 1995, Endo sold 50 trucks and received $2,000 each and purchased 80 more at $20,000 each. What is depreciation expense for 1995?
a. $800,000.   c. $1,600,000.
b. $700,000.   d. $1,500,000.

5. Answer question (4), assuming the replacement system.
a. $1,000,000.   c. $900,000.
b. $1,600,000.   d. $1,500,000.

6. Manara Corporation purchased the following assets January 1, 1995:

Quantity	Type	Unit Cost	Estimated Unit Salvage Value	Unit Useful Life
10	Truck	$ 6,000	$1,000	5 years
5	Bus	12,000	2,000	8 years

Under the composite system of depreciation, what is the composite rate based on cost?
a. 13.54%.   c. 1.88%.
b. 16.25%.   d. 6.15%.

7. Without prejudice to your answer to question (6), assume that the composite rate is 20% and that in 1996, Manara sold two trucks for $4,000 salvage each and replaced them with trucks costing $8,000 each, with $2,000 estimated salvage value each. The new vehicles are considered representative of the group. What is depreciation in 1996?
a. $16,250.   c. $24,800.
b. $24,000.   d. $20,000.

P 12–10
(L.O. 5)

Application of the Composite Depreciation System Operational assets acquired on January 1, 1995, by Sculley Company are to be depreciated under the composite system. Details regarding each asset are given in the schedule below:

Component	Cost	Estimated Residual Value	Estimated Life (years)
A	$90,000	$10,000	10
B	30,000	0	6
C	76,000	16,000	15
D	12,400	400	8

Required
1. Calculate the composite life and annual composite depreciation rate (based on cost) for the asset components listed above. Give the entry to record depreciation after one full year of use. Round the depreciation rate to the nearest two decimal places.
2. During 1996, it was necessary to replace component B, which was sold for $16,000. The replacement component cost $36,000 and will have an estimated residual value of $3,000 at the end of its estimated six-year useful life. Record the disposal and substitution, which was a cash acquisition.
3. Record depreciation at the end of 1996.

P 12–11
(L.O. 5)

Retirement and Replacement Systems Compared Alton Company uses a large number of identical small tools in operations. On January 1, 1995, the first year of operations, 1,200 of these tools were purchased at a cost of $6 each. On December 31, 1995, 150 of the tools were sold or scrapped for $200 and were replaced at a cost of $8.40 each. On December 31, 1996, 300 of the tools were sold or scrapped for $240; they were replaced at a cost of $9.00 each. On December 31, 1997, 160 of the tools were sold or scrapped for $110, each being replaced at a cost of $7.20.

Required
1. Give the entries to record all indicated transactions, assuming that the company employed (a) the retirement system and (b) the replacement system.
2. Compare the results under the two systems by showing periodic depreciation for each year and the balance in the tools account at each December 31, 1995 to 1997.

P 12–12
(L.O. 6)

Impairment of Asset Value Hilltop Mining Company has several mining operations in Northern Ontario. Plant HM-40 has property, plant, and equipment that has been idle for the past three years. Because of continuing weak prices and low demand for the output, the auditor has advised the company that, in view of the probability that the plant will not be opened in the foreseeable future, it should be written down to expected net realizable value. The property, plant, and equipment is shown in the accounts at original cost, $800,000, and accumulated depreciation, $300,000. The estimated net realizable value is $50,000. The assessed property tax for the current year of $6,000 has not been recorded.

Required
1. Give the entries that Hilltop should make to record the decline in use value.
2. Write an appropriate full-disclosure note.

P 12–13
(L.O. 2, 4, 6)

Impairment Loss, Post-Acquisition Cost, Fractional-Year Accelerated Depreciation On October 1, 1995, Flexi-Toys Inc. purchased plastic moulding equipment for $200,000. The equipment has an eight-year useful life and no residual value. The firm uses the double-declining-balance method of depreciation, has a calendar fiscal year, and computes fractional-year depreciation using the exact calculation approach.

On April 1, 1996, the firm added a component to the equipment that increases the production rate. The component cost $20,000 and does not alter the useful life or residual value of the moulding equipment.

On April 1, 1997, the firm decided to write down the recorded value of the moulding equipment to $30,000, its remaining recoverable value in use (fair value), because of a protracted downturn in demand for plastic toys. The total estimated future cash flows from use and disposal of the equipment are estimated to be $45,000.

Required
1. Compute 1995 depreciation on the moulding equipment.
2. Compute 1996 depreciation on the equipment, assuming the firm includes the new component in the moulding equipment account.
3. Compute 1997 depreciation through April 1, and prepare the journal entry to record the impairment loss.

P 12–14
(L.O. 2)

Mathematical Aspects of Depreciation Methods   Several depreciation methods discussed in this chapter can be described algebraically and have certain interesting properties. This problem requires that you explore some of these methods, and it introduces a depreciation method not discussed in this text and not widely used in practice.

Required

Show in general why each of the following statements is true. You may wish to begin by using examples, but finish with a purely algebraic set of assertions leading to each statement. The useful life in years is denoted by n.

1. The SL rate of depreciation is often referred to as a percentage. This percentage is the ratio of annual depreciation to depreciable cost. For example, an asset with a useful life of five years has a 20% depreciation rate. Prove that the double-declining-balance rate, being twice the straight-line rate (based on depreciable cost), is always $2 \div n$.
2. Prove that in the first year of an asset's useful life, DDB depreciation always exceeds SYD.
3. Prove that an alternative way to determine DDB depreciation for year t is:

$$(2 \div n) \times (1 - 2 \div n)^{t-1} \times \text{Cost}$$

4. A depreciation method occasionally discussed by accountants is the fixed rate of declining-balance method. This method applies a rate R to the declining balance of the asset at the beginning of each year to determine depreciation expense. The rate is between $1 \div n$ and $2 \div n$ in magnitude. It therefore produces results between those of the straight-line method and the DDB method. R is defined as:

$$1 - (\text{residual value/cost})^{(1 \div n)}$$

Depreciation in years 1 and 2, $D(1)$ and $D(2)$ below, are computed as follows:

$$D(1) = R \times \text{Cost}$$
$$D(2) = R \times [\text{Cost} - D(1)]$$

One of the more interesting features of this method is that an asset's book value at the end of its useful life equals its residual value. This is the statement you are to prove.

P 12–15
(L.O. 6)

Casualty Losses   Smithson Company suffered a casualty loss to equipment that cost $300,000 and that had been depreciated $40,000 before the casualty. The market value of the asset just before the misfortune was $320,000. Smithson had insured the asset for casualty. The policy has a 90% coinsurance requirement.

Required

1. If the market value of the asset after the casualty is $50,000, what is the minimum policy face value that guarantees full recovery to Smithson? Explain your answer.
2. Answer (1), but assume that the market value is only $20,000 after the casualty.
3. Explain the difference between your answers to (1) and (2).

P 12–16
(L.O. 6)

Fire Loss   South Company operates in a leased building and closes the books each December 31. On April 30, a fire seriously damaged its inventory and fixtures. Inventory was totally destroyed; fixtures were two-thirds destroyed. Different insurance policies cover the assets, but both have a common feature under which they are cancelled for future or remaining coverage to whatever extent a portion of the total potential indemnity is collected by the insured.

The company uses a periodic inventory system, and the accounting records were saved; these reveal that in the past three years, gross margin has averaged 38% of sales price. The January 1 inventory was $73,280. Between January 1 and April 30, purchases were $116,320 and sales were $206,500. Inventory was insured by a $65,000 policy with no coinsurance clause. The latest premium payment covering a one-year period from September 1 of last year amounted to $720 on this policy.

When the books were closed last December 31, the fixtures were two and one-half years old. Accounts related to the fixtures and their insurance policy are set forth below.

Fixtures		Accumulated Depreciated		Prepaid Insurance (on fixtures only)	
Balance $20,000		Year 1 $900		Policy A $42	
		Year 2 1,800		Policy B 480	
		Year 3 1,800			

Policy A on the fixtures expired February 28 of the current year. Policy B was immediately put in force to replace the expired policy on the fixtures; a two-year premium was paid on it. Policy B is for

$10,000 maximum coverage, provides for indemnity on the basis of replacement cost of any loss, and has an 80% coinsurance requirement. It is determined that the replacement cost of the fixtures when the fire occurred was $15,000 and that the damage amounted to a loss of two-thirds of their replacement cost.

Required   Round amounts to nearest dollar.

1. Adjust the books to April 30 and reflect the inventory as of that date.
2. Open a casualty loss account; set up the indemnities collectible as a receivable due from the insurance company.
3. Transfer the net balance in casualty loss to income summary.

P 12–17
(L.O. 2, 4, 6)

Depreciation Calculations   In 1995, Spencer Company purchased an operational asset that experienced several events requiring modification to its ledger account. Spencer has a calendar fiscal year. The events follow:

a. On June 30, 1995, equipment is purchased for $240,000. The equipment has a $40,000 residual value and an expected useful life of five years.
b. A new component is added to the equipment on June 30, 1996, costing $150,000. As a result, the residual value of the original equipment is raised to $60,000. The useful life of the equipment is unchanged and the component has no useful life separate from the equipment.
c. The remaining useful life of the equipment is changed to two years as of January 1, 1997. Residual value is unaffected. (Allocate the remaining book value at Jan. 1/97 over the new remaining useful life.)
d. The equipment becomes totally impaired as a result of a casualty on September 1, 1998. The equipment functions normally through that date. Because the equipment is uninsured, Spencer charges the remaining book value to a loss account.

Required   For the following depreciation methods, (*a*) provide journal entries to completely account for this equipment from acquisition to write-off, and (*b*) prepare a schedule proving that total charges sum to the total cost of the equipment.

1. SL.
2. DDB (assume that the switch to the SL method occurs on January 1, 1997—this is not a change in accounting method but rather a normal event in the DDB method).

ANALYZING FINANCIAL STATEMENTS

All questions in this section are based on information taken from the financial statements of actual companies.

A 12–1
(L.O. 1, 3)

Depreciation and Capital Maintenance   Maritime Telegraph and Telephone Company, Limited (MT&T) is the parent corporation of the Bell companies serving Nova Scotia and PEI. Selected amounts from the firm's 1993 financial statements appear below (thousands of dollars):

Statement of Cash Flows

Net income	$ 59.8
Depreciation	123.9
Net cash provided by operating activities	130.8
Payment of dividends	41.3

Additional assumptions:

a. The average consumer price index for Canada (CPI) was 77 in 1980 and 131 in 1993.
b. MT&T purchased all its property, plant, and equipment in 1980.
c. The CPI provides a reasonable approximation to the increase in replacement cost of MT&T's plant assets since acquisition.

Required   1. Ignoring inflation, or the change in replacement cost of plant assets, has MT&T generated sufficient resources from operations in 1993 to replace its depreciable and amortizable assets?
2. Answer (1), incorporating the effect of inflation in your answer. Comment on your results.

A 12–2
(L.O. 1, 2)

Interpreting Depreciation and Accumulated Depreciation Disclosures   Portions of the 1990 financial statements of Sherwin-Williams Company, a paint manufacturer, are reproduced below (thousands of dollars):

Partial Income Statement
For the Year Ended December 31, 1990

Net sales	$2,266,732
Total expenses.	2,079,455
Income before income taxes	187,277
Income taxes	64,611
Net income	$ 122,666

Note 1. Significant Accounting Policies

Property, Plant and Equipment. Property, plant and equipment is stated on the basis of cost. Depreciation is provided principally by the straight-line method. The major classes of assets and ranges of depreciation rates are as follows:

Buildings	2%–6⅔%
Machinery and equipment	4%–20%
Furniture and fixtures.	5%–20%
Automobiles and trucks	10%–33⅓%

Note 16. Property, Plant, and Equipment Schedules

	Beginning	Additions	Retirements	Other	Ending
Buildings	$191,540	$11,574	$ 960	($7,185)	$194,969
Machinery	404,156	43,968	16,319	466	432,271

Total accumulated depreciation and amortization of property, plant and equipment:

	Beginning	Additions	Retirements	Other	Ending
Buildings	$ 62,843	$ 7,422	$ 769	($4,951)	$ 64,545
Machinery	211,662	37,085	12,302	(845)	235,600

Required

1. What method of depreciation is used by Sherwin-Williams?
2. Assuming that the midpoint of the range of straight-line rates disclosed for buildings is the average straight-line rate, what is the average estimated useful life of buildings owned by Sherwin-Williams?
3. What percentage of the useful life of buildings remains, on average, at the end of the year?
4. What is the book value of machinery and equipment retired in the year?
5. Depreciation on buildings, machinery, and equipment was what percentage of (*a*) total expenses and (*b*) pretax earnings?

A 12–3
(L.O. 6)

Composite Depreciation   Juno Lighting is a manufacturer of track and recessed lighting fixtures. Excerpts from the 1991 balance sheet and disclosure notes to the annual report of Juno Lighting, include the following (thousands of dollars):

Balance Sheet

Property and equipment:

Land	$ 2,311
Building and improvements	12,860
Tools and dies	2,847
Machinery and equipment	2,729
Computer equipment	1,624
Office furniture and equipment	815
Total property and equipment	$23,186

Summary of Accounting Policies

Property, Equipment and Depreciation

Assets are stated at cost. Depreciation of all assets is computed over their estimated useful life by the straight-line method for financial reporting purposes. Useful lives for property and equipment are as follows:

	Years
Building and improvements	40
Tools and dies	5
Machinery and equipment	7
Computer equipment	5
Office furniture and equipment	5

For purposes of this problem, assume that all depreciable plant assets were acquired in 1991 and have no residual value.

Required

1. If Juno Lighting adopts the composite depreciation system for financial reporting purposes in 1991 and plans to use as few asset groups as possible, how would you group the assets?
2. Determine the composite rate of depreciation and the composite life for each group established under (1).
3. Assume that in 1992, new computer equipment costing $400,000, with no residual value and a useful life of five years, is acquired. Also assume that in 1992 the firm retired computer equipment with an original cost of $150,000. Compute depreciation in 1992 under the composite method of depreciation using the two groups established.

A 12–4
(L.O. 4)

Change in Depreciation Estimate   In a disclosure note to its 1991 annual report, Union Camp Corporation, a firm in the timber industry, reported the following information about a change in depreciation estimate:

> In the first quarter of 1991, the company changed the estimated average useful lives used to compute depreciation for most of its pulp and paper mill equipment from 16 years to 20 years. The change better aligns the allocation of equipment cost with its expected use and results in useful lives more consistent with the predominant industry practice for this type of equipment. The effect of this change on income before income tax was $51 million in 1991.

Additional assumptions:

a. The estimate change applies to plant assets acquired on January 1, 1984.
b. The original estimated residual value of these assets was $20 million; the revised estimate in 1991 of the residual value is $8 million.
c. The firm uses SL depreciation.
d. The firm is a calendar-year reporting firm.

Required

1. When a firm changes the useful life of a plant asset, the book value at the beginning of the period of change is allocated over the remaining useful life, as of the beginning of the period of change. What was the original cost of the equipment for which Union Camp's depreciation estimate change was made?
2. What was 1990 depreciation expense?
3. What was 1991 depreciation expense?

A 12–5
(L.O. 1, 3)

 Depreciation and Taxes   Refer to the 1993 financial statements of Magna International Inc., that appear at the end of this text, and respond to the following questions.

1. What method of depreciating plant assets is used by Magna?
2. What is recognized depreciation and amortization as a percentage of 1993 income from continuing operations before taxes? Comment on the magnitude of the adjustment leading to net cash flow from operations in the statement of cash flows.
3. Many firms, including Magna, use different depreciation methods for financial reporting and tax purposes, causing deferred tax liabilities to be recognized. Deferred tax liabilities represent the excess of future income tax payable over income tax expense, based on past transactions. Estimate the difference between expected future deductions for depreciation and expected future depreciation to be recognized for financial reporting at December 31, 1993, for Magna's current portfolio of plant assets. Comment on the magnitude of the difference.

COMPARATIVE ANALYSIS

CA 12-1
(L.O. 2, 3)

Comparative Analysis, Depreciation: Alcan Aluminium Limited, Dofasco Inc., and Stelco Inc.   The depreciation policy disclosure notes for the December 31, 1993, annual report of Alcan Aluminium, Dofasco, and Stelco are reproduced below. Also, summary information from the three annual reports is provided.

Alcan Aluminium Limited

Depreciation

Depreciation is calculated on the straight-line method using rates based on the estimated useful lives of the respective assets. The principal rates are 2½% for buildings and range from 1% to 4% for power assets, and 3% to 6% for chemical, smelter and fabricating assets.

Dofasco Inc.

Fixed Assets—Fixed assets are recorded at their historical cost. Depreciation is computed generally by the straight-line method applied to the cost of assets in service at annual rates based on their estimated useful lives, as follows:

Buildings	2.5 to 5%
Equipment	5 to 7.5%
Mobile equipment	20 to 25%
Mine and quarry	
Processing facilities	4.5 to 5%
Mobile equipment	4.5 to 20%

Stelco Inc.

Fixed Assets and Depreciation

Fixed assets are recorded at historical cost less investment tax credits realized and include construction in progress. Depreciation is provided using the straight-line method applied to the cost of the assets at rates based on their estimated useful life and beginning from the point when production commences.

The following annual depreciation rates are in effect:

Buildings	2½ to 5%
Equipment	6 to 7½%
Automotive and mobile equipment	10 to 20%
Raw material plants and properties	4½ to 5%

	Alcan	Dofasco	Stelco
		(amounts in millions)	
Total assets, Dec. 31/93	$ 9,810	$3,218	$2,364
Average owners' equity, 1993	4,181	1,426	948
Earnings from continuing operations:			
1993	(104)	66	(36)
1992	(112)	(38)	(127)
Depreciation, 1993	443	180	122
Gross plant assets, Jan. 1/93	11,015	3,732	3,332
Gross plant assets, Dec. 31/93	11,092	3,618	3,353
Accumulated depreciation, Dec. 31/93	5,087	1,769	2,179
Capital expenditures, 1993	251	75	8

Required   Discuss the depreciation policy of the three firms relative to their financial results. Make an analysis of the relevant summary financial statement information to support your comments.

13 Intangible Assets and Natural Resources

LEARNING OBJECTIVES

After you have studied this chapter, you will be able to:

1   **Explain the characteristics of intangible assets.**

2   **Describe the general accounting treatment for intangible assets.**

3   **Account for intangible assets, including deferred charges, leaseholds, organization costs, and licensing agreements.**

4   **Explain how goodwill arises; measure, record, and amortize goodwill.**

5   **Explain the accounting treatment required for research and development costs.**

6   **Explain the accounting for the cost of computer software developed for sale.**

7   **Explain the accounting issues and reporting requirements for natural resources.**

8   **Describe the accounting for oil and gas exploration costs (Appendix 13A).**

INTRODUCTION

In 1992, The Thomson Corporation acquired several businesses for an aggregate cash consideration of $336 million. The fair market value of the net assets received was $197 million, leaving $139 million as the excess of the purchase price over the fair value of the assets received. Why did Thomson pay so much more for the assets received? More important from an accounting perspective, how will Thomson account for the $139 million excess amount it paid over the fair value of these assets? Should the $139 million be expensed immediately, or does it constitute an asset?

The Molson Companies 1994 annual report shows the following information:

	1994	1993
	(amounts in thousands)	
Intangible assets:		
Goodwill	$420,704	$372,300
Brand names	61,366	63,029
Hockey franchises	11,100	11,400
	$493,170	$446,729

Intangible assets, which principally include goodwill, brand names, and hockey franchises, are carried at cost less accumulated amortization. Amortization is provided on the straight-line basis, mainly over 40 years.

All of these items, including the $139 million excess of purchase price over net assets acquired paid by Thomson, are intangible assets. Because of their special characteristics, intangible assets are accounted for separately and sometimes differently than the tangible assets covered thus far in this text.

Another type of asset with unusual characteristics is natural resources, such as oil and gas, which first must be discovered and developed before being extracted, processed, and sold. This chapter discusses the accounting for intangible assets and for natural resources.

INTANGIBLE ASSETS

For accounting purposes, **intangible assets** are defined in the same terms as other capital assets. That is, they are held for the use of the entity, have been acquired with the intention of being used on a continuing basis, and are not intended for sale in the ordinary course of business. Section 3060, paragraph .06 of the *CICA Handbook* defines intangible properties as:

> capital assets that lack physical substance. Examples of intangible properties include brand names, copyrights, franchises, licenses, patents, software, subscription lists and trademarks.

There is considerable similarity in the problems of accounting for tangible and intangible assets. In general, however, it is more difficult to identify, measure, and estimate the periods of benefit for intangible assets. In particular, the intangible asset's lack of physical substance makes its value difficult to estimate and may make its useful life indeterminable.

Classification of Intangible Assets

Intangibles appear on the balance sheet under several different labels, such as *intangible assets, intangible operational assets, intangible fixed assets,* and *other assets.* The more common specific intangible assets are patents, copyrights, franchises, trademarks, organizational costs, deferred charges, and goodwill.

Intangible assets can be classified according to four attributes:

1. **Manner of acquisition** Intangible assets can be acquired by purchase from another entity, such as buying a franchise or a patent from someone else. Alternatively, intangible assets can be developed internally in the course of operations; patents and trademarks are examples.
2. **Identifiability** Some intangible assets can be identified separately from the other assets of the firm. Examples include patents, trademarks, and franchises. Other intangible assets are not separable but instead derive their value from their association with the firm. An example is the goodwill of a business, which is based on such factors as the loyalty of its customers or the quality of its products or employees, and not on a specific ownership right.
3. **Exchangeability** Some identifiable intangible assets can be sold or purchased; they are exchangeable. Examples include patents, trademarks, and franchises. Other intangible assets, while separately identifiable, are not exchangeable without selling the firm. Organization costs are an example. No one would be willing to separately purchase the organization costs of another firm. Goodwill is an intangible asset that is neither separately identifiable nor separately exchangeable. Goodwill has value only in combination with the other assets of the firm and cannot be acquired without simultaneous acquisition of the other assets.
4. **Period of expected benefit** Some intangible assets, such as organizational costs, are expected to benefit the firm indefinitely. The period of benefit of other intangibles may be limited either by economic factors or by legal or contractual restrictions. Patents, for example, have a legal life of 17 years, and a leasehold's period of benefit is specified in the lease.

These four characteristics influence the accounting treatment required for the various categories of intangible assets. Before discussing the special accounting

EXHIBIT 13–1
Accounting Treatments for Various Types of Intangible Assets

Type	Manner of Acquisition	
	Purchased	**Internally Generated**
Separately identifiable intangible asset (e.g., patents, copyrights, trademarks, organizational costs).	1. Capitalize at acquisition cost. 2. Amortize over the legal life or the estimated useful life, whichever is shorter, with a maximum of 40 years.	1. Expense or capitalize depending on the specific intangible. 2. If capitalized, amortize as for purchased intangibles.
Intangible asset not separately identifiable (e.g., goodwill).		1. Expense as incurred. 2. There is no option to capitalize, so there is no amortization.

issues associated with intangibles, it is useful to review the basic accounting principles that apply.

Basic Principles of Accounting for Intangible Assets

Accounting for intangible assets involves accounting principles and procedures similar to those that apply to tangible assets such as property, plant, and equipment, including:

1. At acquisition, application of the cost principle.
2. During the period of use, application of the matching principle.
3. At disposition, application of the revenue principle. A gain or loss is recognized on disposal equal to the difference between the consideration received and the book value of the asset sacrificed.

Previously, intangible assets were accounted for on the basis of life expectancy. Intangible assets with limited lives were amortized over their estimated period of future use. Intangible assets with indeterminable lives were not amortized until a realistic determination of their useful life could be made. Often, this determination was never made; thus, the cost of such intangibles was never amortized. The revision to Section 3060, paragraphs .31 and .32 of the *CICA Handbook* stopped this practice and provides the following guidance:

> Amortization should be recognized in a rational and systematic manner appropriate to the nature of a capital asset with a limited life and its use by the enterprise.
>
> When the useful life of a capital asset other than land is expected to exceed 40 years, but cannot be estimated and clearly demonstrated, the amortization period should be limited to 40 years.

Exhibit 13–1 summarizes accounting treatments for various types of intangible assets. The only intangible asset discussed in this chapter that cannot be separately identified is goodwill.

Recording the Cost of Purchased Intangible Assets In conformance with the cost principle, intangible assets should be recorded at acquisition at their current cash equivalent cost. Cost includes purchase price, transfer and legal fees, and any other expenditures related to acquisition. The acquisition cost is the current market value of all consideration given, or of the asset received, whichever is more reliably determinable. When an intangible asset is acquired in whole or in part for non-cash consideration, its cost is any cash paid plus the current market value of the non-cash consideration given. If that value cannot be determined reliably, the market value of the right acquired is used.[1] For example, if a company acquires a patent by issuing

---

[1] If neither the market value of consideration given nor that of the intangible asset acquired can be determined with sufficient reliability, the company may have to assign a value to the intangible asset.

capital stock as the consideration, the cost of the patent should be measured as the current market value of the shares. If the shares issued do not have an established market value, evidence of the market value of the patent itself should be used as the measure of cost of the transaction.

Recording the Costs of Internally Created Intangible Assets   Sometimes a firm develops or self-constructs an intangible asset, such as a patent. Only the costs specifically identifiable with the creation of the intangible asset are capitalized. Thus, even though a firm may incur extensive research costs to develop a patentable item, only the costs of obtaining the patent itself are capitalized as an asset. Because of this constraint, the capitalized cost of an intangible asset developed internally may not reflect its value, whereas the capitalized cost of an intangible asset purchased in an arm's-length transaction presumably does approximate its value, at least at the date of acquisition.

Amortizing the Cost of Intangible Assets   The cost of an intangible asset must be allocated to expense in a rational and systematic manner over the legal life or the estimated useful life of the asset, whichever is shorter, in conformance with the matching principle. This allocation process is called **amortization.** Several factors are to be considered in estimating the life of an intangible asset:[2]

1. Legal, regulatory, or contractual provisions that may limit the maximum useful life.
2. Provisions for renewal or extension that may alter a specified limit on useful life.
3. Effects of obsolescence, demand, and other economic factors that may reduce useful life.
4. The service life expectancies of individuals or groups of employees.
5. Expected actions of competitors and others that may restrict present competitive advantages.
6. Indefiniteness of useful life and benefits that cannot be reasonably projected.
7. Whether an intangible asset is a composite of many individual factors with varying effective useful lives.

By their nature, intangible assets seldom have a residual value. The cost of an intangible asset that does not have a determinable useful life or a definite legal life must nevertheless be amortized on the basis of some estimate of useful life. Section 3060 of the *CICA Handbook* requires that the period of amortization not exceed 40 years. This maximum period of amortization seems arbitrary, but it prevents potential abuses of the matching principle and of the definition of an asset.

Because it is hard to estimate the economic useful life of an intangible asset, periodic evaluations should be made to determine whether the estimate needs revision. A change in estimated useful life is a change in accounting estimate. The unamortized cost is amortized over the revised remaining useful life although never longer than 40 years from the acquisition date.

The method of amortization should reflect the consumption of service potential of the capital asset. Section 3060 allows for the use of the straight-line method, the unit-of-production method, or other methods that may be appropriate in certain situations.

Amortization of an intangible asset usually involves a year-end adjusting entry. The amount to be amortized is recorded as a debit to amortization expense and as a credit either directly to the asset account (because of accounting precedent) or to an accumulated amortization expense account (contra to the asset account).

Impairment of Value of Intangible Assets   Once an intangible asset has been recorded, a periodic assessment of the value of its future benefit must be made to

---

[2] *APB Opinion No. 17,* par. 27.

determine whether its current book value exceeds the estimated future economic benefit. If this is the case, the remaining unamortized cost must be written down to the revised value and a loss recognized to reflect this impairment of value. The new revised value of the asset is to be amortized over the remaining expected useful life of the asset, but the total period of amortization from date of acquisition cannot exceed 40 years.

Disposal of Intangible Assets   When an intangible asset is sold, exchanged, or otherwise disposed of, its unamortized cost must be removed from the accounts and a gain or loss on disposal recognized and recorded. The gain or loss equals the difference between the net proceeds from the disposal and the unamortized cost and is reported as a component of operating income.

| CONCEPT REVIEW

1. Define an intangible asset.
2. How is an intangible asset different from a tangible asset?
3. How can intangible assets be categorized, and how does this categorization influence the accounting?

EXCHANGEABLE INTANGIBLE ASSETS

Exchangeable intangible assets are intangible assets that can be identified apart from the other assets of the firm and can be sold separately. Examples include patents, copyrights, trademarks, and franchises (but not organization costs). Whether acquired by purchase or developed internally, these assets are initially recorded at cost, in conformance with the cost principle. As the economic service value of the asset declines, its cost is amortized and expensed in conformance with the matching principle.

Because there is a wide variety of exchangeable intangible assets, application of the above principles and guidelines varies.

Patents

A **patent** is an exclusive right recognized by law and registered with the Patent Office of Consumer and Corporate Affairs Canada. It enables the holder to use, manufacture, sell, and control the item, process, or activity covered by the patent without interference or infringement by others. Registration of a patent with the Patent Office does not guarantee protection. A patent does not become established until it has been successfully defended in court; thus, there is general agreement that the costs of a successful court defense should be capitalized as part of the cost of the patent. If the suit is lost, the legal cost and the unamortized cost of the patent are written off. An impairment loss should be debited for the amount of any write-down.

The cost of a patent acquired by purchase is determined in conformance with the cost principle. Patents resulting from a company's own research and development activities must be accounted for as specified by *CICA Handbook* Section 3450, discussed more fully later. Laboratory costs leading to the development of the patent must be expensed as incurred. The only costs of an internally developed patent that can be capitalized are legal fees and other costs associated with registration of the patent, such as models and drawings required for the registration, and the legal defense costs.

Patents have a legal life of 17 years, although the useful life of many patents is shorter because technological improvements may cause the products or processes to lose their competitive advantage sooner. The cost of a patent should be amortized over the estimated useful life or legal life, whichever is shorter. Sometimes an old patent is improved or modified, resulting in a new patent. If the new patent takes away the old patent's value, a case can be made for adding the unamortized cost of the old patent to the cost of the new patent and establishing a new amortization period. Most companies, however, rely on the conservatism constraint and immediately write off the unamortized cost of the old patent.

To illustrate the accounting for a typical patent, assume that on January 1, 1995, Alto Company purchased a patent that cost $27,200. The patent had a 17-year legal life that began on January 1, 1994. Alto uses the remaining legal life as the patent's useful life for amortization purposes. During 1996, Alto Company wins a patent infringement suit. Legal costs are $4,750. The entries are as follows:

January 1, 1995—Record purchase of patent:

| Patent | 27,200 | |
| Cash | | 27,200 |

December 31, 1995—Amortization of patent:

| Patent amortization expense | 1,700 | |
| Patent [or accumulated patent amortization] | | 1,700 |

$27,200 ÷ 16 = $1,700

During 1996—Record costs of successful patent infringement suit:

| Patent | 4,750 | |
| Cash | | 4,750 |

December 31, 1996—Amortization of patent:

| Patent amortization expense | 2,017 | |
| Patent [or accumulated patent amortization] | | 2,017 |

($27,200 − $1,700 + $4,750 = $30,250) ÷ 15 = $2,017

Patent owners often contract to let another party use the patent for a stipulated period in return for royalties. In such cases, the patent owner continues to amortize the patent, and recognizes the amounts earned as revenue in conformance with the revenue principle.

Industrial Design Registrations

An **industrial design registration** is similar to a patent but applies to the shape, pattern, or ornamentation applied to an article of manufacture. A patent protects function while industrial design registration protects appearance. For example, a new computer terminal design would be protected by a design registration, whereas a new 486 chip would be protected by a patent. Once registered at the Canadian Industrial Design Office of Consumer and Corporate Affairs Canada, the design is protected for five years and may be renewed for an additional five years.

Copyrights

A **copyright** is a form of protection given by law to the authors of literary, musical, artistic, and similar works (such as the score for the musical *Miss Saigon*). Owners of copyrights have certain exclusive rights, including the right to print, reprint, and copy the work, to sell or distribute copies, and to perform and record the work. The 1987 copyright law protects a copyright for the life of the author plus 50 years. Copyrights can be sold or contractually assigned to others.

The cost of a copyright is measured in accordance with the cost principle. If a copyright does not have economic value for its entire legal life, its cost should be amortized over the period it is expected to produce revenue. In no case should a copyright be amortized over a period in excess of its remaining legal life, or 40 years, whichever is shorter.

Suppose a company acquires a copyright from a second company. The author of the copyrighted item has been deceased for 20 years. Thus, the copyright protection is for an additional 30 years, which would be the maximum period of amortization. If a company acquires a copyright from a living author, the maximum period of amortization would be 40 years, even though the legal life of the copyright is longer. The accounting entries for a copyright are similar to those for a patent.

Trademarks and Trade Names

Trademarks (such as the Blue Jays' team logo) and **trade names** (such as *Coca-Cola*) are names, symbols, or other distinctive identities given to companies, products, and services. They can be registered with the Consumer and Corporate Affairs Canada to help substantiate ownership and provide legal protection. Registered trademarks and trade names can be renewed for successive 20-year periods, extending their lives indefinitely.

The cash equivalent amount paid for the purchase of a trademark is capitalized. Costs directly incurred in the development, protection, expansion, registration, or defense of a trademark should be capitalized and amortized over the useful life of the trademark or 40 years, whichever is shorter.

Franchise Rights

Franchise rights are granted by governmental entities for the right to use public properties or to furnish public utility services (such as cable, in the case of Rogers Cablevision), and by business entities for the right to use a particular name and offer specified service (such as U-Haul Trailers and Canadian Tire). Franchise contracts specify the period of time for which the franchise is valid and the rights and obligations of the franchisor and franchisee. Accounting for franchise revenue by the franchisor is covered in Chapter 7.

The cost of obtaining a franchise can be high; franchise agreements usually require an initial franchise fee to be paid by the franchisee to the franchisor. This initial cost should be capitalized and then amortized as an expense. If the term of the franchise is limited, its cost should be amortized over the term in a rational and systematic manner. If the term is indefinite, amortization should be based on a reliably estimated useful life, with periodic evaluations to determine whether the estimate needs revision. The total amortization period may not exceed 40 years.

Ongoing payments by the franchisee for services such as assistance with promotional campaigns, accounting, and organizational matters should be expensed as incurred. If a franchise becomes worthless or is voided by law, the unamortized amount should be written off immediately.

Leasehold Improvements

A lease is a right granted by one party to a second party to use property, plant, or equipment, usually for a specified period of time. Under some conditions, leases are capitalized as assets by the party receiving the right to use the property, and under other conditions, leases are not capitalized.[3] When a company acquires property through a lease contract, regardless of whether the lease itself is capitalized as an asset, the company may incur costs to modify the leased item. Suppose, for example, a company leases a bare, unpainted office building for a five-year lease period, and then incurs costs to paint and install carpeting. Such costs are usually debited to an account called **leasehold improvements.** Leasehold improvements are classified as intangible assets because the leased property does not belong to the lessee. Leasehold improvements are amortized over the remaining term of the lease or the life of the improvements, whichever is shorter.

SEPARATELY IDENTIFIABLE BUT NOT EXCHANGEABLE INTANGIBLE ASSETS

Some intangibles have two special characteristics: they are essentially prepayments of expenses, and they do not confer rights to the owner that could be sold to a second party. These intangible assets can be identified separately but are not exchangeable. Deferred charges, start-up costs, organization costs, and share issue costs are examples.

---

[3] Accounting for leases is covered in detail in Chapter 18.

Deferred Charges

A **deferred charge** is a general classification in accounting for an expenditure for a service that is expected to contribute to the generation of future revenues. Most are essentially long-term prepaid expenses. Deferred charges are classified as noncurrent assets because their effect on revenues extends beyond the period for current assets. Deferred charges have no physical substance and can rarely be realized through sale.[4] Examples of deferred charges include machinery rearrangement costs, long-term prepaid insurance premiums, and prepaid leasehold costs. When organization expense is capitalized, it is often classified as a deferred charge.

Deferred charges are amortized over the future periods during which they will contribute to the generation of revenues. The 40-year maximum period for amortization of intangible assets applies to deferred charges. However, they seldom have 40-year life spans.

Start-Up Costs

A **start-up cost** is a cost incurred by a newly organized development-stage company before it has significant revenues against which costs can be matched. Some of the recently organized biotechnology firms are prime examples. Often, these costs are capitalized as intangibles and amortized in later years. Development-stage companies can capitalize certain costs as intangible assets that otherwise would be expensed as incurred.

Development-stage enterprises present financial statements prepared in the usual reporting formats. Capitalization of costs is subject to the same assessment of future benefit and recoverability applicable to established businesses. A development-stage enterprise presents a balance sheet showing the "deficit accumulated (from operations) during development stage," an income statement, a statement of cash flows, and a statement of shareholders' equity. The current statements show information for each period covered by the past and present statements and the cumulative amounts. Also, the statements must be specifically identified as those of a development-stage company.

Organization Costs

Organization costs are expenditures incurred in organizing a business. Costs directly related to the organizing activities, such as expenditures for legal, accounting, promotional, and clerical activities, are capitalizable as organization costs. The rationale for capitalizing organization costs is that they benefit future years' operations. To expense the total amount in the first year of operation would result in a mismatching of expense with revenue.

Because the life of a business is usually indefinite, the length of the period receiving the benefits of these costs usually is indeterminate. Therefore, organization costs are usually amortized over an arbitrarily chosen, short period of time.

Share Issuance Costs

Expenditures associated with issuing capital stock are called **share issuance costs.** Such costs include printing share certificates and related items, professional fees, commissions paid for selling capital stock, and the costs of filing with securities commissions. Share issuance costs, as opposed to organizational costs, are accounted for either as an offset to the issuance price of the capital stock to which they relate or as a deferred charge, which is amortized to expense in conformance with the matching principle (usually on a conservative basis).

---

[4] Some deferred charges are reported as current assets where appropriate.

GOODWILL: AN UNIDENTIFIABLE INTANGIBLE ASSET

In 1988, Campeau Corporation acquired Federated Department Stores for a purchase price of approximately $6.6 billion. The fair market value of Federated's net assets that were acquired totalled $4.3 billion. In accordance with GAAP, Campeau recorded the difference, $2.3 billion, as an asset and called it *goodwill*.

Goodwill is the most common and important unidentifiable intangible asset. It represents the value associated with favourable characteristics of a firm that result in earnings in excess of those expected from identifiable assets of the firm. For many firms, the entire intangible asset amount shown is goodwill. Since the middle and late 1980s, goodwill has become a major reported asset of many firms, in large part because of the merger and acquisition activity of that period.

In the Campeau example, goodwill was recorded when one firm acquired another. In fact, goodwill is recorded only when there is an acquisition of one firm by another. Goodwill exists without an acquisition, but it is recorded only when one company is acquired by, or merged with, another.

Conceptual Nature of Goodwill

Essentially, goodwill represents the expected value of future above-normal financial performance. This expectation arises because intangible, favourable characteristics or factors make it likely that the firm will produce higher than average earnings. Examples of such favourable factors are:

- A superior management team.
- An outstanding sales organization.
- A favourable market position due to weakness in the management of one or more major competitors.
- Especially effective advertising.
- A secret manufacturing process.
- Exceptionally good labour relations.
- An outstanding credit rating.
- A top-flight training program for employees.
- An unusually good reputation in its industry for total quality.
- Unfavourable developments in the operations of a competitor.
- A particularly favourable association with a supplier.
- A highly advantageous strategic location.
- Discovery of previously unknown resources or employee skills.
- Favourable tax conditions.
- Favourable government regulations.[5]

Any of these factors may give rise to increased earning power, leading to an increase in value of the firm beyond the value of its individual assets. The increase in value is often reflected in the price of the firm's shares.

Factors that give rise to goodwill derive value from their association with the other assets of the firm. That is, they are not independent of the firm of which they

---

[5] See G. Catlett and N. Olson, "Accounting for Goodwill," *Accounting Research Study No. 10* (New York: AICPA, 1968), pp. 17–18.

	As Reported	Fair Market Value	Difference
Assets			
Cash .	$ 30,000	$ 30,000	
Receivables .	90,000	85,000	($ 5,000)
Inventory .	60,000	60,000	
Other current assets .	33,000	30,000	(3,000)
Plant and equipment (net) .	220,000	235,000	15,000
Other assets .	85,000	90,000	5,000
Total assets .	$518,000	$530,000	
Liabilities			
Short-term notes payable .	$ 85,000	$ 85,000	
Accounts payable .	45,000	45,000	
Other current liabilities .	30,000	30,000	
Long-term debt .	250,000	240,000	(10,000)
Shareholders' equity .	108,000	130,000	22,000
Total equities .	$518,000	$530,000	

are part and cannot be sold separately. This creates a measurement problem because a firm's goodwill cannot be separated from the firm or bought or sold independently. Goodwill can be measured objectively only when the firm is sold. In the absence of a sale, there is no market or arm's-length transaction with which to measure the cost of the goodwill a firm creates as it engages in business activities.

For accounting purposes, goodwill is the difference between the actual purchase price of an acquired firm and the estimated fair market value of the identifiable net assets acquired. *CICA Handbook,* Section 1580, paragraph 44, states that "the excess of the cost of the purchase over the acquiring company's interest in identifiable assets acquired and liabilities assumed should be reflected as goodwill." An acquisition by purchase is the only objective means of measuring the cost of goodwill.

Measuring Goodwill

The value of goodwill is computed only indirectly in an acquisition of a firm, in whole or in significant part. Any method used is indirect. The total value of a firm is first determined or estimated. Second, the current value of the various identifiable assets, both tangible and separately identifiable intangible, and the current value of the liabilities of the firm are determined. The difference between these two is the current value of the net assets acquired:

$$\text{Current fair value of net assets acquired} = \text{Current fair value of tangible and identifiable intangible assets} - \text{Current fair value of liabilities}$$

The value of the goodwill that was purchased is computed as the difference between the total value of the firm usually measured as the purchase price, less the current fair value of the net assets acquired:

$$\text{Purchased goodwill} = \text{Purchase price of firm acquired} - \text{Current fair value of net assets acquired}$$

Example   Assume that Hotel Company is considering the acquisition of Cafe Corporation. Hotel Company obtains financial statements and other financial data on Cafe and estimates the fair market value of Cafe's identifiable assets at $530,000 and the fair market value of the liabilities at $400,000. (See Exhibit 13–2.)

The fair market value column in Exhibit 13–2 shows that several assets have an estimated fair market value different from their cost as reported in the published financial statements. Indeed, there is no reason why amounts shown in the balance sheet should equal fair market values. Accounting is based on recorded historical costs rather than current market values.

The total fair market value of Cafe's net assets is determined to be $130,000 ($530,000 total assets less liabilities of $400,000). This is shown as shareholders' equity in the fair market value column. This value is established not by estimating the value of Cafe as a firm but by summing up the values of individual assets and liabilities. This value is similar to the liquidation value. If the firm were broken up and sold as individual assets and the liabilities were paid off at current market prices, the resulting net cash to be distributed to the owners would be approximately $130,000.

Management of Hotel Company, however, must determine the value of Cafe as a going concern. For now, assume that Hotel negotiates a purchase price with the owners to acquire Cafe as of December 31, 1994, for $202,000. There may be many reasons why Hotel might be willing to pay more than $130,000 for Cafe.

The amount of goodwill in this acquisition can now be computed. The purchase price is $202,000, and the current market value of the identifiable net assets totals $130,000; thus, goodwill is the difference, or $72,000. When Hotel acquires Cafe, it records the various assets and liabilities of Cafe at their current market values, and it records goodwill of $72,000. The entry Hotel Company makes to reflect the acquisition of Cafe is as follows:

Cash	30,000	
Receivables	85,000	
Inventory	60,000	
Other current assets	30,000	
Plant and equipment	235,000	
Other assets	90,000	
Goodwill	72,000	
Short-term notes payable		85,000
Accounts payable		45,000
Other current liabilities		30,000
Long-term debt		240,000
Cash		202,000

The various assets and liabilities of Cafe are recorded at current fair market values in Hotel's financial records. This recording reflects the cost Hotel incurred for these items. These costs will be used in subsequent accounting by Hotel.

In Appendix 13B, several methods for estimating the total current value of a firm and for estimating the value of goodwill are presented. Understanding these topics is not essential to understanding the accounting for purchased goodwill; however, accountants are called on from time to time to help address these valuation issues.

Negative Goodwill

When the fair market value of the net assets acquired is greater than the purchase price of the firm, the acquiring firm has made what is sometimes called a bargain purchase. The amount of goodwill (the difference between the purchase price and fair market value of assets acquired) is negative. This amount is often identified as **negative goodwill.** Even though it would seem that the seller could benefit from selling the assets individually rather than selling the firm as a whole, such situations do occasionally occur. For example, the seller may not have the time or resources to take on the risks of selling the assets separately.

CICA Handbook, Section 1580, paragraph .44, requires that any negative goodwill be allocated to reduce the values assigned to identifiable non-monetary assets to the extent that it is eliminated.

Assume now that Hotel Company purchases Cafe Corp. for $91,500, which is $38,500 less than the fair value of the net assets acquired. The negative goodwill of

$38,500 would be allocated proportionally to reduce the recorded values for plant, equipment, inventory, and other non-monetary assets. Two entries are required. The first records all the assets and liabilities of Cafe at their fair market values and sets up a goodwill account with a credit balance of $38,500. The second entry writes down the plant and equipment and the other non-monetary asset accounts proportionally based on fair value.

The initial entry to reflect this purchase by Hotel of Cafe for $91,500 is as follows:

Cash	30,000	
Receivables	85,000	
Inventory	60,000	
Other current assets (monetary)	30,000	
Plant and equipment	235,000	
Other assets (non-monetary)	90,000	
Goodwill		38,500
Short-term notes payable		85,000
Accounts payable		45,000
Other current liabilities		30,000
Long-term debt		240,000
Cash		91,500

The write-down of the non-monetary asset accounts would be as follows:

Total of non-monetary assets:		
Inventory	$ 60,000	
Plant and equipment	235,000	
Other assets (non-monetary)	90,000	
Total	$385,000	
Negative goodwill or 10% of non-monetary assets	$ 38,500	

The entry to write down these accounts proportionally is:

Goodwill	38,500	
Inventory ($60,000 × 10%)		6,000
Plant and equipment		23,500
Other assets—non-monetary ($90,000 × 10%)		9,000

Amortizing Goodwill

After goodwill has been recorded in a purchase of one firm by another, the next question is what to do with it. Three different treatments have been advocated by accountants at one time or another:

1. **Write off immediately, directly to shareholders' equity.** Because internally generated goodwill is expensed as it is being created, some accountants believe that consistent treatment requires that purchased goodwill also be written off immediately. On the other hand, an objective, reliable measure of the value of this asset occurs with the purchase, and most agree that the objectively measured asset should be recorded. This is not an acceptable accounting treatment under GAAP in Canada, although it is acceptable in the United Kingdom and several other international accountant settings. Some accountants argue that the immediate write-off should not be included in the determination of income, but rather recorded as a direct reduction in owners' equity.

2. **Capitalize as an intangible asset with indefinite life and do not amortize.** Some accountants contend that goodwill has indefinite life and should be maintained as an asset until a definite decline in value occurs. They argue that without evidence that a decline in value has occurred, writing off goodwill over any period is arbitrary.

3. **Capitalize as an intangible asset and amortize over its estimated useful life.** Some accountants argue that goodwill is gradually eroded or used up and that it should be amortized to expense over the periods benefited, thus resulting in a better matching of revenues and expenses. The difficulty with this treatment is determining the period over which the goodwill benefits the firm.

Goodwill would seem to be a fragile asset, and conservatism supports amortizing it over some period. The difficulty of adopting alternative (3) above is determining the appropriate estimated useful life. In resolving this issue, the AcSB came up with a compromise resolution that could appease advocates of any of the three alternatives. *CICA Handbook,* Section 3060, paragraph .3, requires that purchased goodwill be amortized over its estimated useful life (alternative [3] above), but the period of amortization cannot exceed 40 years. Given the difficulty of estimating the useful life of goodwill, firms have considerable flexibility in writing off goodwill. Thus, those that would normally prefer immediate write-off can choose a very short estimated useful life. They must, however, amortize the goodwill as an expense; they cannot write it off directly to shareholders' equity. Advocates of alternative (2), on the other hand, can argue for a long life for goodwill and use the 40-year write-off life. This appears to be the preferred choice.

The amortization period can greatly affect the annual amortization amount. Suppose Hotel estimates a five-year useful life for the $72,000 of purchased goodwill from its acquisition of Cafe. This results in an annual amortization expense of $14,400 ($72,000 ÷ 5 years). If a 40-year amortization period were used, the annual amortization expense drops to $1,800 per year. Some firms use an amortization period as short as three to five years. Using a five-year period, the annual adjusting entry to recognize goodwill amortization is:

Amortization of goodwill (expense).	14,400	
Goodwill		14,400

CONCEPT REVIEW

1. What is goodwill, and how does it arise?
2. When and how is goodwill recorded in the accounting records?
3. Once goodwill is recorded in the accounting records, how is it subsequently treated?

DISCLOSURES AND REPORTING OF INTANGIBLE ASSETS

Intangible assets are reported on the balance sheet under various captions, including *intangible assets, deferred charges,* and *other assets.* Firms sometimes list specific types of intangibles (such as patents). For example, the following is excerpted from the 1993 balance sheet of Moore Corporation Limited:

MOORE CORPORATION LIMITED
Consolidated Balance Sheet
As of December 31

Assets [in part]

	1993	1992
	(in thousands of U.S. dollars)	
Other Assets (Note 4)	$161,045	$134,077

Notes to the Consolidated Financial Statements [in part]

1. Summary of accounting policies
   Goodwill:
   Goodwill is amortized by the straight-line method over periods not exceeding 40 years.

   Amortization of deferred charges:
   Deferred charges are amortized over periods deemed appropriate to match expenses with the related revenues.

MOORE CORPORATION LIMITED (continued)
4. Other Assets

	1993	1992
Long-term receivables	$ 66,890	$ 39,522
Prepaid pension cost	32,008	30,618
Long-term bonds, at cost, which approximates market value	22,810	18,837
Goodwill, net of accumulated amortization of $23,786 (1992—$21,319)	17,776	21,500
Investment in preferred shares, at market value	4,200	4,200
Computer software	4,031	5,184
Other	13,330	14,216
	$161,045	$134,077

RESEARCH AND DEVELOPMENT COSTS

Broadly defined, research and development includes the activities undertaken by firms to create new products and processes, or to improve old ones, and to discover new knowledge that may be of value in the future. R&D costs are not recorded as intangible assets, but they often do result in patents or other types of intangible assets. For many firms, they are a very important part of ongoing activities and can be a large and significant expenditure. The following schedule shows R&D expenses for selected companies as reported in their 1993 financial statements:

Company	R&D Expense (in thousands)	R&D Percentage of Sales
Alcan Aluminium Limited	$99,000	1.4
Bombardier Inc.	73,135	1.6
Cangene Corporation	6,427	171.0
Electrohome Limited	4,796	3.7
Unican Security Systems Ltd.	1,491	1.1
International Verifact Inc.	953	3.6

These expenditures are undertaken because the R&D effort is expected to more than pay for itself in the future by providing the firm with competitive, profitable products and processes.

Prior to the implementation of *CICA Handbook* Section 3450 in 1978, the reporting and accounting for R&D costs varied greatly. Because there was no clear guidance on what constituted R&D activities, different firms included the costs of different activities in R&D costs. R&D costs were sometimes capitalized as intangible assets (and amortized over time); at other times they were expensed immediately. Because of these variations in accounting for R&D costs, financial statements were not comparable among firms, and firms could potentially manipulate income by expensing or capitalizing R&D costs as needed to obtain the desired amount of income. Section 3450 was issued by the AcSB to provide both guidance in defining and standards in accounting for R&D costs.

First, in attempting to distinguish between costs to be included in R&D and similar costs to be excluded from R&D, Section 3450 defines both research and development:[6]

Research is planned investigation undertaken with the hope of gaining new scientific or technical knowledge and understanding. Such investigation may or may not be directed toward a specific practical aim or application.

Development is the translation of research findings or other knowledge into a plan or design for new or substantially improved materials, devices, products, processes, systems, or services prior to the commencement of commercial productions or use.

Because there is considerable similarity between R&D activities and some other activities, Section 3450 goes on to provide examples of activities to be included and of activities to be excluded from R&D costs:

---

[6] "Research and Development Costs," Section 3450, paragraph .02 of the *CICA Handbook*.

Activities Included in Research

Laboratory research aimed at discovery of new knowledge.

Searching for applications of new research findings or other knowledge.

Conceptual formulation and design of possible product or process alternatives.

Activities Included in Development

Testing in search for, or evaluation of, product or process alternatives.

Design, construction, and testing of preproduction prototypes and models.

Design of tools, jigs, molds, and dies involving new technology.

Activities Excluded from Research and Development

Engineering follow-through in an early phase of commercial production.

Quality control during commercial production, including routine testing of products.

Troubleshooting in connection with breakdowns during commercial production.

Routine or periodic alterations to existing products, production lines, manufacturing processes, and other ongoing operations, even though such alterations may represent improvements.

Adaptation of an existing capability to a particular requirement or customer's needs as part of a continuing commercial activity.

Routine design of tools, jigs, molds, and dies.

Activity including design and construction engineering, related to the construction, relocation, rearrangement, or start-up of facilities or equipment other than facilities or equipment whose sole use is for a particular research and development project.[7]

Section 3450 specifies the capitalization of equipment and facilities and of purchased intangibles (such as a purchased patent) when these items can be used in the future. Depreciation and amortization on these items is included in R&D expense in the periods in which the assets are used for R&D purposes. Thus, a firm that builds a research facility at a cost of $40 million with an expected useful life of 20 years and zero salvage value would capitalize the cost of the facility and, assuming straight-line depreciation, include depreciation of $2 million in its R&D expense each year.

Firms sometimes engage in R&D activities on behalf of a second firm under a contractual arrangement. Any costs of R&D performed for other firms are capitalized as part of the work-in-process inventory for the contract. Upon completion of the contract or specified portions of the contract, the capitalized costs are removed from inventory and reported as an expense similar to cost of goods sold. The purchasing firm expenses these costs as it pays or as it accrues the liability for them.

Section 3450 of the *CICA Handbook* provides that some development costs may be capitalized if they meet all of the following criteria:

a. the product or process is clearly defined and the costs attributable thereto can be identified,

b. the technical feasibility of the product or process has been established,

c. the management of the enterprise has indicated its intention to produce and market, or use, the product or process,

d. the future market for the product or process is clearly defined or, if it is to be used internally rather than sold, its usefulness to the enterprise has been established, and

e. adequate resources exist, or are expected to be available, to complete the project.

The effect of these provisions is that all research costs are expensed as incurred as are most development costs. Note that, in order to be deferred to future periods, development costs must meet all of the criteria listed above.

When R&D expense is material, the financial statements must disclose, either in the income statement or in the notes to the financial statements, the total R&D costs included in expense for each period for which an income statement is presented. Alcan Aluminium, for example, shows R&D as a line item on its income statement:

---

[7] "Research and Development Costs," Section 3450, paragraphs .04, .05, and .06.

Year Ended December 31

	1993	1992	1991
	(in millions of U.S. dollars)		
Revenues			
Sales and operating revenues	$7,232	$7,596	$7,748
Other income	75	69	82
	7,307	7,665	7,830
Costs and Expenses			
Cost of sales and operating expenses	6,002	6,300	6,455
Depreciation (note 1)	443	449	429
Selling, administrative and general expenses.	551	596	635
Research and development expenses	99	125	131
Interest	212	254	246
Other expenses.	106	118	163
	7,413	7,842	8,059

An alternative disclosure is to report the amount of R&D expense in a note to the financial statements. Bombardier Inc., for example, provides the following disclosure in note 12 to its 1993 financial statements:

Cost of Sales and Operating Expenses

Cost of sales and operating expenses include research expenses, excluding those incurred under contracts, amounting to $88,749,000 ($73,135,000 in 1993) net of various participative programs and related income tax credits.

Section 3450 has resulted in a consistent, uniform practice of expensing R&D costs. There is some disagreement among accountants, as some continue to believe R&D expenditures should be capitalized rather than expensed when they have expected future economic benefits. Indeed, for some firms, the expensing of R&D means that an item that some consider the firm's most valuable asset is not shown at all on its balance sheet and that current period expenses are overstated. Also, the required expensing of R&D costs does not seem to be consistent with the accounting treatment allowed for exploration costs incurred in the search for oil and gas reserves, which, subject to some constraints, can be capitalized as an asset. Accounting for natural resources is discussed later in this chapter.

Nevertheless, the difficulties associated with measuring R&D as an asset and the potential for abuse are such that the AcSB decided that the most appropriate solution is to require immediate expensing of R&D costs. Section 3450 is an example of the trade-offs that must often be made between relevance and reliability and other cost–benefit considerations in accounting for complex transactions.[8]

CONCEPT REVIEW

1. What are the arguments that support the capitalizing of R&D costs?
2. What are the arguments that support the immediate expensing of R&D costs?
3. How are the costs of an R&D facility to be accounted for?

ACCOUNTING FOR COMPUTER SOFTWARE COSTS

A decade after the AcSB attempted to resolve the problems of accounting for R&D costs, a new industry emerged producing computer software to be sold, leased, or otherwise marketed to others. Computer software development has costs dissimilar to R&D: costs such as designing, coding, testing, debugging the software, and producing master products to be duplicated and sold. As the industry grew, a variety of

---

[8] For an extensive discussion of the conceptual issues and arguments for capitalizing R&D under certain conditions, see H. Bierman, Jr., and R. Dukes, "Accounting for Research and Development Costs," *Journal of Accountancy*, April 1975, pp. 48–55.

accounting procedures developed. Some firms expensed all software development costs, whereas others capitalized nearly all such costs as intangible assets. Because the major asset of some software companies is their investment in software and software development, it became necessary to standardize the accounting for the cost of software development when the software is to be marketed to customers. The basic issue to be resolved was what costs, if any, incurred in the development of a computer software product should be capitalized, and what costs are analogous to R&D and should be expensed.

Capitalization of Computer Software Costs

In 1985, the FASB issued *SFAS No. 86,* "Accounting for the Costs of Computer Software to be Sold, Leased, or Otherwise Marketed." To date, the CICA has not issued a handbook section dealing with this topic. Therefore, many Canadian companies follow the FASB guidelines. The basic provisions of *SFAS No. 86* regarding initial treatment or costs are as follows:

- All costs incurred to establish the *technological feasibility* of a computer software product are to be treated as R&D and expensed as incurred.
- Once the technological feasibility of the software product is established, subsequent costs incurred to obtain *product masters* are to be capitalized as an intangible asset.

The standard defines the establishment of technological feasibility as the completion of a detailed program design or a working model of the product. A detailed program design includes (1) a product design by a firm with the necessary skills, hardware, and software technology to produce the product, (2) confirmation of the completeness of the design by documentation and tracing of design to product specifications, and (3) resolution of any identified high-risk development issues by coding and testing. Alternatively, a firm can establish the technological feasibility of a software product by completing a working model of the product that is consistent with the product design and that has been confirmed by testing.

Exhibit 13–3 is a flow diagram showing the accounting treatment of costs incurred in the development and sale of a software product. Software development costs are to be expensed as incurred until all the planning, designing, coding, and testing activities necessary to establish that the product can be produced to meet its design specifications are completed (or until a working model of the software is completed). Subsequent costs for further coding, testing, debugging, and producing masters of the software product to be duplicated in producing salable products are capitalized. In general, the largest portion of software development costs is incurred before a working model is produced, so the amount of computer software costs capitalized is usually a small portion of the total development costs. The capitalization of these costs stops when the product is available for release to customers.

Costs of producing software from the masters, producing documentation and training materials, and physically packaging the material for distribution are inventoriable production costs. These costs are capitalized as inventory and are recognized as cost of goods sold when sales revenue is recognized.

Amortization of Capitalized Computer Software Costs

The capitalized software costs are amortized to expense on a product-by-product basis. Annual amortization commences when the product begins to be marketed and is the greater of the amount computed according to the revenue method or the straight-line method:

a. **Revenue method** The ratio of current gross product revenue to total current and anticipated future gross product revenue over the remaining estimated economic life of the product, multiplied by the remaining amount to be amortized.
b. **Straight-line method** The amount determined using straight-line amortization over the remaining estimated economic life of the product.

Example Assume that during 1992 and 1993, Supersoft Company spends $3 million developing a working model of a word processing software product that corrects

EXHIBIT 13–3

Diagram of Accounting
Treatment of Computer
Software Costs from Project
Initiation to Sales of Final
Software Products

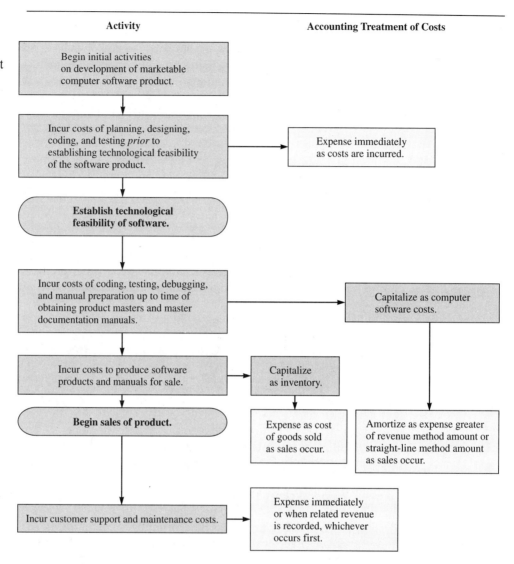

Activity   Accounting Treatment of Costs

spelling as it is being used. During calendar-year 1994, an additional $1 million of costs are incurred on the final coding and testing of the product masters. The product is available for sale as of the beginning of 1995 and is expected to have a four-year economic life. Sales revenues and anticipated future revenues in 1995 and 1996 are as follows:

	1995	1996
	(amounts in millions)	
Current-year revenue	$1.2	$2.4
Anticipated revenue in future years	4.8	2.4
Total	$6.0	$4.8

The costs of development incurred in 1992 and 1993 are prior to establishment of the technological feasibility of the product and are expensed as R&D:

| R&D expense . . . . | 3.0 million | |
| Cash, payables, accruals . . . . | | 3.0 million |

Costs incurred in 1994 are subsequent to the production of a working model and are therefore capitalized as software costs:

Capitalized software costs . . . . 1.0 million
    Cash, payables, accruals. . . . . 1.0 million

To determine the amount of amortization in 1995, compute the amount of amortization under both the revenue and the straight-line methods, and record the larger amount:

1. Revenue method:

$$\text{Amortization} = \frac{\text{Current period revenue}}{\text{Total current and anticipated revenue}} \times \frac{\text{Capitalized}}{\text{amount}}$$

$$= \frac{\$1.2 \text{ million}}{\$1.2 \text{ million} + \$4.8 \text{ million}} \times (\$1.0 \text{ million})$$

$$= \$0.2 \text{ million}$$

2. Straight-line method:

$$\text{Amortization} = \$1.0 \text{ million} \div 4 \text{ years} = \$0.25 \text{ million}$$

The greater amortization amount is given by the straight-line method, therefore, $0.25 million is the amount amortized in 1995:

Software amortization expense . . . . 0.25 million
    Capitalized software costs . . . . 0.25 million

Suppose all aspects of the above example were the same except that 1995 revenues were $3.0 million. Assuming that the total of current and anticipated revenues is still $6.0 million, now the revenue method gives the greater amount:

$$\text{Amortization} = (\$3.0 \text{ million} \div \$6.0 \text{ million}) \times \$1.0 \text{ million} = \$0.5 \text{ million}$$

If the greater portion of total anticipated revenue occurs in the early years of the product's estimated economic life, the revenue method results in the larger amortization. If the product sales revenue is anticipated to increase over time, the straight-line method gives the greater amortization in the early years.

The above calculations must be repeated each year, based on revised estimates of anticipated future sales revenue and on remaining unamortized cost. The computations for 1996 for Supersoft Company, assuming that 1996 revenue is $2.4 million, anticipated future revenue is $2.4 million, and $0.25 million was recorded as amortization in 1995, are as follows:

$$\text{Revenue method amortization} = (\$2.4 \text{ million} \div \$4.8 \text{ million}) \times \$0.75 \text{ million}$$
$$= \$0.375 \text{ million}$$

$$\text{Straight-line method amortization} = (\$1.0 \text{ million} - \$0.25 \text{ million}) \div 3 \text{ years}$$
$$= \$0.25 \text{ million}$$

In 1996, the amount recorded as amortization is $0.375 million, computed using the revenue method.

At each balance sheet date, the capitalized computer software cost is written down to net realizable value if that value is below the remaining unamortized cost. If it is written down to net realizable value, the capitalized software costs cannot be written back up later. Costs of maintenance and customer support for the product are to be expensed as incurred or accrued as the related revenue is recognized, whichever occurs first.

SFAS No. 86 deals only with computer software developed for sale or lease to external parties. There is no specific guidance from the CICA or FASB on accounting for software developed for internal uses. The costs of most software developed for internal purposes are classified as R&D costs and are expensed as incurred.

| *CONCEPT REVIEW*

1. When is it appropriate to capitalize the costs of developing computer software?
2. What is the requirement for amortizing capitalized computer software costs?

ACCOUNTING FOR NATURAL RESOURCES

Natural resources are also called **wasting assets** to indicate that they are consumed physically in production. Wasting assets include timberland, oil and gas, and various types of mineral deposits, such as gold, silver, copper, and coal. Natural resources are classified either as intangible assets or as property, plant, and equipment, and represent rights to exploit a natural resource. Although they may be classified as intangibles, the physical nature of the resource justifies their inclusion in property, plant, and equipment. Such assets present unique accounting problems, including:

1. Determining the cost of such assets when they are developed (as opposed to when they are purchased).
2. Writing off (amortizing) the cost to the income statement.

The cost of the natural resource properties is dependent on which costs are capitalized as the intangible asset. The second problem concerns the rate at which the intangible asset is expensed. The cost of a natural resource that is removed from the natural resource asset account each period is called **depletion.**

Depletion Base

The **depletion base** is the total cost capitalized plus or minus an adjustment for residual value. This amount is the total expense to be recognized over the period of marketing the natural resource. The residual value affects the determination of the asset's depletion base, and it can be positive or negative. A positive residual value is deducted from the total capitalized costs in determining the depletion base. Any costs expected to be incurred in the future in preparing the wasting asset for disposal reduce the residual value. A negative residual value increases the depletion base for purposes of computing depletion. For example, the anticipated cost of restoring the ground surface of a strip mining operation would be added to the depletion base. If the cost of restoring the asset is expected to exceed the asset's residual value, the depletion base will exceed the asset's capitalizable cost.

Section 3060, paragraphs .24 and .25, provide guidance for capitalizing costs for mining properties:

> For a mining property, the cost of the capital asset includes exploration costs if the enterprise considers that such costs have the characteristics of a capital asset. An enterprise applies the method of accounting for exploration costs that it considers to be appropriate to its operations and applies the method consistently to all its properties.

The following describes five categories of costs applicable to natural resources.

1. **Acquisition costs** Costs incurred to purchase, lease, or otherwise acquire the rights to property for purposes of exploring for and producing a natural resource. Acquisition costs are capitalized as part of the depletion base. For example, a mining company may lease property for its mineral resources. The cost of the lease is capitalized and included as acquisition cost.
2. **Exploration costs** Costs incurred to identify areas that may warrant testing or to test specific areas for the presence of a natural resource. If an exploration effort results in discovery of a natural resource in sufficient quantity to be extracted, these costs are capitalized as part of the depletion base. Determination of the appropriate exploration costs to capitalize has been a controversial topic, especially in the oil and gas industries, and is covered in more detail in the next section.
3. **Development costs** Costs incurred to provide facilities for extracting, treating, gathering, and storing the resource. Development costs are capitalized as part of the depletion base. For example, the cost of a mine shaft is a development cost.
4. **Production costs** Costs incurred to extract the natural resource. Production costs are capitalized as part of the cost of the product as they are incurred.
5. **Support equipment and facilities costs** Costs of tangible assets used in the exploration, development, and production of the natural resource. These costs are

EXHIBIT 13–4
Flow Diagram of the
Capitalizing and Expensing of
Costs of Natural Resources

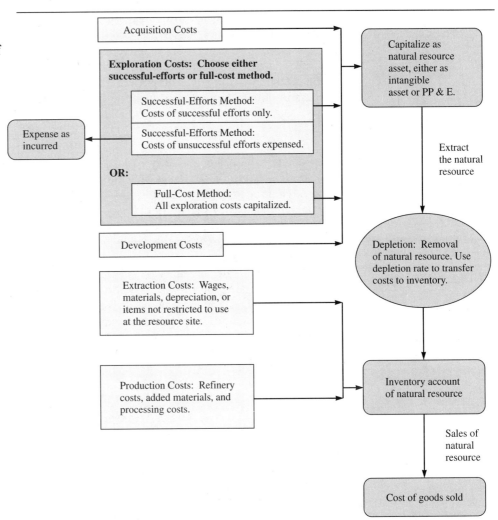

included in the plant and equipment accounts of the firm and are accounted for in the same way as other equipment.

Exhibit 13–4 is a flow diagram of the treatment of these various types of costs to asset and expense accounts. Acquisition costs, certain exploration costs, and development costs are capitalized as the cost of the natural resource. Extraction costs and production costs are capitalized as cost of inventory of the extracted resource and are recognized as cost of goods sold when the product is sold. As the natural resource is extracted from the location where it was found, the capitalized cost is assigned to inventory according to units extracted and a depletion rate. Determination of a depletion rate is discussed in the next section. For example, after crude oil is extracted from an oil well, it is inventory until it is sold. The cost of inventory of crude oil includes not only the cost to extract it but also the amount of depletion assigned to it. As additional costs of refining are incurred to produce marketable oil and gasoline products from the crude oil, these costs are also capitalized as inventory. When the products are sold, the inventory costs become costs of goods sold in the usual manner.

The exploration costs in Exhibit 13–4 are highlighted in the diagram because there are two different acceptable methods of accounting for them. With the successful-efforts method, only the exploration costs incurred that result in the discovery of exploitable resources are capitalized as the cost of the asset; exploration costs that do not directly result in a discovery are expensed as incurred. Under the full-cost method, all exploration costs are capitalized, subject to the constraint that the amount capitalized is not more than the estimated value of the resources discovered. These two accounting alternatives are considered in detail in a following section. Natural resource companies other than oil and gas companies almost always use the successful-efforts method of accounting for exploration costs.

Determining the Depletion Rate

The depletion base includes acquisition, exploration, and development costs, less any residual value of the asset and plus any estimated future cost to return the natural resource property to salable condition. Depletion is the periodic allocation of the depletion base to the units of resource extracted. These extracted units are included in inventory until they are sold, so depletion is generally shown as the reclassification of costs from the capitalized cost of the natural resource account to the inventory account.

The depletion rate allocates the depletion base to the estimated total production of the natural resource over the period of production in conformance with the matching principle. The most common method of calculating depletion is the units-of-production method. The **unit depletion rate** is computed as the depletion base divided by the estimated total number of recoverable units of the resource:

$$\text{Unit depletion rate} = \frac{\text{Capitalized cost of natural resource} - \text{Residual value}}{\text{Estimated recoverable units}}$$

$$= \frac{\text{Depletion base}}{\text{Estimated recoverable units}}$$

The depletion amount for any period is equal to the number of units produced multiplied by the unit depletion rate. This amount is initially debited to the inventory account of the natural resource and credited to the related wasting-asset account. As the inventory is sold, the inventory's cost, including the depletion, is expensed as a cost of the goods sold. At the end of the accounting period a portion of the depletion amount will be included in the inventory account to the extent that units have been produced but not sold during the period.

Example   On January 1, 1995, Burlington Resources, Inc., leases and begins operating a large copper strip mining activity. The firm incurs costs of $4 million to lease, explore, and develop the mine. The company estimates that the property will yield 2 million tonnes of copper ore and uses the full-cost method to account for exploration costs. The account "mine property" is debited for $4 million. In 1995, the firm produces 300,000 tonnes of copper ore. Extraction costs and production costs total $4 per tonne.

The depletion base is the total capitalized cost less any residual value plus any costs to return the strip mine to salable condition. Because the property reverts back to its owners after the mining activity is completed, and there are no costs to be incurred to restore the property, its residual value to Burlington is zero. The unit depletion rate per tonne of production is:

$$\text{Unit depletion rate per tonne} = \frac{\text{Depletion base}}{\text{Estimated recoverable tonnes of ore}}$$

$$= \frac{\$4,000,000}{2,000,000 \text{ tonnes}}$$

$$= \$2 \text{ per tonne}$$

The $2 represents the allocation of acquisition, exploration, and development costs to each tonne of production.

The depletion amount for 1995, when 300,000 tonnes are extracted, is:

Depletion amount = $2 per tonne × 300,000 tonnes

= $600,000

The entry to record the depletion for 1995 is as follows:

Inventory of copper ore ($2 per tonne × 300,000 tonnes) 600,000
    Mine property 600,000

Accountants typically credit the capitalized natural resource property account rather than an accumulated depletion account, although creating a contra account named *accumulated depletion* is also acceptable.

Extraction and production costs are also capitalized as inventory:

Inventory of copper ore ($4 per tonne × 300,000 tonnes) 1,200,000
    Cash, accruals, etc. 1,200,000

Depletion becomes a portion of cost of goods sold when the copper ore is sold. For example, suppose Burlington sells 250,000 of the 300,000 tonnes of copper ore produced in 1995. The journal entry to record cost of goods sold is as follows:

Cost of goods sold (250,000 tonnes × [$2 per tonne + $4 per tonne]) . . 1,500,000
    Inventory of copper ore 1,500,000

Of the $600,000 of depletion recorded, $500,000 has been expensed as cost of goods sold, and $100,000 is included in inventory.

Restoration Costs   Suppose Burlington must restore the land to its original state after mining is completed, and this is expected to cost $1 million. After restoration, the property will revert back to its original owners. The revised depletion base now includes the restoration costs, and the depletion rate increases to $2.50 per tonne:

$$\text{Unit depletion rate} = \frac{\text{Capitalized cost + Restoration costs}}{\text{Estimated recoverable units}}$$

$$= \frac{\$4,000,000 + \$1,000,000}{2,000,000 \text{ tonnes}}$$

$$= \$2.50 \text{ per tonne}$$

The depletion amount for the 1995 production of 300,000 tonnes is $2.50 per tonne × 300,000 tonnes, or $750,000. The entry to record depletion is as follows:

Inventory of copper ore 750,000
    Mine property 600,000
    Accrued liability for mine restoration 150,000

The entry to record the depletion includes an accrued liability because the expenditure to restore the property has not yet been made. When the restoration expenditure is made, the liability is satisfied. The entry at that time, assuming that $1 million is ultimately required, is a debit to the liability ($1 million by that time) and a credit to cash of $1 million.

Change in Estimate

Natural resource operations entail considerable uncertainty regarding the amount of the resource that will be recovered or produced. When new estimates are made of recoverable amounts, a revised depletion rate must be computed based on the amount of cost remaining in the depletion base and the newly estimated number of units to be recovered. This new rate is applied to current and future years' production; there is no revision in the prior depletion charges or in the prior year's income. For example, suppose that in 1996, Burlington revised its estimate of remaining recoverable tonnes of copper ore downward to 1 million tonnes (from the 1.7 million

GLOBAL VIEW

Accounting for intangibles, especially goodwill, is one area where there are important differences in the various international financial reporting environments. In both the Netherlands and Great Britain, for example, there are two options in accounting for purchased goodwill. First, it can be capitalized and amortized, similar to the treatment in Canada. A second option in these countries, and the predominant practice, is to write off any purchased goodwill directly to retained earnings. The effect on both the balance sheet and the income statement can be quite large.

Suppose, for example, a UK airline company with 1 million shares outstanding and a net worth of £100 million acquires another airline for £50 million, which includes £20 million of purchased goodwill. If the acquiring firm chose the first alternative and capitalizes the goodwill, amortizing it over 40 years, the UK firm's earnings would be reduced by £500,000 (£20 million of goodwill divided by 40 years) each year for 40 years as compared with the second option, which is to immediately write off the goodwill to retained earnings. The second option would reduce the amount of shareholders' equity from £100 million to £80 million after the write-off. But, the second option also results in increased earnings and decreased net worth, each of which will have the effect of increasing the return on equity (ROE) for the firm in future years relative to the first option. If investors value securities based primarily on reported earnings and ROE, the second option may be a preferred reporting alternative because of its desirable effects on the financial statements.

There are other important differences across countries in accounting for intangible assets. In some countries (Spain) research and development costs can be capitalized and amortized. Several countries require a much shorter amortization period for goodwill than Canada. In Germany, Italy, and the Netherlands, for example, the maximum amortization period is five years.

The point is that accounting for intangibles is an area where there are important differences across countries. When analyzing financial statements from international companies, it is critically important to understand the accounting treatment of intangibles, especially goodwill.

that would be expected based on the original estimate). The depletion rate for 1996 and thereafter would be the remaining depletion base, or $3.4 million, divided by the remaining estimated recoverable units, or 1 million tonnes, resulting in a depletion rate of $3.40 per tonne.

CONCEPT REVIEW

1. How is the depletion base determined?
2. How is the periodic amount of depletion determined?
3. If a natural resource is extracted during a period but not sold, where is the depletion recorded?

SUMMARY OF KEY POINTS

(L.O. 1)   1. Accounting issues associated with intangible assets are similar to those for other long-lived assets:
- Determining the initial carrying amount of the asset.
- Amortizing the initial carrying amount.
- Writing down the asset when there is a permanent impairment of value.

(L.O. 1)   2. Intangible assets are long-lived assets that:
- Lack physical substance, so they are distinguished from tangible assets.
- Have future economic benefits that are difficult to measure.
- Have a useful life that is difficult to determine.
- Are acquired for operational use.

(L.O. 1)   3. Intangible assets can be categorized according to their:
- Manner of acquisition.
- Identifiability.
- Exchangeability.
- Period of expected benefit.

(L.O. 2)   4. The conceptual guidelines for accounting for intangible assets are similar to those for tangible assets:
- The cost principle is used to determine the initial carrying amount.
- The matching principle is used to determine periodic amortization.
- The revenue principle is used to guide the recording of revenues and gains and losses upon sale or impairment of value.

(L.O. 3)   5. *CICA Handbook* Section 3060 requires that the cost of an intangible asset be allocated to expense in a rational and systematic manner over the asset's estimated useful life, but in no case can the period exceed 40 years. This process is called amortization.

(L.O. 3)   6. The cost of patents, including costs of successfully defending them in court, is capitalized and amortized over the period of their estimated useful life, but no longer than the patent's legal life of 17 years.

(L.O. 3)   7. Copyrights provide protection to the authors of literary, musical, artistic, and similar works. Although a copyright provides protection for the life of the author plus an additional 50 years, *CICA Handbook* Section 3060 requires amortization over the lesser of the estimated useful life or 40 years.

(L.O. 3)   8. Organization costs incurred in organizing a business include costs such as legal, accounting, promotional, and clerical activities. Organization costs should be capitalized and amortized. While the maximum period allowed is 40 years, most firms amortize organization costs over a much shorter period.

(L.O. 4)   9. Development-stage companies should use the same assessment of future benefit and recoverability that established companies use in determining what costs can be capitalized.

(L.O. 4)   10. Goodwill is the most common unidentifiable intangible asset recognized in financial statements, and it is recognized only when there is an acquisition. Goodwill is recorded in an amount equal to the excess of the cost of the acquired company over the sum of values assigned to the net identifiable assets. Goodwill is amortized over its estimated useful life, but in no case should the period exceed 40 years.

(L.O. 4)   11. Negative goodwill (badwill) is allocated proportionally to reduce the values assigned to the nonmonetary assets of the acquired firm.

(L.O. 5)   12. *CICA Handbook* Section 3450 requires firms to expense research and development costs as incurred and to disclose the amount of R&D expense for each period reported.

(L.O. 6)   13. *SFAS No. 86* requires that all computer software costs be expensed until the technical and economic feasibility of the software has been established. *SFAS No. 86* requires capitalization of the costs incurred in the development of computer software to be sold or leased after the technical and economic feasibility has been established.

(L.O. 7)   14. Natural resources are wasting assets that are consumed during production. The major accounting problems for natural resources are determining the depletion base and the depletion rate.

(L.O. 8)   15. Oil and gas companies may use either the successful-efforts or the full-cost method for accounting for exploration costs (see Appendix 13A). Under the successful-efforts method, only the exploration costs of successful exploration are capitalized as the cost of the resource. Under the full-cost method, all costs of exploration can be capitalized as the cost of the resources as long as this amount is less than the estimated value of the resources discovered.

REVIEW PROBLEM

Munn, Inc., reported other noncurrent asset account balances on December 31, 1995, as follows:

Patent	$192,000
Accumulated amortization	(24,000)
Net patent	$168,000

Transactions during 1996 and other information relating to Munn's other noncurrent assets included the following:

a. The patent was purchased from Grey Company on January 2, 1994, when the remaining legal life was 16 years. On January 2, 1996, Munn determined that the remaining useful life of the patent was only eight years from the date of its acquisition.

b. On January 3, 1996, in connection with the purchase of a trademark from Cody Corp., the parties entered into a noncompetition agreement. Munn paid Cody $800,000, of which three-quarters related to the trademark and one-quarter reflected Cody's agreement not to compete for a period of five years in the line of business covered by the trademark. Munn considers the life of the trademark to be indefinite.

c. On January 3, 1996, Munn acquired all the non-cash assets and assumed all liabilities of Amboy Company at a cash purchase price of $1,200,000. Munn determined that the fair value of the net assets acquired in the transaction is $800,000.

Required

1. Prepare a schedule of amortization for 1996 relating to Munn's other noncurrent assets assuming Munn chooses the maximum amortization period for intangibles.
2. Prepare the other noncurrent assets section of the balance sheet for Munn on December 31, 1996.

SOLUTION

1. Schedule of amortization relating to other noncurrent assets for the year ended December 31, 1996:

Amortization of intangibles:	
Patent	$28,000
Trademark	15,000
Noncompetition agreement	40,000
Goodwill	10,000
Total amortization expense	$93,000

2. Other noncurrent assets section of balance sheet, December 31, 1996:

Patent, net of accumulated amortization of $52,000	$140,000
Trademark, net of accumulated amortization of $15,000	585,000
Noncompetition agreement, net of accumulated amortization of $40,000	160,000
Goodwill, net of accumulated amortization of $10,000	390,000

Computations

1. **Patent** On January 3, 1996, Munn determined that the patent has a shorter useful life than originally used in establishing an amortization schedule. This is a change in estimate and is accounted for prospectively. The remaining amortized balance is written off over the new estimate of useful life:

Net patent balance at Jan. 2/96: ($192,000 − $24,000)*	$168,000
Remaining life of patent (divide by)	÷ 6
Amortization for 1996	$ 28,000

* The accumulated amortization at Jan. 2/96 is computed as ($192,000 ÷ 16 years) × 2 years = $24,000.

2. **Trademark** The cost of the trademark is three-quarters of $800,000, or $600,000. Munn considers the trademark to have an indefinite life, but the maximum period over which intangibles can be amortized is 40 years. The trademark need not be amortized over 20 years, even though this is the legal life of a trademark. Trademarks are renewable; hence, in reality they have an indefinite legal life. The amortization for 1996 is $600,000 divided by 40 years, or $15,000.
3. **Noncompetition agreement** The cost of the noncompetition agreement is one-quarter of $800,000, or $200,000. The agreement has a useful life of five years; thus, the amortization for 1996 is $200,000 divided by five years, or $40,000.
4. **Goodwill** First compute the amount of goodwill.

Purchase price of acquired firm	$1,200,000
Less: Fair value of net assets acquired	800,000
Excess of cost over net assets acquired	$ 400,000

The goodwill is $400,000. No mention is made of the period over which the goodwill is expected to yield excess earnings. Munn could select a shorter period, but in this solution, the maximum of 40 years is assumed. The amortization for 1996 is $400,000 divided by 40 years, or $10,000.

Computations of Account Balances at December 31, 1996

	Patent	Trademark	Noncompet. Agreement	Goodwill
Balance, Dec. 31/95	$168,000	0	0	0
Additions, on Jan. 3/96		$600,000	$200,000	$400,000
Deduct 1996 amortization	(28,000)	(15,000)	(40,000)	(10,000)
Balance, Dec. 31/96	$140,000	$585,000	$160,000	$390,000

APPENDIX 13A: *Guidelines for Oil and Gas Companies*

Determining Exploration Costs to Capitalize for Oil and Gas Companies

Oil and gas companies incur large costs exploring for oil and gas deposits. Extensive exploration activities are undertaken when management expects the overall results from such activities not only to repay the costs of the exploration but also to earn a fair return for the company. When a company pursues exploration by drilling test wells in the search for oil and gas reserves, there is considerable risk that some wells will be dry, or unsuccessful. With a large, well-developed exploration program of drilling in areas where there are indications that mineral resources are present, companies expect to have some successful wells that locate recoverable oil and gas, and they expect that these successful efforts will be sufficiently productive to earn the firm a fair return on its overall investment. An important accounting issue is how to record the exploration costs of the discovered mineral resources.

As shown in Exhibit 13–4, there are two methods of determining the amount of exploration costs to capitalize and include in the depletion base:

1. **Successful-efforts method** Under the successful-efforts method, only the exploration costs of successful wells are capitalized in the cost of the natural resource. Exploration costs of wells that are not successful are expensed as incurred. This method is used frequently by the large integrated oil companies.

2. **Full-cost method** Under the full-cost method, all exploration costs are capitalized in the cost of the natural resource as long as the estimated value of the reserves discovered from the successful wells is equal to or greater than the amount to be capitalized. This method tends to be used by smaller companies whose primary business is exploration.

Because exploration costs are often very large in the oil and gas industry, the two methods can result in very different financial statements. The differences are illustrated with the following example.

Example   In year 1, Wildcat Exploration incurs costs of $2 million each in drilling 20 different oil wells exploring for oil and gas. Nineteen of the wells are unsuccessful, but one well does result in the discovery of recoverable oil reserves.

Geological procedures and technology exist with which to estimate the amount of oil that can be extracted from a successful well with reasonable accuracy. Since oil and gas are regularly traded commodities, market prices are readily available, and an estimate of the value of the discovery can be made. Suppose Wildcat's one successful well has estimated reserves of 10 million barrels and the type of crude oil discovered has a current market price of $8 per barrel. The estimated value of the reserves in the successful well is $80 million.

1. **Successful-efforts method** If the successful-efforts method is used, the exploration costs of the 19 unsuccessful wells are expensed, and exploration cost of the 1 successful well of $2 million is recorded as an asset. The entry to record the above exploration activities using the successful-efforts method is as follows:

Cost of oil reserves (included in depletion base)	2,000,000	
Exploration expense	38,000,000	
Cash, payables, accruals, etc.		40,000,000

The capitalized $2 million would be recorded as depletion as oil is extracted from the well at a depletion rate of $0.20 per barrel extracted ($2 million ÷ 10 million barrels).

2. **Full-cost method** If the full-cost method is used, all of the exploration costs, or $40 million, would be capitalized as the cost of the oil reserves as long as the amount capitalized is less than the estimated value of oil discovered from this exploration effort. Since the resources have an estimated value of $80 million, the entry to capitalize the exploration costs under the full-cost method is the following:

Cost of oil reserves (included in depletion base)	40,000,000	
Cash, payables, accruals, etc.		40,000,000

The capitalized $40 million would be recorded as depletion as oil is extracted from the well at a depletion rate of $4 per barrel extracted ($40 million ÷ 10 million barrels).

Suppose that in the year after the above discovery, Wildcat extracts 1 million barrels of crude oil from the successful well at an extraction cost of $0.10 per barrel. Three-quarters of the production is sold without further refining before year-end, and the remaining one-fourth is left in year-end inventory. The entries to record these events for the successful efforts and full-cost methods are as follows:

1. Successful-efforts method:

   To record depletion and extraction costs on extracted reserves:

Inventory of oil [($0.20 + $0.10) × 1 million barrels]	300,000	
Cost of oil reserves (depletion) [$0.20 × 1 million barrels]		200,000
Cash, accruals (extraction costs) [$0.10 × 1 million barrels]		100,000

   To record cost of goods sold for 750,000 barrels sold:

Cost of oil sold ($0.30 per barrel × 750,000 barrels)	225,000	
Inventory of oil		225,000

2. Full-cost method:

   To record depletion and extraction costs on extracted reserves:

Inventory of oil [($4.00 + $0.10) × 1 million barrels]	4,100,000	
Cost of oil reserves (depletion) [$4.00 × 1 million barrels] . . .		4,000,000
Cash, accruals (extraction costs) [$0.10 × 1 million barrels] . .		100,000

   To record cost of goods sold for 750,000 barrels sold:

Cost of oil sold ($4.10 per barrel × 750,000 barrels)	3,075,000	
Inventory of oil		3,075,000

Substantially different income statement and balance sheet effects result from these two methods. For simplicity, assume only exploration costs in the depletion base. Wildcat Exploration would show the following amounts in its financial statements, depending on whether it used the successful-efforts or the full-cost method:

	Successful-Efforts Method		Full-Cost Method	
	Year 1	**Year 2**	**Year 1**	**Year 2**
Balance Sheet				
Inventory of oil	0	$ 75,000	0	$ 1,025,000
Cost of oil reserves	$ 2,000,000	1,800,000	$40,000,000	36,000,000
Income Statement				
Exploration expense	$38,000,000	0	0	0
Cost of oil sold	0	$ 225,000	0	$ 3,075,000

The example illustrates that the two methods of accounting for exploration costs can result in substantially different earnings and total assets. The differences are magnified by increases in exploration expenditures and the proportion of unsuccessful wells. The issue of accounting for exploration costs is controversial. Advocates of the full-cost method argue that the true cost of discovering one successful well is not only the direct cost of finding the one successful well but rather the cost of all exploration. In undertaking an exploration effort in which the success of each well is unknown before it is completed, the firm is willing to invest $40 million into a total exploration effort with the expectation that the effort will result in one or more resource discoveries whose value is greater than the $40 million spent. Thus, full-cost advocates maintain that the cost of the one or more successful wells includes the exploration cost of all wells in the venture and that all such exploration costs are properly recorded as an asset.

Those advocating successful-efforts accounting, on the other hand, argue that only the exploration efforts that result in future benefits are properly capitalized. Exploration costs associated with unsuccessful wells do not provide future benefits, so these costs should be expensed as they are incurred. To capitalize these costs gives the misleading impression that future cash flows are expected from the unsuccessful wells. This results in an overstatement of current period income and understatement of future period income through higher cost of resources sold.

This controversy has been resolved by allowing oil and gas companies to choose either the successful-efforts or the full-costing method. Section 3060, paragraph .25 of the *CICA Handbook* states that:

> For an oil and gas property, the cost of the capital asset comprises acquisition costs, development costs and certain exploration costs depending on whether the enterprise accounts for its oil and gas properties using the full cost method or the successful efforts method. An enterprise applies the method of accounting for acquisition, exploration, and development costs that it considers to be appropriate to its operations and applies the method consistently to all its properties.

Apparently, the method used is not as important as its appropriateness to the enterprise and the application of the chosen method on a consistent basis.

The following are examples of disclosures by oil and gas companies. Note that Imperial Oil Limited uses the successful-efforts method while North Canadian Oils Limited and Rio Alto Exploration Limited use the full-cost method.

Imperial Oil Limited—Summary of Significant Accounting Policies

Property, Plant and Equipment

Property, plant and equipment, including related preoperational and design costs of major projects, are recorded at cost. Cost for property, plant and equipment of acquired companies is the fair market value to the company at the date of acquisition.

The company follows the successful-efforts method of accounting for its exploration and development activities. Under this method, costs of exploration acreage are capitalized and amortized over the period of exploration or until a discovery is made. Costs of exploration wells are initially capitalized until their success can be determined. If the well is successful, the costs remain capitalized; otherwise they are expensed. Capitalized exploration costs are reevaluated annually. All other exploration costs are expensed as incurred. Development costs, including the cost of natural gas and natural-gas liquids used as injectants in enhanced (tertiary) oil recovery projects, are capitalized.

Maintenance and repair costs are expensed as incurred. Improvements that increase or prolong the service capacity of an asset are capitalized.

Investment tax credits and other similar grants are treated as a reduction of the capitalized cost of the assets to which they apply.

Depreciation and depletion of the capitalized costs of producing properties are calculated using the unit-of-production method. Depreciation of other plant and equipment is calculated using the straight-line method, based on the estimated service life of the asset.

Gains or losses on assets sold or otherwise disposed of are included in the consolidated statement of earnings.

North Canadian Oils Limited—Notes to Consolidated Financial Statements

1. Summary of Significant Accounting Policies

Oil and Gas Operations

The Company follows the full-cost method of accounting for oil and natural gas properties and related expenditures, whereby all costs related to the exploration for and development of oil and gas reserves are capitalized in country-by-country cost centres. Such costs include those related to lease acquisitions, geological and geophysical activities, lease rentals on non-producing properties and drilling of productive and non-productive wells. Proceeds from disposal of properties are normally deducted from the full-cost pool without recognition of gain or loss.

Depletion of oil and gas properties and depreciation of production equipment and facilities are calculated using the unit-of-production method based upon estimated proven reserves, before royalties, converted to a common unit of measure using relative energy content of six thousand cubic feet of natural gas equalling one barrel of oil.

The Company applies a ceiling test to capitalized costs to ensure that such costs do not exceed estimated future net revenues from production of proven reserves at year end market prices less future administrative, financing and income tax costs.

Rio Alto Exploration Ltd.—Notes to Consolidated Financial Statements

(b) Exploration and Development Costs

The Company follows the full-cost method of accounting for exploration and development expenditures in accordance with the guideline issued by the Canadian Institute of Chartered Accountants, whereby all costs associated with the exploration for and development of oil and gas reserves are capitalized in cost centres on a country by country basis. Costs capitalized include land acquisitions, drilling, geological and geophysical, interest and overhead expenses related to exploration and development activities. Gains or losses are not recognized upon disposition of oil and gas properties unless crediting the proceeds against accumulated costs would result in a material change in the rate of depletion.

Costs capitalized in the cost centres are depleted using the unit-of-production method, based on estimated proven oil and gas reserves as determined by Company and independent engineers. For purposes of the depletion calculation, oil and gas reserves are converted to a common unit of measure on the basis of their relative energy content which is 6 mcf of gas to 1 bbl of oil.

In applying the full-cost method, the Company performs a ceiling test which restricts the capitalized costs less accumulated depletion and depreciation for each cost centre from exceeding an amount equal to the estimated undiscounted value of future net revenues from proven oil and gas reserves, based on current prices and costs, and after deducting estimated future general and administrative expenses, financing costs and income taxes for each cost centre. For the purposes of the ceiling test the oil and gas prices which were effective at the balance sheet date were used, which in the case of oil, was $23 Cdn. per barrel and $1.54 per mcf for gas.

The Company annually reviews the costs associated with undeveloped properties to determine whether the costs will be recoverable. An impairment allowance is made if the results of the review indicate an impairment has been incurred.

Accounting Guideline for the Oil and Gas Industry

In September 1986, the Accounting Standards Board issued an Accounting Guideline for those companies in the oil and gas industry who elected to use the full-cost method. Guidelines are interpretations of *Handbook Recommendations* or other matters of accounting practice and as such do not have the authority of the *Recommendations*. In this case, therefore, the guideline is the suggested manner for applying the full-cost method of accounting in the oil and gas industry.

The basic characteristics of the guideline for the oil and gas industry follow:

1. Costs capitalized—all costs associated with the property acquisition, exploration, and development activities should be capitalized within the appropriate cost centre.
2. Cost centre—a cost centre comprises the oil and gas activities of an enterprise located within the geographical boundaries of a country. There should be only one cost centre for each country in which an enterprise has oil and gas activity.
3. Depletion and depreciation—capitalized costs within a cost centre should be depleted and depreciated on a unit of production basis.
4. Ceiling test—the ceiling test is designed to limit the aggregate costs which may be carried forward for amortization against future revenues. The test determines if the enterprise will be able to recover the capitalized costs from each cost centre and from the aggregated cost centres. Any excess of the carrying amounts of aggregated costs over estimated future net revenues should be written off to expense. The ceiling test should be conducted at least on an annual basis. The write-offs (if any) are categorized as additional depletion and depreciation.

APPENDIX 13B: *Estimating Goodwill*

A potential purchaser of a company must decide how much to offer for the acquired company. Once the purchase price is determined and estimates of the fair market value of the assets acquired have been made, goodwill can be determined. Goodwill is defined as the difference between the purchase price and the fair market value of the net assets acquired. *CICA Handbook,* Section 1580, paragraph .45, provides guidance on estimating the fair market values of assets acquired. This topic is covered in most texts on advanced accounting; it is not covered further here. Our focus is on determining the purchase price so that goodwill can be computed.

The purchase price is the result of negotiations between a buyer and a seller, and the negotiating skills of these parties can be expected to influence the agreed-on amount. Both parties come to the negotiations with an estimated value for the firm to be exchanged. There are a number of ways that the value of a firm can be estimated. Two relatively straightforward methods for estimating a purchase price, which indirectly yield a value for goodwill, are presented first. This discussion is followed by a more detailed presentation of a method that attempts to estimate the value of goodwill directly. Each approach is used to estimate the purchase price and goodwill for the example given in the chapter involving the purchase of Cafe Corporation by Hotel Company. In each case, the fair market value of the net assets acquired is assumed to be $130,000, as given in the chapter.

Earnings Multiple Approach

Analysts often compute the price to earnings multiple of firms, which is market price per common share divided by the earnings per share. Earnings multiples, also called PE ratios, tend to be approximately the same for the firms in an industry and fairly stable over time. Thus, one way to value a firm is to estimate an appropriate earnings multiplier for the firm's industry and then apply this multiplier to an estimate of the firm's future earnings.[9] Suppose Hotel Company management estimates the earnings multiplier for the restaurant industry to be 7, and that Cafe Corporation's future earnings are expected to be $30,000 per year. The estimated value of Cafe using the earnings multiplier approach is:

$$\text{Estimated value} = \text{Earnings multiplier} \times \text{Estimated future earnings}$$
$$= 7 \qquad\qquad\qquad \times \$30,000$$
$$= \$210,000$$

If Hotel were to acquire Cafe for a purchase price of $210,000, goodwill would be $210,000 less $130,000, or $80,000.

Discounted Present Value of Future Cash Flows

A second approach is to estimate the cash flows that a buyer might expect to receive from the operations of an acquired company and, using an appropriate discount rate, calculate the present value of these cash flows. This is an estimate of the value of the company.[10] Suppose, for example, that Hotel estimates that Cafe will continue to earn $30,000 in cash per year for the next 20 years, and that Hotel desires to earn 15% on its investment in Cafe. The present value of $30,000 per year for 20 years, discounted at 15%, provides an estimate of the total value of Cafe:

$$\text{Estimated value} = (\text{PVA}, 15\%, 20) \times \$30,000$$
$$= 6.25933 \qquad\quad \times \$30,000$$
$$= \$187,780$$

If Hotel were to acquire Cafe for $187,780, goodwill would be $187,780 less $130,000, or $57,780.

---

[9] The earnings multiplier could be based on an average PE across firms in the industry over an appropriate period. Establishing expected future earnings is briefly discussed in a later section of this appendix.

[10] Selecting the appropriate discount rate is a complex decision addressed in courses on finance. It is addressed briefly later in this appendix.

Excess Earnings Approach   With both of the above methods, the amount of goodwill is determined indirectly after an estimate of the total value of the firm is determined. Alternatively, the focus may be placed directly on estimating the value of goodwill using an excess earnings approach.

Briefly, this approach determines the value of goodwill as the present value of the excess earnings a firm is expected to earn over earnings that would usually be expected from a firm of average or normal profitability in the industry:

$$\text{Goodwill} = (\text{PVA}, i, N) \times \text{Excess earnings}$$

where i is the appropriate rate for discounting the excess earnings and N is the number of periods for which the excess earnings are expected. Excess earnings are the difference between expected future earnings and an estimate of the earnings that the net assets being acquired would normally be expected to earn:

$$\text{Excess earnings} = \text{Estimated future earnings} - \text{Normal earnings}$$

Finally, normal earnings are estimated as the product of a normal rate of return on net assets for firms in this industry and the fair value of net assets being acquired:

$$\text{Normal earnings} = \begin{bmatrix} \text{Normal rate of} \\ \text{return on net assets} \\ \text{for firms in this industry} \end{bmatrix} \times \begin{bmatrix} \text{Fair value of} \\ \text{net assets being} \\ \text{acquired} \end{bmatrix}$$

Application of this method requires five steps:

1. Estimate future earnings.
2. Determine a normal rate of return.
3. Determine normal earnings.
4. Determine excess earnings.
5. Compute goodwill.

Step 1. Estimate Future Earnings   Estimates of a firm's future earnings usually begin with an analysis of the firm's past earnings. Past earnings are a useful point of departure because they reflect neither optimistic nor pessimistic thinking about the future. Forecasters will have to justify why they expect earnings to differ from the historical trend.

Suppose Cafe Corp. has the following five-year earnings history:

Year	Earnings
1990	$ 26,000
1991	25,000
1992	30,000
1993	32,000
1994	37,000
Five-year total	$150,000

What should be used as the assessment of the future earnings of the firm? If a simple five-year average is used, the estimate of future earnings is $30,000 ($150,000 ÷ 5 years). However, a five-year average may be too long. Perhaps, because of changes in the business, the average of the most recent three years is more appropriate. If that were the case, the estimate of future earnings would be $33,000 [($30,000 + $32,000 + $37,000) ÷ 3]. Arguments could be advanced in support of other estimates as well. The purpose is to select a realistic and reasonable time frame to use in estimating a value for goodwill. For exposition, assume an annual earnings estimate of $30,000.[11]

Step 2. Determine a Normal Rate of Return   The rate of return on net assets varies across firms, although it is usually reasonably constant within industries. If an industry estimate of a normal rate of return can be obtained, it can be used in the analysis.

---

[11] Adjustments to earnings may be necessary before they are used to forecast future earnings. For example, if the above earnings for Cafe include an after tax extraordinary gain of $5,000 in 1994, the 1994 earnings should be adjusted to $32,000 for purposes of forecasting future earnings. Also, if the acquired firm uses accounting methods different from the acquiring firm and these methods will be changed after the acquisition, forecast earnings should be computed using the new accounting methods. For more on valuing closely held businesses, see W. Rissin and R. Zulli, "Valuation of a Closely Held Business," *Journal of Accountancy*, June 1988, pp. 38–44.

Industry averages are available through various financial services, or they can be determined by an analysis of annual reports and other financial data. One problem is that estimates of normal rates of return are typically computed from historical cost–balance sheet data rather than from data on fair market value. This approach tends to bias the estimate of the normal rate of return upward because fair market values are generally higher than historical cost. For the current example, assume that the industry rate of return for Cafe is 12%.

Step 3. Determine Normal Earnings Once the normal rate of return for the industry and the fair value of the net assets acquired are decided, the expected normal earnings for the firm can be established:

$$
\begin{aligned}
\text{Normal earnings} &= \text{(Rate of return)(Fair value of net assets)} \\
&= (0.12)(\$130,000) \\
&= \$15,600
\end{aligned}
$$

Step 4. Determine Excess Earnings The difference between the computed normal earnings for the firm and the estimate or forecast of future earnings represents the excess earnings of the firm. These are earnings not related specifically or individually to the net identifiable assets. They are considered the earnings resulting from the goodwill of the firm. In this case, the excess earnings are:

$$
\begin{aligned}
\text{Excess earnings} &= \text{Estimated future earnings} - \text{Normal earnings} \\
&= \$30,000 - \$15,600 \\
&= \$14,400
\end{aligned}
$$

Considerable estimation goes into the determination of excess earnings. The estimate depends on estimating the firm's future earnings, assigning an amount as the fair value of the net identifiable assets, and establishing the appropriate rate of return to apply to the fair value of the assets. Rather than proceed with a single figure as the estimate of excess earnings, a range of excess earnings could be used and then a range of goodwill values computed. Despite the appeal of a range of values, only a single value is used in the current example.

Step 5. Compute Goodwill A number of values for goodwill could result depending on what discount rate is used to value the excess earnings stream and on how many periods the excess earnings are assumed to continue in the future. A few examples follow:

a. Excess earnings are expected to continue indefinitely (in perpetuity). If the appropriate discount rate is 12%, the computed present value of the excess earnings stream is:[12]

$$
\text{Value of goodwill} = \frac{\text{Excess earnings}}{\text{Discount rate}} = \frac{\$14,400}{0.12} = \$120,000
$$

b. If the risk associated with the excess earnings is regarded as greater than that of the identifiable assets, a higher discount rate is appropriate for determining the value of the goodwill. If we assume that this rate is appropriately estimated at 20%, the value of the goodwill is:

$$
\text{Value of goodwill} = \frac{\text{Excess earnings}}{\text{Discount rate}} = \frac{\$14,400}{0.20} = \$72,000
$$

The higher the assumed risk, the higher the discount rate and the lower the value of goodwill. Selecting the appropriate discount rate is difficult and can greatly influence the final result. Accountants generally agree that excess earnings are more risky than normal earnings and that a higher discount rate is therefore appropriate. If the value of goodwill is assumed to be $72,000, the purchaser would be willing to pay up to this amount plus the

---

[12] The present value of an ordinary annuity given in Table 6A–4 is:

$$
\left[1 - \frac{1}{(1 + i)^n} \right] \div i.
$$

As n increases without limit, $1 \div (1 + i)^n$ approaches zero and the present value (discount) factor approaches $1 \div i$.

fair market value of the net assets ($130,000), or a total of up to $202,000 to acquire the firm. (This is the value assumed earlier in the Cafe example.)

Excess earnings may not be expected to continue indefinitely. In this situation, determining the periods during which excess earnings might reasonably be expected presents another difficult problem. If a period of 10 years for Cafe Corporation's excess earnings is assumed, present value annuity tables can be used to determine the value of goodwill. Assuming that a discount rate of 12% is appropriate:

$$\text{Value of goodwill} = (\text{PVA}, 12\%, 10)(\text{Excess earnings})$$
$$= (5.65022)(\$14,400)$$
$$= \$81,363$$

The value of goodwill would increase (decrease) if the number of periods the excess earnings are expected to continue is increased (decreased). By a computation analogous to the computation in step (5b) above, if the discount rate is increased, the value of goodwill is reduced.

In the above analysis, several alternative computations of the value for goodwill in the acquisition of Cafe by Hotel Company have been considered. The results range from a low of $57,780 to a high of $120,000. A different range of values would result if different assumptions were made. While the determination of the value of goodwill is a difficult and highly uncertain task, the most important concerns from an accounting point of view are that goodwill is determined for recording purposes after the acquisition purchase price has been set, and that the value of the goodwill equals the purchase price less the fair value of the net identifiable assets acquired.

QUESTIONS

1. What distinguishes intangible assets from tangible assets? How are intangible assets reported on the balance sheet?
2. What outlays are properly considered part of the cost of an intangible asset?
3. Cite the factors that should determine whether an intangible asset is amortized and, if so, over what period of time.
4. What is an identifiable intangible asset? Give some examples of such assets.
5. What is a franchise right? A trademark?
6. Define goodwill and the basis on which goodwill is amortized.
7. What is the role of the accountant in the valuation of goodwill?
8. What is negative goodwill? How does it arise? How is it treated for accounting purposes?
9. What is the maximum number of years over which a patent can be amortized? What determines this maximum? Under what circumstances, if any, should a shorter amortization period be used?
10. Define a deferred charge. Why is it an intangible asset? How are deferred charges distinguished from prepaid expenses? Give two examples of each.
11. What items are properly debited to organization costs? Should organization costs be amortized? Explain.
12. What are the guidelines for accounting for research and development (R&D) costs?
13. Distinguish between trademarks and copyrights.
14. Give examples of situations in which the accounting carrying value of an intangible asset can increase. Does the accounting value of an intangible necessarily bear a close relationship to its economic value?
15. What are the primary characteristics of goodwill?
16. Under what circumstances is goodwill capitalized?
17. Under what circumstances might goodwill not be amortized?
18. Explain impairment of value of an intangible asset. Assume that a patent originally costing $50,000 (accumulated patent amortization, $35,000) will probably not be used further by the company. Its estimated current value is $1,000. Give any indicated entry; if none, explain why.
19. Carter Company owns a trademark that it purchased originally for $40,000; it has been amortized to date in the amount of $26,000. The trademark has just been sold for $10,000 cash. Give any indicated entry; if none is needed, explain why.
20. What are the differences between natural resources and depreciable assets?
21. Describe the types of costs incurred by firms in connection with natural resources. Generally, how is each treated for accounting purposes when incurred?
22. How do firms determine the amount of depletion to be charged as an expense each accounting period?

23. Describe the successful-efforts method and the full-cost method of accounting for exploration costs. Which method is required for financial reporting?
24. Describe the similarities between expenditures for research and development and expenditures for exploration of oil and gas.

25. How is goodwill treated differently in the United Kingdom as compared to Canadian GAAP?

CASES

C 13-1
(L.O. 2, 4)

NBC Settles a Logo Problem   The National Broadcasting Company (NBC) incurred costs of $750,000 in the development of its N logo shown at intervals in its TV broadcasts. Shortly after the N logo was announced and first used by NBC, it was discovered that an educational TV network in Nebraska had already been using a similar logo. To obtain exclusive rights to its already costly logo, NBC agreed, in an out-of-court settlement, to pay $55,000 cash to Nebraska Network and to furnish it with various new and used colour TV equipment without cost (NBC book value, $350,000). The equipment to be transferred was conservatively valued at $500,000 by independent appraisers. A spokesperson for the Nebraska Network said the equipment to be provided by NBC would have cost $750,000 if bought new and that, for the two years preceding the settlement, efforts to get a $750,000 appropriation from the Nebraska legislature to buy such equipment had been unsuccessful. Terms of the settlement provided that $2,500 of the cash settlement was to be paid to William Korbus, who had designed the Nebraska Network's N logo at a cost of $100. Delivery of the equipment to the Nebraska Network was to begin approximately three months after the announced settlement and was to occur over a four-month interval.

Required

1. Briefly explain how you believe NBC should account for its original costs of $750,000 related to the logo. How should it account for the settlement with the Nebraska Network and Korbus?
2. Assuming that accounting principles for not-for-profit organizations such as the Nebraska Network were similar to those for a commercial entity, briefly explain how Nebraska Network should account for the settlement.

C 13-2
(L.O. 2, 7)

Depletion: What Does It Mean in Financial Statements?   A friend of yours recently inherited capital stock in Megamining Corporation. The friend has just received the first annual financial report from the company since the inheritance. One aspect of the report in particular troubles your friend, so you have been asked for an explanation of what the company seems to be saying. The excerpt reads:

> Depletion of mines is computed on the basis of an overall unit rate applied to the amount of principal products sold from mine production. The corporation makes no representation that the annual amount represents the depletion actually sustained or the decline, if any, in mine values attributable to the year's operations, or that it represents anything other than a general provision for the amortization of the remaining book value of mines.

Specifically, your friend asks the following: (1) Is the depletion amount reported on the income statement meaningless? (2) Are the company's mines becoming more or less valuable? (3) What is the significance of the book value of the company's mines?

Required

Write a one-page response to your friend's questions. Identify each element of your response with the three questions your friend has asked.

C 13-3
(L.O. 2, 4)

The Directors Want to Increase Goodwill   Blass Equipment Corporation, a retail farm implements dealer, has increased its annual sales volume to a level 10 times greater than the annual sales of the dealership when purchased in 1968. At that time, a material amount of goodwill was recorded. The goodwill has never been amortized.

The board of directors of Blass recently received an offer to negotiate the sale of the company to a larger competitor. As a result, the majority of the board members want to increase the current amount of goodwill on the balance sheet because of the larger sales volume developed through intensive promotion and the current market prices of the company's products. However, a few of the company's board members would prefer to eliminate goodwill altogether from the balance sheet in order to prevent "possible misinterpretations." Goodwill was properly recorded when the business was acquired eight years ago.

Required

1. *a.* Discuss the meaning of the term *goodwill*. Do not discuss goodwill arising from consolidated statements or the conditions under which goodwill is recorded.

b. What technique is commonly used to estimate the value of goodwill in negotiations to purchase a going concern?

2. Why are the book and market values of the goodwill of Blass Corporation different?

3. Discuss the propriety of:

a. Increasing the stated value of goodwill prior to the negotiations.

b. Eliminating goodwill completely from the balance sheet prior to negotiations.

4. From an ethical point of view, do you believe the goodwill should be written down or left alone? Explain.

(AICPA adapted)

C 13–4
(L.O. 2, 3)

Value of a Trademark   TORONTO[13]—A Federal Court decision that gives Molson Breweries the right to register the trademark Molson's Blue means John Labatt Ltd. may have to change the name of Canada's best-selling brand of beer, say lawyers for Molson.

"It could ultimately mean that Labatt would have to change the name Blue," said trademark lawyer John Macera, acting for Molson.

The 10-page decision—which lawyers for the two major breweries received Wednesday—could cost Labatt up to $15-million in advertising alone, analysts said.

It assures the start of a major court battle between the rival breweries over who has the right to use the name.

The case hinges on Molson's 28-year-old claim to the brand name Blue—once the name of one of the company's ales—and Labatt's failure to ever register the name as its own trademark.

Any setback could mean a drop in a brand's market share—currently around 18 percent for Labatt's Blue, beverage analyst Martin Kaufman said.

Every one percentage point represents $10-million, he said. Changing the name and the repackaging of Blue would cost London, Ont.–based Labatt "10 times" the advertising cost of $15-million, he said.

Registering a trademark gives a company the exclusive right to use that mark in Canada. It also gives a company the right to sue for trademark infringement.

"There's a real probability that if we get this registered, that Labatt will be infringing the trademark if they continue to advertise and sell their product," Molson lawyer Mr. Macera said.

But Labatt says Molson could never win if it tried to stop Labatt from marketing Labatt's Blue.

"It's nonsense. They can't touch Labatt's Blue," said Joe Clark, vice-president of public affairs for Labatt Breweries of Canada.

But Molson says they have a case.

Conceivably, the company could even market another lager under the name Molson's Blue if they succeed in registering the name, Mr. Fremes said.

Molson's case is based on its claim to the name since March, 1962, for a beer then marketed as Molson's Blue.

The ale, now known as Old Stock Ale, still carries the words "The original blue" on its label.

In 1978, Molson applied to register the trademark.

The application was advertised in the Trademark Journal, and Labatt objected, appearing in front of a federal trademark tribunal.

Labatt lost and appealed to the federal court.

On Wednesday, the company lost again—giving Molson the right to register the name after 30 days, if Labatt has not appealed.

If Labatt does appeal, as Mr. Macera expects, a judge will decide who gets to use the name. The case hinges on one point: Labatt has never registered the trademark Blue.

Required

Discuss this article with respect to the possible effects of the legal suit on Labatt's financial statements.

C 13–5
(L.O. 2, 3, 4)

Magna   In its 1993 annual report, Magna shows goodwill in the amounts of $21.3 million and $17.8 million at December 31, 1993 and 1992, respectively.

Required

1. Approximately how much goodwill was acquired in 1993?

2. Approximately how much goodwill did Magna amortize in 1993?

3. What is the period over which goodwill is being amortized by Magna?

EXERCISES

E 13–1
(L.O. 1)

Overview: Characteristics of Intangible Assets   For each of the following independent events, indicate by placing a check mark in the appropriate cells to indicate (*a*) whether the asset involved is identifiable or unidentifiable, (*b*) its manner of acquisition, and (*c*) whether it should be capitalized.

---

[13] Laura Eggerton, "Battle Brewing that May Have Labatt Crying the Blues," *Globe and Mail*, June 22, 1990, p. B5.

Independent Event	Identifiability		Manner of Acquisition		Capitalized?	
	Identifiable	Unidentifiable	External	Internal	Yes	No
a. Purchased a patent.						
b. Purchased a trademark.						
c. During 10 years of operation, a company's goodwill has increased considerably.						
d. Trademark developed by the company.						
e. Patent developed by the company's research program.						
f. Copyright developed by the company over a five-year period.						
g. Prepaid insurance (five-year premium).						
h. Leasehold improvements (operating lease).						
i. Purchased a company (including $1 million of goodwill).						
j. Purchased a copyright.						
k. Franchise received by a public utility company.						
l. Paid legal fees to organize and incorporate a new business.						

E 13–2
(L.O. 2)

Sale and Purchase of a Patent: No Cash   On January 1, 1995, Vox Company sold a patent to Baker Company; the patent had a net carrying value on Vox's books of $20,000. As payment, Baker gave Vox an $80,000 note, which was payable in five equal annual instalments of $16,000, with the first payment payable on December 31, 1995. There was no established exchange price for the patent, and the note had no ready market value. The prevailing rate of interest for a note of this type at January 1, 1995, was 12%. At January 1, 1995, 5 years of the patent's legal life of 17 years had already expired. Disregard income taxes.

Required

1. Give the entry on January 1, 1995, that Vox Company should make. Also, give any related entries that Vox should make on December 31, 1995.
2. Give the entry that Baker Company should make on January 1, 1995.
3. Give the entries for payment of the first annual instalment on the note and for patent amortization that Baker Company should make on December 31, 1995 (end of the annual reporting period).

E 13–3
(L.O. 2)

Reporting Intangible Assets   The adjusted trial balance of United Business Machines Corporation showed the following selected account balances (all debits) at December 31, 1995, the end of the annual reporting period:

Cash.	$44,000
Patent (unamortized balance)	14,000
Accounts receivable (net of allowance)	90,000
Prepaid rent expense	1,000
Marketable equity securities, short term	50,000
Leasehold (rental prepayment)	17,000
Franchise (unamortized balance)	18,000
Rent revenue receivable (current)	3,000
Organization costs (unamortized)	9,000
Goodwill (unamortized)	60,000
Trademark (unamortized)	19,000
Prepaid insurance (two-thirds is long term)	6,000
Copyright (unamortized)	12,000

Equipment (net of accumulated depreciation).	$300,000
Notes receivable, trade (short term)	10,000
Cash in closed bank (percent expected to recover, 40%).	30,000
R&D costs (not capitalizable).	39,000

Required   Prepare the asset section of United's balance sheet at December 31, 1995. Include the proper balance sheet classifications with separate captions for intangible operating assets, deferred charges, and other assets. Assume that all needed amortization entries have been made.

E 13–4
(L.O. 2, 3, 4, 5)

Accounting for Intangible Assets   Select the best answer to each of the following. Briefly justify your choice.

1. Which of the following cost items would be matched with current revenues on a basis other than association of cause and effect?
   - *a.* Goodwill.
   - *b.* Sales commissions.
   - *c.* Cost of goods sold.
   - *d.* Purchases on account.

2. How should R&D costs be accounted for according to Section 3450?
   - *a.* They must be capitalized when incurred and then amortized over their estimated useful lives.
   - *b.* They must be expensed in the period incurred in all but a few instances.
   - *c.* They may be either capitalized or expensed when incurred, depending on the judgment of management.
   - *d.* They must be expensed in the period incurred unless it is expected that the expenditure will have some future benefits.

3. The accounting for a development-stage company:
   - *a.* May be different from that of other companies in numerous ways with regard to expenditures during the development stage.
   - *b.* Must be exactly the same as that of other companies in respect to accounting, reporting, and disclosure.
   - *c.* May capitalize costs that other companies are not permitted to capitalize.
   - *d.* Requires presentation of financial statements on the same basis as other companies and disclosure of certain cumulative amounts, along with disclosure of the fact that the company is a development-stage company.

4. Hilary Company's R&D records contained the following information for 1995:

Materials used in R&D projects.	$ 400,000
Equipment acquired that will have significant alternate future uses including future R&D projects	2,000,000
Depreciation expense for 1995 on above equipment	500,000
Personnel costs involved in R&D projects	1,000,000
Consulting fees paid to outsiders for R&D projects	100,000
Indirect costs reasonably allocable to R&D projects	200,000
	$4,200,000

The amount of R&D costs debited to expense and reported on Hilary's 1995 income statement should be:
   - *a.* $1,500,000.
   - *b.* $1,700,000.
   - *c.* $2,200,000.
   - *d.* $3,500,000.

5. Peter Company has invested $40,000 in a royalty-producing copyright. Peter's expected rate of return from the three-year project is 20%. The cash flow, net of income taxes, was $15,000 for the first year and $18,000 for the second year. Assuming that the rate of return is exactly 20%, what would be the cash flow, net of income taxes, for the third year?
   - *a.* $8,681.
   - *b.* $11,000.
   - *c.* $11,497.
   - *d.* $25,920.

(AICPA adapted)

E 13–5
(L.O. 1, 2, 3, 4)

Accounting for Intangible Assets   Select the best answer to each of the following. Briefly justify your choice.

1. A copyright granted to a composer in 1988 has a legal life of:
   - *a.* 17 years.
   - *b.* 28 years.
   - *c.* The life of the composer plus 50 years.
   - *d.* 40 years.

2. Which of the following is not properly classified as an intangible asset?
   a. A copyright acquired by purchase.
   b. Goodwill.
   c. A patent acquired by purchase.
   d. Losses incurred by a development-stage company.

3. Pan Corporation acquired Company Able in 1969 and Company Baker in 1993. In both instances, the acquired companies were dissolved and their assets and operations merged with other assets and activities of Pan. In both instances, Pan paid more than the current market value of the identifiable net assets for its acquisitions, and most of the difference was attributable to goodwill. In accounting for the goodwill:
   a. Pan must amortize the goodwill related to each company.
   b. Pan need not amortize the goodwill of either company.
   c. Pan need not amortize the goodwill associated with Able but must amortize the goodwill associated with Baker.
   d. Pan need not amortize the goodwill associated with Baker but must amortize the goodwill associated with Able.

4. Patents and copyrights have definite legal lives and should be amortized over:
   a. Their legal life, but not more than 40 years.
   b. Their useful life, but not more than 40 years.
   c. Their legal or useful life, whichever is shorter, but never in excess of 40 years.
   d. A period of 40 years.

5. Xenex Company incurred $50,000 of costs in R&D activities. These costs need not be expensed if:
   a. They give promise of a successful outcome.
   b. The projects are completed and have culminated in a profitable patent for Xenex.
   c. Xenex is doing contract research for another company, and the costs relate to the contract that is still in progress.
   d. The projects were begun before the issuance of *CICA Handbook* Section 3450.

6. Organizational costs:
   a. Are not covered by GAAP and need not be amortized.
   b. Must be amortized over a period not to exceed 40 years.
   c. Should be reported as a contra item under owners' equity.
   d. Should be expensed as soon as they are incurred.

7. Some intangibles are characterized as specifically identifiable, while another classification is unidentifiable. An example of the latter is:
   a. A trademark.   c. A franchise for a limited term.
   b. A perpetual franchise.   d. Goodwill.

8. The legal life of a patent currently is:
   a. 20 years.   c. The life of the holder of the patent.
   b. 17 years.   d. 40 years.

E 13–6
(L.O. 2, 3, 5)

Amortization of Intangibles   Select the best answer to each of the following. Briefly justify your choices.

1. If a company constructs a laboratory building to be used as an R&D facility, the cost of the building is matched against earnings as:
   a. R&D expense during the period(s) of construction.
   b. Depreciation deducted as part of R&D costs.
   c. Depreciation or immediate write-off, depending on company policy.
   d. An expense at such time as productive research and development has been obtained from the facility.

2. Why are certain costs of doing business capitalized when incurred and then depreciated or amortized over subsequent accounting cycles?
   a. To reduce the federal income tax liability.
   b. To aid management in the decision-making process.
   c. To match operating costs with revenues as earned.
   d. To adhere to the accounting concept of conservatism.

3. In January 1992, Idea Company purchased a patent for a new consumer product for $170,000. At the time of purchase the patent was valid for 17 years. Because of the competitive nature of the market, the patent was estimated to have a useful life of 10 years. During 1996, the product was removed from the market in response to a government order because of a potential health hazard

present in the product. What amount should Idea debit to expense during 1996, assuming that amortization is recorded at the end of each reporting year?

a. $10,000.   c. $102,000.

b. $17,000.   d. $130,000.

4. On January 1 of the current year, Melvin Corporation sold a patent. Melvin Corporation originally paid $50,000 for the patent, which now has a book value of $9,000. The terms of sale included cash payments as follows:

$5,000 down payment.

$5,000 per year, payable on December 31 of each of the next two years.

The sale agreement did not specify any interest; however, 10% would be a reasonable rate for this type of transaction. Melvin Corporation should report a gain on disposal of:

a. $4,678.   c. $6,000.

b. $5,000.   d. $5,678.

(AICPA adapted)

E 13–7
(L.O. 4)

Compute Goodwill: Entries   On January 1, 1995, the balance sheet of Nance Toaster Company (a sole proprietorship) was as follows:

Assets

Accounts receivable (net of allowance)	$ 60,000
Inventory	90,000
Plant and equipment (net of depreciation).	200,000
Land	30,000
Total	$380,000

Liabilities

Current	$38,000	
Noncurrent	80,000	$118,000
Owners' equity		262,000
Total		$380,000

On January 1, 1995, Major Appliance Corporation purchased all of the assets and assumed all of the liabilities listed on the above balance sheet for $290,000 cash. The assets, on date of purchase, were valued by Major as follows: accounts receivable (net), $50,000; inventory, $85,000; plant and equipment (net), $200,000; and land, $45,000. The liabilities were valued at their carrying amounts.

Required

1. Compute the amount of goodwill included in the purchase price paid by Major Corporation.
2. Give the entry that Major Corporation should make to record the purchase of Nance Company.
3. What is the minimum amount of goodwill that Major Corporation can amortize at the end of 1995? Give the amortization entry.

E 13–8
(L.O. 3)

Recording a Franchise Contract   On January 1, 1995, Sam's Neighborhood Cleaners (SNC) signed a contract with Super-Cleaners, Incorporated. The agreement provided for the payment of a franchise fee by SNC, and subsequent periodic franchise royalties based on sales. In return for these royalties, Super-Cleaners will provide specified services in the future (e.g., promotional suggestions). The franchise fee was $50,000, payable as $10,000 in cash and the remaining balance payable in three equal annual instalments including interest and principal, starting on December 31, 1995. The market rate of interest for such loans is 10%.

Required

Give the entries that SNC should make on January 1, 1995, and on December 31, 1995. Disregard any franchise royalties based on sales.

E 13–9
(L.O. 7)

Depletion of Gravel Pit: Expense and Reporting the Asset   Miller Company's investment in a gravel quarry was $6,000,000, of which $400,000 represented land value after removal of the gravel. Geologists engaged to estimate the removable gravel reported originally that 5 million units could be extracted. In the first year, 880,000 units were extracted and 820,000 units were sold. In the second year, 830,000 units were extracted and sales were 850,000 units.

At the start of the third year, management of Miller had the quarry examined again, at which time it was determined that the remaining removable gravel was 2 million units. Production and sales for the third year amounted to 400,000 units. In the fourth year, production was 750,000 units and sales amounted to 600,000 units.

Required   1. Calculate the total amount of depletion and the amount of depletion to be reported on Miller's income statement for each of the four years. Assume a FIFO basis and show supporting computations.
2. Show how the gravel inventory and the gravel deposit should be reported on Miller's balance sheet at the end of the fourth year. Assume that an accumulated depletion account is used.

E 13-10   **Depletion: Expense, Reporting, Entries**   Sudbury Mining Company acquired property with copper
(L.O. 7)   ore reserves estimated at 2 million kilos for $1,800,000. The property will have an estimated value of $100,000 after the ore has been extracted. Before any ore could be removed, it was necessary to incur $500,000 of developmental costs. In the first year, 200,000 kilos were removed and 160,000 kilos of ore were sold; in the second year, 400,000 kilos were removed and 410,000 kilos were sold. In the course of the second year's production, discoveries were made that indicated that if an added $1,460,000 is spent on developmental costs during the third year, future removable ore will total 2.5 million kilos. After these added costs were incurred, production for the third year amounted to 510,000 kilos with sales of 450,000 kilos.

Required   1. Calculate the total depletion amount and the depletion expense that Sudbury should report on its income statement for each of the three years. Show supporting computations and round unit costs to the nearest three decimal places (assume FIFO).
2. Show how the resource and the inventory should be reported by Sudbury on its balance sheet at the end of the third year (FIFO basis). Assume that an accumulated depletion account is used.
3. Give the journal entry to record depletion and depletion expense at the end of each of the three years.

E 13-11   **Analyze the Accounting for Depreciation and Depletion**   The accounting treatments of depreci-
(L.O. 7)   ation and depletion have both similarities and differences.

Required   1. In one or two paragraphs, explain the similarities and differences in accounting treatments of depreciation and depletion.
2. In one or two paragraphs, describe depletion and goodwill amortization and explain how they differ.

(AICPA adapted)

E 13-12   **Amortization of Computer Software Costs**   During 1994, the Elephant Software Company capitalizes
(L.O. 6)   computer software costs in the amount of $2,000,000 in accordance with the requirements of *SFAS No. 86*. During 1995, the first year the product is released to sell, sales total $1,000,000. Estimated future sales for the remaining three-year life (through 1998) of the product are $7,000,000.

Required   1. Describe the method that Elephant must use to determine the amount of the capitalized computer software costs to amortize.
2. Compute the amount of amortization of capitalized computer software costs for 1995.

E 13-13   **Capitalization and Amortization of Computer Software Costs**   During 1995, PC Software, Inc., devel-
(L.O. 6)   oped a new personal computer database management software package. Total expenditures on the project were $3,000,000, of which 40% occurred after the technological feasibility of the product had been established. The product was completed and offered for sale on January 1, 1996. During 1996, revenues from sales of the product totalled $4,800,000. The package is expected to be successfully marketable for five years, and the total revenues over the life of the product will be $20,000,000.

Required   1. Prepare the journal entries to account for the development of this product in 1995.
2. Prepare the journal entries to record the amortization of capitalized computer software development costs as of December 31, 1996.
3. What disclosures are required in the December 31, 1996, financial statements regarding computer software costs?
4. Suppose this product were developed for internal use. How would your answers to (1), (2), and (3) change?

E 13-14   **Appendix 13B: Goodwill—Negotiating Price and Valuation**   Dow Corporation is negotiating with
(L.O. 4)   Fox Company to purchase all of Fox's assets and assume its liabilities. You have been asked to help develop a tentative offering price in the negotiations and to evaluate "goodwill on the basis of the latest concepts." Accordingly, you decide to use the present value approach. The following data have been assembled on Fox Company:

	Estimated Current Market Value	Fox Book Value
Total identifiable assets (exclusive of goodwill).	$2,500,000	$2,400,000
Liabilities	1,000,000	1,000,000
Average annual net cash earnings expected (next five years).	520,000	

Dow expects a 16% earnings rate on this investment.

Required

1. Compute (*a*) the tentative offering price and (*b*) the amount of goodwill included in that price.
2. Assume that the deal is consummated on January 1, 1995, at a $1.6 million actual cash price.
   a. Give the acquisition entry for Dow Corporation.
   b. Give the December 31, 1995, adjusting entry for goodwill. Assume a 20-year estimated useful life.

E 13–15
(L.O. 4)

Appendix 13B: Goodwill—Negotiating Price and Valuation Big Company is considering the purchase of Small Company for cash. The following data concerning Small Company have been collected:

	Small Company Book Values	Estimated Current Market Values
Total identifiable assets	$380,000	$400,000
Total liabilities.	280,000	280,000
Owners' equity	$100,000	—

Cumulative total net cash earnings for the past five years is $255,000, which includes extraordinary cash gains of $45,000 and non-recurring cash losses of $30,000.

Big company expects a 20% earnings rate on the investment.

Required

1. Compute (*a*) the maximum offering price that Big would be willing to pay and (*b*) the amount of goodwill included in that price.
2. Compute the amount of goodwill, assuming that the negotiations resulted in an actual purchase price of $140,000 cash.
3. Give the acquisition entry for Big Company, assuming the actual purchase price given in (2).

PROBLEMS

P 13–1
(L.O. 2, 3, 4)

Organization, Franchise, Trademark Costs and Goodwill Transactions during 1995, the first year of the newly organized Jenny's Discount Foods Corporation, included the following:

Jan. 2 Paid $8,000 attorney's fees and other related costs for assistance in securing the corporate charter, drafting bylaws, and advising on operating in other provinces (which the company intends to do). Amortize over five years.

Jan. 31 Paid $2,000 for television commercials advertising the grand opening. In addition, during the grand opening, the company gave away samples of its products, which were taken from inventory; cost $8,000 (perpetual system).

Feb. 1 Paid an invoice received from the financial institution that underwrote the company's $400,000 nopar value shares. Under the contract, the underwriter charged 1% of the gross proceeds from the stock sale. The stock issuance has already been recorded.

Mar. 1 Paid $30,000 to a franchisor for the right to open a Tastee Food lunch counter on the company's premises. The initial franchise runs 10 years from March 1 and can be renewed upon payment of a second amount to be computed later on the basis of sales under the initial franchise.

May 1 Acquired a newly issued patent for $10,200. The patent will not be used in the operations of the Corporation but rather will be held as a long-term investment to produce royalty revenue.

July 1 Paid consultants $6,400 for services in securing a trademark enabling the company to market under the now protected name Jenny's Recipe.

Oct. 1 Obtained a license from the city to conduct operations in a newly opened department. The license, which cost $600, runs for one year and is renewable.

Nov. 1 Acquired another business and paid (among other amounts) $36,000 for its goodwill. Expected useful life, 10 years.

Dec. 31 Apportioned the costs of those assets subject to amortization over their indicated lives. Where no life is indicated, amortize over the longest term possible. Amortization is calculated to the nearest monthly basis; in other words, acquisition of an intangible in July would call for amortization for half of the year.

Required

1. Give the journal entry that Jenny should make for each of the above transactions. December 31 is the end of the annual accounting period; six adjusting entries are required on this date. Ignore closing entries.

2. Classify each of the intangible assets (and their amounts) for balance sheet reporting at the end of 1995. Set deferred charges and any other appropriate items out separately from the other intangibles.

P 13-2
(L.O. 1, 2,
3, 4, 5)

Accounting for Intangibles Select the best answer for each of the following and indicate the basis for your choice.

1. An intangible asset (excluding R&D costs) should be:
   a. Expensed as incurred.
   b. Capitalized and not amortized until it clearly has no value.
   c. Capitalized and amortized over the estimated period benefited.
   d. Capitalized and amortized over the estimated period benefited but not exceeding 40 years.

2. Most R&D costs should be:
   a. Capitalized on a selective basis and not amortized.
   b. Capitalized and then amortized over 40 years.
   c. Expensed in the year in which they are incurred.
   d. Debited directly to retained earnings.

3. Goodwill is amortized over:
   a. Its useful life if it was acquired externally.
   b. A 40-year period if it was acquired externally.
   c. Its useful life, but not to exceed 40 years, if it was acquired externally.
   d. Its useful life, but not to exceed 40 years, if it was developed internally.

4. On January 15, 1991, a corporation was granted a patent. On January 2, 2000, to protect its patent, the corporation purchased another patent that was originally issued on January 10, 1996. Because of its unique plant, the corporation does not believe the competing patent can be used in producing a product. The cost of the competing patent should be:
   a. Amortized over a maximum period of 17 years.
   b. Amortized over a maximum period of 13 years.
   c. Amortized over a maximum period of 8 years.
   d. Expensed in 2000.

5. Goodwill should be written off:
   a. As soon as possible against retained earnings.
   b. As soon as possible as an extraordinary item.
   c. By systematic debits against retained earnings over the period benefited, but not more than 40 years.
   d. By systematic debits to expense over the period benefited, but not more than 40 years.

6. A large, publicly held company registered a trademark during 1995. How should the cost of registering the trademark be accounted for?
   a. Debited to an asset account with no amortization to follow.
   b. Expensed as incurred.
   c. Amortized over 25 years in accordance with management's evaluation of its useful life.
   d. Amortized over its useful life or 17 years, whichever is shorter.

7. Unidentifiable assets include:
   a. Patents, copyrights, franchises, and so on.   c. Deferred charges and goodwill.
   b. Deferred charges only.   d. Goodwill only.

8. Which of the following is not properly reported as a deferred charge?
   a. Stock issue costs.   c. Organization costs.
   b. Discount on bonds payable.   d. Deferred income taxes.

9. Prepaid expenses and deferred charges are alike in that both are:
   a. Reported as current assets on a classified balance sheet.

b. Destined to be debited to expense in some subsequent period in harmony with the matching principle.

c. Reported as other assets.

d. Applicable to the fiscal period immediately following the balance sheet on which they appear.

10. Inger Company bought a patent in January 1995 for $6,800. For the first four years, it was amortized on the assumption that the total useful life would be eight years. At the start of the fifth year, management determined that six years would be the probable total life. Amortization at the end of the fifth year should be:

a. $1,133.   c. $850.

b. $1,700.   d. None of the above.

11. Chance Company has a lease on a site that does not expire for 25 years. With the landowner's permission, Chance erected on the site a building that will last 50 years. Chance should recognize expense in connection with the building's cost:

a. One-fortieth each year.   c. In totality as soon as it is completed.

b. One-twenty-fifth each year.   d. One-fiftieth each year.

(AICPA adapted)

P 13–3
(L.O. 3, 5)

Reporting: Patent, Franchise, R&D   Able Company provided information on its tangible assets as follows:

a. A patent was purchased from East Development Company for $1,500,000 on January 1, 1994. Able estimated the remaining useful life of the patent to be 10 years.

b. On January 1, 1995, a franchise was purchased from the West Company for $500,000. In addition, 5% of revenue from the franchise must be paid to West. Revenue from the franchise for 1995 was $1,200,000. Able Company estimates the useful life of the franchise to be 10 years and records a full year's amortization (straight-line) in the year of purchase.

c. Able incurred R&D costs in 1995 as follows:

Materials (all used during 1995)	$120,000
Personnel	140,000
Indirect costs	60,000
	$320,000

Able estimates that these costs will be recouped by December 31, 1998.

d. On January 1, 1995, Able, based on new events that have occurred in the field, estimates that the remaining life of the patent purchased on January 1, 1994, is only five years from January 1, 1995.

Required

1. Prepare a schedule showing the intangible assets that should be reported on Able Company's balance sheet at December 31, 1995.

2. Prepare an income statement for the year ended December 31, 1995, as a result of the above facts. Ignore income taxes.

(AICPA adapted)

P 13–4
(L.O. 3, 4)

Accounting for Intangibles: Brannen Manufacturing Corporation was incorporated on January 3, 1994. The corporation's financial statements for its first year's operations were not examined by a public accountant. You have been engaged to examine the financial statements for the year ended December 31, 1995, and your examination is substantially completed. The corporation's adjusted trial balance appears as follows:

BRANNEN MANUFACTURING CORPORATION
Adjusted Trial Balance
December 31, 1995

	Debit	Credit
Cash	$ 11,000	
Accounts receivable	68,500	
Allowance for doubtful accounts		$ 500
Inventories	38,500	
Machinery	75,000	
Equipment	29,000	
Accumulated depreciation		10,000
Patents	102,000	
Prepaid expenses	10,500	
Organization costs	29,000	
Goodwill	24,000	
Licensing agreement 1	50,000	
Licensing agreement 2	59,000	
Accounts payable		147,500
Unearned revenue		12,500
Capital stock		317,000
Retained earnings, Jan. 1, 1995	17,000	
Sales revenue		668,500
Cost of goods sold	454,000	
Selling and general expenses	173,000	
Interest expense	3,500	
Extraordinary loss	12,000	
Totals	$1,156,000	$1,156,000

The following information relates to accounts that may still require adjustment:

a. Patents for Brannen's manufacturing process were acquired January 2, 1995, for $68,000. An additional $34,000 was spent in December 1995 to improve machinery covered by the patents and was debited to the patents account. Depreciation on operational assets has been properly recorded for 1995 in accordance with Brannen's practice, which provides a full year's depreciation for property on hand June 30 and no depreciation otherwise. Brannen uses the straight-line method for all depreciation and amortization.

b. The balance in the organization costs account properly includes costs incurred during the organization period. Brannen has exercised its option to amortize organization costs over a five-year period beginning January 1, 1994. No amortization has yet been recorded.

c. On January 3, 1994, Brannen purchased licensing agreement 1, which was believed to have an unlimited useful life. The balance in the licensing agreement 1 account includes its purchase price of $48,000 and costs of $2,000 related to the acquisition. On January 1, 1995, Brannen bought licensing agreement 2, which has a life expectancy of 10 years. The balance in the licensing agreement 2 account includes the $58,000 purchase price and $2,000 in acquisition costs, but it has been reduced by a credit of $1,000 for the advance collection of 1996 revenue from the agreement. No amortization on agreement 2 has been recorded.

   In early 1995, an explosion caused a permanent 60% reduction in the expected revenue-producing value of licensing agreement 1. No entries have been made during 1994 or 1995 for amortization nor for the explosion in 1995.

d. The balance in the goodwill account includes (1) $8,000 paid December 30, 1994, for an advertising program that management believes will assist in increasing Brannen's sales over a period of three to five years following the disbursement, and (2) legal expenses of $16,000 incurred for Brannen's incorporation on January 3, 1994. No amortization has ever been recorded on the goodwill.

Required   Prepare journal entries as of December 31, 1995, as required by the information given above. If the estimated life is not given, use the maximum.

(AICPA adapted)

P 13–5
(L.O. 2, 3, 4, 5)

Accounting for Intangibles   Your new client, Laser Company, is being audited for the first time on December 31, 1995, the end of the accounting period. In the course of your examination, you encounter in the ledger an asset account titled "intangibles" (balance, $85,224), which is presented below:

Intangibles

June 30/1993 Goodwill	9,000	Dec. 31/1994 Amortization, 5%	2,890*
Dec. 31/1993 R&D	10,700	Dec. 31/1995 Amortization, 5%	4,486*
Apr. 1/1994 Goodwill	14,600		
June 30/1994 Patent	9,600		
Dec. 31/1994 R&D	13,900		
June 1/1995 Goodwill	12,900		
July 1/1995 Bond discount	4,800		
Dec. 31/1995 R&D	17,100		

* Offsetting debit was to amortization expense each year.

By tracing entries to the journal and other supporting documents, you ascertain the following facts:

a. The June 30, 1993, entry was made when the first six months' operations were profitable, although a small loss had been anticipated. At the direction of the company president, and with the approval of the board of directors, an entry was made debiting intangibles and crediting retained earnings for $9,000.

b. All debit entries dated December 31 pertaining to R&D arise from the fact that the company has continuously engaged in an extensive R&D program to keep its products competitive and to develop new products. The debits represent half of the costs of the R&D program for each year and were transferred at year-end from the R&D expense account.

c. The April 1, 1994, entry was made after an extensive advertising campaign had seemingly proved successful. Sales rose 8% after the campaign and never dropped again to less than a 4% increase over their former level. The debit represents the expenditures for the campaign.

d. The $9,600 debit on June 30, 1994, represents the purchase price of a patent bought because the company feared that if it fell into other hands, it would damage the company's products competitively. See (g) for amortization information.

e. The debit for June 1, 1995, was made after Laser acquired another company, which will continue to operate as a 100%-owned subsidiary. The price represented an excess payment of $12,900 over the market values of identifiable net assets acquired (which were properly recorded) and was based on an expectation of continued high profitability. See (g) for amortization information.

f. The July 1, 1995, debit for $4,800 represents discount on a 10-year, $100,000 bond issue marketed by the company on that date. The amount is not material; therefore, straight-line amortization is appropriate.

g. The two credits to the intangibles account represent 5% of the ending balance in the intangibles account at the end of 1994 and 1995, respectively; the offsetting debit was to amortization expense. The patent and goodwill costs are to be amortized over 10 years, computed to the nearest month.

Required

1. Give journal entries to clear out the old intangibles account. The accounts at the end of 1995 have been adjusted but not closed. Key your entries with the letters that identify the items in the problem. Explain each entry and give the resulting account balances.

2. Give the 1995 adjusting entries based on your results in (1). Give the final account balances immediately prior to the 1995 closing entries.

P 13–6
(L.O. 3, 4)

Capitalizing and Amortizing Intangible Assets   Select the best answer to each of the following questions:

1. Bye Corporation was organized during 1994 and started operations in 1995. Expenditures during 1994 and early 1995 were professional fees, $25,000; meetings and promotional activities incidental to organization, $11,000; filing and related fees, $2,000; and initial capital stock issuance costs, $3,000. If organization costs are to be amortized over a 10-year period starting in 1995, the amount of organization costs amortized in 1995 would be:

   a. $2,500.   d. $4,100.
   b. $3,600.   e. None of the above; explain.
   c. $3,800.

2. During 1994, Starnes Corporation developed a patent. Expenditures related to the patent were legal fees for patent registration, $7,000; tests to perfect the use of the patent for production processes,

$6,000; research costs in the research laboratory, $21,000; and depreciation on equipment (that has alternative future uses) used in developing the patent, $4,000. Assuming amortization of the patent costs over the legal life of the patent, the annual patent amortization amount would be:

a. $2,000.   d. $1,000.
b. $1,882.   e. None of the above; explain.
c. $1,824.

3. On April 1, 1993, Penn Corporation purchased all the assets and assumed all the liabilities of Suber Company for $140,000 cash. Suber's total identifiable asset values were as follows: Suber's book value, $200,000; estimated market value, $230,000. Suber's total liabilities were $105,000. The amount of goodwill purchased by Penn Corporation was:

a. $75,000.   d. $15,000.
b. $45,000.   e. None of the above; explain.
c. $30,000.

4. On January 1, 1994, Kiker Company purchased a new patent for $10,200 and started amortizing it over the legal life of 17 years. At the start of 1997, Kiker estimated that the total useful life of the patent (from acquisition date) was 12 years. Kiker should record amortization on the patent at the end of 1997 in the amount of:

a. $700.   d. $850.
b. $933.   e. None of the above; explain.
c. $600.

5. On January 1, 1995, Thin Company purchased a patent from the inventor, who asked $110,000 for it. Thin paid for the patent as follows: cash, $40,000; issuance of 1,000 of its own common shares, (market value, $20 per share); and a note payable due at the end of three years, face amount, $50,000, noninterest-bearing. The current interest rate for this type of financing is 12%. Thin Company should record the cost of the patent at:

a. $85,589.   d. $110,000.
b. $95,589.   e. None of the above; explain.
c. $98,800.

P 13–7
(L.O. 7)

Depreciation and Depletion: Schedule, Entries   Gaspe Mining Corporation bought mineral-bearing land for $150,000 that engineers estimate will yield 200,000 kilos of economically removable ore. The land will have a value of $30,000 after the ore is removed.

To work the property, Gaspe built structures and sheds on the site that cost $40,000; these will last 10 years, and because their use is confined to mining and it would be expensive to dismantle and move them, they will have no residual value. Machinery that cost $29,000 was installed at the mine, and the added cost for installation was $7,000. This machinery should last 15 years; like that of the structures, the usefulness of the machinery is confined to these mining operations. Dismantling and removal costs when the property has been fully worked will approximately equal the value of the machinery at that time; therefore, Gaspe does not plan to use the structures or the machinery after the minerals have been removed.

In the first year, Gaspe removed only 15,000 kilos of ore; however, production was doubled in the second year. It is expected that all of the removable ore will be extracted within eight years from the start of operations.

Required

1. Prepare a schedule showing unit and total depletion and depreciation and book value of the operational assets for the first and second years of operation. Use the units-of-production method of depreciation.

2. Assuming that in the first year 80% of production was sold, and that in the second year, the inventory carried over from the first year plus 80% of the second year's production was sold, give the entries to record accumulated depreciation and depletion. To show the effect of these costs, make the offsetting debits to cost of goods sold and inventory. Use accounts labeled *accumulated depreciation* and *accumulated depletion*.

P 13–8
(L.O. 7)

Depletion and Depreciation Expense   On July 1, 1994, Miller Mining, a calendar-year corporation, purchased the rights to a copper mine. Of the total purchase price, $2.8 million was allocable to the copper. Estimated reserves were 800,000 tonnes of copper. Miller expects to extract and immediately sell 10,000 tonnes of copper each month. Production began immediately. The selling price is $25 per tonne. To aid production, Miller also purchased some new equipment on July 1, 1994. The equipment cost $76,000 and had an estimated useful life of eight years. However, after all the copper is removed from this mine, the equipment will be of no use to Miller and will be sold for an estimated $4,000.

Required

1. If sales and production conform to expectations, what is Miller's depletion expense on this mine for financial accounting purposes for the calendar-year 1994?
2. If sales and production conform to expectations, what is Miller's depreciation expense on the new equipment for financial accounting purposes for the calendar-year 1994? Assume straight-line depreciation.

P 13–9
(L.O. 6)

Computer Software Costs   Fox is a new computer software company. In 1994, the firm incurred the following costs in the process of designing, developing, and producing its first new software package, which it expects to begin marketing in 1995:

Designing and planning costs	$150,000
Production of product masters	400,000
Cost of developing code	240,000
Testing	60,000
Production of final product	500,000

The costs of designing and planning, code development, and testing were all incurred before the technological feasibility of the product had been established. Fox estimates that total revenues over the four-year life of the product will be $2,000,000, with $800,000 in revenues expected in 1995.

Required

1. Prepare the entries to account for the costs incurred in 1994.
2. Assuming that 1995 revenues are as estimated, prepare the entry to record the amortization of computer software costs for 1995.
3. Assume that the net realizable value of the product is estimated at December 31, 1995, to be $500,000. What entry, if any, is required? What disclosures are required?

P 13–10
(L.O. 4)

Appendix 13B: Goodwill, Negotiation—Entries   During 1994, Evergreen Corporation has been negotiating to purchase all of Pine Company's non-cash assets and to assume all of its liabilities for a single cash price. The target closing date is January 1, 1995. Evergreen requested, and was provided, considerable data, including the following midyear balance sheet (summarized):

PINE COMPANY
Balance Sheet
At June 30, 1994

Assets

Cash	$ 19,000
Accounts receivable*	60,000
Inventory (LIFO)	140,000
Property, plant, and equipment	300,000
Land	11,000
Franchise (unamortized balance)	20,000
Total	$550,000

Liabilities

Current liabilities	$ 40,000
Bonds payable	200,000
Shareholders' equity	310,000
Total	$550,000

* Net of the allowance for doubtful accounts and accumulated depreciation, respectively.

Based on appraisals, price lists, and specific price level indexes, Evergreen Corporation developed the following estimates of fair market values: cash, not to be purchased; accounts receivable, $60,000 (the allowance account is adequate); inventory (converted to FIFO), $70,000; property, plant, and equipment, $280,000; land, $40,000; and franchise, $22,000. The liabilities are appropriately valued as recorded.

Based on an analysis of the income statements and other data (and excluding all non-recurring and extraordinary gains and losses), Evergreen Corporation's executives projected an average year-end annual net cash inflow from operations (i.e., from the income statement) of $72,000 for each of the next seven years.

Required   1. Compute (*a*) a tentative offering price and (*b*) the amount of goodwill therein, for negotiating purposes. Assume that Evergreen expects a 20% rate of return on this investment. Round to the nearest $1,000.

Negotiations continued throughout the remainder of 1994. During December 1994, a final purchase price of $268,000 was agreed on "to be adjusted upward (for a decrease) or downward (for an increase) for any change from the June 30, 1994, cash account balance (i.e., from $19,000)."

The December 31, 1994, balance sheet prepared by Pine Company is shown below in column *a*, and the revised market values added later by Evergreen Corporation are shown in column *b*.

PINE COMPANY
Balance Sheet
At December 31, 1994

	(*a*) Book Values of Pine Co.	(*b*) Market Values Developed by Evergreen Corp.
Assets		
Cash	$ 20,000	$ —
Accounts receivable (net).	58,000	58,000
Inventory (LIFO)	160,000	90,000
Property, plant, and equipment (net).	309,000	285,000
Land	11,000	40,000
Franchise (unamortized balance)	19,000	21,000
Total	$577,000	
Liabilities		
Current liabilities	$ 37,000	37,000
Bonds payable.	200,000	200,000
Shareholders' equity	340,000	—
Total	$577,000	

Required   2. Compute the amount of goodwill purchased by Evergreen Corporation.
3. Give the entry for Evergreen Corporation to record the purchase of Pine Company.
4. Give the entry at the end of 1995 to record the minimum amount of goodwill that can be amortized.

ANALYZING FINANCIAL STATEMENTS

All questions in this section are based on information taken from the financial statements of actual companies.

A 13–1
(L.O. 4)

Analyzing Goodwill: On the balance sheet of its 1991 annual report, Sequa Corporation reports the following other asset:

	1991	1990
	(in thousands)	
Excess of cost over net assets of companies acquired	$373,012	$381,417

In note 1 to the financial statements, the following disclosure is made:

Excess of cost over net assets of companies acquired is being amortized on a straight-line basis over periods not exceeding forty years. The amortization charged against earnings in 1991, 1990, and 1989 was $10,804,000, $14,645,000, and $11,239,000, respectively. Accumulated amortization at December 31, 1991 and 1990 was $51,934,000 and $41,130,000, respectively.

Required   1. What is another name for excess of cost over net assets of companies acquired?
2. As of December 31, 1991, what is the total or gross amount of excess of cost over net assets of companies acquired?
3. Did Sequa acquire any companies in 1991 for which there was an excess of cost over net assets of companies acquired? If so, how much, if any, was the excess of cost over net assets of the acquired companies?

4. Based on the information for 1991, over what period would you estimate Sequa is amortizing excess of cost over net assets of companies acquired? If Sequa has no further acquisitions of companies and the 1991 amortization amount is used in future years, for how many more years will Sequa be amortizing the excess of cost over net assets of companies acquired?

A 13–2
(L.O. 4)

Analyzing Goodwill: In its 1993 annual report, Maple Leaf Foods Inc. shows the following items in its financial statements for 1993 and 1992:

(thousands)	1993	1992
Balance sheet:		
Goodwill	$185,534	$125,051
Statement of earnings:		
Amortization of goodwill	$ 4,483	$ 3,543

Required

1. Did Maple Leaf acquire any companies at a cost greater than the fair value of net assets acquired between December 31, 1992 and December 31, 1993? Show your work and explain your reasoning.
2. Over what period is Maple Leaf amortizing goodwill?

A 13–3
(L.O. 4)

Recording Goodwill: The Thomson Corporation In its annual report for the fiscal year ending December 31, 1992, The Thomson Corporation provides a note describing its acquisitions of other companies during the year:

In 1992, several businesses were acquired for an aggregate cash consideration of $336 million (1991—$162 million). Details of the net assets acquired are as follows:

	1992	1991
Working capital	(44)	(9)
Property and equipment	14	9
Publishing rights and circulation	236	134
Goodwill.	139	55
Other assets	—	1
Long-term debt and other liabilities	(9)	(28)
Cost.	336	162

Required

1. Show a summary entry Thomson would make to record these acquisitions. Use broadly defined financial statement element accounts (e.g., assets, liabilities) as needed, but use specific account categories (e.g., cash, goodwill) whenever possible.
2. What effect, if any, will the excess of cost over net assets acquired in these acquisitions have on Thomson's earnings in future years? If Thomson's home were Great Britain, what effect might the excess of cost over net assets acquired have on future earnings?

A 13–4
(L.O. 6)

Software Development Costs In the notes to its 1992 financial statements, Unisys Corporation discloses the following regarding its treatment of the cost of software development:

The cost of development of computer software to be sold or leased is capitalized and amortized to cost of net sales over the estimated revenue-producing lives of the products, but not in excess of three years following product release. Unamortized marketable software costs (which are included in other assets) at December 31, 1992 and 1991 were $320.4 and $342.0 million, respectively.

In the statement of cash flows, Unisys shows amortization expense for marketable software for 1992 of $131.8 million.

Required

1. How much cost for the development of marketable software did Unisys capitalize in 1992?
2. Suppose the capitalized marketable software cost shown at December 31, 1991, relates to one software product that was released for sale at that date. The product is expected to produce revenues totalling $1,000.0 million over a three-year useful life.
   a. What would be the minimum amortization amount that would be recorded in 1992?
   b. Suppose revenues from the software product totalled $400.0 million in 1992. What would be the amount of amortization that Unisys would report in 1992?
   c. Given that $131.8 million of amortization was recorded, estimate the amount of revenue generated by this product in 1992.

A 13–5
(L.O. 8)

Natural Resources In a supplemental section of its 1992 annual report, Texaco Inc. provides the following disclosures pertaining specifically to its oil and gas operations:

Costs incurred during fiscal 1992 for (in millions of dollars):

Proved property acquisition	$ 12
Unproved property acquisition.	18
Exploration	416
Development.	1,250
Total	$1,696

Another section of the supplemental section shows for the same period exploration expenses totalling $337 million, and depreciation, depletion, and amortization totalling $1,192 million. Finally, Texaco Inc. reports the amount of capitalized costs for fiscal years ending December 31, 1992 and 1991, as follows:

	1992	1991
	(amounts in millions)	
Proved properties	$23,333	$23,452
Unproved properties	866	869
Support equipment and facilities	659	638
Gross capitalized costs	24,858	24,959
Accumulated depreciation, depletion, and amortization.	15,871	15,891
Net capitalized costs	$ 8,987	$ 9,068

Texaco Inc. uses the successful efforts method to account for exploration costs.

Required

1. What amount of the exploration costs Texaco incurred in 1992 were capitalized?
2. If Texaco were using the full-cost method of accounting for exploration costs, what amount of exploration costs would be capitalized in 1992? Make clear any assumptions needed to answer this question.
3. Based on the information given above, determine the amount of capitalized costs removed (retired or otherwise disposed of) from the capitalized costs account, and the amount of accumulated depreciation, depletion, and amortization related to this item.

14 Investments in Debt and Equity Securities

LEARNING OBJECTIVES

After you have studied this chapter, you will be able to:

1 **Explain why firms invest in debt and equity securities.**

2 **Apply the classification criteria and record the initial investment in securities at the date of acquisition.**

3 **Discuss the conceptual basis for the accounting treatment of various types of investments.**

4 **Account for temporary investments using the allowance method and the direct write-off method.**

5 **Account for long-term investments in debt and equity securities.**

6 **Use the equity method of accounting for long-term investments in equity securities.**

7 **Explain the disclosure requirements for all types of investment securities.**

8 **Account for stock dividends, stock splits, and stock warrants received by the investor.**

INTRODUCTION

Suppose senior management at your employer, GICO Manufacturing Company, asks for your advice on the following accounting matter. GICO had cash available at the beginning of the current fiscal year that was not needed for operations or to acquire fixed assets, so it purchased 10,000 common shares of LTW Corporation at $20 per share. At the end of the year, LTW reported earnings of $3 per share and paid dividends of $1 per share. LTW common shares are traded on a major stock exchange, and at the end of the fiscal year have a market price of $24 per share. Management asks for your advice on (*a*) what amount GICO should report on its balance sheet for its investment in LTW and (*b*) what amount GICO should report as income in the current year from its investment in LTW. For the moment, assume that there is no GAAP on accounting for investments.

Based on the above information, we know the following:

GICO's original investment in LTW shares (10,000 shares × $20 per share)	$200,000
Current value of LTW shares owned by GICO (10,000 shares × $24 per share)	240,000
GICO's share of LTW earnings (10,000 shares × $3 per share)	30,000
Cash dividends received by GICO from LTW (10,000 shares × $1 per share)	10,000

There are several possible methods to report the above information in the financial statements.

1. Maintain the investment at cost ($200,000), and measure investment income as dividends received ($10,000).
2. Report the investment at its current market value ($240,000), and measure investment income as dividends received ($10,000) plus the gain in the market value of the shares held ($40,000), for a total of $50,000 of investment income.
3. Treat the investment in LTW as a special kind of asset that increases in carrying value by the amount of its earnings, less any distribution of those earnings received. Thus, GICO would report investment income equal to its share of LTW earnings ($30,000) and would report the investment at the amount of the original investment ($200,000) plus its share of LTW earnings ($30,000) and less the amount of those earnings that were distributed to GICO ($10,000). The investment would be reported on the balance sheet at $220,000, and investment income at $30,000.

Perhaps you can think of additional ways of accounting for this investment, but these three are readily apparent. The effects on the balance sheet and income statement differ considerably among the three possibilities, as shown in this compilation:

	Method 1	Method 2	Method 3
Investment in LTW common shares	$200,000	$240,000	$220,000
Investment income from investment in LTW common shares.	$ 10,000	$ 50,000	$ 30,000

Which method of reporting the investment do you feel is most appropriate, and why? It turns out that certain conditions require method 1, other conditions require method 2, and still other conditions require method 3.

Many companies invest in the debt and equity securities of other companies and of government agencies for a wide range of reasons. Abitibi-Price, for example, shows short-term investments among its current assets and has a separate subsection of the balance sheet identified as *investments and other assets*. This chapter covers how to account for investments in various types of financial instruments. Investments can include many different types of **financial instruments:**[1] equity securities, debt securities, stock options and warrants, bonds and notes, treasury bills, money market funds, commercial paper, and, in general, any contract that obligates a party to convey financial resources to the investing firm. The accounting procedures and disclosures differ, according to the type of investment and whether the investments are classified as temporary or long term.

Why Invest in Financial Instruments?

Temporary Investment of Idle Cash   Companies invest in the securities of other companies and government agencies for a variety of reasons. Companies often have cash on hand that is not needed at present but will be needed in the near future. Rather than allow the idle cash to remain in a noninterest-bearing account, companies find temporary investments where they can earn a return. These investments are usually low risk and can be quickly and easily converted to cash. These short-term investments are often in the securities of government agencies but can also be the securities of other companies.

Long-Term Investments to Increase Earnings   A second reason firms invest in the securities of other firms, especially in securities representing ownership interest,

---

[1] The CICA has begun using the term *financial instrument* to describe all forms of contracts that convey ownership in firms or obligations to transfer financial resources from one party to another. All the securities and other investments discussed in this chapter are financial instruments.

is to develop a beneficial intercompany relationship that will increase the profitability of the investing company, both directly and indirectly. Maple Leaf Foods Inc. is a good example. The management's financial review and analysis (MFRA) section describes why Maple Leaf engages in such investments:

> Acquisitions by the Company in 1993 amounted to $82 million . . . an increase over the 1992 level of $48 million. All of these acquisitions were strategic additions to core businesses as described below [for one of the acquisitions].
>
> In February, 1993, Corporate Foods, the Company's baking subsidiary, purchased an additional 10% of Circlet Foods Limited, a producer and distributor of pizzas, and pizza shells, to hold 60%. This is part of a planned buyout of shares which will result in a total share holding of 70% in 1996.

Accounting Issues

There are three broad issues in accounting for investments: (1) classification issues, (2) valuation and investment income measurement issues, and (3) disclosure issues.

Classification Classification involves management's intended holding period for an investment. Is it a temporary investment because it would otherwise be idle cash, or is it a long-term investment? If it is a long-term investment in a debt security, does management intend to hold the investment until the debt matures? Classification is important because different accounting valuation methods may be used for different classifications.

Valuation and Investment Income Measurement Various valuation methods are used to determine the carrying value of investments, and this determination in turn affects the measurement of income and owners' equity. Several valuation methods have previously been discussed in this text, including cost, net realizable value, and lower of cost or market. A new valuation method, fair value, is used in the United States to value investments in certain classifications. Because using fair value as a valuation method results in increasing or decreasing the carrying value of investments by the amount of the holding gains and losses associated with the investments, there are consequences for income measurement. Should these holding gains and losses be included in income, or should they be treated as a separate increase or decrease to owners' equity until the investment is sold and they are realized? These issues may eventually affect Canadian companies. At the time of this writing, the AcSB has issued a re-exposure draft, which advocates the use of the fair value method in Canada.

Disclosure Since different classifications of investments are accounted for differently, there are differing disclosure requirements for each.

Our discussion begins with a broad overview of accounting for investments in debt and equity securities for the purpose of clarifying under what conditions (classifications) the different valuation methods are used. This overview is followed by a discussion of accounting for investments in two related classifications: temporary and long-term investments. A later section discusses accounting for investments in temporary debt securities. Because the accounting for long-term debt securities is similar to the accounting by the issuer of the debt, this investment classification is covered in more depth in Chapter 16. The following section covers investments in a final classification: investments in equity securities in which the investor company has significant influence over the investee company. The final section covers special problems in accounting for equity investments: stock dividends, stock splits, and stock rights on investment securities.[2]

---

[2] Appendix 14A covers accounting and reporting for investments other than debt and equity securities: special-purpose funds, cash surrender value of life insurance, and futures contracts.

EXHIBIT 14–1
Accounting Method Used for
Different Types of
Investments

Classification	Investment in Debt Securities	Investment in Equity Securities
Control—greater than 50% ownership of voting shares.	Not applicable	Consolidation
Significant influence—20 to 50% ownership of voting shares.	Not applicable	Equity method
Long-term investments in debt securities and less than 20% ownership of voting shares.	Amortized cost method	Cost method
Debt and equity securities classified as **temporary** investments.	Cost method	Lower of cost or market

**OVERVIEW:
CLASSIFYING
INVESTMENTS**

The accounting for various types of investments in securities is affected by several factors:

1. Is the investment in a debt security or in an equity security?
2. Is the market value of the security readily determinable?
3. Does management intend to hold the investment to maturity or for a long term, or is it a temporary investment?
4. For investments in equity securities with voting rights, what influence or control can the investor company exercise over the investee company?

The answers to these four questions determine the accounting measurement rules to be used. Exhibit 14–1 shows the various classifications of investments in securities and the method of accounting for each classification of investment. Each of the methods shown in Exhibit 14–1 except consolidation is discussed in later sections.

Debt or Equity?

A **security** is a share, participation, or other interest in the property or assets of the issuer, or an obligation of the issuer, that:

1. Is represented by an instrument issued in bearer or registered form or is registered in records maintained to record transfers to and from the issuer.
2. Is of a type commonly dealt with on stock exchanges or is an instrument that is commonly recognized as a medium for investment.
3. Either is one of a class or series of shares, participations, interests, or obligations, or by its terms is divisible into such a class or series.

Securities are either debt securities or equity securities. A **debt security** is any security representing a creditor relationship with an entity. Common examples of debt securities include Canadian government securities, municipal securities, corporate bonds, convertible debt, and commercial paper. Preferred shares that must be redeemed or that are redeemable at the option of the investor are also classified as debt securities.[3] Trade accounts receivable and loan receivables arising from consumer, commercial, and real estate lending activities are not debt securities; they do not meet the definition of a security.

An **equity security** is any security representing an ownership interest in an entity, or the right to acquire or to dispose of an ownership right at a fixed price. Common

---

[3] A number of additional financial instruments are classified as debt securities, including all securitized debt instruments, such as collateralized mortgage obligations (CMOs) and real estate mortgage investment conduits (REMICs). Excluded, however, are option contracts, financial futures contracts, forward contracts, and lease contracts. Accounting for futures contracts is covered later in this chapter. Each of the remaining contracts is covered in the relevant chapter in the text: lease contracts in Chapter 18 on leases, and options in Chapter 21 on shareholders' equity.

examples of equity securities include common, preferred, and other capital stock. Warrants, rights, and options to purchase (call options) or to sell (put options) equity securities at fixed or determinable prices are also classified as equity securities.

Classification of Investments in Equity Securities

The decision process for deciding how to account for investments in equity securities depends on the amount of influence the investor company has over the investee company. This is generally determined by assessing the percentage of voting rights the investor company has of the total voting rights outstanding for the investee company. There are three levels of control or influence that an investor company can have over an investee company:

1. **Controlling interest** A controlling interest is represented by an investment in which the investor owns more than 50% of the voting shares of the investee. The investor has absolute control over the investee. The investor corporation is referred to as the **parent** and the investee as the **subsidiary.** For financial reporting, **consolidated financial statements** are generally prepared. The financial statements of the two corporations are combined into one as if they were one economic entity, with the interest of shareholders of the investee other than the investor reported as a special item called *minority shareholder interest.* When and how to prepare consolidated financial statements is covered in advanced accounting texts.
2. **Significant influence** A significant influence is represented by an investment in equity securities in which the investor holds from 20% to 50% of the voting shares of the investee, although these are not hard and fast percentages. Investments in this category are accounted for using the equity method.
3. **No significant influence** Investments in equity securities in which the investor holds less than 20% of the voting shares of the investee generally do not significantly influence the investee.

For accounting purposes, temporary investments must satisfy the definitional requirements of a current asset. Current assets are those assets that are ordinarily realizable within one year of the balance sheet date or during the normal operating cycle of the firm, if it is longer. Temporary investments must be readily marketable or capable of reasonably prompt liquidation.[4] A security is readily marketable if it is listed on one of the stock exchanges. If an investment is not readily marketable, it does not meet the definition of a current asset and is classified as a long-term investment.

In the case of readily marketable investment securities, the investor's intention determines the classification as temporary or long-term. Thus, temporary investments are those that meet the other criteria of current assets and that managers of the investing firm classify as temporary. The accounting literature does not provide further guidance.

Temporary investments in equity securities often include common shares, preferred shares, warrants, options, and stock rights. Short-term debt securities include corporate and other entity bonds and notes, and other investments such as certificates of deposit, treasury bills, commercial paper, and other types of financial instruments that have a ready market.

Long-term investments include all securities that do not meet the requirements for temporary investments.

---

[4] *CICA Handbook,* Section 3010, paragraph .02, "Temporary Investments."

Classification of Investments in Debt Securities

Investments in debt securities are classified as temporary or long term, depending on the intentions of management. Since debt securities do not typically carry any ownership interest, the issues of significant influence do not apply. Accounting for temporary investments in debt securities will be presented after the sections on equity securities.

CONCEPT REVIEW

1. Why is the classification of investments in debt and equity securities important?
2. What are the alternative methods used in accounting for investments in equity securities?

ACQUISITION OF INVESTMENT SECURITIES

Investments in securities are recorded at cost when acquired. Cost includes the purchase price of the securities and other incidental costs such as brokerage fees, excise taxes, and other transfer costs incurred as part of the purchase. Investments may be purchased for cash, on margin, or for non-cash consideration. When an investment security is acquired on margin, only part of the purchase price is paid initially. The balance is borrowed (usually through a brokerage firm). The investment should be recorded at its cost, including the portion financed with borrowed funds (exclusive of interest).

When non-cash consideration (property or services) is given for an investment, the cost assigned to the securities should be measured by (1) the market value of the consideration given or (2) the market value of the securities received, whichever can be more reliably determined. Inability to determine reliably the market value—for example, an exchange of unlisted securities for property for which no established market value exists—requires appraisals or estimates.

Securities are often purchased between regular interest or dividend dates. For such purchases, accrued interest is recorded on debt securities because interest is a legal obligation. Dividends, however, are not a legal obligation until declared, and dividends are therefore not accrued unless they have been declared.

Example   On November 1, 1995, Able Company purchases (a) 5,000 shares of Baker Company common shares for $20 per share, and (b) a face amount of $30,000 of Charlie Corporation 8% coupon rate bonds that mature on December 31, 2001, at 100, for a total of $30,000, plus accrued interest.[5] Interest is paid semiannually on June 30 and December 31. Commissions on the common share purchase were $500; no commission or fees were charged for the bond purchase; and 30% of the purchase price of the common shares (not including the commissions) was borrowed from the selling brokerage firm. Able classifies both investments as temporary investments.

The entries to record the above purchases are as follows:

1. For the purchase of 5,000 common shares of Baker Company:

Temporary investment: Baker Company common shares	100,500	
Cash [(5,000 shares × $20) × 0.70 + $500]		70,500
Payable to broker		30,000

2. For the purchase of Charlie Corporation bonds:

Temporary investment: Charlie Corporation bonds.	30,000	
Accrued interest receivable ($30,000 × .08 × 4/12).	800	
Cash.		30,800

---

[5] Bond prices are quoted as a price per $100 of face amount of the bond. Thus, a quote of 98 implies that a $1,000 face amount bond has a market price of $980. The quoted price does not include accrued interest, which also must be paid to the seller of the bond.

When interest is received on December 31, a portion of it represents the accrued interest recorded at the acquisition date:

```
Cash ($30,000 × .08 × 6/12) . . . . . . . . . . . . . . . . . . . . .   1,200
        Investment income: Interest . . . . . . . . . . . . . . . . . . . .          400
        Accrued interest receivable . . . . . . . . . . . . . . . . . . . .          800
```

Basket Purchases of Securities

A purchase of two or more classes of securities for a single lump sum is a basket purchase and requires the allocation of the total cost to each class of security. When the market price of each class of security is known, the proportional method is used. If the market price is not known for a class, the incremental method can be used, in which the purchase price is allocated to the class(es) with known prices first, with the remainder of the lump-sum purchase price assigned to the class of investment that does not have a market price.

Example   On September 1, 1995, Balloon Company purchases a basket of securities consisting of 5,000 Red Company common shares; 1,000 shares of Orange Inc.; $5 preferred stock and $40,000 face amount of Green Company 9% coupon rate bonds for a lump-sum payment of $170,000, not including a commission of $1,000, which was also paid. The Green Company bonds pay coupon interest semiannually on August 31 and February 28. At the date of the purchase, Red Company common shares sell for $12 per share, Orange preferred shares sell for $80 per share, and the bonds sell at 100. The allocation of the $171,000 between the three securities acquired using the proportional method is as follows:

Security	Shares Acquired	Market Price per Share	Market Value	Proportion of Market Value	Allocation of Purchase Price
Red Co. common shares.	5,000	$12	$ 60,000	6/18 (×$171,000) =	$ 57,000
Green Co. bonds	—	—	40,000	4/18 (×$171,000) =	38,000
Orange Inc. preferred shares.	1,000	80	80,000	8/18 (×$171,000) =	76,000
Total			$180,000		$171,000

The entry to record the investment is as follows:

```
Temporary Investment: Red Co. common shares. . . . . . . . . . . . .   57,000
Temporary Investment: Green Co. bonds . . . . . . . . . . . . . . .   38,000
Temporary Investment: Orange Inc. preferred shares. . . . . . . . . . .   76,000
        Cash . . . . . . . . . . . . . . . . . . . . . . . . . . . . . .          171,000
```

Multiple Acquisitions and Disposals of Investment Securities

Accounting for investments is facilitated if a consistent system of security cost identification is used. A record of each individual security should be maintained. This record documents units purchased by certificate number, dates, and unit cost. These details are important with respect to the physical safekeeping of the securities.

To illustrate multiple acquisitions and disposal, assume 10 shares of Red Company were purchased at $150 per share, and later an additional 30 shares were purchased at $200 per share. There is a subsequent sale of five shares at $180 per share. If the five shares can be identified by certificate number as a part of the first purchase, a gain of $30 per share is recognized. Alternatively, if they are identified with the second purchase, a loss of $20 per share is recognized. The averaging procedure would report a loss of $7.50 per share computed as follows:

First purchase	10 shares × $150	$1,500
Second purchase	30 shares × $200	6,000
Total	40	$7,500
Average cost per share ($7,500 ÷ 40)		$187.50
Sale price per share		180.00
Loss per share		$ 7.50

To prevent the manipulation of income by choosing the lot from which the shares are taken, the *CICA Handbook,* Section 3050, paragraph .27, requires that "the cost of the investment sold should be calculated on the basis of the average carrying value."

ACCOUNTING FOR HOLDINGS OF TEMPORARY INVESTMENTS IN DEBT AND EQUITY SECURITIES

Temporary investments must be capable of reasonably prompt liquidation. In most cases, this would mean that the investments are actively traded and that their market values fluctuate. The *CICA Handbook* requires that both the basis of valuation and the quoted market, as well as the carrying value of temporary investments, be disclosed. Examples of disclosure for temporary investments follow:

MOORE CORPORATION LIMITED
At December 31

	1993	1992
	(Dollars in thousands)	
Current assets:		
Short-term securities, at cost which approximates market value	$253,930	$299,147

CATHEDRAL GOLD CORPORATION
At December 31

	1993	1992
Current assets:		
Marketable securities (Market value $11,189; 1992—$4,600)	$ 9,622	$ 3,000

Lower of Cost or Market

Section 3010, paragraph .06 of the *CICA Handbook* states that "When the market value of temporary investments has declined below the carrying value, they should be carried at market." Similarly, Section 3050, dealing with long-term investments, requires that they be written down to reflect the loss when there has been a nontemporary decline in value. The *Handbook,* however, does not indicate whether an allowance method or a direct write-off method should be used for recognizing a decline in value for temporary investments. Section 3050, paragraph .20 appears to require that the direct write-off method should be used for long-term investments. Therefore, both methods are described.

Allowance Method   The allowance method for temporary investments is similar to that used for accounts receivable. The investment or portfolio of investments is carried on the balance sheet at cost and, should the market value of the portfolio decline to an amount below the cost at the balance sheet date, an allowance is established to reduce the cost value to market. The following example illustrates the application of the allowance method.

Zero limited invested temporarily idle cash in three short-term investments and made the following entry:

March 1, 1995—to record acquisition:

Temporary investments	24,500*	
Cash		24,500

* Corn common, 500 shares @ $20	$10,000	
Oats common, 300 shares @ $25	7,500	
Rye preferred, 200 shares @ $35	7,000	
Total	$24,500	

November 1, 1995—received a cash dividend of $1 per share on the Rye preferred shares:

Cash	200	
Investment revenue		200

December 31, 1995—Quoted market prices, Corn common, $17; Oats common, $28; Rye preferred, $34. The aggregate cost and aggregate market value for the portfolio of investments needs to be computed:

Stock	Number of Shares	Cost	Market
Corn common	500	@ $20 = $10,000	@ $17 = $ 8,500
Oats common	300	@ 25 = 7,500	@ 28 = 8,400
Rye preferred	200	@ 35 = 7,000	@ 34 = 6,800
Total		$24,500	$23,700

December 31, 1995—to record the required allowance:

Loss on temporary investments	800	
Allowance to reduce temporary investments.		800

Reporting for 1995:

Income Statement

Investment revenue.	$	200
Loss on temporary investments		800

Balance Sheet

Current assets:

Temporary investments, at cost	$24,500	
Less: Allowance to reduce to market	800	$23,700

When a temporary investment is sold, any amount in the allowance account is disregarded because that balance relates to the total portfolio and not to any single part. The allowance account is adjusted only at the balance sheet date.

To illustrate: On January 26, 1996, Zero sold all of its shares in Oats for $26 per share and in Rye for $33 per share. This transaction would be recorded as follows: January 26, 1996:

Cash (300 × $26) + (200 × $33)	14,400	
Loss on sale of securities	100	
Temporary investments (300 × $25) + (200 × $35)		14,500

To conclude this example, assume the following for the balance of 1996: September 18, 1996, Zero Limited purchased 600 common shares of Wheat Corporation for $23 per share.

Temporary investments	13,800	
Cash		13,800

At the end of 1996, the quoted market prices were: Corn shares, $16; and Wheat shares, $25.50. The aggregate cost and aggregate market value for the portfolio are calculated as follows:

Stock	Number of Shares	Cost	Market
Corn common	500	@ $20 = $10,000	@ $16.00 = $ 8,000
Wheat common	600	@ 23 = 13,800	@ 25.50 = 15,300
Total		$23,800	$23,300

The allowance account has a credit balance of $800 carried over from the end of 1995. However, the market value of the portfolio at the end of 1996 is only $500 less than cost. Therefore, the following entry must be made to reduce the allowance account by $300.

December 31, 1996—to adjust allowance:

Allowance to reduce temporary investments	300	
Loss recovery on temporary investments.		300

Reporting for 1996:

Income Statement

Loss recovery on temporary investments.	$ 300
Loss on sales of securities	(100)
Net recovery	$ 200

Balance Sheet

Current assets:

Temporary investments, at cost	$23,800	
Less: Allowance to reduce to market	500	$23,300

The allowance method allows both the individual investments and the portfolio to be carried at cost. Any erosion of the market value of the portfolio below cost is accounted for by the use of the allowance account to reduce the net value of the portfolio to a market value. Because the allowance account cannot have a debit balance, the carrying value of the portfolio never increases to an amount greater than its historical cost. There can, however, be recoveries of previous losses due to increases in market values.

Direct Write-Off Method   The direct write-off method treats each investment in like shares as a separate account. Therefore, if at the balance sheet date the carrying value of those shares is greater than the market value, they are written down to market and a loss is recognized. The new carrying value is not adjusted if the shares subsequently increase in market value, as stipulated by Section 3050, paragraph .21 of the *CICA Handbook*.

Using the same data for Zero Limited, the entries required under the direct write-off method would be as follows:

March 1, 1995—to record acquisition:

Temporary investment, Corn (500 × $20)	10,000	
Temporary investment, Oats (300 × $25)	7,500	
Temporary investment, Rye (200 × $35)	7,000	
Cash		24,500

November 1, 1995—to record receipt of dividend:

Cash	200	
Investment revenue.		200

December 31, 1995—Quoted market prices, Corn common, $17; Oats common, $28; Rye preferred, $34.

Stock	Number of Shares	Carrying Value	Market
Corn common	500	@ $20 = $10,000	@ $17 = $ 8,500
Oats common	300	@ 25 = 7,500	@ 28 = 8,400
Rye preferred	200	@ 35 = 7,000	@ 34 = 6,800

December 31, 1995—to reduce temporary investments to lower of cost or market:

Loss on temporary investments	1,700	
Temporary investment, Corn ($10,000 − $8,500)		1,500
Temporary investment, Rye ($7,000 − $6,800)		200

Reporting for 1995:

Income Statement

Investment revenue	$ 200
Loss on temporary investments	1,700
Net loss	$ 1,500

Balance Sheet

Current assets:

Temporary investments, at lower of cost or market ($8,500 + $7,500 + $6,800)	$22,800

When a temporary investment is sold under the direct write-off method, the gain or loss on sale is the difference between the proceeds and the shares' carrying value. The Oat shares are sold at $26 and the Wheat shares at $33. The sale of the securities is recorded as follows:

January 26, 1996—sale of temporary investments:

Cash (300 × $26) + (200 × $33)	14,400	
Temporary investment, Oat		7,500
Temporary investment, Rye		6,800
Gain on sale of securities		100

September 18, 1996—purchase of Wheat Corporation shares:

Temporary investment, Wheat (600 × $23)	13,800	
Cash		13,800

December 31, 1996—Quoted market prices, Corn, $16; Wheat, $25.50.

Stock	Number of Shares	Carrying Value	Market
Corn common	500	@ $17 = $ 8,500	@ $16.00 = $ 8,000
Wheat common	600	@ 23 = 13,800	@ 25.50 = 15,300

December 31, 1996—to adjust to market:

Loss on temporary investments	500	
Temporary investment, Corn ($8,500 − $8,000)		500

Reporting for 1996:

Income Statement

Gain on sale of securities	$ 100	
Loss on temporary investments ($8,500 − $8,000)	(500)	
Net loss	$ (400)	

Balance Sheet

Current assets:

Temporary investments, at lower of cost or market ($8,000 + $13,800)	$21,800

Realized and Unrealized Gains and Losses

In accounting for both temporary and long-term investments, we must carefully distinguish between realized and unrealized gains and losses.

Realized gains and losses usually relate to the sale of an asset. Unrealized gains and losses relate to the comparison of the market value of the asset to its carrying value. When market value is greater than the carrying value, there is an unrealized gain. When market value is less than the carrying value, there is an unrealized loss. In the context of temporary investments, the following relationships exist:

1. **Realized gain** If, at date of sale, the net proceeds are greater than the carrying value of the securities sold, a *realized gain* in the amount of the difference is recognized.

2. **Realized loss** If at date of sale, the net proceeds are less than the carrying value of the securities sold, a *realized loss* in the amount of the difference is recognized.

3. **Unrealized loss** An unrealized loss occurs when the market value of securities is less than their carrying value. An *unrealized loss* is recognized:
   a. At the end of an accounting period if the current market value of the securities is less than their carrying value.
   b. When individual securities are transferred between the long-term and temporary portfolios and the market value at date of transfer is lower than the carrying value.

4. **Unrealized gain** An unrealized gain occurs when the market value of the securities is greater than their carrying value. *Unrealized gains* are normally not recognized.

When the allowance method is used, unrealized gains are recognized when the allowance to reduce to market account is reduced. The unrealized gain can be recorded only to the extent of the write-downs for unrealized losses. For this reason, it is often called an *unrealized loss recovery*. That is, under the allowance method, the valuation of the portfolio can never exceed the original cost of the total portfolio. An unrealized gain (i.e., reduction of prior unrealized losses) is recorded in an adjusting entry at the end of the accounting period. Under the direct method, previously recorded write-downs are not reversed and unrealized gains are not recognized. Recognition comes about when they are realized through the sale of the securities.

The *CICA Handbook* is silent as to the use of the allowance or direct method. Canadian practice uses both methods, depending on the circumstances. There are some accountants who feel that the allowance method or some variation, which would allow the recognition of unrealized holding gains up to the original cost value, is appropriate because industries such as insurance and pension plans presently use the market approach where unrealized gains and losses are recognized in income. They argue that what is allowed for some industries should be available to all industries. Others, who are more conservative, tend to use the direct method and only recognize unrealized holding losses. This view is supported by Section 3050, paragraph .21, which applies to long-term investments but could be interpreted as applying to temporary investments in the absence of a definitive recommendation. Obviously, the Canadian standards could use some clarification in this area.

| CONCEPT REVIEW

1. How are unrealized losses computed? How are they treated for accounting purposes for temporary investments?
2. Explain the accounting entries that are made when a temporary investment is sold for more than its original cost. What effect does this transaction (by itself) have on any amounts in the allowance to reduce to market account when there is an unrealized loss for the portfolio recorded?
3. What entry would be made at year-end when the aggregate market value has increased to an amount greater than the original cost for a temporary investment portfolio that has previously had a valuation allowance recorded?

Change in Classification between Temporary and Long-Term Marketable Equity Securities

It is possible for management to change the classification of an investment from current to noncurrent, or vice-versa. When this happens, the security involved must be reclassified on the balance sheet. The *CICA Handbook* is silent on this issue. However, *SFAS No. 115* specifies that the security be transferred between two portfolios at the lower of cost or market value at the date of transfer. If market is different than cost, the new cost basis for the security will be the market value. The difference shall be accounted for as if it were a realized gain or loss and included in the determination of net income.

Example   Suppose Alex Company decides as of January 30, 1995, to reclassify its holdings of 5,000 shares of Henry Corporation from long term to temporary. Henry was originally acquired at $7 per share. Assume the market price at January 30, 1995, is $6 per share.

Alex would make the following entry to record the change in classification:

Investments in temporary equity securities	30,000	
Loss on reclassification of equity securities	5,000	
Investments in long-term equity securities		35,000

Because the *CICA Handbook* does not specifically cover this question of reclassification of securities, it may be more likely that the securities would be reclassified at their carrying value. The LCM rule would then be applied at the subsequent balance sheet date and any write-downs, if necessary, would be recorded at that time. This practice could, however, allow management to ignore an unrealized loss at the date of transfer.

Accounting for Nonmarketable, Long-Term Equity Securities At this point, it is appropriate to briefly describe how an equity security is accounted for when (1) it is not readily marketable, and (2) the investor does not have significant influence. When a market value is not determinable, the LCM method cannot be applied. Securities that are not readily marketable and that do not qualify for the equity method are accounted for using the **cost method.** Under the cost method, the investment is carried at the original investment amount, and investment revenue is the dividends received from the investee. Gains and losses on the investment are recorded only when realized, which is when the investment is sold. There are no market values to compare with cost; thus, there are no determinations or any entries for the recording of unrealized losses. This method is more fully described below.

Accounting for Temporary Investments in Marketable Debt Securities

Investments in debt securities are both recorded and carried at their acquisition cost in conformity with the cost principle. If the market value of the securities held temporarily falls below acquisition cost, they are normally not written down to market. A write-down is recommended, however, (1) if the current market value is less than cost by a substantial amount, and (2) if the market value decline is not due to temporary conditions. When both of these conditions exist, the short-term debt security (on a security-by-security basis) should be written down to market value to recognize the permanent impairment of the asset value. There is no direct guidance on how to determine whether the decline in value is a permanent impairment. Changes in value caused by the normal, small changes in the market rate of interest for debt securities would not be viewed as causing a permanent impairment, but a decline in value resulting from a major financial difficulty for the issuer of the debt would most likely be viewed as a permanent impairment. A permanent decline is recorded as a direct credit to the investment account and a debit to a loss (realized) account such as impairment loss on investments in marketable securities.

However, an increasing number of firms have adopted the allowance method for marketable, temporary investments in debt securities. Its application for debt securities is the same as discussed for marketable equity securities—LCM is computed on an aggregate basis, any unrealized loss at the balance sheet date is charged to the income statement, and a valuation allowance account (a contra account) is credited. The unrealized loss can be recovered in the same manner as that for marketable equity securities. When the allowance method is used, usually a separate portfolio is set up for debt securities, and the method is applied to the portfolio in exactly the same way as illustrated earlier for equity securities. In practice, then, marketable debt securities can be carried either at cost or at lower of cost or market. Because the key characteristic is the same for temporary debt and equity securities (i.e., marketability), it makes sense to account for both using the same method.

The acquisition of a debt security is recorded at cost. However, when a debt security is purchased or sold between interest dates, the accrued interest since the last interest date must be computed and recorded separately from cost. On the next interest date, the new owner of the debt security receives the full cash amount of interest for the interest period. On the transaction date, the buyer and seller agree on the price to be paid for the debt and also on the amount of cash that must be transferred to pay the interest accrued from the last interest payment date. This latter amount must be separately recorded to determine correctly the amount of interest revenue that the investor records when interest is received at the next interest payment date.

Example   On May 1, 1995, Laurel Company purchases 100 bonds of Surber Corporation at 96 (face amount $1,000 and stated interest 12%, with interest payable semiannually on July 1 and January 1). Commissions on the purchase are $1,280. Laurel Company has the following cash outlay:

Purchase price of bonds	$ 96,000
Commission	1,280
Cost of bonds acquired	97,280
Accrued interest—January 1 to May 1 ($100,000 × 12% × 4/12)	4,000
Total cash payment	$103,280

To record the preceding transaction, Laurel makes the following entry:

Temporary debt securities	97,280	
Accrued interest receivable	4,000	
Cash		103,280

When the interest payment is received by Laurel on June 1, this entry records the interest revenue:

Cash	6,000	
Accrued interest receivable		4,000
Interest revenue		2,000

Generally, any discount or premium caused by a difference between the maturity value of the debt security and the acquisition price is not separately recorded because the holding period is short. Any discount or premium is usually not amortized. The investment is carried at cost until it is sold.

When the security is sold, the difference between the carrying amount and the selling price, less commissions and other expenses, is recorded as gain or loss. Suppose that on October 1, 1995, Laurel Company sells its holdings of Surber Corporation bonds at a price of 98, plus accrued interest, and incurs commissions and other expenses associated with the sale of the bonds of $560. The gain or loss is computed as:

Selling price of bonds	$98,000
Less: Commission and expenses	560
Net proceeds from bonds	97,440
Carrying amount of bonds	97,280
Gain on sale of bonds	$ 160

Entry to record the sale, including recording the receipt of interest revenue for the period July 1 to the transaction date of October 1:

Cash ($98,000 + $3,000 − $560)	100,440	
Gain on sale of bonds		160
Interest revenue: ($100,000 × 12% × 3/12)		3,000
Temporary debt securities		97,280

Any gain or loss on the disposition of short-term debt securities is included in the determination of income from continuing operations.

As shown in Exhibit 14–1, when management intends to hold securities as long-term investments, the amortized cost method (for debt securities) or the cost method (for equity securities) is used to account for the investment.

Cost Method: For Investments in Equity Securities with No Significant Influence

Investments in equity securities that do not require consolidation or use of the equity method are accounted for using the cost method. An example of such an investment would be one having less than 20% of the voting shares of another corporation. The investment is carried at its original cost on the balance sheet. Ordinary dividends received on the security are recorded as investment income. If the total dividends per share received by an investor since the date of the investment exceed the total earnings per share of the investee company for that time period, the excess is accounted for by the investor as return of investment rather than as investment income. If there is clear evidence that there has been an "other than temporary decline" in market value to below the current carrying value of such investments, a realized loss is recorded and the carrying value is reduced. Examples of value impairment include bankruptcy, depressed market price for a prolonged period, continued losses for a period of years, or severe losses by the investee in the current or prior years. The investment should not be written up if there is a subsequent increase in value.

Example Suppose Tree Corporation acquires 1,000 shares of the 10,000 total common shares outstanding of Peach Company for $20,000 on January 1, 1995. Peach Company shares are not traded, and it is not possible to determine a fair value. During 1995, Peach has earnings per share of $3 and pays dividends of $3 per share. The entry to record this transaction is as follows:

```
Cash . . . . . . . . . . . . . . . . . . . . . . . . . . . . . . . . . . . . . . . . . . . .   3,000
     Investment income: Dividends, Peach Company . . . . . . . . . . . .          3,000
```

Suppose that during 1996, Peach has earnings per share of $2 but continues to pay dividends of $3 per share. The extra dividend over earnings is a liquidating dividend. The entry to record this transaction would be the following:

```
Cash . . . . . . . . . . . . . . . . . . . . . . . . . . . . . . . . . . . . . . . . . . .   3,000
     Investment in Peach Company (liquidating dividend) . . . . . . . . . . .          1,000
     Investment income: Dividends, Peach Company . . . . . . . . . . . . .          2,000
```

At December 31, 1996, the investment in Peach Company is carried at $19,000 ($20,000 original investment less the return of capital in the amount of $1,000). Subsequent increases in earnings over dividends paid do not result in an increase in the investment account. Thus, if in 1997 Peach earns $5 per share and pays dividends of $2 per share, the investment continues to be carried at $19,000.

If at any time the investor determines that there has been a permanent impairment of the value of the investment, a loss is recorded and the carrying value of the investment is permanently reduced to the estimated fair value. Suppose during 1997 in the above example, Tree Corporation management determines that there has been a permanent impairment in the value of Peach Company to $16,000. Since the investment is currently being carried at $19,000, an entry must be made to record the permanent impairment loss:

```
Loss: Permanent impairment of value of Peach Company . . . . . . . . . . .   3,000
     Investment in Peach Company . . . . . . . . . . . . . . . . . . . . . . . .          3,000
```

As with liquidating dividends, once the entry to record the investment at its impaired value is made, subsequent increases in the fair value of the investment security are not recorded.

Amortized Cost Method: For Debt Securities

The amortized cost method applies to investments in debt securities that the investor intends and has the ability to hold to maturity. The investment is recorded at its cost, which may be greater or less than the face amount of the debt. Any premium (discount) the investor paid over (under) the face value of the debt instrument is amortized to income over the period from the investment date to the maturity date, such that the premium (discount) is fully amortized at the maturity date of the security. Since the holder of the debt receives the face amount of the debt as payment at its maturity, the debt is carried at its fair value at maturity. Interest received is included in investment income. Since this procedure is also used in accounting for debt instruments by the issuer, it is covered in detail in Chapter 16. The following is a simplified example of the amortized cost method.

Example   Wooden Company acquires $100,000 face amount of Olsen Corporation 7% bonds for $98,000 on January 1, 1994, and intends to hold the bonds until they mature on December 31, 1997. The bonds pay interest semiannually on June 30 and December 31. Wooden has acquired the bonds at a discount of $2,000. Assume that the discount is amortized over the four years using the straight-line method; thus $2,000 ÷ 4, or $500, of the discount is amortized each year.[6] The entries to record the investment and interest income in 1994 are as follows:

January 1, 1994—To record investment in bonds to be held to maturity:

Long-term investment in debt securities: Olsen bonds   98,000
    Cash   98,000

December 31, 1994—To record receipt of interest and amortization of discount:

Cash ($100,000 × .07).   7,000
Long-term investment in debt securities: Olsen bonds   500
    Investment income: Interest   7,500

At December 31, 1994, the investment in Olsen bonds is carried at $98,500, which is the amortized cost of the investment. The entry to record receipt of interest payments and amortization of discount is repeated from 1995 through 1997. At December 31, 1997, the investment in Olsen Corporation bonds has increased by $500 per year for four years, and hence the carrying value of the investment on this date is its face amount of $100,000. On this date Olsen pays the face amount of the bonds to bond holders and retires the debt. Wooden receives $100,000 in exchange for the Olsen bonds it holds:

Cash   100,000
    Long-term investment in debt securities: Olsen bonds   100,000

Suppose Wooden paid more than the face of the bonds, say $102,000. The excess over the face amount is called a premium. At acquisition, the bonds would be recorded at $102,000, but over the period to their maturity the $2,000 premium would be amortized, reducing the carrying amount each year by the amount of the amortization and decreasing interest income by a like amount.

EQUITY METHOD: INVESTMENTS IN EQUITY SECURITIES RESULTING IN SIGNIFICANT INFLUENCE OVER THE INVESTEE

When an investor company acquires sufficient ownership in the voting shares of an investee company to have "significant influence" over the affairs of the investee company but less than a controlling interest, the investment is accounted for using the equity method. Such investments are made for purposes different from those of temporary investments, so it is not surprising that the accounting requirements are different. When an investor company acquires a significant interest in an investee company, it usually does so because it intends to retain a long-term investment, and through its significant influence it can sometimes affect activities between the two

---

[6] More complex methods for amortizing the premium or discount are required under certain circumstances. They are covered in Chapter 16.

companies that would not be possible otherwise. For example, (1) the investor company might influence the investee company to buy or sell products and services from or to the investor company; (2) the investor company might acquire from or transfer to the investee company various assets such as long-term receivables, perhaps with recourse, such that the balance sheets and income statements of both companies are affected; or (3) an investor company may join with one or more other investor companies to form an investee company that will undertake risky projects that none of the investor companies desires to undertake by itself. In each case, activities result from the unique relationship between the investor and investee companies such that the earnings and balance sheets of each are affected by the relationship. Coca-Cola and its relationship with its bottling company partners is representative of this type of intercompany interaction and relationship.

The equity method of accounting enables this unique relationship to be recognized by the investor. Conceptually, the equity method treats the investee company as if it were condensed into one balance sheet item and one income statement item and then merged into the investor company at the proportion owned by the investor. The equity method is sometimes called the *one-line consolidation method* because it results in the same effect on earnings and retained earnings as would result from consolidating the financial statements of the investor and investee companies but does so without combining both companies' financial statements, as in a complete consolidation.

Before discussing the application of the equity method, we first consider when it is the appropriate method to use. It is useful to again refer to Exhibit 14–1, which shows that when a firm has a significant influence but less than a controlling interest, the investment is accounted for by the equity method. *CICA Handbook,* Section 1590, paragraph .03 defines the conditions under which a controlling interest is deemed to exist and consolidated financial statements combining the investor and investee companies are to be prepared. The usual condition for **control** is the "continuing power to determine [the] strategic operating, investing and financing policies without the co-operation of others." As a general rule, ownership by one company, directly or indirectly, of over 50% of the outstanding voting shares of another company is a condition for control and therefore consolidation. There are two exceptions to this general rule. One occurs when an enterprise is acquired with a clearly demonstrable intention that it be disposed of in the near future or the relationship can be terminated by a decision by someone other than the acquiring enterprise. The second situation occurs when the application of a statute or agreement imposes severe long-term restrictions on the investor to distribute earnings or undertake other transactions. For example, severe foreign exchange or currency export restrictions may indicate that control has been lost.[7]

Short of a controlling interest, a firm can have a significant influence if it has the ability to affect to an important degree the operating and financial policies of an investee company either through ownership of a sufficient portion of voting stock or in some other way. These other ways include representation on the board of directors, interchange of managerial personnel, material intercompany transactions, and technological dependency. To attain a reasonable degree of uniformity on what constitutes significant influence, *CICA Handbook,* Section 3050, paragraph .04 provides an operational rule: In the absence of evidence to the contrary, investments in which the investor company owns 20% or more of the outstanding voting shares of the investee company, the investor company is presumed to have significant influ-

---

[7] *CICA Handbook* Section 1590, "Subsidiaries."

ence over the investee company.[8] Thus, when an investor has an investment in the voting common shares of an investee company that results in significant influence but not control over the investee, the investment is accounted for by the equity method.

Conceptual Basis Underlying the Equity Method

The cost method and the equity method are based on totally different underlying concepts of investment valuation and of investment income measurement. The cost method views the investor and investee companies as two separate entities, whereas the equity method views them as a special type of single entity. The equity method is a modified cost method of valuation and measures investment income as a proportionate share of the investee's income. *CICA Handbook* Section 3050 provides guidance on when and how to implement the equity method.

In its simplest form, the single-entity concept underlying the equity method requires that the investment account represent the investor's proportionate share of the book value of the investee and that the investment income represent the investor's proportionate share of the investee's income. Assume, for initial simplicity, that Tanford Computer Company makes an initial investment of $100,000 for 40% of the voting shares of Rinceton Software on January 1, 1994. The investment amount is exactly equal to the 40% of Rinceton's owners' equity, and this amount also represents 40% of the fair value of net assets of Rinceton. In 1994, Rinceton has earnings of $30,000 and pays dividends of $10,000. The investment is accounted for by the equity method, and the investment account for Rinceton reflects the following:

Investment in Rinceton Software, at Equity

Original investment	100,000		
Proportionate share of earnings of investee ($30,000 × .40)	12,000	Dividends received from investee ($10,000 × .40)	4,000
Ending balance equals original investment plus proportionate share of investee earnings, less dividend paid by investee to investor	108,000		

The difference between investee earnings and investee dividends is the amount of earnings accruing to the investor that the investee retained. Thus, the investment at equity account is equal to the original investment plus the investor's proportionate share of the investee's cumulative retained earnings since the investment was made. In this sense, the equity method represents an extension of accrual accounting to investments in common stock securities.

Investor companies often identify investee companies that are accounted for by the equity method as unconsolidated subsidiaries, associated companies, or affiliated companies. Another name for the proportionate share of earnings of the investee is *equity in the earnings of subsidiary* (or *of equity-basis* or *associated* or *affiliated companies*).

---

[8] An investor may not be able to exercise significant influence over the investee's policies, even though the investor owns more than 20% interest, when:
- Opposition by the investee, such as litigation or complaints to governmental regulatory agencies, challenges the investor's ability to exercise influence.
- The investor and investee sign an agreement under which the investor surrenders significant rights as a shareholder.
- Majority ownership of the investee is concentrated among a small group of shareholders who operate the company without regard to the views of the investor company.
- The investor is unsuccessful in attempts to obtain representation on the investee's board of directors.

Dividends from the investee are not included as investment income. Rather, they represent a disinvestment, a reduction of the investment. Under the equity method, the investor company records its proportionate share of the investee earnings as investment income and increases its investment account by this amount. When the investee pays dividends, its net worth is reduced, and thus the investment account of the investor is reduced.

Under the equity method, the investment is shown on the investor's balance sheet as a single amount. The investor's share of the investee's earnings is shown as a single amount on the investor's income statement except when the investee's earnings includes items reported below income from continuing operations. When the investee reports extraordinary items, discontinued operations, and cumulative effects of accounting changes, the investor company must separately report its proportionate share of these items on its income statement in the same way it would if they were incurred by the investor company.

When an investor company acquires the equity securities of an investee company, it may pay more for the securities than their book value. If it does, the investor's investment income is the proportionate share of investee earnings adjusted for amortization of the difference between the investor's original investment and the underlying fair value of the net assets acquired. In Chapter 13, the process of measuring the fair value of net assets acquired and of determining the amount of goodwill in an acquisition are presented. This process is applicable here. Any difference between the initial cost of an investment and the fair value of the underlying net assets acquired is goodwill and must be amortized according to the requirements of *CICA Handbook* Section 3060.

Equity Method Illustrated

On January 2, 1995, Giant Company purchased 3,600 shares of the 18,000 outstanding common shares of Small Corporation for $300,000 cash. Two Giant Company senior executives were elected to the Small Corporation board of directors. Giant is deemed to be able to exercise significant influence over Small's operating and financial policies, so the equity method of accounting for the investment is appropriate.

At the acquisition of the 20% interest in Small, Giant records its investment as follows:

Investment in Small, at equity 300,000
    Cash   300,000

The balance sheet for Small at January 2, 1995, and estimated market values of its assets and liabilities are as follows:

	Book Value	Market Value	Difference
Cash and receivables	$ 100,000	$ 100,000	0
Inventory (FIFO basis)	400,000	405,000	$ 5,000
Plant and equipment (10-year remaining life).	500,000	700,000	200,000
Land	150,000	165,000	15,000
Total assets	$1,150,000	$1,370,000	$220,000
Liabilities	$ 150,000	$ 150,000	0
Shareholders' equity	1,000,000	1,220,000	$220,000
Total liabilities and equity	$1,150,000	$1,370,000	$220,000

The net book value of the claim Giant has on Small is 20% of Small's shareholders' equity, or $200,000. Since Giant paid $300,000 for its interest in Small, what is required to justify the fact that the purchase price is $100,000 greater than book value? If items can be identified whose market value is greater than their net book value, the $100,000 premium over book value is allocated to these items in accordance with the equity method.

The market value column shows the specific assets whose market value exceeds book value. Giant acquired a portion (20%) of each of these items, including the amount by which market value exceeds book value:

	Book Value	Market Value	Difference	20% of Difference
Inventory.	$400,000	$405,000	$ 5,000	$ 1,000
Plant and equipment (10-year remaining life).	500,000	700,000	200,000	40,000
Land.	150,000	165,000	15,000	3,000
Excess value of assets acquired by Giant				$44,000

Thus, $44,000 of the $100,000 purchase price premium over book value that Giant paid can be identified with these specific assets. The remaining difference, $56,000, cannot be specifically identified with any asset and represents goodwill. Goodwill is defined as the excess of the amount invested in acquiring all or a portion of another firm over the fair value of the net identifiable assets acquired. Goodwill can also be computed as follows:

Computation of Goodwill Purchased by Giant Company

Purchase price (of 20% interest)		$300,000
Market value of identifiable assets	$1,370,000	
Less: Liabilities of Small	(150,000)	
Total market value of identifiable net assets acquired	1,220,000	
Market value of 20% of identifiable net assets acquired: ($1,220,000 × .20).		244,000
Goodwill.		$ 56,000

Giant, then, has acquired a 20% interest in Small at a cost of $300,000, and the items acquired can be represented as follows:

20% of the net book value of Small	$200,000
20% of excess of market value over book value for	
Inventory (.20 × 5,000)	1,000
Plant and equipment (.20 × 200,000)	40,000
Land (.20 × 15,000).	3,000
Goodwill.	56,000
Total	$300,000

The equity method requires that Giant record its initial $300,000 investment in Small as is detailed above. Subsequently, when Small disposes of any of the above items, either in the normal course of business or by asset sales, Giant must record appropriate adjustments to its investment account. For example, since Small uses FIFO to cost its inventory, the beginning inventory is treated as sold first during the coming year. Likewise, its plant and equipment is used and depreciated during the coming year. Since the valuation of these items from Giant's investment perspective is different from that recorded by Small, Giant needs to record adjustments in its investment account and in its investment income account to reflect the using up of the difference between the market value and the book value of these assets.

Assuming that all of Small's beginning inventory is sold during 1995, Small's cost of goods sold for 1995 is understated by $1,000 from the single-entity (Giant) perspective. Also, depreciation is understated. If the plant and equipment has a remaining useful life of 10 years and Small uses straight-line depreciation, Giant needs to increase the depreciation expense for Small by $40,000 divided by 10 years, or $4,000 each year for the next 10 years. Finally, the goodwill must be amortized over a period of 40 years or less. Assuming that Giant amortizes goodwill over the maximum period, the annual charge for goodwill amortization is $56,000 divided by 40, or $1,400 each year for the next 40 years.

No adjustments need be made for the excess of market value over book value for the land. Only if Small disposes of the land would an adjustment need to be made, showing that the cost of 20% of the land from the Giant perspective is understated by $3,000. Giant's proportionate share of any gain (loss) on disposal of the land would be decreased (increased) by $3,000.

Giant's income from its investment in Small requires adjusting entries to reflect the above analysis. Suppose that for the fiscal year ending December 31, 1995, Small reports the following:

Income before extraordinary items	$ 80,000
Extraordinary item	30,000
Net income	$110,000
Cash dividends paid on December 31	$ 50,000

At December 31, Giant would make the following entries to reflect its interest in the earnings of Small:

1. To recognize investment income based on Giant's proportionate share of income reported by Small:

Investment in Small, at equity ($110,000 × .20).	22,000	
Investment income ($80,000 × .20)		16,000
Extraordinary gain ($30,000 × .20)		6,000

2. To record additional costs of goods sold associated with the excess of market value over book value of inventory at the acquisition of Small:

Investment income	1,000	
Investment in Small, at equity		1,000

3. To record depreciation on the $40,000 of depreciable assets implicit in the purchase price paid for Small:

Investment income ($40,000 ÷ 10 years)	4,000	
Investment in Small, at equity		4,000

4. To record periodic amortization of goodwill:

Investment income ($56,000 ÷ 40 years)	1,400	
Investment in Small, at equity		1,400

5. To record the receipt of cash dividends paid by Small:

Cash ($50,000 × .20)	10,000	
Investment in Small, at equity		10,000

After these entries are posted, the balance in the investment in Small account is $305,600:

Beginning balance (acquisition price)	$300,000
Proportionate share of Small's net income	22,000
Additional cost of goods sold adjustment.	(1,000)
Additional depreciation adjustment	(4,000)
Amortization of goodwill	(1,400)
Dividends received	(10,000)
Investment account balance, Dec. 31, 1995	$305,600

The investment revenue for 1995, after all the adjustments, is $9,600 of ordinary income plus an extraordinary item of $6,000:

Investment revenue (ordinary):
Proportionate share of Small's net income $16,000
Additional cost of goods sold adjustment . . . . (1,000)
Additional depreciation adjustment. . . . . (4,000)
Amortization of goodwill . . . . (1,400)
                                                                  9,600

Extraordinary gain:
Extraordinary gain (as recorded by Small) 6,000
Total investment revenue (ordinary and extraordinary) $15,600

The total investment income Giant reports from its investment in Small is $15,600. Since Giant received $10,000 of this in the form of cash dividends, the net increase of its investment is $5,600. This amount is the increase in the investment account from the beginning to the end of the year.

Summary of the Equity Method

The equity basis accounting method for investments can be complex. The investor company must maintain separate records on the transactions of the investee firm and make the appropriate adjusting entries at the appropriate time. In general, six types of entries are involved to account for investment income under the equity method:

1. Record the proportionate share of the investee's reported income. This is a debit to the investment account and a credit to investment revenue (often labelled *equity in the earnings of associated companies*). If the investee firm reports extraordinary items, the investor firm must separately report these items. The rationale is that the investee and the investor are a single entity with respect to the portion of the investee owned by the investor.
2. Record any dividends paid by the investee firm as a debit to cash and a credit to the investment account. The dividends are not income but are rather the conversion of a portion of the investment to cash. Dividends represent a liquidation of the investment.
3. Record the proportionate share of additional expense items related to the investor's cost of the investment over the proportionate share of the book value of the investee firm. In our example, these additional expense items include the cost of goods sold and the depreciation adjustments. Entries made to adjust the investment account and the investment revenue can be complex, and they are covered in detail in advanced accounting courses.
4. Record the amortization of any purchased goodwill. Since the goodwill is associated with the investment, it is recorded as a debit to the investment revenue account and a credit to the investment account. No goodwill is separately identified on the books of the investor firm; the purchased goodwill is included in the investment account.
5. Record any gain or loss on the sale of portions of the investment (any difference between the sale proceeds from disposing of the shares and the carrying amount of the investment). The gain or loss on disposal is separately identified in the income statement accounts of the investor firm.
6. Eliminate any intercompany profits or losses arising from transactions between the investor and investee firms. This topic is also covered in more detail in advanced accounting courses. Because the basic concept being applied is that the investor and investee are a single entity, profits on transactions between the two parties must be eliminated because an entity cannot earn profits in transactions with itself. Thus, when the investor firm sells an asset to the investee firm (or vice versa) at a profit, the item is carried on the books of the buyer at its cost. Its cost, however, is the original cost of the item as was recorded on the books of the selling firm plus the profit that the selling firm records. The profit recorded by the selling firm must be eliminated.

Example   Suppose Giant sells land to Small. The land originally cost Giant $10,000, and the sales price to Small is $15,000. Giant makes the following entry to record the disposal of land:

Cash (or accounts receivable)	15,000	
Land		10,000
Gain on disposal		5,000

The land is recorded by Small at a cost of $15,000, but for the single entity of Giant and Small combined, the land had an original cost of $10,000. To adjust and remove the profit recorded by Giant, the following entry is made at closing (in the year the land is sold):

Gain on disposal	5,000	
Investment in Small.		5,000

With this entry, the profit that would otherwise be reported by Giant is eliminated. The credit is to the investment account because Small has paid $5,000 more to Giant than the original cost of the land. This additional payment is analogous to a dividend, and dividends paid by the investee to the investor are credited to the investment account.

The equity basis method is a modified cost basis method. The investment account is carried at original cost plus the investor's equity in the undistributed earnings of the investee. While the notion of lower of cost or market does not appear to be applicable, some firms do indicate that their equity-basis investments are carried at the lower of cost or market. A permanent impairment in the market value of the investee's shares would require a write-down by the investor to the extent that market value was below carrying value.

|CONCEPT REVIEW

1. What are the components of the carrying amount recorded in an investment account under the equity method?
2. What are the components of investment revenue under the equity method?
3. How are dividends received by the investor firm from the investee firm recorded under the equity method?

Changing between the Cost Method and the Equity Method

An investor's ownership level and therefore level of influence over an investee company can change over time. An investor with a small ownership percentage using the cost method might acquire a sufficient number of additional shares to gain significant influence, thereby necessitating a change in accounting to the equity method. Alternatively, an investor currently using the equity method might sell shares, or the investee might issue additional shares to parties other than the investor, and in either case, the investor's ownership interest might decrease below that considered to have significant influence. The investor would be required to change accounting for its investment from the equity method to the cost method. Both these types of changes are discussed here.

Changes from the Equity Method to the Cost Method   When the ownership level falls below what is necessary to continue using the equity method, the investor must change to the cost method. At the transfer date, the carrying value of the investment under the equity method is regarded as the cost of the investment. Subsequent dividends received are included in investment income. Comparison of the carrying value and market value should be done to determine if an adjustment is necessary to reflect an impairment in value. There is no further accounting for goodwill or differences between the book value and the fair value of the assets of the investee.

Changes to the Equity Method from the Cost Method   When the ownership level in an investee accounted for by the cost method increases to the point where the investor has significant influence, the investment must be accounted for using the equity method. The recorded carrying value at the date of transfer is regarded as the initial cost of the investment, analogous to the purchase price if the investor were to acquire its interest on this date. The investment is recorded in an investment at equity account at this amount, and the original accounts are reduced to zero. From this point on, the accounting proceeds exactly as was described earlier for the equity method. The investor must determine the fair value of the net assets owned and determine the amount of goodwill as the difference between the recorded cost and the fair value of the net assets acquired.[9]

Example   On January 1, 1994, White Company purchased 2,000 shares, or 20% of the outstanding voting shares, of Wong Inc. for $240,000. Because it was not allowed to elect members to the board of directors of Wong nor influence Wong's operating activities in any way, White classified the investment as a long-term investment and used the cost method of accounting for the investment. Two years later, on January 1, 1996, Wong purchases and retires 2,000 of its outstanding shares in the market. The effect of this transaction is to increase White's ownership level to 25% [2,000 shares ÷ (10,000 shares initially outstanding − 2,000 shares retired)]. The restrictions of White's influence are lifted given its level of investment. White reclassifies and accounts for its investment in Wong using the equity method. White is able to determine that the total fair value of the net assets of Wong on January 1, 1996, is $840,000, and that its share is therefore $210,000. The carrying value of the investment in Wong is $240,000, so the amount of goodwill to be accounted for is $240,000 − $210,000, or $30,000. The entries to reclassify the investment are as follows:

```
Long-term investment in Wong Inc., at equity . . . . . . . . . . . . .   240,000
        Long-term investment, Wong Inc.: Cost basis . . . . . . . . . . .          240,000
```

The investment in Wong, at equity of $240,000 includes $30,000 in goodwill and may include additional differences between the book value and the fair value of specific assets and liabilities that must be appropriately accounted for in subsequent periods.

Both changes from and changes to the equity method result in recording the investment at its carrying value at the reclassification date. The reclassification should be disclosed in the notes, including the effect of the reclassification on carrying value of the investment, and the effect on investment income.

Disclosures Required for Investments Accounted for by the Equity Method

The disclosure requirements for long-term investments are detailed in *CICA Handbook,* Section 3050, paragraphs .29 to .33, and include the following:

  a. The basis of valuation of long-term investments should be disclosed.
  b. Investments in companies subject to significant influence, other affiliated companies and other long-term investments should each be shown separately.
  c. Income from investments in companies subject to significant influence, other affiliated companies and other long-term investments should each be shown separately. Income calculated by the equity method should be disclosed separately.
  d. When investments are accounted for by the equity method, disclosure should be made, in the notes to the financial statements, of the amount of any difference between the cost and the underlying net book value of the investee's assets at the

---

[9] The term *fair value* is used several times in this section with two different definitions. The *fair value of the investment* is defined as the market price of the shares multiplied by the number of shares owned. It represents a value for the total investee company, including its goodwill. On the other hand, the *fair value of the net assets owned* refers to sum of the fair values of the identifiable assets and liabilities of the investee company. It does not include goodwill, since goodwill is an unidentifiable asset.

EXHIBIT 14–2
Note Disclosures on
Investments by
Canadian Pacific

11. Investments	December 31, 1993	1992
	(in millions)	
Accounted for on the equity basis:		
Laidlaw Inc.*	$ 656.7	$ 739.8
Unitel Communications Holdings Inc.	173.9	—
Doubletree Hotels†	30.5	
Other	106.3	66.0
Discontinued operations	—	(73.5)
Accounted for on the cost basis:		
United Dominion Industries Limited	170.7	170.7
PacFor Holdings Inc.	86.6	—
Loan to Canadian Pacific Forest Products Limited	39.0	—
Other	62.0	71.9
Discontinued operations	—	214.7
	$1,325.7	$1,189.6

* The Corporation owns 22,500,000 Class A voting shares, which represent 47.2% of Laidlaw's Class A voting shares outstanding, and 29,711,034 Class B non-voting shares, which represent 12.9% of Laidlaw's Class B non-voting shares outstanding. The Corporation's ownership interest in Laidlaw, based on the combined number of Class A and Class B shares outstanding, was 18.8% at December 31, 1993, 1992, and 1991.

At December 31, 1993, the difference of approximately $283 million between the carrying amount of the Corporation's investment in Laidlaw and its share of the underlying equity in net assets of Laidlaw has been assigned to goodwill and is being written off over 40 years.

The quoted market value of the Corporation's investment in Laidlaw at December 31, 1993 was $476.4 million.

The following is a summary of the reported results and financial position of Laidlaw:

For the Year ended August 31

	1993	1992	1991
	(U.S. $ in millions)		
Revenues	$1,993.3	$1,925.6	$1,882.4
Income (loss) from operations	(21.8)	237.7	246.8
Net income (loss)	(291.6)	132.4	(344.4)
Net income (loss) applicable to Class A and Class B shares	(292.1)	131.8	(348.9)

August 31

	1993	1992
	(U.S. $ in millions)	
Total assets	$3,575.1	$3,731.4
Total liabilities	2,021.8	1,771.5
Shareholders' equity	1,553.3	1,959.9

Dividends received by the Corporation from Laidlaw amounted to $8.4 million in 1993, $8.2 million in 1992 and $13.3 million in 1991.

In 1991, the Corporation wrote down the carrying value of its investment in Laidlaw to reflect a decline that management considers to be other than temporary.

† On December 16, 1993 Doubletree Hotels Corporation, an 80%-owned subsidiary of Canadian Pacific Hotels & Resorts Inc. (CP Hotels), merged with Guest Quarters Hotels Partnership to form Doubletree Hotels. CP Hotels accounts for its 32% investment in Doubletree Hotels on the equity method.

date of purchase, as well as the accounting treatment of the components of such difference.

e. When portfolio investments include marketable securities, the quoted market value of such securities as well as their carrying value should be disclosed.

Often, investments accounted for by the equity method are a substantial holding for the investor and require the extensive disclosure described above. An example of such disclosure is shown in Exhibit 14–2 for Canadian Pacific Limited.

Market Value Method for Debt and Equity Securities

Yet another method of accounting for marketable securities is the **market value method.** It is an option only for those firms whose primary line of business includes investing in the securities of others. Some specialized industries, such as investment companies, stock life insurance companies, fire and casualty insurance companies, and brokers and dealers in securities are permitted by the *CICA Handbook* to carry equity securities at market with unrealized gains and losses generally recognized as part of the current year's income (or loss).

The market value method is fundamentally different from the cost or the equity methods. The market value method is based on the concept of current value accounting, not historical cost accounting. Under this method, each individual security investment is revalued at each financial statement date to the current market value of the securities held. The LCM concept is not applied with the market value method.

The market value method is summarized as follows:

1. At date of acquisition, investments are recorded at cost in conformity with the cost principle.
2. After acquisition, each individual investment account balance is adjusted at the end of the accounting year to the current market value of the securities held. The adjusted amount then becomes the new carrying value for subsequent accounting.
3. Interest earned and cash and property dividends declared and paid are recognized by the investor as investment revenue.
4. Increases or decreases in the market value of the securities are recognized at the end of each accounting period. One of the following approaches is used:
   a. Current approach—the price change during the current period is recognized as investment revenue (or loss) in the current income statement clearly labelled as the increase or decrease in market value.
   b. Deferral approach—the price change during the current period is recorded as a deferred item in owners' equity, labelled unrealized market gain or loss. When a security is subsequently sold, the difference between its carrying value in the investment account and its original cost must be removed from its deferred status in the unrealized account and recognized as investment revenue. Any additional difference is recognized as gain or loss on sale of investments.
5. On disposal of the investment, the difference between the carrying value at that date and its sale price is recognized as a gain or loss on disposal.

In May 1993, the FASB issued *SFAS No. 115,* "Accounting for Certain Investments in Debt and Equity Securities," in which securities are divided into three groups:

   a) debt securities that are intended to be held to maturity are classified as *held-to-maturity securities* and reported as amortized cost;
   b) debt and equity securities which are intended to be sold in the near term are classified as *trading securities* and reported at fair (market) value with unrealized gains and losses included in earnings, i.e., the current approach described above; and
   c) debt and equity securities not classified as either of the two previous categories are classified as *available-for-sale securities* and reported at fair (market) value, with unrealized gains and losses excluded from earnings and reported in shareholders' equity i.e., the deferral approach described above.

SFAS No. 115 has adopted the market approach for investments in securities except for debt securities that are being held to maturity and for situations where there is significant influence or control.

RECENT DEVELOPMENTS

In April 1994, the CICA Accounting Standards Board, in a joint project with the International Accounting Standards Committee (IASC), issued the Re-Exposure Draft (RED), "Financial Instruments." The RED contains proposed recommendations for both financial assets and liabilities. A brief summary of the proposals for financial assets in the context of this chapter is presented as follows.

Financial instruments include both primary instruments, such as cash, receivables, payables and equity securities, and secondary derivative instruments, such as financial options, futures and forwards, interest rate swaps and currency swaps. Secondary or derivative instruments create rights and obligations that have the effect of transferring one or more of the financial risks inherent in an underlying primary financial instrument, and the fair value of the contract normally reflects changes in the fair value of the underlying financial instrument. Derivative instruments do not result in a transfer of the underlying financial instrument on inception of the contract and such transfer does not necessarily take place on maturity of the derivative instrument. [RED, par. .010]

A financial instrument is initially measured at the "fair value of the consideration given or received for it," which is the same cost basis on which other assets are acquired. Subsequent to acquisition, the RED classifies financial instruments into three categories, depending on management's intent in entering into the transaction.

For measurement purposes, financial instruments are classified as held for:
- the period to maturity (which may be a relatively short period) or for the long term;
- hedging (when they are held to mitigate an exposure to financial risk, regardless of the expected holding period); or
- purposes other than hedging when there is no intent to hold to maturity or for the long term. [RED, par. .080]

Debt securities held for the long term or to maturity should be carried at amortized cost, and equity securities should be carried at cost. However, if an entity obtains evidence that the financial asset may be impaired, the carrying value of the security should be reduced to an estimated recoverable amount. The carrying amount may be reduced either by writing it down or by means of an allowance account. When the estimated recoverable amount increases, the write-down should be reversed to the extent of the increase. The carrying value should not, however, be greater than the original value assigned to it on acquisition.

The RED provides that "A gain or loss from a change in the fair value of a financial instrument accounted for as a hedge should be recognized in income when the corresponding loss or gain from a change in the fair value of the hedged position is recognized in income." Since the purpose of a hedge is to mitigate the gain or loss in an exposed position, the gain or loss in the one is matched against the loss or gain in the other.

Other financial assets are accounted for initially at cost but subsequently should be remeasured at each balance sheet date and reported at fair value (i.e., market value). Gains and losses from a change in the fair value should be recognized in income as they arise. Thus, financial assets that are not intended to be held for the long term or to maturity and are not classified as hedging instruments are accounted for using the market value method.

The Re-Exposure Draft is a very long and complicated document, with comments accepted until the end of July 1994. It is unlikely that its recommendations will become *Handbook* provisions until the end of 1995 at the earliest. However, should the CICA and the IASC receive reasonable consensus from their constituencies, these recommendations will become part of Canadian and international GAAP.

SPECIAL PROBLEMS IN ACCOUNTING FOR EQUITY INVESTMENTS

Accounting for equity investments poses several special problems relating to acquisition, holding, and sale. They include treatment of:

1. Stock dividends.
2. Stock splits.
3. Stock rights.

ON THE HORIZON

CICA wants derivative disclosure

TORONTO—Canada's Institute of Chartered Accountants (CICA) is asking companies for "immediate implementation" of its proposals on disclosure of financial instruments, even though it will be months before they're finalized.

The CICA financial instruments re-exposure draft calls for the disclosure of the extent and nature of each class of financial instrument and any significant terms and conditions that could affect the amount, timing and certainty of future cash flows. There should be disclosure about interest rate risk and credit risk for each class of financial instruments and its fair value.

For hedging transactions, disclosure should include the nature of the anticipated transaction, the amount of deferred or unrecognized gain or loss and the period of time before the anticipated transaction.

Information should be disclosed on management's attitude to financial risks, the purposes of which the derivatives are used, risk controls—and information about market risk and the adequacy of capital resources.

The Office of the Superintendent of Financial Institutions has already issued draft guidelines on derivative disclosure. The CICA says "it will be some time" before its standards are final, hence the request for advance compliance.

A **derivative financial instrument** is a financial agreement that derives its value from changes in an underlying variable such as interest rates, stock prices, or currency exchange rates. The RED defines a derivative as a future, forward, swap, or option contract or other financial instrument with similar characteristics. Examples of other financial instruments with similar characteristics include interest rate caps or floors, fixed-rate loan commitments, and letters of credit. These instruments provide the holder with the benefits of favourable changes in the price of an underlying asset or index with limited (or no) exposure to losses from unfavourable price movements. Other derivatives can and do cause losses for the holder.

The following **interest rate cap agreement** is an example of a derivative: a manufacturing firm and a bank enter into an agreement entitling the manufacturer to receive from the bank the amount by which the interest payments on $20 million of the manufacturer's floating-rate notes exceed 7 percent of the note's face value. The bank charges a fee of $750,000, which the manufacturer amortizes to interest expense over the 4-year term of the cap agreement. The manufacturer is willing to pay a substantial sum to protect itself from unfavourable changes in market interest rates; the firm is betting that the effect of changes in interest rates will be more unfavourable, at present value, than the cost of the cap agreement.

The Bottom Line, September 1994, p. 20.

Stock Dividends

Cash dividends on investments in capital stock of other companies accounted for by the cost method are recognized as earned at the time of the declaration of the cash dividend. Stock dividends, which provide another way a company can make a distribution to shareholders, are not included as investment revenue.

When a stock dividend is issued, the distributing corporation debits retained earnings and credits the appropriate capital stock accounts. The effect of a stock dividend from the issuing corporation's view is to capitalize a part of retained earnings. Significantly, a stock dividend does not decrease the assets of the issuing corporation.

From the investor's point of view, the nature of a stock dividend is suggested by its effect on the issuing corporation. The investors neither receive assets from the corporation nor own more of the issuing corporation; they merely have more shares to represent the same prior proportional ownership. Thus, the receipt of a stock dividend does not increase the carrying value of the holdings but decreases the carrying value per share.

Assume that XYZ Company purchased 1,000 common shares of ABC Corporation at $90 per share. Subsequently, XYZ Company received a 20% common stock dividend. XYZ later sold 200 of the common shares at $95 per share. Entries are as follows:

At the acquisition date:

Long-term investment in equity securities, ABC Corp. (1,000 × $90). 90,000
    Cash   90,000

At date of stock dividend:

> Memorandum entry only—Received 20% common stock dividend of 200 shares from ABC Corporation, revised cost per share:

$$\$90,000 \div (1,000 + 200 = 1,200 \text{ shares}) = \underline{\$75}.$$

At the date of sale of 200 common shares:

Cash (200 × $95)	19,000	
Long-term investment in equity securities, ABC Corp. (200 × $75) . . .		15,000
Gain on sale of investments		4,000
Remaining shares: 1,300 at $75 cost per share.		

These procedures are followed for the cost, equity, and market value methods; the only difference is in the total carrying value. For all three methods, the appropriate total carrying value is divided by the new total number of shares owned to determine the carrying value per share after the stock dividend.

If the stock dividend is of a different class of stock from that on which the dividend is declared, such as preferred shares received as a dividend on common shares, or vice versa, three methods of accounting for the dividend are possible:

1. **Allocation method** Record the new stock at an amount determined by allocating the carrying value of the old stock between the new stock and the old stock on the basis of the relative market values of the different classes of stock after issuance of the dividend.
2. **Noncost method** Record the new shares in terms of shares only (as a memorandum entry). When they are sold, recognize the total sale price as a gain.
3. **Market value method** Record the new shares at market value upon receipt with an offsetting credit to dividend revenue. This method treats shares of a different class received as a dividend similar to a property dividend (a distribution of a non-cash asset to the shareholders).

The allocation method is the most consistent with the historical cost principle. The noncost method is considered to be conservative, and the market value method is seldom used. Exhibit 14–3 shows the application of the allocation method, which

---

EXHIBIT 14–3

Investor Accounting for a Stock Dividend in a Different Class of Shares: Allocation Method

Case Data

1. CD Corp. purchased 100 common shares of JKL Company at $75 per share (total cost, $7,500).
2. Some time later, CD Corp. received a stock dividend of 40 JKL preferred shares with a market value of $2,500. At that time, the market value of the common shares was $10,000. Using the allocation method, the cost is apportioned, based on the total market value of $12,500, as follows:

$$\text{Cost allocated to common} = \$7,500 \times \frac{\$10,000}{\$12,500} = \underline{\$6,000} \text{ or } \$60 \text{ per share}$$

$$\text{Cost allocated to preferred} = \$7,500 \times \frac{\$2,500}{\$12,500} = \underline{\$1,500} \text{ or } \$37.50 \text{ per share}$$

Total cost allocated . . . . $\underline{\underline{\$7,500}}$

Entry to Record Receipt of Stock Dividend by CD Corp.

Investment in preferred shares of JKL Company (40 × $37.50)	1,500	
Investment in common shares of JKL Company		1,500

assigns the original cost to the two classes of stock. This method would be followed for the cost, equity, and market value methods, with the appropriate carrying value being allocated.

Stock Split of Investment Shares

Although a stock split is different from a stock dividend from the point of view of the issuer, the two are virtually identical from the point of view of the investor. In both cases, the investor has more shares than before the split or dividend, but at the same total cost.[9] The investor's accounting for a stock split is the same as for a stock dividend of the same class of stock. Only a *memorandum entry* is made to record the number of new shares received, and the cost (or carrying value) per share is recomputed.

Stock Split of Investment Shares

Stock rights allow shareholders to purchase additional shares from the issuing corporation at a specific price (called an *exercise price*) and by a specified date. The certificate evidencing one or more rights is called a *stock warrant*. Rights have value when the holder can buy shares through exercise of the rights at a lower price per share than the price on the open market. As the spread between the option price and the market price changes subsequent to issuance of the rights, the value of the rights changes.

The term *stock right* is usually interpreted as one right for each old share. For example, a holder of two shares who receives rights to subscribe for one new share is said to own two stock rights rather than one. There is one right per old share regardless of the entitlement of the right. In this case, each right would entitle the holder to purchase one-half of a share.

When the intention to issue stock rights is declared, the shares with the rights sell *rights on*. The market price of the share includes the value of the share and the value of a right. After the rights are issued, the shares will sell in the market *ex rights*. Rights usually have a separate market from that of the related shares and are separately quoted at a specific market price. After rights are received, the investor has shares and stock rights.

To determine the gain or loss on the sale of either the shares or the rights, the total cost of the investment must be allocated between the shares and the rights. This allocation is usually based on relative market values; that is, the total cost of the old shares is allocated between the old shares and the rights in proportion to their relative market values at the time the rights are issued.

Example   Assume that Garfield Company purchased 500 shares of Franklin Corporation common shares at $93 per share, a total investment of $46,500. The entry to record the investment is as follows:

Investment: Franklin Corporation common shares   46,500
    Cash   46,500

Later in the year of purchase, Garfield Company receives 500 stock rights that entitle it to acquire 100 shares of Franklin Corporation common shares at a price of $100 per share. Each stock right conveys the right to purchase one-fifth of a share of Franklin Corporation common shares. At the date the Franklin Corporation common shares first trade ex rights, they have a market price of $120 per share, and each stock right has a market value of $4. To determine the allocation of the cost of the

---

[9] A reverse split, such as a two-for-three split, reduces rather than increases the number of outstanding shares. Reverse stock splits are rare.

GLOBAL VIEW

Accounting for investments is an area where there are significant differences between Canadian accounting rules and those of many other countries. Many European companies do not consolidate or include the earnings of unconsolidated subsidiaries on an equity basis in their earnings. Moreover, when the operations of a business segment do not go as well as planned, many countries allow the parent to transfer those operations to an unconsolidated subsidiary. Thus, the income statements and balance sheets of many foreign companies often do not provide the same kind of information as those of Canadian-based companies.

The European Union has a priority for standardizing the financial reporting within it and, in particular, requires firms to provide consolidated statements that include subsidiaries over which the firm has a controlling interest. The EU is also moving toward requiring use of the equity method for investments in which the investor has a significant influence, where significant influence is defined similar to Canadian GAAP. As the countries in the EU adopt standards requiring consolidation and the use of the equity method, the financial statements for companies in them will be more comparable to those in Canada. The financial statements of companies in Germany, Luxembourg, and Switzerland will be most affected, because the rules in these countries are currently the least comparable to Canadian GAAP with respect to accounting for investments. In Switzerland, for example, there is no requirement to consolidate controlled subsidiaries, and the equity method is not allowed. Under Swiss accounting rules, all associated companies are reported at cost.

No country has reporting requirements for investments similar to the American (i.e., fair value) method described in this chapter. Some, such as Canada, require a lower-of-cost-or-market valuation basis, and some allow for writing up the value of assets. However, the accounting standards in many jurisdictions allow firms to use the cost method for almost all investments. There is little likelihood that there will be widespread adoption of the fair value method in the reports of other countries anytime soon. A lower-of-cost-or-market method, however, yields results similar to those of the fair value method with respect to holding losses. However, the LCM method would not recognize unrealized holding gains above cost, as is required in the United States under *SFAS No. 115*.

investment to the stock rights and the held common shares, the relative market values are used:

Total market value of common shares held: (500 × $120)	$60,000
Total market value of stock rights held: (500 × $4)	2,000
Total market value of investment	$62,000

$$\text{Cost to be allocated to investments in stock rights} = \frac{\$2,000}{\$62,000} \times \$46,500 = \$1,500$$

$$\text{Cost to be allocated to investments in common shares} = \frac{\$60,000}{\$62,000} \times \$46,500 = \$45,000$$

The cost per share of common stock is now $45,000 ÷ 500 shares, or $90 per share, and the cost per right is $1,500 ÷ 500 rights, or $3 per right.

The entry to record the receipt of the 500 stock rights for Franklin Corporation common stock:

Investment: Franklin Corporation stock rights	1,500	
Investment: Franklin Corporation common shares		1,500

Suppose Garfield exercises 400 rights, acquires an additional 80 shares of Franklin at the exercise price of $100 per share, and sells the remaining 100 stock rights for $4.50 per right.

The entry to record the acquisition of these 80 shares through exercising the rights:

Investment: Franklin Corporation common shares	9,200	
Investment: Franklin Corporation stock rights (400 × $3)		1,200
Cash (80 × $100)		8,000

The entry to record the sale of the 100 stock rights:

Cash (100 × $4.50)	450	
Investment: Franklin Corporation stock rights (100 × $3)		300
Gain on sale of stock rights		150

The 580 common shares acquired by exercising the stock rights have a total cost of $54,200 ($46,500 − $1,500 + $9,200), or $93.45 ($54,200 ÷ 580) per share. If Garfield sells Franklin Corporation common shares in the future, Garfield will determine the gain or loss using this average carrying value.

If stock rights are not sold or exercised, they lapse. In this situation, a loss equivalent to the allocated cost of the rights should theoretically be recognized. As a practical matter, however, the allocation entry is often reversed for the portion that lapses, restoring the cost to the investment account.

| SUMMARY OF KEY POINTS

(L.O. 1)   1. Firms invest in the securities of other firms either to earn a return on otherwise idle cash or to gain influence, control, or some other business advantage.

(L.O. 2)   2. Investment securities are recorded at acquisition using the cost principle.

(L.O. 4)   3. The allowance method values the portfolio of temporary investments at the lower of the aggregate cost or aggregate market value of the portfolio. Subsequent increases in the market value over cost are ignored for accounting purposes.

(L.O. 4)   4. The direct write-off method recognizes a reduction in the market value but ignores any subsequent increase in the market value of an investment.

(L.O. 5)   5. The direct write-off method is also used for long-term investments. Write-downs are only taken, however, when the decline in value is considered to be other than temporary.

(L.O. 6)   6. The equity method must be used for investments in equity securities when the investment results in the investor having a significant influence over the investee company. Significant influence over the investee is presumed to exist if the investor owns at least 20% but not more than 50% of the investee's outstanding voting common stock.

(L.O. 6)   7. Conceptually, the equity method is an extension of accrual accounting to common stock investment. Increases or decreases in the net assets of the investee flow through to the investor as they occur.

(L.O. 6)   8. In the equity method, investor firms must account for any difference between the initial cost of the investment and the net book value acquired. The difference can relate to differences between the fair value and the book value of specific assets and liabilities of the investee and goodwill.

(L.O. 7)   9. Long-term investments require the following disclosures:
   a. Basis of valuation.
   b. Investments subject to significant influence, other affiliates, and other long-term investments should be shown separately.
   c. Income from investments subject to significant influence, other affiliates, and other long-term investments should be shown separately.
   d. Investments accounted for under the equity method should disclose any difference between the cost and the underlying net book value of the investee's assets at date of purchase.
   e. Both the market value and carrying value of marketable securities should be disclosed.

(L.O. 8)   10. Stock dividends and stock splits are accounted for only as a memorandum entry for the number of shares received. The original cost per share of the investment is adjusted to reflect the increased number of shares owned.

(L.O. 8)   11. When stock rights are issued by the investee, the investor must allocate the total carrying amount of the investment between the old stock and the stock rights.

| REVIEW PROBLEM

Suppose that on January 1, 1995, Acme Fruit Company has the following temporary and long-term investments:

Security	Original Cost	Carrying Value at January 1
Temporary investments:		
Apple (2,000 common shares)	$20,000	$19,000
T-bill (matures July 1)	50,000	50,000
Long-term investments:		
Cherry (5,000 shares)	$40,000	40,000

Assume there are no income taxes. The following transactions and reclassifications occur during the year. Acme Fruit uses the allowance method.

a. On February 1, 1995, Acme purchases $30,000 of face amount bonds issued by Plum Inc. for $29,500 plus accrued interest. The bonds have a coupon rate of 8%, pay interest semiannually on June 30 and December 31, and mature on December 31, 1999. The investment is classified as long term. Assume straight-line amortization.

b. Dividends of $0.75 per share are received on the Apple common shares on May 30.

c. Interest on the Plum bonds is received on June 30 and December 31.

d. On July 1, the T-bill matures and is redeemed at its face amount of $54,000. The full amount of proceeds is immediately used to purchase 1,000 common shares of Banana Corporation, and the investment is classified as temporary.

e. On November 1, the investment in Cherry is reclassified as temporary. The stock has a market price of $11 per share on the reclassification date.

f. At December 31, the market value of the various investments is determined to be as follows:

Temporary investments:	
Apple common	$ 15,000
Cherry common	57,500
Banana Corporation.	53,000
	$125,500
Long-term investments:	
Plum bonds (excluding accrued interest).	$ 31,000

Required

1. Show the computation of investment income for 1995.
2. Show the journal entries to record the reclassification of the Cherry common shares on November 1.
3. Show how the above items are reported in the 1995 financial statements of Acme Fruit Company.

SOLUTION

1. Investment income:

Plum bonds:		
Interest—$30,000 × 8% × $^{11}/_{12}$	$2,200	
Amortization of discount—$500 × $^{11}/_{59}$	93	$2,293
Apple dividends—2,000 × $0.75.		1,500
T-bill—$54,000 − $50,000.		4,000
Loss recovery on temporary investments		1,000
Total		$8,793

2. Entry to record reclassification of Cherry shares:

Temporary investment—Cherry common	40,000	
Long-term investment—Cherry common.		40,000

Since the holding gain is unrealized, it is unlikely that it would be recognized on the reclassification. Therefore, the reclassification is recorded at the carrying value of the shares.

3. Partial balance sheet as at December 31, 1995:

Temporary investments (at cost; market value, $125,500)	$114,000
Long-term investments (at amortized cost; market value, $31,000)	$ 29,593

Schedule of cost and market values:

	Cost	Market
Apple common	$ 20,000	$ 15,000
Cherry common.	40,000	57,500
Banana common	54,000	53,000
Total.	$114,000	$125,500
Plum bonds	$ 29,593	$ 31,000

APPENDIX 14: *Other Investments and Funds*

This appendix covers accounting for several unusual types of investments and funds that are less frequently encountered, including special-purpose funds, cash surrender value of life insurance, and futures contracts.

Special-Purpose Funds as Long-Term Investments

Companies sometimes set aside cash or other assets in special-purpose funds for a particular future use. These assets are commonly noncurrent assets and not directly related to current operations. They are reported on the balance sheet under the noncurrent heading classification *investments and funds*.

Funds may be set aside (1) by contract, as in the case of a bond sinking fund; (2) by law, as in the case of rent deposits; or (3) voluntarily, as in the case of a plant expansion fund. Examples of long-term special-purpose funds are:

1. Funds set aside to retire a specific long-term liability, such as a bond, a mortgage payable, or long-term notes payable.
2. Funds set aside to reacquire shares of the company's outstanding stock.
3. Funds set aside to purchase major assets, such as land or buildings.

Typically, special-purpose funds are deposited with an independent trustee, such as a financial institution, which agrees to pay a specified rate of interest each period on the balance in the fund. Accounting for a typical fund is illustrated in Exhibit 14A–1. Special-purpose funds are generally disclosed in the notes to the financial statements.

Cash Surrender Value of Life Insurance

Often a firm insures the lives of its top executives, with the firm as the beneficiary. There are three types of life insurance policies a firm might acquire on the lives of its executives: (1) ordinary or whole-life, (2) limited payment, and (3) term insurance. Only whole-life and limited-payment insurance policies build up value while the policy is in force. They have stipulated loan values and cash surrender values.

The **cash surrender value (CSV)** of a policy is the amount that would be refunded should the policy be terminated at the request of the insured. This value increases over time as the firm pays the insurance premium. The CSV is a form of investment usually reported on the balance sheet under investments and funds as a long-term asset.

Each policy provides a schedule that indicates the cash surrender value and the loan value for each policy year. Because a portion of the premiums paid is refundable in the form of the cash surrender value, only a portion of the periodic premiums is expensed. The firm's life insurance expense each period is the excess of the premium paid over the increase in the cash surrender value for the period.

To illustrate, assume that Zim Corporation purchased a $100,000 whole-life policy on its top executive several years ago. In 1994, which is the fourth year the policy has been in effect, the firm pays an insurance premium in the amount of $2,200. The cash surrender value schedule for the policy shows the following:

Policy Year	Premium	Cash Surrender Value
1991	$2,200	$ 0
1992	2,200	0
1993	2,200	500
1994	2,200	1,500
1995	2,200	2,600

The premium of $2,200 paid in 1994 results in an increase in the cash surrender value of $1,000. This amount is debited to an account called cash surrender value of life insurance, with the remainder being recorded as expense:

Life insurance expense	1,200	
Cash surrender value of life insurance	1,000	
Cash		2,200

At the end of 1994, the cash surrender value of the policy totals $1,500, the amount that should appear in the asset account called cash surrender value of life insurance.

EXHIBIT 14A–1

Accounting for a
Special-Purpose Fund:
Watt Corporation

1. Watt Corporation plans to build a new office building five years hence. The plans estimate
   the total construction cost to be $1,300,000 over a six-month construction period.
2. The company decided to make five $200,000 cash deposits to a special construction fund
   each July 1, starting on July 1, 1991. The fund will be administered by an independent
   trustee. The trustee will increase the fund each June 30 at a 10% interest rate on the fund
   balance at that date.
3. Watt Corporation's accounting period ends December 31.
4. The office building is completed on schedule, the contractor was paid $1,300,000 on July 2,
   1996, and the fund was closed.

Fund Accumulation Schedule (annuity due basis)

Date	Cash Deposits	Interest Revenue Earned	Fund Increases	Fund Balance
July 1, 1991	$ 200,000		$ 200,000	$ 200,000
June 30, 1992		$ 200,000 × .10 = $ 20,000	20,000	220,000
July 1, 1992	200,000		200,000	420,000
June 30, 1993		420,000 × .10 = 42,000	42,000	462,000
July 1, 1993	200,000		200,000	662,000
June 30, 1994		662,000 × .10 = 66,200	66,200	728,200
July 1, 1994	200,000		200,000	928,200
June 30, 1995		928,200 × .10 = 92,820	92,820	1,021,020
July 1, 1995	200,000		200,000	1,221,020
June 30, 1996		1,221,020 × .10 = 122,102	122,102	1,343,122
	$1,000,000	$343,122	$1,343,122	

Selected Journal Entries: First Year and Final Payment

July 1, 1991:		
Special building fund	200,000	
Cash		200,000
Dec. 31, 1991:		
Receivable on building fund	10,000	
Interest revenue ($20,000 × 6/12)		10,000
June 30, 1992:		
Special building fund	20,000	
Receivable on building fund		10,000
Interest revenue		10,000
July 1, 1992:		
Special building fund	200,000	
Cash		200,000
July 2, 1996:		
Cash	43,122	
Office building	1,300,000	
Special building fund		1,343,122

Assume that the insured executive dies on April 1, 1994, after the premium has been
paid and recorded. Most policies refund any premiums paid beyond the life of the insured. Assuming that the policy anniversary date is January 1, the refund in this case is
$2,200 × (9/12), or $1,650. The insurance company pays Zim Corporation the face amount
of the policy ($100,000) plus the refund amount ($1,650). Zim Corporation had recognized
insurance expense of $1,200 for the year. With the policy in effect only three months
before the insured died, the expense recovery is for three-fourths of the year, or $900. A
portion of the $100,000 is recorded as the payment of the cash surrender value, and the
remainder is a gain:

Cash	101,650	
Life insurance expense.		900
Cash surrender value of life insurance		1,500
Gain on settlement of life insurance indemnity		99,250

The gain on life insurance is usually considered ordinary income. Insurance premiums on policies for which the company is the beneficiary are not deductible for tax purposes. The proceeds received from the policy payout are not taxable income.

Accounting for Futures Contracts—An Investment

Futures contracts are purchased as an investment or as a hedge against the risks of future price changes. A futures contract is a contract between a buyer and seller of a commodity or financial instrument executed through the clearinghouse of a futures exchange. Futures contracts have three common characteristics:

1. They obligate the buyer to accept and the seller to make delivery of a commodity or financial instrument at a specified time, or they provide for cash settlement rather than delivery.
2. They can be effectively cancelled by entering into an offsetting contract for the same commodity or financial instrument.
3. All changes in the market value of open contracts are settled on a regular basis, usually daily.

The primary issue in accounting for a futures contract is whether a change in the market value of a futures contract should be recognized as a gain or loss in the reporting period when the market price change takes place, or whether the gain or loss should be deferred to a later date. *SFAS No. 80,* "Accounting for Futures Contracts," specified two approaches for recording and reporting futures contracts. The two approaches are called the *market-value* approach and the *hedge-deferral* approach. There are two criteria for determining the accounting approach for futures contracts:

1. The item to be hedged exposes the company to market price or interest rate risk.
2. The futures contract reduces that risk and is designated a hedge.

The market-value approach must be used if the contract does not meet both these two criteria. The market-value approach requires that all gains and losses due to market price changes be recognized in the reporting period when the market value changes.

The hedge-deferral approach must be used if both criteria are met. The hedge-deferral approach requires that all gains or losses due to market price changes be deferred and recognized at the termination of the futures contract.

Rye Company is a producer of a grain-based product. The following events occur:

October 1994—The company determined that it will need 10,000 bushels of grain near the end of February 1995. The company expects the current price of $3 per bushel of grain to change and does not want to assume the risk of such market price changes.

November 1, 1994—The company decides to purchase a futures contract from Chicago Clearing House Inc. to hedge (that is, shift) the risk of market price changes of grain. The futures contract, which costs $800, provides that the company purchase the grain at the date needed at the then current market price (or pay the equivalent amount in cash if the grain is not purchased). Between the date the futures contract is purchased and the termination date (when the grain is purchased), Chicago Clearing House Inc. must pay the company cash for all market price increases (from the $3 beginning hedge price) and will collect cash from the company for all market price decreases (again, from the hedge price of $3). Thus, for an $800 fee, the company shifts the risk of market price changes to the clearinghouse. Changes in the market price of grain are usually settled daily, and each offset is payable or collectible each weekend.

December 31, 1994—At the end of the reporting period for Rye Company, the market price of grain is $2.80 per bushel.

February 24, 1995—At this date (*a*) The market price of grain is $3.30, (*b*) Rye Company purchases the 10,000 bushels of grain needed for production at $3.30 per bushel, and (*c*) the futures contract is terminated.

Rye Company has transferred the risk of price changes for grain to the clearinghouse. Exhibit 14A–2 presents the required entries for the two approaches. Under the market value approach, the gain is explicitly recognized and the grain acquired is recorded at its current cost. Under the hedge-deferral approach, the gain is not explicitly recognized; rather, the purchase is recorded instead at the cost that was assured by the futures

EXHIBIT 14A–2   Illustration of Entries for Accounting for a Futures Contract under the Market-Value Approach and Hedge-Deferral Approach

Market-Value Approach		Hedge-Deferral Approach	

November 1, 1994—to record the futures contract:

Prepaid expense, futures contract	800		Prepaid expense, futures contract	800	
Cash		800	Cash		800

December 31, 1994—To record cash payment to clearinghouse because of the market price decrease in grain:

Loss on futures contract	2,000		Inventory cost adjustment, futures		
Cash		2,000	contract	2,000	
			Cash		2,000

The $2,000 is the change in price ($3.00 less the current price of $2.80) times the number of bushels, 10,000. The loss on the futures contract is closed to the income statement. The inventory cost adjustment is reported as a deferred charge on the balance sheet.

February 24, 1995—To record the cash payment received from the clearinghouse due to the market price increase in grain:

Cash	5,000		Cash	5,000	
Gain on futures contract.		5,000	Inventory cost adjustment,		
			futures contract		5,000

The payment is computed as the price change since December 31 ($3.30 − $2.80) times the 10,000 bushels covered by the futures contract.

To record the purchase of grain:

Grain inventory	33,000		Grain inventory	30,000	
Cash		33,000	Inventory cost adjustment, futures		
			contract	3,000	
			Cash		33,000

To record termination of the futures contract:

Expenses, futures contract	800		Expenses, futures contract	800	
Prepaid expense, futures contract		800	Prepaid expense, futures contract		800

contract, $30,000. In either case, the firm is better off by $2,200 ($3,000 savings on grain cost less $800 cost of contract).

QUESTIONS

1. Define a security. Distinguish between debt and equity securities.
2. What accounting principle is applied in recording the acquisition of an investment? Explain its application in cash and non-cash acquisitions.
3. Explain the basic features of accounting for temporary investments in equity securities. When are unrealized holding gains and losses included in the determination of earnings? When are they not?
4. An investor purchased 100 shares of Zenics at $20 per share on March 15, 1994. At the end of the 1994 accounting period, December 31, 1994, the stock was quoted at $19 per share. On June 5, 1995, the investor sold the stock for $22 per share. Assuming a temporary investment, show the journal entries to be made at each of the following dates:
   a. March 15, 1994.
   b. December 31, 1994.
   c. June 5, 1995.
5. On August 1, 1994, Baker Company purchased $50,000 face amount of Sugar Company 6% coupon value bonds for $48,000. The bond pays interest semiannually on July 31 and January 31. At the fiscal year-end for Baker, the bonds have a market value of $49,000. Show the journal entries (a) to record the investment, assuming that the bonds are classified as a temporary investment, and (b) to record investment income and any other needed adjustments at December 31.
6. Briefly explain the accounting for temporary investments in debt securities.
7. What is meant by an impairment loss on an investment in securities?

8. Explain why interest revenue is accrued on investments in debt securities, but dividend revenue is not accrued on investments in equity securities.

9. Under the cost method for investments in equity securities, no distinction is made between voting and nonvoting stock, but the distinction is important with respect to the equity method. Explain why.

10. Explain when the LCM method of accounting for equity investments is applicable.

11. How is cost determined when an investment is reclassified from a temporary to a long-term investment?

12. Explain the basic features of the equity method of accounting for long-term investments. When is the equity method applicable?

13. Assume that Company R acquired, as a long-term investment, 30% of the outstanding voting common shares of Company S at a cash cost of $100,000. At date of acquisition, the balance sheet of Company S showed total shareholders' equity of $250,000. The market value of the depreciable assets of Company S was $20,000 greater than their book value at date of acquisition. Compute goodwill purchased, if any. What accounting method should be used in this situation? Explain why.

14. Assume the same facts as in (13), with the addition that the net assets have a remaining estimated life of 10 years and goodwill will be amortized over 20 years (assume no residual values and straight-line depreciation). How much additional depreciation and amortization expense should be reported by the investor, Company R, each year in accounting for this long-term investment? Give the entries to record additional depreciation and amortization of goodwill.

15. Basically, the investor accounts for the receipt of an ordinary stock dividend and a stock split in the same way. Briefly explain the accounting that should be followed by the investor in these situations.

16. What is a stock right (or stock warrant)? If stock rights have a market value, how would the investor account for the receipt of stock rights?

17. What is the cash surrender value of life insurance? How is it accounted for? (Appendix 14A).

18. A firm enters into a futures contract to hedge against losses relating to future receipt of a foreign currency. At fiscal year-end, how is the gain or loss on the futures contract accounted for? If the contract did not qualify as a hedge, how would the gain or loss be accounted for? (Appendix 14A).

19. How would a Swiss-based company report investment income on an equity investment in which it owns 50% of the voting stock?

CASES

C 14-1   **Classification of Investments in Debt and Equity Securities**   Investments in debt securities may be classified as temporary or long-term.

1. At what carrying value are investments in debt securities recorded for each classification? What treatment is given to differences between carrying value and original cost, if any, in terms of how they are reported in the financial statements?

2. Suppose a firm makes an investment in a debt security at the beginning of its fiscal year. The debt security is acquired at face amount (that is, there is no premium or discount), and the security matures in three years. At the purchase of the security, management overlooks the issue of how to classify the investment security.

   a. At year-end, the market price of the security has declined significantly because of a substantial increase in interest rates for investment securities of similar risk. What are some reasons management might wish to classify this investment in either category?

   b. At year-end, the market price of the security has increased significantly because of a substantial decline in interest rates for investment securities of similar risk. What are some reasons management might wish to classify this investment in either category?

C 14-2   **Reclassification and Change in Value of Investments in Equity Securities**   Petersen Company purchased equity securities at a cost of $500,000 on March 1, 1994, and classified them as a long-term investment, as it intended to hold them for more than one year. At December 31, 1994, the fair value of the securities was $470,000. At the end of the third quarter (September 30, 1995), management is considering reclassifying the securities as a temporary investment, because there is now a high likelihood that the securities will be sold during 1996. On this date, the securities have a market value of $485,000.

1. Assuming the decline in value at December 31, 1994, was not temporary, what action should be taken for Petersen's year-end statements?
2. Assuming the decline in value at December 31 was considered to be temporary, what action should be taken at September 30, 1995, when the shares are reclassified? At December 31, 1995, assuming no change in value from September 30?
3. Suppose the securities have a fair value of $495,000 on December 31, 1995, and are sold on May 1, 1996, for $510,000. What are the effects on 1996 income if (*a*) the 1994 decline was not temporary, or (*b*) it was temporary?

C 14-3

Reclassification from Cost to Equity Method   Bell Company acquired a 20% ownership interest in the outstanding voting shares of Harris Inc. on January 1, 1992, at a cost of $800,000. At the time, Bell did not have significant influence over Harris, so Bell classified the investment as a long-term investment. As time has passed, Bell has gained more influence over Harris, culminating in the election of two members of Bell's management to the board of directors of Harris on December 31, 1995. An analysis of Harris Inc. reveals that 20% of its net book value equals $750,000 and that 20% of its net assets measured at fair value equals $820,000.

1. Should Bell continue to account for its investment in Harris using the cost method, or should it use the equity method? What issues would influence the answer to this question?
2. Suppose Bell adopts the equity method effective December 31, 1995. What effect would the decision have on its 1995 income statement and balance sheet?
3. Suppose Bell adopts the equity method effective on January 1, 1996. What effect would the decision have on its 1996 income statement and balance sheet, relative to adoption on December 31, 1995?
4. By adopting the equity method, what are some of the changes that Bell will make in recording its investment income from its investment in Harris?

C 14-4

Cost and Market Value Methods Compared   Ace Investors Company buys and sells various debt and equity securities. These security investments represent approximately 90% of the firm's total assets. Ace has a policy of classifying all its securities as temporary investments, since it has traditionally sold any individual security when management felt it opportune to do so. Ace also operates in an industry where the use of the market value method is allowed.

The following data are taken from their records:

a. January 1, 1994—Purchase securities at a cost of $50 million.
b. December 31—Market value of investment (in millions): 1994, $56.0; 1995, $52.0; 1996, $49.5.
c. Cash dividends received (in millions): 1994, $4.0; 1995, $4.2; 1996, $4.1.
d. December 1, 1996—Sold, for $6.0 million, 10% of the securities from the portfolio that had an original cost of $5.0 million and carrying value $5.2 million.

Ace's accounting period ends December 31.

Required

1. What are the fundamental distinctions between the cost and market value methods for temporary investments?
2. Complete the schedule below using the cost and market value methods.
3. Which method do you think is more appropriate for Ace Investors? Why?

	1994		1995		1996	
Items	**Cost Method**	**Market Value Method**	**Cost Method**	**Market Value Method**	**Cost Method**	**Market Value Method**
Balance Sheet						
Assets:						
Investments						
Shareholders' equity						
Income Statement						
Investment income:						
Dividends						
Unrealized gain or loss						
Gain on sale						

C 14-5   **Magna**   Refer to the Magna financial statements found in back of this text to answer the following questions:

1. What are Magna's accounting policies with respect to its investments?
2. What is Magna's share of total assets of its joint ventures and equity-accounted investments? Its proportionate share of net income from these sources?
3. What investment transactions did Magna engage in during 1993?

EXERCISES

E 14-1
(L.O. 2, 3)

Classification of Investments in Securities   Match the different securities listed below with their usual classification as investments by entering the appropriate letter in each blank space: A, temporary equity investment; B, temporary debt investment; C, investment in equity-basis securities; D, long-term debt investments; E, investment in equity securities of company to be consolidated; and F, none of the above.

Typical Securities

_____ 1. Abbot common shares, nopar; acquired to use temporarily idle cash.
_____ 2. Land acquired for short-term speculation.
_____ 3. Government of Canada Treasury bills, mature in six months.
_____ 4. BCE preferred stock, par $100, mandatory redemption within next 12 months.
_____ 5. Staufer common shares; acquired to attain a continuing controlling interest.
_____ 6. Frazer bonds, 9%, mature at the end of 10 years; intended to be held for 10 years.
_____ 7. Foreign Corporation, common shares; a 30% interest acquired, but difficulties encountered in withdrawing cash earned.
_____ 8. Certificates of deposit (CDs); mature at end of one year.
_____ 9. Savings certificate at Trust Company, mature in 1 year.
_____10. Acorn common shares; acquired as an investment that management plans to hold indefinitely.

E 14-2
(L.O. 2, 4)

Temporary Equity Investments: Entries and Reporting   On November 1, 1994, Decker Company acquired the following temporary investments in equity securities:

X Corporation—500 common shares at $60 per share.

Y Corporation—300 preferred shares at $20 cash per share.

The annual reporting period ends December 31. On December 31, 1994, the quoted market prices were as follows: X Corporation common, $52, and Y Corporation preferred, $24. Following are the data for 1995:

March 2, 1995—Received cash dividends per share as follows: X Corporation, $1, and Y Corporation, $0.50.

Oct. 1, 1995—Sold 100 shares of Y Corporation preferred at $25 per share.

Dec. 31, 1995—Market values were as follows: X common, $46, and Y preferred, $26.

Required

1. Give the entry for Decker Company to record the purchase of the securities.
2. Give any adjusting entry needed at the end of 1994.
3. Give the items and amounts that should be reported on the 1994 income statement and balance sheet.
4. Give all the entries required in 1995.
5. Give the items and amounts that should be reported on the 1995 income statement and balance sheet.

E 14-3
(L.O. 2, 3, 4)

Temporary Equity Investment: Purchase, Sale, Reclassification, Entries, and Reporting   At December 31, 1994, the investments in trading securities of Vista Company were as follows:

Security	Shares	Unit Cost	Unit Market Price
Preferred shares, 80-cent dividend, Knight Corp.	600	$90	$88
Common shares, nopar, Dyer Corp.	200	30	31

The fiscal year ends December 31, and these securities were all purchased during 1994. The transactions that follow all relate to the above equity investments and to those additional securities bought and sold during 1995.

Feb. 2   Received the annual cash dividend from Knight Corporation.
Mar. 1   Sold 150 Dyer shares at $34 per share.
May 1   Sold 400 Knight shares at $89.50 per share.
June 1   Received a cash dividend on Dyer shares of $3.50 per share.
Aug. 1   Purchased 4,000 common shares of Rote Corporation at $45 per share.
Sept. 1 Transferred all shares of Dyer common shares from the temporary portfolio to the long-term portfolio. At this date, the Dyer shares were quoted at $28 per share.

At December 31, 1995, the quoted market prices were as follows: Knight preferred, $98; Dyer common, $28; and Rote common, $44.75.

Required

1. Give the entry that Vista Company should make on December 31, 1994, to record the equity investments at LCM. Use the allowance method.
2. Give the entries for 1995 through September 1.
3. Give the entry(s) required at December 31, 1995.
4. List the items and amounts that should be reported on Vista's 1995 income statement and balance sheet.

E 14–4
(L.O. 2, 4)

Investment in Temporary Debt Security: Entries and Reporting On September 1, 1994, New Company purchased 10 bonds of Old Corporation ($1,000, 6%) as a temporary investment at 96 (i.e., $960) plus accrued interest. The bonds pay annual interest each July 1. New paid cash, including accrued interest. New's annual reporting period ends December 31. At December 31, 1994, the Old bonds were quoted at 95.

Required

1. Give the journal entry for New Company to record the purchase of the bonds.
2. Give any adjusting entries required at December 31, 1994.
3. Give the items and amounts that should be reported on the 1994 income statement and balance sheet.
4. Give the required entry on July 1, 1995.
5. On August 1, 1995, New Company sold four of the bonds at 96.5 plus any accrued interest. Give the required entry(s).
6. At December 31, 1995, the Old Corporation bonds were quoted at 97.5. There were no additional transactions during 1995. Show the entry(s) to be made at December 31, 1995, and list the investment items and amounts that would be reported on the 1995 income statement and balance sheet.

E 14–5
(L.O. 2, 4)

Temporary Investment in Debt Securities: Purchase, Sale, Entries On August 1, 1994, West Company purchased for cash eight $10,000 bonds of Moe Corporation at 98 plus accrued interest. The bonds pay 9% interest, payable on a semiannual basis each May 1 and November 1. The bonds were purchased as a temporary investment. The annual reporting period ends December 31.

Required

1. Give the entries for the following transactions for West Company:

Aug. 1, 1994   Paid $80,200 cash for the bonds including any accrued interest.
Nov. 1, 1994   Collected interest on the bonds.
Dec. 31, 1994   Adjusting entries (if any). The bonds were quoted on the market on this date at 96.

2. Show how this investment should be reported on the 1994 income statement and balance sheet.
3. On February 1, 1995, two of the bonds were sold for $19,950 cash, which includes accrued interest. Give the required entry. Assume that no reversing entries were made on January 1, 1995.
4. Give the entry for the collection of interest on May 1, 1995.

E 14–6
(L.O. 2)

Basket Purchase of Securities: Allocation, Entry On December 1, 1994, Voss Company purchased stock in the three different companies listed below for a lump sum of $113,400, to be held as a long-term investment:

N Corporation, common shares, 300 shares.
O Corporation, preferred shares, 400 shares.
P Corporation common shares, 500 shares.

In addition, Voss paid transfer fees and other costs related to the acquisition amounting to $600. At the time of purchase, the shares were quoted on the local market at the following prices per share: N common, $100; O preferred, $120; and P common, $84.

Required   Give the entry to record the purchase of these investments and payment of the transfer fees and other costs. Record each stock in a separate account and show the cost per share.

E 14–7
(L.O. 2, 3, 4)

Long-Term Investments: Entries and Reporting—Multiple Years   During 1994, Shale Company purchased equity security shares in two corporations and debt securities of a third with the intention of holding them as long-term investments. Transactions were in the following order:

  a. Purchased 200 of the 10,000 common shares outstanding of Tee Corporation at $31 per share plus a 4% brokerage fee and a transfer cost of $52.
  b. Purchased 300 of 4,000 outstanding preferred shares (nonvoting) of Stone Corporation at $78 per share plus a 3% brokerage fee and a transfer cost of $198.
  c. Purchased an additional 20 common shares of Tee Corporation at $35 per share plus a 4% brokerage fee and a transfer cost of $4.
  d. Purchased $10,000 face amount of Container Corporation, 9% bonds at 96.0 plus accrued interest and a transfer fee of $200. The purchase is made on November 1; interest is paid semiannually on January 31 and July 31.
  e. Received $4 per share cash dividend on the Stone Corporation shares (from earnings since acquisition).
  f. Interest payments are made as scheduled.

Required   1. Give the entry in the accounts of Shale Company for each transaction.
  2. The market value of the shares held at the end of 1994 were Tee stock, $34, and Stone stock, $75. The Container Corporation bonds were quoted at 98. Give the appropriate adjusting entry for Shale Company.
  3. The market values of the shares held at the end of 1995 were Tee stock, $36, and Stone stock, $77. The bonds were quoted at 95. Give the appropriate adjusting entry.
  4. Show how the income statement and balance sheet for Shale Company would report relevant data concerning these investments for 1994 and 1995.

E 14–8
(L.O. 2, 5, 7)

Long-Term Investment in Debt Securities, Amortized Cost Method: Entries and Reporting   The Shepard Hydrant Company purchased $50,000 face amount of Beagle Bugler 9% bonds at a price of 98.5 on January 1, 1995. The bonds mature on December 31, 1997, and pay interest annually on December 31. Shepard plans to hold the bonds until maturity. Assume that Shepard uses the straight-line method of amortizing any premium or discount on investments in bonds classified as long-term. At December 31, 1995 and 1996, the bonds are quoted at 98.0 and 99.0, respectively.

Required   1. Show the entry to record the purchase of the bonds.
  2. Show the entry(s) to be made on December 31, 1995.
  3. Show the entry(s) to be made on December 31, 1996.
  4. Show the income statement and balance sheet items and amounts related to the above investment that would be reported for 1995 and 1996.
  5. Show any additional disclosure that would be required for this investment.

E 14–9
(L.O. 6)

Long-Term Equity Investment, Equity Method: Compute Goodwill, Entries   On January 1, 1994, JR Company purchased 400 of the 1,000 outstanding common shares of RV Corporation for $30,000. At that date, the balance sheet of RV showed the following book values:

> Assets not subject to depreciation, $40,000.*
>
> Assets subject to depreciation (net), $26,000.†
>
> Liabilities, $6,000.*
>
> Common shares, $50,000.
>
> Retained earnings, $10,000.
>
> * Same as market value.
>
> † Market value $30,000; the assets have a 10-year remaining life (straight-line depreciation).

Required

1. Assuming that the equity method is appropriate, give the entry by JR Company to record the acquisition at a cost of $30,000. Assume a long-term investment.
2. Show the computation of goodwill purchased at acquisition.
3. Assume that at December 31, 1994 (end of the accounting period), RV Corporation reported a net income of $12,000. Assume goodwill amortization over a 10-year period. Give all entries indicated on the records of JR Company.
4. In February 1995, RV Corporation declared and paid a $2 per share cash dividend. Give the necessary entry for JR Company.

E 14–10
(L.O. 6)

Long-Term Equity Investment, Equity Method: Compute Goodwill, Entries On January 1, 1995, Case Corporation purchased 3,000 of the 10,000 outstanding common shares of Dow Corporation for $28,000 cash. At that date, Dow's balance sheet reflected the following book values:

Assets not subject to depreciation, $25,000.*

Assets subject to depreciation (net), $30,000.†

Liabilities, $5,000.*

Common shares, $40,000.

Retained earnings, $10,000.

* Same as market value.

† Market value $38,000; estimated remaining life of 10 years (straight-line depreciation).

Required

1. If goodwill is relevant to this investment, show the computation of goodwill purchased at acquisition.
2. At the end of 1995, Dow reported income before extraordinary items, $20,000; extraordinary loss, $2,000; and net income, $18,000. In December 1995, Dow Corporation paid a $1 per share cash dividend. Reconstruct the following accounts (use the T-account format) for Case Corporation: cash, investment in Dow Corporation, investment revenue—ordinary, and extraordinary loss. Apply the appropriate method of accounting for long-term investments in equity securities, and assume that straight-line amortization of any goodwill is over 10 years. Date and identify all amounts entered in the accounts.

E 14–11
(L.O. 3, 4, 6)

Long-Term Equity Investment, Cost and Equity Methods Compared: Entries On January 3, 1994, TA Company purchased 2,000 shares of the 10,000 outstanding shares of common stock of UK Corporation for $14,600 cash with the intention of holding the securities indefinitely. At that date, the balance sheet of UK Corporation reflected the following: nondepreciable assets, $50,000 (same as market value); depreciable assets (net), $30,000 (market value, $33,000); total liabilities, $20,000; and shareholders' equity, $60,000. Assume a 10-year remaining life (straight-line depreciation) on the depreciable assets and amortization of goodwill over 10 years.

Required

1. Give the entries, if any are required, on TA's books for each item (*a*) through (*g*) below assuming that the cost method is appropriate.
2. Repeat (1) above assuming that the equity method is appropriate.
   Entries required and other information:
   a. Entry at date of acquisition.
   b. Goodwill purchased—computation only.
   c. Entry on Dec. 31, 1994 to record $15,000 net income reported by UK.
   d. Entry on Dec. 31, 1994 for additional depreciation expense.
   e. Entry on Dec. 31, 1994 for amortization of goodwill.
   f. Entry on Dec. 31, 1994 to recognize decrease in market value of UK stock, quoted market price, $7 per share.
   g. Entry on Mar. 31, 1995 for a cash dividend of $1 per share declared and paid by UK.

E 14–12
(L.O. 4, 8)

Long-Term Equity Investment, Stock Dividend, Investor's Entries Each of the following situations is independent; however, each relates to the receipt of a stock dividend by an investor.

Case A Doe Corporation had 20,000 shares outstanding when the board of directors voted to issue a 25% stock dividend (that is, one additional share for every four shares owned).

Required

Van Company owns 2,000 shares of the Doe Corporation shares (a long-term investment) acquired during the current accounting period at a cost of $65 per share. After receiving the stock dividend, Van Company sold 200 shares of Doe Corporation for $70 per share. Give the entries for Van Company to record (a) acquisition of the 2,000 shares, (b) receipt of the stock dividend, and (c) sale of the 200 shares.

Case B   During the course of an audit, you find two accounts of the investor, May Company, as follows:

Temporary Investments: Yew Company

Debits

Jan. 1	Cost of 100 shares	$17,500
Feb. 1	50 shares received as a stock dividend	5,000

Credits

July 1	25 shares sold at $125	$ 3,125

Income Summary

Credits

Feb. 1	Stock dividend on Yew Company shares	$ 5,000
Aug. 1	Cash dividend on Yew Company shares	3,000

Yew Company common shares have a market price of $150 per share at year-end.

Required   Restate these accounts on a correct basis. Give reasons for each change.

E 14–13
(L.O. 2, 4, 8)

Long-Term Equity Investment: Cash and Stock Dividends, Stock Split, Entries   Hewlett Company purchased common shares (50,000 shares outstanding) of Packard Corporation as a long-term investment. Transactions (which occurred in the order given) related to this investment were as follows:

a. Purchased 600 common shares Packard at $90 per share.
b. Purchased 2,000 common shares Packard at $96 per share.
c. At the end of the first year, Packard Corporation reported net income of $52,000 and the stock was selling at $97.
d. At the end of the year, Packard Corporation declared and paid a cash dividend of $2 per share.
e. After reporting net income of $5,000 for the second year, Packard Corporation issued a stock dividend whereby each shareholder received on additional share for every two shares owned. After the stock dividend at the end of the second year, the stock was selling at $85.
f. Packard Corporation revised its charter to provide for a stock split. The old common shares were turned in, and the holders received in exchange two new shares for each old share turned in.

Required   Give the entries for each transaction as they should be made in the accounts of Hewlett Company. Show computations. Assume that the cost method is appropriate, because less than 20% of Packard's voting stock is held by Hewlett.

E 14–14
(L.O. 8)

Long-Term Equity Investment: Stock Rights, Entries   The Hess Fuel Corporation issued one stock right for each common share owned by investors. The rights provided that for every six rights held, a preferred share could be purchased for $80 cash. When the rights were issued, they had a market value of $7 each, and the common stock was selling at $142 per share (ex rights). Taylor Company owned 300 common shares of Hess Fuel Corporation, acquired earlier in the current accounting period as a long-term investment at a cost of $22,350.

Hess common has a year-end price of $145 per share, and the rights have a quoted market price of $6 each.

Required   1. How many rights did Taylor Company receive?
2. Determine the cost to be allocated of the stock rights received by Taylor Company and give any entry that should be made upon receipt of the rights.
3. Assume that Taylor Company exercised the rights when the market value of the preferred stock of Hess Fuel Corporation was $130. Determine the cost of the new shares and give the entry to record the exercise of the rights.
4. Assume instead that Taylor Company sold its rights for $7.40 each. Give the entry to record the sale.
5. Assume that Taylor Company neither sold nor exercised the rights. Give any year-end entry.

E 14–15

Appendix 14A: Special-Purpose Fund—Accumulation Schedule, Entries   On January 1, 1994, Koke Company decided to create a special-purpose fund to be identified as the special contingency fund.

The resources in the fund will be used to reimburse employees injured while on the job. The company desires to accumulate a $150,000 fund balance by the end of 1996 by making equal annual deposits starting on January 1, 1994. The independent trustee handling the fund will increase the fund by 9% compound interest each December 31.

Required

1. Compute the amount of the annual deposits and prepare a fund accumulations schedule.
2. Give the entries relating to the fund that Koke Company should make each year.
3. Assume that on January 2, 1997, the trustee made the first payment from the fund in the amount of $1,000. Give the entry, if any, that Koke Company should make.

PROBLEMS

P 14–1
(L.O. 2, 4)

Temporary Investments: Entries and Reporting On January 1, 1994, Joy Company acquired the following temporary debt and equity securities:

Co.	Description	Quantity	Unit Cost
T	Common.	1,000 shares	$20
U	Common.	600 shares	15
V	Preferred (nonconvertible)	400 shares	30
W	8% bonds ($1,000 face amount), interest paid on December 31	10 bonds	98

Per share data subsequent to the acquisition are as follows:

Dec. 31/1994	Market values: T stock, $16; U stock, $15; V stock, $34; and W bonds, 97.0.
Feb. 10/1995	Cash dividends received: T stock, $1.50; U stock, $1; and V stock, 50 cents.
Nov. 1/1995	Sold the shares of V stock at $38.
Dec. 31/1995	Market values: T stock, $13; U stock, $17; V stock, $33; and W bonds 99.5.

Required

1. Give all entries indicated for Joy Company for 1994 and 1995. There was no balance in the allowance account on Jan. 1, 1994.
2. Show how the income statement and balance sheet for Joy Company would reflect these investments for 1994 and 1995.

P 14–2
(L.O. 4)

Temporary Equity Investments: Entries and Reporting On December 31, 1994, Raven Company's portfolio of temporary investments in equity securities was as follows (purchased on September 1, 1994):

Security	Shares	Unit Cost	Unit Market
Bic Corp., common shares	50	$186	$187
Cross Corp., $2.40 preferred shares	200	40	35

Transactions relating to this portfolio during 1995 were as follows:

Jan. 25	Received a dividend cheque on the Cross shares.
Apr. 15	Sold 30 Bic Corporation shares at $151 per share.
July 25	Received a $45 dividend cheque on the Bic shares.
Oct. 1	Sold the remaining shares of Bic Corporation at $149.50 per share.
Dec. 1	Purchased 100 Pilot Corporation common shares at $47 per share plus a $30 brokerage fee.
Dec. 5	Purchased 400 Sanford Corporation common shares at $15 per share.
Dec. 31	Transferred the Cross shares to the long-term investment portfolio.

On December 31, 1995, the following unit market prices were available: Bic stock, $140; Cross stock, $38; Pilot stock, $51; and Sanford stock, $14.

Required

1. Give the entries that Raven Company should make on (*a*) September 1, 1994, and (*b*) December 31, 1994. Use the allowance method.
2. Give the investment items and amounts that should be reported on the 1994 income statement and balance sheet.
3. Give the journal entries for 1995 related to the temporary investments.

4. Give the investment items and amounts that should be reported on the 1995 income statement and balance sheet.

P 14–3
(L.O. 5, 6)

Temporary Investment, Debt Securities: Entries and Reporting   On April 1, 1995, Lyn Company purchased for cash eight $1,000, 9% bonds of Star Corporation at 102 plus accrued interest. The bond interest is paid semiannually on each May 1 and November 1. Lyn Company's annual reporting period ends on December 31. Lyn Company uses the direct method.

On December 1, 1995, six of these bonds were sold for cash at 101½ plus any accrued interest. At December 31, 1995, the Star Corporation bonds were quoted at 97.

Required

1. Give the entry for Lyn Company to record the purchase of the bonds on April 1, 1995.
2. Give the entry for interest collected during 1995.
3. Give any adjusting entry(s) required on December 31, 1995.
4. Show what items and amounts should be reported on the 1995 income statement and balance sheet.

P 14–4
(L.O. 2, 4)

Temporary Debt Investment: Entries and Reporting   At December 31, 1994, the portfolio of temporary investments held by Dow Company was as follows:

		Interest				
Security	Par Value	Rate	Payable	Cash Cost*	Date Purchased	Maturity Date
X Corp. bonds.	$10,000	6%	Nov. 1	$10,000	Sept. 1, 1994	Nov. 1, 1999
Y Corp. bonds.	20,000	9%	Dec. 31	20,400	Dec. 31, 1994	Dec. 1, 1996

* Excluding any accrued interest.

Dow's annual reporting period ends on December 31. At December 31, 1994, the X Corporation bonds were selling at 98.5. Dow uses the allowance method.

Transactions relating to the portfolio of temporary investments in debt securities during 1995 were as follows:

June 1	Sold the Y Corporation bonds at 103, plus any accrued interest.
Nov. 1	Collected interest on the X Corporation bonds.
Dec. 1	Purchased $30,000 of Z Corporation bonds at 99½ plus accrued interest. These bonds pay 8% interest semiannually each March 1 and September 1. The investment is classified as temporary investments.
Dec. 31	Transferred the X Corporation bonds, quoted at 99.5, to the portfolio of long-term investments.

Required

1. Give the 1994 entries for Dow Company to record the purchase of the debt securities, collections of interest, and all related adjusting entries.
2. The Z Corporation bonds were quoted at 99 on December 31, 1995. Give all of the 1995 entries, including interest collections and any adjusting entries.
3. List the items and amounts that would be reported on the 1995 income statement and the current section of the balance sheet.

P 14–5
(L.O. 4, 5, 7)

Temporary Equity Investments, Debt Securities, LCM: Entries and Reporting   At December 31, 1995, Piper Company held the following securities in its portfolio of temporary investments:

Description	Quantity	Total Cost	Unit Market Prices
1. Equity securities:			
Damon common shares	50 shares	$ 2,300	$ 47
Martin common shares	100 shares	2,100	19
2. Debt securities:			
Hydro Corp., $1,000 bonds, 9% payable annually on June 1	10 bonds	10,400	103.5

Transactions relating to these investments during 1996 were as follows (the annual reporting period ends December 31):

Mar. 1	Sold 30 Damon common shares at $50 per share.
Apr. 1	Sold 70 Martin common shares at $20 per share.
June 1	Collected interest on the Hydro bonds.
Dec. 31	The Hydro bonds were transferred to long-term investments. The market price at this date was 103.
Sept. 1	Received a cash dividend of $1 per share on the Damon common shares.
Dec. 1	Purchased 300 ATX common shares at $25 cash per share.

Quoted market prices at December 31, 1996, were as follows: Damon common shares, $45; Martin common shares, $21; ATX common shares, $28; and Hydro Corporation bonds, $1,010 per bond (i.e., 101).

Required

1. Show how the investment portfolio should be reported on the 1995 balance sheet. Show computations.
2. Give the entries for the 1996 transactions through December 31, 1996.
3. Give the entry(s) to record fair values on the appropriate securities at December 31, 1996.
4. Give the items and amounts that must be reported on the 1996 income statement and the investments section of the balance sheet.

P 14–6
(L.O. 2, 4, 7)

Long-Term Equity Investments: Entries and Reporting for Two Years On January 1, 1994, Rae Company purchased 4,000 of the 40,000 common shares outstanding of DB Corporation for $80,000 cash, and 3,000 of the 100,000 common shares outstanding of CX Corporation for $7 per share cash as long-term investments. These are the only long-term equity investments held. The accounting periods for all the companies end on December 31.

	DB Corp.	CX Corp.
December 31, 1994:		
Income reported for 1994	$40,000	$20,000
Cash dividend per share declared and paid during 1994	1.00	None
Market price per share of stock	15	8
October 20, 1995:		
Sold 1,000 shares of CX stock at $11 per share.		
December 31, 1995:		
Income reported for 1995	50,000	26,000
Cash dividend per share declared and paid during 1995	1.00	.60
Market price per share of stock	17	6
Reclassified the CX stock as a temporary investment.		

Required

1. Give all of the entries required for Rae Company for 1994 and 1995.
2. Show how the long-term investments in equity securities and the related investment revenue would be reported on the financial statements of Rae Company at the end of each year.

P 14–7
(L.O. 2, 5, 7)

Long-Term Investment in Debt Securities, Amortized Cost Method: Entries and Reporting On July 1, 1994, Wyder Door Company acquired the following bonds, which Wyder intended to hold to maturity:

Security	Price	Face Amount Purchased
Flakey Cement 10% bonds, maturity date July 31, 1999	101.5	$30,000
Green Lawn 8% bonds, maturity date, December 31, 1996	97.0	20,000

Both bonds pay interest annually on December 31. Premium and discount can be amortized on a straight-line basis.

Required

1. Show the entry to record the investment. Assume that cash payments for purchases included accrued interest.
2. Show the entries to be made at December 31, 1994.
3. Show the items and amounts that would be reported in the 1994 income statement and balance sheet related to this investment.
4. Show the entries to be made on December 31, 1995.
5. Show the items and amounts that would be reported in the 1995 income statement and balance sheet related to this investment.

P 14–8
(L.O. 6, 7)

Long-Term Investment, Equity Method, Goodwill: Entries and Reporting for Three Years On January 1, 1994, Parr Company purchased 30% of the 30,000 outstanding common shares of Stub Corporation at $17 per share as a long-term investment (the only long-term equity investment held). The following data relates to Stub Corporation.

a. At acquisition date, January 1, 1994:

	Value At	
	Book	**Market**
Assets not subject to depreciation.	$250,000	$260,000*
Assets subject to depreciation, net (10-year remaining life; straight-line).	200,000	220,000
	$450,000	
Liabilities	$ 50,000	50,000
Common shares.	300,000	
Retained earnings	100,000	
	$450,000	

* Difference is due to inventory, and this inventory is sold during 1994.

b. Selected data available at December 31, 1994 and 1995:

	1994	**1995**
Cash dividends declared and paid by Stub Corporation during the year	$ 8,000	$ 10,000
Income reported by Stub:		
Income (loss) before extraordinary items.	24,000	(5,000)
Extraordinary loss.	(2,000)	
Quoted market price per share, Stub Corporation stock (December 31)	20	18

c. On January 2, 1996, Parr Company sold 500 of the Stub shares at $18 per share.

Required

1. Give all of the appropriate entries for Parr Company during 1994 and 1995. Use straight-line amortization of goodwill over a 30-year period.
2. Give the entry required on January 2, 1996.
3. Show what items and amounts based on (1) and (2) will be reported on the 1994, 1995, and 1996 income statements and on the 1994 and 1995 balance sheets.

P 14–9
(L.O. 4, 7, 8)

Long-Term Investment: Cash and Stock Dividends, Split, Entries, and Reporting Allen Corporation completed the following transactions, in the order given, relative to the portfolio of stocks held as long-term investments:

Year 1994:

a. Purchased 200 MC Corporation common shares at $70 per share plus a brokerage commission of 4% and transfer costs of $20.

b. Purchased, for a lump sum of $96,000, the following shares of NP Corporation:

	Number of Shares	Market Price at Date of Purchase
Class A, common	200	$ 50
Preferred, noncumulative.	300	100
Class B, common	400	150

Year 1995:

c. Purchased 300 MC Corporation common shares at $80 per share plus a brokerage commission of 4% and transfer costs of $60.

d. Received a stock split on the MC Corporation shares; for each share held, an additional share was received.

e. Sold 100 MC Corporation shares at $45 per share.

Year 1996:

f. Received a two-for-one stock split on the class A common shares of NP Corporation (the number of shares doubled).

g. Cash dividends declared and paid:

MC Corporation common—$10 per share.
NP, class A, common—$5 per share.

NP, preferred—$3 per share.
NP, class B, common—$15 per share.

h. Year-end stock prices were as follows:

	1994	1995	1996
MC, common	$ 70	$ 40	$ 39.95
NP, class A, common	51	47	24
NP preferred	98	95	96
NP, class B, common	140	144	144

Required

1. Give entries for Allen Corporation for the above transactions. Show calculations, and assume the cost method is appropriate.
2. What items, amounts, and disclosures would be shown on the 1994, 1995, and 1996 income statements and balance sheets by Allen Corporation with respect to these investments?

P 14–10
(L.O. 2, 3, 4, 6, 7)

Long-Term Equity Investment, Cost and Equity Methods Compared: Entries and Reporting
On January 1, 1995, Redmond Company purchased 3,000 of the 15,000 outstanding common shares of Decca Computer (DC) Corporation for $80,000 cash as a long-term investment (the only long-term equity investment held). At that date, the balance sheet of DC showed the following book values (summarized):

Assets not subject to depreciation	$140,000*
Assets subject to depreciation (net)	100,000†
Liabilities	40,000
Common shares	150,000
Retained earnings	50,000

* Market value, $150,000; difference relates to land held for sale.

† Market value, $140,000, estimated remaining life, 10 years. Use straight-line depreciation with no residual value and amortization of goodwill over 20 years.

Additional subsequent data on DC:

	1995	1996
Income before extraordinary items	$25,000	$26,000
Extraordinary item—gain	—	5,000
Cash dividends declared and paid	10,000	12,000
Market value per share	25	26

Required

1. For Case A, assume that the cost method is appropriate. For Case B, assume the equity method is appropriate. For each case, provide the investor's entries or give the required information for items (a) through (d) in a tabulation similar to the one below.

Entries Required and Other Information	Case A: Cost Method Is Appropriate		Case B: Equity Method Is Appropriate	
a. Entry at date of acquisition.				
b. Amount of goodwill purchased.				
c. Entries at Dec. 31, 1995:				
(1) Investment revenue and dividends.				
(2) Additional depreciation expense.				
(3) Amortization of goodwill.				
(4) Additional entry associated with and held for sale (held by DC) for which market value (i.e., purchase price to Redmond) exceeded book value; the land is sold during 1995.				
(5) Recognition of change in market value of DC stock.				
d. Entries at Dec. 31, 1996:				
(1) Investment revenue and dividends.				
(2) Additional depreciation expense.				
(3) Amortization of goodwill.				
(4) Recognition of change in market value of DC stock.				

2. For each case, reconstruct the investment accounts.
3. Explain why the investment account balance is different between the cost and equity methods.

P 14–11
(L.O. 4, 6)

Reclassification between Equity Method and Cost Method: Entries and Reporting   Refer to Problem 14–10. Assume that all the facts are as given regarding the investment made by Redmond Company in Decca Computer (DC) Corporation, and that Redmond uses the equity method to account for the investment. As of January 1, 1997, however, Redmond management decides it can no longer exert significant influence over the affairs of DC, and elects to reclassify the investment as a long-term (cost-method) investment as of that date. Assume that as of January 1, 1997, the investment in DC, at equity, is recorded at $80,200, and the market price of DC common shares is $26 per share.

Required

1. Prepare the entry to record the reclassification of the investment.
2. Assume the same facts as in Problem 14–10, except that the investment in DC was by the cost method for Redmond from the date of its acquisition through December 31, 1996. On January 1, 1997, management elects to reclassify the DC investments as an equity-basis company. Prepare the entry to record the reclassification from cost method to equity.

P 14–12
(L.O. 4, 6)

Reclassification from Cost Method to Equity Method: Entries and Reporting   At December 31, 1994, Dulls Travel Adventures reported the following regarding its long-term investment:

Long-term investments, at cost $78,000

Dulls has only one security, Scratchee Blanket Company common, classified as a long-term investment. Dulls owns 1,000 of the 5,000 outstanding voting shares of Scratchee common. On January 2, 1995, Dulls purchases an additional 500 shares of Scratchee common for $35,000. At the same time, it determines that it can now exert significant influence over the affairs of Scratchee. Scratchee earnings and dividends during 1995 are $6 and $2 per share, respectively. Assume that the recorded cost of the investment is approximately equal to the net fair value of the assets acquired.

Required

1. Show the entry to record the acquisition of the additional shares and the entry to record the reclassification of the investment in Scratchee from the cost method to the equity method.
2. Show the entry to record equity in earnings and dividends received from Scratchee during 1995.
3. Show the items, amounts, and note disclosures to be presented in the income statement and balance sheet related to this investment for 1995.

P 14–13

Appendix: Special-Purpose Fund—Accumulation Schedule, Entries, and Reporting   On January 1, 1994, Case Corporation created a special building fund by depositing a single sum of $100,000 with an independent trustee. The purpose of the fund is to provide resources to build an addition to the older office building during the latter part of 1998. The company anticipates a total construction cost of $500,000 and completion by January 1, 1999. The company plans to make equal annual deposits each December 31, 1994 through 1998, to accumulate the $500,000. The independent trustee will increase the fund each December 31, at an interest rate of 10 percent. The accounting periods of the company and the fund end on December 31.

Required

1. Compute the amount of the equal annual deposits that will be needed and prepare a fund accumulation schedule through December 31, 1998, for Case Corporation.
2. The total cash outlay by Case will be $_____ .
   Total interest revenue will be $_____ .
   The effective interest rate will be _____ percent.
3. Give the entries for Case on: (*a*) January 1, 1994, and (*b*) December 31, 1994.
4. Give the entries for Case on January 3, 1999, when the addition is completed and the actual cost of $525,000 is paid in full. The trustee paid interest on the fund for two extra days at the fund rate.
5. Show what the 1995 Case income statement, balance sheet, and statement of cash flows should report in regards to the building addition program.
6. Assume that the accounting period of Case Corporation ends on October 31 (instead of December 31) and the fund year-end is unchanged. Give any adjusting entry(s) that Case should make at its 1996 year-end.

ANALYZING FINANCIAL STATEMENTS

All questions in this section are based on information taken from the financial statements of actual companies.

A 14–1 **Equity Method** In its 1993 annual report, Placer Dome Inc. has several items in the financial statements that refer to investments in equity-based companies:

	1993	1992
	(amounts in millions)	
From the Income Statement		
Equity in loss of associates	$ (9)	$(12)
Investment and other income.	79	67
From the Balance Sheet		
Investments	67	81
From the Statement of Cash Flows		
Adjustments to reconcile income to cash flows:*		
Equity in associates, net of dividends received.	9	12
Investment gains	(28)	(23)

* These are amounts added back (subtracted from) net income to obtain cash flow from operations.

Assume that there are no adjustments required for differences between book value and fair value at the date of acquisition, or any goodwill, associated with the equity-based companies.

Required
1. Did Placer Dome make any additional investments in its equity-based companies during 1993 beyond the amount retained by them? If so, how much?
2. Is it possible to determine the amount of dividends Placer Dome received from these investments? Why (not)?
3. Assume that there is only one company in Placer Dome's investment and it is 40% owned. What would you estimate the total shareholders' equity of that company to be at December 31, 1993?

A 14–2   **Equity Method** In its 1993 annual report, Transcanada Pipelines Limited presents the following information from its financial statements with regard to associated operations:

	1993	1992
	(amounts in millions)	
From the Income Statement		
Income from associated operations	$149.4	$128.4
From the Balance Sheet		
Associated operations	945.3	879.5
From the Statement of Changes in Financial Position		
Adjustments to reconcile income to cash flows:*		
Income from associated operations less dividends received.	(56.1)	(46.6)
Investment activities:		
Associated operations	(4.3)	(137.9)

* These are amounts added back (subtracted from) net income to obtain cash flow from operations.

Required
1. How much did Transcanada Pipelines receive in dividends from associated operations in 1993 and 1992?
2. How much did Transcanada Pipelines invest in associated operations in 1993 and 1992?
3. Did Transcanada Pipelines amortize any differences between book value and fair value at date of acquisition, or goodwill in 1993? If so, how much?

A 14–3   **Marketable Securities**   Vencap Equities Alberta Ltd. is a private-sector venture capital fund making equity capital investments in new and existing business enterprises. Vencap has committed $254 million of equity capital to 73 companies in the western regions of Canada and the United States during the past decade. The following information has been taken from Vencap's 1994 annual report.

From the Notes to Financial Statements

1. Summary of significant accounting policies

    Marketable securities

    Marketable securities maturing within one year, consisting of bonds and preferred shares with predetermined maturities, are recorded at cost.

    Marketable securities maturing after one year are recorded at cost unless there has been a permanent impairment in value. A loss associated with a permanent impairment would be reflected in the statement of income.

    Venture investments

    Venture investments having quoted market values and which are publicly traded on a recognized exchange are recorded at values based on the quoted market prices on the balance sheet date.

    Venture investments not having quoted market values are recorded at directors' estimates of fair value. Fair value is defined as the expected realization if venture investments were disposed of in an orderly distribution over a reasonable period of time.

From the Balance Sheet (thousands)

	March 31	
	1994	1993
Current assets:		
Marketable securities maturing in one year	$ 45,115	$ 30,578
Marketable securities maturing after one year	126,633	144,857
Venture investments	114,388	113,486

Required

1. What is your opinion with respect to Vencap's policy of using cost for its marketable securities and market for its venture (long-term) investments? What are your reasons?
2. What alternative methods are available for Vencap in accounting for the unrealized gains and losses in the venture investments? Which accounting method would you recommend?
3. What problems could arise in using the directors' estimates of fair value for the venture investments?

COMPARATIVE ANALYSIS

Dofasco Inc., and Stelco Inc.   In many ways, Dofasco and Stelco are similar companies. Both are engaged in the production of steel and have invested heavily in production facilities. Your task is to identify the important ways in which these two companies are different or similar and to consider what might be the implications of these differences or similarities.

Summarized financial information for both Dofasco and Stelco and relevant notes to the financial statements are presented below:

Summarized Balance Sheets at December 31

	Dofasco		Stelco	
	1993	1992	1993	1992
Current assets	$1,158	$1,111	$ 927	$ 867
Investments and other assets	132	140	193	193
Property, plant, and equipment	1,917	2,004	1,194	1,309
Deferred costs	11	12	50	54
Total assets	$3,218	$3,267	$2,364	$2,423
Current liabilities	$ 295	$ 382	$ 628	$ 588
Long-term debt	833	928	695	767
Other liabilities and deferred taxes	607	588	112	101
Shareholders' equity	1,483	1,369	929	967
Total liabilities and shareholders' equity	$3,218	$3,267	$2,364	$2,423

Summarized Income Statements for Year Ending December 31

	Dofasco		Stelco	
	1993	1992	1993	1992
Sales	$2,103	$1,953	$2,491	$2,203
Cost of sales excluding the following	1,778	1,737	2,166	2,033
Depreciation and amortization	180	167	122	128
Interest	89	91	85	90
Interest income	(17)	(12)		
Other	7	8	157	161
Equity (income) loss	5	11	(9)	3
Loss (gain) on sale of investments	(39)	(14)		(21)
Restructuring (gain) loss	(36)	338		
Total	$1,967	$2,326	$2,521	$2,401
Income (loss) before taxes	$ 136	$ (373)	$ (30)	$ (191)
Income tax (expense) recovery	3	166	(6)	64
Net income (loss)	$ 139	$ (207)	$ (36)	$ (127)

Dofasco's Notes to Financial Statements (excerpts)

1. Accounting Policies

Basis of consolidation—The consolidated financial statements include the accounts of the Corporation, its wholly-owned subsidiaries and the proportionate share of the assets, liabilities and results of operations of its integrated joint venture activities.

Non-integrated investments in which the Corporation has a significant interest but does not have effective control are accounted for by the equity method and the remaining long term investments are carried at cost.

2. Unusual Items

(i) Gain on sale of Algoma preferred shares

Effective June 1, 1992, a restructuring plan of The Algoma Steel Corporation, Limited (a wholly-owned subsidiary) established a new independent company, Algoma Steel Inc. ("Algoma"). Under this restructuring plan, the Corporation received 5.5% distress preferred shares in exchange for its holdings of secured debentures and agreed to loan Algoma an amount equal to the dividend payments on these shares during the period through to the end of 1996. The Corporation relinquished all other rights and claims as a shareholder and creditor of The Algoma Steel Corporation, Limited.

In 1993, the Corporation sold its entire holding of Algoma distress preferred shares for $39.0 million. Prior to the sale of these shares, dividends of $5.3 million were loaned to Algoma as required. There is a further obligation to loan Algoma up to $10.5 million, which is equal to the dividends to be paid on these shares to December 31, 1996. These loans are repayable during the period from 1997 to 2001.

(ii) Restructuring

In 1992, the Corporation announced plans to restructure its Hamilton operations with the closure of the No. 1 ingot production stream and related facilities as well as the closure of the foundry operations. A provision of $338.0 million was recorded in 1992, consisting of $201.6 million for restructuring costs (which included employment reductions, the write-off of fixed assets of $113.2 million and a write-down of other assets) and $136.4 million for the 1992 Early Retirement Program. A major portion of the costs associated with the early retirement programs is funded from the pension plan. In 1993, this provision was reduced by $35.8 million.

In late 1993, the Corporation announced an involuntary indefinite layoff which will impact approximately 650 employees effective April 1994. The costs associated with this program will be charged against the provision for restructuring which was established in 1992.

5. Joint Ventures and Equity Investments

(ii) Non-integrated equity investments

The Corporation's equity investments consist primarily of a 50% interest in the Quebec Cartier Mining Company ("QCM"). The Corporation obtains significantly less than its pro-rata share of QCM's production and therefore the investment is accounted for by the equity method.

18. Subsequent Events

Subsequent to the year end, the Corporation announced a plan to offer to sell to the public all of its holdings of the shares of Prudential Steel Ltd. of Calgary, its wholly-owned subsidiary which produces steel tubular products for the oil, gas and construction industries. Following successful completion of the offering, the Corporation will not retain any ownership interest in Prudential Steel Ltd.

On February 28, 1994 the Corporation announced the sale of its wholly-owned subsidiary National Steel Car Limited, a Hamilton-based manufacturer of railway cars and specialized rolling stock.

Stelco's Notes to Financial Statements (excerpts):

1 Summary of Significant Accounting Policies

Principles of consolidation

The consolidatd financial statements include the accounts of Stelco Inc. and its subsidiaries, all of which are wholly owned. Corporate joint ventures, partnerships, and other corporate interests, in all of which the Corporation does not have effective control, are accounted for by the equity method. (See Note 7.)

7 Long-Term Investments and Related Commitments

(A) Changes affecting investments in 1993:

In 1993, no new investments were made and none were disposed of.

Changes affecting investments in 1992 included the following:

On June 30, 1992, the Corporation sold its wholly-owned Camrose Works to a partnership, the Camrose Pipe Company, for cash of $26 million and a 40 percent continuing interest in this partnership. This 40 percent partnership interest is being accounted for using the equity method and is being carried at $4 million, its original book value.

(B) Long-term investments

	1993	1992
	(millions)	
Corporate joint ventures, partnerships and other corporate interests, at equity	$191	$191
Portfolio investments, at cost	2	2
	$193	$193

Required
a. Analyze and discuss why Dofasco, with almost 50% more total assets than Stelco, would have lower sales but be more profitable.
b. Evaluate the investment strategy of each company. Consider how the business strategy of each company is affecting its profitability.
c. In general terms, evaluate the effects of the differing business strategies on the financial statements of the two companies. Assess the possible risks and rewards associated with each strategy. In your opinion, which company appears to be better situated for the future? Discuss.

Magna International Inc.
1993 Annual Report

FINANCIAL REVIEW

FINANCIAL REVIEW

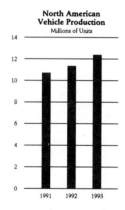

Operating Income
Canadian $ Millions

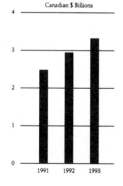

North American Vehicle Production
Millions of Units

Managed Sales
Canadian $ Billions

FINANCIAL HIGHLIGHTS - FISCAL 1993

- Record sales, including joint ventures, of $3.3 billion achieved

- Fully diluted earnings per share of $2.55 achieved, surpassing prior years' levels

- Cash flow from operations of $262 million was generated

- Regular quarterly dividends increased to $0.15 per share in the first quarter of fiscal 1993

- Total debt was reduced by $223 million during the year resulting in a net cash position at July 31, 1993

MANAGEMENT'S DISCUSSION AND ANALYSIS OF RESULTS OF OPERATIONS AND FINANCIAL CONDITION

RESULTS OF OPERATIONS

Overview: Operating income before income taxes and minority interest of $219.9 million in fiscal 1993 was $55.1 million higher than the fiscal 1992 level of $164.8. This 33% improvement over fiscal 1992 was primarily achieved as a result of higher sales, a reduction in interest expense of approximately $33 million and a significant improvement in income from equity investments.

Sales: The Company's consolidated sales increased to $2,606.7 million for fiscal 1993 compared to $2,358.8 million for fiscal 1992. This reflects an increase in production sales of approximately 11% compared to fiscal 1992, attributable to a 9% increase in North American vehicle production to 12.5 million units for fiscal 1993 and a 2% improvement in the Company's average production content per vehicle. Included in consolidated sales are tooling sales which, in fiscal 1993 were $192 million, compared to $190 million in fiscal 1992, reflecting continued new vehicle launches by OEM customers. Sales by joint venture companies totalled $671.5 million for fiscal 1993, bringing managed sales to approximately $3.3 billion.

Substantially all of the Company's revenues are generated from sales of automotive components, assemblies, parts and tooling to North American OEMs. During fiscal 1993, approximately 45% of the Company's sales were in respect of products supplied for inclusion in five vehicle body types (including approximately 23% supplied for the Chrysler minivans).

While both North American vehicle production and sales in fiscal 1993 and the Company's average production content per vehicle were higher than in fiscal 1992, there can be no certainty of the level of North American vehicle production or the Company's average production content per vehicle in fiscal 1994. The Company's sales and profitability are directly affected by such levels of production and average production content per vehicle.

FINANCIAL REVIEW

Facilities: The Company has 67 manufacturing facilities, 62 in North America and 5 in Europe, 9 of which are joint venture operations. During fiscal 1993, the Company commenced production at its first Mexican manufacturing facility, commenced development of a facility in South Carolina and acquired two manufacturing facilities from joint venture partners.

Gross Margin: Gross margin as a percentage of sales declined approximately 0.8% to 19.3% for fiscal 1993 as compared to 20.1% for fiscal 1992, reflecting major new program launch costs, the start-up of the new Mexican manufacturing facility and continued customer pricing pressure, offset partially by higher rates of capacity utilization and improved operating efficiencies.

The competitive environment within the automotive industry has caused OEMs to increase pressure on suppliers for price concessions. While the Company believes that it is, and will remain, competitive, there can be no assurance that the Company will continue to be successful in offsetting required price concessions through cost reductions.

S, G & A: Selling, general and administrative expenses increased by $23.2 million in fiscal 1993 to $179.2 million, as compared to fiscal 1992. The increase is attributable to the higher level of sales activity in fiscal 1993 and retirement and severance costs of approximately $11.3 million incurred in fiscal 1993. Selling, general and administrative expenses, as a percentage of sales, excluding retirement and severance costs, decreased by 0.2% to 6.4% in fiscal 1993, reflecting the effect of spending controls previously put in place by the Company.

Interest Expense: Interest expense in fiscal 1993 decreased by approximately 66% from fiscal 1992 levels, primarily as a result of declining debt levels and a reduction in the average cost of borrowing. Total interest expense for fiscal 1993 amounted to $17.2 million compared to total interest expense for fiscal 1992 of $49.9 million.

Equity Income: Income from equity accounted joint ventures and investments for fiscal 1993 was $18.3 million, an improvement of $19.1 million over the $0.8 million of equity losses for fiscal 1992. Increased sales, the elimination of start-up losses and continued operating improvements at joint ventures contributed to the improvement in results.

Income Taxes: The Company's effective income tax rate, before equity income, of approximately 31% in fiscal 1993 was consistent with fiscal 1992 and lower than the statutory tax rate primarily as a result of the reduction in the income tax provision in fiscal 1993 of $16.8 million ($17.3 million in 1992) due to the benefit of certain losses incurred by subsidiary companies in prior years. Since such losses have been substantially utilized, the Company expects no similar reduction in fiscal 1994 and expects to return in such year to an effective income tax rate, before equity income, approximately equal to the Canadian statutory rate of 36%.

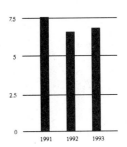
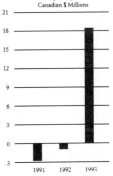
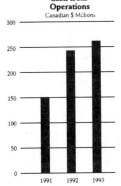

FINANCIAL REVIEW

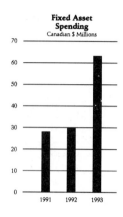

Fixed Asset Spending
Canadian $ Millions

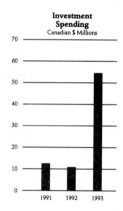

Investment Spending
Canadian $ Millions

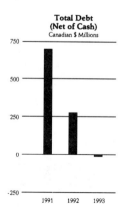

Total Debt (Net of Cash)
Canadian $ Millions

Minority Interest Expense: Minority interest expense increased $1.9 million to $18.9 million for fiscal 1993 reflecting the increased earnings in subsidiaries that have minority interests.

Earnings Per Share: On a fully diluted basis, net income per share was a record $2.55 for fiscal 1993 compared to $2.08 for fiscal 1992. The average number of shares outstanding for fiscal 1993 on a fully diluted basis was approximately 58.6 million shares.

FINANCIAL CONDITION, LIQUIDITY AND CAPITAL RESOURCES

Cash Flow from Operations: In fiscal 1993, the Company generated $262.1 million of cash from operations, an improvement of $16.8 million over the $245.3 million of cash generated from operations in fiscal 1992. The net increase resulted from increases in cash generated from operations of $55.1 million offset by higher cash taxes of $16.3 million, an increase in non-cash equity income of $19.1 million and $2.9 million from other items.

Changes in Non-Cash Working Capital: The Company generated $40.6 million from changes in non-cash working capital for fiscal 1993, primarily due to an increase in accounts payable, partially offset by an increase in accounts receivable.

Capital and Investment Spending: Capital and investment spending totalled $116.8 million in fiscal 1993, compared to $41.6 million in fiscal 1992. The increase is attributable to fixed asset spending at budgeted levels, the purchase of the remaining 50% interests in two manufacturing operations from joint venture partners and additional investments in equity accounted investments and other assets. Capital spending for existing businesses and projects is expected to be between $100 and $150 million for fiscal 1994, the majority of which relates to new production contracts such as the BMW stamping contract, where production is scheduled to commence in January 1995. The Company expects to finance the capital spending program from cash generated from operations.

Debt Reduction: The Company substantially achieved its objective to be free of bank debt, being in a cash position (net of debt) of $2.6 million at July 31, 1993. The Company held cash resources at July 31, 1993 of $105.0 million. Total debt was reduced during fiscal 1993 by $223.0 million to $102.4 million at July 31, 1993, compared to $325.4 million at July 31, 1992. This decrease was mainly a result of applying cash flow from operations to debt reduction and the conversion of $103.6 million principal amount of convertible subordinated bonds and debentures into Class A Subordinate Voting Shares.

Included in the total debt figure at July 31, 1993 is $64.7 million of 10% convertible subordinated debentures which have a conversion price of U.S. $8.525. The Company may call these debentures for redemption on or after May 1, 1994.

Dividends: The Company has declared dividends in respect of fiscal 1993 of $0.60 per Class A Subordinate Voting Share and Class B Share, an increase of $0.30 per share over dividends in respect of fiscal 1992, reflecting the sustained improvement in financial performance. Dividend payments have been financed out of cash flow from operations.

REPORTS TO SHAREHOLDERS

MANAGEMENT'S RESPONSIBILTY FOR FINANCIAL REPORTING

Magna's management is responsible for the preparation and presentation of the consolidated financial statements and all the information in this Annual Report. The consolidated financial statements were prepared by management in accordance with generally accepted accounting principles. Where alternative accounting methods exist, management has selected those it considered to be most appropriate in the circumstances. Financial statements include certain amounts based on estimates and judgements. Management has determined such amounts on a reasonable basis designed to ensure that the consolidated financial statements are presented fairly, in all material respects. Financial information presented elsewhere in this Annual Report has been prepared by management to ensure consistency with that in the consolidated financial statements. The consolidated financial statements have been reviewed by the Audit Committee and approved by the Board of Directors of Magna.

Management is responsible for the development and maintenance of systems of internal accounting and administrative controls of high quality, consistent with reasonable cost. Such systems are designed to provide reasonable assurance that the financial information is accurate, relevant and reliable and that the Company's assets are appropriately accounted for and adequately safeguarded.

The Company's Audit Committee is appointed by its Board of Directors annually and is comprised solely of outside directors. The Committee meets periodically with management, as well as with the independent auditors, to satisfy itself that each is properly discharging its responsibilities, to review the consolidated financial statements and the independent auditors' report to discuss significant financial reporting issues and auditing matters. The Audit Committee reports its findings to the Board of Directors for consideration when approving the consolidated financial statements for issuance to the shareholders.

The consolidated financial statements have been examined by Ernst & Young, the independent auditors, in accordance with generally accepted auditing standards on behalf of the shareholders. The Auditors' Report outlines the nature of their examination and their opinion on the consolidated financial statements of the Company. The independent auditors have full and unrestricted access to the Audit Committee.

September 23, 1993   Magna International Inc.

AUDITORS' REPORT

To the Shareholders of **Magna International Inc.**

We have audited the consolidated balance sheets of Magna International Inc. as at July 31, 1993 and 1992 and the consolidated statements of income and retained earnings (deficit) and cash flows for each of the years in the three-year period ended July 31, 1993. These financial statements are the responsibility of the Company's management. Our responsibility is to express an opinion on these financial statements based on our audits.

We conducted our audits in accordance with generally accepted auditing standards. Those standards require that we plan and perform an audit to obtain reasonable assurance whether the financial statements are free of material misstatement. An audit includes examining, on a test basis, evidence supporting the amounts and disclosures in the financial statements. An audit also includes assessing the accounting principles used and significant estimates made by management, as well as evaluating the overall financial statement presentation.

In our opinion, these consolidated financial statements present fairly, in all material respects, the financial position of the Company as at July 31, 1993 and 1992 and the results of its operations and the changes in its financial position for each of the years in the three-year period ended July 31, 1993 in accordance with accounting principles generally accepted in Canada.

Ernst & Young

Toronto, Canada,
September 8, 1993
(except for Note 17 which is
as of September 23, 1993)

Ernst & Young
Chartered Accountants

SIGNIFICANT ACCOUNTING POLICIES

[a]   Basis of Presentation

The consolidated financial statements have been prepared in Canadian dollars following accounting policies generally accepted in Canada. These policies are also in conformity, in all material respects, with accounting policies generally accepted in the United States except as described in note 2 to the consolidated financial statements.

[b]   Principles of Consolidation

The consolidated financial statements include the accounts of Magna International Inc. and its subsidiaries [the "Company"], some of which have a minority interest. All significant intercompany balances and transactions have been eliminated on consolidation. The Company accounts for its joint ventures and investments in which it has significant influence on the equity basis.

[c]   Cash

Cash includes cash on account, demand deposits and short-term investments with maturities of less than three months and excludes outstanding cheques which are classified as accounts payable.

[d]   Inventories

Inventories are valued at the lower of cost and net realizable value, with cost being determined substantially on a first-in, first-out basis. Cost includes the cost of materials plus direct labour applied to the product and the applicable share of manufacturing overhead.

[e]   Fixed Assets

Fixed assets are recorded at historical cost including interest capitalized on construction in progress and land under development less related investment tax credits.

Depreciation is provided on a straight-line basis over the estimated useful lives of fixed assets at annual rates of 2 1/2% to 5% for buildings, 7% to 10% for general purpose equipment and 10% to 30% for special purpose equipment.

Costs incurred in establishing new facilities which require substantial time to reach commercial production capability are capitalized as deferred preproduction costs. Amortization is being provided over terms ranging from two to five years from the date commercial production is achieved.

[f]   Goodwill

Goodwill, which is the excess of the purchase price of the Company's interest in subsidiary companies over the fair value of the underlying net identifiable assets arising on acquisitions, is amortized over 10 years.

[g]   Revenue Recognition

Revenue from sales of manufactured products is recognized upon shipment to customers. Revenue on major tooling contracts is recognized on a percentage of completion basis.

[h]   Government Financing

The Company makes periodic applications for financial assistance under available government assistance programs in the various jurisdictions in which the Company operates. Grants relating to capital expenditures are reflected as a reduction of the cost of the related assets. Grants and tax credits relating to current operating expenditures are recorded as a reduction of expense at the time the eligible expenses are incurred. The Company also receives loans which are recorded as liabilities in amounts equal to the cash received.

[i]   Foreign Exchange

Assets and liabilities of foreign subsidiaries are translated using the exchange rate in effect at the year-end and revenues and expenses are translated at the average rate during the year. Exchange gains or losses on translation of the Company's net equity investment in these subsidiaries are deferred as a separate component of shareholders' equity. The appropriate amounts of exchange gains or losses accumulated in the separate component of shareholders' equity are reflected in income when there is a reduction in the Company's investment in these subsidiaries as a result of capital transactions.

Foreign exchange gains and losses on transactions during the year are reflected in income except for gains and losses on foreign exchange forward contracts used to hedge specific future commitments payable in foreign currencies. Gains or losses on these contracts are accounted for as a component of the related hedged transaction.

Gains and losses on translation of foreign currency long-term liabilities are deferred and amortized over the period to maturity.

[j]   Income Taxes

The Company follows the deferral method of tax allocation in accounting for income taxes. Under this method, timing differences between accounting and taxable income result in the recording of deferred income taxes.

Investment tax credits relating to fixed asset purchases and research and development expenses are accounted for as a reduction of the cost of such assets and expenses, respectively.

[k]   Earnings per Share

Basic earnings per share are calculated on the weighted average number of shares outstanding during the year. The weighted average number of shares is calculated on the assumption that all convertible subordinated bonds and debentures converted into Class A Subordinate Voting Shares during the year were converted on the dates of the last interest payments.

Fully diluted earnings per share are calculated on the weighted average number of shares that would have been outstanding during the year had all the dilutive options, warrants and convertible subordinated bonds and debentures been exercised or converted into Class A Subordinate Voting Shares at the beginning of the year, or date of issuance, if later. The earnings applicable to the Class A Subordinate Voting Shares and Class B Shares are increased by the amount of interest, net of applicable taxes, that would have been earned on funds received due to the exercise of the options and warrants, and by the amount of interest expense, net of applicable taxes, that would have been eliminated due to the conversion of the convertible subordinated bonds and debentures.

CONSOLIDATED STATEMENTS OF INCOME AND RETAINED EARNINGS (DEFICIT)

[Canadian dollars in millions, except per share figures]	Note	Years ended July 31		
		1993	1992	1991
Sales		$2,606.7	$2,358.8	$2,017.2
Cost of goods sold		2,104.2	1,884.9	1,622.4
Depreciation and amortization		104.5	102.4	105.3
Selling, general and administrative	13	179.2	156.0	154.3
Interest	7	17.2	49.9	82.3
Equity (income) loss	4	(18.3)	0.8	2.7
Income before income taxes and minority interest		219.9	164.8	50.2
Income taxes	6	60.6	49.8	27.0
Minority interest		18.9	17.0	6.7
Net income		140.4	98.0	16.5
Retained earnings (deficit), beginning of year		48.9	(35.0)	(51.5)
		189.3	63.0	(35.0)
Dividends on Class A Subordinate Voting and Class B Shares		25.0	7.4	
Share issue expenses [net of related income taxes]			6.7	
Retained earnings (deficit), end of year		$ 164.3	$ 48.9	$ (35.0)
Earnings per Class A Subordinate Voting or Class B Share:				
Basic		$ 3.09	$ 2.91	$ 0.59
Fully diluted		$ 2.55	$ 2.08	$ 0.58
Cash dividends paid per Class A Subordinate Voting or Class B Share		$ 0.55	$ 0.20	$ Nil
Average number of Class A Subordinate Voting Shares and Class B Shares outstanding during the year [in millions]:				
Basic		45.4	33.6	27.8
Fully diluted		58.6	52.4	29.0

See accompanying notes

CONSOLIDATED STATEMENTS OF CASH FLOWS

[Canadian dollars in millions]   *Years ended July 31*

	Note	1993	1992	1991
Cash provided from (used for):				
OPERATING ACTIVITIES				
Net income		**$140.4**	$ 98.0	$ 16.5
Items not involving current cash flows	12	**121.7**	147.3	135.3
		262.1	245.3	151.8
Changes in non-cash working capital	12	**40.6**	(13.2)	(43.9)
		302.7	232.1	107.9
INVESTMENT ACTIVITIES				
Fixed asset additions		**(63.4)**	(30.8)	(27.9)
Increase in investments and other		**(30.0)**	(10.8)	(11.7)
Purchase of subsidiaries	4	**(23.4)**		
Proceeds from disposition of fixed assets and other		**4.8**	17.8	
Proceeds from restructuring transactions				223.8
		(112.0)	(23.8)	184.2
FINANCING ACTIVITIES				
Issues of debt		**2.3**	233.1	427.4
Repayments of debt		**(129.3)**	(632.4)	(694.7)
Issuance of Class A Subordinate Voting Shares	9	**123.2**	247.8	
Conversion of convertible subordinated bonds and debentures to Class A Subordinate Voting Shares	8,9	**(103.6)**	(35.3)	
Redemption of special share purchase warrant	9		(20.0)	
Dividends paid to [net of capital contribution by] minority interests		**(4.9)**	(2.8)	(13.5)
Dividends		**(25.0)**	(7.4)	
Repurchase of minority interest in subsidiary				(51.0)
		(137.3)	(217.0)	(331.8)
Net increase (decrease) in cash during the year		**53.4**	(8.7)	(39.7)
Cash, beginning of year		**51.6**	60.3	100.0
Cash, end of year		**$105.0**	$ 51.6	$ 60.3

See accompanying notes

CONSOLIDATED BALANCE SHEETS

Incorporated under the laws of Ontario

[Canadian dollars in millions]		As at July 31	
	Note	**1993**	1992
ASSETS			
Current assets:			
Cash		**$ 105.0**	$ 51.6
Accounts receivable		**314.6**	255.7
Inventories	3	**187.1**	172.3
Prepaid expenses and other		**19.9**	20.6
		626.6	500.2
Investments	4,14	**103.9**	80.3
Fixed assets	5	**736.7**	751.7
Goodwill	4	**21.3**	17.8
Other assets	14	**62.6**	51.4
		$ 1,551.1	$1,401.4
LIABILITIES AND SHAREHOLDERS' EQUITY			
Current liabilities:			
Bank indebtedness	7		$ 70.4
Accounts payable		**$ 301.1**	233.3
Accrued salaries and wages		**47.1**	41.2
Other liabilities		**70.8**	48.2
Income taxes payable	6	**11.4**	10.9
Long-term debt due within one year	7	**7.6**	9.3
		438.0	413.3
Long-term debt	7	**30.1**	80.5
Convertible subordinated bonds and debentures	8	**64.7**	165.2
Deferred income taxes	6	**90.8**	81.9
Minority interest	9	**83.1**	70.2
Shareholders' equity:			
Capital stock	9		
Class A Subordinate Voting Shares			
[issued:1993 - 48,807,924; 1992 - 38,755,717]		**668.0**	544.6
Class B Shares [convertible into Class A Subordinate			
Voting Shares] [issued:1993 - 1,128,009; 1992 - 1,288,584]		**1.3**	1.5
Retained earnings		**164.3**	48.9
Currency translation adjustment	10	**10.8**	(4.7)
		844.4	590.3
		$ 1,551.1	$1,401.4

See accompanying notes

On behalf of the Board:

Director

Chairman, Board of Directors

NOTES TO CONSOLIDATED FINANCIAL STATEMENTS — JULY 31, 1993

1.   SIGNIFICANT ACCOUNTING POLICIES

The significant accounting policies followed by the Company are set out under "Significant Accounting Policies" preceding these consolidated financial statements.

2.   UNITED STATES GENERALLY ACCEPTED ACCOUNTING PRINCIPLES

The Company's accounting policies do not differ from accounting principles generally accepted in the United States ["United States GAAP"] except that, under United States GAAP, the gain or loss on translation of the Company's foreign currency denominated debt would be included in income, income tax reductions realized on the utilization of prior years' losses would be disclosed as extraordinary income and the calculation of earnings per share figures would reflect the application of the treasury stock method for outstanding warrants and options. The following table presents net income before extraordinary income, net income and earnings per share information following United States GAAP:

	1993	1992	1991
	[Canadian dollars in millions, except per share figures]		
Net income under			
Canadian GAAP	$140.4	$98.0	$16.5
Adjustments:			
Deferred losses on foreign currency denominated debt	(3.5)	(4.6)	(1.2)
Income tax reduction realized on utilization of prior years' losses	(16.8)	(17.3)	
Net income before extraordinary income under United States GAAP	120.1	76.1	15.3
Extraordinary item:			
Income tax reduction realized on utilization of prior years' losses	16.8	17.3	
Net income under United States GAAP	$136.9	$93.4	$15.3
Earnings per Class A Subordinate Voting or Class B Share under United States GAAP:			
Primary:			
Before extraordinary item	$ 2.60	$2.06	$0.54
After extraordinary item	$ 2.97	$2.52	$0.54
Fully diluted:			
Before extraordinary item	$ 2.21	$1.67	$0.53
After extraordinary item	$ 2.50	$2.00	$0.53

The Financial Accounting Standards Board has issued Statement No. 109, accounting for income taxes, effective for fiscal years beginning after December 15, 1992. The Company has not determined the impact of adopting this standard.

3.   INVENTORIES

Inventories consist of:

	1993	1992
	[Canadian dollars in millions]	
Raw materials and supplies	$ 50.4	$ 51.4
Work-in-process	45.3	40.1
Tooling	64.1	49.5
Finished goods	27.3	31.3
	$187.1	$172.3

4.   JOINT VENTURES AND EQUITY ACCOUNTED INVESTMENTS

The Company conducts certain of its operations through joint ventures. In addition, the Company has made certain investments in other businesses. The Company's current ownership percentage for its joint ventures is 50% to 51% and up to 45% for other investments.

[a]   Summary of transactions

Current year transactions:

During the year, the Company acquired the remaining 50% interests in two manufacturing operations from its joint venture partners. The total purchase price, which was paid in cash, was $23.4 million. These acquisitions have been accounted for under the purchase method of business acquisitions and the net effect on the consolidated balance sheet was an increase in net working capital of $1.8 million, an increase in fixed and other assets of $17.7 million, an increase in goodwill of $5.6 million, a decrease in investments of $2.4 million, a decrease in deferred taxes of $1.0 million and an increase in minority interest of $0.3 million.

In June 1993, the Company and a former senior officer of the Company, who remains a director, entered into an agreement to purchase an automotive fuel systems supply business in Europe. The Company invested $4.5 million in the European business for a 45% ownership interest and accounts for this investment on the equity basis.

Prior years' transactions:

In October 1990, the Company formed a joint venture with the Ford Motor Company with respect to two of its existing operations. The Company transferred assets, net of liabilities, to the joint venture in exchange for net cash proceeds of $87.8 million and $20.4 million of shares of the joint venture corporation.

In November 1990, the Company acquired the remaining 50% interest in a tool and die manufacturing facility from its partner. The purchase price was $3.5 million, payable in instalments over 5 years. This acquisition has been accounted for under the purchase method of business acquisitions and the net effect on the consolidated balance sheet was an increase in net working capital of $4.7 million,

NOTES TO CONSOLIDATED FINANCIAL STATEMENTS — JULY 31, 1993

an increase in fixed and other assets of $11.4 million, a decrease in investments of $13.1 million and an increase in debt of $3.0 million.

[b] Condensed information

The following are condensed combined balance sheets and statements of income (loss) of the joint ventures and equity accounted investments in which the Company has an interest:

Balance Sheets [as at July 31]	1993	1992
	[Canadian dollars in millions]	
Current assets	$169.5	$164.2
Fixed assets	276.8	269.9
Other	12.0	21.6
Total assets	$458.3	$455.7
Current liabilities	$123.6	$134.2
Long-term debt	145.3	160.2
Shareholders' investment	189.4	161.3
Total liabilities and shareholders' investment	$458.3	$455.7

Statements of Income (Loss)	1993	1992	1991
	[Canadian dollars in millions]		
Sales	$671.5	$559.2	$422.5
Gross profit	$144.2	$ 82.5	$ 65.9
Net income (loss)	$ 39.0	$ 0.3	$ (1.0)

The Company's proportionate share of total assets is $227 million [1992 - $226 million], its proportionate share of sales is $350 million [1992 - $274 million; 1991 - $212 million] and its proportionate share of net income (loss) is $18.3 million [1992 - $(0.8) million; 1991 - $(2.7) million].

[c] The Company has guaranteed its pro-rata share of specific bank lines of certain joint ventures. The maximum amount of such guarantees amounts to $71 million.

5. FIXED ASSETS

Fixed assets consist of:

	1993	1992
	[Canadian dollars in millions]	
Land	$ 49.5	$ 46.0
Buildings	210.7	195.8
Machinery and equipment	951.8	883.5
	1,212.0	1,125.3
Accumulated depreciation [i]	504.8	419.1
	707.2	706.2
Deferred preproduction costs [net of accumulated amortization]	29.5	45.5
	$736.7	$751.7

[i] Accumulated depreciation includes $51.8 million for buildings [1992-$43.0 million] and $453.0 million for machinery and equipment [1992 - $376.1 million].

6. INCOME TAXES

[a] The provision for income tax expense differs from the expense that would be obtained by applying Canadian statutory rates as a result of the following:

	1993	1992	1991
Canadian statutory income tax rate	44.3%	44.3%	44.3%
Manufacturing and processing profits deduction	(7.1)	(6.0)	(5.1)
Expected income tax rate	37.2	38.3	39.2
Foreign rate differentials	(0.3)	(0.3)	(1.9)
Earnings and losses of equity investees	(3.1)	0.5	2.1
Large corporation tax	0.3	0.4	3.3
Prior years' losses utilized	(7.6)	(10.5)	
Losses not tax effected			10.8
Other	1.1	1.8	0.3
Effective income tax rate	27.6%	30.2%	53.8%

[b] The details of the income tax provision are as follows:

	1993	1992	1991
	[Canadian dollars in millions]		
Current provision -			
Canadian federal taxes	$16.8	$10.6	$ 8.7
Provincial taxes	19.0	5.9	3.9
Foreign taxes	17.8	20.8	3.6
	53.6	37.3	16.2
Deferred provision -			
Canadian federal taxes	9.5	14.4	2.9
Provincial taxes	(3.2)	8.7	1.6
Foreign taxes	0.7	(10.6)	6.3
	7.0	12.5	10.8
	$60.6	$49.8	$27.0

[c] Deferred income taxes have been provided on timing differences which consist of the following:

	1993	1992	1991
	[Canadian dollars in millions]		
Tax depreciation in excess of book depreciation	$15.3	$18.7	$21.3
Preproduction costs, capitalized for accounting purposes [net of amortization], deducted for tax	(6.4)	(6.8)	(8.8)
Other	(1.9)	0.6	(1.7)
	$ 7.0	$12.5	$10.8

[d] Income taxes paid in cash were $45.2 million for 1993 [1992 - $37.1 million; 1991 - $11.1 million].

[e] Consolidated retained earnings includes approximately $89.2 million at July 31, 1993 [1992 - $39.0 million] of undistributed earnings of United States subsidiaries that may be subject to tax if remitted to the Canadian parent company. No provision has been made for such taxes as these earnings are considered to be reinvested on a long-term basis.

NOTES TO CONSOLIDATED FINANCIAL STATEMENTS — JULY 31, 1993

[f] At July 31, 1993, the Company has losses of $14 million from prior years, the tax benefits of which have not been recognized in the consolidated financial statements. These losses may be available to offset future taxable income and expire between 2004 and 2006. In addition, the Company has losses of approximately $36 million in foreign jurisdictions that it is unlikely to utilize.

7. DEBT AND COMMITMENTS

[a] The Company's long-term debt consists of the following:

	1993	1992
	[Canadian dollars in millions]	
Bank term debt		$39.0
Loans from governments	$15.2	21.8
Mortgages payable at an average interest rate of 11.3% due 1995	18.3	20.7
Other	4.2	8.3
	37.7	89.8
Less due within one year	7.6	9.3
	$30.1	$80.5

[b] Future principal repayments on long-term debt are estimated to be as follows:

	[Canadian dollars in millions]
1995	$18.3
1996	4.2
1997	1.6
1998	1.6
Thereafter	4.4
	$30.1

[c] The Company has operating lines of credit totalling $185.0 million and term lines of credit totalling $95.0 million bearing interest at rates not exceeding the banks' prime rate of interest plus 1/8%. Accounts receivable, inventories and certain assets of subsidiaries have been pledged as collateral under the bank lines of credit. At July 31, 1993, in addition to cash resources of $105.0 million, the Company had unused and available operating lines of credit of approximately $185.0 million and term lines of credit of approximately $74.5 million.

[d] Under the terms of the Company's operating and term credit agreements, it is permitted to make use of bankers' acceptances and commercial paper to borrow at effective interest rates which are, from time to time, lower than those charged under the bank lines of credit.

[e] Interest paid includes:

	1993	1992	1991
	[Canadian dollars in millions]		
Interest expense	$17.2	$49.9	$82.3
Interest payable, beginning of year	6.3	8.6	5.9
Interest payable, end of year	(2.4)	(6.3)	(8.6)
Interest paid for year	$21.1	$52.2	$79.6

[f] At July 31, 1993, the Company had commitments under operating leases requiring annual rental payments as follows:

	[Canadian dollars in millions]
1994	$ 23.9
1995	22.0
1996	18.8
1997	16.7
1998	12.4
Thereafter	28.3
	$122.1

In 1993, payments under operating leases amounted to approximately $21 million [1992 - $25 million; 1991 - $32 million].

[g] The Company has net cash inflows denominated in U.S. dollars, which has averaged approximately $100 million per year for the last three years. The Company utilizes foreign exchange forward contracts to hedge these exposures. At July 31, 1993, the Company had outstanding foreign exchange forward contracts representing a net commitment to sell U.S. dollars aggregating approximately $246.2 million at weighted average rates of exchange of approximately $1.30 Canadian that mature over the next five years. Based on July 31, 1993 foreign exchange rates, these contracts would be converted at weighted average rates of exchange of approximately $1.32 Canadian.

8. CONVERTIBLE SUBORDINATED BONDS AND DEBENTURES

[a] The Company's convertible subordinated bonds and debentures consist of the following:

	1993	1992
	[Canadian dollars in millions]	
10% convertible subordinated debentures [1993 - $57.5 million U.S.; 1992 - $95.5 million U.S.]	$64.7	$105.8
7% convertible subordinated bonds [1992 - $49.6 million U.S.]		59.4
	$64.7	$165.2

[b] The 10% convertible subordinated debentures are convertible into Class A Subordinate Voting Shares at a conversion price of $8.525 U.S. [approximately $10.95 Cdn. as at July 31, 1993] per share and mature on May 1, 2001. From the date of issuance to July 31, 1993, $42.5 million U.S. of the debentures had been converted. The Company has the right to call for redemption the 10% convertible subordinated debentures after April 30, 1994.

[c] As of July 31, 1993, all the 7% convertible subordinated bonds had been converted to Class A Subordinate Voting Shares.

NOTES TO CONSOLIDATED FINANCIAL STATEMENTS — JULY 31, 1993

9. CAPITAL STOCK

[a] The Company's authorized, issued and outstanding capital stock is as follows:

Preference shares - issuable in series -

The Company's authorized capital stock includes 99,760,000 preference shares, issuable in series. None of these shares are currently issued or outstanding.

Class A Subordinate Voting Shares and Class B Shares -

Class A Subordinate Voting Shares without par value [unlimited amount authorized] have the following attributes:

[i] Each share is entitled to one vote per share at all meetings of shareholders.

[ii] Each share shall participate equally as to dividends with each Class B Share.

Class B Shares without par value [authorized - 1,412,341] have the following attributes:

[i] Each share is entitled to 500 votes per share at all meetings of shareholders.

[ii] Each share shall participate equally as to dividends with each Class A Subordinate Voting Share.

[iii] Each share may be converted at any time into a fully-paid Class A Subordinate Voting Share on a one-for-one basis.

In the event that either the Class A Subordinate Voting Shares or the Class B Shares are subdivided or consolidated, the other class shall be similarly changed to preserve the relative position of each class.

[b] Changes in the Class A Subordinate Voting Shares and Class B Shares for the three years ended July 31, 1993 are shown in the following table [Canadian dollars in millions]:

	Class A Subordinate Voting		Class B	
	Number of shares	Stated value	Number of shares	Stated value
Issued and outstanding at July 31, 1990	26,525,210	$290.0	1,294,209	$1.5
Conversion of Class B Shares to Class A Shares	50		(50)	
Issued for cash under the 1987 Incentive Stock Option Plan	30,000	0.1		
Issued and outstanding at July 31, 1991	26,555,260	290.1	1,294,159	1.5

	Class A Subordinate Voting		Class B	
	Number of shares	Stated value	Number of shares	Stated value
Conversion of Class B Shares to Class A Shares	5,575		(5,575)	
Issued for cash	9,570,000	213.4		
Conversion of 7% convertible subordinated bonds	1,222,604	30.1		
Conversion of 10% convertible subordinated debentures	525,278	5.2		
Issued for cash under the 1987 Incentive Stock Option Plan	877,000	5.8		
Issued and outstanding at July 31, 1992	38,755,717	544.6	1,288,584	1.5
Conversion of Class B Shares to Class A Shares	160,575	0.2	(160,575)	(0.2)
Issued for cash on exercise of warrants	2,605,782	10.4		
Conversion of 7% convertible subordinated bonds	2,391,619	60.4		
Conversion of 10% convertible subordinated debentures	4,461,231	43.2		
Issued for cash under the 1987 Incentive Stock Option Plan	433,000	9.2		
Issued and outstanding at July 31, 1993	48,807,924	$668.0	1,128,009	$1.3

[c] Under the 1987 Incentive Stock Option Plan originally approved by the shareholders in December 1987, as amended, the Company may grant options to purchase Class A Subordinate Voting Shares to full-time employees of the Company. The maximum number of shares reserved to be issued for options cannot exceed 10% of the total number of Class A Subordinate Voting Shares outstanding from time to time. The number of unoptioned shares available to be reserved at July 31, 1993 was 2.7 million.

At July 31, 1992, prior to an amendment to the Stock Option Plan approved by the shareholders in September 1992, the number of unoptioned shares available to be reserved was nil.

The following is a continuity schedule of options outstanding:

	1993	1992
Balance, beginning of year	1,093,000	1,970,000
Granted during the year	1,475,000	
Exercised during the year	(433,000)	(877,000)
Balance, end of year	2,135,000	1,093,000
Weighted average exercise price per share on outstanding options at end of year	$21.78	$8.05

NOTES TO CONSOLIDATED FINANCIAL STATEMENTS — JULY 31, 1993

[d] On May 31, 1991, as consideration for the reacquisition of the minority interest in one of the Company's principal subsidiaries, Tesma International Inc., a special share purchase warrant was issued. During 1992, the Company repurchased the warrant for $20 million.

[e] During 1991, the Company granted warrants for the purchase of 2.75 million Class A Subordinate Voting Shares as partial consideration for the restructuring of the Company's debt. These warrants were exercisable at $4.00 per share after August 1, 1992 and were to expire on August 1, 1995. As of July 31, 1993, no warrants remained outstanding.

[f] The following table presents the maximum number of shares that would be outstanding if all the options outstanding at July 31, 1993 were exercised and all the 10% convertible subordinated debentures outstanding at July 31, 1993 were converted into Class A Subordinate Voting Shares:

	[thousands of shares]
Class A Subordinate Voting Shares and Class B Shares outstanding at July 31, 1993	49,936
Options to purchase Class A Subordinate Voting Shares	2,135
10% convertible subordinated debentures	6,744
	58,815

10. CURRENCY TRANSLATION ADJUSTMENT

The following is a continuity schedule of the currency translation adjustment account included in shareholders' equity:

	1993	1992
	[Canadian dollars in millions]	
Balance, beginning of year	$ (4.7)	$ (8.5)
Translation adjustments	15.5	3.8
Balance, end of year	$ 10.8	$ (4.7)

11. RESEARCH AND DEVELOPMENT

The Company carries on various applied research and development programs, certain of which are partially or fully funded by governments or by customers of the Company. Research and development expenditures, net of amounts funded by governments or customers, for 1993 were $14.1 million [1992 - $9.8 million; 1991 - $8.8 million].

12. DETAILS OF CASH FROM OPERATING ACTIVITIES

[a] Items not involving current cash flows:

	1993	1992	1991
	[Canadian dollars in millions]		
Depreciation and amortization	$104.5	$102.4	$105.3
Minority interest	18.9	17.0	6.7
Deferred income taxes	7.0	12.5	10.8
Equity (income) loss	(18.3)	0.8	2.7
Other	9.6	14.6	9.8
	$121.7	$147.3	$135.3

[b] Changes in non-cash working capital.

	1993	1992	1991
	[Canadian dollars in millions]		
Accounts receivable	$(51.9)	$(18.6)	$(14.7)
Inventories	(0.6)	(15.3)	19.2
Prepaid expenses and other	0.9	0.1	(1.4)
Accounts payable and other liabilities	80.3	19.6	(50.9)
Accrued salaries and wages	5.9	0.7	2.6
Income taxes payable	6.0	0.3	1.3
	$ 40.6	$(13.2)	$(43.9)

13. SEGMENTED INFORMATION

The Company's operations are substantially all related to the automotive industry. Operations include the manufacture of automobile parts for the original equipment manufacturers as well as products for the after-market. Substantially all revenue is derived from sales to North American facilities of the major automobile manufacturers. In 1993, sales to the Company's three largest customers amounted to 40%, 27% and 22% [1992 - 37%, 26% and 26%; 1991 - 31%, 28% and 29%] of total sales, respectively.

The following table shows certain information with respect to geographic segmentation [Canadian dollars in millions]:

	1993		
	Canada	United States and Other	Total
Sales	$1,722.3	$884.4	$2,606.7
Income before the following	$ 224.0	$ 62.3	$ 286.3
Corporate expenses [i]			(66.4)
Income before income tax and minority interest			$ 219.9
Assets	$ 920.1	$546.6	$1,466.7
Corporate assets			84.4
Total assets			$1,551.1

	1992		
	Canada	United States and Other	Total
Sales	$1,591.5	$767.3	$2,358.8
Income before the following	$ 179.9	$ 67.5	$ 247.4
Corporate expenses [i]			(82.6)
Income before income tax and minority interest			$ 164.8
Assets	$ 864.7	$471.2	$1,335.9
Corporate assets			65.5
Total assets			$1,401.4

NOTES TO CONSOLIDATED FINANCIAL STATEMENTS — JULY 31, 1993

	1991		
	Canada	United States and Other	Total
Sales	$1,425.2	$592.0	$2,017.2
Income before the following	$ 133.1	$ 27.1	$ 160.2
Corporate expenses [i]			(110.0)
Income before income tax and minority interest			$ 50.2
Assets	$ 947.8	$446.8	$1,394.6
Corporate assets			74.4
Total assets			$1,469.0

Notes:

[i]   Corporate expenses include:

	1993	**1992**	**1991**
	[Canadian dollars in millions]		
Interest expense	$ 17.2	$ 49.9	$ 82.3
Selling, general and administrative	49.2	32.7	27.7
	$ 66.4	$ 82.6	$ 110.0

Selling, general and administrative expense includes $11.3 million [1992 - $0.4 million; 1991 - $1.7 million] for retirement and severance arrangements entered into during the year in respect of former senior officers of the Company and gains (losses) on foreign currency transactions of $(0.7) million in 1993 [1992 - $2.4 million; 1991 - $2.5 million].

[ii]   Canadian sales include export sales of $1,057 million [1992 - $953 million; 1991 - $928 million], substantially all of which are to the United States.

[iii]   Income before income taxes from foreign operations amounts to $57.3 million [1992 - $60.6 million; 1991 - $5.1 million].

14.   TRANSACTIONS WITH RELATED PARTIES

In the year, the Company made a $12 million non-recourse loan, due July 29, 1994, to the Chairman of the Board. Certain options to purchase Class A Subordinate Voting Shares of the Company, which were granted prior to the 1993 fiscal year, have been provided as security for the loan. At the time of granting the loan, the value of these options was in excess of the principal amount of the loan, and such value continues to be in excess of such principal amount. The average annual interest rate charged on the loan during the 1993 fiscal year was approximately 4%.

From time to time, the Company makes advances to officers to assist them in the purchase of shares of the Company and to assist in the purchase of houses following relocations. The maximum amount outstanding under such arrangements during the year was $2.0 million [1992 - $2.0 million; 1991 - $2.8 million]. The balance outstanding at July 31, 1993 was $0.7 million [1992 - $2.0 million; 1991 - $1.9 million]. These amounts are included in accounts receivable.

During the year, trusts which exist to make orderly purchases of the Company's shares for employees, either for transfer to the employees' Deferred Profit Sharing Plan which invests exclusively in such shares, or to recipients of either bonuses or rights to purchase such shares from the trusts, borrowed up to $15.2 million [1992 - $7.2 million; 1991 - $1.4 million] from the Company to facilitate the purchase of Class A Subordinate Voting Shares and Class B Shares of the Company. At July 31, 1993, the trusts' indebtedness to the Company was $14.7 million [1992 - $7.2 million; 1991 - $1.4 million].

Investments include $3.2 million [1992 - $1.3 million], at cost, in respect of an investment in a company that was established to acquire shares of the Company for sale to employees.

The Company obtains services from firms in which non-officer directors and former non-officer directors of the Company are partners or officers. These services include legal services and underwriting of equity and debt issues. On an annual basis, legal fees and underwriters' fees paid to such firms were not in aggregate in excess of three tenths of one percent of revenue.

The Company made an investment with a former senior officer of the Company, who remains a director, which is described in Note 4[a].

15.   CONTINGENCIES

In the ordinary course of business activities, the Company may be contingently liable for litigation and claims with customers, suppliers and former employees. Management believes that adequate provisions have been recorded in the accounts where required. Although it is not possible to estimate the extent of potential costs and losses, if any, management believes that the ultimate resolution of such contingencies will not have a material adverse effect on the consolidated financial position of the Company.

16.   COMPARATIVE FIGURES

Certain comparative figures have been reclassified to conform to the current year's method of presentation.

17.   SUBSEQUENT EVENT

On September 23, 1993, the Company entered into an underwriting agreement with a group of underwriters for the sale of 3,000,000 Class A Subordinate Voting Shares by a short form prospectus for an aggregate consideration of $151.5 million before deducting the underwriters' fees of $6.1 million. The estimated expenses of the issue of $0.4 million are to be paid out of the general funds of the Company.

ELEVEN-YEAR FINANCIAL SUMMARY

[Canadian dollars in millions, except per share figures]

Years ended July 31

	1993	1992	1991	1990	1989	1988	1987	1986	1985	1984	1983
Operations Data											
Sales	$2,606.7	$2,358.8	$2,017.2	$1,927.2	$1,923.7	$1,458.6	$1,152.5	$1,027.8	$690.4	$493.6	$302.5
Net income (loss) (3)	140.4	98.0	16.5	(224.2)	33.6	19.5	40.3	47.3	38.2	29.5	14.3
Basic earnings (loss) per Class A or Class B Share (1,3)	$3.09	$2.91	$0.59	$(8.06)	$1.21	$0.70	$1.56	$1.93	$1.77	$1.81	$1.07
Fully diluted earnings (loss) per Class A or Class B Share (1,3)	$2.55	$2.08	$0.58	$(8.06)	$1.19	$0.70	$1.52	$1.93	$1.71	$1.73	$1.04
Depreciation and amortization (3)	104.5	102.4	105.3	104.2	99.4	74.6	55.0	36.4	23.3	14.7	11.3
Cash flow from operating activities	302.7	232.1	107.9	184.8	90.9	(33.2)	52.3	124.8	19.2	24.3	30.6
Dividends declared per Class A or Class B Share (1,2)	$0.60	$0.30	—	$0.12	$0.48	$0.48	$0.48	$0.48	$0.48	$0.31	$0.13
Cash dividends per Class A or Class B Share (1,2)	$0.55	$0.20	—	$0.24	$0.48	$0.48	$0.48	$0.48	$0.46	$0.26	$0.10
Average number of Class A and Class B Shares outstanding (thousands) (1)	45,443	33,625	27,825	27,819	27,819	27,836	25,860	24,323	21,424	16,105	12,964
Financial Position											
Total assets (3)	1,551.1	1,401.4	1,469.0	1,797.4	1,863.1	1,665.7	1,283.0	908.3	629.6	360.1	204.4
Fixed assets less accumulated depreciation and ammortization (3)	736.7	751.7	841.1	917.8	1,101.2	999.7	881.2	590.3	358.9	173.4	84.8
Working capital (4)	188.6	86.9	13.8	(622.7)	55.6	54.3	58.0	68.3	64.1	79.8	48.3
Capital expenditures (3)	63.4	30.8	27.9	177.9	271.1	250.8	378.5	286.6	212.4	105.7	29.0
Long-term debt (4)	94.8	245.7	581.8	—	685.9	615.5	469.6	280.0	109.1	101.6	47.3
Equity relating to Class A and Class B Shares (1,3,5)	844.4	590.3	268.1	231.1	464.3	446.1	448.9	345.9	289.4	140.1	80.1
Equity per Class A or Class B Share (1,3)	$16.91	$14.74	$8.91	$8.31	$16.69	$16.04	$16.10	$13.63	$12.08	$8.23	$5.48
Long-term debt and convertible subordinated bonds to shareholders' equity ratio (1,3,4,5)	0.11:1	0.42:1	2.17:1	—	1.48:1	1.38:1	1.05:1	0.81:1	0.38:1	0.73:1	0.59:1

(1) 1983 figures adjusted to give effect to the stock dividend issued June 1983.
(2) Stockholders received a special dividend issued June 1983.
(3) 1985 and prior years' figures have been restated to give effect to a change in method of accounting for investment tax credits.
(4) 1990 figures reflect all debt as a current liability defined as "debt to be restructured".
(5) 1991 figures include $20 million of warrants to purchase Class A Subordinate Voting Shares.

SHAREHOLDER AND OTHER FINANCIAL INFORMATION

Supplementary Financial Information

SUPPLEMENTARY QUARTERLY DATA (unaudited)
[Canadian dollars in millions, except per share figures]

Fiscal 1993	October 31	January 31	April 30	July 31	Total
Sales	$ 615.5	$ 600.2	$ 742.3	$ 648.7	$2,606.7
Gross profit	$ 98.2	$ 85.3	$ 121.5	$ 103.5	$ 408.5
Net income	$ 31.7	$ 24.7	$ 44.4	$ 39.6	$ 140.4
Earnings per share:					
Basic	$ 0.76	$ 0.57	$ 1.00	$ 0.79	$ 3.09
Fully diluted	$ 0.59	$ 0.46	$ 0.80	$ 0.70	$ 2.55

Fiscal 1992	October 31	January 31	April 30	July 31	Total
Sales	$ 617.2	$ 484.4	$ 632.2	$ 625.0	$2,358.8
Gross profit	$ 104.8	$ 74.5	$ 106.2	$ 99.0	$ 384.5
Net income	$ 25.5	$ 10.7	$ 30.5	$ 31.3	$ 98.0
Earnings per share:					
Basic	$ 0.92	$ 0.33	$ 0.89	$ 0.82	$ 2.91
Fully diluted	$ 0.59	$ 0.26	$ 0.62	$ 0.61	$ 2.08

Share Information

The Class A Subordinate Voting Shares ("Class A Shares")
are listed and traded in Canada on The Toronto Stock Exchange
("TSE") and the Montreal Exchange and in the United States
on the New York Stock Exchange ("NYSE"). Prior to
October 9, 1992, the Class A Shares were traded on the
NASDAQ National Market System ("NASDAQ") in the United
States. The Class B Shares are listed and traded in Canada
on the TSE. As of September 27, 1993, there were 1,558
registered holders of Class A Shares and 166 registered
holders of Class B Shares.

Distribution of Shares

	Class A	Class B
Canada	24.7%	98.8%
United States	75.3%	1.2%

Price Range of Shares

Canada

The following table sets forth, for the fiscal periods indicated,
the high and low sale prices of the Class A Shares and Class B
Shares and volumes of Class A Shares and Class B Shares traded,
in each case as reported by the TSE.

CLASS A (TSE) ($CDN)

	1993			1992		
Quarter	Volume	High	Low	Volume	High	Low
1st	16,008,700	32.88	22.00	8,771,320	18.88	12.13
2nd	9,421,575	41.00	24.75	9,635,681	23.50	16.38
3rd	5,890,082	43.50	37.00	9,491,841	31.50	22.13
4th	4,461,495	52.13	41.88	8,514,669	32.25	27.50

CLASS B (TSE) ($CDN)

	1993			1992		
Quarter	Volume	High	Low	Volume	High	Low
1st	2,635	31.00	27.75	9,270	19.00	12.75
2nd	7,220	40.38	29.00	13,550	23.00	17.50
3rd	3,837	42.50	37.50	10,584	30.00	22.25
4th	3,525	50.00	45.00	8,791	34.50	28.50

United States

The following table sets forth, for the fiscal periods indicated,
the high and low sale prices of the Class A Shares and volumes
of Class A Shares traded, as reported by NASDAQ or the NYSE.

CLASS A (NASDAQ or NYSE) ($US)

	1993			1992		
Quarter	Volume	High	Low	Volume	High	Low
1st	50,409,400	26.75	17.75	23,794,949	16.75	10.63
2nd	20,757,600	32.25	19.88	26,246,066	20.38	14.50
3rd	14,391,000	34.63	29.25	31,694,868	26.63	19.00
4th	17,877,400	40.75	32.88	31,282,999	29.38	23.38

OTHER SHAREHOLDER INFORMATION

Officers

Frank Stronach
Chairman of the Board

John Doddridge
*Vice-Chairman
& Chief Executive Officer*

Donald Walker
*President
& Chief Operating Officer*

J. Brian Colburn
Executive Vice-President

Donald Amos
*Senior Vice-President
Administration
& Human Resources*

C. Dennis Bausch
*Senior Vice-President
Marketing & Planning*

Graham J. Orr
*Senior Vice-President
Corporate Development
& Investor Relations*

Paul G. Robinson
*Senior Vice-President
Finance*

Guenter Heidbuchel
*Vice-President
International Operations*

Vincent J. Galifi
Controller

Frank Burke
Assistant Treasurer

Brian R. MacLeod
Secretary

Office Locations for Magna and its Automotive Systems Corporations

Magna International Inc.
36 Apple Creek Boulevard
Markham, Ontario, Canada L3R 4Y4
Telephone: (905) 477-7766

Magna International of America, Inc.
26200 Lahser Road, Suite 300
Southfield, Michigan, USA 48034
Telephone: (313) 353-5540

Atoma International Inc.
521 Newpark Boulevard
Newmarket, Ontario, Canada L3Y 4X7
Telephone: (905) 798-7961

Cosma International Inc.
50 Casmir Court
Concord, Ontario, Canada L4K 4J5
Telephone, (905) 669-9000

Decoma International Inc.
50 Casmir Court
Concord, Ontario, Canada L4K 4J5
Telephone: (905) 669-2888

Tesma International Inc.
300 Edgeley Boulevard
Concord, Ontario, Canada L4K 3Y3
Telephone: (905) 669-5444

The 1993 Annual Meeting

The 1993 Annual Meeting of Shareholders will be held at the Metropolitan Club, One East 60th Street, New York, New York on Thursday, December 2 at 10:00 a.m.

Transfer Agents and Registrars

Canada - Class A and B
Montreal Trust Company of Canada, Toronto, Montreal and Vancouver

United States - Class A
The Bank of Nova Scotia Trust Company of New York, New York

Dividends

Dividends on Class A Subordinate Voting and Class B Shares were paid on January 15, April 15, July 15 and October 15, 1993, at the rate of Cdn $0.15 per Share. Dividends on Class A Subordinate Voting and Class B Shares, when payable to holders who are non-residents of Canada, are subject to withholding tax at a rate of 25 per cent unless reduced according to the provisions of an applicable tax treaty. Currently, the reduced rate applicable to dividends paid to a resident of the United States is generally 15 per cent.

Stock Listing

Class A -	The Toronto Stock Exchange	(MG.A)
	Montreal Exchange	(MG.A)
	New York Stock Exchange	(MGA)
Class B -	The Toronto Stock Exchange	(MG.B)

Board of Directors

The Honourable William G. Davis, *Counsel, Tory Tory DesLauriers & Binnington*
John Doddridge, *Vice-Chairman & Chief Executive Officer*
Manfred Gingl, *Managing Director, Blau Ges.m.b.H.*
George C. Hitchman, *Corporate Director*
The Honourable Edward C. Lumley, *Vice-Chairman, Burns Fry Limited*
Donald Resnick, *Corporate Director*
Royden R. Richardson, *Senior Vice-President & Director, Richardson Greenshields of Canada Limited*
Belinda Stronach, *Corporate Director*
Frank Stronach, *Chairman, Board of Directors*

INDEX